D0084943

Chapter 20

Box 3: Why Has There Been a Worldwide Decline in Reserve Requirements?

Chapter 21

Box 1: The Growing European Commitment to Price Stability

Box 2: International Policy Coordination: The Plaza Agreement and the Louvre Accord

Chapter 28

Box 1: Inflation and Money Growth Rates in Latin America, 1983–1993

Box 2: The Budget Deficit and High Inflation In Russia

Chapter 29

Box 3: Why Foreign Exchange Rates Should Follow a Random Walk

Chapter 30

Box 2: Ending the Bolivian Hyperinflation: Case Study of a Successful Anti-inflation Program

BOXES OF GENERAL INTEREST

Chapter 2

Box 1: Different Meaning Used by Academic Economists and by Participants in Financial Markets

Box 2: Mortgage-backed Securities

Chapter 4

Box 1: The Cost of the S&L Bailout: An Application of the Present Value Concept

Box 2: Should Retirees Invest in "Gilt-edged" Long-Term Bonds?

Chapter 5

Box 1: Dangers of not Diversifying: Trump—The Fall

Chapter 7

Box 1: The Stock Market Crash of 1987 and the Junk Bond–Treasury Spread

Box 2: Recent Evidence on Term Structure

Chapter 9

Box 1: Case Study of a Financial Crisis: The Great Depression

Chapter 10

Box 2: What's in a Name?

Box 3: Program Trading and Portfolio Insurance: Were They to Blame for the Stock Market Crash of 1987?

Chapter 11

Box 1: Understand[...]

Box 3: Using an In[...]te Risk

Chapter 13

Box 1: A Tale of Two Bank Collapses: Bank of New England and Freedom National Bank

Box 5: What Went Wrong: Charles Keating and the Lincoln Savings and Loan Scandal

Chapter 14

Box 2: The Perils of Penny Benny: A Repeat of the S&L Bailout?

Chapter 17

Box 1: Recent Bank Panics in Ohio, Maryland, and Rhode Island

Box 2: Why Did the Fed Let the Bank Panics of 1930–1933 Happen?

Chapter 18

Box 2: Games the Fed Plays

Chapter 20

Box 1: Discounting to Troubled Banks: Franklin National Bank and Continental Illinois

Box 2: Discounting to Prevent a Financial Panic: The Black Monday Stock Market Crash of 1987

Chapter 24

Box 1: Meaning of the Word *Investment*

Chapter 27

Box 1: The Perils of Reverse Causation: Should You Become a Moderate Drinker?

Box 2: The Perils of Ignoring an Outside Driving Factor: How to Lose a Presidential Election

Box 3: Consumer's Balance Sheets and the Great Depression

Box 4: Real Business Cycle Theory and the Debate on Money and Economic Activity

Chapter 28

Box 3: The Perils of Accommodating Policy: The Terrorism Dilemma

Chapter 29

Box 1: Should You Hire an Ape as Your Investment Adviser?

Box 2: An Exception That Proves the Rule: Ivan Boesky

Box 4: What Does the Stock Market Crash of 1987 Tell Us About Rational Expectations and Efficient Capital Markets?

Chapter 30

Box 1: A Proof of the Policy Ineffectiveness Proposition

THE ECONOMICS OF MONEY, BANKING, AND FINANCIAL MARKETS

The HarperCollins Series in Economics

Allen
Managerial Economics

Binger/Hoffman
Microeconomics with Calculus

Bowles/Edwards
Understanding Capitalism

Branson
Macroeconomic Theory and Policy

Browning/Browning/Zupan
Microeconomic Theory and
  Applications

Burgess
The Economics of Regulation

Byrns/Stone
Economics

Caniglia
Statistics for Economics

Canterbery
The Literate Economist: A Brief
  History of Economics

Carlton/Perloff
Modern Industrial Organization

Caves/Frankel/Jones
World Trade and Payments

Cooter/Ulen
Law and Economics

Ehrenberg/Smith
Modern Labor Economics

Ekelund/Tollison
Economics

Fusfeld
The Age of the Economist

Gordon
Macroeconomics

Gregory
Essentials of Economics

Gregory/Ruffin
Economics

Gregory/Stuart
Soviet and Post-Soviet Economic
  Structure and Performance

Hamermesh/Rees
The Economics of Work and Pay

Hartwick/Olewiler
The Economics of Natural
  Resource Use

Hogendorn
Economic Development

Hughes/Cain
American Economic History

Hunt
History of Economic Thought

Hunt
Property and Prophets

Husted/Melvin
International Economics

Kohler
Statistics for Business and
  Economics

Krugman/Obstfeld
International Economics: Theory
  and Policy

Kwoka/White
The Antitrust Revolution

Laidler
The Demand for Money

Lardaro
Applied Econometrics

Lipsey/Courant/Purvis/Steiner
Economics

McCafferty
Macroeconomic Theory

McCarty
Dollars and Sense

Melvin
International Money and Finance

Miller
Economics Today

Miller/Benjamin/North
The Economics of Public Issues

Miller/Fishe
Microeconomics: Price Theory in
  Practice

Mills/Hamilton
Urban Economics

Mishkin
The Economics of Money,
  Banking, and Financial Markets

Petersen
Business and Government

Phelps
Health Economics

Ritter/Silber
Principles of Money, Banking, and
  Financial Markets

Ruffin
Intermediate Microeconomics

Ruffin/Gregory
Principles of Economics

Salvatore
Microeconomics

Sargent
Rational Expectations and Inflation

Schotter
Microeconomics: A Modern
  Approach

Studenmund
Using Econometrics

Tietenberg
Environmental and Natural
  Resource Economics

Tietenberg
Environmental Economics and
  Policy

Zerbe/Dively
Benefit-Cost Analysis

THE ECONOMICS OF MONEY, BANKING, AND FINANCIAL MARKETS

FOURTH EDITION

Frederic S. Mishkin

Columbia University

HarperCollinsCollegePublishers

Acquisitions Editor: Bruce Kaplan
Developmental Editor: Jane Tufts
Project Editor: Ellen MacElree
Design Manager: Lucy Krikorian
Text and Cover Designer: Circa 86, Inc.
Cover Images: Telegraph Colour Library/FPG
  International; The Stock Market; © Comstock, Inc.
Art Studio: Interactive Composition Corporation
Electronic Production Manager: Su Levine
Desktop Administrator: Laura Lever
Manufacturing Manager: Willie Lane
Electronic Page Makeup: Interactive Composition Corporation
Printer and Binder: R. R. Donnelley & Sons Company
Cover Printer: Coral Graphic Services, Inc.

The Economics of Money, Banking, and Financial Markets, Fourth Edition
Copyright © 1995 by Frederic S. Mishkin

Library of Congress Cataloging-in-Publication Data

Mishkin, Frederic S.
    The economics of money, banking, and financial markets / Frederic
S. Mishkin. — 4th ed.
        p.   cm — (The HarperCollins series in economics)
    Includes bibliographical references and index.
    ISBN 0-673-52378-0 (Student ed.)—ISBN 0-673-52467-1 (Free Copy Ed.)
    1. Finance. 2. Money. 3. Banks and banking.   I. Title.   II. Series.
HG173.M632 1994
332—dc20   94-20223
                                                                        CIP

94 95 96 97 9 8 7 6 5 4 3 2 1

TO SALLY

Contents in Brief

Contents   ix
Preface   xxix
About the Author   xl
Visual Guide   xli

PART I   INTRODUCTION   1

1 *Why Study Money, Banking, and Financial Markets? 3*
2 *An Overview of the Financial System 21*
3 *What Is Money? 51*

PART II   FINANCIAL MARKETS   67

4 *Understanding Interest Rates 69*
5 *Portfolio Choice: The Theory of Asset Demand 95*
6 *The Behavior of Interest Rates 107*
7 *The Risk and Term Structure of Interest Rates 149*
8 *The Foreign Exchange Market 173*

PART III   FINANCIAL INSTITUTIONS   203

9 *An Economic Analysis of Financial Structure 205*
10 *Financial Innovation 231*
11 *The Banking Firm and Bank Management 251*
12 *The Banking Industry: An Industry in Transition 283*
13 *The Crisis in Banking Regulation 305*
14 *Nonbank Financial Institutions 343*

PART IV   THE MONEY SUPPLY PROCESS   365

15   *Multiple Deposit Creation: Introducing the Money Supply Process   367*

16   *Determinants of the Money Supply   383*

17   *Explaining Depositor and Bank Behavior: The Complete Money Supply Model   407*

PART V   THE FEDERAL RESERVE SYSTEM AND THE CONDUCT OF MONETARY POLICY   435

18   *Structure of the Federal Reserve System   437*

19   *Understanding Movements in the Monetary Base   457*

20   *The Tools of Monetary Policy   477*

21   *The Conduct of Monetary Policy: Goals and Targets   493*

22   *The International Financial System and Monetary Policy   519*

PART VI   MONETARY THEORY   541

23   *The Demand for Money   543*

24   *The Keynesian Framework and the* ISLM *Model   573*

25   *Monetary and Fiscal Policy in the* ISLM *Model   601*

26   *Aggregate Demand and Supply Analysis   625*

27   *Money and Economic Activity: The Empirical Evidence   655*

28   *Money and Inflation   681*

29   *The Theory of Rational Expectations and Efficient Capital Markets   709*

30   *Rational Expectations: Implications for Policy   733*

Mathematical Appendix to Chapter 23   MA-1

Mathematical Appendix to Chapter 25   MA-9

Glossary   G-1

Answers to Selected Questions and Problems   A-1

Credits   C-1

Index   I-1

Contents

Preface xxix
About the Author xl
Visual Guide xli

PART I   **INTRODUCTION**   **1**

Chapter 1   **WHY STUDY MONEY, BANKING, AND FINANCIAL MARKETS?**   **3**

Preview   **3**

Why Study Money?   **3**
    Money and Business Cycles   4
    Money and Inflation   5
    Money and Interest Rates   6
    Conduct of Monetary Policy   7
    Budget Deficits and Monetary Policy   8

Why Study Banking?   **9**
    Financial Intermediation   9
    Banking and the Money Supply   10
    Financial Innovation   10

Why Study Financial Markets?   **11**
    Bond Market   11
    Stock Market   11
    Foreign Exchange Market   13

Concluding Remarks   **14**

* **Summary**   **15**

* **Key Terms**   **15**

* **Questions and Problems**   **15**

  * Summary, Key Terms, and Questions and Problems appear at the end of every chapter.

Appendix to Chapter 1
DEFINING AGGREGATE OUTPUT, INCOME, AND THE PRICE LEVEL   17

Chapter 2   AN OVERVIEW OF THE FINANCIAL SYSTEM   21

Preview   21

Function of Financial Markets   21

Structure of Financial Markets   23
    Debt and Equity Markets   24
    Primary and Secondary Markets   24
    Exchanges and Over-the-Counter Markets   25
    Money and Capital Markets   26

Financial Market Instruments   26
    Money Market Instruments   26

Following the Financial News
Money Market Rates   29
    Capital Market Instruments   30

Box 1 Mortgage-backed Securities   32

Function of Financial Intermediaries   33
    Transactions Costs   33

Box 2 A Global Perspective
The Importance of Financial Intermediaries to Securities Markets: An International Comparison   34
    Asymmetric Information: Adverse Selection and Moral Hazard   35

Box 3 A Global Perspective
Problems of Financial Intermediation in the Countries of Eastern Europe and the Former
Soviet Union   37

Financial Intermediaries   38
    Depository Institutions   38
    Contractual Savings Institutions   40
    Investment Intermediaries   41

Regulation of the Financial System   42
    Increasing Information Available to Investors   42

Box 4 A Global Perspective
Financial Regulation Abroad   43
    Ensuring the Soundness of Financial Intermediaries   43
    Improving Control of Monetary Policy   46

Internationalization of Financial Markets   46
    International Bond Market and Eurobonds   46
    World Stock Markets   47

Following the Financial News
Foreign Stock Market Indexes   47

Chapter 3   WHAT IS MONEY?   51

    Preview   51

    Meaning of *Money*   51

    Functions of Money   52
        Medium of Exchange   52
        Unit of Account   53
        Store of Value   54

    Evolution of the Payments System   55

    Box 1 A Global Perspective
    Monetary Union in Europe?   57

    Measuring Money   58
        Theoretical and Empirical Definitions of Money   59
        The Federal Reserve's Monetary Aggregates   60

    Following the Financial News
    The Monetary Aggregates   62
        Money as a Weighted Aggregate   62

    How Reliable Are the Money Data?   63

PART II   FINANCIAL MARKETS   67

Chapter 4   UNDERSTANDING INTEREST RATES   69

    Preview   69

    Measuring Interest Rates   70
        Present Value   71
        Yield to Maturity   72

    Box 1 The Cost of the S&L Bailout: An Application of the Present Value Concept   73

    Other Measures of Interest Rates   80
        Current Yield   80
        Yield on a Discount Basis   81

    Application Reading the *Wall Street Journal*
    The Bond Page   82

    Following the Financial News
    Bond Prices and Interest Rates   84

    The Distinction Between Interest Rates and Returns   86
        Maturity and the Volatility of Bond Returns: Interest-Rate Risk   88

    Box 2 Should Retirees Invest in "Gilt-edged" Long-Term Bonds?   89
        Summary   90

    The Distinction Between Real and Nominal Interest Rates   90

Chapter 5 PORTFOLIO CHOICE: THE THEORY OF ASSET DEMAND 95

Preview 95

Determinants of Asset Demand 95
Wealth 96
Expected Returns 97
Risk 98
Liquidity 98

Theory of Asset Demand 99

Benefits of Diversification 99

Systematic Risk 101

Box 1 Dangers of Not Diversifying: Trump—The Fall 102

Risk Premiums: Capital Asset Pricing Model and Arbitrage Pricing Theory 103

Chapter 6 THE BEHAVIOR OF INTEREST RATES 107

Preview 107

Loanable Funds Framework: Supply and Demand in the Bond Market 107
Demand Curve 108
Supply Curve 109
Market Equilibrium 110
Supply and Demand Analysis 111

Changes in Equilibrium Interest Rates 113
Shifts in the Demand for Bonds 113
Shifts in the Supply of Bonds 117
Changes in the Equilibrium Interest Rate 119

Application   Reading the *Wall Street Journal*
The "Credit Markets" Column 123

Following the Financial News
The "Credit Markets" Column 124

Liquidity Preference Framework: Supply and Demand in the Market for Money 125

Changes in Equilibrium Interest Rates 128
Shifts in the Demand for Money 128
Shifts in the Supply of Money 129
Changes in the Equilibrium Interest Rate 129

Application
Money and Interest Rates 132

Following the Financial News
Forecasting Interest Rates 134

Appendix to Chapter 6
APPLYING THE ASSET MARKET APPROACH TO A COMMODITY MARKET: THE CASE OF GOLD 141

Application   Reading the *Wall Street Journal*
The "Commodities" Column   145

Following the Financial News
The "Commodities" Column   146

Chapter 7   THE RISK AND TERM STRUCTURE OF INTEREST RATES   149

Preview   149

Risk Structure of Interest Rates   149
Default Risk   150
Liquidity   153

Box 1   The Stock Market Crash of 1987 and the Junk Bond–Treasury Spread   154
Income Tax Considerations   155
Summary   156

Application
Effects of the Clinton Tax Increase on Bond Interest Rates   156

Term Structure of Interest Rates   157

Following the Financial News
Yield Curves   158
Expectations Hypothesis   159
Segmented Markets Theory   162
Preferred Habitat and Liquidity Premium Theories   164

Box 2   Recent Evidence on the Term Structure   167
Summary   167

Application
Interpreting Yield Curves, 1980–1994   168

Chapter 8   THE FOREIGN EXCHANGE MARKET   173

Preview   173

Foreign Exchange Market   173
What Are Foreign Exchange Rates?   175
Why Are Exchange Rates Important?   175

Following the Financial News
Foreign Exchange Rates   176
How Is Foreign Exchange Traded?   177

Exchange Rates in the Long Run   178
Law of One Price   178
Theory of Purchasing Power Parity   178

Why the Theory of Purchasing Power Parity Cannot Fully Explain Exchange Rates   179
Factors That Affect Exchange Rates in the Long Run   180

Exchange Rates in the Short Run   182
Comparing Expected Returns on Domestic and Foreign Deposits   183
Interest Parity Condition   185
Equilibrium in the Foreign Exchange Market   186

Explaining Changes in Exchange Rates   188
Shifts in the Expected-Return Schedule for Foreign Deposits   188
Shifts in the Expected-Return Schedule for Domestic Deposits   190
Changes in the Equilibrium Exchange Rate: Two Examples   191
Exchange Rate Overshooting   194

Application
Why Are Exchange Rates So Volatile?   196

Box 1   A Global Perspective
Forecasting Exchange Rates   196

Application
The Dollar and Interest Rates, 1973–1993   197

Application   Reading the *Wall Street Journal*
The "Foreign Exchange" Column   199

Following the Financial News
The "Foreign Exchange" Column   200

PART III   FINANCIAL INSTITUTIONS   203

Chapter 9   AN ECONOMIC ANALYSIS OF FINANCIAL STRUCTURE   205

Preview   205

Basic Puzzles About Financial Structure Throughout the World   205

Transactions Costs   209
How Transactions Costs Influence Financial Structure   209
How Financial Intermediaries Reduce Transactions Costs   210

Asymmetric Information: Adverse Selection and Moral Hazard   211

The Lemons Problem: How Adverse Selection Influences Financial Structure   212
Lemons in the Stock and Bond Markets   212
Solutions to Adverse Selection Problems   213

How Moral Hazard Affects the Choice Between Debt and Equity Contracts   217
Moral Hazard in Equity Contracts: The Principal-Agent Problem   217
Solutions to the Principal-Agent Problem   219

How Moral Hazard Influences Financial Structure in Debt Markets   220
    Solutions to Moral Hazard in Debt Contracts   221
    Summary   223

Application
Financial Crises and Aggregate Economic Activity   223

Box 1 Case Study of a Financial Crisis: The Great Depression   228

Chapter 10   FINANCIAL INNOVATION   231

Preview   231

An Economic Analysis of Innovation   231

Responses to Changes in Demand Conditions   232
    Adjustable-Rate Mortgages   233
    Financial Futures Market   234

Following the Financial News
Financial Futures   235

Box 1   A Global Perspective
The Globalization of Financial Futures Markets   236
                    Financial Options Market   236

Responses to Changes in Supply Conditions   237
    Bank Credit Cards   238
    Junk Bonds   238
    Rise of the Commercial Paper Market   239
    Internationalization of Financial Markets   239
    Securitization   240

Box 2   What's in a Name?   241
    Discount Brokers and Stock Index Futures   242

Box 3   Program Trading and Portfolio Insurance: Were They to Blame for the Stock Market Crash of 1987?   243

Avoidance of Existing Regulations   244
    Regulations Behind Financial Innovation   244
    Eurodollars and Bank Commercial Paper   245
    NOW Accounts, ATS Accounts, and Overnight Repos   246
    Money Market Mutual Funds   247

Application
Future Evolution of the Financial System   247

Chapter 11   THE BANKING FIRM AND BANK MANAGEMENT   251

Preview   251

The Bank Balance Sheet   251
    Liabilities   252

Assets   254

Box 1 Understanding Loan Loss Reserves   255

Basic Operation of a Bank   257

General Principles of Bank Management   260
Liquidity Management and the Role of Reserves   260
Asset Management   264
Liability Management   264
Managing Capital Adequacy   265
Managing Bank Capital   268

**Application
Did the Capital Crunch Cause a Credit Crunch in the Early 1990s?   268**

Managing Credit Risk   269
Screening and Monitoring   270
Long-Term Customer Relationships   271
Loan Commitments   272

**Box 2 A Global Perspective
Japanese and German Banking Arrangements: A Better Way to Deal with Asymmetric
Information?   273**
Collateral and Compensating Balances   274
Credit Rationing   274

Managing Interest-Rate Risk   275
Gap and Duration Analysis   276
Strategies for Managing Interest-Rate Risk   277

Box 3 Using an Interest-Rate Swap to Eliminate Interest-Rate Risk   278

Off-Balance-Sheet Activities   279

CHAPTER 12   THE BANKING INDUSTRY: AN INDUSTRY IN TRANSITION   283

Preview   283

Historical Development of the Banking System   284

Multiple Regulatory Agencies   286

Structure of the Commercial Banking Industry   286
Branching Regulations and the McFadden Act   287

**Box 1 A Global Perspective
A Comparison of the Banking Structure in the United States and Abroad   288**
Bank Holding Companies   290
Electronic Banking Facilities   291

Thrift Industry: Regulation and Structure   291
Savings and Loan Associations   291
Mutual Savings Banks   292

Credit Unions   292

International Banking   293

Box 2   A Global Perspective
Birth of the Eurodollar Market   294
Eurodollar Market   294
Structure of U.S. Banking Overseas   295

Box 3   A Global Perspective
The Third-World Debt Crisis   296
Foreign Banks in the United States   297

Decline of the U.S. Banking Industry   298
Decline in Cost Advantages in Acquiring Funds (Liabilities)   299
Decline in Income Advantages on Uses of Funds (Assets)   301

Box 4   A Global Perspective
Problems in the Banking Industry Outside the United States   302

Conclusion   303

Chapter 13   THE CRISIS IN BANKING REGULATION   305

Preview   305

Asymmetric Information and Bank Regulation   305
Deposit Insurance and the FDIC   306
Restrictions on Asset Holdings and Bank Capital Requirements   309

Box 1 A Tale of Two Bank Collapses: Bank of
New England and Freedom National Bank   310
Chartering and Examination   310

Box 2 A Global Perspective
The Basel Accord on Risk-based Capital Requirements   312
Separation of the Banking and Securities Industries: The Glass-
Steagall Act   314

International Banking Regulation   314
Problems in Regulating International Banking   314

Box 3 A Global Perspective
Separation of the Banking and Securities Industries in Industrialized Countries   315

Response of Regulation to Financial Innovation   316
Changing Banking Regulation in the 1960s and 1970s   316

Box 4   A Global Perspective
The BCCI Scandal   317
Depository Institutions Deregulation and Monetary Control Act of 1980   318
Depository Institutions (Garn–St Germain) Act of 1982   319

The 1980s Banking Crisis: Why?　320
　Early Stages of the Crisis　320
　Later Stages of the Crisis: Regulatory Forbearance　323
　Competitive Equality in Banking Act of 1987　324

Political Economy of the Savings and Loan Crisis　324
　Principal-Agent Problem for Regulators and Politicians　325

Box 5　A Case Study of What Went Wrong: Charles Keating and the Lincoln Savings and Loan Scandal　326

Savings and Loan Bailout: Financial Institutions Reform, Recovery, and Enforcement Act of 1989　326

Federal Deposit Insurance Corporation Improvement Act of 1991　329

**Application
Evaluating FDICIA　330**

Additional Proposed Reforms of the Banking Regulatory System　333
　Proposed Changes in the Deposit Insurance System　333
　Proposed Changes in Other Banking Regulations　335
　Repeal of the Glass-Steagall Act　337

Chapter 14　NONBANK FINANCIAL INSTITUTIONS　343

Preview　343

Insurance Companies　343
　Insurance Management　344
　Life Insurance Companies　347
　Property and Casualty Insurance Companies　349

**Box 1　A Global Perspective
The Woes of Lloyd's of London　350**

Pension Funds　350
　Private Pension Plans　352
　Public Pension Plans　352

Box 2　The Perils of Penny Benny A Repeat of the S&L Bailout?　353

Finance Companies　354

Mutual Funds　355
　Money Market Mutual Funds　356

Government Financial Intermediation　357
　Federal Credit Agencies　357
　Government Loan Guarantees: Another Crisis Waiting to Happen?　358

Securities Market Institutions　359
　Investment Banks　359

**Following the Financial News
New Securities Issues　360**

Securities Brokers and Dealers   361
Organized Exchanges   362

PART IV   THE MONEY SUPPLY PROCESS   365

Chapter 15   MULTIPLE DEPOSIT CREATION INTRODUCING THE MONEY SUPPLY PROCESS   367

Preview   367
Four Players in the Money Supply Process   367
Overview of the Federal Reserve System   368
Liabilities   369
Assets   370
Multiple Deposit Creation: A Simple Model   370
How the Fed Provides Reserves to the Banking System   371
Deposit Creation: The Single Bank   372
Deposit Creation: The Banking System   374
Multiple Deposit Contraction   377
Deriving the Formula for Multiple Deposit Creation   378
Critique of the Simple Model   379

Chapter 16   DETERMINANTS OF THE MONEY SUPPLY   383

Preview   383
Control of the Monetary Base   384
Federal Reserve Open Market Operations   384
Shifts from Deposits into Currency   387
Discount Loans   388
Overview of the Fed's Ability to Control the Monetary Base   389
The Money Supply Model and the Money Multiplier   390
Deriving the Money Multiplier   391
Intuition Behind the Money Multiplier   393
Factors That Determine the Money Multiplier   394
Additional Factors That Determine the Money Supply   396
Overview   397

 Application
Explaining Movements in the Money Supply, 1980–1993   398

Appendix to Chapter 16
THE *M2* MONEY MULTIPLIER   403

Chapter 17   EXPLAINING DEPOSITOR AND BANK BEHAVIOR THE COMPLETE MONEY SUPPLY MODEL   407

Preview   407

Behavior of the Currency Ratio {C/D}   407
Effect of Changes in Wealth   409
Effect of Changes in Expected Returns   409

Application
Explaining the Historical Record of {C/D}   412

Application
Predicting the Future of {C/D}   414

Explaining Bank Behavior   415
Determinants of the Excess Reserves Ratio {ER/D}   416
Determinants of Discount Loan Borrowing   417

The Complete Money Supply Model   418
Determinants of the Money Supply   420
Interplay of Determinants   422

Anatomy of a Bank Panic   423

Box 1 Recent Bank Panics in Ohio, Maryland, and Rhode Island   424
The Individual Bank   425
The Banking System   426

Box 2 The Bank Panics of 1930–1933: Why Did the Fed Let Them Happen?   427
Bank Panics and the Money Supply   428

Application
The Great Depression Bank Panics, 1930–1933   428

PART V   THE FEDERAL RESERVE SYSTEM AND THE CONDUCT OF MONETARY POLICY   435

Chapter 18   STRUCTURE OF THE FEDERAL RESERVE SYSTEM   437

Preview   437

Origins of the Federal Reserve System   437

Formal Structure of the Federal Reserve System   438
Federal Reserve Banks   438
Member Banks   441
Board of Governors of the Federal Reserve System   442
Federal Open Market Committee (FOMC)   443

Informal Structure of the Federal Reserve System   443

How Independent Is the Fed?   445

Explaining the Fed's Behavior   447

Box 1 A Global Perspective
The Structure and Independence of Foreign Central Banks   448

Box 2 Games the Fed Plays   449

Should the Fed Be Independent?   450
The Case for Independence   450

Box 3 A Global Perspective
Central Bank Independence and Macroeconomic Performance in Seventeen Countries   452
The Case Against Independence   453

Chapter 19   UNDERSTANDING MOVEMENTS IN THE MONETARY BASE   457

Preview   457

The Fed's Balance Sheet and the Monetary Base   457
Assets   457
Liabilities   458
Monetary Base   459

Factors That Affect the Monetary Base   461
Factors That Increase the Monetary Base   461

Box 1 A Global Perspective
Foreign Exchange Rate Intervention and the Monetary Base   462
Factors That Decrease the Monetary Base   465
Summary   466

The Budget Deficit and the Monetary Base   467
The Government Budget Constraint   467

Following the Financial News
Reserves and Sources of Change in the Monetary Base   468
Financing Government Spending   469

Does the Budget Deficit Influence the Monetary Base?   472

Chapter 20   THE TOOLS OF MONETARY POLICY   477

Preview   477

Open Market Operations   477
A Day at the Trading Desk   478
Advantages of Open Market Operations   480

Discount Policy   480
Operation of the Discount Window   480
Lender of Last Resort   481

Box 1 Discounting to Troubled Banks: Franklin National Bank and Continental Illinois   483
Announcement Effect   484

Box 2 Discounting to Prevent a Financial Panic: The Black Monday Stock Market Crash of 1987   485

Advantages and Disadvantages of Discount Policy   486
Proposed Reforms of Discount Policy   487

Reserve Requirements   488
Advantages and Disadvantages of Reserve Requirement Changes   489
Proposed Reforms of Reserve Requirements   489

Box 3   A Global Perspective
Why Has There Been a Worldwide Decline in Reserve Requirements?   490

Chapter 21   THE CONDUCT OF MONETARY POLICY: GOALS AND TARGETS   493

Preview   493

Goals of Monetary Policy   493
High Employment   493
Economic Growth   494
Price Stability   495

Box 1   A Global Perspective
The Growing European Commitment to Price Stability   495
Interest-Rate Stability   496
Stability of Financial Markets   496
Stability in Foreign Exchange Markets   496
Conflict Among Goals   496

The Fed's Strategy: Use of Monetary Targets   497

Choosing the Targets   498
Criteria for Choosing Intermediate Targets   500
Criteria for Choosing Operating Targets   502

Fed Policy Procedures: A Historical Perspective   502
The Early Years: Discount Policy as the Primary Tool   503
Discovery of Open Market Operations   504
The Great Depression   504
Reserve Requirements as a Policy Tool   504
War Finance and the Pegging of Interest Rates: 1942–1951   505
Targeting Money Market Conditions: The 1950s and 1960s   506
Targeting Monetary Aggregates: The 1970s   507
New Fed Operating Procedures: October 1979–October 1982   509
Deemphasis of Monetary Aggregates: October 1982 and Beyond   511
International Considerations   512

How Well Can the Fed Control the Money Supply?   512

Box 2   A Global Perspective
International Policy Coordination: The Plaza Agreement and the Louvre Accord   513

The Conduct of Monetary Policy in Five Other Countries   514
United Kingdom   514
Canada   514

Germany   515
Switzerland   515
Japan   516

Chapter 22   THE INTERNATIONAL FINANCIAL SYSTEM AND MONETARY POLICY   519

Preview   519

Intervention in the Foreign Exchange Market   519
Foreign Exchange Intervention and the Money Supply   519
Unsterilized Intervention   521
Sterilized Intervention   523

Balance of Payments   524
Current Account   524

Following the Financial News
The Balance of Payments   525
Capital Account   527
Official Reserve Transactions Balance   527
Methods of Financing the Balance of Payments   527

Evolution of the International Financial System   528
The Gold Standard   528
The Bretton Woods System and the IMF   529
The Managed Float   533
The European Monetary System (EMS)   534

Application
The September 1992 Foreign Exchange Crisis   535

International Considerations and Monetary Policy   537
Direct Effects of the Foreign Exchange Market on the Money Supply   537
Balance-of-Payments Considerations   537
Exchange Rate Considerations   538

PART VI   MONETARY THEORY   541

Chapter 23   THE DEMAND FOR MONEY   543

Preview   543
Quantity Theory of Money   544
Velocity of Money and the Equation of Exchange   544
Quantity Theory   545
Quantity Theory of Money Demand   546

Cambridge Approach to Money Demand   547

Is Velocity a Constant?   548

Keynes's Liquidity Preference Theory   551
Transactions Motive   551
Precautionary Motive   551
Speculative Motive   552
Putting the Three Motives Together   553

Further Developments in the Keynesian Approach   555
Transactions Demand   555

Precautionary Demand   559

Speculative Demand   559

Friedman's Modern Quantity Theory of Money   560

Distinguishing Between the Friedman and Keynesian Theories   562

Appendix to Chapter 23
EMPIRICAL EVIDENCE ON THE DEMAND FOR MONEY   567

Chapter 24   THE KEYNESIAN FRAMEWORK AND THE *ISLM* MODEL   573

Preview   573

Determination of Aggregate Output   574
Consumer Expenditure and the Consumption Function   575
Investment Spending   577

Box 1 Meaning of the Word *Investment*   577
Equilibrium and the Keynesian Cross Diagram   578
The Expenditure Multiplier   580

Application
The Collapse of Investment Spending and the Great Depression   583
Government's Role   584
Role of International Trade   586
Summary of the Determinants of Aggregate Output   587

The *ISLM* Model   590
Equilibrium in the Goods Market: The *IS* Curve   591
Equilibrium in the Market for Money: The *LM* Curve   595

The *ISLM* Approach to Aggregate Output and Interest Rates   597

Chapter 25   MONETARY AND FISCAL POLICY IN THE *ISLM* MODEL   601

Preview   601

Factors That Cause the *IS* Curve to Shift   602

Factors That Cause the *LM* Curve to Shift   604

Changes in Equilibrium Level of the Interest Rate and Aggregate Output   606
  Response to a Change in Monetary Policy   606
  Response to a Change in Fiscal Policy   608

Application
The Vietnam War Buildup and the Rise in Interest Rates, 1965–1966   609

Effectiveness of Monetary Versus Fiscal Policy   611
  Monetary Policy Versus Fiscal Policy: The Case of Complete
  Crowding Out   612

Application
Targeting on Money Supply Versus Interest Rates   614

The *ISLM* Model in the Long Run   617

The *ISLM* Model and the Aggregate Demand Curve   619
  Deriving the Aggregate Demand Curve   620
  Factors That Cause the Aggregate Demand Curve to Shift   621

Chapter 26   AGGREGATE DEMAND AND SUPPLY ANALYSIS   625

Preview   625

Aggregate Demand   625

Following the Financial News
Aggregate Output, Unemployment, and the Price Level   626
  Monetarist View of Aggregate Demand   626
  Keynesian View of Aggregate Demand   628
  The Crowding-Out Debate   630
  The Money View Versus the Credit View   631

Aggregate Supply   632
  Shifts in the Aggregate Supply Curve   633

Equilibrium in Aggregate Supply and Demand Analysis   633
  Equilibrium in the Short Run   633
  Equilibrium in the Long Run   634
  Shifts in Aggregate Demand   638
  Shifts in Aggregate Supply   640
  Shifts in the Long-Run Aggregate Supply Curve: Real Business Cycle Theory
  and Hysteresis   641
  Conclusions   644

Application
Explaining Past Business Cycle Episodes   645

Application
Predicting Future Economic Activity   648

Appendix to Chapter 26
AGGREGATE SUPPLY AND THE PHILLIPS CURVE: A HISTORICAL PERSPECTIVE 651

Chapter 27   MONEY AND ECONOMIC ACTIVITY: THE EMPIRICAL EVIDENCE   655

Preview   655

Two Types of Empirical Evidence   656
Structural Model Evidence   656
Reduced-Form Evidence   657
Advantages and Disadvantages of Structural Model Evidence   657
Advantages and Disadvantages of Reduced-Form Evidence   658

Box 1   The Perils of Reverse Causation: Should You Become a Moderate Drinker?   659

Box 2   The Perils of Ignoring an Outside Driving Factor: How to Lose a Presidential Election   660
Conclusions   660

Early Keynesian Evidence on the Importance of Money   661

Objections to Early Keynesian Evidence   662

Early Monetarist Evidence on the Importance of Money   664
Timing Evidence   665
Statistical Evidence   668
Historical Evidence   669

Overview of the Monetarist Evidence   670

The Search for New Monetary Transmission Mechanisms   671
Investment Spending   671
Consumer Expenditure   674

Box 3   Consumers' Balance Sheets and the Great Depression   676
International Trade   676

Overview of the Monetarist/Keynesian Debate on Money and Economic Activity   677

Box 4   Real Business Cycle Theory and the Debate on Money and Economic Activity   678

Chapter 28   MONEY AND INFLATION   681

Preview   681

Money and Inflation: The Evidence   682
German Hyperinflation, 1921–1923   682

**Box 1   A Global Perspective
Inflation and Money Growth Rates in Latin America, 1983–1993   683**
Recent Examples of Rapid Inflation   685

The Meaning of *Inflation*   685

Views of Inflation   686
Monetarist View   686
Keynesian View   687
Summary   690

Why Does Inflationary Monetary Policy Come About?   691
  High Employment Targets and Inflation   691
  Budget Deficits and Inflation   695

Box 2   A Global Perspective
The Budget Deficit and High Inflation in Russia and Other Former Members of the Soviet Union   697

Application
Explaining the Rise in U.S. Inflation, 1960–1980   698

The Activist/Nonactivist Policy Debate   701
  Responses to High Unemployment   701
  Activist and Nonactivist Positions   703
  Expectations and the Activist/Nonactivist Debate   704

Box 3 The Perils of Accommodating Policy: The Terrorism Dilemma   706
  Rules Versus Discretion: Conclusions   706

Application
The Importance of Credibility to Volcker's Victory over Inflation   707

Chapter 29   THE THEORY OF RATIONAL EXPECTATIONS AND EFFICIENT CAPITAL MARKETS   709

Preview   709

The Role of Expectations in Economic Activity   710

Theory of Rational Expectations   712
  Formal Statement of the Theory   714
  Rationale Behind the Theory   714
  Implications of the Theory   715

Efficient Markets Theory: Rational Expectations in Financial Markets   716
  Rationale Behind the Theory   718

Application
A Practical Guide to Investing in the Stock Market   719

Following the Financial News
Stock Prices   720

Box 1 Should You Hire an Ape as Your Investment Adviser?   721

Box 2 An Exception That Proves the Rule: Ivan Boesky   722

Box 3 A Global Perspective
Why Foreign Exchange Rates Should Follow a Random Walk   724

Evidence on Rational Expectations in Other Markets   728

Box 4 What Does the Stock Market Crash of 1987 Tell Us About Rational Expectations and Efficient Markets?   729

Chapter 30   RATIONAL EXPECTATIONS: IMPLICATIONS FOR POLICY   733

Preview   733

The Lucas Critique of Policy Evaluation   734
Econometric Policy Evaluation   734
An Example: The Term Structure of Interest Rates   735

The New Classical Macroeconomic Model   736
Effect of Unanticipated and Anticipated Policy   736

Box 1   A Proof of the Policy Ineffectiveness Proposition   739
Can an Expansionary Policy Lead to a Decline in Aggregate Output?   739
Implications for Policymakers   740

The New Keynesian Model   742
Effects of Unanticipated and Anticipated Policy   743
Implications for Policymakers   743

Comparison of the Two New Models with the Traditional Model   745
Short-Run Output and Price Responses   745
Stabilization Policy   748
Anti-inflation Policies   749
The Role of Credibility in Fighting Inflation   751

Box 2   A Global Perspective
Ending the Bolivian Hyperinflation: Case Study of a Successful Anti-inflation Program   753

Application
Credibility and the Reagan Budget Deficits   753

Impact of the Rational Expectations Revolution   754

MATHEMATICAL APPENDIX TO CHAPTER 23: A MATHEMATICAL TREATMENT OF THE BAUMOL-TOBIN AND TOBIN MEAN-VARIANCE MODELS   MA-1

MATHEMATICAL APPENDIX TO CHAPTER 25: ALGEBRA OF THE *ISLM* MODEL   MA-9

GLOSSARY   G-1

ANSWERS TO SELECTED QUESTIONS AND PROBLEMS   A-1

CREDITS   C-1

INDEX   I-1

Preface

The study of money, banking, and financial markets has become one of the most exciting areas in economics. Financial markets are changing rapidly, and new financial instruments appear almost daily; the once staid banking industry has become highly dynamic, and the difficulties in the savings and loan and commercial banking industries are continually featured in the media. Well-functioning international trade and financial markets have created an integrated world economy in which events in one country's financial markets have a major impact on financial markets in other countries, the conduct of monetary policy is at center stage in debates about economic policy, and new developments in monetary theory have changed the way we think about the role of money in the economy.

This fourth edition of *The Economics of Money, Banking, and Financial Markets* is a major revision that conveys these exciting developments and addresses issues of concern to instructors and students alike.

BASIC FEATURES

In writing this edition, I have continued to be guided by several basic features that have always distinguished this book from its competitors: a unifying analytic framework that stresses the economic way of thinking; careful, step-by-step development of models; an applications-oriented perspective; a thorough integration of an international perspective throughout the text; flexibility; and pedagogical aids and supplementary materials that make it easier for students to learn and instructors to teach money and banking.

A Unifying Analytic Framework

Instead of focusing on a mass of dull facts that will soon become obsolete, this textbook stresses the economic way of thinking by developing a unifying analytic framework for the study of money, banking, and financial markets. This framework uses a few basic economic principles to organize students' thinking about the structure of financial markets, the foreign exchange market, bank management, and the role of money in the economy. The basic principles are a simplified approach to portfolio choice (what I call the *theory of asset demand*), the concept of equilibrium, an asset market approach that uses basic supply and demand analysis to explain behavior in financial markets, profit maximization, a transactions cost and asymmetric information approach to financial structure, and aggregate supply and demand analysis.

The unifying framework developed in this book not only makes the material more interesting and keeps students' knowledge from becoming obsolete, but it also discourages them from memorizing a mass of facts that will be forgotten soon after the final exam. The framework also provides students with the tools for understanding trends in the financial marketplace and in variables such as interest rates, exchange rates, inflation, and aggregate output.

An additional benefit of teaching money, banking, and financial markets with unifying analytic models is that instructors can teach the material using a modern approach based on the latest research. The model used to analyze interest rate and exchange rate determination, for example, is based on a modern asset market approach. Many other textbooks take an older approach that stresses flows rather than stocks of assets. Because the modern asset market approach is much better suited to explaining the high volatility we see in asset prices such as interest rates, exchange rates, and stock prices, it has been adopted by the economics profession in the professional literature.

To reinforce the models' usefulness, this text emphasizes the interaction of theoretical analysis and empirical data. The text and numerous special-interest boxes present evidence that supports or casts doubt on the theories being discussed. This exposure to real-life events and data should dissuade students from thinking that all economists make abstract assumptions and develop theories that have nothing to do with actual behavior.

Careful, Step-by-Step Development of Models

To help students understand and apply the unifying analytic framework, the text adopts an approach found in the best principles-of-economics textbooks: Simple models are constructed in which the variables being held constant are carefully delineated, each step in the derivation of the model is clearly and carefully laid out, and the models are then used to explain various phenomena by focusing on changes in one variable at a time, holding all other variables constant.

No other book in this market spends as much time and effort as this one does to make the models clear and easy to learn. Not only does the careful, step-by-step development of models improve students' performance in the course, but it also makes the instructor's job easier because students are less likely to have to seek extra help.

Applications-oriented Perspective

In teaching money, banking, and financial markets over the past 20 years, I have found that students get more out of the course if it is applications-oriented. This book contains more than 25 major applications that demonstrate how the analysis in the book can be used to explain many important real-world situations. There are applications on the following topics, among others: explaining the relationship between money and interest rates (Chapter 6), explaining the rise and fall of the dollar in the foreign exchange market (Chapter 8), predicting the future evolution of the financial system (Chapter 10), evaluating the Federal Deposit Insurance Corporation Improvement Act (FDICIA) of 1991 (Chapter 13), explaining why foreign exchange crises such as the one in September 1992 occur (Chapter 22), and examining the role of credibility in recent successes in controlling inflation (Chapter 28).

To function better in the real world outside the classroom, students must be given the tools to follow the financial news that appears in leading financial publications such as the *Wall Street Journal*. Encouraging students to read the financial section of the newspaper helps them understand and apply the material covered in the money and banking course. To this end, this book contains two special features.

The first is a set of special boxed inserts titled "Following the Financial News" that contain relevant columns and data from the *Wall Street Journal* that typically appear daily or periodically. These self-contained boxes give students the detailed information and definitions they need to evaluate the data being presented.

The second feature is a set of special applications titled "Reading the *Wall Street Journal*" that elaborate on a "Following the Financial News" box. These applications show students how the analytic framework in the book can be used directly to understand the daily columns in the United States' leading financial newspaper. They include reading the bond page (Chapter 4), the "Credit Markets" column (Chapter 6), the "Commodities" column (appendix to Chapter 6), and the "Foreign Exchange" column (Chapter 8). Once students see how to use the analytic framework by working through these applications in the textbook, they can do this analysis every day when they read the newspaper. In teaching, I bring the previous day's *Wall Street Journal* columns into class and use them to conduct a case discussion along the lines of the "Reading the *Wall Street Journal*" applications in the text.

One important characteristic of the "Following the Financial News" boxes and the "Reading the *Wall Street Journal*" applications is that they never go out of date. Because the columns or data analyzed in these two special features typically appear daily or periodically, the information or analysis provided in these two special features will continue to prove useful to the student well into the future.

In addition to these applications, this book also contains 450 end-of-chapter problems that ask students to apply the economic concepts they have learned to other real-world issues. Particularly relevant to students are a special class of problems headed "Using Economic Analysis to Predict the Future." The problems, half of which are answered at the back of the book, should further stimulate interest among students and help them learn the subject matter.

Thorough Integration of an International Perspective

In recent years, financial markets throughout the world have become highly integrated across national borders. In light of this development, both students and professors want to see the study of money, banking, and financial markets thoroughly internationalized. This book integrates an international perspective throughout the text.

Many books cover international material in separate chapters that are usually placed later in the book. This book, by contrast, integrates an international perspective right at the outset with discussions starting as early as Chapter 1. These self-contained sections cover issues such as the growing internationalization of financial markets (Chapter 2), basic puzzles of financial structure throughout the world (Chapter 9), international banking (Chapters 11 and 13), the conduct of monetary policy in other countries (Chapter 21), and the September 1992 foreign exchange rate crisis (Chapter 22). An additional vehicle for integrating an international perspective throughout the text is a distinctive set of more than 20 special-interest boxes (not found in other money and banking texts) titled "A Global Perspective." These boxes continually give students an international perspective by comparing the financial system and monetary policy in the United States to those in other countries. They discuss topics such as problems of financial intermediation in the countries of Eastern Europe and the former Soviet Union (Chapter 2), the globalization of financial futures markets (Chapter 10), Japanese and German banking arrangements (Chapter 11), problems in the banking industry outside of the United States (Chapter 12), the woes of Lloyd's of London (Chapter 14), and a comparison of central bank independence and macroeconomic performance in 17 countries (Chapter 18).

The book also includes two chapters that are devoted exclusively to international issues and are not relegated to the back. The discussion of the foreign exchange market appears early in the book in Chapter 8 because the early placement of this material allows a more coherent discussion of an international perspective in later chapters. Chapter 22 on the international financial system and monetary policy deals with closely related topics such as how developments in the foreign exchange market and other international financial markets affect the U.S. economy and the conduct of monetary policy.

Flexibility

In using previous editions, adopters, reviewers, and survey respondents have continually praised this text's flexibility. There are as many ways to teach money, banking, and financial markets as there are instructors, and to satisfy the diverse needs of educators, the text achieves flexibility in a variety of ways:

- Core chapters provide the basic analysis used throughout the book, and other chapters or sections of chapters can be used or omitted according to instructor preferences. For example, Chapter 2 provides an introductory view of the financial system and basic concepts such as transactions costs, adverse selection, and moral hazard. After covering Chapter 2, an instructor can decide to teach a more detailed coverage of financial structure in Chapter 9 or choose to skip this chapter or take any of a number of different paths through the book.
- The text has also been designed to allow instructors to cover the most important issues in monetary theory and policy without having to use the *ISLM* model in Chapters 24 and 25, while more complete treatments of monetary theory make use of the *ISLM* chapters.
- The approach to internationalizing the text using both the "Global Perspective" boxes, separate international sections within chapters, and separate chapters on the foreign exchange market and the international monetary system is comprehensive yet flexible. Although many instructors will teach all the international material, others will choose not to. Instructors who want less emphasis on international topics can easily skip Chapter 8 (foreign exchange market) and Chapter 22 (international financial system and monetary policy). Instructors who would like to teach material on the foreign exchange market later in the course can easily teach Chapter 8 on the foreign exchange market just before Chapter 22 on the international financial system and monetary policy.
- In addition, because the "Global Perspective" boxes are self-contained, as are the chapter sections on international banking, internationalization of financial markets, and the conduct of monetary policy in other countries, they can also be skipped without any loss of continuity.

To illustrate how this book can be used for courses with a different emphasis, several course outlines are suggested for a semester teaching schedule. More detailed information about how the text can be used flexibly in your course is available in the *Instructor's Manual.*

General Money and Banking Course: Chapters 1–6, 11–13, 18, 20–21, 26, 28, with a choice of 6 of the remaining 16 chapters.

General Money and Banking Course with International Emphasis: Chapters 1–6, 8, 11–13, 18, 20–22, 26, 28, with a choice of 4 of the remaining 14 chapters.

Financial Markets and Institutions Course: Chapters 1–7, 9–14, 29 with a choice of 6 of the remaining 16 chapters.

Monetary Theory and Policy Course: Chapters 1–6, 15–16, 18, 20–21, 23, 26–28, with a choice of 5 of the remaining 15 chapters.

NEW TO THE FOURTH EDITION

Although the basic features and material of the previous edition have been retained, the fourth edition represents a major revision.

Further Development of an International Dimension

Because of events such as the foreign exchange crisis in September 1992 and the debate over NAFTA, professors and students have increased their demand for further internationalization of the text. To meet this demand, I have added many new major sections on international topics including international banking regulation (Chapter 13), the conduct of monetary policy in five other countries (Chapter 21), the European Monetary System (Chapter 22), and a new application on the September 1992 foreign exchange crisis (Chapter 22). In addition, I have added seven new "Global Perspective" boxes, on the globalization of financial futures markets (Chapter 10), the BCCI scandal (Chapter 13), the woes of Lloyd's of London (Chapter 14), the structure and independence of foreign central banks (Chapter 18), why there has been a worldwide decline in reserve requirements (Chapter 20), the growing European commitment to price stability (Chapter 21), and budget deficits and high inflation in Russia and other former members of the Soviet Union (Chapter 28).

Another major change is the placement of the chapter on the foreign exchange market early in the book (Chapter 8). This early placement is more logical because the foreign exchange market *is* a financial market. In addition, the early placement of this material enables instructors to give a more international slant to their course if they so choose. However, because some instructors might prefer to teach this chapter later in their course (typically right before Chapter 22 on the international financial system and monetary policy), the book has been written to make this possible with no loss of continuity.

An Integrated Approach for Understanding Financial Structure and Institutions

In the third edition of this book, I introduced the concepts of transactions costs and asymmetric information to explain the structure of our financial system and the operations of financial institutions. Reviewers and users of the book have found this new approach to thinking about financial markets and institutions quite exciting. However, because this material was so new, I did not fully integrate it into the chapters on financial institutions. With further thought, I have realized that by using an integrated approach for understanding financial structure and institutions, I could reorganize the text to make the flow of information more logical, thereby making it easier for students to see how financial institutions and markets all fit together. As a result, I have thoroughly reorganized Part III of the text.

- Transactions costs, adverse selection, and moral hazard are now introduced at the beginning of the text in Chapter 2 so that instructors can use the book more flexibly.
- The chapter on financial innovation has now been moved from the end of this part of the book to Chapter 10 in order to show how the process of financial innovation has contributed to major changes in the banking industry and to the crisis in banking regulation. It has also been revised to emphasize how changes in demand and supply conditions related to changes in information collection technology have led to financial innovation and the growth of such markets as the commercial paper and junk bond markets.
- Chapter 11 on the banking firm and bank management has a new section on capital adequacy, an increasing concern for bank managers in recent years. The link between increases in capital requirements and the credit crunch (which helped cause the 1990–1991 recession and led to a slow recovery) is also covered in this chapter.
- Chapter 12 on the banking industry has been made more dynamic with new sections on the historical development of the banking system and on how developments in transactions cost and information technology have led to a decline of the banking industry.
- The discussion of regulation is no longer spread out over several chapters as in the previous edition. Now it is discussed primarily in Chapter 13, which describes the current regulatory system and its problems. It has new sections on how asymmetric information explains the regulatory structure, international banking regulation, the response of regulation to financial innovation, the Federal Deposit Insurance Corporation Improvement Act (FDICIA) of 1991, and the Glass-Steagall separation of the banking and securities industries.
- Chapter 14 on nonbank financial institutions now has a more dynamic focus to reflect how changes in information technology have led to the rapid growth of nonbank financial institutions at the expense of banks.

Other New Material

- New material in the financial markets section of the book includes the new applications mentioned earlier on reading the *Wall Street Journal,* which teach students how to read that paper's bond page (Chapter 4), "Credit Markets" column (Chapter 6), "Commodities" column (appendix to Chapter 6), and "Foreign Exchange" column (Chapter 8), and a new appendix to Chapter 6 on applying the asset market approach to a commodities market, gold.
- The monetary theory part of the book also has new material on how developments in financial markets affect the business cycle. New sections focus on the money view versus the credit view and on the credit crunch and the slow recovery from the 1990–1991 recession.
- A new section on the *ISLM* model in the long run has been added to Chapter 25.
- Boxes, discussions of empirical evidence, and all figures and tables have been thoroughly updated, at least through the end of 1993.

An Easier Way to Teach Money, Banking, and Financial Markets

From my experience, the demands for good teaching have increased dramatically in recent years. To meet this demand, I have worked hard to provide instructors with new supplementary materials for this edition, unavailable with any competing text, that should make teaching this course substantially easier.

This edition of the book not only comes with over 200 full-color transparencies of all the figures and tables in the book (as in the previous edition) but now also makes available a full set of lecture notes on overhead transparencies. Furthermore, the *Instructor's Manual* has been thoroughly reorganized to make it easier to use and contains transparency masters of the lecture notes that are perforated so that they can be easily detached from the manual for use in class.

The lecture notes are comprehensive and outline all the major points covered in the text. They have been class-tested successfully—they are in fact the ones that I use in my class—and they should help other instructors prepare their lectures as these notes have helped me. Some instructors might use these lecture notes as their own class notes but prefer to teach from a chalkboard. Others might prefer to teach with transparencies, and the lecture notes on transparencies in combination with the full-color transparencies of the figures and tables provide the flexibility to do this.

I am also aware that many instructors want to make variations in their lectures that depart somewhat from material covered in the text. To make this easy to do, the entire set of lecture notes has been put on diskette using WordPerfect 5.1, and the diskette is included with the *Instructor's Manual*. This will allow instructors to modify the lecture notes as they see fit for their own use, for class handouts, or for transparencies to be used with an overhead projector.

The diskette also contains the entire contents of the *Instructor's Manual,* which includes chapter outlines, overviews and teaching tips, answers to the end-of-chapter problems that are not answered in the text, and discussion questions. This will make it easier for instructors to prepare handouts for their students, such as solutions to problem sets made up of end-of-chapter problems, outlines of the lecture of the day, or essay questions for homework. I have used handouts of this type in my teaching and have found them to be very effective. Instructors have my permission and are encouraged to photocopy all of the materials on the diskette and use them as they see fit in class.

PEDAGOGICAL AIDS

A textbook must be a solid motivational tool. To this end, a wide variety of pedagogical features are incorporated into this textbook.

1. *Previews* at the beginning of each chapter tell students where the chapter is heading, why specific topics are important, and how they relate to other topics in the book.

2. *Applications* demonstrate how the analysis in the book can be used to explain many important real-world situations. A special set of applications, called "Reading the *Wall Street Journal*," shows students how to read daily columns in this leading financial newspaper.

3. *"Following the Financial News" boxes* introduce students to relevant news articles and data that are reported daily in the press and explain how to read them.

4. *"Global Perspective" boxes* give students an international perspective by comparing the financial system and monetary policy in the United States to those in other countries.

5. *Special-interest boxes* highlight dramatic historical episodes, noteworthy ideas, and interesting facts related to the subject matter.

6. *Study guides,* scattered throughout the text, provide hints on how to think about or approach a topic as students work their way through it.

7. *Summary tables* serve as a useful study aid when reviewing material.

8. *Key statements* are important points set in boldface type so that students can easily find them for later reference.

9. Over 120 *graphs* with captions help students understand the interrelationship of the variables plotted and the principles of analysis.

10. A *summary* at the end of each chapter reviews the main points.

11. *Key terms* are important words or phrases, boldfaced when they are defined for the first time and listed at the end of the chapter.

12. End-of-chapter *questions and problems,* 450 of them, help students learn the subject matter by applying economic concepts, including a special class of problems that students find particularly relevant, under the heading "Using Economic Analysis to Predict the Future."

13. The *glossary* at the back of the book provides the definitions for all key terms.

14. An *answer section* at the back of the book provides the solutions to half of the questions and problems (marked by *).

SUPPLEMENTARY MATERIALS

This fourth edition of *The Economics of Money, Banking, and Financial Markets* includes the most comprehensive package of supplementary materials of any textbook in its field.

1. The *Study Guide and Workbook,* prepared by John McArthur of Wofford College and myself, includes chapter synopses and completions, exercises, problems, self-tests, and answers to the exercises, problems, and self-tests.

2. The *Instructor's Manual,* prepared by myself, includes sample course outlines, chapter outlines, answers to questions and problems in the text, and transparency masters for the lecture notes.

3. A *diskette* with the entire contents of the *Instructor's Manual* (including the lecture notes) contains WordPerfect files that can be modified to fit any particular course.

4. *Readings in Money, Banking, and Financial Markets,* edited by James W. Eaton of Bridgewater College and myself, is updated annually with over half the articles new each year to enable instructors to keep the content of their course current throughout the three-year life of an edition of the text; it will be sold with the text at a particularly low price.

5. *Custom publishing option* of the readings

6. *Money Game Computer Software,* prepared for IBM-compatible PCs by Richard Alston and Wan Fu Chi of Weber State College, provides students with hands-on experience with the analytic concepts of the text.

7. *Full-color transparencies,* numbering over 150, are provided for *all* figures, tables, and summary tables.

8. *Lecture note transparencies,* numbering over 150, comprehensively outline all points covered in the text.

9. *Electronic transparencies*

10. A *test bank,* available both in print form and on computer disks, includes over 2500 multiple-choice test items, many with graphs. The test bank is computerized so that the instructor can easily produce exams automatically.

ACKNOWLEDGMENTS

As always in so large a project, there are many people to thank. Special thanks go to Bruce Kaplan, economics editor at HarperCollins, who has been especially valuable to both this and the previous edition, and to Jane Tufts, the best development editor in the business. I also have been assisted by comments from my colleagues at Columbia University—Frank Edwards, Alberto Giovannini, Glenn Hubbard, and Bob Shay—and from my students.

I have also been helped in this edition by outside reviewers as well as correspondents who have made this a better book. I thank the following:

John Bay, University of Southern Maine
John Beuhler, University of Arizona
W. Carl Biven, Georgia Institute of Technology
Steven Bovee, Oral Roberts University
Mary Bumgarner, Kennesaw State College
Steve Cobb, Xavier University
Frank Corcione, University of Scranton
Eleanor Craig, University of Delaware
Jacob De Rooy, Pennsylvania State University at Harrisburg

John Dominguez, University of Wisconsin—Whitewater
Richard Douglas, Bowling Green State University
Donald Dutkowsky, Syracuse University
Robert Elliot, Northwestern State University of Louisiana
Michael Ellis, Kent State University
David Gillette, Northeast Missouri State University
Stuart Glosser, University of Wisconsin—Whitewater
David Hammes, University of Hawaii at Hilo
Berch Haroian, William Patterson College of New Jersey
Michael Jenkins, Pennsylvania State University
Frederick Joutz, George Washington University
Maryann Keating, Valparaiso University
Richard Keehn, University of Wisconsin—Parkside
Elizabeth Sawyer Kelly, University of Wisconsin—Madison
Ruby Pandey Kishan, Southwest Texas State University
Kishore Kulkarni, Metropolitan State College of Denver
Thomas Lee, California State University, Northridge
Serpil Leveen, Montclair State College
Kara Lown, Federal Reserve Bank of New York
W. Douglas McMillan, Lousiana State University
Robert Mettlen, University of Texas—Austin
Scott Moore, John Carroll University
Robert Mulligan, Providence College
Dennis Petruska, Youngstown State University
Joseph M. Phillips, Eppley College of Business Administration
Ronald Ratti, University of Missouri—Columbia
Duane Rosa, West Texas State University
Ibrahim el-Saify, State University of New York at Albany
Alden Shiers, California Polytechnic State University—San Luis Obispo
Harinder Singh, San Diego State University
Pam Whalley, Western Washington University
James Wible, University of New Hampshire

Finally, I want to thank my wife, Sally; my son, Matthew; and my daughter, Laura, who provide me with a warm and happy environment that enables me to do my work, and my father, Sydney, now deceased, who a long time ago put me on the path that led to this book.

Frederic S. Mishkin

ABOUT THE AUTHOR

Frederic S. Mishkin is currently an executive vice president and director of research at the Federal Reserve Bank of New York. He is on leave from the Graduate School of Business at Columbia, where he is the A. Barton Hepburn Professor of Economics. He is also a Research Associate at the National Bureau of Economic Research. Since receiving his Ph.D. from the Massachusetts Institute of Technology in 1976, he has taught at the University of Chicago, Northwestern University, Princeton University, and Columbia.

Professor Mishkin's research focuses on monetary policy and its impact on financial markets and the aggregate economy. He is the author of *A Rational Expectations Approach to Macroeconometrics: Testing Policy Ineffectiveness and Efficient Markets Models* (Chicago: University of Chicago Press, 1983) and *Money, Interest Rates, and Inflation* (London: Edward Elgar, 1993). In addition he has published over 50 articles in such journals as the *American Economic Review,* the *Journal of Political Economy, Econometrica,* the *Quarterly Journal of Economics,* the *Journal of Finance,* and the *Journal of Monetary Economics.*

Similarly, Professor Mishkin has served on the editorial board of the *American Economic Review* and has been an associate editor at the *Journal of Business and Economic Statistics.* He is currently an associate editor at the *Journal of Applied Econometrics,* the *Journal of International Money and Finance,* the *Journal of Money, Credit and Banking,* and the *Journal of Economic Perspectives.* He has been an academic consultant to the Board of Governors of the Federal Reserve System, a member of the Academic Advisory Panel of the Federal Reserve Bank of New York, and a visiting scholar at the Ministry of Finance in Japan and the Reserve Bank of Australia.

A Visual Guide To:

The Economics of Money, Banking and Financial Markets

Fourth Edition

Frederic S. Mishkin
Columbia University

ISBN 0-673-52378-0

The fourth edition of Frederic Mishkin's *The Economics of Money, Banking, and Financial Markets* continues to build upon the foundation that has made it a market leader. Rather than giving students a mass of quickly dated facts, Mishkin provides students with simple economic concepts that build a unifying analytic framework for interpretation. This framework enables students to critically evaluate and understand such things as why and how markets are set up, as well as what role money and information play in the economy. Mishkin also provides careful, step-by-step development of models that aid in student learning. To help students apply this knowledge to the everyday world, this text is filled with applications of financial events and policy issues. This fourth edition represents a major revision that now fully prepares students to enter the global financial arena with an increased integration and focus on international events and issues. Mishkin also includes a more integrated approach for understanding financial structure and institutions, making it easier to see the dynamic nature of the financial system and the pressure for innovation. This edition also includes a revised bank management chapter that brings in the consequences of the new rules on capital adequacy, and many new real-world applications.

Chapter 5

PORTFOLIO CHOICE: THE THEORY OF ASSET DEMAND

PREVIEW

Suppose you suddenly struck it rich. Maybe you've just won $25 million in the lottery and your first payment of $600,000 has arrived. Or your dear departed Aunt Thelma has remembered you with a $200,000 bequest. There are a lot of things you might want to do with this windfall: put a down payment on a mansion, buy a Ferrari, or invest in gold coins, land, Treasury bills, or AT&T stock. How will you decide what portfolio of assets you should hold to store your new-found wealth? What criteria should you use to decide among these various stores of wealth? Should you buy only one type of asset or several different types?

This chapter helps answer these questions by developing an economic theory known as the *theory of asset demand* (or the *theory of portfolio choice*). This theory outlines criteria that are important when deciding which assets are worth buying. In addition, it gives us an idea why it is good to diversify and not to put ___ one basket.

UNIFYING ANALYTICAL FRAMEWORK

Rather than memorizing a mass of facts that will soon go out of date, Mishkin provides students with tools for understanding which they can use during and after the course. This framework helps them organize their thinking about money, banking, and financial markets.

...riods (such as three months). However, given the recent breakdown of a stable relationship between monetary aggregates and economic activity, there are doubts as to whether tighter control of the money supply is desirable.

COMPLETE INTEGRATION OF INTERNATIONAL ISSUES

Integrating a more extensive international dimension—both in topic coverage and additional Global Perspective boxes—this fourth edition provides students with a sense of global forces and ramifications by comparing the financial system and monetary policy in the U.S. to those of other nations.

THE CONDUCT OF MONETARY POLICY IN FIVE OTHER COUNTRIES

To understand how well a central bank can control the money supply, it is worth examining how monetary policy has been conducted in other countries besides the United States. Here we look at the conduct of monetary policy in recent decades in five other countries: the United Kingdom, Canada, Germany, Switzerland, and Japan.

United Kindgom

As in the United States, the British introduced monetary targeting in late 1973 in response to mounting concerns about inflation. The Bank of England used a broader monetary target than the Fed did in the United States, $M3$, but did not pursue it seriously, resulting in greater volatility of British monetary aggregates than American ones. After inflation accelerated in the late 1970s, Prime Minister Margaret Thatcher in 1980 introduced the Medium-Term Financial Strategy, which proposed a gradual deceleration of $M3$ growth. Unfortunately, the $M3$ targets ran into problems similar to those of the $M1$ targets in the United States: They were not reliable indicators of the tightness of monetary policy. Subsequent to 1983, arguing that financial innovation was wreaking havoc with the relationship between $M3$ and income, the Bank of England began to deemphasize $M3$ in favor of a narrower monetary aggregate, $M0$ (the monetary base). The target for $M3$ was temporarily suspended in October 1985 and was completely dropped in 1987, leaving $M0$ as the only monetary aggregate targeted. Since 1984, target ranges for the growth in $M0$ have been reduced over time, and actual $M0$ growth has fallen within or close to the target ranges.

Canada

The Canadian experience with monetary policy closely parallels that of the United States. This is not surprising given the strong ties between the two economies and the fact that the value of the Canadian dollar has been closely linked to the U.S dollar.

In response to the rise in inflation in the early 1970s, the Bank of Canada introduced a program of "monetary gradualism," under which $M1$ growth would be controlled within a gradually falling target range. Monetary gradualism was

---

A Global Perspective

Box 1

PROBLEMS OF FINANCIAL INTERMEDIATION IN THE COUNTRIES OF EASTERN EUROPE AND THE FORMER SOVIET UNION

Under the communist regimes, the only financial intermediaries in the countries of Eastern Europe and the Soviet Union were state-owned banks, which lent directly to state enterprises. In the communist system, the banks did not have to worry whether their loans were being used to support productive investments because even if a firm was unprofitable, it would still be allowed to stay in business by being given subsidies from the state. Thus the state-owned banks did not need to acquire expertise to solve the adverse selection and moral hazard problems that prevent financial markets from operating efficiently.

With the collapse of communism and the breakup of the Soviet Union, the state-owned banks and newly created private banks were completely unprepared to promote economic efficiency by lending to borrowers with the most productive investment opportunities. As a result, funds continue to be channeled to unproductive firms, and inefficiency is rampant in these economies. A major objective of economic reform in these countries is to establish a set of financial intermediaries that will perform the essential functions of screening out good from bad credit risks and monitoring borrowers to make sure that they take actions that will make it likely that they can pay off their loans. Not surprisingly, countries in Eastern Europe and the former Soviet Union have been seeking out Western help to set up well-functioning financial intermediaries.

GLOBAL PERSPECTIVE BOXES

To further reinforce the text's international perspective, Mishkin integrates special-interest boxes which compare U.S. financial institutions and structure to those in other countries. These boxes enable students to learn more about global interaction.

Not surprisingly, given the similarity of the economic system here and in Japan, Canada, and the nations of Western Europe, financial regulation in these countries is similar to financial regulation in the United States. The provision of information is improved by requiring corporations issuing securities to report details about assets and liabilities, earnings, and sales of stock and by prohibitions on insider trading. The soundness of intermediaries is ensured by licensing, periodic inspection of financial intermediaries' books, and the provision of deposit insurance (although its coverage is smaller and its existence is often purposely not advertised).

The major differences between financial regulation in the United States and abroad relate to bank regulation. Only the United States currently prevents a national banking system by restricting branches to certain regions. Indeed, this difference between the United States and Europe will widen because new banking directives for the European Union (EU), formerly the European Community (EC), will enable a bank licensed in one EU country to offer a full range of services in all other EEC countries. U.S. banks are also the most restricted in the range of financial services they may provide and the assets they may hold. Banks abroad frequently hold shares in commercial firms; in

REAL-WORLD APPLICATIONS

The text offers more than twenty-five different in-depth applications based on today's pressing issues to help students understand and apply financial and economic theories to familiar, real-world events.

APPLICATION

EFFECTS OF THE CLINTON TAX INCREASE ON BOND INTEREST RATES

As part of the Clinton administration's 1993 deficit reduction plan, the top income tax bracket was raised from 31% to 40% and the corporate income tax rate was raised from 34% to 35%. What was the effect of this income tax increase on interest rates in the municipal bond market relative to those in the Treasury bond market?

The supply and demand analysis in Figure 3 provides the answer. The increased income tax rate for rich people and corporations means that the tax-free status of municipal bonds raises their after-tax expected return relative to that on Treasury bonds because the interest on Treasury bonds is now taxed at a higher rate. Because municipal bonds now become more desirable, their demand increases, shifting the demand curve to the right as in Figure 3, which raises their price and lowers their interest rate. Conversely, the higher income tax rates make Treasury bonds less desirable; that shifts their demand curve to the left, lowers their price, and raises their interest rates, as indicated in Figure 3.

Our analysis thus shows that the Clinton tax increase lowered the interest rates on municipal bonds relative to interest rates on Treasury bonds.

APPLICATION

DID THE CAPITAL CRUNCH CAUSE A CREDIT CRUNCH IN THE EARLY 1990'S?

During the 1990–1991 recession and the year following, there occurred a slow-down in the growth of credit that was unprecedented in the post–World War II era. Many economists and politicians have claimed that there was a "credit crunch" during this period in which credit was hard to get, and as a result, the performance of the economy in 1990–1992 was very weak. Was the slowdown in credit growth a manifestation of a credit crunch, and if so, what caused it?

Our analysis of how a bank manages bank capital suggests that a credit crunch was likely to have occurred in 1990–1992 and that it was caused at least in part by the so-called capital crunch in which shortfalls of bank capital led to slower credit growth.

The period of the late 1980s saw a boom and then a major bust in the real estate market that led to huge losses for banks on their real estate loans. As our example on how bank capital helps prevent bank failures demonstrates, the loan losses caused a substantial fall in the amount of bank capital. At the same time, regulators were raising capital requirements (a subject discussed in Chapter 13). The resulting capital shortfalls meant that banks had either to raise new capital or to restrict their asset growth by cutting back on lending. Because of the weak economy at the time, raising new capital was extremely difficult for banks, so they chose the latter course. Banks did restrict their lending, and borrowers found it harder to obtain loans, leading to complaints by banks and their customers that the resulting credit crunch was creating a drag on the economy. Not surprisingly, these complaints encouraged politicians, including the Clinton administration, to call for policies to encourage bank

APPLICATION

WHY ARE EXCHANGE RATES SO VOLATILE?

The high volatility of foreign exchange rates surprises many people. Thirty or so years ago, economists generally believed that allowing exchange rates to be determined in the free market would not lead to large fluctuations in their values. Recent experience has proved them wrong. If we return to Figure 1, we see that exchange rates over the 1973–1993 period have been very volatile.

The asset market approach to exchange rate determination that we have outlined here gives a straightforward explanation of volatile exchange rates. Because expected appreciation of the domestic currency affects the expected return on foreign deposits, expectations about the price level, inflation, tariffs and quotas, productivity, import demand, export demand, and the money supply play important roles in determining the exchange rate. When expectations about any of these variables change, our model indicates that there will be an immediate effect on the expected return on foreign deposits and therefore on the exchange rate. Since expectations on all these variables change with just about every bit of news that appears, it is not surprising that the exchange rate is volatile. In addition, we have seen that our exchange rate analysis produces exchange rate overshooting when the money supply increases. Exchange rate overshooting is an additional reason for the high volatility of exchange rates.

Because earlier models of exchange rate behavior focused on goods markets rather than asset markets, they did not emphasize changing expectations as a source of exchange rate movements, and so these earlier models could not predict substantial fluctuations in exchange rates. The failure of earlier models to explain volatility is one reason why they are no longer so popular. The more modern approach developed here emphasizes that the foreign exchange market is like any other asset market in which expectations of the future matter. The foreign exchange market, like other asset markets such as the stock market, displays substantial price volatility, and foreign exchange rates are notoriously hard to forecast (see Box 1).

FOLLOWING THE FINANCIAL NEWS

Bond Prices and Interest Rates

Bond prices and interest rates are published daily. In the *Wall Street Journal* they can be found in the "NYSE/AMEX Bonds" and "Treasury/Agency Issues" section of the paper. Three basic formats for quoting bond prices and yields are illustrated below.

(a) Treasury bonds and notes

(b) Treasury bills

(c) New York Stock Exchange bonds

Wall Street Journal, March 2, 1994, pp. C16 and C17.

Chapter 8   The Foreign Exchange Market

APPLICATION   READING THE *WALL STREET JOURNAL*:

THE "FOREIGN EXCHANGE" COLUMN

Now that we have an understanding of how exchange rates are determined, we can use our analysis to understand discussions about developments in the foreign exchange market reported in the financial press.

The column focuses on U.S monetary and trade policy as the source of the decline in the dollar in the foreign exchange markets.

The column discusses the surprise resignation of David Mullins, the vice chairman of the Federal Reserve, and the departure of Federal Reserve Governor Wayne Angell, both of whom are considered avid inflation fighters, as important news events to the foreign exchange markets. The departure of these two figures from the Federal Reserve leads to concerns that President Clinton's replacement for these Fed officials might be less hawkish on inflation, leading to a more inflationary monetary policy in the future.

Our analysis of the foreign exchange market explains why these developments result in a decline in the dollar. The higher expected U.S. inflation leads to a larger expected depreciation of the dollar because it raises the expected future price level in the United States relative to foreign countries. The larger expected depreciation of the dollar implies a higher expected appreciation of foreign currencies, thereby increasing the expected return on foreign deposits, which shifts the RET^F schedule to the right as in Figure 4, and the value of the dollar falls.

The column also indicates that the departure of the two Fed officials makes it more likely that U.S. interest rates will be lower in the future. Our analysis indicates that lower U.S. interest rates in the future are another reason for the fall in the dollar. The lower U.S. interest rates will shift the RET^D schedule to the left and will thereby cause the exchange rate

FOREIGN EXCHANGE

Dollar Falls Against Major Currencies
On Concern Over U.S. Rates and Trade

By GARY ROSENBERGER
Special to THE WALL STREET JOURNAL
NEW YORK — The dollar tumbled to new lows for this year against the yen on fresh concerns over the future direction of U.S. interest rates and over stalled trade negotiations with Japan.

The dollar fell heavily against most other major currencies, but recovered some lost ground on promising new U.S. economic data and a spate of short-covering and bargain-hunting.

Late in New York, the dollar was quoted at 1.7220 marks, down from 1.7345 marks late Monday in New York. The U.S. currency also was changing hands at 107.70 yen, down from 108.70 yen. Sterling was trading at $1.5010, down from $1.5060.

About midday Wednesday in Tokyo, the dollar was trading at 108.20 yen and at 1.7336 marks.

The surprise resignation of David Mullins, vice chairman of the Federal Reserve, yesterday roused speculation that U.S. interest rates, long thought to be headed for higher ground, will stay flat.

The departure of Mullins, considered an anti-inflation hawk, opens the way for President Clinton to appoint an inflation dove as his successor.

The move also countered somewhat warnings on Monday by Alan Greenspan, the Fed's chairman, that short-term U.S. rates will move higher eventually in order to prevent any return of inflation.

Mr. Mullins, who will resign Feb. 14, said he won't attend the meeting of the Federal Open Market Committee tomorrow and Friday. Traders said that may diminish the likelihood of a panel vote in favor of higher rates at this week's meeting.

In addition, Mr. Mullins' leave-taking coincides with the departure Feb. 10 of Federal Reserve Governor Wayne Angell, a far more resolute anti-inflation hawk.

"You have two people that historically have been inflation fighters leaving at the same time," said Alan Leslie, chief economist for Discount Corp. of New York.

"They were both appointed by more conservative administrations, and expectations are that Clinton will appoint more growth-oriented people as opposed to anti-inflation people—which means lower interest rates and a lower dollar," he said.

The Mullins announcement brought the dollar to its intraday low of 107.55 yen, the lowest level since Dec. 8.

Traders also said the slide was pushed along by concerns that U.S. trade representative Mickey Kantor's trip to Japan to further trade negotiations will be too little, too late.

"The dollar-yen is reacting to Mickey Kantor," said Carl Porcheski, a trader at Chemical Bank. "There are worries that nothing will come of his visit."

Indeed, Japan is under the gun to produce a viable trade agreement prior to Prime Minister Morihiro Hosokawa's meeting with Mr. Clinton Feb. 11, and traders fear that lack of an agreement will prompt more U.S. pressure for a strong yen.

Meanwhile, the dollar made a partial recovery from its fall against the mark on a combination of short-covering and promising U.S. economic data.

The National Association of Purchasing Management's January report showed its overall index of business activity rose to 57.7% from 57.1% in December. Economists had predicted a decline to 56%.

Shifts in the Expected-Return Schedule for Domestic Deposits

Since the expected return on domestic (dollar) deposits is just the interest rate on these deposits $i^\$$, this interest rate is the only factor that shifts the schedule for the expected return on dollar deposits.

Changes in the Domestic Interest Rate $i^\$$ A rise in $i^\$$ raises the expected return on dollar deposits, shifts the $RET^\$$ schedule to the right, and leads to a rise in the exchange rate, as is shown in Figure 5. Another way of seeing this is to recognize that a rise in $i^\$$, which raises the expected return on dollar deposits, creates an excess demand for dollar deposits at the original equilibrium exchange rate, and the resulting purchases of dollar deposits cause an appreciation of the dollar. *A rise in the domestic interest rate $i^\$$ shifts the $RET^\$$ schedule to the right and causes an appreciation of the domestic currency; a fall in $i^\$$ shifts the $RET^\$$ schedule to the left and causes a depreciation of the domestic currency.*

FIGURE 5
Shifts in the Expected Return on Domestic Deposits Schedule ($RET^\$$)
An increase in the expected return on dollar deposits ($i^\$$) shifts the expected return on domestic (dollar) deposits.

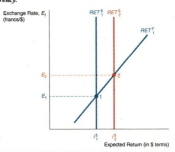

STUDY GUIDE

As a study aid, the factors that shift the RET^F and $RET^\$$ schedules and lead to changes in the current exchange rate E_t are listed in Table 2. The table shows what happens to the exchange rate when there is an increase in each of these variables, holding everything else constant. To give yourself practice, see if you can work out what happens to the RET^F and $RET^\$$ schedules and to the exchange rate if each of these factors falls rather than rises. Check your answers by seeing if you get the opposite change in the exchange rate to those indicated in Table 2.

Just as prices rise and fall, so do interest rates fluctuate. In fact, interest rate fluctuations have been greater since the 1960s than in any other period in U.S. history. For example, the interest rate on long-term U.S. Treasury bonds was about 4% in 1963, rose to close to 15% in 1981, and fell below 6% for a short time in 1993. In the preceding 30-year period, from 1933 to 1963, the rate fluctuated between 2% and 5%.

What do these fluctuations mean, and what causes them? In addition to other factors, money plays an important role in interest-rate fluctuations. Figure 4 shows the changes in the interest rate on long-term Treasury bonds and the rate of money growth. As the money growth rate rose in the 1960s and 1970s, the long-term bond rate rose with it. However, the relationship between money growth and interest rates has been less clear-cut in the 1980s and 1990s. We analyze the relationship between money and interest rates when we examine the behavior of interest rates.

FIGURE 4
Money Growth (M2 Annual Rate) and Interest Rates (Long-term U.S. Treasury Bonds):
1951–1993 Sources: Feeeral Reserve Bulletin and Citibase databank

Conduct of Monetary Policy

Because money can affect many economic variables that are important to the well-being of our economy, politicians and policymakers in the federal government care about the conduct of **monetary policy,** the management of money and interest rates. The organization responsible for the conduct of monetary policy in the United States is the central bank, the **Federal Reserve System** (also called the **Fed**). In later chapters we study how the Federal Reserve System can affect the quantity of money in the economy and then look at how monetary

SUMMARY TABLES

Summary Tables highlight important relationships within a chapter, providing students with useful study aids for reviewing material.

SUMMARY

TABLE 2 Factors That Shift the RET^F and RET^S Schedules and Affect the Exchange Rate

Factor	Change in Factor		Response of Exchange Rate, E_t
Domestic interest rate, i^S	↑	↑	
Foreign interest rate, i^F	↑	↓	
Expected domestic price level*	↑	↓	
Expected tariffs and quotas*	↑	↑	
Expected import demand	↑	↓	
Expected export demand	↑	↑	
Expected productivity*	↑	↑	

Note: Only increases (↑) in the factors are shown; the effects of decreases in the variables on the exchange rate are the opposite of those indicated in the "Response" column.

State and local governments and other government agencies also issue bonds to finance their expenditures, and this can also affect the supply of bonds. We will see in later chapters that the conduct of monetary policy involves the purchase and sale of bonds, which in turn influences the supply of bonds.

Changes in the Equilibrium Interest Rate

We now can use our knowledge of how supply and demand curves shift to analyze how the equilibrium interest rate can change. The best way to do this is to pursue several applications that are particularly relevant to our understanding of how monetary policy affects interest rates.

STUDY GUIDE

Supply and demand analysis for the bond market is best learned by practicing applications. When there is an application in the text and we look at how the interest rate changes because some economic variable increases, see if you can draw the appropriate shifts in the supply and demand curves when this same economic variable decreases. While you are practicing applications, keep two things in mind:

1. When you examine the effect of a variable change, remember that we are assuming that all other variables are unchanged; that is, we are making use of the *ceteris paribus* assumption.
2. Remember that the interest rate is negatively related to the bond price, so when the equilibrium bond price rises, the equilibrium interest rate falls. Conversely, if the equilibrium bond price moves downward, the equilibrium interest rate rises.

Changes in Expected Inflation: The Fisher Effect

We have already done most of the work to evaluate how a change in expected inflation affects the nominal interest rate in that we have already analyzed how a change in expected inflation shifts the supply and demand curves. Figure 5 shows the effect on the equilibrium interest rate of an increase in expected inflation.

Suppose that expected inflation is initially 5% and the initial supply and demand curves B^s_1 and B^d_1 intersect at point 1, where the equilibrium bond price is P_1 and the equilibrium interest rate is i_1. If expected inflation rises to 10%, the expected return on bonds relative to real assets falls for any given bond price and interest rate. As a result, the demand for bonds falls, and the demand curve shifts to the left from B^d_1 to B^d_2. The rise in expected infla-

IN-TEXT STUDY GUIDES

Sprinkled generously throughout the book, these in-text Study Guides provide students with hints on how to think about or approach a topic as they work.

QUESTIONS AND PROBLEMS

Four-hundred and fifty chapter-ending problems let students test and apply the economic concepts they have learned.

SUMMARY

1. The theory of asset demand tells us that the quantity demanded of an asset is (a) positively related to wealth, (b) positively related to the expected return on the asset relative to alternative assets, (c) negatively related to the riskiness of the asset relative to alternative assets, and (d) positively related to the liquidity of the asset relative to alternative assets.
2. Diversification (the holding of more than one asset) benefits investors because it reduces the risk they face, and the benefits are greater the less returns on securities move together.
3. An asset's risk is made up of two components: systematic risk, which cannot be diversified away, and nonsystematic risk, which can. An asset's systematic risk is measured by beta, and the higher an asset's beta and hence its systematic risk, the less desirable the asset.
4. Both the capital asset pricing model and arbitrage pricing theory provide an explanation for an asset's risk premium, the difference between the asset's expected return and the risk-free interest rate. The capital asset pricing model indicates that an asset's risk premium is positively related to the asset's beta, the sensitivity to the market return; arbitrage pricing theory indicates that an asset's risk premium is positively related to the asset's sensitivity to many factors that represent sources of nondiversifiable risk in the economy.

KEY TERMS

assets
wealth
expected return
risk
liquidity
wealth elasticity of demand
necessity
luxury
theory of asset demand
diversification
systematic risk
nonsystematic risk
beta

QUESTIONS AND PROBLEMS

1. In terms of the theory of asset demand, explain why you would be more or less willing to buy a share of Polaroid stock in the following situations:
   Your wealth falls.
   You expect it to appreciate in value.
   The bond market becomes more liquid.
   You expect gold to appreciate in value.
   Prices in the bond market become more volatile.
2. In terms of the theory of asset demand, explain why you would be more or less willing to buy a house under the following circumstances:
   You just inherited $100,000.
   Real estate commissions fall from 6% of the sales price to 4% of the sales price.
   You expect Polaroid stock to double in value next year.
   Prices in the stock market become more volatile.
   You expect housing prices to fall.
3. In terms of the theory of asset demand, explain why you would be more or less willing to buy gold under the following circumstances:
   Gold again becomes acceptable as a medium of exchange.
   Prices in the gold market become more volatile.
   You expect inflation to rise, and gold prices tend to move with the aggregate price level.
   You expect interest rates to rise.
4. In terms of the theory of asset demand, explain why you would be more or less willing to buy AT&T bonds under the following circumstances:

---

3. Check in a newspaper the exchange rates for the foreign currencies listed in the "Following the Financial News" box. Which of these currencies have appreciated and which have depreciated since March 2, 1994?
4. If the French price level rises by 5% relative to the price level in the United States, what does the theory of purchasing power parity predict will happen to the value of the French franc in terms of dollars?

5. If the demand for a country's exports falls at the same time that tariffs on imports are raised, will the country's currency tend to appreciate or depreciate in the long run?
6. In the mid-to-late 1970s, the yen appreciated relative to the dollar even though Japan's inflation rate was higher than America's. How can this be explained by an improvement in the productivity of Japanese industry relative to American indus-

Using Economic Analysis to Predict the Future

Answer the remaining questions by drawing the appropriate exchange market diagrams.
7. The president of the United States announces that he will reduce inflation with a new anti-inflation program. If the public believes him, predict what will happen to the U.S. exchange rate.
8. If the British central bank prints money to reduce unemployment, what will happen to the value of the pound in the short run and the long run?
9. If the French government unexpectedly announces that it will be imposing higher tariffs and quotas on foreign goods one year from now, what will happen to the value of the franc today?
10. If nominal interest rates in America rise but real interest rates fall, predict what will happen to the U.S. exchange rate.
11. If American auto companies make a breakthrough in automobile technology and are able to produce a car that gets 60 miles to the gallon, what will happen to the U.S. exchange rate?
12. If Americans go on a spending spree and buy twice as much French perfume, Japanese TVs, English sweaters, Swiss watches, and Italian wine, what will happen to the value of the U.S. dollar?
13. If expected inflation drops in Europe so that interest rates fall there, predict what will happen to the U.S. exchange rate.
14. If the German central bank decides to contract the money supply in order to fight inflation, what will happen to the value of the U.S. dollar?
15. If there is a strike in France, making it harder to buy French goods, what will happen to the value of the franc?

"USING ECONOMIC ANALYSIS TO PREDICT THE FUTURE"

These unique chapter-ending problems, half of which are answered at the back of the book, ask students to evaluate chapter material and apply concepts to future real-world issues.

PART I

INTRODUCTION

Chapter 1

WHY STUDY MONEY, BANKING, AND FINANCIAL MARKETS?

PREVIEW On the evening news you have just heard that the money supply has declined by $4 billion. What effect might this have on the interest rate of an automobile loan when you finance your purchase of a sleek new sports car? Does it mean that a house will be more or less affordable in the future? Will it make it easier or harder for you to get a job next year?

This book provides answers to these questions by exploring the role of money in the economy and by examining how financial institutions (banks, insurance companies, mutual funds, and so on) and financial markets (such as those for bonds, stocks, and foreign exchange) work. Financial markets and institutions not only affect your everyday life but also involve huge flows of funds (trillions of dollars) throughout our economy, which in turn affect business profits, the production of goods and services, and even the economic well-being of countries other than the United States. What happens to money, financial institutions, and financial markets is of great concern to our politicians and can even have a major impact on our elections. The study of money, banking, and financial markets will reward you with an understanding of many exciting issues. In this chapter we outline what these issues are and why they are worth studying.

WHY STUDY MONEY?

Money, or the **money supply,** is defined as anything that is generally accepted in payment for goods or services or in the repayment of debts. Money is linked to changes in economic variables that affect all of us and are important to the health of the economy.

Money and Business Cycles

In 1981–1982, total production of goods and services (called **aggregate output**) in the economy fell, the number of people out of work rose to more than 10 million (over 10% of the labor force), and more than 25,000 businesses failed. After 1982, the economy began to expand rapidly, and by 1989, the **unemployment rate** (the percentage of the available labor force unemployed) had declined from over 10% to 5%. In 1990, the eight-year expansion came to an end, and the economy began to decline again, with unemployment rising above the 7% level. Although the economy bottomed out in 1991, the subsequent recovery was a sluggish one.

Why did the economy contract in 1981–1982, boom thereafter, and begin to contract again in 1990? Evidence suggests that money plays an important role in generating **business cycles,** the upward and downward movement of aggregate output produced in the economy. Business cycles affect all of us in immediate and important ways. When output is rising, for example, it is easier to find a good job; when output is falling, finding a good job might be difficult. Figure 1 shows the movements of the rate of money growth over the 1950–1993 period, with the shaded areas representing **recessions,** periods when aggregate output is declining. What we see is that the rate of money growth has declined before every recession. Indeed, every recession in the twentieth century has been preceded by a decline in the rate of money growth, indicating that changes in

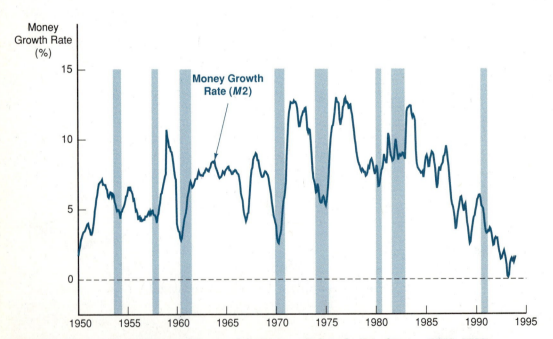

FIGURE 1   Money Growth (*M*2 Annual Rate) and the Business Cycle in the United States, 1950–1993
Shaded areas represent recessions. *Sources*: Federal Reserve *Bulletin;* Citibase databank.

money might also be a driving force behind business cycle fluctuations. However, not every decline in the rate of money growth is followed by a recession.

We explore how money might affect aggregate output when we study **monetary theory,** the theory that relates changes in the quantity of money to changes in aggregate economic activity and the price level.

Money and Inflation

Thirty years ago, the $7 movie you might have seen last week would have set you back only a dollar or two. In fact, for $7 you could probably have had dinner, seen the movie, and bought yourself a big bucket of hot buttered popcorn. As seen in Figure 2, which illustrates the movement of average prices in the U.S. economy from 1950 to 1993, the prices of most items are quite a bit higher now than they were then. The average price of goods and services in an economy is called the **aggregate price level** or, more simply, the *price level* (a more precise definition is found in the appendix to this chapter). From 1950 to 1993, the price level has more than quintupled. **Inflation,** a continual increase in the price level, affects individuals, businesses, and the government. Inflation is generally regarded as an important problem to be solved and has often been a primary concern of politicians and policymakers. To solve the inflation problem, we need to know something about its causes.

What explains inflation? One clue to answering this question is found in Figure 2, which plots the money supply and the price level. As we can see, the price level and the money supply generally move closely together. These data seem to indicate that a continuing increase in the money supply might be an important factor in causing the continuing increase in the price level that we call inflation.

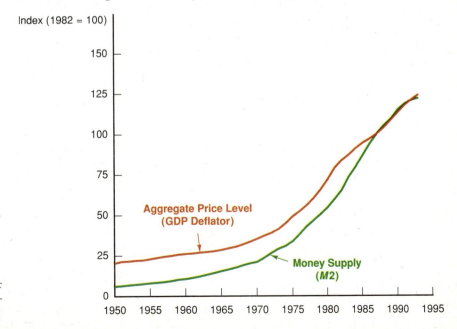

FIGURE 2
Aggregate Price Level and the Money Supply in the United States, 1950–1993
Source: Economic Report of the President.

Index (1982 = 100)

Aggregate Price Level (GDP Deflator)

Money Supply (*M2*)

Further evidence that inflation may be tied to continuing increases in the money supply is found in Figure 3. For a number of countries, it plots the average **inflation rate** (the rate of change of the price level, usually measured as a percentage change per year) over the ten-year period 1983–1993 against the average rate of money growth over the same period.[1] As you can see, there is a positive association between inflation and the growth rate of the money supply: The countries with the highest inflation rates are also the ones with the highest money growth rates. Argentina, for example, has experienced very high inflation, and its rate of money growth was high. By contrast, Switzerland and Germany have had very low inflation rates over the same period, and their rates of money growth have been low.

Such evidence led Milton Friedman, a Nobel laureate in economics, to make the famous statement "Inflation is always and everywhere a monetary phenomenon."[2] This statement suggests a good reason for studying money because its rate of growth may be a driving force behind inflation. We look at money's role in creating inflation by studying the relationship between changes in the quantity of money and changes in the price level.

Money and Interest Rates

An **interest rate** is the cost of borrowing or the price paid for the rental of funds (usually expressed as a percentage of the rental of $100 per year). There are many interest rates in the economy—mortgage interest rates, car loan rates, and interest rates on many different types of bonds. Interest rates are important on a number of levels. On a personal level, high interest rates could deter you from buying a house or a car because the cost of financing it would be high. Conversely, high interest rates could encourage you to save because you can earn more interest income by putting aside some of your earnings as savings.

On a more general level, interest rates have an impact on the overall health of the economy because they affect not only consumers' willingness to spend or save but also businesses' investment decisions. High interest rates, for example, may cause a corporation to postpone building a new plant that would ensure more jobs.

Just as prices rise and fall, so do interest rates fluctuate. In fact, interest rate fluctuations have been greater since the 1960s than in any other period in U.S. history. For example, the interest rate on long-term U.S. Treasury bonds was about 4% in 1963, rose to close to 15% in 1981, and fell below 6% for a short time in 1993. In the preceding 30-year period, from 1933 to 1963, the rate fluctuated between 2% and 5%.

---

[1] If the aggregate price level at time t is denoted by P_t, the inflation rate from time $t-1$ to t, denoted as π_t, is defined as

$$\pi_t = \frac{P_t - P_{t-1}}{P_{t-1}}$$

[2] Milton Friedman, *Dollars and Deficits* (Englewood Cliffs, N.J.: Prentice Hall, 1968), p. 39.

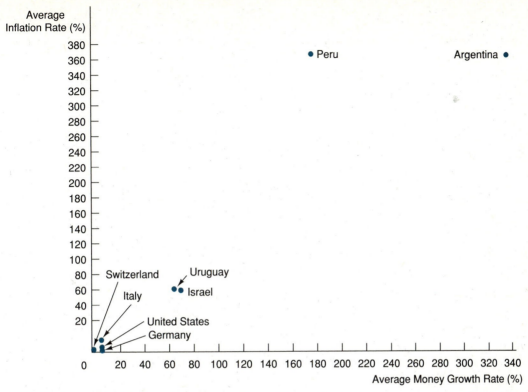

FIGURE 3 Average Inflation Rate Versus Average Rate of Money Growth for Selected Countries, 1983–1993
Source: International Financial Statistics.

What do these fluctuations mean, and what causes them? In addition to other factors, money plays an important role in interest-rate fluctuations. Figure 4 shows the changes in the interest rate on long-term Treasury bonds and the rate of money growth. As the money growth rate rose in the 1960s and 1970s, the long-term bond rate rose with it. However, the relationship between money growth and interest rates has been less clear-cut in the 1980s and 1990s. We analyze the relationship between money and interest rates when we examine the behavior of interest rates.

Conduct of Monetary Policy

Because money can affect many economic variables that are important to the well-being of our economy, politicians and policymakers in the federal government care about the conduct of **monetary policy,** the management of money and interest rates. The organization responsible for the conduct of monetary policy in the United States is the central bank, the **Federal Reserve System** (also called the **Fed**). In later chapters we study how the Federal Reserve System can

FIGURE 4   Money Growth (*M*2 Annual Rate) and Interest Rates (Long-Term U.S. Treasury Bonds), 1950 –1993
Sources: Federal Reserve *Bulletin;* Citibase databank.

affect the quantity of money in the economy and then look at how monetary policy is actually conducted.

Budget Deficits and Monetary Policy

The **budget deficit** is the excess of government expenditures over tax revenues for a particular time period, typically a year, a deficit that the government must finance by borrowing. As Figure 5 shows, the budget deficit, relative to the size of our economy, peaked in 1983 at 6% of national output (as calculated by the gross domestic product measure of aggregate output described in the appendix to this chapter). Since then, the budget deficit at first declined to less than 3% of GDP by 1989 but had risen again to over the 5% level four years later. Budget deficits have been the subject of legislation and bitter battles between the president and Congress in recent years. Indeed, the vote on President Clinton's 1993 budget deficit reduction package was so close in the Senate that the vice president's tiebreaking vote was needed to pass the legislation.

You may have seen or heard statements in newspapers or on TV that such deficits are undesirable because they will ultimately lead to inflation. We explore the accuracy of such statements by first examining the impact of financing these deficits on the conduct of monetary policy and then by exploring why deficits might lead to a higher rate of money growth, a higher rate of inflation, and higher interest rates.

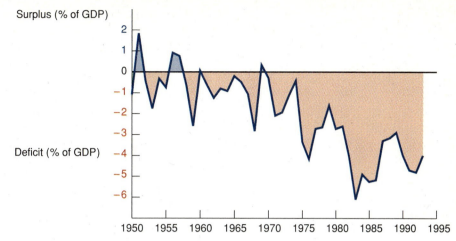

FIGURE 5
Government Budget
Surplus (+) or
Deficit (−) as a
Percentage of
Gross Domestic
Product,
1950–1993
Source: Economic
Report of the Pres-
ident.

WHY STUDY BANKING?

The second major topic of this book is the business of banking. **Banks** are financial institutions that accept money deposits and make loans. Included under the term *banks* are firms such as commercial banks, savings and loan associations, mutual savings banks, and credit unions. The banking industry has been much in the news of late. Failures of commercial banks have been running at the highest rates since the Great Depression, and the savings and loan industry has required a massive bailout, costing taxpayers over $150 billion. Banks are important to our study of money and the economy for three reasons:

1. They provide a channel for linking people who want to save with those who want to invest.
2. They play an important role in determining the money supply and in transmitting the effects of monetary policy to the economy.
3. They have been a source of the rapid financial innovation that is expanding the ways in which we can invest our savings.

Financial Intermediation

If you wanted to make a loan to IBM or General Motors, you would not go directly to the president of the company and offer a loan. Instead, you would lend your money to such companies indirectly through **financial intermediaries,** institutions such as commercial banks, savings and loan associations, mutual savings banks, credit unions, insurance companies, mutual funds, pension funds, and finance companies that borrow funds from people who have saved and in turn make loans to others.

Banks are the financial intermediaries that the average person interacts with most frequently. A person who needs a loan to buy a house or a car usually obtains it from a local bank. Most Americans keep a large proportion of their financial wealth in banks in the form of checking accounts, savings accounts, or other types of bank deposits.

Financial intermediation is an important activity in the economy because it allows funds to be channeled from people who might otherwise not put them to productive use to people who will. In this way, financial intermediaries help promote a more efficient and dynamic economy.

Because banks are the largest financial intermediaries in our economy, they deserve careful study. We examine how they manage their assets and liabilities to make profits, how they are regulated by the government, and why the banking industry has recently run into problems. In addition, we discuss the operation and regulation of other financial intermediaries such as insurance companies, pension funds, and mutual funds.

Banking and the Money Supply

Banks play a critical role in the creation of money, not by printing $20 bills but by lending; a bank's loans create checking account deposits, a large component of the money supply. We study how banks decide to make loans in order to understand how the money supply is determined and why conducting monetary policy may be a complicated task.

Financial Innovation

Until around 1970, people without a substantial amount of wealth were unable to obtain high interest rates on their savings. If you were an average wage earner, your only choice was to put your savings in a savings account that earned a low interest rate. Nowadays, small savers have a larger number of options. For example, they can put their funds in negotiable order of withdrawal (NOW) accounts and money market mutual funds, both of which allow them to write checks on their accounts and yet earn higher rates of interest. To see why these options have been developed, we study why and how financial innovation takes place.

We also study financial innovation because it shows us how creative thinking on the part of financial institutions can lead to higher profits. By seeing how and why financial institutions have been creative in the past, we obtain a better grasp of how they may be creative in the future. This knowledge provides us with useful clues about how the financial system may change over time.

The rapid pace of financial innovation has meant that many regulations imposed on the banking system by government have become obsolete or, even worse, have been damaging the health of the financial system. Rapid changes in the regulatory environment have accompanied rapid financial innovation. Understanding the how and why of regulations allows us to understand how banks may evolve in the future and keeps our knowledge about banks and their role in determining the money supply from becoming obsolete.

WHY STUDY FINANCIAL MARKETS?

Financial markets are markets in which funds are transferred from people who have an excess of available funds to people who have a shortage. Financial markets such as the bond and stock markets are important in channeling funds from people who do not have a productive use for them to those who do, resulting in greater economic efficiency. Activities in financial markets also have direct effects on personal wealth and on the behavior of businesses.

Bond Market

A **security** (also called a *financial instrument*) is a claim on the issuer's future income or **assets** (any financial claim or piece of property that is subject to ownership), and a **bond** is a debt security that promises to make payments periodically for a specified period of time.[3] The bond market is especially important to economic activity because it enables corporations or governments to borrow to finance their activities and because it is where interest rates are determined.

Because different interest rates have a tendency to move in unison, economists frequently lump interest rates together and refer to "the" interest rate. As Figure 6 shows, however, interest rates on several types of bonds can differ substantially. The interest rate on three-month Treasury bills, for example, fluctuates more than the other interest rates and is lower, on average. The interest rate on Baa (medium-quality) corporate bonds is higher, on average, than the other interest rates, and the spread between it and the other rates became larger in the 1970s.

We study how the common movements in these interest rates come about and why interest rates on different bonds vary.

Stock Market

The stock market, in which claims on the earnings of corporations (shares of stock) are traded, is the most widely followed financial market in America (that's why it is often called simply "the market"). A big swing in the prices of shares in the stock market is always a big story on the evening news. People often express

---

[3]The definition of *bond* used throughout this book is the broad one in common use by academics, which covers short- as well as long-term debt instruments. However, some practitioners in financial markets use the word *bond* only to describe specific long-term debt instruments such as corporate bonds or U.S. Treasury bonds.

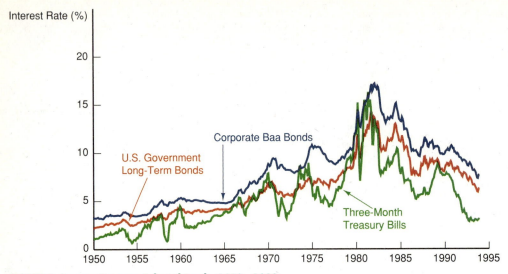

FIGURE 6 Interest Rates on Selected Bonds, 1950–1993
Sources: Federal Reserve *Bulletin;* Citibase databank.

their opinion on where the market is heading and will frequently tell you about their latest "big killing" (although you seldom hear about their latest "big loss"!). The attention that the market receives can probably be best explained by one simple fact: It is a place where people can get rich quickly.

As Figure 7 indicates, stock prices have been extremely volatile. They climbed steadily in the 1950s, reached a peak in 1966, then fluctuated up and down until 1973, when they fell sharply. Stock prices had recovered sub- stantially by the early 1980s when a major stock market boom began, send- ing the Dow Jones Industrial Average (DJIA) to a peak of 2722 on August 25, 1987. After a 17% decline over the next month and a half, the stock market experienced the worst one-day drop in its entire history on "Black Monday," October 19, 1987, when the DJIA fell by more than 500 points, a 22% decline. The stock market then recovered, climbing almost to the 4000 level by early 1994. These considerable fluctuations in stock prices affect the size of people's wealth and as a result may affect their willingness to spend.

The stock market is also an important factor in business investment deci- sions because the price of shares affects the amount of funds that can be raised by selling newly issued stock to finance investment spending. A higher price for a firm's shares means that it can raise a larger amount of funds, which can be used to buy production facilities and equipment.

We explore how stock prices behave and respond to information in the mar- ketplace. We will also see that monetary policy can affect stock prices, which can in turn have an effect on the business cycle.

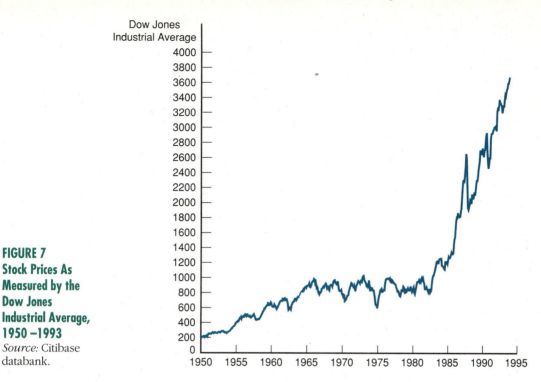

FIGURE 7
Stock Prices As Measured by the Dow Jones Industrial Average, 1950–1993
Source: Citibase databank.

Foreign Exchange Market

The price of one country's currency in terms of another's is called the **foreign exchange rate.** Figure 8 shows the exchange rate for the U.S. dollar from 1970 to 1993 (measured as the value of the American dollar in terms of a basket of foreign currencies). The fluctuations in prices in this market have also been substantial: The dollar weakened considerably from 1971 to 1973, rose slightly in value until 1976, and then reached a low point in the 1978–1980 period. From 1980 to early 1985, the dollar dramatically appreciated in value, but since then it has fallen substantially.

What have these fluctuations in the exchange rate meant to the American public and businesses? A change in the exchange rate has a direct effect on American consumers because it affects the cost of foreign goods. In 1985, when the British currency, the pound sterling, cost approximately $1.30, £100 of British goods (say, Shetland sweaters) would cost $130. When a weaker dollar raised the cost of a pound to $1.50 in 1994, the same £100 of Shetland sweaters cost $150. Thus a weaker dollar leads to more expensive foreign goods, makes vacationing abroad more expensive, and raises the cost of indulging your yen for imported delicacies. When the value of the dollar drops, Americans will decrease their purchases of foreign goods and increase their consumption of domestic goods (such as travel in the United States or American-made sweaters).

FIGURE 8 Exchange Rate of the U.S. Dollar, 1970 – 1993
Sources: Federal Reserve *Bulletin;* Citibase databank.

Conversely, a strong dollar means that U.S. goods exported abroad will cost more in foreign countries, and hence foreigners will buy fewer of them. Exports of steel, for example, declined sharply when the dollar strengthened in the 1980–1985 period. A strong dollar benefited American consumers by making foreign goods cheaper but hurt American businesses and eliminated some jobs by cutting both domestic and foreign sales of their products. The recent weakness of the dollar has had the opposite effect: It has made foreign goods more expensive but has made American businesses more competitive. Fluctuations in the foreign exchange markets have major consequences for the American economy.

We study how exchange rates are determined in the foreign exchange market in which dollars are bought and sold for foreign currencies. Finally, we will see how the foreign exchange rate can affect the money supply in the United States and how U.S. monetary policy can affect the foreign exchange rate.

CONCLUDING REMARKS

The field of money, banking, and financial markets is an exciting one. We not only discuss issues that directly affect your life—interest rates on loans and on your savings and how monetary policy may affect your job prospects and the price of goods in the future—but also gain a clearer understanding of economic phenomena you frequently hear about in the news media. Our study of money, banking, and financial markets will also introduce you to many of the controversies about the conduct of economic policy that are currently the subject of hot debate in the political arena.

SUMMARY

1. Money appears to be a major influence on inflation, business cycles, and interest rates. Because these economic variables are so important to the health of the economy, we need to understand how monetary policy is and should be conducted. We also need to study government budget deficits because they can be an influential factor in the conduct of monetary policy.

2. Banks are the most important of a number of financial intermediaries that channel funds from people who might not put them to productive use to people who can do so. Banks also play a critical role in the creation of money and have been important in the rapid pace of recent financial innovation.

3. Activities in financial markets have direct effects on individuals' wealth, the behavior of businesses, and the efficiency of our economy. Three financial markets deserve particular attention: the bond market (where interest rates are determined), the stock market (which has a major effect on people's wealth and on firms' investment decisions), and the foreign exchange market (because fluctuations in the foreign exchange rate have major consequences for the American economy).

KEY TERMS

money (money supply)

aggregate output

unemployment rate

business cycles

recessions

monetary theory

aggregate price level

inflation

inflation rate

interest rate

monetary policy

Federal Reserve System (the Fed)

budget deficit

banks

financial intermediaries

financial markets

security

assets

bond

foreign exchange rate

QUESTIONS AND PROBLEMS

Questions marked with an asterisk are answered at the end of the book in an appendix, "Answers to Selected Questions and Problems."

1. Has the inflation rate in the United States increased or decreased in the past few years? What about interest rates?

*2. If history repeats itself and we see a decline in the rate of money growth, what might you expect to happen to (a) real output, (b) the inflation rate, and (c) interest rates?

3. When was the most recent recession?

*4. When interest rates fall, how might you change your economic behavior?

5. Can you think of any financial innovation in the past ten years that has affected you personally? Has it made you better or worse off? Why?

*6. Is everybody worse off when interest rates rise?

7. What is the basic activity of banks?

*8. Why are financial markets important to the health of the economy?

9. What is the typical relationship between interest rates on three-month Treasury bills, long-term Treasury bonds, and Baa corporate bonds?

*10. What effect might a fall in stock prices have on business investment?

11. What effect might a rise in stock prices have on consumers' decisions to spend?

*12. How does a depreciation of the pound sterling affect British consumers?

13. How does an appreciation of the pound sterling affect American businesses?

*14. Looking at Figure 8, in what years would you have chosen to visit the Grand Canyon in Arizona rather than the Tower of London?

15. When the dollar is worth more in relation to currencies of other countries, are you more likely to buy American-made or foreign-made jeans? Are U.S. companies that make jeans happier when the dollar is strong or when it is weak? What about an American company that is in the business of importing jeans into the United States?

Appendix to Chapter 1

DEFINING AGGREGATE OUTPUT, INCOME, AND THE PRICE LEVEL

Because these terms are used so frequently throughout the text, we need to have a clear understanding of the definitions of *aggregate output, income,* and the *price level.*

AGGREGATE OUTPUT AND INCOME

The most commonly reported measure of aggregate output, the **gross domestic product (GDP),** is the value of all final goods and services produced in a country during the course of the year.[1] This measure excludes two sets of items that at first glance you might think would be included. Purchases of goods that have been produced in the past, whether a Rembrandt painting or a house built 20 years ago, are not counted as part of GDP, nor are purchases of stocks or bonds. None of these enter into GDP because they are not goods and services produced during the course of the year. Intermediate goods, which are used up in producing final goods and services, such as the sugar in a candy bar or the energy used to produce steel, are also not counted separately as part of GDP. They are not counted separately because to do so would be to count them twice, as the value of the final goods *already* includes the value of the intermediate goods.

Aggregate income, the total income of factors of production (land, labor, and capital) from producing goods and services in the economy during the course of the year, is best thought of as being equal to aggregate output. Because the payments for final goods and services must eventually flow back to the owners of the factors of production as income, income payments must equal payments for final goods and services. For example, if the economy has an aggregate output of $5 trillion, total income payments in the economy (aggregate income) are also $5 trillion.

---

[1]Another measure of aggregate output is *gross national product (GNP),* the value of all final goods and services produced by domestically owned factors of production during a year. It differs from GDP in that part of U.S. GNP is earned abroad by American individuals and corporations. Also, earnings by foreign companies in the United States are excluded from U.S. GNP but are included in GDP.

REAL VERSUS NOMINAL MAGNITUDES

When the total value of final goods and services is calculated using current prices, the resulting GDP measure is referred to as *nominal GDP*. The word *nominal* indicates that values are measured using current prices. If all prices doubled but actual production of goods and services remained the same, nominal GDP would double even though people do not enjoy the benefits of twice as many goods and services. As a result, nominal variables can be misleading measures of economic well-being.

A more reliable measure of economic well-being measures values in terms of prices for an arbitrary base year, currently 1987. GDP measured with constant prices is referred to as *real GDP,* the word *real* indicating that values are measured in terms of fixed prices. Real variables thus measure the quantities of goods and services and do not change because prices have changed but rather only if actual quantities have changed.

A brief example will make the distinction clearer. Suppose that you have a nominal income of $30,000 in 1995 and that your nominal income was $15,000 in 1987. If all prices doubled between 1987 and 1995, are you better off? The answer is no: Although your income has doubled, your $30,000 buys you only the same amount of goods because prices have also doubled. A real income measure indicates that your income in terms of the goods it can buy is the same. Measured in 1987 prices, the $30,000 of nominal income in 1995 turns out to be only $15,000 of real income. Because your real income is actually the same in the two years, you are no better or worse off in 1995 than you were in 1987.

Because real variables measure quantities in terms of real goods and services, they are typically of more interest than nominal variables. In this text, discussion of aggregate output or aggregate income always refers to real measures (such as real GDP).

AGGREGATE PRICE LEVEL

In the chapter we defined the aggregate price level as a measure of average prices in the economy. Two measures of the aggregate price level are commonly encountered in economic data. The first is the *GDP deflator,* which is defined as nominal GDP divided by GDP. Thus if 1995 nominal GDP is $6 trillion but 1995 real GDP in 1987 prices is $4 trillion,

$$\text{GDP deflator} = \frac{\$6 \text{ trillion}}{\$4 \text{ trillion}} = 1.50$$

The GDP deflator indicates that, on average, prices have risen 50% since 1987. Typically, measures of the price level are presented in the form of a price index, which expresses the price level for the base year (in our example, 1987) as 100. Thus the GDP deflator for 1995 would be 150.

Another popular measure of the aggregate price level (and the one that is most frequently reported in the press) is the *consumer price index (CPI)*. The CPI is measured by pricing a "basket" list of goods and services bought by a typical urban household over a given period, say, one month. If over the course of the year the cost of this basket of goods and services rises from $500 to $600, the CPI has risen by 20%. The CPI is also expressed as a price index with the base year equal to 100.

Both the CPI and GDP deflator measures of the price level can be used to convert or deflate a nominal magnitude into a real magnitude. This is accomplished by dividing the nominal magnitude by the price index. In our example, in which the GDP deflator for 1995 is 1.50 (expressed as an index value of 150), real GDP for 1995 equals

$$\frac{\$6 \text{ trillion}}{1.50} = \$4 \text{ trillion in 1987 prices}$$

which corresponds to the real GDP figure for 1995 mentioned earlier.

Chapter 2

AN OVERVIEW OF THE FINANCIAL SYSTEM

PREVIEW   Inez the Inventor has designed a low-cost robot that cleans house (even does windows), mows the lawn, and washes the car, but she has no funds to put her wonderful invention into production. Walter the Widower has plenty of savings, which he and his wife accumulated over the years. If we could get Inez and Walter together so that Walter could provide funds to Inez, Inez's robot would see the light of day, and the economy would be better off: We would have cleaner houses, shinier cars, and more beautiful lawns.

Financial markets (bond and stock markets) and financial intermediaries (banks, insurance companies, pension funds) have the basic function of getting people such as Inez and Walter together by moving funds from those who have a surplus of funds (Walter) to those who have a shortage of funds (Inez). More realistically, when Apple invents a better computer, it may need funds to bring it to market, or a local government may need funds to build a road or a school. Well-functioning financial markets and financial intermediaries are needed to improve our economic well-being and are crucial to our economic health.

To study the effects of financial markets and financial intermediaries on the economy, we must first acquire an understanding of their general structure and operation. In this chapter we learn about the major financial intermediaries and the instruments that are traded in financial markets as well as how these markets are regulated.

This chapter is meant to be a preliminary overview of the fascinating study of financial markets and institutions. We return to a more detailed treatment of the regulation, structure, and evolution of financial markets in Chapters 9 through 14.

FUNCTION OF FINANCIAL MARKETS

Financial markets perform the essential economic function of channeling funds from people who have saved surplus funds by spending less than their income to people who have a shortage of funds because they wish to spend more than their income. This function is shown schematically in Figure 1. Those who have saved and are lending funds, the lender-savers, are at the left, and those who must borrow funds to finance their spending, the borrower-spenders, are at the right. The principal lender-savers are households, but business enterprises and the government (particularly state and local government), as well as foreigners and their governments, sometimes also find themselves with excess funds and so lend them out. The most important borrower-spenders are businesses and the government (particularly the federal government), but households and foreigners also borrow to finance their purchases of cars, furniture, and houses. The arrows show that funds flow from lender-savers to borrower-spenders via two routes.

In direct finance (the route at the bottom of Figure 1), borrowers borrow funds directly from lenders in financial markets by selling them *securities* (also called *financial instruments*), which are claims on the borrower's future income or assets. Whereas securities are assets for the person who buys them, they are **liabilities** (IOUs or debts) for the individual or firm that sells (issues) them. For example, if General Motors needs to borrow funds to pay for a new factory to manufacture computerized cars, it might borrow the funds from a saver by selling the saver a *bond,* a debt security that promises to make payments periodically for a specified period of time.

Why is this channeling of funds from savers to spenders so important to the economy? The answer is that the people who save are frequently not the same people who have profitable investment opportunities available to them, the entrepreneurs. Let's first think about this on a personal level. Suppose that you

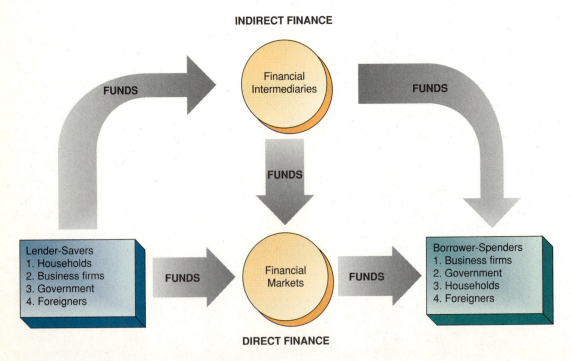

FIGURE 1 Flows of Funds Through the Financial System

have saved $1000 this year, but no borrowing or lending is possible because there are no financial markets. If you do not have an investment opportunity that will permit you to earn income with your savings, you will just hold on to the $1000 and will earn no interest. However, Carl the Carpenter has a productive use for your $1000: He can use it to purchase a new tool that will shorten the time it takes him to build a house, thereby earning an extra $200 per year. If you could get in touch with Carl, you could lend him the $1000 at a rental fee (interest) of $100 per year, and both of you would be better off. You would earn $100 per year on your $1000, instead of the zero amount that you would earn otherwise, while Carl would earn $100 more income per year (the $200 extra earnings per year minus the $100 rental fee for the use of the funds).

In the absence of financial markets, you and Carl the Carpenter might never get together. Without financial markets, it is hard to transfer funds from a person who has no investment opportunities to one who has them; you would both be stuck with the status quo, and both of you would be worse off. Financial markets are thus essential to promoting economic efficiency.

The existence of financial markets is also beneficial even if someone borrows for a purpose other than increasing production in a business. Say that you are recently married, have a good job, and want to buy a house. You earn a good salary, but because you have just started to work, you have not yet saved much. Over time you would have no problem saving enough to buy the house of your dreams, but by then you would be too old to get full enjoyment from it. Without financial markets, you are stuck; you cannot buy the house and will continue to live in your tiny apartment.

If a financial market were set up so that people who had built up savings could lend you the money to buy the house, you would be more than happy to pay them some interest in order to own a home while you are still young enough to enjoy it. Then, when you had saved up enough funds, you would pay back your loan. The overall outcome would be such that you would be better off, as would the persons who made you the loan. They would now earn some interest, whereas they would not if the financial market did not exist.

Now we can see why financial markets have such an important function in the economy. They allow funds to move from people who lack productive investment opportunities to people who have such opportunities. By so doing, financial markets contribute to higher production and efficiency in the overall economy. They also directly improve the well-being of consumers by allowing them to time their purchases better. They provide funds to young people to buy what they need and can eventually afford without forcing them to wait until they have saved up the entire purchase price. Financial markets that are operating efficiently improve the economic welfare of everyone in the society.

STRUCTURE OF FINANCIAL MARKETS

Now that we understand the basic function of financial markets, let's look at their structure. The following descriptions of several categorizations of financial markets illustrate essential features of these markets.

Debt and Equity Markets

A firm or an individual can obtain funds in a financial market in two ways. The most common method is to issue a debt instrument, such as a bond or a mortgage, which is a contractual agreement by the borrower to pay the holder of the instrument fixed dollar amounts at regular intervals (interest payments) until a specified date (the maturity date), when a final payment is made. The **maturity** of a debt instrument is the time (term) to that instrument's expiration date. A debt instrument is **short-term** if its maturity is less than a year and **long-term** if its maturity is ten years or longer. Debt instruments with a maturity between one and ten years are said to be **intermediate-term.**

The second method of raising funds is by issuing **equities**, such as common stock, which are claims to share in the net income (income after expenses and taxes) and the assets of a business. If you own one share of common stock in a company that has issued one million shares, you are entitled to 1 one-millionth of the firm's net income and 1 one-millionth of the firm's assets. Equities usually make periodic payments **(dividends)** to their holders and are considered long-term securities because they have no maturity date.

The main disadvantage of owning a corporation's equities rather than its debt is that an equity holder is a *residual claimant;* that is, the corporation must pay all its debt holders before it pays its equity holders. The advantage of holding equities is that equity holders benefit directly from any increases in the corporation's profitability or asset value because equities confer ownership rights on the equity holders. Debt holders do not share in this benefit because their dollar payments are fixed. We examine the pros and cons of debt versus equity instruments in more detail in Chapter 9, which provides an economic analysis of financial structure.

The total value of equities in the United States has typically fluctuated between \$1 and \$7.5 trillion since the early 1970s, depending on the prices of shares. Although the average person is more aware of the stock market than any other financial market, the size of the debt market greatly exceeds that of the equities market: The value of debt instruments (\$12.7 trillion at the end of 1993) is more than 50% larger than the value of equities (\$7.5 trillion at the end of 1993).

Primary and Secondary Markets

A **primary market** is a financial market in which new issues of a security, such as a bond or a stock, are sold to initial buyers by the corporation or government agency borrowing the funds. A **secondary market** is a financial market in which securities that have been previously issued (and are thus secondhand) can be resold.

The primary markets for securities are not well known to the public because the selling of securities to initial buyers takes place behind closed doors. An important financial institution that assists in the initial sale of securities in the primary market is the **investment bank.** It does this by **underwriting** securities; that is, it guarantees a price for a corporation's securities and then sells them to the public.

The New York and American stock exchanges, in which previously issued stocks are traded, are the best-known examples of secondary markets, although the bond markets, in which previously issued bonds of major corporations and the U.S. government are bought and sold, actually have a larger trading volume. Other examples of secondary markets are foreign exchange markets, futures markets, and options markets. Securities brokers and dealers are crucial to a well-functioning secondary market. **Brokers** are agents of investors who match buyers with sellers of securities; **dealers** link buyers and sellers by buying and selling securities at stated prices.

When an individual buys a security in the secondary market, the person who has sold the security receives money in exchange for the security, but the corporation that issued the security acquires no new funds. A corporation acquires new funds only when its securities are first sold in the primary market. Nonetheless, secondary markets serve two functions. First, they make it easier to sell these financial instruments in order to raise cash; that is, they make the financial instruments more **liquid.** The increased liquidity of these instruments then makes them more desirable and thus easier for the issuing firm to sell in the primary market. Second, they determine the price of the security that the issuing firm sells in the primary market. The firms that buy securities in the primary market will pay the issuing corporation no more than the price that they think the secondary market will set for this security. The higher the security's price in the secondary market, the higher will be the price that the issuing firm will receive for a new security in the primary market and hence the greater the amount of capital it can raise. Conditions in the secondary market are therefore the most relevant to corporations issuing securities. It is for this reason that books like this one, which deal with financial markets, focus on the behavior of secondary markets rather than primary markets.

Exchanges and Over-the-Counter Markets

Secondary markets can be organized in two ways. One is to organize **exchanges,** where buyers and sellers of securities (or their agents or brokers) meet in one central location to conduct trades. The New York and American stock exchanges for stocks and the Chicago Board of Trade for commodities (wheat, corn, silver, and other raw materials) are examples of organized exchanges.

The other method of organizing a secondary market is to have an **over-the-counter (OTC) market,** in which dealers at different locations who have an inventory of securities stand ready to buy and sell securities "over the counter" to anyone who comes to them and is willing to accept their prices. Because over-the-counter dealers are in computer contact and know the prices set by one another, the OTC market is very competitive and not very different from a market with an organized exchange.

Many common stocks are traded over-the-counter, although the largest corporations have their shares traded at organized stock exchanges such as the New York Stock Exchange. The U.S. government bond market, with a larger trading volume than the New York Stock Exchange, is set up as an over-the-counter market. Forty or so dealers establish a "market" in these securities by standing ready to buy and sell U.S. government bonds. Other over-the-counter markets include those that trade negotiable certificates of deposit, federal funds, banker's acceptances, and foreign exchange.

Money and Capital Markets

Another way of distinguishing between markets is on the basis of the maturity of the securities traded in each market. The **money market** is a financial market in which only short-term debt instruments (maturity of less than one year) are traded; the **capital market** is the market in which longer-term debt (maturity of one year or greater) and equity instruments are traded. Money market securities are usually more widely traded than longer-term securities and so tend to be more liquid. In addition, as we will see in Chapter 4, short-term securities have smaller fluctuations in prices than long-term securities, making them safer investments. As a result, corporations and banks actively use this market to earn interest on surplus funds that they expect to have only temporarily. Capital market securities, such as stocks and long-term bonds, are often held by financial intermediaries such as insurance companies and pension funds, which have little uncertainty about the amount of funds they will have available in the future.

FINANCIAL MARKET INSTRUMENTS

To complete our understanding of how financial markets perform the important role of channeling funds from lender-savers to borrower-spenders, we need to examine the securities (instruments) traded in financial markets. We first focus on the instruments traded in the money market and then turn to those traded in the capital market.

Money Market Instruments

Because of their short terms to maturity, the debt instruments traded in the money market undergo the least price fluctuations and so are the least risky investments. The money market has undergone great changes in the past three decades, with the amount of some financial instruments growing at a far more rapid rate than others. Why this has been happening is a fascinating topic discussed in Chapter 10, which examines the forces that have been driving the rapid pace of financial innovation in recent years.

The principal money market instruments are listed in Table 1 along with the amount outstanding at the end of 1970, 1980, 1990, and 1993.

United States Treasury Bills These short-term debt instruments of the U.S. government are issued in 3-, 6-, and 12-month maturities to finance the deficits of the federal government. They pay a set amount at maturity and have no interest payments, but they effectively pay interest by initially selling at a discount, that is, at a price lower than the set amount paid at maturity. For instance, you might buy a one-year Treasury bill in May 1995 for $9000 that can be redeemed for $10,000 in May 1996.

U.S. Treasury bills are the most liquid of all the money market instruments because they are the most actively traded. They are also the safest of all money market instruments because there is no possibility of **default,** a situation in which the party issuing the debt instrument (the federal government in this case) is unable to make interest payments or pay off the amount owed when the instrument matures. The federal government is always able to meet its debt obligations because it can raise taxes or issue **currency** (paper money or coins) to pay off its debts. Treasury bills are held mainly by banks, although small amounts are held by households, corporations, and other financial intermediaries.

Negotiable Bank Certificates of Deposit A *certificate of deposit (CD)* is a debt instrument sold by a bank to depositors that pays annual interest of a given amount and at maturity pays back the original purchase price. Before 1961, CDs were nonnegotiable; that is, they could not be sold to someone else and could not be redeemed from the bank before maturity without paying a substantial penalty. In 1961, to make CDs more liquid and more attractive to investors, Citibank introduced the first negotiable CD in large denominations (over $100,000) that could

TABLE 1 Principal Money Market Instruments

Type of Instrument	Amount Outstanding ($ billions, end of year)			
	1970	1980	1990	1993
U.S. Treasury bills	81	216	527	715
Negotiable bank certificates of deposit (large denominations)	55	317	543	381
Commercial paper	33	122	557	550
Banker's acceptances	7	42	52	32
Repurchase agreements	3	57	144	168
Federal funds*	16	18	61	62
Eurodollars	2	55	92	63

*Figures after 1970 are for large banks only.

Sources: Federal Reserve Flow of Funds Accounts; Federal Reserve *Bulletin; Banking and Monetary Statistics, 1945–1970; Annual Statistical Digest, 1971–1975; Economic Report of the President;* Board of Governors of the Federal Reserve System, Statistical Release H.6, April 1994.

be resold in a secondary market. This instrument is now issued by almost all the major commercial banks and has been extremely successful, with the amount outstanding currently exceeding $350 billion.. CDs are an extremely important source of funds for commercial banks, from corporations, money market mutual funds, charitable institutions, and government agencies.

Commercial Paper   *Commercial paper* is a short-term debt instrument issued by large banks and well-known corporations, such as General Motors or AT&T. Before the 1960s, corporations usually borrowed their short-term funds from banks, but since then they have come to rely more heavily on selling commercial paper to other financial intermediaries and corporations for their immediate borrowing needs; that is, they engage in direct finance. Growth of the commercial paper market has been substantial: The amount of commercial paper outstanding has increased by over 1500% (from $33 billion to $550 billion) in the period 1970–1993. We will discuss why the commercial paper market has had such tremendous growth in Chapter 10 when we discuss financial innovation,

Banker's Acceptances   These money market instruments are created in the course of carrying out international trade and have been in use for hundreds of years. A *banker's acceptance* is a bank draft (a promise of payment similar to a check) issued by a firm, payable at some future date, and guaranteed for a fee by the bank that stamps it "accepted." The firm issuing the instrument is required to deposit the required funds into its account to cover the draft. If the firm fails to do so, the bank's guarantee means that it is obligated to make good on the draft. The advantage to the firm is that the draft is more likely to be accepted when purchasing goods abroad because the foreign exporter knows that even if the company purchasing the goods goes bankrupt, the bank draft will still be paid off. These "accepted" drafts are often resold in a secondary market at a discount and so are similar in function to Treasury bills. Typically, they are held by many of the same parties that hold Treasury bills, and the amount outstanding has also experienced substantial growth, rising by 400% ($7 billion to $32 billion) from 1970 to 1993.

Repurchase Agreements   *Repurchase agreements (repos)* are effectively short-term loans (usually with a maturity of less than two weeks) in which Treasury bills serve as collateral, an asset that the lender receives if the borrower does not pay back the loan. Repos are made as follows: A large corporation, such as General Motors, may have some idle funds in its bank account, say, $1 million, which it would like to lend overnight. GM uses this excess $1 million to buy Treasury bills from a bank, which agrees to repurchase them the next morning at a price slightly above GM's purchase price. The effect of this agreement is that GM makes a loan of $1 million to the bank and holds $1 million of the bank's Treasury bills until the bank repurchases the bills to pay off the loan. Repurchase agreements are a fairly recent innovation in financial markets, having been introduced in 1969. They are now an important source of bank funds (over $160 billion), and the most important lenders in this market are large corporations.

Money Market Rates

The *Wall Street Journal* publishes daily a listing of interest rates on many different financial instruments in its "Money Rates" column. (See "Today's Contents" on page 1 of the *Journal* for the location.)

The four interest rates in the "Money Rates" column that are discussed most frequently in the media are these:

Prime rate: The base interest rate on corporate bank loans, an indicator of the cost of business borrowing from banks

Federal funds rate: The interest rate charged on overnight loans in the federal funds market, a sensitive indicator of the cost to banks of borrowing funds from other banks and the stance of monetary policy

Treasury bill rate: The interest rate on U.S. Treasury bills, an indicator of general interest-rate movements

Federal Home Loan Mortgage Corporation rates: Interest rates on "Freddie Mac" guaranteed mortgages, an indicator of the cost of financing residential housing purchases

Source: Wall Street Journal, Wednesday, March 2, 1994, p. C21.

MONEY RATES

Tuesday, March 1, 1994

The key U.S. and foreign annual interest rates below are a guide to general levels but don't always represent actual transactions.

PRIME RATE: 6%. The base rate on corporate loans posted by at least 75% of the nation's 30 largest banks.

FEDERAL FUNDS: 3⅜% high, 3⅛% low, 3 3/16% near closing bid, 3¼% offered. Reserves traded among commercial banks for overnight use in amounts of $1 million or more. Source: Prebon Yamane (U.S.A.) Inc.

DISCOUNT RATE: 3%. The charge on loans to depository institutions by the Federal Reserve Banks.

CALL MONEY: 5%. The charge on loans to brokers on stock exchange collateral. Source: Dow Jones Telerate Inc.

COMMERCIAL PAPER placed directly by General Electric Capital Corp.: 3.48% 30 to 59 days; 3.55% 60 to 89 days; 3.60% 90 to 129 days; 3.68% 130 to 179 days; 3.78% 180 to 239 days; 3.85% 240 to 270 days.

COMMERCIAL PAPER: High-grade unsecured notes sold through dealers by major corporations: 3.52% 30 days; 3.67% 60 days; 3.74% 90 days.

CERTIFICATES OF DEPOSIT: 2.84% one month; 2.93% two months; 3.04% three months; 3.20% six months; 3.46% one year. Average of top rates paid by major New York banks on primary new issues of negotiable C.D.s, usually on amounts of $1 million and more. The minimum unit is $100,000. Typical rates in the secondary market: 3.45% one month; 3.63% three months; 3.85% six months.

BANKERS ACCEPTANCES: 3.43% 30 days; 3.50% 60 days; 3.55% 90 days; 3.70% 120 days; 3.67% 150 days; 3.73% 180 days. Offered rates of negotiable, bank-backed business credit instruments typically financing an import order.

LONDON LATE EURODOLLARS: 3 9/16% - 3 7/16% one month; 3 11/16% - 3 9/16% two months; 3¾% - 3⅝% three months; 3⅞% - 3¾% four months; 3 15/16% - 3 13/16% five months; 4% - 3⅞% six months.

LONDON INTERBANK OFFERED RATES (LIBOR): 3 9/16% one month; 3 11/16% three months; 3 15/16% six months; 4 5/16% one year. The average of interbank offered rates for dollar deposits in the London market based on quotations at five major banks. Effective rate for contracts entered into two days from date appearing at top of this column.

FOREIGN PRIME RATES: Canada 5.50%; Germany 5.93%; Japan 3%; Switzerland 7.50%; Britain 5.25%. These rate indications aren't directly comparable; lending practices vary widely by location.

TREASURY BILLS: Results of the Monday, February 28, 1994, auction of short-term U.S. government bills, sold at a discount from face value in units of $10,000 to $1 million: 3.40% 13 weeks; 3.61% 26 weeks.

FEDERAL HOME LOAN MORTGAGE CORP. (Freddie Mac): Posted yields on 30-year mortgage commitments. Delivery within 30 days 7.42%, 60 days 7.47%, standard conventional fixed-rate mortgages; 3.875%, 2% rate capped one-year adjustable rate mortgages. Source: Dow Jones Telerate Inc.

FEDERAL NATIONAL MORTGAGE ASSOCIATION (Fannie Mae): Posted yields on 30 year mortgage commitments (priced at par) for delivery within 30 days 7.41%, 60 days 7.50%, standard conventional fixed rate-mortgages; 5.50%, 6/2 rate capped one-year adjustable rate mortgages. Source: Dow Jones Telerate Inc.

MERRILL LYNCH READY ASSETS TRUST: 2.75%. Annualized average rate of return after expenses for the past 30 days; not a forecast of future returns.

Federal (Fed) Funds These are typically overnight loans between banks of their deposits at the Federal Reserve. The *federal funds* designation is somewhat confusing because these loans are not made by the federal government or by the Federal Reserve but rather by banks to other banks. One reason why a bank might borrow in the federal funds market is that it might find that the deposits it has at the Fed do not meet the amount required by regulations. It can then borrow these deposits from another bank, which transfers them to the borrowing bank using the Fed's wire transfer system. This market is very sensitive to the credit needs of the banks, so the interest rate on these loans, called the **federal funds rate,** is a closely watched barometer of the tightness of credit market conditions in the banking system and the stance of monetary policy; when it is high, it indicates that the banks are strapped for funds, whereas when it is low, banks' credit needs are low.

Eurodollars U.S. dollars deposited in foreign banks outside the United States or in foreign branches of U.S. banks are called **Eurodollars.** American banks can borrow these deposits from other banks or from their own foreign branches when they need funds. Eurodollars have become an important source of funds for banks (over $60 billion).

Capital Market Instruments

Capital market instruments are debt and equity instruments with maturities of greater than one year. They have far wider price fluctuations than money market instruments and are considered to be fairly risky investments. The principal capital market instruments are listed in Table 2, which shows the amount outstanding at the end of 1970, 1980, 1990, and 1993.

Stocks *Stocks* are equity claims on the net income and assets of a corporation. Their value of over $7 trillion at the end of 1993 exceeds that of any other type of security in the capital market. The amount of new stock issues in any given

TABLE 2 Principal Capital Market Instruments				
	Amount Outstanding ($ billions, end of year)			
Type of Instrument	**1970**	**1980**	**1990**	**1993**
Corporate stocks (market value)	906	1601	4146	7548
Residential mortgages	355	1106	2886	3403
Corporate bonds	167	366	1008	1226
U.S. government securities (marketable long-term)	160	407	1653	2260
State and local government bonds	146	310	870	1057
U.S. government agency securities	51	193	435	545
Bank commercial loans	152	459	818	781
Consumer loans	134	355	813	858
Commercial and farm mortgages	116	352	829	771

Sources: Federal Reserve Flow of Funds Accounts; Federal Reserve *Bulletin; Banking and Monetary Statistics, 1941–1970.*

year is typically quite small, less than 1% of the total value of shares outstanding. Individuals hold around half of the value of stocks; the rest are held by pension funds, mutual funds, and insurance companies.

Mortgages   *Mortgages* are loans to individuals or firms to purchase housing, land, or other real structures, where the structure, or land, then in turn serves as collateral for the loans. The mortgage market is the largest debt market in the United States, with the amount of residential mortgages (used to purchase residential housing) outstanding more than quadruple the amount of commercial and farm mortgages. Savings and loan associations and mutual savings banks have been the primary lenders in the residential mortgage market, although commercial banks have started to enter this market more aggressively. The majority of commercial and farm mortgages are made by commercial banks and life insurance companies. The federal government has played an active role in the mortgage market via the three government agencies—the Federal National Mortgage Association (FNMA, "Fannie Mae"), the Government National Mortgage Association (GNMA, "Ginnie Mae"), and the Federal Home Loan Mortgage Corporation (FHLMC, "Freddie Mac")—that provide funds to the mortgage market by selling bonds and using the proceeds to buy mortgages. An important development in the residential mortgage market in recent years is the mortgage-backed security (see Box 1).

Corporate Bonds   These are long-term bonds issued by corporations with very strong credit ratings. The typical *corporate bond* sends the holder an interest payment twice a year and pays off the face value when the bond matures. Some corporate bonds, called *convertible bonds,* also have the additional feature of allowing the holder to convert them into a specified number of shares of stock at any time up to the maturity date. This feature makes these convertible bonds more desirable to prospective purchasers than bonds without it and allows the corporation to reduce its interest payments because these bonds can increase in value if the price of the stock appreciates sufficiently. Because the outstanding amount of both convertible and nonconvertible bonds for any given corporation is small, they are not nearly as liquid as other securities such as U.S. government bonds.

   Although the size of the corporate bond market is substantially smaller than that of the stock market, with the amount of corporate bonds outstanding less than one-fifth that of stocks, the volume of new corporate bonds issued each year is substantially greater than the volume of new stock issues. Thus the behavior of the corporate bond market is probably far more important to a firm's financing decisions than the behavior of the stock market. The principal buyers of corporate bonds are life insurance companies; pension funds and households are other large holders.

U.S. Government Securities   These long-term debt instruments are issued by the U.S. Treasury to finance the deficits of the federal government. Because they are the most widely traded bonds in the United States (the volume of transactions on average exceeds $100 billion daily), they are the most liquid security traded in the

Box 1

MORTGAGE-BACKED SECURITIES

A major change in the residential mortgage market in recent years has been the creation of an active secondary market for mortgages. Because mortgages have different terms and interest rates, they were not sufficiently liquid to trade as securities on secondary markets. To stimulate mortgage lending, in 1970, the Government National Mortgage Association (GNMA, called "Ginnie Mae") developed the concept of a pass-through, mortgage-backed security when it began a program in which it guaranteed interest and principal payments on bundles of standardized mortgages. Under this program, private financial institutions such as savings and loans and commercial banks were now able to gather a group of GNMA-guaranteed mortgages into a bundle of, say, $1 million and then sell this bundle as a security to a third party (usually a large institutional investor such as a pension fund). When individuals make their mortgage payments on the GNMA-guaranteed mortgage to the financial institution, the financial institution passes the payments through to the owner of the security by sending a check for the total of all the payments. Because GNMA guarantees the payments, these pass-through securities have a very low default risk and are very popular, with amounts outstanding exceeding $400 billion.

Mortgage-backed securities are issued not only by the government agencies but also by private financial institutions. Indeed, mortgage-backed securities have been so successful that they have completely transformed the residential mortgage market. Throughout the 1970s, over 80% of residential mortgages were owned outright by savings and loans, mutual savings banks, and commercial banks. Now only one-third are owned outright by these institutions, with two-thirds held as mortgage-backed securities.

capital market. They are held by the Federal Reserve, banks, households, and foreigners.

U.S. Government Agency Securities These are long-term bonds issued by various government agencies. Many of these securities are guaranteed by the federal government. They function much like U.S. government bonds and are held by similar parties.

State and Local Government Bonds State and local bonds, also called *municipal bonds,* are long-term instruments issued by state and local governments to finance expenditures on schools, roads, and other large programs. An important feature of these bonds is that their interest payments are exempt from federal income tax and generally from state taxes in the issuing state. Commercial banks, with their high income tax rate, are the biggest buyers of these securities, owning over one-half the total amount outstanding. The next biggest group of holders are wealthy individuals in high income brackets, followed by insurance companies.

Consumer and Bank Commercial Loans These are loans to consumers and businesses made principally by banks but, in the case of consumer loans, also by finance companies. There are often no secondary markets in these loans, which makes them the least liquid of the capital market instruments listed in Table 2.

FUNCTION OF FINANCIAL INTERMEDIARIES

As shown in Figure 1, funds can move from lenders to borrowers by a second route, called indirect finance because it involves a financial intermediary that stands between the lender-savers and the borrower-spenders and helps transfer funds from one to the other. A financial intermediary does this by borrowing funds from the lender-savers and then in turn making loans to borrower-spenders. For example, a bank might acquire funds by issuing a liability to the public in the form of savings deposits. It might then use the funds to acquire an asset by making a loan to General Motors or by buying a GM bond in the financial market. The ultimate result is that funds have been transferred from the public (the lender-savers) to GM (the borrower-spender) with the help of the financial intermediary (the bank).

The process of indirect finance using financial intermediaries, called **financial intermediation,** is the primary route for moving funds from lenders to borrowers. Indeed, although the media focus much of their attention on securities markets, particularly the stock market, financial intermediaries are a far more important source of financing for corporations than securities markets are. This is true not only for the United States but for other industrialized countries as well (see Box 2). Why are financial intermediaries and indirect finance so important in financial markets? To answer this question, we need to understand the role of transactions costs and information costs in financial markets.

Transactions Costs

Transactions costs, the time and money spent in carrying out financial transactions, are a major problem for people who have excess funds to lend. As we have seen, Carl the Carpenter needs $1000 for his new tool, and you know that it is an excellent investment opportunity. You have the cash and would like to lend him the money, but to protect your investment, you have to hire a lawyer to write up the loan contract that specifies how much interest Carl will pay you, when he will make these interest payments, and when he will repay you the $1000. Obtaining the contract will cost you $500. When you figure in this transactions cost for making the loan, you realize that you can't earn enough from the deal (you spend $500 to make perhaps $100) and reluctantly tell Carl that he will have to look elsewhere.

This example illustrates that small savers like you or potential borrowers like Carl might be frozen out of financial markets and thus be unable to benefit from them. Can anyone come to the rescue? Financial intermediaries can.

A Global Perspective

Box 2

THE IMPORTANCE OF FINANCIAL INTERMEDIARIES TO SECURITIES MARKETS: AN INTERNATIONAL COMPARISON

Patterns of financing corporations differ across countries, but one key fact emerges. Studies of the major developed countries, including the United States, Canada, Great Britain, Japan, Italy, Germany, and France, show that when businesses go looking for funds to finance their activities, they usually obtain them from financial intermediaries.* Not surprisingly, the United States and Canada, which have the most developed securities markets in the world, also make the greatest use of them in financing corporations. Even so, in the United States, loans from financial intermediaries are almost twice as important for corporate finance as securities markets are. The countries that have made the least use of securities markets are Germany and Japan; in these two countries, financing from financial intermediaries has been almost ten times greater than that from securities markets. However, with the deregulation of Japanese securities markets in recent years, the share of corporate financing by financial intermediaries has been declining relative to the use of securities markets.

Although the dominance of financial intermediaries over securities markets is clear in all countries, the relative importance of bond versus stock markets differs widely across countries. In the United States, the bond market is far more important as a source of corporate finance: On average, the amount of new financing raised using bonds is ten times the amount using stocks. By contrast, countries such as France and Italy make use of equities markets more than the bond market to raise capital.

*See, for example, Colin Mayer, "Financial Systems, Corporate Finance, and Economic Development," in *Asymmetric Information, Corporate Finance, and Investment,* ed. R. Glenn Hubbard (Chicago: University of Chicago Press, 1990), pp. 307–332.

Financial intermediaries can substantially reduce transactions costs because they have developed expertise in lowering them and because their large size allows them to take advantage of **economies of scale,** the reduction in transactions costs per dollar of transactions as the size (scale) of transactions increases. For example, a bank knows how to find a good lawyer to produce an airtight loan contract, and this contract can be used over and over again in its loan transactions, thus lowering the legal cost per transaction. Instead of a loan contract (which may not be all that well written) costing $500, a bank can hire a topflight lawyer for $5000 to draw up an airtight loan contract that can be used for 2000 loans at a cost of $2.50 per loan. At a cost of $2.50 per loan, it now becomes profitable for the financial intermediary to loan Carl the $1000.

Because financial intermediaries are able to reduce transactions costs substantially, they make it possible for you to provide funds indirectly to people with productive investment opportunities like Carl. In addition, a financial intermediary's low transactions costs mean that it can provide its customers with liquidity services, services that make it easier for customers to conduct transactions. Banks, for example, provide depositors with checking accounts that enable them to pay their bills easily. In addition, depositors can earn interest on checking and savings accounts and yet still convert them into goods and services whenever necessary.

Asymmetric Information: Adverse Selection and Moral Hazard

The presence of transactions costs in financial markets explains, in part, why financial intermediaries and indirect finance play such an important role in financial markets. An additional reason is that in financial markets, one party often does not know enough about the other party to make accurate decisions. This inequality is called **asymmetric information.** For example, a borrower who takes out a loan usually has better information about the potential returns and risk associated with the investment projects for which the funds are earmarked than the lender does. Lack of information creates problems in the financial system on two fronts: before the transaction is entered into and after.

Adverse selection is the problem created by asymmetric information *before* the transaction occurs. Adverse selection in financial markets occurs when the potential borrowers who are the most likely to produce an undesirable *(adverse)* outcome—the bad credit risks—are the ones who most actively seek out a loan and are thus most likely to be *selected*. Because adverse selection makes it more likely that loans might be made to bad credit risks, lenders may decide not to make any loans even though there are good credit risks in the marketplace.

To understand why adverse selection occurs, suppose that you have two aunts to whom you might make a loan—Aunt Sheila and Aunt Louise. Aunt Louise is a conservative type who borrows only when she has an investment that she is quite sure will pay off. Aunt Sheila, by contrast, is an inveterate gambler who has just come across a get-rich-quick scheme that will make her a millionaire if she can just borrow $1000 to invest in it. Unfortunately, as with most get-rich-quick schemes, there is a high probability that the investment won't pay off and that Aunt Sheila will lose the $1000.

Which of your aunts is more likely to call you to ask for a loan? Aunt Sheila, of course, because she has so much to gain if the investment pays off. You, however, would not want to make a loan to her because there is a high probability that her investment will turn sour and she will be unable to pay you back.

If you knew both your aunts very well—that is, if information was not asymmetric—you wouldn't have a problem because you would know that Aunt Sheila is a bad risk and so you would not lend to her. Suppose, though, that you don't know your aunts well. You are more likely to lend to Aunt Sheila than to Aunt Louise because Aunt Sheila would be hounding you for the loan. Because of the possibility of adverse selection, you might decide not to lend to either of your aunts, even though there are times when Aunt Louise, who is an excellent credit risk, might need a loan for a worthwhile investment.

Moral hazard is the problem created by asymmetric information *after* the transaction occurs. Moral hazard in financial markets is the risk *(hazard)* that the borrower might engage in activities that are undesirable *(immoral)* from the lender's point of view because they make it less likely that the loan will be paid back. Because moral hazard lowers the probability that the loan will be repaid, lenders may decide that they would rather not make a loan.

As an example of moral hazard, suppose that you made a $1000 loan to another relative, Uncle Melvin, who needs the money to purchase a word processor so that he can set up a business typing students' term papers. Once you have made the loan, however, Uncle Melvin is more likely to slip off to the track and play the horses. If he bets on a 20-to-1 long shot and wins with your money, he is able to pay you back your $1000 and live high on the hog with the remaining $19,000. But if he loses, as is likely, you don't get paid back, and all he has lost is his reputation as a reliable, upstanding uncle. Uncle Melvin therefore has an incentive to go to the track because his gains ($19,000) if he bets correctly may be much greater than the cost to him (his reputation) if he bets incorrectly. *If you knew* what Uncle Melvin was up to, you would prevent him from going to the track, and he would not be able to increase the moral hazard. However, because it is hard for you to keep informed about his whereabouts—that is, because information is asymmetric—there is a good chance that Uncle Melvin will go to the track and you will not get paid back. The risk of moral hazard might therefore discourage you from making the $1000 loan to Uncle Melvin, even if you were sure that you would be paid back if he used it to set up his business.

STUDY GUIDE

Because the concepts of adverse selection and moral hazard are extremely useful in understanding the behavior we examine in this and many of the later chapters, you must understand them fully. One way to distinguish between them is to remember that adverse selection is a problem of asymmetric information *before* entering into a transaction, whereas moral hazard is a problem of asymmetric information *after* the transaction has occurred. A helpful way to nail down these concepts is to think of other examples, for financial or other types of transactions, in which adverse selection or moral hazard plays a role. Several problems at the end of the chapter also provide additional examples of situations involving adverse selection and moral hazard.

The problems created by adverse selection and moral hazard are an important impediment to well-functioning financial markets. Again, financial intermediaries can alleviate these problems.

With financial intermediaries in the economy, small savers can provide their funds to the financial markets by lending these funds to a trustworthy intermediary, say, the Honest John Bank, which in turn lends the funds out either by making loans or by buying securities such as stocks or bonds. Successful financial intermediaries have higher earnings on their investments because they are better equipped than individuals for screening out good from bad credit risks, thereby reducing losses due to adverse selection. In addition, financial intermediaries have high earnings because they develop expertise to monitor the parties they lend to, thus reducing losses due to moral hazard. The result is that financial intermediaries can afford to pay lender-savers interest or provide substantial services and still earn a profit.

The success of financial intermediaries is evidenced by the fact that most Americans invest their savings with them and also obtain their loans from them. Financial intermediaries play a key role in improving economic efficiency because they help financial markets channel funds from lender-savers to people with productive investment opportunities. Without a well-functioning set of financial intermediaries, it is very hard for an economy to reach its full potential, as the countries of Eastern Europe and the former Soviet Union have found out (see Box 3). We will explore further the role of financial intermediaries in the economy in Chapters 9 through 14.

A Global Perspective

Box 3

PROBLEMS OF FINANCIAL INTERMEDIATION IN THE COUNTRIES OF EASTERN EUROPE AND THE FORMER SOVIET UNION

Under the communist regimes, the only financial intermediaries in the countries of Eastern Europe and the Soviet Union were state-owned banks, which lent directly to state enterprises. In the communist system, the banks did not have to worry whether their loans were being used to support productive investments because even if a firm was unprofitable, it would still be allowed to stay in business by being given subsidies from the state. Thus the state-owned banks did not need to acquire expertise to solve the adverse selection and moral hazard problems that prevent financial markets from operating efficiently.

With the collapse of communism and the breakup of the Soviet Union, the state-owned banks and newly created private banks were completely unprepared to promote economic efficiency by lending to borrowers with the most productive investment opportunities. As a result, funds continue to be channeled to unproductive firms, and inefficiency is rampant in these economies. A major objective of economic reform in these countries is to establish a set of financial intermediaries that will perform the essential functions of screening out good from bad credit risks and monitoring borrowers to make sure that they take actions that will make it likely that they can pay off their loans. Not surprisingly, countries in Eastern Europe and the former Soviet Union have been seeking out Western help to set up well-functioning financial intermediaries.

TABLE 3 Primary Assets and Liabilities of Financial Intermediaries

Type of Intermediary	Primary Liabilities (Sources of Funds)	Primary Assets (Uses of Funds)
Depository institutions (banks)		
Commercial banks	Deposits	Business and consumer loans, mortgages, U.S. government securities and municipal bonds
Savings and loan associations	Deposits	Mortgages
Mutual savings banks	Deposits	Mortgages
Credit unions	Deposits	Consumer loans
Contractual savings institutions		
Life insurance companies	Premiums from policies	Corporate bonds and mortgages
Fire and casualty insurance companies	Premiums from policies	Municipal bonds, corporate bonds and stock, U.S. government securities
Pension funds, government retirement funds	Employer and employee contributions	Corporate bonds and stock
Investment intermediaries		
Finance companies	Commercial paper, stocks, bonds	Consumer and business loans
Mutual funds	Shares	Stocks, bonds
Money market mutual funds	Shares	Money market instruments

FINANCIAL INTERMEDIARIES

We have seen why financial intermediaries play such an important role in the economy. Now we look at the principal financial intermediaries and how they perform the intermediation function. There are three categories: depository institutions (banks), contractual savings institutions, and investment intermediaries. Table 3 provides a guide to the discussion of the financial intermediaries that fit into these three categories by describing their primary liabilities (sources of funds) and assets (uses of funds). The relative size of these intermediaries in the United States is indicated by Table 4, which lists the amount of their assets at the end of 1970, 1980, 1990, and 1993.

Depository Institutions

Depository institutions (which for simplicity we refer to as *banks* throughout this text) are financial intermediaries that accept deposits from individuals and institutions and make loans. The study of money and banking focuses special attention on this group of financial institutions because they are involved in the cre-

TABLE 4   Principal Financial Intermediaries

Type of Intermediary	Value of Assets ($ billions, end of year)			
	1970	1980	1990	1993
Depository institutions (banks)				
Commercial banks	517	1481	3334	3869
Savings and loan associations and mutual savings banks	250	792	1365	1033
Credit unions	18	67	215	281
Contractual savings institutions				
Life insurance companies	201	464	1367	1792
Fire and casualty insurance companies	50	182	533	637
Pension funds (private)	112	504	1629	2336
State and local government retirement funds	60	197	737	1065
Investment intermediaries				
Finance companies	64	205	610	658
Mutual funds	47	70	654	1523
Money market mutual funds	0	76	498	559

Source: Federal Reserve Flow of Funds.

ation of deposits, an important component of the money supply. These institutions include commercial banks and the so-called **thrift institutions (thrifts):** savings and loan associations, mutual savings banks, and credit unions. Their behavior plays an important role in determining the money supply.

Commercial Banks These financial intermediaries raise funds primarily by issuing checkable deposits (deposits on which checks can be written), savings deposits (deposits that are payable on demand but do not allow their owner to write checks), and time deposits (deposits with fixed terms to maturity). They then use these funds to make commercial, consumer, and mortgage loans and to buy U.S. government securities and municipal bonds. There are approximately 12,000 commercial banks in the United States, and as a group, they are the largest financial intermediary and have the most diversified portfolios (collections) of assets.

Savings and Loan Associations Savings and loan associations (S&Ls) obtain funds primarily through savings deposits (often called shares) and time and checkable deposits. The acquired funds have traditionally been used to make mortgage loans. S&Ls are the second-largest group of financial intermediaries, numbering around 2000. In the 1950s and 1960s, S&Ls grew much more rapidly than commercial banks, but when interest rates climbed sharply from the late 1960s to the early 1980s, S&Ls encountered difficulties that slowed their rapid growth. Because many mortgages are long-term loans, with maturities in excess of 25 years, many in existence today were made years ago when interest rates were substantially lower. When interest rates rose, S&Ls frequently found that the income from their mortgages was well below the cost of acquiring funds. Many of them began to suffer large losses, and many have gone out of business.

Until 1980, savings and loans were restricted to making mortgage loans and could not establish checking accounts. Their troubles encouraged Congress to pass legislation in the early 1980s allowing them to offer checking accounts, make consumer loans, and pursue many activities previously restricted to commercial banks. In addition, they are now subject to the same requirements as the commercial banks regarding deposits with the Federal Reserve. The net result of this legislation is that the distinction between savings and loans and commercial banks is being blurred, and these intermediaries have become more competitive with each other.

Mutual Savings Banks Mutual savings banks are very similar to savings and loans. They raise funds by accepting deposits (often called shares) and use them primarily to make mortgage loans. Their corporate structure is somewhat different from that of S&Ls in that they are always structured as "mutuals," which means that they function as cooperatives: The depositors own the bank. There are around 500 of these institutions, located primarily in New York State and New England. Like savings and loans, until 1980 they were restricted to making mortgage loans, and they suffered similar problems when interest rates rose from the late 1960s to the early 1980s. They were similarly affected by the banking legislation in the 1980s and can now issue checkable deposits and make loans other than mortgages.

Credit Unions These financial institutions, numbering about 13,000, are very small cooperative lending institutions organized around a particular group: union members, employees of a particular firm, and so forth. They acquire funds from deposits called shares and primarily make consumer loans. Thanks to the banking legislation in the 1980s, credit unions too are allowed to issue checkable deposits and can make mortgage loans in addition to consumer loans.

Contractual Savings Institutions

Contractual savings institutions, such as insurance companies and pension funds, are financial intermediaries that acquire funds at periodic intervals on a contractual basis. Because they can predict with reasonable accuracy how much they will have to pay out in benefits in the coming years, they do not have to worry as much as depository institutions about losing funds. As a result, the liquidity of assets is not as important a consideration for them as it is for depository institutions, and they tend to invest their funds primarily in long-term securities such as corporate bonds, stocks, and mortgages.

Life Insurance Companies Life insurance companies insure people against financial hazards following a death and sell annuities (annual income payments upon retirement). They acquire funds from the premiums that people pay to keep their policies in force and use them mainly to buy corporate bonds and mortgages. They also purchase stocks but are restricted in the amount that they can hold. Currently, with $1.8 trillion of assets, they are among the largest of the contractual savings institutions.

Fire and Casualty Insurance Companies These companies insure their policyholders against loss from theft, fire, and accidents. They are very much like life insurance companies, receiving funds through premiums for their policies, but they have a greater possibility of loss of funds if major disasters occur. For this reason, they use their funds to buy more liquid assets than life insurance companies do. Their largest holding of assets is municipal bonds; they also hold corporate bonds and stocks and U.S. government securities.

Pension Funds and Government Retirement Funds Private pension funds and state and local retirement funds provide retirement income in the form of annuities to employees who are covered by a pension plan. Funds are acquired by contributions from employers or from employees, who either have a contribution automatically deducted from their paychecks or contribute voluntarily. The largest asset holdings of pension funds are corporate bonds and stocks. The establishment of pension funds has been actively encouraged by the federal government both through legislation requiring pension plans and through tax incentives to encourage contributions.

Investment Intermediaries

This category of financial intermediaries includes finance companies, mutual funds, and money market mutual funds.

Finance Companies Finance companies raise funds by selling commercial paper (a short-term debt instrument) and by issuing stocks and bonds. They lend these funds to consumers, who make purchases of such items as furniture, automobiles, and home improvements, and to small businesses. Some finance companies are organized by a parent corporation to help sell its product. For example, Ford Motor Credit Company makes loans to consumers who purchase Ford automobiles.

Mutual Funds These financial intermediaries acquire funds by selling shares to many individuals and use the proceeds to purchase diversified portfolios of stocks and bonds. Mutual funds allow shareholders to pool their resources so that they can take advantage of lower transactions costs when buying large blocks of stocks or bonds. In addition, mutual funds allow shareholders to hold more diversified portfolios than they otherwise would. Shareholders can sell (redeem) shares at any time, but the value of these shares will be determined by the value of the mutual fund's holdings of securities. Because these fluctuate greatly, the value of mutual fund shares will too; therefore, investments in mutual funds can be risky.

Money Market Mutual Funds These relatively new financial institutions have the characteristics of a mutual fund but also function to some extent as a depository institution because they offer deposit-type accounts. Like most mutual funds, they sell shares to acquire funds that are then used to buy money market instruments that are both safe and very liquid. The interest on these assets is then paid out to the shareholders.

A key feature of these funds is that shareholders can write checks against the value of their shareholdings. There generally are, however, restrictions on the use of the check-writing privilege; checks frequently cannot be written for amounts less than a set minimum, such as $500, and a substantial amount of money is required initially to open an account. In effect, shares in a money market mutual fund function like checking account deposits that pay interest, but with some restrictions on the check-writing privilege. Money market mutual funds have experienced extraordinary growth since 1971, when they first appeared. By 1993, their assets had climbed to over $500 billion.

REGULATION OF THE FINANCIAL SYSTEM

The financial system is among the most heavily regulated sectors of the American economy. (This is also the case in foreign countries; see Box 4.) The government regulates financial markets for three main reasons: to increase the information available to investors, to ensure the soundness of the financial system, and to improve control of monetary policy. We will examine how these three reasons have led to the present regulatory environment. As a study aid, the principal regulatory agencies of the U.S. financial system are listed in Table 5.

Increasing Information Available to Investors

Asymmetric information in financial markets means that investors may be subject to adverse selection and moral hazard problems that may hinder the efficient operation of financial markets. Risky firms or outright crooks may be the most eager to sell securities to unwary investors, and the resulting adverse selection problem may keep investors out of financial markets. Furthermore, once an investor has bought a security, thereby lending money to a firm, the borrower may have incentives to engage in risky activities or to commit outright fraud. The presence of this moral hazard problem may also keep investors away from financial markets. Government regulation can reduce adverse selection and moral hazard problems in financial markets and increase their efficiency by increasing the amount of information available to investors.

As a result of the stock market crash in 1929 and revelations of widespread fraud in the aftermath, political demands for regulation culminated in the Securities Act of 1933 and the establishment of the Securities and Exchange Commission (SEC). The SEC requires corporations issuing securities to disclose certain

A Global Perspective

Box 4

FINANCIAL REGULATION ABROAD

Not surprisingly, given the similarity of the economic system here and in Japan, Canada, and the nations of Western Europe, financial regulation in these countries is similar to financial regulation in the United States. The provision of information is improved by requiring corporations issuing securities to report details about assets and liabilities, earnings, and sales of stock and by prohibiting insider trading. The soundness of intermediaries is ensured by licensing, periodic inspection of financial intermediaries' books, and the provision of deposit insurance (although its coverage is smaller and its existence is often purposely not advertised).

The major differences between financial regulation in the United States and abroad relate to bank regulation. Only the United States currently prevents a national banking system by restricting branches to certain regions. Indeed, this difference between the United States and Europe will widen because new banking directives for the European Union (EU), formerly the European Community (EC), will enable a bank licensed in one EU country to offer a full range of services in all other EU countries. U.S. banks are also the most restricted in the range of financial services they may provide and the assets they may hold. Banks abroad frequently hold shares in commercial firms; in Japan and Germany, those stakes can be sizable.

information about their sales, assets, and earnings to the public and restricts trading by the largest stockholders (known as *insiders*) in the corporation. By requiring disclosure of this information and by discouraging insider trading, which could be used to manipulate security prices, the SEC hopes that investors will be better informed and be protected from some of the abuses in financial markets that occurred before 1933. Indeed, in recent years, the SEC has been particularly active in prosecuting people involved in insider trading.

Ensuring the Soundness of Financial Intermediaries

Asymmetric information can also lead to widespread collapse of financial intermediaries, referred to as a **financial panic.** Because providers of funds to financial intermediaries may not be able to assess whether the institutions holding their funds are sound or not, if they have doubts about the overall health of financial intermediaries, they may want to pull their funds out of both sound and unsound institutions. The possible outcome is a financial panic that produces large losses for the public and causes serious damage to the economy. To protect the public and the economy from financial panics, the government has implemented six types of regulations.

TABLE 5 Principal Regulatory Agencies of the U.S. Financial Sytem

Regulatory Agency	Subject of Regulation	Nature of Regulations
Securities and Exchange Commission (SEC)	Organized exchanges and financial markets	Requires disclosure of information, restricts insider trading
Commodities Futures Trading Commission (CFTC)	Futures market exchanges	Regulates procedures for trading in futures markets
Office of the Comptroller of the Currency	Federally chartered commercial banks	Charters and examines the books of federally chartered commercial banks and imposes restrictions on assets they can hold
National Credit Union Administration (NCUA)	Federally chartered credit unions	Charters and examines the books of federally chartered credit unions and imposes restrictions on assets they can hold
State banking and insurance commissions	State-chartered depository institutions	Charter and examine the books of state-chartered banks and insurance companies, impose restrictions on assets they can hold, impose restrictions on branching
Federal Deposit Insurance Corporation (FDIC)	Commercial banks, mutual savings banks, savings and loan associations	Provides insurance of up to $100,000 for each depositor at a bank, examines the books of insured banks and imposes restrictions on assets they can hold
Federal Reserve System	All depository institutions	Examines the books of commercial banks that are members of the system, sets reserve requirements for all banks
Office of Thrift Supervision	Savings and loan associations	Examines the books of savings and loan associations, imposes restrictions on assets they can hold

1. State banking and insurance commissions, as well as the Office of the Comptroller of the Currency (an agency of the federal government), have created very tight regulations as to who is allowed to set up a financial intermediary. Individuals or groups that want to establish a financial intermediary, such as a bank or an insurance company, must obtain a charter from the state or the federal government. Only if they are upstanding citizens with impeccable credentials and a large amount of initial funds will they be given a charter.

2. There are stringent reporting requirements for financial intermediaries. Their bookkeeping must follow certain strict principles, their books are subject to periodic inspection, and they must make certain information available to the public.

3. There are restrictions on what financial intermediaries are allowed to do and what assets they can hold. Before you put your funds into a bank or some other such institution, you would want to know that your funds are safe and that the bank or other financial intermediary will be able to meet its obligations to you. One way of doing this is to restrict the financial intermediary from engaging in certain risky activities. Legislation passed in 1933 separates commercial banking from the securities industry so that banks do not engage in risky ventures associated with this industry. Another way is to restrict financial intermediaries from holding certain risky assets, or at least from holding a greater quantity of these risky assets than is prudent. For example, commercial banks and other depository institutions are not allowed to hold common stock because stock prices experience substantial fluctuations. Insurance companies are allowed to hold common stock, but their holdings cannot exceed a certain fraction of their total assets.

4. The government can insure people providing funds to a financial intermediary from any financial loss if the financial intermediary should fail. The most important government agency that provides this type of insurance is the Federal Deposit Insurance Corporation (FDIC), which insures each depositor at a commercial bank or mutual savings bank up to losses of $100,000. All commercial and mutual savings banks, with a few minor exceptions, make contributions into the FDIC, which are used to pay off depositors in the case of a bank's failure. The FDIC was created in 1934 after the massive bank failures of 1930–1933 in which the savings of many depositors at commercial banks were wiped out. Similar government agencies exist for other depository institutions: The Savings Association Insurance Fund (part of the FDIC) provides deposit insurance for savings and loan associations, and the National Credit Union Share Insurance Fund (NCUSIF) does the same for credit unions.

5. Politicians have often declared that unbridled competition among financial intermediaries promotes failures that will harm the public. Although the evidence that competition does this is extremely weak, it has not stopped the state and federal governments from imposing many restrictive regulations. These regulations have taken two forms. First are the restrictions on the opening of additional locations (branches). Banks have not been allowed to open up branches in other states, and in some states banks are restricted from opening additional locations.

6. Competition has also been inhibited by regulations that impose restrictions on interest rates that can be paid on deposits. After 1933, banks were prohibited from paying interest on checking accounts. In addition, until 1986, the Federal Reserve System had the power under **Regulation Q** to set maximum interest rates that banks could pay on savings deposits. These regulations were instituted because of the widespread belief that unrestricted interest-rate competition helped encourage bank failures during the Great Depression. Later evidence does not seem to support this view.

Improving Control of Monetary Policy

Banks play a very important role in determining the supply of money: Much regulation of these financial intermediaries is intended to improve its control. One such regulation is **reserve requirements,** which make it obligatory for all depository institutions to keep a certain fraction of their deposits in accounts with the Federal Reserve System (the Fed), the central bank in the United States. Reserve requirements help the Fed exercise more precise control over the money supply. Deposit insurance regulation can also be rationalized along these lines: The FDIC gives depositors confidence in the banking system and eliminates widespread bank failures, which can in turn cause large, uncontrollable fluctuations in the quantity of money.

In later chapters we will look more closely at government regulation of financial markets and will see whether it has improved the functioning of financial markets.

INTERNATIONALIZATION OF FINANCIAL MARKETS

The growing internationalization of financial markets has become an important trend. Before the 1980s, U.S. financial markets were much larger than financial markets outside the United States, but in recent years the dominance of U.S. markets has been disappearing. The extraordinary growth of foreign financial markets has been the result of both large increases in the pool of savings in foreign countries such as Japan and the deregulation of foreign financial markets, which has enabled them to expand their activities. American corporations and banks are now more likely to tap international capital markets to raise needed funds, and American investors often seek investment opportunities abroad. Similarly, foreign corporations and banks raise funds from Americans, and foreigners are becoming important investors in the United States. A look at international bond markets and world stock markets will give us a picture of how this globalization of financial markets is taking place.

International Bond Market and Eurobonds

The traditional instruments in the international bond market are known as **foreign bonds.** Foreign bonds are sold in a foreign country and are denominated in that country's currency. For example, if the Swedish automaker Volvo sells a bond in the United States denominated in U.S. dollars, it is classified as a foreign bond. Foreign bonds have been an important instrument in the international capital market for centuries. In fact, a large percentage of U.S. railroads built in the nineteenth century were financed by sales of foreign bonds in Britain.

A more recent innovation in the international bond market is the **Eurobond,** a bond denominated in a currency other than that of the country in which it is sold—for example, a bond denominated in U.S. dollars sold in London. Currently, over 80% of the new issues in the international bond market are Eurobonds, and the market for these securities has grown very rapidly. As a result, the Eurobond market has passed the U.S. corporate bond market as a source of new funds.

World Stock Markets

Until recently, the U.S. stock market was by far the largest in the world, but foreign stock markets have been growing in importance. Now the United States is not always number one: Starting in the mid-1980s, the value of stocks traded in Japan has at times exceeded the value of stocks traded in the United States. The increased interest in foreign stocks has prompted the development in the United States of mutual funds specializing in trading in foreign stock markets. American investors now pay attention not only to the Dow Jones Industrial Average but

FOLLOWING THE FINANCIAL NEWS

Foreign Stock Market Indexes

Foreign stock market indexes are published daily in the *Wall Street Journal* next to the "World Markets" column, which reports developments in foreign stock markets.

The first column identifies the foreign stock exchange and the market index; for example, the first entry is for the Nikkei 225 Average for the Tokyo Stock Exchange. The second column, "CLOSE," gives the closing value of the index, which was 20,216.62 for the Nikkei 225 Average on March 1, 1994. The "NET CHG" column indicates the change in the index from the previous trading day, +219.42, and the "PCT CHG" column indicates the percentage change in the index, +1.10%.

Source: Wall Street Journal, Wednesday, March 2, 1994, p. C12.

Stock Market Indexes

EXCHANGE	3/1/94 CLOSE	NET CHG	PCT CHG
Tokyo Nikkei 225 Average	20216.62 +	219.42	+ 1.10
Tokyo Nikkei 300 Index	304.25 +	2.02	+ 0.67
Tokyo Topix Index	1645.48 +	13.77	+ 0.84
London FT 30-share	2536.0 −	28.1	− 1.10
London 100-share	3270.6 −	57.5	− 1.73
London Gold Mines	210.8 +	1.4	+ 0.67
Frankfurt DAX	2067.05 −	24.52	− 1.17
Zurich Swiss Market	2847.7 −	39.1	− 1.35
Paris CAC 40	2183.12 −	54.94	− 2.45
Milan MIBtel Index	10367 −	112	− 1.07
Amsterdam ANP-CBS General	281.3 −	2.4	− 0.85
Stockholm Affarsvarlden	1522.5 −	16.4	− 1.07
Brussels Bel-20 Index	1516.9 +	1.1	+ 0.07
Australia All Ordinaries	2181.7 +	1.6	+ 0.07
Hong Kong Hang Seng	10148.36 −	261.87	− 2.52
Singapore Straits Times	2312.79 −	29.93	− 1.28
Johannesburg J'burg Gold	1976 −	19	− 0.95
Madrid General Index	332.68 −	6.78	− 2.00
Mexico I.P.C.	2514.15 −	71.29	− 2.76
Toronto 300 Composite	4390.43 −	33.41	− 0.76
Euro, Aust, Far East MSCI-p	1049.9 −	4.3	− 0.41

p-Preliminary
na-Not available

also to stock price indexes for foreign stock markets such as the Nikkei 225 Average (Tokyo) and the Financial Times–Stock Exchange 100-Share Index (London).

The internationalization of financial markets is having profound effects on the United States. Foreigners, particularly the Japanese, are not only providing funds to corporations in the United States, but they are also helping finance a significant fraction of the federal government's huge budget deficit. Without these foreign funds, the U.S. economy would have grown far less rapidly in the 1980s and 1990s. The internationalization of financial markets is also leading the way to a more integrated world economy in which flows of goods and technology between countries are more commonplace. In later chapters we will encounter many examples of the important roles that international factors play in our economy.

SUMMARY

1. The basic function of financial markets is to channel funds from savers who have an excess of funds to spenders who have a shortage of funds. This channeling improves the economic welfare of everyone in the society because it allows funds to move from people who have no productive investment opportunities to those who have such opportunities, thereby contributing to increased efficiency in the economy. In addition, it directly benefits consumers by allowing them to make purchases when they need them most.

2. Financial markets can be classified as debt and equity markets, primary and secondary markets, exchanges and over-the-counter markets, and money and capital markets.

3. The principal money market instruments (debt instruments with maturities of less than one year) are U.S. Treasury bills, negotiable bank certificates of deposit, commercial paper, banker's acceptances, repurchase agreements, federal funds, and Eurodollars. The principal capital market instruments (debt and equity instruments with maturities greater than one year) are stocks, mortgages, corporate bonds, U.S. government securities, U.S. government agency securities, state and local government bonds, and consumer and bank commercial loans.

4. Financial intermediaries are financial institutions that acquire funds by issuing liabilities and in turn use those funds to acquire assets by purchasing securities or making loans. Financial intermediaries play such an important role in the financial system because they reduce transactions costs and

solve problems created by adverse selection and moral hazard. As a result, financial intermediaries allow small savers and borrowers to benefit from the existence of financial markets, thereby increasing the efficiency of the economy.

5. The principal financial intermediaries fall into three categories: (a) banks—commercial banks, savings and loan associations, mutual savings banks, and credit unions, (b) contractual savings institutions—life insurance companies, fire and casualty insurance companies, and pension funds; and (c) investment intermediaries—finance companies, mutual funds, and money market mutual funds.

6. The government regulates financial markets for three main reasons: to increase the information available to investors, to ensure the soundness of the financial system, and to improve control of monetary policy. Regulations include requiring disclosure of information to the public, restrictions on who can set up a financial intermediary, restrictions on what assets financial intermediaries can hold, the provision of deposit insurance, reserve requirements, and the setting of maximum interest rates that can be paid on checking accounts and savings deposits.

7. An important trend in recent years is the growing internationalization of financial markets. Eurobonds, which are denominated in a currency other than that of the country in which they are sold, are now the dominant security in the international bond market and have passed U.S. corporate bonds as a source of new funds.

KEY TERMS

liabilities	investment bank	capital market	adverse selection
maturity	underwriting	default	moral hazard
short-term	brokers	currency	thrift institutions (thrifts)
long-term	dealers	federal funds rate	financial panic
intermediate-term	liquid	Eurodollars	Regulation Q
equities	exchanges	financial intermediation	reserve requirements
dividends	over-the-counter (OTC) market	transactions costs	foreign bonds
primary market		economies of scale	Eurobond
secondary market	money market	asymmetric information	

QUESTIONS AND PROBLEMS

*1. Why is a share of IBM common stock an asset for its owner and a liability for IBM?

2. If I can buy a car today for $5000 and it is worth $10,000 in extra income next year to me because it enables me to get a job as a traveling anvil seller, should I take out a loan from Larry the Loan Shark at a 90% interest rate if no one else will give me a loan? Will I be better or worse off as a result of taking out this loan? Can you make a case for legalizing loan-sharking?

*3. Some economists suspect that one of the reasons that economies in developing countries grow so slowly is that they do not have well-developed financial markets. Does this argument make sense?

4. The U.S. economy borrowed heavily from the British in the nineteenth century to build a railroad system. What was the principal debt instrument used? Why did this make both countries better off?

*5. "Because corporations do not actually raise any funds in secondary markets, they are less important to the economy than primary markets." Comment.

6. If you suspect that a company will go bankrupt next year, which would you rather hold, bonds issued by the company or equities issued by the company? Why?

*7. How can the adverse selection problem explain why you are more likely to make a loan to a family member than to a stranger?

8. Think of one example in which you have had to deal with the adverse selection problem.

*9. Why do loan sharks worry less about moral hazard in connection with their borrowers than some other lenders do?

10. If you are an employer, what kinds of moral hazard problems might you worry about with your employees?

*11. If there were no asymmetry in the information that a borrower and a lender had, could there still be a moral hazard problem?

12. "In a world without information and transactions costs, financial intermediaries would not exist." Is this statement true, false, or uncertain? Explain.

*13. Why might you be willing to make a loan to your neighbor by putting funds in a savings account earning a 5% interest rate at the bank and having the bank loan her the funds at a 10% interest rate, rather than loan her the funds yourself?

14. In two lists, rank the following money market instruments in terms of their liquidity and their safety:
  (a) U.S. Treasury bills
  (b) Negotiable CDs
  (c) Repurchase agreements
  (d) Commercial paper

*15. Discuss some of the manifestations of the globalization of world capital markets.

Chapter 3

WHAT IS MONEY?

PREVIEW If you had lived in America before the Revolutionary War, your money might have primarily consisted of Spanish doubloons (silver coins that were also called *pieces of eight*). Before the Civil War, the principal forms of money in the United States were not only gold and silver coins but also paper notes, called *banknotes,* issued by private banks. Today you use not only coins and dollar bills issued by the government as money but also checks written on accounts held at banks. Money has been different things at different times; however, it has *always* been important to people and to the economy.

To understand the effects of money on the economy, we must understand exactly what money is. In this chapter we develop precise definitions by exploring the functions of money, looking at why and how it promotes economic efficiency, tracing how its forms have evolved over time, and examining how money is currently measured.

MEANING OF MONEY

As the word *money* is used in everyday conversation, it can mean many things, but to economists it has a very specific meaning. To avoid confusion, we must clarify how economists' use of the word *money* differs from conventional usage.

Economists define *money* (or, equivalently, the *money supply*) as anything that is generally accepted in payment for goods or services or in the repayment of debts. Currency, which is dollar bills and coins, clearly fits this definition and is one type of money. When most people talk about "money," they're talking about currency. If, for example, someone comes up to you and says, "Your money or your life," you should quickly hand over all your currency rather than ask, "What exactly do you mean by 'money'?"

To define money merely as currency is much too narrow for economists. Because checks are also accepted as payment for purchases, checking account deposits are considered money as well. An even broader definition of money is often needed because other items such as savings deposits can in effect function as money if they can be quickly and easily converted into currency or checking account deposits. As you can see, there is no single, precise definition of money or the money supply, even for economists.

To complicate matters further, the word *money* is frequently used synonymously with *wealth*. When people say, "Joe sure is rich—he has an awful lot of money," they probably mean that Joe not only has a lot of currency and a high balance in his checking account but also has stocks, bonds, four cars, three houses, and a yacht. Thus while "currency" is too narrow a definition of money, this other popular usage is much too broad. Economists make a distinction between money in the form of currency, demand deposits, and other items that are used to make purchases and **wealth,** the total collection of pieces of property that are a store of value. Wealth includes not only money but also other assets such as bonds, common stock, art, land, furniture, cars, and houses.

People also use the word *money* to describe what economists call *income,* as in the sentence "Sheila would be a wonderful catch; she has a good job and earns a lot of money." **Income** is a *flow* of earnings per unit of time. Money, by contrast, is a *stock;* that is, it is a certain amount at a given point in time. If someone tells you that he has an income of $1000, you cannot tell whether he earned a lot or a little without knowing whether this $1000 is earned per year, per month, or even per day. But if someone tells you that she has $1000 in her pocket, you know exactly how much this is.

Keep in mind that the money discussed in this book refers to anything that is generally accepted in payment for goods and services or in the repayment of debts and is distinct from income and wealth.

FUNCTIONS OF MONEY

Whether money is shells or rocks or gold or paper, it has three primary functions in any economy: as a medium of exchange, a unit of account, and a store of value. Of the three functions, its function as a medium of exchange is what distinguishes money from other assets such as stocks, bonds, and houses.

Medium of Exchange

In almost all market transactions in our economy, money in the form of currency or checks is a **medium of exchange;** that is, it is used to pay for goods and services. The use of money as a medium of exchange promotes economic efficiency by eliminating much of the time spent in exchanging goods and services. To see why, let's look at a barter economy, one without money, in which goods and services are exchanged directly for other goods and services.

Take the case of Ellen the Economics Professor, who can do just one thing well: give brilliant economics lectures. In a barter economy, if Ellen wants to eat, she must find a farmer who not only produces the food she likes but also wants to learn economics. As you might expect, this search will be difficult and time-consuming, and Ellen may spend more time looking for such an economics-hungry farmer than she will teaching. It is even possible that she will have to quit lecturing and go into farming herself. Even so, she may still starve to death.

The time spent trying to exchange goods or services is called a transactions cost. In a barter economy, transactions costs are high because people have to satisfy a "double coincidence of wants"—they have to find someone who has a good or service they want and who also wants the good or service they have to offer.

Let's see what happens if we introduce money into Ellen the Economics Professor's world. Ellen can teach anyone who is willing to pay money to hear her lecture. She can then go to any farmer (or his representative at the supermarket) and buy the food she needs with the money she has been paid. The problem of the double coincidence of wants is avoided, and Ellen saves a lot of time, which she may spend doing what she does best: teach.

As this example shows, money promotes economic efficiency by eliminating much of the time spent exchanging goods and services. It also promotes efficiency by allowing people to specialize in what they do best. Money is therefore essential in an economy: It is a lubricant that allows the economy to run more smoothly by lowering transactions costs, thereby encouraging specialization and the division of labor.

The need for money is so strong that almost every society, except the most primitive, invents it. For a commodity to function effectively as money, it has to meet several criteria: (1) It must be easily standardized, making it simple to ascertain its value; (2) it must be widely accepted; (3) it must be divisible so that it is easy to "make change"; (4) it must be easy to carry; and (5) it must not deteriorate quickly. Forms of money that have satisfied these criteria have taken many unusual forms throughout human history, ranging from wampum (strings of beads), used by American Indians, to tobacco and whiskey, used by the early American colonists, to cigarettes, used in prisoner-of-war camps during World War II or currently in Russia.[1] The diversity of forms of money that have been developed over the years is as much a testament to the inventiveness of the human race as the development of tools and language.

Unit of Account

The second role of money is to provide a **unit of account;** that is, it is used to measure value in the economy. We measure the values of goods and services in terms of money, just as we measure weight in terms of pounds or distance in terms of miles. To see why this function is important, let's look again at a barter

---

[1]An extremely entertaining article on the development of money in a prisoner-of-war camp during World War II is R. A. Radford, "The Economic Organization of a P.O.W. Camp," *Economica* 12 (November 1945): 189–201.

economy where money does not perform this function. If the economy has only three goods, say, peaches, economics lectures, and movies, then we need to know only three prices to tell us how to exchange one for another: the price of peaches in terms of economics lectures (that is, how many economics lectures you have to pay for a peach), the price of peaches in terms of movies, and the price of economics lectures in terms of movies. If there were ten goods, we would need to know 45 prices in order to exchange one good for another; with 100 goods, we would need 4950 prices; and with 1000 goods, 499,500 prices.[2]

Imagine how hard it would be to shop in a supermarket with 1000 different items on its shelves; deciding whether chicken or fish is cheaper would be difficult if the price of a pound of chicken were quoted as 4 pounds of butter and the price of a pound of fish were quoted as 8 pounds of tomatoes. To make sure that you can compare the prices of all items, the price tags of each item would have to list up to 999 different prices, and the time spent reading them would result in very high transactions costs.

The solution to the problem is to introduce money into the economy and have all prices quoted in terms of units of that money, enabling us to quote the price of economics lectures, peaches, and movies in terms of, say, dollars. If there were only three goods in the economy, this would not be a great advantage over the barter system because we still would need three prices to conduct transactions. But for ten goods we now need only ten prices; for 100 goods, 100 prices; and so on. At the 1000-good supermarket, there are now only 1000 prices to look at, not 499,500!

We can see that using money as a unit of account reduces transactions costs in an economy by reducing the number of prices that need to be considered. The benefits of this function of money grow as the economy becomes more complex.

Store of Value

Money also functions as a **store of value;** it is a repository of purchasing power over time. A store of value is used to save purchasing power from the time income is received until the time it is spent. This function of money is useful because most of us do not want to spend our income immediately upon receiving it but rather prefer to wait until we have the time or the desire to shop.

Money is not unique as a store of value; any asset, be it money, stocks, bonds, land, houses, art, or jewelry, can be used to store wealth. Many such as-

---

[2]The formula for telling us the number of prices we need when we have N goods is the same formula that tells us the number of pairs when there are N items. It is

$$\frac{N(N-1)}{2}$$

In the case of ten goods, for example, we would need

$$\frac{10(10-1)}{2} = \frac{90}{2} = 45$$

sets have advantages over money as a store of value: They often pay the owner a higher interest rate than money, experience price appreciation, and deliver services such as providing a roof over one's head. If these assets are a more desirable store of value than money, why do people hold money at all?

The answer to this question relates to the important economic concept of **liquidity,** the relative ease and speed with which an asset can be converted into a medium of exchange. Liquidity is highly desirable. Money is the most liquid asset of all because it *is* the medium of exchange; it does not have to be converted into anything else in order to make purchases. Other assets involve transactions costs when they are converted into money. When you sell your house, for example, you have to pay a brokerage commission (usually 5% to 7% of the sales price), and if you need cash immediately to pay some pressing bills, you might have to settle for a lower price in order to sell the house quickly. The fact that money is the most liquid asset, then, explains why people are willing to hold it even if it is not the most attractive store of value.

How good a store of value money is depends on the price level because its value is fixed in terms of the price level. A doubling of all prices, for example, means that the value of money has dropped by half; conversely, a halving of all prices means that the value of money has doubled. In an inflation, when the price level is increasing rapidly, money loses value rapidly, and people will be more reluctant to hold their wealth in this form. This is especially true during periods of extreme inflation, known as **hyperinflation,** in which the inflation rate exceeds 50% per month.

Hyperinflation occurred in Germany after World War I, with inflation rates sometimes exceeding 1000% per month. By the end of the hyperinflation in 1923, the price level had risen to more than 30 billion times what it had been just two years before. The quantity of money needed to purchase even the most basic items became excessive. There are stories, for example, that near the end of the hyperinflation, a wheelbarrow of cash would be required to pay for a loaf of bread. Money was losing its value so rapidly that workers were paid and given time off several times during the day to spend their wages before the money became worthless. No one wanted to hold on to money, and so the use of money to carry out transactions declined and barter became more and more dominant. Transactions costs skyrocketed, and as we would expect, output in the economy fell sharply.

EVOLUTION OF THE PAYMENTS SYSTEM

We can obtain a better picture of the functions of money and the forms it has taken over time by looking at the evolution of the **payments system,** the method of conducting transactions in the economy. The payments system has been evolving over centuries, and with it the form of money. At one point, precious metals such as gold were used as the principal means of payment and were the main form of money. Later, paper assets such as checks and currency began to be used in the payments system and viewed as money. Where the payments system is heading has an important bearing on how money will be defined in the future.

To obtain perspective on where the payments system is heading, it is worth exploring how it has evolved. For any object to function as money, it must be universally acceptable; everyone must be willing to take it in payment for goods and services. An object that clearly has value to everyone is a likely candidate to serve as money, and a natural choice is a precious metal such as gold or silver. Money made up of precious metals or another valuable commodity is called **commodity money,** and from ancient times until several hundred years ago, commodity money functioned as the medium of exchange in all but the most primitive societies. The problem with a payments system based exclusively on precious metals is that such a form of money is very heavy and is hard to transport from one place to another. Imagine the holes you'd wear in your pockets if you had to buy things only with coins! Indeed, for large purchases such as a house, you'd have to rent a truck to transport the money payment.

The next development in the payments system was paper currency (pieces of paper that function as a medium of exchange). Initially, paper currency embodied a promise that it was convertible into coins or into a quantity of precious metal. In most countries, however, currency has evolved into **fiat money,** paper currency decreed by governments as legal tender (meaning that legally it must be accepted as payment for debts) but not convertible into coins or precious metal. Paper currency has the advantage of being much lighter than coins or precious metal, but it can be accepted as a medium of exchange only if there is some trust in the authorities who issue it and printing has reached a sufficiently advanced stage that counterfeiting is extremely difficult. Because paper currency has evolved into a legal arrangement, countries can change the currency that they use at will. Indeed, this is currently a hot topic of debate in Europe, which is contemplating a unified currency (see Box 1).

Major drawbacks of paper currency and coins are that they are easily stolen and can be expensive to transport because of their bulk if there are large amounts. To combat this problem, another step in the evolution of the payments system occurred with the development of modern banking: the invention of checks. Checks are a type of IOU payable on demand that allows transactions to take place without the need to carry around large amounts of currency. The introduction of checks was a major innovation that improved the efficiency of the payments system. Frequently, payments made back and forth cancel each other; without checks, this would involve the movement of a lot of currency. With checks, payments that cancel each other can be settled by canceling the checks, and no currency need be moved. The use of checks thus reduces the transportation costs associated with the payments system and improves economic efficiency. Another advantage of checks is that they can be written for any amount up to the balance in the account, making transactions for large amounts much easier. Checks are advantageous in that loss from theft is greatly reduced, and they provide convenient receipts for purchases.

There are, however, two problems with a payments system based on checks. First, it takes time to get checks from one place to another, a particularly

A Global Perspective

Box 1

MONETARY UNION IN EUROPE?

As part of the December 1991 Maastricht Treaty of European Union, the European Economic Commission (EEC) outlined a plan to achieve the creation of a single European currency based on the ECU, the European currency unit. Advocates of monetary union point to the advantages that a single currency has in eliminating the transactions costs involved in having to exchange the currency of one country for the currency of another. However, the motive behind monetary union is not just gains in efficiency resulting from lower transactions costs; it is also the push that such a monetary union gives toward the integration of Europe's various economies.

Growing disquiet among the European populace about the benefits of monetary unification and political and economic events in the summer and fall of 1992, discussed in more detail in Chapter 22, have made the European union plan for a single European currency less likely. No one knows for sure whether the monetary union in Europe will occur in the near future, but for the first time in history, a serious plan for a single European currency is now on the table.

serious problem if you are paying someone in a different location who needs to be paid quickly. In addition, if you have a checking account, you know that it takes several business days before a bank will allow you to make use of the funds from a check that you have deposited. If your need for cash is urgent, this feature of paying by check can be frustrating. Second, all the paper shuffling required to process checks is costly; it is estimated that it currently costs over $5 billion per year to process all the checks written in the United States.

With the development of the computer and advanced telecommunications technology, there would seem to be a better way to organize our payments system. All paperwork could be eliminated by converting completely to what is known as an electronic funds transfer system (EFTS), in which all payments are made using electronic telecommunications. Let's see how such a system might work.

All stores would have a computer system, typically referred to as a point-of-sale (POS) or debit card system, that would allow you to make purchases without cash or checks. When you select your purchase—say, a new pair of jeans—you would put your debit card into a computer terminal, punch in your secret code number, and be able to move funds from your bank account to the store's to pay for the jeans. If you had a bill to pay, you would just turn on your personal computer and dial into a special electronic network where you could transfer funds from your bank account to the account of the person or firm whom you owed. These transactions would occur instantaneously, and no humans would be required to process any paper.

Does EFTS sound farfetched? It isn't; indeed, to a great extent, such a system is already in operation. The Federal Reserve has a telecommunications system, called Fedwire, that allows all financial institutions that maintain accounts with the Federal Reserve to wire (transfer) funds to each other without having to send checks. In addition, CHIPS (Clearing House Interbank Payment System), a private electronic funds transfer system, is used to wire funds among banks internationally. Now banks, money market mutual funds, securities dealers, and corporations can wire funds using these systems. Wire transfers are typically for amounts greater than $1 million, so even though fewer than 1% of the number of transactions use electronic funds transfers, over 80% of the dollar value of transactions is conducted electronically. Indeed, when we say that a corporation is paying for something with a check, it is frequently paying by an electronic wire transfer.

Lately, EFTS has been touching the lives of the public at large directly. Some stores allow you to make purchases with debit cards: Funds are immediately deducted from your checking account to pay for purchases. Certain recurrent debts such as utility bills and mortgage payments can now be paid automatically every month out of your checking account. Many companies pay salaries by wiring them directly into their employees' bank accounts. Some banks offer their customers a service whereby they can plug their personal computers in to a network that allows them to conduct certain transactions such as moving funds from their savings accounts into their checking accounts.

Although it has been predicted that checks will soon disappear from America's economy, the movement to a checkless society has been far slower than many people expected. Although EFTS may be more efficient than a payments system based on paper, several factors work against the complete disappearance of the paper system. Paper has advantages in that it provides receipts and may make it harder to commit fraud. By contrast, we often hear that an unauthorized person has been able to access a computer database and has been able to alter information entered there. The fact that this occurs means that unscrupulous persons might be able to access bank accounts in an electronic payments system and steal funds by moving them from someone else's account into their own. The prevention of this activity is no easy task, and a whole new field is developing to improve computer security. Another problem with the electronic payments system is that many tricky legal issues remain to be sorted out. For example, can you stop payment on a wire transfer as you can with checks? Who is responsible if someone gets access to your secret code number and removes funds illegally from your account?

The conclusion from this discussion seems to be that we are moving toward a payments system in which the use of paper will diminish, although the development of new forms of electronic money may be a gradual process because of obstacles such as the provision of adequate security.

MEASURING MONEY

The definition of money as anything that is generally accepted in payment for goods and services tells us that money is defined by people's behavior. What makes an asset money is that people believe it will be accepted by others when making payment. As we have seen, many different assets have performed this role over the centuries, ranging from gold to paper currency to checking accounts. For that reason, this behavioral definition does not tell us exactly what assets in our economy should be considered money.

To measure money, we need a precise definition that tells us exactly what assets should be included. There are two ways of obtaining a precise definition of money: the theoretical approach and the empirical approach.

Theoretical and Empirical Definitions of Money

The theoretical approach defines money by using economic theory to decide which assets should be included in its measure. As we have seen, the key feature of money is that it is used as a medium of exchange. Therefore, the theoretical approach focuses on this aspect and suggests that only assets that clearly act as a medium of exchange belong in a measure of the money supply. Currency, checking account deposits, and traveler's checks can all be used to pay for goods and services and clearly function as a medium of exchange. The theoretical approach suggests that a measure of the money supply should include only these assets.

Unfortunately, the theoretical approach is not as clear-cut as we would like. Other assets function like a medium of exchange but are not quite as liquid as currency and checking account deposits. Customers of brokerage firms, for example, can write checks against the value of the securities held for them by the firm. (Because there are often restrictions on the check-writing privilege—for example, a minimum amount for which you can write a check—it is not clear whether these accounts really function as a medium of exchange.) Other assets (such as savings accounts at banks) can similarly be turned quickly into cash without incurring appreciable costs.

The ambiguities inherent in the theoretical approach in determining which assets should be included in a measure of money have led many economists to suggest that money should be defined with a more empirical approach; that is, the decision about what to call money should be based on which measure of money works best in predicting movements of variables that money is supposed to explain. For example, we might look at which measure of money does the best job of predicting the inflation rate or the business cycle and then officially designate it as the preferred measure of the money supply. Unfortunately, the empirical evidence on which measure of money is best is mixed; a measure that predicts well in one period may not predict well in another, and a measure that predicts inflation may not be the best predictor of the business cycle.

As you can see, neither approach to choosing an exact definition of money is entirely satisfactory. The theoretical approach is not specific enough to tell us which assets should be included in or excluded from the appropriate measure of money. The empirical approach encounters difficulties because the evidence on which is the preferred measure of money is mixed, and even if it weren't, we could not be sure that a measure that has worked well in the past would work well in the future. The ambiguity about the precise definition of money is not a very satisfactory state of affairs because policymakers who are responsible for managing the economy need to know exactly what the components of the money supply are if they are to conduct policy by trying to control it.

The Federal Reserve's Monetary Aggregates

The Federal Reserve System (the Fed), the central banking authority responsible for monetary policy in the United States, has conducted many studies on how to define money. The problem of defining money has become especially crucial because extensive financial innovation has produced new types of assets that might properly belong in a measure of money. Since 1980, the Fed has modified its definitions of money several times and has settled on the following measures of the money supply, which are also referred to as **monetary aggregates** (see Table 1).

The narrowest definition of money that the Fed reports is **M1**, which corresponds to the definition proposed by the theoretical approach and includes currency, checking account deposits, and traveler's checks. These assets are clearly money because they can be used directly as a medium of exchange. Until the mid-1970s, only commercial banks were permitted to establish checking accounts, and they were not allowed to pay any interest on them. With the financial innovation that has occurred (discussed more extensively in Chapter 10), regulations have changed so that other types of banks, such as savings and loan associations, mutual savings banks, and credit unions, can also offer checking accounts. In addition, banking institutions can offer other checkable deposits, such as NOW (negotiated order of withdrawal) accounts and ATS (automatic transfer from savings) accounts, that do pay interest on their balances. Table 1 lists the assets included in the measures of the monetary aggregates; both demand deposits (checking accounts that pay no interest) and these other checkable deposits are included in the $M1$ measure.

The **M2** monetary aggregate adds to $M1$ other assets that have check-writing features (money market deposit accounts and money market mutual fund shares) and other assets (small-denomination time deposits, savings deposits, overnight repurchase agreements, and overnight Eurodollars) that are extremely liquid because they can be turned into cash quickly at very little cost.

The **M3** monetary aggregate adds to $M2$ somewhat less liquid assets such as large-denomination time deposits, term repurchase agreements, term Eurodollars, and institutional money market mutual fund shares.

The final measure, **L**, which is really not a measure of money at all but rather a measure of highly liquid assets, adds to $M3$ several types of securities that are essentially highly liquid bonds, such as short-term Treasury securities, commercial paper, savings bonds, and banker's acceptances.

Because we cannot be sure which of the monetary aggregates is the true measure of money, it is logical to wonder if their movements closely parallel each other. If they do, then using one monetary aggregate to conduct policy will be the same as using another, and the fact that we are not sure of the appropriate definition of money (for a given policy decision) is not too costly. However, if the monetary aggregates do not move together, then what one monetary ag-

TABLE 1 Measures of the Monetary Aggregates

	Value as of December 1993 ($ billions)
M1 = Currency	321.4
+ Traveler's checks	7.9
+ Demand deposits	384.8
+ Other checkable deposits	414.3
Total M1	1128.4
M2 = M1	
+ Small-denomination time deposits	782.9
+ Savings deposits and money market deposit accounts	1215.5
+ Money market mutual fund shares (noninstitutional)	348.8
+ Overnight repurchase agreements	72.5
+ Overnight Eurodollars	17.0
+ Consolidation adjustment*	−2.0
Total M2	3563.1
M3 = M2	
+ Large-denomination time deposits	338.9
+ Money market mutual fund shares (institutional)	197.0
+ Term repurchase agreements	95.4
+ Term Eurodollars	45.7
+ Consolidation adjustment*	−15.3
Total M3	4224.8
L = M3	
+ Short-term Treasury securities	323.4
+ Commercial paper	386.8
+ Savings bonds	171.7
+ Banker's acceptances	16.3
Total L	5123.0

*An adjustment to avoid double counting. For example, the M2 consolidation adjustment subtracts short-term repurchase agreements and Eurodollars held by money market mutual funds (which are already included in money market mutual fund balances).

Source: Board of Governors of the Federal Reserve System, Statistical Release H.6, April 1994.

gregate tells us is happening to the money supply might be quite different from what another monetary aggregate would tell us. The conflicting stories might present a confusing picture that would make it hard for policymakers to decide on the right course of action.

Figure 1 plots the growth rates M1, M2, and M3 over the 1960–1993 period. The growth rates of these three monetary aggregates do have some tendency to move together; the timing of their rise and fall is roughly similar, and all of them show a higher rate of growth on average in the 1970s than in the 1960s.

The Monetary Aggregates

Data for the Federal Reserve's monetary aggregates (*M*1, *M*2, and *M*3) are published every Friday. In the *Wall Street Journal,* the data are found in the "Federal Reserve Data" column, an example of which is presented here.

The third entry indicates that the money supply (*M*2) averaged $3564.3 billion for the week ending February 21, 1994. The notation "sa" for this entry indicates that the data are seasonally adjusted; that is, seasonal movements, such as those associated with Christmas shopping, have been removed from the data. The notation "nsa" indicates that the data have not been seasonally adjusted.

Source: Wall Street Journal, Friday, March 4, 1994, p. C17.

FEDERAL RESERVE DATA

MONETARY AGGREGATES
(daily average in billions)

	One week ended:	
	Feb. 21	Feb. 14
Money supply (M1) sa	1139.0	1139.2
Money supply (M1) nsa	1120.6	1127.8
Money supply (M2) sa	3564.3	3573.7
Money supply (M2) nsa	3549.3	3564.1
Money supply (M3) sa	4196.4	4210.3
Money supply (M3) nsa	4182.6	4205.9
	Four weeks ended:	
	Feb. 21	Jan. 24
Money supply (M1) sa	1137.5	1132.5
Money supply (M1) nsa	1123.2	1154.6
Money supply (M2) sa	3569.5	3573.0
Money supply (M2) nsa	3554.9	3591.8
Money supply (M3) sa	4211.9	4234.5
Money supply (M3) nsa	4198.9	4243.6
	Month	
	Jan.	Dec.
Money supply (M1) sa	1133.6	1128.5
Money supply (M2) sa	3572.9	3566.0
Money supply (M3) sa	4232.7	4228.5

nsa-Not seasonally adjusted. sa-Seasonally adjusted.

There are, however, some glaring discrepancies in the movements of these aggregates. According to *M*1, the growth rate of money did not accelerate from 1968, when it was in the 6% to 7% range, to 1971, when it was at a similar level. In the same period, the *M*2 and *M*3 measures tell a different story; they show a marked acceleration from the 8% to 10% range to the 12% to 15% range. Similarly, while the growth rate of *M*1 actually increased from 1989 to 1993, the growth rates of *M*2 and *M*3 in this same period instead showed a downward trend. To this extent, the different measures of money tell a different story about the course of monetary policy from the 1980s to the early 1990s.

From the data in Figure 1, you can see that obtaining a single precise, correct definition of money does seem to matter and that it *does* make a difference which monetary aggregate policymakers and economists choose as the true measure of money.

Money as a Weighted Aggregate

The measures of the money supply listed in Table 1 make black-and-white decisions about whether a given asset is money by including it or excluding it. This distinction, however, is not always so clear-cut. Because all assets have some degree of "moneyness" or liquidity, we might want to say that some fraction of any

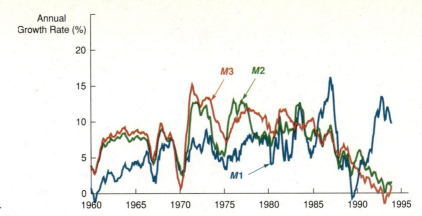

**FIGURE 1
Growth Rates of
the Three Money
Aggregates,
1960–1993**
Sources: Federal
Reserve *Bulletin;*
Citibase databank.

asset functions as money. For example, a share in a money market fund that allows you to write checks with some restrictions against your shares might be viewed as being 60% like money, while a savings account deposit is viewed as 40% like money. Then you might want to define the money supply to include not only the items in $M1$ but also 60% of money market fund shares and 40% of savings deposits:

$$M1 + 0.60 \text{ (money market fund shares)} + 0.40 \text{ (savings deposits)}$$

A measure of the money supply using this approach is called a *weighted* monetary aggregate because each asset receives a different weight (for example, 1.00 for $M1$, 0.60 for the money market fund shares, and 0.40 for savings deposits) when added together. Research along these lines has produced measures of money that seem to predict inflation and business cycles somewhat better than more conventional measures.[3] How successful the monetary aggregates created by this approach will be in the future, only time will tell.

HOW RELIABLE ARE THE MONEY DATA?

The difficulties of measuring money arise not only because it is hard to decide what is the best definition of money but also because the Fed frequently revises earlier estimates of the monetary aggregates by large amounts later on. There are two reasons why the Fed revises its figures. First, because small depository institutions need to report the amounts of their deposits only infrequently, the Fed has to estimate these amounts until the small depository institutions provide the actual figures at some future date. Second, the adjustment of the data for seasonal

---

[3]For example, see William Barnett, Edward Offenbacher, and Paul Spindt, "New Concepts of Aggregate Money," *Journal of Finance* 36 (1981): 487–505, and K. Alec Chrystal, "Empirical Evidence on the Recent Behavior and Usefulness of Simple Sum and Weighted Measures of the Money Stock," *Federal Reserve Bank of St. Louis Review,* forthcoming.

variation is revised substantially as more data become available. To see why this happens, let's look at an example of the seasonal variation of the money data around Christmastime. The monetary aggregates always rise around Christmas because of increased spending during the holiday season; the rise is greater in some years than in others. This means that the factor that adjusts the data for the seasonal variation due to Christmas must be estimated from several years of data, and the estimates of this seasonal factor become more precise only as more data become available. When the data on the monetary aggregates are revised, it often means that the seasonal adjustments change dramatically from the initial calculation.

Table 2 shows how severe a problem data revisions can be. It provides the rates of money growth from one-month periods calculated from initial estimates of the $M2$ monetary aggregate, along with the rates of money growth calculated from a major revision of the $M2$ numbers published in April 1994. As the table shows, for one-month periods the initial versus the revised data can give a different picture of what is happening to monetary policy. For March 1993, for example, the initial data indicated that the growth rate of $M2$ at an annual rate was −0.8%, whereas the revised data indicate a much higher growth rate of +0.2%.

A distinctive characteristic shown in Table 2 is that the differences between the initial and revised $M2$ series tend to cancel out. You can see this by looking at the last row of the table, which shows the average rate of $M2$ growth for the two series and the average difference between them. The average $M2$ growth for the initial calculation of $M2$ is 1.6%, and the revised number is 1.6%, a difference

TABLE 2 Growth Rate of M2: Initial and Revised Series, 1993 (%, compounded annual rate)

Period	Initial Rate	Revised Rate	Difference (Revised Rate − Initial Rate)
January	−4.1	−2.1	2.0
February	−4.2	−2.9	1.3
March	−0.8	0.2	1.0
April	0.1	1.1	1.0
May	10.8	8.2	−2.6
June	2.2	2.3	0.1
July	1.8	1.7	−0.1
August	1.4	1.4	0.0
September	4.3	2.7	−1.6
October	0.7	0.5	−0.2
November	4.2	3.7	−0.5
December	2.3	2.3	0.0
Average	1.6	1.6	0.0

Sources: Federal Reserve *Bulletin,* various issues; Board of Governors of the Federal Reserve System, Statistical Release H.6, April 1994.

of 0.0%. The conclusion that we can draw is that the initial data on the monetary aggregates reported by the Fed are not a reliable guide to what is happening to short-run movements in the money supply, such as the one-month growth rates. However, the initial money data are reasonably reliable for longer periods, such as a year. ***The moral is that we probably should not pay much attention to short-run movements in the money supply numbers but should be concerned only with longer-run movements.***

SUMMARY

1. To economists, the word *money* has a different meaning from *income* or *wealth*. Money is anything that is generally accepted as payment for goods or services or in the repayment of debts.

2. Money serves three primary functions: as a medium of exchange, as a unit of account, and as a store of value. Money as a medium of exchange avoids the problem of double coincidence of wants that arises in a barter economy by lowering transactions costs and encouraging specialization and the division of labor. Money as a unit of account reduces the number of prices needed in the economy, which also reduces transactions costs. Money also functions as a store of value but performs this role poorly if it is rapidly losing value due to inflation.

3. The payments system has evolved over time. Until several hundred years ago, the payments system in all but the most primitive societies was based primarily on precious metals. The introduction of paper currency lowered the cost of transporting money. The next major advance was the introduction of checks, which lowered transactions costs still further. We are currently moving toward an electronic payments system in which paper is eliminated and all transactions are handled by computers. Despite the potential efficiency of such a system, obstacles are slowing the movement to the checkless society and the development of new forms of electronic money.

4. There are two approaches to the measurement of money: theoretical and empirical. The theoretical approach defines the money supply by using economic reasoning, whereas the empirical approach decides on the best measure of money by seeing which measure best predicts inflation and business cycles. Neither approach is completely adequate: the theoretical is not specific enough, and the empirical suffers from the problem that a measure that predicts well in one period will not necessarily continue to predict well in the future. The Federal Reserve System has defined three different measures of the money supply—*M*1, *M*2, and *M*3—and a measure of liquid assets, *L*. These measures are not equivalent and do not always move together, so they cannot be used interchangeably by policymakers. Obtaining the precise, correct definition of money does seem to matter and has implications for the conduct of monetary policy.

5. Another problem in the measurement of money is that the data are not always as accurate as we would like. Substantial revisions in the data do occur; they indicate that initially released money data are not a reliable guide to short-run (say, month-to-month) movements in the money supply, although they are more reliable over longer periods of time, such as a year.

KEY TERMS

wealth	medium of exchange	store of value	hyperinflation
income	unit of account	liquidity	payments system

commodity money　　　　monetary aggregates　　　*M2*　　　　　　　　*L*

fiat money　　　　　　　*M1*　　　　　　　　　　*M3*

QUESTIONS AND PROBLEMS

1. Which of the following three expressions uses economists' definition of *money?*
   (a) "How much money did you earn last week?"
   (b) "When I go to the store, I always make sure that I have enough money."
   (c) "The love of money is the root of all evil."

*2. There are three goods produced in an economy by three individuals:

Good	Producer
Apples	Orchard owner
Bananas	Banana grower
Chocolate	Chocolatier

   If the orchard owner likes only bananas, the banana grower likes only chocolate, and the chocolatier likes only apples, will any trade between these three persons take place in a barter economy? How will introducing money into the economy benefit these three producers?

3. Why did cavemen not need money?

*4. Was money a better store of value in the United States in the 1950s than it was in the 1970s? Why or why not? In which period would you have been more willing to hold money?

5. Rank the following assets from most liquid to least liquid:
   (a) Checking account deposits
   (b) Houses
   (c) Currency
   (d) Washing machines
   (e) Savings deposits
   (f) Common stock

*6. Why have some economists described money during a hyperinflation as a "hot potato" that is quickly passed from one person to another?

7. In Brazil, a country that has been undergoing a rapid inflation, many transactions are conducted in dollars rather than in cruzado reals, the domestic currency. Why?

*8. Suppose that a researcher discovers that a measure of the total amount of debt in the U.S. economy over the past 20 years was a better predictor of inflation and the business cycle than *M1*, *M2*, or *M3*. Does this discovery mean that we should define money as equal to the total amount of debt in the economy?

9. Look up the *M1*, *M2*, and *M3* numbers in the Federal Reserve *Bulletin* for the most recent one-year period. Have their growth rates been similar? What implications do their growth rates have for the conduct of monetary policy?

*10. Which of the Federal Reserve's measures of the monetary aggregates, *M1*, *M2*, or *M3*, is composed of the most liquid assets? Which is the largest measure?

11. In a weighted monetary aggregate, which of the following assets would probably receive the highest weights? Which would receive the lowest weights?
   (a) Currency
   (b) Savings account deposits
   (c) NOW accounts
   (d) U.S. savings bonds
   (e) Houses
   (f) Furniture

*12. Why are revisions of monetary aggregates less of a problem for measuring long-run movements of the money supply than they are for measuring short-run movements?

13. In ancient Greece, why was gold a more likely candidate for use as money than wine was?

*14. Why were people in the United States in the nineteenth century sometimes willing to be paid by check rather than with gold, even though they knew that there was a possibility that the check might bounce?

15. Would you be willing to give up your checkbook and instead use an electronic funds transfer system if it were made available? Why or why not?

PART II

FINANCIAL MARKETS

Chapter 4

UNDERSTANDING INTEREST RATES

PREVIEW   Interest rates are among the most closely watched variables in the economy. Their movements are reported almost daily by the news media because they directly affect our everyday lives and have important consequences for the health of the economy. They affect personal decisions such as whether to consume or save, whether to buy a house, and whether to purchase bonds or put funds into a savings account. Interest rates also affect the economic decisions of businesses and households, such as whether to use their funds to invest in new equipment for factories or to save their money in a bank.

Before we can go on with the study of money, banking, and financial markets, we must understand exactly what the phrase *interest rates* means. In this chapter we see that a concept known as the *yield to maturity* is the most accurate measure of interest rates; the yield to maturity is what economists mean when they use the term *interest rate*. We discuss how the yield to maturity is measured on many of the credit market instruments mentioned in Chapter 2 and examine alternative (but less accurate) ways in which interest rates are quoted. We also see that a bond's interest rate does not necessarily indicate how good an investment the bond is because what it earns (its rate of return) can differ from its interest rate. Finally, we explore the distinction between real interest rates, which are adjusted for changes in the price level, and nominal interest rates, which are not.

Although learning definitions is not always the most exciting of pursuits, it is important to read carefully and understand the concepts presented in this chapter. Not only are they continually used throughout the remainder of this text, but a clear grasp of these terms will give you a clearer understanding of the role that interest rates play in your life as well as in the general economy.

MEASURING INTEREST RATES

In Chapter 2 you were introduced to a number of credit market instruments, which fall into four types:

1. A **simple loan** provides the borrower with an amount of funds (principal) that must be repaid to the lender at the maturity date along with an additional amount known as an *interest* payment. For example, if a bank made you a simple loan of $100 for one year, you would have to repay the principal of $100 in one year's time along with an additional interest payment of, say, $10. Commercial loans to businesses are often of this type.

2. A **fixed-payment loan** provides a borrower with an amount of funds that is to be repaid by making the same payment every month, consisting of part of the principal and interest for a set number of years. For example, if you borrowed $1000, a fixed-payment loan might require you to pay $126 every year for 25 years. Installment loans (such as auto loans) and mortgages are frequently of the fixed-payment type.

3. A **coupon bond** pays the owner of the bond a fixed interest payment (coupon payment) every year until the maturity date, when a specified final amount **(face value or par value)** is repaid. The coupon payment is so named because the bond-holder used to obtain payment by clipping a coupon off the bond and sending it to the bond issuer, who then sent the payment to the holder. Nowadays, for most coupon bonds it is no longer necessary to send in coupons to receive these payments. A coupon bond with $1000 face value, for example, might pay you a coupon payment of $100 per year for ten years and at the maturity date repay you the face value amount of $1000. (The face value of a bond is usually in $1000 increments.)

A coupon bond is identified by three pieces of information. First is the corporation or government agency that issues the bond. Second is the maturity date of the bond. Third is the bond's **coupon rate,** the dollar amount of the yearly coupon payment expressed as a percentage of the face value of the bond. In our example, the coupon bond has a yearly coupon payment of $100 and a face value of $1000. The coupon rate is then $100/$1000 = 0.10, or 10%. Treasury bonds and notes and corporate bonds are examples of coupon bonds.

4. A **discount bond** (also called a **zero-coupon bond**) is bought at a price below its face value (at a discount), and the face value is repaid at the maturity date. Unlike a coupon bond, a discount bond does not make any interest payments; it just pays off the face value. For example, a discount bond with a face value of $1000 might be bought for $900 and in a year's time the owner would be repaid the face value of $1000. U.S. Treasury bills, U.S. savings bonds, and long-term zero-coupon bonds are examples of discount bonds.

These four types of instruments require payments at different times: Simple loans and discount bonds make payment only at their maturity dates, whereas fixed-payment loans and coupon bonds have payments periodically until maturity. How would you decide which of these instruments provides you with more income? They all seem so different because they make payments at different times. To solve this problem, we use the concept of *present value* to provide us with a procedure for measuring interest rates on these different types of instruments.

Present Value

The concept of **present value** is based on the commonsense notion that a dollar paid to you one year from now is less valuable to you than a dollar today; this notion is true because you can deposit the dollar in a savings account and have more than a dollar in one year. We will now define this concept more formally.

In the case of a simple loan, the interest payment divided by the amount of the loan is a natural and sensible way to measure the cost of borrowing funds: The measure of the cost is the *simple interest rate*. In the example we used to describe the simple loan, a loan of $100 today requires the borrower to repay the $100 a year from now and to make an additional interest payment of $10. Hence, using the definition just given, the simple interest rate i is

$$i = \frac{\$10}{\$100} = 0.10 = 10\%$$

If you make this $100 loan, at the end of the year you would receive $110, which can be rewritten as

$$\$100 \times (1 + 0.10) = \$110$$

If you then loaned out the $110, at the end of the second year you would receive

$$\$110 \times (1 + 0.10) = \$121$$

or, equivalently,

$$\$100 \times (1 + 0.10) \times (1 + 0.10) = \$100 \times (1 + 0.10)^2 = \$121$$

Continuing with the loan again, you would receive at the end of the third year

$$\$121 \times (1 + 0.10) = \$100 \times (1 + 0.10)^3 = \$133.10$$

These calculations of the proceeds from a simple loan can be generalized as follows: If the simple interest rate i is expressed as a decimal fraction (such as 0.10 for the 10% interest rate in our example), then after making these loans for n years, you will receive a total payment of

$$\$100 \times (1 + i)^n$$

We can also work these calculations backward. Because $100 today will turn into $110 next year when the simple interest rate is 10%, we could say that $110 next year is worth only $100 today. Or we could say that no one would pay more than $100 to get $110 next year. Similarly, we could say that $121 two years from now or $133.10 three years from now is worth $100 today. This process of calculating what dollars received in the future are worth today is called *discounting the future.* We have been implicitly solving our forward-looking equations for today's value of a future dollar amount. For example, in the case of the $133.10 received three years from now, when $i = 0.10$,

Current	**Future**
$\$100 \times (1 + i)^3$ =	$133.10

so that

$$\$100 = \frac{\$133.10}{(1 + i)^3}$$

More generally, we can solve this equation to tell us the present value *(PV)*, or **present discounted value,** of the future $1, that is, today's value of a $1 payment received n years from now when the simple interest rate is i:

$$PV \text{ of future } \$1 = \frac{\$1}{(1+ i)^n} \tag{1}$$

Intuitively, what Equation 1 tells us is that if you are promised $1 for certain ten years from now, this dollar would not be as valuable to you as $1 is today because you can earn interest on the dollar.

The concept of present value is extremely useful (see Box 1) because it allows us to figure out today's value of a credit market instrument at a given simple interest rate i by just adding up the present value of all the future payments received. This information allows us to compare the value of two instruments with very different timing of their payments, such as a discount bond and a coupon bond. As we will see, this concept also allows us to obtain an equivalent measure of the interest rate on all four types of credit market instruments discussed here.

Yield to Maturity

Although there are several common ways of calculating interest rates, the most important is the **yield to maturity,** the interest rate that equates the present value of payments received from a debt instrument with its value today. Because the concept behind the calculation of the yield to maturity makes good economic sense, economists consider it the most accurate measure of interest rates.

To understand the yield to maturity better, we now look at how it is calculated for the four types of credit market instruments.

Simple Loan Using the concept of present value, the yield to maturity on a simple loan is easy to calculate. For the one-year loan we discussed, today's value is

Box 1

THE COST OF THE S&L BAILOUT: AN APPLICATION OF THE PRESENT VALUE CONCEPT

The government bailout of the savings and loan industry has been one of the major news stories of the past decade. Statements frequently appeared in the press that the cost of the bailout to taxpayers would exceed $500 billion, more than $2000 for every man, woman, and child in the United States. The $500 billion–plus figure makes for wonderful political rhetoric, but is the cost really this high?

The answer is no, and the concept of present value tells us why. The $500 billion figure includes bond payments over the next 40 years. The present value concept tells us that to figure out the cost of these payments in today's dollars, we have to discount them back to the present. When we do this, the present value of these payments is on the order of $150 billion, not $500 billion. It is still true that a present value of the bailout of $150 billion is nothing to sneeze at, but it is not quite as scary as a figure more than three times this size. (Chapter 13 contains an extensive discussion of the S&L crisis and bailout.)

$100, and the payments in one year's time would be $110 (the repayment of $100 plus the interest payment of $10). We can use this information to solve for the yield to maturity i by recognizing that the present value of the future payments must equal today's value of a loan. Making today's value of the loan ($100) equal to the present value of the $110 payment in a year (using Equation 1) gives us

$$\$100 = \frac{\$110}{1+i}$$

Solving for i,

$$i = \frac{\$110 - \$100}{\$100} = \frac{\$10}{\$100} = 0.10 = 10\%$$

This calculation of the yield to maturity should look familiar because it equals the interest payment of $10 divided by the loan amount of $100; that is, it equals the simple interest rate on the loan. An important point to recognize is that *for simple loans, the simple interest rate equals the yield to maturity.* Hence the same term i is used to denote both the yield to maturity and the simple interest rate.

STUDY GUIDE

The key to understanding the calculation of the yield to maturity is equating today's value of the debt instrument with the present value of all of its future payments. The best way to learn this principle is to apply it to other specific examples of the four types of credit market instruments in addition to those we discuss here. See if you can develop the equations that would allow you to solve for the yield to maturity in each case.

Fixed-Payment Loan Recall that this type of loan has the same payment every year throughout the life of the loan. On a fixed-rate mortgage, for example, the borrower makes the same payment to the bank every month until the maturity date, when the loan will be completely paid off. To calculate the yield to maturity for a fixed-payment loan, we follow the same strategy we used for the simple loan—we equate today's value of the loan with its present value. Because the fixed-payment loan involves more than one payment, the present value of the fixed-payment loan is calculated as the sum of the present values of all payments (using Equation 1).

In the case of our earlier example, the loan is $1000 and the yearly payment is $126 for the next 25 years. The present value is calculated as follows: At the end of one year, there is a $126 payment with a *PV* of $126/(1 + i); at the end of two years there is another $126 payment with a *PV* of $126/(1 + i)^2$; and so on until at the end of the twenty-fifth year, the last payment of $126 with a *PV* of $126/(1 + i)^{25}$ is made. Making today's value of the loan ($1000) equal to the sum of the present values of all the yearly payments gives us

$$\$1000 = \frac{\$126}{1 + i} + \frac{\$126}{(1 + i)^2} + \frac{\$126}{(1 + i)^3} + \cdots + \frac{\$126}{(1 + i)^{25}}$$

More generally, for any fixed-payment loan,

$$LOAN = \frac{FP}{1 + i} + \frac{FP}{(1 + i)^2} + \frac{FP}{(1 + i)^3} + \cdots + \frac{FP}{(1 + i)^N} \qquad (2)$$

where *LOAN* = amount of the loan
    FP = fixed yearly payment
    N = number of years until maturity

For a fixed-payment loan amount, the fixed yearly payment and the number of years until maturity are known quantities, and only the yield to maturity is not. So we can solve this equation for the yield to maturity *i*. Because this calculation is not easy, tables have been created that allow you to find *i* given the loan's values for *LOAN, FP,* and *N*. For example, in the case of the 25-year loan with yearly payments of $126, the yield to maturity taken from the table that solves equation 2 is 12%. Real estate brokers always have such a table handy (or a pocket calculator that can solve such equations) so that they can immediately

12%	Monthly Payment Necessary to Amortize a Loan						
	Term (years)						
Amount ($)	19	20	21	22	23	24	25
25	.28	.28	.28	.27	.27	.27	.27
50	.56	.56	.55	.54	.54	.54	.53
75	.84	.83	.82	.81	.81	.80	.79
100	1.12	1.11	1.09	1.08	1.07	1.07	1.06
200	2.24	2.21	2.18	2.16	2.14	2.13	2.11
300	3.35	3.31	3.27	3.24	3.21	3.19	3.16
400	4.47	4.41	4.36	4.32	4.28	4.25	4.22
500	5.58	5.51	5.45	5.39	5.35	5.31	5.27
600	6.70	6.61	6.54	6.47	6.42	6.37	6.32
700	7.81	7.71	7.63	7.55	7.48	7.43	7.38
800	8.93	8.81	8.71	8.63	8.55	8.49	8.43
900	10.04	9.91	9.80	9.71	9.62	9.55	9.48
1000	11.16	11.02	10.89	10.78	10.69	10.61	10.54
2000	22.31	22.03	21.78	21.56	21.38	21.21	21.07
3000	33.47	33.04	32.67	32.34	32.06	31.82	31.60
4000	44.62	44.05	43.55	43.12	42.75	42.42	42.13
5000	55.77	55.06	54.44	53.90	53.43	53.02	52.67

FIGURE 1 A Mortgage Payment Table

This table is for loans with a 12% interest rate. To find the monthly payment for the loan, you pick out the amount of the loan in the first column and then follow that row across to the entry in the column with the number of years to maturity of the loan. For a $1000, 25-year fixed-payment loan with a 12% interest rate, following this procedure indicates that the monthly payment is $10.54 ($126 per year).

tell the prospective house buyer exactly what the yearly (or monthly) payments will be if the house purchase is financed by taking out a mortgage (see Figure 1).[1]

Coupon Bond To calculate the yield to maturity for a coupon bond, follow the same strategy used for the fixed-payment loan: Equate today's value of the bond with its present value. Because coupon bonds also have more than one payment, the present value of the bond is calculated as the sum of the present values of all the coupon payments plus the present value of the final payment of the face value of the bond.

The present value of a $1000-face-value bond with ten years to maturity and yearly coupon payments of $100 (a 10% coupon rate) can be calculated as follows: At the end of one year, there is a $100 coupon payment with a *PV* of $100/(1 + i); at the end of the second year there is another $100 coupon payment with a *PV* of $100/(1 + i)^2$; and so on until at maturity, there is a $100

---

[1]The calculation with a pocket calculator programmed for this purpose requires simply that you enter the amount of the loan *LOAN*, the number of years to maturity *N*, and the interest rate *i* and then run the program.

coupon payment with a *PV* of $100/(1 + i)^{10} plus the repayment of the $1000 face value with a *PV* of $1000/(1 + i)^{10}. Setting today's value of the bond (its current price, denoted by P_b) equal to the sum of the present values of all the payments for this bond gives

$$P_b = \frac{\$100}{1 + i} + \frac{\$100}{(1 + i)^2} + \frac{\$100}{(1 + i)^3} + \cdots + \frac{\$100}{(1 + i)^{10}} + \frac{\$1000}{(1 + i)^{10}}$$

More generally, for any coupon bond,[2]

$$P_b = \frac{C}{1 + i} + \frac{C}{(1 + i)^2} + \frac{C}{(1 + i)^3} + \cdots + \frac{C}{(1 + i)^N} + \frac{F}{(1 + i)^N} \qquad (3)$$

where C = yearly coupon payment
  F = face value of the bond
  N = years to maturity date
  P_b = price of coupon bond

In Equation 3, the coupon payment, the face value, the years to maturity, and the price of the bond are known quantities, and only the yield to maturity is not. Hence we can solve this equation for the yield to maturity i.[3] Just as in the case of the fixed-payment loan, this calculation is not easy, so bond tables (see Figure 2) have been created that allow you to read off the yield to maturity for a bond given its coupon rate, its years to maturity, and its price. Some business-oriented pocket calculators have built-in programs that solve this equation for you.[4]

Let's look at some examples of the solution for the yield to maturity on our 10%-coupon-rate bond that matures in ten years. If the purchase price of the bond is $1000, then either using a pocket calculator with the built-in program or looking at a bond table, we will find that the yield to maturity is 10%. If the price is $900, we find that the yield to maturity is 11.75%. Table 1 shows the yields to maturity calculated for several bond prices.

Three interesting facts are illustrated by Table 1:

1. When the coupon bond is priced at its face value, the yield to maturity equals the coupon rate.

2. The price of a coupon bond and the yield to maturity are negatively related; that is, as the yield to maturity rises, the price of the bond falls. If the yield to maturity falls, the price of the bond rises.

3. The yield to maturity is greater than the coupon rate when the bond price is below its face value.

---

[2]Most coupon bonds actually make coupon payments on a semiannual basis rather than once a year as assumed here. The effect on the calculations is only very slight and will be ignored here.

[3]In other contexts, it is also called the *internal rate of return.*

[4]The calculation of a bond's yield to maturity with the programmed pocket calculator requires simply that you enter the amount of the yearly coupon payment C, the face value F, the number of years to maturity N, and the price of the bond P_b and then run the program.

| 10.00% | Bond Values per $100 of Face Value | | | | | | | | | |

| | Years to Maturity | | | | | | | | | |
Yield (%)	1	2	3	4	5	6	7	8	9	10
10.00	100.00	100.00	100.00	100.00	100.00	100.00	100.00	100.00	100.00	100.00
10.25	99.77	99.56	99.37	99.20	99.04	98.90	98.77	98.66	98.55	98.46
10.50	99.54	99.12	98.74	98.40	98.09	97.82	97.56	97.34	97.13	96.95
10.75	99.31	98.68	98.12	97.61	97.16	96.75	96.38	96.04	95.74	95.47
11.00	99.08	98.25	97.50	96.83	96.23	95.69	95.21	94.77	94.38	94.02
11.25	98.85	97.82	96.89	96.06	95.32	94.65	94.05	93.52	93.04	92.61
11.50	98.62	97.39	96.28	95.30	94.41	93.63	92.92	92.29	91.72	91.22
11.75	98.39	96.96	95.68	94.54	93.52	92.61	91.80	91.08	90.44	89.86
12.00	98.17	96.53	95.08	93.79	92.64	91.62	90.71	89.89	89.17	88.53
12.25	97.94	96.11	94.49	93.05	91.77	90.63	89.62	88.73	87.93	87.23
12.50	97.72	95.69	93.90	92.31	90.91	89.66	88.56	87.58	86.72	85.95
12.75	97.49	95.28	93.32	91.59	90.06	88.71	87.51	86.46	85.52	84.70

FIGURE 2 A Bond Table

This table is for bonds with a 10% coupon rate. To find the price of the bond, you pick out its yield to maturity in the first column and then follow that row across to the entry in the column with the number of years to maturity for the bond. For a ten-year, 10%-coupon-rate bond with a yield to maturity of 11.75%, following this procedure indicates that the price of the bond is $89.86 per $100 of face value (which means that a $1000-face-value bond sells for approximately $900).

These three facts are true for any coupon bond and are really not surprising if you think about the reasoning behind the calculation of the yield to maturity. When you put $1000 in a bank account with an interest rate of 10%, you can take out $100 every year and you will be left with the $1000 at the end of ten years. This is similar to buying the $1000 bond with a 10% coupon rate analyzed in Table 1, which pays a $100 coupon payment every year and then repays $1000 at the end of ten years. If the bond is purchased at the par value of $1000, its yield to maturity must equal the interest rate of 10%, which is also equal to the coupon rate of 10%. The same reasoning applied to any coupon bond

TABLE 1 Yields to Maturity on a 10% Coupon Rate Bond Maturing in Ten Years (Face Value = $1000)	
Price of Bond ($)	**Yield to Maturity (%)**
1200	7.13
1100	8.48
1000	10.00
900	11.75
800	13.81

demonstrates that if the coupon bond is purchased at its par value, the yield to maturity and the coupon rate must be equal.

It is straightforward to show that the bond price and the yield to maturity are negatively related. As i, the yield to maturity, rises, all denominators in the bond price formula must necessarily rise. Hence a rise in the interest rate as measured by the yield to maturity means that the price of the bond must fall. Another way to explain why the bond price falls when the interest rises is that a higher interest rate implies that the future coupon payments and final payment are worth less when discounted back to the present; hence the price of the bond must be lower.

There is one special case of a coupon bond that is worth discussing because its yield to maturity is particularly easy to calculate. This bond is called a **consol;** it is a perpetual bond with no maturity date and no repayment of principal that makes fixed coupon payments of $\$C$ forever. Consols were first sold by the British Treasury during the Napoleonic Wars and are still traded today; however, they are quite rare in American capital markets. The formula in Equation 3 for the price of the consol P_c simplifies to the following:[5]

$$P_c = \frac{C}{i} \qquad (4)$$

One nice feature of consols is that you can immediately see that as i goes up, the price of the bond falls. For example, if a consol pays $\$100$ per year forever and the interest rate is 10%, its price will be $\$1000 = \$100/0.10$. If the interest rate rises to 20%, its price will fall to $\$500 = \$100/0.20$. We can also rewrite this formula as

$$i = \frac{C}{P_c} \qquad (5)$$

---

[5]The bond price formula for a consol is

$$P_c = \frac{C}{1 + i} + \frac{C}{(1 + i)^2} + \frac{C}{(1 + i)^3} + \cdots$$

which can be written as

$$P_c = C(x + x^2 + x^3 + \cdots)$$

in which

$$x = \frac{1}{1 + i}$$

From your high school algebra you might remember the formula for an infinite sum:

$$1 + x + x^2 + x^3 + \cdots = \frac{1}{1 - x} \quad \text{for} \quad x < 1$$

and so

$$P_c = C\left(\frac{1}{1 - x} - 1\right) = C\left[\frac{1}{1 - 1/(1 + i)} - 1\right]$$

which by suitable algebraic manipulation becomes

$$P_c = C\left(\frac{1 + i}{i} - \frac{i}{i}\right) = \frac{C}{i}$$

We see then that it is also easy to calculate the yield to maturity for the consol (despite the fact that it never matures). For example, with a consol that pays $100 yearly and has a price of $2000, the yield to maturity is easily calculated to be 5% (= $100/$2000).

Discount Bond The yield-to-maturity calculation for a discount bond is similar to that for the simple loan. Let us consider a discount bond such as a one-year U.S. Treasury bill, which pays off a face value of $1000 in one year's time. If the current purchase price of this bill is $900, then equating this price to the present value of the $1000 received in one year, using Equation 1, gives

$$\$900 = \frac{\$1000}{1 + i}$$

and solving for i,

$$i = \frac{\$1000 - \$900}{\$900} = 0.111 = 11.1\%$$

More generally, for any one-year discount bond, the yield to maturity can be written as

$$i = \frac{F - P_d}{P_d} \tag{6}$$

where F = face value of the discount bond
  P_d = current price of the discount bond

In other words, the yield to maturity equals the increase in price over the year $F - P_d$ divided by the initial price P_d.

An important feature of this equation is that it indicates that for a discount bond, the yield to maturity is negatively related to the current bond price. This is the same conclusion that we reached for a coupon bond. For example, Equation 6 shows that a rise in the bond price from $900 to $950 means that the bond will have a smaller increase in its price over its lifetime, and the yield to maturity falls from 11.1% to 5.3%. Similarly, a fall in the yield to maturity means that the price of the discount bond has risen.

Summary The concept of present value tells you that a dollar in the future is not as valuable to you as a dollar today because you can earn interest on this dollar. Specifically, a dollar received n years from now is worth only $\$1/(1 + i)^n$ today. The present value of a set of future payments on a debt instrument equals the sum of the present values of each of the future payments. The yield to maturity for an instrument is the interest rate that equates the present value of the future payments on that instrument to its value today. Because the procedure for calculating the yield to maturity is based on sound economic principles, this is the measure that economists think most accurately describes the interest rate.

Our calculations of the yield to maturity for a variety of bonds reveal the important fact that *current bond prices and interest rates are negatively related: When the interest rate rises, the price of the bond falls, and vice versa.*

OTHER MEASURES OF INTEREST RATES

The yield to maturity is the most accurate measure of interest rates and is what economists mean when they use the term *interest rate*. Unless otherwise specified, the terms *interest rate* and *yield to maturity* are used synonymously in this book. However, because the yield to maturity is sometimes difficult to calculate, other, less accurate measures of interest rates have come into common use in bond markets. You will frequently encounter two of these measures, the *current yield* and the *yield on a discount basis,* when reading the newspaper, and it is important for you to understand what they mean and how they differ from the more accurate measure of interest rates, the yield to maturity.

Current Yield

The **current yield** is an approximation of the yield to maturity on coupon bonds that is often reported because in contrast to the yield to maturity, it is easily calculated. It is defined as the yearly coupon payment divided by the price of the security,

$$i_c = \frac{C}{P_b} \tag{7}$$

where i_c = current yield
P_b = price of the coupon bond
C = yearly coupon payment

This formula is identical to the formula in Equation 5, which describes the calculation of the yield to maturity for a consol. Hence, for a consol, the current yield is an exact measure of the yield to maturity. When a coupon bond has a long term to maturity (say, 20 years or more), it is very much like a consol, which pays coupon payments forever. Thus you would expect the current yield to be a rather close approximation of the yield to maturity for a long-term coupon bond, and you can safely use the current-yield calculation instead of looking up the yield to maturity in a bond table. However, as the time to maturity of the coupon bond shortens (say, it becomes less than five years), it behaves less and less like a consol and so the approximation afforded by the current yield becomes worse and worse.

We have also seen that when the bond price equals the par value of the bond, the yield to maturity is equal to the coupon rate (the coupon payment divided by the par value of the bond). Because the current yield equals the coupon payment divided by the bond price, the current yield is also equal to the coupon rate when the bond price is at par. This logic leads us to the conclusion that when the bond price is at par, the current yield equals the yield to maturity. This means that the nearer the bond price is to the bond's par value, the better the current yield will approximate the yield to maturity.

The current yield is negatively related to the price of the bond. In the case of our 10%-coupon-rate bond, when the price rises from $1000 to $1100, the current yield falls from 10% (= $100/$1000) to 9.09% (= $100/$1100). As Table 1 indicates, the yield to maturity is also negatively related to the price of the bond; when the price rises from $1000 to $1100, the yield to maturity falls from 10% to 8.48%. In this we see an important fact: The current yield and the yield to maturity always move together; a rise in the current yield always signals that the yield to maturity has also risen.

The general characteristics of the current yield (the yearly coupon payment divided by the bond price) can be summarized as follows: The current yield better approximates the yield to maturity when the bond's price is nearer to the bond's par value and the maturity of the bond is longer. It becomes a worse approximation when the bond's price is further from the bond's par value and the bond's maturity is shorter. Regardless of whether the current yield is a good approximation of the yield to maturity, a change in the current yield *always* signals a change in the same direction of the yield to maturity.

Yield on a Discount Basis

Before the advent of calculators and computers, dealers in U.S. Treasury bills found it difficult to calculate interest rates as a yield to maturity. Instead, they quoted the interest rate on bills as a **yield on a discount basis** (or **discount yield**), and they still do so today. Formally, the yield on a discount basis is defined by the following formula:

$$i_{db} = \frac{F - P_d}{F} \times \frac{360}{\text{days to maturity}} \tag{8}$$

where i_{db} = yield on a discount basis
F = face value of the discount bond
P_d = purchase price of the discount bond

This method for calculating interest rates has two peculiarities. First, it uses the percentage gain on the face value of the bill $(F - P_d)/F$ rather than the percentage gain on the purchase price of the bill $(F - P_d)/P_d$ used in calculating the yield to maturity. Second, it puts the yield on an annual basis by taking the year to be 360 days long rather than 365 days.

Because of these peculiarities, the discount yield understates the interest rate on bills as measured by the yield to maturity. On our one-year bill, which is selling for $900 and has a face value of $1000, the yield on a discount basis would be as follows:

$$i_{db} = \frac{\$1000 - \$900}{\$1000} \times \frac{360}{365} = 0.099 = 9.9\%$$

whereas the yield to maturity for this bill, which we calculated before, is 11.1%. The discount yield understates the yield to maturity by a factor of over 10%. A little more than 1% can be attributed to the understatement of the length of the year: When the bill has one year to maturity, the second term on the right-hand side of the formula is 360/365 = 0.986 rather than 1.0, as it should be.

The more serious source of the understatement, however, is the use of the percentage gain on the face value rather than on the purchase price. Because, by definition, the purchase price of a discount bond is always less than the face value, the percentage gain on the face value is necessarily smaller than the percentage gain on the purchase price. The greater the difference between the purchase price and the face value of the discount bond, the more the discount yield understates the yield to maturity. Because the difference between the purchase price and the face value gets larger as maturity gets longer, we can draw the following conclusion about the relationship of the yield on a discount basis to the yield to maturity: The yield on a discount basis always understates the yield to maturity, and this understatement becomes more severe the longer the maturity of the discount bond.

Another important feature of the discount yield is that, like the yield to maturity, it is negatively related to the price of the bond. For example, when the price of the bond rises from $900 to $950, the formula indicates that the yield on a discount basis declines from 9.9% to 4.9%. At the same time, the yield to maturity declines from 11.1% to 5.3%. Here we see another important factor about the relationship of yield on a discount basis to yield to maturity: They always move together; that is, a rise in the discount yield always means that the yield to maturity has risen, and a decline in the discount yield means that the yield to maturity has declined as well.

The characteristics of the yield on a discount basis can be summarized as follows: Yield on a discount basis understates the more accurate measure of the interest rate, the yield to maturity; and the longer the maturity of the discount bond, the greater this understatement becomes. Even though the discount yield is a somewhat misleading measure of the interest rates, however, a change in the discount yield always indicates a change in the same direction for the yield to maturity.

APPLICATION   READING THE *WALL STREET JOURNAL*

THE BOND PAGE

Now that we understand the different interest-rate definitions, let's apply our knowledge and take a look at what kind of information appears on the bond page of a typical newspaper, in this case the *Wall Street Journal*. The "Following the Financial News" box contains the *Journal*'s listing for three different types of bonds on Wednesday, March 2, 1994. Panel (a) contains the information on U.S. Treasury bonds and notes. Both are coupon bonds, the only difference being their time to maturity from when they were originally issued: Notes have a time to maturity of less than ten years; bonds have a time to maturity of more than ten years.

The information found in the "Rate" and "Maturity" columns identifies the bond by coupon rate and maturity date. For example, T-bond 1 has a coupon rate of 4% indicating that it pays out $40 per year on a $1000-face-value bond and matures in September 1994. The next three columns tell us about the bond's price. By convention, all prices in the bond market are quoted per $100 of face value. Furthermore, the numbers after the colon represent thirty-seconds. In the case of T-bond 1, the first price of 100:01 represents 100½₂ = 100.031, or an actual price of $1000.31 for a $1000-face-value bond. The bid price tells you what price you will receive if you sell the bond, and the asked price tells you what you must pay for the bond. (You might want to think of the bid price as the "wholesale" price and the asked price as the "retail" price.) The "Chg." column indicates how much the bid price has changed in 32nds (i.e., minus 3 32nds) from the previous trading day.

Notice that for all the bonds and notes, the asked price is more than the bid price. Can you guess why this is so? The difference between the two (the *spread*) provides the bond dealer who trades these securities with a profit. For T-bond 1, the dealer who buys it at 100½₂ and sells it for 100³⁄₂ makes a profit of ²⁄₃₂ = ¹⁄₁₆. This profit is what enables the dealer to make a living and provide the service of allowing you to buy and sell bonds at will.

The "Ask Yld." column provides the yield to maturity, which is 3.83% for T-bond 1. It is calculated with the method described earlier in this chapter using the asked price as the price of the bond. The asked price is used in the calculation because the yield to maturity is most relevant to a person who is going to buy and hold the security and thus earn the yield. The person selling the security is not going to be holding it and is thus less concerned with the yield.

The figure for the current yield is not usually included in the newspaper's quotations for Treasury securities, but it has been added in panel (a) to give you some real-world examples of how well the current yield approximates the yield to maturity. Our previous discussion provided us with some rules for deciding when the current yield is likely to be a good approximation and when it is not.

T-bonds 3 and 4 mature in more than 20 twenty years, meaning that their characteristics are like those of a consol. The current yields should then be a good approximation of the yields to maturity, and they are: The current yields are within two-tenths of a percentage point of the values for the yields to maturity. This approximation is reasonable even for T-bond 3, which has a price more than 10% above its face value.

Now let's take a look at T-bonds 1 and 2, which have a much shorter time to maturity. The current yield is a good approximation when the price is very near the par price of 100, as it is for T-bond 1. However, the price of T-bond 2 differs by only 3% from the par value, and look how poor an approximation the current yield is for the yield to maturity; it overstates the yield to maturity by

Bond Prices and Interest Rates

Bond prices and interest rates are published daily. In the *Wall Street Journal* they can be found in the "NYSE/AMEX Bonds" and "Treasury/Agency Issues" section of the paper. Three basic formats for quoting bond prices and yields are illustrated below.

(a) Treasury bonds and notes

Tuesday, March 1, 1994

Representative Over-the-Counter quotations based on transactions of $1 million or more.

Treasury bond, note and bill quotes are as of mid-afternoon. Colons in bid-and-asked quotes represent 32nds; 101:01 means 101 1/32. Net changes in 32nds. n-Treasury note. Treasury bill quotes in hundredths, quoted on terms of a rate of discount. Days to maturity calculated from settlement date. All yields are to maturity and based on the asked quote. Latest 13-week and 26-week bills are boldfaced. For bonds callable prior to maturity, yields are computed to the earliest call date for issues quoted above par and to the maturity date for issues below par. *-When issued.

Source: Federal Reserve Bank of New York.

GOVT. BONDS & NOTES

	Rate	Maturity Mo/Yr	Bid	Asked	Chg.	Ask Yld.	
T-bond 1		Sep 94n	100:01	100:03	– 3	3.83	Current Yield = 3.99%
	8½	Sep 94n	102:19	102:21	– 3	3.81	
T-bond 2	9½	Oct 94n	103:10	103:12	– 3	3.93	Current Yield = 9.19%
T-bond 3	8	Nov 21	113:04	113:06	–44	6.92	Current Yield = 7.07%
	7¼	Aug 22	104:00	104:02	–43	6.92	
	7⅝	Nov 22	108:29	108:31	–43	6.90	
	7⅛	Feb 23	102:31	103:01	–42	6.88	
T-bond 4	6¼	Aug 23	93:07	93:09	–44	6.78	Current Yield = 6.70%

(b) Treasury bills

TREASURY BILLS

Maturity	Days to Mat.	Bid	Asked	Chg.	Ask Yld.
Mar 03 '94	0	3.17	3.07	+0.08	0.00
Mar 10 '94	7	3.16	3.06	+0.07	3.10
Mar 17 '94	14	2.95	2.85	+0.18	2.89
Mar 24 '94	21	2.89	2.79	+0.18	2.83
Mar 31 '94	28	2.96	2.86	+0.08	2.91
Apr 07 '94	35	3.19	3.15	+0.08	3.20
Apr 14 '94	42	3.19	3.15	+0.09	3.21
Apr 21 '94	49	3.33	3.29	+0.13	3.35
Apr 28 '94	56	3.37	3.33	+0.14	3.39
May 05 '94	63	3.41	3.39	+0.10	3.46
May 12 '94	70	3.42	3.40	+0.10	3.47
May 19 '94	77	3.42	3.40	+0.09	3.47
May 26 '94	84	3.46	3.44	+0.10	3.52
Jun 02 '94	**91**	**3.50**	**3.48**	**+0.11**	**3.56**
Jun 09 '94	98	3.50	3.48	+0.11	3.56
Jun 16 '94	105	3.50	3.48	+0.11	3.56
Jun 23 '94	112	3.50	3.48	+0.10	3.57
Jun 30 '94	119	3.49	3.47	+0.10	3.56
Jul 07 '94	126	3.57	3.55	+0.09	3.64
Jul 14 '94	133	3.58	3.56	+0.10	3.66
Jul 21 '94	140	3.59	3.57	+0.10	3.67
Jul 28 '94	147	3.62	3.60	+0.10	3.70
Aug 04 '94	154	3.64	3.62	+0.10	3.73
Aug 11 '94	161	3.65	3.63	+0.10	3.74
Aug 18 '94	168	3.67	3.65	+0.10	3.76
Aug 25 '94	175	3.69	3.67	+0.11	3.79
Sep 01 '94	**182**	**3.70**	**3.68**	**+0.09**	**3.80**
Sep 22 '94	203	3.72	3.70	+0.10	3.82
Oct 20 '94	231	3.81	3.79	+0.11	3.92
Nov 17 '94	259	3.85	3.83	+0.12	3.97
Dec 15 '94	287	3.87	3.85	+0.12	4.00
Jan 12 '95	315	3.92	3.90	+0.12	4.06
Feb 09 '95	343	3.95	3.93	+0.12	4.10

(c) New York Stock Exchange bonds

CORPORATION BONDS
Volume, $45,740,000

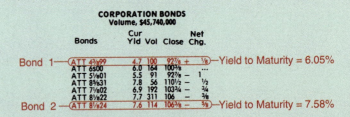

	Bonds	Cur Yld	Vol	Close	Net Chg.	
Bond 1	ATT 4⅜99	4.7	100	92⅞	+ ⅛	Yield to Maturity = 6.05%
	ATT 6s00	6.0	164	100⅜	...	
	ATT 5⅛01	5.5	91	92⅞	– 1	
	ATT 8⅝31	7.8	56	110½	– ½	
	ATT 7⅛02	6.9	192	103¾	– ¾	
	ATT 8⅛22	7.7	311	106	– ⅜	
Bond 2	ATT 8⅛24	7.6	114	106⅜	– ⅝	Yield to Maturity = 7.58%

Source: Wall Street Journal, Wednesday, March 2, 1994, pp. C16 and C17.

more than 5 percentage points. This bears out what we learned earlier about the current yield: It can be a very misleading guide to the value of the yield to maturity for a short-term bond if the bond price is not very close to par.

Two other categories of bonds are reported much like the Treasury bonds and notes in the newspaper. Government agency and miscellaneous securities include securities issued by U.S. government agencies such as the Government National Mortgage Association, which makes loans to savings and loan institutions, and international agencies such as the World Bank. Tax-exempt bonds are the other category reported in a manner similar to panel (a), except that yield to maturity calculations are not usually provided. Tax-exempt bonds include bonds issued by local government and public authorities whose interest payments are exempt from federal income taxes.

Panel (b) quotes yields on U.S. Treasury bills, which, as we have seen, are discount bonds. Since there is no coupon, these securities are identified solely by their maturity dates, which you can see in the first column. The next column, "Days to Mat.," provides the number of days to maturity of the bill. Dealers in these markets always refer to prices by quoting the yield on a discount basis. The "Bid" column gives the discount yield for people selling the bills to dealers, and the "Asked" column gives the discount yield for people buying the bills from dealers. As with bonds and notes, the dealers' profits are made by the asked price being higher than the bid price, leading to the asked discount yield being lower than the bid discount yield.

The "Chg." column indicates how much the asked discount yield changed from the previous day. When financial analysts talk about changes in the yield, they frequently describe the changes in terms of **basis points,** which are hundredths of a percentage point. For example, a financial analyst would describe the +0.08 change in the asked discount yield for the March 3, 1994, T-bill by saying that it had risen by eight basis points.

As we learned earlier, the yield on a discount basis understates the yield to maturity, which is reported in the column of panel (b) headed "Ask Yld." This is evident from a comparison of the "Ask Yld." and "Asked" columns. As we would also expect from our discussion of the calculation of yields on a discount basis, the understatement grows as the maturity of the bill lengthens.

Panel (c) has quotations for corporate bonds traded on the New York Stock Exchange. Corporate bonds traded on the American Stock Exchange are reported in like manner. The first column identifies the bond by indicating the corporation that issued it. The bonds we are looking at have all been issued by American Telephone and Telegraph (AT&T). The next column tells the coupon rate and the maturity date (4⅜ and 1999 for Bond 1). The "Cur. Yld." column reports the current yield (4.7%), and "Vol." gives the volume of trading in that bond (100 bonds of $1000 face value traded that day). The "Close" price is the last traded price that day per $100 of face value. The price of 92⅞ represents $928.75 for a $1000-face-value bond. The "Net Chg." is the change in the closing price from the previous trading day.

The yield to maturity is also given for two bonds. This information is not usually provided in the newspaper, but it is included here because it shows how misleading the current yield can be even for a bond with a maturity of five years such as the 4 3/8 of 1999. The current yield of 4.7% is a misleading measure of the interest rate because the yield to maturity is actually 6.05%.

THE DISTINCTION BETWEEN INTEREST RATES AND RETURNS

Many people think that the interest rate on a bond tells them all they need to know about how well off they are as a result of owning it. If Irving the Investor thinks he is better off when he owns a long-term bond yielding a 10% interest rate and the interest rate rises to 20%, he will have a rude awakening: As we will shortly see, Irving has lost his shirt! How well a person does by holding a bond or any other security over a particular time period is accurately measured by the **return** or, in more precise terminology, the **rate of return.** For any security, the rate of return is defined as the payments to the owner plus the change in its value, expressed as a fraction of its purchase price. To make this definition clearer, let us see what the return would look like for a $1000-face-value coupon bond with a coupon rate of 10% that is bought for $1000, held for one year, and then sold for $1200. The payments to the owner are the yearly coupon payments of $100, and the change in its value is $1200 − $1000 = $200. Adding these together and expressing them as a fraction of the purchase price of $1000 gives us the one-year holding-period return for this bond:

$$\frac{\$100 + \$200}{\$1000} = \frac{\$300}{\$1000} = 0.30 = 30\%$$

You may have noticed something quite surprising about the return that we have just calculated: It equals 30%, yet as Table 1 indicates, initially the yield to maturity was only 10%. This demonstrates that ***the return on a bond will not necessarily equal the interest rate on that bond.*** We now see that the distinction between interest rate and return can be important, although for many securities the two may be closely related.

STUDY GUIDE

The concept of return discussed here is extremely important because it is used continually throughout the book. Make sure that you understand how a return is calculated and why it can differ from the interest rate. This understanding will make the material presented later in the book easier to follow.

More generally, the return on a bond held from time t to time $t+1$ can be written as

$$RET = \frac{C + P_{t+1} - P_t}{P_t} \qquad (9)$$

where RET = return from holding the bond from time t to time $t + 1$
P_t = price of the bond at time t
P_{t+1} = price of the bond at time $t + 1$
C = coupon payment

A convenient way to rewrite the return formula in Equation 9 is to recognize that it can be split up into two separate terms. The first is the current yield i_c (the coupon payment over the purchase price):

$$\frac{C}{P_t} = i_c$$

The second term is the **rate of capital gain,** or the change in the bond's price relative to the initial purchase price:

$$\frac{P_{t+1} - P_t}{P_t} = g$$

where g = rate of capital gain. Equation 9 can then be rewritten as

$$RET = i_c + g \qquad (10)$$

which shows that the return on a bond is the current yield i_c plus the rate of capital gain g. This rewritten formula illustrates the point we just discovered. Even for a bond for which the current yield i_c is an accurate measure of the yield to maturity, the return can differ substantially from the interest rate. Returns will differ from the interest rate especially if there are sizable fluctuations in the price of the bond that produce substantial capital gains or losses.

To understand this point even further, let's look at what happens to the returns on bonds of different maturities when interest rates rise. Table 2 calculates the one-year return on several 10%-coupon-rate bonds all purchased at par

TABLE 2 One-Year Returns on Different-Maturity 10% Coupon Rate Bonds When Interest Rates Rise

(1) Years to Maturity When Bond Is Purchased	(2) Initial Yield to Maturity (%)	(3) Initial Price ($)	(4) Yield to Maturity Next Year (%)	(5) Price Next Year* ($)	(6) Initial Current Yield (%)	(7) Rate of Capital Gain (%)	(8) Rate of Return (6 + 7) (%)
30	10	1000	20	503	10	– 49.7	– 39.7
20	10	1000	20	516	10	– 48.4	– 38.4
10	10	1000	20	597	10	– 40.3	– 30.3
5	10	1000	20	741	10	– 25.9	– 15.9
2	10	1000	20	917	10	– 8.3	+ 1.7
1	10	1000	20	1000	10	0.0	+ 10.0

*Calculated using Equation 3.

when interest rates on all these bonds rise from 10% to 20%. Several key findings in this table are generally true of all bonds:

1. The only bond whose return equals the initial yield to maturity is one whose time to maturity is the same as the holding period (see the last bond in Table 2).

2. A rise in interest rates is associated with a fall in bond prices, resulting in capital losses on bonds whose terms to maturity are longer than the holding period.

3. The more distant a bond's maturity, the greater the size of the price change associated with an interest-rate change.

4. The more distant a bond's maturity, the lower the rate of return that occurs as a result of the increase in the interest rate.

5. Even though a bond has a substantial initial interest rate, its return can turn out to be negative if interest rates rise.

At first it frequently puzzles students that a rise in interest rates can mean that a bond has been a poor investment (as it puzzles poor Irving the Investor). The trick to understanding this is to recognize that a rise in the interest rate means that the price of a bond has fallen. A rise in interest rates therefore means that a capital loss has occurred, and if this loss is large enough, the bond can be a poor investment indeed.[6] For example, we see in Table 2 that the bond that has 30 years to maturity when purchased has a capital loss of 49.7% when the interest rate rises from 10% to 20%. This loss is so large that it exceeds the current yield of 10%, resulting in a negative return (loss) of −39.7%.

Maturity and the Volatility of Bond Returns: Interest-Rate Risk

The finding that the prices of longer-maturity bonds respond more dramatically to changes in interest rates helps explain an important fact about the behavior of bond markets: ***Prices and returns for long-term bonds are more volatile than those for shorter-term bonds.*** Price changes of +20% and −20% within a year, with corresponding variations in returns, are common for bonds more than 20 years away from maturity (the U.S. Treasury, 11¼s of 2015 in Box 2, for example.)

We now see that changes in interest rates make investments in long-term bonds quite risky. Indeed, the riskiness of an asset's return that results from interest-rate changes is so important that it has been given a special name, **interest-rate risk.** Dealing with interest-rate risk is a major concern of managers of financial institutions, as we will see in later chapters.

---

[6]If Irving does not sell the bond, his capital loss is often referred to as a "paper loss." This is a loss nonetheless because if he had not bought this bond and had instead put his money in the bank, he would now be able to buy more bonds than he presently owns.

B o x   2

SHOULD RETIREES INVEST IN "GILT-EDGED" LONG-TERM BONDS?

A common bit of conventional wisdom is that retirees should invest their money in "gilt-edged" securities like long-term U.S Treasury bonds because this will provide them with a safe return. Is this good advice given today's financial markets? The accompanying table provides the prices and one-year returns on Treasury 11¼s of 2015, from 1985 to 1993.

As you can see, there have been big swings in the returns on this supposedly safe investment, with low returns and even losses occurring in some years. If retirees at times need to sell bonds to pay bills, they may find themselves in financial difficulties when the bonds decline in value. Conclusion: Retirees beware!

Prices and One-Year Returns on U.S. Treasury 11¼s of 2015; 1985–1993		
Year	Price at End of Year	Return (%)
1985	117²⁹₃₂	
1986	138⁴₃₂	+26.7
1987	121³¹₃₂	−3.6
1988	121³¹₃₂	+9.2
1989	133²⁶₃₂	+18.9
1990	129²⁴₃₂	+5.4
1991	141²⁷₃₂	+18.0
1992	141¹⁴₃₂	+7.6
1993	154⁶₃₂	+17.0

Although long-term debt instruments have substantial interest-rate risk, short-term debt instruments do not. Indeed, bonds with a maturity that is as short as the holding period have no interest-rate risk.[7] We see this for the coupon bond at the bottom of Table 2, which has no uncertainty about the rate of return because it equals the yield to maturity, which is known at the time the bond is purchased. The key to understanding why there is no interest-rate risk

---

[7]The statement that there is no interest-rate risk for any bond whose time to maturity matches the holding period is only literally true for discount bonds and zero-coupon bonds that make no intermediate cash payments before the holding period is over. A coupon bond that makes an intermediate cash payment before the holding period is over requires that this payment be reinvested at some future date. Since the interest rate at which this payment can be reinvested is uncertain, there is some uncertainty about the return on this coupon bond even when the time to maturity equals the holding period. However, the riskiness of the return on a coupon bond from reinvesting the coupon payments is typically quite small, and so the basic point that a coupon bond with a time to maturity equaling the holding period has very little risk still holds true.

for *any* bond whose time to maturity matches the holding period is to recognize that (in this case) the price at the end of the holding period is already fixed at the face value. The change in interest rates can then have no effect on the price at the end of the holding period for these bonds, and the return will therefore be equal to the yield to maturity known at the time the bond is purchased.[8]

Summary

The return on a bond, which tells you how good an investment it has been over the holding period, is equal to the yield to maturity in only one special case: when the holding period and the maturity of the bond are identical. Bonds whose term to maturity is longer than the holding period are subject to interest-rate risk: Changes in interest rates lead to capital gains and losses that produce substantial differences between the return and the yield to maturity known at the time the bond is purchased. Interest-rate risk is especially important for long-term bonds, where the capital gains and losses can be substantial. This is why long-term bonds are not considered to be safe assets with a sure return over short holding periods.

THE DISTINCTION BETWEEN REAL AND NOMINAL INTEREST RATES

So far in our discussion of interest rates we have ignored the effects of inflation on the cost of borrowing. What we have up to now been calling the interest rate makes no allowance for inflation, and it is more precisely referred to as the

---

[8]In the text, we are assuming that all holding periods are as short as the maturity on short-term bonds and are thus not subject to interest-rate risk. However, if an investor's holding period is longer than the term to maturity of the bond, the investor is exposed to a type of interest-rate risk called *reinvestment risk*. Reinvestment risk occurs because the proceeds from the short-term bond need to be reinvested at a future interest rate that is uncertain.

To understand reinvestment risk, suppose that Irving the Investor has a holding period of two years and decides to purchase a $1000 one-year bond and will then purchase another one at the end of the first year. If the initial interest rate is 10%, Irving will have $1100 at the end of the year. If the interest rate rises to 20%, as in Table 2, Irving will find that buying $1100 worth of another one-year bond will leave him at the end of the second year with $1100 × (1 + 0.20) = $1320. Thus Irving's two-year return will be ($1320 − $1000)/$1000 = 0.32 = 32% which equals 14.9% at an annual rate. In this case, Irving has earned more by buying the one-year bonds than if he had initially purchased the two-year bond with an interest rate of 10%. Thus when Irving has a holding period that is longer than the term to maturity of the bonds he purchases, he benefits from a rise in interest rates. Conversely, if interest rates fall to 5%, Irving will have only $1155 at the end of two years [$1100 × (1 + 0.05)]. Thus his two-year return will be ($1155 − $1000)/$1000 = 0.155 = 15.5%, which is 7.2% at an annual rate. Now with a holding period greater than the term to maturity of the bond, Irving loses from a fall in interest rates.

We have thus seen that when the holding period is longer than the term to maturity of a bond, the return is uncertain because the future interest rate when reinvestment occurs is also uncertain: In short, there is reinvestment risk. We also see that if the holding period is longer than the term to maturity of the bond, the investor benefits from a rise in interest rates and is hurt by a fall in interest rates.

nominal interest rate, which is to distinguish it from the **real interest rate,** the interest rate that is adjusted for expected changes in the price level so that it more accurately reflects the true cost of borrowing.[9] The real interest rate is more accurately defined by the *Fisher equation,* named after Irving Fisher, one of the great monetary economists of the twentieth century. The Fisher equation states that the nominal interest rate i equals the real interest rate i_r plus the expected rate of inflation π^e:[10]

$$i = i_r + \pi^e \qquad (11)$$

Rearranging terms, we find that the real interest rate equals the nominal interest rate minus the expected inflation rate:

$$i_r = i - \pi^e \qquad (12)$$

To see why this definition makes sense, let us first consider a situation in which you have made a one-year simple loan with a 5% interest rate ($i = 5\%$) and you expect the price level to rise by 3% over the course of the year ($\pi^e = 3\%$). As a result of making the loan, at the end of the year you will have 2% more in **real terms,** that is, in terms of real goods and services you can buy. In this case, the interest rate you have earned in terms of real goods and services is 2%; that is,

$$i_r = 5\% - 3\% = 2\%$$

as indicated by the Fisher definition.

Now what if the interest rate rises to 8%, but you expect the inflation rate to be 10% over the course of the year? Although you will have 8% more dollars at the end of the year, you will be paying 10% more for goods; the result is that you will be able to buy 2% fewer goods at the end of the year and you are 2% worse off *in real terms.* This is also exactly what the Fisher definition tells us because

$$i_r = 8\% - 10\% = -2\%$$

---

[9] The real interest rate defined in the text is more precisely referred to as the *ex ante real interest rate* because it is adjusted for *expected* changes in the price level. This is the real interest rate that is most important to economic decisions, and typically it is what economists mean when they make reference to the "real" interest rate. The interest rate that is adjusted for *actual* changes in the price level is called the *ex post real interest rate.* It describes how well a lender has done in real terms *after the fact.*

[10] A more precise formulation of the Fisher equation is

$$i = i_r + \pi^e + (i_r \times \pi^e)$$

because

$$1 + i = (1 + i_r)(1 + \pi^e) = 1 + i_r + \pi^e + (i_r \times \pi^e)$$

and subtracting 1 from both sides gives us the first equation. For small values of i_r and π^e, the term

As a lender, you are clearly less eager to make a loan in this case because in terms of real goods and services you have actually earned a negative interest rate of 2%. By contrast, as the borrower, you fare quite well because at the end of the year, the amounts you will have to pay back will be worth 2% less in terms of goods and services—you as the borrower will be ahead by 2% in real terms. ***When the real interest rate is low, there are greater incentives to borrow and fewer incentives to lend.***

A similar distinction can be made between nominal returns and real returns. Nominal returns, which do not allow for inflation, are what we have been referring to as simply "returns." When inflation is subtracted from a nominal return, we have the real return, which indicates the amount of extra goods and services that can be purchased as a result of holding the security.

The distinction between real and nominal interest rates is important because the real interest rate, which reflects the real cost of borrowing, is likely to be a better indicator of the incentives to borrow and lend. It appears to be a better guide to how people will be affected by what is happening in credit markets. Figure 3, which presents estimates from 1953 to 1993 of the real and nominal interest rates on three-month U.S. Treasury bills, shows us that nominal and real rates often do not move together. (This is also true for nominal and real interest rates in the rest of the world.) In particular, when nominal rates in the United States were high in the 1970s, real rates were actually extremely low, often negative. By the standard of nominal interest rates, you would have thought that credit market conditions were tight in this period because it was expensive to borrow. However, the estimates of the real rates indicate that you would have been mistaken. In real terms, the cost of borrowing was actually quite low.[11]

---

[11]Since most interest income in the United States is subject to federal income taxes, the true earnings in real terms from holding a debt instrument is not the real interest rate defined by the Fisher equation but rather the *after-tax real interest rate,* which equals the nominal interest rate *after income tax payments have been subtracted,* minus the expected inflation rate. For a person facing a 30% tax rate, the after-tax interest rate earning on a bond yielding 10% is only 7% because 30% of the interest income must be paid to the Internal Revenue Service. Thus the after-tax real interest rate on this bond when expected inflation is 20% equals −13% (= 7% − 20%). More generally, the after-tax real interest rate can be expressed as

$$i(1 - \tau) - \pi^e$$

where τ = the income tax rate.

This formula for the after-tax real interest rate also provides a better measure of the effective cost of borrowing for many corporations and individuals in the United States because in calculating income taxes, they can deduct interest payments on loans from their income. Thus if you face a 30% tax rate and take out a mortgage loan with a 10% interest rate, you are able to deduct the 10% interest payment and thus lower your taxes by 30% of this amount. Your after-tax nominal cost of borrowing is then 7% (10% minus 30% of the 10% interest payment), and when the expected inflation rate is 20%, the effective cost of borrowing in real terms is again −13% (= 7% − 20%).

As the example (and the formula) indicates, after-tax real interest rates are always below the real interest rate defined by the Fisher equation. For a further discussion of measures of after-tax real interest rates, see Frederic S. Mishkin, "The Real Interest Rate: An Empirical Investigation," *Carnegie-Rochester Conference Series on Public Policy* 15 (1981): 151–200.

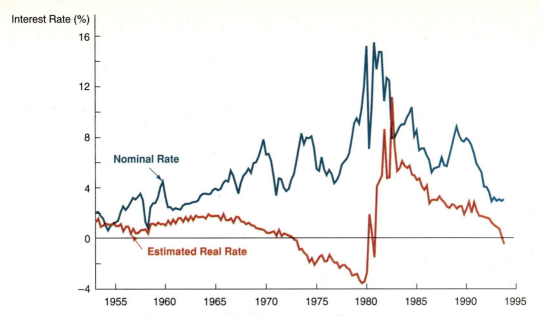

FIGURE 3 Real and Nominal Interest Rates (Three-Month Treasury Bill), 1953–1993
Source: Nominal rates from the Citibase databank. The real rate is constructed using the procedure outlined in Frederic S. Mishkin, "The Real Interest Rate: An Empirical Investigation," *Carnegie-Rochester Conference Series on Public Policy* 15 (1981): 151–200. This involves estimating expected inflation as a function of past interest rates, inflation, and time trends and then subtracting the expected inflation measure from the nominal interest rate.

SUMMARY

1. The yield to maturity, which is the measure that most accurately describes interest rates, is the interest rate that equates the present value of future payments of a debt instrument with its value today. Application of this principle reveals that bond prices and interest rates are negatively related: When the interest rate rises, the price of the bond must fall, and vice versa.

2. Two less accurate measures of interest rates are commonly used to quote interest rates on coupon and discount bonds. The current yield, which equals the coupon payment divided by the price of a coupon bond, is a less accurate measure of the yield to maturity the shorter the maturity of the bond and the greater the gap between the price and the par value. The yield on a discount basis (also called the discount yield) understates the yield to maturity on a discount

bond, and the understatement worsens the more distant the maturity of the discount security. Even though these measures are misleading guides to the size of the interest rate, a change in them always signals a change in the same direction for the yield to maturity.

3. The return on a security, which tells you how well you have done by holding this security over a stated period of time, can differ substantially from the interest rate as measured by the yield to maturity. Long-term bond prices have substantial fluctuations when interest rates change and thus bear interest-rate risk. The resulting capital gains and losses can be large, which is why long-term bonds are not considered to be safe assets with a sure return.

4. The real interest rate is defined as the nominal interest rate minus the expected rate of inflation. It

is a better measure of the incentives to borrow and lend than the nominal interest rate, and it is a more accurate indicator of the tightness of credit market conditions than the nominal interest rate.

KEY TERMS

simple loan

fixed-payment loan

coupon bond

face value (par value)

coupon rate

discount bond (zero-coupon bond)

present value (present discounted value)

yield to maturity

consol

current yield

yield on a discount basis (discount yield)

basis points

return (rate of return)

rate of capital gain

interest-rate risk

nominal interest rate

real interest rate

real terms

QUESTIONS AND PROBLEMS

*1. Would a dollar tomorrow be worth more or less to you today when the interest rate is 20% or when it is 10%?

2. You have just won $20 million in the state lottery, which promises to pay you $1 million (tax free) every year for the next 20 years. Have you really won $20 million?

*3. If the interest rate is 10%, what is the present value of a security that pays you $1100 next year, $1210 the year after, and $1331 the year after that?

4. If the security in Problem 3 sold for $4000, is the yield to maturity greater or less than 10%? Why?

*5. Write down the formula that is used to calculate the yield to maturity on a 20-year 10% coupon bond with $1000 face value that sells for $2000.

6. What is the yield to maturity on a $1000-face-value discount bond maturing in one year that sells for $800?

*7. What is the yield to maturity on a simple loan for $1 million that requires a repayment of $2 million in five years' time?

8. To pay for college, you have just taken out a $1000 government loan that makes you pay $126 per year for 25 years. However, you don't have to start making these payments until you graduate from college two years from now. Why is the yield to maturity necessarily less than 12%, the yield to maturity on a normal $1000 fixed-payment loan in which you pay $126 per year for 25 years?

*9. Which $1000 bond has the higher yield to maturity, a 20-year bond selling for $800 with a cur-

rent yield of 15% or a one-year bond selling for $800 with a current yield of 5%?

10. Pick five U.S. Treasury bonds from the bond page of the newspaper and calculate the current yield. Note when the current yield is a good approximation of the yield to maturity.

*11. You are offered two bonds, a one-year U.S. Treasury bond with a yield to maturity of 9% and a one-year U.S. Treasury bill with a yield on a discount basis of 8.9%. Which would you rather own?

12. If there is a decline in interest rates, which would you rather be holding, long-term bonds or short-term bonds? Why? Which type of bond has the greater interest-rate risk?

*13. Francine the Financial Adviser has just given you the following advice: "Long-term bonds are a great investment because their interest rate is over 20%." Is Francine necessarily right?

14. If mortgage rates rise from 5% to 10% but the expected rate of increase in housing prices rises from 2% to 9%, are people more or less likely to buy houses?

*15. Interest rates were lower in the mid-1980s than they were in the late 1970s, yet many economists have commented that real interest rates were actually much higher in the mid-1980s than in the late 1970s. Does this make sense? Do you think that these economists are right?

Chapter 5

PORTFOLIO CHOICE: THE THEORY OF ASSET DEMAND

PREVIEW Suppose you suddenly struck it rich. Maybe you've just won $25 million in the lottery and your first payment of $600,000 has arrived. Or your dear departed Aunt Thelma has remembered you with a $200,000 bequest. There are a lot of things you might want to do with this windfall: put a down payment on a mansion, buy a Ferrari, or invest in gold coins, land, Treasury bills, or AT&T stock. How will you decide what portfolio of assets you should hold to store your new-found wealth? What criteria should you use to decide among these various stores of wealth? Should you buy only one type of asset or several different types?

This chapter helps answer these questions by developing an economic theory known as the *theory of asset demand* (or the *theory of portfolio choice*). This theory outlines criteria that are important when deciding which assets are worth buying. In addition, it gives us an idea why it is good to diversify and not to put all our eggs in one basket.

The theory of asset demand plays a pivotal role in the study of money, banking, and financial markets and is a building block for much of the analysis in the remainder of the text. In later chapters, for example, we use the theory of asset demand to examine the behavior of interest rates, bank asset and liability management, the money supply process, the evolution of the banking system, financial innovation, the demand for money, and theories of financial market behavior.

DETERMINANTS OF ASSET DEMAND

An **asset** is a piece of property that is a store of value. Items such as money, bonds, stocks, art, land, houses, farm equipment, and manufacturing machinery are all assets. Faced with the question of whether to buy and hold an asset or whether to buy one asset rather than another, an individual must consider the following factors:

1. **Wealth,** the total resources owned by the individual, including all assets

2. **Expected return** (the return expected over the next period) on one asset relative to alternative assets

3. **Risk** (the degree of uncertainty associated with the return) on one asset relative to alternative assets

4. **Liquidity** (the ease and speed with which an asset can be turned into cash) relative to alternative assets

---

STUDY GUIDE

As we discuss each factor that influences asset demand, remember that we are always holding all the other factors constant. Also, think of additional examples of how changes in each factor would influence your decision to purchase a particular asset, say, a house or a share of common stock. This intuitive approach will help you understand how the theory works in practice.

Wealth

When we find that our wealth has increased, we have more resources available with which to purchase assets and so, not surprisingly, the quantity of assets we demand increases.[1] The demands for different assets do have different responses to changes in wealth, however, the quantity demanded of some assets grows more rapidly with a rise in wealth than the quantity demanded of others. The degree of this response is measured by a concept known as the **wealth elasticity of demand** (which is similar to the concept of income elasticity of demand, which you might have learned in an earlier economics course). The wealth elasticity of demand measures how much, with everything else unchanged, the quantity demanded of an asset changes in percentage terms in response to a percentage change in wealth:

$$\frac{\% \text{ change in quantity demanded}}{\% \text{ change in wealth}} = \text{wealth elasticity of demand}$$

If, for example, the quantity of currency demanded increases only by 50% when wealth increases by 100%, we say that currency has a wealth elasticity of demand of ½. If, for a common stock, the quantity demanded increases by 200% when wealth increases by 100%, the wealth elasticity of demand equals 2.

Assets can be sorted into two categories, depending on the value of their wealth elasticity of demand. An asset is a **necessity** if there is only so much that

---

[1]Although it is possible that some assets (called *inferior assets*) might have the property that the quantity demanded does not increase as wealth increases, such assets are rare. Hence we will always assume that demand for an asset increases as wealth increases.

people want to hold, so that as wealth grows, the percentage increase in the quantity demanded of the asset is less than the percentage increase in wealth—in other words, its wealth elasticity is less than 1. Because the quantity demanded of a necessity does not grow proportionally with wealth, the amount of this asset that people want to hold relative to their wealth falls as wealth grows. An asset is a **luxury** if its wealth elasticity is greater than 1, and as wealth grows, the quantity demanded of this asset grows more than proportionally, and the amount that people hold relative to their wealth grows. Common stocks and municipal bonds are examples of luxury assets, and currency and checking account deposits are necessities.

The effect of changes in wealth on the quantity demanded of an asset can be summarized in this way: ***Holding everything else constant, an increase in wealth raises the quantity demanded of an asset, and the increase in the quantity demanded is greater if the asset is a luxury than if it is a necessity.***

Expected Returns

In Chapter 4 we saw that the return on an asset (such as a bond) measures how much we gain from holding that asset. When we make a decision to buy an asset, we are influenced by what we expect the return on that asset to be. If a Mobil Oil Corporation bond, for example, has a return of 15% half of the time and 5% the other half of the time, its expected return (which you can think of as the average return) is 10%.[2] If the expected return on the Mobil Oil bond rises relative to expected returns on alternative assets, holding everything else constant, then it becomes more desirable to purchase it, and the quantity demanded increases. This can occur in either of two ways: (1) when the expected return on the Mobil Oil bond rises while the return on an alternative asset—say, stock in American Broadcasting Corporation—remains unchanged or (2) when the return on the alternative asset, the ABC stock, falls while the return on the Mobil Oil bond remains unchanged. To summarize, ***an increase in an asset's expected***

---

[2]More generally, the expected return equals a weighted sum of each possible realized return multiplied by the probability of its occurring:

$$RET^e = \sum p_i \times RET_i$$

where RET^e = expected return
$\quad p_i \quad$ = probability of getting the realization RET_i
$\quad RET_i$ = realization of the return

For a Mobil Oil bond,

$$RET^e = \left(\frac{1}{2} \times 15\%\right) + \left(\frac{1}{2} \times 5\%\right) = 10\%$$

return relative to that of an alternative asset, holding everything else un-
changed, raises the quantity demanded of the asset.

Risk

The degree of risk or uncertainty of an asset's returns also affects the demand for the asset. Consider two assets, stock in Fly-by-Night Airlines and stock in Feet-on-the-Ground Bus Company. Suppose that Fly-by-Night stock has a return of 15% half the time and 5% the other half of the time, making its expected return 10%, while stock in Feet-on-the-Ground has a fixed return of 10%. Fly-by-Night stock has uncertainty associated with its returns and so has greater risk than stock in Feet-on-the-Ground, whose return is a sure thing.[3]

A *risk-averse* person prefers stock in Feet-on-the-Ground (the sure thing) to Fly-by-Night stock (the riskier asset), even though the stocks have the same expected return, 10%. By contrast, a person who prefers risk is a *risk preferrer* or *risk lover*. Most people are risk-averse: Everything else being equal, they prefer to hold the less risky asset. Hence, **holding everything else constant, if an asset's risk rises relative to that of alternative assets, its quantity demanded will fall.**

Liquidity

Another factor that affects the demand for an asset is how quickly it can be converted into cash without incurring large costs—its liquidity. An asset is liquid if the market in which it is traded has depth and breadth, that is, if the market has many buyers and sellers. A house is not a very liquid asset because it may be hard to find a buyer quickly; if a house must be sold to pay off bills, it might have to be sold for a much lower price. And the transactions costs in selling a house (broker's commissions, lawyer's fees, and so on) are substantial. A U.S. Treasury bill, by contrast, is a highly liquid asset. It can be sold in a well-orga-

---

[3]One frequently used formal measure of risk is the standard deviation, σ:

$$\sigma = \sqrt{\sum p_i \times (RET_i - RET^e)^2}$$

where all the variables are as defined in footnote 2. For Fly-by-Night Airlines stock it equals $\sqrt{0.5 \times (15\% - 10\%)^2 + 0.5 \times (5\% - 10\%)^2} = 5\%$, while for stock in Feet-on-the-Ground Bus Company it is $\sqrt{1 \times (10\% - 10\%)^2} = 0\%$. As you would expect, Fly-by-Night stock, the riskier asset, has a higher standard deviation of its returns. If there is another asset, such as High Flyer, Inc., stock with a return of 0% half of the time and 20% the other half of the time, its expected return is also 10%. This asset is riskier than either of the other two assets, as the standard deviation of its returns shows. For High Flyer stock, the standard deviation is $\sqrt{0.5 \times (0\% - 10\%)^2 + 0.5 \times (20\% - 10\%)^2} = 10\%$, which is higher than the standard deviations for stock in Fly-by-Night or Feet-on-the-Ground.

nized market where there are many buyers, so it can be sold quickly at low cost. ***The more liquid an asset is relative to alternative assets, holding everything else unchanged, the more desirable it is, and the greater will be the quantity demanded.***

THEORY OF ASSET DEMAND

All the determining factors we have just discussed can be assembled into the **theory of asset demand,** which states that, holding all of the other factors constant:

1. The quantity demanded of an asset is usually positively related to wealth, with the response being greater if the asset is a luxury rather than a necessity.

2. The quantity demanded of an asset is positively related to its expected return relative to alternative assets.

3. The quantity demanded of an asset is negatively related to the risk of its returns relative to alternative assets.

4. The quantity demanded of an asset is positively related to its liquidity relative to alternative assets.

These results are summarized in Table 1.

BENEFITS OF DIVERSIFICATION

Our discussion of the theory of asset demand indicates that most people like to avoid risk; that is, they are risk-averse. Why, then, do many investors hold many risky assets rather than just one? Doesn't holding many risky assets expose the investor to more risk?

SUMMARY

TABLE 1 Response of the Demand for an Asset to Changes in Income or Wealth, Expected Returns, Risk, and Liquidity		
Variable	**Change in Variable**	**Change in Quantity Demanded**
Income or wealth	↑	↑
Expected return relative to other assets	↑	↑
Risk relative to other assets	↑	↓
Liquidity relative to other assets	↑	↑

Note: Only increases (↑) in the variables are shown. The effect of decreases in the variables on the change in demand would be the opposite of those indicated in the rightmost column.

The old warning about not putting all your eggs in one basket holds the key to the answer: Because holding many risky assets (called **diversification**) reduces the overall risk an investor faces, diversification is beneficial. To see why this is so, let's look at some specific examples of how an investor fares when holding two risky securities.

Consider two assets, common stock of Frivolous Luxuries, Inc., and common stock of Bad Times Products, Unlimited. When the economy is strong, which we'll assume is half of the time, Frivolous Luxuries has high sales and the return on the stock is 15%; when the economy is weak, the other half of the time, sales are low and the return on the stock is 5%. In contrast, suppose that Bad Times Products thrives when the economy is weak so that its stock has a return of 15%, but it earns less when the economy is strong and has a return on the stock of 5%. Both stocks have a return of 15% half of the time and 5% the other half of the time, and both have an expected return of 10%. However, both stocks carry a fair amount of risk because there is uncertainty about their actual returns.

Suppose now that instead of buying one stock or the other, Irving the Investor puts half his savings in Frivolous Luxuries stock and the other half in Bad Times Products stock. When the economy is strong, Frivolous Luxuries stock has a return of 15% and Bad Times Products has a return of 5%. The result is that Irving earns a return of 10% (the average of 5% and 15%) on his holdings of the two stocks. When the economy is weak, Frivolous Luxuries has a return of only 5% and Bad Times Products has a return of 15%, so Irving still earns a return of 10%. If Irving diversifies by buying both stocks, he earns a return of 10% regardless of whether the economy is strong or weak. Irving is better off from this strategy of diversification because his expected return is 10%, the same as from holding either Frivolous Luxuries or Bad Times Products alone, yet he is not exposed to *any* risk.

Although the case we have described demonstrates the benefits of diversification, it is somewhat unrealistic. It is hard to find two securities with the characteristic that when the return of one is high, the return of the other is always low.[4] In the real world, we are more likely to find at best returns on securities that are independent of each other; that is, when one is high, the other is just as likely to be high as to be low.

Suppose that both securities have an expected return of 10%, with a return of 5% half of the time and 15% the other half of the time. Sometimes both securities will earn the higher return, and sometimes both will earn the lower return. In this case, if Irving holds equal amounts of each security, he will on average earn the same return as if he had just put all his savings into one of the securities. However, because the returns on these two securities are independent, it is just as likely that when one earns the high 15% return, the other earns the low 5% return, and vice versa, giving Irving a return of 10% (equal to the expected

---

[4]Such a case is described by saying that the returns on the two securities are perfectly *negatively* correlated.

return). Because Irving is more likely to earn what he expected to earn when he holds both securities instead of just one, we can see that Irving has again reduced his risk through diversification.[5]

The one case in which Irving will not benefit from diversifying occurs when the returns on the two securities move perfectly together. In this case, when the first security has a return of 15%, the other also has a return of 15%, and holding both securities results in a return of 15%. When the first security has a return of 5%, the other has a return of 5%, and holding both results in a return of 5%. The result of diversifying by holding both securities is a return of 15% half of the time and 5% the other half of the time, which is exactly the same returns that are earned by holding only one of the securities. Consequently, diversification in this case does not lead to any reduction of risk.

The examples we have just examined illustrate the following important points about diversification:

1. Diversification is almost always beneficial to the risk-averse investor because it reduces risk except in the extremely rare case where returns on securities move perfectly together.

2. The less the returns on two securities move together, the more benefit (risk reduction) there is from diversification.

For a real-world perspective on diversification, see Box 1.

SYSTEMATIC RISK

Given the benefits of diversification, you might think that by holding enough different securities in a portfolio, you could eliminate risk entirely. Unfortunately, this is not possible because securities have **systematic risk,** risk that cannot be eliminated through diversification. To understand systematic risk better, we need to recognize that we can divide the risk of an asset into two components, systematic risk and **nonsystematic risk,** the risk unique to an asset that can be diversified away:

$$\text{Asset risk} = \text{systematic risk} + \text{nonsystematic risk}$$

---

[5]We can also see that diversification in our example leads to lower risk by examining the standard deviation of returns when Irving diversifies and when he doesn't. The standard deviation of returns if Irving holds only one of the two securities is $\sqrt{0.5 \times (15\% - 10\%)^2 + 0.5 \times (5\% - 10\%)^2} = 5\%$. When Irving holds equal amounts of each security, there is a probability of 1/4 that he will earn 5% on both (for a total return of 5%), a probability of 1/4 that he will earn 15% on both (for a total return of 15%), and a probability of ½ that he will earn 15% on one security and 5% on the other security (for a total return of 10%). The standard deviation of returns when Irving diversifies is thus $\sqrt{0.25 \times (15\% - 10\%)^2 + 0.25 \times (5\% - 10\%)^2 + 0.5 \times (10\% - 10\%)^2} = 3.5\%$. Since the standard deviation of returns when Irving diversifies is lower than when he holds only one security, we can see that diversification has reduced risk.

Box 1

DANGERS OF NOT DIVERSIFYING: TRUMP—THE FALL

The saga of Donald Trump, a symbol of arrogant wealth in the 1980s, illustrates the dangers of not diversifying. Trump, the author of the best-seller *Trump: The Art of the Deal,* made one deal too many in real estate. Trump's real estate holdings included the Plaza Hotel, a 74-acre plot of undeveloped land on Manhattan's West Side, and two casinos in Atlantic City, at which point he plunged further into the real estate market and borrowed heavily to buy and refurbish another casino in Atlantic City, the Taj Mahal, at a cost of $1 billion.

With Trump's lack of diversification, any softening of the real estate and casino markets could prove disastrous, and this is exactly what happened. Due to the weakening of the real estate market in the Northeast beginning in the late 1980s and lower revenues than expected in Atlantic City casinos, by mid-1990 Trump found himself unable to meet his debt payments. Only with a $65 million bailout loan from four New York City banks and a group of 70 other banks that held pieces of his loans was Trump able to avoid bankruptcy. Continuing troubles at his prized Taj Mahal forced Trump to give up half his stake in the casino in late 1990.

Under the arrangements with the banks, Trump had to give up much of his autonomy in running his businesses; what's worse, he was even put on a budget. His personal spending was restricted to $450,000 *a month* in 1990, $375,000 a month in 1991, and $300,000 a month in 1992 and thereafter. Although these restrictions would not be a hardship for you or me, the free-spending Trump has found them to be a serious hindrance to his lifestyle. The 110-room mansion in Florida and the $29 million yacht have had to go. What may even be more galling to "The Donald," as he is called by those close to him, is that the magic of the Trump name may be no more. In 1989, Trump's net worth was reported to be $1.7 billion, while in August 1990 the New Jersey Casino Control Commission disclosed that he might have a *negative* net worth of $294 million. In 1993, Trump made a new deal with the banks that he hopes will allow him to get rid of his personal debts within two years, but he is still far from out of the woods.

Nonsystematic risk is unique to an asset because it is related to the part of an asset's return that does not vary with returns on other assets. With many assets in a portfolio, nonsystematic risk becomes less important because when the non-systematic part of one asset's return goes up, it is likely that the nonsystematic part of another asset's return has gone down, movements that cancel each other out. Hence with enough diversification as a result of a portfolio containing a large number of different assets, the nonsystematic risk contributes nothing to the total risk of the portfolio. In other words, ***the risk of a well-diversified portfolio is due solely to the systematic risk of assets in the portfolio.***

This fact is very important because it tells us that if we diversify sufficiently, the only component of an asset's risk that we have to worry about is its systematic risk. Systematic risk of an asset is measured by a concept called **beta,** a measure of the sensitivity of an asset's return to changes in the value of the entire market of assets. When on average a 1% rise in the value of the market portfolio leads to a 2% rise in the value of an asset, the beta for this asset is calculated to be 2.0. If, conversely, the value of the asset on average rises by only 0.5% when the market rises by 1%, the asset's beta is 0.5.

The first asset, with a beta of 2.0, has much more systematic risk than the asset with a beta of 0.5. To see this, we first recognize that the portfolio made up of the entire market is a completely diversified portfolio and hence has only systematic risk. When the value of the market fluctuates by a certain amount, the asset with a beta of 2.0 fluctuates twice as much. Therefore, its return has twice as much systematic risk. By contrast, the asset with a beta of 0.5 fluctuates less than the market and so has less systematic risk. Because an asset with a higher beta has more systematic risk, this asset is less desirable because the systematic risk cannot be diversified away. Thus, holding everything else constant, an asset with a higher beta has a lower quantity demanded. We have reached the following conclusion, which is of great importance to participants in financial markets: ***The greater an asset's beta, the greater the asset's systematic risk and the less desirable the asset.***

RISK PREMIUMS: CAPITAL ASSET PRICING MODEL AND ARBITRAGE PRICING THEORY

Our recognition that greater systematic risk makes an asset less desirable can be used to understand the *capital asset pricing model (CAPM),* a widely used theory developed by William Sharpe, John Litner, and Jack Treynor. The CAPM is useful because it provides an explanation for the magnitude of an asset's *risk premium,* the difference between the asset's expected return and the risk-free interest rate (the interest rate on a security that has no possibility of default).

We have seen that an asset contributes risk to a well-diversified portfolio in the amount of its systematic risk as measured by beta. When an asset has a high beta, meaning that it has a large amount of systematic risk and is therefore less desirable, we would expect that investors would be willing to hold this asset only if it yielded a higher expected return. This is exactly what the CAPM tells us in the equation

$$\text{Risk premium} = R^e - R_f = \beta(R_m^e - R_f) \qquad (1)$$

where R^e = expected return for the asset

         R_f = risk-free interest rate

         β = beta of the asset

         R_m^e = expected return for the market portfolio

The CAPM equation provides the commonsense result that when an asset's beta is zero, meaning that it has no systematic risk, its risk premium will be zero. If its beta is 1.0, meaning that it has the same systematic risk as the entire market, it will have the same risk premium as the market, $R_m^e - R_f$. If the asset has an even higher beta, say, 2.0, its risk premium will be greater than that of the market. For example, if the expected return on the market is 8% and the risk-free rate is 2%, the risk premium for the market is 6%. The asset with the beta of 2.0 would then be expected to have a risk premium of 12% (= $2 \times 6\%$).

Although the capital asset pricing model has proved to be useful in real-world applications, it assumes that there is only one source of systematic risk, that found in the market portfolio. However, an alternative theory, the *arbitrage pricing theory (APT)*, developed by Stephen Ross of Yale University, takes the view that there are several sources of risk in the economy that cannot be eliminated by diversification. These sources of risk can be thought of as related to economywide factors such as inflation and aggregate output. Instead of calculating a single beta, like the CAPM, arbitrage pricing theory calculates many betas by estimating the sensitivity of an asset's return to changes in each factor. The arbitrage pricing theory equation is

$$\text{Risk premium} = R^e - R_f = \beta_1 (R_{factor\,1}^e - R_f) \tag{2}$$

$$+ \beta_2 (R_{factor\,2}^e - R_f)$$

$$+ \cdots + \beta_k (R_{factor\,k}^e - R_f)$$

Arbitrage pricing theory thus indicates that the risk premium for an asset is related to the risk premium for each factor and that as the asset's sensitivity to each factor increases, its risk premium will increase as well.

Which of these theories provides a better explanation of risk premiums is still uncertain. Both agree that an asset has a higher risk premium when it has higher systematic risk, and both are considered valuable tools for explaining risk premiums.

With our understanding of the factors that influence investors' decisions to buy and hold different assets, we are ready to explore in the next chapter how the price of a particular asset, bonds, is determined.

SUMMARY

1. The theory of asset demand tells us that the quantity demanded of an asset is (a) positively related to wealth, (b) positively related to the expected return on the asset relative to alternative assets, (c) negatively related to the riskiness of the asset relative to alternative assets, and (d) positively related to the liquidity of the asset relative to alternative assets.

2. Diversification (the holding of more than one asset) benefits investors because it reduces the risk they face, and the benefits are greater the less returns on securities move together.

3. An asset's risk is made up of two components: systematic risk, which cannot be diversified away, and nonsystematic risk, which can. An asset's systematic risk is measured by beta, and the higher an asset's beta and hence its systematic risk, the less desirable the asset.

4. Both the capital asset pricing model and arbitrage pricing theory provide an explanation for an asset's risk premium, the difference between the asset's expected return and the risk-free interest rate. The capital asset pricing model indicates that an asset's risk premium is positively related to the asset's beta, the sensitivity to the market return; arbitrage pricing theory indicates that an asset's risk premium is positively related to the asset's sensitivity to many factors that represent sources of nondiversifiable risk in the economy.

KEY TERMS

asset	liquidity	luxury	nonsystematic risk
wealth	wealth elasticity of demand	theory of asset demand	beta
expected return		diversification	
risk	necessity	systematic risk	

QUESTIONS AND PROBLEMS

1. In terms of the theory of asset demand, explain why you would be more or less willing to buy a share of Polaroid stock in the following situations:
   (a) Your wealth falls.
   (b) You expect it to appreciate in value.
   (c) The bond market becomes more liquid.
   (d) You expect gold to appreciate in value.
   (e) Prices in the bond market become more volatile.

*2. In terms of the theory of asset demand, explain why you would be more or less willing to buy a house under the following circumstances:
   (a) You just inherited $100,000.
   (b) Real estate commissions fall from 6% of the sales price to 4% of the sales price.
   (c) You expect Polaroid stock to double in value next year.
   (d) Prices in the stock market become more volatile.
   (e) You expect housing prices to fall.

3. In terms of the theory of asset demand, explain why you would be more or less willing to buy gold under the following circumstances:
   (a) Gold again becomes acceptable as a medium of exchange.
   (b) Prices in the gold market become more volatile.
   (c) You expect inflation to rise, and gold prices tend to move with the aggregate price level.

   (d) You expect interest rates to rise.

*4. In terms of the theory of asset demand, explain why you would be more or less willing to buy AT&T bonds under the following circumstances:
   (a) Trading in these bonds increases, making them easier to sell.
   (b) You expect a bear market in stocks (stock prices are expected to decline).
   (c) Brokerage commissions on stocks fall.
   (d) You expect interest rates to rise.
   (e) Brokerage commissions on bonds fall.

5. What would happen to the demand for Rembrandts if the stock market undergoes a boom? Why?

*6. If stocks are suddenly expected to yield a higher return, would this affect the demand for bonds? Explain.

7. "The more risk-averse a person is, the more likely that person is to diversify." Is this statement true, false, or uncertain? Explain.

*8. I own a pro football team, and I plan to diversify by purchasing shares in either a company that owns a pro basketball team or a pharmaceutical company. Which of these two investments is more likely to reduce the overall risk I face? Why?

9. "No one who is risk-averse will ever buy a security that has a lower expected return, more risk, and less liquidity than another security." Is this statement true, false, or uncertain? Explain.

*10. "The demand for an asset will be lower, everything else being equal, if its beta is higher." Is this statement true, false, or uncertain? Explain.

11. If on average a stock falls by 3% when the market rises by 2%, what is its beta?

*12. Which stock would you prefer to hold, everything else being equal: a stock that on average rises by 0.5% when the market rises by 1% or a stock that on average rises by 1% when the market rises by 2%?

13. "The higher a security's beta, the lower its risk premium." Is this statement true, false or uncertain? Explain.

*14. If the expected return for the market portfolio is 8% and the risk-free rate is 5%, what does the capital asset pricing model predict the expected return on a security with a beta of 3.0 to be?

15. What is the basic difference between arbitrage pricing theory and the capital asset pricing model?

Chapter 6

THE BEHAVIOR OF INTEREST RATES

PREVIEW In the early 1950s, nominal interest rates on three-month Treasury bills were about 1% at an annual rate; by 1981, they had reached over 15%, then fell to below 6% in the mid-1980s, rose beyond 7% in 1990, and then fell to the 3% level in 1993. What explains these substantial fluctuations in interest rates? One reason why we study money, banking, and financial markets is to provide some answers to this question.

In this chapter we examine how the overall level of *nominal* interest rates (which we refer to as simply "interest rates") is determined and the factors that influence their behavior. We learned in Chapter 4 that interest rates are negatively related to the price of bonds, so if we can explain why bond prices change, we can also explain why interest rates fluctuate. Here we will apply supply and demand analysis to examine how bond prices and interest rates change.

LOANABLE FUNDS FRAMEWORK: SUPPLY AND DEMAND IN THE BOND MARKET

We first approach the analysis of interest-rate determination by studying the supply of and demand for bonds. Because interest rates on different securities tend to move together, in this chapter we will act as if there is only one type of security and a single interest rate in the entire economy. In the chapter following, we will expand our analysis to look at why interest rates on different securities differ.

The first step in the analysis is to use the theory of asset demand discussed in Chapter 5 to obtain a **demand curve,** which shows the relationship between the quantity demanded and the price when all other economic variables are held constant (that is, values of other variables are taken as given). You may recall from previous economics courses that the assumption that all other economic variables are held constant is called *ceteris paribus,* which means "other things being equal" in Latin.

Demand Curve

To clarify our analysis, let us consider the demand for one-year discount bonds, which make no coupon payments but pay the owner the $1000 face value in a year. If the holding period is one year, then as we have seen in Chapter 4, the return on the bonds is known absolutely and is equal to the interest rate as measured by the yield to maturity. This means that the expected return on this bond is equal to the interest rate i, which, using Equation 6 in Chapter 4, is

$$i = RET^e = \frac{F - P_d}{P_d}$$

where i = interest rate = yield to maturity
RET^e = expected return
F = face value of the discount bond
P_d = initial purchase price of the discount bond

This formula shows that a particular value of the interest rate corresponds to each bond price. If the bond sells for $950, the interest rate and expected return is

$$\frac{\$1000 - \$950}{\$950} = 0.053 = 5.3\%$$

At this 5.3% interest rate and expected return corresponding to a bond price of $950, let us assume that the quantity of bonds demanded is $100 billion, which is plotted as point A in Figure 1. To display both the bond price and the corresponding interest rate, Figure 1 has two vertical axes. The left vertical axis shows the bond price, with the price of bonds increasing from $750 near the bottom of the axis toward $1000 at the top. The right vertical axis shows the interest rate, which increases in the *opposite* direction from 0% at the top of the axis to 33% near the bottom. The right and left vertical axes run in opposite directions because, as we learned in Chapter 4, bond price and interest rate are always negatively related: As the price of the bond rises, the interest rate on the bond necessarily falls.

At a price of $900, the interest rate and expected return equals

$$\frac{\$1000 - \$900}{\$900} = 0.111 = 11.1\%$$

Since the expected return on these bonds is higher, with all other economic variables (such as income, expected returns on other assets, risk, and liquidity) held constant, the quantity demanded of bonds will be higher as predicted by the theory of asset demand. Point B in Figure 1 shows that the quantity of bonds demanded at the price of $900 has risen to $200 billion. Continuing with this reasoning, if the bond price is $850 (interest rate and expected return = 17.6%), the quantity of bonds demanded (point C) will be greater than at point B. Similarly,

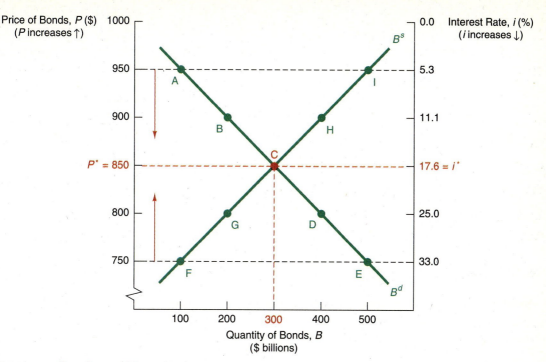

FIGURE 1 Supply and Demand for Bonds
Equilibrium in the bond market occurs at the intersection of the demand curve B^d and the bond supply curve B^s at point C. The equilibrium price is $P^* = \$850$, and the equilibrium interest rate is $i^* = 17.6\%$. (*Note: P* and *i* increase in opposite directions. *P* on the left vertical axis increases as we go up the axis from \$750 near the bottom to \$1000 at the top, while *i* on the right vertical axis increases as we go down the axis from 0% at the top to 33% near the bottom.)

at the lower prices of \$800 (interest rate = 25%) and \$750 (interest rate = 33.3%), the quantity of bonds demanded will be even higher (points D and E). The curve B^d, which connects these points, is the demand curve for bonds. It has the usual downward slope, indicating that at lower prices of the bond (everything else being equal), the quantity demanded is higher.[1]

Supply Curve

An important assumption behind the demand curve for bonds in Figure 1 is that all other economic variables besides the bond's price and interest rate are held constant. We use the same assumption in deriving a **supply curve,** which

[1]Note that although our analysis indicates that the demand curve is downward-sloping, it does not imply that the curve is a straight line. For ease of exposition, however, we will draw demand curves and supply curves as straight lines.

shows the relationship between the quantity supplied and the price when all other economic variables are held constant.

When the price of the bonds is $750 (interest rate = 33.3%), point F shows that the quantity of bonds supplied is $100 billion for the example we are considering. If the price is at $800, the interest rate is at the lower rate of 25%. Since at this interest rate it is now less costly to borrow by issuing bonds, firms will be willing to borrow more through bond issues, and the quantity of bonds supplied is at the higher level of $200 billion (point G). An even higher price of $850, corresponding to a lower interest rate of 17.6%, results in a larger quantity of bonds supplied of $300 billion (point C). Higher prices of $900 and $950 result in even greater quantities of bonds supplied (points H and I). The B^s curve, which connects these points, is the supply curve for bonds. It has the usual upward slope found in supply curves, indicating that as the price increases (everything else being equal), the quantity supplied increases.

Market Equilibrium

In economics, **market equilibrium** occurs when the amount that people are willing to buy *(demand)* equals the amount that people are willing to sell *(supply)* at a given price. In the bond market, this is achieved when the quantity of bonds demanded equals the quantity of bonds supplied:

$$B^d = B^s \tag{1}$$

In Figure 1, equilibrium occurs at point C, where the demand and supply curves intersect at a bond price of $850 (interest rate of 17.6%) and a quantity of bonds of $300 billion. The price of $P^* = 850$, where the quantity demanded equals the quantity supplied, is called the *equilibrium* or *market-clearing* price. Similarly, the interest rate of $i^* = 17.6\%$ that corresponds to this price is called the equilibrium or market-clearing interest rate.

The concepts of market equilibrium and equilibrium price or interest rate are useful because there is a tendency for the market to head toward them. We can see that it does in Figure 1 by first looking at what happens when we have a bond price that is above the equilibrium price. When the price of bonds is set too high, at, say, $950, the quantity of bonds supplied at point I is greater than the quantity of bonds demanded at point A. A situation like this, in which the quantity of bonds supplied exceeds the quantity of bonds demanded, is called a condition of **excess supply.** Because people want to sell more bonds than others want to buy, the price of the bonds will fall, and this is why the downward arrow is drawn in the figure at the bond price of $950. As long as the bond price remains above the equilibrium price, there will continue to be an excess supply of bonds, and the price will continue to fall. This will stop only when the price has reached the equilibrium price of $850, where the excess supply of bonds has been eliminated.

Now let's look at what happens when the price of bonds is below the equilibrium price. If the price of the bonds is set too low, at, say, $750, the quantity demanded at point E is greater than the quantity supplied at point F. This is called a condition of **excess demand.** People now want to buy more bonds than others are willing to sell, and so the price of bonds will be driven up. This is illustrated by the upward arrow drawn in the figure at the bond price of $750. Only when the excess demand for bonds is eliminated by the price rising to the equilibrium level of $850 is there no further tendency for the price to rise.

We can see that the concept of equilibrium price is a useful one because it indicates where the market will settle. Because each price on the left vertical axis of Figure 1 corresponds to a value of the interest rate on the right vertical axis, the same diagram also shows that the interest rate will head toward the equilibrium interest rate of 17.6%. When the interest rate is below the equilibrium interest rate, as it is when it is at 5.3%, the price of the bond is above the equilibrium price, and there will be an excess supply of bonds. The price of the bond then falls, leading to a rise in the interest rate toward the equilibrium level. Similarly, when the interest rate is above the equilibrium level, as it is when it is at 33.3%, there is excess demand for bonds, and the bond price will rise, driving the interest rate back down to the equilibrium level of 17.6%.

Supply and Demand Analysis

Our Figure 1 is a conventional supply and demand diagram with price on the left vertical axis and quantity on the horizontal axis. Because the interest rate that corresponds to each bond price is also marked on the right vertical axis, this diagram allows us to read the equilibrium interest rate, giving us a model that describes the determination of interest rates. It is important to recognize that a supply and demand diagram like Figure 1 can be drawn for *any* type of bond because the interest rate and price of a bond are *always* negatively related for any type of bond, be it a discount bond or a coupon bond.

One disadvantage of the diagram in Figure 1 is that interest rates run in an unusual direction on the right vertical axis: As we go up the right axis, interest rates fall. Because economists are typically more concerned with the value of interest rates rather than the price of bonds, we could plot the supply of and demand for bonds on a diagram that has only a left vertical axis that provides the values of the interest rates running in the usual direction, rising as we go up the axis. Figure 2 is such a diagram, in which points A through I match the corresponding points in Figure 1.

However, making interest rates run the "usual" direction on the vertical axis presents us with a problem. Our demand curve for bonds, points A through E, now looks peculiar because it has an upward slope. This upward slope is, however, completely consistent with our usual demand analysis, which produces a negative relationship between price and quantity. The inverse relationship between bond prices and interest rates means that in moving from point A to point B to point C, bond prices are falling and, consistent with usual demand analysis, the quantity demanded is rising. Similarly, our supply curve for bonds, points F through I, has an unusual-looking downward slope but is completely consistent with the usual view that price and the quantity supplied are positively related.

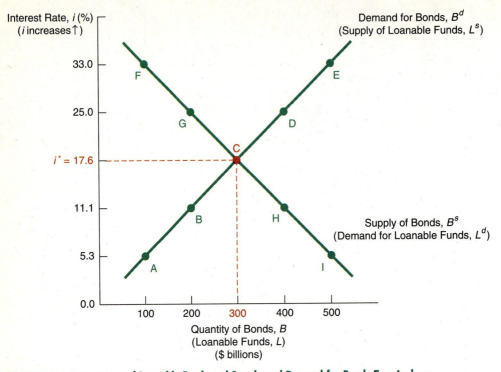

FIGURE 2 A Comparison of Loanable Funds and Supply and Demand for Bonds Terminology
The demand for bonds is equivalent to the *supply of loanable funds,* and the supply of bonds is equivalent to the *demand for loanable funds.* (*Note:* i increases as we go up the vertical axis, in contrast to Figure 1, in which the opposite occurs.)

One way to give the demand curve the usual downward slope and the supply curve the usual upward slope is to rename the horizontal axis and the demand and supply curves. Because a firm supplying bonds is in fact taking out a loan from a person buying a bond, "supplying a bond" is equivalent to "demanding a loan." Thus the supply curve for bonds can be reinterpreted as indicating the quantity of loans demanded for each value of the interest rate. If we rename the horizontal axis **loanable funds,** defined as the quantity of loans, the supply of bonds can be reinterpreted as the *demand for loanable funds.* Similarly, the demand curve for bonds can be reidentified as the *supply of loanable funds* because buying (demanding) a bond is equivalent to supplying a loan. Figure 2 relabels the curves and the horizontal axis using the loanable funds terminology in parentheses, and now the renamed loanable funds demand curve has the usual downward slope and the renamed loanable funds supply curve the usual upward slope.

Because supply and demand diagrams that explain how interest rates are determined in the bond market most commonly use the loanable funds terminology, this analysis is frequently referred to as the **loanable funds framework.** However, because in later chapters describing the conduct of monetary policy we focus on how the demand for and supply of bonds is affected, we will continue to conduct supply and demand analysis in terms of bonds, as in Figure 1, rather than loanable funds. Whether the analysis is done in terms of loanable funds or in terms of the demand for and supply of bonds, the results are the same; the two ways of analyzing the determination of interest rates are equivalent.

An important feature of the analysis here is that supply and demand are always in terms of *stocks* (amounts at a given point in time) of assets, not in terms of *flows*. This approach is somewhat different from certain loanable funds analyses, which are conducted in terms of flows (loans per year). The **asset market approach** for understanding behavior in financial markets—which emphasizes stocks of assets rather than flows in determining asset prices—is now the dominant methodology used by economists because correctly conducting analyses in terms of flows is very tricky, especially when we encounter inflation. (See the appendix to this chapter for an application of the asset market approach to another market.)

CHANGES IN EQUILIBRIUM INTEREST RATES

We will now use the supply and demand framework for bonds to analyze why interest rates change. To avoid confusion, it is important to make the distinction between *movements along* a demand (or supply) curve and *shifts in* a demand (or supply) curve. When quantity demanded (or supplied) changes as a result of a change in the price of the bond (or, equivalently, a change in the interest rate), we have a *movement along* the demand (or supply) curve. The change in the quantity demanded when we move from point A to B to C in Figure 1 or Figure 2, for example, is a movement along a demand curve. A *shift in* the demand (or supply) curve, by contrast, occurs when the quantity demanded (or supplied) changes *at each given price (or interest rate)* of the bond in response to a change in some other factor besides the bond's price or interest rate. When one of these factors changes, causing a shift in the demand or supply curve, there will be a new equilibrium value for the interest rate.

In the following pages we will look at how the supply and demand curves shift in response to changes in variables, such as expected inflation and wealth, and what effects these changes have on the equilibrium value of interest rates.

Shifts in the Demand for Bonds

The theory of asset demand developed in Chapter 5 provides a framework for deciding what factors cause the demand curve for bonds to shift. These factors include changes in four parameters:

1. Wealth
2. Expected returns on bonds relative to alternative assets

3. Risk of bonds relative to alternative assets

4. Liquidity of bonds relative to alternative assets

To see how a change in each of these factors (holding all other factors constant) can shift the demand curve, let us look at some examples. (As a study aid, Table 1 summarizes the effects of changes in these factors on the bond demand curve.)

Wealth When the economy is growing rapidly in a business cycle expansion and wealth is increasing, the quantity of bonds demanded at each bond price (or interest rate) increases as shown in Figure 3. To see how this works, consider point B on the initial demand curve for bonds B_1^d. It tells us that at a bond price of $900 and an interest rate of 11.1%, the quantity of bonds demanded is $200 billion. With higher wealth, the quantity of bonds demanded at the same interest rate must rise, say, to $400 billion (point B'). Similarly, the higher wealth causes the quantity demanded at a bond price of $800 and an interest rate of 25% to rise from $400 billion to $600 billion (point D to D'). Continuing with this reasoning for every point on the initial demand curve B_1^d, we can see that the demand curve shifts to the right from B_1^d to B_2^d as is indicated by the arrows.

The conclusion we have reached is that ***in a business cycle expansion with growing wealth, the demand for bonds rises and the demand curve for bonds shifts to the right.*** However, how much demand will shift (increase)

FIGURE 3
Shift in the Demand Curve for Bonds
When the demand for bonds increases, the demand curve shifts to the right as shown. (*Note: P* and *i* increase in opposite directions. *P* on the left vertical axis increases as we go up the axis, while *i* on the right vertical axis increases as we go down the axis.)

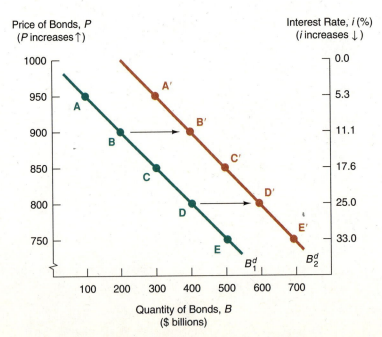

SUMMARY

TABLE 1 Factors That Shift the Demand Curve for Bonds

Variable	Change in Variable	Change in Quantity Demanded	Shift in Demand Curve	
Wealth	↑	↑	P (increases ↑)	i (increases ↓)
Expected interest rate	↑	↓	P (increases ↑)	i (increases ↓)
Expected inflation	↑	↓	P (increases ↑)	i (increases ↓)
Riskiness of bonds relative to other assets	↑	↓	P (increases ↑)	i (increases ↓)
Liquidity of bonds relative to other assets	↑	↑	P (increases ↑)	i (increases ↓)

Note: Only increases (↑) in the variables are shown. The effect of decreases in the variables on the change in demand would be the opposite of those indicated in the remaining columns.

will depend on the extent to which bonds are luxuries rather than necessities. Using the same reasoning, ***in a recession, when income and wealth are falling, the demand for bonds falls, and the demand curve shifts to the left.***

Expected Returns For a one-year discount bond and a one-year holding period, the expected return and the interest rate are identical. No component of the expected return is unrelated to the bond price or the interest rate.

For bonds with maturities of greater than one year, the expected return may differ from the interest rate. For example, we saw in Chapter 4, Table 2, that a rise in the interest rate on a long-term bond from 10% to 20% would lead to a sharp decline in price and a very negative return. Hence if people begin to think that interest rates will be higher next year than they had originally anticipated, the expected return on long-term bonds would fall, and the quantity demanded would fall at each interest rate. ***Higher expected interest rates in the future decrease the demand for long-term bonds and shift the demand curve to the left.***

By contrast, a revision downward of expectations of future interest rates would mean that long-term bond prices would be expected to rise more than originally anticipated, and the resulting higher expected return would raise the quantity demanded at each bond price and interest rate. ***Lower expected interest rates in the future increase the demand for long-term bonds and shift the demand curve to the right*** (as in Figure 3).

Changes in expected returns on other assets can also shift the demand curve for bonds. If people suddenly became more optimistic about the stock market and began to expect higher stock prices in the future, both expected capital gains and expected returns on stocks would rise. With the expected return on bonds held constant, the expected return on bonds relative to stocks would fall, lowering the demand for bonds and shifting the demand curve to the left.

A change in expected inflation is likely to alter expected returns on physical assets (also called *real assets*) such as automobiles and houses, which affect the demand for bonds. An increase in expected inflation, say, from 5% to 10%, will lead to higher prices on cars and houses in the future and hence higher nominal capital gains. The resulting rise in the expected returns on these real assets will lead to a fall in the expected return on bonds relative to the expected return on real assets and thus cause the demand for bonds to fall. Alternatively, we can think of the rise in expected inflation as lowering the real interest rate on bonds, and the resulting decline in the relative expected return on bonds causes the demand for bonds to fall. ***An increase in the expected rate of inflation will cause the demand for bonds to decline and the demand curve to shift to the left.***

Risk If prices in the bond market become more volatile, the risk associated with bonds increases, and bonds become a less attractive asset. ***An increase in the riskiness of bonds causes the demand for bonds to fall and the demand curve to shift to the left.***

Conversely, an increase in the volatility of prices in another asset market, such as the stock market, would make bonds more attractive. ***An increase in the riskiness of alternative assets causes the demand for bonds to rise and the demand curve to shift to the right*** (as in Figure 3).

Liquidity If more people started trading in the bond market and as a result it became easier to sell bonds quickly, the increase in their liquidity would cause the quantity of bonds demanded at each interest rate to rise. ***Increased liquidity of bonds results in an increased demand for bonds, and the demand curve shifts to the right*** (see Figure 3). ***Similarly, increased liquidity of alternative assets lowers the demand for bonds and shifts the demand curve to the left.*** The reduction of brokerage commissions for trading common stocks that occurred when the fixed-rate commission structure was abolished in 1975, for example, increased the liquidity of stocks relative to bonds, and the resulting lower demand for bonds shifted the demand curve to the left.

Shifts in the Supply of Bonds

Certain factors can cause the supply curve for bonds to shift, among them these:

1. Expected profitability of investment opportunities
2. Expected inflation
3. Government activities

We will look at how the supply curve shifts when each of these factors changes (when all others remain constant). (As a study aid, Table 2 summarizes the effects of changes in these factors on the bond supply curve.)

Expected Profitability of Investment Opportunities The more profitable investments that a firm expects it can make, the more willing it will be to borrow and increase the amount of its outstanding debt in order to finance these investments. When the economy is growing rapidly, as in a business cycle expansion, investment opportunities that are expected to be profitable abound, and the quantity of bonds supplied at any given bond price and interest rate will increase (see Figure 4). Therefore, in a business cycle expansion, the supply of bonds increases, and the supply curve shifts to the right. Likewise, in a recession, when there are far fewer expected profitable investment opportunities, the supply of bonds falls, and the supply curve shifts to the left.

Expected Inflation As we saw in Chapter 4, the real cost of borrowing is more accurately measured by the real interest rate, which equals the (nominal) interest rate minus the expected inflation rate. For a given interest rate, when expected inflation increases, the real cost of borrowing falls; hence the quantity of bonds supplied increases at any given bond price and interest rate. ***An increase in expected inflation causes the supply of bonds to increase and the supply curve to shift to the right*** (see Figure 4).

SUMMARY

TABLE 2 Factors That Shift the Supply of Bonds

Variable	Change in Variable	Change in Quantity Supplied	Shift in Supply Curve
Profitability of investments	↑	↑	
Expected inflation	↑	↑	
Government deficit	↑	↑	

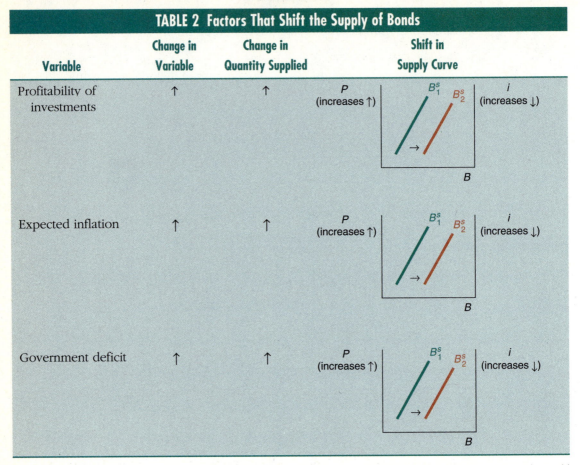

Note: Only increases (↑) in the variables are shown. The effect of decreases in the variables on the change in supply would be the opposite of those indicated in the remaining columns.

Government Activities The activities of the government can influence the supply of bonds in several ways. The U.S. Treasury issues bonds to finance government deficits, the gap between the government's expenditures and its revenues. When these deficits are large, as they have been recently, the Treasury sells more bonds, and the quantity of bonds supplied at each bond price and interest rate increases. *Higher government deficits increase the supply of bonds and shift the supply curve to the right* (see Figure 4).

State and local governments and other government agencies also issue

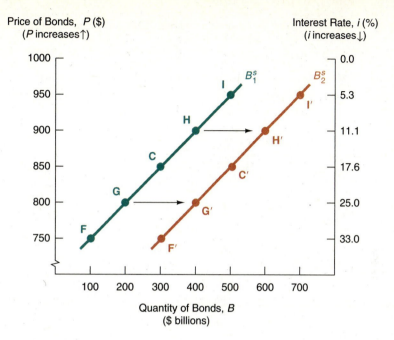

FIGURE 4
Shift in the Supply Curve for Bonds
When the supply of bonds increases, the supply curve shifts to the right. (*Note: P* and *i* increase in opposite directions. *P* on the left vertical axis increases as we go up the axis, while *i* on the right vertical axis increases as we go down the axis.)

bonds to finance their expenditures, and this can also affect the supply of bonds. We will see in later chapters that the conduct of monetary policy involves the purchase and sale of bonds, which in turn influences the supply of bonds.

Changes in the Equilibrium Interest Rate

We now can use our knowledge of how supply and demand curves shift to analyze how the equilibrium interest rate can change. The best way to do this is to pursue several applications that are particularly relevant to our understanding of how monetary policy affects interest rates.

STUDY GUIDE

Supply and demand analysis for the bond market is best learned by practicing applications. When there is an application in the text and we look at how the interest rate changes because some economic variable increases, see if you can draw the appropriate shifts in the supply and demand curves when this same economic variable decreases. While you are practicing applications, keep two things in mind:

1. When you examine the effect of a variable change, remember that we are assuming that all other variables are unchanged; that is, we are making use of the *ceteris paribus* assumption.

2. Remember that the interest rate is negatively related to the bond price, so when the equilibrium bond price rises, the equilibrium interest rate falls. Conversely, if the equilibrium bond price moves downward, the equilibrium interest rate rises.

Changes in Expected Inflation: The Fisher Effect We have already done most of the work to evaluate how a change in expected inflation affects the nominal interest rate in that we have already analyzed how a change in expected inflation shifts the supply and demand curves. Figure 5 shows the effect on the equilibrium interest rate of an increase in expected inflation.

Suppose that expected inflation is initially 5% and the initial supply and demand curves B_1^s and B_1^d intersect at point 1, where the equilibrium bond price is P_1 and the equilibrium interest rate is i_1. If expected inflation rises to 10%, the expected return on bonds relative to real assets falls for any given bond price and interest rate. As a result, the demand for bonds falls, and the demand curve shifts to the left from B_1^d to B_2^d. The rise in expected inflation also shifts the supply curve. At any given bond price and interest rate, the real cost of borrowing

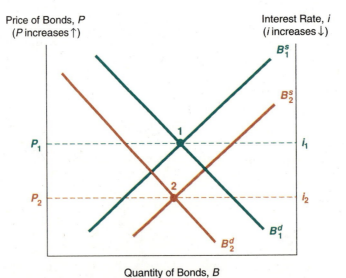

FIGURE 5 Response to a Change in Expected Inflation
When expected inflation rises, the supply curve shifts from B_1^s to B_2^s, and the demand curve shifts from B_1^d to B_2^d. The equilibrium moves from point 1 to point 2, with the result that the equilibrium bond price (left axis) falls from P_1 to P_2 and the equilibrium interest rate (right axis) rises from i_1 to i_2. (*Note:* P and i increase in opposite directions. P on the left vertical axis increases as we go up the axis, while i on the right vertical axis increases as we go down the axis.)

has declined, causing the quantity of bonds supplied to increase, and the supply curve shifts to the right from B_1^s to B_2^s.

When the demand and supply curves shift in response to the change in expected inflation, the equilibrium moves from point 1 to point 2, which is the intersection of B_2^d and B_2^s. The equilibrium bond price has fallen from P_1 to P_2, and since the bond price is negatively related to the interest rate (as is indicated by the interest rate rising as we go down the right vertical axis), this means that the interest rate has risen from i_1 to i_2. Note that Figure 5 has been drawn so that the equilibrium quantity of bonds remains the same for both point 1 and point 2. However, depending on the size of the shifts in the supply and demand curves, the equilibrium quantity of bonds could either rise or fall when expected inflation rises.

Our supply and demand analysis has led us to an important observation: ***When expected inflation rises, interest rates will rise.*** This result has been named the **Fisher effect,** after Irving Fisher, the economist who first pointed out the relationship of expected inflation to interest rates. The accuracy of this prediction is shown in Figure 6. The interest rate on three-month Treasury bills has usually moved along with the expected inflation rate. Consequently, it is understandable that many economists recommend that the fight against inflation must be won if we want to lower interest rates.

Business Cycle Expansion   Figure 7 analyzes the effects of a business cycle expansion on interest rates. In a business cycle expansion, the amount of goods and services being produced in the economy rises, so national income increases. When this occurs, businesses will be more willing to borrow because they are likely to have many profitable investment opportunities for which they need financing. Hence at a given bond price and interest rate, the quantity of bonds that firms

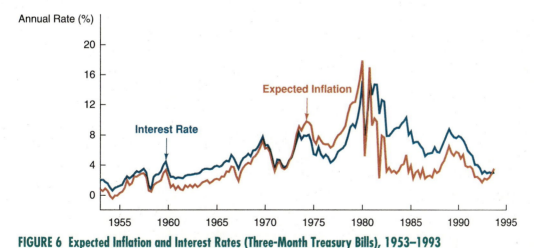

FIGURE 6   Expected Inflation and Interest Rates (Three-Month Treasury Bills), 1953–1993
Source: Expected inflation calculated using procedures outlined in Frederic S. Mishkin, "The Real Interest Rate: An Empirical Investigation," *Carnegie-Rochester Conference Series on Public Policy* 15 (1981): 151–200. This involves estimating expected inflation as a function of past interest rates, inflation, and time trends.

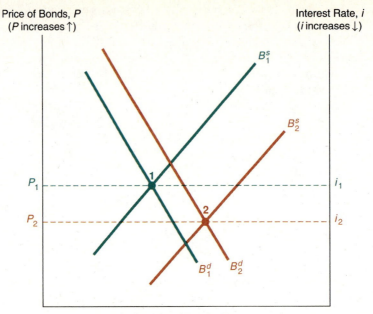

Price of Bonds, P
(P increases ↑)

Interest Rate, i
(i increases ↓)

Quantity of Bonds, B

FIGURE 7 Response to a Business Cycle Expansion
In a business cycle expansion, when income and wealth are rising, the demand curve shifts rightward from B_1^d to B_2^d, and the supply curve shifts rightward from B_1^s to B_2^s. If the supply curve shifts to the right more than the demand curve, as in this figure, the equilibrium bond price (left axis) moves down from P_1 to P_2, and the equilibrium interest rate (right axis) rises from i_1 to i_2. (*Note: P* and *i* increase in opposite directions. *P* on the left vertical axis increases as we go up the axis, while *i* on the right vertical axis increases as we go down the axis.)

want to sell (that is, the supply of bonds) will increase. This means that in a business cycle expansion, the supply curve for bonds shifts to the right (see Figure 7) from B_1^s to B_2^s.

The expanding economy will also affect the demand for bonds. The theory of asset demand tells us that as the business cycle expands and wealth increases, the demand for bonds will rise as well. We see this in Figure 7, where the demand curve has shifted to the right from B_1^d to B_2^d.

Given that both the supply and demand curves have shifted to the right, we know that the new equilibrium reached at the intersection of B_2^d and B_2^s must also move to the right. However, depending on whether the supply curve shifts more than the demand curve or vice versa, the new equilibrium interest rate can either rise or fall.

The supply and demand analysis used here gives us an ambiguous answer to the question of what will happen to interest rates in a business cycle expansion. The figure has been drawn so that the shift in the supply curve is greater

FIGURE 8   Business Cycle and Interest Rates (Three-Month Treasury Bills), 1951–1993
Shaded areas indicate periods of recession. *Sources:* Federal Reserve *Bulletin;* Citibase databank.

than the shift in the demand curve, causing the equilibrium bond price to fall to P_2, leading to a rise in the equilibrium interest rate to i_2. The reason the figure has been drawn so that a business cycle expansion and a rise in income lead to a higher interest rate is because this is the outcome we actually see in the data.Figure 8 plots the movement of the interest rate on three-month U.S. Treasury bills from 1951 to 1993 and indicates when the business cycle is undergoing recessions (shaded areas). As you can see, the interest rate rises during business cycle expansions and falls during recessions, which is what the supply and demand diagram indicates.

APPLICATION   **READING THE *WALL STREET JOURNAL***

THE "CREDIT MARKETS" COLUMN

Now that we have an understanding of how supply and demand determines prices and interest rates in the bond market, we can use our analysis to understand discussions about bond prices and interest rates appearing in the financial press. Every day, the *Wall Street Journal* reports on developments in the bond market on the previous business day in its "Credit Markets" column, an example of which is found in the "Following the Financial News" box. Let's see how

The "Credit Markets" Column

The "Credit Markets" column appears daily in the *Wall Street Journal;* an example is pre- sented here. It is found in the third section, "Money and Investing."

CREDIT MARKETS

Sharp Increase in National Purchasing Index Fuels Inflation Fears, Pushing Down Bond Prices

By THOMAS D. LAURICELLA
Staff Reporter of THE WALL STREET JOURNAL
NEW YORK — The bond market sell-off turned into a rout yesterday as prices of Treasury securities suffered their biggest losses in months on worrisome inflation news.

The violent downdraft left investors unwilling to take advantage of the higher yields resulting from the sell-off. Traders are looking to the Federal Reserve to signal its resolve against inflation by raising short-term interest rates a second time.

"Until we get the market to stabilize ... customers won't buy," said Mead Briggs, head of risk trading at Deutsche Bank Securities Corp. "And you won't get some stability until the Fed does what it has to do." The Fed raised short-term rates in early February.

The collapse in prices briefly took the yield on the 6¼% 30-year bond to 6.81%, its highest level since June. The yield on the 10-year note reached a 12-month high. For short-term yields, one has to look even further back. The yield on the new two-year note reached 4.82%, its loftiest perch since early December 1992.

Prices managed to creep back from their worst levels, however. The benchmark 30-year Treasury bond dropped 1½ points, or $15 for a bond with $1,000 face value, to yield 6.77%, up from 6.65% on Monday.

The bulk of yesterday's selling was caused by troublesome data on inflation contained in a National Association of Purchasing Management report released at midmorning. The association said its prices-paid index jumped to 67 in February from 59.8 in January. The overall NAPM index slipped to 56.6 in February from 57.7, depressed by harsh winter weather. Also troubling for the bond market was a rise in the NAPM employment index to an lmost five-year high of 50 from 48.3.

"The story of the day was the price index and a little bit the employment index," said Mr. Briggs.

A reading above 50 on the price index reflects rising prices—the higher the index level, the faster the increase in prices. Bond investors fear inflation because it reduces the value of investments with a fixed rate of return.

Earlier in the day, the Commerce Department revised fourth-quarter gross-do- mestic-product growth up sharply to a 7.5% rate from an originally reported 5.9% pace. Analysts said the fourth-quarter data indicate the economy began the current year with a great deal of momentum.

In addition to the economic news, market watchers also reported widespread nervousness over weakness in other major bond markets around the world. Many of those declines were actually sparked by concerns over what was happening with U.S. interest rates. Participants also say the market has reached a stage where selling only breeds more selling, especially by traders who end up making short sales of Treasurys as a hedge against losses on holdings of other securities. A trader executes a short sale by selling a borrowed security in hopes of buying it back at a later date at a lower price and pocketing the difference.

By the time the NAPM report was released yesterday, the market had already given up a portion of the gains it eked out Monday. And once traders and investors saw the details of the report, the floor fell out from underneath the bond market.

Source: Wall Street Journal, Wednesday March 2, 1994, p. C21.

---

statements in the "Credit Markets" column can be explained using our supply and demand framework.

The column opens by stating that bond market sell-off occurred because of worrisome inflation news. This is exactly what our supply and demand analysis predicts would happen. The jump in the prices-paid index in the National Association of Purchasing Management report caused bond investors to raise their assessment of expected inflation. As we have seen in this chapter, the rise in expected inflation causes the expected return on bonds relative to real assets to fall, which shifts the demand curve to the left. In addition, the higher expected inflation lowers the real cost of borrowing at any given interest rate, which increases the quantity of bonds supplied at each interest rate and shifts the supply curve to the right. The outcome is exactly the one we have seen in Figure 5, a decline in bond prices and a rise in interest rates.

The column also mentions that both the National Association of Purchasing Management report and the Commerce Department released data that suggested a stronger economy. The NAPM employment index reached a five-year high, while the growth in the gross domestic product in the fourth quarter was revised upward to 7.5% from an originally reported 5.9%. An upward revision in the strength of the economy indicates that investment opportunities are improving, so businesses are more likely to issue bonds. The result is that the quantity of bonds supplied increases at each interest rate and the supply curve shifts to the right. Meanwhile, the strong economy suggests that wealth is increasing and hence the quantity of bonds demanded at each interest rate rises, shifting the demand curve to the right. Because, as is shown in Figure 7, the rightward shift in the supply curve is likely to be greater than the rightward shift in the demand curve, equilibrium bond prices fall. Our analysis shows that the news of a stronger economy thus also contributed to the bond market sell-off.

LIQUIDITY PREFERENCE FRAMEWORK: SUPPLY AND DEMAND IN THE MARKET FOR MONEY

Whereas the loanable funds framework determines the equilibrium interest rate using the supply of and demand for bonds, an alternative model developed by John Maynard Keynes and known as the **liquidity preference framework** determines the equilibrium interest rate in terms of the supply of and demand for money. Although the two frameworks look different, the liquidity preference analysis of the market for money is closely related to the loanable funds framework of the bond market.[2]

The starting point of Keynes's analysis is his assumption that there are two main categories of assets that people use to store their wealth: money and bonds. Therefore, total wealth in the economy must equal the total quantity of bonds plus money in the economy, which equals the quantity of bonds supplied B^s plus the quantity of money supplied M^s. The quantity of bonds B^d and money M^d that people want to hold and thus demand must also equal the total amount of wealth because people cannot purchase more assets than their available resources allow. The conclusion is that the quantity of bonds and money supplied must equal the quantity of bonds and money demanded:

---

[2]Note that the term *market for money* refers to the market for money, the medium of exchange. This market differs from the *money market* referred to by finance practitioners, which is the financial market in which short-term debt instruments are traded.

$$B^s + M^s = B^d + M^d \tag{2}$$

Collecting the bond terms on one side of the equation and the money terms on the other, this equation can be rewritten as

$$B^s - B^d = M^d - M^s \tag{3}$$

The rewritten equation tells us that if the market for money is in equilibrium $(M^s = M^d)$, the right-hand side of Equation 3 equals zero, implying that $B^s = B^d$, meaning that the bond market is also in equilibrium.

Thus it is the same to think about determining the equilibrium interest rate by equating the supply and demand for bonds or by equating the supply and demand for money. In this sense, the liquidity preference framework, which analyzes the market for money, is equivalent to the loanable funds framework, which analyzes the bond market. In practice, the approaches differ because by assuming that there are only two kinds of assets, money and bonds, the liquidity preference approach implicitly ignores any effects on interest rates that arise from changes in the expected returns on real assets such as automobiles and houses. In most instances, both frameworks yield the same predictions.

The reason that we approach the determination of interest rates with both frameworks is that the loanable funds framework is easier to use when analyzing the effects from changes in expected inflation, whereas the liquidity preference framework provides a simpler analysis of the effects from changes in income, the price level, and the supply of money.

Because the definition of money that Keynes used includes currency (which earns no interest) and checking account deposits (which in his time typically earned little or no interest), he assumed that money has a zero rate of return. Bonds, the only alternative asset to money in Keynes's framework, have an expected return equal to the interest rate i.[3] As this interest rate rises (holding everything else unchanged), the expected return on money falls relative to the expected return on bonds, and as the theory of asset demand tells us, this causes the demand for money to fall.

We can also see that the demand for money and the interest rate should be negatively related by using the concept of ***opportunity cost,*** the amount of interest (expected return) sacrificed by not holding the alternative asset—in this case, a bond. As the interest rate on bonds i rises, the opportunity cost of holding money rises, and so money is less desirable and the quantity of money demanded must fall.

Figure 9 shows the quantity of money demanded at a number of interest rates, with all other economic variables, such as income and the price level, held constant. At an interest rate of 25%, point A shows that the quantity of money demanded is $100 billion. If the interest rate is at the lower rate of 20%, the op-

---

[3]Keynes did not actually assume that the expected returns on bonds equaled the interest rate but rather argued that they were closely related (see Chapter 23). This distinction makes no appreciable difference in our analysis.

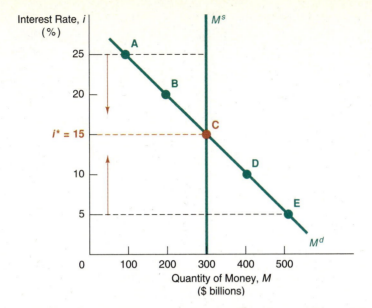

FIGURE 9
Equilibrium in the
Market for Money

portunity cost of money is lower, and the quantity of money demanded rises to $200 billion, as indicated by the move from point A to point B. If the interest rate is even lower, the quantity of money demanded is even higher, as is indicated by points C, D, and E. The curve M^d connecting these points is the demand curve for money, and it slopes downward.

At this point in our analysis, we will assume that a central bank controls the amount of money supplied at a fixed quantity of $300 billion, so the supply curve for money M^s in the figure is a vertical line at $300 billion. The equilibrium where the quantity of money demanded equals the quantity of money supplied occurs at the intersection of the supply and demand curves at point C, where

$$M^d = M^s \qquad (4)$$

The resulting equilibrium interest rate is at $i^* = 15\%$.

We can again see that there is a tendency to approach this equilibrium by first looking at the relationship of money demand and supply when the interest rate is above the equilibrium interest rate. When the interest rate is 25%, the quantity of money demanded at point A is $100 billion, yet the quantity of money supplied is $300 billion. The excess supply of money means that people are holding more money than they desire, so they will try to get rid of their excess money balances by trying to buy bonds. Accordingly, they will bid up the price of bonds, and as the bond price rises, the interest rate will fall toward the equilibrium interest rate of 15%. This tendency is shown by the downward arrow drawn at the interest rate of 25%.

Likewise, if the interest rate is 5%, the quantity of money demanded at point E is $500 billion, but the quantity of money supplied is only $300 billion. There is now an excess demand for money because people want to hold more money than they currently have. To try to get the money, they will sell their only other asset—bonds—and the price will fall. As the price of bonds falls, the interest rate will rise toward the equilibrium rate of 15%. Only when the interest rate is at its equilibrium value will there be no tendency for it to move further, and the interest rate will settle to its equilibrium value.

CHANGES IN EQUILIBRIUM INTEREST RATES

Analyzing how the equilibrium interest rate changes using the liquidity preference framework requires that we understand what causes the demand and supply curves for money to shift.

STUDY GUIDE

Learning the liquidity preference framework also requires practicing applications. When there is an application in the text to examine how the interest rate changes because some economic variable increases, see if you can draw the appropriate shifts in the supply and demand curves when this same economic variable decreases. And remember to use the *ceteris paribus* assumption: When examining the effect of a change in one variable, hold all other variables constant.

Shifts in the Demand for Money

In Keynes's liquidity preference analysis, two factors cause the demand curve for money to shift: income and the price level.

Income Effect   In Keynes's view, there were two reasons why income would affect the demand for money. First, as an economy expands and income rises, wealth increases and people will want to hold more money as a store of value. Second, as the economy expands and income rises, people will want to carry out more transactions using money, with the result that they will also want to hold more money. The conclusion is that *a higher level of income causes the demand for money to increase and the demand curve to shift to the right.*

Price-Level Effect   Keynes took the view that people care about the amount of money they hold *in real terms,* that is, in terms of the goods and services that it can buy. When the price level rises, the same nominal quantity of money is no longer as valuable; it cannot be used to purchase as many real goods or services. To restore their holdings of money in real terms to its former level, people will want to hold a greater nominal quantity of money, so *a rise in the price level causes the demand for money to increase and the demand curve to shift to the right.*

Shifts in the Supply of Money

We will assume that the supply of money is completely controlled by the central bank, which in the United States is the Federal Reserve. (Actually, the process that determines the money supply is substantially more complicated and involves banks, depositors, and borrowers from banks. We will study it in more detail later in the book.) For now, all we need to know is that *an increase in the money supply engineered by the Federal Reserve will shift the supply curve for money to the right.*

Changes in the Equilibrium Interest Rate

To see how the liquidity preference framework can be used to analyze the movement of interest rates, we will again look at several applications that will be useful in evaluating the effect of monetary policy on interest rates. (As a study aid, Table 3 summarizes the shifts in the demand and supply curves for money.)

Changes in Income   When income is rising during a business cycle expansion, we have seen that the demand for money will rise. It is shown in Figure 10 by the shift rightward in the demand curve from M_1^d to M_2^d. The new equilibrium is reached at point 2 at the intersection of the M_2^d curve with the money supply curve M^s. As you can see, the equilibrium interest rate rises from i_1 to i_2. The liquidity preference framework thus generates the conclusion that *when income is rising during a business cycle expansion (holding other economic variables constant), interest rates will rise.* This conclusion is unambiguous when contrasted to the conclusion reached about the effects of a change in income on interest rates using the loanable funds framework.

Changes in the Price Level   When the price level rises, the value of money in terms of what it can purchase is lower. To restore their money holdings in real terms to its former level, people will want to hold a greater nominal quantity of money. A higher price level shifts the demand curve for money to the right from M_1^d to M_2^d (see Figure 11). The equilibrium moves from point 1 to point 2, where the

SUMMARY

	TABLE 3 Factors That Shift the Demand for and Supply of Money		
Variable	**Change in Variable**	**Change in Money Demand (Md) or Supply (Ms)**	**Change in Interest Rate**
Income	↑	M^d ↑	↑
Price level	↑	M^d ↑	↑
Money supply	↑	M^s ↑	↓

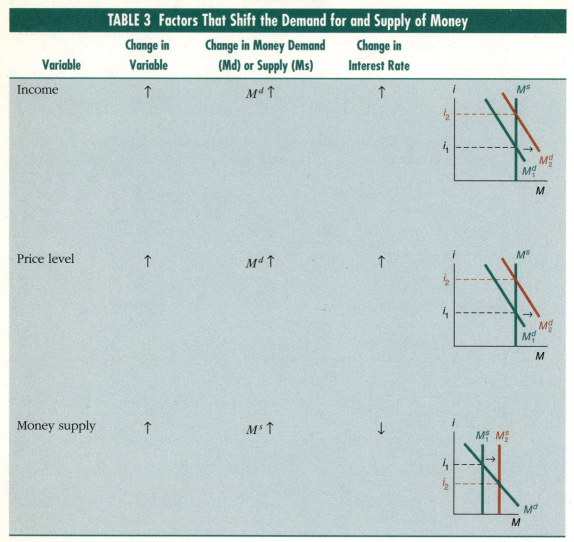

Note: Only increases (↑) in the variables are shown. The effect of decreases in the variables on the change in demand would be the opposite of those indicated in the remaining columns.

equilibrium interest rate has risen from i_1 to i_2, illustrating that ***when the price level increases, with the supply of money and other economic variables held constant, interest rates will rise.***

Changes in the Money Supply An increase in the money supply due to expansionary monetary policy by the Federal Reserve implies that the supply curve for money shifts to the right. As is shown in Figure 12 by the movement of the supply curve

FIGURE 10
Response to a
Change in Income
In a business
cycle expansion,
when income is
rising, the de-
mand curve shifts
from M_1^d to M_2^d.
The supply curve
is fixed at $M^s = \overline{M}$.
The equilibrium
interest rate rises
from i_1 to i_2.

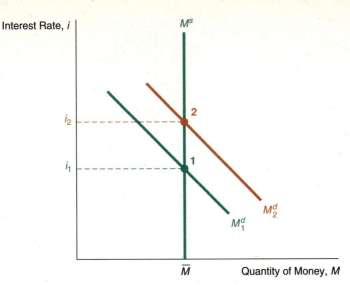

from M_1^s to M_2^s, the equilibrium moves from point 1 down to point 2, where the
M_2^s supply curve intersects with the demand curve M^d and the equilibrium interest rate has fallen from i_1 to i_2. **When the money supply increases (everything else remaining equal), interest rates will decline.**[4]

FIGURE 11
Response to a
Change in the
Price Level
An increase in
price level shifts
the money de-
mand curve from
M_1^d to M_2^d, and
the equilibrium
interest rate rises
from i_1 to i_2.

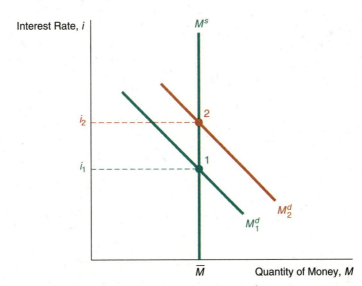

[4]This same result can be generated using the loanable funds framework. As we will see in Chapters
15 and 16, the primary way that a central bank produces an increase in the money supply is by buying bonds and thereby decreasing the supply of bonds to the public. The resulting shift to the left of
the supply curve for bonds will lead to a decline in the equilibrium interest rate.

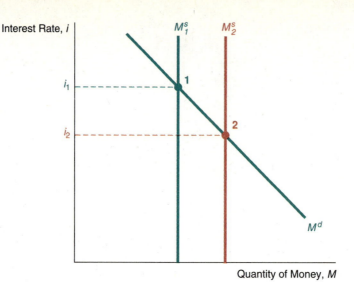

FIGURE 12

Response to a Change in the Money Supply

When the money supply increases, the supply curve shifts from M_1^s to M_2^s, and the equilibrium interest rate falls from i_1 to i_2.

APPLICATION

MONEY AND INTEREST RATES

The liquidity preference analysis in Figure 12 seems to lead to the conclusion that an increase in the money supply will lower interest rates. This conclusion has important policy implications because it has frequently caused politicians to call for a more rapid growth of the money supply in order to drive down interest rates.

But is this conclusion that money and interest rates should be negatively related correct? Might there be other important factors left out of the liquidity preference analysis in Figure 12 that would reverse this conclusion? We will provide answers to these questions by applying the supply and demand analysis we have learned in this chapter to obtain a deeper understanding of the relationship between money and interest rates.

An important criticism of the conclusion that a rise in the money supply lowers interest rates has been raised by Milton Friedman, a Nobel laureate in economics. He acknowledges that the liquidity preference analysis is correct and calls the result that an increase in the money supply (*everything else remaining equal*) lowers interest rates the *liquidity effect*. However, he views the liquidity effect as merely part of the story: An increase in the money supply might not leave "everything else equal" and will have other effects on the economy that may make interest rates rise. If these effects are substantial, it is entirely possible that when the money supply rises, interest rates

We have already laid the groundwork to discuss these other effects because we have shown how changes in income, the price level, and expected inflation affect the equilibrium interest rate.

STUDY GUIDE

To get further practice with the loanable funds and liquidity preference frameworks, show how the effects discussed here work by drawing the supply and demand diagrams that explain each effect. This exercise will also help you understand better the effect of money on interest rates.

1. *Income Effect*. Because an increasing money supply is an expansionary influence on the economy, it should raise national income and wealth. Both the liquidity preference and loanable funds frameworks indicate that interest rates will then rise (see Figures 7 and 10). Thus ***the income effect of an increase in the money supply is a rise in interest rates in response to the higher level of income.***

2. *Price-Level Effect*. An increase in the money supply can also cause the overall price level in the economy to rise. The liquidity preference framework predicts that this will lead to a rise in interest rates. So ***the price-level effect from an increase in the money supply is a rise in interest rates in response to the rise in the price level.***

3. *Expected-Inflation Effect*. The rising price level (the higher inflation rate) that results from an increase in the money supply also affects interest rates by affecting the expected inflation rate. Specifically, an increase in the money supply may lead people to expect a higher price level in the future—hence the expected inflation rate will be higher. The loanable funds framework has shown us that this increase in expected inflation will lead to a higher level of interest rates. Therefore, ***the expected-inflation effect of an increase in the money supply is a rise in interest rates in response to the rise in the expected inflation rate.***

At first glance it might appear that the price-level effect and the expected-inflation effect are the same thing. They both indicate that increases in the price level induced by an increase in the money supply will raise interest rates. However, there is a subtle difference between the two, and this is why they are discussed as two separate effects.

Suppose there is a one-time increase in the money supply today that leads to a rise in prices to a permanently higher level by next year. As the price level rises over the course of this year, the interest rate will rise via the price-level effect. Only at the end of the year, when the price level has risen to its peak, will the price-level effect be at a maximum.

The rising price level will also raise interest rates via the expected-inflation effect because people will expect that inflation will be higher over the course of the year. However, when the price level stops rising next year, inflation and the expected inflation rate will fall back down to zero. Any rise in interest rates as a result of the earlier rise in expected inflation will then be reversed. We thus see that, in contrast to the price-level effect, which reaches its greatest impact next year, the expected-inflation effect will have its smallest impact (zero impact) next year. The basic difference between the two effects, then, is that the

FOLLOWING THE FINANCIAL NEWS

Forecasting Interest Rates

Forecasting interest rates is a time-honored profession. Economists are hired (sometimes at very high salaries) to forecast interest rates because businesses need to know what they will be to plan their future spending, while banks and investors require interest rate forecasts in order to decide which assets to buy. Interest-rate forecasters predict what will happen to the factors that affect the supply and demand for bonds and for money—factors such as the strength of the economy, the profitability of investment opportunities, the expected inflation rate, and the size of government budget deficits and borrowing. They then use the supply and demand analysis we have outlined in this chapter to come up with their interest-rate forecasts.

The *Wall Street Journal* reports interest-rate forecasts by leading prognosticators twice a year (early January and July) in its "Economy" column or in its "Credit Markets" column, which surveys developments in the bond market daily. Forecasting interest rates is a perilous business. To their embarrassment, even the top experts are frequently far off in their forecasts.

A Sampling of Interest-Rate, Economic and Currency Forecasts
(In percent except for the dollar vs. yen)

	JUNE 1993 SURVEY					NEW FORECASTS FOR 1994									
	3-MO. TREASURY BILLS-a 12/31	30-YR. BONDS 12/31	GDP-b 2nd HALF 1993	CPI-c 2nd HALF 1993	DLR. vs. YEN 12/31	3-MONTH TREASURY BILLS-a 6/30	12/31	30-YEAR TREASURY BONDS 6/30	12/31	GDP-d 1st HALF	2nd HALF	INFLATION RATE-e MAY 1994	NOV 1994	DOLLAR vs. YEN JUNE	DEC
Maureen Allyn, Scudder Stevens Clark	3.30	6.75	3.4	3.0	114	3.55	4.60	5.90	6.90	0.7	2.9	2.8	3.2	119	126
Robert Barbera, Lehman Brothers	3.50	6.80	3.5	3.5	118	3.70	4.20	6.40	6.60	3.6	3.4	3.0	3.3	115	125
Richard Berner, Mellon Bank	3.75	6.80	3.6	2.9	110	3.55	3.75	5.75	5.90	2.5	3.2	2.0	3.0	112	115
David Berson, Fannie Mae	3.20	7.10	3.6	3.0	115	3.50	3.90	6.40	6.55	3.1	2.5	2.9	3.2	113	120
Paul Boltz, T. Rowe Price	3.30	6.90	3.0	3.1	105	3.63	4.13	6.63	6.88	3.1	3.2	2.7	2.8	108	103
David Bostian, Herzog, Heine, Geduld	N.A.	N.A.	N.A.	N.A.	N.A.	3.45	3.60	6.40	6.75	2.4	3.2	3.2	3.4	109	114
Philip Braverman, DKB Securities	2.9	6.25	2.3	3.0	105	2.95	2.60	5.75	5.50	1.5	1.8	2.2	2.0	100	95
William Brown, J.P. Morgan	3.50	6.50	3.5	2.8	115	3.90	4.40	6.40	6.50	3.1	3.5	2.5	2.8	117	120
Ed Campbell, Brown Bros.	N.A	N.A.	N.A.	N.A.	N.A.	3.10	3.25	6.00	6.25	3.2	3.4	2.5	2.7	110	115
Gary Ciminero, Fleet Financial Group	3.19	6.98	2.4	3.4	115	3.36	3.59	6.51	6.77	2.2	2.7	2.8	3.2	112	114
James Coons, Huntington Natl Bank	N.A.	N.A.	N.A.	N.A.	N.A.	3.15	3.15	6.10	5.85	3.0	3.0	2.4	2.6	115	118
Michael Cosgrove, The Econoclast	3.40	7.36	3.3	3.3	120	3.40	3.70	6.50	6.90	2.2	2.5	3.5	4.0	112	110
Dewey Daane, Vanderbilt Univ.	3.50	7.25	3.2	3.4	110	3.70	3.95	6.85	7.25	3.4	3.1	3.3	3.7	115	108
Robert Dederick, Northern Trust	3.60	6.85	3.4	3.0	110	3.70	4.20	6.25	6.40	3.3	3.1	2.4	2.8	115	120
Michael Englund, MMS Intl	N.A.	N.A.	N.A.	N.A.	N.A.	3.35	3.60	5.50	6.00	3.3	3.5	2.9	2.9	115	116

(con't.)

price-level effect remains even after prices have stopped rising, whereas the expected-inflation effect disappears.

An important point is that the expected-inflation effect will persist only as long as the price level continues to rise. As we will see in our discussion of monetary theory in subsequent chapters, a one-time increase in the money supply will not produce a continually rising price level; only a higher rate of money supply growth will. Thus a higher rate of money supply growth is needed if the expected-inflation effect is to persist.

FOLLOWING THE FINANCIAL NEWS

Forecasting Interest Rates (cont.)

Michael Evans, Evans Group	N.A.	N.A.	N.A.	N.A.	N.A.	3.00	3.15	6.10	6.30	1.7	1.8	2.9	3.4	105	110
Gail Fosler, Conference Board	3.10	6.80	2.6	3.5	105	3.50	3.80	6.50	6.50	3.4	3.0	3.5	3.9	110	113
Lyle Gramley, Mortg. Bankers Assn.	3.60	7.00	3.7	3.1	115	3.70	4.30	6.40	6.60	3.1	2.9	2.9	3.1	110	112
Maury Harris, PaineWebber Inc.	3.30	6.50	3.0	2.5	110	3.10	3.20	5.70	6.20	2.1	3.1	2.5	2.5	110	115
H.E. Heinemann, Ladenburg, Thal.	3.50	7.50	2.5	3.9	104	3.60	4.50	6.70	7.70	2.4	1.8	3.1	4.6	109	104
Richard Hoey, Dreyfus Corp.	3.30	6.80	3.2	2.7	110	3.35	3.60	6.30	6.50	2.9	2.2	2.6	3.4	115	118
William Hummer, Wayne Hummer	3.30	7.00	2.8	3.2	111	3.80	4.10	6.80	7.10	3.3	3.4	3.2	3.6	113	120
Edward Hyman, ISI Group Inc.	3.10	6.30	3.0	2.0	110	3.80	3.80	5.50	5.50	2.5	3.0	2.0	2.0	118	120
Saul Hymans, Univ. of Michigan	3.12	6.80	1.9	3.1	105	3.07	3.19	6.51	6.54	2.6	1.9	2.6	3.2	107	108
Mieczyslaw Karczmar, Deutsche Bank	3.30	7.15	3.1	3.5	110	3.50	4.00	7.00	7.25	3.2	2.7	3.2	3.5	115	125
Kurt Karl, WEFA Group	N.A.	N.A.	N.A.	N.A.	N.A.	3.30	3.50	6.40	6.50	2.9	3.0	2.6	3.3	120	124
Irwin Kellner, Chemical Bank	3.30	7.00	2.3	2.8	100	3.15	3.25	6.10	6.00	2.1	1.7	1.5	1.5	105	100
Michael Keran, Prudential Insurance	N.A.	N.A.	N.A.	N.A.	N.A.	3.06	2.80	5.80	5.80	2.5	2.5	2.4	2.5	110	110
Lawrence Kudlow, Bear Stearns	4.00	7.40	4.5	3.8	120	3.40	3.60	6.90	7.30	3.5	2.3	2.7	3.7	112	115
Carol Leisenring, CoreStates Fin'l	3.70	6.90	3.3	2.4	115	3.40	4.00	6.10	6.50	2.7	2.8	2.4	2.5	115	108
Mickey Levy, NationsBank Cap.Mkts	3.20	6.50	2.9	3.2	107	3.30	3.60	5.90	6.10	3.1	3.0	2.2	3.0	115	112
John Lonski, Moody's Investors Svc	N.A.	N.A.	N.A.	N.A.	N.A.	3.37	3.68	6.50	6.80	3.2	3.6	3.0	3.4	112	115
Arnold Moskowitz, Moskowitz Capital	3.50	6.75	3.2	3.3	114	3.20	3.30	5.75	5.70	2.2	1.7	2.6	2.4	106	105
David Munro, High Frequency Econ.	N.A.	N.A.	N.A.	N.A.	N.A.	3.50	3.80	6.10	5.90	2.8	2.9	2.1	2.2	N.A	N.A.
Elliott Platt, Donaldson Lufkin	3.06	7.00	3.5	3.3	115	3.30	3.30	6.38	5.75	3.5	3.0	3.0	3.0	117	115
Donald Ratajczak, Georgia State Univ.	3.20	7.07	3.3	2.9	105	3.42	4.05	6.45	6.65	2.7	3.5	2.7	2.9	109	107
Lynn Reaser, First Interstate Bancorp	3.62	6.70	3.5	3.5	112	3.55	3.75	6.30	6.40	3.1	2.7	2.7	3.2	114	117
David Resler, Nomura Securities Int'l	3.10	6.50	3.2	2.8	115	3.30	3.60	6.00	5.75	3.0	2.7	2.5	2.7	111	115
Alan Reynolds, Hudson Institute	4.00	7.50	3.7	4.0	115	3.60	4.00	6.90	7.30	3.3	2.3	2.9	3.8	112	116
Richard Rippe, Prudential Securities	3.60	7.00	3.2	2.8	115	3.55	4.10	6.50	6.75	3.0	2.7	2.6	3.2	115	110
Norman Robertson, Carnegie Mellon	3.30	6.70	2.8	3.0	115	3.60	4.00	6.30	6.40	2.9	3.1	2.9	3.2	110	115
A. Gary Shilling, Shilling & Co.	2.50	6.00	2.0	2.2	130	2.50	2.50	5.50	5.00	1.5	2.0	1.9	2.0	140	160
Allen Sinai, Lehman Bros.	3.18	6.50	2.3	3.0	107	3.20	3.47	6.35	6.64	2.4	3.5	2.2	2.7	117	121
Neal Soss, First Boston Corp.	3.25	5.99	3.0	3.2	100	3.50	3.75	6.25	6.50	2.8	3.4	2.8	3.2	115	125
Susan Sterne, Economic Analysis	N.A.	N.A.	N.A.	N.A.	N.A.	4.00	3.50	7.00	6.50	3.4	1.1	3.2	3.7.	N.A.	N.A.
Donald Straszheim, Merrill Lynch	3.10	6.65	3.6	2.5	110	3.65	3.90	6.15	5.90	2.9	3.2	2.3	2.7	106	100
Anthony Vignola, Kidder Peabody	3.50	7.00	3.3	3.2	113	3.50	4.00	6.50	6.75	3.2	2.8	2.8	3.3	114	117
John Williams, Bankers Trust	3.00	6.30	2.8	2.5	100	3.10	3.15	6.15	6.00	2.7	2.8	2.6	2.8	125	135
Raymond Worseck, A.G. Edwards	3.80	7.00	3.5	3.7	120	3.30	3.60	6.10	6.40	2.8	2.8	3.0	3.0	117	122
David Wyss, DRI/McGraw-Hill	3.50	6.90	3.1	3.2	103	3.25	3.70	6.20	6.30	2.9	2.7	2.7	3.2	111	105
Edward Yardeni, C.J. Lawrence	3.50	7.08	3.0	2.0	120	3.00	3.00	5.75	5.25	3.0	3.2	2.0	2.0	115	119
AVERAGE-f	3.36	6.83	3.1	3.1	111	3.40	3.67	6.26	6.39	2.8	2.8	2.7	3.0	113	115
Closing Rates as of 12/31/93-g	3.05	6.34	N.A.	N.A.	112										

N.A.-Not available, did not participate in prior survey. a-Treasury bill rates are on a bond-equivalent basis. b-Gross domestic product, annualized rate. c-Consumer price index, annual rate. d-Annualized rate based on rounded average of quarter to prior quarter estimates. e-CPI vs. 12 months earlier. f-Averages for the June survey are for the analysts polled at that time. g-Government estimates of second half gross domestic product and inflation are not yet available.

Source: *Wall Street Journal,* Monday, January 3, 1994, p. A2.

Does a Higher Rate of Growth of the Money Supply Lower Interest Rates?

We can now put together all the effects we have discussed to help us decide whether our analysis supports the politicians who advocate a greater rate of growth of the money supply when they feel that interest rates are too high. Of all the effects, only the liquidity effect indicates that a higher rate of money growth will cause a decline in interest rates. In contrast, the income, price-level, and expected-inflation effects indicate that interest rates will rise when money growth is higher. Which of these effects are largest, and how quickly do they take effect? The answers are critical in determining whether interest rates will rise or fall when money supply growth is increased.

Generally, the liquidity effect from the greater money growth takes effect immediately because the rising money supply leads to an immediate decline in the equilibrium interest rate. The income and price-level effects take time to work because the increasing money supply takes time to raise the price level and income, which in turn raise interest rates. The expected-inflation effect, which also raises interest rates, can be slow or fast, depending on whether people adjust their expectations of inflation slowly or quickly when the money growth rate is increased

Three possibilities are outlined in Figure 13; each shows how interest rates respond over time to an increased rate of money supply growth starting at time *T.* Panel (a) shows a case in which the liquidity effect dominates the other effects so that the interest rate falls from i_1 at time *T* to a final level of i_2. The liquidity effect operates quickly to lower the interest rate, but as time goes by, the other effects start to reverse some of the decline. Because the liquidity effect is larger than the others, however, the interest rate never rises back to its initial level.

Panel (b) has a lesser liquidity effect than the other effects, with the expected-inflation effect operating slowly because expectations of inflation are slow to adjust upward. Initially, the liquidity effect drives down the interest rate. Then the income, price-level, and expected-inflation effects begin to raise it. Because these effects are dominant, the interest rate eventually rises above its initial level to i_2. In the short run, lower interest rates result from increased money growth, but eventually they end up climbing above the initial level.

Panel (c) has the expected-inflation effect dominating as well as operating rapidly because people quickly raise their expectation of inflation when the rate of money growth increases. The expected-inflation effect begins immediately to overpower the liquidity effect, and the interest rate immediately starts to climb. Over time, as the income and price-level effects start to take hold, the interest rate rises even higher, and the eventual outcome is an interest rate that is substantially above the initial interest rate. The result shows clearly that increasing money supply growth is not the answer to reducing interest rates but rather that money growth should be reduced in order to lower interest rates!

An important issue for economic policymakers is which of these three scenarios is closest to reality. If a decline in interest rates is desired, then an increase in money supply growth is called for when the liquidity effect dominates the other effects, as in panel (a). A decrease in money growth is appropriate if the other effects dominate the liquidity effect and expectations of inflation adjust rapidly, as in panel (c). If the other effects dominate the liquidity effect but expectations of inflation adjust only slowly, as in panel (b), then whether you want to increase or decrease money growth depends on whether you care more about what happens in the short run or the long run.

Which scenario is supported by the evidence? The relationship of interest rates and money growth from 1951 to 1993 is plotted in Figure 14. When the rate of money supply growth began to climb in the mid-1960s, interest rates rose, indicating that the liquidity effect was dominated by the price-level, income, and expected-inflation effects. By the 1970s, interest rates reached levels unprecedented

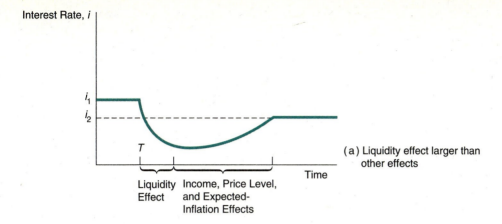

(a) Liquidity effect larger than other effects

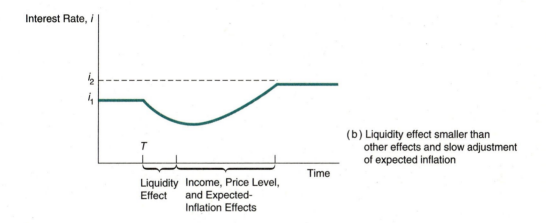

(b) Liquidity effect smaller than other effects and slow adjustment of expected inflation

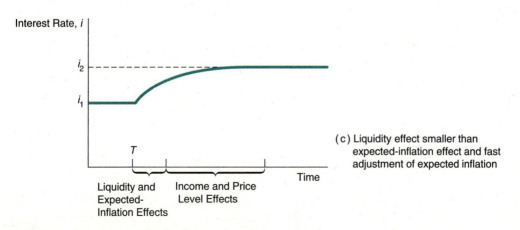

(c) Liquidity effect smaller than expected-inflation effect and fast adjustment of expected inflation

FIGURE 13 Response over Time to an Increase in Money Supply Growth

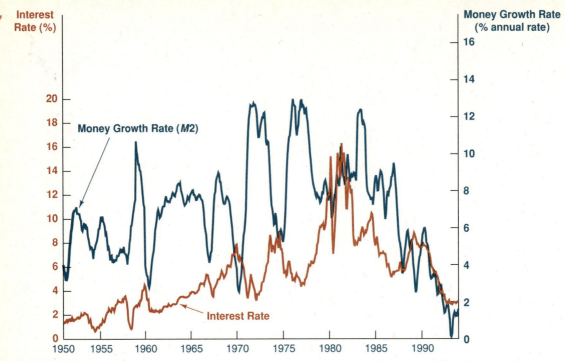

FIGURE 14 Money Growth (M2, Annual Rate) and Interest Rates (Three-Month Treasury Bills), 1950–1993
Sources: Federal Reserve *Bulletin;* Citibase databank.

in the period after World War II, as did the rate of money supply growth.

The scenario depicted in panel (a) of Figure 13 seems doubtful, and the case for lowering interest rates by raising the rate of money growth is much weakened. Looking back at Figure 6, which shows the relationship between interest rates and expected inflation, you should not find this too surprising. The rise in the rate of money supply growth in the 1960s and 1970s is matched by a large rise in expected-inflation, which would lead us to predict that the expected-inflation effect would be dominant. It is the most plausible explanation for why interest rates rose in the face of higher money growth. However, Figure 14 does not really tell us which one of the two scenarios, panel (b) or panel (c) of Figure 13, is more accurate. It depends critically on how fast people's expectations about inflation adjust. How expectations are formed and whether they adjust rapidly is an important topic that is under active study by economists and is dealt with in Chapter 29.[5]

---

[5]Recent research provides mixed evidence on whether a higher rate of money growth leads immediately to higher or lower interest rates. For example, see Lawrence J. Christiano and Martin Eichenbaum, *Liquidity Effects, Monetary Policy and the Business Cycle,* Working Paper Series, WP-92-15 (Chicago: Federal Reserve Bank of Chicago, 1992); Eric M. Leeper and David B. Gordon, "In Search of the Liquidity Effect," *Journal of Monetary Economics* 29 (1992): 341–370; and Steven Strongin, *The Identification of Monetary Policy Disturbances: Explaining the Liquidity Puzzle,* Working Paper Series, WP-91-24 (Chicago: Federal Reserve Bank of Chicago, 1991).

SUMMARY

1. The supply and demand analysis for bonds, known as the loanable funds framework, provides one theory of how interest rates are determined. It predicts that interest rates will change when there is a change in demand because of changes in income (or wealth), expected returns, risk, or liquidity, or when there is a change in supply because of changes in the attractiveness of investment opportunities, the real cost of borrowing, or government activities.

2. An alternative theory of how interest rates are determined is provided by the liquidity preference framework, which analyzes the supply of and demand for money. It shows that interest rates will change when there is a change in the demand for money because of changes in income or the price level or when there is a change in the supply of money.

3. There are four possible effects of an increase in the money supply on interest rates: the liquidity effect, the income effect, the price-level effect, and the expected-inflation effect. The liquidity effect indicates that a rise in money supply growth will lead to a decline in interest rates; the other effects work in the opposite direction. The evidence seems to indicate that the income, price-level, and expected-inflation effects dominate the liquidity effect such that an increase in money supply growth leads to higher rather than lower interest rates.

KEY TERMS

demand curve	excess supply	loanable funds framework	liquidity preference framework
supply curve	excess demand	asset market approach	opportunity cost
market equilibrium	loanable funds	Fisher effect	

QUESTIONS AND PROBLEMS

Answer each question by drawing the appropriate supply and demand diagrams.

*1. As we will see in Chapter 16, an important way in which the Federal Reserve decreases the money supply is by selling bonds to the public. Using the loanable funds framework, show what effect this action has on interest rates. Is your answer consistent with what you would expect to find with the liquidity preference framework?

2. Using both the liquidity preference and loanable funds frameworks, show why interest rates are *procyclical* (rising when the economy is expanding and falling during recessions).

*3. Why should a rise in the price level (but *not* in expected inflation) cause interest rates to rise when the nominal money supply is fixed?

4. Find the "Credit Markets" column in the *Wall Street Journal*. Underline the statements in the column that explain bond price movements, and draw the appropriate supply and demand diagrams that support these statements.

5. What effect will a sudden increase in the volatility of gold prices have on interest rates?

*6. How might a sudden increase in people's expectations of future real estate prices affect interest rates?

7. Explain what effect a large federal deficit might have on interest rates.

*8. Using both the loanable funds and liquidity preference frameworks, show what the effect is on interest rates when the riskiness of bonds rises. Are the results the same in the two frameworks?

9. If the price level falls next year, remaining fixed thereafter, and the money supply is fixed, what is likely to happen to interest rates over the next two years? (*Hint:* Take account of both the price-level effect and the expected-inflation effect.)

*10. Will there be an effect on interest rates if brokerage commissions on stocks fall? Why?

Using Economic Analysis to Predict the Future

11. The president of the United States announces in his press conference that he will fight the higher inflation rate with a new anti-inflation program. Predict what will happen to interest rates if the public believes him.

*12. The chairman of the Fed announces that interest rates will rise sharply next year, and the market believes him. What will happen to today's interest rate on the AT&T bonds, such as the 8⅛s of 2022?

13. Predict what will happen to interest rates if the public suddenly expects a large increase in stock prices.

*14. Predict what will happen to interest rates if prices in the bond market become more volatile.

15. If the next chairperson of the Federal Reserve Board has a reputation for advocating an even slower rate of money growth than the current chairperson, what will happen to interest rates? Discuss the possible resulting situations.

Appendix to Chapter 6

APPLYING THE ASSET MARKET APPROACH TO A COMMODITY MARKET: THE CASE OF GOLD

Both models of interest rate determination in Chapter 6 make use of an asset market approach in which supply and demand are always considered in terms of stocks of assets (amounts at a given point in time). The asset market approach is useful in understanding not only why interest rates fluctuate but also how any asset's price is determined.

One asset that has fascinated people for thousands of years is gold. It has been a driving force in history: The conquest of the Americas by Europeans was to a great extent the result of the quest for gold, to cite just one example. The fascination with gold continues to the present day, and developments in the gold market are followed closely by financial analysts and the media. This appendix shows how the asset market approach can be applied to understanding the behavior of commodity markets, in particular the gold market. (The analysis in this appendix can also be used to understand behavior in many other asset markets.)

SUPPLY AND DEMAND IN THE GOLD MARKET

The analysis of a commodity market, such as the gold market, proceeds in a similar fashion to the analysis of the bond market by examining the supply of and demand for the commodity. We again use the theory of asset demand to obtain a demand curve for gold, which shows the relationship between the quantity of gold demanded and the price when all other economic variables are held constant.

Demand Curve

To derive the relationship between the quantity of gold demanded and its price, we again recognize that an important determinant of the quantity demanded is its expected return:

$$RET^e = \frac{P^e_{t+1} - P_t}{P_t} = g^e$$

where RET^e = expected return
    P_t = price of gold today
    P^e_{t+1} = expected price of gold next year
    g^e = expected capital gain

In deriving the demand curve, we hold all other variables constant, particularly the expected price of gold next year P^e_{t+1}. With a given value of the expected price of gold next year P^e_{t+1}, a lower price of gold today P_t means that there will be a greater appreciation in the price of gold over the coming year. The result is that a lower price of gold today implies a higher expected capital gain over the coming year and hence a higher expected return: $RET^e = (P^e_{t+1} - P_t)/P_t$. Thus because the price of gold today (which for simplicity we will denote as P) is lower, the expected return on gold is higher, and the quantity demanded is higher. Consequently, the demand curve G^d_1 slopes downward in Figure A1.

Supply Curve

To derive the supply curve, expressing the relationship between the quantity supplied and the price, we again assume that all other economic variables are held constant. A higher price of gold will induce producers to mine for extra gold and also possibly induce governments to sell some of their gold stocks to

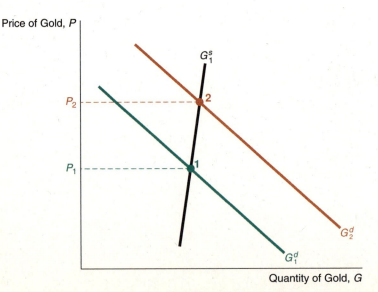

FIGURE A1
A Change in the Equilibrium Price of Gold
When the demand curve shifts rightward from G^d_1 to G^d_2, say, because expected inflation rises, equilibrium moves from point 1 to point 2, and the equilibrium price of gold rises from P_1 to P_2.

the public, thus increasing the quantity supplied. Hence the supply curve G_1^s in Figure A1 slopes upward. Notice that the supply curve in the figure is drawn to be very steep. The reason for this is that the actual amount of gold produced in any year is only a tiny fraction of the outstanding stock of gold that has been accumulated over hundreds of years. Thus the increase in the quantity of the gold supplied in response to a higher price is only a small fraction of the stock of gold, resulting in a very steep supply curve.

Market Equilibrium

Market equilibrium in the gold market occurs when the quantity of gold demanded equals the quantity of gold supplied:

$$G^d = G^s$$

With the initial demand and supply curves of G_1^d and G_1^s, equilibrium occurs at point 1, where these curves intersect at a gold price of P_1. At a price above this equilibrium, the amount of gold supplied exceeds the amount demanded, and this condition of excess supply leads to a decline in the gold price until it reaches P_1, the equilibrium price. Similarly, if the price is below P_1, there is excess demand for gold, which drives the price upward until it settles at the equilibrium price P_1.

CHANGES IN THE EQUILIBRIUM PRICE OF GOLD

Changes in the equilibrium price of gold occur when there is a shift in either the supply curve or the demand curve, that is, when the quantity demanded or supplied changes at each given price of gold in response to a change in some other factor besides today's gold price.

Shift in the Demand Curve for Gold

The theory of asset demand provides the factors that shift the demand curve for gold: wealth, expected return on gold relative to alternative assets, riskiness of gold relative to alternative assets, and liquidity of gold relative to alternative assets. The analysis of how changes in each of these factors shift the demand curve for gold is the same as that found in the chapter.

When wealth rises, at a given price of gold, the quantity demanded increases, and the demand curve shifts to the right, as in Figure A1. When the expected return on gold relative to other assets rises—either because speculators think that the future price of gold will be higher or because the expected return on other assets declines—gold becomes more desirable; the quantity demanded therefore increases at any given price of gold, and the demand curve shifts to the right, as in Figure A1. When the relative riskiness of gold declines, either because gold prices become less volatile or because returns on other assets become more volatile, gold becomes more desirable, the quantity demanded at every given price rises, and the demand curve again shifts to the right. When the gold market becomes relatively more liquid and gold therefore becomes more desirable, the quantity demanded at any given price rises, and the demand curve also shifts to the right, as in Figure A1.

Shifts in the Supply Curve for Gold

The supply curve for gold shifts when there are changes in technology that make gold mining more efficient or when governments at any given price of gold decide to increase sales of their holdings of gold. In these cases, the quantity of gold supplied at any given price increases, and the supply curve shifts to the right.

Changes in the Equilibrium Price of Gold

To illustrate how changes in the equilibrium price of gold occur when supply and demand curves shift, let's look at what happens when there is a change in expected inflation.

Suppose that expected inflation is 5% and the initial supply and demand curves are at G_1^s and G_1^d so that the equilibrium price of gold is at P_1 in Figure A1. If expected inflation now rises to 10%, prices of goods and commodities next year will be expected to be higher than they otherwise would have been, and the price of gold next year P_{t+1}^e will also be expected to be higher than otherwise. Now at any given price of gold today, gold is expected to have a greater rate of appreciation over the coming year and hence a higher expected capital gain and return. The greater expected return means that the quantity demanded of gold increases at any given price, thus shifting the demand curve from G_1^d to G_2^d. Equilibrium therefore moves from point 1 to point 2, and the price of gold rises from P_1 to P_2.

By using a supply and demand diagram like that in Figure A1, you should be able to see that if the expected rate of inflation falls, the price of gold today will also fall. We thus reach the following conclusion: ***The price of gold should be positively related to the expected inflation rate.***

Because the gold market responds immediately to any changes in expected inflation, it is considered a good barometer of the trend of inflation in the future. Indeed, Alan Greenspan, the chairman of the Board of Governors of the Federal Reserve System, has advocated using the price of gold as an indicator of inflationary pressures in the economy. Not surprisingly, then, the gold market is followed closely by financial analysts and monetary policymakers.

STUDY GUIDE

To give yourself practice with supply and demand analysis in the gold market, see if you can analyze what happens to the price of gold for the following situations, remembering that all other things are held constant: (1) Interest rates rise, (2) the gold market becomes more liquid, (3) the volatility of gold prices increases, (4) the stock market is expected to turn bullish in the near future, (5) investors suddenly become fearful that there will be a collapse in real estate prices, and (6) Russia sells a lot of gold in the open market to raise hard currency to feed its people.

The analysis in this appendix can also be applied to many other asset markets. See if you can apply the analysis here to understand fluctuations in the prices of classic comic books, old baseball cards, oil, Rembrandt paintings, or other commodities mentioned in the following application.

APPLICATION   **READING THE *WALL STREET JOURNAL***

THE "COMMODITIES" COLUMN

The supply and demand analysis in this appendix can help you evaluate events in commodity markets that are reported in the media. Every day, the *Wall Street Journal* reports on developments in the commodities markets on the previous business day in its "Commodities" column, an example of which is found in the "Following the Financial News" box.

The column focuses on the price rise for precious metals as a result of concerns about the clash between U.S. and Serbian jets and in general worries about a resurgence of inflation. Our supply and demand analysis explains why these factors would boost the prices of precious metals.

The renewed fears of inflation indicate that the prices of goods and commodities like gold are expected to rise in the future, so P_{t+1}^e for gold is expected to be higher than otherwise. The resulting higher expected appreciation of gold implies that its expected return will rise, which means that the quantity demanded will increase at any given price, shifting the demand curve to the right as in Figure A1. As we see in Figure A1, the equilibrium price of gold therefore rises.

The column also points out that concerns about international conflict increase the demand for gold because it is considered to be a "safe-haven" investment. The analysis in Figure A1 also demonstrates why this would lead to a rise in the price of gold. The increased demand for gold shifts the gold demand curve to the right as in Figure A1, and as shown there, the equilibrium price would therefore rise.

The column also points out that the price of wheat sank because of forecasts for rain in dry areas of the Southern Plains. Our supply and demand

The "Commodities" Column

The "Commodities" column appears daily in the *Wall Street Journal;* an example is pre- sented here. It is typically found in the third section, "Money and Investing."

COMMODITIES

Prices of Precious Metals Rise Amid Concerns Over U.S.-Serbia Clash, Prospect for Inflation

By JEFFREY TAYLOR
Staff Reporter of THE WALL STREET JOURNAL

Precious-metals prices rose on nervous-ness about clashes between Serbian and U.S. jet fighters in Bosnia and general worries about a potential return of infla-tion to the economy.

At New York's Commodity Exchange, gold for April delivery was up $2.70 to $382.50 an ounce, while the actively traded May silver-futures contract rose 12.8 cents to $5.39 an ounce. At the New York Mercantile Exchange, meanwhile, plati-num for April delivery climbed $4.30 to $397.70 an ounce.

The downing of four Serbian jets by U.S. F-16 fighters "supposedly triggered buying of gold as a 'safe-haven' invest-ment," said Bernard Savaiko, senior ana-lyst for PaineWebber Inc. But Mr. Savaiko and other analysts said the buying proba-bly would have occurred anyway because of liquidation of "short" positions, or wa-gers that gold prices would fall, amid renewed fears of increasing inflation.

The Journal of Commerce index of 18 industrial commodities, a popular barome-ter of inflation among economists, has been rising lately. Yesterday, the Knight-Ridder Commodity Research Bureau index also rose, settling at 227.55. Surges in the prices of commodities in general — and especially gold — are viewed as early indi-cators of inflation.

"Gold is a hedge against economic and political uncertainty," said Fred Demler, metals economist for E,D & F Man. "There's a lot of political unrest simmer-ing around the world, and a lot speculation about an upturn of inflation. That gave people reason to buy precious metals."

For weeks, the price of gold has been trading in a tight $375-to-$390 range.

"If the CRB index were to shoot through 229 or 230, inflation fears would grow and lead to an advance in gold prices," Mr. Savaiko said. "If, however, the CRB can't clear that level, it would indicate the Federal Reserve is keeping inflation con-cerns in check, and precious-metals prices might fall."

In other commodity markets yester-day:

GRAINS AND SOYBEANS: Wheat prices sank amid forecasts for rain in some dry areas of the Southern Plains, where the hard red winter-wheat crop is begin-ning to emerge from dormancy. In trading at the Kansas City Board of Trade, the wheat contract for March delivery slipped 1.25 cents a bushel to settle at $3.55 a bushel. Soybean prices settled mostly lower while corn prices settled mixed. Speculation is growing that the U.S. gov-ernment might offer grain-buying credit guarantees to Mexico, which is a major importer of U.S. corn. Bill Biedermann, vice president of research at Allendale Inc., Crystal Lake, Ill., said he expects Mexican purchases of U.S. corn to rise by about one million metric tons this year over 1993.

ENERGY: Heating-oil futures prices rose as renewed cold weather across the Midwest and the Northeast propped up prices. Otherwise, market participants said, there was little news to move energy contracts in either direction. Traders noted that the March heating-oil contract, which expired yesterday, was the only heating-oil contract to rise. Thus, they questioned whether the strong price envi-ronment would last much longer, particu-larly as warmer weather is bound to arrive some time soon. Natural gas prices fell despite the cold weather. Meanwhile, crude oil and gasoline prices slid.

Source: Wall Street Journal, Tuesday, March 1, 1994, p. C16.

analysis predicts that this is exactly what would occur because the rain in the parched areas would increase production and the supply of wheat in the future, which would lower its future price. The lower future price implies a smaller expected return on wheat, so the current demand for it would shrink at any given price, which would shift the demand curve to the left. The result would be that the equilibrium price of wheat would fall just as is described in the column.

The column also points out that renewed cold weather in the Midwest and the Northeast caused heating-oil prices to rise. The cold weather increases the demand for heating oil, thereby shifting the demand curve to the right as in Figure A1, thereby raising the equilibrium price. Thus our analysis also provides an explanation for the link between cold weather and higher heating-oil prices.

Chapter 7

THE RISK AND TERM STRUCTURE OF INTEREST RATES

PREVIEW In our supply and demand analysis of interest-rate behavior in Chapter 6, we examined the determination of just one interest rate. Yet we saw earlier that there are enormous numbers of bonds on which the interest rates can and do differ. In this chapter we complete the interest-rate picture by examining the relationship of the various interest rates to each other. Understanding why they differ from bond to bond can help businesses, banks, insurance companies, and private investors decide which bonds to purchase as investments or which ones to sell.

We first look at why bonds with the same term to maturity have different interest rates. The relationship among these interest rates is called the **risk structure of interest rates,** although risk, liquidity, and income tax rules all play a role in determining the risk structure. A bond's term to maturity also affects its interest rate, and the relationship among interest rates on bonds with different terms to maturity is called the **term structure of interest rates.** In this chapter we examine the sources and causes of fluctuations in interest rates relative to one another and look at a number of theories that explain these fluctuations.

RISK STRUCTURE OF INTEREST RATES

Figure 1 shows the yields to maturity for several categories of long-term bonds from 1919 to 1993. It shows us two important features of interest-rate behavior for bonds of the same maturity: Interest rates on different categories of bonds differ from one another in any given year, and the spread (or difference) between the interest rates varies over time. The interest rates on municipal bonds, for example, are above those on U.S. government (Treasury) bonds in the late 1930s but lower thereafter. In addition, the spread between the interest rates on Baa corporate bonds (riskier than Aaa corporate bonds) and U.S. government

149

**FIGURE 1
Long-Term
Bond Yields,
1919–1993**
Sources: Board of
Governors of the
Federal Reserve
System, *Banking
and Monetary
Statistics,
1941–1970*; Fed-
eral Reserve *Bul-
letin*.

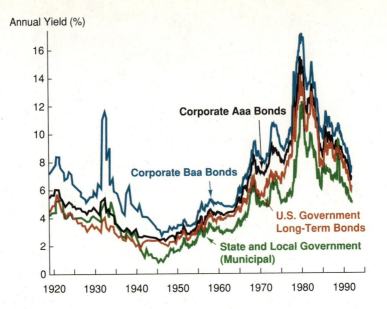

bonds is very large during the Great Depression years 1930–1933, is smaller during the 1940s–1960s, and then widens again in the 1970s–1990s. What factors are responsible for these phenomena?

Default Risk

One attribute of a bond that influences its interest rate is its **default risk,** the chance that the issuer of the bond will default, that is, be unable to make interest payments or pay off the face value when the bond matures. A corporation suffering big losses, such as Chrysler Corporation did in the 1970s, might be more likely to suspend interest payments on its bonds.[1] The default risk on its bonds would therefore be quite high. By contrast, U.S. Treasury bonds have no default risk because the federal government can always increase taxes or even print money to pay off its obligations. Bonds like these with no default risk are called **default-free bonds.** The spread between the interest rates on bonds with default risk and default-free bonds, called the **risk premium,** indicates how much additional interest people must earn in order to be willing to hold a risky bond. Our supply and demand analysis of the bond market in Chapter 6 can be used to explain why a bond with default risk always has a positive risk premium and why the higher the default risk is, the larger the risk premium will be.

[1]Chrysler did not default on its loans in this period, but it would have were it not for a government bailout plan intended to preserve jobs that in effect provided Chrysler with funds that were used to pay off creditors.

STUDY GUIDE

Two exercises will help you gain a better understanding of the risk structure:

1. Put yourself in the shoes of an investor—see how your purchase decision would be affected by changes in risk and liquidity.

2. Practice drawing the appropriate shifts in the supply and demand curves when risk and liquidity change. For example, see if you can draw the appropriate shifts in the supply and demand curves when, in contrast to the examples in the text, a corporate bond has a decline in default risk or an improvement in its liquidity.

To examine the effect of default risk on interest rates, let us look at the supply and demand diagrams for the default-free (U.S. Treasury) and corporate long-term bond markets in Figure 2. To make the diagrams somewhat easier to read, let's assume that initially there is no possibility of default on the corporate bonds, so they are default-free like U.S. Treasury bonds. In this case, these two bonds have the same attributes (identical risk and maturity); their equilibrium prices and interest rates will initially be equal ($P_1^c = P_1^T$ and $i_1^c = i_1^T$), and the risk premium on corporate bonds ($i_1^c - i_1^T$) will be zero.

If the possibility of a default increases because a corporation begins to suffer large losses, the default risk on corporate bonds will increase, and the expected

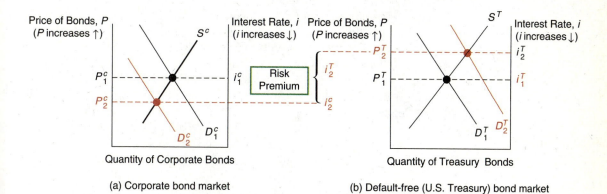

(a) Corporate bond market   (b) Default-free (U.S. Treasury) bond market

FIGURE 2 Response to an Increase in Default Risk on Corporate Bonds

An increase in default risk on corporate bonds shifts the demand curve from D_1^c to D_2^c. Simultaneously, it shifts the demand curve for Treasury bonds from D_1^T to D_2^T. The equilibrium price for corporate bonds (left axis) falls from P_1^c to P_2^c, and the equilibrium interest rate on corporate bonds (right axis) rises from i_1^c to i_2^c. In the Treasury market, the equilibrium bond price rises from P_1^T to P_2^T, and the equilibrium interest rate falls from i_1^T to i_2^T. The brace indicates the difference between i_2^c and i_2^T, the risk premium on corporate bonds. (*Note: P* and *i* increase in opposite directions. *P* on the left vertical axis increases as we go up the axis, while *i* on the right vertical axis increases as we go down the axis.)

return on these bonds will decrease. In addition, the corporate bond's return will be more uncertain as well. The theory of asset demand predicts that because the expected return on the corporate bond falls relative to the expected return on the default-free Treasury bond while its relative riskiness rises, the corporate bond is less desirable (holding everything else equal), and demand for it will fall. The demand curve for corporate bonds in panel (a) of Figure 2 then shifts to the left from D_1^c to D_2^c.

At the same time, the expected return on default-free Treasury bonds increases relative to the expected return on corporate bonds while their relative riskiness declines. The Treasury bonds thus become more desirable, and demand rises, as shown in panel (b) by the rightward shift in the demand curve for these bonds from D_1^T to D_2^T.

As we can see in Figure 2, the equilibrium price for corporate bonds (left axis) falls from P_1^c to P_2^c, and since the bond price is negatively related to the interest rate, the equilibrium interest rate on corporate bonds (right axis) rises from i_1^c to i_2^c. At the same time, however, the equilibrium price for the Treasury bonds rises from P_1^T to P_2^T, and the equilibrium interest rate falls from i_1^T to i_2^T. The spread between the interest rates on corporate and default-free bonds—that is, the risk premium on corporate bonds—has risen from zero to $i_2^c - i_2^T$. We can now conclude that ***a bond with default risk will always have a positive risk premium, and an increase in its default risk will raise the risk premium.***

Because default risk is so important to the size of the risk premium, purchasers of bonds need to know whether a corporation is likely to default on its bonds. Two major investment advisory firms, Moody's Investors Service and Standard and Poor's Corporation, provide default risk information by rating the quality of corporate and municipal bonds in terms of the probability of default. The ratings and their description are contained in Table 1. Bonds with relatively low risk of default are called *investment-grade* securities and have a rating of Baa (or BBB) and above. Bonds with ratings below Baa (or BBB) have higher default risk and have been aptly dubbed **junk bonds.**

Next let's look back at Figure 1 and see if we can explain the relationship between interest rates on corporate and U.S. Treasury bonds. Corporate bonds always have higher interest rates than U.S. Treasury bonds because they always have some risk of default, whereas U.S. Treasury bonds do not. Because Baa-rated corporate bonds have a greater default risk than the higher-rated Aaa bonds, their risk premium is greater, and the Baa rate therefore always exceeds the Aaa rate.

We can use the same analysis to explain the huge jump in the risk premium on Baa corporate bond rates during the Great Depression years 1930–1933 and the rise in the risk premium in the 1970s, 1980s, and 1990s (see Figure 1). The Great Depression period saw a very high rate of business failures and defaults. As we would expect, these factors led to a substantial increase in default risk for bonds issued by vulnerable corporations, and the risk premium for Baa bonds reached unprecedentedly high levels. The 1970s, 1980s, and 1990s again saw higher levels of business failures and defaults, although they were still well below Depression levels. Again, as expected, default risks and risk premiums for

TABLE 1   Bond Ratings by Moody's and Standard and Poor's

Rating			
Moody's	**Standard and Poor's**	**Descriptions**	**Examples of Corporations with Bonds Outstanding in 1994**
Aaa	AAA	Highest quality (lowest default risk)	General Electric, Johnson and Johnson, Wisconsin Bell
Aa	AA	High quality	McDonalds, Mobil Oil, Wal-Mart
A	A	Upper medium grade	Anheuser-Busch, Ford Motor, Xerox
Baa	BBB	Medium grade	Chrysler, General Motors, Wendy's
Ba	BB	Lower medium grade	McDonnell Douglas, RJR-Nabisco, Time-Warner
B	B	Speculative	Marriott, Revlon, Turner Broadcasting
Caa	CCC, CC	Poor (high default risk)	
Ca	C	Highly speculative	
C	D	Lowest grade	

corporate bonds rose, widening the spread between interest rates on corporate bonds and Treasury bonds. Our analysis also explains the sharp rise in the spread between interest rates on junk bonds and Treasury bonds after the stock market crash in October 1987 (see Box 1).

Liquidity

Another attribute of a bond that influences its interest rate is its liquidity. As we learned in Chapter 5, a liquid asset is one that can be quickly and cheaply converted into cash if the need arises. The more liquid an asset is, the more desirable it is (holding everything else constant). U.S. Treasury bonds are the most liquid of all long-term bonds because they are so widely traded that they are the easiest to sell quickly and the cost of selling them is low. Corporate bonds are not as liquid because fewer bonds for any one corporation are traded; thus it can be costly to sell these bonds in an emergency because it may be hard to find buyers quickly.

B o x   1

THE STOCK MARKET CRASH OF 1987 AND THE JUNK BOND–TREASURY SPREAD

The stock market crash on "Black Monday," October 19, 1987, had a major impact on bond markets that is well explained by the supply and demand analysis in Figure 2. As a consequence of the Black Monday crash, many investors began to doubt the financial health of corporations with lower credit ratings that had issued junk bonds. The increase in default risk for junk bonds made them less desirable at any given interest rate, decreased the quantity demanded, and shifted the demand curve for junk bonds to the left. As shown in panel (a) of Figure 2, the interest rate on junk bonds should have risen, which is indeed what happened: Interest rates on junk bonds shot up by about one percentage point. But the increase in the perceived default risk for junk bonds after the crash made default-free U.S. Treasury bonds relatively more attractive and shifted the demand curve for these securities to the right—an outcome described by some analysts as a "flight to quality." Just as our analysis predicts in Figure 2, interest rates on Treasury securities fell by about one percentage point. The overall outcome was that the spread between interest rates on junk bonds and government bonds rose by two percentage points, from 4% before the crash to 6% immediately after.

How does the reduced liquidity of the corporate bonds affect their interest rates relative to the interest rate on Treasury bonds? We can use supply and demand analysis with the same figure that was used to analyze the effect of default risk, Figure 2, to show that the lower liquidity of corporate bonds relative to Treasury bonds increases the spread between the interest rates on these two bonds. Let us start the analysis by assuming that initially corporate and Treasury bonds are equally liquid and all their other attributes are the same. As shown in Figure 2, their equilibrium prices and interest rates will initially be equal: $P_1^c = P_1^T$ and $i_1^c = i_1^T$. If the corporate bond becomes less liquid than the Treasury bond because it is less widely traded, then, as the theory of asset demand indicates, its demand will fall, shifting its demand curve from D_1^c to D_2^c as in panel (a). The Treasury bond now becomes relatively more liquid in comparison with the corporate bond, so its demand curve shifts rightward from D_1^T to D_2^T as in panel (b). The shifts in the curves in Figure 2 show that the price of the less liquid corporate bond falls and its interest rate rises, while the price of the more liquid Treasury bond rises and its interest rate falls.

The result is that the spread between the interest rates on the two bond types has risen. Therefore, the differences between interest rates on corporate bonds and Treasury bonds (that is, the risk premiums) reflect not only the corporate bond's default risk but its liquidity too. This is why a risk premium is sometimes called a *liquidity premium*. Most accurately, it should be called a "risk and liquidity premium," but convention dictates that it be called a *risk premium*.

Income Tax Considerations

Returning to Figure 1, we are still left with one puzzle—the behavior of municipal bond rates. Municipal bonds are certainly not default-free: State and local governments have defaulted on the municipal bonds they have issued in the past, particularly during the Great Depression and even more recently in the case of the Washington State Public Power Supply System in 1983. Also, municipal bonds are not as liquid as U.S. Treasury bonds.

Why is it, then, that these bonds have had lower interest rates than U.S. Treasury bonds for at least 40 years, as indicated in Figure 1? The explanation lies in the fact that interest payments on municipal bonds are exempt from federal income taxes, a factor that has the same effect on the demand for municipal bonds as an increase in their expected return.

Let us imagine that you have a high enough income to put you in the 40% income tax bracket, where for every extra dollar of income you have to pay 40 cents to the government. If you own a $1000-face-value U.S. Treasury bond that sells for $1000 and has a coupon payment of $100, you get to keep only $60 of the payment after taxes. Although the bond has a 10% interest rate, you actually earn only 6% after taxes.

Suppose, however, that you put your savings into a $1000-face-value municipal bond that sells for $1000 and pays only $80 in coupon payments. Its interest rate is only 8%, but because it is a tax-exempt security, you pay no taxes on the $80 coupon payment, so you earn 8% after taxes. Clearly, you earn more on the municipal bond after taxes, so you are willing to hold the riskier and less liquid municipal bond even though it has a lower interest rate than the U.S. Treasury bond. (This was not true before World War II because the tax-exempt status of municipal bonds did not convey much of an advantage, in that income tax rates were extremely low in that period.)

Another way of understanding why municipal bonds have lower interest rates than Treasury bonds is to use the supply and demand analysis displayed in Figure 3. To begin with, we assume that municipal and Treasury bonds have identical attributes and so have the same bond prices and interest rates as drawn in the figure: $P_1^m = P_1^T$ and $i_1^m = i_1^T$. Once the municipal bonds are given a tax advantage that raises their after-tax expected return relative to Treasury bonds and makes them more desirable, demand for them rises, and their demand curve shifts to the right from D_1^m to D_2^m. The result is that their equilibrium bond price rises from P_1^m to P_2^m, and their equilibrium interest rate falls from i_1^m to i_2^m. By contrast, Treasury bonds have now become less desirable relative to municipal bonds, demand for Treasury bonds decreases, and D_1^T shifts to D_2^T. The Treasury bond price falls from P_1^T to P_2^T, and the interest rate rises from i_1^T to i_2^T. The resulting lower interest rates for municipal bonds and higher interest rates for

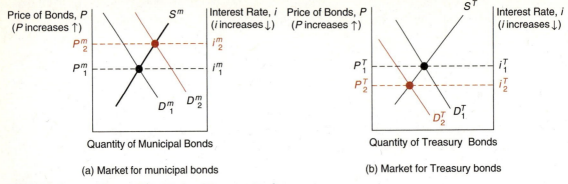

FIGURE 3   Interest Rates on Municipal and Treasury Bonds

When the municipal bond is given tax-free status, demand for the municipal bond shifts rightward from D_1^m to D_2^m and demand for the Treasury bond shifts leftward from D_1^T to D_2^T. The equilibrium price of the municipal bond (left axis) rises from P_1^m to P_2^m, so its interest rate (right axis) falls from i_1^m to i_2^m, while the equilibrium price of the Treasury bond falls from P_1^T to P_2^T, and its interest rate rises from i_1^T to i_2^T. The result is that municipal bonds end up with lower interest rates than those on Treasury bonds. (*Note:* P and i increase in opposite directions. P on the left vertical axis increases as we go up the axis, while i on the right vertical axis increases as we go down the axis.)

Treasury bonds explains why municipal bonds can have interest rates below those of Treasury bonds.[2]

Summary

The risk structure of interest rates (the relationship among interest rates on bonds with the same maturity) is explained by three factors: default risk, liquidity, and the income tax treatment of the bond's interest payments. As a bond's default risk increases, the risk premium on that bond (the spread between its interest rate and the interest rate on a default-free Treasury bond) rises. The greater liquidity of Treasury bonds also explains why their interest rates are lower than interest rates on less liquid bonds. If a bond has a favorable tax treatment, as do municipal bonds, whose interest payments are exempt from federal income taxes, its interest rate will be lower.

APPLICATION

EFFECTS OF THE CLINTON TAX INCREASE ON BOND INTEREST RATES

As part of the Clinton administration's 1993 deficit reduction plan, the top income tax bracket was raised from 31% to 40% and the corporate income tax rate was raised from 34% to 35%. What was the effect of this income tax in-

---

[2]In contrast to corporate bonds, Treasury bonds are exempt from state and local income taxes. Using the analysis in the text, you should be able to show that this feature of Treasury bonds provides an additional reason why interest rates on corporate bonds are higher than those on Treasury bonds.

crease on interest rates in the municipal bond market relative to those in the Treasury bond market?

The supply and demand analysis in Figure 3 provides the answer. The increased income tax rate for rich people and corporations means that the tax-free status of municipal bonds raises their after-tax expected return relative to that on Treasury bonds because the interest on Treasury bonds is now taxed at a higher rate. Because municipal bonds now become more desirable, their demand increases, shifting the demand curve to the right as in Figure 3, which raises their price and lowers their interest rate. Conversely, the higher income tax rate makes Treasury bonds less desirable; that shifts their demand curve to the left, lowers their price, and raises their interest rates, as in Figure 3.

Our analysis thus shows that the Clinton tax increase lowered the interest rates on municipal bonds relative to interest rates on Treasury bonds.

TERM STRUCTURE OF INTEREST RATES

We have seen how risk, liquidity, and tax considerations (collectively embedded in the risk structure) can influence interest rates. Another factor that influences the interest rate on a bond is its term to maturity: Bonds with identical risk, liquidity, and tax characteristics may have different interest rates because the time remaining to maturity is different. A plot of the yields on bonds with differing terms to maturity but the same risk, liquidity, and tax considerations is called a **yield curve,** and it describes the term structure of interest rates for particular types of bonds, such as government bonds. The "Following the Financial News" box shows several yield curves for Treasury securities that were published in the *Wall Street Journal*. Yield curves can be classified as upward-sloping, flat, and downward-sloping. When yield curves are upward-sloping, as in the "Following the Financial News" box, the long-term interest rates are above the short-term interest rates; when yield curves are flat, short- and long-term interest rates are the same; and when yield curves are downward-sloping, long-term interest rates are below short-term interest rates. Yield curves can also have more complicated shapes in which they first slope up and then down, or vice versa. Why do we usually see upward slopes of the yield curve as in the "Following the Financial News" box but sometimes other shapes?

Besides explaining why yield curves take on different shapes at different times, a good theory of the term structure of interest rates must explain the following three important empirical facts.

1. As we see in Figure 4 on page 159, interest rates on bonds of different maturities move together over time.

2. When short-term interest rates are low, yield curves are more likely to have an upward slope; when short-term interest rates are high, yield curves are more likely to slope downward.

3. Yield curves almost always slope upward, as in the "Following the Financial News" box.

FOLLOWING THE FINANCIAL NEWS

Yield Curves

The *Wall Street Journal* publishes a daily plot of the yield curves for Treasury securities, an example of which is presented here. It is typically found next to the "Credit Markets" column.

The numbers on the vertical axis indicate the interest rate for the Treasury security, with the maturity given by the numbers on the horizontal axis. For example, the yield curve marked "Yesterday" indicates that the interest rate on the three-month Treasury bill yesterday was 3.50%, while the one-year bill had an interest rate of 4.10% and the ten-year bond had an interest rate of 6.25%. As you can see, the yield curves in the plot have the typical upward slope.

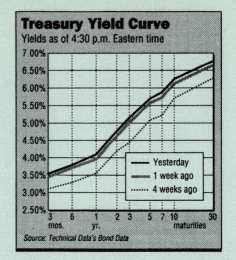

Source: Wall Street Journal, Thursday, March 3, 1994, p. C23.

Three theories have been put forth to explain the term structure of interest rates, that is, the relationship among interest rates on bonds of different maturities reflected in yield curve patterns: (1) the expectations hypothesis, (2) segmented markets theory, and (3) the preferred habitat theory (which is closely related to the liquidity premium theory). The expectations hypothesis does a good job of explaining the first two facts on our list but not the third. Segmented markets theory can explain fact 3 but not the other two facts, which are well explained by the expectations hypothesis. Because each theory explains facts that the other cannot, a natural way to seek a better understanding of the term structure is to combine features of both theories, which leads us to the preferred habitat theory and closely related liquidity premium theory, which can explain all three facts.

If the preferred habitat and liquidity premium theories do a better job of explaining the facts and are hence the most widely accepted theories, why do we spend time discussing the other two theories? There are two reasons. First, the ideas in these two theories provide the groundwork for the preferred habitat and liquidity premium theories. Second, it is important to see how economists modify theories to improve them when they find that the predicted results are inconsistent with the empirical evidence.

FIGURE 4
Movements over Time of Interest Rates on U.S. Government Bonds with Different Maturities
Sources: Board of Governors of the Federal Reserve System, *Banking and Monetary Statistics, 1941–1970;* Federal Reserve *Bulletin;* Citibase databank.

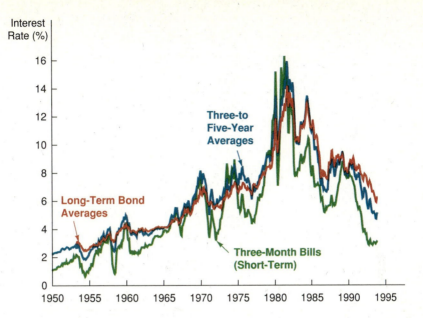

Expectations Hypothesis

The **expectations hypothesis** of the term structure states the following commonsense proposition: The interest rate on a long-term bond will equal an average of short-term interest rates that people expect to occur over the life of the long-term bond. For example, if people expect that short-term interest rates will be 10% on average over the coming five years, the expectations hypothesis predicts that the interest rate on bonds with five years to maturity will be 10% too. If short-term interest rates were expected to rise even higher after this five-year period, so that the average short-term interest rate over the coming 20 years is 11%, then the interest rate on 20-year bonds would equal 11% and would be higher than the interest rate on five-year bonds. We can see that the explanation provided by the expectations hypothesis for why interest rates on bonds of different maturities differ is that short-term interest rates are expected to have different values at future dates.

The key assumption behind this theory is that buyers of bonds do not prefer bonds of one maturity over another, so they will not hold any quantity of a bond if its expected return is less than that of another bond with a different maturity. Bonds that have this characteristic are said to be *perfect substitutes*. What this means in practice is that if bonds with different maturities are perfect substitutes, the expected return on these bonds must be equal.

To see how the assumption that bonds with different maturities are perfect substitutes leads to the expectations hypothesis, let us consider the following two investment strategies:

1. Purchasing a one-year bond and, when it matures in one year, purchasing another one-year bond

2. Purchasing a two-year bond and holding it until maturity

Because both strategies must have the same expected return if people are holding both one- and two-year bonds, the interest rate on the two-year bond must equal the average of the two one-year interest rates. For example, let's say that the current interest rate on the one-year bond is 9% and you expect the interest rate on the one-year bond next year to be 11%. If you pursue the first strategy of buying the two one-year bonds, the expected return over the two years will average out to be (9% + 11%)/2 = 10% per year. You will be willing to hold both the one- and two-year bonds only if the expected return per year of the two-year bond equals this. Therefore, the interest rate on the two-year bond must equal 10%, the average interest rate on the two one-year bonds.

We can make this argument more general. For an investment of $1, consider the choice of holding, for two periods, a two-period bond or two one-period bonds. Using the definitions

i_t = today's (time t) interest rate on a one-period bond
i^e_{t+1} = interest rate on a one-period bond expected for next period (time $t+1$)
i_{2t} = today's (time t) interest rate on the two-period bond

the expected return over the two periods from investing $1 in the two-period bond and holding it for the two periods can be calculated as

$$(1 + i_{2t})(1 + i_{2t}) - 1 = 1 + 2i_{2t} + (i_{2t})^2 - 1$$

After the second period, the $1 investment is worth $(1 + i_{2t}) (1 + i_{2t})$. Subtracting the $1 initial investment from this amount and dividing by the initial $1 investment gives the rate of return calculated in the first equation. Because $(i_{2t})^2$ is extremely small—if $i_{2t} = 10\% = 0.10$, then $(i_{2t})^2 = 0.01$—we can simplify the expected return for holding the two-period bond for the two periods to

$$2i_{2t}$$

With the other strategy, in which one-period bonds are bought, the expected return on the $1 investment over the two periods is

$$(1 + i_t)(1 + i^e_{t+1}) - 1$$

After the first period, the $1 investment becomes $1 + i_t$ and this is reinvested in the one-period bond for the next period, yielding an amount $(1 + i_t)(1 + i^e_{t+1})$. Subtracting the $1 initial investment from this amount and dividing by the initial investment of $1 gives the expected return for the strategy of holding one-period bonds for the two periods. Because $i_t(i_{t+1}^e)$ is also extremely small—if $i_t = i_{t+1}^e = 0.10$, then $i_t(i_{t+1}^e) = 0.01$—we can simplify this to

$$i_t + i_{t+1}^e$$

Both bonds will be held only if these expected returns are equal, that is, when

$$2i_{2t} = i_t + i_{t+1}^e$$

Solving for i_{2t} in terms of the one-period rates, we have

$$i_{2t} = \frac{i_t + i_{t+1}^e}{2} \tag{1}$$

which tells us that the two-period rate must equal the average of the two one-period rates. We can conduct the same steps for bonds with a longer maturity so that we can examine the whole term structure of interest rates. Doing so, we will find that the interest rate of i_{nt} on an n-period bond must equal

$$i_{nt} = \frac{i_t + i_{t+1}^e + i_{t+2}^e + \cdots + i_{t+(n-1)}^e}{n} \tag{2}$$

Equation 2 states that the n-period interest rate equals the average of the one-period interest rates expected to occur over the n-period life of the bond. This is a restatement of the expectations hypothesis in more precise terms.[3]

A simple numerical example might clarify what the expectations theory in Equation 2 is saying. If the one-year interest rate over the next five years is expected to be 5%, 6%, 7%, 8%, and 9%, Equation 2 indicates that the interest rate on the two-year bond would be

$$\frac{5\% + 6\%}{2} = 5.5\%$$

while for the five-year bond it would be

$$\frac{5\% + 6\% + 7\% + 8\% + 9\%}{5} = 7\%$$

Doing a similar calculation for the one-, three-, and four-year interest rates, you should be able to verify that the one- to five-year interest rates are 5.0%, 5.5%, 6.0%, 6.5%, and 7.0%, respectively. Thus we see that the rising trend in short-term interest rates produces an upward-sloping yield curve along which interest rates rise as maturity lengthens.

---

[3]The analysis here has been conducted for discount bonds. Formulas for interest rates on coupon bonds would differ slightly from those used here but would convey the same principle.

The expectations hypothesis is an elegant theory that provides an explanation of why the term structure of interest rates (as represented by yield curves) changes at different times. When the yield curve is upward-sloping, the expectations hypothesis suggests that short-term interest rates are expected to rise in the future, as we have seen in our numerical example. In this situation, in which the long-term rate is currently above the short-term rate, the average of future short-term rates is expected to be higher than the current short-term rate, which can occur only if short-term interest rates are expected to rise. This is what we see in our numerical example. When the yield curve slopes downward, the average of future short-term interest rates is expected to be below the current short-term rate, implying that short-term interest rates are expected to fall, on average, in the future. Only when the yield curve is flat does the expectations hypothesis suggest that short-term interest rates are not expected to change, on average, in the future.

The expectations hypothesis also explains fact 1 that interest rates on bonds with different maturities move together over time. Historically, short-term interest rates have had the characteristic that if they increase today, they will tend to be higher in the future. Hence a rise in short-term rates will raise people's expectations of future short-term rates. Because long-term rates are related to the average of expected future short-term rates, a rise in short-term rates will also raise long-term rates, causing short- and long-term rates to move together.

The expectations hypothesis also explains fact 2 that yield curves tend to have an upward slope when short-term interest rates are low and a downward slope when short-term rates are high. When short-term rates are low, people generally expect them to rise to some normal level in the future, and the average of future expected short-term rates is high relative to the current short-term rate. Therefore, long-term interest rates will be substantially above current short-term rates, and the yield curve would then have an upward slope. Conversely, if short-term rates are high, people usually expect them to come back down. Long-term rates would then drop below short-term rates because the average of expected future short-term rates would be below current short-term rates and the yield curve would slope downward.

The expectations hypothesis is an attractive theory because it provides a simple explanation of the behavior of the term structure, but unfortunately it has a major shortcoming: It cannot explain fact 3 that yield curves usually slope upward. The typical upward slope of yield curves implies that short-term interest rates are usually expected to rise in the future. In practice, short-term interest rates are just as likely to fall as they are to rise, and so the expectations hypothesis suggests that the typical yield curve should be flat rather than upward-sloping.

Segmented Markets Theory

As the name suggests, the **segmented markets theory** of the term structure sees markets for different-maturity bonds as completely separate and segmented. The interest rate for each maturity bond is then determined by the supply of and demand for that maturity bond with no effects from expected returns on other maturity bonds.

The key assumption in the segmented markets theory is that bonds of different maturities are not substitutes at all, so the expected return from holding a bond of one maturity has no effect on the demand for a bond of another maturity. This theory of the term structure is at the opposite extreme to the expectations hypothesis, which assumes that bonds of different maturities are perfect substitutes.

The argument for why bonds of different maturities are not substitutes is that investors have strong preferences for bonds of one maturity but not for another, so they will be concerned with the expected returns only for bonds of the maturity they prefer. This might occur because they have a particular holding period in mind, and if they match the maturity of the bond to the desired holding period, they can obtain a certain return with no risk at all.[4] (We have seen in Chapter 4 that if the term to maturity equals the holding period, the return is known for certain because it equals the yield exactly, and there is no interest-rate risk.) For example, people who have a short holding period would prefer to hold short-term bonds. Conversely, if you were putting funds away for your young child to go to college, your desired holding period might be much longer, and you would want to hold longer-term bonds.

In the segmented markets theory, differing yield curve patterns are accounted for by supply and demand differences associated with bonds of different maturities. If, as seems sensible, on average investors prefer bonds with shorter maturities that have less interest-rate risk, segmented markets theory can explain fact 3 that yield curves typically slope upward. Because the demand for long-term bonds is relatively lower than for short-term bonds in the typical situation, long-term bonds will have lower prices and higher interest rates, and hence the yield curve will typically slope upward.

Although the segmented markets theory can explain why yield curves usually tend to slope upward, it has a major flaw in that it cannot explain facts 1 and 2. Because it views the market for bonds of different maturities as completely segmented, there is no reason for a rise in interest rates on a bond of one maturity to affect the interest rate on a bond of another maturity. Therefore, it cannot explain why interest rates on bonds of different maturities tend to move together (fact 1). Second, because it is not clear how demand and supply for short- versus long-term bonds changes with the level of short-term interest rates, the theory cannot explain why yield curves tend to slope upward when short-term interest rates are low and downward when short-term interest rates are high (fact 2).

---

[4]The statement that there is no uncertainty about the return if the term to maturity equals the holding period is literally true only for a discount bond. For a coupon bond with a long holding period, there is some risk because coupon payments must be reinvested before the bond matures. Our analysis here is thus being conducted for discount bonds. However, the gist of the analysis remains the same for coupon bonds because the amount of this risk from reinvestment is small when coupon bonds have the same term to maturity as the holding period.

Because each of our two theories explains empirical facts that the other cannot, a logical step is to combine the theories, which leads us to the preferred habitat theory and closely related liquidity premium theory.

Preferred Habitat and Liquidity Premium Theories

The **preferred habitat theory** of the term structure states that the interest rate on a long-term bond will equal an average of short-term interest rates expected to occur over the life of the long-term bond plus a term (liquidity) premium that responds to supply and demand conditions for that bond.

The preferred habitat theory's key assumption is that bonds of different maturities are substitutes, which means that the expected return on one bond *does* influence the expected return on a bond of a different maturity, but it allows investors to prefer one bond maturity over another. In other words, bonds of different maturities are assumed to be substitutes but not perfect substitutes. We might think of investors as having a preference for bonds of one maturity over another, a particular bond market where they are most comfortable to reside; we might then say that they have a preferred habitat. Investors still care about the expected returns on bonds with a maturity other than their preferred maturity, and so they will not allow expected returns on one bond to get too far out of line with that on another bond with a different maturity. Because they prefer bonds of one maturity over another, they will be willing to buy bonds that do not have the preferred maturity only if they earn a somewhat higher expected return.

If investors prefer the habitat of short-term bonds over longer-term bonds, for example, they might be willing to hold short-term bonds even though they have a lower expected return. This means that investors would have to be paid a positive term premium to be willing to hold a long-term bond. Such an outcome would modify the expectations hypothesis story by adding a positive term premium to the equation that describes the relationship between long- and short-term interest rates. The preferred habitat theory is thus written as

$$i_{nt} = \frac{i_t + i^e_{t+1} + i^e_{t+2} + \cdots + i^e_{t+(n-1)}}{n} + k_{nt} \tag{3}$$

where k_{nt} = the term premium for the n-period bond at time t.

Closely related to the preferred habitat theory is the **liquidity premium theory,** which takes a somewhat more direct approach to modifying the expectations hypothesis. It reasons that a positive term (liquidity) premium must be offered to buyers of longer-term bonds to compensate them for their increased risk. This reasoning leads to the same Equation 3 implied by the preferred habitat theory, with the proviso that the term premium k_{nt} is always positive and rises with the term to maturity of the bond.

A simple numerical example similar to the one we used for the expectations hypothesis further clarifies what the preferred habitat and liquidity premium theories in Equation 3 are saying. Again suppose that the one-year interest rate over the next five years is expected to be 5%, 6%, 7%, 8%, and 9%, while investors' preferences for holding short-term bonds means that the term premiums for one- to five-year bonds are 0%, 0.25%, 0.5%, 0.75%, and 1.0%, respectively. Equation 3 then indicates that the interest rate on the two-year bond would be

$$\frac{5\% + 6\%}{2} + 0.25\% = 5.75\%$$

while for the five-year bond it would be

$$\frac{5\% + 6\% + 7\% + 8\% + 9\%}{5} + 1\% = 8\%$$

Doing a similar calculation for the one-, three-, and four-year interest rates, you should be able to verify that the one- to five-year interest rates are 5.0%, 5.75%, 6.5%, 7.25%, and 8.0%, respectively. Comparing these findings with those for the expectations hypothesis, we see that the preferred habitat and liquidity premium theories produce yield curves that slope more steeply upward because of investors' preferences for short-term bonds.

Let's see if the preferred habitat and liquidity premium theories are consistent with all three empirical facts we have discussed. They explain fact 1 that interest rates on different-maturity bonds move together over time: A rise in short-term interest rates indicates that short-term interest rates will, on average, be higher in the future, and the second term in Equation 3 then implies that long-term interest rates will rise along with them.

They also explain why yield curves tend to have an especially steep upward slope when short-term interest rates are low and a downward slope when short-term rates are high (fact 2). Because investors generally expect short-term interest rates to rise to some normal level when they are low, the average of future expected short-term rates will be high relative to the current short-term rate. With the additional boost of a positive term premium, long-term interest rates will be substantially above current short-term rates, and the yield curve would then have a steep upward slope. Conversely, if short-term rates are high, people usually expect them to come back down. Long-term rates would then drop below short-term rates because the average of expected future short-term rates would be so far below current short-term rates that despite positive term premiums, the yield curve would slope dowward.

The preferred habitat and liquidity premium theories explain fact 3 that yield curves typically slope upward by recognizing that the term premium rises with a bond's maturity because of investors' preferences for short-term bonds. Even if short-term interest rates are usually expected to stay the same on average in the future, long-term interest rates will be above short-term interest rates, and yield curves will typically slope upward.

How can the preferred habitat and liquidity premium theories explain the occasional appearance of downward-sloping yield curves if the term premium is positive? It must be that at times short-term interest rates are expected to fall so much in the future that the average of the expected short-term rates is well

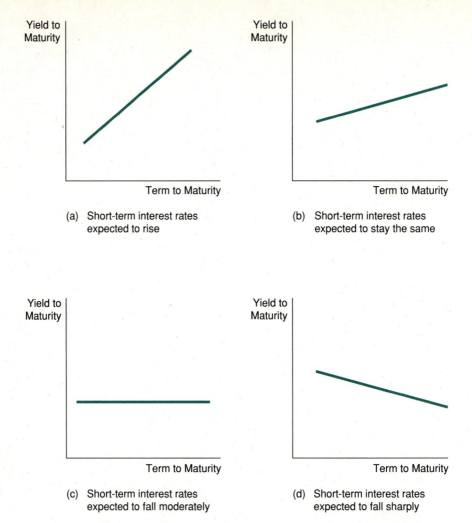

FIGURE 5
Yield Curves and the Market's Expectations of Future Short-Term Interest Rate

below the current short-term rate. Even when the positive term premium is added to this average, the resulting long-term rate will still be below the current short-term interest rate.

As our discussion indicates, a particularly attractive feature of the preferred habitat and liquidity premium theories is that they tell you what the market is predicting about future short-term interest rates by just looking at the slope of the yield curve. A steeply rising yield curve, as in panel (a) of Figure 5, indicates that short-term interest rates are expected to rise in the future. A moderately steep yield curve, as in panel (b), indicates that short-term interest rates are not expected to rise or fall much in the future. A flat yield curve, as in panel (c), indicates that short-term rates are expected to fall moderately in the future. Finally, a downward-sloping yield curve, as in panel (d), indicates that short-term interest rates are expected to fall sharply in the future. See Box 2 for the evidence on what the slope of the yield curve tells us about future movements of short-term interest rates.

Box 2

RECENT EVIDENCE ON THE TERM STRUCTURE

Some researchers examining the term structure of interest rates in the 1980s questioned whether the slope of the yield curve provides information about movements of future short-term interest rates.* They found that the spread between long- and short-term interest rates does not always help predict future short-term interest rates, a finding that may stem from substantial fluctuations in the term premium for long-term bonds. More recent research, however, using more sophisticated tests, finds that the term structure does contain information about the future movements of interest rates.[†]

*Robert J. Shiller, John Y. Campbell, and Kermit L. Schoenholtz, "Forward Rates and Future Policy: Interpreting the Term Structure of Interest Rates," *Brookings Papers on Economic Activity* 1 (1983): 173–217; N. Gregory Mankiw and Lawrence H. Summers, "Do Long-Term Interest Rates Overreact to Short-Term Interest Rates?" *Brookings Papers on Economic Activity* 1 (1984): 243–247.

[†]Eugene Fama, "The Information in the Term Structure," *Journal of Financial Economics* 13 (1984): 509–528; Eugene Fama and Robert Bliss, "The Information in Long-Maturity Forward Rates," *American Economic Review* 77 (1987): 680–692; John Y. Campbell and Robert J. Shiller, "Cointegration and Tests of the Present Value Models," *Journal of Political Economy* 95 (1987): 1062–1088; "Yield Spreads and Interest Rate Movements: A Bird's Eye View," *Review of Economic Studies* 58 (1991): 495–514.

Summary

The preferred habitat and liquidity premium theories are the most widely accepted theories of the term structure of interest rates because they explain the major empirical facts about the term structure so well. They combine the features of both the expectations hypothesis and the segmented markets theory by asserting that a long-term interest rate will be the sum of a term premium (liquidity) and of the average of the short-term interest rates that are expected to occur over the life of the bond.

The preferred habitat and liquidity premium theories explain the following facts: (1) Interest rates on bonds of different maturities tend to move together over time, (2) yield curves usually slope upward, and (3) when short-term interest rates are low, yield curves are more likely to have a steep upward slope, whereas when short-term interest rates are high, yield curves are more likely to slope downward.

The theories also show how to tell what the market is predicting for the movement of short-term interest rates in the future. A steep upward slope of the yield curve means that short-term rates are expected to rise, a mild upward slope means that short-term rates are expected to remain the same, a flat slope means that short-term rates are expected to fall moderately, and a downward slope means that short-term rates are expected to fall sharply.

APPLICATION

INTERPRETING YIELD CURVES, 1980–1994

Figure 6 illustrates several yield curves that have appeared for U.S. government bonds in recent years. What do these yield curves tell us about the public's expectations of future movements of short-term interest rates?

STUDY GUIDE

Try to answer the question before reading further in the text. If you have trouble answering it with the preferred habitat and liquidity premium theories, first try answering it with the expectations hypothesis (which is simpler because you don't have to worry about the term premium). When you understand what the expectations of future interest rates are in this case, modify your analysis by taking the term premium into account.

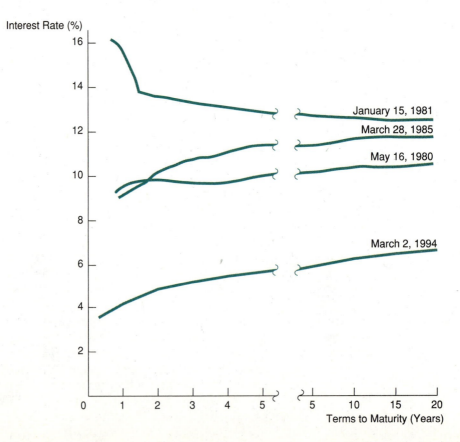

FIGURE 6
Yield Curves for
U.S. Government
Bonds
Sources: Federal
Reserve Bank of
St. Louis; *U.S. Fi-*
nancial Data,
various issues;
Wall Street Jour-
nal, various dates.

The steep downward-sloping yield curve that occurred on January 15, 1981, indicated that short-term interest rates were expected to decline sharply in the future. In order for longer-term interest rates with their positive term premium to be well below the short-term interest rate, short-term interest rates must be expected to decline so sharply that their average is far below the current short-term rate. Indeed, the public's expectations of sharply lower short-term interest rates evident in the yield curve were realized soon after January 15; by March, three-month Treasury bill rates had declined from the 16% level to 13%.

The steep upward-sloping yield curves on March 28, 1985, and March 2, 1994, indicated that short-term interest rates would climb in the future. The long-term interest rate is above the short-term interest rate when short-term interest rates are expected to rise because their average plus the term premium will be above the current short-term rate. The moderately upward-sloping yield curve on May 16, 1980, indicated that short-term interest rates were expected neither to rise nor to fall in the near future. In this case, their average remains the same as the current short-term rate, and the positive term premium for longer-term bonds explains the moderate upward slope of the yield curve.

SUMMARY

1. Bonds with the same maturity will have different interest rates because of three factors: default risk, liquidity, and tax considerations. The more default risk a bond has, the higher will be its interest rate relative to other bonds. The more liquid a bond is, the lower will be its interest rate. Bonds with tax-exempt status will have lower interest rates than they otherwise would. The relationship among interest rates on bonds with the same maturity that arise because of these three factors is known as the risk structure of interest rates.

2. There are three theories of the term structure that provide explanations of how interest rates on bonds with different terms to maturity are related. The expectations hypothesis views long-term interest rates as equaling the average of future short-term interest rates expected to occur over the life of the bond, whereas the segmented markets theory treats the determination of interest rates for each bond's maturity as the outcome of supply and demand in that market only. Neither of these theories can explain both the fact that interest rates on bonds of different maturities move together over time and that yield curves usually slope upward.

3. The preferred habitat and liquidity premium theories combine the features of the other two theories and by so doing are able to explain the facts just mentioned. They view long-term interest rates as equaling the average of future short-term interest rates expected to occur over the life of the bond plus a term premium that reflects the supply of and demand for bonds of different maturities. These theories allow us to infer the market's expectations about the movement of future short-term interest rates from the yield curve. A steeply upward-sloping curve indicates that future short-term rates are expected to rise, a mildly upward-sloping curve indicates that short-term rates are expected to stay the same, a flat curve indicates that short-term rates are expected to decline slightly, and a downward-sloping curve indicates that a substantial decline in short-term rates is expected in the future.

KEY TERMS

risk structure of interest rates

term structure of interest rates

default risk

default-free bonds

risk premium

junk bonds

yield curve

expectations hypothesis

segmented markets theory

preferred habitat theory

liquidity premium theory

QUESTIONS AND PROBLEMS

1. Which should have the higher risk premium on its interest rates, a corporate bond with a Moody's Baa rating or a corporate bond with a C rating? Why?

*2. Why do U.S. Treasury bills have lower interest rates than large-denomination negotiable bank CDs?

3. Risk premiums on corporate bonds are usually anticyclical; that is, they decrease during business cycle expansions and increase during recessions. Why is this so?

*4. "If bonds of different maturities are close substitutes, their interest rates are more likely to move together." Is this statement true, false, or uncertain? Explain.

5. If yield curves, on average, were flat, what would this say about the term premiums in the term structure? Would you be more or less willing to accept the expectations hypothesis?

*6. Assuming that the expectations hypothesis is the correct theory of the term structure, calculate the interest rates in the term structure for maturities of one to five years, and plot the resulting yield curves for the following series of one-year interest rates over the next five years:
   (a) 5%, 7%, 7%, 7%, 7%
   (b) 5%, 4%, 4%, 4%, 4%
   How would your yield curves change if people preferred shorter-term bonds over longer-term bonds?

7. Assuming that the expectations hypothesis is the correct theory of the term structure, calculate the interest rates in the term structure for maturities of one to five years, and plot the resulting yield curves for the following path of one-year interest rates over the next five years:

   (a) 5%, 6%, 7%, 6%, 5%
   (b) 5%, 4%, 3%, 4%, 5%
   How would your yield curves change if people preferred shorter-term bonds over longer-term bonds?

*8. If the yield curve looks like the accompanying one, what is the market predicting about the movement of future short-term interest rates? What might the yield curve indicate about the market's predictions about the inflation rate in the future?

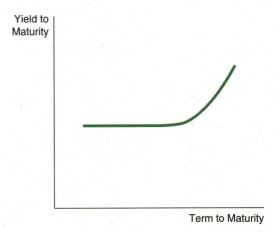

9. If the yield curve looks like the accompanying one, what is the market predicting about the movement of future short-term interest rates? What might the yield curve indicate about the

market's predictions about the inflation rate in the future?

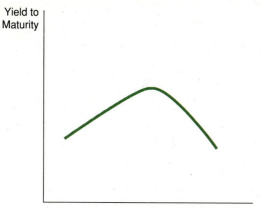

Yield to Maturity

Term to Maturity

*10. What effect would reducing income tax rates have on the interest rates of municipal bonds? Would interest rates of Treasury securities be affected, and if so, how?

Using Economic Analysis to Predict the Future

11. Predict what will happen to interest rates on a corporation's bonds if the federal government guarantees that it will pay creditors if the corporation goes bankrupt. What will happen to the interest rates on Treasury securities?

*12. Predict what would happen to the risk premiums on corporate bonds if brokerage commissions were lowered in the corporate bond market.

13. If the income tax exemption on municipal bonds were abolished, what would happen to the interest rates on these bonds? What effect would it have on interest rates on U.S. Treasury securities?

*14. If the yield curve suddenly becomes steeper, how would you revise your predictions of interest rates in the future?

15. If expectations of future short-term interest rates suddenly fall, what would happen to the slope of the yield curve?

Chapter 8

THE FOREIGN EXCHANGE MARKET

PREVIEW   Fewer Americans have traveled abroad in recent years than in the early to mid-1980s. The decrease in foreign travel did not occur because Americans suddenly lost their taste for adventure. The decrease occurred because American dollars had become worth less in terms of foreign currencies—a change that made it more expensive for Americans to travel abroad.

The price of one currency in terms of another is called the **exchange rate.** It affects the economy and our daily lives because when the U.S. dollar becomes less valuable relative to foreign currencies, foreign goods and travel become more expensive. When the U.S. dollar rises in value, foreign goods and travel become cheaper. We begin our study of international finance by examining the **foreign exchange market,** which is where exchange rates are determined.

In the 1980s, exchange rates were highly volatile. As shown in Figure 1, from the beginning of 1980 to early 1985, the dollar strengthened, and its value relative to many other currencies climbed sharply—100% against the pound sterling, 90% against the German mark, and 75% against the Swiss franc. From early 1985 to the end of 1993, the dollar weakened and fell in value relative to other currencies—over 50% against the Japanese yen, 40% against the German mark and the Swiss franc, and 15% against the pound sterling. What factors explain the former strength and later weakness of the dollar that has caused foreign goods to be more expensive since 1985 and has made overseas travel less of a bargain? Why are exchange rates so volatile from day to day?

To answer these questions, we develop a modern view of exchange rate determination that explains recent behavior in the foreign exchange market.

FOREIGN EXCHANGE MARKET

Most countries of the world have their own currencies: The United States has its dollar; France, its franc; Brazil, its cruzeiro real; and India, its rupee. Trade between countries involves the mutual exchange of different currencies (or, more usually, bank deposits denominated in different currencies). When an American

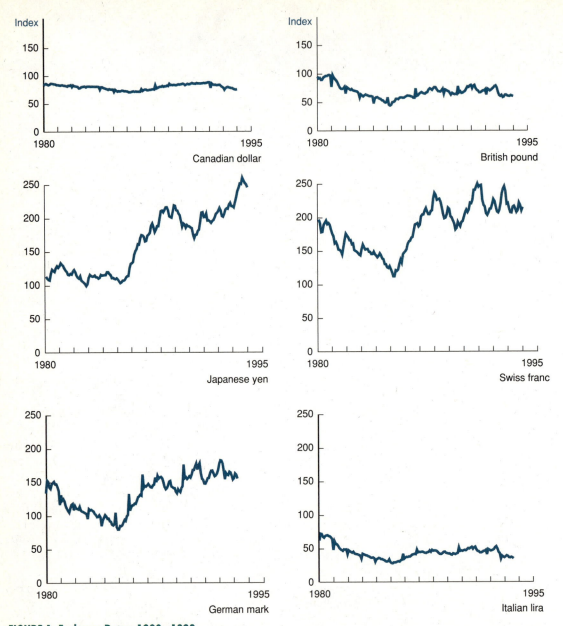

FIGURE 1 Exchange Rates, 1980–1993

Dollar prices of selected foreign currencies (monthly averages; index: March 1973 = 100). Note that a decline in these plots means a strengthening of the dollar, and an increase indicates a weakening of the dollar. *Sources: International Financial Statistics;* Citibase databank.

firm buys foreign goods, services, or financial assets, for example, U.S. dollars (typically, bank deposits denominated in U.S. dollars) must be exchanged for foreign currency (bank deposits denominated in the foreign currency).

The trading of currency and bank deposits denominated in particular currencies takes place in the foreign exchange market. The volume of these transactions worldwide averages over $1 trillion daily. Transactions conducted in the foreign exchange market determine the rates at which currencies are exchanged, which in turn determine the cost of purchasing foreign goods and financial assets.

What Are Foreign Exchange Rates?

There are two kinds of exchange rate transactions. The predominant ones, called **spot transactions,** involve the immediate (two-day) exchange of bank deposits. **Forward transactions** involve the exchange of bank deposits at some specified future date. The **spot exchange rate** is the exchange rate for the spot transaction, and the **forward exchange rate** is the exchange rate for the forward transaction.

When a currency increases in value, it experiences **appreciation;** when it falls in value and is worth fewer U.S. dollars, it undergoes **depreciation.** At the beginning of 1980, for example, the French franc was valued at 24 cents, and as indicated in the "Following the Financial News" box, on March 2, 1994, it was valued at 17.2 cents. The franc *depreciated* by 28% [= (17.2 − 24)/24 = −0.28 = −28%]. Conversely, we could say that the U.S. dollar, which went from a value of 4.23 francs per dollar in 1980 to a value of 5.81 francs per dollar in March 1994 *appreciated* by 37% [= (5.81 − 4.23)/4.23 = 0.37 = 37%].

Why Are Exchange Rates Important?

Exchange rates are important because they affect the relative price of domestic and foreign goods. The dollar price of French goods to an American is determined by the interaction of two factors: the price of French goods in francs and the franc/dollar exchange rate.

Suppose that Wanda the Winetaster, an American, decides to buy a bottle of 1961 (a very good year) Château Lafite Rothschild to complete her wine cellar. If the price of the wine in France is 2000 francs and the exchange rate is $0.17226 to the franc, the wine will cost Wanda $345 (= 2000 francs × 0.17226). Now suppose that Wanda delays her purchase by two months, at which time the French franc has appreciated to $0.20 per franc. If the domestic price of the bottle of Lafite Rothschild remains 2000 francs, its dollar cost will have risen from $345 to $400.

The same currency appreciation, however, makes the price of foreign goods in that country less expensive. At an exchange rate of $0.17226 per franc, an Apple computer priced at $2000 costs Claude the Programmer 11,610 francs; if the exchange rate increases to $0.20 per franc, the computer will cost only 10,000 francs.

A depreciation of the franc lowers the cost of French goods in America but raises the cost of American goods in France. If the franc drops in value to $0.10,

FOLLOWING THE FINANCIAL NEWS

Foreign Exchange Rates

Foreign exchange rates are published daily and appear in the "Currency Trading" column of the *Wall Street Journal*. The entries from one such column, shown here, are explained in the text.

The first entry for the French franc lists the exchange rate for the spot transaction (the spot exchange rate) on Wednesday and is quoted in two ways: $0.17226 per franc or 5.8053 francs per dollar. Americans generally

regard the exchange rate with France as $0.17226 per franc, while the French think of it as 5.8053 francs per dollar. The three entries immediately below the spot exchange rates give the rates for forward transactions (the forward exchange rates) that will take place 30, 90, and 180 days in the future. For example, Wednesday's 180-day forward rate for the French franc is $0.17047 per franc or, equivalently, 5.8663 francs per dollar.

CURRENCY TRADING

EXCHANGE RATES

Wednesday, March 2, 1994

The New York foreign exchange selling rates below apply to trading among banks in amounts of $1 million and more, as quoted at 3 p.m. Eastern time by Bankers Trust Co., Dow Jones Telerate Inc. and other sources. Retail transactions provide fewer units of foreign currency per dollar.

Country	U.S. $ equiv. Wed.	U.S. $ equiv. Tues.	Currency per U.S. $ Wed.	Currency per U.S. $ Tues.
Argentina (Peso)	1.01	1.01	.99	.99
Australia (Dollar)	.7059	.7130	1.4166	1.4025
Austria (Schilling)	.08340	.08325	11.99	12.01
Bahrain (Dinar)	2.6529	2.6529	.3770	.3770
Belgium (Franc)	.02848	.02845	35.11	35.15
Brazil (Cruzeiro real) .	.0015298	.0015518	653.70	644.40
Britain (Pound)	1.4970	1.4896	.6680	.6713
30-Day Forward	1.4951	1.4875	.6689	.6723
90-Day Forward	1.4920	1.4845	.6702	.6736
180-Day Forward	1.4890	1.4812	.6716	.6751
Canada (Dollar)	.7389	.7403	1.3533	1.3508
30-Day Forward	.7388	.7402	1.3536	1.3510
90-Day Forward	.7384	.7400	1.3542	1.3514
180-Day Forward	.7376	.7394	1.3557	1.3524
Czech. Rep. (Koruna)				
Commercial rate	.0334795	.0334795	29.8690	29.8690
Chile (Peso)	.002400	.002400	416.59	416.59
China (Renminbi)	.114882	.114882	8.7046	8.7046
Colombia (Peso)	.001220	.001220	819.71	819.71
Denmark (Krone)	.1497	.1494	6.6795	6.6928
Ecuador (Sucre)				
Floating rate	.000493	.000493	2030.00	2030.00
Finland (Markka)	.17982	.18056	5.5613	5.5382
France (Franc)	.17226	.17191	5.8053	5.8170
30-Day Forward	.17183	.17147	5.8196	5.8320
90-Day Forward	.17117	.17082	5.8423	5.8540
180-Day Forward	.17047	.17008	5.8663	5.8795
Germany (Mark)	.5866	.5855	1.7046	1.7080
30-Day Forward	.5853	.5841	1.7085	1.7121
90-Day Forward	.5834	.5822	1.7140	1.7175
180-Day Forward	.5816	.5802	1.7195	1.7234
Greece (Drachma)	.004046	.004034	247.15	247.90
Hong Kong (Dollar)	.12938	.12939	7.7290	7.7287
Hungary (Forint)	.0096852	.0096740	103.2500	103.3700
India (Rupee)	.03216	.03216	31.09	31.09
Indonesia (Rupiah)	.0004664	.0004664	2144.04	2144.04
Ireland (Punt)	1.4358	1.4289	.6965	.6998
Israel (Shekel)	.3339	.3339	2.9945	2.9945
Italy (Lira)	.0005935	.0005910	1685.01	1691.96

Country	U.S. $ equiv. Wed.	U.S. $ equiv. Tues.	Currency per U.S. $ Wed.	Currency per U.S. $ Tues.
Japan (Yen)	.009598	.009565	104.19	104.55
30-Day Forward	.009609	.009575	104.07	104.44
90-Day Forward	.009636	.009600	103.77	104.17
180-Day Forward	.009685	.009646	103.26	103.67
Jordan (Dinar)	1.4620	1.4620	.6840	.6840
Kuwait (Dinar)	3.3634	3.3634	.2973	.2973
Lebanon (Pound)	.000588	.000588	1701.00	1701.00
Malaysia (Ringgit)	.3680	.3670	2.7175	2.7245
Malta (Lira)	2.5608	2.5608	.3905	.3905
Mexico (Peso)				
Floating rate	.3076923	.3144654	3.2500	3.1800
Netherland (Guilder) ..	.5227	.5213	1.9133	1.9182
New Zealand (Dollar) ..	.5712	.5759	1.7507	1.7364
Norway (Krone)	.1351	.1348	7.4019	7.4170
Pakistan (Rupee)	.0330	.0330	30.33	30.33
Peru (New Sol)	.4759	.4759	2.10	2.10
Philippines (Peso)	.03670	.03670	27.25	27.25
Poland (Zloty)	.00004570	.00004560	21881.00	21931.00
Portugal (Escudo)	.005722	.005737	174.77	174.30
Saudi Arabia (Riyal) ..	.26702	.26702	3.7450	3.7450
Singapore (Dollar)	.6333	.6317	1.5790	1.5830
Slovak Rep. (Koruna) .	.0301841	.0301841	33.1300	33.1300
South Africa (Rand)				
Commercial rate	.2891	.2896	3.4588	3.4525
Financial rate	.2136	.2133	4.6825	4.6875
South Korea (Won)	.0012364	.0012376	808.80	808.00
Spain (Peseta)	.007137	.007160	140.12	139.66
Sweden (Krona)	.1247	.1248	8.0176	8.0131
Switzerland (Franc) ...	.6985	.6962	1.4317	1.4364
30-Day Forward	.6980	.6957	1.4326	1.4373
90-Day Forward	.6978	.6955	1.4331	1.4378
180-Day Forward	.6982	.6957	1.4323	1.4374
Taiwan (Dollar)	.037756	.037756	26.49	26.49
Thailand (Baht)	.03954	.03954	25.29	25.29
Turkey (Lira)	.0000526	.0000527	19023.95	18977.00
United Arab (Dirham) .	.2723	.2723	3.6725	3.6725
Uruguay (New Peso)				
Financial	.211864	.211864	4.72	4.72
Venezuela (Bolivar)				
Floating rate	.00896	.00896	111.59	111.59
SDR	1.40689	1.40248	.71079	.71302
ECU	1.13320	1.13070	....	....

Special Drawing Rights (SDR) are based on exchange rates for the U.S., German, British, French and Japanese currencies. Source: International Monetary Fund.

European Currency Unit (ECU) is based on a basket of community currencies.

Source: Wall Street Journal, Thursday, March 3, 1994, p. C15.

Wanda's bottle of Lafite Rothschild will cost her only $200 instead of $345, and the Apple computer will cost Claude 20,000 francs rather than 11,610.

Such reasoning leads to the following conclusion: ***When a country's currency appreciates (rises in value relative to other currencies), the country's goods abroad become more expensive and foreign goods in that country become cheaper (holding domestic prices constant in the two countries). Conversely, when a country's currency depreciates, its goods abroad become cheaper and foreign goods in that country become more expensive.***

Appreciation of a currency can make it harder for domestic manufacturers to sell their goods abroad and can increase competition at home from foreign goods because they cost less. From 1980 to early 1985, the appreciating dollar hurt U.S. industries. For instance, the U.S. steel industry was hurt not just because sales abroad of the more expensive American steel declined but also because sales of relatively cheap foreign steel in the United States increased. Although appreciation of the U.S. dollar hurt some domestic businesses, American consumers benefited because foreign goods were less expensive. Japanese videocassette recorders and cameras and the cost of vacationing in Europe fell in price as a result of the strong dollar.

How Is Foreign Exchange Traded?

You cannot go to a centralized location to watch exchange rates being determined; currencies are not traded on exchanges such as the New York Stock Exchange. Instead, the foreign exchange market is organized as an over-the-counter market in which several hundred dealers (mostly banks) stand ready to buy and sell deposits denominated in foreign currencies. Because these dealers are in constant telephone and computer contact, the market is very competitive; in effect, it functions no differently from a centralized market.

An important point to note is that while banks, companies, and governments talk about buying and selling currencies in foreign exchange markets, they do not take a fistful of dollar bills and sell them for British pound notes. Rather, most trades involve the buying and selling of bank deposits denominated in different currencies. So when we say that a bank is buying dollars in the foreign exchange market, what we actually mean is that the bank is buying deposits *denominated in dollars*.

Trades in the foreign exchange market consist of transactions in excess of $1 million. The market that determines the exchange rates in the "Following the Financial News" box is not where one would buy foreign currency for a trip abroad. Instead, we buy foreign currency in the retail market from dealers such as American Express or from banks. Because retail prices are higher than wholesale, when we buy foreign exchange, we obtain fewer units of foreign currency per dollar than exchange rates in the box indicate.

EXCHANGE RATES IN THE LONG RUN

Like the price of any good or asset in a free market, exchange rates are determined by the interaction of supply and demand. To simplify our analysis of exchange rates in a free market, we divide it into two parts. First, we examine how exchange rates are determined in the long run; then we use our knowledge of the long-run determinants of the exchange rate to help us understand how they are determined in the short run.

Law of One Price

The starting point for understanding how exchange rates are determined is a simple idea called the **law of one price:** If two countries produce an identical good, the price of the good should be the same throughout the world no matter which country produces it. Suppose that American steel costs $100 per ton and identical Japanese steel costs 10,000 yen per ton. The law of one price suggests that the exchange rate between the yen and the dollar must be 100 yen per dollar ($0.01 per yen) in order for one ton of American steel to sell for 10,000 yen in Japan (the price of Japanese steel) and one ton of Japanese steel to sell for $100 in the United States. If the exchange rate were 200 yen to the dollar, Japanese steel would sell for $50 per ton in the United States or $50 less than the American steel, and American steel would sell for 20,000 yen per ton in Japan, twice the price of the Japanese steel. Because American steel would be more expensive than Japanese steel in both countries and it is identical to Japanese steel, the demand for American steel would go to zero. Given a fixed dollar price for the American steel, the resulting excess supply of American steel will be eliminated only if the exchange rate falls to 100 yen per dollar, making the price of American steel and Japanese steel the same in both countries.

Theory of Purchasing Power Parity

One of the most prominent theories of how exchange rates are determined is the **theory of purchasing power parity (PPP).** It states that exchange rates between any two currencies will adjust to reflect changes in the price levels of the two countries. The theory of PPP is simply an application of the law of one price to national price levels rather than to individual prices. Suppose that the yen price of Japanese steel rises 10% (to 11,000 yen) relative to the dollar price of American steel (unchanged at $100). For the law of one price to hold, the exchange rate must rise to 110 yen to the dollar, a 10% appreciation of the dollar. Applying the law of one price to the price levels in the two countries produces the theory of purchasing power parity, which maintains that if the Japanese *price level* rises 10% relative to the U.S. *price level,* the dollar will appreciate by 10%.

As our U.S./Japanese example demonstrates, the theory of PPP suggests that if one country's price level rises relative to another's, its currency should depreciate (the other country's currency should appreciate). As you can see in Figure 2, this prediction is borne out in the long run. From 1973 to early 1993, the British price level rose 82% percent relative to the U.S. price level, and as the theory of PPP predicts, the dollar appreciated against sterling, though by 65%, an amount smaller than the 82% increase predicted by PPP.

Yet, as the same figure indicates, PPP theory often has little predictive power in the short run. From early 1985 to the end of 1987, for example, the British price level rose relative to that of the United States. Instead of appreciating, as PPP theory predicts, the U.S. dollar actually depreciated by 40%. So even though PPP theory provides *some* guidance to the long-run movement of exchange rates, it is not perfect and in the short run is a particularly poor predictor. What explains PPP theory's failure to predict well?

Why the Theory of Purchasing Power Parity Cannot Fully Explain Exchange Rates

The PPP conclusion that exchange rates are determined solely by changes in relative price levels rests on the assumption that all goods are identical in both countries. When this assumption is true, the law of one price states that the relative prices of all these goods (that is, the relative price level between the two countries) will determine the exchange rate. The assumption that goods are identical may not be too unreasonable for American and Japanese steel, but is it a reasonable assumption for American and Japanese cars? Is a Toyota the equivalent of a Chevrolet?

Because Toyotas and Chevys are obviously not identical, their prices do not have to be equal. Toyotas can be more expensive relative to Chevys and both Americans and Japanese will still purchase Toyotas. Because the law of one

FIGURE 2
Purchasing Power Parity, United States/United Kingdom, 1973–1993
(Index: March 1973 = 100.)
Source: International Financial Statistics.

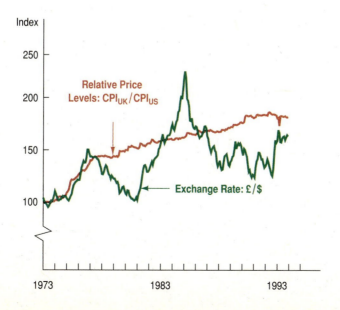

price does not hold for all goods, a rise in the price of Toyotas relative to Chevys will not necessarily mean that the yen must depreciate by the amount of the relative price increase of Toyotas over Chevys.

PPP theory furthermore does not take into account that many goods and services (whose prices are included in a measure of a country's price level) are not traded across borders. Housing, land, and services such as restaurant meals, haircuts, and golf lessons are not traded goods. So even though the prices of these items might rise and lead to a higher price level relative to another country's, there would be little direct effect on the exchange rate.

Factors That Affect Exchange Rates in the Long Run

Our analysis indicates that relative price levels and additional factors affect the exchange rate. In the long run, there are four major ones: relative price levels, tariffs and quotas, preferences for domestic versus foreign goods, and productivity. We examine how each of these factors affects the exchange rate while holding the others constant.

The basic reasoning proceeds along the following lines: Anything that increases the demand for domestic goods relative to foreign goods tends to appreciate the domestic currency because domestic goods will continue to sell well even when the value of the domestic currency is higher. Similarly, anything that increases the demand for foreign goods relative to domestic goods tends to depreciate the domestic currency because domestic goods will continue to sell well only if the value of the domestic currency is lower.

Relative Price Levels In line with PPP theory, when prices of American goods rise (holding prices of foreign goods constant), the demand for American goods falls and the dollar tends to depreciate so that American goods can still sell well. By contrast, if prices of Japanese goods rise so that the relative prices of American goods fall, the demand for American goods increases, and the dollar tends to appreciate because American goods will continue to sell well even with a higher value of the domestic currency. *In the long run, a rise in a country's price level (relative to the foreign price level) causes its currency to depreciate, and a fall in the country's relative price level causes its currency to appreciate.*

Tariffs and Quotas Barriers to free trade such as **tariffs** (taxes on imported goods) and **quotas** (restrictions on the quantity of foreign goods that can be imported) can affect the exchange rate. Suppose that the United States imposes a tariff or a quota on Japanese steel. These trade barriers increase the demand for American steel, and the dollar tends to appreciate because American steel will still sell well even with a higher value of the dollar. *Tariffs and quotas cause a country's currency to appreciate in the long run.*

Preferences for Domestic Versus Foreign Goods If the Japanese develop an appetite for American goods, say, for Florida oranges and American movies, then the increased demand for American goods (exports) tends to appreciate the dollar because the American goods will continue to sell well even at a higher value for the dollar. Likewise, if Americans decide that they prefer Japanese cars to American cars, the increased demand for Japanese goods (imports) tends to depreciate the dollar. ***Increased demand for a country's exports causes its currency to appreciate in the long run; conversely, increased demand for imports causes its currency to depreciate.***

Productivity If one country becomes more productive than other countries, businesses in that country can lower the prices of domestic goods relative to foreign goods and still earn a profit. As a result, the demand for domestic goods rises, and the domestic currency tends to appreciate because domestic goods will continue to sell well at a higher value for the currency. If, however, its productivity lags behind that of other countries, its goods become relatively more expensive, and the currency tends to depreciate. ***In the long run, as a country becomes more productive relative to other countries, its currency appreciates.***[1]

STUDY GUIDE

The trick to figuring out what long-run effect a factor has on the exchange rate is to remember the following: ***If a factor increases the demand for domestic goods relative to foreign goods, the domestic currency will appreciate, and if a factor decreases the relative demand for domestic goods, the domestic currency will depreciate.*** See how this works by explaining what happens to the exchange rate when any of the factors in Table 1 declines rather than increases.

Our long-run theory of exchange rate behavior is summarized in Table 1. We use the convention that the exchange rate E is quoted so that an appreciation of the currency corresponds to a rise in the exchange rate. In the case of the United States, this means that we are quoting the exchange rate as units of foreign currency per dollar (say, yen per dollar).[2]

---

[1]A country might be so small that a change in productivity or the preferences for domestic or foreign goods would have no effect on prices of these goods relative to foreign goods. In this case, changes in productivity or changes in preferences for domestic or foreign goods affect the country's income but will not necessarily affect the value of the currency. In our analysis, we are assuming that these factors can affect relative prices and consequently the exchange rate.

[2]In their professional writings, many economists quote exchange rates as units of domestic currency per foreign currency so that an appreciation of the domestic currency is portrayed as a fall in the exchange rate. The opposite convention is used in the text here because it is more intuitive to think of an appreciation of the domestic currency as a rise in the exchange rate.

SUMMARY

TABLE 1   Factors That Affect Exchange Rates in the Long Run

Factor	Change in Factor	Response of the Exchange Rate, E*
Domestic price level[†]	↑	↓
Tariffs and quotas[†]	↑	↑
Import demand	↑	↓
Export demand	↑	↑
Productivity[†]	↑	↑

*Units of foreign currency per dollar: ↑ indicates currency appreciation; ↓, depreciation.

†Relative to other countries.

Note: Only increases (↑) in the factors are shown; the effects of decreases in the variables on the exchange rate are the opposite of those indicated in the "Response" column.

EXCHANGE RATES IN THE SHORT RUN

We have developed a theory of the long-run behavior of exchange rates. However, if we are to understand why exchange rates exhibit such large changes (sometimes several percent) from day to day, we must develop a theory of how current exchange rates (spot exchange rates) are determined in the short run.

The key to understanding the short-run behavior of exchange rates is to recognize that an exchange rate is the price of domestic bank deposits (those denominated in the domestic currency) in terms of foreign bank deposits (those denominated in the foreign currency). Because the exchange rate is the price of one asset in terms of another, the natural way to investigate the short-run determination of exchange rates is through an asset market approach that relies heavily on the theory of asset demand developed in Chapter 5. As you will see, however, the long-run determinants of the exchange rate we have just outlined also play an important role in the short-run asset market approach.[3]

Earlier approaches to exchange rate determination emphasized the role of import and export demand. The more modern asset market approach used here does not emphasize the flows of purchases of exports and imports over short periods because these transactions are quite small relative to the amount of do-

---

[3]For a further description of the modern asset market approach to exchange rate determination that we use here, see Paul Krugman and Maurice Obstfeld, *International Economics,* 3rd ed. (New York: HarperCollins, 1994).

mestic and foreign bank deposits at any given time. For example, foreign exchange transactions in the United States each year are well over 25 times greater than the amount of U.S. exports and imports. Thus over short periods such as a year, decisions to hold domestic or foreign assets play a much greater role in exchange rate determination than the demand for exports and imports does.

Comparing Expected Returns on Domestic and Foreign Deposits

In this analysis, we treat the United States as the home country, so domestic bank deposits are denominated in dollars. For simplicity, we use francs to stand for any foreign country's currency, so foreign bank deposits are denominated in francs. The theory of asset demand suggests that the most important factor affecting the demand for domestic (dollar) deposits and foreign (franc) deposits is the expected return on these assets relative to each other. When Americans or foreigners expect the return on dollar deposits to be high relative to the return on foreign deposits, there is a higher demand for dollar deposits and a correspondingly lower demand for franc deposits. To understand how the demands for dollar and foreign deposits change, we need to compare the expected returns on dollar deposits and foreign deposits.

To illustrate further, suppose that dollar deposits have an interest rate (expected return payable in dollars) of $i^\$$, and foreign bank deposits have an interest rate (expected return payable in the foreign currency, francs) of i^F. To compare the expected returns on dollar deposits and foreign deposits, investors must convert the returns into the currency unit they use.

First let us examine how François the Foreigner compares the returns on dollar deposits and foreign deposits denominated in his currency, the franc. When he considers the expected return on dollar deposits in terms of francs, he recognizes that it does not equal $i^\$$; instead, the expected return must be adjusted for any expected appreciation or depreciation of the dollar. If the dollar were expected to appreciate by 7%, for example, the expected return on dollar deposits in terms of francs would be 7% higher because the dollar has become worth 7% more in terms of francs. Thus if the interest rate on dollar deposits is 10%, with an expected appreciation of the dollar of 7%, the expected return on dollar deposits in terms of francs is 17%: the 10% interest rate plus the 7% expected appreciation of the dollar. Conversely, if the dollar were expected to depreciate by 7% over the year, the expected return on dollar deposits in terms of francs would be only 3%: the 10% interest rate minus the 7% expected depreciation of the dollar.

Writing the currency exchange rate (the spot exchange rate) as E_t and the expected exchange rate for the next period as E^e_{t+1}, we can write the expected rate of appreciation of the dollar as $(E^e_{t+1} - E_t)/E_t$. Our reasoning indicates that the expected return on dollar deposit $RET^\$$ in terms of foreign currency can be written as the sum of the interest rate on dollar deposits plus the expected appreciation of the dollar:[4]

$$RET^\$ \text{ in terms of francs} = i^\$ + \frac{E^e_{t+1} - E_t}{E_t}$$

However, François's expected return on foreign deposits RET^F in terms of francs is just i^F. Thus in terms of francs, the relative expected return on dollar deposits (that is, the difference between the expected return on dollar deposits and franc deposits) is calculated by subtracting i^F from the expression just given to yield

$$\text{Relative } RET^\$ = i^\$ - i^F + \frac{E^e_{t+1} - E_t}{E_t} \tag{1}$$

As the relative expected return on dollar deposits increases, foreigners will want to hold more dollar deposits and fewer foreign deposits.

Next let us look at the decision to hold dollar deposits versus franc deposits from Al the American's point of view. Following the same reasoning we used to evaluate the decision for François, we know that the expected return on foreign deposits RET^F in terms of dollars is the interest rate on foreign deposits i^F plus the expected appreciation of the foreign currency, equal to minus the expected appreciation of the dollar, $-(E^e_{t+1} - E_t)/E_t$, that is,

$$RET^F \text{ in terms of dollars} = i^F - \frac{E^e_{t+1} - E_t}{E_t}$$

If the interest rate on franc deposits is 5%, for example, and the dollar is expected to appreciate by 4%, then the expected return on franc deposits in terms of dollars is 1%. Al earns the 5% interest rate, but he expects to lose 4% because he expects the franc to be worth 4% less in terms of dollars as a result of the dollar's appreciation.

---

[4]This expression is actually an approximation of the expected return in terms of francs, which can be more precisely calculated by thinking how a foreigner invests in the dollar deposit. Suppose that François decides to put one franc into dollar deposits. First he buys $1/E_t$ of U.S. dollar deposits (recall that E_t, the exchange rate between dollar and franc deposits, is quoted in francs per dollar), and at the end of the period he is paid $(1 + i^\$) (1/E_t)$ in dollars. To convert this amount into the number of francs he expects to receive at the end of the period, he multiplies this quantity by E^e_{t+1}. François's expected return on his initial investment of one franc can thus be written as $(1 + i^\$) (E^e_{t+1}/E_t)$ minus his initial investment of one franc:

$$(1 + i^\$)\left(\frac{E^e_{t+1}}{E_t}\right) - 1$$

which can be rewritten as

$$i^\$\left(\frac{E^e_{t+1}}{E_t}\right) + \frac{E^e_{t+1} - E_t}{E_t}$$

which is approximately equal to the expression in the text because E^e_{t+1}/E_t is typically close to 1.

Al's expected return on the dollar deposits $RET^\$$ in terms of dollars is just $i^\$$. Hence in terms of dollars, the relative expected return on dollar deposits is calculated by subtracting the expression just given from $i^\$$ to obtain

$$\text{Relative } RET^\$ = i^\$ - \left(i^F - \frac{E^e_{t+1} - E_t}{E_t} \right) = i^\$ - i^F + \frac{E^e_{t+1} - E_t}{E_t}$$

This equation is the same as the one describing François's relative expected return on dollar deposits (calculated in terms of francs). The key point here is that the relative expected return on dollar deposits is the same whether it is calculated by François in terms of francs or by Al in terms of dollars. Thus as the relative expected return on dollar deposits increases, both foreigners and domestic residents respond in exactly the same way—both will want to hold more dollar deposits and fewer foreign deposits.

Interest Parity Condition

We currently live in a world in which there is **capital mobility:** Foreigners can easily purchase American assets such as dollar deposits, and Americans can easily purchase foreign assets such as franc deposits. Because foreign bank deposits and American bank deposits have similar risk and liquidity and because there are few impediments to capital mobility, it is reasonable to assume that the deposits are perfect substitutes (that is, equally desirable). When capital is mobile and when bank deposits are perfect substitutes, if the expected return on dollar deposits is above that on foreign deposits, both foreigners and Americans will want to hold only dollar deposits and will be unwilling to hold foreign deposits. Conversely, if the expected return on foreign deposits is higher than on dollar deposits, both foreigners and Americans will not want to hold any dollar deposits and will want to hold only foreign deposits. For existing supplies of both dollar deposits and foreign deposits to be held, it must therefore be true that there is no difference in their expected returns; that is, the relative expected return in Equation 1 must equal zero. This condition can be rewritten as

$$i^\$ = i^F - \frac{E^e_{t+1} - E_t}{E_t} \tag{2}$$

This equation is called the **interest parity condition,** and it states that the domestic interest rate equals the foreign interest rate minus the expected appreciation of the domestic currency. Equivalently, this condition can be stated in a more intuitive way: The domestic interest rate equals the foreign interest rate plus the expected appreciation of the foreign currency. If the domestic interest rate is above the foreign interest rate, this means that there is a positive expected appreciation of the foreign currency, which compensates for the lower foreign interest rate. A domestic interest rate of 15% versus a foreign interest rate of 10% means that the expected appreciation of the foreign currency must be 5% (or, equivalently, that the expected depreciation of the dollar must be 5%).

There are several ways to look at the interest parity condition. First, we should recognize that interest parity means simply that the expected returns are the same on both dollar deposits and foreign deposits. To see this, note that the left side of the interest parity condition (Equation 2) is the expected return on dollar deposits, while the right side is the expected return on foreign deposits, both calculated in terms of a single currency, the U.S. dollar. Given our assumption that domestic and foreign bank deposits are perfect substitutes (equally desirable), the interest parity condition is an equilibrium condition for the foreign exchange market. Only when the exchange rate is such that expected returns on domestic and foreign deposits are equal—that is, when interest parity holds—will the outstanding domestic and foreign deposits be willingly held.

Equilibrium in the Foreign Exchange Market

To see how the interest parity equilibrium condition works in determining the exchange rate, our first step is to examine how the expected returns on franc and dollar deposits change as the current exchange rate changes.

Expected Return on Franc Deposits As we demonstrated earlier, the expected return in terms of dollars on foreign deposits, RET^F is the foreign interest rate minus the expected appreciation of the domestic currency: $i^F - (E_{t+1}^e - E_t)/E_t$. Suppose that the foreign interest rate i^F is 10% and that the expected exchange rate next period E_{t+1}^e is 10 francs per dollar. When the current exchange rate E_t is 9.5 francs per dollar, the expected appreciation of the dollar is $(10.0 - 9.5)/9.5 = 0.052 = 5.2\%$, so the expected return on franc deposits RET^F in terms of dollars is 4.8% (equal to the 10% foreign interest rate minus the 5.2% dollar appreciation). This expected return when $E_t = 9.5$ francs per dollar is plotted as point A in Figure 3. At a higher current exchange rate of $E_t = 10$ francs per dollar, the expected appreciation of the dollar is zero because E_{t+1}^e also equals 10 francs per dollar. Hence RET^F, the expected dollar return on franc deposits, is now just $i^F = 10\%$. This expected return on franc deposits when $E_t = 10$ francs per dollar is plotted as point B. At an even higher exchange rate of $E_t = 10.5$ francs per dollar, the expected change in the value of the dollar is now -4.8% [$= (10.0 - 10.5)/10.5 = -0.048$], so the expected dollar return on foreign deposits RET^F has now risen to 14.8% [$= 10\% - (-4.8\%)$]. This combination of exchange rate and expected return on franc deposits is plotted as point C.

The curve connecting these points is the schedule for the expected return on franc deposits in Figure 3, labeled RET^F, and as you can see, it slopes upward; that is, as the exchange rate E_t rises, the expected return on franc deposits rises. The intuition for this upward slope is that because the expected next-period exchange rate is held constant as the current exchange rate rises, there is less ex-

FIGURE 3
Equilibrium in the Foreign Exchange Market

Equilibrium in the foreign exchange market occurs at the intersection of the schedules for the expected return on franc deposits (RET^F) and the expected return on dollar deposits ($RET^\$$) at point B. The equilibrium exchange rate is $E^* = 10$ francs per dollar.

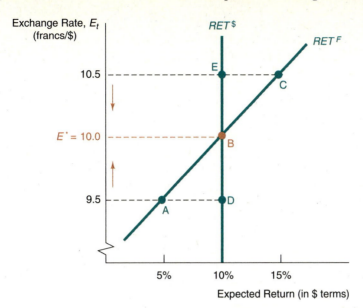

pected appreciation of the dollar. Hence a higher current exchange rate means a greater expected appreciation of the foreign currency in the future, which increases the expected return on foreign deposits in terms of dollars.

Expected Return on Dollar Deposits The expected return on dollar deposits in terms of dollars $RET^\$$ is always the interest rate on dollar deposits $i^\$$ no matter what the exchange rate is. Suppose that the interest rate on dollar deposits is 10%. The expected return on dollar deposits whether at an exchange rate of 9.5, 10.0, or 10.5 francs per dollar is always 10% (points D, B, and E). The line connecting these points is the schedule for the expected return on dollar deposits, labeled $RET^\$$ in Figure 3.

Equilibrium The intersection of the schedules for the expected return on dollar deposits $RET^\$$ and the expected return on franc deposits RET^F is where equilibrium occurs in the foreign exchange market; in other words,

$$RET^\$ = RET^F$$

At the equilibrium point B where the exchange rate E^* is 10 francs per dollar, the interest parity condition is satisfied because the expected returns on dollar deposits and on franc deposits are equal.

   To see that the exchange rate actually heads toward the equilibrium exchange rate E^*, let's see what happens if the exchange rate is 10.5 francs per dollar, a value above the equilibrium exchange rate. As we can see in Figure 3, the expected return on franc deposits at point C is greater than the expected return on dollar deposits at point E. Since dollar and franc deposits are equally desirable, people will not want to hold any dollar deposits, and holders of dollar deposits will try to sell them for franc deposits in the foreign exchange market (which is referred to as "selling dollars" and "buying francs"). However, because the expected return on these dollar deposits is below that on franc deposits, no one holding francs will be willing to exchange them for dollar deposits. The resulting excess supply of dollar deposits means that the price of the dollar deposits relative to franc deposits must fall; that is, the exchange rate (amount of francs per dollar) falls as is illustrated by the downward arrow drawn in the figure at the exchange rate of 10.5 francs per dollar. The decline in the exchange rate will continue until point B is reached at the equilibrium exchange rate of 10 francs per dollar, where the expected return on dollar and franc deposits is now equalized.

Now let us look at what happens when the exchange rate is 9.5 francs per dollar, a value below the equilibrium level. Here the expected return on dollar deposits is greater than that on franc deposits. No one will want to hold franc deposits, and everyone will try to sell them to buy dollar deposits (sell francs and buy dollars), thus driving up the exchange rate as illustrated by the upward arrow. As the exchange rate rises, there is a smaller expected appreciation of the dollar and so a higher expected appreciation of the franc, thereby increasing the expected return on franc deposits. Finally, when the exchange rate has risen to $E^* = 10$ francs per dollar, the expected return on franc deposits has risen enough so that it again equals the expected return on dollar deposits.

EXPLAINING CHANGES IN EXCHANGE RATES

To explain how an exchange rate changes over time, we have to understand the factors that shift the expected-return schedules for domestic (dollar) deposits and foreign (franc) deposits.

Shifts in the Expected-Return Schedule for Foreign Deposits

As we have seen, the expected return on foreign (franc) deposits depends on the foreign interest rate i^F minus the expected appreciation of the dollar ($E_{t+1}^e - E_t)/E_t$. Because a change in the current exchange rate E_t results in a *movement along* the expected-return schedule for franc deposits, factors that *shift* this schedule must work through the foreign interest rate i^F and the expected future exchange rate E_{t+1}^e. We examine the effect of changes in these factors on the expected-return schedule for franc deposits RET^F, holding everything else constant.

STUDY GUIDE

To grasp how the expected-return schedule for franc deposits shifts, just think of yourself as an investor who is considering putting funds into foreign deposits. When a variable changes (i^F for example), decide whether at a given level of the current exchange rate, holding all other variables constant, you would earn a higher or lower expected return on franc deposits.

Changes in the Foreign Interest Rate i^F   If the interest rate on foreign deposits i^F increases, holding everything else constant, the expected return on these deposits must also increase. Hence at a given exchange rate, the increase in i^F leads to a rightward shift in the expected-return schedule for franc deposits from RET_1^F to RET_2^F in Figure 4. As you can see in the figure, the outcome is a depreciation of the dollar from E_1 to E_2. An alternative way to see this is to recognize that the increase in the expected return on franc deposits at the original equilibrium exchange rate resulting from the rise in i^F means that people will want to buy francs and sell dollars, so the value of the dollar must fall. Our analysis thus generates the following conclusion: *An increase in the foreign interest rate i^F shifts the RET^F schedule to the right and causes the domestic currency to depreciate ($E\downarrow$).*

Conversely, if i^F falls, the expected return on franc deposits falls, the RET^F schedule shifts to the left, and the exchange rate rises. This yields the following conclusion: *A decrease in i^F shifts the RET^F schedule to the left and causes the domestic currency to appreciate ($E\uparrow$).*

Changes in the Expected Future Exchange Rate E_{t+1}^e   Any factor that causes the expected future exchange rate to fall decreases the expected appreciation of the dollar

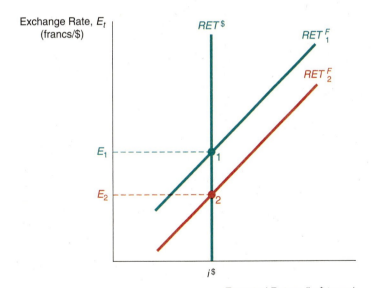

FIGURE 4   **Shifts in the Schedule for the Expected Return on Foreign Deposits RET^F**
An increase in the expected return on foreign deposits, which occurs when either the foreign interest rate rises or the expected future exchange rate falls, shifts the schedule for the expected return on foreign deposits from RET_1^F to RET_2^F, and the exchange rate falls from E_1 to E_2.

and hence raises the expected appreciation of the franc. The result is a higher expected return on franc deposits, which shifts the schedule for the expected return on franc deposits to the right and leads to a decline in the exchange rate as in Figure 4. Conversely, a rise in E^e_{t+1} raises the expected appreciation of the dollar, lowers the expected return on foreign deposits, shifts the RET^F schedule to the left, and raises the exchange rate. To summarize, *a rise in the expected future exchange rate shifts the RET^F schedule to the left and causes an appreciation of the domestic currency; a fall in the expected future exchange rate shifts the RET^F schedule to the right and causes a depreciation of the domestic currency.*

Our analysis of the long-run determinants of the exchange rate indicates the factors that influence the expected future exchange rate: the relative price level, relative tariffs and quotas, import demand, export demand, and relative productivity (refer to Table 1). The theory of purchasing power parity suggests that if a higher American price level relative to the foreign price level is expected to persist, the dollar will depreciate in the long run. A higher expected relative American price level should thus have a tendency to raise the expected return on franc deposits, shift the RET^F schedule to the right, and lower the current exchange rate.

Similarly, the other long-run determinants of the exchange rate we discussed earlier can also influence the expected return on franc deposits and the current exchange rate. Briefly, the following changes will increase the expected return on franc deposits, shift the RET^F schedule to the right, and cause a depreciation of the domestic currency, the dollar: (1) expectations of a rise in the American price level relative to the foreign price level, (2) expectations of lower American tariffs and quotas relative to foreign tariffs and quotas, (3) expectations of higher American import demand, (4) expectations of lower foreign demand for American exports, and (5) expectations of lower American productivity relative to foreign productivity.

Shifts in the Expected-Return Schedule for Domestic Deposits

Since the expected return on domestic (dollar) deposits is just the interest rate on these deposits $i^\$$, this interest rate is the only factor that shifts the schedule for the expected return on dollar deposits.

Changes in the Domestic Interest Rate $i^\$$ A rise in $i^\$$ raises the expected return on dollar deposits, shifts the $RET^\$$ schedule to the right, and leads to a rise in the exchange rate, as is shown in Figure 5. Another way of seeing this is to recognize that a rise in $i^\$$, which raises the expected return on dollar deposits, creates an excess demand for dollar deposits at the original equilibrium exchange rate, and the resulting purchases of dollar deposits cause an appreciation of the dollar. *A rise in the domestic interest rate $i^\$$ shifts the $RET^\$$ schedule to the right*

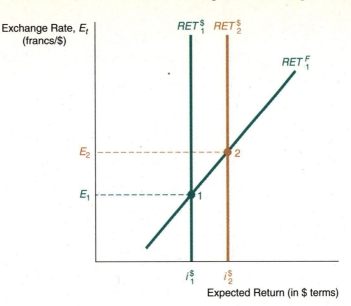

FIGURE 5
Shifts in the
Schedule for the
Expected Return on
Domestic Deposits
($RET^\$$)
An increase in the
expected return
on dollar deposits
$i^\$$ shifts the ex-
pected return on
domestic (dollar)
deposits from
$RET_1^\$$ to $RET_2^\$$
and the exchange
rate from E_1 to E_2.

and causes an appreciation of the domestic currency; a fall in $i^\$$ shifts the $RET^\$$ schedule to the left and causes a depreciation of the domestic currency.

STUDY GUIDE

As a study aid, the factors that shift the RET^F and $RET^\$$ schedules and lead to changes in the current exchange rate E_t are listed in Table 2. The table shows what happens to the exchange rate when there is an increase in each of these variables, holding everything else constant. To give yourself practice, see if you can work out what happens to the RET^F and $RET^\$$ schedules and to the exchange rate if each of these factors falls rather than rises. Check your answers by seeing if you get the opposite change in the exchange rate to those indicated in Table 2.

Changes in the Equilibrium Exchange Rate: Two Examples

Our analysis has revealed the factors that affect the value of the equilibrium exchange rate. Now we use this analysis to take a close look at the response of the exchange rate to changes in interest rates and money growth.

SUMMARY

TABLE 2   Factors That Shift the RET^F and RET^S Schedules and Affect the Exchange Rate

Factor	Change in Factor	Response of Exchange Rate, E_t	
Domestic interest rate, $i^{\$}$	↑	↑	
Foreign interest rate, i^F	↑	↓	
Expected domestic price level*	↑	↓	
Expected tariffs and quotas*	↑	↑	
Expected import demand	↑	↓	
Expected export demand	↑	↑	
Expected productivity*	↑	↑	

*Relative to other countries.

Note: Only increases (↑) in the factors are shown; the effects of decreases in the variables on the exchange rate are the opposite of those indicated in the "Response" column.

Changes in Interest Rates Changes in domestic interest rates $i^\$$ are often cited as a major factor affecting exchange rates. For example, we see headlines in the financial press like this one: "Dollar Recovers As Interest Rates Edge Upward." But is the view presented in this headline always correct?

Not necessarily, because to analyze the effects of interest rate changes, we must carefully distinguish the sources of the changes. The Fisher equation (Chapter 4) states that a (nominal) interest rate equals the *real* interest rate plus expected inflation: $i = i_r + \pi^e$. The Fisher equation indicates that an interest rate i can change for two reasons: Either the real interest rate i_r changes or the expected inflation rate π^e changes. The effect on the exchange rate is quite different, depending on which of these two factors is the source of the change in the nominal interest rate.

Suppose that the domestic real interest rate increases so that the nominal interest rate $i^\$$ rises while expected inflation remains unchanged. In this case, it is reasonable to assume that the expected appreciation of the dollar will be unchanged because expected inflation is unchanged, and so the expected return on foreign deposits will remain unchanged for any given exchange rate. The result is that the RET^F schedule stays put and the $RET^\$$ schedule shifts to the right, and we end up with the situation depicted in Figure 5, which analyzes an increase in $i^\$$, holding everything else constant. Our model of the foreign exchange market produces the following result: ***When domestic real interest rates rise, the domestic currency appreciates.***

When the nominal interest rate rises because of an increase in expected inflation, we get a different result from the one shown in Figure 5. The rise in expected domestic inflation leads to a decline in the expected appreciation of the dollar (a higher appreciation of the franc), which is typically thought to be larger than the increase in the domestic interest rate $i^\$$.[5] As a result, at any given exchange rate, the expected return on foreign deposits rises more than the expected return on dollar deposits. Thus, as we see in Figure 6, the RET^F schedule shifts to the right more than the $RET^\$$ schedule, and the exchange rate falls. Our analysis leads to this conclusion: ***When domestic interest rates rise due to an expected increase in inflation, the domestic currency depreciates.***

Since this conclusion is completely different from that reached when the rise in the domestic interest rate is associated with a higher real interest rate, we must always distinguish between *real* and *nominal* measures when analyzing the effects of interest rates on exchange rates.

---

[5]This conclusion is standard in asset market models of exchange rate determination; see Rudiger Dornbusch, "Expectations and Exchange Rate Dynamics," *Journal of Political Economy* 84 (1976): 1061–1076. It is also consistent with empirical evidence that suggests that nominal interest rates do not rise one-for-one with increases in expected inflation. See Frederic S. Mishkin, "The Real Interest Rate: An Empirical Investigation," *Carnegie-Rochester Conference Series on Public Policy* 15 (1981): 151–200; and Lawrence Summers, "The Nonadjustment of Nominal Interest Rates: A Study of the Fisher Effect," in *Macroeconomics, Prices and Quantities,* ed. James Tobin (Washington, D.C.: Brookings Institution, 1983), pp. 201–240.

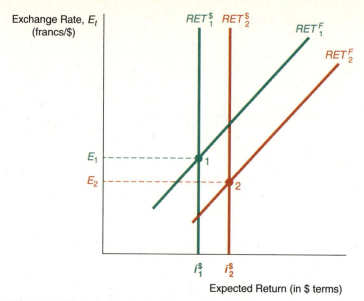

FIGURE 6   Effect of a Rise in the Domestic Nominal Interest Rate as a Result of an Increase in Expected Inflation
Because a rise in domestic expected inflation leads to a decline in expected dollar appreciation that is larger than the resulting increase in the domestic interest rate, the expected return on foreign deposits rises by more than the expected return on domestic (dollar) deposits. RET^F shifts to the right more than $RET^\$$, and the equilibrium exchange rate falls from E_1 to E_2.

Changes in the Money Supply Suppose that the Federal Reserve decides to increase the level of the money supply in order to reduce unemployment, which it believes to be excessive. The higher money supply will lead to a higher American price level in the long run (as we will see in Chapters 23 and 26) and hence to a lower expected future exchange rate. The resulting decline in the expected appreciation of the dollar increases the expected return on foreign deposits at any given current exchange rate and so shifts the RET^F schedule rightward from RET^F_1 to RET^F_2 in Figure 7. In addition, the higher money supply will lead to a higher real money supply M/P because the price level does not immediately increase in the short run. As suggested in Chapter 6, the resulting rise in the real money supply causes the domestic interest rate to fall from $i^\$_1$ to $i^\$_2$, which lowers the expected return on domestic (dollar) deposits, shifting the $RET^\$$ schedule in from $RET^\$_1$ to $RET^\$_2$. As we can see in Figure 7, the result is a decline in the exchange rate from E_1 to E_2. The conclusion is this: ***A higher domestic money supply causes the domestic currency to depreciate.***

Exchange Rate Overshooting

Our analysis of the effect of a money supply increase on the exchange rate is not yet over—we still need to look at what happens to the exchange rate in the long run. A basic proposition in monetary theory, called **monetary neutrality,** states

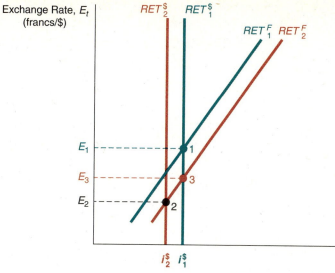

FIGURE 7   Effect of a Rise in the Money Supply

A rise in the money supply leads to a higher domestic price level in the long run, which in turn leads to a lower expected future exchange rate. The resulting decline in the expected appreciation of the dollar raises the expected return on foreign deposits, shifting the RET^F schedule rightward from RET^F_1 to RET^F_2. In the short run, the domestic interest rate $i^\$$ falls, shifting $RET^\$$ from $RET^\$_1$ to $RET^\$_2$. The short-run outcome is that the exchange rate falls from E_1 to E_2. In the long run, however, the interest rate returns to $i^\$_1$, and $RET^\$$ returns to $RET^\$_1$. The exchange rate thus rises from E_2 to E_3 in the long run.

that in the long run, a one-time percentage rise in the money supply is matched by the same one-time percentage rise in the price level, leaving unchanged the real money supply and all other economic variables such as interest rates. An intuitive way to understand this proposition is to think of what would happen if our government announced overnight that an old dollar would now be worth 100 new dollars. The money supply in new dollars would be 100 times its old value and the price level would also be 100 times higher, but nothing in the economy would really have changed; interest rates and the real money supply would remain the same. Monetary neutrality tells us that in the long run, the rise in the money supply would not lead to a change in the domestic interest rate and so it would return to $i^\$_1$ in the long run, and the schedule for the expected return on domestic deposits would return to $RET^\$_1$. As we can see in Figure 7, this means that the exchange rate would rise from E_2 to E_3 in the long run.

The phenomenon we have described here in which the exchange rate falls by more in the short run than it does in the long run when the money supply increases is called **exchange rate overshooting.** It is important because, as we will see in the following application, it can help explain why exchange rates exhibit so much volatility.

Another way of thinking about why exchange rate overshooting occurs is to recognize that when the domestic interest rate falls in the short run, equilibrium in the foreign exchange market means that the expected return on foreign deposits must be lower. With the foreign interest rate given, this lower expected return on foreign deposits means that there must be an expected appreciation of the dollar (depreciation of the franc) in order for the expected return on foreign deposits to decline when the domestic interest rate falls. This can occur only if the current exchange rate falls below its long-run value.

APPLICATION

WHY ARE EXCHANGE RATES SO VOLATILE?

The high volatility of foreign exchange rates surprises many people. Thirty or so years ago, economists generally believed that allowing exchange rates to be determined in the free market would not lead to large fluctuations in their values. Recent experience has proved them wrong. If we return to Figure 1, we see that exchange rates over the 1980–1993 period have been very volatile.

The asset market approach to exchange rate determination that we have outlined here gives a straightforward explanation of volatile exchange rates. Because expected appreciation of the domestic currency affects the expected return on foreign deposits, expectations about the price level, inflation, tariffs and quotas, productivity, import demand, export demand, and the money supply play important roles in determining the exchange rate. When expectations

A Global Perspective

Box 1

FORECASTING EXCHANGE RATES

Businesses and financial institutions care a great deal about what foreign exchange rates will be in the future because these rates affect the value of assets on their balance sheet that are denominated in foreign currencies. In addition, financial institutions often engage in trading foreign exchange, both for their own account and for their customers. Businesses and financial institutions therefore need accurate predictions of exchange rates.

Financial institutions and businesses obtain foreign exchange forecasts either by hiring their own staff economists to generate them or by purchasing forecasts from other financial institutions or economic forecasting firms. In predicting exchange rate movements, forecasters look at the factors mentioned in this chapter. For example, if they expect domestic real interest rates to rise, they will predict, in line with our analysis, that the domestic currency will appreciate; conversely, if they expect domestic inflation to increase, they will predict that the domestic currency will depreciate. Exchange rate forecasters are no more or less accurate than other economic forecasters, and they often make large errors. Reports on foreign exchange rate forecasts and how well forecasters are doing appear from time to time in the *Wall Street Journal* and in the trade magazine *Euromoney*.

about any of these variables change, our model indicates that there will be an immediate effect on the expected return on foreign deposits and therefore on the exchange rate. Since expectations on all these variables change with just about every bit of news that appears, it is not surprising that the exchange rate is volatile. In addition, we have seen that our exchange rate analysis produces exchange rate overshooting when the money supply increases. Exchange rate overshooting is an additional reason for the high volatility of exchange rates.

Because earlier models of exchange rate behavior focused on goods markets rather than asset markets, they did not emphasize changing expectations as a source of exchange rate movements, and so these earlier models could not predict substantial fluctuations in exchange rates. The failure of earlier models to explain volatility is one reason why they are no longer so popular. The more modern approach developed here emphasizes that the foreign exchange market is like any other asset market in which expectations of the future matter. The foreign exchange market, like other asset markets such as the stock market, displays substantial price volatility, and foreign exchange rates are notoriously hard to forecast (see Box 1).

APPLICATION

THE DOLLAR AND INTEREST RATES, 1973–1993

In the chapter preview we mentioned that the dollar was weak in the late 1970s, rose substantially from 1980 to 1985, and declined thereafter. We can use our analysis of the foreign exchange market to understand exchange rate movements and help explain the dollar's rise and fall in the 1980s.

Some important information for tracing the dollar's changing value is presented in Figure 8, which plots measures of real and nominal interest rates and the value of the dollar in terms of a basket of foreign currencies (called an **effective exchange rate index**). We can see that the value of the dollar and the measure of real interest rates rise and fall together. In the late 1970s, real interest rates were at low levels, and so was the value of the dollar. Beginning in 1980, however, real interest rates in the United States began to climb sharply, and at the same time so did the dollar. After 1984, the real interest rate declined substantially, as did the dollar.

Our model of exchange rate determination helps explain the rise and fall in the dollar in the 1980s. As Figure 5 indicates, a rise in the U.S. real interest rate raises the expected return on dollar deposits while leaving the expected return on foreign deposits unchanged. The resulting increased demand for dollar deposits then leads to purchases of dollar deposits (and sales of foreign deposits), which raise the exchange rate. This is exactly what occurred in the 1980–1984 period. The subsequent fall in U.S. real interest rates then lowered the expected return on dollar deposits relative to foreign deposits, and the resulting sales of dollar deposits (and purchases of foreign deposits) lowered the exchange rate.

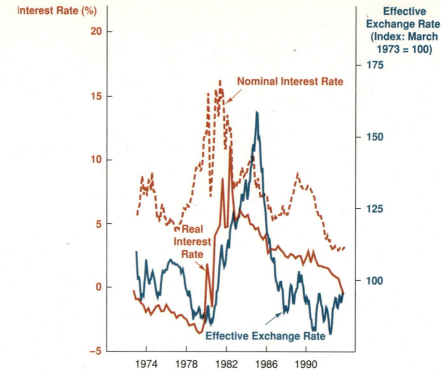

FIGURE 8
Value of the
Dollar and
Interest Rates,
1973–1993
Sources: International Financial Statistics;
Figure 3 in
Chapter 4 of this
text.

The plot of nominal interest rates in Figure 8 also demonstrates that the correspondence between *nominal* interest rates and exchange rate movements is not nearly as close as that between *real* interest rates and exchange rate movements. This is also exactly what our analysis predicts. The rise in nominal interest rates in the late 1970s was not reflected in a corresponding rise in the value of the dollar; indeed, the dollar actually fell in the late 1970s. Figure 8 explains why the rise in nominal rates in the late 1970s did not produce a rise in the dollar. As a comparison of the real and nominal interest rates in the late 1970s indicates, the rise in nominal interest rates reflected an increase in expected inflation and not an increase in real interest rates. As our analysis in Figure 6 demonstrates, the rise in nominal interest rates stemming from a rise in expected inflation should lead to a decline in the dollar, and that is exactly what transpired.

If there is a moral to the story, it is that a failure to distinguish between real and nominal interest rates can lead to poor predictions of exchange rate movements: The weakness of the dollar in the late 1970s and the strength of the dollar in the early 1980s can be explained by movements in *real* interest rates but not *nominal* interest rates.

APPLICATION	READING THE *WALL STREET JOURNAL*

THE "FOREIGN EXCHANGE" COLUMN

Now that we have an understanding of how exchange rates are determined, we can use our analysis to understand discussions about developments in the foreign exchange market reported in the financial press.

Every day, the *Wall Street Journal* reports on developments in the foreign exchange market on the previous business day in its "Foreign Exchange" column, an example of which is presented in the "Following the Financial News" box.

The column focuses on U.S monetary and trade policy as the source of the decline in the dollar in the foreign exchange markets.

The column discusses the surprise resignation of David Mullins, the vice chairman of the Federal Reserve, and the departure of Federal Reserve Governor Wayne Angell, both of whom are considered avid inflation fighters, as important news events to the foreign exchange markets. The departure of these two figures from the Federal Reserve leads to concerns that President Clinton's replacements for these Fed officials might be less hawkish on inflation, leading to a more inflationary monetary policy in the future.

Our analysis of the foreign exchange market explains why these developments result in a decline in the dollar. The higher expected U.S. inflation leads to a larger expected depreciation of the dollar because it raises the expected future price level in the United States relative to foreign countries. The larger expected depreciation of the dollar implies a higher expected appreciation of foreign currencies, thereby increasing the expected return on foreign deposits, which shifts the RET^F schedule to the right as in Figure 4, and the value of the dollar falls. The column also indicates that the departure of the two Fed officials makes it more likely that U.S. interest rates will be lower in the future. Our analysis indicates that lower U.S. interest rates in the future are another reason for the fall in the dollar. The lower U.S. interest rates will shift the $RET^\$$ schedule to the left and will thereby cause the exchange rate to fall in the future. The resulting expected depreciation of the dollar, which implies an appreciation of foreign currencies, increases the expected return on foreign currency deposits and again shifts the RET^F schedule to the right as in Figure 4. The lower future U.S. interest rates thus provide an additional reason why the dollar would decline in value.

The column suggests a third reason for the decline in the dollar. Pessimism about the outcome of trade talks with Japan leads traders to expect that there will be more U.S. pressure to increase the value of the yen. Our analysis shows why this development leads to the dollar decline. Expectations of a higher future value of the yen imply a higher expected appreciation of the yen. The re-

FOLLOWING THE FINANCIAL NEWS

The "Foreign Exchange" Column

The "Foreign Exchange" column appears daily in the *Wall Street Journal;* an example is presented here. It is found in the third section, "Money and Investing."

FOREIGN EXCHANGE

Dollar Falls Against Major Currencies On Concern Over U.S. Rates and Trade

By GARY ROSENBERGER

Special to THE WALL STREET JOURNAL

NEW YORK — The dollar tumbled to new lows for this year against the yen on fresh concerns over the future direction of U.S. interest rates and over stalled trade negotiations with Japan.

The dollar fell heavily against most other major currencies, but recovered some lost ground on promising new U.S. economic data and a spate of short-covering and bargain-hunting.

Late in New York, the dollar was quoted at 1.7320 marks, down from 1.7345 marks late Monday in New York. The U.S. currency also was changing hands at 107.70 yen, down from 108.70 yen. Sterling was trading at $1.5010, down from $1.5060.

About midday Wednesday in Tokyo, the dollar was trading at 108.20 yen and at 1.7336 marks.

The surprise resignation of David Mullins, vice chairman of the Federal Reserve, yesterday roused speculation that U.S. interest rates, long thought to be headed for higher ground, will stay flat.

The departure of Mullins, considered an anti-inflation hawk, opens the way for President Clinton to appoint an inflation dove as his successor.

The move also countered somewhat warnings on Monday by Alan Greenspan, the Fed's chairman, that short-term U.S. rates will move higher eventually in order to prevent any return of inflation.

Mr. Mullins, who will resign Feb. 14, said he won't attend the meeting of the Federal Open Market Committee tomorrow and Friday. Traders said that may diminish the likelihood of a panel vote in favor of higher rates at this week's meeting.

In addition, Mr. Mullins' leave-taking coincides with the departure Feb. 10 of Federal Reserve Governor Wayne Angell, a far more resolute anti-inflation hawk.

"You have two people that historically have been inflation fighters leaving at the same time," said Alan Leslie, chief economist for Discount Corp. of New York.

"They were both appointed by more conservative administrations, and expectations are that Clinton will appoint more growth-oriented people as opposed to anti-inflation people—which means lower interest rates and a lower dollar," he said.

The Mullins announcement brought the dollar to its intraday low of 107.55 yen, the lowest level since Dec. 8.

Traders also said the slide was pushed along by concerns that U.S. trade representative Mickey Kantor's trip to Japan to further trade negotiations will be too little, too late.

"The dollar-yen is reacting to Mickey Kantor," said Carl Forcheski, a trader at Chemical Bank. "There are worries that nothing will come of his visit."

Indeed, Japan is under the gun to produce a viable trade agreement prior to Prime Minister Morihiro Hosokawa's meeting with Mr. Clinton Feb. 11, and traders fear that lack of an agreement will prompt more U.S. pressure for a strong yen.

Meanwhile, the dollar made a partial recovery from its fall against the mark on a combination of short-covering and promising U.S. economic data.

The National Association of Purchasing Management's January report showed its overall index of business activity rose to 57.7% from 57.1% in December. Economists had predicted a decline to 56%.

Source: Wall Street Journal, Wednesday, February 2, 1994, p. C18.

sulting increase in the expected return on yen deposits shifts the RET^F schedule to the right and results in a decline in the dollar.

SUMMARY

1. Foreign exchange rates (the price of one country's currency in terms of another's) are important because they affect the price of domestically produced goods sold abroad and the cost of foreign goods bought domestically.

2. The theory of purchasing power parity suggests that long-run changes in the exchange rate between two countries are determined by changes in the relative price levels of the two countries. Other factors that affect exchange rates in the long run are tariffs and quotas, import demand, export demand, and productivity.

3. Exchange rates are determined in the short run by the interest parity condition, which states that the expected return on domestic deposits is equal to the expected return on foreign deposits.

4. Any factor that changes the expected returns on domestic and foreign deposits will lead to changes in the exchange rate. Such factors include changes in the interest rates on domestic and foreign deposits as well as changes in any of the factors that affect the long-run exchange rate and hence the expected future exchange rate. Changes in the money supply lead to exchange rate overshooting, causing the exchange rate to change by more in the short run than in the long run.

5. The asset market approach to exchange rate determination can explain both the volatility of exchange rates and the rise of the dollar in the 1980–1984 period and its subsequent fall.

KEY TERMS

exchange rate

foreign exchange market

spot transactions

forward transactions

spot exchange rate

forward exchange rate

appreciation

depreciation

law of one price

theory of purchasing power parity (PPP)

tariffs

quotas

capital mobility

interest parity condition

monetary neutrality

exchange rate overshooting

effective exchange rate index

QUESTIONS AND PROBLEMS

1. When the French franc appreciates, are you more likely to drink California or French wine?

*2. "A country is always worse off when its currency is weak (falls in value)." Is this statement true, false, or uncertain? Explain.

3. Check in a newspaper the exchange rates for the foreign currencies listed in the "Following the Financial News" box. Which of these currencies have appreciated and which have depreciated since February 2, 1994?

*4. If the French price level rises by 5% relative to the price level in the United States, what does the theory of purchasing power parity predict will happen to the value of the French franc in terms of dollars?

5. If the demand for a country's exports falls at the same time that tariffs on imports are raised, will the country's currency tend to appreciate or depreciate in the long run?

*6. In the mid- to late 1970s, the yen appreciated relative to the dollar even though Japan's inflation rate was higher than America's. How can this be explained by an improvement in the productivity of Japanese industry relative to American industry?

Using Economic Analysis to Predict the Future

Answer the remaining questions by drawing the appropriate exchange market diagrams.

7. The president of the United States announces that he will reduce inflation with a new anti-inflation program. If the public believes him, predict what will happen to the U.S. exchange rate.

*8. If the British central bank prints money to reduce unemployment, what will happen to the value of the pound in the short run and the long run?

9. If the French government unexpectedly announces that it will be imposing higher tariffs and quotas on foreign goods one year from now, what will happen to the value of the franc today?

*10. If nominal interest rates in America rise but real interest rates fall, predict what will happen to the U.S. exchange rate.

11. If American auto companies make a breakthrough in automobile technology and are able to produce a car that gets 60 miles to the gallon, what will happen to the U.S. exchange rate?

*12. If Americans go on a spending spree and buy twice as much French perfume, Japanese TVs, English sweaters, Swiss watches, and Italian wine, what will happen to the value of the U.S. dollar?

13. If expected inflation drops in Europe so that interest rates fall there, predict what will happen to the U.S. exchange rate.

*14. If the German central bank decides to contract the money supply in order to fight inflation, what will happen to the value of the U.S. dollar?

15. If there is a strike in France, making it harder to buy French goods, what will happen to the value of the franc?

PART III

FINANCIAL INSTITUTIONS

Chapter 9

AN ECONOMIC ANALYSIS OF FINANCIAL STRUCTURE

PREVIEW   A healthy and vibrant economy requires a financial system that moves funds from people who save to people who have productive investment opportunities. But how does the financial system make sure that your hard-earned savings get channeled to Paula the Productive Investor rather than to Benny the Bum?

This chapter answers that question by providing an economic analysis of how our financial structure is designed to promote economic efficiency. The analysis focuses on a few simple but powerful economic concepts that enable us to explain features of our financial markets such as why financial contracts are written as they are, why financial intermediaries are more important than securities markets for getting funds to borrowers, and why financial crises occur and have such severe consequences for the health of the economy.

BASIC PUZZLES ABOUT FINANCIAL STRUCTURE THROUGHOUT THE WORLD

The financial system is complex in structure and function throughout the world. There are many different types of institutions: banks, insurance companies, mutual funds, stock and bond markets, and so on—all of which are regulated by government. The financial system channels billions of dollars per year from savers to people with productive investment opportunities. If we take a close look at financial structure all over the world, we find eight basic puzzles that we need to solve in order to understand how the financial system works.

The pie chart in Figure 1 indicates how American businesses financed their activities using external funds (those obtained from outside the business itself) in the period 1970–1985. The *loans* category is made up primarily of bank loans, but it also includes loans made by other financial intermediaries; the *bonds* category includes marketable debt securities such as corporate bonds and commercial paper; *stock* consists of stock market shares; and *other* includes other loans such as government loans, loans by foreigners, and trade debt (loans made by

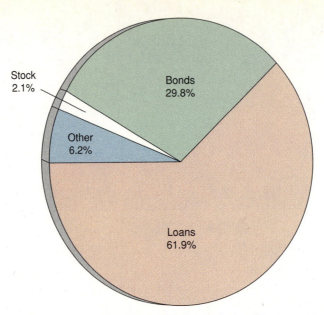

FIGURE 1   Sources of External Funds for Nonfinancial Businesses in the United States
The categories of external funds are as follows: *Loans* is made up primarily of bank
loans, but it also includes loans made by other financial intermediaries. *Bonds* includes
marketable debt securities such as corporate bonds and commercial paper. *Stock* consists
of stock market shares. *Other* includes other loans such as government loans, loans by
foreigners, and trade debt (loans made by businesses to other businesses when they purchase goods). *Source:* Colin Mayer, "Financial Systems, Corporate Finance, and Economic Development," in *Asymmetric Information, Corporate Finance, and Investment,*
ed. R. Glenn Hubbard (Chicago: University of Chicago Press, 1990), p. 312.

businesses to other businesses when they purchase goods). Figure 2 uses the
same classifications as Figure 1 and compares the U.S. data to those of five other
industrialized countries.

Now let us explore the eight financial puzzles.

**1. *Stocks are not the most important source of financing for busi-
nesses.*** Because so much attention in the media is focused on the stock market,
many people have the impression that stocks are the most important sources of
financing for American corporations. However, as we can see from the pie chart
in Figure 1, the stock market accounted for only a small fraction of the external
financing of American businesses in the 1970–1985 period, 2.1%.[1] (Indeed, since

---

[1]The 2.1% figure for the percentage of external financing provided by stocks is based on the flows of
external funds to corporations. However, this flow figure is somewhat misleading because when a
share of stock is issued, it raises funds permanently, whereas when a bond is issued, it raises funds
only temporarily until they are paid back at maturity. To see this, suppose that a firm raises $1000 by
selling a share of stock and another $1000 by selling a $1000 one-year bond. In the case of the stock
issue, the firm can hold on to the $1000 it raised this way, but to hold on to the $1000 it raised

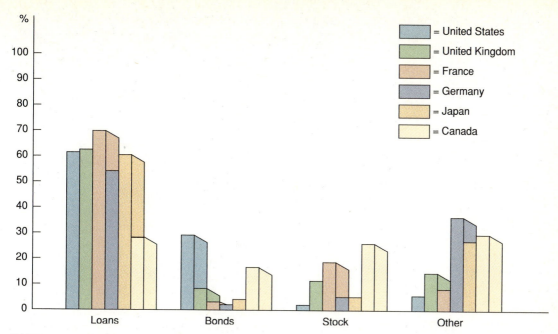

FIGURE 2 Sources of External Funds for Nonfinancial Businesses: A Comparison of the United States and Five Other Industrialized Countries

The categories of external funds are the same as in Figure 1. *Sources:* U.S. figures from Figure 1; others from Colin Mayer, "Financial Systems, Corporate Finance, and Economic Development," in *Asymmetric Information, Corporate Finance, and Investment,* ed. R. Glenn Hubbard (Chicago: University of Chicago Press, 1990), p. 312.

1984, American corporations have generally stopped issuing shares to finance their activities; instead they have purchased large numbers of shares, meaning that the stock market has actually been a *negative* source of corporate finance in recent years.) Similarly small figures apply in the other countries presented in Figure 2 as well. Why is the stock market less important than other sources of financing in the United States and other countries?

2. Issuing marketable securities is not the primary way in which businesses finance their operations. Figure 1 shows that bonds are a far more important source of financing than stocks in the United States (29.8% versus 2.1%). However, stocks and bonds combined (31.9%), which make up the total share of marketable securities, still supply less than one-third of the external funds corporations need to finance their activities. The fact that issuing marketable securities is not the most important source of financing is true elsewhere

through debt, it has to issue a new $1000 bond every year. If we look at the flow of funds to corporations over a 15-year period, as in Figure 1, the firm will have raised $1000 with a stock issue only once in the 15-year period, while it will have raised $1000 with debt 15 times, once in each of the 15 years. Thus it will look like debt is 15 times more important than stocks in raising funds, even though our example indicates that they are actually equally important for the firm.

in the world as well. Indeed, as we see in Figure 2, most countries, with the exception of Canada, have a much smaller share of external financing supplied by marketable securities than the United States. Why don't businesses use marketable securities more extensively to finance their activities?

3. Indirect finance, which involves the activities of financial intermediaries, is many times more important than direct finance, in which businesses raise funds directly from lenders in financial markets. Direct finance involves the sale to households of marketable securities such as stocks and bonds. The 31.9% share of stocks and bonds as a source of external financing for American businesses actually greatly overstates the importance of direct finance in our financial system. Since 1970, less than 5% of newly issued corporate bonds and commercial paper and around 50% of stocks have been sold directly to American households. The rest of these securities have been bought primarily by financial intermediaries such as insurance companies, pension funds, and mutual funds. These figures indicate that direct finance is used in less than 5% of the external funding of American business. Because in most countries marketable securities are an even less important source of finance than in the United States, direct finance is also far less important than indirect finance in the rest of the world. Why are financial intermediaries and indirect finance so important in financial markets?

4. Banks are the most important source of external funds used to finance businesses. As we can see in Figures 1 and 2, the primary sources of external funds for businesses throughout the world are loans (61.9% in the United States). Most of these loans are bank loans, so the data suggest that banks have the most important role in financing business activities. An extraordinary fact that surprises most people is that in an average year in the United States, 25 times more funds are raised with bank loans than with stocks. What makes banks so important to the workings of the financial system?

5. The financial system is among the most heavily regulated sectors of the economy. You learned in Chapter 2 that the financial system is heavily regulated, not only in the United States but in all other developed countries as well. Governments regulate financial markets primarily to promote the provision of information and to ensure the soundness of the financial system. Why are financial markets so extensively regulated throughout the world?

6. Only large, well-established corporations have access to securities markets to finance their activities. Individuals and smaller businesses that are not well established almost never raise funds by issuing marketable securities. Instead, they obtain their financing from banks. Why do only large, well-known corporations have the ability to raise funds in securities markets?

***7. Collateral is a prevalent feature of debt contracts for both households and businesses.* Collateral** is property that is pledged to the lender to guarantee payment in the event that the borrower should be unable to make debt payments. Collateralized debt (which is also known as **secured debt** to contrast it with **unsecured debt,** which is not collateralized) is the predominant form of household debt and is widely used in business borrowing as well. The majority of household debt in the United States consists of collateralized loans: Your automobile is collateral for your auto loan, and your house is collateral for your mortgage. Commercial and farm mortgages, for which property is pledged as collateral, make up one-quarter of borrowing by nonfinancial businesses; corporate bonds and other bank loans also often involve pledges of collateral. Why is collateral such an important feature of debt contracts?

8. Debt contracts are typically extremely complicated legal documents that place substantial restrictions on the behavior of the borrower. Many students think about a debt contract as a simple IOU that can be written on a single piece of paper. The reality of debt contracts is far different, however. In all countries, bond or loan contracts are typically long legal documents with provisions (called **restrictive covenants**) that restrict and specify certain activities that the borrower can engage in. Restrictive covenants are not just a feature of debt contracts for businesses; for example, personal automobile loan and home mortgage contracts have restrictive covenants that require the borrower to maintain sufficient insurance on the automobile or house purchased with the loan. Why are debt contracts so complex and restrictive?

As you might recall from Chapter 2, an important feature of financial markets is that they have substantial transactions and information costs. An economic analysis of how these costs affect financial markets provides us with solutions to the eight puzzles, which in turn provide us with a much deeper understanding of how our financial system works. In the next section we examine the impact of transactions costs on the structure of our financial system. Then we turn to how information costs affect financial structure.

TRANSACTIONS COSTS

Transactions costs are a major problem in financial markets. An example will make this clear.

How Transactions Costs Influence Financial Structure

Say you have $5000 you would like to invest, and you think about investing in the stock market. Because you have only $5000, you can buy only a small number of shares. The stockbroker tells you that your purchase is so small that the brokerage commission for buying the stock you picked will be a large percentage of the purchase price of the shares. If instead you decide to buy a bond, the problem is even worse because the smallest denomination for some bonds you might want to buy is as much as $10,000 and you do not have that much to invest. Indeed, the broker may not even be interested in your business at all because the small size of your account doesn't make spending time on it worthwhile. You are disappointed and realize that you will not be able to use financial markets to earn a return on your hard-earned savings. You can take some consolation, however, in the fact that you are not alone in being stymied by high transactions costs. This is a fact of life for most of us: Most American households never own any securities.

You also face another problem because of transactions costs. Because you have only a small amount of funds available, you can make only a restricted number of investments. That is, you have to put all your eggs in one basket, and your inability to diversify will subject you to a lot of risk.

How Financial Intermediaries Reduce Transactions Costs

This example of the problems posed by transactions costs and the example outlined in Chapter 2 when legal costs kept you from making a loan to Carl the Carpenter illustrate that small savers like you are frozen out of financial markets and are unable to benefit from them. Fortunately, financial intermediaries, an important part of the financial structure, have evolved to reduce transactions costs and allow small savers and borrowers to benefit from the existence of financial markets.

Economies of Scale One solution to the problem of high transactions costs is to bundle the funds of many investors together so that they can take advantage of *economies of scale,* the reduction in transactions costs per dollar of investment as the size (scale) of transactions increases. By bundling investors' funds together, transactions costs for each individual investor are far smaller. Economies of scale exist because the total cost of carrying out a transaction in financial markets increases only a little as the size of the transaction grows. For example, the cost of arranging a purchase of 10,000 shares of stock is not much greater than the cost of arranging a purchase of 50 shares of stock.

The presence of economies of scale in financial markets helps explain why financial intermediaries developed and are such an important part of our financial structure. The clearest example of a financial intermediary that arose because of economies of scale is a mutual fund. A *mutual fund* is a financial intermediary that sells shares to individuals and then invests the proceeds in bonds or stocks. Because it buys large blocks of stocks or bonds, a mutual fund can take advantage of lower transactions costs. These cost savings are then passed on to individual investors after the mutual fund has taken its cut in the form of management fees for administering their accounts. An additional benefit for individual investors is that a mutual fund is large enough to purchase a widely diversified portfolio of securities. The increased diversification for individual investors reduces their risk, thus making them better off.

Economies of scale are also important in lowering the costs of things such as computer technology that financial institutions need to accomplish their tasks. Once a large mutual fund has invested a lot of money in setting up a telecommunications system, for example, it can be used for a huge number of transactions at a low cost per transaction.

Expertise   Financial intermediaries also arise because they are better able to develop expertise to lower transactions costs. Mutual funds, banks, and other financial intermediaries develop expertise in computer technology so that they can cheaply provide convenient services such as toll-free numbers that allow you to check on how well your investments are doing or the ability to write checks on your account.

An important outcome of a financial intermediary's low transactions costs is that they allow a financial intermediary to provide its customers with *liquidity services,* services that make it easier for customers to conduct transactions. Money market mutual funds, for example, allow shareholders to write checks that enable them to pay their bills easily while at the same time paying them high interest rates.

ASYMMETRIC INFORMATION: ADVERSE SELECTION AND MORAL HAZARD

The presence of transactions costs in financial markets explains in part why financial intermediaries and indirect finance play such an important role in financial markets (puzzle 3). To understand financial structure more fully, however, we turn to the role of information in financial markets.[2]

Asymmetric information—one party's having insufficient knowledge about the other party involved in a transaction to make accurate decisions—is an important aspect of financial markets. For example, managers of a corporation know whether they are honest or have better information about how well their business is doing than the stockholders do. The presence of asymmetric information leads to adverse selection and moral hazard problems, which were introduced in Chapter 2.

Adverse selection is an asymmetric information problem that occurs *before* the transaction occurs: Potential bad credit risks are the ones who most actively seek out loans. Thus the parties who are the most likely to produce an undesirable outcome are most likely to want to engage in the transaction. For example, big risk takers or outright crooks might be the most eager to take out a loan because they know that they are unlikely to pay it back. Because adverse selection increases the chances that a loan might be made to a bad credit risk, lenders may decide not to make any loans even though there are good credit risks in the marketplace.

Moral hazard arises *after* the transaction occurs: The lender runs the risk that the borrower will engage in activities that are undesirable from the lender's point of view because they make it less likely that the loan will be paid back. For example, once borrowers have obtained a loan, they may take on big risks (which have possible high returns but also run a greater risk of default) because

---

[2]An excellent survey of the literature on information and financial structure that expands on the topics discussed in the rest of this chapter is contained in Mark Gertler, "Financial Structure and Aggregate Economic Activity: An Overview," *Journal of Money, Credit and Banking* 20 (1988): 559–588.

they are playing with someone else's money. Because moral hazard lowers the probability that the loan will be repaid, lenders may decide that they would rather not make a loan.

THE LEMONS PROBLEM: HOW ADVERSE SELECTION INFLUENCES FINANCIAL STRUCTURE

A particular characterization of the adverse selection problem and how it interferes with the efficient functioning of a market was outlined in a famous article by George Akerlof. It is referred to as the "lemons problem" because it resembles the problem created by lemons in the used-car market.[3] Potential buyers of used cars are frequently unable to assess the quality of the car; that is, they can't tell whether a particular used car is a good car that will run well or a lemon that will continually give them grief. The price that a buyer pays must therefore reflect the *average* quality of the cars in the market, somewhere between the low value of a lemon and the high value of a good car.

The owner of a used car, by contrast, is more likely to know whether the car is a peach or a lemon. If the car is a lemon, the owner is more than happy to sell it at the price the buyer is willing to pay, which, being somewhere between the value of a lemon and a good car, is greater than the lemon's value. However, if the car is a peach, the owner knows that the car is undervalued by the price the buyer is willing to pay, and so the owner may not want to sell it. As a result of this adverse selection, very few good used cars will come to the market. Because the average quality of a used car available in the market will be low and because very few people want to buy a lemon, there will be few sales. The used-car market will then function poorly, if at all.

Lemons in the Stock and Bond Markets

A similar lemons problem arises in securities markets, that is, the debt (bond) and equity (stock) markets. Suppose that our friend Irving the Investor, a potential buyer of securities such as common stock, can't distinguish between good firms with high expected profits and low risk and bad firms with low expected profits and high risk. In this situation, Irving will be willing to pay only a price that reflects the *average* quality of firms issuing securities—a price that lies between the value of securities from bad firms and the value of those from good firms. If the owners or managers of a good firm have better information than Irv-

---

[3]George Akerlof, "The Market for 'Lemons': Quality, Uncertainty and the Market Mechanism," *Quarterly Journal of Economics* 84 (1970): 488–500. Two important papers that have applied the lemons problem analysis to financial markets are Stewart Myers and N. S. Majluf, "Corporate Financing and Investment Decisions When Firms Have Information That Investors Do Not Have," *Journal of Financial Economics* 13 (1984): 187–221, and Bruce Greenwald, Joseph E. Stiglitz, and Andrew Weiss, "Information Imperfections in the Capital Market and Macroeconomic Fluctuations," *American Economic Review* 74 (1984): 194–199.

ing and *know* that they are a good firm, they know that their securities are undervalued and will not want to sell them to Irving at the price he is willing to pay. The only firms willing to sell Irving securities will be bad firms (because the price is higher than the securities are worth). Our friend Irving is not stupid; he does not want to hold securities in bad firms, and hence he will decide not to purchase securities in the market. In an outcome similar to that in the used-car market, this securities market will not work very well because few firms will sell securities in it to raise capital.

The analysis is similar if Irving considers purchasing a corporate debt instrument in the bond market rather than an equity share. Irving will buy a bond only if its interest rate is high enough to compensate him for the average default risk of the good and bad firms trying to sell the debt. The knowledgeable owners of a good firm realize that they will be paying a higher interest rate than they should, and so they are unlikely to want to borrow in this market. Only the bad firms will be willing to borrow, and because investors like Irving are not eager to buy bonds issued by bad firms, they will probably not buy any bonds at all. Few bonds are likely to sell in this market, and so it will not be a good source of financing.

The analysis we have just conducted explains puzzle 2—why marketable securities are not the primary source of financing for businesses in any country in the world. It also partly explains puzzle 1—why stocks are not the most important source of financing for American businesses. The presence of the lemons problem keeps securities markets such as the stock and bond markets from being effective in channeling funds from savers to borrowers.

Solutions to Adverse Selection Problems

In the absence of asymmetric information, the lemons problem goes away. If buyers know as much about the quality of used cars as sellers so that all involved can tell a good car from a bad one, buyers will be willing to pay full value for good used cars. Because the owners of good used cars can now get a fair price, they will be willing to sell them in the market. The market will have many transactions and will do its intended job: channeling good cars to people who want them.

Similarly, if purchasers of securities can distinguish good firms from bad, they will pay the full value of securities issued by good firms, and good firms will sell their securities in the market. The securities market will then be able to move funds to the good firms that have the most productive investment opportunities.

Private Production and Sale of Information The solution to the adverse selection problem in financial markets is to eliminate asymmetric information by furnishing people supplying funds with full details about the individuals or firms seeking to finance their investment activities. One way to get this material to saver-lenders is to have private companies collect and produce information that distinguishes good from bad firms and then sell it to purchasers of securities. In the United States, companies such as Standard and Poor's, Moody's, and Value Line gather information on firms' balance sheet positions and investment activities, publish these data, and sell them to subscribers (individuals, libraries, and financial intermediaries involved in purchasing securities).

The system of private production and sale of information does not completely solve the adverse selection problem in securities markets, however, because of the so-called **free-rider problem.** The free-rider problem occurs when people who do not pay for information take advantage of the information that other people have paid for. The free-rider problem suggests that the private sale of information will be only a partial solution to the lemons problem. To see why, suppose that you have just purchased information that tells you which firms are good and which are bad. You believe that this purchase is worthwhile because you can make up the cost of acquiring this information, and then some, by purchasing the securities of good firms that are undervalued. However, when our savvy (free-riding) investor Irving sees you buying certain securities, he buys right along with you, even though he has not paid for any information. If many other investors act as Irving does, the increased demand for the undervalued good securities will cause their low price to be bid up immediately to reflect the securities' true value. As a result of all these free riders, you can no longer buy the securities for less than their true value. Now because you will not gain any extra profits from purchasing the information, you realize that you never should have paid for this information in the first place. If other investors come to the same realization, private firms and individuals may not be able to sell enough of this information to make it worth their while to gather and produce it. The weakened ability of private firms to profit from selling information will mean that less information is produced in the marketplace, and so adverse selection (the lemons problem) will still interfere with the efficient functioning of securities markets.

Government Regulation The free-rider problem prevents the private market from producing enough information to eliminate all the asymmetric information that leads to adverse selection. Could financial markets benefit from government intervention? The government could, for instance, produce information to help investors distinguish good from bad firms and provide it to the public free of charge. This solution, however, would involve the government in releasing negative information about firms, a practice that might be politically difficult. A second possibility (and one followed by the United States and most governments throughout the world) is for the government to regulate securities markets in a way that encourages firms to reveal honest information about themselves so that investors can determine how good or bad the firms are. In the United States, the Securities and Exchange Commission (SEC) is the government agency that requires firms selling their securities in public markets to adhere to standard accounting principles and to disclose information about their sales, assets, and earnings. Similar regulations are found in other countries.

The asymmetric information problem of adverse selection in financial markets helps explain why financial markets are among the most heavily regulated sectors in the economy (puzzle 5). Government regulation to increase information for investors is needed to reduce the adverse selection problem, which interferes with the efficient functioning of securities (stock and bond) markets.

Although government regulation lessens the adverse selection problem, it does not eliminate it. Even when firms provide information to the public about their sales, assets, or earnings, they *still* have more information than investors: There is a lot more to knowing the quality of a firm than is provided by statistics. Furthermore, bad firms have an incentive to make themselves look like good firms because this would enable them to fetch a higher price for their securities. Bad firms will slant the information they are required to transmit to the public, thus making it harder for investors to sort out the good firms from the bad.

Financial Intermediation So far we have seen that private production of information and government regulation to encourage provision of information do not eliminate the adverse selection problem in financial markets. How, then, can the financial structure help promote the flow of funds to people with productive investment opportunities when there is asymmetric information? A clue is provided by the structure of the used-car market.

An important feature of the used-car market is that most used cars are not sold directly by one individual to another. An individual considering buying a used car might pay for privately produced information by subscribing to a magazine like *Consumer Reports* to find out if a particular make of car has a good repair record. Nevertheless, reading *Consumer Reports* does not solve the adverse selection problem because even if a particular make of car has a good reputation, the actual car someone is trying to sell could be a lemon. The prospective buyer might also bring the used car to a mechanic for a once-over. But what if the prospective buyer doesn't know a mechanic who can be trusted or if the mechanic would charge a high fee to evaluate the car?

Because these roadblocks make it hard for individuals to acquire enough information about used cars, most used cars are not sold directly by one individual to another. Instead, they are sold by an intermediary, a used-car dealer who purchases used cars from individuals and resells them to other individuals. Used-car dealers produce information in the market by becoming experts in determining whether a car is a peach or a lemon. Once they know that a car is good, they can sell it with some form of a guarantee: either a guarantee that is explicit, such as a warranty, or an implicit guarantee in which they stand by their reputation for honesty. People are more likely to purchase a used car because of a dealer's guarantee, and the dealer is able to make a profit on the production of information about automobile quality by being able to sell the used car at a higher price than the dealer paid for it. If dealers purchase and then resell cars on which they have produced information, they avoid the problem of other people free-riding on the information they produced.

Just as used-car dealers help solve adverse selection problems in the automobile market, financial intermediaries play a similar role in financial markets. A financial intermediary such as a bank becomes an expert in the production of information about firms so that it can sort out good credit risks from bad ones. Then it can acquire funds from depositors and lend them to the good firms. Because the bank is able to lend mostly to good firms, it is able to earn a higher return on its loans than the interest it has to pay to its depositors. As a result, the bank earns a profit, which allows it to engage in this information production activity.

An important element in the ability of the bank to profit from the information it produces is that it avoids the free-rider problem by primarily making private loans rather than by purchasing securities that are traded in the open market. Because a private loan is not traded, other investors cannot watch what the bank is doing and bid up the loan's price to the point that the bank receives no compensation for the information it has produced. The bank's role as an intermediary that holds mostly nontraded loans is the key to its success in reducing asymmetric information in financial markets.

Our analysis of adverse selection indicates that financial intermediaries in general, and banks in particular because they hold a large fraction of nontraded loans, should play a greater role in moving funds to corporations than securities markets do. Our analysis thus explains puzzles 3 and 4: why indirect finance is so much more important than direct finance and why banks are the most important source of external funds for financing businesses.

Our analysis of adverse selection also explains which firms are more likely to obtain funds from banks and financial intermediaries rather than from the securities markets. The better known a corporation is, the more information about its activities is available in the marketplace. Thus it is easier for investors to evaluate the quality of the corporation and determine whether it is a good firm or a bad one. Because investors have fewer worries about adverse selection with well-known corporations, they will be willing to invest directly in their securities. Hence we have an explanation for puzzle 6: The larger and more mature a corporation is, the more information investors have about it, and the more likely it is that the corporation can raise funds in securities markets.

Collateral and Net Worth Adverse selection interferes with the functioning of financial markets only if a lender suffers a loss when a borrower is unable to make loan payments and thereby defaults. Collateral, property promised to the lender if the borrower defaults, reduces the consequences of adverse selection because it reduces the lender's losses in the event of a default. If a borrower defaults on a loan, the lender can sell the collateral and use the proceeds to make up for the losses on the loan. For example, if you fail to make your mortgage payments, the lender can take title to your house, auction it off, and use the receipts to pay off the loan. Lenders are thus more willing to make loans secured by collateral, and borrowers are willing to supply collateral because the reduced risk for the lender makes it more likely they will get the loan in the first place and perhaps at a better loan rate. The presence of adverse selection in credit markets thus provides an explanation for why collateral is an important feature of debt contracts (puzzle 7).

Net worth (also called **equity capital**), the difference between a firm's assets (what it owns or is owed) and its liabilities (what it owes), can perform a similar role to collateral. If a firm has a high net worth, then even if it engages in investments that cause it to have negative profits and so defaults on its debt payments, the lender can take title to the firm's net worth, sell it off, and use the proceeds to recoup some of the losses from the loan. In addition, the more net worth a firm has in the first place, the less likely it is to default because the firm has a cushion of assets that it can use to pay off its loans. Hence when firms seeking credit have high net worth, the consequences of adverse selection are less important and lenders are more willing to make loans. This analysis lies behind the often-heard lament, "Only the people who don't need money can borrow it!"

Summary So far we have used the concept of adverse selection to explain seven of the eight puzzles about financial structure introduced earlier: The first four emphasize the importance of financial intermediaries and the relative unimportance of securities markets for the financing of corporations; the fifth, that financial markets are among the most heavily regulated sectors of the economy; the sixth, that only large, well-established corporations have access to securities markets; and the seventh, that collateral is an important feature of debt contracts. In the next section we will see that the other asymmetric information concept of moral hazard provides additional reasons for the importance of financial intermediaries and the relative unimportance of securities markets for the financing of corporations, the prevalence of government regulation, and the importance of collateral in debt contracts. In addition, the concept of moral hazard can be used to explain our final puzzle (puzzle 8) of why debt contracts are complicated legal documents that place substantial restrictions on the behavior of the borrower.

HOW MORAL HAZARD AFFECTS THE CHOICE BETWEEN DEBT AND EQUITY CONTRACTS

Moral hazard is the asymmetric information problem that occurs after the financial transaction takes place, when the seller of a security may have incentives to hide information and engage in activities that are undesirable for the purchaser of the security. Moral hazard has important consequences for whether a firm finds it easier to raise funds with debt rather than equity contracts.

Moral Hazard in Equity Contracts: The Principal-Agent Problem

Equity contracts, such as common stock, are claims to a share in the profits and assets of a business. Equity contracts are subject to a particular type of moral hazard called the **principal-agent problem.** When managers own only a small fraction of the firm they work for, the stockholders who own most of the firm's equity (called the *principals*) are separate from the managers of the firm, who are the *agents* of the owners. This separation of ownership and control involves moral hazard in that the managers in control (the agents) may act in their own interest rather than in the interest of the stockholder-owners (the principals) because the managers have less incentive to maximize profits than the stockholder-owners do.

To understand the principal-agent problem more fully, suppose that your friend Steve asks you to become a silent partner in his ice-cream store. The store requires an investment of $10,000 to set up, but Steve has only $1000. So you purchase an equity stake (stock shares) for $9000, which entitles you to 90% of the ownership of the firm, while Steve owns only 10%. If Steve works hard to make tasty ice cream, keeps the store clean, smiles at all the customers, and hustles to wait on tables quickly, after all expenses (including Steve's salary), the store will have $50,000 in profits per year, of which Steve receives 10% ($5000) and you receive 90% ($45,000).

But if Steve doesn't provide quick and friendly service to his customers, uses the $50,000 in income to buy artwork for his office, and even sneaks off to the beach while he should be at the store, the store will not earn any profit. Steve can only earn the additional $5000 (his 10% share of the profits) over his salary if he works hard and forgoes unproductive investments (such as art for his office). Steve might decide that the extra $5000 just isn't enough to make him want to expend the effort to be a good manager; he might decide that it would be worth his while only if he earned an extra $10,000. If Steve feels this way, he does not have enough incentive to be a good manager and will end up with a beautiful office, a good tan, and a store that doesn't show any profits. Because the store won't show any profits, Steve's decision not to act in your interest will cost you $45,000 (your 90% of the profits if he had chosen to be a good manager instead).

The moral hazard arising from the principal-agent problem might be even worse if Steve were not totally honest. Because his ice-cream store is a cash business, Steve has the incentive to pocket $50,000 in cash and tell you that the profits were zero. He now gets a return of $50,000, but you get nothing.

Further indications that the principal-agent problem created by equity contracts can be severe are provided by examples of managers who build luxurious offices for themselves or drive high-priced corporate automobiles. Besides pursuing personal benefits, managers might also pursue corporate strategies (such as the acquisition of other firms) that enhance their personal power but do not increase the corporation's profitability.

The principal-agent problem would not arise if the owners of a firm had complete information about what the managers were up to and could prevent wasteful expenditures or fraud. The principal-agent problem, which is an example of moral hazard, arises only because a manager, like Steve, has more information about his activities than the stockholder does—that is, there is asymmetric information. The principal-agent problem would also not arise if Steve alone owned the store and there were no separation of ownership and control. If this were the case, Steve's hard work and avoidance of unproductive investments would yield him a profit (and extra income) of $50,000, an amount that would make it worth his while to be a good manager.

Solutions to the Principal-Agent Problem

Production of Information: Monitoring You have seen that the principal-agent problem arises because managers have more information about their activities and actual profits than stockholders do. One way for stockholders to reduce this moral hazard problem is for them to engage in a particular type of information production, the monitoring of the firm's activities: auditing the firm frequently and checking on what the management is doing. The problem is that the monitoring process can be expensive in terms of time and money, as reflected in the name economists give it, **costly state verification.** Costly state verification makes the equity contract less desirable, and it explains, in part, why equity is not a more important element in our financial structure.

As with adverse selection, the free-rider problem decreases the amount of information production that would reduce the moral hazard (principal-agent) problem. In this example, the free-rider problem decreases monitoring. If you know that other stockholders are paying to monitor the activities of the company you hold shares in, you can take a free ride on their activities. Then you can use the money you save by not engaging in monitoring to vacation on a Caribbean island. If you can do this, though, so can other stockholders. Perhaps all the stockholders will go to the islands, and no one will spend any resources on monitoring the firm. The moral hazard problem for shares of common stock will then be severe, making it hard for firms to issue them to raise capital.

Government Regulation to Increase Information As with adverse selection, the government has an incentive to try to reduce the moral hazard problem created by asymmetric information. Governments everywhere have laws to force firms to adhere to standard accounting principles that make profit verification easier. They also pass laws to impose stiff criminal penalties on people who commit the fraud of hiding and stealing profits. However, these measures can only be partly effective. Catching this kind of fraud is not easy; fraudulent managers have the incentive to make it very hard for government agencies to find or prove fraud.

Financial Intermediation Financial intermediaries have the ability to avoid the free-rider problem in the face of moral hazard. One financial intermediary that helps reduce the moral hazard arising from the principal-agent problem is the **venture capital firm.** Venture capital firms pool the resources of their partners and use the funds to help budding entrepreneurs start new businesses. In exchange for the use of the venture capital, the firm receives an equity share in the new business. Because verification of earnings and profits is so important in eliminating moral hazard, venture capital firms usually insist on having several of their own people participate as members of the managing body of the firm, the board of directors, so that they can keep a close watch on the firm's activities. When a venture capital firm supplies start-up funds, the equity in the firm is not marketable to anyone *but* the venture capital firm. Thus other investors are unable to free-ride on the verification activities of the venture capital firm. As a result of this arrangement, the venture capital firm is able to garner the full benefits of its verification activities and is given the appropriate incentives to minimize the moral hazard problem.

Debt Contracts Moral hazard arises with an equity contract, which is a claim on profits in all situations, whether the firm is making or losing money. If a contract could be structured so that moral hazard would exist only in certain situations, there would be a reduced need to monitor managers, and the contract would be more attractive than the equity contract. The debt contract has exactly these attributes because it is a contractual agreement by the borrower to pay the lender *fixed* dollar amounts at periodic intervals. When the firm has high profits, the lender receives the contractual payments and does not need to know the exact profits of the firm. If the managers are hiding profits or are pursuing activities that are personally beneficial but don't increase profitability, the lender doesn't care as long as these activities do not interfere with the ability of the firm to make its debt payments on time. Only when the firm cannot meet its debt payments, thereby being in a state of default, is there a need for the lender to verify the state of the firm's profits. Only in this situation do lenders involved in debt contracts need to act more like equity holders; now they need to know how much income the firm has in order to get their fair share.

The advantage of a less frequent need to monitor the firm, and thus a lower cost of state verification, helps explain why debt contracts are used more frequently than equity contracts to raise capital. The concept of moral hazard thus helps explain puzzle 1, why stocks are not the most important source of financing for businesses.[4]

HOW MORAL HAZARD INFLUENCES FINANCIAL STRUCTURE IN DEBT MARKETS

Even with the advantages just described, debt contracts are still subject to moral hazard. Because a debt contract requires the borrowers to pay out a fixed amount and lets them keep any profits above this amount, the borrowers have an incentive to take on investment projects that are riskier than the lenders would like.

For example, suppose that because you are concerned about the problem of verifying the profits of Steve's ice-cream store, you decide not to become an equity partner. Instead, you lend Steve the $9000 he needs to set up his business and have a debt contract that pays you an interest rate of 10%. As far as you are concerned, this is a surefire investment because there is a strong and steady demand for ice cream in your neighborhood. However, once you give Steve the funds, he might use them for purposes other than you intended. Instead of opening up the ice-cream store, Steve might use your $9000 loan to invest in

---

[4]Another factor that encourages the use of debt contracts rather than equity contracts in the United States is our tax code. Debt interest payments are a deductible expense for American firms, whereas dividend payments to equity shareholders are not.

chemical research equipment because he thinks he has a 1-in-10 chance of inventing a diet ice cream that tastes every bit as good as the premium brands but has no fat or calories.

Obviously, this is a very risky investment, but if Steve is successful, he will become a multimillionaire. He has a strong incentive to undertake the riskier investment because the gains to him would be so large if he succeeded. You would clearly be very unhappy if Steve used your loan for the riskier investment because if he were unsuccessful, which is highly likely, you would lose most, if not all, of the money you gave him. And if he were successful, you wouldn't share in his success—you would still get only a 10% return on the loan because the principal and interest payments are fixed. Because of the potential moral hazard (Steve might use your money to finance a very risky venture), you would probably not make the loan to Steve, even though an ice-cream store in the neighborhood is a good investment that would provide benefits for everyone.

Solutions to Moral Hazard in Debt Contracts

Net Worth When borrowers have more at stake because their net worth (the difference between their assets and their liabilities) is high, the risk of moral hazard—the temptation to act in a manner that lenders find objectionable—will be greatly reduced because the borrowers themselves have a lot to lose. Let's return to Steve and his ice-cream business. Suppose that the cost of setting up either the ice-cream store or the research equipment is $100,000 instead of $10,000. So Steve needs to put $91,000 of his own money into the business (instead of $1000) in addition to the $9000 supplied by your loan. Now if Steve is unsuccessful in inventing the no-calorie nonfat ice cream, he has a lot to lose, the $91,000 of net worth ($100,000 in assets minus the $9000 loan from you). He will think twice about undertaking the riskier investment and is more likely to invest in the ice-cream store, which is more of a sure thing. Hence when Steve has more of his own money (net worth) in the business, you are more likely to make him the loan.

One way of describing the solution that high net worth provides to the moral hazard problem is to say that it makes the debt contract **incentive-compatible;** that is, it aligns the incentives of the borrower with those of the lender. The greater the borrower's net worth, the greater the borrower's incentive to behave in the way that the lender expects and desires, the smaller is the moral hazard problem in the debt contract, and the easier it is for the firm to borrow. Conversely, when the borrower's net worth is lower, the moral hazard problem is greater, and it is harder for the firm to borrow.

Monitoring and Enforcement of Restrictive Covenants As the example of Steve and his ice-cream store shows, if you could make sure that Steve doesn't invest in anything riskier than the ice-cream store, it would be worth your while to make him the loan. You can ensure that Steve uses your money for the purpose *you* want it to be used for by writing provisions (restrictive covenants) into the debt contract that restrict his firm's activities. By monitoring Steve's activities to see whether he is complying with the restrictive covenants and enforcing the covenants if he is not, you can make sure that he will not take on risks at your expense.

Restrictive covenants are directed at reducing moral hazard by either ruling out undesirable behavior or by encouraging desirable behavior. There are four types of restrictive covenants that achieve this objective:

1. Covenants can be designed to minimize moral hazard by keeping the borrower from engaging in the undesirable behavior of undertaking risky investment projects. Some such covenants mandate that a loan can be used only to finance specific activities, such as the purchase of particular equipment or inventories. Others restrict the borrowing firm from engaging in certain risky business activities, such as purchasing other businesses.

2. Restrictive covenants can encourage the borrower to engage in desirable activities that make it more likely that the loan will be paid off. One restrictive covenant of this type requires the breadwinner in a household to carry life insurance that pays off the mortgage upon that person's death. Restrictive covenants of this type for businesses focus on encouraging the borrowing firm to keep its net worth high because higher borrower net worth reduces moral hazard and makes it less likely that the lender will suffer losses. These restrictive covenants typically specify that the firm must maintain minimum holdings of certain assets relative to the firm's size.

3. Because collateral is an important protection for the lender, restrictive covenants can encourage the borrower to keep the collateral in good condition and make sure that it stays in the possession of the borrower. This is the type of covenant ordinary people encounter most often. Automobile loan contracts, for example, require the car owner to maintain a minimum amount of collision and theft insurance and prevent the sale of the car unless the loan is paid off. Similarly, the recipient of a home mortgage must have adequate insurance on the home and must pay off the mortgage when the property is sold.

4. Restrictive covenants also require a borrowing firm to provide information about its activities periodically in the form of quarterly accounting and income reports, thereby making it easier for the lender to monitor the firm and reduce moral hazard. This type of covenant may also stipulate that the lender has the right to audit and inspect the firm's books at any time.

We now see why debt contracts are often complicated legal documents with numerous restrictions on the borrower's behavior (puzzle 8): Debt contracts require complicated restrictive covenants to minimize moral hazard.

Financial Intermediation Although restrictive covenants help reduce the moral hazard problem, they do not eliminate it completely. It is almost impossible to write covenants that rule out *every* risk-taking activity. Furthermore, borrowers may be clever enough to find loopholes in restrictive covenants that make them ineffective.

Another problem with restrictive covenants is that they must be monitored and enforced. A restrictive covenant is meaningless if the borrower can violate it knowing that the lender won't check up or is unwilling to pay for legal recourse.

Because monitoring and enforcement of restrictive covenants are costly, the free-rider problem arises in the debt securities (bond) market just as it does in the stock market. If you know that other bondholders are monitoring and enforcing the restrictive covenants, you can free-ride on their monitoring and enforcement. But other bondholders can do the same thing, so the likely outcome is that not enough resources are devoted to monitoring and enforcing the restrictive covenants. Moral hazard therefore continues to be a severe problem for marketable debt.

As we have seen before, financial intermediaries, particularly banks, have the ability to avoid the free-rider problem as long as they primarily make private loans. Private loans are not traded, so no one else can free-ride on the intermediary's monitoring and enforcement of the restrictive covenants. The intermediary making private loans thus receives the benefits of monitoring and enforcement and will work to shrink the moral hazard problem inherent in debt contracts. The concept of moral hazard has provided us with additional reasons why financial intermediaries play a more important role in channeling funds from savers to borrowers than marketable securities do, as described in puzzles 1 through 4.

Summary

The presence of asymmetric information in financial markets leads to adverse selection and moral hazard problems that interfere with the efficient functioning of those markets. Solutions to these problems involve the private production and sale of information, government regulation to increase information in financial markets, the importance of collateral and net worth to debt contracts, and the use of monitoring and restrictive covenants. A key finding from our analysis is that the existence of the free-rider problem for traded securities such as stocks and bonds indicates that financial intermediaries, particularly banks, should play a greater role than securities markets in financing the activities of businesses. Economic analysis of the consequences of adverse selection and moral hazard has helped explain the basic features of our financial system and has provided solutions to the eight puzzles about our financial structure outlined at the beginning of this chapter.

APPLICATION

FINANCIAL CRISES AND AGGREGATE ECONOMIC ACTIVITY

Our economic analysis of the effects of adverse selection and moral hazard can help us understand **financial crises,** major disruptions in financial markets that are characterized by sharp declines in asset prices and the failures of many financial and nonfinancial firms. Financial crises have been common in most countries throughout history. The United States has had major financial crises in 1819, 1837, 1857, 1873, 1884, 1893, 1907, and 1929–1933, but none since then.[5] Studying financial crises is worthwhile because they have led to severe economic downturns in the past and have the potential for doing so in the future.

Financial crises occur when adverse selection and moral hazard problems in financial markets increase so much that the markets are unable to channel funds efficiently from savers to people with productive investment opportunities. As a result of this inability of financial markets to function efficiently, economic activity contracts sharply.

Factors Causing Financial Crises

Five factors in the economic environment can lead to the substantial worsening of adverse selection and moral hazard problems in financial markets, which then cause a financial crisis: increases in interest rates, stock market declines, unanticipated declines in the aggregate price level, increases in uncertainty, and bank panics.

Increases in Interest Rates As we saw earlier, individuals and firms with the riskiest investment projects are exactly those who are willing to pay the highest interest rates. If market interest rates are driven up sufficiently because of increased demand for credit or because of a decline in the money supply, good credit risks are less likely to want to borrow while bad credit risks are still willing to borrow. Because of the resulting increase in adverse selection, lenders will no longer want to make loans. The substantial decline in lending will lead to a substantial decline in investment and aggregate economic activity.

Stock Market Declines A sharp decline in the stock market can increase adverse selection and moral hazard problems in financial markets and provoke a financial crisis. A decline in the stock market means that the net worth of corporations has fallen because share prices are the valuation of a corporation's net worth. The decline in net worth as a result of a stock market decline makes lenders less willing to lend because, as we have seen, the net worth of a firm plays a role similar to that of collateral. When the value of collateral declines, it provides less protection to lenders, meaning that losses on loans are likely to be more severe. Because lenders are now less protected against the consequences

---

[5]Although we in the United States have not experienced any financial crises since the Great Depression, we have had several close calls—the October 1987 stock market crash, for example. An important reason why we have escaped financial crises is the timely action of the Federal Reserve to prevent them during episodes like that of October 1987. We look at the issue of the Fed's role in preventing financial crises in Chapter 20.

of adverse selection, they decrease their lending, which in turn causes investment and aggregate output to decline.

In addition, the decline in corporate net worth as a result of a stock market decline increases moral hazard by providing incentives for borrowing firms to make risky investments, as they now have less to lose if their investments go sour. The resulting increase in moral hazard makes lending less attractive—another reason why a stock market decline and hence a decline in net worth leads to decreased lending and economic activity.

Unanticipated Declines in the Aggregate Price Level   Unanticipated declines in the aggregate price level also decrease the net worth of firms. Because debt payments are contractually fixed in nominal terms, an unanticipated decline in the price level raises the value of firms' liabilities in *real* terms (increases the burden of the debt) but does not raise the real value of firms' assets. The result is that net worth in *real* terms (the difference between assets and liabilities in *real* terms) declines. A sharp drop in the price level, therefore, causes a substantial decline in real net worth and an increase in adverse selection and moral hazard problems facing lenders. An unanticipated decline in the aggregate price level thus leads to a drop in lending and economic activity.

Increases in Uncertainty   A dramatic increase in uncertainty in financial markets, due perhaps to the failure of a prominent financial or nonfinancial institution, a recession, or a stock market crash, makes it harder for lenders to screen good from bad credit risks. The resulting inability of lenders to solve the adverse selection problem makes them less willing to lend, which leads to a decline in lending, investment, and aggregate activity.

Bank Panics   Banks perform an important financial intermediation role by engaging in information-producing activities that facilitate productive investment for the economy. Consequently, a financial crisis in which many banks go out of business (called a **bank panic**) reduces the amount of financial intermediation undertaken by banks and so leads to a decline in investment and aggregate economic activity. A decrease in the number of banks during a financial crisis also decreases the supply of funds to borrowers, which in turn leads to higher interest rates. Since a rise in interest rates also increases adverse selection in credit markets, bank panics further intensify the decrease in economic activity through this channel as well.

Anatomy of a Financial Crisis

Now that we have examined the five factors that can produce serious disruptions in financial markets, we are ready to look at the anatomy of a financial crisis.

STUDY GUIDE

To understand fully what takes place in a financial crisis, make sure that you can state the reasons why each of the five factors—increases in interest rates, stock market declines, unanticipated declines in the aggregate price level, increases in uncertainty, and bank panics—increases adverse selection and moral hazard problems, which in turn lead to a decline in economic activity. To help you with the topic to which we turn next, you might want to refer to Figure 3, a diagram that traces the sequence of events in a financial crisis.

Most financial crises in the United States have begun with a sharp rise in interest rates, a steep stock market decline, and an increase in uncertainty resulting from a failure of major financial or nonfinancial firms (the Ohio Life Insurance & Trust Company in 1857, the Northern Pacific Railroad and Jay Cooke & Company in 1873, Grant & Ward in 1884, the National Cordage Company in 1893, the Knickerbocker Trust Company in 1907, and the Bank of the United States in 1930). During these crises, the increase in uncertainty, the rise in interest rates, and the stock market decline increased the severity of adverse selection problems in credit markets; the stock market decline also increased moral hazard problems. The rise in adverse selection and moral hazard problems then made it less attractive for lenders to lend and led to a decline in investment and aggregate economic activity.

Because of the worsening business conditions and uncertainty about their bank's health (perhaps banks would go broke), depositors began to withdraw their funds from banks. As we will see in Chapter 17, such massive withdrawals of deposits led to bank panics. The resulting decline in the number of banks raised interest rates even further and decreased the amount of financial intermediation by banks. Worsening of the problems created by adverse selection and moral hazard led to further economic contraction.

Finally, there was a sorting out of insolvent (truly bankrupt) firms from healthy firms by bankruptcy proceedings. The same process occurred for banks, often with the help of public and private authorities. Once this sorting out was complete, uncertainty in financial markets declined, the stock market underwent a recovery, and interest rates fell. The overall result was that adverse selection and moral hazard problems diminished and the financial crisis subsided. With the financial markets able to operate well again, the stage was set for the recovery of the economy.

If, however, the economic downturn led to a sharp decline in prices, the recovery process was short-circuited. In this situation, a process called **debt deflation** occurred in which a substantial decline in the price level set in, leading to a further deterioration in firms' net worth because of the increased burden of indebtedness. When debt deflation set in, the adverse selection and moral hazard problems continued to increase so that lending, investment spending, and aggregate economic activity remained depressed for a long time. The most significant financial crisis that included debt deflation was the Great Depression, the worst economic contraction in U.S. history (see Box 1).

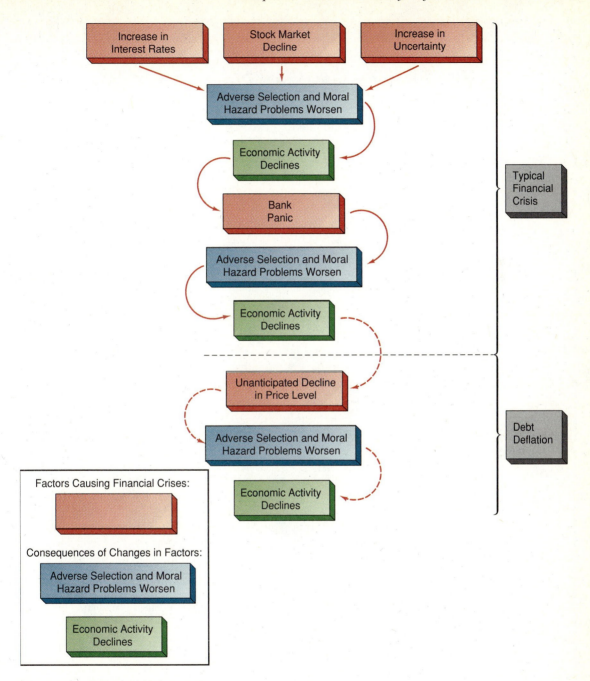

FIGURE 3 Anatomy of a Financial Crisis
The solid arrows trace the sequence of events in a typical financial crisis; the dotted arrows show the additional set of events that occur if the crisis develops into a debt deflation.

Box 1

CASE STUDY OF A FINANCIAL CRISIS: THE GREAT DEPRESSION

Federal Reserve officials viewed the stock market boom of 1928 and 1929, during which stock prices doubled, as excessive speculation. To curb it, they pursued a tight monetary policy to raise interest rates. The Fed got more than it bargained for with the stock market crash in October 1929.

Although the 1929 crash had a great impact on the minds of a whole generation, most people forget that by the middle of 1930, more than half of the stock market decline had been reversed. What might have been a normal recession turned into something far different, however, with adverse shocks to the agricultural sector, a continuing decline in the stock market after the middle of 1930, and a sequence of bank failures from October 1930 until March 1933 in which over one-third of the banks in the United States went out of business (events described in more detail in Chapter 17).

The continuing decline in stock prices after mid-1930 (by mid-1932 stocks had declined to 10% of their value at the 1929 peak) and the increase in uncertainty from the unsettled business conditions created by the economic contraction made adverse selection and moral hazard problems worse in the credit markets. The loss of one-third of the banks reduced the amount of financial intermediation. This intensified adverse selection and moral hazard problems, thereby decreasing the ability of financial markets to channel funds to firms with productive investment opportunities. As our analysis predicts, the amount of outstanding commercial loans fell by half from 1929 to 1933, and investment spending collapsed, declining by 90% from its 1929 level.

The short-circuiting of the process that kept the economy from recovering quickly, which it does in most recessions, occurred because of a fall in the price level by 25% in the 1930–1933 period. This huge decline in prices triggered a debt deflation in which net worth fell because of the increased burden of indebtedness borne by firms. The decline in net worth and the resulting increase in adverse selection and moral hazard problems in the credit markets led to a prolonged economic contraction in which unemployment rose to 25% of the labor force. The financial crisis in the Great Depression was the worst ever experienced in the United States, and it explains why this economic contraction was also the most severe one ever experienced in the nation.*

*See Ben Bernanke, "Nonmonetary Effects of the Financial Crisis in the Propagation of the Great Depression," *American Economic Review* 73 (1983): 257–276, for a discussion of the role of asymmetric information problems in the Great Depression period.

SUMMARY

1. There are eight basic puzzles about our financial structure. The first four emphasize the importance of financial intermediaries and the relative unimportance of securities markets for the financing of corporations; the fifth recognizes that financial markets are among the most heavily regulated sectors of the economy; the sixth states that only large, well-established corporations have access to securities markets; the seventh indicates that collateral is an important feature of debt contracts; and the eighth presents debt contracts as complicated legal documents that place substantial restrictions on the behavior of the borrower.

2. Transactions costs freeze many small savers and borrowers out of direct involvement with financial markets. Financial intermediaries can take advantage of economies of scale and are better able to develop expertise to lower transactions costs, thus enabling their savers and borrowers to benefit from the existence of financial markets.

3. Asymmetric information results in two problems: adverse selection, which occurs before the transaction, and moral hazard, which occurs after the transaction. Adverse selection refers to the fact that bad credit risks are the ones most likely to seek loans, and moral hazard refers to the risk of the borrower's engaging in activities that are undesirable from the lender's point of view.

4. Adverse selection interferes with the efficient functioning of financial markets. Solutions to the adverse selection problem include private production and sale of information, government regulation to increase information, financial intermediation, and collateral and net worth. The free-rider problem occurs when people who do not pay for information take advantage of information that other people have paid for. This problem explains why financial intermediaries, particularly banks, play a more important role in financing the activities of businesses than securities markets do.

5. Moral hazard in equity contracts is known as the principal-agent problem because managers (the agents) have less incentive to maximize profits than stockholders (the principals). The principal-agent problem explains why debt contracts are so much more prevalent in financial markets than equity contracts. Solutions to the principal-agent problem include monitoring, government regulation to increase information, and financial intermediation.

6. Solutions to the moral hazard problem in debt contracts include net worth, monitoring and enforcement of restrictive covenants, and financial intermediaries.

7. Financial crises are major disruptions in financial markets. They are caused by increases in adverse selection and moral hazard problems that prevent financial markets from channeling funds to people with productive investment opportunities, leading to a sharp contraction in economic activity. The five factors that lead to financial crises are increases in interest rates, stock market declines, unanticipated declines in the aggregate price level, increases in uncertainty, and bank panics.

KEY TERMS

collateral	free-rider problem	costly state verification	bank panic
secured debt	net worth (equity capital)	venture capital firm	debt deflation
unsecured debt		incentive-compatible	
restrictive covenants	principal-agent problem	financial crises	

QUESTIONS AND PROBLEMS

1. How can economies of scale help explain the existence of financial intermediaries?

*2. Describe two ways in which financial intermediaries help lower transactions costs in the economy.

3. Would moral hazard and adverse selection still arise in financial markets if information were not asymmetric? Explain.

*4. How do standard accounting principles required by the government help financial markets work more efficiently?

5. Do you think the lemons problem would be more severe for stocks traded on the New York Stock Exchange or those traded over-the-counter? Explain.

*6. Which firms are most likely to use bank financing rather than to issue bonds or stocks to finance their activities? Why?

7. How can the existence of asymmetric information provide a rationale for government regulation of financial markets?

*8. Would you be more willing to lend to a friend who has put all of her life savings into her business than if she had not done so? Why?

9. Rich people often worry that someone will marry them for their money. Is this a problem of adverse selection?

*10. The more collateral backing a loan, the less the lender has to worry about adverse selection." Is this statement true, false, or uncertain? Explain.

11. How does the free-rider problem aggravate adverse selection and moral hazard problems in financial markets?

*12. Explain how the separation of ownership and control in American corporations might lead to poor management.

13. Is a financial crisis more likely to occur when the economy is experiencing deflation or inflation? Explain.

*14. How can a stock market crash provoke a financial crisis?

*15. How can a sharp rise in interest rates provoke a financial crisis?

Chapter 10

FINANCIAL INNOVATION

PREVIEW   Twenty-five years ago, many of the financial instruments that we now take for granted did not exist. For example, checking accounts that earn interest (such as NOW accounts) were not available until 1972. Today the number of financial instruments available to people with large, medium, or small amounts to invest has expanded rapidly, and a number of new financial institutions (like money market mutual funds) have come into existence. What explains this revolutionary change in our financial system and the proliferation of new financial products available to consumers?

Like other industries, the financial industry is in business to earn profits by selling its products. If a soap company perceives that there is a need in the marketplace for a laundry detergent with fabric softener, it develops a product to fit the need. Similarly, financial institutions develop products to satisfy their own needs as well as those of their customers. Innovations in this industry are stimulated by many of the same factors (changes in demand and supply conditions) that stimulate innovation in other industries. Because financial institutions face more restrictive regulations than most firms in other industries, the desire to avoid burdensome regulations is an additional important factor producing financial innovation.

In this chapter we use economic analysis to explain why various innovations have occurred. Then we try to predict the course of future financial innovation—an important task for understanding what may happen to our financial system in the future. Given the current rapid pace of financial innovation, the financial system we face in the future will surely be different from the one we know today.

AN ECONOMIC ANALYSIS OF INNOVATION

Any analysis that explains innovation must address the incentives that cause innovations to appear. Economists contend that innovation is produced by the desire of individuals and businesses to maximize profits; in other words, innovation—which can be extremely beneficial to the economy—is driven by the desire to get (or stay) rich. This view leads to the following simple economic analysis: ***A change in the economic environment will stimulate a search for innovations that are likely to be profitable.***

Starting in the 1960s, individuals and financial institutions operating in financial markets were confronted with drastic changes in the economic environment: Inflation and interest rates climbed sharply and became harder to predict, a situation that changed demand conditions in financial markets. Computer technology advanced rapidly, which changed supply conditions. In addition, financial regulations became more burdensome. Financial institutions found that many of the old ways of doing business were no longer profitable; the financial services and products they had been offering to the public were not selling. Many financial intermediaries found that they were no longer able to acquire funds with their traditional financial instruments, and without these funds they would soon be out of business. To survive in the new economic environment, financial institutions had to research and develop new products and services that would meet customer needs and prove profitable, a process referred to as **financial engineering.** In their case, necessity was the mother of innovation.

Even in businesses (financial and otherwise) that were not threatened by the new economic environment, entrepreneurs recognized that changes in the financial environment could be exploited to make them rich. They began the search for new financial products and services that would be profitable. Their efforts produced many multimillionaires and led to the development of many of our present financial innovations.

STUDY GUIDE

To understand more clearly why the financial innovations discussed in this chapter have appeared, keep in mind the simple idea that each of these innovations grew out of the search for profits.

Our discussion of why financial innovation occurs suggests that there are three basic types of financial innovations: responses to changes in demand conditions, responses to changes in supply conditions, and avoidance of regulations. Now that we have an economic framework for understanding innovation, let's look at examples of financial innovations of the three basic types.

RESPONSES TO CHANGES IN DEMAND CONDITIONS

The most significant change in the economic environment that altered the demand for financial products in recent years has been the dramatic increase in the volatility of interest rates. In the 1950s, the interest rate on three-month Treasury bills fluctuated between 1.0% and 3.5%; in the 1970s, it fluctuated between 4.0%

and 11.5%. This volatility became even more pronounced in the 1980s, during which the three-month T-bill rate ranged from 5% to over 15%. We have seen in Chapter 4 (Table 2) that a rise in the interest rate from 10% to 20% would result in a capital loss of nearly 50% on a 30-year bond and a negative return of almost 40%. Large fluctuations in interest rates lead to substantial capital gains or losses and greater uncertainty about returns on investments. Recall that the risk that is related to the uncertainty about interest-rate movements and returns is called *interest-rate risk*, and high volatility of interest rates, such as we saw in the 1970s and 1980s, leads to a higher level of interest-rate risk.

We would expect the increase in interest-rate risk to increase the demand for financial products and services that could reduce that risk. This change in the economic environment would thus stimulate a search for profitable innovations that meet this new demand and would spur the creation of new financial instruments that help lower interest-rate risk. Three examples of financial innovations in the 1970s confirm this prediction: the development of adjustable-rate mortgages, the creation of the financial futures market, and the creation of an options market for financial instruments.[1]

Adjustable-Rate Mortgages

Like other investors, financial institutions find that lending is more attractive if interest-rate risk is lower. They would not want to make a mortgage loan at a 10% interest rate and two months later find that they could obtain a 12% interest rate on the same mortgage. To reduce interest-rate risk, in 1975 savings and loans in California began to issue adjustable-rate mortgages, mortgage loans on which the interest rate changes when a market interest rate (usually the Treasury bill rate) changes. Initially, an adjustable-rate mortgage might have a 5% interest rate. In six months, this interest rate might increase or decrease by the amount of the increase or decrease in, say, the six-month Treasury bill rate, and the mortgage payment would change. Because adjustable-rate mortgages allow mortgage-issuing institutions to earn higher interest rates on mortgages when rates rise, profits are kept higher during these periods.

This attractive feature of adjustable-rate mortgages has encouraged mortgage-issuing institutions to issue adjustable-rate mortgages with lower initial interest rates than on conventional fixed-rate mortgages, making them popular with many households. However, because the mortgage payment can increase with variable-rate mortgages, many households continue to prefer fixed-rate mortgages. Hence both types of mortgages are widespread.

---

[1]Interest-rate swaps, which first appeared in the early 1980s, were another important financial innovation created to reduce interest-rate risk for financial institutions, particularly banks. We discuss this financial innovation in Chapter 11.

Financial Futures Market

A futures market conducts trades of **futures contracts,** in which the seller agrees to provide a certain standardized commodity to the buyer on a specified future date at an agreed-on price.[2]. Futures markets for commodities such as wheat or pork bellies (the source of bacon) have been around for a long time, but futures contracts in which the standardized commodity is a particular type of financial instrument **(financial futures contracts)** did not appear until 1975. To understand why futures markets in financial instruments developed, we must first understand what a financial futures contract is and how it enables investors to **hedge** (protect themselves) against interest-rate risk.

For example, in December 1995, a financial futures contract for certificates of deposit (CDs) might specify that $1 million of CDs with a maturity of three months will be delivered by the seller of the contract to the buyer in June 1996. On this date, the buyer will have to purchase the $1 million of CDs with a discount yield that is stipulated in the contract price. The contract price for CDs (and also Treasury bills) is quoted as a price index that equals 100 minus the discount yield on the CD; a price of 90, for example, indicates a 10% discount yield.

To see how the financial futures contract described here can help a buyer hedge against interest-rate risk, suppose that in December 1995, Michelle the Money Manager expects that the money market mutual funds she manages will have an inflow of $1 million in June 1996. If Michelle purchases the CD futures contract in December 1995 at 90, then even if interest rates on CDs fall below 10% by June 1996, Michelle has *guaranteed* her mutual fund a 10% interest rate on the $1 million it will receive—she has been able to hedge against any interest-rate risk.[3]

Similarly, in December 1995, the First National Bank may make a commitment to loan $1 million to one of its customers in June 1996 at an interest rate of 10.5%. If interest rates on CDs rose in June 1996 to 11%, the bank would suffer a loss on the loan because the interest cost of acquiring funds would be 11%, while the interest earned on the loan would be only 10.5%. The bank can protect itself from this interest-rate risk by being the one to sell Michelle the futures contract, which promises delivery of the CDs in June 1996 with a 10% interest rate. Now the bank knows that the CDs it will deliver to Michelle in June 1996 will have an interest cost of 10% —it has *locked in* a 10% interest rate on the cost of acquiring funds to make its loan. The financial futures contract has enabled the bank to hedge against any interest-rate risk, and it definitely will make a profit on its loan.

---

[2]An important feature of trading in futures contracts is that any gains or losses in the price of the contract are settled after each day of trading. If at the end of a trading day, the price of the contract falls by $100, the buyer must immediately pay $100 into the seller's account; if the price rises by $100, the seller must immediately pay $100 into the buyer's account. On the specified day when the commodity is finally delivered, the purchaser of the contract pays the seller the difference between the agreed-on purchase price and the funds already paid into the seller's account, for a total that equals the originally agreed-on price.

[3]To simplify the discussion, the interest rates in our example are quoted on a discount yield basis.

So a financial futures market can enable both buyers and sellers of financial futures contracts to hedge against interest-rate risk. When interest-rate risk increased in the 1970s, the ability to hedge against it became especially valuable, making it more likely that a large number of investors would be willing to trade in financial futures markets. Because large trading volume would result in higher profits for those who set up a financial futures market, our economic analysis of financial innovation predicts that such a market would develop. This prediction was realized in 1975 when the Chicago Board of Trade (in which futures contracts for commodities such as wheat, corn, soybeans, and oats were already traded) created a futures market in Government National Mortgage Association (GNMA) securities.

The GNMA financial futures market was so successful that the Chicago Board of Trade (CBT) later opened futures markets in long-term U.S. Treasury

FOLLOWING THE FINANCIAL NEWS

Financial Futures

The prices for financial futures contracts are published daily. In the *Wall Street Journal,* these prices are found in the "Commodities" section under the "Interest Rate" heading of the "Futures Prices" columns. An excerpt is reproduced below.

INTEREST RATE

TREASURY BILLS (CME) – $1 mil.; pts. of 100%

	Open	High	Low	Settle	Chg	Discount Settle	Chg	Open Interest
Mar	96.55	96.55	96.49	96.53	+ .02	3.47	− .02	6,570
June	96.14	96.19	96.14	96.17	+ .02	3.83	− .02	25,792
Sept	95.83	95.89	95.79	95.84	+ .01	4.16	− .01	5,337
Dec	95.50	95.52	95.48	95.50	+ .02	4.50	− .02	2,940

Est vol 11,751; vol Tues 10,250; open int 40,639, −443.

Source: Wall Street Journal, Thursday, March 3, 1994, p. C14

Information for each contract is presented in columns, as follows. (The contract for delivery of T-bills in March 1994 is used as an example.)

Open: Opening price, which equals 100.00 minus the discount yield of the T-bills—96.55 for the March contract

High: Highest traded price that day—96.55 for the March contract

Low: Lowest traded price that day—96.49 for the March contract

Settle: Settlement price, the closing price that day—96.53 for the March contract

Chg: Change in the settlement price from the previous trading day—plus 0.02 change for the March contract

Discount Settle: Interest rate on a discount basis for delivered securities, calculated from settlement price—3.47% on T-bills delivered in March

Discount Chg: Change in interest rate (discount basis) for delivered securities from previous trading day—minus 0.02 for the March contract

Open Interest: Number of contracts outstanding—6570 for the March contract

A Global Perspective

THE GLOBALIZATION OF FINANCIAL FUTURES MARKETS

Because American futures exchanges were the first to develop financial futures, they dominated the trading of financial futures in the early 1980s. For example, in 1985, all of the top ten futures contracts were traded at exchanges in the United States. With the rapid growth of financial futures markets and the resulting high profits made by the American exchanges, foreign exchanges saw a profit opportunity and began to enter this business. By the 1990s, Eurodollar contracts traded at the London International Financial Futures Exchange, Japanese government bond contracts and Euroyen contracts traded at the Tokyo Stock Exchange, French government bond contracts traded in Le Marché à Terme des Instruments Financiers, and Nikkei 225 contracts traded at the Osaka Securities Exchange became among the most widely traded futures contracts in the world.

Foreign competition has also spurred knockoffs of the most popular financial futures contracts initially developed in the United States. These contracts traded in foreign exchanges are virtually identical to those traded in the United States and have the advantage that they can be traded when the American exchanges are closed. The movement to 24-hour-a-day trading in financial futures has been further stimulated by the development of the Globex electronic trading system, developed by the Chicago Mercantile Exchange, which allows traders throughout the world to trade futures even when the exchanges are not officially open. Financial futures trading is thus well on the way to being completely internationalized, and competition between U.S. and foreign exchanges will continue to be intense in the future.

bonds and notes, while the International Monetary Market (IMM), a subsidiary of the Chicago Mercantile Exchange (CME), organized a futures market in U.S. Treasury bills, bank CDs, and Eurodollars. The volume of trading in financial futures markets has grown to an extraordinary extent, and Treasury bonds and Eurodollars are now among the top 10 of the 100 or so standardized commodities traded in both financial and nonfinancial futures markets. Given the globalization of other financial markets in recent years, it is not surprising that increased competition from abroad has been occurring in financial futures markets as well (see Box 1).

Financial Options Market

Another financial innovation that enables investors to reduce interest-rate risk is an option contract on financial instruments. An option contract provides the right to buy (a **call option**) or sell (a **put option**) a security at a specified price, called the *exercise* or *strike price*. A call option that expires in six months' time to buy $1 million face value of three-month Treasury bills at an exercise price of $975,000 is one example; a six-month put option to sell a $100,000-face-value Treasury bond at an exercise price of $102,000 is another.

An option contract is like a form of insurance against interest-rate risk. To understand this, let us consider two examples. Suppose that Irving the Investor owns a $100,000-face-value Treasury bond that has a yield of 10% and buys a three-month put option for the bond, which gives him the right to sell the bond at an exercise price of $102,000 (which corresponds to a yield of 10%). Even if interest rates rise above 10% and the price of the bond falls below the exercise price of $102,000, Irving is protected from a loss because the option contract gives him the right to sell the bond for $102,000. Similarly, if Irving is thinking about buying the Treasury bond, he can ensure that at a minimum he will be able to obtain a 10% interest rate by buying a three-month call for the bond with an exercise price of $102,000. Now if interest rates fall below 10%, his option contract allows him to buy the bond for $102,000, providing him with a 10% interest rate.

Because option contracts provide a form of insurance, purchasers must pay a price for them called, naturally enough, a *premium*. As you would expect, the increased volatility of interest rates in the 1980s increased the demand for this type of insurance, making an option market in debt instruments potentially profitable. The Chicago Board Options Exchange (CBOE), where options for stocks had been traded since 1973, initiated trading in options for debt instruments in 1981. Currently, the CBOE and other exchanges offer options not only for Treasury bonds and bills but also for financial futures contracts.

RESPONSES TO CHANGES IN SUPPLY CONDITIONS

The most important source of the changes in supply conditions that stimulate financial innovation has been the improvement in computer and telecommunications technology. These changes have made it profitable to supply new financial products and services to the public. When computer technology that substantially lowered the cost of processing financial transactions became available, financial institutions conceived new financial products and instruments dependent on this technology that might appeal to the public. One such product was the bank credit card. Advances in computer technology and telecommunications have also improved the ability of the marketplace to acquire information about securities. These advances in information technology have led to further financial innovation, such as junk bonds, the rise in the commercial paper market, and the internationalization of financial markets. An important example of a financial innovation arising from improvements in both transaction and information technology is securitization, one of the most important financial innovations in the past two decades. Changes in supply conditions can also result from changes in government regulations. Examples of innovation in response to such changes are the appearance of discount brokers and stock index futures. These and other products and services that arose in response to supply condition changes are described in the following discussion.

Bank Credit Cards

Credit cards have been around since well before World War II. Many individual stores (Sears, Macy's, Goldwater's) institutionalized charge accounts by providing customers with credit cards that allowed them to make purchases at these stores without cash. Nationwide credit cards were not established until after World War II, when Diners Club developed one to be used in restaurants all over the country (and abroad). Similar credit card programs were started by American Express and Carte Blanche, but because of the high cost of operating these programs, cards were issued only to select persons and businesses who could afford expensive purchases.

A firm issuing credit cards earns income from loans it makes to credit card holders and from payments made by stores on credit card purchases (a percentage of the purchase price, say, 5%). A credit card program's costs arise from loan defaults, stolen cards, and the expense involved in processing credit card transactions.

Bankers saw the success of Diners Club, American Express, and Carte Blanche and wanted to share in the profitable credit card business. Several commercial banks attempted to expand the credit card business to a wider market in the 1950s, but the cost per transaction when running these programs was so high that their early attempts failed.

In the late 1960s, improved computer technology, which lowered the transactions costs for providing credit card services, made it more likely that bank credit card programs would be profitable. The banks tried to enter this business again, and this time their efforts led to the creation of two successful bank credit card programs: BankAmericard (originally started by the Bank of America but now an independent organization called VISA) and MasterCharge (now Master-Card, run by the Interbank Card Association). These programs have become phenomenally successful; more than 200 million of their cards are in use. Indeed, bank credit cards have been so profitable that nonfinancial institutions such as Sears (with its Discover card), General Motors, and AT&T have also entered the credit card business. Consumers have benefited because credit cards are more widely accepted than checks when paying for purchases (particularly abroad), and they allow consumers to take out loans more easily.

Junk Bonds

Before the advent of computers and advanced telecommunications, it was difficult to acquire information about the financial situation of firms that might want to sell securities. Because of the difficulty in screening out good from bad credit risks, the only firms that were able to sell bonds were very well established corporations that had high credit ratings.[4] Before the 1980s, then, only corporations

---

[4] The discussion of adverse selection problems in Chapter 9 provides a more detailed analysis of why only well-established firms with high credit ratings were able to sell securities.

that could issue bonds with ratings of Baa or above could raise funds selling newly issued bonds. Some firms that had fallen on bad times, so-called *fallen angels,* had previously issued long-term corporate bonds that now had ratings that had fallen below Baa, bonds that were pejoratively dubbed "junk bonds."

With the improvement in information technology in the 1970s, it became easier for investors to screen out good from bad credit risks, thus making it more likely that they would buy long-term debt securities from less well known corporations with lower credit ratings. With this change in supply conditions, we would expect that some smart individual would pioneer the concept of selling new public issues of junk bonds, not for fallen angels but for companies that had not yet achieved investment-grade status. This is exactly what Michael Milken of Drexel Burnham, an investment banking firm, started to do in 1977. Junk bonds became an important factor in the corporate bond market, with the amount outstanding exceeding $200 billion by the late 1980s. Although there was a sharp slowdown in activity in the junk bond market after Milken was indicted for securities law violations in 1989, it has heated up again in the 1990s.

Rise of the Commercial Paper Market

Recall that *commercial paper* is a short-term debt security issued by large banks and corporations. As we saw in Chapter 2, the commercial paper market has undergone tremendous growth since 1970, when there was $33 billion outstanding, to over $500 billion outstanding at the end of 1993. Indeed, commercial paper has been one of the fastest-growing money market instruments.

Improvements in information technology provide an explanation for the rapid rise of the commercial paper market. We have seen that the improvement in information technology made it easier for investors to screen out good from bad credit risks, thus making it easier for corporations to issue debt securities. Not only did this make it easier for corporations to issue long-term debt securities as in the junk bond market, but it also meant that they could raise funds by issuing short-term debt securities like commercial paper more easily. Many corporations that used to do their short-term borrowing from banks now frequently raise short-term funds in the commercial paper market instead. As we will see in later chapters when we discuss trends in the banking industry, the resulting growth of the commercial paper market has had important consequences for the health of the banking industry.

Internationalization of Financial Markets

Computers and advanced telecommunications have been a driving force behind the internationalization of financial markets. Technology to transmit share prices and information instantaneously around the world has freed dealers in New York or Tokyo from the constraints of business hours on the organized exchanges; they can now trade at any time of the day or night. The low cost of international communications is making it easier to invest abroad, and we are rapidly moving toward a world in which stocks and bonds are traded internationally 24 hours a day.

The impact of advanced telecommunications on the internationalization of financial markets was most dramatically illustrated by the Black Monday crash of 1987. Just before the crash on October 19, 1987, foreign stock markets declined substantially. As a result, when the U.S. markets opened on October 19, huge sell orders were waiting, and stock prices on the U.S. exchanges plummeted. The crash in U.S. stocks was then transmitted to foreign markets, which experienced declines of similar magnitude. For better or for worse, we now live in a world of highly integrated financial markets in which we all boom or bust together.

Securitization

Securitization is the process of transforming otherwise illiquid financial assets (such as residential mortgages) into marketable capital market securities, and its existence is the result of advances in both information and transactions technology. As we have seen, improvements in the ability to acquire information have made it easier to sell marketable capital market securities. In addition, with low transactions costs because of improvements in computer technology, financial institutions find that they can cheaply bundle together a portfolio of loans (such as mortgages) with varying small denominations (often less than $100,000), collect the interest and principal payments on the mortgages in the bundle, and then "pass them through" (pay them out) to third parties. By dividing the portfolio of loans into standardized amounts, the financial institution can then sell the claims to these interest and principal payments to third parties as securities. The standardized amounts of these securitized loans make them liquid securities, and the fact that they are made up of a bundle of loans helps diversify risk, making them desirable. The financial institution selling the securitized loans makes a profit by servicing the loans (collecting the interest and principal payments and paying them out) and charging a fee to the third party for this service.

Securitization first started in 1970 when the GNMA began a program in which it guaranteed interest and principal payments on bundles of standardized mortgages, thereby encouraging the creation of a new financial instrument, the mortgage-backed security. The guarantee of the interest and principal payments made it easy for private financial institutions such as savings and loans and commercial banks to sell a bundle of GNMA-guaranteed mortgages as a security and to pass through these payments to the owner of the security.

In the usual GNMA pass-through security, the buyer has direct ownership of a pro rata share of the portfolio of mortgage loans. Other types of mortgage-backed securities do not provide ownership of the mortgage portfolio to the buyer but are instead debt obligations of the mortgage-lending institution for which the mortgage loans are the collateral. Mortgage-backed securities continue to be the most common form of securitization. Securitization of mortgages has expanded enormously; two-thirds of all residential mortgages are now securitized, and over $1 trillion of securitized mortgages are currently outstanding.

Securitization has not stopped with mortgages, however: Securitization of automobile loans, credit card receivables, and commercial and computer leases began in the mid-1980s. Securitized automobile loans, called CARs or FASTBACs (see Box 2), with only $900 million issued in 1985, grew to a market of $10 billion the very next year. By 1989, securitized credit card receivables had surpassed $30 billion. Nonmortgage securitization is now a market in excess of $100 billion.

Computer technology has also enabled financial institutions to tailor securitization to produce securities that have payment streams considered especially desirable by the market. Collateralized mortgage obligations (CMOs), which are bonds that pass through the payments from a portfolio of mortgages, are a good example of such tailoring. Computerization enables a CMO to be split into four classes or *tranches.* The first three classes receive interest payments according to the coupon rate on the CMO, with class 1 first receiving all principal payments and prepayments from the collateralized pool of mortgages. After the class 1 bonds have been paid off, the principal payments and prepayments are used to retire the remaining classes sequentially. The fourth class, called *accrual* or *Z bonds,* receives interest and principal payments only after the other classes have been paid off. The CMO has the advantage of containing bonds of both short maturity (class 1) and long maturity (the later classes or the Z bond), thus increasing its potential market.

Although securitization could not take place without modern computer technology (think of the cost of collecting payments and paying them out by hand), technology is not the only factor encouraging it; the government has played an important role too. Securitization first started with GNMA guarantees of mortgage

WHAT'S IN A NAME?

As anyone in the advertising business knows, it's not enough to have a good product; a catchy name is a must. Even Wall Street now recognizes that a security's name can be a marketing tool. Merrill Lynch started the trend when it named its deep-discount bonds TIGRs, for Treasury Investment Growth Receipts. Salomon Brothers soon followed with its CATS, for Certificates of Accrual on Treasury Securities, and Merrill Lynch with its LYONs, for Liquid-Yield Option Notes. Securitization has spawned its own set of names too. Salomon Brothers named its securitized automobile loans backed by automobile loans CARs (Certificates of Automobile Receivables), while Drexel Burnham called its version FASTBACs (First Automotive Short-Term Bonds and Certificates). Securitized credit card receivables have been named, naturally enough, CARDs, for Certificates for Amortizing Revolving Debts. Who knows what nifty names they'll think up next?

payments and even today involves mostly assets directly or indirectly guaranteed by the government. Tax rules have also stimulated new securitized instruments. A change in IRS regulations made possible real estate mortgage investment conduits (REMICs), which are essentially CMOs with a more favorable tax treatment.

Discount Brokers and Stock Index Futures

As the securitization examples suggest, changes in supply conditions can result from changes in government regulations and can result in financial innovation. Before 1975, the stock exchanges had rules that fixed brokerage commission rates at a high level. Because brokerage firms were not allowed to compete on the basis of price, they competed instead on the quality of the services they provided. Brokerage firms supplied their customers with frequent reports on securities, had large research departments to do financial analysis, and even had fancy offices in which their customers could watch price quotations.

In 1975, the SEC changed the regulatory environment by disallowing the rules that set the high brokerage commissions, and profits could now be made in the brokerage industry by competing on price. As our analysis of financial innovation predicts, a new type of brokerage emerged—the *discount broker*. Like discount stores that have lower prices and provide fewer services, discount brokers have lower brokerage commissions but reduce the services they provide to their customers. For example, they lack large research departments to provide financial analysis and frequent reports for their customers. These discount brokers (the largest is Charles Schwab and Company) have carved out a substantial chunk of the brokerage business and have been an important factor in the drop in brokerage commission rates that has occurred since the 1975 regulatory change.

The sharp drop in brokerage commissions that occurred after 1975 was especially pronounced for traders of large blocks of stocks, pension funds, and mutual funds. The cheaper costs for these institutional investors meant that they could attract more customers, with the result that institutional investors became a more important force in the marketplace. In addition, many small investors recognized that mutual funds have a hard time beating the market, and index funds (mutual funds that focus on producing returns similar to those on broad market indexes) became increasingly popular. The increased importance of institutional investors along with the increased focus on tracking market indexes led to an increased demand for a more liquid market in a basket of stocks that track the market.

Given this need in the marketplace, a natural extension to the already successful markets in financial futures occurred in 1982. The financial innovation was futures trading in stock price indexes at the Chicago Board of Trade (CBT), the Chicago Mercantile Exchange (CME), the Kansas City Board of Trade (KCBT), and the New York Futures Exchange (NYFE), a subsidiary of the New York Stock Exchange. The futures trading in stock price indexes is now quite controversial (see Box 3) because critics assert that it has led to substantial increases in market volatility, especially in such episodes as 1987's Black Monday crash and the 190-point decline in the Dow Jones Industrial Average on Friday, October 13, 1989 (most of which occurred in the last hour of trading).

Box 3

PROGRAM TRADING AND PORTFOLIO INSURANCE: WERE THEY TO BLAME FOR THE STOCK MARKET CRASH OF 1987?

In the aftermath of the Black Monday crash on October 19, 1987, in which the stock market declined by over 20% in one day, trading strategies involving stock price index futures markets have been accused (by the Brady Commission, for example) of being culprits in the market collapse. One such strategy, called *program trading,* involves computer-directed trading between the stock index futures and the stocks whose prices are reflected in the index. Program trades are conducted to keep stock index futures and stock prices in line with each other (a process called *arbitrage*). For example, when the price of the stock index futures contract is far below the prices of the underlying stocks in the index, program traders buy index futures and sell the stocks. Critics of program trading assert that the sharp fall in stock index futures prices on Black Monday led to massive selling in the stock market to keep stock prices in line with the stock index futures prices.

Another trading strategy, called *portfolio insurance,* involves hedging against stock market declines by selling stock index futures. The idea behind this strategy is that when stock prices fall, stock index futures prices fall with them, so investors can obtain capital gains on the futures that offset the losses on the stocks they are holding. Some experts blame portfolio insurance for amplifying the crash because they feel that an increased desire to hedge stocks led to massive selling of stock index futures, which precipitated large price declines in these contracts, which in turn led to massive selling of stocks by program traders to keep prices in line.

Because they view program trading and portfolio insurance as causes of the October 1987 market collapse, critics of stock index futures have advocated restrictions on their trading. In response, certain brokerage firms, as well as organized exchanges, have placed limits on program trading. For example, the New York Stock Exchange has curbed computerized program trading when the Dow Jones Industrial Average moves by more than 50 points in one day. However, some prominent financial economists (Nobel laureate Merton Miller of the University of Chicago, for example) do not accept the hypothesis that program trading and portfolio insurance provoked the stock market crash. They believe that the prices of stock index futures primarily reflect the same economic forces that move stock prices—changes in the market's underlying assessment of the value of stocks.

AVOIDANCE OF EXISTING REGULATIONS

The process of financial innovation we have discussed so far is much like innovation in other areas of the economy: It occurs in response to changes in demand and supply conditions. However, because the financial industry is more heavily regulated than other industries, government regulation is a much greater source of innovation in this industry. Government regulation leads to financial innovation by creating incentives for firms to skirt regulations that restrict their ability to earn profits. Edward Kane describes this process of avoiding regulations as "loophole mining."[5] The economic analysis of innovation suggests that when the economic environment changes such that regulatory constraints are so burdensome that large profits can be made by avoiding them, loophole mining and innovation are more likely to occur.

Because banking is one of the most heavily regulated industries in America, loophole mining is especially likely to occur. The rise in inflation and interest rates from the late 1960s to 1980 made the regulatory constraints imposed on this industry even more burdensome. Under these circumstances, we would expect the pace of financial innovation in banking to be rapid, and, indeed, it has been.

Regulations Behind Financial Innovation

Two sets of regulations have seriously restricted the ability of banks to make profits: reserve requirements that force banks to keep a certain fraction of their deposits as reserves (deposits in the Federal Reserve System) and restrictions on the interest rates that can be paid on deposits. For the following reasons, these regulations have been among the major forces behind financial innovation in recent years.

Reserve Requirements The key to understanding why reserve requirements affect financial innovation is to recognize that they act, in effect, as a tax on deposits. Because the Fed does not pay interest on reserves, the opportunity cost of holding them is the interest that a bank could otherwise earn by lending the reserves out. For each dollar of deposits, reserve requirements therefore impose a cost on the bank equal to the interest rate that could be earned if the reserves could be lent out i times the fraction of deposits required as reserves r_D. The cost of $i \times r_D$ imposed on the bank is just like a tax on bank deposits of $i \times r_D$.

It is a great tradition to avoid taxes if possible, and banks do not act differently. Just as taxpayers look for loopholes to lower their tax bills, banks seek to in-

---

[5]Edward J. Kane, "Accelerating Inflation, Technological Innovation, and the Decreasing Effectiveness of Bank Regulation," *Journal of Finance* 36 (1981): 355–367.

crease their profits by mining loopholes and by producing new financial innovations that allow them to escape the tax on deposits imposed by reserve requirements.

Restrictions on Interest Paid on Deposits Until 1980, legislation prohibited banks in most states from paying interest on checking account deposits, and through Regulation Q, the Fed set maximum limits on the interest rate that could be paid on time deposits. The desire to avoid these **deposit rate ceilings** also produced financial innovations.

If market interest rates rose above the maximum rates that banks paid on time deposits under Regulation Q, depositors withdrew funds from banks to put them into higher-yielding securities. This loss of deposits from the banking system restricted the amount of funds that banks could lend (called **disintermediation**) and thus limited bank profits. Banks had an incentive to get around deposit rate ceilings because by so doing, they could acquire more funds to make loans and earn higher profits.

We can now look at how the desire to avoid restrictions on interest payments and the tax effect of reserve requirements led to several important financial innovations.

Eurodollars and Bank Commercial Paper

In the late 1960s, inflation was accelerating, and (as we would expect from our analysis of the Fisher effect in Chapter 6) interest rates began to rise. The tax on deposits from reserve requirements $i \times r_D$ also began to rise, and the incentives to avoid this tax increased. In addition, higher interest rates meant that market interest rates exceeded the maximum rate payable on time deposits under Regulation Q, and as market interest rates climbed to then record highs in 1969, investors reduced their time deposits to invest in higher-yielding securities. By the late 1960s, commercial banks had a strong incentive to search for new funds that would not be subject to reserve requirements and so escape the tax of $i \times r_D$ and not be subject to the interest rate ceiling set by Regulation Q.

As the economic analysis of innovation predicts, the banks began to mine loopholes and discovered two sources of funds that avoided both reserve requirements and deposit rate ceilings: Eurodollars and bank commercial paper. Because Eurodollars (deposits abroad denominated in dollars) were borrowed from banks outside the United States, they were not subject to reserve requirements or to Regulation Q. Similarly, commercial paper issued by a bank's parent holding company was not treated as deposits and so was also exempt from these regulations. Not surprisingly, the markets for Eurodollars and bank commercial paper began to expand rapidly in the late 1960s.

NOW Accounts, ATS Accounts, and Overnight Repos

The rise in interest rates in the late 1960s, which made the avoidance of restrictions on deposit rates profitable, stimulated the development of new types of checking accounts. Because of Regulation Q ceilings, savings and loans and mutual savings banks were hit especially hard by the rise in interest rates in the late 1960s. They lost large amounts of funds to financial instruments that paid higher interest rates, and they needed to find new sources of funds to continue to make profitable loans.

In 1970, as a result of diligent loophole mining, a mutual savings bank in Massachusetts struck gold by discovering a loophole in the prohibition of interest payments on checking accounts. In effect, by calling a check a negotiable order of withdrawal (NOW), accounts on which these NOWs could be written were not legally checking accounts. Hence NOW accounts were not subject to regulations on checking accounts and could pay interest. In May 1972, after two years of litigation, mutual savings banks in Massachusetts were allowed to issue NOW accounts that paid interest. Subsequently, in September 1972, the courts approved NOW accounts in New Hampshire.

NOW accounts were immediately successful in Massachusetts and New Hampshire, and they enabled savings and loans and mutual savings banks in those states to earn higher profits because they were able to attract more funds that could be loaned out. Since commercial banks did not want competition from other financial intermediaries for checking account deposits (at the time only commercial banks were legally allowed to issue checking accounts), they mounted a campaign to prevent the spread of these accounts to other states. The result was congressional legislation enacted in January 1974 that limited NOW accounts to New England. Legislation in 1980 finally authorized NOW accounts nationwide for savings and loans, mutual savings banks, and commercial banks, and similar accounts **(share draft accounts)** were authorized for credit unions.

Another innovation that enables banks to pay interest on checking accounts is the ATS (automatic transfer from savings) account. Balances above a certain amount in a checking account are automatically transferred into a savings account that pays interest. When a check is written on the ATS account, the necessary funds to cover the check are automatically transferred from the savings account into the checking account. Thus balances earning interest in a savings account are effectively part of the depositor's checking account because they are available for writing checks. Legally, however, it is the savings account and not the checking account that pays interest to the depositor.

Commercial banks provide a variant of the ATS account to their corporate depositors, which involves the use of a so-called *sweep account* to engage in overnight repurchase agreements (repos). In this type of arrangement, any balances above a certain amount in a corporation's checking account at the end of a business day are "swept out" of the account and invested in overnight repos that pay the corporation interest. (As you may recall from Chapter 2, the repo is an agreement whereby a corporation purchases Treasury bills that the bank agrees to repurchase the next day at a slightly higher price.) Again, although the checking account does not legally pay interest, in effect the corporation is receiving interest on balances that are available for writing checks.

The financial innovations of ATS accounts and overnight repo arrangements were stimulated not only by deposit rate ceilings but also by new technology. Without low-cost computers to process inexpensively the additional transactions required by these accounts, neither of these innovations would be profitable and therefore would not have been developed. Technological factors often combine with other incentives, such as the desire to get around restrictions on deposit rates, to produce financial innovation.

Money Market Mutual Funds

The desire to avoid deposit rate ceilings and the tax on deposits imposed by reserve requirements led to the development of money market mutual funds. Money market mutual funds issue shares that are redeemable at a fixed price (usually $1) by writing checks. For example, if you buy 5000 shares for $5000, the money market fund uses these funds to invest in short-term money market securities (Treasury bills, certificates of deposit, commercial paper) that provide you with interest payments. In addition, you are able to write checks up to the $5000 held as shares in the money market fund. Although money market fund shares effectively function as checking account deposits that earn interest, they are not legally deposits and so are not subject to reserve requirements or prohibitions on interest payments. For this reason they can pay higher interest rates than deposits at banks.

The first money market mutual fund was created by two Wall Street mavericks, Bruce Bent and Henry Brown, in 1971. However, the low market interest rates from 1971 to 1977 (which were just slightly above Regulation Q ceilings of 5.25% to 5.5%) kept them from being particularly advantageous relative to bank deposits. In early 1978, the situation changed rapidly as market interest rates began to climb over 10%, well above the 5.5% maximum interest rates payable on savings accounts and time deposits under Regulation Q. In 1977, money market mutual funds had assets under $4 billion; in 1978, their assets climbed to close to $10 billion; in 1979, to over $40 billion; and in 1982, to $230 billion. Currently, their assets are around $500 billion. To say the least, money market mutual funds have been a successful financial innovation, which is exactly what we would have predicted for the late 1970s and early 1980s when interest rates soared beyond Regulation Q ceilings.

APPLICATION

FUTURE EVOLUTION OF THE FINANCIAL SYSTEM

Although the evolution of our financial system is well explained by our analysis of financial innovation, useful economic analysis must also help us predict the future. This is crucial because, unfortunately, economists do not have access to crystal balls. Now we will use the economic analysis of financial innovation to explain what may happen to the financial system in years to come.

STUDY GUIDE

In the examples that follow, try to use the analysis outlined earlier in the chapter to predict what *you* think will happen to the financial system before reading the explanation in the text. This will reinforce earlier material and at the same time give you some feel for how economic analysis is applied to the real world.

What If Interest-Rate Risk Falls in the Future?

Over the past 25 years, we have witnessed an unprecedented rise in interest-rate risk. Since "what goes up must come down," it is possible that interest-rate risk will decline in the future. What effect would a decline have on the financial system?

With lower interest-rate risk, investors would have less need to protect themselves against it. As a result, less hedging would occur in financial futures markets, and so less trading of financial futures contracts would take place. In addition, there would be less demand for the insurance against interest-rate risk provided by options for debt instruments. The growth experienced in both of these markets in the late 1970s and the 1980s would slow, and the markets might even shrink. If trading volume declined sufficiently, some financial futures and options markets could disappear.[6]

What If Inflation Declines in the Future?

We have recently been through a period in which the inflation rate has declined from the very high levels in the early 1980s. If inflation should decline even further to a level that is permanently lower than it is now, how will the financial system respond?

A decline in inflation would, through the Fisher effect we described in Chapter 6, lower interest rates. The fall in interest rates would then lower the tax on deposits imposed by reserve requirements, $i \times r_D$. Since there would be

---

[6]There would also be a slowing in the growth of adjustable-rate mortgages and interest-rate swaps (discussed in Chapter 11), which are also used to protect financial institutions from interest-rate risk.

less incentive for banks to avoid this tax, they might borrow less from the bank commercial paper or Eurodollar markets, which currently have no reserve requirements, and would look for deposit business instead. Another factor that would increase the quantity of deposits is that the lower tax on deposits would allow banks to pay a higher interest rate on them and so make them more competitive with money market funds. Depositors would now find deposits more attractive relative to money market funds, deposits would rise further, and money market funds would decline.

The examples here indicate that our economic analysis of financial innovation can help us predict how the financial system may respond to possible changes. Additional examples of the usefulness of this analysis appear in the problems at the end of the chapter. However, the analysis cannot precisely predict every financial innovation of the future because the actual form an innovation takes reflects the mysterious process of human ingenuity. Technological change also plays an important role in financial innovation, and predicting technological change is notoriously difficult. Who could have imagined 30 years ago that computers that once filled large rooms would be outperformed by personal computers that fit on a lap?

The fact that economic analysis does not tell us everything we want to know about the phenomenon of financial innovation does not reduce its value. Economic analysis is a useful tool, but it has limitations, and a large part of the art of using economics to understand what is happening around us is recognizing the purposes for which it will be useful.

SUMMARY

1. The economic analysis of innovation suggests that a change in the economic environment will stimulate the search for innovations that are likely to be profitable.
2. Changes in demand conditions, especially the rise in interest-rate risk, have stimulated a search for profits that has resulted in financial innovations such as adjustable-rate mortgages, financial futures, and options for debt instruments.
3. Changes in supply conditions of three basic types have led to financial innovations. The improvement in transactions technology promoted the development of bank credit cards, while the improvement of information technology led to junk bonds, the rise of the commercial paper market, and the internationalization of financial markets. An important example of a financial innovation arising from improvements in both transactions and information technology is securitization. Changes in supply conditions stemming from changes in government regulation have produced such innovations as discount brokers and stock index futures.
4. Regulation leads to financial innovation by encouraging loophole mining. Starting in the late 1960s, for example, higher interest rates (resulting from higher inflation) combined with deposit rate ceilings and the "tax" on deposits to limit bank profits. The desire to avoid these regulations encouraged financial innovations, including NOW accounts, ATS accounts, overnight repos, and money market mutual funds.

KEY TERMS

financial engineering   hedge   securitization   disintermediation

futures contracts   call option   deposit rate ceilings   share draft accounts

financial futures contracts   put option

QUESTIONS AND PROBLEMS

*1. "Rather than view greed as a vice, we should view it as a positive element in our society that improves our well-being." Discuss this statement in the context of financial innovation.

2. What explains the appearance of futures markets for financial instruments and options markets for debt instruments in the 1970s and early 1980s?

*3. If you plan to take out a three-month loan nine months from now, how can you use the financial futures market to reduce your interest-rate risk?

4. Your rich uncle has just died and left you $1 million, but you will not receive your inheritance for six months. If interest rates are currently high, how can you use the financial futures market to make sure that you will earn a high interest rate on the $1 million when you get it? How can you use the options market?

*5. If high-speed computers had been developed ten years earlier, would the first attempts by banks to mass-merchandise credit cards have met with failure? Why or why not?

6. Why did banks devote more resources to loophole mining in the late 1960s and the 1970s than they did in the 1950s?

*7. "An important source of growth in the Eurodollar market has been government regulations." Is this statement true, false, or uncertain?

8. Why was it more likely that NOW accounts would be developed by a savings and loan or a mutual savings bank than by a commercial bank?

*9. What changes in supply conditions helped lead to the innovation of junk bonds?

10. What forces helped stimulate the growth of the commercial paper market?

Using Economic Analysis to Predict the Future

*11. If the Federal Reserve begins to pay interest on reserves in order to improve monetary control, what effect would this have on the financial system?

12. If the stock exchanges were again allowed to set minimum brokerage commissions, what would happen to the employment of financial analysts?

*13. If inflation becomes more variable in the future, would you expect to see a rise or a fall in the volume of trading in financial futures markets? In options markets for debt instruments?

14. If reserve requirements were eliminated in the future, as some economists advocate, what effects would this have on money market mutual funds?

*15. Predict what would happen to the financial system if Regulation Q ceilings were reimposed.

Chapter 11

THE BANKING FIRM AND BANK MANAGEMENT

PREVIEW Because banks (depository institutions) play such a major role in channeling funds to borrowers with productive investment opportunities, they are important in ensuring that the financial system and the economy run smoothly and efficiently. In the United States, banks supply over $5 trillion of credit: They provide loans to businesses, help us finance our college educations or the purchase of a new car or home, and provide us with services such as checking and savings accounts.

In this chapter we examine how banks, the most important of all the financial intermediaries, operate to earn the highest profits possible: how and why they make loans, how they acquire funds and manage their assets and liabilities (debts), and how they earn income. Although we focus on commercial banks because they hold over two-thirds of the assets in the banking system, the principles are equally applicable to other types of banking institutions, such as savings and loans, mutual savings banks, and credit unions.

THE BANK BALANCE SHEET

To understand how a bank operates, first we need to examine its **balance sheet,** a list of the bank's assets and liabilities. As the name implies, this list balances; that is, it has the characteristic that

$$\text{Total assets} = \text{total liabilities} + \text{capital}$$

Furthermore, a bank's balance sheet lists *sources* of bank funds (liabilities) and *uses* to which they are put (assets). Banks obtain funds by borrowing and by issuing other liabilities such as deposits. They then use these funds to acquire assets such as securities and loans. Banks make profits by charging an interest rate on their holdings of securities and loans that is higher than the expenses on their

TABLE 1 Balance Sheet of All Commercial Banks (items as % of total, end of 1993)			
Assets (Uses of Funds)*		**Liabilities (Sources of Funds)**	
Reserves	2	Checkable deposits	23
Cash items in process of collection	2	Nontransaction deposits	
Deposits at other banks	2	Savings deposits	20
Securities		Small-denomination (<$100,000) time deposits	16
U.S. government and agency	19	Large-denomination time deposits	9
State and local government and other securities	5	Borrowings	24
Loans		Bank capital	8
Commercial and industrial	16		
Real estate	25		
Consumer	10		
Interbank	4		
Other	8		
Other assets (for example, physical capital)	7		
Total	100	Total	100

*In order of decreasing liquidity.

Source: Federal Reserve *Bulletin*.

liabilities. The balance sheet of all commercial banks at the end of 1993 appears in Table 1.

Liabilities

A bank acquires funds by issuing (selling) liabilities, which are consequently also referred to as *sources of funds*. The funds obtained from issuing liabilities are used to purchase income-earning assets.

Checkable Deposits These are bank accounts that allow the owner of the account to write checks to third parties. Checkable deposits include all accounts on which checks can be drawn: non-interest-bearing checking accounts (demand deposits), interest-bearing NOW (negotiable order of withdrawal) accounts, and money market deposit accounts (MMDAs). Introduced in 1982, MMDAs have similar features to money market mutual funds and are included in the checkable deposits category. However, MMDAs differ from checkable deposits in that they are not subject to reserve requirements (discussed later in the chapter) like checkable deposits and are not included in the $M1$ definition of money. Table 1 shows that the category of checkable deposits is an important source of bank funds, making up 23% of bank liabilities. Once checkable deposits were the most important source of bank funds (over 60% of bank liabilities in 1960), but with the appearance of the new, more attractive financial instruments discussed in Chapter 10 (such as money market mutual funds), the share of checkable deposits in total bank liabilities has shrunk over time.

Checkable deposits and money market deposit accounts are payable on demand; that is, if a depositor shows up at the bank and requests payment by making a withdrawal, the bank must pay the depositor immediately. Similarly, if a person receives a check written on an account from a bank, when the bank is presented with the check it must transfer funds immediately to that person's account.

A checkable deposit is an asset for the depositor because it is part of his or her wealth. Conversely, because the depositor can withdraw funds from his or her account that the bank is obligated to pay, checkable deposits are a liability for the bank. They are usually the lowest-cost source of bank funds because depositors are willing to forgo some interest in order to have access to a liquid asset that can be used to make purchases. The bank's costs of maintaining checkable deposits include interest payments and the costs incurred in servicing these accounts—processing and storing canceled checks, preparing and sending out monthly statements, providing efficient tellers (human or otherwise), maintaining an impressive building and conveniently located branches, and advertising and marketing to entice customers to deposit their funds with a given bank. In recent years, interest paid on deposits (checkable and time) have accounted for around 40% of total bank operating expenses, while the costs involved in servicing accounts (employee salaries, building rent, and so on) have been approximately 45% of operating expenses.

Nontransaction Deposits Nontransaction deposits are the primary source of bank funds (45% of bank liabilities in Table 1). Owners cannot write checks on nontransaction deposits, but their interest rates are usually higher than those on checkable deposits. There are two basic types of nontransaction deposits: savings accounts and time deposits (also called certificates of deposit, CDs).

Savings accounts were once the most common type of nontransaction deposit. In these accounts, to which funds can be added or withdrawn at any time, transactions and interest payments are recorded in a monthly statement or in a small book (the passbook) held by the owner of the account. Technically, this form of deposit is not payable on demand (the bank *can* wait up to 30 days to pay); however, because of competition for deposits, banks allow depositors to make withdrawals from their savings accounts without delay.

Time deposits have a fixed maturity length ranging from several months to over five years and have substantial penalties for early withdrawal (the forfeiture of several months' interest). Small-denomination time deposits (deposits of less than $100,000) are less liquid for the depositor than passbook savings, earn higher interest rates, and are a more costly source of funds for the banks.

Large-denomination time deposits (CDs) are available in denominations of $100,000 or over and are typically bought by corporations or other banks. Large-denomination CDs are negotiable; like bonds, they can be resold in a secondary market before they mature. For this reason, negotiable CDs are held by corporations, money market mutual funds, and other financial institutions as alternative assets to Treasury bills and other short-term bonds. Since 1961, when they first appeared, negotiable CDs have become an important source of bank funds (9%).

Borrowings Banks obtain funds by borrowing from the Federal Reserve System, other banks, and corporations. Borrowings from the Fed are called **discount loans** (also known as *advances*). Banks also borrow reserves overnight in the federal (fed) funds market from other U.S. banks and financial institutions. Other sources of borrowed funds are loans made to banks by their parent companies (bank holding companies), loan arrangements with corporations (such as repurchase agreements), and borrowings of Eurodollars (deposits denominated in U.S. dollars residing in foreign banks or foreign branches of U.S. banks). Borrowings have become a more important source of bank funds over time: In 1960, they were only 2% of bank liabilities, whereas currently they exceed 20% of bank liabilities.

Bank Capital The final category on the liabilities side of the balance sheet is bank capital, the bank's net worth, which equals the difference between total assets and liabilities (8% of total bank assets in Table 1). The funds are raised by selling new equity (stock) or from retained earnings. Bank capital is a cushion against a drop in the value of its assets, which could force the bank into insolvency (when the value of bank assets falls below its liabilities, meaning that the bank is bankrupt). One important component of bank capital is loan loss reserves, which are described in Box 1.

Assets

A bank uses the funds that it has acquired by issuing liabilities to purchase income-earning assets. Bank assets are thus naturally referred to as *uses of funds,* and the interest payments earned on them are what enable banks to make profits.

Reserves All banks hold some of the funds they acquire as deposits in an account at the Fed. **Reserves** are these deposits plus currency that is physically held by banks (called **vault cash** because it is stored in bank vaults overnight). Although reserves currently do not pay any interest, banks hold them for two reasons. First, some reserves, called **required reserves,** are held because, by law, the Fed requires that for every dollar of checkable deposits at a bank, a certain fraction (10 cents, for example) must be kept as reserves. This fraction (10% in the example) is called the **required reserve ratio.** Additional reserves, called **excess reserves,** are held because they are the most liquid of all bank

Box 1

UNDERSTANDING LOAN LOSS RESERVES

Perhaps you have seen headlines in the press about a bank's large increase in loan loss (bad debt) reserves. Often there is confusion about loan loss reserves, perhaps because they have a similar-sounding name to the "Reserves" item on a bank's balance sheet. Actually, loan loss reserves have nothing to do with the reserves shown on the assets side of the balance sheet; rather they are a component of the liabilities item known as bank capital.

To see how loan loss reserves work, suppose that a bank suspects that some of its loans, say, $1 million worth, might prove to be bad debts that will have to be written off (valued at zero) in the future. The bank can set aside $1 million of its earnings and put it into its loan loss reserves account. Because the $1 million is now retained earnings, it adds to the difference between the bank's assets and liabilities and so increases bank capital. The fact that adding to loan loss reserves increases bank capital explains why loan loss reserves are counted as a component of capital. As a result of adding to loan loss reserves, the bank reduces its reported earnings by $1 million, even though it has not yet actually lost the $1 million—in effect, taking its lumps even before the bad debt is written off.

If the bank eventually determines that the $1 million loan will never be paid back and formally writes it off, it reduces the value of its assets by $1 million. The resulting $1 million decline in bank capital is reflected as a decrease in the loan loss reserves account by $1 million. At this time, however, reported earnings are unaffected by the loan write-off because they were reduced earlier when the bank set aside $1 million of earnings as loan loss reserves.

Banks add to loan loss reserves before a bad loan has to be written off because it is better for them to allow for the loss when they have plenty of earnings rather than to wait and find that they must take the loss when they have little in earnings to write the loan off against. In addition, adding to loan loss reserves, which reduces reported earnings, can reduce the amount of taxes a bank has to pay and is also a way of informing the bank's stockholders, depositors, and regulators about potential future losses on loans.

assets and can be used by a bank to meet its obligations when funds are withdrawn, either directly by a depositor or indirectly when a check is written on an account.

Cash Items in Process of Collection   Suppose that a check written on an account at another bank is deposited in your bank and the funds for this check have not yet been received (collected) from the other bank. The check is classified as a cash item in process of collection, and it is an asset for your bank because it is a claim on another bank for funds that will be paid within a few days.

Deposits at Other Banks Many small banks hold deposits in larger banks in exchange for a variety of services, including check collection, foreign exchange transactions, and help with securities purchases. This is an aspect of a system called *correspondent banking*.

Collectively, reserves, cash items in process of collection, and deposits at other banks are often referred to as *cash items*. In Table 1 they constitute only 6% of total assets, and their importance has been shrinking over time: In 1960, for example, they accounted for 20% of total assets.

Securities A bank's holdings of securities are an important income-earning asset: Securities (made up entirely of debt instruments for commercial banks because banks are not allowed to hold stock) are 24% of bank assets in Table 1, and they provide commercial banks with about 15% of their revenue. These securities can be classified into three categories: U.S. government and agency securities, state and local government securities, and other securities. U.S. government and agency securities are the most liquid because they can be easily traded and converted into cash with low transactions costs. Because of their high liquidity, short-term U.S. government securities are called **secondary reserves.**

State and local government securities are desirable for banks to hold not only because of their tax advantages (their interest payments are deductible from federal and sometimes state income taxes) but also because state and local governments are more likely to do business with banks that hold their securities. State and local government and other securities are less marketable (hence less liquid) and are also riskier than U.S. government securities, primarily because of default risk: There is some possibility that the issuer of the securities may not be able to make its interest payments or pay back the face value of the securities when they mature. Because these securities are less liquid and riskier than U.S. government and agency ones, their expected returns (after taxes) are highest, as the theory of asset demand predicts.

Loans Banks make their profits primarily by issuing loans. In Table 1, 63% of bank assets are in the form of loans and in recent years they have generally produced more than half of bank revenues. A loan is a liability for the individual or corporation receiving it but an asset for a bank because it provides income to the bank. Loans are typically less liquid than other assets because they cannot be turned into cash until the loan matures. If the bank makes a one-year loan, for example, it cannot get its funds back until the loan comes due in one year. Loans also have a higher probability of default than other assets. Because of the lack of liquidity and higher default risk, the bank earns its highest return on loans.

As you can see in Table 1, the largest categories of loans for commercial banks are commercial and industrial loans made to businesses and real estate loans. Commercial banks also make consumer loans and lend to each other. The bulk of these interbank loans are overnight loans lent in the federal funds market. The major difference in the balance sheets of the various depository institutions is primarily in the type of loan in which they specialize. Savings and loans and mutual savings banks, for example, specialize in residential mortgages, while credit unions tend to make consumer loans.

Other Assets   The physical capital (bank buildings, computers, and other equipment) owned by the banks is included in this category.

BASIC OPERATION OF A BANK

Before proceeding to more detailed study of how a bank manages its assets and liabilities in order to make the highest profit, you should understand the basic operation of a bank.

In general terms, banks make profits by selling liabilities with one set of characteristics (a particular combination of liquidity, risk, and return) and using the proceeds to buy assets with a different set of characteristics. This process is often referred to as *asset transformation.* Instead of making a mortgage loan directly to a neighbor, a person can hold a savings deposit that enables a bank to use the funds provided by the deposit to make the loan to the neighbor. The bank has, in effect, transformed the savings deposit (an asset held by the depositor) into a mortgage loan (an asset held by the bank).

The process of transforming assets and providing a set of services (check clearing, record keeping, credit analysis, and so forth) is like any other production process in a firm. If the bank produces desirable services at low cost and earns substantial income on its assets, it earns profits; if not, the bank suffers losses.

To make our analysis of the operation of a bank more concrete, we use a tool called a **T-account.** A T-account is a simplified balance sheet, with lines in the form of a T, that lists only the changes that occur in balance sheet items starting from some initial balance sheet position. Let's say that Jane Brown has heard that the First National Bank provides excellent service, so she opens a checking account with a $100 bill. She now has a $100 checkable deposit at the bank, which shows up as a $100 liability on the bank's balance sheet. The bank now puts her $100 bill into its vault so that the bank's assets rise by the $100 increase in vault cash. The T-account for the bank looks like this:

First National Bank			
Assets		Liabilities	
Vault cash	+ $100	Checkable deposits	+ $100

Since vault cash is also part of the bank's reserves, we can rewrite the T-account as follows:

Assets		Liabilities	
Reserves	+ $100	Checkable deposits	+ $100

Note that Jane Brown's opening of a checking account leads to *an increase in the bank's reserves equal to the increase in checkable deposits.*

If Jane had opened her account with a $100 check written on an account at another bank, say, the Second National Bank, we would get the same result. The initial effect on the T-account of the First National Bank is as follows:

Assets		Liabilities	
Cash items in process of collection	+ $100	Checkable deposits	+ $100

Checkable deposits increase by $100 as before, but now the First National Bank is owed $100 by the Second National Bank. This asset for the First National Bank is entered in the T-account as $100 of cash items in process of collection because the First National Bank will now try to collect the funds that it is owed. It could go directly to the Second National Bank and ask for payment of the funds, but if the two banks are in separate states, that would be a time-consuming and costly process. Instead, the First National Bank deposits the check in its account at the Fed, and the Fed collects the funds from the Second National Bank. The result is that the Fed transfers $100 of reserves from the Second National Bank to the First National Bank, and the final balance sheet positions of the two banks are as follows:

First National Bank			**Second National Bank**		
Assets		Liabilities	Assets		Liabilities
Reserves	+ $100	Checkable deposits + $100	Reserves	− $100	Checkable deposits − $100

The process initiated by Jane Brown can be summarized as follows: When a check written on an account at one bank is deposited in another, the bank receiving the deposit gains reserves equal to the amount of the check, while the bank on which the check is written sees its reserves fall by the same amount. Therefore, **when a bank receives additional deposits, it gains an equal amount of reserves; when it loses deposits, it loses an equal amount of reserves.**

STUDY GUIDE

T-accounts are used to study various topics throughout this text. Whenever you see a T-account, try to analyze what would happen if the opposite action were taken; for example, what would happen if Jane Brown decided to close her $100 account at the First National Bank by writing a $100 check and depositing it in a new checking account at the Second National Bank?

Now that you understand how banks gain and lose reserves, we can examine how a bank rearranges its balance sheet to make a profit when it experiences a change in its deposits. Let's return to the situation when the First National Bank has just received the extra $100 of checkable deposits. As you know, the bank is obliged to keep a certain fraction of its checkable deposits as required reserves. If the fraction (the required reserve ratio) is 10%, the First National Bank's required reserves have increased by $10, and we can rewrite its T-account as follows:

First National Bank			
Assets		Liabilities	
Required reserves	+ $10	Checkable deposits	+ $100
Excess reserves	+ $90		

Let's see how well the bank is doing as a result of the additional checkable deposits. Because reserves pay no interest, it has no income from the additional $100 of assets. But servicing the extra $100 of checkable deposits is costly because the bank must keep records, pay tellers, return canceled checks, pay for check clearing, and so forth. The bank is making a loss! The situation is even worse if the bank makes interest payments on the deposits, as with NOW accounts. If it is to make a profit, the bank must put to productive use all or part of the $90 of excess reserves it has available.

Let us assume that the bank chooses not to hold any excess reserves but to make loans instead. The T-account then looks like this:

Assets		Liabilities	
Required reserves	+ $10	Checkable deposits	+ $100
Loans	+ $90		

The bank is now making a profit because it holds short-term liabilities such as checkable deposits and uses the proceeds to buy longer-term assets such as loans with higher interest rates. This process of asset transformation is frequently described by saying that banks are in the business of "borrowing short and lending long." For example, if the loans have an interest rate of 10% per year, the bank earns $9 in income from its loans over the year. If the $100 of checkable deposits is in a NOW account with a 5% interest rate and it costs another $3 per year to service the account, the cost per year of these deposits is $8. The bank's profit on the new deposits is then $1 per year (a 1% return on assets).

GENERAL PRINCIPLES OF BANK MANAGEMENT

Now that you have some idea of how a bank operates, let's look at how a bank manages its assets and liabilities in order to earn the highest possible profit. The bank manager has four primary concerns. The first is to make sure that the bank has enough ready cash to pay its depositors when there are **deposit outflows,** that is, when deposits are lost because depositors make withdrawals and demand payment. To keep enough cash on hand, the bank must engage in **liquidity management,** the acquisition of sufficiently liquid assets to meet the bank's obligations to depositors. Second, the bank manager must minimize risk by acquiring assets that have a low rate of default and by diversifying asset holdings **(asset management)**. The third concern is to acquire funds at low cost **(liability management)**. Finally, the manager must decide the amount of capital the bank should maintain and then acquire the needed capital **(managing capital adequacy)**.

To understand bank management fully, we must go beyond the general principles of bank asset and liability management described next and look in more detail at how a bank manages its assets. The two sections following this one provide an in-depth discussion of how a bank manages **credit risk,** the risk arising because borrowers may default, and how it manages **interest-rate risk,** the riskiness of earnings and returns on bank assets that results from interest-rate changes.

Liquidity Management and the Role of Reserves

Let us see how a typical bank, the First National Bank, can deal with deposit outflows that occur when its depositors withdraw cash from checking or savings accounts or write checks that are deposited in other banks. In the example that follows, we assume that the bank has ample excess reserves and that all deposits have the same required reserve ratio of 10% (the bank is required to keep 10% of its time and checkable deposits as reserves). Suppose that the First National Bank's initial balance sheet is as follows:

Assets		Liabilities	
Reserves	$20 million	Deposits	$100 million
Loans	$80 million	Bank capital	$ 10 million
Securities	$10 million		

The bank's required reserves are 10% of $100 million, or $10 million. Since it holds $20 million of reserves, the First National Bank has excess reserves of $10 million. If a deposit outflow of $10 million occurs, the bank's balance sheet becomes

Assets		Liabilities	
Reserves	$10 million	Deposits	$90 million
Loans	$80 million	Bank capital	$10 million
Securities	$10 million		

The bank loses $10 million of deposits *and* $10 million of reserves, but since its required reserves are now 10% of only $90 million ($9 million), its reserves still exceed this amount by $1 million. In short, ***if a bank has ample reserves, a deposit outflow does not necessitate changes in other parts of its balance sheet.***

The situation is quite different when a bank holds insufficient excess reserves. Let's assume that instead of initially holding $10 million in excess reserves, the First National Bank makes loans of $10 million, so that it holds no excess reserves. Its initial balance sheet would be

Assets		Liabilities	
Reserves	$10 million	Deposits	$100 million
Loans	$90 million	Bank capital	$ 10 million
Securities	$10 million		

When it suffers the $10 million deposit outflow, its balance sheet becomes

Assets		Liabilities	
Reserves	$ 0	Deposits	$90 million
Loans	$90 million	Bank capital	$10 million
Securities	$10 million		

After $10 million has been withdrawn from deposits and hence reserves, the bank has a problem: It has a reserve requirement of 10% of $90 million, or $9 million, but it has no reserves! To eliminate this shortfall, the bank has four basic options. One is to acquire reserves to meet a deposit outflow by borrowing them from other banks in the federal funds market or by borrowing from corporations.[1] If the First National Bank acquires the $9 million shortfall in reserves by borrowing it from other banks or corporations, its balance sheet becomes

Assets		Liabilities	
Reserves	$ 9 million	Deposits	$90 million
Loans	$90 million	Borrowings from other	
Securities	$10 million	banks or corporations	$ 9 million
		Bank capital	$10 million

The cost of this activity is the interest rate on these loans, such as the federal funds rate.

A second alternative is for the bank to sell some of its securities to help cover the deposit outflow. For example, it might sell $9 million of its securities and deposit the proceeds with the Fed, resulting in the following balance sheet:

Assets		Liabilities	
Reserves	$ 9 million	Deposits	$90 million
Loans	$90 million	Bank capital	$10 million
Securities	$ 1 million		

The bank incurs some brokerage and other transactions costs when it sells these securities. The U.S. government securities that are classified as secondary reserves are very liquid, so the transactions costs of selling them are quite modest. However, the other securities the bank holds are less liquid and the transactions costs can be appreciably higher.

A third way that the bank can meet a deposit outflow is to acquire reserves by borrowing from the Fed. In our example, the First National Bank could leave its security and loan holdings the same and borrow $9 million in discount loans from the Fed. Its balance sheet would be

Assets		Liabilities	
Reserves	$ 9 million	Deposits	$90 million
Loans	$90 million	Discount loans from the Fed	$ 9 million
Securities	$10 million	Bank capital	$10 million

There are two costs associated with discount loans. First is the interest rate that must be paid to the Fed (called the **discount rate**). The second is a nonexplicit cost resulting from the Fed's discouragement of too much borrowing from it. If a bank takes out too many discount loans, the Fed may refuse to let it borrow further. In popular parlance, the Fed can "close down the discount window" for that bank.

---

[1]One way that the First National Bank can borrow from other banks and corporations is by selling negotiable certificates of deposit. This method for obtaining funds is discussed in the section on liability management.

Finally, a bank can acquire the $9 million of reserves to meet the deposit outflow by reducing its loans by this amount and depositing the $9 million it then receives with the Fed, thereby increasing its reserves by $9 million. This transaction changes the balance sheet as follows:

Assets		Liabilities	
Reserves	$ 9 million	Deposits	$90 million
Loans	$81 million	Bank capital	$10 million
Securities	$10 million		

The First National Bank is once again in good shape because its $9 million of reserves satisfies the reserve requirement.

However, this process of reducing its loans is the bank's costliest way of acquiring reserves when there is a deposit outflow. If the First National Bank has numerous short-term loans renewed at fairly short intervals, it can reduce its total amount of loans outstanding fairly quickly by *calling in* loans—that is, by not renewing some loans when they come due. Unfortunately for the bank, this is likely to antagonize the customers whose loans are not being renewed because they have not done anything to deserve such treatment. Indeed, they are likely to take their business elsewhere in the future, a very costly consequence for the bank.

A second method for reducing its loans is for the bank to sell them off to other banks. Again, this is very costly because other banks do not personally know the customers who have taken out the loans and so may not be willing to buy the loans at their full value.

The foregoing discussion explains why banks hold excess reserves even though loans or securities earn a higher return. When a deposit outflow occurs, holding excess reserves allows the bank to escape the costs of (1) borrowing from other banks or corporations, (2) selling securities, (3) borrowing from the Fed, or (4) calling in or selling off loans. ***Excess reserves are insurance against the costs associated with deposit outflows. The higher the costs associated with deposit outflows, the more excess reserves banks will want to hold.***

Just as you and I would be willing to pay an insurance company to insure us against a casualty loss such as the theft of a car, a bank is willing to pay the cost of holding excess reserves (the opportunity cost, which is the earnings forgone by not holding income-earning assets such as loans or securities) in order to insure against losses due to deposit outflows. Because excess reserves, like insurance, have a cost, banks also take other steps to protect themselves; for example, they might shift their holdings of assets to more liquid securities (secondary reserves).

STUDY GUIDE

Bank management is easier to grasp if you put yourself in the banker's shoes and imagine what you would do in the situations described. To understand a bank's possible responses to deposit outflows, imagine how you as a banker might respond to two successive deposit outflows of $10 million.

Asset Management

Now that you understand why a bank has a need for liquidity, we can examine the basic strategy a bank pursues in managing its assets. To maximize its profits, a bank must simultaneously seek the highest returns possible on loans and securities, minimize risk, and make adequate provisions for liquidity by holding liquid assets. Banks try to accomplish these three goals in four basic ways.

First, banks try to find borrowers who will pay high interest rates and are unlikely to default on their loans. They seek out loan business by advertising their borrowing rates and by approaching corporations directly to solicit loans. It is up to the bank's loan officer to decide if potential borrowers are good credit risks who will make interest and principal payments on time. Typically, banks are conservative in their loan policies; the default rate is usually less than 1%. It is important, however, that banks not be so conservative that they miss out on attractive lending opportunities that earn high interest rates.

Second, banks try to purchase securities with high returns and low risk. Third, in managing their assets, banks must attempt to minimize risk by diversifying. They accomplish this by purchasing many different types of assets (short- and long-term, U.S. Treasury, and municipal bonds) and approving many types of loans to a number of customers. Banks that have not sufficiently sought the benefits of diversification often come to regret it later. For example, banks that had overspecialized in making loans to energy companies, real estate developers, or farmers suffered huge losses in the 1980s with the slump in energy, property, and farm prices. Indeed, many of these banks went broke because they had "put too many eggs in one basket."

Finally, the bank must manage the liquidity of its assets so that it can satisfy its reserve requirements without bearing huge costs. This means that it will hold liquid securities even if they earn a somewhat lower return than other assets. The bank must decide, for example, how much excess reserves must be held to avoid costs from a deposit outflow. In addition, it will want to hold U.S. government securities as secondary reserves so that even if a deposit outflow forces some costs on the bank, these will not be terribly high. Again, it is not wise for a bank to be too conservative. If it avoids all costs associated with deposit outflows by holding only excess reserves, losses are suffered because reserves earn no interest, while the bank's liabilities are costly to maintain. The bank must balance its desire for liquidity against the increased earnings that can be obtained from less liquid assets such as loans.

Liability Management

Before the 1960s, liability management was a staid affair: For the most part, banks took their liabilities as fixed and spent their time trying to achieve an optimal mix of assets. There were two main reasons for the emphasis on asset management. First, over 60% of the sources of bank funds were obtained through checkable (demand) deposits that by law could not pay any interest. Thus banks could not actively compete with one another for these deposits, and so their amount was effectively a given for an individual bank. Second, because the markets for making overnight loans between banks were not well developed, banks rarely borrowed from other banks to meet their reserve needs.

Starting in the 1960s, however, large banks (called **money center banks**) in key financial centers began to explore ways in which the liabilities on their balance sheets could provide them with reserves and liquidity. This led to an expansion of overnight loans markets, such as the federal funds market, and the development of new financial instruments such as negotiable CDs (first developed in 1961), which enabled money center banks to acquire funds quickly.[2]

This new flexibility in liability management meant that banks could take a different approach to bank management. They no longer needed to depend on checkable deposits as the primary source of bank funds and as a result no longer treated their sources of funds (liabilities) as given. Instead, they aggressively set target goals for their asset growth and tried to acquire funds (by issuing liabilities) as they were needed.

For example, today when a money center bank finds an attractive loan opportunity, it can acquire funds by selling a negotiable CD. Or if it has a reserve shortfall, funds can be borrowed from another bank in the federal funds market without incurring high transactions costs. The federal funds market can also be used to finance loans.

The emphasis on liability management explains some of the important changes over the past three decades in the composition of banks' balance sheets. While negotiable CDs and bank borrowings have greatly increased in importance as a source of bank funds in recent years (rising from 2% of bank liabilities in 1960 to 33% by the end of 1993), checkable deposits have decreased in importance (from 61% of bank liabilities in 1960 to 23% by the end of 1993). Newfound flexibility in liability management and the search for higher profits have also stimulated banks to increase the proportion of their assets held in loans, which earn higher income (from 46% of bank assets in 1960 to 63% by the end of 1993).

Managing Capital Adequacy

Banks have to make decisions about the amount of capital they need to hold for three reasons. First, bank capital helps prevents **bank failure,** a situation in which the bank cannot satisfy its obligations to pay its depositors and other creditors. Second, the amount of capital affects returns for the owners (equity holders) of the bank. And third, a minimum amount of bank capital (bank capital requirements) is required by regulatory authorities.

---

[2]Because small banks are not as well known as money center banks and so might be a higher credit risk, they find it harder to raise funds in the negotiable CD market. Hence they do not engage nearly as actively in liability management.

How Bank Capital Helps Prevent Bank Failure Let's consider two banks with identical balance sheets, except that the High Capital Bank has a ratio of capital to assets of 10% while the Low Capital Bank has a ratio of 4%.

High Capital Bank				Low Capital Bank			
Assets		Liabilities		Assets		Liabilities	
Reserves	$10 million	Deposits	$90 million	Reserves	$10 million	Deposits	$96 million
Loans	$90 million	Bank		Loans	$90 million	Bank	
		capital	$10 million			capital	$ 4 million

Suppose that both banks got caught up in the euphoria of the real estate market in the 1980s, only to find that $5 million of their real estate loans became worthless in the 1990s. When these bad loans are written off (valued at zero), the total value of assets declines by $5 million, and so bank capital, which equals total assets minus liabilities, also declines by $5 million. The balance sheets of the two banks now look like this:

High Capital Bank				Low Capital Bank			
Assets		Liabilities		Assets		Liabilities	
Reserves	$10 million	Deposits	$90 million	Reserves	$10 million	Deposits	$96 million
Loans	$85 million	Bank		Loans	$85 million	Bank	
		capital	$ 5 million			capital	− $ 1 million

The High Capital Bank takes the $5 million loss in stride because its initial cushion of $10 million in capital means that it still has a positive net worth (bank capital) of $5 million after the loss. The Low Capital Bank, however, is in big trouble. Now the value of its assets has fallen below its liabilities, and its net worth is now −$1 million. Because the bank has a negative net worth, it is **insolvent** (bankrupt): It does not have sufficient assets to pay off all holders of its liabilities (creditors). When a bank becomes insolvent, government regulators close the bank, its assets are sold off, and its managers are fired. Since the owners of the Low Capital Bank will find their investment wiped out, they would clearly have preferred the bank to have had a larger cushion of bank capital to absorb the losses, as was the case for the High Capital Bank. We therefore see an important rationale for a bank to maintain a high level of capital: ***A bank maintains bank capital to lessen the chance that it will become insolvent.***

How the Amount of Bank Capital Affects Returns to Equity Holders Because owners of a bank must know whether their bank is being managed well, they need good measures of bank profitability. A basic measure of bank profitability is the **return on assets (ROA)**, the net profit after taxes per dollar of assets:

$$ROA = \frac{\text{net profit after taxes}}{\text{assets}}$$

The return on assets provides information on how efficiently a bank is being run because it indicates how much profits are generated on average by each dollar of assets.

However, what the bank's owners (equity holders) care about most is how much the bank is earning on their equity investment. This information is provided by the other basic measure of bank profitabilty, the **return on equity *(ROE)***, the net profit after taxes per dollar of equity capital:

$$ROE = \frac{\text{net profit after taxes}}{\text{equity capital}}$$

There is a direct relationship between the return on assets (which measures how efficiently the bank is run) and the return on equity (which measures how well the owners are doing on their investment). This relationship is determined by the so-called **equity multiplier** *(EM)*, which is the amount of assets per dollar of equity capital:

$$EM = \frac{\text{assets}}{\text{equity capital}}$$

To see this, we note that

$$\frac{\text{Net profit after taxes}}{\text{Equity capital}} = \frac{\text{net profit after taxes}}{\text{assets}} \times \frac{\text{assets}}{\text{equity capital}}$$

which, using our definitions, yields

$$ROE = ROA \times EM \qquad (1)$$

The formula in Equation 1 tells us what happens to the return on equity when a bank holds a smaller amount of capital (equity) for a given amount of assets. As we have seen, the High Capital Bank initially has $100 million of assets and $10 million of equity, which gives it an equity multiplier of 10 (= $100 million/$10 million). The Low Capital Bank, by contrast, has only $4 million of equity, so its equity multiplier is higher, equaling 25 (= $100 million/$4 million). Suppose that these banks have been equally well run so that they both have the same returns on assets of 1%. The return on equity for the High Capital Bank equals $1\% \times 10 = 10\%$, while the return on equity for the Low Capital Bank equals $1\% \times 25 = 25\%$. The equity holders in the Low Capital Bank are clearly a lot happier than the equity holders in the High Capital Bank because they are earning more than twice as high a return. We now see why owners of a bank may not want it to hold a lot of capital. ***Given the return on assets, the lower the bank capital, the higher the return for the owners of the bank.***

Trade-off Between Safety and Returns to Equity Holders We now see that bank capital has benefits and costs. Bank capital benefits the owners of a bank in that it makes their investment safer by reducing the likelihood of bankruptcy. But bank capital is costly because the higher it is, the lower will be the return on equity for a given return on assets. In determining the amount of bank capital, managers must decide how much of the increased safety that comes with higher capital (the benefit) they are willing to trade off against the lower return on equity that comes with higher capital (the cost).

In more uncertain times, when the possibility of large losses on loans increases, bank managers might want to hold more capital to protect the equity holders. Conversely, if they have confidence that loan losses won't occur, they might want to reduce the amount of bank capital, have a high equity multiplier, and thereby increase the return on equity.

Bank Capital Requirements Banks also hold capital because they are required to do so by regulatory authorities. Because of the high costs of holding capital for the reasons just described, bank managers often want to hold less bank capital than is required by the regulatory authorities. In this case, the amount of bank capital is determined by the bank capital requirements. We will discuss the details of bank capital requirements and why they are such an important part of bank regulation in Chapter 13.

Managing Bank Capital

If a bank finds that it has too high an equity multiplier and is short on bank capital, either because it feels that it doesn't have enough of a cushion to prevent bank failure or because its capital falls below capital requirements, it can deal with this problem in three ways: It can raise capital by issuing equity (common stock); it can raise capital by reducing its dividends to shareholders, thereby increasing retained earnings which it can put into its capital account; or it can keep capital at the same level but reduce the amount of its assets by making fewer loans or by selling off securities and then using the proceeds to reduce its liabilities. In recent years, many banks have experienced capital shortfalls and have had to restrict asset growth. This has had important consequences for the credit markets, discussed in the application that follows.

If a bank has a capital surplus and would like to increase its equity multiplier in order to increase the return on equity, it can achieve this by reducing its capital by paying out higher dividends to its shareholders, reducing its capital by buying back some of its shares, or keeping its capital constant but increasing the amount of its assets by acquiring new funds and then seeking out new loan business or purchasing more securities with these new funds.

APPLICATION

DID THE CAPITAL CRUNCH CAUSE A CREDIT CRUNCH IN THE EARLY 1990s?

During the 1990–1991 recession and the year following, there occurred a slow-down in the growth of credit that was unprecedented in the post–World War II era. Many economists and politicians have claimed that there was a "credit crunch" during this period in which credit was hard to get, and as a result the performance of the economy in 1990–1992 was very weak. Was the slowdown in credit growth a manifestation of a credit crunch, and if so, what caused it?

Our analysis of how a bank manages bank capital suggests that a credit crunch was likely to have occurred in 1990–1992 and that it was caused at least in part by the so-called capital crunch in which shortfalls of bank capital led to slower credit growth.

The period of the late 1980s saw a boom and then a major bust in the real estate market that led to huge losses for banks on their real estate loans. As our example on how bank capital helps prevent bank failures demonstrates, the loan losses caused a substantial fall in the amount of bank capital. At the same time, regulators were raising capital requirements (a subject discussed in Chapter 13). The resulting capital shortfalls meant that banks had either to raise new capital or to restrict their asset growth by cutting back on lending. Because of the weak economy at the time, raising new capital was extremely difficult for banks, so they chose the latter course. Banks did restrict their lending, and borrowers found it harder to obtain loans, leading to complaints by banks and their customers that the resulting credit crunch was creating a drag on the economy.[3] Not surprisingly, these complaints encouraged politicians, including the Clinton administration, to call for policies to encourage bank lending.

MANAGING CREDIT RISK

As seen in the earlier discussion of general principles of asset management, banks must make successful loans that are paid back in full (and so subject the bank to little credit risk) in order to earn high profits. The economic concepts of adverse selection and moral hazard (introduced in Chapter 2) provide a framework for understanding the principles that banks have to follow to minimize credit risk and make successful loans.[4]

Adverse selection in loan markets occurs because bad credit risks (those most likely to default on their loans) are the ones who usually line up for loans: In other words, those who are most likely to produce an *adverse* outcome are the most likely to be *selected*. Borrowers with very risky investment projects have much to gain if their projects are successful, and so they are the most eager

---

[3]As we will see in Chapter 13, not only were capital requirements raised, but also risk-based capital requirements were imposed that required even more capital if loans were made but not if banks bought government securities. The risk-based capital requirements thus encouraged banks to switch out of loans and into government securities, and this was an additional factor that led to a decline in bank lending. For a discussion of the evidence on how the capital crunch caused the credit crunch of 1990–1992, see the symposium "The Role of the Credit Slowdown in the Recent Recession" in the *Federal Reserve Bank of New York Quarterly Review,* Spring 1993.

[4]Other financial intermediaries such as insurance companies, pension funds, and finance companies also make private loans, and the credit-risk management principles we outline here apply to them as well.

to obtain loans. Clearly, however, they are the least desirable borrowers because of the greater possibility that they will be unable to pay back their loans.

Moral hazard exists in loan markets because borrowers may have incentives to engage in activities that are undesirable from the lender's point of view. In such situations, it is more likely that the lender will be subjected to the *hazard* of default. Once borrowers have obtained a loan, they are more likely to invest in high-risk investment projects—projects that pay high returns to the borrowers if successful. The high risk, however, makes it less likely that they will be able to pay the loan back.

To be profitable, banks must overcome the adverse selection and moral hazard problems that make loan defaults more likely. The attempts of banks to solve these problems help explain a number of principles for managing credit risk: screening and monitoring, establishment of long-term customer relationships, loan commitments, collateral, compensating balance requirements, and credit rationing.

Screening and Monitoring

Asymmetric information is present in loan markets because lenders have less information about the investment opportunities and activities of borrowers than borrowers do. This situation leads to two information-producing activities by banks, screening and monitoring. Indeed, Walter Wriston, a former head of Citicorp, the largest bank corporation in the United States, was often quoted as stating that the business of banking is the production of information.

Screening Adverse selection in loan markets requires that banks screen out the good credit risks from the bad ones so that loans are profitable to the banks. To accomplish effective screening, banks must collect reliable information from prospective borrowers. Effective screening and information collection together form an important principle of credit risk management.

When you go into a bank to apply for a consumer loan (such as a car loan or a mortgage to purchase a house), the first thing you are asked to do is fill out forms that elicit a great deal of information about your personal finances. You are asked about your salary, bank accounts, other assets (such as cars, insurance policies, and furnishings), and outstanding loans; your record of loan, credit card, and charge account repayments; the number of years you've worked and who your employers have been. You also are asked personal questions such as your age, marital status, and number of children. The bank uses this information to evaluate how good a credit risk you are by calculating your "credit score," a statistical measure derived from your answers that predicts whether you are likely to have trouble making your loan payments. Deciding on how good a risk you are cannot be entirely scientific, so the bank must also use judgment. The loan officer, whose job is to decide whether you should be given the loan, might call your employer or talk to some of the personal references you supplied. The officer might even make a judgment based on your demeanor or your appearance. (This is why most people dress neatly and conservatively when they go to the bank to apply for a loan.)

The process of screening and collecting information is similar when a bank makes a business loan. It collects information about the company's profits and losses (income) and about its assets and liabilities. The bank also has to evaluate the likely future success of the business. So in addition to obtaining information on such items as sales figures, a loan officer might ask questions about the company's future plans, how the loan will be used, and the competition in the industry. The officer may even visit the company to obtain a firsthand look at its operations. The bottom line is that, whether for personal or business loans, bankers need to be nosy.

Specialization in Lending   One puzzling feature of bank lending is that a bank often specializes in lending to local firms or to firms in particular industries, such as energy. In one sense, this behavior seems surprising because it means that the bank is not diversifying its portfolio of loans and thus is exposing itself to more risk. But from another perspective such specialization makes perfect sense. The adverse selection problem requires that the bank screen out bad credit risks. It is easier for the bank to collect information about local firms and determine their creditworthiness than to collect comparable information on firms that are far away. Similarly, by concentrating its lending on firms in specific industries, the bank becomes more knowledgeable about these industries and is therefore better able to predict which firms will be able to make timely payments on their debt.

Monitoring and Enforcement of Restrictive Covenants   Once a loan has been made, the borrower has an incentive to engage in risky activities that make it less likely that the loan will be paid off. To reduce this moral hazard, banks must adhere to the principle for managing credit risk that a bank should write provisions (restrictive covenants) into loan contracts that restrict borrowers from engaging in risky activities. By monitoring borrowers' activities to see whether they are complying with the restrictive covenants and by enforcing the covenants if they are not, banks can make sure that borrowers are not taking on risks at the bank's expense. The need for banks to engage in screening and monitoring explains why successful banks spend so much money on auditing and information-collecting activities.

Long-Term Customer Relationships

An additional way for banks to obtain information about their borrowers is through long-term customer relationships, another important principle of credit risk management.

If a prospective borrower has had a checking or savings account or other loans with the bank over a long period of time, a loan officer can look at past activity on the accounts and learn quite a bit about the borrower. The balances in the checking and savings accounts tell the banker how liquid the potential borrower is and at what time of year the borrower has a strong need for cash. A review of the checks the borrower has written reveals the borrower's suppliers. If the borrower has borrowed previously from the bank, the bank has a record of the loan payments. Thus long-term customer relationships reduce the costs of information collection and make it easier to screen out bad credit risks.

The need for monitoring by banks adds to the importance of long-term customer relationships. If the borrower has borrowed from the bank before, the bank has already established procedures for monitoring that customer. Therefore, the costs of monitoring long-term customers are lower than those for new customers.

Long-term relationships benefit the customers as well as the bank. A firm with a previous relationship will find it easier to obtain a loan at a low interest rate because the bank has an easier time determining if the prospective borrower is a good credit risk and incurs fewer costs in monitoring the borrower.

A long-term customer relationship has another advantage for the bank. No bank can think of every contingency when it writes a restrictive covenant into a loan contract; there will always be risky borrower activities that are not ruled out. However, what if a borrower wants to preserve a long-term relationship with a bank because it will be easier to get future loans at low interest rates? The borrower then has the incentive to avoid risky activities that would upset the bank, even if restrictions on these risky activities are not specified in the loan contract. Indeed, if a bank doesn't like what a borrower is doing even when the borrower isn't violating any restrictive covenants, it has some power to discourage the borrower from such activity: The bank can threaten not to let the borrower have new loans in the future. Long-term customer relationships therefore enable banks to deal with even unanticipated moral hazard contingencies.

The advantages of establishing long-term customer relationships suggest that closer ties between corporations and banks might be beneficial to both. One way to create these ties is for banks to hold equity stakes in companies they lend to and for banks to have members on the boards of directors of these companies. Currently, such financial arrangements do not exist in the United States. They were outlawed by legislation passed in the 1930s for reasons described in Chapter 13. They are, however, an important feature of the Japanese and German financial systems. Box 2 discusses how financial ties work in these countries to help banks cope with asymmetric information.

Loan Commitments

Banks also create long-term relationships and gather information by issuing a **loan commitment** to a commercial customer. A loan commitment is a bank's commitment (for a specified future period of time) to provide a firm with loans up to a given amount at an interest rate that is tied to some market interest rate.

A Global Perspective

Box 2

JAPANESE AND GERMAN BANKING ARRANGEMENTS: A BETTER WAY TO DEAL WITH ASYMMETRIC INFORMATION?

An important feature of the Japanese economic system is the *keiretsu,* or industrial group. Each *keiretsu* is made up of a core group of banks and other financial intermediaries that are linked to a group of industrial firms, many of which trade with each other. Linkages between firms and banks are cemented by each group member's holding equity shares in the other members. Because of their equity holdings, banks have memberships on their *keiretsu* firms' supervisory boards (boards of directors), and former bank executives are often placed in top managerial positions at these firms. Not surprisingly, banks favor firms of their *keiretsu* when making loans and hold a large fraction of these firms' debt.

Although nothing as formal or extensive as the *keiretsu* exists in Germany, German banks also hold shares in industrial firms and sit on their boards of directors.

The Japanese and German banking arrangements give banks tremendous advantages in collecting information and monitoring activities. Long-term customer relationships are strengthened because banks have ownership rights in firms to which they lend. For the reasons we discussed in the text, these stronger long-term relationships make it easier for banks to collect information and monitor firms, thus enabling banks to reduce adverse selection and moral hazard problems. In addition, because the banks have a role in the management of firms, they have timely access to information and the ability to influence management to act in the banks' interest by not investing in projects deemed too risky.

You can see that Japanese and German banking arrangements give their banks a tremendous advantage that American banks do not have. Their financial systems might be better able to channel funds to firms with the most productive investment opportunities. Should similar banking arrangements be allowed in the United States? We will return to this question when we discuss banking regulation in Chapter 13.

The majority of commercial and industrial loans are made under the loan commitment arrangement. The advantage for the firm is that it has a source of credit when it needs it. The advantage for the bank is that the loan commitment promotes a long-term relationship, which in turn facilitates information collection. In addition, provisions in the loan commitment agreement require that the firm continually supply the bank with information about the firm's income, asset and liability position, business activities, and so on. A loan commitment arrangement is a powerful method for reducing the bank's costs for screening and information collection.

Collateral and Compensating Balances

Collateral requirements for loans are important credit risk management tools. Collateral, which is property promised to the lender as compensation if the borrower defaults, lessens the consequences of adverse selection because it reduces the lender's losses in the case of a loan default. If a borrower defaults on a loan, the bank can sell the collateral and use the proceeds to make up for its losses on the loan. One particular form of collateral required when a bank makes commercial loans is called **compensating balances:** A firm receiving a loan must keep a required minimum amount of funds in a checking account at the bank. For example, a business getting a $10 million loan may be required to keep compensating balances of at least $1 million in its checking account at the bank. This $1 million in compensating balances can then be taken by the bank to make up some of the losses on the loan if the borrower defaults.

Besides serving as collateral, compensating balances help increase the likelihood that a loan will be paid off. They do this by helping the bank monitor the borrower and consequently minimize moral hazard. Specifically, by requiring the borrower to use a checking account at the bank, the bank can observe the firm's check payment practices, which may yield a great deal of information about the borrower's financial condition. For example, a sustained drop in the borrower's checking account balance may signal that the borrower is having financial trouble, or account activity may suggest that the borrower is engaging in risky activities; perhaps a change in suppliers means that the borrower is pursuing new lines of business. Any significant change in the borrower's payment procedures is a signal to the bank that it should make inquiries. Compensating balances therefore make it easier for banks to monitor borrowers more effectively and are another important credit risk management tool.

Credit Rationing

Another way in which successful banks deal with adverse selection and moral hazard is through **credit rationing:** Lenders refuse to make loans even though borrowers are willing to pay the stated interest rate or even a higher rate. Credit rationing takes two forms. The first occurs when a bank refuses to make a loan *of any amount* to a borrower, even when the borrower is willing to pay a higher interest rate. The second occurs when a bank is willing to make a loan but restricts the size of the loan to less than the borrower would like.

At first you might be puzzled by the first type of credit rationing. After all, even if the potential borrower is a credit risk, why doesn't the bank just extend the loan but at a higher interest rate? The answer is that adverse selection prevents this solution. Individuals and firms with the riskiest investment projects are exactly those that are willing to pay the highest interest rates. If a borrower took on a high-risk investment and succeeded, the borrower would become extremely rich. But a bank wouldn't want to make such a loan precisely because the investment risk is high; the likely outcome is that the borrower will *not* succeed and the bank will not be paid back. Charging a higher interest rate just makes adverse selection worse for the bank; that is, it increases the likelihood that the bank is lending to a bad credit risk. The bank would therefore rather not make any loans at a higher interest rate; instead, it would engage in the first type of credit rationing and would turn down loans.

Banks engage in the second type of credit rationing to guard against moral hazard: They grant loans to borrowers, but not loans as large as the borrowers want. Such credit rationing is necessary because the larger the loan, the greater the benefits from moral hazard. If a bank gives you a $1000 loan, for example, you are likely to take actions that enable you to pay it back because you don't want to hurt your credit rating for the future. However, if the bank lends you $10 million, you are more likely to fly off to Rio to celebrate. The larger your loan, the greater your incentives to engage in activities that make it less likely that you will repay the loan. Since more borrowers repay their loans if the loan amounts are small, banks ration credit by providing borrowers with smaller loans than they seek.

MANAGING INTEREST-RATE RISK

With the increased volatility of interest rates that occurred in the 1980s, banks became more concerned about their exposure to interest-rate risk, the riskiness of earnings and returns that is associated with changes in interest rates. To see what interest-rate risk is all about, let's again take a look at the First National Bank, which has the following balance sheet:

First National Bank			
Assets		Liabilities	
Rate-sensitive assets	$20 million	Rate-sensitive liabilities	$50 million
Variable-rate loans		Variable-rate CDs	
Short-term securities		Money market deposit	
Federal funds		accounts	
Fixed-rate assets	$80 million	Fixed-rate liabilities	$50 million
Reserves		Checkable deposits	
Long-term loans		Savings deposits	
Long-term securities		Long-term CDs	
		Equity capital	

A total of $20 million of its assets are rate-sensitive with interest rates that change frequently (at least once a year), and $80 million of its assets are fixed-rate with interest rates that remain unchanged for a long period (over a year). On the liabilities side, the First National Bank has $50 million of rate-sensitive liabilities and $50 million of fixed-rate liabilities. Suppose that interest rates rise by 5 percentage points, say, on average from 10% to 15%. The income on the assets rises by $1 million (= 5% × $20 million of rate-sensitive assets), while the payments on the liabilities rise by $2.5 million (= 5% × $50 million of rate-sensitive liabilities). The First National Bank's profits now decline by $1.5 million (= $1 million − $2.5 million). Conversely, if interest rates fall by 5 percentage points, similar reasoning tells us that the First National Bank's profits rise by $1.5 million. This example illustrates the following point: ***If a bank has more rate-sensitive liabilities than assets, a rise in interest rates will reduce bank profits and a decline in interest rates will raise bank profits.***

Gap and Duration Analysis

The sensitivity of bank profits to changes in interest rates can be measured more directly using **gap analysis,** in which the amount of rate-sensitive liabilities is subtracted from the amount of rate-sensitive assets. In our example, this calculation (called the "gap") is −$30 million (= $20 million − $50 million). By multiplying the gap times the change in the interest rate, we can immediately obtain the effect on bank profits. For example, when interest rates rise by 5 percentage points, the change in profits is 5% × −$30 million, which equals −$1.5 million, as we saw.

The analysis we just conducted is known as *basic gap analysis,* and it can be refined in two ways. Clearly, not all assets and liabilities in the fixed-rate category have the same maturity. One refinement, the *maturity bucket approach,* is to measure the gap for several maturity subintervals, called *maturity buckets,* so that effects of interest-rate changes over a multiyear period can be calculated. The second refinement, called *standardized gap analysis,* accounts for the differing degrees of rate sensitivity for different rate-sensitive assets and liabilities.

An alternative method for measuring interest-rate risk, called **duration analysis,** examines the sensitivity of the market value of the bank's total assets and liabilities to changes in interest rates. Duration analysis is based on Macaulay's concept of *duration,* which measures the average lifetime of a security's stream of payments.[5] Duration is a useful concept because it provides a good approximation of the sensitivity of a security's market value to a change in its interest rate:

---

[5]Algebraically, Macaulay's duration, *D,* is defined as

$$D = \frac{\displaystyle\sum_{\tau=1}^{N} \tau \left[CP_\tau / (1 + i)^\tau \right]}{\displaystyle\sum_{\tau=1}^{N} CP_\tau / (1 + i)^\tau}$$

where τ = time until cash payment is made
  CP_τ = cash payment (interest plus principal) at time τ
  i = interest rate
  N = time to maturity of the security

$$\begin{array}{ll} \text{Percent change} & - \text{(percentage-point change} \\ \text{in market value} \approx & \text{in interest rate)} \times \\ \text{of security} & \text{(duration in years)} \end{array}$$

where ≈ denotes "approximately equals."

Duration analysis involves using the average duration of the bank's assets and of its liabilities to see how the bank's net worth responds to a change in interest rates. Going back to our example of the First National Bank, suppose that the average duration of its assets is three years (that is, the average lifetime of the stream of payments is three years), while the average duration of its liabilities is two years. In addition, the First National Bank has $100 million of assets and $90 million of liabilities, so its bank capital is 10% of assets. With a 5-percentage-point increase in interest rates, the market value of the bank's assets falls by 15% (= −5% × 3 years), a decline of $15 million on the $100 million of assets. However, the market value of the liabilities falls by 10% (= −5% × 2 years), a decline of $9 million on the $90 million of liabilities. The net result is that the net worth (the market value of the assets minus the liabilities) has declined by $6 million, or 6% of the total original asset value. Similarly, a 5-percentage-point decline in interest rates increases the net worth of the First National Bank by 6% of the total asset value.

As our example makes clear, both duration analysis and gap analysis indicate that the First National Bank will suffer from a rise in interest rates but will gain from a fall in interest rates. Duration analysis and gap analysis are thus useful tools for telling a bank manager the bank's degree of exposure to interest-rate risk.

Strategies for Managing Interest-Rate Risk

Once Mona the Bank Manager has done her duration and gap analysis for the First National Bank, she needs to decide what alternative strategies she should pursue. If she firmly believes that interest rates will fall in the future, she may be willing to take no action because she knows that the bank has more rate-sensitive liabilities than rate-sensitive assets and so will benefit from the expected interest-rate decline. However, Mona also realizes that the First National Bank is subject to substantial interest-rate risk because there is always a possibility that interest rates will rise rather than fall. She might try to shorten the duration of the bank's assets to increase their rate sensitivity or, alternatively, lengthen the duration of the liabilities. By this adjustment of the bank's assets and liabilities, the bank will be less affected by interest-rate swings.

One problem with eliminating the First National Bank's interest-rate risk by altering the balance sheet is that doing so might be very costly in the short run. The bank may be locked into assets and liabilities of particular durations because of where its expertise lies. Financial instruments have been developed that help banks manage their interest-rate risk more easily. The *interest-rate swap,* which first appeared in the Eurobond market in 1981, is an example of such a financial instrument. Interest-rate swaps enable a financial institution that has more rate-sensitive assets than rate-sensitive liabilities to "swap" payment streams with a financial institution that has more rate-sensitive liabilities than rate-sensitive assets, thereby reducing interest-rate risk for both parties (see Box 3). The beauty of this arrangement is that it does not require either financial institution to rearrange its balance sheet; thus interest-rate swaps are a relatively low-cost way of reducing interest-rate risk.

Banks can also use the financial futures market and the options market for debt instruments to reduce interest-rate risk by hedging. Although financial futures markets and the options market for debt instruments have the advantage that they have lower transactions costs than the interest-rate swap market, they do have an important disadvantage: Contracts in these markets are standardized and cannot be tailored to the

---

Box 3

USING AN INTEREST-RATE SWAP TO ELIMINATE INTEREST-RATE RISK

To eliminate its interest-rate risk and match up the rate sensitivity of its assets and liabilities, First National Bank would, in effect, like to convert $30 million of its fixed-rate assets into $30 million of rate-sensitive assets. Suppose that another financial intermediary, say, the Friendly Finance Company, has $30 million of fixed-rate liabilities and $30 million of rate-sensitive assets, so that it would like to eliminate its interest-rate risk by, in effect, converting its $30 million of rate-sensitive assets into fixed-rate assets. An intermediary, say, an investment bank, would get these two parties together for a fee and set up an agreement whereby the First National Bank would pay the Friendly Finance Company the interest earned on the $30 million of fixed-rate assets and, in return, the Friendly Finance Company would pay the First National Bank the interest earned on the $30 million of rate-sensitive assets. This interest-rate swap would result in the complete elimination of interest-rate risk for both parties: The First National Bank would now have rate-sensitive income on $50 million of assets, which would exactly match the rate-sensitive payments on $50 million of its liabilities, and the Friendly Finance Company would have fixed-rate income on $30 million of assets, which would exactly match the fixed-rate payments on $30 million of liabilities.

precise needs of a bank. Thus interest-rate swaps, financial futures, and options for debt instruments are all used by banks to manage their interest-rate risk.

OFF-BALANCE-SHEET ACTIVITIES

Although asset and liability management has traditionally been the major concern of banks, in the more competitive environment of recent years banks have been aggressively seeking out profits by engaging in off-balance-sheet activities. **Off-balance-sheet activities** involve trading financial instruments and the generation of income from fees and loan sales, all of which affect bank profits but are not visible on bank balance sheets. Indeed, off-balance-sheet activities have been growing in importance for banks: The income from these activities as a percentage of assets has doubled since 1979.

We have already seen that banks' attempts to manage interest-rate risk have led to trading in financial futures, options for debt instruments, and interest-rate swaps. Banks engaged in international banking also conduct transactions in the foreign exchange market. All transactions in these markets are off-balance-sheet activities because they do not have a direct effect on the bank's balance sheet. Although bank trading in these markets is usually directed toward reducing risk or facilitating other bank business, banks sometimes do try to outguess the markets and engage in speculation. This speculation can be a very risky business and indeed has led to bank insolvencies—the most dramatic being the failure in 1974 of the Franklin National Bank, which collapsed because of losses in the foreign exchange market.

A second type of off-balance-sheet activity that has grown in importance in recent years involves income generated by loan sales. A **loan sale,** also called a *secondary loan participation,* involves a contract that sells all or part of the cash stream from a specific loan and thereby removes the loan from the bank's balance sheet. Banks earn profits by selling loans for an amount slightly greater than the amount of the original loan. Because the high interest rate on these loans makes them attractive, institutions are willing to buy them even though the higher price means that they earn a slightly lower interest rate than the original interest rate on the loan, usually on the order of 0.15 percentage point.

A third type of off-balance-sheet activity involves the generation of income from fees that banks receive for providing specialized services to their customers, such as making foreign exchange trades on a customer's behalf, servicing a mortgage-backed security by collecting interest and principal payments and then paying them out, guaranteeing debt securities such as banker's acceptances (the bank promises to make interest and principal payments if the party issuing the security cannot), and providing backup lines of credit. There are several types of backup lines of credit. The most important is a loan commitment, in which for a fee, the bank agrees that for a specified period of time it will provide a loan at the customer's request, up to a given dollar amount. Credit lines are also now available to bank depositors, who can write checks in excess of their deposit balances and, in effect, write themselves a loan. Other lines of credit for which banks get fees include standby letters of credit to back up issues of commercial paper and other securities and credit lines for underwriting Euronotes (called *note issuance facilities* [NIFs] and *revolving underwriting facilities* [RUFs]).

Off-balance-sheet activities involving guarantees of securities and backup credit lines increase the risk a bank faces. Even though a guaranteed security does not appear on a bank balance sheet, it still exposes the bank to default risk: If the issuer of the security defaults, the bank is left holding the bag and must pay off the security's owner. Backup credit lines also expose the bank to risk because the bank may be forced to provide loans when it does not have sufficient liquidity or when the borrower is a very poor credit risk.

Because of the increased risk that banks are facing from their off-balance-sheet activities, many are carefully scrutinizing their risk assessment procedures and are using the latest computer technology to overhaul them. As we will see in Chapter 13, bank regulators have also become concerned about increased risk from banks' off-balance-sheet activities. Banking is no longer the staid profession it once was, prompting one banker to state, "Despite all the dark suits worn by its leaders, banking is a very dynamic industry."[6]

---

[6]"Banking Takes a Beating," *Time,* December 3, 1984, p. 49.

SUMMARY

1. The balance sheet of commercial banks can be thought of as a list of the sources and uses of bank funds. The bank's liabilities are its sources of funds, which include checkable deposits, time deposits, discount loans from the Fed, borrowings from other banks and corporations, and bank capital. The bank's assets are its uses of funds, which include reserves, cash items in process of collection, deposits at other banks, securities, loans, and other assets (mostly physical capital).

2. Banks make profits through the process of asset transformation: They borrow short (accept deposits) and lend long (make loans). When a bank takes in additional deposits, it gains an equal amount of reserves; when it pays out deposits, it loses an equal amount of reserves.

3. Although more liquid assets tend to earn lower returns, banks still desire to hold them. Specifically, banks hold excess and secondary reserves because they provide insurance against the costs of a deposit outflow. Banks manage their assets to maximize profits by seeking the highest returns possible on loans and securities while at the same time trying to minimize risk and making adequate provisions for liquidity. Although liability management was once a staid affair, large (money center) banks now actively seek out sources of funds by issuing liabilities such as negotiable CDs or by actively borrowing from other banks and corporations. Banks manage the amount of capital they hold to prevent bank failure and to meet bank capital requirements set by the regulatory authorities. However, they do not want to hold too much

capital because by so doing they will lower the returns to equity holders.

4. The concepts of adverse selection and moral hazard explain many credit risk management principles involving loan activities: screening and monitoring, establishment of long-term customer relationships and loan commitments, collateral and compensating balances, and credit rationing.

5. With the increased volatility of interest rates that occurred in the 1980s, banks became more concerned about their exposure to interest-rate risk. Gap and duration analyses tell a bank if it has more rate-sensitive liabilities than assets (in which case a rise in interest rates will reduce bank profits and a fall in interest rates will raise bank profits). Banks manage their interest-rate risk not only by modifying their balance sheets but also by trading interest-rate swaps, financial futures, and options for financial instruments.

6. Off-balance-sheet activities consist of trading financial instruments and generating income from fees and loan sales, all of which affect bank profits but are not visible on bank balance sheets. Because these off-balance-sheet activities expose banks to increased risk, many banks are using the latest computer technology to update their risk assessment procedures.

KEY TERMS

balance sheet	T-account	discount rate	compensating balances
discount loans	deposit outflows	money center banks	credit rationing
reserves	liquidity management	bank failure	gap analysis
vault cash	asset management	insolvent	duration analysis
required reserves	liability management	return on assets *(ROA)*	off-balance-sheet activities
required reserve ratio	managing capital adequacy	return on equity *(ROE)*	loan sale
excess reserves		equity multiplier	
secondary reserves	credit risk	loan commitment	
	interest-rate risk		

QUESTIONS AND PROBLEMS

1. Why might a bank be willing to borrow funds from other banks at a higher rate than it can borrow from the Fed?

*2. Rank the following bank assets from most to least liquid:
  (a) Commercial loans
  (b) Securities
  (c) Reserves
  (d) Physical capital

3. Using the T-accounts of the First National Bank and the Second National Bank, describe what happens when Jane Brown writes a $50 check on her account at the First National Bank to pay her friend Joe Green, who in turn deposits the check in his account at the Second National Bank.

*4. What happens to reserves at the First National Bank if one person withdraws $1000 of cash and another person deposits $500 of cash? Use T-accounts to explain your answer.

5. The bank you own has the following balance sheet:

Assets		Liabilities	
Reserves	$ 75 million	Deposits	$500 million
Loans	$525 million	Bank capital	$100 million

If the bank suffers a deposit outflow of $50 million with a required reserve ratio on deposits of 10%, what actions must you take to keep your bank from failing?

*6. If a deposit outflow of $50 million occurs, which balance sheet would a bank rather have initially, the balance sheet in Problem 5 or the following balance sheet? Why?

Assets		Liabilities	
Reserves	$100 million	Deposits	$500 million
Securities	$500 million	Bank capital	$100 million

7. Why has the development of overnight loan markets made it more likely that banks will hold fewer excess reserves?

*8. If the bank you own has no excess reserves and a sound customer comes in asking for a loan, should you automatically turn the customer down, explaining that you don't have any excess reserves to loan out? Why or why not? What options are available for you to provide the funds your customer needs?

9. If a bank finds that its *ROE* is too low because it has too much bank capital, what can it do to raise its *ROE?*

*10. If a bank is falling short of meeting its capital requirements by $1 million, what three things can it do to rectify the situation?

11. Why is being nosy a desirable trait for a banker?

*12. A bank almost always insists that the firms it lends to keep compensating balances at the bank. Why?

13. "Because diversification is a desirable strategy for avoiding risk, it never makes sense for a bank to specialize in making specific types of loans." Is this statement true, false, or uncertain? Explain.

*14. Suppose that you are the manager of a bank whose $75 billion of assets have an average duration of four years, while its $75 billion of liabilities have an average duration of six years. Conduct a duration analysis for the bank, and show what will happen to the net worth of the bank if interest rates rise by 2 percentage points. What actions could you take to reduce the bank's interest-rate risk?

15. Suppose that you are the manager of a bank that has $15 million of fixed-rate assets, $30 million of rate-sensitive assets, $25 million of fixed-rate liabilities, and $20 million of rate-sensitive liabilities. Conduct a gap analysis for the bank, and show what will happen to bank profits if interest rates rise by 5 percentage points. What actions could you take to reduce the bank's interest-rate risk?

Chapter 12

THE BANKING INDUSTRY: AN INDUSTRY IN TRANSITION

PREVIEW The operations of individual banks (how they acquire, use, and manage funds to make a profit) are roughly similar throughout the world. In all countries, banks are financial intermediaries in the business of earning profits. When you consider the structure and operation of the banking industry as a whole, however, the United States is in a class by itself. In most countries, four or five large banks typically dominate the banking industry, but in the United States there are on the order of 12,000 commercial banks, 2000 savings and loan associations, 500 mutual savings banks, and 13,000 credit unions.

Is more better? Does this diversity mean that the American banking system is more competitive and therefore more economically efficient and sound than banking systems in other countries? What in the American economic and political system explains this large number of banking institutions? In this chapter we try to answer these questions by examining the historical trends in and overall structure of the banking industry. We see that in recent years, the banking industry has been in a transition to a smaller industry. An important task of this chapter is to explain why this decline in the industry has occurred.

We start the chapter by examining the commercial banking industry in detail and then go on to look at the thrift industry, which includes savings and loan associations, mutual savings banks, and credit unions. We spend more time on commercial banks because they are by far the largest depository institutions, accounting for over two-thirds of the deposits in the banking system. In addition to looking at our domestic banking system, we also examine the forces behind the growth in international banking to see how it has affected us in the United States. Finally, we examine trends in the banking industry and explore why this industry has been in decline.

HISTORICAL DEVELOPMENT OF THE BANKING SYSTEM

The modern commercial banking industry began in America when the Bank of North America was chartered in Philadelphia in 1782. With the success of this bank, other banks opened for business, and the banking industry was off and running. (As a study aid, Figure 1 provides a time line of the most important dates in the history of American banking before World War II.)

A major controversy involving the industry in its early years was whether the federal government or the states should charter banks. The Federalists, particularly Alexander Hamilton, advocated greater centralized control of banking and federal chartering of banks. Their efforts led to the creation in 1791 of the Bank of the United States, which had elements of both a private and a **central bank,** a government institution that has responsibility for the amount of money and credit supplied in the economy as a whole. Agricultural and other interests, however, were quite suspicious of centralized power and hence advocated chartering by the states. Furthermore, their distrust of moneyed interests in the big cities led to political pressures to eliminate the Bank of the United States, and in 1811 their efforts met with success when its charter was not renewed. Because of abuses by state banks and the clear need for a central bank to help the federal government raise funds during the War of 1812, Congress was stimulated to create the Second Bank of the United States in 1816. The tensions between advocates and opponents of centralized banking power were a recurrent theme during the operation of this second attempt at central banking in the United States, and with the election of Andrew Jackson, a strong advocate of states' rights, the fate of the Second Bank was sealed. After the election in 1832, Jackson vetoed the rechartering of the Second Bank of the United States as a national bank, and its charter lapsed in 1836.

Until 1863, all commercial banks in the United States were chartered by the

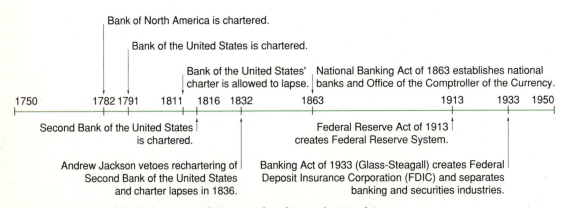

FIGURE 1 Time Line of the Early History of Commercial Banking in the United States

banking commission of the state in which each operated. No national currency existed, and banks obtained funds primarily by issuing *banknotes* (currency circulated by the banks that could be redeemed for gold). Because banking regulations were extremely lax in many states, banks regularly failed due to fraud or lack of sufficient bank capital; their banknotes became worthless.

To eliminate the abuses of the state-chartered banks (called **state banks**), the National Banking Act of 1863 (and subsequent amendments to it) created a new banking system of federally chartered banks (called **national banks**), supervised by the Office of the Comptroller of the Currency, a department of the U.S. Treasury. This legislation was originally intended to dry up sources of funds to state banks by imposing a prohibitive tax on their banknotes while leaving the banknotes of the federally chartered banks untaxed. The state banks cleverly escaped extinction by acquiring funds by accepting deposits. As a result, today the United States has a **dual banking system** in which banks supervised by the federal government and banks supervised by the states operate side by side.

Central banking did not reappear in this country until the Federal Reserve System (the Fed) was created in 1913 to promote an even safer banking system. All national banks were required to become members of the Federal Reserve System and became subject to a new set of regulations issued by the Fed. State banks could choose (but were not required) to become members of the system, and most did not because of the high costs of membership stemming from the Fed's regulations.

During the Great Depression years from 1930 to 1933, some 9000 bank failures wiped out the savings of many depositors at commercial banks. To prevent future depositor losses from such failures, banking legislation in 1933 established the Federal Deposit Insurance Corporation (FDIC), which provided federal insurance on bank deposits. Member banks of the Federal Reserve System were required to purchase FDIC insurance for their depositors, and non–Federal Reserve commercial banks could choose to buy this insurance (almost all of them did). The purchase of FDIC insurance made banks subject to another set of regulations imposed by the FDIC.

Because investment banking activities of the commercial banks were blamed for many bank failures, the banking legislation in 1933 (also known as the Glass-Steagall Act) prohibited commercial banks from underwriting or dealing in corporate securities (commercial banks were allowed to sell new issues of government securities, however) and limited banks to the purchase of debt securities approved by the bank regulatory agencies. Likewise it prohibited investment banks from engaging in commercial banking activities. In effect, the Glass-Steagall Act separated the activities of commercial banks from those of the securities industry.

Under the conditions of the Glass-Steagall Act, commercial banks had to sell off their investment banking operations. The First National Bank of Boston, for example, spun off its investment banking operations into the First Boston Corporation, now one of the largest investment banking firms in America. Investment banking firms typically discontinued their deposit business, although J. P. Morgan discontinued its investment banking business and reorganized as a commercial bank; however, some senior officers of J. P. Morgan went on to organize Morgan Stanley, one of the largest investment banking firms today.

MULTIPLE REGULATORY AGENCIES

Commercial bank regulation in the United States has developed into a crazy-quilt system of multiple regulatory agencies with overlapping jurisdictions. The Office of the Comptroller of the Currency has the primary supervisory responsibility for the 3000 national banks that own more than half of the assets in the commercial banking system. The Federal Reserve and the state banking authorities jointly have primary responsibility for the 1000 state banks that are members of the Federal Reserve System. The Fed also has sole regulatory responsibility over companies that own one or more banks (called **bank holding companies**) and secondary responsibility for the national banks. The FDIC and the state banking authorities jointly supervise the 7000 state banks that have FDIC insurance but are not members of the Federal Reserve System. The state banking authorities have sole jurisdiction over the fewer than 500 state banks without FDIC insurance. (Such banks hold less than 0.2% of the deposits in the commercial banking system.)

If you find the U.S. bank regulatory system confusing, imagine how confusing it is for the banks, which have to deal with several regulatory agencies. To rectify this situation, the Clinton administration has proposed that regulation of all depository institutions be centralized under a new independent agency, the Federal Banking Commission. The Bush administration also proposed a similar centralization of banking regulation but was unsuccessful in getting it passed in Congress. The outcome of the Clinton administration's proposal is uncertain.

STRUCTURE OF THE COMMERCIAL BANKING INDUSTRY

There are around 12,000 commercial banks in the United States, far more than in any other country in the world (see Box 1). As Table 1 indicates, we have an extraordinary number of small banks. Twenty-two percent of the banks have less than $25 million in assets. Far more typical is the size distribution in Canada or the United Kingdom, where five or fewer banks dominate the industry. In contrast, the ten largest commercial banks in the United States (listed in Table 2) together hold just 30% of the assets in their industry.

Most industries in the United States have far fewer firms than the commercial banking industry; typically, large firms tend to dominate these industries to a greater extent than in the commercial banking industry. (Consider, for example, the computer industry, which is dominated by IBM, or the automobile industry,

TABLE 1 Size Distribution of Insured Commercial Banks, End of 1992

Assets	Number of Banks	Share of Banks (%)	Share of Assets Held (%)
Less than $25 million	2,556	22.3	1.2
$25–$50 million	2,949	25.7	3.1
$50–$100 million	2,785	24.3	5.6
$100–$500 million	2,539	22.2	14.3
$500 million–$1 billion	252	2.2	5.1
$1–$10 billion	329	2.9	29.5
More than $10 billion	51	0.4	41.2
Total	11,461	100.0	100.0

Source: Federal Deposit Insurance Corporation, *1992 Statistics on Banking.*

TABLE 2 Ten Largest U.S. Banks, 1993

Bank	Assets ($ billions)	Share of All Commercial Bank Assets (%)
1. Citicorp, New York	210.0	6.0
2. BankAmerica Corp., San Francisco	170.0	5.1
3. Chemical Bank Corp., New York	138.0	3.9
4. Nations Bank, Charlotte, N.C.	119.2	3.4
5. J. P. Morgan & Co., New York	101.9	2.9
6. Chase Manhattan Corp., New York	95.3	2.7
7. Bankers Trust Corp., New York	72.2	2.1
8. Banc One Corp., Columbus, Ohio	61.2	1.7
9. Wells Fargo & Co., San Francisco	52.4	1.5
10. PNC Financial Corp., Pittsburgh, Pa.	51.4	1.5
Total	1,082.6	30.8

Source: The Banker, July 1993.

which is dominated by General Motors.) Does the large number of banks in the commercial banking industry and the absence of a few dominant firms suggest that the commercial banking industry is more competitive than other industries?

Branching Regulations and the McFadden Act

The presence of so many commercial banks in the United States actually reflects regulations that restrict the ability of these financial institutions to open **branches** (additional offices that conduct banking operations). Each state has its

A Global Perspective

Box 1

A COMPARISON OF THE BANKING STRUCTURE IN THE UNITED STATES AND ABROAD

The structure of the commercial banking industry in the United States is radically different from that in other industrialized nations. The United States is the only country without a true national banking system in which banks have branches throughout the country. In contrast to other countries, the United States has ended up with a crazy-quilt pattern of state and federal regulations governing interstate banking that has blocked a national banking system. One result is that there are many more banks in the United States than in other industrialized countries. In contrast to the United States, which has on the order of 12,000 commercial banks, every other industrialized country has well under 1000. Japan, for example, has around 150 commercial banks—just 1% of the number in the United States, even though its economy and population are half the size of the United States'.

Another result of the restrictions on branching in the United States is that on average our banks are much smaller than those in other countries. The uniqueness of the banking structure in the United States will stand out in even sharper contrast to the rest of the world as Europe furthers its economic integration. Since January 1, 1993, all banks licensed in any European Union country have been freely able to provide complete banking services in any other EU country. The result will be a Europe-wide banking system, with even larger European banks.

own regulations on the type and number of branches that a bank can open. Regulations on the West and East Coasts, for example, tend to allow banks to open branches throughout their state, while in the middle part of the country, regulations on branching are more restrictive (see Figure 2). Some states, marked as "limited branching" states, put limits on the amount of branching permitted. The McFadden Act of 1927, which was designed to put national banks and state banks on an equal footing, effectively prohibited banks from branching across state lines and forced all national banks to conform to the branching regulations in the state of their location.

The result of the McFadden Act and the state branching regulations is that many small banks stay in existence because a large bank capable of driving them out of business is often restricted from opening a branch nearby. Indeed, it is often easier for a U.S. bank to open a branch in a foreign country than it is for it to open a branch in another state!

Advocates of restrictive state branching regulations say that these regulations foster competition by keeping so many banks in business. But the existence of

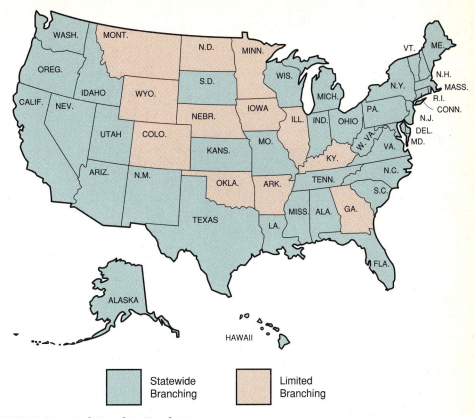

FIGURE 2 **State Bank Branching Regulations**
Source: Conference of State Bank Supervisors, December 1993.

large numbers of banks in the United States must be seen as an indication of a
lack of competition, *not* the presence of vigorous competition. Inefficient banks
can remain in business because their customers cannot find a conveniently located branch of another bank where they can conduct their business.

The McFadden Act and state branching regulations constitute strong anticompetitive forces in the commercial banking industry. If competition is beneficial to society, why have regulations restricting branching arisen in America? The
simplest explanation is that the American public has historically been hostile to
large banks. States with the most restrictive branching regulations are typically
ones in which populist antibank sentiment was strongest in the nineteenth century. (These states usually had large farming populations whose relations with
banks periodically became tempestuous when banks would foreclose on farmers
who couldn't pay their debts.) The legacy of nineteenth-century politics is a
banking system with restrictive branching regulations and hence an inordinate
number of small banks. However, as we will see later in this chapter, branching
restrictions have been breaking down, and we are likely to be heading toward
nationwide banking in the near future.

Bank Holding Companies

An important feature of the U.S. banking industry is that competition can be repressed by regulation but not completely quashed. In Chapter 10 we discussed how the search for profits has led to financial innovation that skirts restrictive regulations. The growth of bank holding companies is one example of how competitive forces have weakened the impact of restrictive branching regulations.

A holding company is a corporation that owns several different companies. This form of corporate ownership has important advantages for banks in that (1) it allows them to circumvent restrictive branching regulations, because the holding company can own a controlling interest in several banks even if branching is not permitted; (2) a bank holding company can engage in other activities related to banking, such as the provision of investment advice, data processing and transmission services, leasing, credit card services, and servicing of loans in other states; and (3) the holding company can issue commercial paper, allowing the bank to tap into nondeposit sources of funds.

Bank holding companies are restricted to owning businesses that are "closely related to banking." Permissible activities, which are specified by the Federal Reserve's Regulation Y, include the activities mentioned here as well as others, ranging from providing courier services to real estate appraisal. In the past, the Fed and congressional legislation have prohibited bank holding companies from engaging in activities such as brokering real estate, underwriting securities, operating travel agencies, and general management consulting. However, in their continuing search for profits, bank holding companies have been seeking ways to get around these regulations and have been entering previously prohibited areas.

Significantly, more states now allow bank holding companies headquartered in other states to purchase banks in their state. In addition, since 1982, banks have been permitted to purchase out-of-state banks that are failing. For example, bank holding companies headquartered in New York, Ohio, North Carolina, Michigan, and California have all gained entry into the Texas market by purchasing failing institutions in that state. The result is that the McFadden Act's restrictions on branching no longer prevent these companies from providing banking services in other states. In addition, bank holding companies have opened limited-service banks that either don't make commercial loans or don't take in deposits. These so-called **nonbank banks** are often not subject to branching regulations and so allow bank holding companies effectively to branch across state lines. However, banking legislation passed in 1987 placed a moratorium on new nonbank banks. In response to the weakening of restrictions on branching across state lines, most states now allow some interstate branching.

The growth of the bank holding companies has been dramatic over the past three decades. Today bank holding companies (including Citicorp, BankAmerica, Chase Manhattan, NCNB, and Wells Fargo) own almost all large banks, and over 90% of all commercial bank deposits are held in banks owned by holding companies.

Electronic Banking Facilities

The wonders of modern computer technology have led to the important financial innovation of electronic banking facilities (automated teller machines, ATMs) through which bank customers are able to obtain banking services at locations other than a bank or one of its branches. Indeed, it is now as easy to get foreign currency from an ATM when you are traveling in Europe as it is to get cash from your local bank.

The regulatory agencies and courts in most states have determined that if an electronic banking facility is owned by a bank, it is considered a branch of that bank and is subject to a state's branching regulations. However, states typically have special provisions that allow wider establishment of electronic banking facilities than is permissible for traditional "brick and mortar" branches.

A farther-reaching development arising from computer technology is the use of shared electronic banking facilities that often span state lines. As long as a facility is not owned or rented by a bank but is paid for on a transaction fee basis, it is not considered a branch of a bank and, as such, is not subject to branching regulations. Because they enable banks to widen their markets, a number of these shared facilities (such as Cirrus and NYCE) have been established nationwide. As electronic banking becomes more prevalent in the future, the McFadden Act and state branching regulations will prove less of a barrier to competition in the banking industry. Indeed, the McFadden Act may soon be a dead letter: Proposals have been raised in Congress and by the Clinton administration to abolish restrictions on branching across state lines entirely.

THRIFT INDUSTRY: REGULATION AND STRUCTURE

Not surprisingly, the regulation and structure of the thrift industry (savings and loan associations, mutual savings banks, and credit unions) closely parallels the regulation and structure of the commercial banking industry.

Savings and Loan Associations

Just as there is a dual banking system for commercial banks, savings and loan associations (S&Ls) can be chartered either by the federal government or by the states. Most S&Ls, whether state or federally chartered, are members of the Federal Home Loan Bank System (FHLBS). Established in 1932, the FHLBS was styled after the Federal Reserve System. It has 12 district Federal Home Loan banks, which are supervised by the Office of Thrift Supervision.

Federal deposit insurance (up to $100,000 of deposits per account) for S&Ls is provided by the Savings Association Insurance Fund, a subsidiary of the FDIC. The Office of Thrift Supervision regulates federally insured S&Ls by setting minimum capital requirements, requiring periodic reports, and examining the S&Ls. It is also the chartering agency for federally chartered S&Ls, and for these S&Ls it approves mergers and sets the rules for branching.

The branching regulations for S&Ls have been more liberal than for commercial banks: Almost all states permit branching, and since 1980, federally chartered S&Ls have been allowed to branch statewide in all states. Since 1981, mergers of financially troubled S&Ls have also been allowed across state lines, and nationwide branching of S&Ls may soon become common. A result of the less restrictive regulations on S&L branching is that the percentage of S&Ls with under $25 million in assets (3%) is less than the percentage of commercial banks with under $25 million in assets (22%).

The FHLBS, like the Fed, makes loans to the members of the system (the FHLBS obtains funds for this purpose by issuing bonds). However, in contrast to the Fed's discount loans, which are expected to be repaid quickly, the loans from the FHLBS often need not be repaid for long periods of time. In addition, the rates charged to S&Ls for these loans are often below the rates that the S&Ls must pay when they borrow in the open market. In this way, the FHLBS loan program provides a subsidy to the savings and loan industry (and implicitly to the housing industry, since most of the S&Ls' loans are for residential mortgages).

Mutual Savings Banks

Of the 500 or so mutual savings banks, around half are chartered by the states. Although the mutual savings banks are primarily regulated by the states in which they are located, the majority have their deposits insured by the FDIC up to the limit of $100,000 per account; these banks are also subject to many of the FDIC's regulations for state-chartered banks. As a rule, the mutual savings banks whose deposits are not insured by the FDIC have their deposits insured by state insurance funds.

The branching regulations for mutual savings banks are determined by the states in which they operate. Because these regulations are not too restrictive, there are few mutual savings banks with assets of less than $25 million.

Credit Unions

Credit unions are small cooperative lending institutions that are organized around a particular group (union members or employees of a particular firm). They can be chartered either by the states or by the federal government; over half are federally chartered. The National Credit Union Administration (NCUA) issues federal charters and regulates federally chartered credit unions by setting minimum capital requirements, requiring periodic reports, and examining the credit unions. Federal deposit insurance (up to the $100,000-per-account limit) is provided to both federally chartered and state-chartered credit unions by a subsidiary of the NCUA, the National Credit Union Share Insurance Fund (NCUSIF). Since the majority of credit union lending is for consumer loans with fairly short terms to maturity, they have not suffered the recent financial difficulties of the S&Ls and mutual savings banks.

Because their members share a common bond, credit unions are typically quite small; most hold less than $10 million of assets. In addition, their ties to a particular industry or company make them more likely to fail when large numbers of workers in that industry or company are laid off and have trouble making loan payments. Recent regulatory changes allow individual credit unions to cater to a more diverse group of people, and this has encouraged an expansion in the size of credit unions and may help reduce credit union failures in the future.

Often a credit union's shareholders are dispersed over many states, some even worldwide, so branching across state lines and into other countries is permitted for federally chartered credit unions. The Navy Federal Credit Union, for example, whose shareholders are members of the U.S. Navy and Marine Corps, has branches throughout the world.

INTERNATIONAL BANKING

In 1960, only eight U.S. banks operated branches in foreign countries, and their total assets were less than $4 billion. Currently over 100 American banks have branches abroad, with assets totaling over $500 billion. The spectacular growth in international banking can be explained by three factors.

First is the rapid growth in international trade and multinational (worldwide) corporations that has occurred since 1960. When American firms operate abroad, they need banking services in foreign countries. Although these firms could use foreign banks, many of them prefer to do business with the U.S. banks with which they have established long-term relationships and which understand American business customs and practices. As international trade has grown, international banking has grown with it.

Second, when American banks go abroad, they are allowed to pursue activities that are prohibited in the United States under the Glass-Steagall Act. American banks such as Citicorp are very active in underwriting securities and selling insurance abroad and derive substantial profits from these activities. The desire to escape burdensome regulations, an important factor that has stimulated financial innovations, has also been a major spur to international banking.

Third, American banks have wanted to tap into the large pool of dollar-denominated deposits in foreign countries known as Eurodollars. To understand the structure of U.S. banking overseas, let us first look at the Eurodollar market, an important source of growth for international banking.

Box 2

A Global Perspective

BIRTH OF THE EURODOLLAR MARKET

One of capitalism's great ironies is that the Eurodollar market, one of the most important financial markets used by capitalists, was fathered by the Soviet Union. In the early 1950s, during the height of the Cold War, the Soviets had accumulated a substantial amount of dollar balances held by banks in the United States. Because the Russians feared that the U.S. government might freeze these assets in the United States, they wanted to move the deposits to Europe, where they would be safe from expropriation. (This fear was not un-justified—consider the U.S. freeze on Iranian assets in 1979 and Iraqi assets in 1990.) However, they also wanted to keep the deposits in dollars to be used in their international transactions. The solution to the problem was to transfer the deposits to European banks but to keep the deposits denominated in dollars. When the Soviets did this, the Eurodollar was born.

Eurodollar Market

Eurodollars are created when deposits in accounts in the United States are trans-ferred to a bank outside the country and are kept in the form of dollars. For ex-ample, if Rolls-Royce Corporation deposits a $1 million check, written on an ac-count at an American bank, in its bank in London—specifying that the deposit is payable in dollars—$1 million of Eurodollars are created.[1] Over 90% of Eurodol-lar deposits are time deposits, more than half of them certificates of deposit with maturities of 30 days or more. The total amount of Eurodollars outstanding ex-ceeds $2 trillion, making the Eurodollar market one of the most important finan-cial markets in the world economy (see Box 2).

Why would companies like Rolls-Royce want to hold dollar deposits outside the United States? First, the dollar is the most widely used currency in interna-tional trade, so Rolls-Royce might want to hold deposits in dollars to conduct its international transactions. Second, Eurodollars are "offshore" deposits—they are held in countries that will not subject them to regulations such as reserve re-quirements or restrictions (called *capital controls*) on taking the deposits outside the country.[2]

---

[1]Note that the London bank has acquired the deposit at the American bank formerly owned by Rolls-Royce, so the creation of Eurodollars has not caused a reduction in the amount of bank deposits in the United States.

[2]Although most offshore deposits are denominated in dollars, some are also denominated in other currencies. Collectively, these offshore deposits are referred to as Eurocurrencies. A German mark–denominated deposit held in London, for example, is called a Euromark, and a French franc–denominated deposit held in London is called a Eurofranc.

The main center of the Eurodollar market is London, a major international financial center for hundreds of years. Eurodollars are also held outside of Europe in locations that provide offshore status to these deposits—for example, Hong Kong, Singapore, and the Caribbean (the Bahamas and the Cayman Islands).

The minimum-sized transaction in the Eurodollar market is typically $1 million, and approximately 75% of these deposits are held by banks. Plainly, you and I are unlikely to come into direct contact with Eurodollars. The Eurodollar market is, however, an important source of funds to U.S. banks, whose borrowing of these deposits is over $60 billion. Rather than using an intermediary and borrowing all the deposits from foreign banks, American banks decided that they could earn higher profits by opening their own branches abroad to attract these deposits. Consequently, the Eurodollar market has been an important stimulus to U.S. banking overseas.

Structure of U.S. Banking Overseas

U.S. banks have most of their foreign branches in Latin America, the Far East, the Caribbean, and London. The largest volume of assets is held by branches in London because it is a major international financial center and the central location for the Eurodollar market. Latin America and the Far East have many branches because of the importance of U.S. trade with these regions. The Caribbean (the Bahamas and the Cayman Islands) has become an important location for international banking because it is a tax haven, with minimal taxation and few restrictive regulations. In actuality, the branches in the Bahamas and the Cayman Islands are "shell operations" because they function primarily as bookkeeping centers and do not provide normal banking services.

An alternative corporate structure for U.S. banks that operate overseas is the **Edge Act corporation,** which is a special subsidiary engaged primarily in international banking. This corporate structure, created by the Edge Act of 1919, allows American banks to compete more effectively against foreign banks by exempting Edge Act corporations from certain U.S. banking regulations. For example, Edge Act corporations are exempt from the prohibition on branching across state lines; they can have branches in different states to facilitate the financing of trade with different parts of the world—an office on the West Coast to handle the financing of trade with Japan, an office in Miami to handle the financing of trade with Latin America, and so forth.

U.S. banks (through their holding companies) can also own a controlling interest in foreign banks and in foreign companies that provide financial services, such as finance companies. The international activities of member banks of the Federal Reserve System, bank holding companies, and Edge Act corporations (which account for almost all international banking conducted by U.S. banks) are regulated by the Federal Reserve's Regulation K. As in the case of bank holding companies, these international activities must be "closely related to banking."

In late 1981, the Federal Reserve approved the creation of **international banking facilities (IBFs)** within the United States that can accept time deposits

THE THIRD-WORLD DEBT CRISIS

An important aspect of international banking is the loans made to third-world countries—particularly Argentina, Brazil, and Mexico. In the aftermath of the sharp rise in oil prices in 1973–1974, developing countries found their import bills rising dramatically due to increased costs for energy, while the OPEC countries found themselves with huge amounts of idle funds due to increased revenue from oil. U.S. banks were in the forefront of "recycling" these funds from those countries by accepting deposits from those countries and in turn lending out the proceeds to developing countries. In contrast to earlier loans to developing countries, which were used for special development projects (for example, highway systems and dams), these new loans were often made to governments to pay for the higher level of imports.

This recycling of funds proceeded smoothly until the worldwide recession of 1980–1982, which led to a sharp fall in the exports of the third-world countries, which had trouble meeting their debt (interest and principal) payments. When Mexico encountered difficulties with its debt payments in late 1982, the banks and international financial agencies (such as the International Monetary Fund) stepped in to help restructure the debt, that is, to change the terms of repayment and the interest rates. The magnitude of the debt crisis has been immense; since the crisis began in 1982, about 40 developing countries with $300 billion of debt to commercial banks have been involved in restructuring their debt.

U.S. banks held more than $100 billion of third-world debt, mostly of Latin American countries, particularly of Brazil and Mexico (over $20 billion each). Citicorp, Manufacturers Hanover, BankAmerica, Chase Manhattan, Chemical, J. P. Morgan, Bankers Trust, and First Chicago were among the largest lenders to third-world countries. In 1982, when the first fears of third-world default arose, there were worries that the U.S. banking system could be threatened with collapse, since many money center banks held amounts of third-world debt well in excess of their bank capital. Although the losses incurred on third-world debt have been substantial and have been a major drag on bank profits, particularly at large money center banks, the banking system has weathered the storm. Encouraged by regulators, money center banks have increased their primary capital from 4.2% of assets in 1981 to over 7% today. In addition, these banks have been continually setting aside income to increase their loan loss reserves to cover the losses on this debt.

The third-world debt crisis is mostly behind us, and fears of a financial collapse have subsided. However, banks that hoped to make substantial profits on their international banking business have come to regret this foray into interna-

from foreigners but are not subject to either reserve requirements or restrictions on interest payments. IBFs are also allowed to make loans to foreigners, but they are not allowed to make loans to domestic residents. States have encouraged the establishment of IBFs by exempting them from state and local taxes. In essence, IBFs are treated like foreign branches of U.S. banks and are not subject to domestic regulations and taxes. The purpose of establishing IBFs is to encourage American and foreign banks to do more banking business in the United States rather than abroad. From this point of view, IBFs have been a success: Their assets climbed to nearly $200 billion in the first two years and currently exceed this amount.

Foreign Banks in the United States

The growth in international trade has not only encouraged U.S. banks to open offices overseas but has also encouraged foreign banks to establish offices in the United States. More than 500 offices of foreign banks are now operating in America, and they hold more than 20% of the total U.S. bank assets.

Foreign banks engage in banking activities in the United States by operating an agency office of the foreign bank, a subsidiary U.S. bank, or a branch of the foreign bank. An agency office can lend and transfer funds in the United States, but it cannot accept deposits from domestic residents. Agency offices have the advantage of not being subject to regulations that apply to full-service banking offices (such as requirements for FDIC insurance and restrictions on branching). A subsidiary U.S. bank is just like any other U.S. bank (it may even have an American-sounding name) and is subject to the same regulations, but it is owned by the foreign bank. A branch of a foreign bank bears the foreign bank's name and is usually a full-service office. Foreign banks may also form Edge Act corporations and IBFs.

Before 1978, foreign banks were not subject to many regulations that applied to domestic banks: They could open branches across state lines and were not expected to meet reserve requirements, for example. The passage of the International Banking Act of 1978, however, put foreign and domestic banks on a more equal footing. Now foreign banks may open new full-service branches only in the state they designate as their home state or in states that allow the entry of out-of-state banks. Limited-service branches and agency offices in any other state are permitted, however, and foreign banks are allowed to retain any full-service branches opened before the International Banking Act of 1978.

The internationalization of banking, both by U.S. banks going abroad and by foreign banks entering the United States, has meant that financial markets throughout the world have become more integrated. As a result, there is a growing trend toward international coordination of bank regulation, one example of which is the 1988 Basel agreement to standardize minimum capital requirements in industrialized countries, discussed in Chapter 13. Another trend is the increasing dominance of Japanese banks in international banking. By 1993, eight of the ten largest banks in the world were Japanese, with Dai-Ichi Kangyo taking over the top spot. The implications of this financial market integration for the operation of our economy is examined further in Chapter 22 when we discuss the international financial system in more detail.

DECLINE OF THE U.S. BANKING INDUSTRY

The past few decades have not been good ones for the American banking industry. As Figure 3 shows, the importance of commercial banks as a source of funds for borrowers has shrunk dramatically, from a peak of 35% of total credit advanced in 1974 to around 22% in the early 1990s.[3] Thrifts have also seen a decline in market share, from 20% in the 1960s and 1970s to below 15% in the early 1990s. Furthermore, bank profitability has also declined, as we can see in Figure 4, which shows bank profits as a percentage of GDP. Although bank profits did improve sharply in 1992 and 1993, many bank analysts believe that profits in that year were temporarily high because of favorable interest-rate developments that would not be long-lasting.

The dismal performance of the banking industry has led to a large number of bank failures (which have been running at rates more than ten times that of the 1945–1981 period; see Figure 5 on p. 300) and to a shrinkage of the number of commercial banks from around 15,000 in the 1970s to 12,000 today. What explains the decreasing importance of banks and the dramatic decline in this industry?

To understand why the banking industry has declined in both size and profitability, we need to look at how the financial innovation process described in Chapter 10 has made banks less competitive with other financial institutions. Financial innovation has caused banks to suffer declines in their cost advantages in acquiring funds, that is, on the liabilities side of their balance sheet, while at

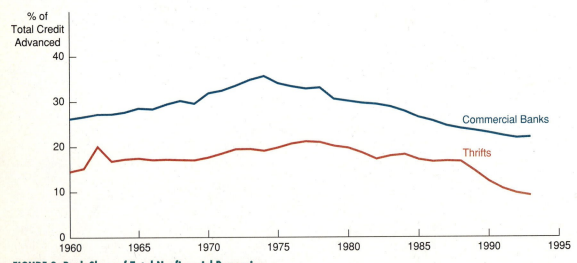

FIGURE 3 Bank Share of Total Nonfinancial Borrowing
Source: Federal Reserve Flow of Funds Accounts.

---

[3]Looking at the decline in the market share of credit advanced by banks overstates somewhat the decline of the banking industry in credit markets because, as pointed out in Chapter 11, banks have increased their off-balance-sheet activities in credit markets.

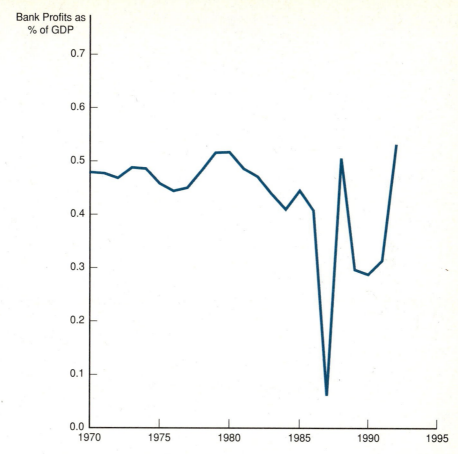

FIGURE 4
Commercial Bank Profitability
Sources: Federal Deposit Insurance Corporation, *Historical Statistics on Banking; Economic Report of the President.*

the same time they have lost income advantages on the assets side of their balance sheet. The simultaneous decline of cost and income advantages has caused the industry to shrink and its profitability to decline.

Decline in Cost Advantages in Acquiring Funds (Liabilities)

Until 1980, banks were subject to deposit rate ceilings that restricted them from paying any interest on checkable deposits and (under Regulation Q) limited them to paying a maximum interest rate of a little over 5% on time deposits. Until the 1960s, these restrictions worked to the banks' advantage because their major source of funds was checkable deposits (over 60%) and the zero interest cost on these deposits meant that the banks had a very low cost of funds. Unfortunately, this cost advantage for banks did not last. The rise in inflation from the late 1960s on led to higher interest rates, which made investors more sensitive to yield differentials on different assets. The result was the disintermediation process described in Chapter 10: People began to take their money out of banks,

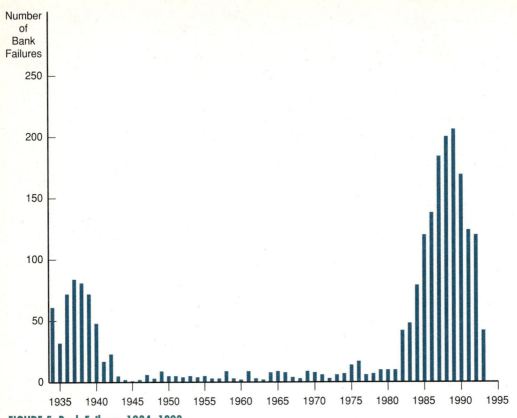

FIGURE 5 Bank Failures, 1934–1993
Source: Federal Deposit Insurance Corporation.

with their low interest rates on both checkable and time deposits, and began to seek out higher-yielding investments. At the same time, attempts to get around deposit rate ceilings and reserve requirements led to financial innovation that produced money market mutual funds, which put the banks at an even further disadvantage because depositors could now obtain checking-like services while earning high interest on their money market mutual fund accounts. One manifestation of these changes in the financial system was that the low-cost source of funds, checkable deposits, declined dramatically in importance for banks, falling from over 60% of bank liabilities to around 20% today.

The growing difficulty for banks in raising funds led to their supporting legislation in the 1980s that eliminated Regulation Q ceilings on time deposit interest rates and allowed checkable deposits like NOW accounts that paid interest. Although these changes in regulation helped make banks more competitive in their quest for funds, it also meant that their cost of acquiring funds had risen substantially, thereby reducing their earlier cost advantage over other financial institutions.

Our discussion of international banking earlier in the chapter documented the increasing encroachment of foreign (particularly Japanese) banks in U.S. financial markets. The loss of cost advantages of American banks helps explain this trend. With the growing success of the Japanese economy and the high savings by the Japanese public, Japanese banks were able to tap a large savings pool and thus had access to a cheaper source of funds than American banks. This cost advantage for Japanese banks meant that they could more aggressively seek out loan business in the United States, which is exactly what they did. As a result, they have grown at the expense of American banks. Before 1980, two U.S. banks, Citicorp and BankAmerica, were at the top of the heap, whereas in the 1990s, neither even ranks in the top 20 of the world's largest banks.

Decline in Income Advantages on Uses of Funds (Assets)

The loss of cost advantages on the liabilities side of the balance sheet for American banks is one reason that they have become less competitive, but they have also been hit by a decline in income advantages on the assets side. The three most important developments that have reduced banks' income advantage are the growth of the commercial paper market, the junk bond market, and securitization, all of which were discussed in Chapter 10.

There we saw that improvements in information technology have made it easier for firms to issue securities directly to the public. This has meant that instead of going to banks to finance short-term credit needs, many of the banks' best business customers now find it cheaper to go to the commercial paper market for funds instead. The loss of this competitive advantage for banks is evident in the fact that before 1970, the amount of nonfinancial commercial paper was less than 5% of commercial and industrial bank loans, whereas this percentage has grown to over 20% today.

The rise of money market mutual funds has been another factor in the rapid growth in the commercial paper market. Because money market mutual funds need to hold liquid, high-quality, short-term assets such as commercial paper, the growth of assets in these funds to over $500 billion has created a ready market in commercial paper. This growth in the commercial paper market has allowed finance companies, which depend primarily on commercial paper to acquire funds, to expand their operations at the expense of banks. Finance companies, which lend to many of the same businesses that borrow from banks, have increased their market share relative to banks: Before 1980, finance company loans to business were around 30% of commercial and industrial loans, whereas currently they account for over 60%.

The rise of the junk bond market has also eaten into banks' loan business, as the following headline from the *Wall Street Journal* indicates: "Wall Street Is Using Junk Bonds to Take Another Slice of Banks' Lending Pie."[4] Improvements in information technology have made it easier for corporations to sell their

---

[4]May 18, 1993, p. C1.

bonds to the public directly, thereby bypassing banks. Although *Fortune* 500 companies started taking this route in the 1970s, now lower-quality corporate borrowers are using banks less often because they have access to the junk bond market.

We also saw in Chapter 10 that improvements in computer technology have led to securitization, whereby illiquid financial assets such as bank loans or mortgages are transformed into marketable securities. Computers enable other financial institutions to originate loans because they can now accurately evaluate credit risk with statistical methods, while computers have lowered transactions costs, making it possible to bundle these loans and sell them as securities. As a result, banks no longer have an advantage in making loans when default risk can be easily evaluated with computers. Without their former advantages, banks have lost loan business to other financial institutions even though the banks themselves are involved in the process of securitization. Securitization has been a particular problem for mortgage-issuing institutions such as S&Ls because most residential mortgages are now securitized.

A Global Perspective

Box 4

PROBLEMS IN THE BANKING INDUSTRY OUTSIDE THE UNITED STATES

Because of differences in national accounting and disclosure rules, it is difficult to make comparisons on the state of the banking industry in other countries. However, since 1980, bank profitability appears to have declined in the United Kingdom, Australia, and the Scandinavian countries.

Even in countries like Switzerland and Germany, banks have been running into trouble. For example, in January 1993, BfG Bank, a German bank, needed a capital infusion from its parent company, Crédit Lyonnais, because it suffered huge losses in 1992. Japanese banks, which have come to dominate the international banking scene, are also in big trouble. The collapse of real estate values in Japan has left many banks such as Sumitomo Trust and Banking Company, one of the world's largest, with huge losses. Private analysts have estimated that in 1993, Japanese banks were holding over $150 billion worth of nonperforming loans—loans on which interest payments have not been made for over six months. The troubles in the Japanese banking industry have slowed their lending, and Japan's banking federation has even been working on a bank bailout plan.

The United States is not unique in seeing its banks face a more difficult competitive environment, which can lead to bank failures. The problems for the banking industry in other countries thus present challenges for the international regulation of banking, a subject we discuss further in the next chapter.

Conclusion

The process of financial innovation that has eroded banks' cost advantages in raising funds and income advantages in making loans is the source of the industry's lower profitability and shrinkage. The same technological forces that have hurt the competitiveness of banks in the United States also seem to be at work abroad (see Box 4). The decline of the banking industry is important not only because it is a major change in our financial structure but also because it has helped produce a high number of bank failures in recent years. This, in turn, has created a crisis for banking regulation, a topic we turn to in the next chapter.

SUMMARY

1. The history of banking in the United States has left us with a dual banking system with commercial banks chartered by the states and the federal government. Multiple agencies regulate commercial banks: the Office of the Comptroller, the Federal Reserve, the FDIC, and the state banking authorities.

2. Restrictive state branching regulations and the McFadden Act, which prohibits branching across state lines, have led to a large number of small commercial banks. The large number of commercial banks in the United States reflects the *lack* of competition, not the presence of vigorous competition. Bank holding companies and electronic banking facilities are important forces that are weakening the anticompetitive effect of restrictive branching regulations.

3. The regulation and structure of the thrift industry (savings and loan associations, mutual savings banks, and credit unions) parallel closely the regulation and structure of the commercial banking industry. Savings and loans are primarily regulated by the Office of Thrift Supervision, and deposit insurance is administered by the FDIC. Mu-

tual savings banks are regulated by the states, and federal deposit insurance is provided by the FDIC. Credit unions are regulated by the National Credit Union Administration, and deposit insurance is provided by the National Credit Union Share Insurance Fund.

4. With the rapid growth of world trade since 1960, international banking has grown dramatically. U.S. banks engage in international banking activities by opening branches abroad, owning controlling interests in foreign banks, forming Edge Act corporations, and operating international banking facilities (IBFs) located in the United States. Foreign banks operate in the United States by owning a subsidiary American bank or by operating branches or agency offices in the United States.

5. Banks have been decreasing in importance in recent years. Financial innovation has caused banks to suffer declines in cost advantages in acquiring funds and in income advantages on their assets. The resulting squeeze has hurt bank profitability and led to a shrinkage of the industry.

KEY TERMS

central bank

state banks

national banks

dual banking system

bank holding
companies

branches

nonbank banks

Edge Act corporation

international banking
facilities (IBFs)

QUESTIONS AND PROBLEMS

1. Why was the United States one of the last of the major industrialized countries to have a central bank?

*2. Which regulatory agency has the primary responsibility for supervising the following categories of commercial banks?
   (a) National banks
   (b) Bank holding companies
   (c) Non–Federal Reserve state banks
   (d) Federal Reserve member state banks

3. "The commercial banking industry in Canada is less competitive than the commercial banking industry in the United States because in Canada only a few large banks dominate the industry, while in the United States there are around 12,000 commercial banks." Is this statement true, false, or uncertain? Explain.

*4. Why has new technology made it harder to enforce limitations on bank branching?

5. Why has there been such a dramatic increase in bank holding companies?

*6. Why is there a higher percentage of banks with under $25 million of assets among commercial banks than among savings and loans and mutual savings banks?

7. Unlike commercial banks, savings and loans, and mutual savings banks, credit unions do not have restrictions on locating branches in other states. Why, then, are credit unions typically smaller than the other depository institutions?

*8. What incentives have regulatory agencies created to encourage international banking? Why have they done this?

9. How could the approval of international banking facilities (IBFs) by the Fed in 1981 have reduced employment in the banking industry in Europe?

*10. If the bank at which you keep your checking account is owned by Saudi Arabians, should you worry that your deposits are less safe than if the bank were owned by Americans?

11. What facts indicate that the American banking industry has been declining in recent years?

*12. Why have banks been losing cost advantages in acquiring funds in recent years?

13. "If inflation had not risen in the 1960s and 1970s, the banking industry might be healthier today." Is this statement true, false, or uncertain? Explain.

*14. Why have banks been losing income advantages on their assets in recent years?

15. "The invention of the computer is the major factor behind the decline of the banking industry." Is this statement true, false, or uncertain? Explain.

Chapter 13

THE CRISIS IN BANKING REGULATION

PREVIEW Banking regulation in the United States has encountered a crisis of massive proportions. As we saw in Chapter 12, in recent years commercial banks have been failing at rates more than ten times those of the 1945–1981 period. As a result of these bank failures, the FDIC's bank insurance fund spent more than it took in for four straight years, from 1988 to 1991, an unprecedented set of deficits since the FDIC started operations in 1934. Because of these problems, the FDIC required an infusion of cash in 1991. Yet if we find the problems in the commercial banking industry troubling, they are nothing compared to the mess in the savings and loan industry. Losses in this industry were close to $20 billion in 1989, and legislation passed in that year to bail out the industry has cost taxpayers in excess of $150 billion.

In Chapter 12, we saw that one source of problems in the banking industry has been a decline in the competitiveness of American banks. Another source of problems has been the bank regulatory system itself. In this chapter we develop an economic analysis of how banking regulation, and particularly federal deposit insurance, affects the behavior of banking institutions. This analysis will help us understand not only why the crisis in banking regulation has occurred but also how the regulatory system might be reformed to prevent future disasters.

Our first step in understanding the crisis in banking regulation is to look more closely at the nature of banking regulation in the United States and abroad and to understand why it has taken the general form that it has. We then need to see how banking regulation responded to the financial innovation in the 1960s, 1970s, and early 1980s that set the stage for the banking crisis that followed. With all these pieces in place, we can go on to analyze why the crisis occurred and what might be done to prevent another occurrence in the future.

ASYMMETRIC INFORMATION AND BANK REGULATION

In earlier chapters we have seen how asymmetric information, the fact that different parties in a financial contract do not have the same information, leads to adverse selection and moral hazard problems that have an important impact on our financial system. The concepts of asymmetric information, adverse selection, and moral hazard are especially useful in understanding why government has chosen the form of banking regulation we see in both the United States and in other countries. There are four basic categories of banking regulation: deposit insurance, restrictions on bank asset holdings and capital requirements, chartering and bank examination, and separation of the banking and securities industries.

Deposit Insurance and the FDIC

Before the FDIC started operations in 1934, asymmetric information was a basic problem for depositors in banks in that they were unable to determine the quality of the assets, particularly loans, held by the bank. A bank failure meant that depositors would have to wait to get their deposit funds until the bank was liquidated (that is, until its assets had been turned into cash), and at that time they would be paid only a fraction of the value of their deposits. Unable to learn if bank managers were taking on too much risk or were outright crooks, depositors would be reluctant to put money in the bank. The government realized that it could solve this problem by providing a guarantee that depositors would be paid off in full no matter what happened to the bank, and so it created the FDIC. That is how the government came to provide deposit insurance.

Another important rationale for government deposit insurance is that depositors' lack of information about the quality of bank assets can lead to bank panics, which, as we saw in Chapter 9, can have serious harmful consequences for the economy. To see this, consider the following situation. There is no deposit insurance, and an adverse shock hits the economy. As a result of the shock, 5% of the banks have such large losses on loans that they become insolvent. Because of asymmetric information, depositors are unable to tell whether their bank is a good bank or one of the 5% of insolvent banks. Depositors at bad *and* good banks recognize that they may not get back 100 cents on the dollar for their deposits and will want to withdraw them. Indeed, because banks operate on a "sequential service constraint" (a first-come, first-served basis), depositors have a very strong incentive to show up at the bank first because if they are last on line, the bank may run out of funds and they will get nothing. Uncertainty about the health of the banking system in general can lead to runs on banks both good and bad, and the failure of one bank can hasten the failure of others (referred to as the *contagion effect*). If nothing is done to restore the public's confidence, a bank panic can ensue.

Indeed, bank panics were a fact of American life in the nineteenth and early twentieth centuries, with major ones occurring every 20 years or so in 1837, 1857, 1873, 1884, 1893, 1907, and 1930–1933. Bank failures were a serious problem even during the boom years of the 1920s, when the number of bank failures averaged around 600 per year.

Government deposit insurance effectively short-circuits runs on banks and bank panics. With fully insured deposits, depositors don't need to run to the bank to make withdrawals–even if they are worried about the bank's health–

because their deposits will be worth 100 cents on the dollar no matter what. From 1930 to 1933, the years immediately preceding the creation of the FDIC, the number of bank failures averaged over 2000 per year. After the establishment of the FDIC in 1934, bank failures averaged less than 15 per year until 1981.

The FDIC uses two primary methods to handle a failed bank. In the first, called the *payoff method,* the FDIC allows the bank to fail and pays off deposits up to the $100,000 insurance limit (with funds acquired from the insurance premiums paid by the banks who have bought FDIC insurance). After the bank has been liquidated, the FDIC lines up with other creditors of the bank and is paid its share of the proceeds from the liquidated assets. Typically, when the payoff method is used, account holders with deposits in excess of the $100,000 limit get back more than 90 cents on the dollar, although the process can take several years to complete.

In the second method, called the *purchase and assumption method,* the FDIC reorganizes the bank, typically by finding a willing merger partner who assumes (takes over) all of the failed bank's deposits so that none of the depositors loses a penny. The FDIC may help the merger partner by providing it with subsidized loans or by buying some of the failed bank's weaker loans. The net effect of the purchase and assumption method is that the FDIC has guaranteed *all* deposits, not just those under the $100,000 limit. The purchase and assumption method was the FDIC's most common procedure for dealing with a failed bank before new banking legislation in 1991.

Moral Hazard and Deposit Insurance Although federal deposit insurance has been successful at protecting depositors and preventing bank panics, it is a mixed blessing. The most serious drawback of deposit insurance stems from moral hazard, the incentives of one party to a transaction to engage in activities detrimental to the other party. Moral hazard is an important concern in insurance arrangements in general because the existence of insurance provides increased incentives for taking risks that might result in an insurance payoff. For example, some drivers with automobile collision insurance that has a low deductible might be more likely to drive recklessly because if they get into an accident, the insurance company pays most of the costs for damage and repairs.

Moral hazard is a prominent concern in government arrangements to provide deposit insurance. Because insured depositors know that they will not suffer losses if a bank fails, they do not impose the discipline of the marketplace on banks by withdrawing deposits when they suspect that the bank is taking on too much risk. Consequently, banks with deposit insurance can (and do) take on greater risks than they otherwise would.

Adverse Selection and Deposit Insurance A further problem for deposit insurance arises because of adverse selection, the fact that the people who are most likely to produce the adverse outcome insured against (bank failure) are those who most want to take advantage of the insurance. For example, bad drivers are more likely than good drivers to take out automobile collision insurance with a low deductible. Because insured depositors have little reason to impose discipline on the bank, risk-loving entrepreneurs find the banking industry a particularly attractive one to enter—they know that they will be able to engage in highly risky activities. Even worse, because insured depositors have so little reason to monitor the bank's activities, outright crooks also find banking an attractive industry for their activities because it is easy for them to get away with fraud and embezzlement.

"Too Big to Fail"   The moral hazard created by deposit insurance and the desire to prevent bank failures have presented bank regulators with a particular quandary. Because the failure of a very large bank makes it more likely that a major financial disruption will occur, bank regulators are naturally reluctant to allow a big bank to fail and cause losses to its depositors. Indeed, consider Continental Illinois, one of the ten largest banks in the United States when it became insolvent in May 1984. Not only did the FDIC guarantee depositors up to the $100,000 insurance limit, but it also guaranteed accounts exceeding $100,000 and even prevented losses for Continental Illinois bondholders. Shortly thereafter, the Comptroller of the Currency (the regulator of national banks) testified to Congress that the FDIC's policy was to regard the 11 largest banks as "too big to fail"—in other words, the FDIC would bail them out so that no depositor or creditor would suffer a loss. The FDIC would do this by using the purchase and assumption method, giving the insolvent bank a large infusion of capital and then finding a willing merger partner to take over the bank and its deposits. As Box 1 indicates, the too-big-to-fail policy has been extended to big banks that are not even among the 11 largest. (Note that "too big to fail" is somewhat misleading because when a bank is closed or merged into another bank, the managers are usually fired and the stockholders in the bank lose their investment.)

One problem with the too-big-to-fail policy is that it increases the moral hazard incentives for big banks. If the FDIC were willing to close a bank using the alternative payoff method, paying depositors only up to the $100,000 limit, large depositors with more than $100,000 would suffer losses if the bank failed. Thus they would have an incentive to monitor the bank by examining closely the bank's balance-sheet and off-balance-sheet activities and then pulling their money out if the bank was taking on too much risk. To prevent such a loss of deposits, the bank would be more likely to engage in less risky activities. However, once large depositors know that a bank is too big to fail, they have no incentive to monitor the bank and pull out their deposits when it takes on too much risk: No matter what the bank does, large depositors will not suffer any losses. The result of the too-big-to-fail policy is that big banks take on even greater risks, thereby making bank failures more likely.[1]

Another serious problem with the too-big-to-fail policy is that it is basically unfair. Small banks are put at a competitive disadvantage because they will be allowed to fail, creating potential losses for their large depositors, while big banks' large depositors are immune from losses. The unfairness of the too-big-

---

[1]Recent evidence reveals, as our analysis predicts, that large banks have taken on riskier loans than smaller banks and that this has led to higher loan losses for big banks; see John Boyd and Mark Gertler, "U.S. Commercial Banking: Trends, Cycles and Policy," *NBER Macroeconomics Annual 1993*, pp. 319–368.

to-fail doctrine came to a head with the different FDIC treatment of two insolvent banks in late 1990 and early 1991 (see Box 1).

Restrictions on Asset Holdings and Bank Capital Requirements

As we have seen, the moral hazard associated with deposit insurance encourages too much risk taking on the part of banks. Bank regulations that restrict asset holdings and bank capital requirements are directed at minimizing this moral hazard, which can cost the taxpayers dearly.

Even in the absence of deposit insurance, banks still have the incentive to take on too much risk. Risky assets may provide the bank with higher earnings when they pay off; but if they do not pay off and the bank fails, depositors are left holding the bag. If depositors were able to monitor the bank easily by acquiring information on its risk-taking activities, they would immediately withdraw their deposits if the bank was taking on too much risk. To prevent such a loss of deposits, the bank would be more likely to reduce its risk-taking activities. Unfortunately, acquiring the information on a bank's balance-sheet and off-balance-sheet activities that indicates how much risk the bank is taking is a difficult task. Hence most depositors are incapable of imposing discipline that might prevent banks from engaging in risky activities. A strong rationale for government regulation to reduce risk taking on the part of banks therefore existed even before the establishment of federal deposit insurance.

Bank regulations that restrict banks from holding risky assets such as common stock are a direct means of making banks avoid too much risk. Bank regulations also promote diversification, which reduces risk by limiting the amount of loans in particular categories or to individual borrowers. Requirements that banks have sufficient bank capital are another way to change the bank's incentives to take on less risk. When a bank is forced to hold a large amount of equity capital, the bank has more to lose if it fails and is thus more likely to pursue less risky activities.

Bank capital requirements take two forms. The first type is based on the so-called **leverage ratio,** the amount of capital divided by the bank's total assets. (The leverage ratio is the inverse of the equity multiplier described in Chapter 11.) To be classified as well capitalized, a bank's leverage ratio must exceed 5%; a lower leverage ratio, especially one below 3%, triggers increased regulatory restrictions on the bank. Until recently, minimum bank capital in the United States was set solely by specifying a minimum leverage ratio. But in the wake of the Continental Illinois and savings and loans bailouts, regulators in the United States and the rest of the world have become increasingly worried about banks' holdings of risky assets and about the increase in banks' off-balance-sheet activities, which also expose banks to risk. Under an agreement among banking officials from 12 industrialized nations (who met under the auspices of the Bank for International Settlements in Basel, Switzerland), the Federal Reserve, the FDIC, and the Office of the Comptroller of the Currency have implemented an additional risk-based capital requirement which was fully phased in by December

Box 1

A TALE OF TWO BANK COLLAPSES: BANK OF NEW ENGLAND AND FREEDOM NATIONAL BANK

The FDIC's procedures for handling two bank collapses, those of the Bank of New England and Freedom National Bank, illustrate how the too-big-to-fail policy works.

The Bank of New England, based in Boston, was the thirty-third-largest bank holding company in the United States, with over $20 billion of assets. In the 1980s, it was the region's most aggressive real estate lender; over 30% of its loan portfolio was in commercial real estate. With the collapse of real estate prices in New England beginning in the late 1980s (commercial real estate values dropped by more than 25%), many of the bank's loans went sour. On Friday, January 4, 1991, the bank announced a projected $450 million fourth-quarter loss that exceeded the bank's capital of $255 million. Expecting the failure of the bank, in the next 48 hours depositors lined up at the bank and withdrew over $1 billion in funds, much of it from automatic teller machines.

The chairman of the FDIC, William Seidman, expressed his concern over the ramifications of the potential failure: "Given the condition of the financial system in New England, it would be unwise to send a signal that large depositors weren't going to be protected."* The FDIC followed its too-big-to-fail policy. Sunday night, January 6, the FDIC moved in to stop the run on the bank and agreed to guarantee all Bank of New England deposits, including those in excess of the $100,000 insurance limit. To keep the bank in operation until a buyer could be found and the purchase and assumption method could be used to make sure that no depositors would suffer any loss, the FDIC created what is called a *bridge bank*. In this arrangement, the FDIC creates a new corporation to run the bank and immediately injects capital ($750 million in the case of the

*Quoted in John Meehan, "A Shock to the System: How Far Will Banking's Crisis of Confidence Spread?" *Business Week,* January 21, 1991, p. 26.

(cont.)

1992. Under this risk-based capital requirement, which the banks must meet along with the leverage ratio capital requirement, minimum capital standards are linked to off-balance-sheet activities such as interest-rate swaps and trading positions in futures and options. Box 2 outlines the structure of these capital requirements in more detail.

Chartering and Examination

Because banks can be used by crooks or high-flying entrepreneurs to engage in highly speculative activities, such undesirable people are the most likely ones to

A TALE OF TWO BANK COLLAPSES: BANK OF NEW ENGLAND AND FREEDOM NATIONAL BANK (cont.)

Bank of New England). The FDIC and the buyer of the bank then put additional capital into the bank over time, and eventually the acquirer buys out the FDIC's share. The net result of these transactions was that the FDIC spent $2.3 billion bailing out the Bank of New England, the third-costliest bailout in the FDIC's history. However, when all was said and done and spent, none of the depositors lost a penny.

The very different FDIC treatment of a small insolvent bank in Harlem several months earlier raised serious questions of fairness. The Freedom National Bank was founded in 1964 by baseball great Jackie Robinson and other minority investors. Despite its small size (under $100 million of deposits), it was one of the most prominent black-owned banks.

As a result of numerous speculative loans that went bad, the bank became insolvent in November 1990. Because of the bank's small size, the FDIC was not concerned that the failure of the bank would have serious repercussions for the rest of the banking system, so it decided to close the bank on November 9 using the payoff method. The Freedom National Bank was liquidated, and large depositors were paid only 50 cents on the dollar for deposits in excess of $100,000. Not only fat cats suffered losses when this bank failed: Charitable organizations like the United Negro College Fund, the National Urban League, and several churches were among the large depositors at the bank. Seidman described the unfairness of the treatment of the Freedom National Bank to Congress: "My first testimony when I came to this job was that it's unfair to treat big banks in a way that covers all depositors but not small banks. I promised to do my best to change that. Five years later, I can report that my best wasn't good enough."[†]

[†]Quoted in Kenneth H. Bacon, "Failures of a Big Bank and a Little Bank Bring Fairness of Deposit-Security Policy into Question," *Wall Street Journal,* December 5, 1990, p. A18.

want to run a bank. (Charles Keating, Jr., discussed in Box 5 later in this chapter, is one such person.) Chartering of banks is one method for preventing this adverse selection problem; through chartering, proposals for new banks are screened to prevent undesirable people from controlling them.

Regular bank examinations, which allow regulators to monitor whether the bank is complying with capital requirements and restrictions on asset holdings, also function to limit moral hazard. Bank examiners give banks a so-called *CAMEL rating* (the acronym is based on the five areas assessed: capital adequacy, asset quality, management, earnings, and liquidity). With this information about a bank's activities, regulators can enforce regulations and close a bank if its CAMEL rating is low. Actions taken to reduce moral hazard by preventing

Box 2

THE BASEL ACCORD ON RISK-BASED CAPITAL REQUIREMENTS

The increased integration of financial markets across countries and the need to make the playing field level for banks from different countries led to the Basel accord in June 1988 to standardize bank capital requirements internationally. The stated purposes of the agreement were (1) to promote world financial stability by coordinating supervisory definitions of capital, risk assessments, and standards for capital adequacy across countries and (2) to link a bank's capital requirements systematically to the riskiness of its activities, including various off-balance-sheet forms of risk exposure.

The Basel capital requirements work as follows. Assets and off-balance-sheet activities are allocated into four categories, each with a different weight to reflect the degree of credit risk. The lowest risk category carries a zero weight and includes items that have no default risk, such as reserves and government securities. The next lowest risk category has a weight of 20% and includes assets with a low default risk, such as interbank deposits, fully backed mortgage bonds, and securities issued by government agencies. The third category has a weight of 50% and includes municipal bonds and residential mortgages. The last risk category has the maximum weight of 100% and includes all remaining securities (such as commercial paper), loans (such as commercial and real estate construction loans), and fixed assets (bank building, computers, and other property). Off-balance-sheet activities are treated in a similar manner by assigning a credit equivalent percentage that converts them to on-balance-sheet items, and then the appropriate risk weight applies. For example, a standby letter of credit backing a customer's commercial paper is assigned a 100% credit equivalent percentage and then has a risk weight of 100% because it exposes the bank to the same risk as a direct loan to this customer.

Once all the bank's assets and off-balance-sheet items have been assigned to a risk category, they are weighted by the corresponding risk factor and are added up to compute the total "risk-adjusted assets." The bank must then meet two capital requirements: It must have "core" or Tier 1 capital (stockholder equity capital) of at least 4% of total risk-adjusted assets, and total capital (Tier 1 capital plus Tier 2 capital, which is made up of loan loss reserves and subordinated debt) must come to 8% of total risk-adjusted assets. (Subordinated debt is debt that is paid off only after depositors and other creditors have been paid.) For the Federal Reserve to classify a bank as well capitalized, it must meet an even more stringent total-capital requirement of 10% of risk-adjusted assets and Tier 1 capital of 6% of risk-adjusted assets.

banks from taking on too much risk help reduce the adverse selection problem further because with less of an opportunity for risk-taking, risk-loving entrepreneurs will be less likely to be attracted to the banking industry.[2]

A commercial bank obtains a charter either from the Comptroller of the Currency (in the case of a national bank) or from a state banking authority (in the case of a state bank). To obtain a charter, the people planning to organize the bank must submit an application that shows how they plan to operate the bank. In evaluating the application, the regulatory authority looks at whether the bank is likely to be sound by examining the quality of the bank's intended management, the likely earnings of the bank, and the amount of the bank's initial capital. Before 1980, the chartering agency typically explored the issue of whether the community needed a new bank. Often a new bank charter would not be granted if existing banks in a community would be severely hurt by its presence. Today this anticompetitive stance (justified by the desire to prevent bank failures of existing banks) is no longer as strong in the chartering agencies.

Once a bank has been chartered, it is required to file periodic (usually quarterly) reports that reveal the bank's assets and liabilities, income and dividends, ownership, foreign exchange operations, and other details. The bank is also subject to examination by the bank regulatory agencies to ascertain its financial condition at least once a year. To avoid duplication of effort, the three federal agencies work together and usually accept each other's examinations. This means that, typically, national banks are examined by the Office of the Comptroller of the Currency, the state banks that are members of the Federal Reserve System are examined by the Fed, and nonmember state banks are examined by the FDIC.

Bank examinations are conducted by bank examiners, who make unannounced visits to the bank (so that nothing can be "swept under the rug" in anticipation of their examination). The examiners study a bank's books to see whether it is complying with the rules and regulations that apply to its holdings of assets. If a bank is holding securities or loans that are too risky, the bank examiner can force the bank to get rid of them. If a bank examiner decides that a loan is unlikely to be repaid, the examiner can force the bank to declare the loan worthless (to write off the loan). If, after examining the bank, the examiner feels that it does not have sufficient capital or has engaged in dishonest practices, the bank can be declared a "problem bank" and will be subject to more frequent examinations.

---

[2]Note that the methods regulators use to cope with adverse selection and moral hazard have their counterparts in private financial markets (see Chapters 9 and 11). Chartering is similar to the screening of potential borrowers, regulations restricting risky asset holdings are similar to restrictive covenants that prevent borrowing firms from engaging in risky investment activities, bank capital requirements act like restrictive covenants that require minimum amounts of net worth for borrowing firms, and regular bank examinations are similar to the monitoring of borrowers by lending institutions.

Separation of the Banking and Securities Industries: The Glass-Steagall Act

Before 1933, commercial banks engaged in investment banking activities as well as traditional banking activities. Because investment banking is inherently risky, allowing banks to pursue these activities increased their moral hazard opportunities for risk taking. After sensational congressional hearings documenting abuses of commercial banks in their securities activities during the Great Depression collapse—which were as widely followed by the public as the Watergate or Iran-*contra* hearings in recent years—Congress passed the Glass-Steagall Act in 1933. Glass-Steagall allowed commercial banks to sell new offerings of government securities but prohibited them from underwriting corporate securities or from engaging in brokerage activities. It also prohibited investment banks from engaging in commercial banking activities. Additional regulation has prohibited the banks from selling insurance and engaging in other nonbank activities that are considered risky.

Not many other countries have followed the lead of the United States in separating the banking and securities industries (see Box 3). This separation is the most prominent difference between banking regulation in the United States and in other countries.

INTERNATIONAL BANKING REGULATION

Because asymmetric information problems in the banking industry are a fact of life throughout the world, bank regulation in other countries is similar to that in the United States. Banks are chartered and examined by government regulators, just as they are in the United States—for example, by the Ministry of Finance in Japan and by the Bank of England in the United Kingdom. Deposit insurance is also a feature of the regulatory systems in most other developed countries, although its coverage often is smaller than in the United States and is purposely not advertised. We have also seen that bank capital requirements are in the process of being standardized across countries with agreements like the Basel accord.

Problems in Regulating International Banking

Particular problems in bank regulation occur when banks are engaged in international banking and thus can readily shift their business from one country to another. Bank regulators closely examine the domestic operations of banks in their country, but they often do not have the knowledge or ability to keep a close watch on bank operations in other countries, either by domestic banks'

SEPARATION OF THE BANKING AND SECURITIES INDUSTRIES IN INDUSTRIALIZED COUNTRIES

Major industrialized countries allow different relationships between the banking and securities industries. There are three basic frameworks for the separation of the banking and the securities industries.

The first framework is *universal banking,* which exists in Germany, the Netherlands, and Switzerland. It provides no separation at all between the banking and securities industries. In a universal banking system, commercial banks provide a full range of banking, securities, and insurance services, all within a single legal entity. Banks are allowed to own sizable equity shares in commercial firms, and often they do.

The British-style universal banking system, the second framework, is found in the United Kingdom and countries with close ties to it, such as Canada and Australia. The British-style universal bank engages in securities underwriting, but it differs from the German-style universal bank in three ways: Separate legal subsidiaries are more common, bank equity holdings of commercial firms are less common, and combinations of banking and insurance firms are less common.

The third framework features legal separation of the banking and securities industries, as in the United States and Japan. A major difference between the U.S. and Japanese banking systems is that Japanese banks are allowed to hold substantial equity stakes in commercial firms, whereas American banks cannot. In addition, most American banks use a bank-holding-company structure, but bank holding companies are illegal in Japan. Although the banking and securities industries are legally separated under the Glass-Steagall Act in the United States and Section 65 of the Japanese Securities Act, in both countries commercial banks are increasingly engaging in securities activities and are thus becoming more like British-style universal banks.

foreign affiliates or by foreign banks with domestic branches. In addition, when a bank operates in many countries, it is not always clear which national regulatory authority should have the primary responsibility for keeping that bank from engaging in overly risky activities. The difficulties inherent in regulating international banking have been recently highlighted by the BCCI scandal discussed in Box 4. Cooperation among regulators in different countries and standardization of regulatory requirements provide potential solutions to the problems of regulating international banking. The world has been moving in this direction through agreements like the Basel accord on capital requirements in 1988 and the new regulatory oversight procedures announced by the Basel Committee in

July 1992 (see Box 4). However, whether agreements of this type will solve the problem of regulating international banking in the future is an open question.

RESPONSE OF REGULATION TO FINANCIAL INNOVATION

To understand fully why the crisis in banking regulation has occurred, we need to see how banking regulation changed in response to financial innovation that occurred in the 1960s, 1970s, and early 1980s. Just as financial institutions change and financial innovation occurs in response to regulation, the regulatory authorities change their regulations in response to financial innovation. This process can be thought of as a cat-and-mouse game between the financial institutions and the regulators, each side continually adapting to the other.

Two major objectives of the regulatory authorities have governed their response to financial innovation in the past 25 years: the desire to encourage home ownership, reflected in attempts by the regulatory authorities to ensure flows of funds into mortgage-issuing institutions, and the desire to encourage stability in the financial system, reflected in attempts to prevent bank failures.

Changing Banking Regulation in the 1960s and 1970s

When market interest rates began to rise above the Regulation Q ceilings on deposit rates in the mid-1960s, funds began to leave depository institutions, particularly savings and loans and mutual savings banks. Because these latter institutions were the most important issuers of residential mortgages, their loss of deposits meant that fewer funds were available to loan out on home mortgages. Therefore, to encourage the flow of funds into these mortgage-issuing institutions, the Fed adjusted its Regulation Q ceilings to allow savings and loans and mutual savings banks to pay slightly higher interest rates (by 0.25%) on their time deposits than commercial banks could pay on theirs. In addition, to put everyone on a more equal footing, deposit rate ceilings were extended to previously unregulated institutions such as credit unions.

Regulators also pursued a second strategy to discourage financial market instruments that would compete with deposits. They convinced the U.S. Treasury in 1970 to raise the minimum denomination on Treasury bills to $10,000 so that small savers would be forced to put their savings into savings and loans and mutual savings banks. In addition, they encouraged bank holding companies and corporations not to issue small-denomination debt. This strategy discriminated against small savers (typically with low incomes), who were prevented from earning market interest rates. Large savers (typically with high incomes) had sufficient resources to buy large-denomination securities and earn market interest rates. This strategy of discrimination against lower-income people is both pecu-

A Global Perspective

Box 4

THE BCCI SCANDAL

The Bank of Credit and Commerce International (BCCI) was chartered in Luxembourg in 1972 by a Pakistani businessman, Agha Hasan Abedi. The bank grew rapidly to $20 billion in assets and by 1991 was operating in more than 70 countries. Unfortunately, the bank was siphoning off funds to secret accounts in the Cayman Islands, where much of this money was stolen. Indeed, estimates suggest that nearly half of the bank's assets may have "disappeared." Fraud was not the only shady activity BCCI engaged in. BCCI supposedly helped dictators such as Saddam Hussein of Iraq, Manuel Noriega of Panama, and Ferdinand Marcos of the Philippines steal huge sums from their countries, helped the CIA channel funds to the *contras* in Nicaragua, and acted as a banker for the notorious Abu Nidal terrorist group. Not surprisingly, BCCI has been dubbed the "Bank of Crooks and Criminals, Inc."

How did BCCI get away with these fraudulent activities for so long? The answer illustrates the difficulties in regulating banks with operations in many countries. Although BCCI's headquarters were in London, regulatory oversight fell to the chartering country, Luxembourg, whose tiny bank regulator, the Institut Monétaire Luxembourgeois (IML), was not up to the task. As a result, BCCI effectively operated free of government regulatory oversight for 15 years. In 1987, the IML reached an agreement with seven other countries' regulators to oversee BCCI jointly, but even this larger group was unable to keep track of the bank's activities. Only in spring 1990 did these regulators uncover some evidence of fraud, and not until July 1991 did Price Waterhouse document the pervasiveness of the fraud to the Bank of England, which then closed BCCI down.

The losses to depositors and stockholders from the BCCI collapse were immense, and national regulators, particularly the Bank of England, have been severely criticized for their slowness in uncovering the scandal. A year after the BCCI collapse, in July 1992, the Basel Committee announced an agreement to standardize further the regulation of international banks. Now a bank's worldwide operations will be under the scrutiny of a single home-country regulator with enhanced powers to acquire information on the bank's activities. Furthermore, regulators in other countries will have the right to restrict operations of a foreign bank if they feel that it lacks effective oversight. Despite this improvement in the regulation of international banks, there are still fears that another BCCI-like scandal could happen again.

liar and somewhat paradoxical; most of us do not advocate the "Robin Hood in reverse" policy of taking from the poor to give to the rich.

Although deposit rate ceilings worked in the short run to provide low-cost funds to the mortgage-issuing institutions, financial innovation ultimately got around these regulations. By the late 1970s, the success of money market mutual funds and overnight repurchase agreements was causing mortgage-issuing institutions to lose so many deposits that their financial health was severely threatened. One temporary solution was to allow these institutions to issue money market certificates (MMCs), which paid market interest rates. An interesting feature of this regulatory change is that it continued to discriminate against small savers because these certificates were issued in denominations of $10,000. The large-denomination MMCs kept small savers from shifting their deposits into these certificates. This enabled the mortgage-issuing institutions to hold on to their low-cost deposits and thus have an overall lower cost of funds.

By 1980, despite all of these regulatory changes, continually rising interest rates had left savings and loans and mutual savings banks in even deeper financial trouble and threatened commercial banks as well. A major financial reform was needed, and it came in the form of congressional legislation: the Depository Institutions Deregulation and Monetary Control Act of 1980.

Depository Institutions Deregulation and Monetary Control Act of 1980

When attempting to pass major legislation, it is usually necessary to try to please as many opposing parties as possible. An important intent of the Depository Institutions Deregulation and Monetary Control Act (DIDMCA) was to help the mortgage-issuing institutions (savings and loan associations and mutual savings banks). These institutions were allowed to compete more effectively against commercial banks by being given wider latitude in the loans they could make. For example, savings and loans, whose loans had effectively been restricted to mortgages, were now allowed to invest up to 20% of their assets in consumer loans, commercial paper, and corporate bonds. Mutual savings banks were allowed to make commercial loans up to 5% of their assets and were allowed to open checking accounts in connection with these loans. In addition, savings and loans were allowed to expand into new lines of business such as trust services and credit cards.

DIDMCA also approved NOW and ATS accounts nationwide at all depository institutions, thereby allowing all of these institutions to compete more effectively against money market mutual funds, and it also mandated a phaseout of Regulation Q, to be completed by 1986. The provisions of DIDMCA benefited not only the mortgage-issuing institutions but also commercial banks and credit unions, thus garnering their support for this legislation. These provisions were popular with the public because they allowed depositors to earn higher interest payments on their deposits.

Other provisions of DIDMCA involved eliminating the usury ceilings (maximum interest rates) on loans and increasing the amount of deposit insurance to $100,000. Finally, DIDMCA imposed uniform reserve requirements on all depository institutions and allowed all of these institutions access to Federal Reserve facilities, such as the discount window and Fed check-clearing services. This final set of provisions put all of these institutions on an equal footing and made them more subject to control by the Fed. The Fed argued strenuously for provisions of this type to stem the loss of members from the Federal Reserve System and to improve monetary control.

Impact of DIDMCA The expansion of NOW and ATS account deposits after they were authorized by DIDMCA was dramatic, with the amount of these deposits increasing from $27 billion to $101 billion from 1980 to 1982. However, because Regulation Q deposit rate ceilings were being phased out gradually and market interest rates climbed to record levels in 1981–1982, money market funds continued to grow rapidly (averaging $76 billion in 1980 and $230 billion in 1982). As a result, savings and loans and mutual savings banks were losing deposits at the same time that the cost of their acquired funds climbed higher. The result was a number of failures of these institutions, unprecedented in the postwar era. Further reform legislation was needed to help these institutions.

Depository Institutions (Garn–St Germain) Act of 1982

In October 1982, the Depository Institutions Act, also known as the Garn–St Germain Act, was passed to deal with the immediate emergency stemming from the mounting number of failures of savings and loans and mutual savings banks (over 250 in 1982). To compete more effectively with money market funds, depository institutions were allowed to offer money market deposit accounts (MMDAs), which provided services comparable to money market mutual funds and were not subject to Regulation Q ceilings or reserve requirements. Because depository institutions were able to pay high interest rates on these accounts, they became immensely popular: By the end of 1983, MMDA deposits had grown to almost $400 billion.

The Garn–St Germain Act had additional provisions to help savings and loans and mutual savings banks. By 1984, federally chartered savings and loans and mutual savings banks were allowed to invest up to 10% of their assets in commercial loans, and the maximum amount of consumer lending was raised to 30% of their assets. Because the provisions put these institutions on a more equal footing with commercial banks, the Garn–St Germain Act required that from 1984 on, Regulation Q ceilings should apply equally to all depository institutions until these ceilings expired in 1986.

A final set of provisions was designed to assist the FDIC and its S&L counterpart, the FSLIC, in dealing with the emergency situation due to bank failures. For example, the FDIC and FSLIC were given emergency powers to merge troubled institutions across state lines or to merge thrift institutions (mutual savings banks and savings and loans) into commercial banks.

Impact of the Garn–St Germain Act The net effect of the Garn–St Germain Act and the DIDMCA legislation of 1980 has been to make the banking system as a whole more competitive: All depository institutions are treated more equally, and the distinctions among the various depository institutions have become blurred. Although the deregulation in DIDMCA and the Garn–St Germain Act produced the benefit of a more competitive banking system, it also helped increase risk taking on the part of savings and loans, which resulted in the S&L crisis discussed in the next section.

STUDY GUIDE

Because there has been so much legislation on banking regulation, it is hard to keep track of it all. As a study aid, Table 1 lists the major banking legislation in the twentieth century and its key provisions.

THE 1980s BANKING CRISIS: WHY?

Before the 1980s, federal deposit insurance seemed to work exceedingly well. In contrast to the pre-1934 period, when bank failures were common and depositors frequently suffered losses, the period from 1934 to 1980 was one in which bank failures were a rarity, averaging 15 a year for commercial banks and fewer than 5 a year for savings and loans. After 1981, this rosy picture changed dramatically. Failures in both commercial banks and savings and loans climbed to levels more than ten times greater than in earlier years. Why did this happen? How did a deposit insurance system that seemed to be working well for half a century find itself in so much trouble?

Early Stages of the Crisis

The story starts with the burst of financial innovation in the 1960s, 1970s, and early 1980s discussed in Chapters 11 and 12. As we have seen, financial innovation decreased the profitability of certain traditional business for commercial banks. Banks now faced increased competition for their sources of funds from new financial institutions such as money market mutual funds while they were losing commercial lending business to the commercial paper market and securitization.

With the decreasing profitability of their traditional business, commercial banks were forced to seek out new and potentially risky business to keep their profits up. For example, in recent years commercial banks increased their risk taking by placing a greater percentage of their total loans in real estate and in credit extended to assist corporate takeovers and leveraged buyouts (called *highly leveraged transaction loans*).

The existence of deposit insurance increased moral hazard for banks because insured depositors had little incentive to keep the banks from taking on

TABLE 1   Major Banking Legislation in the United States in the Twentieth Century

Federal Reserve Act (1913)
Created the Federal Reserve System

Banking Act of 1933 (Glass-Steagall) and 1935
Created the FDIC
Separated commercial banking from the securities industry
Prohibited interest on checkable deposits and restricted such deposits to commercial banks
Put interest-rate ceilings on other deposits

Bank Holding Company Act (1956) and Douglas Amendment (1970)
Clarified the status of bank holding companies (BHCs)
Gave the Federal Reserve regulatory responsibility for BHCs

Bank Merger Acts (1960, 1966)
Provided guidelines for bank mergers

Depository Institutions Deregulation and Monetary Control Act (DIDMCA) of 1980
Gave thrift institutions wider latitude in activities
Approved NOW and ATS accounts nationwide
Phased out deposit rate ceilings
Imposed uniform reserve requirements on depository institutions
Eliminated usury ceilings on loans
Increased deposit insurance to $100,000 per account

Depository Institutions Act of 1982 (Garn–St Germain)
Gave the FDIC and the FSLIC emergency powers to merge banks and thrifts across state lines
Allowed depository institutions to offer money market deposit accounts (MMDAs)
Granted thrifts wider latitude in commercial and consumer lending

Competitive Equality in Banking Act (CEBA) of 1987
Provided $10.8 billion to the FSLIC
Made provisions for regulatory forbearance in depressed areas

Financial Institutions Reform, Recovery, and Enforcement Act (FIRREA) of 1989
Provided funds to resolve S&L failures
Eliminated the FSLIC and the Federal Home Loan Bank Board
Created the Office of Thrift Supervision to regulate thrifts
Created the Resolution Trust Corporation to resolve insolvent thrifts
Raised deposit insurance premiums
Reimposed restrictions on S&L activities

Federal Deposit Insurance Corporation Improvement Act (FDICIA) of 1991
Recapitalized the FDIC
Limited brokered deposits and the too-big-to-fail policy
Set provisions for prompt corrective action
Instructed the FDIC to establish risk-based premiums
Increased examinations, capital requirements, and reporting requirements
Included the Foreign Bank Supervision Enhancement Act (FBSEA), which strengthened the Fed's
   authority to supervise foreign banks

too much risk. Regardless of how much risk banks were taking, deposit insurance guaranteed that depositors would not suffer any losses.

Adding fuel to the fire, financial innovation produced new financial instruments that widened the scope for risk taking. New markets in financial futures, junk bonds, swaps, and other instruments made it easier for banks to take on extra risk—making the moral hazard problem more severe. New legislation that deregulated the banking industry in 1980 and 1982 opened up even more avenues to savings and loans and mutual savings banks to take on more risk. These thrift institutions, which had been restricted almost entirely to making loans for home mortgages, now were allowed to have up to 40% of their assets in commercial real estate loans, up to 30% in consumer lending, and up to 10% in commercial loans and leases. In the wake of this legislation, savings and loans regulators allowed up to 10% of assets to be in junk bonds or in direct investments (common stocks, real estate, service corporations, and operating subsidiaries).

In addition, the 1980 legislation increased the mandated amount of federal deposit insurance from $40,000 per account to $100,000 and phased out Regulation Q deposit rate ceilings. Banks and S&Ls that wanted to pursue rapid growth and take on risky projects could now attract the necessary funds by issuing larger-denomination insured certificates of deposit with interest rates much higher than those being offered by their competitors. Without deposit insurance, high interest rates would not have induced depositors to provide the high-rolling banks with funds because of the realistic expectation that they might not get the funds back. But with deposit insurance, the government was guaranteeing that the deposits were safe, so depositors were more than happy to make deposits in banks with the highest interest rates.

A financial innovation that made it even easier for high-rolling banks to raise funds is known as **brokered deposits,** which enable depositors to circumvent the $100,000 limit on deposit insurance. Brokered deposits work as follows: A large depositor with $10 million goes to a broker, who breaks the $10 million into 100 packages of $100,000 each and then buys $100,000 CDs at 100 different banks. Because the amount of each CD is within the $100,000 limit for deposits at each bank, the large depositor has in effect obtained deposit insurance on all $10 million. The federal deposit insurance agencies did pass a regulation to ban brokered deposits in 1984, but a federal court judgment overturned the ban.

Financial innovation and deregulation in the permissive atmosphere of the Reagan years made the moral hazard problem more severe. In addition, the incentives of moral hazard were increased dramatically by a historical accident: the combination of the sharp increases in interest rates from late 1979 until 1981 and the severe recession in 1981–1982, both of which were engineered by the Federal Reserve to bring down inflation. The sharp rises in interest rates produced rapidly rising costs of funds for the savings and loans that were not matched by higher earnings on the S&Ls' principal asset, long-term residential mortgages (whose rates had been fixed at a time when interest rates were far lower). Then the 1981–1982 recession and the collapse in the prices of energy and farm products hit the economies of certain parts of the country such as Texas very hard. As a result, there were defaults on many S&Ls' loans. Losses for savings and loan institutions mounted to $10 billion in 1981–1982, and by some estimates over half of the S&Ls in the United States had a negative net worth and were thus insolvent by the end of 1982.

Later Stages of the Crisis: Regulatory Forbearance

At this point, a logical step might have been for the S&L regulators—the Federal Home Loan Bank Board and its deposit insurance subsidiary, the Federal Savings and Loan Insurance Fund (FSLIC), both now abolished—to close the insolvent S&Ls. Instead, these regulators adopted the stance of **regulatory forbearance:** They refrained from exercising their regulatory right to put the insolvent S&Ls out of business. To sidestep their responsibility to close ailing S&Ls, they adopted irregular regulatory accounting principles that in effect substantially lowered capital requirements. For example, they allowed S&Ls to include in their capital calculations a high value for intangible capital, called *goodwill.*

There were three main reasons why the Federal Home Loan Bank Board and FSLIC opted for regulatory forbearance. First, the FSLIC did not have sufficient funds in its insurance fund to close the insolvent S&Ls and pay off their deposits. Second, the Federal Home Loan Bank Board was established to encourage the growth of the savings and loan industry, so the regulators were probably too close to the people they were supposed to be regulating. Third, because bureaucrats do not like to admit that their own agency is in trouble, the Federal Home Loan Bank Board and the FSLIC preferred to sweep their problems under the rug in the hope that they would go away.

Regulatory forbearance increases moral hazard dramatically because an operating but insolvent S&L (nicknamed a "zombie S&L" by Edward Kane of Ohio State University because it is the "living dead") has almost nothing to lose by taking on great risk and "betting the bank": If it gets lucky and its risky investments pay off, it gets out of insolvency. Unfortunately, if, as is likely, the risky investments don't pay off, the zombie S&L's losses will mount, and the deposit insurance agency will be left holding the bag.

This strategy is similar to the "long bomb" strategy in football. When a football team is almost hopelessly behind and time is running out, it often resorts to a high-risk play: the throwing of a long pass to try to score a touchdown. Of course, the long bomb is unlikely to be successful, but there is always a small chance that it will work. If it doesn't, the team has lost nothing since it would have lost the game anyway.

Given the sequence of events we have discussed here, it should be no surprise that savings and loans began to take huge risks: They built shopping centers in the desert, bought manufacturing plants to convert manure to methane, and purchased billions of dollars of high-risk, high-yield junk bonds. The S&L industry was no longer the staid industry that once operated on the so-called *3-6-3 rule:* You took in money at 3%, lent it at 6%, and played golf at 3 P.M. Although many savings and loans were making money, losses at other S&Ls were colossal.

Another outcome of regulatory forbearance was that with little to lose, zombie S&Ls attracted deposits away from healthy S&Ls by offering higher interest rates. Because there were so many zombie S&Ls in Texas pursuing this strategy, above-market interest rates on deposits at Texas S&Ls were said to have a "Texas premium." Potentially healthy S&Ls now found that to compete for deposits, they had to pay higher interest rates, which made their operations less profitable and frequently pushed them into the zombie category. Similarly, zombie S&Ls in pursuit of asset growth made loans at below-market interest rates, thereby lowering loan interest rates for healthy S&Ls, and again made them less profitable. The zombie S&Ls had actually taken on attributes of vampires—their willingness to pay above-market rates for deposits and take below-market interest rates on loans was sucking the lifeblood (profits) out of healthy S&Ls.

Competitive Equality in Banking Act of 1987

Toward the end of 1986, the growing losses in the savings and loan industry were bankrupting the insurance fund of the FSLIC. The Reagan administration sought $15 billion in funds for the FSLIC, a completely inadequate sum considering that many times this amount was needed to close down insolvent S&Ls. The legislation passed by Congress, the Competitive Equality in Banking Act (CEBA) of 1987, did not even meet the administration's requests. It provided only $10.8 billion to the FSLIC and, what was worse, included provisions that directed the Federal Home Loan Bank Board to continue to pursue regulatory forbearance (allow insolvent institutions to keep operating), particularly in economically depressed areas such as Texas.

The failure of Congress to deal with the savings and loan crisis was not going to make the problem go away and, consistent with our analysis, the situation deteriorated rapidly. Losses in the savings and loan industry surpassed $10 billion in 1988 and approached $20 billion in 1989. The crisis was reaching epidemic proportions.

POLITICAL ECONOMY OF THE SAVINGS AND LOAN CRISIS

Although we now have a grasp of the regulatory and economic forces that created the S&L crisis, we still need to understand the political forces that produced the regulatory structure and activities that led to it. The key to understanding the political economy of the S&L is to recognize that the relationship between voter-taxpayers and the regulators and politicians creates a particular type of moral hazard problem, discussed in Chapter 9: the *principal-agent problem,* which occurs when representatives (agents) such as managers have incentives that differ from those of their employer (the principal) and so act in their own interest rather than in the interest of the employer.

Principal-Agent Problem for Regulators and Politicians

Regulators and politicians are ultimately agents for voter-taxpayers (principals) because in the final analysis, taxpayers bear the cost of any losses by the deposit insurance agency. The principal-agent problem occurs because the agent (a politician or regulator) does not have the same incentives to minimize costs to the economy as the principal (the taxpayer).

To act in the taxpayer's interest and lower costs to the deposit insurance agency, regulators have several tasks, as we have seen. They must set tight restrictions on holding assets that are too risky, must impose high capital requirements, and must not adopt a stance of regulatory forbearance, which allows insolvent institutions to continue to operate. However, because of the principal-agent problem, regulators have incentives to do the opposite. Indeed, as our sad saga of the S&L debacle indicates, they have often loosened capital requirements and restrictions on risky asset holdings and pursued regulatory forbearance. One important incentive for regulators that explains this phenomenon is their desire to escape blame for poor performance by their agency. By loosening capital requirements and pursuing regulatory forbearance, regulators hide the problem of an insolvent bank and hope that the situation will improve. Edward Kane characterizes such behavior on the part of regulators as "bureaucratic gambling."

Another important incentive for regulators is that they want to protect their careers by acceding to pressures from the people who most influence their careers. These people are not the taxpayers but the politicians who try to keep regulators from imposing tough regulations on institutions that are major campaign contributors. Members of Congress have often lobbied regulators to ease up on a particular S&L that contributed large sums to their campaigns (see Box 5).

In addition, both Congress and the presidential administration promoted banking legislation in 1980 and 1982 that made it easier for savings and loans to engage in risk-taking activities. After the legislation passed, the need for monitoring the S&L industry increased because of the expansion of permissible activities. The S&L regulatory agencies needed more resources to carry out their monitoring activities properly, but Congress (successfully lobbied by the S&L industry) was unwilling to allocate the necessary funds. As a result, the S&L regulatory agencies became so short-staffed that they actually had to cut back on their on-site examinations just when these were needed most. In the period from January 1984 to July 1986, for example, several hundred S&Ls were not examined once. Even worse, spurred on by the intense lobbying efforts of the S&L industry, Congress passed the Competitive Equality in Banking Act of 1987, which, as we have seen, provided inadequate funding to close down the insolvent S&Ls and also hampered the S&L regulators from doing their job properly by including provisions encouraging regulatory forbearance.

As these examples indicate, the structure of our political system has created a serious principal-agent problem; politicians have strong incentives to act in their own interests rather than in the interests of taxpayers. Because of the high

B o x   5

A CASE STUDY OF WHAT WENT WRONG: CHARLES KEATING AND THE LINCOLN SAVINGS AND LOAN SCANDAL

The scandal associated with Charles H. Keating, Jr., and the Lincoln Savings and Loan Association provides a graphic example of why the savings and loan crisis occurred. As Edwin Gray, a former chairman of the Federal Home Loan Bank Board, stated, "This is a story of incredible corruption. I can't call it anything else."*

Charles Keating was allowed to acquire Lincoln Savings and Loan of Irvine, California, in early 1984, even though he had been accused of fraud by the SEC only 4½ years earlier. For Keating, whose construction firm, American Continental, planned to build huge real estate developments in Arizona, the S&L was a gold mine: In the lax regulatory atmosphere at the time, controlling the S&L gave his firm easy access to funds without being scrutinized by outside bankers. Within days of acquiring control, Keating got rid of Lincoln's conservative lending officers and internal auditors, even though he had promised regulators he would keep them. Lincoln then plunged into high-risk investments such as currency futures, junk bonds, common stock, hotels, and vast tracts of desert land in Arizona.

Because of the shortage of savings and loan examiners that existed at the time, Lincoln was able to escape a serious examination until 1986, whereupon examiners from the Federal Home Loan Bank of San Francisco discovered that Lincoln had exceeded the 10% limit on equity investments by $600 million. Because of these activities and some evidence that Lincoln was deliberately trying to mislead the examiners, the examiners recommended federal seizure of the bank and all its assets. Keating was not about to take this lying down; he engaged hordes of lawyers—eventually 77 law firms—and accused the bank examiners of bias. He also sued unsuccessfully to overturn the 10% equity limit. Keating is said to have bragged that he spent $50 million fighting regulators.

(cont.)

cost of running campaigns, American politicians must raise substantial contributions. This situation may provide lobbyists and other campaign contributors with the opportunity to influence politicians to act against the public interest.

SAVINGS AND LOAN BAILOUT: FINANCIAL INSTITUTIONS REFORM, RECOVERY, AND ENFORCEMENT ACT OF 1989

Immediately after taking office, the Bush administration proposed new legislation to provide adequate funding to close down the insolvent S&Ls. The resulting legislation, the Financial Institutions Reform, Recovery, and Enforcement Act

A CASE STUDY OF WHAT WENT WRONG: CHARLES KEATING AND THE LINCOLN SAVINGS AND LOAN SCANDAL (cont.)

Lawyers were not Keating's only tactic for keeping regulators off his back. After receiving $1.3 million of contributions to their campaigns from Keating, five senators—Dennis De Concini and John McCain of Arizona, Alan Cranston of California, John Glenn of Ohio, and Donald Riegle of Michigan (subsequently nicknamed the "Keating Five")—met with Edwin Gray, the chairman of the Federal Home Loan Board, and later with four top regulators from San Francisco in April 1987. They complained that the regulators were being too tough on Lincoln and urged the regulators to quit dragging out the investigation. After Gray was replaced by M. Danny Wall, Wall took the unprecedented step of removing the San Francisco examiners from the case in September 1987 and transferred the investigation to the bank board's headquarters in Washington. No examiners called on Lincoln for the next ten months, and as one of the San Francisco examiners described it, Lincoln dropped into a "regulatory black hole."

Lincoln Savings and Loan finally failed in early 1989, with estimated costs to taxpayers of $2.6 billion, making it possibly the most costly S&L failure in history. Keating was convicted for abuses (such as having Lincoln pay him and his family $34 million) and is now serving a lengthy jail term, and Wall was forced to resign as head of the Office of Thrift Supervision because of his involvement in the Keating scandal. As a result of their activities on behalf of Keating, the Keating Five senators were made the object of a congressional ethics investigation, but given Congress's propensity to protect its own, they were subjected only to minor sanctions.

*Quoted in Tom Morganthau, Rich Thomas, and Eleanor Clift, "The S&L Scandal's Biggest Blowout," *Newsweek,* November 6, 1989, p. 35.

(FIRREA), was signed into law on August 9, 1989. It was the most significant legislation to affect the thrift industry since the 1930s. FIRREA's major provisions were as follows: The regulatory apparatus was significantly restructured without the Federal Home Loan Bank Board and the FSLIC, both of which had failed in their regulatory tasks. The regulatory role of the Federal Home Loan Bank Board was relegated to the Office of Thrift Supervision (OTS), a bureau within the U.S. Treasury Department, and its responsibilities are similar to those that the Office of the Comptroller of the Currency has over the national banks. The regulatory responsibilities of the FSLIC were given to the FDIC, and the FDIC became the sole administrator of the federal deposit insurance system with two separate insurance funds: the Bank Insurance Fund (BIF) and the Savings Association Insurance Fund (SAIF). Another new agency, the Resolution Trust Corporation

(RTC), was established to manage and resolve insolvent thrifts placed in conservatorship or receivership. It was made responsible for selling more than $300 billion of real estate owned by failed institutions. The RTC is managed by the FDIC and is under the general supervision of the RTC Oversight Board (composed of the secretary of the Treasury, the chairman of the Board of Governors of the Federal Reserve, the secretary of Housing and Urban Development, and two other members).

Initially, the total cost of the bailout was estimated to be $159 billion over the ten-year period through 1999, but more recent estimates indicate that the cost will be far higher. Indeed, the General Accounting Office placed a cost for the bailout at more than $500 billion over 40 years. However, as pointed out in Box 1 in Chapter 4, this estimate is misleading because, for example, the value of a payment 30 years from now is worth much less in today's dollars. The present value of the bailout cost is on the order of $150 billion. The funding for the bailout comes partly from capital in the Federal Home Loan Banks (owned by the S&L industry) but mostly from the sale of government debt by both the Treasury and the Resolution Funding Corporation (RefCorp).

To replenish the reserves of the Savings Association Insurance Fund, insurance premiums for S&Ls were increased from 20.8 cents per $100 of deposits to 23 cents and can rise as high as 32.5 cents. Premiums for banks immediately rose from 8.3 cents to 15 cents per $100 of deposits and were raised further to 23 cents in 1991.

FIRREA also imposed new restrictions on thrift activities that in essence reregulated the S&L industry to the asset choices it had before 1982. S&Ls can no longer purchase junk bonds and had to sell their holdings by 1994. Commercial real estate loans are restricted to four times capital rather than the previous limit of 40% of assets, and so this new restriction is a reduction for all institutions whose capital is less than 10% of assets. S&Ls must also hold at least 70%—up from 60%—of their assets in investments that are primarily housing-related. Troubled thrifts are not allowed to accept brokered deposits. Among the most important provisions of FIRREA was the increase in the core-capital leverage requirement from 3% to 8% and the eventual adherence to the same risk-based capital standards imposed on commercial banks.

FIRREA also enhanced the enforcement powers of thrift regulators by making it easier for them to remove managers, issue cease and desist orders, and impose civil penalties. The Justice Department was also given $75 million per year for three years to uncover and prosecute fraud in the banking industry, and maximum fines rose substantially.

FIRREA was a serious attempt to deal with some of the problems created by the banking crisis in that it provided substantial funds to close insolvent thrifts. However, the losses that continued to mount for the FDIC in 1990 and 1991 would have depleted its Bank Insurance Fund by 1992, requiring that this fund be recapitalized. In addition, FIRREA did little to cope with the underlying adverse selection and moral hazard problems created by deposit insurance. FIRREA did, however, mandate that the U.S. Treasury produce a comprehensive study and plan for reform of the federal deposit insurance system. After this study appeared in 1991, Congress passed the Federal Deposit Insurance Corporation Improvement Act (FDICIA), which engendered major reforms in the bank regulatory system.

FEDERAL DEPOSIT INSURANCE CORPORATION IMPROVEMENT ACT OF 1991

FDICIA's provisions were designed to serve two purposes: to recapitalize the Bank Insurance Fund of the FDIC and to reform the deposit insurance and regulatory system so that taxpayer losses would be minimized.

FDICIA recapitalized the Bank Insurance Fund by increasing the FDIC's ability to borrow from the Treasury to $30 billion (up from $5 billion). FDICIA also allowed the FDIC to borrow $45 billion for working capital—money that would be repaid as the FDIC sold the assets of failed banks. FDICIA also mandated that the FDIC assess higher deposit insurance premiums to pay back its loans and to achieve a level of reserves in its insurance funds that would equal 1.25% of insured deposits within 15 years.

The bill reduced the scope of deposit insurance in several ways. First, the FDIC is allowed to insure brokered deposits or accounts only if they are established under pension plans at well-capitalized banks. Second, and more important, the too-big-to-fail doctrine has been substantially limited: The FDIC must now close failed banks using the least-cost method, thus making it far more likely that uninsured depositors will suffer losses. An exception to this provision, whereby a bank would be declared too big to fail so that all depositors, both insured and uninsured, would be fully protected, would be allowed only if not doing so would "have serious adverse effects on economic conditions or financial stability." Furthermore, to invoke the too-big-to-fail policy, a two-thirds majority of both the Board of Governors of the Federal Reserve System and the directors of the FDIC, as well as the approval of the secretary of the Treasury, would be required. Furthermore, FDICIA requires that the Fed share in the FDIC's losses if long-term Fed lending to a bank that fails increases the FDIC's losses.

Probably the most important feature of FDICIA is its prompt corrective action provisions, which require the FDIC to intervene earlier and more vigorously when a bank gets into trouble. Banks are now classified into five groups based on bank capital. Group 1, classified as "well capitalized," are banks that significantly exceed minimum capital requirements and are allowed privileges such as insurance on brokered deposits and the ability to do some securities underwriting. Banks in group 2, classified as "adequately capitalized," meet minimum capital requirements and are not subject to corrective actions but are not allowed the privileges of the well-capitalized banks. Banks in group 3, "undercapitalized," fail to meet any relevant capital measure. Banks in groups 4 and 5 are "significantly undercapitalized" and "critically undercapitalized," respectively, and are not allowed to pay interest on their deposits at rates that are higher than average. In addition, for group 3 banks, the FDIC is required to take prompt corrective actions such as requiring them to submit a capital restoration plan, restrict their asset growth, and seek regulatory approval to open new branches or develop new lines of business. Banks that are so undercapitalized as to have equity capital less than 2% of assets fall into group 5, and the FDIC must take steps to close them down.

FDICIA also instructed the FDIC to come up with risk-based insurance premiums. The system the FDIC has put in place uses the bank capital classifications just outlined and other supervisory criteria to assess these premiums. For example, in 1993 and 1994, well-capitalized banks with the best supervisory rating only had to pay an insurance premium of 23 cents per $100, while undercapitalized banks with a low supervisory rating had to pay 31 cents per $100. These premiums were scheduled to rise by 1 cent on January 1, 1995.

Other provisions of FDICIA require regulators to perform annual on-site examinations, restrict real estate lending, and mandate stricter and more burdensome reporting requirements. The act also requires that the existing risk-based capital standards, which focus solely on credit risk, be modified to take account of interest-rate risk as well. FDICIA also provides securities firms with access to Federal Reserve discount lending during a financial crisis.

FDICIA also includes the Foreign Bank Supervision Enhancement Act (FBSEA), which in the wake of the BCCI scandal gives supervisory responsibility for foreign banks to the Federal Reserve and gives the Fed increased powers to acquire information on the foreign banks' activities. In addition, the Fed now has the right to prevent the operation of a foreign bank in the United States if it feels that the home country's supervision is not adequate or if the foreign bank is engaging in unsound banking practices.

APPLICATION

EVALUATING FDICIA

FDICIA is a major step in reforming the banking regulatory system. How well will it work to solve the adverse selection and moral hazard problems of the bank regulatory system? Let's use the analysis in the chapter to evaluate the most important provisions of this legislation to answer this question.

STUDY GUIDE

Before looking at the evaluation for each set of provisions, reread their description in the text. Then try to reason out how well the provisions will solve the current problems with banking regulation. This exercise will help you develop a deeper understanding of the material in this chapter.

Limits on the Scope of Deposit Insurance

Reducing the scope of deposit insurance by limiting insurance on brokered deposits and restricting the use of the too-big-to-fail policy have increased the incentives for uninsured depositors to monitor banks and to withdraw funds if the bank is taking on too much risk. Because banks will now fear the loss of deposits when they engage in risky activities, they have less incentive to take on too much risk. Limitations on the use of the too-big-to-fail policy starting in 1992 have resulted in increased losses to uninsured depositors as planned.

Some experts do not believe that depositors are capable of monitoring banks and imposing discipline on the banks, but it must be remembered that uninsured deposits exceed $100,000, a substantial amount. Many, though not all, holders of these large deposit amounts are pretty sophisticated and so do have the capability of monitoring and disciplining banks. Evidence that the largest banks benefiting from the too-big-to-fail policy before 1991 were also the ones that took on the most risk (see footnote 1) suggests that limiting its application may substantially reduce risk taking.

Prompt Corrective Action

The prompt corrective action provisions in FDICIA should also substantially reduce incentives for bank risk taking and reduce taxpayer losses. FDICIA uses a carrot-and-stick approach to get banks to hold more capital. If they are well capitalized, they receive valuable privileges; if their capital ratio falls, they are subject to more and more onerous regulation. Increased bank capital reduces moral hazard incentives for the bank because the bank now has more to lose if it fails and so is less likely to take on too much risk.

In addition, encouraging banks to hold more capital reduces potential losses for the FDIC because increased bank capital is a cushion that makes bank failure less likely. Furthermore, forcing the FDIC to close banks once their net worth is less than 2% (group 5) rather than waiting until net worth has fallen to zero makes it more likely that when a bank is closed, it will still have a positive net worth, thus limiting FDIC losses.

Prompt corrective action, which requires regulators to intervene early when bank capital begins to fall, is a serious attempt to reduce the principal-agent problem for politicians and regulators. With prompt corrective action provisions, regulators no longer have the option of regulatory forbearance, which, as we have seen, can greatly increase moral hazard incentives for banks.

Some critics of FDICIA feel that there are too many loopholes in the bill that still allow regulators too much discretion, thus leaving open the possibility of regulatory forbearance. However, an often overlooked part of the bill increases the accountability of regulators. FDICIA requires a mandatory review of any bank failure that imposes costs on the FDIC. The resulting report must be made available to any member of Congress and to the general public upon request, and the General Accounting Office must do an annual review of these reports. Opening up the actions of the regulators to public scrutiny will make regulatory forbearance less attractive to them, thereby reducing the principal-agent problem. It will also reduce the incentives of politicians to lean on regulators to relax their regulatory supervision of banks.

Risk-based Insurance Premiums

Under FDICIA, banks deemed to be taking on greater risk, in the form of lower capital or riskier assets, will be subjected to higher insurance premiums. Risk-based insurance premiums will consequently reduce the moral hazard incentives for banks to take on higher risk because if they do so, they will have to pay higher premiums. In addition, the fact that risk-based premiums drop as the bank's capital increases encourages the bank to hold more capital, which has the benefits already mentioned.

One problem with risk-based premiums is that the scheme for determining the amount of risk the bank is taking may not be very accurate. For example, it might be hard for regulators to determine when a bank's loans are risky. Some critics have also pointed out that the classification of banks by such measures as the Basel risk-based standard solely reflects credit risk and does not take sufficient account of interest-rate risk. The regulatory authorities, however, are encouraged by FDICIA to modify existing risk-based standards to include interest-rate risk. In 1993, the Office of Thrift Supervision and the Federal Reserve outlined possible additional risk-based standards that take account of interest-rate risk, and the Basel Committee of bank regulators agreed to propose for the member countries new capital standards that are linked to interest-rate and exchange rate risk.

Other Provisions

Requirements that regulators perform bank examinations at least once a year are necessary for monitoring banks' compliance with bank capital requirements and asset restrictions. As the S&L debacle illustrates, frequent supervisory examinations of banks are necessary to keep them from taking on too much risk or committing fraud. Similarly, beefing up the ability of the Federal Reserve to monitor foreign banks might help dissuade international banks from engaging in these undesirable activities.

The stricter and more burdensome reporting requirements for banks have the advantage of providing more information to regulators to help them monitor bank activities. However, these reporting requirements have been criticized by banks, which claim that the requirements make it harder to lend to small businesses, a limitation that the banks claim has helped produce a credit crunch. To counter these criticisms, in 1993 the Clinton administration proposed legislation to ease these reporting requirements for loans to small businesses.

Overall Evaluation

FDICIA appears to be an important step in the right direction because it increases the incentives for banks to hold capital and decreases their incentives to take on excessive risk. However, some critics feel that FDICIA does not go far enough and that additional reforms are needed for the bank regulatory system. We look at some of these suggestions in the next section.

ADDITIONAL PROPOSED REFORMS OF THE BANKING REGULATORY SYSTEM

The central issue in preventing further losses to the taxpayer is the reform of the banking regulatory system so that it reduces the adverse selection and moral hazard problems created by deposit insurance. Next we look at nine proposed reforms and evaluate whether they are feasible and would improve the performance of the banking system.

Proposed Changes in the Deposit Insurance System

Elimination of Deposit Insurance A simple solution to the adverse selection and moral hazard problems of deposit insurance would be to eliminate the insurance entirely. Then depositors would have the incentive to monitor banks and withdraw deposits when they thought a bank was taking on too much risk. Although elimination of deposit insurance removes many of the incentives for banks to engage in excessive risk taking, it creates another set of problems.

The basic problem with abolishing deposit insurance is that banks would be subject to runs, sudden withdrawals by nervous depositors. Such runs could by themselves lead to bank failures. In addition to protecting individual depositors, the purpose of deposit insurance is to prevent a large number of bank failures, which would lead to an unstable banking system and an unstable economy as occurred periodically before the establishment of federal deposit insurance in 1934. From this perspective, federal deposit insurance has been a resounding success. Bank panics, in which there are simultaneous failures of many banks and consequent disruption of the financial system, have not occurred since federal deposit insurance was established.

The ability of deposit insurance to prevent bank panics makes many economists uncomfortable with the idea of abolishing it entirely. Perhaps even more important, deposit insurance is extremely popular with the American public. Few Americans would want to return to the hardships associated with bank panics before the establishment of federal deposit insurance. Hence abolishing deposit insurance does not seem to be a feasible political strategy.

Lower Limits   Other reform proposals suggest reducing the amount of deposit insurance from the current $100,000 limit to, say, $50,000 or $20,000. With a smaller amount of deposit insurance, depositors with an amount in excess of the insurance limit would have the incentive to monitor the amount of risk a bank takes on. However, depositors with less than $100,000 in deposits are usually not the best equipped to monitor a bank's activities. Because they are not necessarily well informed, these depositors are more likely to get nervous and cause a run on the bank. The outcome could be a less stable banking system.

Abandonment of the Too-Big-to-Fail Policy   Some critics of FDICIA still think that there is still too much scope for the too-big-to-fail policy in this legislation. Because the Fed, the Treasury, and the FDIC can still agree to implement too-big-to-fail and thus bail out uninsured as well as insured depositors, big banks will not be subjected to enough discipline by uninsured depositors. These critics advocate eliminating the too-big-to-fail policy entirely, thereby decreasing the incentives of big banks to take on too much risk.

Abandoning too-big-to-fail, however, would also cause some of the same problems that would occur if deposit insurance were eliminated or reduced: The probability of bank panics would increase. If a big bank were allowed to fail, the repercussions in the financial system might be immense. Other banks with a correspondent relationship with the failed bank (those that have deposits at the bank in exchange for a variety of services) would suffer large losses and might fail in turn, leading to a full-scale panic. In addition, the problem of liquidating the big bank's loan portfolio might create a major disruption in the financial market.

Coinsurance   Another proposed reform would institute a system of **coinsurance** in which only a percentage of a deposit, say, 90%, would be covered by insurance. In this system, the insured depositor would suffer a percentage of the losses along with the deposit insurance agency. Because depositors would suffer losses if the bank goes broke, they will have an incentive to monitor the bank's activities. However, we again face the problem that most depositors are not well informed, so banks will be subject to runs, and the banking system will be less stable.

Narrow-Bank Deposit Insurance   Another proposal suggests that deposit insurance be allowed only on deposits at so-called *narrow banks*—banks that restrict their assets to ones that are virtually free of risk, such as Treasury bills. The fact that insured depositors would not monitor these narrow banks would encourage little moral hazard because the assets of the narrow banks bear almost no risk anyway. Although this proposal would eliminate the adverse selection and moral hazard problems from deposit insurance, it would leave deposits at *wider banks,* the ones that will make loans, uninsured. These wider banks would be subject to bank runs by nervous depositors, and a less stable banking system might be the result.

Private Deposit Insurance Other proposals suggest that deposit insurance might be provided by private insurers or that private insurance might be provided for deposit amounts that exceed the limits for federal deposit insurance. The advantage of private insurance is that the insurer would have the incentive to monitor the bank whose deposits it is insuring. A private insurance scheme is under study by bank regulators.

The problem with this option is that private insurers can fail, leading to bank panics like the ones we have seen in Ohio, Maryland, and Rhode Island in recent years (see Box 1 in Chapter 17). Thus there still might be a need for a federal agency to guarantee that the private insurer won't fail. Without such a guarantee, fears about the health of the private insurer might lead depositors to withdraw their deposits and precipitate bank runs. Private insurance by itself would not prevent an unstable banking system.

Proposed Changes in Other Banking Regulations

Nationwide Banking Restrictions on branching, particularly interstate branching, have also contributed to the deposit insurance crisis. Because of these regulations, banks remain tied to economic conditions in their local area and are less able to diversify their loans. It is no coincidence that a higher proportion of bank failures have occurred in economically depressed states where farming and oil production are primary industries (Texas, Louisiana, Colorado, Kansas). Although branching across state lines is becoming more common, faster movement toward a nationwide banking system by eliminating branching restrictions altogether would decrease bank failures by promoting increased diversification. Although nationwide banking was proposed by the Bush administration in 1991, it did not find its way into the FDICIA. However, nationwide banking has strong support from economists, bankers, and the Clinton administration, so it may come to pass in the near future.

Regulatory Consolidation The current bank regulatory system in the United States has banking institutions supervised by four federal agencies: the FDIC, the Office of the Comptroller of the Currency, the Office of Thrift Supervision, and the Federal Reserve. Critics of this system of multiple regulatory agencies with overlapping jurisdictions believe that it creates a system that is too complex and too costly because it is rife with duplication. The Clinton administration has proposed a consolidation in which the duties of the four regulatory agencies would be given to a new Federal Banking Commission governed by a five-member board with one member from the Treasury, one from the Federal Reserve, and three independent members appointed by the president and confirmed by the Senate. The Federal Reserve has strongly opposed this proposal because it believes that it needs to have hands-on supervision of the largest banks through their bank holding companies (as is the case currently) in order for the Fed to have the information that will enable it to respond sufficiently quickly in a crisis. The Fed has also pointed out that a monolithic regulator might be less effective than two or more regulators in providing checks and balances for regulatory supervision. Because regulatory consolidation is so controversial, the passage of the Clinton administration's proposal is unlikely. However, some form of regulatory consolidation is likely to occur in the near future.

Market-Value Accounting for Capital Requirements We have seen that the requirement that a bank have substantial equity capital makes the bank less likely to fail. The requirement is also advantageous because a bank with high equity capital has more to lose if it takes on risky investments and so will have less incentive to hold risky assets. Unfortunately, capital requirements, including new risk-based measures, are calculated on a historical-cost (book value) basis in which the value of an asset is set at its initial purchase price. The problem with historical-cost accounting is that changes in the value of assets and liabilities because of changes in interest rates or default risk are not reflected in the calculation of the firm's equity capital. Yet changes in the market value of assets and liabilities and hence changes in market value of equity capital are what indicate if a firm is really insolvent. Furthermore, it is the market value of capital that determines the incentives for a bank to hold risky assets.

Market-value accounting when calculating capital requirements is another reform that receives wide support from economists. All assets and liabilities could be updated to market value periodically, say, every three months, to determine if a bank's capital is sufficient to meet the minimum requirements. This market-value accounting information would let the deposit insurance agency know quickly when a bank was falling below its capital requirement. The bank could then be closed down before its net worth fell below zero, thus preventing a loss to the deposit insurance agency. The market-value-based capital requirement would also ensure that banks would not be operating with negative capital, thereby preventing the bet-the-bank strategy of taking on excessive risk.

Using market values to calculate equity capital would also have the advantage of making bank insolvency more transparent. As we saw from our discussion of the political economy of the savings and loan fiasco, regulators and politicians are subject to a principal-agent problem because they often have incentives to hide insolvencies, even though taxpayers would be better off if they didn't. Market-value accounting would make hiding insolvencies more difficult, and so it would help taxpayers monitor regulators and politicians, who would have a harder time arguing for regulatory forbearance. Market-value accounting could therefore make regulators and politicians more accountable and give them better incentives to act in the interests of taxpayers. Indeed, critics of FDICIA suggest that the legislation's greatest failing is that it does not institute market-value accounting. Without it, they feel that the prompt corrective action and risk-based insurance premiums provisions of FDICIA will not work well enough.

Objections to market-value-based capital requirements center on the difficulty of making accurate and straightforward market-value estimates of capital. Historical-cost accounting has an important advantage in that accounting rules are easier to define and standardize when the value of an asset is simply set at its purchase price. Market-value accounting, by contrast, requires estimates and approximations that are harder to standardize. For example, it might be hard to assess the market value of your friend Joe's car loan, whereas it would be quite easy to value a government bond. In addition, conducting market-value accounting would prove costly to banks because estimation of market values requires the collection of more information about the characteristics of assets and liabilities.

Nevertheless, proponents of market-value accounting for capital requirements point out that although market-value accounting involves some estimates and approximations, it would still provide regulators with more accurate assessment of bank equity capital than historical-cost accounting does. They also point out that although opponents of market-value accounting claim that it would be too costly to collect the necessary information, market participants routinely evaluate the market value of bank assets when they purchase bank equity or debt. Furthermore, many banks already calculate market values of their assets in order to make business decisions, and market-value accounting is already standard for investment securities held by banks. Greater movement toward market-value accounting appears to be entirely feasible and could help decrease the likelihood of a future crisis in banking.

Repeal of the Glass-Steagall Act

The Case for Allowing Banks to Enter the Securities Business   As we have seen, the Glass-Steagall Act of 1933 prohibited banks from engaging in securities market activities such as securities underwriting or the sale of mutual funds. Advocates of allowing banks to participate in securities market activities argue that it is unfair to keep commercial banks from pursuing these activities in competition with investment banking and brokerage firms. Brokerage firms have been able to pursue traditional banking activities with the development of money market mutual funds and cash management accounts. Why shouldn't banks be allowed to compete with brokerage firms in those firms' traditional areas of business, the selling of corporate securities and the management of mutual funds?

Another argument in favor of allowing banks to enter the securities business is increased competition. Bank entry will mean that, in the case of a new issue of securities, there will be more bidders to underwrite the issue. As a result, the spread between the price guaranteed to the issuer of the security and the price paid for the security by the general public will fall. This reduction in the spread will mean that both borrowers and lenders in financial markets will be better off: Issuers of securities (borrowers) will receive a higher price for their securities and will thus bear a lower interest cost, while the purchasers of securities (lenders) will be able to buy the securities at a lower price, thereby giving them a higher interest rate. The fact that underwriting spreads for investment-grade bonds have dropped substantially since commercial banks have been allowed to underwrite these securities is powerful evidence in support of this view. If banks were also allowed to enter the brokerage business, increased competition in this industry would reduce brokerage commissions—another advantage to investors.

The Case Against Allowing Banks to Enter the Securities Business   Opponents of bank entry into the securities business argue that banks have an unfair advantage in competing against brokerage firms. Deposits provide banks with an artificially low cost of funds because they are insured by the FDIC.[3] Brokerage firms have higher costs on the funds they acquire, which are usually obtained with loans from banks.

The securities business, particularly investment banking, involves more risk than traditional banking activities. An investment bank can suffer substantial losses if it is unable to sell securities it has underwritten for the price that it has agreed to pay the issuer. So allowing commercial banks to engage in investment banking might produce more bank failures and a less stable financial system. This problem would be even more acute because of the existence of federal deposit insurance. Allowing commercial banks to take advantage of additional risky activities increases the potential for moral hazard and adverse selection problems to arise. So it is more likely that taxpayers would be subjected to a high-cost bailout of the commercial banking industry like the one we experienced in the savings and loan industry.

Another argument against allowing banks to enter the securities business is that commercial banks face a potential conflict of interest if they engage in underwriting of securities. Congressional hearings prior to enactment of the Glass-Steagall Act in 1933 turned up many abuses that were tied to commercial banking's activities in the investment banking area. Banks that were underwriting new issues of securities sold them to trust funds that they managed when they could not sell them to anyone else, and these trust funds often took substantial losses when the securities were sold later. Cases surfaced in which the bank itself would buy securities that it was underwriting when the securities could not be sold elsewhere. The resulting lower quality of the bank's assets could have contributed to a failure later on.

Proponents of allowing banks to enter the securities business counter this argument by saying that the securities markets and commercial banking are very different industries today from what they were before 1933. Bank regulation and the SEC could probably prevent many of the abuses that occurred before the Glass-Steagall Act. Regulatory authorities now have much greater power than before 1933 to find and punish people who would abuse commercial banking's se-

---

[3]Note that the cost of funds will be artificially low only if the FDIC subsidizes the insurance by charging premiums that are too low. The past losses to the FDIC suggest that this was the case until 1991, but with the large increases in insurance premiums in recent years, it is no longer clear that the FDIC is subsidizing deposit insurance. So the argument that banks have an unfair advantage because they have an artificially low cost of funds is no longer as persuasive.

curities activities. Although proponents do not guarantee that no abuses would occur, they suggest that abuses would be infrequent enough that any costs associated with them would be far smaller than the benefits of increased competition in the securities industry.

Future Prospects The debate about whether banks should be involved in securities activities has not been resolved. However, the pursuit of profits has stimulated both banks and other financial institutions to bypass the intent of the Glass-Steagall Act and encroach on each other's traditional territory. In addition, even primarily nonfinancial corporations have entered the banking and securities business. Companies like General Motors, Ford, and General Electric provide installment loans to their customers through their finance company subsidiaries, and retailers like J. C. Penney, Montgomery Ward, and Sears have experimented with selling insurance, securities, money market mutual funds, and real estate in their stores. (However, in 1992, Sears decided that this business was not sufficiently profitable and sold off some of its financial services businesses.)

Because commercial banks' market share in financial services had been falling, in January 1989 the Federal Reserve allowed bank holding companies to underwrite corporate debt securities and also to sell first-mortgage life insurance. The chairman of the Federal Reserve Board, Alan Greenspan, favors allowing banks to affiliate with securities firms, and in September 1990 the Federal Reserve took the historic step of allowing a commercial bank, J. P. Morgan, to underwrite stocks, with the privilege subsequently extended to other banks. The FDIC has also allowed banks to invest in real estate and to engage in some insurance activities.

The regulatory trend seems to be accepting what has already been occurring in the marketplace. An important factor is that foreign commercial banks are often allowed to engage in the securities business, giving them a competitive edge over American banks (see Box 3). Regulators may thus be reluctant to restrict commercial banks' securities activities if it puts American banks at a competitive disadvantage relative to foreign banks. The trend away from the separation of banking and the securities industry is therefore likely to continue, and the demise of the Glass-Steagall Act may not be far off.

SUMMARY

1. The concepts of asymmetric information, adverse selection, and moral hazard help explain the four types of banking regulation that we see in the United States and other countries: deposit insurance, restrictions on bank asset holdings and capital requirements, chartering and bank examination, and the separation of the banking and securities industries.

2. Because asymmetric information problems in the banking industry are a fact of life throughout the world, bank regulation in other countries is similar to that in the United States. It is particularly problematic to regulate banks engaged in international banking because they can readily shift their business from one country to another.

3. Just as financial institutions change in response to regulation, regulatory authorities change their regulations in response to financial innovations. In the 1960s and 1970s, the regulatory authorities' objective of ensuring flows of funds into mortgage-issuing institutions led them to encourage discrimination against small savers and to plug loopholes in Regulation Q. Although this strategy worked well in the short run, it led eventually to severe financial difficulties for depository institutions. To encourage a more stable financial system, major reform legislation was passed in 1980 and 1982 that allowed nationwide NOW accounts, money market deposit accounts (MMDAs), uniform reserve requirements for all depository institutions, and the phaseout of deposit rate ceilings.

4. Because of financial innovation, deregulation, and a set of historical accidents, adverse selection and moral hazard problems increased in the 1980s and resulted in huge losses for the savings and loan industry and for taxpayers.

5. Regulators and politicians are subject to the principal-agent problem, meaning that they may not have sufficient incentives to minimize the costs of deposit insurance to taxpayers. As a result, regulators and politicians relaxed capital standards, removed restrictions on holdings of risky assets, and relied on regulatory forbearance, thereby increasing the costs of the S&L bailout.

6. The Financial Institutions Reform, Recovery, and Enforcement Act (FIRREA) of 1989 provided funds for the S&L bailout; created the Resolution Trust Corporation to manage the resolution of insolvent thrifts; eliminated the Federal Home Loan Bank Board and gave its regulatory role to the Office of Thrift Supervision; eliminated the FSLIC, whose insurance role and regulatory responsibilities were taken over by the FDIC; imposed restrictions on thrift activities similar to those in effect before 1982; increased the capital requirements to those adhered to by commercial banks; and increased the enforcement powers of thrift regulators.

7. The Federal Deposit Insurance Corporation Improvement Act (FDICIA) of 1991 recapitalized the Bank Insurance Fund of the FDIC and included reforms for the deposit insurance and regulatory system so that taxpayer losses would be minimized. This legislation limited brokered deposits and the use of the too-big-to-fail policy, mandated prompt corrective action to deal with troubled banks, and instituted risk-based deposit insurance premiums. These provisions have helped reduce the incentives of banks to take on excessive risk and so should help reduce taxpayer exposure in the future.

8. Proposals for reforming the banking regulatory system include elimination of deposit insurance, lower limits on the amount of deposit insurance, outright elimination of the too-big-to-fail policy, coinsurance, narrow-bank deposit insurance, private deposit insurance, nationwide banking, regulatory consolidation, market-value accounting for capital requirements, and repeal of the Glass-Steagall Act.

KEY TERMS

leverage ratio

brokered deposits

regulatory forbearance

coinsurance

QUESTIONS AND PROBLEMS

1. Give one example each of moral hazard and adverse selection in private insurance arrangements.

*2. If casualty insurance companies provided fire insurance without any restrictions, what kind of adverse selection and moral hazard problems might result?

3. What bank regulation is designed to reduce adverse selection problems for deposit insurance? Will it always work?

*4. What bank regulations are designed to reduce moral hazard problems created by deposit insurance? Will they completely eliminate the moral hazard problem?

5. What are the costs and benefits of a too-big-to-fail policy?

*6. Why did the S&L crisis not occur until the 1980s?

7. Why is regulatory forbearance a dangerous strategy for a deposit insurance agency?

*8. The FIRREA legislation of 1989 is the most comprehensive banking legislation since the 1930s. Describe its major features.

9. What steps were taken in the FDICIA legislation of 1991 to improve the functioning of federal deposit insurance?

*10. Some advocates of campaign reform believe that government funding of political campaigns and restrictions on campaign spending might reduce the principal-agent problem in our political system. Do you agree? Explain.

11. How can the S&L crisis be blamed on the principal-agent problem?

*12. Do you think that eliminating or limiting the amount of deposit insurance would be a good idea? Explain.

13. Do you think that removing the impediments to a nationwide banking system will be beneficial to the economy? Explain.

*14. How could higher deposit insurance premiums for banks with riskier assets benefit the economy?

15. How could market-value accounting for bank capital requirements benefit the economy? How difficult would it be to implement?

Chapter 14

NONBANK FINANCIAL INSTITUTIONS

PREVIEW Although banks may be the financial institutions we deal with most often, they are not the only financial institutions we come in contact with. Suppose that you purchase insurance from an insurance company, take out an installment loan on your new car from a finance company, or buy a share of common stock with the help of a broker. In each of these transactions, you are dealing with a nonbank financial institution. In our economy, nonbank financial institutions also play an important role in channeling funds from lender-savers to borrower-spenders. Furthermore, the process of financial innovation has increased the importance of nonbank financial institutions. Through innovation, nonbank financial institutions now compete more directly with banks by providing banking-like services to their customers. This chapter examines in more detail how the major nonbank financial institutions operate, how they are regulated, and recent trends in the nonbank financial industry.

INSURANCE COMPANIES

Every day we face the possibility of the occurrence of certain catastrophic events that could lead to large financial losses. A spouse's earnings might disappear due to death or illness; a car accident might result in costly repair bills or payments to an injured party. Because financial losses from crises could be large relative to our financial resources, we protect ourselves against them by purchasing insurance coverage that will pay a sum of money if catastrophic events occur. Life insurance companies sell policies that provide income if a person dies, is incapacitated by illness, or retires. Property and casualty companies specialize in policies that pay for losses incurred as a result of accidents, fire, or theft.

Insurance Management

Insurance companies, like banks, are in the financial intermediation business of transforming one type of asset into another for the public. Insurance companies use the premiums paid on policies to invest in assets such as bonds, stocks, mortgages, and other loans; the earnings from these assets are then used to pay out claims on the policies. In effect, insurance companies transform assets such as bonds, stocks, and loans into insurance policies that provide a set of services (for example, claim adjustments, savings plans, friendly insurance agents). If the insurance company's production process of asset transformation efficiently provides its customers with adequate insurance services at low cost and if it can earn high returns on its investments, it will make profits; if not, it will suffer losses.

In Chapter 11, the economic concepts of adverse selection and moral hazard allowed us to understand principles of bank management related to managing credit risk; many of these same principles also apply to the lending activities of insurance companies. Here again we use the adverse selection and moral hazard concepts to explain many management practices specific to the insurance industry.

In the case of an insurance policy, moral hazard arises when the existence of insurance encourages the insured party to take risks that increase the likelihood of an insurance payoff. For example, a person covered by burglary insurance might not take as many precautions to prevent a burglary because the insurance company will reimburse most of the losses if a theft occurs. Adverse selection holds that the people most likely to receive large insurance payoffs are the ones who will want to purchase insurance the most. For example, a person suffering from a terminal disease would want to take out the biggest life and medical insurance policies possible, thereby exposing the insurance company to potentially large losses. Both adverse selection and moral hazard can result in large losses to insurance companies because they lead to higher payouts on insurance claims. Minimizing adverse selection and moral hazard to reduce these payouts is therefore an extremely important goal for insurance companies, and this goal explains the insurance practices we will discuss here.

Screening To reduce adverse selection, insurance companies try to screen out good insurance risks from poor ones. Effective information collection procedures are therefore an important principle of insurance management.

When you apply for auto insurance, the first thing your insurance agent does is ask you questions about your driving record (the number of speeding tickets and accidents), the type of car you are insuring, and certain personal matters (age, marital status). If you are applying for life insurance, you go through a similar grilling, but you are asked even more personal questions about such things as your health, smoking habits, and drug and alcohol use. The life insurance company even orders a medical evaluation (usually done by an independent company) that involves taking blood and urine samples. Just as a bank calculates a credit score to evaluate a potential borrower, the insurance company uses the information you provide to allocate you to a risk class—a statistical estimate of how likely you are to have an insurance claim. Based on this information, the insurance company can decide whether to accept you for the insurance or to turn you down because you pose too high an insurance risk and thus would be an unprofitable customer for the insurance company.

Risk-based Premiums Charging insurance premiums on the basis of how much risk a policyholder poses for the insurance company is a time-honored principle of insurance management. Adverse selection explains why this principle is so important to insurance company profitability.

To understand why an insurance company finds it necessary to have risk-based premiums, let's examine an example of risk-based insurance premiums that at first glance seems unfair. Harry and Sally, both college students with no accidents or speeding tickets, apply for auto insurance. Normally, Harry will be charged a much higher premium than Sally. Insurance companies do this because young males have a much higher accident rate than young females. Suppose, though, that one insurance company did not base its premiums on a risk classification but rather just charged a premium based on the average combined risk for males and females. Then Sally would be charged too much and Harry too little. Sally could go to another insurance company and get a lower rate, while Harry would sign up for the insurance. Because Harry's premium isn't high enough to account for the accidents he is likely to have, on average the company would lose money on Harry. Only with a premium based on a risk classification, so that Harry is charged more, can the insurance company make a profit.[1]

Restrictive Provisions Restrictive provisions in policies are another insurance management tool for reducing moral hazard. Such provisions discourage policyholders from engaging in risky activities that make an insurance claim more likely. One type of restrictive provision keeps the policyholder from benefiting from behavior that makes a claim more likely. For example, life insurance companies have provisions in their policies that eliminate death benefits if the insured person commits suicide within the first two years that the policy is in effect. Restrictive provisions may also require certain behavior on the part of the insured that makes a claim less likely. A company renting motor scooters may be required to provide helmets for renters in order to be covered for any liability associated with the rental. The role of restrictive provisions is not unlike that of restrictive covenants on debt contracts described in Chapter 9: Both serve to reduce moral hazard by ruling out undesirable behavior.

Prevention of Fraud Insurance companies also face moral hazard because an insured person has an incentive to lie to the company and seek a claim even if the claim is not valid. For example, a person who has not complied with the restrictive provisions of an insurance contract may still submit a claim. Even worse, a person may file claims for events that did not actually occur. Thus an important

---

[1]You might recognize that the example here is in fact the *lemons problem* described in Chapter 9.

management principle for insurance companies is conducting investigations to prevent fraud so that only policyholders with valid claims receive compensation.

Cancellation of Insurance Being prepared to cancel policies is another insurance management tool. Insurance companies can discourage moral hazard by threatening to cancel a policy when the insured person engages in activities that make a claim more likely. If your auto insurance company makes it clear that if a driver gets too many speeding tickets, coverage will be canceled, you will be less likely to speed.

Deductibles A **deductible** is the fixed amount by which the insured's loss is reduced when a claim is paid off. A $250 deductible on an auto policy, for example, means that if you suffer a loss of $1000 because of an accident, the insurance company pays you only $750. Deductibles are an additional management tool that helps insurance companies reduce moral hazard. With a deductible, you experience a loss along with the insurance company when you make a claim. Because you also stand to lose when you have an accident, you have an incentive to drive more carefully. A deductible thus makes a policyholder act more in line with what is profitable for the insurance company; moral hazard has been reduced. And because moral hazard has been reduced, the insurance company can lower the premium by more than enough to compensate the policyholder for the existence of the deductible.

Coinsurance When a policyholder shares a percentage of the losses along with the insurance company, their arrangement is called *coinsurance*. For example, some medical insurance plans provide coverage for 80% of medical bills, and the insured person pays 20% after a certain deductible has been met. Coinsurance works to reduce moral hazard in exactly the same way that a deductible does. A policyholder who suffers a loss along with the insurance company has less incentive to take actions, such as going to the doctor unnecessarily, that involve higher claims. Coinsurance is thus another useful management tool for insurance companies.

Limits on the Amount of Insurance Another important principle of insurance management is that there should be limits on the amount of insurance provided, even though a customer is willing to pay for more coverage. The higher the insurance coverage, the more the insured person can gain from risky activities that make an insurance payoff more likely and hence the greater the moral hazard. For example, if Zelda's car were insured for more than its worth, she might not take proper precautions to prevent its theft, such as making sure that the key is always removed or putting in an alarm system. If it were stolen, she comes out ahead because the excessive insurance payments allow her to buy an even better car. By contrast, when the insurance payments are lower than the value of her car, she will suffer a loss if it is stolen and will thus take the proper precautions to prevent this from happening. Insurance companies must always make sure that their coverage is not so high that moral hazard leads to large losses.

Summary Effective insurance management requires several practices: information collection and screening of potential policyholders, risk-based premiums, restrictive provisions, prevention of fraud, cancellation of insurance, deductibles, coinsurance, and limits on the amount of insurance. All of these practices reduce moral hazard and adverse selection by making it harder for policyholders to benefit from engaging in activities that increase the amount and likelihood of claims. With smaller benefits available, the poor insurance risks (those who are more likely to engage in the activities in the first place) see less benefit from the insurance and are thus less likely to seek it out.

Now that we have a general understanding of how insurance companies must operate, we will look in more detail at the two different categories of companies: life insurance companies and property and casualty insurance companies.

Life Insurance Companies

The first life insurance company in the United States (Presbyterian Ministers' Fund in Philadelphia) was established in 1759 and is still in existence. There are currently about 2000 life insurance companies, which are organized in two forms: as stock companies or as mutuals. Stock companies are owned by stockholders; mutuals are technically owned by the policyholders. Although over 90% of life insurance companies are organized as stock companies, the largest ones (including Prudential Insurance Company and Metropolitan Life) are organized as mutuals; indeed, over half the assets in the industry are owned by mutual companies.

Life insurance companies have never experienced widespread failures like commercial banks, so the federal government has not seen the need to regulate the industry. Instead, regulation is left to the states in which a company operates. State regulation is directed at sales practices, the provision of adequate liquid assets to cover losses, and restrictions on the amount of risky assets (such as common stock) that the companies can hold. The regulatory authority is typically a state insurance commissioner.

Because death rates for the population as a whole are predictable with a high degree of certainty, life insurance companies can accurately predict what their payouts to policyholders will be in the future. Consequently, they hold long-term assets that are not particularly liquid—corporate bonds and commercial mortgages as well as some corporate stock.

There are two principal forms of life insurance policies: permanent life insurance (such as whole, universal, and variable life) and temporary insurance (such as term). Permanent life insurance policies have a constant premium throughout the life of the policy. In the early years of the policy, the size of this premium exceeds the amount needed to insure against death because the probability of death is low. Thus the policy builds up a cash value in its early years, but in later years the cash value declines because the constant premium falls below the amount needed to insure against death, the probability of which is now higher. The policyholder can borrow against the cash value of the permanent life policy or can claim it by canceling the policy.

Term insurance, by contrast, has a premium that is matched every year to the amount needed to insure against death during the period of the term (such as one year or five years). As a result, term policies have premiums that rise over time as the probability of death rises (or level premiums with a decline in the amount of death benefits). Term policies have no cash value and thus, in contrast to permanent life policies, are pure insurance with no savings aspect.

Weak investment returns on permanent life insurance in the 1960s and 1970s led to slow growth of demand for life insurance products. The result was a shrinkage in the size of the life insurance industry relative to other financial intermediaries, with their share of total financial intermediary assets falling from 19.6% at the end of 1960 to 11.5% at the end of 1980. (See Table 1, which shows the relative shares of financial intermediary assets for each of the financial intermediaries discussed in this chapter.)

Beginning in the mid-1970s, life insurance companies began to restructure their business to become managers of assets for pension funds. An important factor behind this restructuring was 1974 legislation that encouraged pension funds to turn over fund management to life insurance companies. Now more than half of the assets managed by life insurance companies are for pension funds and not for life insurance. The result has been that the market share of life

TABLE 1 Relative Shares of Total Financial Intermediary Assets, 1960–1993 (%)

	1960	1970	1980	1990	1993
Insurance companies					
Life insurance	19.6	15.3	11.5	12.5	13.0
Property and casualty	4.4	3.8	4.5	4.9	4.6
Pension funds					
Private	6.4	8.4	12.5	14.9	17.0
Public (state and local government)	3.3	4.6	4.9	6.7	7.7
Finance companies	4.7	4.9	5.1	5.6	4.8
Mutual funds					
Stock and bond	2.9	3.6	1.7	5.9	11.1
Money market	0.0	0.0	1.9	4.6	4.1
Depository institutions (banks)					
Commercial banks	38.6	38.5	36.7	30.4	28.1
S&Ls and mutual savings banks	19.0	19.4	19.6	12.5	7.5
Credit unions	1.1	1.4	1.6	2.0	2.1
Total	100.0	100.0	100.0	100.0	100.0

Source: Federal Reserve Flow of Funds Accounts.

insurance companies as a percentage of total financial intermediary assets has increased since 1980.

Property and Casualty Insurance Companies

There are over 3000 property and casualty insurance companies in the United States, the two largest of which are State Farm and Allstate. Property and casualty companies are organized as both stock and mutual companies and are regulated by the states in which they operate.

Although property and casualty insurance companies have seen a moderate increase in their share of total financial intermediary assets since 1960 (see Table 1), in recent years they have not fared well, and insurance rates have skyrocketed. With the high interest rates in the 1970s, insurance companies had high investment income that enabled them to keep insurance rates low. Since then, however, investment income has fallen with the decline in interest rates, while the growth in lawsuits involving property and casualty insurance and the explosion in amounts awarded in such cases have produced substantial losses for companies.

To return to profitability, insurance companies have raised their rates dramatically—sometimes doubling or even tripling premiums—and refused to provide coverage for some people. They have also campaigned actively for limits on insurance payouts, particularly for medical malpractice. In the search for profits, insurance companies are also branching out into uncharted territory by insuring the payment of interest on municipal and corporate bonds and on mortgage-backed securities. One worry is that the insurance companies may be taking on excessive risk in order to boost their profits. One result of the concern about the health of the property and casualty insurance industry is that insurance regulators have proposed new rules that would impose risk-based capital requirements for these companies based on the riskiness of their assets and operations.

The investment policies of these companies are affected by two basic facts. First, because they are subject to federal income taxes, the largest share of their assets is held in tax-exempt municipal bonds. Second, because property losses are more uncertain than the death rate in a population, these insurers are less able to predict how much they will have to pay policyholders than life insurance companies are. Natural disasters such as the Los Angeles earthquake in 1994 or the two major hurricanes in 1992, Andrew and Iniki, that devastated parts of Florida and Hawaii, respectively, exposed the property and casualty insurance companies to billions of dollars of losses. Therefore, property and casualty insurance companies hold more liquid assets than life insurance companies; municipal bonds and U.S. government securities amount to over half their assets, and most of the remainder are held in corporate bonds and corporate stock.

Property and casualty insurance companies will insure against losses from almost any type of event, including fire, theft, negligence, malpractice, earthquakes, and automobile accidents. If a possible loss being insured is too large for any one firm, several firms may join together to write a policy in order to

A Global Perspective

THE WOES OF LLOYD'S OF LONDON

In June 1993, Lloyd's of London announced the biggest loss in its history, $4.33 billion for the year 1990 (Lloyd's waits three years to allow all claims to be processed before reporting profits or losses). The chairman of Lloyd's stated that the 1990 deficit "represents in every way the low point of Lloyd's history in the last 305 years."*

Lloyd's began in 1688 in a London coffeehouse owned by Edward Lloyd, which was a meeting place for merchants, shipowners, and sea captains. Lloyd's became a marketplace in which members, known as "names," trade pieces of insurance policies in order to spread the risk, a process called *re-insurance.* An unusual feature of Lloyd's is that names are directly exposed to losses because they accept unlimited personal liability for any claims they have to pay. Many of those participating in Lloyd's have come to regret it in recent years, having lost their entire personal fortunes. Indeed, the average loss per name was over $150,000 in 1990. The losses at Lloyd's have also resulted in a slew of lawsuits, with members suing each other right and left over who should be responsible for paying claims.

To survive, the basic structure of Lloyd's has had to change. Lloyd's has opened itself up to corporate capital with only limited liability, has taken measures to lower central spending by the organization, and has altered the way it is governed. Victim of the worldwide woes of the property and casualty insurance industry, Lloyd's of London, after three centuries, will never be the same.

*"Lloyd's of London Posts Big Loss, Raising Fears on Market's Viability," *Wall Street Journal,* June 23, 1993, p. A10.

share the risk. The most famous risk-sharing operation is Lloyd's of London, an association in which different insurance companies can underwrite a fraction of an insurance policy. Lloyd's of London has claimed that it will insure against any contingency—for a price. Unfortunately, the problems in the insurance industry have not been restricted to the United States, and even the venerable Lloyd's of London has recently found itself in trouble (see Box 1).

PENSION FUNDS

In performing the financial intermediation function of asset transformation, pension funds provide the public with another kind of protection: income payments on retirement. Employers, unions, or private individuals can set up pension plans, which acquire funds through contributions paid in by the plan's participants. As we can see in Table 1, pension plans both public and private have grown in importance, with their share of total financial intermediary assets rising from 10% at the end of 1960 to close to 25% at the end of 1993. Federal tax policy has been a major factor behind the rapid growth of pension funds because employer contributions to employee pension plans are tax-deductible. Furthermore, tax policy has also encouraged employee contributions to pension funds by making them tax-deductible as well and enabling self-employed individuals to open up their own tax-sheltered pension plans, Keogh plans, and individual retirement accounts (IRAs).

Because the benefits paid out of the pension fund each year are highly predictable, pension funds invest in long-term securities, with the bulk of their asset holdings in bonds, stocks, and long-term mortgages. The key management issues for pension funds revolve around asset management: Pension fund managers try to hold assets with high expected returns and minimize risk through diversification. They also use techniques we have already discussed in Chapter 11 to manage credit and interest-rate risk. The investment strategies of pension plans have changed radically over time. In the aftermath of World War II, most pension fund assets were held in government bonds, with less than 1% held in stock. However, the strong performance of stocks in the 1950s and 1960s afforded pension plans higher returns, causing them to shift their portfolios into stocks, currently on the order of 40% of their assets. As a result, pension plans now have a much stronger presence in the stock market: In the early 1950s, they held on the order of 1% of corporate stock outstanding, while currently they hold on the order of 25%.

Although the purpose of all pension plans is the same, they can differ in a number of attributes. First is the vesting of the plan, that is, the length of time that a person must be enrolled in the pension plan (by being a member of a union or an employee of a company) before being entitled to receive benefits. Typically, firms require that an employee work five years for the company before being vested and qualifying to receive pension benefits; if the employee leaves the firm before the five years are up, either by quitting or being fired, all rights to benefits are lost.

A second characteristic is the method by which payments are made: If the benefits are determined by the contributions into the plan and their earnings, the pension is a *defined-contribution plan;* if future income payments (benefits) are set in advance, the pension is a *defined-benefit plan.* In the case of a defined-benefit plan, a further attribute is related to how the plan is funded.

A defined-benefit plan is **fully funded** if the contributions into the plan and their earnings over the years are sufficient to pay out the defined benefits when they come due. If the contributions and earnings are not sufficient, the plan is **underfunded.** For example, if Jane Brown contributes $100 per year into her pension plan and the interest rate is 10%, after ten years the contributions and their earnings would be worth $1753.[2] If the defined benefit on her pension plan

---

[2]The $100 contributed in year one would become worth $100 \times (1 + 0.10)^{10} = \$259.37$ at the end of ten years; the $100 contributed in year 2 would become worth $100 \times (1 + 0.10)^9 = \$235.79$; and so on until the $100 contributed in year 10 would become worth $100 \times (1 + 0.10) = \$110$. Adding these together, we get the total value of these contributions and their earnings at the end of ten years:

$$\$259.37 + \$235.79 + \$214.36 + \$194.87 + \$177.16$$
$$+ \$161.05 + \$146.41 + \$133.10 + \$121.00 + \$110.00 = \$1753.11$$

pays her $1753 or less after ten years, the plan is fully funded because her contributions and earnings will fully pay for this payment. But if the defined benefit is $2000, the plan is underfunded because her contributions and earnings do not cover this amount.

Private Pension Plans

Private pension plans are administered by a bank, a life insurance company, or a pension fund manager. In employer-sponsored pension plans, contributions are usually shared between employer and employee. Many companies' pension plans are underfunded because they plan to meet their pension obligations out of current earnings when the benefits come due. As long as companies have sufficient earnings, underfunding creates no problems, but if not, they may not be able to meet their pension obligations. Because of potential problems caused by corporate underfunding, mismanagement, fraudulent practices, and other abuses of private pension funds (Teamsters pension funds are notorious), Congress enacted the Employee Retirement Income Security Act (ERISA) in 1974. This act established minimum standards for the reporting and disclosure of information, set rules for vesting and the degree of underfunding, placed restrictions on investment practices, and assigned the responsibility of regulatory oversight to the Department of Labor.

ERISA also created the Pension Benefit Guarantee Corporation (called "Penny Benny"), which performs a role similar to that of the FDIC. It insures pension benefits up to a limit (currently just over $30,000 per year per person) if a company with an underfunded pension plan goes bankrupt or is unable to meet its pension obligations for other reasons. Penny Benny charges pension plans premiums to pay for this insurance, and it can also borrow funds up to $100 million from the U.S. Treasury. Unfortunately, the problem of pension plan underfunding has been growing worse in recent years. In 1993, the secretary of labor indicated that underfunding had reached levels in excess of $45 billion, with one company's pension plan alone, that of General Motors, underfunded to the tune of $11.8 billion. As a result, Penny Benny, which insures the pensions of one of every three workers, is encountering severe financial difficulties that may necessitate a federal bailout (see Box 2).

Public Pension Plans

The most important public pension plan is Social Security (Old Age and Survivors' Insurance Fund), which covers virtually all individuals employed in the private sector. Funds are obtained from workers through Federal Insurance Contribution Act (FICA) deductions from their paychecks and from employers

Box 2

THE PERILS OF PENNY BENNY: A REPEAT OF THE S&L BAILOUT?

The current woes of "Penny Benny," the government pension insurance agency, unfortunately display many of the characteristics of the savings and loan crisis we discussed in Chapter 13. When an insured company with an underfunded pension plan files for bankruptcy, Penny Benny must pay the company's workers their retirement benefits. Again, we see the moral hazard principle at work: A company is more likely to risk underfunding its pension plan if Penny Benny will foot the pension bill if it goes bankrupt. For example, the LTV Steel Company's bankruptcy in February 1987 resulted in Penny Benny's paying out $400 million per year to LTV pensioners alone, even though Penny Benny was taking in only $280 million in premiums in total.

As we have seen, to keep the costs of government insurance programs from getting out of hand, the insurance agency must reduce moral hazard by monitoring the firms it is insuring to make sure that they are not subjecting the agency to too much risk. In the case of Penny Benny, this means that Penny Benny must audit pension plans to make sure that they are not becoming too severely underfunded. The decrease in the amount of monitoring of S&Ls was one reason for the huge losses to their government insurance agency, the FSLIC; unfortunately, we see a similar pattern for Penny Benny. Since the establishment of Penny Benny, the number of pension funds has more than doubled, and yet the number of federal audits of pension plans has declined. As a result, fewer than 1% of private plans insured by Penny Benny are audited each year. Not surprisingly, given the failure of Penny Benny to control moral hazard, the liabilities arising from its responsibility for troubled pension plans have grown at an alarming rate and are now estimated to exceed its assets by more than $15 billion. Taxpayers are likely to be hit with another massive government bailout, the size of which will keep growing unless the government makes a concerted effort to reduce the underfunding of corporate pension plans.

The Clinton administration has proposed legislation to deal with some of these problems. It would require underfunded pension plans to make larger insurance contributions, thereby providing Penny Benny with more funding and making it less attractive for companies to underfund their pension plans. In addition, the legislation would tighten the rules for calculating the degree of underfunding and would also give Penny Benny greater powers to enforce compliance with its regulations, thus making it easier for it to discourage underfunding.

through payroll taxes. Social Security benefits include retirement income, Medicare payments, and aid to the disabled.

When Social Security was established in 1935, the federal government intended to operate it like a private pension fund. However, unlike a private pension plan, paid-out benefits are not tied closely to a participant's past contributions, so typically they are paid out from current contributions. This "pay as you go" system at one point led to a massive underfunding, estimated at over $1 trillion.

The problems of the Social Security system could become worse in the future because today's aging American population will lead to a higher number of retired people relative to the working population. Congress has been grappling with the problems of the Social Security system for years, and progress has been made on reducing the underfunding by raising FICA contributions and limiting benefits.

State and local governments and the federal government, like private employers, have also set up pension plans for their employees. These plans are almost identical in operation to private pension plans and hold similar assets. Underfunding of the plans is also prevalent, and some investors in municipal bonds worry that it may lead to future difficulties in the ability of state and local governments to meet their debt obligations.

FINANCE COMPANIES

Finance companies acquire funds by issuing commercial paper or stocks and bonds or borrowing from banks, and they use the proceeds to make loans (often for small amounts) that are particularly well suited to consumer and business needs. The financial intermediation process of finance companies can be described by saying that they borrow in large amounts but often lend in small amounts—a process quite different from that of commercial banks, which collect deposits in small amounts and then often make large loans.

A key feature of finance companies is that although they lend to many of the same customers that borrow from banks, they are virtually unregulated compared to commercial banks and thrift institutions. States regulate the maximum amount they can loan to individual consumers and the terms of the debt contract, but there are no restrictions on branching, the assets they hold, or how they raise their funds. The lack of restrictions enables finance companies to tailor their loans to customer needs better than banking institutions can.

As we can see in Table 1, while banking institutions have shrunk dramatically relative to other financial intermediaries, finance companies have held their own in the 1980s and 1990s. Finance companies have benefited from the rapid growth of the commercial paper market because it has given them access to a low-cost source of funds. This access has in turn given them competitive advantages over banks. (Chapters 10 and 12 explain in more detail why the commercial paper market has grown so rapidly and how this has benefited finance companies.)

There are three types of finance companies: sales, consumer, and business.

1. *Sales finance companies* make loans to consumers to purchase items from a particular retailer or manufacturer. Sears Roebuck Acceptance Corporation, for example, finances consumer purchases of all goods and services at Sears stores, and General Motors Acceptance Corporation finances purchases of GM cars. Sales finance companies compete directly with banks for consumer loans and are used by consumers because loans can frequently be obtained faster and more conveniently at the location where an item is purchased.

2. *Consumer finance companies* make loans to consumers to buy particular items such as furniture or home appliances, to make home improvements, or to help refinance small debts. Consumer finance companies are separate corporations (like Household Finance Corporation) or are owned by banks (Citicorp owns Person-to-Person Finance Company, which operates offices nationwide). Typically, these companies make loans to consumers who cannot obtain credit from other sources and charge higher interest rates.

3. *Business finance companies* provide specialized forms of credit to businesses by making loans and purchasing accounts receivable (bills owed to the firm) at a discount; this provision of credit is called *factoring*. For example, a dressmaking firm might have outstanding bills (accounts receivable) of $100,000 owed by the retail stores that have bought its dresses. If this firm needs cash to buy 100 new sewing machines, it can sell its accounts receivable for, say, $90,000 to a finance company, which is now entitled to collect the $100,000 owed to the firm. Besides factoring, business finance companies also specialize in leasing equipment (such as railroad cars, jet planes, and computers), which they purchase and then lease to businesses for a set number of years.

MUTUAL FUNDS

Mutual funds are financial intermediaries that pool the resources of many small investors by selling them shares and using the proceeds to buy securities. Through the asset transformation process of issuing shares in small denominations and buying large blocks of securities, mutual funds can take advantage of volume discounts on brokerage commissions and purchase diversified holdings (portfolios) of securities. Mutual funds allow the small investor to obtain the benefits of lower transactions costs in purchasing securities and to take advantage of the reduction of risk by diversifying the portfolio of securities held.

Mutual funds have had a large increase in their market share since 1980 (see Table 1), which has resulted primarily from the booming stock market. Another source of growth has been mutual funds that specialize in debt instruments (which first appeared in the 1970s): Before 1970, mutual funds invested almost solely in common stocks. Funds that purchase common stocks may specialize even further and invest solely in foreign securities or in specialized industries, such as energy or high technology. Funds that purchase debt instruments may specialize further in corporate, U.S. government, or tax-exempt municipal bonds or in long-term or short-term securities.[3]

Mutual funds are structured in two ways. The more common structure is an **open-end fund,** from which shares can be redeemed at any time at a price that is tied to the asset value of the fund. Mutual funds also can be structured as a **closed-end fund,** in which a fixed number of nonredeemable shares are sold at an initial offering and are then traded in the over-the-counter market like a common stock. The market price of these shares fluctuates with the value of the assets held by the fund. In contrast to the open-end fund, however, the price of the shares may be above or below the value of the assets held by the fund, depending on factors such as the liquidity of the shares or the quality of the management. The greater popularity of the open-end funds is explained by the greater liquidity of their redeemable shares relative to the nonredeemable shares of closed-end funds.

Originally, shares of most open-end mutual funds were sold by salespeople (usually brokers) who were paid a commission. Since this commission is paid at the time of purchase and is immediately subtracted from the redemption value of the shares, these funds are called **load funds.** Most mutual funds are currently **no-load funds;** they are sold directly to the public with no sales commissions. In both types of funds, the managers earn their living from management fees paid by the shareholders. These fees amount to approximately 0.5% of the asset value of the fund per year.

Mutual funds are regulated by the Securities and Exchange Commission, which was given the ability to exercise almost complete control over investment companies in the Investment Company Act of 1940. Regulations require periodic disclosure of information on these funds to the public and restrictions on the methods of soliciting business.

Money Market Mutual Funds

An important addition to the family of mutual funds resulting from the financial innovation process described in Chapter 10 is the money market mutual fund. Recall that this type of mutual fund invests in short-term debt (money market) instruments of very high quality, such as Treasury bills, commercial paper, and bank certificates of deposit. There is some fluctuation in the market value of these securities, but because their maturity is typically less than six months, the change in the market value is small enough that these funds allow their shares to

---

[3] Tax-exempt bond funds did not appear until after 1976, when a change in the tax law allowed mutual funds to pass through to shareholders the tax exemption on the interest income from municipal bonds.

be redeemed at a fixed value. (Changes in the market value of the securities are figured into the interest paid out by the fund.) Because these shares can be redeemed at a fixed value, the funds allow shareholders to redeem shares by writing checks above some minimum amount (usually $500) on the fund's account at a commercial bank. In this way, shares in money market mutual funds effectively function as checkable deposits that earn market interest rates on short-term debt securities.

In 1977, the assets in money market mutual funds were less than $4 billion; by 1980 they had climbed to over $50 billion and now are $500 billion, with a share of financial intermediary assets that has grown to over 4% (see Table 1). Currently, money market mutual funds account for around one-quarter of the asset value of all mutual funds.

GOVERNMENT FINANCIAL INTERMEDIATION

The government has become involved in financial intermediation in two basic ways: first, by setting up federal credit agencies that directly engage in financial intermediation and, second, by supplying government guarantees for private loans.

Federal Credit Agencies

To promote residential housing, the government has created three government agencies that provide funds to the mortgage market by selling bonds and using the proceeds to buy mortgages: the Federal National Mortgage Association (FNMA, called "Fannie Mae"), the Government National Mortgage Association (GNMA, or "Ginnie Mae"), and the Federal Home Loan Mortgage Company (FHLMC, or "Freddie Mac"). Except for GNMA, which is a federal agency and is thus an entity of the U.S. government, the other agencies are federally sponsored agencies that function as private corporations with close ties to the government. As a result, the debt of sponsored agencies is not explicitly backed by the U.S. government, as is the case for Treasury bonds. As a practical matter, however, it is unlikely that the federal government would allow a default on the debt of these sponsored agencies.

Agriculture is another area in which financial intermediation by government agencies plays an important role. The Farm Credit System (composed of Banks for Cooperatives, Farm Credit banks, and various farm credit associations) issues securities and then uses the proceeds to make loans to farmers.

Students also benefit from government financial intermediation. The Student Loan Marketing Association (called "Sallie Mae") provides funds for higher education primarily by purchasing student loans granted by private financial institutions under the Guaranteed Student Loan Program.

In recent years, government financial intermediaries have been experiencing financial difficulties. The Farm Credit System is one example. The rising tide of farm bankruptcies meant losses in the billions of dollars for the Farm Credit System, and as a result it required a bailout from the federal government in 1987. The agency was authorized to borrow up to $4 billion to be repaid over a 15-year period and to date has received over $1 billion in assistance. Sallie Mae has also experienced losses on some of its loan portfolio. There is growing concern in Washington about the health of the federal credit agencies. To head off government bailouts like that for the Farm Credit System, there has been a push for new rules that require such agencies to increase their capital to provide a greater cushion to offset any potential losses.

Government Loan Guarantees: Another Crisis Waiting to Happen?

Another important government role in promoting financial intermediation has been the provision of government loan guarantees. A government loan guarantee acts just like insurance: It insures the lender, say, a bank, from any loss if the borrower defaults. In the housing market, government loan guarantees are provided by the Federal Housing Administration (FHA), the Veterans Administration (VA), and the Department of Housing and Urban Development (HUD). The Education Department guarantees student loans, and the Farmer's Home Administration guarantees loans to farmers.

Government loan guarantees have grown at a rapid rate, increasing tenfold between 1973 and 1993. They have been particularly attractive to Congress because they subsidize activities that our politicians believe in, like going to college and owning a home, and yet do not involve any direct expenditures on the part of the government. An important economic principle that you hear all the time is "You don't get something for nothing," and this is just as true for the government. The problem with government loan guarantees is the same as that with government deposit insurance: Both are insurance schemes that create moral hazard problems that result in losses to the government. Because banks and other institutions making the loans don't suffer any losses if the loans default, they have little incentive to be careful about to whom they make their loans.

The resulting lax lending practices can cause substantial losses for the government agencies that provide the loan guarantees. Notorious is the over 30% default rate on government-guaranteed loans for students in trade schools. The costs of loan guarantees have recently been hitting the government hard. In 1990, the General Accounting Office startled Congress by predicting that losses on government loan guarantees could end up exceeding $100 billion, and the problem seems only to be getting worse. For example, an audit of the Department of Housing and Urban Development's loan guarantee program in 1993 increased the projected losses to the government from loan defaults to $11.9 billion from an estimate of $5.5 billion just two years earlier. Unless the government tries to solve the adverse selection and moral hazard problems inherent in their loan guarantees, taxpayers may be hit with another costly bailout of the same magnitude as that required for the savings and loan industry.

SECURITIES MARKET INSTITUTIONS

The smooth functioning of securities markets, in which bonds and stocks are traded, involves several financial institutions, including securities brokers and dealers, investment banks, and organized exchanges. None of these institutions were included in our list of financial intermediaries because they do not perform the intermediation function of acquiring funds by issuing liabilities and then using the funds to acquire financial assets. Nonetheless, they are important in the process of channeling funds from savers to spenders.

First, however, we must recall the distinction between primary and secondary securities markets discussed in Chapter 2. In a primary market, new issues of a security are sold to buyers by the corporation or government agency borrowing the funds. A secondary market then trades the securities that have been sold in the primary market (and so are secondhand). *Investment banks* assist in the initial sale of securities in the primary market; *securities brokers* and *dealers* assist in the trading of securities in the secondary markets, some of which are organized into exchanges.

Investment Banks

When a corporation wishes to borrow (raise) funds, it normally hires the services of an investment bank to help sell its securities. (Despite its name, an investment bank is not a bank in the ordinary sense; that is, it is not a financial intermediary that takes in deposits and then lends them out.) Some of the well-known U.S. investment banking firms are Morgan Stanley, Merrill Lynch, Salomon Brothers, First Boston Corporation, and Goldman, Sachs.

Investment bankers assist in the sale of securities as follows. First, they advise the corporation on whether it should issue bonds or stock. If they suggest that the corporation issue bonds, investment bankers give advice on what the maturity and interest payments on the bonds should be. When the corporation decides which kind of financial instrument it will issue, it offers them to **underwriters**—investment banks that guarantee the corporation a price on the securities and then sell them to the public. If the issue is small, only one investment bank underwrites it (usually the original investment banking firm hired to provide advice on the issue). If the issue is large, several investment banking firms form a syndicate to underwrite the issue jointly, thus limiting the risk that any one investment bank must take. The underwriters sell the securities to the

FOLLOWING THE FINANCIAL NEWS

New Securities Issues

Information about new securities being issued is presented in distinctive advertisements published in the *Wall Street Journal* and other newspapers. These advertisements, called "tombstones" because of their appearance, are typically found in the "Money and Investing section" of the *Wall Street Journal*.

The tombstone indicates the number of shares of stock being issued (15 million shares for Bethlehem Steel Corporation) and the investment banks involved in selling them. Three of the most important investment banks (listed in the middle of the advertisement) are involved in underwriting these securities. As you can also see from the bottom of the advertisement, a portion of the shares are being sold abroad, a demonstration of the continuing internationalization of financial markets.

Source: Wall Street Journal, March 14, 1994, p. C19.

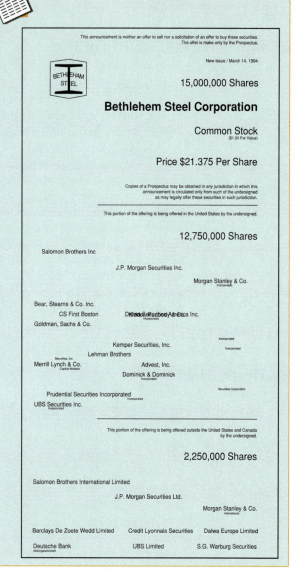

This announcement is neither an offer to sell nor a solicitation of an offer to buy these securities. The offer is make only by the Prospectus.

New Issue / March 14, 1994

15,000,000 Shares

Bethlehem Steel Corporation

Common Stock
($1.00 Par Value)

Price $21.375 Per Share

Copies of a Prospectus may be obtained in any jurisdiction in which this announcement is circulated only from such of the undersigned as may legally offer these securities in such jurisdiction.

This portion of the offering is being offered in the United States by the undersigned.

12,750,000 Shares

Salomon Brothers Inc

J.P. Morgan Securities Inc.

Morgan Stanley & Co.
Incorporated

Bear, Stearns & Co. Inc.
CS First Boston
Goldman, Sachs & Co.

Donaldson, Lufkin & Jenrette
Securities Corporation

Dillon, Read & Co. Inc.

Kidder, Peabody & Co.
Incorporated

Incorporated

Kemper Securities, Inc.
Lehman Brothers

Merrill Lynch & Co.
Capital Markets

Advest, Inc.

Dominick & Dominick
Incorporated

Securities Corporation

Prudential Securities Incorporated
Incorporated
UBS Securities Inc.
Incorporated

This portion of the offering is being offered outside the United States and Canada by the undersigned.

2,250,000 Shares

Salomon Brothers International Limited

J.P. Morgan Securities Ltd.

Morgan Stanley & Co.
International

Barclays De Zoete Wedd Limited   Credit Lyonnais Securities   Daiwa Europe Limited

Deutsche Bank
Aktiengesellschaft   UBS Limited   S.G. Warburg Securities

general public by contacting potential buyers, such as banks and insurance companies, directly and by placing advertisements in newspapers like the *Wall Street Journal* (see the "Following the Financial News" box).

The activities of investment banks and the operation of primary markets are heavily regulated by the Securities and Exchange Commission (SEC), which was created by the Securities and Exchange Acts of 1933 and 1934 to ensure that adequate information reaches prospective investors. Issuers of new securities to the general public (for amounts greater than $1.5 million in a year with a maturity longer than 270 days) must file a registration statement with the SEC and must provide to potential investors a prospectus containing all relevant information on the securities. The issuer must then wait 20 days after the registration statement is filed with the SEC before it can sell any of the securities. If the SEC does not object during the 20-day waiting period, the securities can be sold.

Securities Brokers and Dealers

Securities brokers and dealers conduct trading in secondary markets. Brokers are pure middlemen who act as agents for investors in the purchase or sale of securities. Their function is to match buyers with sellers, a function for which they are paid brokerage commissions. In contrast to brokers, dealers link buyers and sellers by standing ready to buy and sell securities at given prices. Therefore, dealers hold inventories of securities and make their living by selling these securities for a slightly higher price than they paid for them—that is, on the "spread" between the bid price and the asked price. This is a high-risk business because dealers hold securities that can rise or fall in price; in recent years, several firms specializing in bonds have collapsed. Brokers, by contrast, are not as exposed to risk because they do not own the securities involved in their business dealings.

Brokerage firms engage in all three securities market activities, acting as brokers, dealers, and investment bankers. The largest in the United States is Merrill Lynch; other well-known ones are Paine Webber, Dean Witter Reynolds, and Smith Barney Shearson. The SEC not only regulates the investment banking operation of the firms but also restricts brokers and dealers from misrepresenting securities and from trading on *insider information,* nonpublic information known only to the management of a corporation.

The forces of competition led to an important development: Brokerage firms started to engage in activities traditionally conducted by commercial banks. In 1977, Merrill Lynch developed the cash management account (CMA), which provides a package of financial services that includes credit cards, immediate loans, check-writing privileges, automatic investment of proceeds from the sale of securities into a money market mutual fund, and unified record keeping. CMAs were adopted by other brokerage firms and spread rapidly. The result is that the distinction between banking activities and the activities of nonbank financial institutions has become blurred. Walter Wriston, former head of Citicorp (the largest bank holding company in the country), has been quoted as saying, "The bank of the future already exists, and it's called Merrill Lynch."[4]

---

[4]"Banking Takes a Beating," *Time,* December 3, 1984, p. 50.

Organized Exchanges

As discussed in Chapter 2, secondary markets can be organized either as over-the-counter markets, in which trades are conducted using dealers, or as organized exchanges, in which trades are conducted in one central location. The New York Stock Exchange (NYSE), trading thousands of securities, is the largest organized exchange in the world, and the American Stock Exchange (AMEX) is a distant second. A number of smaller regional exchanges, which trade only a small number of securities (under 100), exist in places such as Boston and Los Angeles.

Organized stock exchanges actually function as a hybrid of an auction market (in which buyers and sellers trade with each other in a central location) and a dealer market (in which dealers make the market by buying and selling securities at given prices). Securities are traded on the floor of the exchange with the help of a special kind of dealer-broker called a **specialist.** A specialist matches buy and sell orders submitted at the same price and so performs a brokerage function. However, if buy and sell orders do not match up, the specialist buys stocks or sells from a personal inventory of securities, in this manner performing a dealer function. By assuming both functions, the specialist maintains orderly trading of the securities for which he or she is responsible.

Organized exchanges in which securities are traded are also regulated by the SEC. Not only does the SEC have the authority to impose regulations that govern the behavior of brokers and dealers involved with exchanges, but it also has the authority to alter the rules set by exchanges. In 1975, for example, the SEC disallowed rules that set minimum brokerage commission rates. The result was a sharp drop in brokerage commission rates, especially for institutional investors (mutual funds and pension funds), which purchase large blocks of stock. The Securities Amendments Act of 1975 confirmed the SEC's action by outlawing the setting of minimum brokerage commissions.

Furthermore, the Securities Amendments Act directed the SEC to facilitate a national market system that consolidates trading of all securities listed on the national and regional exchanges as well as those traded in the over-the-counter market using the National Association of Securities Dealers' automated quotation system (NASDAQ). Computers and advanced telecommunications, which reduce the costs of linking these markets, have encouraged the expansion of a national market system. We thus see that legislation and modern computer technology are leading the way to a more competitive securities industry.

The growing internationalization of capital markets has encouraged another trend in securities trading. Increasingly, foreign companies are being listed on U.S. stock exchanges, and the markets are moving toward trading stocks internationally, 24 hours a day.

SUMMARY

1. Insurance companies, which are regulated by the states, acquire funds by selling policies that pay out benefits if catastrophic events occur. Property and casualty insurance companies hold more liquid assets than life insurance companies because of greater uncertainty regarding the benefits they will have to pay out. All insurance companies face moral hazard and adverse selection problems that explain the use of insurance management tools, such as information collection and screening of potential policyholders, risk-based premiums, restrictive provisions, prevention of fraud, cancellation of insurance, deductibles, coinsurance, and limits on the amount of insurance.

2. Pension plans provide income payments to people when they retire after contributing to the plans for many years. Pension funds have experienced very rapid growth as a result of encouragement by federal tax policy and now play an important role in the stock market. Many pension plans are underfunded, which means that in future years they will have to pay out higher benefits than the value of their contributions and earnings. The problem of underfunding is especially acute for public pension plans such as Social Security. To prevent abuses, Congress enacted the Employee Retirement Income Security Act (ERISA), which established minimum standards for reporting, vesting, and degree of underfunding of private pension plans. This act also created the Pension Benefit Guarantee Corporation, which insures pension benefits.

3. Finance companies raise funds by issuing commercial paper and stocks and bonds, then use the proceeds to make loans that are particularly suited to consumer and business needs. Virtually unregulated in comparison to commercial banks and thrift institutions, finance companies have been able to enter new credit arrangements (such as equipment leasing) very quickly and have grown rapidly.

4. Mutual funds sell shares and use the proceeds to buy securities. Open-end funds issue shares that can be redeemed at any time at a price tied to the asset value of the firm. Closed-end funds issue nonredeemable shares, which are traded like common stock. They are less popular than open-end funds because their shares are not as liquid. Money market mutual funds hold only short-term, high-quality securities, allowing shares to be redeemed at a fixed value using checks. Shares in these funds effectively function as checkable deposits that earn market interest rates. All mutual funds are regulated by the SEC.

5. Investment banks are firms that assist in the initial sale of securities in primary markets, whereas securities brokers and dealers assist in the trading of securities in the secondary markets, some of which are organized into exchanges. The SEC regulates the financial institutions in the securities markets and ensures that adequate information reaches prospective investors.

KEY TERMS

deductible	open-end fund	no-load funds	brokerage firms
fully funded	closed-end fund	underwriters	specialist
underfunded	load funds		

QUESTIONS AND PROBLEMS

*1. If death rates were to become less predictable than they are, how would life insurance companies change the types of assets they hold?

2. Why do property and casualty insurance companies have large holdings of municipal bonds while life insurance companies do not?

*3. Why are all defined contribution pension plans fully funded?

4. How can favorable tax treatment of pension plans encourage saving?

*5. "In contrast to private pension plans, government pension plans are rarely underfunded." Is this statement true, false, or uncertain? Explain.

6. What explains the widespread use of deductibles in insurance policies?

*7. Why might insurance companies restrict the amount of insurance a policyholder can buy?

8. Why are restrictive provisions a necessary part of insurance policies?

*9. If you needed to take out a loan, why might you first go to your local bank rather than to a finance company?

10. Explain why shares in closed-end mutual funds typically sell for less than the market value of the stocks they hold.

*11. Why might you buy a no-load mutual fund instead of a load fund?

12. Why can a money market mutual fund allow its shareholders to redeem shares at a fixed price while other mutual funds cannot?

*13. Why might government loan guarantees be a high-cost way for the government to subsidize certain activities?

14. If you like to take risks, would you rather be a dealer, a broker, or a specialist? Why?

*15. Is investment banking a good career for someone who is afraid of taking risks? Why or why not?

PART IV

THE MONEY SUPPLY PROCESS

MULTIPLE DEPOSIT CREATION: INTRODUCING THE MONEY SUPPLY PROCESS

PREVIEW   On the evening news you hear that last week the money supply rose by $5 billion. The news immediately sets off a chain reaction. Interest rates may rise because people expect that the increase in the money supply will lead to inflation, the stock market may boom because financial markets expect a stronger economy in the future, and firms may decide to invest more and consumers to spend more. Politicians also react to the news: Some berate the Fed for promoting inflation by letting the money supply expand *too much,* and others berate the Fed for *not* expanding the money supply *enough* to reduce unemployment.

Because movements in the money supply affect the health of the economy and thus affect us all, we need to understand how the money supply is determined. Who controls it? What causes it to change? How might control of it be improved? In this and subsequent chapters we answer these questions by providing a detailed description of the money supply process, the mechanism that determines the level of the money supply.

Because deposits at banks are by far the largest component of the money supply, understanding how these deposits are created is the first step in understanding the money supply process. This chapter provides an overview of how the banking system creates deposits. In addition, it outlines the basic building blocks needed in later chapters for you to understand in greater depth how the money supply is determined.

FOUR PLAYERS IN THE MONEY SUPPLY PROCESS

The "cast of characters" in the money supply story is as follows:

1. The **central bank:** the government agency that oversees the banking system and is responsible for the conduct of monetary policy; in the United States, the Federal Reserve System

2. Banks (depository institutions): the financial intermediaries that accept deposits from individuals and institutions and make loans—commercial banks, savings and loan associations, mutual savings banks, and credit unions

3. Depositors: individuals and institutions that hold deposits in banks

4. Borrowers from banks: individuals and institutions that borrow from the depository institutions, or institutions that issue bonds that are purchased by the depository institutions

Of the four players, the central bank, the Federal Reserve System, is the most important. To explore the money supply process, we must first understand its function.[1]

OVERVIEW OF THE FEDERAL RESERVE SYSTEM

The **Federal Reserve System,** commonly called **the Fed** or the Federal Reserve, is the central bank of the United States. It consists of 12 Federal Reserve banks in major cities (for example, New York, Chicago, Boston, Dallas, Atlanta, and San Francisco) and the Board of Governors of the Federal Reserve System, located in Washington, D.C.

The Federal Reserve System performs several essential functions:

1. It conducts monetary policy by affecting the behavior of banks, thereby affecting the money supply.

2. It clears checks—that is, it transfers funds between banks to settle claims that arise as a result of the depositing of checks in one bank that have been written on an account at another bank.

3. It performs a regulatory function by setting rules for how banks can operate.

The operation of the Fed and its conduct of monetary policy involve actions that affect its balance sheet (holdings of assets and liabilities). Here we discuss a simplified balance sheet, which includes just four items that are essential to our analysis of the money supply process. (The complete balance sheet appears in Chapter 19.)

Federal Reserve System	
Assets	Liabilities
Government securities Discount loans	Currency in circulation Reserves

---

[1]The Fed's structure and operation are discussed in greater detail in Chapters 18–21.

Liabilities

The two liabilities on the balance sheet, currency in circulation and reserves, are often referred to as the *monetary liabilities* of the Fed. They are an important part of the money supply story because increases in either or both will lead to an increase in the money supply (everything else being constant). The sum of the Fed's monetary liabilities (currency in circulation and reserves) and the U.S. Treasury's monetary liabilities (Treasury currency in circulation, primarily coins) is called the **monetary base.** When discussing the monetary base, we will focus only on the monetary liabilities of the Fed because the monetary liabilities of the Treasury account for less than 10% of the base.[2]

1. Currency in circulation. The Fed issues currency (those green and gray pieces of paper in your wallet that say "Federal Reserve note" at the top). Currency in circulation is the amount of currency in the hands of the public (outside of banks)—an important component of the money supply. (Currency held by depository institutions is also a liability of the Fed but is counted as part of reserves.)

Federal Reserve notes are IOUs from the Fed to the bearer and are also liabilities, but unlike most, they promise to pay back the bearer solely with Federal Reserve notes; that is, they pay off IOUs with other IOUs. Accordingly, if you bring a $100 bill to the Federal Reserve and demand payment, you will receive two $50s, five $20s, ten $10s, or one hundred $1 bills.

People are more willing to accept IOUs from the Fed than from you or me because Federal Reserve notes are a recognized medium of exchange; that is, they are accepted as a means of payment and so function as money. Unfortunately, neither you nor I can convince people that our IOUs are worth anything more than the paper they are written on.[3]

2. Reserves. All banks have an account at the Fed in which they hold deposits. **Reserves** consist of deposits at the Fed plus currency that is physically

---

[2]It is also safe to ignore the Treasury's monetary liabilities when discussing the monetary base because the Treasury cannot actively supply its monetary liabilities to the economy due to legal restrictions (see Chapter 19).

[3]The currency item on our balance sheet refers only to currency *in circulation,* that is, the amount in the hands of the public. Currency that has been printed by the U.S. Bureau of Printing and Engraving is not automatically a liability of the Fed. For example, consider the importance of having $1 million of your own IOUs printed up. You give out $100 worth to other people and keep the other $999,900 in your pocket. The $999,900 of IOUs does not make you richer or poorer and does not affect your indebtedness. You care only about the $100 of liabilities from the $100 of circulated IOUs. The same reasoning applies for the Fed in regard to its Federal Reserve notes.

For similar reasons, the currency component of the money supply, no matter how it is defined, includes only currency in circulation. It does not include any additional currency that is not yet in the hands of the public. The fact that currency has been printed but is not circulating means that it is not anyone's asset or liability and thus cannot affect anyone's behavior. Therefore, it makes sense not to include it in the money supply.

held by banks (called *vault cash* because it is stored in bank vaults). Reserves are assets for the banks but liabilities for the Fed because the banks can demand payment on them at any time and the Fed is obliged to satisfy its obligation by paying Federal Reserve notes. As you will see, an increase in reserves leads to an increase in the level of deposits and hence in the money supply.

Total reserves can be divided into two categories: reserves that the Fed requires banks to hold **(required reserves)** and any additional reserves the banks choose to hold **(excess reserves).** For example, the Fed might require that for every dollar of deposits at a depository institution, a certain fraction (say, 10 cents) must be held as reserves. This fraction (10%) is called the **required reserve ratio.** Currently, the Fed pays no interest on reserves.

Assets

The two assets on the Fed's balance sheet are important for two reasons. First, changes in the asset items lead to changes in reserves and consequently to changes in the money supply. Second, because these assets (government securities and discount loans) earn interest while the liabilities (currency in circulation and reserves) do not, the Fed makes billions of dollars every year—its assets earn income, and its liabilities cost nothing. Although it returns most of its earnings to the federal government, the Fed does spend some of it on "worthy causes," such as supporting economic research.

1. Government securities. This category of assets covers the Fed's holdings of securities issued by the U.S. Treasury. As you will see, the Fed provides reserves to the banking system by purchasing securities, thereby increasing its holdings of these assets. An increase in government securities held by the Fed leads to an increase in the money supply.

2. Discount loans. The Fed can provide reserves to the banking system by making discount loans to banks. An increase in discount loans can also be the source of an increase in the money supply. The interest rate charged banks for these loans is called the **discount rate.**

MULTIPLE DEPOSIT CREATION: A SIMPLE MODEL

With our understanding of the basic functions of the Federal Reserve and how banks operate (Chapter 11), we now have the tools necessary to explain how deposits are created. When the Fed supplies the banking system with $1 of additional reserves, deposits increase by a multiple of this amount—a process called **multiple deposit creation.** Let us begin with the Fed and see how its actions lead to an increase in reserves.

How the Fed Provides Reserves to the Banking System

The Fed can provide additional reserves to the banking system in two ways: It can make loans to the banks, and it can purchase government bonds.

Loans to Banks Suppose that the Fed makes a $100 discount loan to the First National Bank. To understand what occurs as a result of this transaction, we look at *T-accounts,* which list only the changes that occur in balance sheet items starting from the initial balance sheet position. When the Fed makes the loan, it immediately credits the proceeds from the loan to the account of the First National Bank at the Fed. The bank's reserves rise by $100, while its borrowings from the Fed have increased by $100, resulting in the following T-account:

First National Bank			
Assets		Liabilities	
Reserves	+ $100	Discount loan from the Fed	+ $100

The same items appear in the Fed's T-account but in the opposite columns, because for the Fed reserves are a liability (payable on demand) and the discount loan is an asset (earning income for the Fed):

Federal Reserve System			
Assets		Liabilities	
Discount loan to First National Bank	+ $100	Reserves	+ $100

You can see that the Fed can provide reserves to the banking system by loaning them to the banks.

Purchase of Government Bonds The Fed's buying or selling of bonds in the open market is called an **open market operation.** Suppose that the Fed buys $100 worth of bonds from the First National Bank and pays for them with a check written on the Federal Reserve Bank of New York. The First National Bank then deposits the check with the Fed, and it is credited to the First National Bank's reserves account. The net result of the open market operation on the First National Bank's balance sheet is that it has reduced its holdings of securities by $100 and increased its reserves by $100:

First National Bank			
Assets		Liabilities	
Securities	− $100		
Reserves	+ $100		

The Fed finds that its liabilities have increased by $100 because reserves have increased by this amount, yet it now finds itself holding an extra $100 of bonds, which appears in its assets column as an increase of $100 in government securities. Its T-account is

Federal Reserve System			
Assets		Liabilities	
Government securities	+ $100	Reserves	+ $100

You can see that the Fed can exercise control over the size of reserves by varying its holdings of government securities via open market operations.[4]

With this information in mind, we now examine how an increase in reserves can create deposits.

Deposit Creation: The Single Bank

After the Fed has bought the $100 bond from the First National Bank, the bank finds that it has an increase in reserves of $100. To analyze what the bank will do with these additional reserves, assume that the bank does not want to hold excess reserves because it earns no interest on them. We begin the analysis with the following T-account:

First National Bank			
Assets		Liabilities	
Securities	− $100		
Reserves	+ $100		

Because the bank has no increase in its checkable deposits, required reserves remain the same, and the bank finds that its additional $100 of reserves means that

---

[4]Chapter 16 details further how the Fed uses open market operations to affect reserves. For example, we show that an open market operation has the same effect on reserves if bonds are purchased from the nonbank public rather than from banks.

its excess reserves have increased by $100. Let's say that the bank decides to make a loan equal in amount to the $100 increase in excess reserves. When the bank makes the loan, it sets up a checking account for the borrower and puts the proceeds of the loan into this account. In this way the bank alters its balance sheet by increasing its liabilities with $100 of checkable deposits and at the same time increasing its assets with the $100 loan. The resulting T-account looks like this

First National Bank			
Assets		Liabilities	
Securities	− $100	Checkable deposits	+ $100
Reserves	+ $100		
Loans	+ $100		

The bank has created checkable deposits by its act of lending. Because checkable deposits are part of the money supply, the bank's act of lending has in fact created money.

In its current balance sheet position, the First National Bank still has excess reserves and so might want to make additional loans. However, these reserves will not stay at the bank for very long. The borrower took out a loan not to leave $100 idle at the First National Bank but to purchase goods and services from other individuals and corporations. When the borrower makes these purchases by writing checks, they will be deposited at other banks, and the $100 of reserves will leave the First National Bank. *A bank cannot safely make loans for an amount greater than the excess reserves it has before it makes the loan.*

The final T-account of the First National Bank is

First National Bank			
Assets		Liabilities	
Securities	− $100		
Loans	+ $100		

The increase in reserves of $100 has been converted into additional loans of $100 at the First National Bank, plus an additional $100 of deposits that have made their way to other banks. (All the checks written on account at the First National Bank are deposited in banks rather than converted into cash because we are assuming that the public does not want to hold any additional currency.) Now let's see what happens to these deposits at the other banks.

Deposit Creation: The Banking System

To simplify the analysis, let us assume that the $100 of deposits created by First National Bank's loan is deposited at Bank A and that this bank and all other banks hold no excess reserves. Bank A's T-account becomes

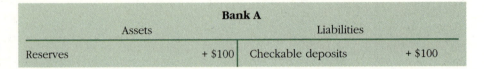

Bank A			
Assets		Liabilities	
Reserves	+ $100	Checkable deposits	+ $100

If the required reserve ratio is 10%, this bank will now find itself with a $10 increase in required reserves, leaving it $90 of excess reserves. Because Bank A (like the First National Bank) does not want to hold on to excess reserves, it will make loans for the entire amount. Its loans and checkable deposits will then increase by $90, but when the borrower spends the $90 of checkable deposits, they and the reserves at Bank A will fall back down by this same amount. The net result is that Bank A's T-account will look like this:

Bank A			
Assets		Liabilities	
Reserves	+ $10	Checkable deposits	+ $100
Loans	+ $90		

If the money spent by the borrower to whom Bank A lent the $90 is deposited in another bank, such as Bank B, the T-account for Bank B will be

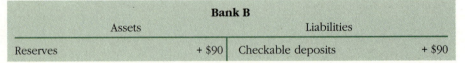

Bank B			
Assets		Liabilities	
Reserves	+ $90	Checkable deposits	+ $90

The checkable deposits in the banking system have increased by another $90, for a total increase of $190 ($100 at Bank A plus $90 at Bank B). In fact, the distinction between Bank A and Bank B is not necessary to obtain the same result on the overall expansion of deposits. If the borrower from Bank A writes checks to someone who deposits them at Bank A, the same change in deposits would occur. The T-accounts for Bank B would just apply to Bank A, and its checkable deposits would increase by the total amount of $190.

Bank B will want to modify its balance sheet further. It must keep 10% of $90 ($9) as required reserves and has 90% of $90 ($81) in excess reserves and so can make loans of this amount. Bank B will make an $81 loan to a borrower, who spends the proceeds from the loan. Bank B's T-account will be

	Bank B		
Assets		Liabilities	
Reserves	+ $ 9	Checkable deposits	+ $90
Loans	+ $81		

The $81 spent by the borrower from Bank B will be deposited in another bank (Bank C). Consequently, from the initial $100 increase of reserves in the banking system, the total increase of checkable deposits in the system so far is $271 (= $100 + $90 + $81).

Following the same reasoning, if all banks make loans for the full amount of their excess reserves, further increments in checkable deposits will continue (at Banks C, D, E, and so on), as depicted in Table 1. Therefore, the total increase in deposits from the initial $100 increase in reserves will be $1000: The increase is tenfold, the *reciprocal* of the reserve requirement.

	TABLE 1 Creation of Deposits (assuming 10% reserve requirement and a $100 increase in reserves)		
Bank	Increase in Deposits ($)	Increase in Loans ($)	Increase in Reserves ($)
First National	0.00	100.00	0.00
A	100.00	90.00	10.00
B	90.00	81.00	9.00
C	81.00	72.90	8.10
D	72.90	65.61	7.29
E	65.61	59.05	6.56
F	59.05	53.14	5.91
.	.	.	.
.	.	.	.
.	.	.	.
Total for all banks	1000.00	1000.00	100.00

If the banks choose to invest their excess reserves in securities, the result is the same. If Bank A had taken its excess reserves and purchased securities instead of making loans, its T-account would have looked like this:

	Bank A		
Assets		Liabilities	
Reserves	+ $10	Checkable deposits	+ $100
Securities	+ $90		

When the bank buys $90 of securities, it writes a $90 check to the seller of the securities, who in turn deposits the $90 at a bank such as Bank B. Bank B's checkable deposits rise by $90, and the deposit expansion process is the same as before. ***Whether a bank chooses to use its excess reserves to make loans or to purchase securities, the effect on deposit expansion is the same.***

You can now see the difference in deposit creation for the single bank versus the banking system as a whole. Because a single bank can create deposits equal only to the amount of its excess reserves, it cannot by itself generate multiple deposit expansion. A single bank cannot make loans greater in amount than its excess reserves because the bank will lose these reserves as the deposits created by the loan find their way to other banks. However, the banking system as a whole can generate a multiple expansion of deposits because when a bank loses its excess reserves, these reserves do not leave the banking system even though they are lost to the individual bank. So as each bank makes a loan and creates deposits, the reserves find their way to another bank, which uses them to make additional loans and create additional deposits. As you have seen, this process continues until the initial increase in reserves results in a multiple increase in deposits.

The multiple increase in deposits generated from an increase in the banking system's reserves is called the **simple deposit multiplier**.[5] In our example with a 10% required reserve ratio, the simple deposit multiplier is 10. More generally, the simple deposit multiplier equals the reciprocal of the required reserve ratio, expressed as a fraction (10 = 1/0.10), so that the formula for the multiple expansion of deposits can be written as[6]

$$\Delta D = \frac{1}{r_D} \times \Delta R \qquad (1)$$

where ΔD = change in total checkable deposits in the banking system
r_D = required reserve ratio (0.10 in the example)
ΔR = change in reserves for the banking system ($100 in the example)

---

[5] This multiplier should not be confused with the Keynesian multiplier, which is derived through a similar step-by-step analysis. That multiplier relates an increase in income to an increase in investment, whereas the simple deposit multiplier relates an increase in deposits to an increase in reserves.

[6] A formal derivation of this formula follows. Using the reasoning in the text, the change in checkable deposits is $100 (= $\Delta R \times 1$) plus $90 [= $\Delta R \times (1 - r_D)$] plus $81 [= $\Delta R \times (1 - r_D)^2$] and so on, which can be rewritten as

$$\Delta D = \Delta R \times [1 + (1 - r_D) + (1 - r_D)^2 + (1 - r_D)^3 + \cdots]$$

Using the formula for the sum of an infinite series found in footnote 5 in Chapter 4, this can be rewritten as

$$\Delta D = \Delta R \times \frac{1}{1 - (1 - r_D)} = \frac{1}{r_D} \times \Delta R$$

Multiple Deposit Contraction

The multiple deposit creation process should also work in reverse; that is, when the Fed withdraws reserves from the banking system, there should be a multiple contraction of deposits. To prove this, let us trace the effect of a reduction of reserves in the banking system when again we assume that banks do not hold any excess reserves.

STUDY GUIDE

Test your understanding of multiple deposit creation by writing down the appropriate T-account for each step in the process of multiple deposit contraction before you look at the T-accounts in the text.

Let's start our analysis with a $100 reduction in the reserves of the First National Bank (by the Fed's sale of a $100 bond to the bank). The First National Bank finds that it has lost $100 of reserves, and because it has not been holding any excess reserves, its holdings of reserves are $100 short of the required amount. It can obtain the reserves needed by selling $100 of securities or by demanding repayment of $100 of loans. When it sells the securities, it will receive $100 of checks written on an account with another bank that will be deposited at the Fed, thus raising its reserves by the same amount. Similarly, the repayment of the loan will also be made with checks written on an account with another bank. In both cases, the reserves at the First National Bank will be increased by $100, but the bank on which the checks are drawn (such as Bank A) will lose $100 of checkable deposits and $100 of reserves. Bank A's T-account will be

Bank A			
Assets		Liabilities	
Reserves	− $100	Checkable deposits	− $100

Bank A will now find that it cannot meet its reserve requirements—it will be $90 short. Its reserves have fallen by $100, but its required reserves have also fallen by $10 (10% of the $100 decline in checkable deposits). To meet this reserve shortfall, Bank A will reduce its holdings of loans or securities by $90, transforming its T-account to

Bank A			
Assets		Liabilities	
Reserves	− $10	Checkable deposits	− $100
Loans and securities	− $90		

If the checks that Bank A receives as a result of reducing its loans or securities were written on accounts at Bank B, Bank B would then find itself with the following T-account:

	Bank B		
Assets		Liabilities	
Reserves	− $90	Checkable deposits	− $90

Bank B now has a reserve shortfall of $81 ($90 minus 10% of $90), and so it reduces its loans and securities by this amount, lowering another bank's checkable deposits by $81. This process keeps on going, with the level of checkable deposits in the banking system changing by

$$ - \$100 - \$90 - \$81 - \$72.90 - \$65.61 - \$59.05 - \cdots = -\$1000 $$

You can see that the process of multiple deposit contraction is symmetrical to the process of multiple deposit creation.

Deriving the Formula for Multiple Deposit Creation

The formula for the multiple creation of deposits can also be derived directly using algebra. We obtain the same answer for the relationship between a change in deposits and a change in reserves, but more quickly.

Our assumption that banks do not hold on to any excess reserves means that the total amount of required reserves for the banking system RR will equal the total reserves in the banking system R:

$$ RR = R $$

The total amount of required reserves equals the required reserve ratio r_D times the total amount of checkable deposits D:

$$ RR = r_D \times D $$

Substituting $r_D \times D$ for RR in the first equation,

$$ r_D \times D = R $$

and dividing both sides of the preceding equation by r_D gives us

$$ D = \frac{1}{r_D} \times R $$

Taking the change in both sides of this equation and using delta to indicate a change,

$$ \Delta D = \frac{1}{r_D} \times \Delta R $$

which is the same formula for deposit creation found in Equation 1.

This derivation provides us with another way of looking at the multiple creation of deposits because it forces us to look directly at the banking system as a whole rather than one bank at a time. For the banking system as a whole, deposit creation (or contraction) will stop only when all excess reserves in the banking system are gone; that is, the banking system will be in equilibrium when the total amount of required reserves equals the total amount of reserves, as seen in the equation $RR = R$. When $r_D \times D$ is substituted for RR, the resulting equation $R = r_D \times D$ tells us how high checkable deposits will have to be in order for required reserves to equal total reserves. Accordingly, a given level of reserves in the banking system determines the level of checkable deposits when the banking system is in equilibrium (when $ER = 0$); put another way, the given level of reserves supports a given level of checkable deposits.

In our example, the required reserve ratio is 10%. If reserves increase by $100, checkable deposits must rise to $1000 in order for total required reserves also to increase by $100. If the increase in checkable deposits is less than this, say, $900, then the increase in required reserves of $90 remains below the $100 increase in reserves, so there are still excess reserves somewhere in the banking system. The banks with the excess reserves will now make additional loans, creating new deposits, and this process will continue until all reserves in the system are used up. This occurs when checkable deposits have risen to $1000.

We can also see this by looking at the T-account of the banking system as a whole (including the First National Bank) that results from this process:

Banking System			
Assets		Liabilities	
Securities	− $ 100	Checkable deposits	+ $1000
Reserves	+ $ 100		
Loans	+ $1000		

The procedure of eliminating excess reserves by loaning them out means that the banking system (First National Bank and Banks A, B, C, D, and so on) continues to make loans up to the $1000 amount until deposits have reached the $1000 level. In this way, $100 of reserves supports $1000 (ten times the quantity) of deposits.

CRITIQUE OF THE SIMPLE MODEL

Our model of multiple deposit creation seems to indicate that the Federal Reserve is able to exercise complete control over the level of checkable deposits by setting the required reserve ratio and the level of reserves. The actual creation of deposits is much less mechanical than the simple model indicates. If proceeds from Bank A's $90 loan are not deposited but are kept in cash, nothing is deposited in Bank B, and the deposit creation process stops dead in its tracks. The total increase in checkable deposits is only $100—considerably less than the

$1000 we calculated. So if some proceeds from loans are used to raise the holdings of currency, checkable deposits will not increase by as much as our streamlined model of multiple deposit creation tells us.

Another situation ignored in our model is one in which banks do not make loans or buy securities in the full amount of their excess reserves. If Bank A decides to hold on to all $90 of its excess reserves, no deposits would be made in Bank B, and this would also stop the deposit creation process. The total increase in deposits would again be only $100 and not the $1000 increase in our example. Hence if banks choose to hold all or some of their excess reserves, the full expansion of deposits predicted by the simple model of multiple deposit creation does not occur.

Our examples rightly indicate that the Fed is not the only player whose behavior influences the level of deposits and therefore the money supply. Banks' decisions regarding the amount of excess reserves they wish to hold and depositors' decisions regarding how much currency to hold can cause the money supply to change. In later chapters we stress the behavior and interactions of the four players in constructing a more realistic model of the money supply process.

SUMMARY

1. There are four players in the money supply process: the central bank, banks (depository institutions), depositors, and borrowers from banks.

2. The central bank in the United States is the Federal Reserve System (the Fed). It conducts monetary policy, clears checks, and performs a regulatory function. The Fed has monetary liabilities (currency in circulation and reserves), which make up the bulk of the monetary base; it has assets of government securities and the discount loans it grants to banks.

3. The Fed provides reserves to the banking system by purchasing bonds or by making loans to the banks. A single bank can make loans up to the amount of its excess reserves, thereby creating an equal amount of deposits. The banking system can create a multiple expansion of deposits be-

cause as each bank makes a loan and creates deposits, the reserves find their way to another bank, which uses them to make loans and create additional deposits. In the simple model of multiple deposit creation in which banks do not hold on to excess reserves and the public holds no currency, the multiple increase in checkable deposits (simple deposit multiplier) equals the reciprocal of the required reserve ratio.

4. The simple model of multiple deposit creation has serious deficiencies. Decisions by depositors to increase their holdings of currency or of banks to hold excess reserves will result in a smaller expansion of deposits than the simple model predicts. All four players—the Fed, banks, depositors, and borrowers from banks—are important in the determination of the money supply.

KEY TERMS

central bank	reserves	required reserve ratio	open market operation
Federal Reserve Sytem (the Fed)	required reserves	discount rate	simple deposit multiplier
monetary base	excess reserves	multiple deposit creation	

QUESTIONS AND PROBLEMS

*1. "When a bank takes some of its cash and deposits it at the Fed, its reserves increase." Is this statement true, false, or uncertain? Explain.

2. Show what happens to the T-accounts of the Fed and the First National Bank when the Fed sells $1000 of securities to the First National Bank. What happens to reserves at the First National Bank?

*3. If the Fed loans the First National Bank $1 million and the First National Bank uses the proceeds to buy $1 million of bonds from the Fed, what happens to reserves at the First National Bank? Explain your answer using T-accounts for the Fed and the First National Bank.

4. The First National Bank receives an extra $100 of reserves but decides not to loan any of these reserves out. How much deposit creation takes place for the entire banking system?

Unless otherwise noted, the following assumptions are made in all the remaining problems: The required ratio on checkable deposits is 10%, banks do not hold on to excess reserves, and the public's holdings of currency do not change.

*5. Using T-accounts, show what happens to checkable deposits in the banking system when the Fed loans an additional $1 million to the First National Bank.

6. Using T-accounts, show what happens to checkable deposits in the banking system when the Fed sells $2 million of bonds to the First National Bank.

*7. Suppose that the Fed buys $1 million of bonds from the First National Bank. If the First National Bank and all other banks use the resulting increase in reserves to purchase securities only and not to make loans, what will happen to checkable deposits?

8. If the Fed buys $1 million of bonds from the First National Bank, but an additional 10% of any deposit is held as excess reserves, what is the total increase in checkable deposits? (*Hint:* Use T-accounts to show what happens at each step of the multiple expansion process.)

*9. If a bank depositor withdraws $1000 of currency from an account, what happens to reserves and checkable deposits?

10. If reserves in the banking system increase by $1 billion as a result of discount loans of $1 billion and checkable deposits increase by $9 billion, why isn't the banking system in equilibrium? What will continue to happen in the banking system until equilibrium is reached? Show the T-account for the banking system in equilibrium.

*11. If the Fed reduces reserves by selling $5 million worth of bonds to the banks, what will the T-account of the banking system look like when the banking system is in equilibrium? What will have happened to the level of checkable deposits?

12. If the required reserve ratio on checkable deposits increases to 20%, how much multiple deposit creation will take place when reserves are increased by $100?

*13. If a bank decides that it wants to hold $1 million of excess reserves, what effect will this have on checkable deposits in the banking system?

14. If a bank sells $10 million of bonds back to the Fed in order to pay back $10 million on the discount loan it owes, what will be the effect on the level of checkable deposits?

*15. If you decide to hold $100 less cash than usual and therefore deposit $100 in cash in the bank, what effect will this have on checkable deposits in the banking system if the rest of the public keeps its holdings of currency constant?

Chapter 16

DETERMINANTS OF THE MONEY SUPPLY

PREVIEW
In Chapter 15 we developed a simple model of multiple deposit creation that showed how the Fed can control the level of checkable deposits by setting the required reserve ratio and the level of reserves. Unfortunately for the Fed, life isn't that simple; control of the money supply is far more complicated. Our critique of this model indicated that decisions by depositors about their holdings of currency and by banks about their holdings of excess reserves also affect the money supply. To deal with these criticisms, in this chapter we develop a money supply model in which depositors and banks assume their important roles. The resulting framework provides an in-depth description of the money supply process to help you understand the complexity of the Fed's role.

To simplify the analysis, we separate the development of our model into several steps. First we see that the Fed can exert more precise control over the monetary base (currency in circulation plus total reserves in the banking system) than it can over total reserves alone. So our model links changes in the money supply to changes in the monetary base. This link is achieved by deriving a **money multiplier** (a ratio that relates the change in the money supply to a given change in the monetary base). Finally, we examine the determinants of the money multiplier.

STUDY GUIDE

One reason for breaking the money supply model into its component parts is to help you answer questions using intuitive step-by-step logic rather than memorizing how changes in the behavior of the Fed, depositors, or banks will affect the money supply.

In deriving a model of the money supply process, we focus here on a simple definition of money (currency plus checkable deposits), which corresponds to the $M1$ definition. Although other broader definitions of money are frequently used in policymaking, particularly *M2*, we conduct the analysis with an *M1* definition because it is less complicated and yet provides a basic understanding of the money supply process. Furthermore, all analyses and results using the *M1* definition apply equally well to the *M2* definition. A somewhat more complicated money supply model for the *M2* definition is developed in the appendix to this chapter.

CONTROL OF THE MONETARY BASE

The *monetary base* (also called **high-powered money**) equals currency in circulation C plus the total reserves in the banking system R.[1] The monetary base *MB* is expressed as

$$MB = C + R$$

Chapter 15 showed how the Fed provides additional reserves to the banking system by purchasing government bonds or making loans to banks. We will see shortly that in actuality, though these actions are sure to increase the monetary base, their effect on reserves is more uncertain. This is why models describing the determination of the money supply and the Fed's role in this process normally focus on the monetary base rather than reserves.

Federal Reserve Open Market Operations

One way in which the Fed causes changes in the monetary base is purchasing or selling government bonds in an open market operation. A purchase of bonds by the Fed is called an **open market purchase**, and a sale of bonds by the Fed is called an **open market sale.**

Open Market Purchase from a Bank   As described in Chapter 15, the Fed purchases $100 of bonds from a bank and pays for them with a $100 check. The bank will either deposit the check in its account with the Fed or cash it in for currency, which will be counted as vault cash. Either action means that the bank will find itself with $100 more reserves and a reduction in its holdings of securities of $100. The T-account for the banking system, then, is

Banking System		
Assets		Liabilities
Securities	− $100	
Reserves	+$100	

---

[1]Currency in circulation includes both Federal Reserve currency (Federal Reserve notes) and Treasury currency (primarily coins).

The Fed meanwhile finds that its liabilities have increased by the additional $100 of reserves, while its assets have increased by the $100 of additional securities that it now holds. Its T-account is

Federal Reserve System				
Assets		Liabilities		
Securities	+ $100	Reserves		+ $100

The net result of this open market purchase is that reserves have increased by $100, the amount of the open market purchase. Because there has been no change of currency in circulation, the monetary base has also risen by $100.

Open Market Purchase from the Nonbank Public To understand what happens when there is an open market purchase from the nonbank public, we must look at two cases. First, let's assume that the person or corporation that sells the $100 of bonds to the Fed deposits the Fed's check in the local bank. The nonbank public's T-account after this transaction is

Nonbank Public			
Assets		Liabilities	
Securities	− $100		
Checkable deposits	+ $100		

When the bank receives the check, it credits the depositor's account with the $100 and then deposits the check in its account with the Fed, thereby adding to its reserves. The banking system's T-account becomes

Banking System			
Assets		Liabilities	
Reserves	+ $100	Checkable deposits	+ $100

The effect on the Fed's balance sheet is that it has gained $100 of securities in its assets column, while it has an increase of $100 of reserves in its liabilities column:

Federal Reserve System			
Assets		Liabilities	
Securities	+ $100	Reserves	+ $100

As you can see in this T-account, when the Fed's check is deposited in a bank, the net result of the Fed's open market purchase from the nonbank public is identical to the effect of its open market purchase from a bank: Reserves increase by the amount of the open market purchase, and the monetary base increases by the same amount.

If, however, the person or corporation selling the bonds to the Fed cashes the Fed's check either at a local bank or at a Federal Reserve bank for currency, the effect on reserves is different.[2] This seller will receive currency of $100 while reducing holdings of securities by $100. The bond seller's T-account will be

Nonbank Public		
Assets		Liabilities
Securities	− $100	
Currency	+ $100	

The Fed now finds that it has exchanged $100 of currency for $100 of securities, so that its T-account is

Federal Reserve System		
Assets		Liabilities
Securities	+ $100	Currency in circulation + $100

The net effect of the open market purchase in this case is that reserves are unchanged, while currency in circulation increases by the $100 of the open market purchase. Thus the monetary base increases by the $100 amount of the open market purchase, while reserves do not. This contrasts with the case in which the seller of the bonds deposits the Fed's check in a bank; in that case, reserves increase by $100, and so does the monetary base.

The analysis reveals that ***the effect of an open market purchase on reserves depends on whether the seller of the bonds keeps the proceeds from the sale in currency or in deposits.*** If the proceeds are kept in currency, the open market purchase has no effect on reserves; if the proceeds are kept as deposits, reserves increase by the amount of the open market purchase.

The effect of an open market purchase on the monetary base, however, is always the same (the monetary base increases by the amount of the purchase) whether the seller of the bonds keeps the proceeds in deposits or in currency. The impact of an open market purchase on reserves is much more uncertain than its impact on the monetary base.

Open Market Sale If the Fed sells $100 of bonds to a bank or the nonbank public, the monetary base will decline by $100. For example, if the Fed sells the bonds

---

[2]If the bond seller cashes the check at the local bank, its balance sheet will be unaffected because the $100 of vault cash that it pays out will be exactly matched by the deposit of the $100 check at the Fed. Thus its reserves will remain the same, and there will be no effect on its T-account. That is why a T-account for the banking system does not appear here.

to an individual who pays for them with currency, the buyer exchanges $100 of currency for $100 of bonds, and the resulting T-account is

Nonbank Public			
Assets		Liabilities	
Securities	+ $100		
Currency	− $100		

The Fed, for its part, has reduced its holdings of securities by $100 and has also lowered its monetary liability by accepting the currency as payment for its bonds, thereby reducing the amount of currency in circulation by $100:

Federal Reserve System			
Assets		Liabilities	
Securities	− $100	Currency in circulation	- $100

The effect of the open market sale of $100 of bonds is to reduce the monetary base by an equal amount, although reserves remain unchanged. Manipulations of T-accounts in cases in which the buyer of the bonds is a bank or the buyer pays for the bonds with a check written on a checkable deposit account at a local bank lead to the same $100 reduction in the monetary base, although the reduction occurs because the level of reserves has fallen by $100.

STUDY GUIDE

The best way to learn how open market operations affect the monetary base is to use T-accounts. Using T-accounts, try to verify that an open market sale of $100 of bonds to a bank or to a person who pays with a check written on a bank account leads to a $100 reduction in the monetary base.

The following conclusion can now be drawn from our analysis of open market purchases and sales: ***The effect of open market operations on the monetary base is much more certain than the effect on reserves.*** Therefore, the Fed can control the monetary base with open market operations more effectively than it can control reserves.

Shifts from Deposits into Currency

Even if the Fed does not conduct open market operations, a shift from deposits to currency will affect the reserves in the banking system. However, such a shift will have no effect on the monetary base, another reason why the Fed has more control over the monetary base than over reserves.

Let's suppose that Jane Brown (who opened a $100 checking account at the First National Bank in Chapter 11) decides that tellers are so abusive in all banks that she closes her account by withdrawing the $100 balance in cash and vows never to deposit it in a bank again. The effect on the T-account of the nonbank public is

Withdrawal:

Nonbank Public		
Assets		Liabilities
Checkable deposits	− $100	
Currency	+ $100	

The banking system loses $100 of deposits and hence $100 of reserves:

Banking System		
Assets		Liabilities
Reserves	− $100	Checkable deposits - $100

For the Fed, Jane Brown's action means that there is $100 of additional currency circulating in the hands of the public, while reserves in the banking system have fallen by $100. The Fed's T-account is

Federal Reserve System		
Assets		Liabilities
		Currency in circulation + $100
		Reserves − $100

The net effect on the monetary liabilities of the Fed is a wash; the monetary base is unaffected by Jane Brown's disgust at the banking system. But reserves *are* affected. Random fluctuations of reserves can occur as a result of random shifts into currency and out of deposits, and vice versa. The same is not true for the monetary base, making it a more stable variable.

Discount Loans

In this chapter so far we have seen changes in the monetary base solely as a result of open market operations. However, the monetary base is also affected when the Fed makes a discount loan to a bank. In Chapter 15, when the Fed made a $100 discount loan to the First National Bank, the bank was credited with $100 of reserves from the proceeds of the loan. The effects on the balance sheet of the banking system and the Fed are illustrated by the following T-accounts:

Banking System				Federal Reserve System			
Assets		Liabilities		Assets		Liabilities	
Reserves	+ $100	Discount loans	+ $100	Discount loans	+ $100	Reserves	+ $100

The monetary liabilities of the Fed have now increased by $100, and the monetary base, too, has increased by this amount. However, if a bank pays off a loan from the Fed, thereby reducing its borrowings from the Fed by $100, the T-accounts of the banking system and the Fed are as follows:

Banking System				Federal Reserve System			
Assets		Liabilities		Assets		Liabilities	
Reserves	− $100	Discount loans	− $100	Discount loans	− $100	Reserves	− $100

The net effect on the monetary liabilities of the Fed, and hence on the monetary base, is then a reduction of $100. We see that the monetary base changes one-for-one with the change in the borrowings from the Fed.

Overview of the Fed's Ability to Control the Monetary Base

The general conclusion from the foregoing analysis is that the Fed can control the monetary base better than it can control reserves. However, whereas the amount of open market purchases or sales is completely controlled by the Fed's placing orders with dealers in bond markets, the central bank lacks complete control over the monetary base because it cannot unilaterally determine, and therefore perfectly predict, the amount of borrowing by banks from the Fed. The Federal Reserve sets the discount rate (interest rate on discount loans), and then banks make a decision about whether to borrow. The amount of discount loans, though influenced by the Fed's setting of the discount rate, is not completely controlled by the Fed; banks' decisions play a role too.[3]

Therefore, we might want to split the monetary base into two components: one that the Fed can control completely and another that is less tightly controlled. The less tightly controlled component is the amount of the base that is

---

[3]The Fed, like any banker, can also decide whether or not to make such a loan, thus giving it further control over the amount of borrowings from the Fed. The key point, however, is not altered by this fact. Decisions of the banks as well as the Fed are important to the level of discount loans from the Fed.

created by discount loans from the Fed. The remainder of the base (called the **nonborrowed monetary base**) is under the Fed's control because it results primarily from open market operations.[4] The nonborrowed monetary base is formally defined as the monetary base minus discount loans from the Fed:

$$MB_n = MB - DL$$

where MB_n = nonborrowed monetary base
  MB = monetary base
  DL = discount loans from the Fed

The reason for distinguishing the nonborrowed monetary base MB_n from the monetary base MB is that the nonborrowed monetary base, which is tied to open market operations, is directly under control of the Fed, whereas the monetary base, which is also influenced by discount loans from the Fed, is not.

THE MONEY SUPPLY MODEL AND THE MONEY MULTIPLIER

Because the Fed can control the monetary base better than it can control reserves, it makes sense to link the money supply M to the monetary base MB through a relationship such as the following:

$$M = m \times MB \tag{1}$$

The variable m is the money multiplier, which tells us how much the money supply changes for a given change in the monetary base MB. This multiplier tells us what multiple of the monetary base is transformed into the money supply. Because the money multiplier is larger than 1, the alternative name for the monetary base, *high-powered money,* is logical; a $1 change in the monetary base leads to more than a $1 change in the money supply.

The money multiplier reflects the effect on the money supply of other factors besides the monetary base, and the following model will explain the factors that determine the size of the money multiplier. Depositors' decisions about their holdings of currency and checkable deposits are one set of factors affecting the money multiplier. Another involves the reserve requirements imposed by the Fed on the banking system. Banks' decisions about excess reserves also affect the money multiplier.

---

[4]Actually, there are other items on the Fed's balance sheet (discussed in Chapter 19) that affect the magnitude of the nonborrowed monetary base. Since their effects on the nonborrowed base relative to open market operations are both small and predictable, these other items do not present the Fed with difficulties in controlling the nonborrowed base.

Deriving the Money Multiplier

In our model of multiple deposit creation in Chapter 15, we ignored the effects on deposit creation of changes in the public's holdings of currency and banks' holdings of excess reserves. Now we incorporate these changes into our model of the money supply process by assuming that the level of currency C and excess reserves ER grows proportionally with checkable deposits D; in other words, we assume that the ratios of these items to checkable deposits are constants:

$$\{C/D\} = \text{currency ratio}$$
$$\{ER/D\} = \text{excess reserves ratio}$$

where the braces indicate that we are treating the ratio as a constant.

We will now derive a formula that describes how the currency ratio set by depositors, the excess reserves ratio set by banks, and the required reserve ratio set by the Fed affect the multiplier m. We begin the derivation of the model of the money supply with the equation

$$R = RR + ER$$

which states that the total amount of reserves in the banking system R equals the sum of required reserves RR and excess reserves ER. (Note that this equation corresponds to the equilibrium condition $RR = R$ in Chapter 15, where excess reserves were assumed to be zero.)

The total amount of required reserves equals the required reserve ratio r_D times the amount of checkable deposits D:

$$RR = r_D \times D$$

Substituting $r_D \times D$ for RR in the first equation yields an equation that links reserves in the banking system to the amount of checkable deposits and excess reserves they can support:

$$R = (r_D \times D) + ER$$

A key point here is that the Fed sets the required reserve ratio r_D to be less than 1. Thus $1 of reserves can support more than $1 of deposits, and the multiple expansion of deposits can occur.

Let's see how this works in practice. If excess reserves are held at zero ($ER = 0$), the required reserve ratio is set at $r_D = 0.10$, and the level of checkable deposits in the banking system is $800 billion, then the amount of reserves needed to support these deposits is $80 billion (= $0.10 \times$ $800 billion). The $80 billion of reserves can support ten times this amount in checkable deposits, just as in Chapter 15, because multiple deposit creation will occur.

Because the monetary base *MB* equals currency *C* plus reserves *R*, we can generate an equation that links the amount of monetary base to the levels of checkable deposits and currency by adding currency to both sides of the equation:

$$MB = R + C = (r_D \times D) + ER + C$$

Another way of thinking about this equation is to recognize that it reveals the amount of the monetary base that is needed to support the existing amounts of checkable deposits, currency, and excess reserves.

An important feature of this equation is that an additional dollar of *MB* that arises from an additional dollar of currency does not support any additional deposits. This occurs because such an increase leads to an identical increase in the right-hand side of the equation with no change occurring in *D*. The currency component of *MB* does not lead to multiple deposit creation as the reserves component does. Put another way, *an increase in the monetary base that goes into currency is not multiplied, whereas an increase that goes into supporting deposits is multiplied.*

Another important feature of this equation is that an additional dollar of *MB* that goes into excess reserves *ER* does not support any additional deposits or currency. The reason for this is that when a bank decides to hold excess reserves, it does not make additional loans, so these excess reserves do not lead to the creation of deposits. Therefore, if the Fed injects reserves into the banking system and they are held as excess reserves, there will be no effect on deposits or currency and hence no effect on the money supply. In other words, you can think of excess reserves as an idle component of reserves that are not being used to support any deposits (although they are important for bank liquidity management, as we saw in Chapter 11). This means that for a given level of reserves, a higher amount of excess reserves implies that the banking system in effect has fewer reserves to support deposits.

To derive the money multiplier formula in terms of the currency ratio {*C/D*} and the excess reserves ratio {*ER/D*}, we rewrite the last equation, specifying *C* as {*C/D*} × *D* and *ER* as {*ER/D*} × *D*:

$$MB = (r_D \times D) + (\{ER/D\} \times D) + (\{C/D\} \times D) = (r_D + \{ER/D\} + \{C/D\}) \times D$$

We next divide both sides of the equation by the term inside the parentheses to get an expression linking checkable deposits *D* to the monetary base *MB*:

$$D = \frac{1}{r_D + \{ER/D\} + \{C/D\}} \times MB \qquad (2)$$

Using the definition of the money supply as currency plus checkable deposits (*M = D + C*) and again specifying *C* as {*C/D*} × *D*,

$$M = D + (\{C/D\} \times D) = (1 + \{C/D\}) \times D$$

Substituting in this equation the expression for *D* from Equation 2, we have

$$M = \frac{1 + \{C/D\}}{r_D + \{ER/D\} + \{C/D\}} \times MB \qquad (3)$$

Finally, we have achieved our objective of deriving an expression in the form of our earlier Equation 1. As you can see, the ratio that multiplies *MB* is the money multiplier that tells how much the money supply changes in response to a given change in the monetary base (high-powered money). The money multiplier *m* is thus

$$m = \frac{1 + \{C/D\}}{r_D + \{ER/D\} + \{C/D\}} \qquad (4)$$

and it is a function of the currency ratio set by depositors $\{C/D\}$, the required reserve ratio set by the Fed r_D, the excess reserves ratio set by banks $\{ER/D\}$.

Although the algebraic derivation we have just completed shows you how the money multiplier is constructed, you need to understand the basic intuition behind it in order to be able to understand and apply the money multiplier concept without having to memorize it.

Intuition Behind the Money Multiplier

To get a feel for what the money multiplier means, let us again construct a numerical example with realistic numbers for the following variables:

r_D = required reserve ratio = 0.10
C = currency in circulation = $400 billion
D = checkable deposits = $800 billion
ER = excess reserves = $0.8 billion
M = money supply (*M*1) = $C + D$ = $1200 billion

From these numbers we can calculate the values for the currency ratio $\{C/D\}$ and the excess reserves ratio $\{ER/D\}$:

$$\{C/D\} = \frac{\$400 \text{ billion}}{\$800 \text{ billion}} = 0.5$$

$$\{ER/D\} = \frac{\$0.8 \text{ billion}}{\$800 \text{ billion}} = 0.001$$

The resulting value of the money multiplier is

$$m = \frac{1 + 0.5}{0.1 + 0.001 + 0.5} = \frac{1.5}{0.601} = 2.5$$

The money multiplier of 2.5 tells us that given the required reserve ratio of 10% on checkable deposits and the behavior of depositors as represented by

$\{C/D\}$ = 0.5 and banks as represented by $\{ER/D\}$ = 0.001, a $1 increase in the monetary base leads to a $2.50 increase in the money supply ($M1$).

An important characteristic of the money multiplier is that it is less than the simple deposit multiplier of 10 found in Chapter 15. The key to understanding this result and our money supply model is to realize that **although there is multiple expansion of deposits, there is no such expansion for currency.** Thus if some portion of the increase in high-powered money finds its way into currency, this portion does not undergo multiple deposit expansion. In our analysis in Chapter 15, we did not allow for this possibility, and so the increase in reserves led to the maximum amount of multiple deposit creation. However, in our current model of the money multiplier, the level of currency *does* increase when the monetary base MB and checkable deposits D increase because $\{C/D\}$ is greater than zero. As previously stated, any increase in MB that goes into an increase in currency is not multiplied, so only part of the increase in MB is available to support checkable deposits that undergo multiple expansion. The overall level of multiple deposit expansion must be lower, meaning that the increase in M, given an increase in MB, is smaller than the simple model in Chapter 15 indicated.[5]

Factors That Determine the Money Multiplier

To develop our intuition of the money multiplier even further, let us look at how this multiplier changes in response to changes in the variables in our model: $\{C/D\}$, r_D, and $\{ER/D\}$. The "game" we are playing is a familiar one in economics: We ask what happens when one of these variables changes, leaving all other variables the same *(ceteris paribus)*.

Changes in the Required Reserve Ratio r_D If the required reserve ratio on checkable deposits increases while all the other variables stay the same, the same level of reserves cannot support as large an amount of checkable deposits; more reserves are needed because required reserves for these checkable deposits have risen. The resulting deficiency in reserves then means that banks must contract their loans, causing a decline in deposits and hence in the money supply. The reduced money supply relative to the level of MB, which has remained unchanged, indicates that the money multiplier has declined as well. Another way to see this is to realize that when r_D is higher, less multiple expansion of check-

_____

[5]Another reason that the money multiplier is smaller is that $\{ER/D\}$ is a constant fraction greater than zero, indicating that an increase in MB and D leads to higher excess reserves. The resulting higher amount of excess reserves means that the amount of reserves used to support checkable deposits will not increase as much as it otherwise would. Hence the increase in checkable deposits and the money supply will be lower, and the money multiplier will be smaller. However, because $\{ER/D\}$ is currently so tiny, around 0.001, the impact of this ratio on the money multiplier is now quite small. But there have been periods when the $\{ER/D\}$ ratio has been much larger and so has had a more important role in lowering the money multiplier.

able deposits occurs. With less multiple deposit expansion, the money multiplier must fall.[6]

We can verify that the foregoing analysis is correct by seeing what happens to the value of the money multiplier in our numerical example when r_D increases from 10% to 15%. The money multiplier becomes

$$m = \frac{1 + 0.5}{0.15 + 0.001 + 0.5} = \frac{1.5}{0.651} = 2.3$$

which, as we would expect, is less than 2.5.

The analysis just conducted can also be applied to the case in which the required reserve ratio falls. In this case, there will be more multiple expansion for checkable deposits because the same level of reserves can now support more checkable deposits, and the money multiplier will rise. For example, if r_D falls from 10% to 5%, plugging this value into our money multiplier formula (leaving all the other variables unchanged) yields a money multiplier of

$$m = \frac{1 + 0.5}{0.05 + 0.001 + 0.5} = \frac{1.5}{0.551} = 2.72$$

which is above the initial value of 2.5.

We can now state the following result: ***The money multiplier and the money supply are negatively related to the required reserve ratio r_D.***[7]

Changes in the Currency Ratio {C/D} Next, what happens to the money multiplier when depositor behavior causes {C/D} to increase with all other variables unchanged? An increase in {C/D} means that depositors are converting some of their checkable deposits into currency. As shown before, checkable deposits undergo multiple expansion while currency does not. Hence when checkable deposits are being converted into currency, there is a switch from one component of the money supply that undergoes multiple expansion to one that does not. The overall level of multiple expansion declines, and so must the multiplier.[8]

---

[6] This result can be demonstrated from the Equation 4 formula as follows: When r_D rises, the denominator of the money multiplier rises, and therefore the money multiplier must fall.

[7] Before December 1990, the Federal Reserve required reserves on time deposits as well as on checkable deposits. A modification of the analysis to reflect the situation before 1990 is straightforward. If we assume that time deposits T grow proportionally with checkable deposits so that {T/D} is a constant, we need only recognize that the required reserve ratio r_D should be replaced in our formulas by $r_D + (r_T \times \{T/D\})$, where r_T is the required reserve ratio for time deposits. The intuition behind this replacement is that for every dollar of checkable deposits there are {T/D} dollars of time deposits, which have required reserves of $r_T \times \{T/D\}$. Thus the total amount of required reserves that banks must have per dollar of checkable deposits is the Fed's requirement of r_D plus the additional amount arising from time deposits, $r_T \times \{T/D\}$. Note that either a rise in the required reserve ratio for time deposits r_T or a rise in {T/D} in effect raises the amount of required reserves per dollar of checkable deposits and thus lowers the money multiplier and the money supply.

[8] As long as $r_D + \{ER/D\}$ is less than 1 (as is the case using the realistic numbers we have used), an increase in {C/D} raises the denominator of the money multiplier proportionally by more than it raises the numerator. The increase in {C/D} causes the multiplier to fall.

This reasoning is confirmed by our numerical example, where {C/D} rises from 0.50 to 0.75. The money multiplier then falls from 2.5 to

$$m = \frac{1 + 0.75}{0.1 + 0.001 + 0.75} = \frac{1.75}{0.851} = 2.06$$

withdrawal/
↑ in currency in
circulation →
↓ $ supply

We have now demonstrated another result: **The money multiplier and the money supply are negatively related to the currency ratio {C/D}.**

Changes in the Excess Reserves Ratio {ER/D}   When banks increase their holdings of excess reserves relative to checkable deposits, the banking system in effect has fewer reserves to support checkable deposits. This means that given the same level of *MB*, banks will contract their loans, causing a decline in the level of checkable deposits and a decline in the money supply, and the money multiplier will fall.[9]

This reasoning is supported in our numerical example when {ER/D} rises from 0.001 to 0.005. The money multiplier declines from 2.5 to

$$m = \frac{1 + 0.5}{0.1 + 0.005 + 0.5} = \frac{1.5}{0.605} = 2.48$$

↑ ER ⟹ ↓ $ supply

Note that although the excess reserves ratio has risen fivefold, there has been only a small decline in the money multiplier. This decline is small because in recent years the {ER/D} ratio has been extremely small, so changes in it have only a small impact on the money multiplier. However, there have been times, particularly during the Great Depression, when this ratio was far higher, and its movements had a substantial effect on the money supply and the money multiplier. Thus our final result is still an important one: **The money multiplier and the money supply are negatively related to the excess reserves ratio {ER/D}.**

Additional Factors That Determine the Money Supply

To complete the money supply model, we must remember that the monetary base is made up of two components: the nonborrowed monetary base MB_n, which is directly controlled by the Fed through open market operations, and discount loans *DL*, in which banks' decisions play a role along with the Fed's set-

---

[9]This result can be demonstrated from the Equation 4 formula as follows: When {ER/D} rises, the denominator of the money multiplier rises, and so the money multiplier must fall.

ting of the discount rate. Using the fact that $MB = MB_n + DL$, we can rewrite the money supply model as

$$M = m \times (MB_n + DL) \tag{5}$$

where the money multiplier m is defined as in Equation 4. Thus in addition to the effects on the money supply of the required reserve ratio, currency ratio, and excess reserves ratio, the expanded model stipulates that the money supply is also affected by changes in MB_n and DL. Because the money multiplier is positive, Equation 5 immediately tells us that the money supply is positively related to both the nonborrowed monetary base and discount loans. However, it is still worth developing the intuition for these results.

Changes in the Nonborrowed Monetary Base MB_n As shown at the beginning of this chapter, the Fed's open market purchases increase the nonborrowed monetary base, and its open market sales decrease it. Holding all other variables constant, an increase in MB_n arising from an open market purchase increases the amount of the monetary base that is available to support currency and deposits, so the money supply will increase. Similarly, an open market sale that decreases MB_n will shrink the amount of the monetary base available to support currency and deposits, thereby causing the money supply to decrease.

We have the following result: ***The money supply is positively related to the nonborrowed monetary base MB_n.***

Changes in Discount Loans DL from the Fed With the nonborrowed monetary base MB_n unchanged, more discount loans from the Fed provide additional reserves (hence higher MB) to the banking system, and these are used to support more currency and deposits. As a result, the increase in DL will lead to a rise in the money supply. If banks reduce the level of their discount loans, with all other variables held constant, the amount of MB available to support currency and deposits will decline, causing the money supply to decline.

Our final result is this: ***The money supply is positively related to the level of discount loans DL from the Fed.***

Overview

We now have a model of the money supply process in which three of the "players"—the Federal Reserve System, depositors, and the banks—directly influence the money supply. The Federal Reserve is an important player because it controls both the nonborrowed monetary base MB_n and the required reserve ratio r_D. Depositors matter because they decide on the $\{C/D\}$ ratio. The banks are important through their decisions about the excess reserves ratio $\{ER/D\}$ and their

SUMMARY

Variable	Change in Variable	Response of *M1* Money Supply	Reason
MB_n	↑	↑	More *MB* to support *C* and *D*
DL	↑	↑	More *MB* to support *C* and *D*
r_D	↑	↓	Less multiple deposit expansion
{*ER/D*}	↑	↓	Fewer reserves to support *C* and *D*
{*C/D*}	↑	↓	Less overall deposit expansion

TABLE 1 Response of the *M1* Money Supply to Changes in MB_n, *DL*, r_D, {*ER/D*}, and {*C/D*}

Note: Only increases (↑) in the variables are shown; the effects of decreases in the variables on the money supply would be the opposite of those indicated in the "Response" column.

borrowing of discount loans *DL* from the Fed. As we will see in Chapter 17, the fourth player, borrowers from banks, enters indirectly by affecting bank decisions about {*ER/D*} and *DL*.

As a study aid, Table 1 summarizes the response of the money supply (*M1*) to changes in all these variables. An upward arrow (↑) indicates an increase, and a downward arrow (↓) indicates a decrease.

STUDY GUIDE

To improve your understanding of the money supply process, slowly work through the logic behind the results in Table 1 rather than just memorizing the results. Then see if you can construct your own table in which all the variables decrease rather than increase.

APPLICATION

EXPLAINING MOVEMENTS IN THE MONEY SUPPLY, 1980–1993

To complete your understanding of the money supply process, you must understand what motivates depositors' and bankers' decisions. But before examining bank and depositor behavior in Chapter 17, you should see whether the model of the money supply process developed here helps you understand recent movements of the money supply. We look at money supply movements from 1980 to 1993, a particularly interesting period because the growth rate of the money supply displayed unusually high variability.

Figure 1 shows the movements of the money supply (*M1*) from 1980 to 1993, with the percentage next to each bracket representing the annual growth rate for the bracketed period: From January 1980 to October 1984, for example,

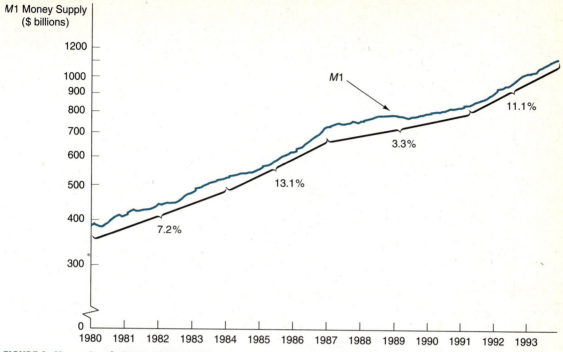

FIGURE 1 Money Supply (M1), 1980–1993
Source: Citibase databank.

the money supply grew at a 7.2% annual rate. The variability of money growth in the 1980–1993 period is quite apparent, swinging from 7.2% to 13.1%, down to 3.3%, and then back up to 11.1%. What explains these sharp swings in the growth rate of the money supply?

Our money supply model, as represented by Equation 5, suggests that the movements in the money supply that we see in Figure 1 are explained by either changes in $MB_n + DL$ (the nonborrowed monetary base plus discount loans) or by changes in m (the money multiplier). Figure 2 plots these variables and shows their growth rates for the same bracketed periods as in Figure 1. Notice that the money multiplier m fluctuates within a fairly narrow band between 2.7 and 3.3.

Over the whole period, the average growth rate of the money supply (7.7%) is well explained by the average growth rate of the nonborrowed monetary base MB_n (7.8%). In addition, we see that the term DL is rarely an important source of fluctuations in the money supply since $MB_n + DL$ is closely tied to MB_n, except for the unusual period in 1984 when discount loans increased dramatically (the Fed extended $5 billion of loans to the financially troubled Continental Illinois National Bank).

The conclusion drawn from our analysis is this: ***Over long periods, the primary determinant of movements in the money supply is the nonborrowed monetary base MB_n, which is controlled by Federal Reserve open market operations.***

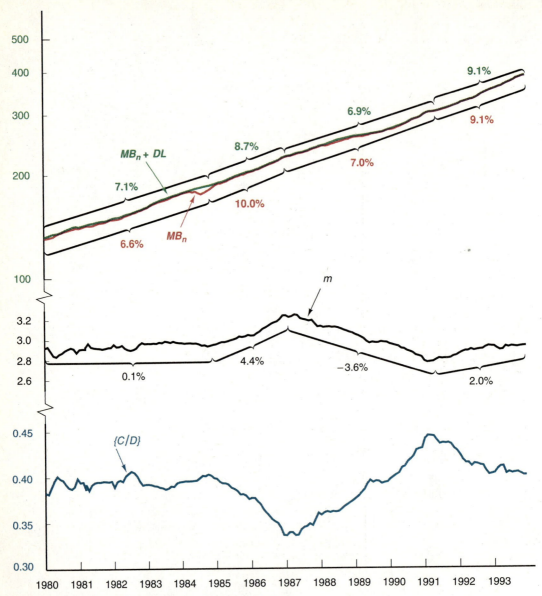

FIGURE 2 Determinants of the *M1* Money Supply, 1980–1993
Source: Citibase databank.

For shorter time periods, the link between the growth rates of the non-borrowed monetary base and the money supply is not always close, primarily because the money multiplier *m* experiences substantial short-run swings that have a major impact on the growth rate of the money supply. The currency ratio {*C*/*D*}, which is also plotted in Figure 2, explains most of these movements in the money multiplier.

From January 1980 until October 1984, {*C*/*D*} is relatively constant. Not surprisingly, there is almost no trend in the money multiplier *m,* so the growth rate of the money supply and the nonborrowed monetary base have similar magnitudes. The upward movement in the money multiplier from October 1984 to January 1987 is explained by the downward trend in the currency ratio. The decline in {*C*/*D*} meant that there was a shift from one component of the money supply with less multiple expansion (currency) to one with more (checkable deposits), so the money multiplier rose. In the period from January 1987 to April 1991, {*C*/*D*} underwent a substantial rise. The rise led to a fall in the money multiplier because there was a shift from checkable deposits, with more multiple expansion, to currency, which had less. From April 1991 to December 1993, {*C*/*D*} fell somewhat. The decline in {*C*/*D*} should have led to a rise in the money multiplier because there was again a shift from the currency component of the money supply with less multiple expansion to the checkable deposits component with more. As our money supply model predicts, the money multiplier did indeed rise in this period, and there was an acceleration of money growth.

Although our examination of the 1980–1993 period indicates that factors such as changes in the {*C*/*D*} ratio can have a major impact on the money supply over short periods, we must not forget that over the entire period, the growth rate of the money supply is closely linked to the growth rate of the nonborrowed monetary base MB_n. Indeed, empirical evidence suggests that more than three-fourths of the fluctuations in the money supply can be attributed to Federal Reserve open market operations, which determine MB_n.

SUMMARY

1. We developed a model to describe how the money supply is determined. First, we saw how the monetary base is determined and why it is easier to control than reserves in the banking system. Second, we linked the monetary base to the money supply using the concept of the money multiplier, which tells us how much the money supply changes when there is a change in the monetary base.

2. An open market purchase increases the monetary base, and an open market sale decreases it. The monetary base also changes one-for-one with changes in discount loans from the Fed. The

monetary base can be broken up into two components. The first, the nonborrowed monetary base, is directly under the control of the Fed because it is the result of open market operations; the second, which results from discount loans, is not as closely controlled by the Fed because banks' decisions play an important role in determining this component.

3. The money supply is negatively related to the required reserve ratio r_D, the currency ratio {*C*/*D*} and the excess reserves ratio {*ER*/*D*}. It is positively related to the level of discount loans *DL* from the Fed and the nonborrowed base MB_n,

which is determined by Fed open market operations. The money supply model therefore allows for the behavior of all four players in the money supply process: the Fed through its setting of the required reserve ratio and open market operations, depositors through their decisions about the currency ratio, the banks through their decisions about the excess reserves ratio and discount loans from the Fed, and borrowers from banks indirectly through their effect on bank decisions regarding the excess reserves ratio and borrowings from the Fed.

KEY TERMS

money multiplier

high-powered money

open market purchase

open market sale

nonborrowed monetary base

QUESTIONS AND PROBLEMS

1. If the Fed sells $2 million of bonds to the First National Bank, what happens to reserves and the monetary base? Use T-accounts to explain your answer.

*2. If the Fed sells $2 million of bonds to Irving the Investor, who pays for the bonds with a briefcase filled with currency, what happens to reserves and the monetary base? Use T-accounts to explain your answer.

3. If the Fed lends five banks an additional $100 million but depositors withdraw $50 million and hold it as currency, what happens to reserves and the monetary base? Use T-accounts to explain your answer.

*4. "The money multiplier is necessarily greater than 1." Is this statement true, false, or uncertain? Explain.

5. "If reserve requirements on checkable deposits were set at zero, the amount of multiple deposit expansion would go on indefinitely." Is this statement true, false, or uncertain? Explain.

* 6. During the Great Depression years 1930–1933, the currency ratio {C/D} rose dramatically. What do you think happened to the money supply? Why?

7. During the Great Depression, the excess reserves ratio {ER/D} ratio rose dramatically. What do you think happened to the money supply? Why?

*8. Traveler's checks have no reserve requirements and are included in the $M1$ measure of the money supply. When people travel during the summer and convert some of their checking account deposits into traveler's checks, what happens to the money supply? Why?

9. If Jane Brown closes her account at the First National Bank and uses the money instead to open up a money market mutual fund account, what happens to $M1$ and $M2$? Why?

*10. Some economists have suggested that reserve requirements on checkable deposits and time deposits should be set equal because this would improve control of $M2$. Does this argument make sense? (*Hint:* Think about what happens when checkable deposits are converted into time deposits or vice versa.)

Using Economic Analysis to Predict the Future

11. Predict what will happen to the money supply if the Fed increases r_D.

*12. The Fed buys $100 million of bonds from the public and also lowers r_D. What will happen to the money supply?

13. Predict what will happen to the money supply if there is a sharp rise in the currency ratio.

*14. If the Fed sells $1 million of bonds and banks reduce their discount loans by $1 million, predict what will happen to the money supply.

15. If banks borrow an additional $1 million from the Fed and also reduce {ER/D}, what will happen to the money supply?

Appendix to Chapter 16

THE *M*2 MONEY MULTIPLIER

The derivation of a money multiplier for the $M2$ definition of money requires only slight modifications to the analysis in the chapter. The definition of $M2$ is

$$M2 = D + C + T + MMF$$

where C = currency in circulation
          D = checkable deposits
          T = time deposits
          MMF = primarily money market mutual fund shares and money market deposit accounts, plus overnight repurchase agreements and overnight Eurodollars

We again assume that all these variables rise proportionally with checkable deposits so that the ratios $\{C/D\}$, $\{T/D\}$, and $\{MMF/D\}$ set by depositors are treated as constants. Replacing C by $\{C/D\} \times D$, T by $\{T/D\} \times D$, and MMF by $\{MMF/D\} \times D$ in the definition of $M2$ just given, we get

$$M2 = D + (\{C/D\} \times D) + (\{T/D\} \times D) + (\{MMF/D\} \times D)$$
$$= (1 + \{C/D\} + \{T/D\} + \{MMF/D\}) \times D$$

Substituting in the expression for D from Equation 2 in the chapter,[1] we have

$$M2 = \frac{1 + \{C/D\} + \{T/D\} + \{MMF/D\}}{r_D + \{ER/D\} + \{C/D\}} \times MB \qquad (1)$$

To see what this formula implies about the $M2$ money multiplier, we continue with the same numerical example in the chapter, with the additional information

---

[1]From the derivation here it is clear that the quantity of checkable deposits D is unaffected by the depositor ratios $\{T/D\}$ and $\{MMF/D\}$ even though time deposits and money market mutual fund shares are included in $M2$. This is just a consequence of the absence of reserve requirements on time deposits and money market mutual fund shares, so T and MMF do not appear in any of the equations in the derivation of D earlier in the chapter.

that $T = \$2400$ billion and $MMF = \$400$ billion so that $\{T/D\} = 3$ and $\{MMF/D\} = 0.5$. The resulting value of the multiplier for $M2$ is

$$m_2 = \frac{1 + 0.5 + 3 + 0.5}{0.10 + 0.001 + 0.5} = \frac{5.0}{0.601} = 8.32$$

An important feature of the $M2$ multiplier is that it is substantially above the $M1$ multiplier of 2.5 that we found in the chapter. The crucial concept in understanding this difference is that a lower required reserve ratio for time deposits or money market mutual fund shares means that they undergo more multiple expansion because fewer reserves are needed to support the same amount of them. Time deposits and MMFs have a lower required reserve ratio than checkable deposits—zero—and they will therefore have more multiple expansion than checkable deposits will. Thus the overall multiple expansion for the sum of these deposits will be greater than for checkable deposits alone, and so the $M2$ money multiplier will be greater than the $M1$ money multiplier.

FACTORS THAT DETERMINE THE *M2* MONEY MULTIPLIER

Changes in r_D, $\{C/D\}$, and $\{ER/D\}$

The economic reasoning analyzing the effect of changes in the required reserve ratio and the currency ratio on the $M2$ money multiplier is identical to that used for the $M1$ multiplier in the chapter. An increase in the required reserve ratio r_D will decrease the amount of multiple deposit expansion, thus lowering the $M2$ money multiplier. An increase in $\{C/D\}$ means that depositors have shifted out of checkable deposits into currency, and since currency has no multiple deposit expansion, the overall level of multiple deposit expansion for $M2$ must also fall, lowering the $M2$ multiplier. An increase in the excess reserves ratio, $\{ER/D\}$, means that banks use fewer reserves to support deposits, so deposits and the $M2$ money multiplier fall.

We thus have the same results we found for the $M1$ multiplier: ***The M2 money multiplier and M2 money supply are negatively related to the required reserve ratio r_D, the currency ratio $\{C/D\}$, and the excess reserves ratio $\{ER/D\}$.***

Response to Changes in $\{T/D\}$ and $\{MMF/D\}$

An increase in either $\{T/D\}$ or $\{MMF/D\}$ leads to an increase in the $M2$ multiplier because the required reserve ratios on time deposits and money market mutual fund shares are zero and hence are lower than the required reserve ratio on checkable deposits.

Both time deposits and money market mutual fund shares undergo more multiple expansion than checkable deposits. Thus a shift out of checkable deposits into time deposits or money market mutual funds, increasing $\{T/D\}$ or $\{MMF/D\}$, implies that the overall level of multiple expansion will increase, raising the $M2$ money multiplier.

A decline in $\{T/D\}$ or $\{MMF/D\}$ will result in less overall multiple expansion, and the $M2$ money multiplier will decrease, leading to the following conclusion: ***The M2 money multiplier and M2 money supply are positively related to both the time deposit ratio $\{T/D\}$ and the money market fund ratio $\{MMF/D\}$.***

The response of the $M2$ money supply to all the depositor and required reserve ratios is summarized in Table A1.

SUMMARY

TABLE A1   Response of the $M2$ Money Supply to Changes in MB_n, DL, r_D, $\{ER/D\}$, $\{C/D\}$, $\{T/D\}$, and $\{MMF/D\}$

Variable	Change in Variable	M2 Money Supply Response	Reason
MB_n	↑	↑	More MB to support C and D
DL	↑	↑	More MB to support C and D
r_D	↑	↓	Less multiple deposit expansion
$\{ER/D\}$	↑	↓	Fewer reserves to support C and D
$\{C/D\}$	↑	↓	Less overall deposit expansion
$\{T/D\}$	↑	↑	More multiple deposit expansion
$\{MMF/D\}$	↑	↑	More multiple deposit expansion

Note: Only increases (↑) in the variables are shown; the effects of decreases in the variables on the money multiplier would be the opposite of those indicated in the "Response" column.

Chapter 17

EXPLAINING DEPOSITOR AND BANK BEHAVIOR: THE COMPLETE MONEY SUPPLY MODEL

PREVIEW In Chapters 15 and 16 we developed, step by step, the building blocks necessary to understand the money supply process. We saw first how deposits are created, and then we developed a money multiplier to reflect the important role of depositor and bank behavior in the deposit creation process. Although we now understand what effect depositor and bank behavior has on the money supply, we do not yet know *why* depositors or banks choose to behave in one way or another. This chapter completes the development of the money supply model by explaining depositor and bank behavior.

Although fairly simple in structure, the complete model is the basis of much of the money supply analysis performed by practicing economists in the private sector and the government. The model is used, for example, by the Federal Reserve Board of Governors for forecasting and policy analysis. In this and the following chapters, we use the model to understand the difficulties that the Federal Reserve faces in conducting monetary policy. The model will provide answers to some of the questions that policymakers in the United States must answer when formulating their economic policies: How do money market conditions affect the money supply? How can the Federal Reserve control the money supply? What factors make the control of the money supply a difficult problem for the Fed? How do bank panics occur, and what is their effect on the money supply? How do expectations about the future affect the money supply?

BEHAVIOR OF THE CURRENCY RATIO {C/D}

The general outline of the movements of the currency ratio {C/D} since 1892 is shown in Figure 1. As you can see, several episodes stand out:

1. The declining trend in the ratio from 1892 until 1917, when the United States entered World War I

Currency Ratio,
{C/D}

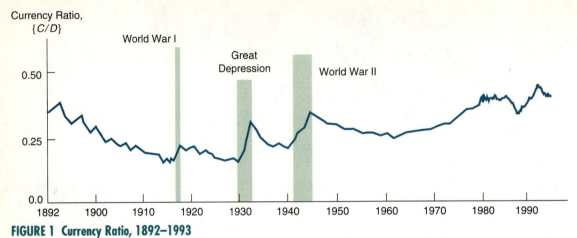

FIGURE 1 Currency Ratio, 1892–1993
Sources: Federal Reserve *Bulletin; Banking and Monetary Statistics.*

2. The sharp increase in the ratio during World War I and the decline thereafter

3. The steepest increase in the ratio that we see in the figure, during the Great Depression years 1930–1933

4. The increase in the ratio during World War II

5. The reversal in the early 1960s of the downward trend in the ratio and the persistent upward trend from the 1960s to 1980

6. The halt in the upward trend after 1980

To be worthwhile, our analysis of {C/D} must be able to explain these movements. They will help us develop our analysis because they provide clues to the factors that influence {C/D}.

A natural way to approach the analysis of the relative amount of assets (currency and checkable deposits) that people want to hold, and hence the currency ratio, is to use the theory of asset demand developed in Chapter 5. Recall that the theory states that four factors influence the demand for an asset such as currency or checkable deposits: (1) the total resources available to individuals, that is, wealth; (2) the expected return on one asset relative to the expected return on alternative assets; (3) the degree of uncertainty or risk associated with the return from this asset relative to alternative assets; and (4) the liquidity of one asset relative to alternative assets. In our analysis, we focus only on the first two factors, wealth and expected returns. The reason for this is that the other two factors, risk and liquidity, have not changed independently of wealth and expected returns and lead to similar conclusions on the historical movements of {C/D}.

Effect of Changes in Wealth

What is the relative response of currency to checkable deposits when an individual's resources change? Currency is a necessity because it is used extensively by people with low incomes and little wealth, which means that the demand for currency grows proportionally less with accumulation of wealth. In contrast, checkable deposits are held by people with greater wealth, so checkable deposits are less of a necessity. Put another way, as wealth grows, the holdings of checkable deposits relative to the holdings of currency increase, and the amount of currency relative to checkable deposits falls, causing the currency ratio {C/D} to decline. A decrease in income will lead to an increase in the amount of currency relative to checkable deposits, causing {C/D} to increase. **The currency ratio is negatively related to income or wealth.**

Effect of Changes in Expected Returns

The second factor that influences the decision to hold currency versus checkable deposits involves the expected returns on checkable deposits relative to currency and other assets. Three primary factors influence expected returns (and hence the currency ratio): interest rates on checkable deposits, bank panics, and illegal activity.[1]

Interest Rates on Checkable Deposits By its very nature, currency cannot pay interest. Yet banks can and do pay interest on checkable deposits. One measure of the expected return on checkable deposits relative to currency is the interest rate on checkable deposits. As this interest rate increases, the theory of asset demand tells us that people will want to hold less currency relative to checkable deposits, and {C/D} will fall. Conversely, a decline in this interest rate will cause {C/D} to rise. **The currency ratio is negatively related to the interest rate paid on checkable deposits.**

Between 1933 and 1980, regulations prevented banks from paying interest on most checkable deposits,[2] and before 1933, these interest rates were low and did not undergo substantial fluctuations. However, since 1980, banks have been

---

[1]Changes in interest rates on other alternative assets (such as U.S. Treasury bills) could have a differential effect on the demand for currency versus checkable deposits, resulting in some effect on {C/D}. However, the evidence for this effect is weak.

[2]Although banks could not pay interest on checkable deposits, they provided services to their checking account customers that can be thought of as implicit interest payments. Because these services changed only slowly over time, these implicit interest payments were not a major factor causing the demand for checkable deposits to fluctuate.

allowed to pay any interest rate they choose on checkable deposits, suggesting that fluctuations in these rates can now be an important factor influencing {C/D} movements.

Bank Panics Our discussion of interest-rate effects suggests that they did not have a substantial impact on {C/D} before 1980. You might conclude that expected returns have had little importance in determining this ratio for most of its history. Figure 1 provides us with a clue that we are overlooking an important factor when measuring expected returns solely by the interest rates on assets. The steepest rise in {C/D} occurred during the Great Depression years 1930–1933, when the banking system nearly collapsed. Legend has it that during this period, people stuffed their mattresses with cash rather than keep it in banks because they had lost confidence in them as a safe haven for their hard-earned savings. Can the theory of asset demand explain this phenomenon?

A bank failure occurs when the bank is no longer able to pay back its depositors. Before creation of the FDIC in 1933, if you had an account at a bank that failed, you would suffer a substantial loss—you could not withdraw your savings and might receive only a small fraction of the value of your deposits sometime in the future. The simultaneous failure of many banks is called a *bank panic,* and the Great Depression years 1930–1933 witnessed the worst set of bank panics in U.S. history. From the end of 1930 to the bank holiday in March 1933, more than one-third of the banks in the United States failed.

Bank panics can have a devastating effect on the expected returns from holding deposits. When a bank is likely to fail during a bank panic, depositors know that if they have deposits in this bank, they are likely to suffer substantial losses, and the expected return on deposits can be negative. The theory of asset demand predicts that depositors will shift their holdings from checkable deposits to currency by withdrawing currency from their bank accounts, and {C/D} will rise. This is exactly what we see in Figure 1 during the bank panics of the Great Depression period 1930–1933 and to a lesser extent in 1893 and 1907, when smaller-scale bank panics occurred. The conclusion is that **bank panics lead to a sharp increase in the currency ratio.** Bank panics have been an important source of fluctuations in this ratio in the past and could be important in the future.

Illegal Activity Expected returns on checkable deposits relative to currency can also be affected by the amount of illegal activity conducted in an economy. U.S. law allows government prosecutors access to bank records when conducting a criminal investigation. So if you were engaged in some illegal activity, you would not conduct your transactions with checks because they are traceable and therefore a potentially powerful piece of evidence against you. Currency, however, is much harder to trace. The expected return on currency relative to checkable deposits is higher when you are engaged in illegal transactions. Hence when illegal activity in a society increases, there is an increase in the use of currency relative to checkable deposits, and {*C/D*} rises. ***There is a positive association between illegal activity and the currency ratio.***[3]

Looking at Figure 1, what types of increases in illegal activity would lead to an increase in {*C/D*}? Beginning in the 1960s, {*C/D*} began to climb—just when the illegal drug trade began to experience phenomenal growth. Because illegal drug transactions are always carried out with currency, it is likely that the rise in drug trade is related to the rise in {*C/D*}. Supporting evidence is the current huge flow of currency into southern Florida, the major center for illegal drug importing in the United States.[4] Other illegal activities—prostitution, black markets, gambling, loan sharking, fencing of stolen goods, the employment of illegal aliens—could also be sources of a higher currency ratio.

Another interesting set of movements in {*C/D*} are the two increases during both world wars, which are associated with large increases in income taxes. Income taxes were raised substantially in 1917 to help finance America's entry into World War I. Although income tax rates were reduced after the war, they were again raised substantially during World War II to finance that conflict—never to return to prewar levels.

Increases in {*C/D*} when income tax rates rise can be explained in the following manner: Higher tax rates promote the evasion of taxes. When income tax rates rise, the incentive is high to evade taxes by conducting transactions in cash. If you receive an unreported cash payment for some service (say, as a cab driver, waiter, or doctor), it is less likely that the Internal Revenue Service can prove that you are understating your income. If you are paid with a check or credit card, you would be wise to declare the income. The conclusion is clear: ***Higher tax rates will lead to a rise in {C/D}.***

Not only does income tax evasion explain the rise in {*C/D*} during the two world wars, but it also helps explain the rise in the 1960s and 1970s. This may seem surprising because the income tax rate schedule was not raised during this period. However, the burden of income taxes was increasing because the American income tax system is progressive (as income increases, the tax rate rises). A rising price level in the 1960s and 1970s raised nominal income and pushed more individuals into higher tax brackets (a phenomenon called *bracket creep*). This meant that the effective tax rate increased even though the tax schedule was unchanged. As a result, incentives increased to evade paying taxes by not

---

[3]One exception to this is an increase in street crime. Checkable deposits have the advantage over currency that if you are mugged, the loss from carrying checks is likely to be far less than the loss from carrying currency. So if muggings are on the rise, the expected return on currency will fall relative to the expected return on checkable deposits, and you would hold less currency relative to checkable deposits. The resulting negative association of the illegal activity of street crime and {*C/D*} is ignored in the text because it is not an important source of fluctuations in {*C/D*}.

[4]The Drug Enforcement Agency has estimated that the retail value of the illegal drug trade exceeds $100 billion, making it one of the largest businesses in the United States. Evidence that the drug trade has affected {*C/D*} is found in Ralph C. Kimball, "Trends in the Use of Currency," *New England Economic Review,* September–October 1981, pp. 43–53.

declaring income, and people would avoid the use of checkable deposits. In other words, the expected return on checkable deposits fell, so $\{C/D\}$ rose.

Increased tax evasion and other illegal activities not only reflect an increase in the currency ratio but also imply that more income will go unreported to the government. The result is an understatement of statistics on economic activity such as gross domestic product (GDP), which measures the total production of goods and services in the economy.

This unreported economic activity has been labeled the **underground economy.** Evidence of its scope is the fact that the amount of currency for every man, woman, and child in the United States (as measured by currency in circulation in 1993 divided by the population) is around $1000. Very few people hold this amount of currency; the likelihood is that much is used to conduct transactions in the underground economy. Calculations of the size of the underground economy indicate that it may exceed 10% of total economic activity. If this is true, and unreported income could be taxed, America would solve its budget deficit problems overnight!

APPLICATION

EXPLAINING THE HISTORICAL RECORD OF {C/D}

The interaction of historical data with the theory of asset demand has helped us identify the factors that influence the currency ratio. We have seen that the theory of asset demand developed in Chapter 5 can help us understand how these different factors influence $\{C/D\}$.

To put our analysis in perspective, let us proceed to explain the major movements of $\{C/D\}$ in Figure 1 by time periods.

STUDY GUIDE

An excellent way to test your understanding of the factors influencing $\{C/D\}$ is to explain the movements in Figure 1 before reading this section of the text. This exercise will give you practice in using the ideas developed in the preceding discussion and should help make the abstract analysis clearer.

1892–1917 The general decline in $\{C/D\}$ reflected in this period is explained by the increase in wealth. Because checkable deposits have a higher wealth elasticity than currency, the general trend of rising wealth over this span implies that the holdings of currency will grow more slowly than the holdings of checkable deposits, thus lowering $\{C/D\}$.

The upward blips in the ratio seen in 1893 and 1907 were due to bank panics, which temporarily reduced the expected return on checkable deposits and increased the risk—these factors led to a temporary increase in the holdings of currency relative to checkable deposits, temporarily increasing $\{C/D\}$.

1917–1919 The upward surge in {C/D} when America entered World War I is explained by the use of the income tax to help finance the war. The resulting attempts at tax evasion encouraged people to avoid the use of checks, which would make their income visible to the IRS; put another way, the increased desire to avoid taxes lowered the expected return on checkable deposits, resulting in a lower demand for them. The resulting increase in the use of currency relative to checkable deposits raised {C/D}.

1919–1921 When income taxes were reduced after the war, the demand for currency relative to checkable deposits began to fall back toward its old level, and the rise in {C/D} that occurred during the war was reversed. However, a severe recession in 1920–1921 led to a decline in wealth along with an increased number of bank failures, both of which might have caused a rise in {C/D} at that time. The decline in wealth led to a decline in the demand for both currency and checkable deposits, but the higher wealth elasticity of checkable deposits meant that they declined more than currency, raising the currency ratio. The increased number of bank failures also made checkable deposits less desirable because it lowered their expected return, also leading to a rise in {C/D}.

1921–1929 During the prosperous period of the Roaring Twenties, we would expect to see the downward trend in {C/D} reasserting itself. The rise in wealth would lead to a fall in {C/D} because the holdings of currency would grow more slowly than the holdings of checkable deposits.

1929–1933 The decline in income during the Great Depression was one factor in the rise in {C/D}, but far more important were the bank panics that began in late 1930 and ended in March 1933. The consequent sharp rise in {C/D} from 1930 to 1933 was a major factor in the financial and economic collapse. These panics (the most severe in all of U.S. history) lowered the expected return on deposits, thereby raising the demand for currency relative to checkable deposits.

1933–1941 With the end of the bank panics and some restoration of the confidence in banks (helped by establishment of the FDIC), {C/D} fell. This decline was strengthened by a rise in wealth. However, {C/D}, did not return to pre-Depression levels primarily because a loss of confidence in the U.S. banking system lingered in the public mind. As a result, expected returns on deposits did not return to their pre-Depression levels, leaving a high level of {C/D}.

1941–1945 When income tax rates were raised to unprecedented levels to finance combat in World War II, {C/D} underwent a substantial rise. The incentive to evade taxes was especially strong; hence the expected return on checkable deposits fell. Price controls imposed during the war may also have contributed to the rise in {C/D} because they stimulated illegal black market activity, whose transactions could be hidden using currency.

1945–Early 1960s After the war, income tax rates were reduced slightly, but not to anywhere near their prewar levels. Income taxes remained at permanently higher levels because of the revenue needed to support an expanded role for the U.S. military as the "world's police force" and enlarged social programs such as welfare, unemployment insurance, housing and urban development, and Social Security. Although some decline in {C/D} occurred after the war due to a reduction in tax rates, permanently higher income tax rates left strong incentives for tax evasion, and {C/D} remained high. The steady rise in wealth after the war promoted the return to a declining trend in {C/D}, but its effect was not sufficiently strong to reduce the ratio below prewar levels.

Early 1960s–1980 The declining trend beginning at the end of World War II began to reverse in the early 1960s for a number of reasons. Most important was the growth of the underground economy, both because of the spectacular rise in illegal drug trade and because of the increased desirability of evading taxes due to bracket creep, which raised the effective tax rates. The increase in illegal activity lowered the expected return on checkable deposits, leading to an increased use of currency in relation to checkable deposits, thereby raising {C/D}.

1980–1993 A halt in the upward trend in {C/D} can be attributed to the deregulation of the banking system that allowed banks to pay interest on checkable deposits. This raised the expected return on checkable deposits relative to currency, and the resulting reduced demand for currency helped lower {C/D}.

APPLICATION

PREDICTING THE FUTURE OF {C/D}

A good economic model not only explains the past but also helps predict the response of economic variables to new events. The analysis of factors that influence the currency ratio outlined here has this capability. Let us consider two possible changes in the economic environment of the future and ask what our analysis would predict will happen to the currency ratio as a result. These predictions could be of interest to policymakers, who would want to know how the money supply might be affected in each of these cases.

STUDY GUIDE

Try to provide the reasoning for the predictions here without having to refer to the text. This will give you excellent practice with the economic analysis of {C/D} that we have developed in this chapter. You can get additional practice by answering problems at the end of the chapter, which also ask you to predict future movements in {*C/D*}.

A Rise in Income Tax Rates to Balance the Budget

Much talk is circulating about balancing the budget by increasing taxes. What would happen to the currency ratio if income tax rates were raised?

Higher tax rates would increase the incentives to evade taxes. The expected return on checkable deposits would then effectively decline. The use of currency would increase relative to checkable deposits (if other factors are held constant), and we would predict a rise in {*C/D*}.

Abolishment of Interest Payments on Checking Accounts

There have always been swings back and forth from deregulation to increased regulation. What if the present tide of deregulation is reversed and regulations were imposed that returned us to the situation when banks were not allowed to pay interest on checkable deposits? What would happen to the currency ratio in this case?

This policy would mean that the expected return on checkable deposits would fall below its current level, and the expected return on checkable deposits relative to currency would also fall. The resulting decreased attractiveness of checkable deposits relative to currency would mean that holdings of currency relative to checkable deposits would increase, raising {*C/D*}.

The usefulness of the foregoing analysis is not restricted to the predictions of the response of {*C/D*} to the events discussed here. With this framework, many other possible changes in our economic environment that would have an impact on {*C/D*} can be analyzed (a few are discussed in the problems at the end of the chapter).

EXPLAINING BANK BEHAVIOR

In Chapter 16 we saw that the money supply increases when banks decrease the excess reserves ratio {*ER/D*} or increase the amount of discount loans they borrow from the Fed. To understand the money supply process completely, we need to understand the determinants of {*ER/D*} and discount loans from the Fed. Here we outline a model of bank behavior that explains movements in {*ER/D*} and discount loans.

Determinants of the Excess Reserves Ratio {*ER/D*}

To understand the factors that determine the level of {*ER/D*} in the banking system, we must look at the costs and benefits to banks of holding excess reserves. When the costs of holding excess reserves rise, we would expect the level of excess reserves and hence {*ER/D*} to fall; conversely, when the benefits of holding excess reserves rise, we would expect the level of excess reserves and {*ER/D*} to rise. Two primary factors affect these costs and benefits and hence affect the excess reserves ratio: market interest rates and expected deposit outflows.

Market Interest Rates As you may recall from our analysis of bank management in Chapter 11, the cost to a bank of holding excess reserves is its opportunity cost: the interest that could have been earned on loans or securities if they had been held instead of excess reserves. For the sake of simplicity, we assume that loans and securities earn the same interest rate *i*, which we call the market interest rate. If *i* increases, the opportunity cost of holding excess reserves rises, and the desired ratio of excess reserves to deposits will fall. A decrease in *i*, by contrast, will reduce the opportunity cost of excess reserves, and {*ER/D*} will rise. **The banking system's excess reserves ratio {ER/D} is negatively related to the market interest rate i.**

Another way of understanding the negative effect of market interest rates on {*ER/D*} is again to use the theory of asset demand, which states that if the expected returns on alternative assets rise relative to the expected returns on an asset, the demand for it will decrease. As the market interest rate increases, the expected return on loans and securities rises relative to the zero return on excess reserves, and the excess reserves ratio falls.

Figure 2 shows us (as the theory of asset demand predicts) that there is a negative relationship between the excess reserves ratio and a representative market interest rate, the federal funds rate. In the period shown, there has been a declining trend in {*ER/D*} and an upward trend in the federal funds rate. In addition, there is a tendency for the level of {*ER/D*} to hit its peaks when the federal funds rate is falling to its depths, and vice versa. The empirical evidence supports our analysis that the excess reserves ratio is negatively related to market interest rates.

Expected Deposit Outflows Our earlier analysis of bank management showed us that the primary benefit to a bank of holding excess reserves is that they provide insurance against losses due to deposit outflows; that is, they enable the bank experiencing deposit outflows to escape the costs of borrowing from other banks or corporations, selling securities, borrowing from the Fed, or calling in or selling off loans. If banks fear that deposit outflows are likely to increase (that is, if *expected* deposit outflows increase), they will want more insurance against this possibility and will increase the excess reserves ratio. Another way to put it is, if

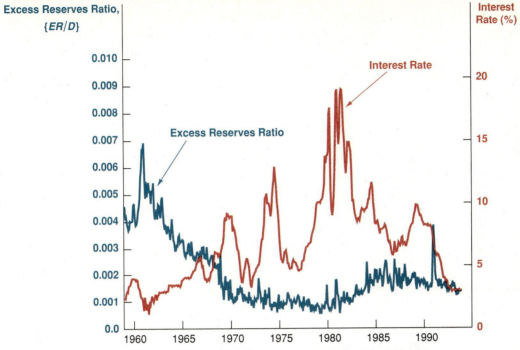

FIGURE 2 The Excess Reserves Ratio, {*ER/D*} and the Interest Rate (Federal Funds Rate)
Sources: Federal Reserve *Bulletin;* Citibase databank.

expected deposit outflows rise, the expected benefits, and hence the expected returns for holding excess reserves, increase. As the theory of asset demand predicts, excess reserves will then rise. Conversely, a decline in expected deposit outflows will reduce the insurance benefit of excess reserves, and their level should fall. We have the following result: ***The excess reserves ratio {ER/D} is positively related to expected deposit outflows.***

Determinants of Discount Loan Borrowing

Our analysis of what determines discount loan borrowing from the Federal Reserve again relies on identifying the costs and benefits of borrowing from the Fed. Two primary factors affect these costs and benefits and subsequently the volume of discount loans: market interest rates and the discount rate.

The principal benefit of borrowing from the Fed is straightforward. With additional borrowed reserves, a bank can acquire loans and securities, which earn the market interest rate i. The primary cost of borrowing, however, is the discount rate i_d, the interest rate the Fed charges on its loans to banks.[5] The greater the difference between the benefits (earnings) obtained from the use of borrowed funds i and the cost of borrowing i_d, the more a bank will borrow from the Fed. Thus discount loan borrowing is positively related to $i - i_d$. This relationship in turn implies that ***the amount of discount loans DL is positively related to the market interest rate i and negatively related to the discount rate i_d.***

Again, empirical evidence strongly confirms this economic analysis. Figure 3 shows a strong positive relationship between the volume of discount loans and the difference between a representative market interest rate (the federal funds rate) and the discount rate.

THE COMPLETE MONEY SUPPLY MODEL

Using the analysis of depositor and bank behavior, we can now summarize the complete money supply ($M1$) model, which has the following form:

$$M = m \times (MB_n + DL) \tag{1}$$

where M = money supply (currency plus checkable deposits)
m = money multiplier = $(1 + \{C/D\})/(r_D + \{ER/D\} + \{C/D\})$
MB_n = nonborrowed monetary base
DL = discount loans from the Fed

Our money supply analysis has focused on the following nine variables that influence the money supply by affecting the money multiplier or the monetary base:

1. Required reserve ratio r_D

2. Nonborrowed monetary base MB_n

3. Discount rate i_d

---

[5] The "cost" of the Fed's disapproval of borrowing and potential termination of future discount privileges (discussed in Chapter 11) is ignored here because it is hard to quantify. Changes in the discount rate i_d can also have an effect on the excess reserves ratio $\{ER/D\}$. The cost to a bank experiencing a deposit outflow rises when i_d rises because it is more costly to borrow from the Fed when an outflow occurs. Thus a rise in i_d increases the benefits of holding excess reserves, and $\{ER/D\}$ rises. This effect of the discount rate on the excess reserves ratio has not been emphasized in the text because it is believed to be small.

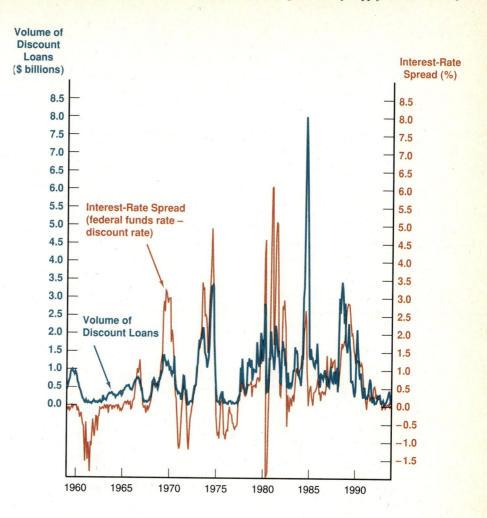

FIGURE 3
Discount Loans and the Interest-Rate Spread
Sources: Federal Reserve *Bulletin;* Citibase databank.

4. Wealth

5. Illegal activity

6. Interest rates on checkable deposits

7. Bank panics

8. Expected deposit outflows

9. Representative market interest rate i

Variables 1 and 4–9 influence the money supply by affecting the money multiplier m; variables 2 and 3 influence the money supply by affecting the monetary base MB.

Determinants of the Money Supply

To see how the money supply model works, let's analyze the effect of changes in each of these variables on the money supply, holding all the others constant.

STUDY GUIDE

The analysis in this and earlier chapters should enable you to reason out the effects of changes in these nine variables on the money supply. It is important not simply to memorize these effects but rather to use intuitive reasoning to work out the response of the money supply to a change in each variable.

Required Reserve Ratio on Checkable Deposits r_D If r_D increases, the required reserves on checkable deposits increase, and so the same level of reserves cannot support as large an amount of checkable deposits. Because of the resulting deficiency in reserves, banks must contract their loans, causing a decline in deposits and in the money supply. A more insightful explanation is that a rise in r_D lowers the amount of multiple deposit expansion, reducing the money supply. If r_D decreases, more multiple expansion occurs, and the money supply will increase. *The money supply, then, is negatively related to r_D the required reserve ratio on checkable deposits.*

Nonborrowed Monetary Base MB_n An increase in MB_n (as a result of an open market purchase) increases the amount of the monetary base available to support currency and checkable deposits, raising the money supply. A decline in MB_n (as a result of an open market sale) reduces the monetary base, lowering the money supply. *The money supply is positively related to MB_n the nonborrowed monetary base.*

Discount Rate i_d If the discount rate i_d rises, the cost of borrowing from the Fed increases, and the amount of discount loans decreases; a smaller monetary base will be available to support currency and checkable deposits, lowering the money supply. If i_d falls, discount loans from the Fed and the monetary base increase, and the money supply increases. Consequently, *the money supply is negatively related to i_d the discount rate.*

Wealth An increase in wealth increases the demand for checkable deposits more than the demand for currency, so the currency ratio {C/D} falls. Because of the shift from currency, which does not undergo multiple expansion, to checkable deposits, which do, the overall level of multiple expansion rises, and the money supply rises. If wealth falls, {C/D} rises, the overall level of multiple expansion falls, and the money supply falls. ***The money supply is positively related to wealth.***

Illegal Activity Because checkable deposits make illegal activity easier to detect, if illegal activity climbs—say, because higher tax rates lead to increased tax evasion or because of an increase in the drug trade—there is a shift into currency, which does not undergo multiple expansion, from checkable deposits, which do. The resulting rise in {C/D} and fall in multiple deposit expansion causes the money supply to fall. A decline in illegal activity causes {C/D} to fall, multiple expansion to rise, and the money supply to rise. ***The money supply is negatively related to illegal activity.***

Interest Rates on Checkable Deposits If the interest rates on checkable deposits rise, there is a shift from currency to checkable deposits because the relative expected return on currency has fallen. The resulting decline in {C/D} and rise in multiple expansion leads to an increase in the money supply. Alternatively, if the interest rate on checkable deposits falls, {C/D} rises, multiple expansion falls, and the money supply falls. ***The money supply is positively related to the interest rate on checkable deposits.***

Bank Panics When a bank panic occurs, depositors shift into currency from checkable deposits because they are more likely to suffer losses on their deposits; thus the relative expected return on currency increases. The resulting rise in {C/D} reduces multiple expansion and lowers the money supply. When the bank panic subsides, depositors shift back into checkable deposits, {C/D} falls, multiple expansion increases, and the money supply rises. ***The money supply falls during a bank panic and rises when the panic subsides.***

Expected Deposit Outflows If expected deposit outflows rise because banks fear that deposit withdrawals are more likely, they will want to have more insurance against this possibility by holding more excess reserves. The resulting increase in the excess reserves ratio {ER/D} means that the banking system uses fewer reserves to support checkable deposits, and the levels of checkable deposits and the money supply fall. Conversely, if expected deposit outflows fall, {ER/D} falls, and the money supply rises. Therefore, ***the money supply is negatively related to expected deposit outflows.***

Market Interest Rates *i* If the interest rate on loans and securities, represented by the market interest rate i, rises, the opportunity cost of holding excess reserves increases and {ER/D} falls. As a result, more reserves will be available to support checkable deposits, and the money supply rises. In addition, the rise in i will increase the benefits of borrowing from the Fed because banks can earn higher profits by taking out discount loans and using the proceeds to acquire loans and securities. The rise in i then leads to an increase in discount loans, a higher level of the monetary base, and hence a higher money supply. Because both effects of an increase in i on the money supply are in the same direction, we see that an increase in i raises the money supply. If i decreases, the excess reserves ratio rises and the volume of discount loans falls, both of which lower the money supply. Consequently, ***the money supply is positively related to the market interest rate.***[6]

As a study aid, Table 1 charts the money supply ($M1$) response to all nine variables discussed and gives a brief synopsis of the reasoning behind the result. The variables are grouped by the "players" that either influence the variable or are most influenced by it. The Federal Reserve, for example, influences the money supply by controlling the first three variables—r_D, MB_n, and i_d—also known as the *tools of the Fed* (these will be discussed extensively in subsequent chapters).

Interplay of Determinants

Depositors influence the money supply through their decisions about the currency ratio {C/D}, which is affected by wealth, illegal activity, the interest rate on checkable deposits, and bank panics. Banks influence the money supply by their decisions about {ER/D}, which reflect their expectations about deposit outflows, and by their decisions about the interest rate on checkable deposits, which in turn affects {C/D}. Because depositors' behavior also influences bankers' expectations about deposit outflows and bankers' decisions affect the probability that bank panics will occur, both these variables also reflect the role of both depositors and bankers in the money supply process.

Market interest rates, as represented by i, affect the money supply through the excess reserves ratio {ER/D}. As shown in Chapter 6, the demand for loans by borrowers influences market interest rates, as does the supply of money. Therefore, all four players are important in the determination of i.

The most important of these variables to money supply movements is the nonborrowed monetary base MB_n. More than three-fourths of the fluctuations in the money supply can be attributed to Federal Reserve open market operations, which determine MB_n. The other tools of the Fed, the required reserve ratio r_D and the discount rate i_d, have normally not been as important a source of money supply fluctuations, nor have the other six variables. However, as you will see in the next section, during periods such as the Great Depression, bank panics and expected deposit outflows have been the most important variables affecting the money supply.

We have now completed our study of the money supply model. In Chapter 15 you learned that the money supply resulted from the interaction of four players: the Fed, depositors, banks, and borrowers from banks. The complete money supply model summarized in Table 1 shows you how these players interact and what the outcomes of their actions are.

---

[6]There are other possible effects of i on the money supply through {C/D}, but they are small enough to be ignored here.

SUMMARY

TABLE 1 Money Supply Response in the Complete Model

Player	Variable	Change in Variable	Money Supply Response	Reason
Federal Reserve System	r_D	↑	↓	Less multiple deposit expansion
	MB_n	↑	↑	More MB to support currency and checkable deposits
	i_d	↑	↓	DL ↓ so less MB to support D and C
Depositors	Wealth	↑	↑	$\{C/D\}$ ↓ so more overall multiple expansion
	Illegal activity	↑	↓	$\{C/D\}$ ↑ so less overall multiple expansion
Depositors and banks	Interest rates on checkable deposits	↑	↑	$\{C/D\}$ ↓ so more overall multiple expansion
	Bank panics	↑	↓	$\{C/D\}$ ↑so less overall multiple expansion
	Expected deposit outflows	↑	↓	$\{ER/D\}$ ↑ so fewer reserves to support D
Borrowers from banks and the other three players	i	↑	↑	$\{ER/D\}$ ↓ so more reserves to support D; DL ↑ so more MB to support D and C

Note: Only increases (↑) in the variables are shown. The effect of decreases on the money supply would be the opposite of those indicated in the "Response" column.

ANATOMY OF A BANK PANIC

The money supply model we have developed is a powerful tool; we will use it in later chapters to examine many issues that arise about how monetary policy operates and how it might be improved. To apply the model, let's use it to analyze a particularly interesting economic phenomenon, a bank panic in which a large number of banks fail at one time. Bank panics have had a major historical

Box 1

RECENT BANK PANICS IN OHIO, MARYLAND, AND RHODE ISLAND

Until the 1980s, most people believed that bank panics were a thing of the past, the last occurring during the Great Depression. Events in Ohio, Maryland, and Rhode Island in recent years, however, have demonstrated that bank panics are still a danger to the health of the financial system.

In all three states, deposits were guaranteed not by federal deposit insurance but by a private state insurance fund: in Ohio by the Ohio Deposit Guarantee Fund, in Maryland by the Maryland Savings-Share Insurance Corporation, and in Rhode Island by the Rhode Island Share and Deposit Indemnity Corporation. When the reserves held in these insurance funds were exceeded by losses at failed insured institutions, depositors feared that they would suffer losses on their deposits at other banking institutions. As our analysis in this chapter predicts, bank panics reminiscent of those in the 1930s ensued when runs on these other institutions began to occur.

The first bank panic since the Great Depression occurred in Ohio after the Ohio Deposit Guarantee Fund was depleted by losses from the failure of the Home State Savings Bank of Cincinnati in March 1985 because of bad loans to a securities firm that was engaged in fraudulent activities. To gain time to sort out solvent from insolvent banks, the governor of Ohio declared a bank holiday, temporarily closing 70 savings institutions. These banks were reopened with the help of the Federal Reserve and the Federal Home Loan Bank Board after they obtained federal deposit insurance.

Soon afterward, in May 1985, the failure of two insured Maryland S&Ls bank-

(cont.)

impact; they have been blamed for some of our most severe economic contractions, including the Great Depression. The danger of bank panics has appeared in the news lately because of recent bank panics in Ohio, Maryland, and Rhode Island (see Box 1) and the collapse of several of our largest banking institutions—Continental Illinois, First Republic Bank of Texas, and Bank of New England. Although rare, the possibility of bank panics affects the way we conduct monetary policy because their prevention requires an active role on the part of the Federal Reserve.

Because most bank panics involve only a few banks at first, it is helpful to begin with a look at why an individual bank fails during such a crisis.

RECENT BANK PANICS IN OHIO, MARYLAND, AND RHODE ISLAND (cont.)

rupted the Maryland Savings-Share Insurance Corporation. A panic at 100 Maryland S&Ls was finally stopped by the governor's temporary decree establishing a $1000-per-month withdrawal limit and by the replacement of private deposit insurance by a newly created, state-backed deposit insurance fund.

The most damaging bank panic occurred in Rhode Island in January 1991. After the failure of a bank in Providence due to embezzlement, the governor was forced to declare a bank holiday on New Year's Day, closing 45 small banks and credit unions. The result was the freezing of $1.3 billion in 359,000 accounts in a state with only 1 million people. The governor's bailout proposal gave each depositor at failed institutions up to only $12,500 in cash and, for the remainder of deposits up to the $100,000 insured limit, non-interest-bearing state scrip (small-denomination paper IOUs) that would be paid back over several years. (Scrip like this was last issued during the bank panics of the 1930s.) Any deposit amount over $100,000 at a failed bank was unlikely to be paid back. It took 18 months to resolve the banking crisis in Rhode Island. The last group of insured depositors received 90% of their deposits in June 1992, with the remaining 10% to be paid back over 20 years.

The economic hardship imposed on Rhode Island has been severe. The state government has had to increase sales taxes permanently by 1 percentage point to pay for the bailout, and the bank panic worsened the recession in the state. In the aftermath of the bank panic, the state lost 6.1% of its jobs in 1992, the highest percentagewise job loss in the country.

The Individual Bank

In an economy without federal deposit insurance, a bank failure means that depositors will not recover the full value of their deposits. If depositors suspect for any reason (unfounded or not) that a bank might fail, they will immediately withdraw their deposits. The bank loses reserves and is even more vulnerable to future deposit outflows. Other depositors who see this happening will begin to question the bank's health and withdraw their funds too. The more depositors who withdraw funds, the fewer reserves the bank will have, and the more likely it is to fail. The more likely it is to fail, the more likely depositors will show up to withdraw their deposits. This snowballing process, called a *run on the bank,* usually ends in the failure of the bank unless something can be done to restore the public's confidence.

Fear of a bank's failing can feed on itself and force even a healthy bank to fail. Although it may be in the best interest of the individual depositor to withdraw funds, it is not necessarily in the best interest of the bank's depositors as a whole. Depositors' attempts to withdraw their funds lead to what they fear most—closing of the bank and the reality of not being able to recover their deposits.

The Banking System

The failure of one bank could cause depositors at another bank to suspect that their bank could also fall victim to a run and fail, setting in motion a run on this second bank. The failure of this bank can trigger runs on other banks, and the whole process can multiply until there is a full-fledged bank panic in which a large number of banks fail.

Oddly enough, the desire of banks to protect themselves can increase the panic. If a bank is experiencing a run or fears that one will occur in the near future, it needs to acquire excess reserves to avoid the costs associated with expected deposit outflows. To increase excess reserves in a bank panic (known as a *scramble for liquidity*), the bank sells securities and calls in loans, keeping the proceeds as excess reserves for protection. The scramble for liquidity results in deposit outflows from other banks and multiple deposit contraction, with the net result that other banks are more likely to fail. As with depositors, the desire of individual banks to protect themselves, even though in their best personal interest, may be damaging to the banking system as a whole.

Bank runs and a bank panic can be stopped by restoring depositors' as well as bankers' confidence in the health of the banks. It is not surprising that Franklin Delano Roosevelt's statement "The only thing we have to fear is fear itself" was made after the United States had already experienced the most severe bank panics in its history.

To eliminate the climate of fear, banks have sometimes banded together in an attempt to prevent bank failures by lending the troubled bank enough reserves to survive the run. Why would a group of banks want to save a competitor who potentially takes away some of their business? Because it is in their self-interest to prevent a bank panic.

Another way to prevent a panic is for the central bank to supply substantial reserves to the banking system when bank failures occur so that other banks have enough reserves to handle the potential deposit outflows. It can do this either by increasing the nonborrowed monetary base MB_n or by freely lending to banks in this time of crisis. If the central bank's policy of preventing a panic becomes known, depositors will no longer feel the need to withdraw their deposits, and bankers will not feel the need to call in loans and build up their excess reserves. The knowledge alone that the central bank will attempt to prevent a panic is often enough to stop a bank panic in its tracks.

As you will see in Chapter 18, the central bank in the United States, the Federal Reserve System, was created in response to the bank panic of 1907. Its intended role was to be the **lender of last resort** in a banking crisis; that is, the Fed was supposed to provide reserves to banks when no one else would in order to prevent bank failures. Unfortunately, the Fed did not fulfill its role during the Great Depression (see Box 2), a failure that had dire consequences for the U.S. economy.

Box 2

THE BANK PANICS OF 1930–1933—WHY DID THE FED LET THEM HAPPEN?

The Federal Reserve System was totally passive during the bank panics of the Great Depression period and did not perform its intended role of lender of last resort to prevent them. In retrospect, the Fed's behavior seems quite extraordinary, but then hindsight is always clearer than foresight.

The primary reason for the Fed's inaction was that Federal Reserve officials did not understand the negative impact bank failures could have on the money supply and economic activity. Friedman and Schwartz report that the Federal Reserve officials "tended to regard bank failures as regrettable consequences of bank management or bad banking practices, or as inevitable reactions to prior speculative excesses, or as a consequence but hardly a cause of the financial and economic collapse in process." In addition, bank failures in the early stages of the bank panics "were concentrated among smaller banks and, since the most influential figures in the system were big-city bankers who deplored the existence of smaller banks, their disappearance may have been viewed with complacency."[*]

Friedman and Schwartz also point out that political infighting may have played an important role in the passivity of the Fed during this period. The Federal Reserve Bank of New York, which until 1928 was the dominant force in the Federal Reserve System, strongly advocated an active program of open market purchases to provide reserves to the banking system during the bank panics. However, other powerful figures in the Federal Reserve System opposed the New York bank's position, and the bank was outvoted. (Friedman and Schwartz's discussion of the politics of the Federal Reserve System during this period makes for fascinating reading, and you might enjoy their highly readable book.)

[*]Milton Friedman and Anna Jacobson Schwartz, *A Monetary History of the United States, 1867–1960* (Princeton, N.J.: Princeton University Press, 1963), p. 358.

A final and most important way to prevent bank panics is to provide federal insurance for bank deposits. If depositors know that they will recover the full value of their deposits if their bank fails, suspicion of a bank failure will no longer cause them to make a run on the bank. As a result of the bank panics during the Great Depression, the Federal Deposit Insurance Corporation (FDIC) was put into operation on January 1, 1934. Since its birth, federal deposit insurance has been successful in sharply reducing the number of bank failures in the United States, although, as we saw in Chapter 13, it has created other problems.

STUDY GUIDE

To test your knowledge of the money supply model, see if you can analyze (without referring to the text) the effects of a bank panic on the money supply as a result of depositor and bank behavior.

Bank Panics and the Money Supply

We can now apply the model to determine the effect of a bank panic on the money supply.

When a bank panic occurs, depositors will try to avoid the losses due to bank failures by turning their deposits into currency, and $\{C/D\}$ will rise. As the money supply model predicts, the overall level of multiple expansion will then decline, and the money supply will fall. In addition, deposit outflows will be expected to be higher and banks will want to hold more insurance in the form of excess reserves. The resulting scramble for liquidity, which raises the level of the excess reserves ratio $\{ER/D\}$, will reduce the amount of reserves available to support checkable deposits, and this will also cause the money supply to fall. So a bank panic will have very negative effects on the money supply.

The following application examines the worst episode of bank panics in the United States, which started in late 1930 and ended with the bank holiday of March 1933. Not surprisingly, the largest decline of the money supply ever recorded in U.S. history occurred in this same period.

APPLICATION

THE GREAT DEPRESSION BANK PANICS, 1930–1933

We have used our model of the money supply process to understand the dynamics of a bank panic. To put this model to the test, we look here at a particu-

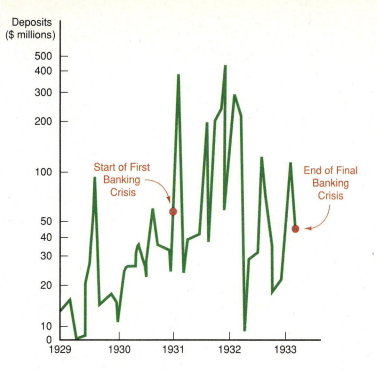

FIGURE 4
Deposits of Failed Commercial Banks, 1929–1933
Source: Milton Friedman and Anna Jacobson Schwartz, *A Monetary History of the United States, 1867–1960* (Princeton, N.J.: Princeton University Press, 1963), p. 309.

lar historical period, the Great Depression. Figure 4 traces the banking crisis in this period by showing the volume of deposits at failed commercial banks from 1929 to 1933. In their classic book *A Monetary History of the United States, 1867–1960,* Milton Friedman and Anna Schwartz describe the onset of the first banking crisis in late 1930 as follows:

> Before October 1930, deposits of suspended [failed] commercial banks had been somewhat higher than during most of 1929 but not out of line with experience during the preceding decade. In November 1930, they were more than double the highest value recorded since the start of monthly data in 1921. A crop of bank failures, particularly in Missouri, Indiana, Illinois, Iowa, Arkansas, and North Carolina, led to widespread attempts to convert checkable and time deposits into currency, and also, to a much lesser extent, into postal savings deposits. A contagion of fear spread among depositors, starting from the agricultural areas, which had experienced the heaviest impact of bank failures in the twenties. But failure of 256 banks with $180 million of deposits in November 1930 was followed by the failure of 532 with over $370 million of deposits in December (all figures seasonally unadjusted), the most dramatic being the failure on December 11 of the Bank of the United States with over $200 million of deposits. That failure was especially important. The Bank of United States was the largest commercial bank, as measured by volume of deposits, ever to have failed up to that time in U.S. history. Moreover, though it was

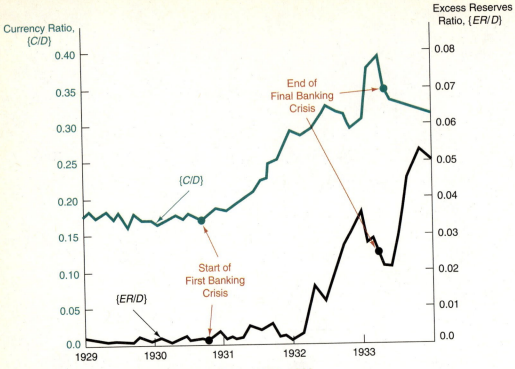

FIGURE 5 The Excess Reserves and Currency Ratios, 1929–1933
Sources: Federal Reserve *Bulletin;* Milton Friedman and Anna Jacobson Schwartz, *A Monetary History of the United States, 1867–1960* (Princeton, N.J.: Princeton University Press, 1963), p. 333.

just an ordinary commercial bank, the Bank of the United States's name had led many at home and abroad to regard it somehow as an official bank, hence its failure constituted more of a blow to confidence than would have been administered by the fall of a bank with a less distinctive name.[7]

The first bank panic, from October 1930 until January 1931, is clearly visible in Figure 4 at the end of 1930, when there is a rise in the amount of deposits at failed banks. According to the money supply model, {C/D} should have risen sharply with the onset of the first banking crisis, and the banks should have tried to protect themselves by substantially increasing their excess reserves ratio {ER/D}. Both these predictions are borne out by the data in Figure 5. {C/D} began to climb during the first bank panic (October 1930–January 1931). Even more striking is the behavior of {ER/D}, which more than doubled from Novem-

---

[7]Milton Friedman and Anna Jacobson Schwartz, *A Monetary History of the United States, 1867–1960* (Princeton, N.J.: Princeton University Press, 1963), pp. 308–311.

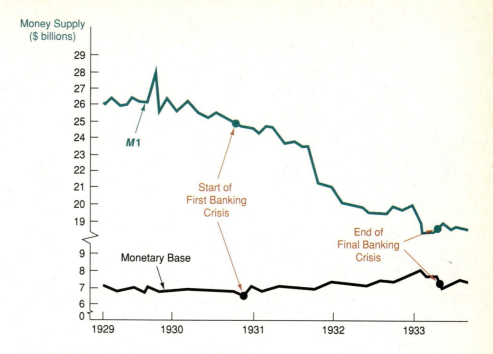

FIGURE 6 *M*1 **and the Monetary Base, 1929–1933**
Source: Milton Friedman and Anna Jacobson Schwartz, *A Monetary History of the United States, 1867–1960* (Princeton, N.J.: Princeton University Press, 1963), p. 333.

ber 1930 to January 1931. The money supply model also predicts that when {*ER/D*} and {*C/D*} increase, the money supply will fall—a prediction borne out by the evidence in Figure 6. The money supply declined sharply in December 1930 and January 1931 during the first bank panic.

Banking crises continued to occur from 1931 to 1933, and the pattern predicted by our model persisted: {*C/D*} continued to rise, and so did {*ER/D*}. By the end of the banking crises in March 1933, the money supply (*M*1) had declined by over 25%—by far the largest decline in all of American history—and it coincided with the nation's worst economic contraction (see Chapter 9). Even more remarkable is that this decline occurred despite a 20% rise in the level of the monetary base—which illustrates how important the changes in {*C/D*} and {*ER/D*} during bank panics can be in the determination of the money supply. It also illustrates that the Fed's job of conducting monetary policy can be complicated by depositor and bank behavior (see Box 2 on p. 427).

SUMMARY

1. The interaction between the theory of asset demand and empirical data provides a framework that allows us to identify four primary factors that influence the currency ratio {C/D}: wealth, interest rates on checkable deposits, bank panics, and illegal activity. The currency ratio is positively related to bank panics and illegal activity and negatively related to wealth and interest rates on checkable deposits.
2. The desired level of the excess reserves ratio {ER/D} is negatively related to interest rates and positively related to expected deposit outflows. Discount loan borrowing from the Fed is positively related to market interest rates and negatively related to the discount rate.
3. The complete money supply model focuses on

the effects of nine factors. The results are summarized in Table 1, which shows how the money supply is affected by changes in these factors.
4. The phenomenon of a bank panic illustrates many of the principles of money supply analysis. Fearing bank failures, depositors turn their deposits into currency, causing a sharp rise in {C/D} and a contraction in the money supply. Banks, trying to protect themselves against the resulting deposit outflows, increase their excess reserves ratio {ER/D}, resulting in a further decline in the money supply. This is exactly what occurred in the Great Depression period, when the money supply declined by 25% (even though the monetary base rose by 20%).

KEY TERMS

underground economy

lender of last resort

QUESTIONS AND PROBLEMS

1. If the currency ratio rises from its current level, what might this imply about the growth of the underground economy?
*2. Why might the procyclical behavior of interest rates (rising during business cycle expansions and falling during recessions) lead to procyclical movements in the money supply?
3. "Self-preservation can be self-destructive during a bank panic." Is this statement true, false, or uncertain? Explain.

Using Economic Analysis to Predict the Future

*4. In contrast to procedures in the United States, Swiss government investigations are not allowed to access bank records of individuals or corporations. If the United States decided to adopt this attribute of the Swiss system, what do you predict would happen to the currency ratio?

5. Predict what would happen to the currency ratio if cigarette smoking were made illegal.
*6. With all other factors held constant, predict what will happen to the currency ratio over the next 20 years if wealth continues to rise.
7. If the government reinstituted regulations to prevent the payment of interest on checkable deposits, what would happen to the currency ratio?
*8. The Fed has been discussing the possibility of paying interest on excess reserves. If this occurred, what would happen to the level of {ER/D}?
9. If the FDIC were abolished, what would happen to the money supply as a result of bank behavior? Depositor behavior?

*10. What do you predict would happen to the money supply if expected inflation suddenly increased?

11. If the economy starts to boom and loan demand picks up, what do you predict will happen to the money supply?

*12. Milton Friedman once suggested that Federal Reserve discount lending should be abolished. Predict what would happen to the money supply if Friedman's suggestion were put into practice.

13. If the Fed paid a market interest rate on reserves and also set its discount rate equal to this rate, what do you predict would happen to the money supply if interest rates were to rise?

*14. If Congress reduced the penalties for check forgery, what would happen to the money supply?

15. Predict what would happen to the money supply if the Fed makes open market purchases of bonds at the same time that market interest rates are rising.

PART V

THE FEDERAL RESERVE SYSTEM AND THE CONDUCT OF MONETARY POLICY

Chapter 18

STRUCTURE OF THE FEDERAL RESERVE SYSTEM

PREVIEW   Our money supply analysis in earlier chapters attests to the critical role in the money supply process played by the Federal Reserve System—the U.S. government authority in charge of the country's monetary policy. Indeed, over three-quarters of the fluctuations in the money supply can be attributed to changes in the monetary base (currency in circulation plus reserves), which can be controlled by the Fed. The Fed is clearly the lead player in the money supply process, and others are supporting characters. But who controls the Fed and determines its actions? What motivates its behavior? Who holds the reins of power?

In this chapter we look at the formal institutional structure of the Fed and the more relevant informal structure that determines where the true power within the Federal Reserve System lies. By understanding who makes the decisions, we will have a better idea of how they are made. Consequently, the actual conduct of monetary policy described in the following chapters will be more comprehensible.

ORIGINS OF THE FEDERAL RESERVE SYSTEM

Of all the central banks throughout the world, the Federal Reserve System probably has the most unusual structure. To understand why this structure arose, we must go back before 1913, when the Federal Reserve System was created.

Before the twentieth century, a major characteristic of American politics was the fear of centralized power, as seen in the checks and balances of the Constitution and the preservation of states' rights. This fear of centralized power was one source of the American resistance to the establishment of a central bank (see Chapter 12). Another source was the traditional American distrust of moneyed interests, the most prominent symbol of which was a central bank. The open hostility of the American public to the existence of a central bank resulted in the demise of the first two experiments in central banking, whose function was to police the banking system: The First Bank of the United States was disbanded in

1811, and the national charter of the Second Bank of the United States expired in 1836 after its renewal was vetoed in 1832 by President Andrew Jackson.

The termination of the Second Bank's national charter in 1836 created a severe problem for American financial markets because there was no lender of last resort who could provide reserves to the banking system to avert a bank panic. Hence in the nineteenth and early twentieth centuries, nationwide bank panics became a regular event, occurring in 1837, 1857, 1873, 1884, 1893, and 1907. The 1907 panic resulted in such widespread bank failures and such substantial losses to depositors that the public was finally convinced that a central bank was needed to prevent future panics.

The hostility of the American public to banks and centralized authority created great opposition to the establishment of a single central bank like the Bank of England. Fear was rampant that the moneyed interests on Wall Street (including the largest corporations and banks) would be able to manipulate such an institution to gain control over the economy and that federal operation of the central bank might result in too much government intervention in the affairs of private banks. Serious disagreements existed over whether the central bank should be a private bank or a government institution. Because of the heated debates on these issues, a compromise was struck. In the great American tradition, Congress wrote an elaborate system of checks and balances into the Federal Reserve Act of 1913, which created the Federal Reserve System with its 12 regional Federal Reserve banks.

FORMAL STRUCTURE OF THE FEDERAL RESERVE SYSTEM

The formal structure of the Federal Reserve System was intended by designers of the Federal Reserve Act to diffuse power along regional lines, between the private sector and the government, and among bankers, businesspeople, and the public. This initial diffusion of power has resulted in the evolution of the Federal Reserve System to include the following entities: the **Federal Reserve banks,** the **Board of Governors of the Federal Reserve System,** the **Federal Open Market Committee (FOMC),** the Federal Advisory Council, and around 4000 member commercial banks. Figure 1 outlines the relationships of these entities to one another and to the three policy tools of the Fed (open market operations, the discount rate, and reserve requirements).

Federal Reserve Banks

Each of the 12 Federal Reserve districts has one main Federal Reserve bank, which may have branches in other cities in the district. The locations of these districts, the Federal Reserve banks, and their branches are shown in Figure 2. The three largest Federal Reserve banks in terms of assets are those of New York, Chicago, and San Francisco—combined they hold over 50% of the assets (discount loans, securities, and other holdings) of the Federal Reserve System. The New York bank, with over 30% of the assets, is the most important of the

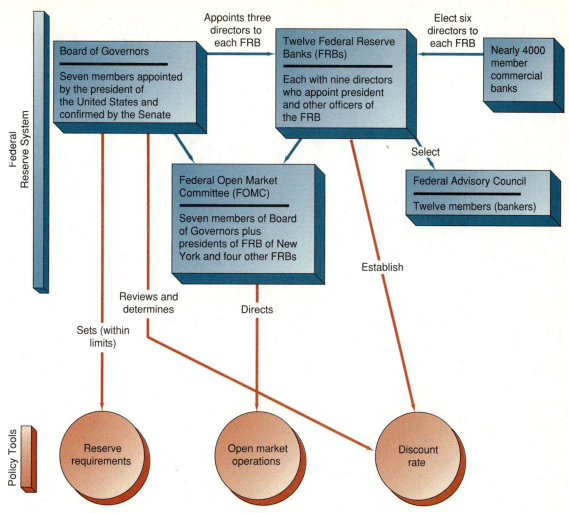

FIGURE 1 Formal Structure and Allocation of Policy Tools in the Federal Reserve

Federal Reserve banks because its district contains many of the largest commercial banks in the United States and because it is in direct contact with the major financial markets, which operate out of New York City.

Each of the Federal Reserve banks is a quasi-public incorporated institution owned by the private commercial banks in the district who are members of the Federal Reserve System. These member banks have purchased stock in their district Federal Reserve bank (a requirement of membership), and the dividends paid by that stock are limited to 6% annually. The member banks elect six directors for each district bank; three more are appointed by the Board of Governors. Together, these nine directors appoint the president of the bank (subject to the approval of the Board of Governors).

The directors of a district bank are classified into three categories (A, B, and C): the three A directors (elected by the member banks) are professional

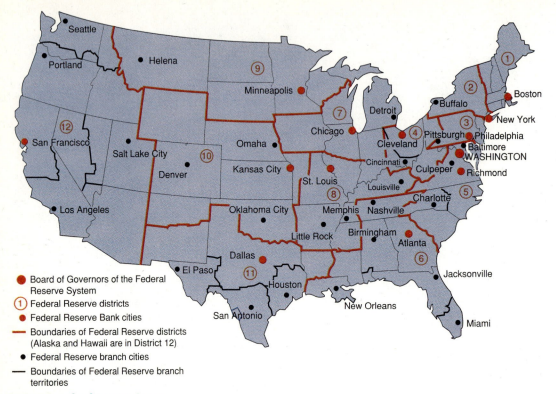

FIGURE 2 Federal Reserve System
Source: Federal Reserve *Bulletin.*

bankers, and the three B directors (also elected by the member banks) are prominent businesspeople in the areas of industry, commerce, and agriculture. The three C directors, who are appointed by the Board of Governors to represent the public interest, are not allowed to be officers, employees, or stockholders of banks. This design of choosing directors was intended by the Federal Reserve Act to ensure that the directors of each Federal Reserve bank would reflect all constituencies of the American public.

The 12 Federal Reserve banks perform the following functions:

1. Clear checks

2. Issue new currency

3. Withdraw damaged currency from circulation

4. Evaluate some merger applications

5. Administer and make discount loans to banks in their districts

6. Act as liaisons between the business community and the Federal Reserve System

7. Examine state member banks

8. Collect data on local business conditions

9. Use their large staffs of professional economists to research topics related to the conduct of monetary policy and publish reviews (a good source of supplemental material for money and banking students) that present the staffs' views

The 12 Federal Reserve banks are involved in monetary policy in several ways:

1. They "establish" the discount rate (although the discount rate in each district is reviewed and determined by the Board of Governors).

2. They decide which banks, member and nonmember alike, can obtain discount loans from the Federal Reserve Bank.

3. They each select one commercial banker to serve on the Federal Advisory Council, which consults with the Board of Governors and makes recommendations on the conduct of monetary policy.

4. Five bank presidents each have a vote in the Federal Open Market Committee (FOMC), which directs open market operations (the purchase and sale of government securities that affect the monetary base). The president of the New York Fed always has a vote in the FOMC, making it the most important of the banks; the other four votes allocated to the district banks rotate among the remaining 11 presidents.

Member Banks

All *national banks* (commercial banks chartered by the Office of the Comptroller of the Currency) are required to be members of the Federal Reserve System. Commercial banks chartered by the states are not required to be members, but they can choose to join. Currently, around one third of the commercial banks in the United States are members of the Federal Reserve System, having declined from a peak figure of 49% in 1947.

Before 1980, only member banks were required to keep reserves as deposits at the Federal Reserve banks. Nonmember banks were subject to reserve requirements determined by their states, which typically allowed them to hold much of their reserves in interest-bearing securities. Because no interest is paid on reserves deposited at the Federal Reserve banks, it was costly to be a member of the system, and as interest rates rose, the relative cost of membership rose, and more and more banks left the system.

This decline in Fed membership was a major concern of the Board of Governors (one reason was that it lessened the Fed's control over the money supply, making it more difficult for the Fed to conduct monetary policy). The chairman of the Board of Governors repeatedly called for new legislation that required all commercial banks to be members of the Federal Reserve System. One result of the Fed's pressure on Congress was a provision in the Depository Institutions

Deregulation and Monetary Control Act of 1980: All banks became subject (by 1987) to the same requirements to keep deposits at the Fed, so member and nonmember banks would be on an equal footing in terms of their reserve requirements. In addition, all banks were given access to the Federal Reserve facilities, such as the discount window and Fed check clearing, on an equal basis. These provisions ended the decline in Fed membership and reduced the distinction between member and nonmember banks.

Board of Governors of the Federal Reserve System

At the head of the Federal Reserve System is the seven-member Board of Governors, headquartered in Washington, D.C. Each governor is appointed by the president of the United States and confirmed by the Senate. To limit a particular president's control over the Fed and insulate the Fed from other political pressures, the governors serve one nonrenewable 14-year term, with one governor's term expiring every other January.[1] The governors (many are professional economists) are required to come from different Federal Reserve districts to prevent the interests of one region of the country from being overrepresented. The chairman of the Board of Governors is chosen from among the seven governors and serves a four-year term. Traditionally, once a new chairman is chosen, the old chairman resigns from the Board of Governors, even if there are many years left to his or her term as a governor.

The Board of Governors is actively involved with decisions concerning the conduct of monetary policy. All seven governors are members of the FOMC and vote on the conduct of open market operations. Because there are only 12 voting members on this committee (seven governors and five presidents of the district banks), the board has the majority of the votes. The board also sets reserve requirements (within limits imposed by legislation) and effectively controls the discount rate by the "review and determination" process, whereby it approves or disapproves the discount rate "established" by the Federal Reserve banks. The chairman of the board advises the president of the United States on economic policy, testifies in Congress, and speaks for the Federal Reserve System to the media. The chairman and other governors may also represent the United States in negotiations with foreign governments on economic matters. The board has a staff of professional economists (larger than those of individual Federal Reserve banks), which provides economic analysis that the board uses in making its decisions.

Through legislation, the Board of Governors has often been given duties not directly related to the conduct of monetary policy. In the past, for example, the board set the maximum interest rates payable on certain types of time deposits

---

[1]Although technically a governor's term is nonrenewable, a governor can resign just before the term expires and then be reappointed by the president. This explains how one governor, William McChesney Martin, Jr., served for 28 years. Since Martin, the chairman from 1951 to 1970, retired from the board in 1970, the practice of extending a governor's term beyond 14 years has become a rarity.

under Regulation Q. (Since Regulation Q was eliminated in 1986, the board no longer has this authority.) Under the Credit Control Act of 1969 (which expired in 1982), the board had the ability to regulate and control credit once the president of the United States approved. The Board of Governors also sets margin requirements, the fraction of the purchase price of the securities that has to be paid for with cash rather than borrowed funds. It also sets the salary of the president and all officers of each Federal Reserve bank and reviews each bank's budget. Finally, the board has substantial bank regulatory functions: It approves bank mergers, specifies the permissible activities of bank holding companies, and supervises the activities of foreign banks in the United States.

Federal Open Market Committee (FOMC)

The FOMC usually meets eight times a year (about every six weeks) and makes decisions regarding the conduct of open market operations, which influence the monetary base. The committee consists of the seven members of the Board of Governors, the president of the Federal Reserve Bank of New York, and presidents of four other Federal Reserve banks. The chairman of the Board of Governors also presides as the chairman of the FOMC. Even though only presidents of five of the Federal Reserve banks are voting members of the FOMC, the other seven presidents of the district banks attend FOMC meetings and participate in discussions. Hence they have some input into the committee's decisions.

Because open market operations are the most important policy tool that the Fed has for controlling the money supply, the FOMC is necessarily the focal point for policymaking in the Federal Reserve System. Although reserve requirements and the discount rate are not actually set by the FOMC, decisions in regard to these policy tools are effectively made here. The FOMC does not actually carry out securities purchases or sales. Rather it issues directives to the trading desk at the Federal Reserve Bank of New York, where the manager for domestic open market operations supervises a roomful of people who execute the purchases and sales of the government or agency securities.[2] The manager communicates daily with the FOMC members and their staffs concerning the activities of the trading desk.

INFORMAL STRUCTURE OF THE FEDERAL RESERVE SYSTEM

The Federal Reserve Act and other legislation give us some idea of the formal structure of the Federal Reserve System and who makes decisions at the Fed. What is written in black and white, however, does not necessarily reflect the reality of the power and decision-making structure.

---

[2]The decisions contained in the directive are often not unanimous, and the dissenting views are made public. However, except in rare cases, the chairman's vote is always on the winning side.

As envisioned in 1913, the Federal Reserve System was to be a highly decentralized system designed to function as 12 separate, cooperating central banks. In the original plan, the Fed was not responsible for the health of the economy through its control of the money supply and its ability to affect interest rates. Over time it has acquired the responsibility for promoting a stable economy, and this responsibility has caused the Federal Reserve System to evolve slowly into a more unified central bank.

The designers of the Federal Reserve Act of 1913 intended the Fed to have only one basic tool of monetary policy, the control of discount loans to member banks. The use of open market operations as a tool for monetary control was not yet well understood, and reserve requirements were fixed by the Federal Reserve Act. The discount tool was to be controlled by the joint decision of the Federal Reserve banks and the Federal Reserve Board (which later became the Board of Governors), so that both would share equally in the determination of monetary policy. However, the board's ability to "review and determine" the discount rate effectively allowed it to dominate the district banks in setting this policy.

Banking legislation during the Great Depression years centralized power within the newly created Board of Governors by giving it effective control over the remaining two tools of monetary policy, open market operations and changes in reserve requirements. The Banking Act of 1933 granted the FOMC authority to determine open market operations, and the Banking Act of 1935 gave the board the majority of votes in the FOMC. The Banking Act of 1935 also gave the board authority to change reserve requirements.

Over time, then, the Board of Governors has acquired the reins of control over the tools for conducting monetary policy. In recent years, the power of the board has become even greater. It frequently suggests a choice (often a professional economist) for president of a Federal Reserve bank to the directors of the bank, who normally follow the board's suggestions. Since the board sets the salary of the bank's president and reviews the budget of each Federal Reserve bank, it has further influence over the district banks' activities.

If the Board of Governors has so much power, what power do the Federal Advisory Council and the "owners" of the Federal Reserve banks—the member banks—actually have within the Federal Reserve System? The answer is almost none. Although member banks own stock in the Federal Reserve banks, they have none of the usual benefits of ownership. First, they have no claim on the earnings of the Fed and get paid only a 6% annual dividend, regardless of how much the Fed earns. Second, they have no say over how their property is used by the Federal Reserve System, in contrast to stockholders of private corporations. Third, there is usually only a single candidate for each of the six A and B directorships "elected" by the member banks, and this candidate is frequently suggested by the president of the Federal Reserve bank (who, in turn, is usually suggested by the Board of Governors, although on paper the directors of the bank elect the president). The net result is that member banks are essentially frozen out of the political process at the Fed and have no effective power. Fourth, the Federal Advisory Council has little impact on Federal Reserve policymaking and serves mostly a ceremonial function.

A fair characterization of the Federal Reserve System as it has evolved is that it functions as a central bank, headquartered in Washington, D.C., with branches in 12 cities. Because all aspects of the Federal Reserve System are essentially controlled by the Board of Governors, who controls the board? Although the chairman of the Board of Governors does not have legal authority to exercise control over this body, the chairman effectively does so through the ability to set the agenda of board and FOMC meetings, act as spokesperson for the Fed, and negotiate with Congress and the president of the United States. The chairman also influences the board through the force of stature and personality. Chairmen of the Board of Governors (including Marriner S. Eccles; William McChesney Martin, Jr.; Arthur Burns; Paul A. Volcker; and Alan Greenspan) have typically had strong personalities and have wielded great power.

The chairman also exercises power by supervising the board's staff of professional economists and advisers. Because the staff gathers information for the board and conducts the analyses that the board uses in its decisions, it also has some influence over monetary policy. In addition, several recent appointments to the board itself have come from within the ranks of its professional staff, making the chairman's influence even farther-reaching and longer-lasting than a four-year term.

The informal power structure of the Fed, in which power is centralized in the chairman of the Board of Governors, is summarized in Figure 3.

HOW INDEPENDENT IS THE FED?

When we look, in the next three chapters, at how the Federal Reserve conducts monetary policy, we will want to know why it decides to take certain policy actions but not others. To understand its actions, we must understand the incentives that motivate the Fed's behavior. How free is the Fed from presidential and congressional pressures? Do economic, bureaucratic, or political considerations guide it? Is the Fed truly independent of outside pressures?

The Federal Reserve appears to be remarkably free of the political pressures that influence other government agencies. Not only are the members of the Board of Governors appointed for a 14-year term (and so cannot be ousted from office), but also the term is technically not renewable, eliminating some of the incentive for the governors to curry favor with the president and Congress.

Probably even more important to its independence from the whims of Congress is the Fed's independent and substantial source of revenue from its holdings of securities and, to a lesser extent, from its loans to banks. In recent years, for example, the Fed has had net earnings after expenses of over $15 billion per year—not a bad living if you can find it! Because it returns the bulk of these earnings to the Treasury, it does not get rich from its activities, but this income gives the Fed an important advantage over other government agencies: It is not subject to the appropriations process usually controlled by Congress. Indeed, the Fed can refuse audits by the General Accounting Office, the auditing agency of the federal government. Because the power to control the purse strings is usually

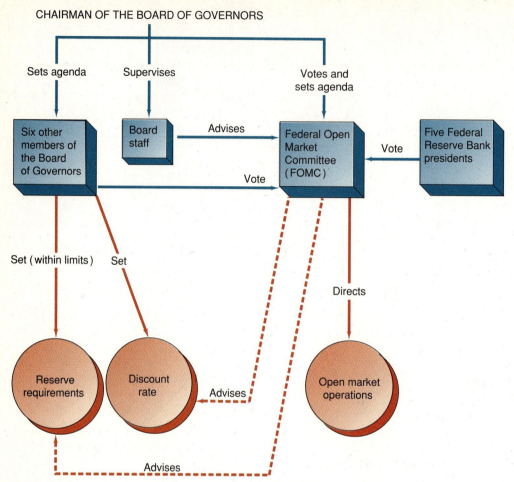

FIGURE 3 Informal Power Structure of the Federal Reserve System

synonymous with the power of overall control, this feature of the Federal Reserve System contributes to its independence more than any other factor.

Yet the Federal Reserve is still subject to the influence of Congress because the legislation that structures it is written by Congress and is subject to change at any time. When legislators are upset with the Fed's conduct of monetary policy, they frequently threaten to take control of the Fed's finances and force it to submit a budget request like other government agencies. (Often you will spot newspaper articles reporting calls by members of Congress for tighter supervision of the Fed.) This is a powerful club to wave, and it certainly has some effect in keeping the Fed from straying too far from congressional wishes.

Congress has also passed legislation to make the Federal Reserve more accountable for its actions. In 1975, Congress passed House Concurrent Resolution 133, which requires the Fed to announce its objectives for the growth rates of the monetary aggregates. In the Full Employment and Balanced Growth Act of 1978 (the Humphrey-Hawkins Bill), the Fed is required to explain how these objectives are consistent with the economic plans of the president of the United States. In recent years, Representative Henry Gonzalez, the chairman of the House Banking Committee, has pressured the Fed to be less secretive in its deliberations about monetary policy.

The president can also influence the Federal Reserve. Because congressional legislation can affect the Fed directly or affect its ability to conduct monetary policy, the president can be a powerful ally through his influence on Congress. Second, although ostensibly a president might be able to appoint only one or two members to the Board of Governors during each presidential term, in actual practice the president appoints members far more often. One reason is that most governors do not serve out a full 14-year term. (One explanation is that governors' salaries are substantially below what they can earn in the private sector, thus providing them with an incentive to take a private sector job before their term expires.) In addition, the president is able to appoint a new chairman of the Board of Governors every four years, and traditionally a chairman who is not reappointed resigns from the board so that a new member can be appointed.

The power that the president enjoys through his appointments to the Board of Governors is limited, however. Because the term of the chairman is not necessarily concurrent with that of the president, a president may have to deal with a chairman of the Board of Governors appointed by a previous administration. Paul Volcker, for example, was appointed chairman in 1979 by President Jimmy Carter, and his term did not expire until 1983—three years into President Reagan's term. Republican Reagan was put under tremendous pressure to reappoint Volcker when his term expired. Reagan then did reappoint Volcker, even though Volcker was first appointed by a Democrat.[3]

You can see that the Federal Reserve has extraordinary independence for a government agency and is one of the most independent central banks in the world (see Box 1). Nonetheless, the Fed is not free from political pressures. Indeed, to understand the Fed's behavior, we must recognize that politics plays a very important role.

EXPLAINING THE FED'S BEHAVIOR

One view of government bureaucratic behavior is that bureaucracies serve the public interest (this is the *public interest view*). Yet some economists have developed a theory of bureaucratic behavior that suggests other factors that influence how bureaucracies operate. The *theory of bureaucratic behavior* suggests that the objective of a bureaucracy is to maximize its own welfare, just as a consumer's behavior is motivated by the maximization of personal welfare and a

---

[3]Similarly, William McChesney Martin, Jr., the chairman from 1951 to 1970, was appointed by President Truman (Dem.) but was reappointed by Presidents Eisenhower (Rep.), Kennedy (Dem.), and Nixon (Rep.).

A Global Perspective

Box 1

THE STRUCTURE AND INDEPENDENCE OF FOREIGN CENTRAL BANKS

In contrast to the Federal Reserve System, which is decentralized into 12 district banks, central banks in other industrialized countries consist of one centralized unit. As in the United States, most heads of foreign central banks (with the title of president or governor rather than chairman of the board, as in the United States) are appointed by the government. Canada provides an interesting exception, in that its central bank's governor is appointed by the governing board of the bank. The governing boards of foreign central banks (including Canada's) are usually appointed by the government, as is the case in the United States, but their terms are typically quite a bit shorter than the 14-year stint in the United States; they average around five years. The size of the governing boards, excluding the governor, vice governor, and government representatives, varies; for most countries, it ranges from 3 to 15, but Switzerland has a board of 40 members.

Many central banks do not have as much independence as the Fed. Representatives of the government attend meetings or are members of the governing board of foreign central banks; this is not the case for the Fed. In countries such as Japan and France, representatives of the Ministry of Finance have the right to advise the governing board. Furthermore, many foreign central banks are required to provide credit facilities that enable the government to borrow from them, which is not the case for the Fed.

The most independent central banks in the industrialized world are in Germany, Switzerland, Canada, the Netherlands, and the United States; the least independent are in Portugal, Greece, and Spain. Proposals for a European central bank envision it as being highly independent.

firm's behavior is motivated by the maximization of profits. The welfare of a bureaucracy is related to its power and prestige. Thus this theory suggests that an important factor affecting the Fed's behavior is its attempt to increase its power and prestige.

What predictions does this view of the Fed's behavior suggest? One is that the Federal Reserve will fight vigorously to preserve its autonomy, a prediction verified time and time again as the Fed has continually counterattacked congressional attempts to control its budget. In fact, it is extraordinary how effectively the Fed has been able to mobilize a lobby of bankers and businesspeople to preserve its independence when threatened.

Another prediction is that the Federal Reserve will try to avoid conflict with powerful groups that may threaten to curtail its power and reduce its autonomy.

The Fed's behavior may take several forms. To avoid a conflict with the president and Congress over increases in interest rates, the Fed often tries to prevent the increases. The desire to avoid conflict with Congress and the president may also explain why the Fed (particularly the chairman of the Board of Governors) has become so expert at avoiding blame for its past mistakes and why Fed officials have devised clever stratagems to obscure what they have been doing in the past and what they plan to do in the future (see Box 2).

Box 2

GAMES THE FED PLAYS

As the theory of bureaucratic behavior predicts, the Fed may play games to obscure its actions in order to avoid congressional interference in its activities. In 1975, Congress passed House Concurrent Resolution 133, which instructed the Fed to report quarterly to the banking committees of the House and the Senate its target ranges for the growth in the monetary aggregates over the next 12 months and how successful it had been in achieving its previous targets. One game that the Fed played was to report on several monetary aggregates (such as $M1$, $M2$, and $M3$) rather than on one: When the Fed testified to Congress on its success in achieving its past targets, it would focus on the particular monetary aggregate whose growth rate was closest to the target range.

In addition to this clever tactic, the Fed devised a procedure for setting its target for monetary aggregates (called *base drift*) that made it more likely that it would hit its targets, thereby avoiding conflict with Congress. Every quarter the Fed would revise the target values for monetary aggregates by applying target growth rates to the amount at which the aggregate had *ended up* (a new base). When the Fed overshot its targets, as frequently occurred after 1975, it revised future target values upward, making it less likely that the monetary aggregates would exceed target ranges in the future. Similarly, if the Fed undershot its targets, it revised future target values downward, making it less likely that the monetary aggregates would fall below the target ranges in the future. Subsequent legislation now restricts the Fed to changing the base for its target ranges only once a year, reducing the extent of base drift.

Another indication that the Fed actively wants to obscure its actions is its desire for secrecy, as reflected in the active defense of its continual delay in releasing FOMC directives to Congress or to the public. A former Fed official has stated that "a lot of staffers would concede that [secrecy] is designed to shield the Fed from political oversight."*

*"Monetary Zeal: How Federal Reserve Under Volcker Finally Slowed Down Inflation," *Wall Street Journal,* December 7, 1984, p. 23. The official also stated that this was not a bad thing because "most politicians have a shorter time horizon than is optimal for monetary policy."

The desire of the Fed to hold as much power as possible also explains why it vigorously pursued a campaign to gain control over more banks. The campaign culminated in legislation that expanded jurisdiction of the Fed's reserve requirements to *all* banks (not just the member commercial banks) by 1987.

The theory of bureaucratic behavior seems applicable to the Federal Reserve's actions, but we must recognize that this view of the Fed as being solely concerned with its own self-interest is too extreme. Maximizing one's welfare does not rule out altruism. (You might give generously to the Salvation Army because it makes you feel good about yourself, but in the process you *are* helping a worthy cause.) The Fed is surely concerned that it conduct monetary policy on behalf of the public interest. However, much uncertainty and disagreement exist over what monetary policy should be.[4] When it is unclear what is in the public interest, other motives may influence the Fed's behavior. In these situations, the theory of bureaucratic behavior may be a useful guide to predicting what motivates the Fed.

SHOULD THE FED BE INDEPENDENT?

As we have seen, the Federal Reserve is probably the most independent government agency in the United States. Every few years, the question arises in Congress as to whether the independence of the Fed should be curtailed. Politicians who strongly oppose a Fed policy often want to bring it under their supervision in order to change the policy more to their liking. Should the Fed be independent, or would we be better off with a central bank under the control of the president or Congress?

The Case for Independence

The strongest argument for an independent Federal Reserve rests on the view that subjecting the Fed to more political pressures would impart an inflationary bias to monetary policy. In the view of many observers, politicians in a democatic society are shortsighted because they are driven by the need to win their next election. With this as the primary goal, they are unlikely to focus on long-run objectives, such as promoting a stable price level. Instead, they will seek short-run solutions to problems, like high unemployment and high interest rates, even if the short-run solutions have undesirable long-run consequences. For example, we saw in Chapter 6 that high money growth might lead initially to a

---

[4]One example of the uncertainty over how best to conduct monetary policy was discussed in Chapter 3: Economists are not sure how to measure money. So even if economists agreed that controlling the quantity of money is the appropriate way to conduct monetary policy (a controversial position, as we will see in later chapters), the Fed cannot be sure which monetary aggregate it should control.

drop in interest rates but might cause an increase later as inflation heats up. Would a Federal Reserve under the control of Congress or the president be more likely to pursue a policy of excessive money growth when interest rates are high, even though it would eventually lead to inflation and even higher interest rates in the future? The advocates of an independent Federal Reserve say yes. They believe that a politically insulated Fed is more likely to be concerned with long-run objectives and thus be a defender of a sound dollar and a stable price level. Evidence supporting this view is found in Box 3.

A variation on the preceding argument is that the political process in America leads to the so-called **political business cycle,** in which just before an election, expansionary policies are pursued to lower unemployment and interest rates. After the election, the bad effects of these policies—high inflation and high interest rates—come home to roost, requiring contractionary policies that politicians hope the public will forget before the next election. There is some evidence that such a political business cycle exists in the United States, and a Federal Reserve under the control of Congress or the president might make the cycle even more pronounced.

Putting the Fed under the control of the president (making it more subject to influence by the Treasury) is also considered dangerous because the Fed can be used to facilitate Treasury financing of large budget deficits by its purchases of Treasury bonds.[5] As we saw in Chapter 16, the Fed's purchase of Treasury bonds leads to an expansion in the monetary base and hence in the money supply. Treasury pressure on the Fed to "help out" might lead to a more inflationary bias in the economy. An independent Fed is better able to resist this pressure from the Treasury.

Another argument for Fed independence is that control of monetary policy is too important to leave to politicians, a group that has repeatedly demonstrated a lack of expertise at making hard decisions on issues of great economic importance, such as reducing the budget deficit or reforming the banking system.[6] Indeed, some politicians may prefer to have an independent Fed, which can be used as a public "whipping boy" to take some of the heat off their shoulders. It is possible that a politician who in private opposes an inflationary monetary policy will be forced to support such a policy in public for fear of not being reelected. An independent Fed can pursue policies that are politically unpopular yet in the public interest.

---

[5] The Federal Reserve Act prohibited the Fed from buying Treasury bonds directly from the Treasury (except to roll over maturing securities); instead the Fed buys Treasury bonds on the open market. One possible reason for this prohibition is consistent with the foregoing argument: The Fed would find it harder to facilitate Treasury financing of large budget deficits.

[6] Another way to state this argument is in terms of the principal-agent problem discussed in Chapters 9 and 13. Both the Federal Reserve and politicians are agents of the public (the principals), and as we have seen, both politicians and the Fed have incentives to act in their own interest rather than in the interest of the public. The argument supporting Federal Reserve independence is that the principal-agent problem is worse for politicians than for the Fed because politicians have fewer incentives to act in the public interest.

A Global Perspective

CENTRAL BANK INDEPENDENCE AND MACROECONOMIC PERFORMANCE IN SEVENTEEN COUNTRIES

Advocates of an independent central bank believe that macroeconomic performance will be improved by making the central bank more independent. Recent research seems to support this conjecture: When central banks are ranked from 1 (least independent) to 4 (most independent), the inflation performance is found to be the best for countries with the most independent central banks.* As you can see in the bar graph, Germany and Switzerland, with the two most independent central banks, are also the countries with the lowest inflation rates in the 1973–1988 period. By contrast, the countries with the highest inflation—Spain, New Zealand, Australia, and Italy—are also the countries with the least independent central banks. Although a more independent central bank appears to lead to a lower inflation rate, this is not achieved at the expense of poorer real economic performance. Countries with independent central banks are not more likely to have high unemployment or greater output fluctuations than countries with less independent central banks.

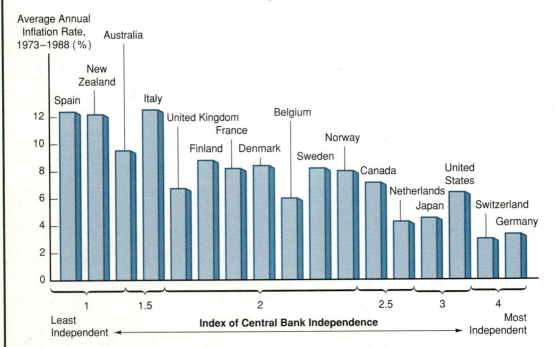

*Alberto Alesina and Lawrence H. Summers, "Central Bank Independence and Macroeconomic Performance: Some Comparative Evidence," *Journal of Money, Credit and Banking* 25 (1993): 151–162.

The Case Against Independence

Proponents of a Fed under the control of the president or Congress argue that it is undemocratic to have monetary policy (which affects almost everyone in the economy) controlled by an elite group responsible to no one. The current lack of accountability of the Federal Reserve has serious consequences: If the Fed performs badly, there is no provision for replacing members (as there is with politicians). True, the Fed needs to pursue long-run objectives, but elected officials of Congress vote on long-run issues also (foreign policy, for example). If we push the argument further that policy is always performed better by elite groups like the Fed, we end up with such conclusions as the Joint Chiefs of Staff should determine military budgets or the IRS should set tax policies with no oversight from the president or Congress. Would you advocate this degree of independence for the Joint Chiefs or the IRS?

The public holds the president and Congress responsible for the economic well-being of the country, yet they lack control over the government agency that may well be the most important factor in determining the health of the economy. In addition, to achieve a cohesive program that will promote economic stability, monetary policy must be coordinated with fiscal policy (management of government spending and taxation). Only by placing monetary policy under the control of the politicians who also control fiscal policy can these two policies be prevented from working at cross-purposes.

Another argument against Federal Reserve independence is that an independent Fed has not always used its freedom successfully. As shown in Chapter 17, the Fed failed miserably in its stated role as lender of last resort during the Great Depression, and its independence certainly didn't prevent it from pursuing an overly expansionary monetary policy in the 1960s and 1970s that contributed to rapid inflation in this period.

Our earlier discussion also suggests that the Federal Reserve is not immune from political pressures.[7] Its independence may encourage it to pursue a course of narrow self-interest rather than the public interest.

No widespread consensus currently exists on whether Federal Reserve independence is a good thing. As you might expect, people who like the Fed's policies support its independence, while those who dislike its policies advocate a less independent Fed.

---

[7]For evidence on this issue, see Robert E. Weintraub, "Congressional Supervision of Monetary Policy," *Journal of Monetary Economics* 4 (1978): 341–362. Some economists suggest that lessening the independence of the Fed might even reduce the incentive for politically motivated monetary policy; see Milton Friedman, "Monetary Policy: Theory and Practice," *Journal of Money, Credit and Banking* 14 (1982): 98–118.

SUMMARY

1. The Federal Reserve System was created in 1913 to lessen the frequency of bank panics. Because of public hostility to central banks and the centralization of power, the Federal Reserve System was created with many checks and balances to diffuse power.
2. The formal structure of the Federal Reserve System consists of 12 regional Federal Reserve banks, around 4000 member commercial banks, the Board of Governors of the Federal Reserve System, the Federal Open Market Committee, and the Federal Advisory Council.
3. Although on paper the Federal Reserve System appears to be decentralized, in practice it has come to function as a unified central bank controlled by the Board of Governors, especially the board's chairman.
4. The Federal Reserve is more independent than most agencies of the U.S. government, but it is still subject to political pressures because the legislation that structures the Fed is written by Congress and can be changed at any time. The theory of bureaucratic behavior indicates that one factor driving the Fed's behavior is its attempt to increase its power and prestige. This view explains many of the Fed's actions, although it may also try to act in the public interest.

5. The case for an independent Federal Reserve rests on the view that curtailing the Fed's independence and subjecting it to more political pressures would impart an inflationary bias to monetary policy. An independent Fed can afford to take the long view and not respond to short-run problems that will result in expansionary monetary policy and a political business cycle. The case against an independent Fed holds that it is undemocratic to have monetary policy (so important to the public) controlled by an elite that is not accountable to the public. An independent Fed also makes the coordination of monetary and fiscal policy difficult, and in any case it is by no means clear that the Fed has used its independence wisely: The Fed may be no less shortsighted than politicians and may still pursue its own narrow self-interest.

KEY TERMS

Federal Reserve banks

Board of Governors of the Federal Reserve System

Federal Open Market Committee (FOMC)

political business cycle

QUESTIONS AND PROBLEMS

*1. Why was the Federal Reserve System set up with 12 regional Federal Reserve Banks rather than one central bank, as in other countries?
2. What political realities might explain why the Federal Reserve Act of 1913 placed two Federal Reserve banks in Missouri?
*3. "The Federal Reserve System resembles the U.S. Constitution in that it was designed with many checks and balances." Discuss.
4. In what ways can the regional Federal Reserve banks influence the conduct of monetary policy?

*5. Which entities in the Federal Reserve System control the discount rate? Reserve requirements? Open market operations?
6. Do you think that the 14-year nonrenewable terms for governors effectively insulate the Board of Governors from political pressure?
*7. Over time, which entities have gained power in the Federal Reserve System and which have lost power? Why do you think this has happened?
8. The Fed is the most independent of all government agencies. What is the main difference be-

tween it and other government agencies that explains its greater independence?

*9. What is the primary tool that Congress uses to exercise some control over the Fed?

10. In the 1960s and 1970s, the Federal Reserve System lost member banks at a rapid rate. How can the theory of bureaucratic behavior explain the Fed's campaign for legislation to require all commercial banks to become members? Was the Fed successful in this campaign?

*11. "The theory of bureaucratic behavior indicates that the Fed never operates in the public interest." Is this statement true, false, or uncertain? Explain.

12. Why might eliminating the Fed's independence lead to a more pronounced political business cycle?

*13. "The independence of the Fed leaves it completely unaccountable for its actions." Is this statement true, false, or uncertain? Explain.

14. "The independence of the Fed has meant that it takes the long view and not the short view." Is this statement true, false, or uncertain? Explain.

*15. The Fed promotes secrecy by not releasing FOMC directives to Congress or the public immediately. Discuss the pros and cons of this policy.

Chapter 19

UNDERSTANDING MOVEMENTS IN THE MONETARY BASE

PREVIEW Now that we have examined the structure of the Federal Reserve System, in this chapter and the next two we will look at how the Fed actually conducts monetary policy. Our analysis of the money supply process demonstrated that movements in the monetary base (also called *high-powered money*) are the main driving force behind changes in the money supply and that the Fed influences the monetary base through the policy tools of open market operations (the purchase and sale of government securities) or changes in the discount rate. Although these two policy tools are the primary determinants of the monetary base, other factors also affect it. In this chapter we examine these other factors because the Fed must take account of them if it is to exercise accurate control over the money supply.

THE FED'S BALANCE SHEET AND THE MONETARY BASE

We first examine the balance sheet of the Federal Reserve System because it can be used to identify factors that affect the monetary base.

Assets

1. Securities. These are the Fed's holdings of securities, which consist primarily of Treasury securities but in the past have also included banker's acceptances. The total amount of securities is controlled by open market operations (the Fed's purchase and sale of these securities). As shown in Table 1, it is by far the largest category of assets in the Fed's balance sheet.

2. Discount loans. These are loans the Fed makes to banks, and the amount is affected by the Fed's setting of the interest rate on these loans (the discount rate).

TABLE 1 Consolidated Balance Sheet of the Federal Reserve System ($ billions, end of 1993)

Assets		Liabilities	
Securities: U.S. government and agency securities and banker's acceptances	344.2	Federal Reserve notes outstanding	343.9
Discount loans	0.9	Bank deposits	35.0
Gold and SDR certificate accounts	19.1	U.S. Treasury deposits	14.8
Coin	0.4	Foreign and other deposits	0.8
Cash items in process of collection	6.5	Deferred-availability cash items	5.5
Other Federal Reserve assets	38.2	Other Federal Reserve liabilities and capital accounts	9.3
Total	409.3	Total	409.3

Source: Federal Reserve *Bulletin*.

3. *Gold and SDR certificate accounts.* Special drawing rights (SDRs) are issued to governments by the International Monetary Fund (IMF) to settle international debts and have replaced gold in international financial transactions. When the Treasury acquires gold or SDRs, it issues certificates to the Fed that are claims on the gold or SDRs and is in turn credited with deposit balances at the Fed. The gold and SDR accounts are made up of these certificates issued by the Treasury.

4. *Coin.* This is the smallest item in the balance sheet, and it consists of Treasury currency (mostly coins) held by the Fed.

5. *Cash items in process of collection.* These arise from the Fed's check-clearing process described in Chapter 11. When a check is given to the Fed for clearing, the Fed will present it to the bank on which it is written and will collect funds by deducting the amount of the check from the bank's deposits (reserves) with the Fed. Before these funds are collected, the check is a cash item in process of collection and is a Fed asset.

6. *Other Federal Reserve assets.* These include deposits and bonds denominated in foreign currencies as well as physical goods such as computers, office equipment, and buildings owned by the Federal Reserve.

Liabilities

1. *Federal Reserve notes outstanding.* These are the Federal Reserve notes (currency) issued by the Fed.

2. *Bank deposits.* These are the deposits that banks have made at the Fed. These deposits plus vault cash at the banks equal reserves.

3. *U.S. Treasury deposits.* These are deposits that the Treasury keeps at the Fed, which it uses to write all its checks.

4. *Foreign and other deposits.* These include the deposits with the Fed owned by foreign governments, foreign central banks, international agencies (such as the World Bank and the United Nations), and U.S. government agencies (such as the FDIC and Federal Home Loan banks).

5. *Deferred-availability cash items.* Like cash items in process of collection, these also arise from the Fed's check-clearing process. When a check is submitted for clearing, the Fed does not immediately credit the bank that submitted the check. Instead, it promises to credit the bank within a certain prearranged time limit, which never exceeds two days. These promises are the deferred availability items and are a liability of the Fed.

6. *Other Federal Reserve liabilities and capital accounts.* This item includes all the remaining Federal Reserve liabilities not included elsewhere on the balance sheet. For example, stock in the Federal Reserve System purchased by member banks is included here.

Monetary Base

As you may recall, the monetary base *MB* consists of the monetary liabilities (currency in circulation *C* plus reserves *R*), which equal Federal Reserve notes outstanding, plus bank deposits with the Fed and Treasury currency not held at the Fed (Treasury currency outstanding minus the "Coin" asset in the Fed's balance sheet):[1]

$$MB = C + R + \text{Federal Reserve notes} + \text{bank deposits}$$
$$+ \text{Treasury currency outstanding} - \text{coin}$$

The items on the right-hand side of this equation indicate how the base is used and are called the **uses of the base.** Unfortunately, this equation does not tell us the factors that determine the base (the **sources of the base**), but the Federal Reserve balance sheet in Table 1 comes to the rescue because like all balance sheets, it has the property that the total assets on the left-hand side must equal the total liabilities on the right-hand side. Because the "Federal Reserve notes" and "bank deposits" items in the uses of the base are Federal Reserve liabilities, the "assets equals liabilities" property of the Fed balance sheet enables us to solve for these items in terms of the Fed balance sheet items that are included in the sources of the base: Specifically, Federal Reserve notes and bank deposits equal the sum of all the Fed assets minus all the other Fed liabilities:

---

[1]In the member bank reserves data that the Fed publishes every week, Treasury currency outstanding is actually defined to include Treasury currency that is held at the Treasury (called "Treasury cash holdings"). What we have defined as "Treasury currency outstanding" is actually equal to the Fed's definition of "Treasury currency outstanding" minus "Treasury cash holdings."

Federal Reserve notes + bank deposits = securities + discount loans + gold and SDRs + coin + cash items in process of collection + other Federal Reserve assets − Treasury deposits − foreign and other deposits − deferred-availability cash items − other Federal Reserve liabilities

The two balance sheet items related to check clearing can be collected into one term called **float,** defined as "cash items in process of collection" minus "deferred-availability cash items." Then, substituting all the right-hand-side items in the equation for "Federal Reserve notes + bank deposits" in the uses-of-the-base equation, we obtain the following expression describing the sources of the monetary base:

MB = securities + discount loans + gold and SDRs + float + other Federal Reserve assets + Treasury currency oustanding − Treasury deposits − foreign and other deposits − other Federal Reserve liabilities   (1)

Accounting logic has led us to a useful equation that clearly identifies the nine factors affecting the monetary base listed in Table 2. As Equation 1 and Table 2 depict, increases in the first six factors increases the monetary base, and increases in the last three reduce the monetary base.[2]

Now that we have identified these nine factors and their effect on the monetary base, let's look more carefully at *why* they affect the monetary base. To do this, we will go on playing accountant and make use of T-accounts.

STUDY GUIDE

It is not hard to understand how each of the following factors affects the monetary base if you work through the effects of a particular transaction on the T-acount of each individual or institution in the transaction. Having done this, you will know what has happened to reserves or to currency and can then see what has happened to the monetary base. To test your understanding, work through what happens to the T-accounts when the factor falls rather than rises.

---

[2]Some bank deposits with the Fed are not included in reserves and hence in the monetary base because they are service-related deposits. These balances are included in an entry, "service-related balances and adjustments," that should be subtracted from the right-hand side of the expression describing the sources of the base in order to obtain the correct measure of the monetary base. The "service-related balances and adjustments" entry ($6.9 billion at the end of 1993) is ignored in the expression in the text.

SUMMARY

TABLE 2 Factors Affecting the Monetary Base

Factor	Value ($ billions, end of 1993)	Change in Factor	Change in Monetary Base
Factors That Increase the Monetary Base			
1. Securities: U.S. government and agency securities and banker's acceptances	344.2	↑	↑
2. Discount loans	0.9	↑	↑
3. Gold and SDR certificate accounts	19.1	↑	↑
4. Float	1.0	↑	↑
5. Other Federal Reserve assets	38.2	↑	↑
6. Treasury currency outstanding	22.0	↑	↑
Subtotal 1	425.4		
Factors That Decrease the Monetary Base			
7. Treasury deposits with the Fed	14.8	↑	↓
8. Foreign and other deposits with the Fed	0.8	↑	↓
9. Other Federal Reserve liabilities and capital accounts	9.3	↑	↓
Subtotal 2	24.9		
Monetary Base			
Subtotal 1 − Subtotal 2	400.5		

Source: Federal Reserve *Bulletin.*

FACTORS THAT AFFECT THE MONETARY BASE

As we examine the effect of changes in each factor on the monetary base, we assume that there are no changes elsewhere in the Fed's balance sheet. Let us look first at the factors whose increase adds to the monetary base.

Factors That Increase the Monetary Base

Securities and Discount Loans We have already described in detail in Chapters 15 and 16 how changes in discount loans and the Fed's holding of securities via open market operations affect the monetary base, so we will simply restate our conclusions here: ***An increase in the Fed's holding of securities or in discount***

loans leads to an equal increase in the monetary base (as shown in Table 2).

Gold and SDR Accounts and Other Federal Reserve Assets   A Fed purchase of gold, SDRs, deposits denominated in a foreign currency, or any other asset is just an open market purchase of these assets. Thus the effect on the monetary base is the same as an open market purchase of bonds (as Box 1 demonstrates). *An increase in gold and SDR accounts or in other Federal Reserve assets leads to an equal increase in the monetary base.*

Float   As shown in Chapter 11, the Federal Reserve's check-clearing process involves the deposit of a check received by a bank into its Fed account, the crediting of the amount of its check to its reserves, and an equal debit to the reserves of the bank on which the check is drawn. We might assume that these transactions occur simultaneously and immediately, but in reality the Fed frequently credits the amount of a check to a bank that has deposited it (increases the bank's reserves) before it debits (decreases the reserves of) the bank on which

---

A Global Perspective

Box 1

FOREIGN EXCHANGE RATE INTERVENTION AND THE MONETARY BASE

It is common to read in the newspaper about a Federal Reserve intervention in the foreign exchange market to buy or sell dollars. Can this also be a factor that affects the monetary base? The answer is yes because a Federal Reserve intervention in the foreign exchange market involves a purchase or sale of assets denominated in a foreign currency, which is included in the "Other Federal Reserve assets" category in the Fed's balance sheet.

Suppose that the Fed purchases $10 million of deposits denominated in French francs in exchange for $10 million of dollar deposits at the Fed (a sale of dollars for francs). As discussed in the text, a Federal Reserve purchase of any asset, whether it be a U.S. government bond or a deposit denominated in a foreign currency, is just an open market purchase and so leads to an equal rise in the monetary base. Hence the purchase of the $10 million in franc deposits leads to a $10 million increase in "Other Federal Reserve assets" and a $10 million increase in the monetary base. Similarly, a sale of foreign currency deposits leads to a decline in "Other Federal Reserve assets" and a decline in the monetary base. Federal Reserve interventions in the foreign exchange market are thus an important influence on the monetary base, a topic that we discuss further in Chapter 22.

the check is drawn.[3] The resulting net increase in the total amount of reserves in the banking system is called *float,* and it equals the difference between the asset "Cash items in process of collection" (checks on which the Fed has not yet collected payment) and the liability "Deferred-availability cash items" (checks that have not yet been credited to the bank depositing them).

Float occurs because sometimes the Fed cannot present checks for payment as fast as it credits the bank depositing the check; float fluctuates when weather conditions and other factors cause delays in presenting checks for payment. For example, if a severe snowstorm hits New York City, the Fed will not be able to move some checks that it wants to present for payment, and float will rise sharply. When the weather clears, the checks will be presented for payment, and float will fall back down again.[4]

To understand the concept better, let's return to our example from Chapter 11 in which Jane Brown takes a $100 check written on an account at the Second National Bank (in Los Angeles) and deposits it in her account at the First National Bank (in New York City). The First National Bank takes the check to the Fed for clearing, with the following effect on the Fed balance sheet:

Federal Reserve System			
Assets		Liabilities	
Cash items in process of collection	+ $100	Deferred-availability cash items	+ $100

The $100 of deferred-availability cash items is the liability incurred by the Fed when it accepts the checks from the First National Bank because it promises to credit the First National Bank with $100 of deposits within a certain prearranged time limit (never exceeding two days). The $100 of cash items in process of collection is a Fed asset because the Fed will deduct this amount from the Second National Bank's deposits when it presents the check to the Second National Bank for payment.

At this point, reserves have not changed anywhere in the banking system, and because cash items in process of collection equal deferred-availability cash items, their difference—equal to float—is also unchanged. Because of possible delays due to bad weather conditions, the Fed may not be able to move the

---

[3]Many people take advantage of the fact that it takes time for a check they have written to be debited from their account: They write a check on Friday for money they don't have, thinking it won't clear till Tuesday after they have gone to the bank and deposited the necessary funds. This is called *taking advantage of the float.*

[4]Note that although float is usually positive, occasionally it turns negative. This occurs if the Fed has been able to present checks for payment faster than it has credited the banks depositing the checks.

check to Los Angeles before the prearranged time limit is up. However, it still dutifully does as it promised and credits the First National Bank with $100 of deposits (reserves) and cancels out its liability of $100 of deferred-availability cash items. The Fed's T-account now becomes

Federal Reserve System		
Assets	Liabilities	
Cash items in process of collection + $100	Reserves (of First National Bank) + $100	

Float, the difference between cash items in process of collection ($100) and deferred-availability cash items ($0), is now +$100, and reserves in the banking system have also increased by this same amount. What has happened is that the Fed has not yet been able to collect what is owed by the Second National Bank but has credited the First National Bank anyway. The result is that, in effect, the Fed has extended the First National Bank an interest-free loan equal to the amount of the float, thus raising reserves and hence the monetary base.

This "loan" will be only temporary, however, because when the Fed finally gets the check to Los Angeles and presents it to the Second National Bank, it deducts $100 from the Second National Bank's deposits (reserves) and cancels out the $100 of cash items in process of collection. The Fed's T-account ends up as follows:

Federal Reserve System		
Assets	Liabilities	
	Reserves (of First National Bank) + $100	
	Reserves (of Second National Bank) − $100	

The end result of the check-clearing process is that total reserves in the banking system have not changed, even though reserves have moved from one bank to another. In the process of clearing the Second National Bank's check, however, reserves and the monetary base have been *temporarily increased*. If you multiply these temporary increases in the monetary base by the millions of checks cleared each day, it can lead to sizable week-to-week fluctuations in the monetary base. Yet since most fluctuations in float are temporary, they are not a major source of fluctuations in the monetary base over longer periods of time (such as a month or three months).

Our conclusion from the manipulations of these T-accounts is consistent with Table 2: *An increase in float leads to an equal increase in the monetary base.*

Treasury Currency Outstanding   Although this term is not on the Federal Reserve's balance sheet, it has an effect on the monetary base. An increase in Treasury currency outside the Treasury finds its way either into bank vaults (where it counts as reserves) or into the hands of the public (where it counts as currency in circulation). Thus, as Table 2 indicates, ***the monetary base rises when there is an increase in Treasury currency outstanding.***[5]

Factors That Decrease the Monetary Base

Treasury Deposits with the Fed The funds that the Treasury gets from tax payments and the proceeds from the sale of government bonds are initially held in accounts at commercial banks called *tax and loan accounts* and are then deposited in accounts with the Fed used by the Treasury to write all its checks. Suppose that the Treasury intends to pay for a $100 million supercomputer, and it transfers $100 million from its tax and loan accounts to its account with the Fed, resulting in the following T-account:

U.S. Treasury		
Assets		Liabilities
Deposits in commercial banks	− $100 million	
Deposits with the Fed	+ $100 million	

The commercial banks now find that they have lost $100 million in deposits and hence $100 million in reserves, so their T-account looks like this:

Commercial Banks		
Assets		Liabilities
Reserves	− $100 million	U.S. Treasury deposits − $100 million

For the Fed, reserves decrease by $100 million and Treasury deposits increase by $100 million:

Federal Reserve System		
Assets		Liabilities
		Reserves − $100 million
		U.S. Treasury deposits + $100 million

---

[5]Although an increase in Treasury currency outstanding will increase the monetary base *if all other balance sheet items are held constant,* most increases in Treasury currency are accompanied by offsetting changes in other balance sheet items so that the monetary base remains unchanged. For example, if the public uses more coins because of a video game craze, the Treasury has more coins minted, which it sends to the Fed, and in exchange the Fed credits the dollar amount of the coins to Treasury deposits at the Fed. When these coins are distributed to the public, Treasury currency outstanding has increased, but Treasury deposits have increased by an equal amount. The net result, then, is that the monetary base will remain unchanged (the increase from higher Treasury currency outstanding is exactly offset by the decrease from higher Treasury deposits). We thus see that a change in the public's preference for Treasury currency (mostly coins) relative to Federal Reserve notes (paper currency) will have no effect on the monetary base.

Consequently, *an increase in U.S. Treasury deposits reduces reserves and the monetary base* (as shown in Table 2).

When the Treasury pays for the supercomputer, the process is reversed. U.S. Treasury deposits with the Fed fall by $100 million, and the computer maker deposits the check received from the Treasury in its bank, whose reserves rise by $100 million. The T-account for the Federal Reserve is now

Federal Reserve System		
Assets	Liabilities	
	Reserves	+ $100 million
	U.S. Treasury deposits	− $100 million

We again see that the monetary base moves in a direction opposite that of Treasury deposits with the Federal Reserve.

Because Treasury purchases and receipts change dramatically during the course of a year, Treasury deposits with the Fed experience large swings and consequently can be an important source of weekly fluctuations in the monetary base. Fluctuations are fairly predictable, though, because the Treasury usually knows in advance when it plans to move funds from its tax and loan accounts into its accounts with the Fed. In addition, because most of the variations in Treasury deposits are temporary, they are not a major source of fluctuations in the monetary base over longer periods of time (such as three months or a year).

Foreign and Other Deposits with the Fed When these deposits rise, either because funds from accounts at commercial banks are transferred into accounts with the Fed or because checks written on U.S. banks are being deposited, the T-accounts are identical to the one described for Treasury deposits with the Fed. Therefore, *an increase in foreign and other deposits leads to a decline in the monetary base.*

Other Liabilities and Capital Accounts Suppose that a bank has just joined the Federal Reserve System and buys the required amount of stock in it, raising the capital accounts with the Fed. Its deposits with the Fed will be reduced by the dollar value of the stock, and reserves in the banking system will decline by this amount. Therefore, *an increase in other liabilities and capital leads to a decline in the monetary base.*

Summary

Our analysis of the Fed's balance sheet identifies nine factors that affect the monetary base. Increases in six factors increase the monetary base (the Fed's holdings of securities, discount loans, gold and SDR accounts, float, other Federal Reserve assets, and Treasury currency outstanding), and increases in three factors reduce the monetary base (Treasury deposits with the Fed, foreign and other deposits with the Fed, and other Federal Reserve liabilities and capital accounts).

The factor that most affects the monetary base is the Fed's holdings of securities, which are completely controlled by the Fed through its open market operations. Factors not controlled by the Fed (for example, float and Treasury deposits with the Fed) undergo substantial short-run variations and can be important sources of fluctuations in the monetary base over time periods as short as a week. However, these fluctuations are usually quite predictable and so can be offset through open market operations. ***Although float and Treasury deposits with the Fed undergo substantial short-run fluctuation, which complicates control of the monetary base, they do not prevent the Fed from accurately controlling it.***

THE BUDGET DEFICIT AND THE MONETARY BASE

Although we now understand what factors affect the monetary base directly, another important factor affects it indirectly: government budget deficits. To see why budget deficits can matter to the monetary base, we must look at how spending by the government is financed.

The Government Budget Constraint

Because the government has to pay its bills just as we do, it has a budget constraint. There are two ways we can pay for our spending: raise revenue (by working) or borrow. The government also enjoys these two options: raise revenue by levying taxes or go into debt by issuing government bonds. Unlike us, however, it has a third option: The government can create money and use it to pay for the goods and services it buys.

Methods of financing government spending are described by an expression called the **government budget constraint,** which states the following: The government budget deficit *DEF,* which equals the excess of government spending *G* over tax revenue *T,* must equal the sum of the change in the monetary base ΔMB and the change in government bonds held by the public ΔB. Algebraically, this expression can be written as

$$DEF = G - T = \Delta MB + \Delta B \qquad (2)$$

To see what the government budget constraint means in practice, let's look at the case in which the only government purchase is a $100 million supercomputer. If the government convinces the electorate that such a computer is worth paying for, it will probably be able to raise the $100 million of taxes to pay for it, and the budget deficit will equal zero. The government budget constraint then tells us that no issue of money or bonds is needed to pay for the computer because the budget is balanced. If taxpayers think that supercomputers are too expensive and refuse to pay taxes for them, the budget constraint indicates that the government must pay for it by selling $100 million of new bonds to the public or by printing $100 million of currency to pay for the computer. In either case, the budget constraint is satisfied; the $100 million deficit is balanced by the change in the stock of government bonds held by the public (ΔB = $100 million) or by the change in the monetary base (ΔMB = $100 million). A combination of all three methods of financing can be used to pay for spending. The $100 million supercomputer could be financed, for example, by raising $50 million in taxes, printing $25 million of currency, and selling $25 million of bonds.

FOLLOWING THE FINANCIAL NEWS

Reserves and Sources of Change in the Monetary Base

Data for bank reserves and the sources of changes in the monetary base (which are the same as the sources of changes in reserves) are published every Friday or Monday. In the *Wall Street Journal* they are found in the "Federal Reserve Data" column, an example of which appears here.

"Member Bank Reserve Changes" shows the sources of changes in bank reserves (the sources of changes in the monetary base described in the chapter). Float, for example, averaged $323 million for the week ending March 16, 1994, and changed –$1085 million from the week ending March 9, 1994, and –$1895 million from the week ending March 17, 1993 (one year earlier).

"Reserve Aggregates" provides data on different measures of reserves and the monetary base. For example, the monetary base averaged $396,233 million for the two weeks ended March 16, 1994, and $394,891 million for the two weeks ended March 2.

Source: Wall Street Journal, March 18, 1994, p. C17.

FEDERAL RESERVE DATA

MEMBER BANK RESERVE CHANGES

Changes in weekly averages of reserves and related items during the week and year ended March 16, 1994 were as follows (in millions of dollars)

	Mar. 16, 1994	Chg fm wk end Mar. 9, 1994	Mar. 17, 1993
Reserve bank credit:			
U.S. Gov't securities:			
Bought outright	334,014	+ 169	+35,342
Held under repurch agreemt	4,494	+ 1,855	+ 2,866
Federal agency issues:			
Bought outright	4,237	....	– 928
Held under repurch agreemt	291	+ 54	+ 255
Acceptances			
Borrowings from Fed:			
Adjustment credit	35	+ 26	– 102
Seasonal borrowings	18	+ 3	– 7
Extended credit	....	....	....
Float	323	– 1,085	– 1,895
Other Federal Reserve Assets	32,266	+ 303	+ 2,218
Total Reserve Bank Credit	375,679	+ 1,325	+37,749
Gold Stock	11,053	....	– 2
SDR certificates	8,018	....	....
Treasury currency			
outstanding	22,244	+ 14	+ 691
Total	416,994	+ 1,339	+38,438
Currency in circulation	366,638	+ 843	+34,749
Treasury cash holdings	378	+ 3	– 133
Treasury dpts with F.R. Bnks	5,463	+ 241	– 100
Foreign dpts with F.R. Bnks	171	– 22	– 204
Other dpts with F.R. Bnks	354	– 9	+ 10
Service related balances, adj	6,744	+ 355	+ 439
Other F.R. liabilities			
& capital	10,015	– 152	+ 922
Total	389,762	+ 1,259	+35,682

RESERVE AGGREGATES
(daily average in millions)

	Two weeks ended:	
	Mar. 16	Mar. 2
Total Reserves (sa)	60,658	60,736
Nonborrowed Reserves (sa)	60,619	60,691
Required Reserves (sa)	59,521	59,588
Excess Reserves (nsa)	1,137	1,148
Borrowings from Fed (nsa)-a	39	45
Free Reserves (nsa)	1,098	1,103
Monetary Base (sa)	396,233	394,891

a-Excluding extended credit. nsa-Not seasonally adjusted. sa-Seasonally adjusted.

Financing Government Spending

Now that you recognize the three methods for financing government spending, you need to know the effect of each method on the monetary base, holding everything else constant. Therefore, we will use T-accounts to examine the mechanics of using each method to pay for the government purchase of the supercomputer.

Tax Financing Suppose that when the government levies $100 million of taxes to pay for the computer, the public sends the Treasury $100 million of checks. After the Treasury receives its tax payment checks from the public, it deposits them into its tax and loan accounts and then transfers them to its account with the Fed. The result is that $100 million of deposits have left the banking system, reducing reserves by $100 million, and the Treasury finds itself with $100 million of deposits with the Fed. The T-accounts of the nonbank public, the Treasury, the banking system, and the Fed are as follows:

Nonbank Public		U.S. Treasury	
Assets	Liabilities	Assets	Liabilities
Deposits at banks − $100 million	Taxes due − $100 million	Deposits with Fed + $100 million Taxes due − $100 million	

Banking System		Federal Reserve System	
Assets	Liabilities	Assets	Liabilities
Reserves − $100 million	Deposits − $100 million		Reserves − $100 million Treasury deposits + $100 million

When the Treasury pays for the supercomputer, it writes a check for $100 million and gives it to the public (the computer maker), who then deposits it in a bank. The overall balance sheet changes for the four groups are then

Nonbank Public		U.S. Treasury	
Assets	Liabilities	Assets	Liabilities
Deposits at banks 0 Computer − $100 million	Taxes due − $100 million	Deposits with Fed 0 Taxes due − $100 million Computer + $100 million	

Banking System		Federal Reserve System	
Assets	Liabilities	Assets	Liabilities
Reserves 0	Deposits 0		Reserves 0 Treasury deposits 0

Because the net effect of these transactions is that the monetary base is unaffected, we can conclude that *financing government spending with taxes has no effect on the monetary base.*

Suppose (somewhat less realistically) that when the government levies $100 million of taxes to pay for the computer, the public sends the Treasury $100 million of currency rather than checks. Then the T-accounts for the Treasury and public will be as follows:

U.S. Treasury		Nonbank Public	
Assets	Liabilities	Assets	Liabilities
Currency + $100 million		Currency − $100 million	Taxes due − $100 million
Taxes due − $100 million			

The currency in the hands of the public (and hence in circulation) declines by $100 million, and the Treasury uses the $100 million to pay for the computer. The public receives back the $100 million of currency and, in exchange, gives the government the computer it ordered. The overall balance sheet changes of the Treasury and the public are as follows:

U.S. Treasury		Nonbank Public	
Assets	Liabilities	Assets	Liabilities
Currency 0		Currency 0	Taxes due − $100 million
Taxes due − $100 million		Computer − $100 million	
Computer + $100 million			

The net effect on the monetary base is the same as when checks are used to pay taxes—there is none.

Because results are the same and are easier to follow when transactions are carried out with currency, we will examine only currency transactions in the analysis of debt financing that follows.

Debt Financing (ΔB) Now suppose that the government finances its purchase of the computer by selling $100 million of bonds to the public, which in turn pays for them with $100 million of currency. The T-accounts of the Treasury and the public are as follows:

U.S. Treasury		Nonbank Public	
Assets	Liabilities	Assets	Liabilities
Currency + $100 million	Securities + $100 million	Currency − $100 million	
		Securities + $100 million	

The currency in circulation declines by $100 million, and the Treasury uses the currency to pay for the computer. The public receives back the $100 million of currency and gives the government the computer. The overall balance sheet changes for the Treasury and public then are as follows:

U.S. Treasury		Nonbank Public	
Assets	Liabilities	Assets	Liabilities
Currency 0 Computer + $100 million	Securities + $100 million	Currency 0 Securities + $100 million Computer − $100 million	

Because the net effect of these transactions is that the items in the monetary base are unaffected, we can conclude that ***the financing of government spending by issuing debt has no effect on the monetary base.***

Financing with Money Creation (ΔMB) Finally, we look at the case in which the government finances the purchase of the supercomputer by creating money. In many countries, this is a straightforward operation because the treasury has the legal right to issue currency with which it can pay for government spending. Thus, as the budget constraint indicates, this method of financing government spending leads to an increase in the monetary base (high-powered money). In the United States, the process is somewhat more complicated because the Treasury does not have the legal right to issue currency to pay for goods and services; it can only issue securities.[6] Financing government spending with money creation thus takes a more circuitous route whereby the Treasury sells bonds to the public that are then purchased by the Federal Reserve.

This method of financing government spending proceeds in two steps. First, the Treasury purchases the computer and finances it by selling $100 million of bonds to the public. As we have just seen, this results in a T-account in which the monetary base remains unchanged. Second, the Fed buys an equivalent dollar amount of bonds from the public through an open market purchase, which (as we saw earlier in the chapter) raises the monetary base by $100 million. The outcome is that the monetary base has increased by $100 million, yielding this conclusion: ***The financing of government spending through a Treasury sale of bonds that are then purchased by the Fed increases the monetary base.***

This last method of financing government spending is called **monetizing the debt** because, as the two-step process described indicates, government debt issued to finance government spending has been removed from the hands of the public and has been replaced by high-powered money. This method of financing is also, somewhat misleadingly, referred to as **printing money** because high-powered money (the monetary base) is created in the process. However,

---

[6]The Treasury does have the legal right to mint coins, but it cannot issue them to pay for goods and services. It is restricted to supplying coins to the public passively in exchange for deposits or Federal Reserve notes.

use of the word *printing* is misleading because what is essential to this method of financing government spending is not the actual printing of money but rather the issuing of monetary liabilities to the public after the money has been printed.

Summary   What does the foregoing discussion tell us about the various methods of financing the government budget deficit? When government spending is fully financed by taxes, resulting in a balanced budget, there is no effect on the monetary base. When government spending is greater than tax revenues, the resulting budget deficit can be financed by selling government bonds to the public or by creating money, which (in the United States) involves the purchase of government bonds by the Federal Reserve. The first method, debt financing, has no effect on the monetary base, whereas the second method, money creation, leads to an expansion of the monetary base (high-powered money).

DOES THE BUDGET DEFICIT INFLUENCE THE MONETARY BASE?

In some countries, the government can simply decide to print money to finance the deficit by having its treasury issue currency to pay for goods and services. This option is not open to the U.S. Treasury; a government budget deficit can lead to an expansion of the monetary base only if the Fed allows this to happen by willingly purchasing bonds issued by the Treasury to finance the deficit. Because the decision to create money to finance a deficit is not automatic but rather is up to the Fed, a natural question arises: Which method of financing is most used and why? Why do we read so much about "the deficit"?

Whether the budget deficit influences the monetary base or not depends critically on how the Federal Reserve chooses to conduct monetary policy. If the Fed pursues a policy goal of preventing high interest rates (a likely possibility, as we will see in Chapter 21), many economists contend that a budget deficit will lead to the printing of money. Their reasoning, using the supply and demand analysis of the bond market we learned in Chapter 6, is as follows: When the Treasury issues bonds to the public, the supply of bonds rises (from B_1^s to B_2^s in Figure 1), causing interest rates to rise from i_1 to i_2 and bond prices to fall. If the Fed considers the rise in interest rates undesirable, it will buy bonds to prop up bond prices and reduce interest rates. The net result is that the government budget deficit has led to Federal Reserve open market purchases, which raise the monetary base (create high-powered money).

Economists such as Robert Barro of Harvard University, however, do not agree that budget deficits influence the monetary base in the manner just described. Their analysis (which Barro named *Ricardian equivalence* after the nineteenth-century British economist David Ricardo) contends that when the government runs deficits and issues bonds, the public recognizes that it will be subject to higher taxes in the future in order to pay off these bonds. The public then saves more in anticipation of these future taxes, with the net result that the public demand for bonds increases to match the increased supply. The demand

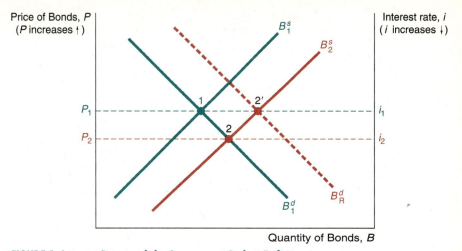

FIGURE 1   Interest Rates and the Government Budget Deficit
When the Treasury issues bonds to finance the budget deficit, the supply curve for bonds shifts rightward from B_1^s to B_2^s. Many economists take the position that the equilibrium moves to point 2 because the bond demand curve remains unchanged, with the result that the bond price falls from P_1 to P_2 and the interest rate rises from i_1 to i_2. Adherents of *Ricardian equivalence*, however, suggest that the demand curve for bonds also increases to B_R^d, moving the equilibrium to point 2', where the interest rate is unchanged at i_1. (*Note: P* and *i* increase in opposite directions. *P* on the left vertical axis increases as we go up the axis, whereas *i* on the right vertical axis increases as we go down the axis.)

curve for bonds shifts rightward to B_R^d in Figure 1, leaving the interest rate unchanged at i_1. There is now no need for the Fed to purchase bonds to keep the interest rate from rising.

The effect of budget deficits on interest rates and monetary policy is controversial, and we will return to the issue of budget deficits and their effect on the monetary base and the money supply when we look at the more general issue of budget deficits and inflation in Chapter 28. For now, the important point to remember is that budget deficits *may* lead to money creation.

SUMMARY

1. Nine factors affect the monetary base: the Fed's holdings of securities, discount loans, gold and SDR accounts, float, other Federal Reserve assets, Treasury currency outstanding, Treasury deposits with the Fed, foreign and other deposits with the Fed, and other Federal Reserve liabilities and capital accounts. Increases in the first six add to the monetary base; increases in the last three reduce the monetary base.

2. The most important of these factors is the Fed's holdings of securities, which it controls completely through its open market operations. Treasury deposits with the Fed and float (factors that cannot be controlled by the Fed) can undergo substantial short-run variations and can be important sources of fluctuations in the monetary base in time periods as short as a week. However, because changes in these factors are predictable,

they can be offset by open market operations, so they do not prevent the Fed from accurately controlling the monetary base.

3. A budget deficit can be financed by debt financing, that is, selling government debt to the public, and by money creation (printing money), which in the United States involves selling government securities to the Federal Reserve. Debt financing has no effect on the monetary base, whereas money creation leads to an expansion of the monetary base.

4. Budget deficits do not have to influence the monetary base because the decision to finance a deficit by money creation is up to the Fed. However, budget deficits *can* lead to money creation if the Fed pursues a policy goal of preventing high interest rates. When the Treasury sells bonds to the public to finance a deficit, bond prices might fall and interest rates rise. To prevent the rise in interest rates, the Fed would buy bonds to prop up bond prices, and the open market purchases would raise the monetary base (high-powered money).

KEY TERMS

uses of the base

sources of the base

float

government budget constraint

monetizing the debt

printing money

QUESTIONS AND PROBLEMS

Answer the questions using T-accounts when possible.

1. During its financial difficulties in 1984, Continental Illinois National Bank borrowed several billion dollars from the Federal Reserve. What effect did this have on the monetary base?

*2. What happens to the monetary base when the Fed sells $200 billion of bonds to commercial banks? To private investors?

3. Milton Friedman has proposed abolishing Fed discounting. If that were done, what would happen to the monetary base?

4. Because the price of gold soars from $400 to $800 an ounce, the U.S. government decides to sell one million ounces of gold in the open market. What will happen to the monetary base?

*5. If an earthquake hits California, what effect will this have on float and the monetary base?

6. If the Fed puts in a new electronic mail system that allows it to present checks for payment on average a day faster than at present, what will happen to float and the monetary base?

*7. The Federal Reserve Board of Governors decides that its building in Washington, D.C., is shabby and needs a thorough renovation. If the board spends $100 million to renovate it, what effect will this have on the monetary base?

8. If the Treasury gets ready to buy a $100 million computer by adding to its deposits at the Fed but then decides at the last minute not to buy it, what will happen to the monetary base?

*9. If the Treasury were better able to predict when it needed to make payments out of its Fed account and so only made deposits at the Fed at the same time it wrote checks to pay for goods and services, what would happen to the average level of Treasury deposits at the Fed and the monetary base?

10. People make $1 million in UNICEF donations to the United Nations, which deposits the donations in its account at the Fed. What happens to the monetary base?

*11. What would happen to the monetary base when the Treasury financed a $200 billion deficit by selling bonds to the public? To commercial banks? To the Fed?

12. "An increase in the budget deficit will not necessarily lead to a higher level of the monetary base

in the future." Is this statement true, false, or uncertain? Explain.

*13. If the deficit falls from $200 billion to $100 billion, will the monetary base rise by more or less than it otherwise would? Explain how the Fed's desire to prevent higher interest rates affects your answer.

14. With a supply and demand diagram of the bond market, show why Ricardian equivalence implies that a fall in the deficit will not lower interest rates.

*15. Why does Ricardian equivalence suggest that there should be no relationship between the deficit and the monetary base?

Chapter 20

THE TOOLS OF MONETARY POLICY

PREVIEW In the chapters describing the money supply process and the structure of the Federal Reserve System, we mentioned three policy tools that the Fed can use to manipulate the money supply: open market operations, which affect the monetary base; changes in the discount rate, which affect the monetary base by influencing the quantity of discount loans; and changes in reserve requirements, which affect the money multiplier. Because the Fed's use of these policy tools has such impact on economic activity, it is important to understand how the Fed wields them in practice and how relatively useful each tool is. In this chapter we also seek an answer to the following question: How can the use of these policy tools be modified to improve control over the money supply?

OPEN MARKET OPERATIONS

Open market operations are the most important monetary policy tool because they are the primary determinant of changes in the monetary base, the main source of fluctuations in the money supply. Open market purchases expand the monetary base, thereby raising the money supply, and open market sales shrink the monetary base, lowering the money supply. (Details and T-accounts for this mechanism are found in Chapter 16.) Now that we understand the factors that influence the monetary base, we can examine how the Federal Reserve conducts open market operations with the object of controlling the money supply.

There are two types of open market operations: **Dynamic open market operations** are intended to change the level of reserves and the monetary base, and **defensive open market operations** are intended to offset movements in other factors that affect the monetary base, such as changes in Treasury deposits with the Fed or float. The Fed conducts open market operations in U.S. Treasury and government agency securities, especially U.S. Treasury bills.[1] The Fed conducts most of its open market operations in Treasury securities because the market for these securities is the most liquid and has the largest trading volume. It has the capacity to absorb the Fed's substantial volume of transactions without experiencing excessive price fluctuations that would disrupt the market.

As we saw in Chapter 18, the decision-making authority for open market operations is the Federal Open Market Committee (FOMC). The actual execution of these operations, however, is conducted by the trading desk at the Federal Reserve Bank of New York. The best way to see how these transactions are executed is to look at a typical day at the trading desk, located in a room on the eighth floor of the Federal Reserve Bank of New York.

A Day at the Trading Desk

The manager for domestic operations supervises the traders who execute the purchases and sales of securities. Let's call this manager Jim. He starts his workday by reading a report that estimates the total amount of reserves in the banking system as of the night before. This information on reserves helps him decide how large a change in reserves is needed to obtain a desired level of the money supply. He also examines the current federal funds rate, which provides information about the amount of reserves in the banking system. If the banking system has a large amount of reserves, many banks will have excess reserves to lend to other banks, and the federal funds rate will probably fall. If the level of reserves is low, few banks will have excess reserves to lend, and the federal funds rate will probably rise.

At 9:00 A.M. Jim has discussions with several government securities dealers (who operate out of private firms or commercial banks) to get a feel for what may happen to the prices of these securities in the course of the day. After the meeting with the dealers, at around 10:00 A.M., he receives a report from the research staff with a detailed forecast of what will be happening to some of the short-term factors affecting the monetary base (discussed in Chapter 19). For example, if float is predicted to decrease because good weather throughout the country is speeding up check delivery, Jim knows that he will have to conduct a defensive open market operation (a purchase of securities) to offset the expected decline in the monetary base from the decreased float. However, if Treasury deposits or foreign deposits with the Fed are predicted to fall, a defensive open market sale would be needed to offset the expected increase in the monetary base. The report also predicts the change in the public's holding of cur-

---

[1] The Fed does not conduct open market operations in privately issued securities in order to avoid conflicts of interest. (For example, think of the conflict of interest if the Federal Reserve purchased bonds issued by a company owned by the chairman's brother-in-law.)

rency. If currency holdings are expected to rise, then, as we have seen in our money supply model of Part IV, an open market purchase is needed to raise the monetary base to prevent the money supply from falling.

At 10:15 A.M. Jim or a member of his staff telephones the U.S. Treasury to compare his staff's forecasts on such items as Treasury deposits with the Treasury's forecasts. Because the Treasury may have additional information on the changes in its own deposits, its forecasts help Jim refine his staff's forecasts. The call to the Treasury is also used to procure other pieces of helpful information—for example, the timing of future Treasury sales of securities—that provide clues as to what will be happening in the bond market.

After collecting all these data, Jim looks at the directive he has received from the FOMC, which indicates the desired growth rate of several monetary aggregates (expressed as a range, say, 4% to 6% at an annual rate) and the range on the federal funds rate (say, 10% to 14%) that the FOMC would like to achieve. He then figures out the dynamic open market operations that are needed to satisfy the FOMC directive. By combining the necessary defensive open market operations with the desired dynamic open market operations, the manager puts together the "game plan" for open market operations that day.

The whole process is completed by 11:15 A.M., at which time Jim makes daily conference calls to several members of the FOMC and outlines his strategy. After the plan is approved, normally a little after 11:30 A.M., he has the traders in the trading room call the primary dealers (private bond dealers numbering around 40) who trade government securities and request selling price quotations (if open market purchases are planned). For instance, if Jim wants to purchase $250 million of Treasury bills in order to increase the monetary base, the traders list on a large board the quantity of bills at the selling prices that dealers are asking, with the offers ranked from the lowest to the highest price. Since the Fed wants to get the best prices possible, it goes down the list and purchases bills until the desired amount of $250 million has been bought.

Collecting quotations and executing trades is completed around 12:15 P.M. The trading room then quiets down, but the traders continue to monitor conditions in the money market and in bank reserves in the rare instance Jim decides that additional trades are necessary.

Sometimes the open market operations are conducted by straightforward purchases or sales of securities. But ordinarily the trading desk engages in two other types of transactions. In a **repurchase agreement** (often called a **repo**), the Fed purchases securities with an agreement that the seller will repurchase them in a short period of time, usually less than a week. A repo is actually a temporary open market purchase and is an especially desirable way of conducting a defensive open market purchase that will be reversed shortly. When the Fed wants to conduct a temporary open market sale, it engages in a **matched sale-purchase transaction** (sometimes called a **reverse repo**) in which the Fed sells securities and the buyer agrees to sell them back to the Fed in the near future.

Advantages of Open Market Operations

Open market operations have several advantages over the other tools of monetary policy.

1. Open market operations occur at the initiative of the Fed, which has complete control over their volume. This control is not found, for example, in discount operations in which the Fed can encourage or discourage banks to take out discount loans by altering the discount rate but cannot directly control the volume of discounting.

2. Open market operations are flexible and precise; they can be used to any extent. No matter how small a change in reserves or the monetary base is desired, open market operations can achieve it with a small purchase or sale of securities. Conversely, if the desired change in reserves or the base is very large, the open market operations tool is strong enough to do the job through a very large purchase or sale of securities.

3. Open market operations are easily reversed. When a mistake is made in conducting an open market operation, the Fed can immediately reverse its use of this tool. If the Fed decides that the money supply is growing too fast because it has made too many open market purchases, it can immediately make a correction by conducting open market sales.

4. Open market operations can be implemented quickly; they involve no administrative delays. When the Fed decides that it wants to change the monetary base or reserves, it just places an order with a securities dealer, and the trade is executed immediately.

DISCOUNT POLICY

Discount policy, which primarily involves changes in the discount rate, affects the money supply by affecting the volume of discount loans and the monetary base. A rise in discount loans adds to the monetary base and expands the money supply; a fall in discount loans reduces the monetary base and shrinks the money supply. The Federal Reserve facility at which discount loans are made to banks is called the **discount window.** It is easiest to understand how the Fed affects the volume of discount loans by looking at how the discount window operates.

Operation of the Discount Window

The Fed can affect the volume of discount loans in two ways: by affecting the *price* of the loans (the discount rate) or by affecting the *quantity* of the loans through its administration of the discount window.[2]

---

[2]Each Federal Reserve bank administers its own discount window facility. In our discussion here of discount policy, when we discuss the Fed's administration of the discount window, we are actually referring to the district banks' administration of their discount window facilities.

The mechanism through which the Fed's discount rate affects the volume of discount loans is straightforward: A higher discount rate raises the cost of borrowing from the Fed, so banks will take out fewer discount loans; a lower discount rate makes discount loans more attractive to banks, and loan volume will increase.

To examine how the Fed affects the quantity of discount loans through its administration of the discount window, we have to examine more closely how these loans are made.

The Fed's discount loans to the banks are of three types: adjustment credit, seasonal credit, and extended credit. *Adjustment credit loans,* the most common type, are intended to be used by banks to help them with short-term liquidity problems that may result from a temporary deposit outflow. Adjustment credit, which can be obtained with a phone call, is expected to be repaid fairly quickly—by the end of the next business day for the larger banks. *Seasonal credit* is given to meet the seasonal needs of a limited number of banks in vacation and agricultural areas that have a seasonal pattern. *Extended credit,* given to banks that have experienced severe liquidity problems because of deposit outflows, is not expected to be repaid quickly. Banks obtaining this type of credit have to submit a proposal outlining the need for extended credit and a plan for restoring the liquidity of the bank. The most important example of extended credit to a bank was the Fed's loans to Continental Illinois in 1984, which exceeded $5 billion.

The Fed administers the discount window in several ways to prevent its credit funds from being misused and to limit this borrowing. In recent years, as depicted in Figure 1, the discount rate has frequently been below market interest rates, so there is a great incentive for banks to take out low-interest discount loans from the Fed and use the proceeds to make loans or purchase securities with higher interest rates. (Figure 3 in Chapter 17 shows that the volume of discount loans rises abruptly when the discount rate falls below market interest rates.) Banks are not supposed to make a profit from discount loans, and the Fed tries to prevent that by setting rules for individual banks that limit how often they can take out discount loans. If a bank comes to the discount window too frequently, the Fed will deny it loans in the future. Its position is that coming to the discount window is a privilege, not a right.

A bank faces three costs when it borrows from the discount window: the interest cost represented by the discount rate, the cost of complying with Fed investigations of the soundness of the bank when it borrows at the discount window, and the cost of being more likely to be turned down for a discount loan in the future because of too frequent trips to the discount window. The Fed's setting of rules for use of the discount window is frequently referred to as *moral suasion.*

Lender of Last Resort

In addition to its use as a tool to influence the monetary base and the money supply, discounting is important in preventing financial panics. When the Federal Reserve System was created, its most important role was intended to be as

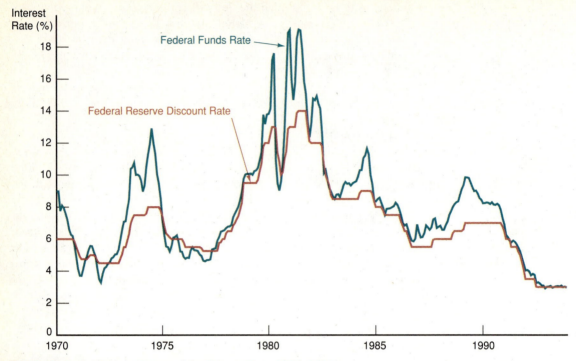

FIGURE 1 Market Interest Rates and the Discount Rate, 1970–1993
Source: Federal Reserve *Bulletin*.

the lender of last resort; it was to provide reserves to the banking system when bank failures threatened to get out of control, thereby preventing bank and financial panics. Discounting is a particularly effective way to provide reserves to the banking system during a banking crisis because reserves are immediately channeled to the banks that need them most.

Using the discount tool to avoid financial panics by performing the role of lender of last resort is an extremely important requirement of successful monetary policymaking. As we demonstrated with our money supply analysis in Chapter 17, the bank panics in the 1930–1933 period were the cause of the sharpest decline in the money supply in U.S. history, which many economists see as the driving force behind the collapse of the economy during the Great Depression. Financial panics can also severely damage the economy because they interfere with the ability of these markets to move funds to people with productive investment opportunities (Chapter 9).

Unfortunately, the discount tool has not always been used by the Fed to prevent financial panics, as our discussion of massive bank failures during the Great Depression in Chapter 17 indicated. The Fed learned from its mistakes of that period and has performed admirably in its role of lender of last resort in the post–World War II period. Two examples of the use of the Fed's discount

Box 1

DISCOUNTING TO TROUBLED BANKS: FRANKLIN NATIONAL BANK AND CONTINENTAL ILLINOIS

In May 1974, the public learned that Franklin National Bank, the twentieth-largest bank in the United States, with deposits close to $3 billion, had suffered large losses in foreign exchange trading and had made many bad loans. Large depositors, whose deposits exceeded the $100,000 limit insured by the FDIC, began to withdraw their deposits, and the failure of the bank was imminent. Because the immediate failure of Franklin National would have had repercussions on other vulnerable banks, possibly leading to more bank failures, the Fed announced that discount loans would be made available to Franklin National so that depositors, including the largest, would not suffer any losses. By the time that Franklin National was merged into the European-American Bank in October 1974, the Fed had lent Franklin National the sum of $1.75 billion, nearly 5% of the total amount of reserves in the banking system. The quick Fed action was completely successful in preventing any other bank failures, and a possible bank panic was avoided.

A 1984 episode involved Continental Illinois National Bank and the Fed in a similar action. Continental Illinois had made many bad loans (primarily to businesses in the energy industry and to foreign countries), and rumors of financial trouble in early May 1984 caused large depositors to withdraw over $10 billion of deposits from the bank. The FDIC arranged a rescue effort in July 1984, which culminated in a $4.5 billion commitment of funds to save the bank; still, the Fed had to lend Continental Illinois over $5 billion—making its $1.75 billion loan to Franklin National look like small potatoes! The Fed's action prevented further bank failures, and again a potential bank panic was averted.

weapon to avoid bank panics are the provisions of huge loans to Franklin National Bank in 1974 and to Continental Illinois ten years later (see Box 1).

At first glance it might appear as though the presence of the FDIC, which insures depositors from losses due to a bank's failure up to a limit of $100,000 per depositor, would make the lender-of-last-resort function of the Fed superfluous. (The FDIC is described in detail in Chapter 13.) There are two reasons why this is not the case. First, it is important to recognize that the FDIC's insurance fund (which guarantees deposits under $100,000) amounts to less than 1% of the amount of these deposits outstanding. If a large number of bank failures occurred, the FDIC would not be able to cover all the depositors' losses. Indeed, the large number of bank failures in recent years, described in Chapter 13, has led to large losses and a shrinkage in the FDIC's insurance fund, which has reduced the FDIC's ability to cover depositors' losses. This fact has not weakened the confidence of small depositors in the banking system because the Fed has been ready to stand behind the FDIC and to provide whatever reserves the banking system needs to prevent bank panics. Second, more than $300 billion of large-denomination deposits in the banking system are not guaranteed by the FDIC because they exceed the $100,000 limit. A loss of confidence in the banking system could still lead to runs on banks from the large-denomination depositors, and bank panics could still occur despite the existence of the FDIC. The importance of the Federal Reserve's role as lender of last resort is, if anything, more important today because of the growing number of bank failures experienced in the 1980s and 1990s.

Not only can the Fed be a lender of last resort to banks, but it can also play the same role for the financial system as a whole. The Fed's discount policy can be used to prevent financial panics that are not triggered by bank failures. The Black Monday stock market crash of 1987 provides a clear-cut example of how the Fed can prevent a financial panic by using the discount window to keep markets operating (see Box 2).

Although the Fed's role as the lender of last resort has the benefit of preventing bank and financial panics, it does have a cost. If a bank expects that the Fed will provide it with discount loans when it gets into trouble, as occurred with Continental Illinois, it will be willing to take on more risk knowing that the Fed will come to the rescue. The Fed's lender-of-last-resort role has thus created a moral hazard problem similar to the one created by deposit insurance (discussed in Chapter 13): Banks take on more risk, thus exposing the deposit insurance agency, and hence taxpayers, to greater losses. The moral hazard problem is most severe for large banks, which may believe that the Fed and the FDIC view them as "too big to fail"; that is, they will always receive Fed loans when they are in trouble because their failure would be likely to precipitate a bank panic.

Similarly, Federal Reserve actions to prevent financial panic, as occurred after the October 1987 stock market crash, may encourage financial institutions other than banks to take on greater risk. They, too, expect the Fed to ensure that they could get loans if a financial panic seemed imminent. When the Fed considers using the discount weapon to prevent panics, it therefore needs to consider the trade-off between the moral hazard cost of its role as lender of last resort and the benefit of preventing financial panics. This trade-off explains why the Fed must be careful not to perform its role as lender of last resort too frequently.

Announcement Effect

Discount policy serves another function for the Federal Reserve: It can be used to signal the Fed's intentions about future monetary policy. Hence if the Fed decides to slow down expansion in the economy by letting interest rates rise, it can

Box 2

DISCOUNTING TO PREVENT A FINANCIAL PANIC: THE BLACK MONDAY STOCK MARKET CRASH OF 1987

Although October 19, 1987, dubbed "Black Monday," will go down in the history books as the largest one-day decline in stock prices to date, it was on Tuesday, October 20, 1987, that financial markets almost stopped functioning. Felix Rohatyn, one of the most prominent men on Wall Street, stated flatly: "Tuesday was the most dangerous day we had in 50 years."* Much of the credit for prevention of a market meltdown after Black Monday must be given to the Federal Reserve System and the chairman of the Board of Governors, Alan Greenspan.

The stress of keeping markets functioning during the sharp decline in stock prices on Monday, October 19, meant that many brokerage houses and specialists (dealer-brokers who maintain orderly trading on the stock exchanges) were severely in need of additional funds to finance their activities. However, understandably enough, New York banks, as well as foreign and regional U.S. banks, growing very nervous about the financial health of securities firms, began to cut back credit to the securities industry at a time when it was most needed. Panic was in the air. One chairman of a large specialist firm commented that on Monday, "from 2 P.M. on, there was total despair. The entire investment community fled the market. We were left alone on the field." It was time for the Fed, like the cavalry, to come to the rescue.

Upon learning of the plight of the securities industry, Greenspan and E. Gerald Corrigan, president of the Federal Reserve Bank of New York and the Fed official most closely in touch with Wall Street, became fearful of a spreading collapse of securities firms. To prevent this from occurring, Greenspan announced before the market opened on Tuesday, October 20, the Federal Reserve System's "readiness to serve as a source of liquidity to support the economic and financial system." In addition to this extraordinary announcement, the Fed made it clear that it would provide discount loans to any bank that would make loans to the securities industry. As one New York banker said, the Fed's message was, "We're here. Whatever you need, we'll give you."

The outcome of the Fed's timely action was that a financial panic was averted. The markets kept functioning on Tuesday and a market rally ensued that day with the Dow Jones Industrial Average climbing over 100 points.

*"Terrible Tuesday: How the Stock Market Almost Disintegrated a Day After the Crash," *Wall Street Journal,* Friday, November 20, 1987, p. 1. This article provides a fascinating and more detailed view of the events described here and is the source of all the quotations cited.

signal its intent to do so by raising the discount rate. This signal may help slow the economic expansion because the public will expect monetary policy to be less expansionary in the future.

The problem with the announcement effect is that it is subject to misinterpretation. In Chapter 17 we saw that if market interest rates are rising relative to the discount rate, the volume of discount loans will rise. In such a situation, the Fed may have no intention of changing its policy to be less expansionary, but to keep the amount of discounting from becoming excessive, it may raise the discount rate to keep it more in line with market interest rates. When the discount rate rises, the market may interpret this as a signal that the Fed is moving to a contractionary policy when that is not the case. The announcement effect may be a hindrance rather than a help. A more sensible approach is probably for the Fed to communicate directly with the public by announcing its intentions outright and then carrying them out. Fed announcements would be believed, and the market would respond accordingly.

Advantages and Disadvantages of Discount Policy

The most important advantage of discount policy is that the Fed can use it to perform its role of lender of last resort. Experiences with Continental Illinois, Franklin National Bank, and the Black Monday crash indicate that this role has become more important in the past couple of decades. Yet two significant disadvantages of discount policy cause many economists to suggest that it should not be used as a tool of monetary control. First is the confusion about the Federal Reserve's intentions that may be created by the announcement of discount rate changes. Second, when the Fed sets the discount rate at a particular level, large fluctuations will occur in the spread between market interest rates and the discount rate $(i - i_d)$ as market interest rates change. As we have seen in Chapter 17 (see Figure 3), these fluctuations lead to large unintended fluctuations in the volume of discount loans and hence in the money supply. Discount policy can make it harder to control the money supply.

The use of discount policy to control the money supply seems to have little to recommend it. Not only does it suffer from the two disadvantages described, but it is also less effective than open market operations in controlling the money supply for two additional reasons. Open market operations are completely at the discretion of the Fed, whereas the volume of discount loans is not—the Fed can change the discount rate, but it can't make banks borrow. In addition, open market operations are more easily reversed than changes in discount policy. The disadvantages of discount policy as a tool of monetary control have prompted economists to suggest several proposed reforms of discount policy.

Proposed Reforms of Discount Policy

Should Discounting Be Abolished? Milton Friedman and other economists have proposed that the Fed should terminate its discount facilities in order to establish better monetary control.[3] Friedman has contended that the presence of the FDIC eliminates the possibility of bank panics; therefore, the use of discounting is no longer as necessary. Abolishing discounting would eliminate fluctuations in the monetary base due to changes in the volume of discount loans and so would reduce unintended fluctuations in the money supply.

Critics of Friedman's proposal emphasize that the FDIC is effective at preventing bank panics only because the Fed stands behind it and plays the role of lender of last resort. Furthermore, as we have seen in the case of the Black Monday crash, the Federal Reserve's discount facilities can be used to avert a financial panic unrelated to bank failures. Because of the increased number of bank failures in recent years, the need for the Fed's use of the discount facility to preserve the health of the financial system has become more apparent. Hence most economists do not support Friedman's proposal.

Should the Discount Rate Be Tied to a Market Rate of Interest? An alternative proposal, much less radical than abolishing discounting, is that the discount rate be tied to a market rate of interest, such as the three-month U.S. Treasury bill rate or the federal funds rate. One version of this proposal, called the *penalty discount rate concept,* involves setting the discount rate at a fixed amount above the market interest rate—say, at 3 percentage points above the three-month bill rate—and allowing banks to borrow all the funds they want at that rate.

The advantages of tying the discount rate to a market rate of interest are many. First, the Fed could continue to use discounting to perform its role of lender of last resort. Second, most fluctuations in the spread between market interest rates and the discount rate $(i - i_d)$ would be eliminated, removing a major source of fluctuations in the volume of discount loans. Third, if the penalty discount rate concept were used, the administration of the discount window would be greatly simplified because banks would no longer be borrowing from the discount window to make a profit. Fourth, because discount rate changes would be automatic, there would be no false signals about the Federal Reserve's intentions, and the announcement effect would disappear.

Tying the discount rate to a market rate of interest is supported by many professional economists. However, the Federal Reserve has opposed this proposed reform, and a possible reason is provided by the theory of bureaucratic behavior discussed in Chapter 18. By tying the discount rate to a market interest

---

[3]Milton Friedman, *A Program for Monetary Stability* (New York: Fordham University Press, 1960); Marvin Goodfriend and Robert G. King, "Financial Deregulation, Monetary Policy, and Central Banking," *Federal Reserve Bank of Richmond Review* 74 (1988): 3–22.

rate, the Fed would be giving up one of its policy tools, and this it may be reluctant to do because it implies giving up some of its power. Another reason why the Fed might want to keep the discount rate fixed when market interest rates change is that it thinks that this would reduce fluctuations in market interest rates. Such a policy would cause discount loans and hence reserves to rise when market interest rates rise, possibly countering some of the rise in market interest rates.

Despite the Federal Reserve's objections to tying the discount rate to a market rate of interest, we can see in Figure 1 that the Fed already pursues a discount policy that is not too far removed from this proposal. It does not let the discount rate move too far away from market rates of interest because it does not want to let the volume of discount loans get out of hand.

RESERVE REQUIREMENTS

As we saw in Chapter 16, changes in reserve requirements affect the money supply by causing the money supply multiplier to change. A rise in reserve requirements reduces the amount of deposits that can be supported by a given level of the monetary base and will lead to a contraction of the money supply. Conversely, a decline in reserve requirements leads to an expansion of the money supply because more multiple deposit creation can take place. The Fed has had the authority to vary reserve requirements since the 1930s, and this is a powerful way of affecting the money supply. Indeed, changes in reserve requirements have such large effects on the money supply that the Fed rarely resorts to using this tool to control it.

The Depository Institutions Deregulation and Monetary Control Act of 1980 provided a simpler scheme for setting reserve requirements. All depository institutions, including commercial banks, savings and loan associations, mutual savings banks, and credit unions, are now subject to the same reserve requirements, as follows: Required reserves on all checkable deposits—including non-interest-bearing checking accounts, NOW accounts, super-NOW accounts, and ATS (automatic transfer savings) accounts—are equal to 3% of the bank's first $51.9 million of checkable deposits[4] and 10% of the checkable deposits over $51.9 million, and the percentage set initially at 10% can be varied between 8% and 14% at the Fed's discretion. In extraordinary circumstances, the percentage can be raised as high as 18%.

---

[4]The $51.9 million figure is as of the end of 1993. Each year, the figure is adjusted upward by 80% of the percentage increase in checkable deposits in the United States.

Advantages and Disadvantages of Reserve Requirement Changes

The main advantage of using reserve requirements to control the money supply is that they affect all banks equally and have a powerful effect on the money supply. The fact that changing reserve requirements is a powerful tool, however, is probably more of a curse than a blessing because small changes in the money supply are hard to engineer by varying reserve requirements. With checkable deposits currently hovering near the $800 billion level, a $\frac{1}{2}$ percentage-point increase in the reserve requirement on these deposits would reduce excess reserves by $4 billion. Because this decline in excess reserves would result in multiple deposit contraction, the decline in the money supply would be even greater. It is true that small changes in the money supply could be obtained by extremely small changes in reserve requirements (say, by 0.001 percentage point), but because it is so expensive to administer changes in reserve requirements, such a strategy is not practical. Using reserve requirements to fine-tune the money supply is like trying to use a jackhammer to cut a diamond.

Another disadvantage of using reserve requirements to control the money supply is that raising the requirements can cause immediate liquidity problems for banks with low excess reserves. When the Fed has raised these requirements in the past, it has usually softened the blow by conducting open market purchases or by making the discount window more available, thus providing reserves to banks that needed them. Continually fluctuating reserve requirements would also create more uncertainty for banks and make their liquidity management more difficult.

The policy tool of changing reserve requirements does not have much to recommend it, and it is rarely used.

Proposed Reforms of Reserve Requirements

Two extreme proposals have been suggested to reform reserve requirements. One is to abolish reserve requirements entirely, and the other is to set required reserves at 100% of deposits.

Should Reserve Requirements Be Abolished? As we see in Box 3, central banks in many countries have been reducing reserve requirements, and some have eliminated them entirely. If you had studied only the simple deposit multiplier (Chapter 15), you might think that abolishing reserve requirements would result in an infinite money supply. However, as our more sophisticated money supply model (Chapters 16 and 17) indicates, this reasoning would be incorrect. Banks would still want to hold reserves to protect themselves against deposit outflows, and there

A Global Perspective

WHY HAS THERE BEEN A WORLDWIDE DECLINE IN RESERVE REQUIREMENTS?

In recent years, central banks in many countries in the world have been reducing or eliminating their reserve requirements. In the United States, the Federal Reserve eliminated reserve requirements on time deposits in December 1990 and lowered reserve requirements on checkable deposits from 12% to 10% in April 1992. Canada has gone a step further: Financial market legislation taking effect in June 1992 eliminated all reserve requirements over a two-year period. The central banks of Switzerland, New Zealand, and Australia have also eliminated reserve requirements entirely. What explains the downward trend for reserve requirements in most countries?

You may recall from Chapter 10 that reserve requirements act as a tax on banks. Because central banks typically do not pay interest on reserves, the bank earns nothing on them and loses the interest that could have been earned if the bank held loans instead. The cost imposed on banks from reserve requirements means that banks, in effect, have a higher cost of funds than intermediaries not subject to reserve requirements, making them less competitive. We have already seen in Chapter 12 that additional market forces have been making banks less competitive, weakening the health of banking systems throughout the world. Central banks have thus been reducing reserve requirements to make banks more competitive and stronger.* The Federal Reserve was explicit about this rationale for its April 1992 reduction when it announced it on February 18, 1992, stating in its press release that "the reduction . . . will reduce funding costs for depositories and strengthen their balance sheets. Over time, it is expected that most of these cost savings will be passed on to depositors and borrowers."

*Many economists believe that the Fed should pay market interest rates on reserves, another suggestion for dealing with this problem.

would still be a demand for currency. Both these factors would limit the size of the money supply.

The case for keeping reserve requirements must rest on the proposition that having reserve requirements results in a more stable money multiplier and hence a more controllable money supply. Since the evidence for or against this view is limited, the desirability of this proposed reform remains an open question.

Should Reserve Requirements Be Raised to 100%? At the same time that Milton Friedman suggested abolishing discounting, he also suggested that required reserves be set equal to 100% of deposits.[5] With 100% reserve requirements, the money supply could be strictly controlled by the Fed because it would be equal to the monetary base. The advantage of this proposal is clear, but several major disadvantages surface. Banks would no longer be able to make loans because with a 100% reserve requirement, no excess reserves would be available. Loans would have to be made by other financial intermediaries. Not only would this restructuring of the banking system be extremely costly, but the financial intermediaries not subject to reserve requirements might develop ways of making their liabilities function more like checkable deposits in order to attract funds.[6] The outcome might be that the Fed would enjoy complete control of the *official* money supply, but the *economically relevant* money supply might be even less under the Fed's control because it is affected by the activities of the nonbank financial intermediaries. In addition, the Fed's control over the financial system could be weakened further because all the loan activity would be in the hands of financial institutions not subject to the Fed's reserve requirements.

---

[5] Friedman, *Program for Monetary Stability*. This proposal was outlined earlier by Henry Simons in *Economic Policy for a Free Society* (Chicago: University of Chicago Press, 1948).

[6] We would expect this to happen because it would trigger the process of financial innovation discussed in Chapter 10.

SUMMARY

1. The number of open market operations conducted in any given day by the trading desk of the Federal Reserve Bank of New York is determined by the number of dynamic open market operations intended to change the monetary base and by the number of defensive open market operations used to offset other factors that affect the monetary base. Open market operations are the primary tool used by the Fed to control the money supply because they occur at the initiative of the Fed, are flexible, are easily reversed, and can be implemented quickly.

2. The volume of discount loans is determined by the discount rate and the discouragement of borrowing by moral suasion. Besides its effect on the monetary base and the money supply, discounting allows the Fed to perform its role as the lender of last resort. However, discount policy does make control of the money supply more difficult because it results in unintended fluctuations in the volume of discount loans and hence in the money supply. Many economists support tying the discount rate to a market interest rate to reduce these unintended fluctuations in the volume of discount loans.

3. Changing reserve requirements is too blunt a tool to use for controlling the money supply, and hence it is rarely used.

KEY TERMS

dynamic open market operations

defensive open market operations

repurchase agreement (repo)

matched sale-purchase transaction (reverse repo)

discount window

QUESTIONS AND PROBLEMS

*1. If the manager of domestic operations hears that a snowstorm is about to strike New York City, making it difficult to present checks for payment there, what defensive open market operations will the manager undertake?

2. During Christmastime, when the public's holdings of currency increase, what defensive open market operations typically occur? Why?

*3. If the Treasury has just paid for a supercomputer and as a result its deposits with the Fed fall, what defensive open market operations will the manager of domestic operations undertake?

4. If float decreases below its normal level, why might the manager of domestic operations consider it more desirable to use repurchase agreements to affect the monetary base rather than an outright purchase of bonds?

*5. Most open market operations are currently repurchase agreements. What does this tell us about the likely volume of defensive open market operations relative to dynamic open market operations?

6. "The only way that the Fed can affect the level of discount loans is by adjusting the discount rate." Is this statement true, false, or uncertain? Explain.

*7. If the Fed did not administer the discount window to limit borrowing, what do you predict would happen to the money supply if the discount rate were several percentage points below the interest rate on loans?

8. "If the discount rate were always kept above the interest rate on loans, the Fed would rarely have to administer the discount window to limit borrowing." Is this statement true, false, or uncertain? Explain.

*9. "Discounting is no longer needed because the presence of the FDIC eliminates the possibility of bank panics." Discuss.

10. The benefits of using Fed discount operations to prevent bank panics are straightforward. What are the costs?

*11. You often read in the newspaper that the Fed has just lowered the discount rate. Does this signal that the Fed is moving to a more expansionary monetary policy? Why or why not?

*12. How can the procyclical movement of interest rates (rising during business cycle expansions and falling during business cycle contractions) lead to a procyclical movement in the money supply as a result of Fed discounting? Why might this movement of the money supply be undesirable?

*13. Which proposal would lead to tighter control of the money supply: abolishing discounting or tying the discount rate to a market rate of interest? Which of the two proposals would you prefer and why?

14 "Considering that raising reserve requirements to 100% makes complete control of the money supply possible, Congress should authorize the Fed to raise reserve requirements to this level." Discuss.

*15. Compare the use of open market operations, discounting, and changes in reserve requirements to control the money supply on the following criteria: flexibility, reversibility, effectiveness, and speed of implementation.

Chapter 21

THE CONDUCT OF MONETARY POLICY: GOALS AND TARGETS

PREVIEW In earlier chapters you have seen how the Fed can use its tools to affect the money supply. Although we have hinted that the conduct (planning and implementation) of monetary policy is an inexact procedure, an examination of the Fed's conduct of monetary policy gives rise to an important question: Given the tools at its disposal, how well can the Fed actually control the money supply?

To explore this subject, we look at the goals the Fed establishes for its monetary policy and its strategies for attaining them. After examining the goals and strategies, we can evaluate the Fed's and other countries' central banks' conduct of monetary policy in the past, with the hope that it will give us some clues to where monetary policy may head in the future.

GOALS OF MONETARY POLICY

Six basic goals are continually mentioned by personnel at the Federal Reserve and other central banks when they discuss the objectives of monetary policy: (1) high employment, (2) economic growth, (3) price stability, (4) interest-rate stability, (5) stability of financial markets, and (6) stability in foreign exchange markets.

High Employment

The Employment Act of 1946 and the Full Employment and Balanced Growth Act of 1978 (more commonly called the Humphrey-Hawkins Act) commit the U.S. government to promoting high employment consistent with a stable price level. High employment is a worthy goal for two main reasons: (1) the alternative situation, high unemployment, causes much human misery, with families suffering financial distress, loss of personal self-respect, and increases in crime (though this last conclusion is highly controversial), and (2) when unemployment is high,

493

the economy has not only idle workers but also idle resources (closed factories and unused equipment), resulting in a loss of output (lower GDP).

Although it is clear that high employment is desirable, how high should it be? At what point can we say that the economy is at full employment? At first it might seem that full employment is the point at which no worker is out of a job, that is, when unemployment is zero. But this definition ignores the fact that some unemployment, called *frictional unemployment,* is beneficial to the economy. For example, a worker who decides to look for a better job might be unemployed for a while during the job search. Workers often voluntarily decide to leave work temporarily to pursue other activities (raising a family, travel, returning to school), and when they decide to reenter the job market, it again takes some time for them to find the right job. The benefit of having some unemployment is similar to the benefit of having a nonzero vacancy rate in the market for rental apartments. As many of you who have looked for an apartment have discovered, when the vacancy rate in the rental market is too low, you will have a difficult time finding the right apartment.

The goal for high employment should therefore not seek an unemployment level of zero but rather a level above zero consistent with full employment at which the demand for labor equals the supply of labor. Economists call this the **natural rate of unemployment.**

Although this definition sounds neat and authoritative, it isn't because it leaves a troublesome question unanswered: What unemployment rate is consistent with full employment? On the one hand, in some cases, it is obvious that the unemployment rate is too high: The unemployment rate in excess of 20% during the Great Depression, for example, was clearly far too high. In the early 1960s, on the other hand, economists thought that a reasonable goal was 4%, a level that was probably too low because it led to accelerating inflation. Current estimates of the natural rate of unemployment place it around 6%, but even this estimate is subject to uncertainty and disagreement. In addition, it is possible that appropriate government policy, such as the provision of better information about job vacancies or job training programs, might decrease the natural rate of unemployment.

Economic Growth

The goal of steady economic growth is closely related to the high employment goal because businesses are more likely to invest in capital equipment to increase productivity and economic growth when unemployment is low. Conversely, if unemployment is high and factories are idle, it does not pay for a firm to invest in additional plants and equipment. Although the two goals are closely related, policies can be specifically aimed at promoting economic growth by directly encouraging firms to invest or by encouraging people to save, which provides more funds for firms to invest. In fact, this was the stated purpose of Ronald Reagan's supply-side economics policies, which were intended to spur economic growth by providing tax incentives for businesses to invest in plants and equipment and for taxpayers to save more.

Price Stability

Over the past two decades, American economists have become more aware of the social and economic costs of inflation and more concerned with a stable price level as a goal of economic policy. (The growing commitment to price stability is also evident in Europe; see Box 1.) Price stability is desirable because a rising price level (inflation) creates uncertainty in the economy. For example, the information conveyed by the prices of goods and services is harder to interpret when the overall level of prices is changing, which complicates decision making for consumers, businesses, and government. The most extreme example of unstable prices is hyperinflation, such as Germany experienced in 1921–1923. In the last two years of hyperinflation, Germany's economic activity (as measured by GDP) underwent a sharp slowdown because of the costs imposed by the rising price level.

Inflation also makes it hard to plan for the future. For example, it is more difficult to decide how much funds should be put aside to provide for one's children's college education in an inflationary environment. Further, inflation may strain a country's social fabric: Conflict may result because each group in the society may compete with other groups to make sure that its wages keep up with the rising level of prices.

A Global Perspective

Box 1

THE GROWING EUROPEAN COMMITMENT TO PRICE STABILITY

Not surprisingly, given Germany's experience with hyperinflation, its central bank has the strongest commitment to price stability. In contrast to statutes for the German central bank, the statutes of other central banks in Europe set various objectives for policy, including all the goals outlined here in the text. However, European policymakers have been coming around to the view that the primary objective for a central bank should be price stability. The increased importance of this goal is reflected in the December 1991 Treaty of European Union, known as the Maastricht Treaty, which proposed the creation of the European System of Central Banks, which would function very much like the Federal Reserve System. The statute of the European System of Central Banks sets price stability as the primary objective of this system and indicates that the general economic policies of the European Union are to be supported only if they are not in conflict with price stability.

Interest-Rate Stability

Interest-rate stability is desirable because fluctuations in interest rates can create uncertainty in the economy and make it harder to plan for the future. Fluctuations in interest rates that affect consumers' willingness to buy houses, for example, make it more difficult both for consumers to decide when to purchase a house and for construction firms to plan how many houses to build. The Fed may also want to reduce upward movements in interest rates for the reasons we discussed in Chapter 18: Upward movements in interest rates generate hostility toward the Fed and lead to demands that its power be curtailed.

Stability of Financial Markets

An explicit reason for the creation of the Federal Reserve System was that it could promote a more stable financial system. One way in which the Fed promotes stability is helping prevent financial panics (particularly bank panics) through its role as lender of last resort. The Fed has performed this role many times since the 1970s.

The stability of financial markets is also promoted by interest-rate stability because fluctuations in interest rates create great uncertainty for financial institutions. An increase in interest rates produces large capital losses on long-term bonds and mortgages, losses that can cause the failure of the financial institutions holding them. In recent years, more pronounced interest-rate fluctuations have been a particularly severe problem for savings and loan associations and mutual savings banks, many of which have gotten into serious financial trouble (as we have seen in Chapter 13).

Stability in Foreign Exchange Markets

With the increasing importance of international trade to the U.S. economy, the value of the dollar relative to other currencies has become a major consideration for the Fed. As we saw in Chapter 8, a rise in the value of the dollar makes American industries less competitive with those abroad, and declines in the value of the dollar stimulate inflation in the United States. In addition, preventing large changes in the value of the dollar makes it easier for firms and individuals purchasing or selling goods abroad to plan ahead. Stabilizing extreme movements in the value of the dollar in foreign exchange markets is thus viewed as a worthy goal of monetary policy.

Conflict Among Goals

Although many of the goals mentioned are consistent with each other—high employment with economic growth, interest-rate stability with financial market stability—this is not always the case. The goal of price stability often conflicts with the goals of interest-rate stability and high employment in the short run. For example, when the economy is expanding and unemployment is falling, both inflation and interest rates may start to rise. If the Fed tries to prevent a rise in interest rates by buying bonds, bidding up their price and thus causing interest rates to fall, the resulting open market purchases will cause the monetary base and the money supply to rise, stimulating inflation. But if the Fed slows down money supply growth to prevent inflation, in the short run both interest rates and unemployment may rise. The conflict among goals may thus present the Fed with some hard choices. We return to the issue of how the Fed should choose between conflicting goals in later chapters when we examine how monetary policy affects the economy.

THE FED'S STRATEGY: USE OF MONETARY TARGETS

The Fed's problem is that it wishes to achieve certain goals such as price stability with high employment, but it does not directly influence the goals. It has a set of tools to employ (open market operations, changes in the discount rate, and changes in reserve requirements) that can affect the goals indirectly after a period of time (typically more than a year). If the Fed waits to see what the price level and employment will be one year later, it will be too late to make any corrections to its policy—mistakes will be irreversible.

The Fed consequently pursues a different strategy for conducting monetary policy by aiming at variables that lie between its tools and the achievement of its goals. The Fed's strategy is as follows: After deciding on its goals for employment and the price level, it chooses a set of variables to aim for, called **intermediate targets,** such as the monetary aggregates ($M1$, $M2$, or $M3$) or interest rates (short- or long-term), which have a direct effect on employment and the price level. However, even these intermediate targets are not directly affected by the Fed's policy tools. Therefore, it chooses another set of variables to aim for, called **operating targets,** such as reserve aggregates (reserves, nonborrowed reserves, monetary base, or nonborrowed base) or interest rates (federal funds rate or Treasury bill rate), which are more responsive to its policy tools. (Recall that nonborrowed reserves are total reserves minus borrowed reserves, which are the amount of discount loans; the nonborrowed base is the monetary base minus borrowed reserves; and the federal funds rate is the interest rate on funds loaned overnight between banks.)[1]

The Fed pursues this strategy because it is easier to hit a goal by aiming at targets than by aiming at the goal directly. Specifically, by using intermediate and operating targets, it can more quickly judge whether its policies are on the right

---

[1]There is some ambiguity as to whether to call a particular variable an operating target or an intermediate target. Some economists view the monetary base and the Treasury bill rate as possible intermediate targets, even though they may function as operating targets as well. In addition, if the Fed wants to pursue a goal of interest-rate stability, an interest rate can be both a goal variable and a target variable.

track, rather than waiting until it sees the final outcome of its policies on employment and the price level.[2] By analogy, NASA employs the strategy of using targets when it is trying to send a spaceship to the moon. It will check to see whether the spaceship is positioned correctly as it leaves the atmosphere (we can think of this as NASA's "operating target"). If the spaceship is off course at this stage, NASA engineers will adjust its thrust (a policy tool) to get it back on target. NASA may check the position of the spaceship again when it is halfway to the moon (NASA's "intermediate target") and can make further midcourse corrections if necessary.

The Fed's strategy works in a similar way. Suppose that the Fed's employment and price-level goals are consistent with a nominal GDP growth rate of 5%. If the Fed feels that the 5% nominal GDP growth rate will be achieved by a 4% growth rate for *M2* (its intermediate target), which will in turn be achieved by a growth rate of 3½% for the monetary base (its operating target), it will carry out open market operations (its tool) to achieve the 3½% growth in the monetary base. Within days after implementing this policy, the Fed may find that the monetary base is growing too slowly, say, at a 2% rate; then it can correct this too slow growth by increasing the amount of its open market purchases. Somewhat later, the Fed will begin to see how its policy is affecting the growth rate of the money supply. If *M2* is growing too fast, say, at a 7% rate, the Fed may decide to reduce its open market purchases or make open market sales to reduce the *M2* growth rate.

One way of thinking about the Fed's strategy (illustrated in Figure 1) is that it is using its operating and intermediate targets to direct monetary policy (the spaceship) toward the achievement of its goals. After the initial setting of the policy tools (the liftoff), an operating target such as the monetary base, which the Fed can control fairly directly, is used to reset the tools so that monetary policy is channeled toward achieving the intermediate target of a certain rate of money supply growth. Midcourse corrections in the policy tools can be made again when the Fed sees what is happening to its intermediate target, thus directing monetary policy so that it will achieve its goals of high employment and price stability (the spaceship reaches the moon).

CHOOSING THE TARGETS

As we see in Figure 1, there are two different types of target variables: interest rates and aggregates (monetary aggregates and reserve aggregates). In our example, the Fed chose a 4% growth rate for *M2* to achieve a 5% rate of growth for nominal GDP. It could have chosen to lower the interest rate on the three-month Treasury bills to, say, 3% to achieve the same goal. Can the Fed choose to pursue both of these targets at the same time? The answer is no. The application of

---

[2]This reasoning for the use of monetary targets has come under fire because information on employment and the price level can be useful in evaluating policy. See Benjamin M. Friedman, "The Inefficiency of Short-Run Monetary Targets for Monetary Policy," *Brookings Papers on Economic Activity* 2 (1977): 292–346.

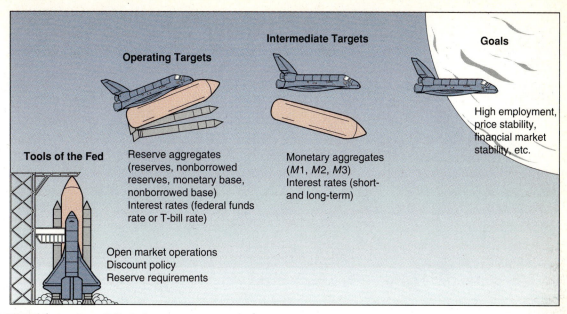

FIGURE 1 Strategy of the Fed

the supply and demand analysis of the money market that we covered in Chapter 6 explains why the Fed must choose one or the other.

Let's first see why a monetary aggregate target involves losing control of the interest rate. Figure 2 contains a supply and demand diagram for the money market. Although the Fed expects the demand curve for money to be at M^{d^*}, it fluctuates between $M^{d'}$ and $M^{d''}$ because of unexpected increases or decreases in output or changes in the price level. The money demand curve might also shift unexpectedly because the public's preferences about holding bonds versus money may change. If the Fed's monetary aggregate target of a 4% growth rate in $M2$ results in a money supply of M^*, it expects that the interest rate will be i^*. However, as the figure indicates, the fluctuations in the money demand curve between $M^{d'}$ and $M^{d''}$ will result in an interest rate fluctuating between i' and i''. Pursuing a monetary aggregate target implies that interest rates will fluctuate.

The supply and demand diagram in Figure 3 shows the consequences of an interest rate target set at i^*. Again, the Fed expects the money demand curve to be at M^{d^*}, but it fluctuates between $M^{d'}$ and $M^{d''}$ due to unexpected changes in output, the price level, or the public's preferences toward holding money. If the demand curve falls to $M^{d'}$, the interest rate will begin to fall below i^* and the price of bonds will rise. With an interest-rate target, the Fed will prevent the interest rate from falling by selling bonds to drive their price back down and the interest rate back up to its former level. The Fed will make open market sales until the money supply declines to $M^{s'}$, at which point the equilibrium interest rate is again i^*. Conversely, if the demand curve rises to $M^{d''}$ and drives up the interest rate, the Fed would keep interest rates from rising by buying bonds to keep their prices from falling. The Fed will make open market purchases until

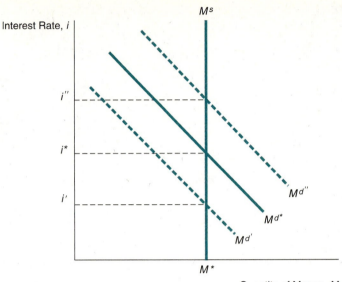

FIGURE 2
Result of Targeting on the Money Supply
The Federal Reserve's targeting on the money supply at M^* will lead to fluctuations in the interest rate between i' and i'' because of fluctuations in the money demand curve between $M^{d'}$ and $M^{d''}$.

the money supply rises to $M^{s''}$ and the equilibrium interest rate is i^*. The Fed's adherence to the interest rate target thus leads to a fluctuating money supply as well as fluctuations in reserve aggregates such as the monetary base.

The conclusion from the supply and demand analysis is that interest-rate and monetary aggregate targets are incompatible: The Fed can hit one or the other but not both. Because a choice between them has to be made, we need to examine what criteria should be used to decide on the target variable.

Criteria for Choosing Intermediate Targets

The rationale behind the Fed's strategy of using targets suggests three criteria for choosing an intermediate target: It must be measurable, it must be controllable by the Fed, and it must have a predictable effect on the goal.

Measurability Quick and accurate measurement of an intermediate target variable is necessary because the intermediate target will be useful only if it signals when policy is off track more rapidly than the goal. What good does it do for the Fed to plan to hit a 4% growth rate for $M2$ if it has no way of quickly and accurately measuring $M2$? Data on the monetary aggregates are obtained after a two-week delay, and interest-rate data are available almost immediately. Data on a goal variable like GDP, by contrast, are compiled quarterly and are made available with a month's delay. In addition, the GDP data are less accurate than data on the monetary aggregates or interest rates. On these grounds alone, focusing on interest rates and monetary aggregates as intermediate targets rather than on a goal like GDP can provide clearer signals about the status of the Fed's policy.

At first glance, interest rates seem to be more measurable than monetary aggregates and hence more useful as intermediate targets. Not only are the data on

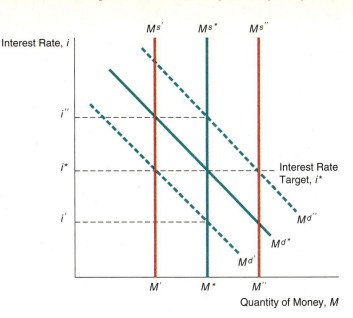

FIGURE 3
Result of Targeting on the Interest Rate
The Federal Reserve's targeting on the interest rate at i^* will lead to fluctuations in the money supply between M' and M'' because of fluctuations in the money demand curve between $M^{d'}$ and $M^{d''}$.

interest rates available more quickly than on monetary aggregates, but they are also measured more precisely and are rarely revised, in contrast to the monetary aggregates, which are subject to a fair amount of revision (as we saw in Chapter 3). However, as we learned in Chapter 4, the interest rate that is quickly and accurately measured, the nominal interest rate, is typically a poor measure of the real cost of borrowing, which indicates with more certainty what will happen to GDP. This real cost of borrowing is more accurately measured by the real interest rate—the interest rate adjusted for expected inflation ($i_r = i - \pi^e$). Unfortunately, the real interest rate is extremely hard to measure because we have no direct way to measure *expected* inflation. Since both interest rate and monetary aggregates have measurability problems, it is not clear whether one should be preferred to the other as an intermediate target.

Controllability   The Fed must be able to exercise effective control over a variable if it is to function as a useful target. If the Fed cannot control an intermediate target, knowing that it is off track does little good because the Fed has no way of getting it back on track. Some economists have suggested that nominal GDP should be used as an intermediate target, but since the Fed has little direct control over nominal GDP, it will not provide much guidance on how the Fed should set its policy tools. The Fed does, however, have a good deal of control over the monetary aggregates and interest rates.

Our discussion of the money supply process and the Fed's policy tools indicates that the Fed does have the ability to exercise a powerful effect on the money supply, although its control is not perfect. We have also seen that open market operations can be used to set interest rates by directly affecting the price of bonds. Because the Fed can set interest rates directly whereas it cannot completely control the money supply, it might appear that interest rates dominate the monetary aggregates on the controllability criterion. However, the Fed cannot set *real* interest rates because it does not have control over expectations of inflation.

So again, a clear-cut case cannot be made that interest rates are preferable to monetary aggregates as an intermediate target, or vice versa.

Predictable Effect on Goals   The most important characteristic a variable must have to be useful as an intermediate target is that it have a *predictable* impact on a goal. If the Fed can accurately and quickly measure the price of tea in China and can completely control its price, what good will it do? The Fed cannot use the price of tea in China to affect unemployment or the price level in the United States. Because the ability to affect goals is so critical to the usefulness of an intermediate target variable, the linkage of the money supply and interest rates with the goals—output, employment, and the price level—is a matter of much debate in the economics profession. The evidence on whether these goals have a closer (more predictable) link with the money supply than with interest rates is mixed. We discuss the evidence on this issue extensively in Chapter 27.

Criteria for Choosing Operating Targets

The choice of an operating target can be based on the same criteria used to evaluate intermediate targets. Both the federal funds rate and reserve aggregates are measured accurately and are available daily with almost no delay; both are easily controllable using the policy tools that we discussed in Chapter 20. When we look at the third criterion, however, we can think of the intermediate target as the goal for the operating target. An operating target that has a more predictable impact on the most desirable intermediate target is preferred. If the desired intermediate target is an interest rate, the preferred operating target will be an interest-rate variable like the federal funds rate because interest rates are closely tied to each other (as we saw in Chapter 7). However, if the desired intermediate target is a monetary aggregate, our money supply model of Part IV shows that a reserve aggregate operating target such as the monetary base will be preferred. Because there does not seem to be much reason to choose an interest rate over a reserve aggregate on the basis of measurability or controllability, the choice of which operating target is better rests on the choice of the intermediate target (the goal of the operating target).

FED POLICY PROCEDURES: A HISTORICAL PERSPECTIVE

The well-known adage "The road to hell is paved with good intentions" applies as much to the Federal Reserve as it does to human beings. Understanding the Fed's goals and the strategies it can use to pursue its goals cannot tell us *how* monetary policy is actually conducted. To understand the practical results of the theoretical underpinnings, we have to look at the Fed's past policy procedures: its choice of goals, policy tools, operating targets, and intermediate targets. This historical perspective will not only show us how our central bank carries out its duties but will also help us interpret the Fed's activities and see where monetary policy may be heading in the future.

STUDY GUIDE

The following discussion of the Fed's policy procedures and their effect on the money supply provides a review of the money supply process and how the Fed's policy tools work. If you have trouble understanding how the particular policies described affect the money supply, it might be helpful to review the material in Part IV.

The Early Years: Discount Policy as the Primary Tool

When the Fed was created, changing the discount rate was the primary tool of monetary policy—the Fed had not yet discovered that open market operations were a more powerful tool for influencing the money supply, and the Federal Reserve Act made no provisions for changes in reserve requirements. The guiding principle for the conduct of monetary policy was that as long as loans were being made for "productive" purposes—that is, to support the production of goods and services—providing reserves to the banking system to make these loans would not be inflationary.[3] This theory, now thoroughly discredited, became known as the **real bills doctrine.** In practice, it meant that the Fed would make loans to member commercial banks when they showed up at the discount window with *eligible paper,* loans to facilitate the production and sale of goods and services. (Note that since the 1920s, the Fed has not conducted discount operations in this way.) The Fed's act of making loans to member banks was initially called *rediscounting* because the original bank loans to businesses were made by discounting (loaning less than) the face value of the loan, and the Fed would be discounting them again. (Over time, when the Fed's emphasis on eligible paper diminished, the Fed's loans to banks became known as *discounts* and the interest rate on these loans the *discount rate,* which is the terminology we use today.)

By the end of World War I, the Fed's policy of rediscounting eligible paper and keeping interest rates at low levels to help the Treasury finance the war had led to a raging inflation; in 1919 and 1920, the inflation rate averaged 14%. The Fed decided that it could no longer follow the passive policy prescribed by the real bills doctrine because it was inconsistent with the goal of price stability, and for the first time the Fed accepted the responsibility of playing an active role in influencing the economy. In January 1920, the Fed raised the discount rate from

---

[3]Another guiding principle was the maintenance of the gold standard, which we will discuss in Chapter 22.

4¾% to 6%, the largest jump in its history, and eventually raised it further to 7% in June 1920, where it remained for nearly a year. The result of this policy was a sharp decline in the money supply and an especially sharp recession in 1920–1921. Although the blame for this severe recession can clearly be laid at the Fed's doorstep, in one sense the Fed's policy was very successful: After an initial decline in the price level, the inflation rate went to zero, paving the way for the prosperous Roaring Twenties.

Discovery of Open Market Operations

In the early 1920s, a particularly important event occurred: The Fed accidentally discovered open market operations. When the Fed was created, its revenue came exclusively from the interest it received on the discount loans that it made to member banks. After the 1920–1921 recession, the volume of discount loans shrank dramatically, and the Fed was hard pressed for income. It solved this problem by purchasing income-earning securities. In doing so, the Fed noticed that reserves in the banking system grew and there was a multiple expansion of bank loans and deposits. This result is obvious to us now (we studied the multiple deposit creation process in Chapter 15), but to the Fed at that time it was a revelation. A new monetary policy tool was born, and by the end of the 1920s, it was the most important weapon in the Fed's arsenal.

The Great Depression

The stock market boom in 1928 and 1929 created a dilemma for the Fed. It wanted to temper the boom by raising the discount rate, but it was reluctant to do so because that would have meant raising interest rates to businesses and individuals who had legitimate needs for credit. (The Fed did not yet have the authority to set margin requirements as it does today.) Finally, in August 1929, the Fed raised the discount rate, but by then it was too late; the speculative excesses of the market boom had already occurred, and the Fed's action only hastened the stock market crash and pushed the economy into recession. In Chapter 17 we discussed the Fed's many policy blunders from 1930 to 1933, when its failure to perform its role as lender of last resort allowed over a third of the commercial banks in the United States to fail. The resulting unprecedented decline in the money supply during this period is thought by many economists to have been the major contributing factor to the severity of the depression, which has never been equaled before or since.

Reserve Requirements as a Policy Tool

The Thomas Amendment to the Agricultural Adjustment Act of 1933 provided the Board of Governors with emergency power to alter reserve requirements with the approval of the president of the United States. In the Banking Act of

1935, this emergency power was expanded to allow the Fed to alter reserve requirements unilaterally without the president's approval.

The first use of reserve requirements as a tool of monetary control proved that the Federal Reserve was capable of adding to the blunders that it had made during the bank panics of the early 1930s. By the end of 1935, banks had increased their holdings of excess reserves to unprecedented levels, a sensible strategy considering their discovery during the 1930–1933 period that the Fed would not always perform its intended role as lender of last resort. Bankers now understood that they would have to protect themselves against a bank run by holding substantial amounts of excess reserves. The Fed viewed these excess reserves as a nuisance that made it harder to exercise monetary control. Specifically, the Fed worried that these excess reserves might be loaned out and would produce "an uncontrollable expansion of credit in the future."[4]

To improve monetary control, the Fed raised reserve requirements in three steps: August 1936, January 1937, and May 1937. The result of this action was, as we would expect from our money supply model, a slowdown of money growth toward the end of 1936 and an actual decline in 1937. The recession of 1937–1938, which commenced in May 1937, was a severe one and was especially upsetting to the American public because even at its outset, unemployment was intolerably high. So not only does it appear that the Fed was at fault for the severity of the Great Depression contraction in 1929–1933, but to add insult to injury, it appears that it was also responsible for aborting the subsequent recovery. The Fed's disastrous experience with varying its reserve requirements made it far more cautious in the use of this policy tool in the future.

War Finance and the Pegging of Interest Rates: 1942–1951

With the entrance of the United States into World War II in late 1941, government spending skyrocketed, and to finance it, the Treasury issued huge amounts of bonds. The Fed agreed to help the Treasury finance the war cheaply by pegging interest rates at the low levels that had prevailed before the war: ⅜% on Treasury bills and 2½% on long-term Treasury bonds. Whenever interest rates would rise above these levels and the price of bonds would begin to fall, the Fed would make open market purchases, thereby bidding up bond prices and driving interest rates down again. The Fed had thus in effect relinquished its control of monetary policy to meet the financing needs of the government. The result was a substantial monetization of the debt and a rapid growth in the monetary base and the money supply.

When the war ended, the Fed continued to peg interest rates, and because there was little pressure on them to rise, this policy did not result in an explosive growth in the money supply. When the Korean War broke out in 1950, however, interest rates began to climb, and the Fed found that it was again forced to expand the monetary base at a rapid rate. Because inflation began to heat up (the

---

[4]Milton Friedman and Anna Jacobson Schwartz, *A Monetary History of the United States, 1867–1960,* (Princeton, N.J.: Princeton University Press, 1963), p. 524.

consumer price index rose 8% between 1950 and 1951), the Fed decided that it was time to reassert its control over monetary policy by abandoning the interest-rate peg. An often bitter debate ensued between the Fed and the Treasury, which wanted to keep its interest costs down and so favored a continued pegging of interest rates at low levels. In March 1951, the Fed and the Treasury came to an agreement known as the Accord, in which pegging was abandoned but the Fed promised that it would not allow interest rates to rise precipitously. After Eisenhower's election as president in 1952, the Fed was given complete freedom to pursue its monetary policy objectives.

Targeting Money Market Conditions: The 1950s and 1960s

With its freedom restored, the Federal Reserve, then under the chairmanship of William McChesney Martin, Jr., took the view that monetary policy should be grounded in intuitive judgment based on a feel for the money market. The policy procedure that resulted can be described as one in which the Fed targeted on money market conditions, a vague collection of variables that were supposed to describe supply and demand conditions in the money market. Included among these variables were short-term interest rates and **free reserves** *FR*, equal to excess reserves in the banking system *ER* minus the volume of discount loans *DL*:

$$FR = ER - DL$$

The Fed considered free reserves a particularly good indicator of money market conditions because it thought that they represented the amount of slack in the banking system. The Fed viewed banks as having a first priority in using their excess reserves to repay their discount loans, so only the excess reserves not borrowed from the Fed represented the *free* reserves that could be used to make loans and create deposits. The Fed interpreted an increase in free reserves as an easing of money market conditions and used open market sales to withdraw reserves from the banking system. A fall in free reserves meant a tightening of money market conditions, and the Fed made open market purchases.

An important characteristic of this policy procedure is that it led to more rapid growth in the money supply when the economy was expanding and a slowing of money growth when the economy was in recession. The so-called *procyclical monetary policy* (that is, a positive association of money supply growth with the business cycle) is explained by the following step-by-step reasoning. As we learned in Chapter 6, a rise in national income ($Y\uparrow$) leads to a rise in market interest rates ($i\uparrow$), thus raising the opportunity cost of holding excess reserves and causing excess reserves to decline ($ER\downarrow$). The rise in interest rates also increases the incentives to borrow from the discount window because bank loans become more profitable and so the volume of discount loans will rise ($DL\uparrow$). The decline in excess reserves and the rise in the volume of discount loans then imply that free reserves will fall ($FR\downarrow = ER\downarrow - DL\uparrow$). When the Fed reacts to the decline in free reserves by making open market purchases, it raises the monetary base ($MB\uparrow$) and hence the money supply ($M\uparrow$). The reasoning outlined can be summarized as follows:

$$Y\uparrow \rightarrow i\uparrow \rightarrow ER\downarrow, DL\uparrow \rightarrow FR\downarrow \rightarrow MB\uparrow \rightarrow M\uparrow$$

A business cycle contraction causes the opposite chain of events so that the fall in income leads to a fall in the money supply ($Y\downarrow \rightarrow M\downarrow$). Thus the Fed's use of a free reserves target results in a positive association of money supply movements with national income and hence a procyclical monetary policy.

During this period, many economists, especially Karl Brunner and Allan Meltzer, criticized the Fed's use of free reserves as a target variable because of the procyclical monetary policy that it created. When the money supply grows more rapidly during a business cycle expansion, it can add to inflationary pressures; when it grows more slowly during a recession, it is likely to make the economic contraction worse. Indeed, a stated objective of the Fed during this period was that monetary policy should "lean against the wind": In other words, monetary policy should be anticyclical—contractionary when there is a business cycle expansion and expansionary when there is a business cycle contraction.

The Fed's other primary operating target, short-term interest rates, performed no better as a target variable than free reserves and also led to procyclical monetary policy. If the Fed saw interest rates rising as a result of a rise in income, it would purchase bonds to bid their price up and lower interest rates to their target level. The resulting increase in the monetary base caused the money supply to rise and the business cycle expansion to be accompanied by a faster rate of money growth. In summary,

$$Y\uparrow \rightarrow i\uparrow \rightarrow MB\uparrow \rightarrow M\uparrow$$

In a recession, the opposite sequence of events would occur, and the decline in income would be accompanied by a slower rate of growth in the money supply ($Y\downarrow \rightarrow M\downarrow$).

By the late 1960s, the rising chorus of criticism of procyclical monetary policy finally led the Fed to abandon its focus on money market conditions.

Targeting Monetary Aggregates: The 1970s

In 1970, Arthur Burns was appointed chairman of the Board of Governors, and soon thereafter the Fed stated that it was committing itself to the use of monetary aggregates as intermediate targets. Did monetary policy cease to be procyclical? A glance at Figure 1 in Chapter 1 indicates that monetary policy was as procyclical in the 1970s as in the 1950s and 1960s. What went wrong? Why did the conduct of monetary policy not improve? The answers to these questions lie in the Fed's operating procedures during the period, which suggest that its commitment to targeting monetary aggregates was not very strong.

Every six weeks, the Federal Open Market Committee would set target ranges for the growth rate of various monetary aggregates and would determine what federal funds rate (the interest rate on funds loaned overnight between banks) it thought consistent with these aims. The target ranges for the growth in monetary aggregates were fairly broad—a typical range for $M1$ growth might be 3% to 6%; for $M2$, 4% to 7%—while the range for the federal funds rate was a narrow band, say, from 7½% to 8¼%. The trading desk at the Federal Reserve Bank of New York was then instructed to meet both sets of targets, but as we saw earlier, interest-rate targets and monetary aggregate targets might not be compatible. If the two targets were incompatible, say, the federal funds rate began to climb higher than the top of its target band when $M1$ was growing too rapidly, the trading desk was instructed to give precedence to the federal funds rate target. In the situation we have just described, this would mean that although $M1$ growth was too high, the trading desk would make open market purchases to keep the federal funds rate within its target range.

The Fed was actually using the federal funds rate as its operating target. During the six-week period between FOMC meetings, an unexpected rise in income (which would cause the federal funds rate to hit the top of its target band) would then induce open market purchases and a too rapid growth of the money supply. When the FOMC met again, it would try to bring money supply growth back on track by raising the target range on the federal funds rate. However, if income continued to rise unexpectedly, money growth would overshoot again. This is exactly what occurred from June 1972 to June 1973, when the economy boomed unexpectedly: $M1$ growth greatly exceeded its target, increasing at approximately an 8% rate, while the federal funds rate climbed from 4½% to 8½%. The economy soon became overheated, and inflationary pressures began to mount.

The opposite chain of events occurred at the end of 1974, when the economic contraction was far more severe than anyone had predicted. The federal funds rate fell precipitously from over 12% to 5% and persistently bumped against the bottom of its target range. The trading desk conducted open market sales to keep the federal funds rate from falling, and money growth dropped precipitously, actually turning negative by the beginning of 1975. Clearly, this sharp drop in money growth when the United States was experiencing one of the worst economic contractions of the postwar era was a serious mistake.

Using the federal funds rate as an operating target promoted a procyclical monetary policy despite the Fed's lip service to monetary aggregate targets. If the Federal Reserve really intended to pursue monetary aggregate targets, it seems peculiar that it would have chosen an interest rate for an operating target rather than a reserve aggregate. (However, as the discussion of the conduct of Japanese monetary policy later in this chapter makes clear, more effective monetary control can be achieved even when an interest rate is used as an operating target.) The explanation for why the Fed chose an interest rate as an operating target is that it was still very concerned with achieving interest-rate stability and was reluctant to relinquish control over interest-rate movements. The incompatibility of the Fed's policy procedure with its stated intent of targeting on the monetary aggregates had become very clear by October 1979, when the Fed's policy procedures underwent drastic revision.

New Fed Operating Procedures: October 1979–October 1982

In October 1979, two months after Paul Volcker became chairman of the Board of Governors, the Fed finally deemphasized the federal funds rate as an operating target by widening its target range more than fivefold: A typical range might be from 10% to 15%. The primary operating target became nonborrowed reserves, which the Fed would set after estimating the volume of discount loans the banks would borrow. Figure 4 shows what happened to the federal funds rate and the growth rate of the M1 money supply both before and after October 1979. Not surprisingly, the federal funds rate underwent much greater fluctuations after it was deemphasized as an operating target. What is surprising, however, is that the deemphasis of the federal funds target did not result in improved monetary control: After October 1979, the fluctuations in the rate of money supply growth *increased* rather than decreased as would have been expected. In addition, the Fed missed its M1 growth target ranges in all three years of the 1979–1982 period.[5] What went wrong?

There are several possible answers to this question. The first is that the economy was exposed to several shocks during this period that made monetary control more difficult: the acceleration of financial innovation and deregulation, which added new categories of deposits such as NOW accounts to the measures of monetary aggregates; the imposition of credit controls from March to July 1980, which restricted the growth of consumer and business loans; and the back-to-back recessions of 1980 and 1981–1982.[6]

A more persuasive explanation for poor monetary control, however, is that controlling the money supply was never really the intent of Volcker's policy shift. Despite Volcker's statements about the need to target monetary aggregates, he was not committed to these targets. Rather, he was far more concerned with using interest-rate movements to wring inflation out of the economy. Volcker's primary reason for changing the Fed's operating procedure was to free his hand

---

[5]The M1 target ranges and actual growth rates for 1980 through 1982 were as follows:

Year	Range(%)	Actual(%)
1980	4.5–7.0	7.5
1981	6.0–8.5	5.1
1982	2.5–5.5	8.8

Source: Board of Governors of the Federal Reserve System, *Monetary Policy Objectives, 1981–1983*.

[6]Another explanation focuses on the technical difficulties of monetary control when using a nonborrowed reserves operating target under a system of lagged reserve requirements, in which required reserves for a given week are calculated on the basis of the level of deposits two weeks earlier. See David Lindsey, "Nonborrowed Reserve Targeting and Monetary Control," in *Improving Money Stock Control*, ed. Laurence Meyer (Boston: Kluwer-Nijhoff, 1983), pp. 3–41.

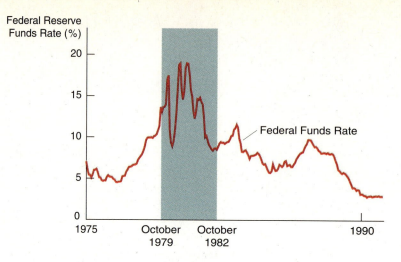

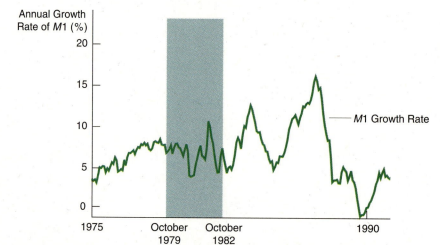

FIGURE 4
Federal Funds Rate and Growth Rate of the Money Supply, Before and After October 1979
Source: Federal Reserve *Bulletin.*

to manipulate interest rates in order to fight inflation. It was necessary to abandon interest-rate targets if Volcker were to be able to raise interest rates sharply when a slowdown in the economy was required to dampen inflation. This view of Volcker's strategy suggests that the Fed's announced attachment to monetary aggregate targets may have been a smokescreen to keep the Fed from being blamed for the high interest rates that would result from the new policy.

The interest-rate movements in Figure 4 support this interpretation of Fed strategy. After the October 1979 announcement, short-term interest rates were driven up by nearly 5%, until in March 1980 they exceeded 15%. With the imposition of credit controls in March 1980 and the rapid decline in real GDP in the second quarter of 1980, the Fed eased up on its policy and allowed interest rates to decline sharply. With the recovery starting in July 1980, inflation remained persistent, still exceeding a 10% rate. Because the inflation fight was not yet won, the Fed tightened the screws again, sending short-term rates above the 15% level for a second time. Finally, the 1981–1982 recession, with its large decline in output and high unemployment, began to bring inflation down. With the inflationary psychology apparently broken, interest rates were allowed to fall.

The Fed's anti-inflation strategy during the October 1979–October 1982 period was neither intended nor likely to produce smooth growth in the monetary aggregates. Indeed, the large fluctuations in interest rates and the business cycle, along with financial innovation, helped generate volatile money growth.

Deemphasis of Monetary Aggregates: October 1982 and Beyond

In October 1982, with inflation in check, the Fed returned, in effect, to a policy of smoothing interest rates. It did this by placing less emphasis on monetary aggregate targets and shifting to borrowed reserves (discount loan borrowings) as an operating target. To see how a borrowed reserves target produces interest rate smoothing, let's consider what happens when the economy expands ($Y\uparrow$) so that interest rates are driven up. The rise in interest rates ($i\uparrow$) increases the incentives for banks to borrow more from the Fed, so borrowed reserves rise ($DL\uparrow$). To prevent the resulting rise in borrowed reserves from exceeding the target level, the Fed must lower interest rates by bidding up the price of bonds through open market purchases. The outcome of targeting on borrowed reserves, then, is that the Fed prevents a rise in interest rates. In doing so, however, the Fed's open market purchases increase the monetary base ($MB\uparrow$) and lead to a rise in the money supply ($M\uparrow$), which produces a positive association of money and national income ($Y\uparrow \rightarrow M\uparrow$). Schematically,

$$Y\uparrow \rightarrow i\uparrow \rightarrow DL\uparrow \rightarrow MB\uparrow \rightarrow M\uparrow$$

A recession causes the opposite chain of events: The borrowed reserves target prevents interest rates from falling and results in a drop in the monetary base, leading to a fall in the money supply ($Y\downarrow \rightarrow M\downarrow$).

The deemphasis of monetary aggregates and the change to a borrowed reserves target are visible in Figure 4, where we see much smaller fluctuations in the federal funds rate after October 1982 but continue to have large fluctuations in money supply growth. Finally, in February 1987, the Fed announced that it would no longer even set $M1$ targets. The abandonment of $M1$ targets has been defended on two grounds. The first is that the rapid pace of financial innovation and deregulation has made the definition and measurement of money very difficult. The second is that there has been a breakdown in the stable relationship between $M1$ and economic activity (discussed in Chapter 23). These two arguments suggest that a monetary aggregate such as $M1$ may no longer be a reliable guide for monetary policy. As a result, the Fed switched its focus to the broader monetary aggregate $M2$, which it felt had a more stable relationship with economic activity. However, in the early 1990s, this relationship also broke down, and in July 1993, the Board of Governors' chairman, Alan Greenspan, testified in Congress that the Fed would no longer use any monetary targets, including $M2$, as a guide for conducting monetary policy.

The Fed's continuing deemphasis of monetary aggregates suggests that the Fed has returned to interest-smoothing operating procedures that, as we have seen, are likely to produce procyclical money supply growth in the future.

International Considerations

The increasing importance of international trade to the American economy has brought international considerations to the forefront of Federal Reserve policy-making in recent years. By 1985, the strength of the dollar had contributed to a deterioration in American competitiveness with foreign businesses. In public pronouncements, Volcker and other Fed officials made it clear that the dollar was at too high a value and needed to come down. Because, as we saw in Chapter 8, expansionary monetary policy is one way to lower the value of the dollar, it is no surprise that the Fed engineered an acceleration in the growth rates of the monetary aggregates in 1985 and 1986 and that the value of the dollar declined. By 1987, policymakers at the Fed agreed that the dollar had fallen sufficiently, and sure enough, monetary growth in the United States slowed. These monetary policy actions by the Fed were encouraged by the process of **international policy coordination** (agreements among countries to enact policies cooperatively) that led to the Plaza Agreement in 1985 and the Louvre Accord in 1987 (see Box 2). International considerations are likely to be a major factor in the conduct of American monetary policy in the future.

HOW WELL CAN THE FED CONTROL THE MONEY SUPPLY?

Our examination of the historical record of the Fed's conduct of monetary policy comes to the conclusion that the Fed has not been able to exercise effective control over the money supply. Does this mean that the Fed cannot control the money supply? Some economists, particularly those at the Fed, contend that the Fed's failure to control the money supply in the past implies that this objective is unachievable. Our analysis of the money supply process since Chapter 15 gives some credence to this position because we have seen that several factors outside of the Fed's control affect both the monetary base and money multiplier. Empirical evidence, however, supports a strong link between the monetary base, which is easily controlled through open market operations, and the money supply, suggesting that over longer time periods—six months to a year—the money supply can be controlled quite accurately.

Many economists contend that the Fed's failure to control the money supply in the past has occurred because, despite Fed statements to the contrary, the Fed really did not want to control it. Specifically, the Fed was not willing to commit

A Global Perspective

Box 2

INTERNATIONAL POLICY COORDINATION: THE PLAZA AGREEMENT AND THE LOUVRE ACCORD

By 1985, the decrease in the competitiveness of American corporations as a result of the strong dollar was raising strong sentiment in Congress for restricting imports. This protectionist threat to the international trading system stimulated finance ministers and the heads of central banks from the Group of Five (G-5) industrial countries—the United States, the United Kingdom, France, West Germany, and Japan—to reach an agreement at New York's Plaza Hotel in September 1985 to bring down the value of the dollar. From September 1985 until the beginning of 1987, the value of the dollar did indeed undergo a substantial decline, falling by 35% on average relative to foreign currencies. At this point, there was growing controversy over the decline in the dollar, and another meeting of the economic policymakers from the G-5 countries plus Canada took place in February 1987 at the Louvre Museum in Paris. There the policymakers agreed that exchange rates should be stabilized around the levels currently prevailing. Although the value of the dollar did continue to fluctuate relative to foreign currencies after the Louvre Accord, its downward trend had been checked as intended.

Because exchange rate movements were pretty much in line with the Plaza Agreement and the Louvre Accord, these attempts at international policy coordination have been considered successful. However, other aspects of the agreements were not adhered to by all signatories. For example, West German and Japanese policymakers agreed that their countries should pursue more expansionary policies by increasing government spending and cutting taxes, and the United States agreed to try to bring down its budget deficit. The United States has not been particularly successful in lowering its deficit, and the Germans have been reluctant to pursue expansionary policies because of their concerns about inflation.

itself to policy procedures that would ensure better control.[7] They suggest that the Fed could obtain far better control if it were willing to do two things: tie the discount rate to a market interest rate to decrease unwanted fluctuations in the volume of discount loans and focus less on stabilizing interest rates and more on control of the monetary base and the money supply. There is some evidence that policy procedures incorporating these suggestions could result in greatly improved control of the money supply over even shorter time periods (such as

---

[7]One possible reason is that such policy procedures would make the Fed more accountable for its actions, something that the theory of bureaucratic behavior suggests the Fed may want to avoid.

three months).[8] However, given the recent breakdown of a stable relationship between monetary aggregates and economic activity, there are doubts as to whether tighter control of the money supply is desirable.

THE CONDUCT OF MONETARY POLICY IN FIVE OTHER COUNTRIES

To understand how well a central bank can control the money supply, it is worth examining how monetary policy has been conducted in other countries besides the United States. Here we look at the conduct of monetary policy in recent decades in five other countries: the United Kingdom, Canada, Germany, Switzerland, and Japan.[9]

United Kindgom

As in the United States, the British introduced monetary targeting in late 1973 in response to mounting concerns about inflation. The Bank of England used a broader monetary target than the Fed did in the United States, $M3$, but did not pursue it seriously, resulting in greater volatility of British monetary aggregates than American ones. After inflation accelerated in the late 1970s, Prime Minister Margaret Thatcher in 1980 introduced the Medium-Term Financial Strategy, which proposed a gradual deceleration of $M3$ growth. Unfortunately, the $M3$ targets ran into problems similar to those of the $M1$ targets in the United States: They were not reliable indicators of the tightness of monetary policy. Subsequent to 1983, arguing that financial innovation was wreaking havoc with the relationship between $M3$ and income, the Bank of England began to deemphasize $M3$ in favor of a narrower monetary aggregate, $M0$ (the monetary base). The target for $M3$ was temporarily suspended in October 1985 and was completely dropped in 1987, leaving $M0$ as the only monetary aggregate targeted. Since 1984, target ranges for the growth in $M0$ have been reduced over time, and actual $M0$ growth has fallen within or close to the target ranges.

Canada

The Canadian experience with monetary policy closely parallels that of the United States. This is not surprising given the strong ties between the two economies and the fact that the value of the Canadian dollar has been closely linked to the U.S dollar.

---

[8]See, for example, James Johannes and Robert Rasche, "Predicting the Money Multiplier," *Journal of Monetary Economics* 5 (1979): 301–325.

[9]The discussion here is based on Ben Bernanke and Frederic S. Mishkin, "Central Bank Behavior and the Strategy of Monetary Policy: Observations from Six Industrialized Countries," in *NBER Macroeconomics Annual, 1992,* ed. O. Blanchard and S. Fischer (Cambridge: MIT Press, 1992), pp. 183–228.

In response to the rise in inflation in the early 1970s, the Bank of Canada introduced a program of "monetary gradualism," under which $M1$ growth would be controlled within a gradually falling target range. Monetary gradualism was no more successful in Canada than the initial attempts at monetary targeting in the United States and the United Kingdom. By 1978, only three years after monetary targeting had begun, the Bank of Canada began to distance itself from this strategy out of concern for the exchange rate. Because of the conflict with exchange rate goals, as well as the uncertainty about $M1$ as a reliable guide to monetary policy, the $M1$ targets were abandoned in November 1982. In a dramatic reversal of the subsequent ad hoc monetary strategy, in January 1988, John Crow, the governor (head) of the Bank of Canada, announced that the Bank of Canada would subsequently pursue an objective of price stability. The Bank and the Ministry of Finance have jointly announced a series of declining inflation targets in which $M2$ would be used as the guide to policy, along with an index of monetary conditions based on interest rates and exchange rates.

Germany

Germany's central bank, the Bundesbank, also responded to rising inflation in the early 1970s by adopting monetary targets in 1975. The monetary aggregate chosen was a narrow one known as *central bank money,* the sum of currency in circulation and bank deposits weighted by the 1974 required reserve ratios. The Bundesbank has allowed growth outside of its target ranges for periods of two to three years, and overshoots of its targets have subsequently been reversed. The primary reason for allowing deviations from its targets has been exchange rate considerations, which have been important to international agreements such as the European Exchange Rate Mechanism, the Plaza Agreement, and the Louvre Accord. In 1988, the Bundesbank switched targets from central bank money to $M3$. German monetary policy using monetary targeting has been quite successful in maintaining a low and stable inflation rate.

The reunification of Germany in 1990 created some difficult problems for monetary policy. The Bundesbank has been torn between trying to restrain the inflationary pressures created by reunification and keeping its exchange rate in line with those in other European countries. These strains contributed to an exchange rate crisis in Europe in September 1992, which will be discussed further in Chapter 22.

Switzerland

The Swiss National Bank, the central bank, began to announce monetary targets, with $M1$ as the targeted aggregate, at the end of 1974. The Swiss approach has been unusual in two ways: Targets are expressed as precise values rather than ranges, and the monetary base serves as the operating target. (Interest rates have been the operating target for the other countries discussed here, except for brief periods such as 1979–1982 in the United States.) The approach to hitting targets has been similar to that followed by Germany, with deviations to deal with exchange rate considerations reversed at a later date. Beginning in 1980, the Swiss National Bank switched to $M0$, the monetary base, as its targeted aggregate, thus using it as both its operating and intermediate target. In recent years, the relationship between the monetary aggregates and inflation have become quite unstable in Switzerland, leading the Swiss National Bank to deemphasize monetary targeting.

Japan

The increase in oil prices in late 1973 was a major shock for Japan, which experienced a huge jump in the inflation rate to greater than 20% in 1974—a surge facilitated by money growth in 1973 in excess of 20%. The Bank of Japan, like the other central banks discussed here, began to pay more attention to money growth rates. In 1978, the Bank of Japan began to announce "forecasts" at the beginning of each quarter for $M2 + CDs$. Although the Bank of Japan was not officially committed to monetary targeting, after 1978 monetary policy appeared to be more money-focused. For example, after the second oil price shock in 1979, the Bank of Japan quickly reduced $M2 + CDs$ growth, rather than allowing it to shoot up as occurred after the first oil shock. The Bank of Japan conducted monetary policy with operating procedures that are similar in many ways to those that the Federal Reserve has used in the United States. The Bank of Japan uses the interest rate in the Japanese interbank market (which has a function similar to that of the federal funds market in the United States) as its daily operating target, just as the Fed has done.

The Bank of Japan's monetary policy performance during the 1978–1987 period was much better than the Fed's. Money growth in Japan slowed gradually, beginning in the mid-1970s, and was much less variable than in the United States. The outcome was a more rapid braking of inflation and an average inflation rate that was lower in Japan. These excellent results on inflation were achieved with lower variability in real output in Japan than in the United States. The success of Japanese monetary policy in the 1978–1987 period using an interest rate as an operating target, in contrast to the lack of success in the 1970–1979 period in the United States when the Fed used a similar operating procedure, suggests that using an interest rate as an operating target is not necessarily a barrier to successful monetary policy. More important might be a commitment to a low inflation rate, something that was true for the Bank of Japan in this period.

In parallel with the United States, financial innovation and deregulation in Japan began to reduce the usefulness of the $M2 + CDs$ monetary aggregate as an indicator of monetary policy. Because of concerns about the appreciation of the yen, the Bank of Japan significantly increased the rate of money growth from 1987 to 1989. Many observers blame speculation in Japanese land and stock prices (the so-called *bubble economy*) on the increase in money growth, and to reduce this speculation, the Bank of Japan switched to a tighter monetary policy aimed at slower money growth. The aftermath has been a substantial decline in land and stock prices and the end of the bubble economy.

SUMMARY

1. There are six basic goals of monetary policy: high employment, economic growth, price stability, interest-rate stability, stability of financial markets, and stability in foreign exchange markets.

2. By using intermediate and operating targets, the Fed can more quickly judge whether its policies are on the right track and make midcourse corrections, rather than waiting to see the final outcome of its policies on such goals as employment and the price level. The Fed's policy tools directly affect its operating targets, which in turn affect the intermediate targets, which in turn affect the goals.

3. Because interest-rate and monetary aggregate targets are incompatible, the Fed must choose between them on the basis of three criteria: measurability, controllability, and the ability to affect goal variables predictably. Unfortunately, these criteria do not establish an overwhelming case for one set of targets over another.

4. The historical record of the Fed's conduct of monetary policy suggests that the Fed has not been able to exercise effective control over the money supply.

5. Some economists contend that the historical record indicates that the Fed cannot control the money supply, while other economists contend the Fed could obtain better control over the money supply if it wanted to. Empirical evidence supports a strong link between open market operations and the money supply, suggesting that over longer time periods, such as six months to a year, the money supply can be controlled quite effectively.

6. In response to the rise in inflation in the early 1970s, central banks around the world began to target monetary aggregates.

KEY TERMS

natural rate of unemployment

intermediate targets

operating targets

real bills doctrine

free reserves

international policy coordination

QUESTIONS AND PROBLEMS

*1. "Unemployment is a bad thing, and the government should make every effort to eliminate it." Do you agree or disagree? Explain.

2. Classify each of the following as either an operating target or an intermediate target, and explain why.
    (a) The three-month Treasury bill rate
    (b) The monetary base
    (c) M2

*3. "If the demand for money did not fluctuate, the Fed could pursue both a money supply target and an interest-rate target at the same time." Is this statement true, false, or uncertain? Explain.

4. If the Fed has an interest-rate target, why will an increase in money demand lead to a rise in the money supply?

*5. What procedures can the Fed use to control the three-month Treasury bill rate? Why does control of this interest rate imply that the Fed will lose control of the money supply?

6. Compare the monetary base to *M2* on the grounds of controllability and measurability. Which do you prefer as an intermediate target? Why?

*7. "Interest rates can be measured more accurately and more quickly than the money supply. Hence an interest rate is preferred over the money supply as an intermediate target." Do you agree or disagree? Explain.

8. Explain why the rise in the discount rate in 1920 led to a sharp decline in the money supply.

*9. How did the Fed's failure to perform its role as the lender of last resort contribute to the decline of the money supply in the 1930–1933 period?

10. Excess reserves are frequently called *idle reserves,* suggesting that they are not useful. Does the episode of the rise in reserve requirements in 1936–1937 bear out this view?

*11. "When the economy enters a recession, either a free reserves target or an interest-rate target will lead to a slower rate of growth for the money supply." Explain why this statement is true. What does it say about the use of free reserves or interest rates as targets?

12. "The failure of the Fed to control the money supply in the 1970s and 1980s suggests that the Fed is not able to control the money supply." Do you agree or disagree? Explain.

*13. Which is more likely to produce smaller fluctuations in the federal funds rate, a nonborrowed reserves target or a borrowed reserves target? Why?

14. How can bank behavior and the Fed's behavior cause money supply growth to be procyclical (rising in booms and falling in recessions)?

*15. Why might the Fed say that it wants to control the money supply but in reality not be serious about doing so?

Chapter 22

THE INTERNATIONAL FINANCIAL SYSTEM AND MONETARY POLICY

PREVIEW   The growing interdependence between the U.S. economy and the economies of the rest of the world means that a country's monetary policy can no longer be conducted without taking international considerations into account. In this chapter we examine how international financial transactions and the structure of the international financial system affect monetary policy. We also examine the evolution of the international financial system during the past half century and where it may be heading in the future.

INTERVENTION IN THE FOREIGN EXCHANGE MARKET

In Chapter 8 we analyzed the foreign exchange market as if it were a completely free market that responds to all market pressures. However, the foreign exchange market, like many others, is not free of government intervention; central banks regularly engage in international financial transactions called **foreign exchange interventions** in order to influence exchange rates. In our current international financial arrangement, called a **managed float regime** (or a **dirty float**), exchange rates fluctuate from day to day, but central banks attempt to influence their countries' exchange rates by buying and selling currencies. The exchange rate analysis we developed in Chapter 8 is used here to explain the impact this central bank intervention has on the foreign exchange market.

Foreign Exchange Intervention and the Money Supply

The first step in understanding how central bank intervention in the foreign exchange market affects exchange rates is to see the impact on the monetary base from a central bank sale in the foreign exchange market of some of its holdings of assets denominated in a foreign currency (called **international reserves**).

519

Suppose that the Fed decides to sell $10 billion of its foreign assets in exchange for $10 billion of currency. The Fed's purchase of dollars has two effects. First, it reduces the Fed's holding of international reserves by $10 billion. Second, because its purchase of currency removes it from the hands of the public, currency in circulation falls by $10 billion. We can see this in the following T-account for the Federal Reserve:

Federal Reserve System			
Assets		Liabilities	
Foreign assets (international reserves)	– $10 billion	Currency in circulation	– $10 billion

Because the monetary base is made up of currency in circulation plus reserves, this decline in currency implies that the monetary base has fallen by $10 billion.

If instead of paying for the foreign assets sold by the Fed with currency, the persons buying the foreign assets pay for them by checks written on accounts at domestic banks, the Fed deducts the $10 billion from the deposit accounts these banks have with the Fed. The result is that deposits with the Fed (reserves) decline by $10 billion, as shown in the following T-account:

Federal Reserve System			
Assets		Liabilities	
Foreign assets (international reserves)	– $10 billion	Deposits with the Fed (reserves)	– $10 billion

In this case, the outcome of the Fed sale of foreign assets and the purchase of dollar deposits is a $10 billion decline in reserves and a $10 billion decline in the monetary base because reserves are also a component of the monetary base.

We now see that the outcome for the monetary base is exactly the same when a central bank sells foreign assets to purchase domestic bank deposits or domestic currency. This is why when we say that a central bank has purchased its domestic currency, we do not have to distinguish whether it actually purchased currency or bank deposits denominated in the domestic currency. We have thus reached an important conclusion: ***A central bank's purchase of domestic currency and corresponding sale of foreign assets in the foreign exchange market leads to an equal decline in its international reserves and the monetary base.***

We could have reached the same conclusion by a more direct route. A central bank sale of a foreign asset is no different from an open market sale of a government bond. We learned in our exploration of the money supply process that an open market sale leads to an equal decline in the monetary base; therefore, a sale of foreign assets also leads to an equal decline in the monetary base. By similar reasoning, a central bank purchase of foreign assets paid for by selling domestic currency, like an open market purchase, leads to an equal rise in the monetary base. Thus we reach the following conclusion: ***A central bank's sale***

of domestic currency to purchase foreign assets in the foreign exchange market results in an equal rise in its international reserves and the monetary base.

The intervention we have just described, in which a central bank allows the purchase or sale of domestic currency to have an effect on the monetary base, is called an **unsterilized foreign exchange intervention.** But what if the central bank does not want the purchase or sale of domestic currency to affect the monetary base? All it has to do is to counter the effect of the foreign exchange intervention by conducting an offsetting open market operation in the government bond market. For example, in the case of a $10 billion purchase of dollars by the Fed and a corresponding $10 billion sale of foreign assets, which we have seen would decrease the monetary base by $10 billion, the Fed can conduct an open market purchase of $10 billion of government bonds, which would increase the monetary base by $10 billion. The resulting T-account for the foreign exchange intervention and the offsetting open market operation leaves the monetary base unchanged:

Federal Reserve System			
Assets		Liabilities	
Foreign assets (international reserves)	- $10 billion	Monetary base (reserves)	0
Government bonds	+ $10 billion		

A foreign exchange intervention with an offsetting open market operation that leaves the monetary base unchanged is called a **sterilized foreign exchange intervention.**

Now that we understand that there are two types of foreign exchange interventions, unsterilized and sterilized, let's look at how each of these interventions affects the exchange rate.

Unsterilized Intervention

Your intuition might lead you to suspect that if a central bank wants to lower the value of the domestic currency, it should sell its currency in the foreign exchange market and purchase foreign assets. Indeed, this intuition is correct for the case of an unsterilized intervention.

Recall that in an unsterilized intervention, if the Federal Reserve decides to sell dollars in order to buy foreign assets in the foreign exchange market, this works just like an open market purchase of bonds to increase the monetary base. Hence the sale of dollars leads to an increase in the money supply, and we find ourselves analyzing exactly the situation already described in Figure 7 of Chapter 8, which is reproduced here as Figure 1. The higher money supply leads to a higher U.S. price level in the long run and so to a lower expected future exchange rate. The resulting decline in the expected appreciation of the dollar increases the expected return on foreign deposits and shifts the RET^F schedule to the right. In addition, the increase in the money supply will lead to a higher real money supply in the short run, which causes the interest rate on dollar deposits to fall. The resulting lower expected return on dollar deposits translates as a leftward shift in the $RET^\$$ schedule. The fall in the expected return on dollar deposits and the increase in the expected return on foreign deposits means that foreign assets have a higher expected return than dollar deposits at the old equilibrium exchange rate. Hence people will try to sell their dollar deposits, and the exchange rate will fall. Indeed, as we saw in Chapter 8, the increase in the money supply will lead to exchange rate overshooting, whereby the exchange rate falls by more in the short run than it does in the long run.

Our analysis leads us to the following conclusion about unsterilized interventions in the foreign exchange market: ***An unsterilized intervention in which domestic currency is sold to purchase foreign assets leads to a gain in international reserves, an increase in the money supply, and a depreciation of the domestic currency.***

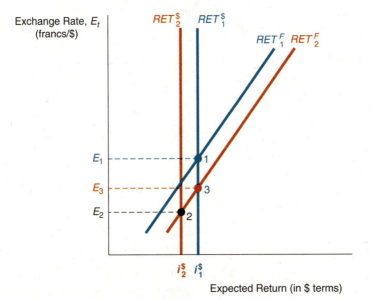

FIGURE 1 Effect of a Sale of Dollars and a Purchase of Foreign Assets
A sale of dollars and the consequent open market purchase of foreign assets increase the monetary base. The resulting rise in the money supply leads to a higher domestic price level in the long run, which leads to a lower expected future exchange rate. The resulting decline in the expected appreciation of the dollar raises the expected return on foreign deposits, shifting the RET^F schedule rightward from RET_1^F to RET_2^F. In the short run, the domestic interest rate $i^\$$ falls, shifting $RET^\$$ from $RET_1^\$$ to $RET_2^\$$. The short-run outcome is that the exchange rate falls from E_1 to E_2. In the long run, however, the interest rate returns to $i_1^\$$, and $RET^\$$ returns to $RET_1^\$$. The exchange rate therefore rises from E_2 to E_3 in the long run.

The reverse result is found for an unsterilized intervention in which domestic currency is purchased by selling foreign assets. The purchase of domestic currency by selling foreign assets (reducing international reserves) works like an open market sale to reduce the monetary base and the money supply. The decrease in the money supply raises the interest rate on dollar deposits and shifts $RET^\$$ rightward while causing RET^F to shift leftward because it leads to a lower U.S. price level in the long run and thus to a higher expected appreciation of the dollar and hence a lower expected return on foreign deposits. The increase in the expected return on dollar deposits relative to foreign deposits will mean that people will want to buy more dollar deposits, and the exchange rate will rise. ***An unsterilized intervention in which domestic currency is purchased by selling foreign assets leads to a drop in international reserves, a decrease in the money supply, and an appreciation of the domestic currency.***

Sterilized Intervention

The key point to remember about a sterilized intervention is that the central bank engages in offsetting open market operations so that there is no impact on the monetary base and the money supply. In the context of the model of exchange rate determination we have developed here, it is straightforward to show that a sterilized intervention has *no effect* on the exchange rate. Remember that in our model, foreign and domestic deposits are perfect substitutes, so equilibrium in the foreign exchange market occurs when the expected returns on foreign and domestic deposits are equal. A sterilized intervention leaves the money supply unchanged and so has no way of directly affecting interest rates or the expected future exchange rate.[1] Because the expected returns on dollar and foreign deposits are unaffected, the expected return schedules remain at $RET^\$_1$ and RET^F_1 in Figure 1, and the exchange rate remains unchanged at E_1.

At first it might seem puzzling that a central bank purchase or sale of domestic currency that is sterilized does not lead to a change in the exchange rate. A sterilized central bank purchase of domestic currency cannot raise the exchange rate because with no effect on the domestic money supply or interest rates, any resulting rise in the exchange rate would mean that the expected re-

---

[1]Note that a sterilized intervention could indicate what central banks want to happen to the future exchange rate and so might provide a signal about the course of future monetary policy. In this way, a sterilized intervention could lead to shifts in the RET^F schedule, but in reality it is the future change in monetary policy, not the sterilized intervention, that is the ultimate source of exchange rate effects. For a discussion of the signaling effect, see Maurice Obstfeld, "The effectiveness of Foreign Exchange Intervention: Recent Experience, 1985–1988," in *International Policy Coordination and Exchange Rate Fluctuations,* ed. William H. Branson, Jacob A. Frenkel, and Morris Goldstein (Chicago: University of Chicago Press, 1990), pp. 197–237.

turn on foreign deposits would be greater than the expected return on domestic deposits. Given our assumption that foreign and domestic deposits are perfect substitutes (equally desirable), this would mean that no one would want to hold domestic deposits.[2] So the exchange rate would have to fall back to its previous level where the expected returns on domestic and foreign deposits were equal.

BALANCE OF PAYMENTS

Because international financial transactions such as foreign exchange interventions have considerable effect on monetary policy, it is worth knowing how these transactions are measured. The **balance of payments** is a bookkeeping system for recording all payments that have a direct bearing on the movement of funds between a nation (private sector and government) and foreign countries.

The balance-of-payments account in the accompanying "Following the Financial News" box uses a standard double-entry bookkeeping system much like one that you or I might use to keep a record of payments and receipts. All payments from foreigners to Americans are entered in the "Receipts" column with a plus (+) sign to reflect that they are credits; that is, they result in a flow of funds to Americans. Receipts include foreign purchases of American products such as computers and wheat (exports), payments from foreign tourists (services), income earned from American investment abroad (investment income), foreign gifts and pensions paid to Americans (unilateral transfers), and foreign payments for American assets (capital inflows).

All payments to foreigners are entered in the "Payments" column with a minus (−) sign to reflect that they are debits because they result in flows of funds to other countries. Payments include American purchases of foreign products such as French wine and Japanese cars (imports), American travel abroad (services), income earned by foreigners from investments in the United States (investment income), foreign aid and gifts and pensions paid to foreigners (unilateral transfers), and American payments for foreign assets (capital outflows).

Current Account

The **current account** shows international transactions that involve currently produced goods and services. The difference between merchandise exports (line

---

[2]If domestic and foreign deposits are not perfect substitutes, a sterilized intervention can affect the exchange rate. However, most studies by both academic and government economists find little evidence to support the position that sterilized intervention has a significant impact on foreign exchange rates. For a further discussion of the effects of sterilized versus unsterilized intervention, see Paul Krugman and Maurice Obstfeld, *International Economics,* 3rd ed. (New York: HarperCollins, 1994).

FOLLOWING THE FINANCIAL NEWS

The Balance of Payments

Newspapers periodically report information on the balance of payments. Balance-of-trade figures (merchandise exports minus imports) are reported monthly in the last week of the month. The complete set of items in the balance of payments is published on a quarterly basis with the previous quarter's figures published between the eighteenth and twentieth day of the last month of the following quarter. An example of the balance-of-payments accounts for the United States appears here.

U.S. Balance of Payments, 1993 ($ billions)

	Receipts (+)	Payments (−)	Balance
Current Account			
(1) Merchandise exports	+457		
(2) Merchandise imports		−589	
Trade balance			−132
(3) Net investment income	+0		
(4) Net services	+56		
(5) Net unilateral transfers		−33	
Current account balance:			
(1) + (2) + (3) + (4) + (5)			−109
Capital Account			
(6) Capital outflows		−142	
(7) Capital inflows	+155		
(8) Statistical discrepancy	+26		
Official reserve transactions balance:			
(1) + (2) + (3) + (4) + (5) + (6) + (7) + (8)			−70
Method of Financing			
(9) Increase in U.S. official reserve assets		−1	
(10) Increase in foreign official assets	+71		
Total financing of surplus			+70
Balance of Payments			
Sum: (1) through (10)			0

Source: Survey of Current Business, March 1994.

1) and imports (line 2) is called the **trade balance.** When merchandise imports are greater than exports (here by $132 billion), we have a trade balance deficit; if exports are greater than imports, we have a trade balance surplus.

The next three items in the current account are the net payments or receipts that arise from investment income, the purchase and sale of services, and unilateral transfers (gifts, pensions, and foreign aid). In 1993, for example, net investment income was essentially zero (in line 3) for the United States because Americans received the same amount of investment income that they paid out. Americans bought less in services from foreigners than foreigners bought from Americans, so net services generated $56 billion in receipts (line 4). Since Americans made more unilateral transfers to foreign countries (especially foreign aid) than foreigners made to the United States, a $33 billion payment is shown in line 5.

The sum of the items in lines 1 through 5 is the current account balance, which in 1993 showed a deficit of $109 billion. The current account balance is an important balance-of-payments concept for several reasons. As we can see from the balance-of-payments account, any surplus or deficit in the current account must be balanced either by capital account transactions (lending or borrowing abroad) or by changes in government reserve asset items:

Current account + capital account = change in government reserve assets

The current account balance tells us whether the United States (private sector and government combined) is increasing or decreasing its claims on foreign wealth. A surplus indicates that America is increasing its claims on foreign wealth, and a deficit, as in 1993, indicates that the country is reducing its claims on foreign wealth.[3]

Economists follow the current account balance closely because they believe that it can provide information on the future movement of exchange rates. The current account balance provides some indication of what is happening to the demand for imports and exports, which, as we saw in Chapter 8, can affect the exchange rate. In addition, the current account balance provides information about what will be happening to U.S. claims on foreign wealth in the long run. Because a movement of foreign wealth to American residents can affect the demand for dollar assets, changes in U.S. claims on foreign wealth, reflected in the current account balance, can affect the exchange rate over time.[4]

---

[3]The current account balance can also be viewed as showing by how much total saving exceeds private sector and government investment in the United States. We can see this by noting that total U.S. saving equals the increase in total wealth held by the U.S. private sector and government. Total investment equals the increase in the U.S. capital stock (wealth physically in the United States). The difference between them is the increase in U.S. claims on foreign wealth.

[4]If American residents have a greater preference for dollar assets than foreigners do, a movement of foreign wealth to American residents when there is a balance-of-payments surplus will increase the demand for dollar assets over time and will cause the dollar to appreciate.

Capital Account

The **capital account** describes the flow of capital between the United States and other countries. Capital outflows are American purchases of foreign assets (a "Payments" item), and capital inflows are foreign purchases of American assets (a "Receipts" item). The capital outflows (line 6) are less than the capital inflows (line 7), resulting in a net flow of $13 billion in funds from foreigners in exchange for claims against American individuals and corporations.

The statistical discrepancy (line 8) represents errors due to unrecorded transactions involving smuggling and other capital flows. The statistical discrepancy, which keeps the balance-of-payments account in balance, is +$26 billion, which suggests that some of the other items in the balance of payments may not be measured very accurately. Many experts believe that the statistical discrepancy is primarily the result of large hidden capital flows, and so the item has been placed in the capital account part of the balance of payments.

Official Reserve Transactions Balance

The sum of lines 1 through 8, called the **official reserve transactions balance,** equals the current account balance plus the items in the capital account. When we refer to a surplus or a deficit in the balance of payments, we actually mean a surplus or deficit in the official reserve transactions balance. Because the balance-of-payments account must balance, the official reserve transactions balance tells us the net amount of international reserves that must move between central banks to finance international transactions. One reason we are particularly interested in the movements of international reserves is that, as we saw earlier in the chapter, these movements have an important impact on the money supply and exchange rates.

Methods of Financing the Balance of Payments

Because most countries' currencies are not held by other countries as international reserves, these countries must finance an excess of payments over receipts (a deficit in the balance of payments) by providing international reserves to foreign governments and central banks. A balance-of-payments deficit is associated with a loss of international reserves; likewise, a balance-of-payments surplus is associated with a gain.

In contrast to other countries' currencies, the U.S. dollar and dollar-denominated assets are the major component of international reserves held by other countries. Thus a U.S. balance-of-payments deficit can be financed by a decrease in U.S. international reserves, an increase in foreign central banks' holdings of international reserves (dollar assets), or both. Conversely, a U.S. balance-of-payments surplus can be financed by an increase in U.S. international reserves, a decrease in foreign central banks' international reserves, or both.

For the United States in 1993, the official reserve transactions deficit of $70 billion was financed by a $1 billion increase in U.S. international reserves (−1 in the "Payments" column of line 9)[5] and a $71 billion increase of foreign holdings of dollars (in the "Receipts" column of line 10). On net, the United States' indebtedness to foreign governments (central banks) increased by $70 billion (the $71 billion foreign increase in holdings of U.S. dollars minus the $1 billion increase in U.S. holdings of international reserves). This $70 billion increase in net U.S. government indebtedness just matches the $70 billion official reserve transactions deficit, so the sum of lines 1 through 10 is zero, and the account balances.

EVOLUTION OF THE INTERNATIONAL FINANCIAL SYSTEM

Before examining the impact of international financial transactions on monetary policy, we need to understand the past and current structure of the international financial system.

The Gold Standard

Before World War I, the world economy operated under a **gold standard,** in which the currency of most countries was convertible directly into gold. American dollar bills, for example, could be turned in to the U.S. Treasury and exchanged for approximately ¹⁄₂₀ ounce of gold. Likewise, the British Treasury would exchange ¼ ounce of gold for £1 sterling. Because an American could convert $20 into 1 ounce of gold, which could be used to buy £4, the exchange rate between the pound and the dollar was effectively fixed at $5 to the pound. Tying currencies to gold resulted in an international financial system with fixed exchange rates between currencies. The fixed exchange rates under the gold standard had the important advantage of encouraging world trade by eliminating the uncertainty that occurs when exchange rates fluctuate.

To see how the gold standard operated in practice, let us see what occurs if, under a gold standard, the British pound begins to appreciate above the $5 par value. If an American importer of £100 of English tweed tries to pay for the tweed with dollars, it costs more than the $500 it cost before. Nevertheless, the

---

[5]At first it may appear strange that when the United States gains $4 billion of international reserves, it is entered in the balance of payments as a payment with a negative sign. Recall, however, that when a central bank gains international reserves, it has bought foreign assets. Thus an increase in international reserves is just like an outflow of capital in the capital account and appears as a payment with a negative sign.

importer has another option involving the purchase of gold that can reduce the cost of the tweed. Instead of using dollars to pay for the tweed, the American importer can exchange the $500 for gold, ship the gold to Britain, and convert it into £100. The shipment of gold to Britain is cheaper as long as the British pound is above the $5 par value (plus a small amount to pay for the cost of shipping the gold).

The appreciation of the pound leads to a British gain of international reserves (gold) and an equal U.S. loss. Because a change in a country's holdings of international reserves (gold) leads to an equal change in its monetary base, the movement of gold from the United States to Britain causes the British monetary base to rise and the American monetary base to fall. The resulting rise in the British money supply raises the British price level, while the fall in the U.S. money supply lowers the U.S. price level. The resulting increase in the British price level relative to the United States then causes the pound to depreciate. This process will continue until the value of the pound falls back down to its $5 par value.

A depreciation of the pound below the $5 par value, on the contrary, stimulates gold shipments from Britain to the United States. These shipments raise the American money supply and lower the British money supply, causing the pound to appreciate back toward the $5 par value. We thus see that under a gold standard, a rise or fall in the exchange rate sets in motion forces that return it to the par value.

As long as countries abided by the rules under the gold standard and kept their currencies backed by and convertible into gold, exchange rates remained fixed. However, adherence to the gold standard meant that a country had no control over its monetary policy because its money supply was, for the most part, determined by gold flows between countries. Furthermore, monetary policy throughout the world was greatly influenced by the production of gold and gold discoveries. When gold production was low in the 1870s and 1880s, the money supply throughout the world grew slowly and did not keep pace with the growth of the world economy. The result was deflation (falling price levels). Gold discoveries in Alaska and South Africa in the 1890s then greatly expanded gold production, which in turn caused money supplies to increase rapidly and price levels to rise (inflation) until World War I.

The Bretton Woods System and the IMF

With the coming of World War I, which led to massive trade disruptions, countries could no longer convert their currencies into gold. The gold standard collapsed. Despite attempts to revive it in the interwar period, the worldwide depression, beginning in 1929, led to its permanent demise. As the Allied victory in World War II was becoming certain in 1944, the Allies met in Bretton Woods, New Hampshire, to develop a new international monetary system to promote world trade and prosperity after the war. In the agreement worked out among the Allies, central banks bought and sold their own currencies to keep their exchange rates fixed at a certain level (called a **fixed exchange rate regime**). The agreement lasted from 1945 to 1971 and was known as the **Bretton Woods system.**

The Bretton Woods agreement created the **International Monetary Fund (IMF),** which had 30 original member countries in 1945 and currently has over 150. The IMF was given the task of promoting the growth of world trade by setting rules for the maintenance of fixed exchange rates and by making loans to countries that were experiencing balance-of-payments difficulties.[6] As part of its role of monitoring the compliance of member countries with its rules, the IMF also took on the job of collecting and standardizing international economic data.

The Bretton Woods agreement also set up the International Bank for Reconstruction and Development, commonly referred to as the **World Bank,** which provides long-term loans to assist developing countries to build dams, roads, and other physical capital that would contribute to their economic development. The funds for these loans are obtained primarily by issuing World Bank bonds, which are sold in the capital markets of the developed countries.[7]

Because the United States emerged from World War II as the world's largest economic power with over half of the world's manufacturing capacity and the greater part of the world's gold, the Bretton Woods system of fixed exchange rates was based on the convertibility of U.S. dollars into gold (for foreign governments and central banks only) at $35 per ounce. The fixed exchange rates were to be maintained by intervention in the foreign exchange market by central banks in countries besides the United States who bought and sold dollar assets, which they held as international reserves. The U.S. dollar, which was used by other countries to denominate the assets that they held as international reserves, was called a **reserve currency.** Thus an important feature of the Bretton Woods system was the establishment of the United States as the reserve currency country.

How a Fixed Exchange Rate Regime Works   The most important feature of the Bretton Woods system was that it set up a fixed exchange rate regime. Figure 2 shows how a fixed exchange rate regime works in practice using the model of exchange rate determination we learned in Chapter 8. Panel (a) describes a situation in which the domestic currency is initially overvalued: The schedule for the expected return on foreign deposits RET_1^F intersects the schedule for the expected return on domestic deposits RET_1^D at exchange rate E_1, which is lower than the par (fixed) value of the exchange rate E_{par}. To keep the exchange rate

---

[6]Rules for the conduct of trade between countries (the setting of tariffs and quotas) were given to the General Agreement on Tariffs and Trade (GATT), headquartered in Geneva. For a discussion of how this agency operates, see John Williamson, *The Open Economy and the World Economy* (New York: Basic Books, 1983).

[7]In 1960, the World Bank established an affiliate, the International Development Association (IDA), which provides particularly attractive loans to third-world countries (with 50-year maturities and zero interest rates, for example). Funds for these loans are obtained by direct contributions of member countries.

at E_{par}, the central bank must intervene in the foreign exchange market to purchase domestic currency by selling foreign assets, and this action, like an open market sale, means that the monetary base and the money supply decline. Because the exchange rate will continue to be fixed at E_{par}, the expected future exchange rate remains unchanged, and so the schedule for the expected return on foreign deposits remains at RET_1^F. However, the purchase of domestic currency, which leads to a fall in the money supply, also causes the interest rate on domestic deposits i^D to rise. This increase in turn shifts the expected return on domestic deposits RET^D to the right. The central bank will continue purchasing domestic currency and selling foreign assets until the RET^D curve reaches RET_2^D and the equilibrium exchange rate is at E_{par} at point 2 in panel (a).

We have thus come to the conclusion that ***when the domestic currency is overvalued, the central bank must purchase domestic currency to keep the exchange rate fixed, but as a result it loses international reserves.***

Panel (b) in Figure 2 shows how a central bank intervention keeps the exchange rate fixed at E_{par} when the exchange rate is initially undervalued, that is, when RET_1^F and the initial RET_1^D intersect at exchange rate E_1 which is above E_{par}. Here the central bank must sell domestic currency and purchase foreign assets, and this works like an open market purchase to raise the money supply and to lower the interest rate on domestic deposits i^D. The central bank keeps

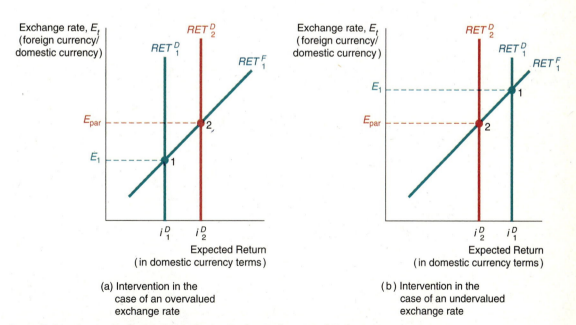

(a) Intervention in the
case of an overvalued
exchange rate

(b) Intervention in the
case of an undervalued
exchange rate

Figure 2 Intervention in the Foreign Exchange Market Under a Fixed Exchange Rate Regime
In panel (a), the exchange rate at E_{par} is overvalued. To keep the exchange rate at E_{par} (point 2), the central bank must purchase domestic currency to shift the schedule for the expected return on domestic deposits to RET_2^D. In panel (b), the exchange rate at E_{par} is undervalued, so a central bank sale of domestic currency is needed to shift RET^D to RET_2^D to keep the exchange rate at E_{par} (point 2).

selling domestic currency and lowers i^D until RET^D shifts all the way to RET_2^D where the equilibrium exchange rate is at E_{par}—point 2 in panel (b). Our analysis thus leads us to the following result: ***When the domestic currency is undervalued, the central bank must sell domestic currency to keep the exchange rate fixed, but as a result it gains international reserves.***

As we have seen, if a country's currency has an overvalued exchange rate, its central bank's attempts to keep the currency from depreciating will result in a loss of international reserves. If the country's central bank eventually runs out of international reserves, it cannot keep its currency from depreciating, and a **devaluation** must occur, meaning that the par exchange rate is reset at a lower level.

If, by contrast, a country's currency has an undervalued exchange rate, its central bank's intervention to keep the currency from appreciating leads to a gain of international reserves. Because, as we will see shortly, the central bank might not want to acquire these international reserves, it might want to reset the par value of its exchange rate at a higher level (a **revaluation**).

Note that if domestic and foreign deposits are perfect substitutes, as is assumed in the model of exchange rate determination used here, a sterilized exchange rate intervention would not be able to keep the exchange rate at E_{par} because, as we have seen in Chapter 8, neither RET^F or RET^D will shift. For example, if the exchange rate is overvalued, a sterilized purchase of domestic currency will still leave the expected return on domestic deposits below the expected return on foreign deposits at the par exchange rate—so pressure for a depreciation of the domestic currency is not removed. If the central bank keeps on purchasing its domestic currency but continues to sterilize, it will just keep on losing international reserves until it finally runs out of them and is forced to let the value of the currency seek a lower level.

The Bretton Woods System of Fixed Exchange Rates   Under the Bretton Woods system, exchange rates were supposed to change only when a country was experiencing a "fundamental disequilibrium," that is, large persistent deficits or surpluses in its balance of payments. To maintain fixed exchange rates when countries had balance-of-payments deficits and were losing international reserves, the IMF would loan deficit countries international reserves contributed by other members. As a result of its power to dictate loan terms to borrowing countries, the IMF could encourage deficit countries to pursue contractionary monetary policies that would strengthen their currency or eliminate their balance-of-payment deficits. If the IMF loans were not sufficient to prevent depreciation of a currency, the country was allowed to devalue its currency by setting a new, lower exchange rate.

A notable weakness of the Bretton Woods system was that although deficit countries losing international reserves could be pressured into devaluing their currency or pursuing contractionary policies, the IMF had no way to force surplus countries to revise their exchange rates upward or pursue more expansionary policies. Particularly troublesome in this regard was the fact that the reserve currency country, the United States, could not devalue its currency under the Bretton Woods system even if the dollar was overvalued. When the United States attempted to reduce domestic unemployment in the 1960s by pursuing an inflationary monetary policy (described in Chapter 28), a fundamental disequilibrium of an overvalued dollar developed. Because surplus countries were not willing to revise their exchange rates upward, adjustment in the Bretton Woods system did not take place, and the system collapsed in 1971. Attempts to patch up the Bretton Woods system with the Smithsonian Agreement in December 1971 proved unsuccessful, and by 1973, America and its trading partners had agreed to allow exchange rates to float.

The Managed Float

Although exchange rates are currently allowed to change daily in response to market forces, central banks have not been willing to give up their option of intervening in the foreign exchange market. Preventing large changes in exchange rates makes it easier for firms and individuals purchasing or selling goods abroad to plan into the future. Furthermore, countries with surpluses in their balance of payments frequently do not want to see their currencies appreciate because it makes their goods more expensive abroad and foreign goods cheaper in their country. Because an appreciation might hurt sales for domestic businesses and increase unemployment, surplus countries have often sold their currency in the foreign exchange market and acquired international reserves.

Countries with balance-of-payments deficits do not want to see their currency lose value because it makes foreign goods more expensive for domestic consumers and can stimulate inflation. To keep the value of the domestic currency high, deficit countries have often bought their own currency in the foreign exchange market and given up international reserves.

The current international financial system is a hybrid of a fixed and a flexible exchange rate system. Rates fluctuate in response to market forces but are not determined solely by them. Furthermore, many countries continue to keep the value of their currency fixed against other currencies, as in the European Monetary System (to be described shortly).

The IMF continues to function as a data collector and international lender but does not attempt to encourage fixed exchange rates. The IMF's role of international lender has also become important recently because of the third-world debt crisis (discussed in Chapter 12). The IMF has been directly involved in helping developing countries that are experiencing difficulties in repaying their loans come to terms with lenders in the West.

Another important feature of the current system is the continuing deemphasis of gold in international financial transactions. Not only has the United States suspended convertibility of dollars into gold for foreign central banks, but since

1970 the IMF has been issuing a paper substitute for gold, called **special draw-ing rights (SDRs).** Like gold in the Bretton Woods system, SDRs function as international reserves. Unlike gold, whose quantity is determined by gold discoveries and the rate of production, SDRs can be created by the IMF whenever it decides that there is a need for additional international reserves to promote world trade and economic growth.

The use of gold in international transactions was further deemphasized by the IMF's elimination of the official gold price in 1975 and by the sale of gold by the U.S. Treasury and the IMF to private interests in order to demonetize it. Currently, the price of gold is determined in a free market. Investors who want to speculate in it are able to purchase and sell at will, as are jewelers and dentists who use gold in their businesses.

The European Monetary System (EMS)

In March 1979, eight members of the European Economic Community (West Germany, France, Italy, the Netherlands, Belgium, Luxembourg, Denmark, and Ireland) set up the European Monetary System (EMS) in which they agreed to fix their exchange rates vis-à-vis one another and to float jointly against the U.S. dollar. Spain joined the EMS in June 1989, the United Kingdom in October 1990, and Portugal in April 1992. The EMS has created a new monetary unit, the European Currency Unit (ECU), whose value is tied to a basket of specified amounts of European currencies. Each member of the EMS is required to contribute 20% of its holdings of gold and dollars to the European Monetary Cooperation Fund and in return receives an equivalent amount of ECUs.

The exchange rate mechanism (ERM) of the European Monetary System works as follows. The exchange rate between every pair of currencies of the participating countries is not allowed to fluctuate outside narrow limits around a fixed exchange rate. (The limits were typically ±2.25% but were raised to ±15% after the September 1992 foreign exchange crisis to be discussed shortly.) When the exchange rate between two countries' currencies moves outside of these limits, the central banks of both countries are supposed to intervene in the foreign exchange market. If, for example, the French franc depreciates below its lower limit against the German mark, the Bank of France must buy francs and sell marks, thereby giving up international reserves. Similarly, the German central bank must also intervene to buy marks and sell francs and consequently increase its international reserves. The EMS thus requires that intervention be symmetric when a currency falls outside the limits, with the central bank with a weak currency giving up international reserves and the one with a strong currency gaining them. Central bank intervention is also very common even when the exchange rate is within the limits, but in this case, if one central bank intervenes, others are not required to intervene as well.

A serious shortcoming of fixed exchange rate systems such as the Bretton Woods system or the European Monetary System is that they can lead to foreign exchange crises involving a "speculative attack" on a currency—massive sales of a weak currency or purchases of a strong currency to cause a sharp change in the exchange rate. In the following application, we use our model of exchange rate determination to understand how the September 1992 exchange rate crisis that rocked the European Monetary System came about.

APPLICATION

THE SEPTEMBER 1992 FOREIGN EXCHANGE CRISIS

In the aftermath of German reunification in October 1990, the German central bank, the Bundesbank, faced rising inflationary pressures, with inflation having accelerated from below 3% to near 5% by 1992. To get monetary growth under control and to dampen inflation, the Bundesbank raised German interest rates to near double-digit levels. Figure 3 shows the consequences of these actions by the Bundesbank in the foreign exchange market for sterling. Note that in the diagram, the pound sterling is the domestic currency and RET^D is the expected return on sterling deposits, while the foreign currency is the German (deutsche mark, DM) so RET^F is the expected return on mark deposits.

The increase in German interest rates i^F shifted the RET^F schedule rightward to RET^F_2 in Figure 3, so that the intersection of the RET^D_1 and the RET^F_2 schedules at point 1' was below the lower exchange rate limit (2.778 marks per

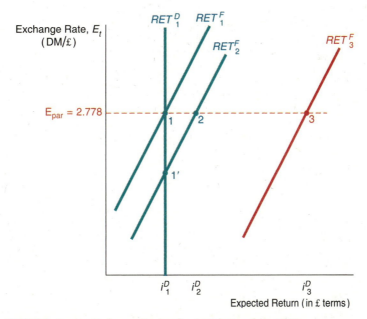

FIGURE 3 Foreign Exchange Market for British Pounds in 1992
The realization by speculators that Great Britain would soon devalue the pound increased the expected return on foreign (German mark, DM) deposits and shifted RET^F_2 rightward to RET^F_3. The result was the need for a much greater purchase of pounds by the British central bank to raise the interest rate to i^D_3 to keep the exchange rate at 2.778 German marks per pound.

pound, denoted E_{par}) under the exchange rate mechanism. To lower the value of the mark relative to the pound and restore the pound/mark exchange rate to within the ERM limits, either the Bank of England had to pursue a contractionary monetary policy, thereby raising British interest rates to i_2^D and shifting the RET^D schedule to the right to point 2, or the Bundesbank could pursue an expansionary monetary policy, thereby lowering German interest rates, which would shift the RET^F schedule to the left to move back to point 1. (The shifts in RET^D to point 2 or RET^F to point 1 are not shown in the figure.)

The catch was that the Bundesbank, whose primary goal is fighting inflation, was unwilling to pursue an expansionary monetary policy, while the British, who were facing their worst recession in the postwar period, were unwilling to pursue a contractionary monetary policy to prop up the pound. This impasse became clear when in response to great pressure from other members of the EMS, the Bundesbank was willing to lower its lending rates by only a token amount on September 14 after a speculative attack was mounted on the currencies of the Scandinavian countries. So at some point in the near future, the value of the pound would have to decline to point 1. Speculators now knew that the appreciation of the mark was imminent and hence that the value of foreign (mark) deposits would rise in value relative to the pound. As a result, the expected return on mark deposits increased sharply, shifting the RET^F schedule to RET_3^F in Figure 3.

The huge potential losses on pound deposits and potential gains on mark deposits caused a massive sell-off of pounds (and purchases of marks) by speculators. The need for the British central bank to intervene to raise the value of the pound now became much greater and required a huge rise in British interest rates all the way to i_3^D. After a major intervention effort on the part of the Bank of England, which included a rise in its lending rate from 10% to 15% that still wasn't enough, the British were finally forced to give up on September 16: They pulled out of the ERM indefinitely, allowing the pound to depreciate by 10% against the mark.

Speculative attacks on other currencies forced devaluation of the Spanish peseta by 5% and the Italian lira by 15%. To defend its currency, the Swedish central bank was forced to raise its daily lending rate to the astronomical level of 500%! By the time the crisis was over, the British, French, Italian, Spanish, and Swedish central banks had intervened to the tune of $100 billion; the Bundesbank alone had laid out $50 billion for foreign exchange intervention.

The attempt to prop up the European Monetary System was not cheap for these central banks. It is estimated that they lost $4 to $6 billion as a result of exchange rate intervention during the crisis. What the central banks lost, the speculators gained. A speculative fund run by George Soros ran up $1 billion of profits during the crisis, and Citibank traders are reported to have made $200 million. When an exchange rate crisis comes, life can certainly be sweet for exchange rate speculators!

The September 1992 crisis has created great uncertainty for the future of the European Monetary System. Europeans are now questioning whether the dreams of monetary union and a European central bank envisioned in the December 1991 Treaty of European Union will ever come true.

INTERNATIONAL CONSIDERATIONS AND MONETARY POLICY

Our analysis in this chapter so far has suggested several ways in which monetary policy can be affected by international considerations. These considerations can have significant implications for the way monetary policy is conducted.

Direct Effects of the Foreign Exchange Market on the Money Supply

When central banks intervene in the foreign exchange market, they acquire or sell off international reserves, and their monetary base is affected. When a central bank intervenes in the foreign exchange market, it gives up some control of its money supply. For example, in the early 1970s, the German central bank faced a dilemma. In attempting to keep the German mark from appreciating too much against the U.S. dollar, the Germans acquired huge quantities of international reserves, leading to a rapid rate of money growth that the German central bank considered inflationary.

The Bundesbank could have tried to eliminate the growth of the money supply by stopping its intervention in the foreign exchange market and reasserting control over its own money supply. Such strategy has a major drawback when the central bank is under pressure not to allow its currency to appreciate: The lower price of imports and higher price of exports as a result of an appreciation in its currency will hurt domestic producers and increase unemployment.

Because the U.S. dollar has been treated as a reserve currency, the U.S. monetary base and money supply have been less affected by developments in the foreign exchange market. As long as foreign central banks, rather than the Fed, intervene to keep the value of the dollar from changing, American holdings of international reserves are unaffected. The ability to conduct monetary policy is typically easier when a country's currency is a reserve currency.[8]

Balance-of-Payments Considerations

Under the Bretton Woods system, balance-of-payments considerations were more important than they are under the current managed float system. When a nonreserve currency country is running balance-of-payments deficits, it necessarily gives up international reserves. To keep from running out of these reserves, under the Bretton Woods system it had to implement a contractionary monetary policy to strengthen its currency. Exactly that occurred in Britain before its devaluation in 1967. When policy became expansionary, the balance of payments deteriorated, and the British were forced to "slam on the brakes" by implementing a contractionary policy. Once the balance of payments improved, policy became

---

[8]However, the central bank of a reserve currency country must worry about a shift away from the use of its currency as international reserves.

more expansionary until the deteriorating balance of payments again forced the British to pursue a contractionary policy. Such on-again, off-again actions became known as a "stop-go" policy, and the domestic instability it created was criticized severely.

Because the United States is a major reserve currency country, it can run large balance-of-payments deficits without losing huge amounts of international reserves. This does not mean, however, that the Federal Reserve is never influenced by developments in the U.S. balance of payments. Current account deficits in the United States suggest that American businesses may be losing some of their ability to compete because the value of the dollar is too high. In addition, large U.S. balance-of-payments deficits lead to balance-of-payments surpluses in other countries, which can lead to large increases in their holdings of international reserves (which was especially true under the Bretton Woods system). Because such increases put a strain on the international financial system and may stimulate world inflation, the Fed worries about U.S. balance-of-payments and current account deficits. Sometimes it tries to shrink them through more contractionary monetary policy.

Exchange Rate Considerations

Unlike balance-of-payments considerations, which have become less important under the current managed float system, exchange rate considerations now play a more important role in the conduct of monetary policy. If a central bank does not want to see its currency fall in value, it may pursue a more contractionary monetary policy of reducing the money supply to raise the domestic interest rate, thereby strengthening its currency. Similarly, if a country experiences an appreciation in its currency, domestic industry may suffer from increased foreign competition and may pressure the central bank to pursue a higher rate of money growth in order to lower the exchange rate.

The pressure to manipulate exchange rates seems to be greater for central banks in countries other than the United States, but even the Federal Reserve is not completely immune. The growing tide of protectionism stemming from the inability of American firms to compete with foreign firms because of the strengthening dollar from 1980 to early 1985 stimulated congressional critics of the Fed to call for a more expansionary monetary policy to lower the value of the dollar. As we saw in Chapter 21, the Fed then did let money growth surge to very high levels. A policy to bring the dollar down was confirmed in the Plaza Agreement of September 1985, in which the finance ministers from the five most important industrial nations in the free world (the United States, Japan, West Germany, the United Kingdom, and France) agreed to intervene in foreign exchange markets to achieve a decline in the dollar. The dollar continued to fall rapidly after the Plaza Agreement, and the Fed played an important role in this decline by continuing to expand the money supply at a rapid rate.

SUMMARY

1. An unsterilized central bank intervention in which the domestic currency is sold to purchase foreign assets leads to a gain in international reserves, an increase in the money supply, and a depreciation of the domestic currency. Available evidence suggests, however, that sterilized central bank interventions have little effect on the exchange rate.

2. The balance of payments is a bookkeeping system for recording all payments between a country and foreign countries that have a direct bearing on the movement of funds between them. The official reserve transactions balance is the sum of the current account balance plus the items in the capital account. It indicates the amount of international reserves that must move between countries to finance international transactions.

3. Before World War I, the gold standard was predominant. Currencies were convertible into gold, thus fixing exchange rates between countries. After World War II, the Bretton Woods system and the IMF were established to promote a fixed exchange rate system in which the U.S. dollar was convertible into gold. The Bretton Woods system collapsed in 1971. We now have an international financial system which has elements of a managed float and a fixed exchange rate system. Some exchange rates fluctuate from day to day, although central banks intervene in the foreign exchange market, while other exchange rates are fixed, as in the European Monetary System.

4. Three international considerations affect the conduct of monetary policy: direct effects of the foreign exchange market on the money supply, balance-of-payments considerations, and exchange rate considerations. Because the United States has been a reserve currency country in the post–World War II period, U.S. monetary policy has been less affected by developments in the foreign exchange market and its balance of payments than is true for other countries. However, in recent years, exchange rate considerations have been playing a more prominent role in in-

KEY TERMS

foreign exchange interventions

managed float regime (dirty float)

international reserves

unsterilized foreign exchange intervention

sterilized foreign exchange intervention

balance of payments

current account

trade balance

capital account

official reserve transactions balance

gold standard

fixed exchange rate regime

Bretton Woods system

International Monetary Fund (IMF)

World Bank

reserve currency

devaluation

revaluation

special drawing rights (SDRs)

QUESTIONS AND PROBLEMS

1. If the Federal Reserve buys dollars in the foreign exchange market but conducts an offsetting open market operation to sterilize the intervention, what will be the impact on international reserves, the money supply, and the exchange rate?

*2. If the Federal Reserve buys dollars in the foreign exchange market but does not sterilize the intervention, what will be the impact on international reserves, the money supply, and the exchange rate?

3. For each of the following, identify in which part of the balance-of-payments account it appears (current account, capital account, or method of financing) and whether it is a receipt or a payment.
   (a) A British subject's purchase of a share of Johnson & Johnson stock
   (b) An American's purchase of an airline ticket from Air France
   (c) The Swiss government's purchase of U.S. Treasury bills
   (d) A Japanese's purchase of California oranges
   (e) $50 million of foreign aid to Honduras
   (f) A loan by an American bank to Mexico
   (g) An American bank's borrowing of Eurodollars

*4. Why does a balance-of-payments deficit for the United States have a different effect on its international reserves than a balance-of-payments deficit for the Netherlands?

5. Under a gold standard, if Britain became more productive relative to the United States, what would happen to the money supply in the two countries? Why would the changes in the money supply help preserve a fixed exchange rate between the United States and Britain?

*6. What is the exchange rate between dollars and francs if one dollar is convertible into 1/20 ounce of gold and one franc is convertible into 1/40 ounce of gold?

7. If a country's par exchange rate was undervalued during the Bretton Woods fixed exchange rate regime, what kind of intervention would that country's central bank be forced to undertake, and what effect would it have on its international reserves and the money supply?

* 8. How can a large balance-of-payments surplus contribute to the country's inflation rate?

9. "If a country wants to keep its exchange rate from changing, it must give up some control over its money supply." Is this statement true, false, or uncertain? Explain.

*10. Why can balance-of-payments deficits force some countries to implement a contractionary monetary policy?

11. "Balance-of-payments deficits always cause a country to lose international reserves." Is this statement true, false, or uncertain? Explain.

*12. How can persistent U.S. balance-of-payments deficits help stimulate world inflation?

13. "Inflation is not possible under a gold standard." Is this statement true, false, or uncertain? Explain.

*14. Why is it that in a pure flexible exchange rate system, the foreign exchange market has no direct effects on the money supply? Does this mean that the foreign exchange market has no effect on monetary policy?

15. "The abandonment of fixed exchange rates after 1973 has meant that countries have pursued more independent monetary policies." Is this statement true, false, or uncertain? Explain.

PART VI

MONETARY THEORY

Chapter 23

THE DEMAND FOR MONEY

PREVIEW   In earlier chapters we spent a lot of time and effort learning what the money supply is, how it is determined, and what role the Federal Reserve System plays in it. Now we are ready to explore the role of the money supply in determining the price level and total production of goods and services (aggregate output) in the economy. The study of the effect of money on the economy is called **monetary theory,** and we examine this branch of economics in the chapters of Part VI.

When economists mention *supply,* the word *demand* is sure to follow, and the discussion of money is no exception. The supply of money is an essential building block in understanding how monetary policy affects the economy because it suggests the factors that influence the quantity of money in the economy. Not surprisingly, another essential part of monetary theory is the demand for money.

This chapter describes how the theories of the demand for money have evolved. We begin with the classical theories refined at the start of the twentieth century by economists such as Irving Fisher, Alfred Marshall, and A. C. Pigou; then we move to the Keynesian theories of the demand for money. We end with Milton Friedman's modern quantity theory.

A central question in monetary theory is whether or to what extent the quantity of money demanded is affected by changes in interest rates. Because this issue is crucial to how we view money's effects on aggregate economic activity, we focus on the role of interest rates in the demand for money.[1]

---

[1]In Chapter 25 we will also see that the responsiveness of the quantity of money demanded to changes in interest rates has important implications for the relative effectiveness of monetary policy and fiscal policy in influencing aggregate economic activity.

QUANTITY THEORY OF MONEY

Developed by the classical economists in the nineteenth and early twentieth centuries, the quantity theory of money is a theory of how the nominal value of aggregate income is determined. Because it also tells us how much money is held for a given amount of aggregate income, it is also a theory of the demand for money. The most important feature of this theory is that it suggests that interest rates have no effect on the demand for money.

Velocity of Money and the Equation of Exchange

The clearest exposition of the classical quantity theory approach is found in the work of the American economist Irving Fisher, in his influential book *The Purchasing Power of Money,* published in 1911. Fisher wanted to examine the link between the total quantity of money M (the money supply) and the total amount of spending on final goods and services produced in the economy $P \times Y$, where P is the price level and Y is aggregate output. (Total spending $P \times Y$ is also thought of as aggregate nominal income for the economy or as nominal GDP.) The concept that provides the link between M and $P \times Y$ is called the **velocity of money** (or more simply, *velocity*), the rate of turnover of money, that is, the average number of times per year that a dollar is spent in buying the total amount of goods and services produced in the economy. Velocity V is defined more precisely as total spending $P \times Y$ divided by the quantity of money M:

$$V = \frac{P \times Y}{M} \tag{1}$$

If, for example, nominal GDP ($P \times Y$) in a year is \$5 trillion and the quantity of money is \$1 trillion, then velocity is 5, meaning that the average dollar bill is spent five times in purchasing final goods and services in the economy.

By multiplying both sides of this definition by M, we obtain the **equation of exchange,** which relates nominal income to the quantity of money and velocity:

$$M \times V = P \times Y \tag{2}$$

The equation of exchange thus states that the quantity of money multiplied by the number of times that this money is spent in a given year must be equal to the nominal income (that is, the total nominal amount spent on goods and services in that year).[2]

As it stands, Equation 2 is nothing more than an identity—a relationship that is true by definition. It does not tell us, for instance, that when the money supply M changes, nominal income ($P \times Y$) changes in the same direction; a rise in M, for example, could be offset by a fall in V that leaves $M \times V$ (and therefore $P \times Y$) unchanged. To convert the equation of exchange (an *identity*) into a *theory* of how nominal income is determined requires an understanding of the factors that determine velocity.

Irving Fisher reasoned that velocity is determined by the institutions in an economy that affect the way individuals conduct transactions. If people use charge accounts and credit cards to conduct their transactions and consequently use money less often when making purchases, less money is required to conduct the transactions generated by nominal income ($M\downarrow$ relative to $P \times Y$), and velocity ($P \times Y$)/M will increase. Conversely, if it is more convenient for purchases to be paid for with cash or checks (both of which are money), more money is used to conduct the transactions generated by the same level of nominal income, and velocity will fall. Fisher took the view that the institutional and technological features of the economy would affect velocity only slowly over time, so velocity would normally be reasonably constant in the short run.

Quantity Theory

Fisher's view that velocity is fairly constant in the short run transforms the equation of exchange into the **quantity theory of money,** which states that nominal income is determined solely by movements in the quantity of money: When the quantity of money M doubles, $M \times V$ doubles and so must $P \times Y$, the value of nominal income. To see how this works, let's assume that velocity is 5 and initially nominal income (GDP) is \$5 trillion and the money supply is \$1 trillion. If

---

[2]Irving Fisher actually first formulated the equation of exchange in terms of the nominal value of transactions in the economy PT:

$$MV_T = PT$$

where P = average price per transaction
T = number of transactions conducted in a year
$V_T = PT/M$ = transactions velocity of money

Because the nominal value of transactions T is difficult to measure, the quantity theory has been formulated in terms of aggregate output Y, as follows: T is assumed to be proportional to Y so that $T = vY$, where v is the constant of proportionality. Substituting vY for T in Fisher's equation of exchange yields $MV_T = vPY$, which can be written as Equation 2 in the text in which $V = V_T/v$.

the money supply doubles to $2 trillion, the quantity theory of money tells us that nominal income will double to $10 trillion (= 5 × $2 trillion).

Because the classical economists (including Fisher) thought that wages and prices were completely flexible, they believed that the level of aggregate output Y produced in the economy during normal times would remain at the full employment level, so Y in the equation of exchange could also be treated as reasonably constant in the short run. The quantity theory of money then implies that if M doubles, P must also double because V and Y are constant. In our example, if aggregate output is $5 trillion, the velocity of 5 and a money supply of $1 trillion indicate that the price level equals 1 because 1 times $5 trillion equals the nominal income of $5 trillion. When the money supply doubles to $2 trillion, the price level must also double to 2 because 2 times $5 trillion equals the nominal income of $10 trillion.

For the classical economists, the quantity theory of money provided an explanation of movements in the price level: ***Movements in the price level result solely from changes in the quantity of money.***

Quantity Theory of Money Demand

Because the quantity theory of money tells us how much money is held for a given amount of aggregate income, it is in fact a theory of the demand for money. We can see this by dividing both sides of the equation of exchange by V, thus rewriting it as

$$M = \frac{1}{V} \times PY$$

where nominal income $P \times Y$ is written as PY. When the money market is in equilibrium, the quantity of money M that people hold equals the quantity of money demanded M^d, so we can replace M in the equation by M^d. Using k to represent the quantity $1/V$ (a constant because V is a constant), we can rewrite the equation as

$$M^d = k \times PY \tag{3}$$

Equation 3 tells us that because k is a constant, the level of transactions generated by a fixed level of nominal income PY determines the quantity of money M^d that people demand. Therefore, ***Fisher's quantity theory of money suggests that the demand for money is purely a function of income, and interest rates have no effect on the demand for money.***

Fisher came to this conclusion because he believed that people hold money only to conduct transactions and have no freedom of action in terms of the amount they want to hold. The demand for money is determined (1) by the level of transactions generated by the level of nominal income PY and (2) by the institutions in the economy that affect the way people conduct transactions that determine velocity and hence *k*.

CAMBRIDGE APPROACH TO MONEY DEMAND

While Fisher was developing his quantity theory approach to the demand for money, a group of classical economists in Cambridge, England, which included Alfred Marshall and A. C. Pigou, were studying the same topic. Although their analysis led them to an equation identical to Fisher's money demand equation ($M^d = k \times PY$), their approach differed significantly. Instead of studying the demand for money by looking solely at the level of transactions and the institutions that affect the way people conduct transactions as the key determinants, the Cambridge economists asked how much money individuals would want to hold, given a set of circumstances. In the Cambridge model, then, individuals are allowed some flexibility in their decision to hold money and are not completely bound by institutional constraints such as whether they can use credit cards to make purchases. Accordingly, the Cambridge approach did not rule out the effects of interest rates on the demand for money.

The classical Cambridge economists recognized that money has two properties that motivate people to want to hold it.

1. *Medium of Exchange.* Money functions as a medium of exchange that people can use to carry out transactions. The Cambridge economists agreed with Fisher that the demand for money would be *related to* (but not determined solely by) the level of transactions and that there would be a transactions component of money demand proportional to nominal income.

2. *Store of Wealth.* That money functions as a store of wealth led the Cambridge economists to suggest that the level of people's wealth also affects the demand for money. As wealth grows, an individual needs to store it by holding a larger quantity of assets—one of which is money. Because the Cambridge economists believed that wealth in nominal terms is proportional to nominal income, they also believed that the wealth component of money demand is proportional to nominal income.

The Cambridge economists concluded that the demand for money would be proportional to nominal income and expressed the demand for money function as

$$M^d = k \times PY$$

where *k* is the constant of proportionality. Because this equation looks just like Fisher's (Equation 3), it seems that the Cambridge group agreed with Fisher that interest rates play no role in the demand for money in the short run. However, this is not the case.

Although the Cambridge economists often treated *k* as a constant and agreed with Fisher that nominal income is determined by the quantity of money, their approach allowed individuals to choose how much money they wished to hold. It allowed for the possibility that k could fluctuate in the short run because the decisions about using money to store wealth would depend on the yields and expected returns on other assets that also function as stores of wealth. If these characteristics of other assets changed, k might change too. Although this seems a minor distinction between the Fisher and Cambridge approaches, you will see that when John Maynard Keynes (a later Cambridge economist) extended the Cambridge approach, he arrived at a very different view from the quantity theorists on the importance of interest rates to the demand for money.

To summarize, both Irving Fisher and the Cambridge economists developed a classical approach to the demand for money in which the demand for money is proportional to income. However, the two approaches differ in that Fisher's emphasized technological factors and ruled out any possible effect of interest rates on the demand for money in the short run, whereas the Cambridge approach emphasized individual choice and did not rule out the effects of interest rates.

IS VELOCITY A CONSTANT?

The classical economists' conclusion that nominal income is determined by movements in the money supply rested on their belief that velocity PY/M could be treated as reasonably constant.[3] Is it reasonable to assume that velocity is constant? To answer this, let's look at Figure 1, which shows the value of velocity from 1915 to 1993 (nominal income is represented by nominal GDP and the money supply by $M1$ and $M2$), and Table 1, which shows the year-to-year changes in velocity from 1915 to 1993.

What we see in Figure 1 and Table 1 is that even in the short run, velocity fluctuates too much to be viewed as a constant. Prior to 1950, velocity exhibited large swings up and down. This may reflect the substantial instability of the economy in this period, which included two world wars and the Great Depression. (Velocity actually falls, or at least its rate of growth declines, in years when recessions are taking place.) After 1950, velocity appears to have more moderate fluctuations, yet there are large differences in the growth rate of velocity from year to year. The percentage change in $M1$ velocity (GDP/$M1$) from 1981 to 1982, for example, was -2.5%, whereas from 1980 to 1981 velocity grew at a rate of 4.2%. This difference of 6.7% means that nominal GDP was 6.7% lower than it otherwise would have been if velocity had kept growing at the same rate as in

---

[3]Actually, the classical conclusion still holds if velocity grows at some uniform rate over time that reflects changes in transactions technology. Hence the concept of a constant velocity should more accurately be thought of here as a lack of upward and downward fluctuations in velocity.

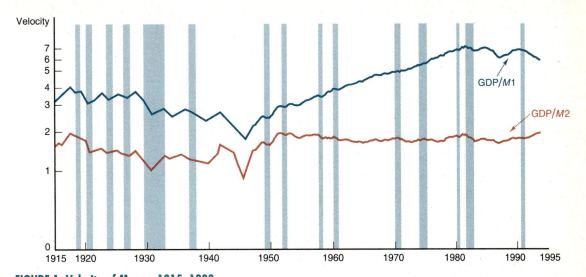

FIGURE 1 Velocity of Money, 1915–1993
Shaded areas indicate recessions. *Sources: Economic Report of the President; Banking and Monetary Statistics;* Citibase databank. Velocities before 1959 are calculated using nominal GNP; for 1959 and after, using nominal GDP.

1980–1981.[4] The drop is enough to account for the severe recession that took place in 1981–1982. After 1982, $M1$ velocity appears to have become even more volatile, a fact that has puzzled researchers when they examine the empirical evidence on the demand for money (see the appendix to this chapter). $M2$ velocity remained more stable than $M1$ velocity after 1982, with the result that the Federal Reserve dropped its $M1$ targets in 1987 and began to focus more on $M2$ targets. However, instability of $M2$ velocity in the early 1990s has resulted in the Fed's announcement in July 1993 that it no longer felt that monetary aggregates, including $M2$, were a reliable guide for monetary policy.

Until the Great Depression, economists did not recognize that velocity declines sharply during severe economic contractions. Why did the classical economists not recognize this fact when it is easy to see in the predepression period in Figure 1? Unfortunately, accurate data on GDP and the money supply did not exist before World War II. (Only after the war did the government start to collect these data.) Economists had no way of knowing that their view of velocity as a

---

[4]We reach a similar conclusion if we use $M2$ velocity. The percentage change in $M2$ velocity (GDP/$M2$) from 1981 to 1982 was −5.0%, while from 1980 to 1981 it was +2.3%. This difference of 7.3% means that nominal GDP was 7.3% lower than it would have been otherwise if $M2$ velocity had kept growing at the same rate as in 1980–1981.

TABLE 1· Change in Velocity from Year to Year, 1915–1993

Year	Change in M1 Velocity (%)	Change in M2 Velocity (%)	Year	Change in M1 Velocity (%)	Change in M2 Velocity (%)
1915–1916	− 0.5	1.9	1954–1955	6.7	6.5
1916–1917	9.0	9.3	1955–1956	4.2	3.2
1917–1918	10.4	12.5	1956–1957	6.1	2.9
1918–1919	− 6.1	− 5.0	1957–1958	− 2.4	− 5.0
1919–1920	− 2.5	5.7	1958–1959	6.8	6.9
1920–1921	−13.4	−17.7	1959–1960	4.0	− 0.1
1921–1922	3.7	− 4.9	1960–1961	1.6	− 3.0
1922–1923	7.1	10.6	1961–1962	5.0	− 0.2
1923–1924	− 7.2	− 7.7	1962–1963	2.4	− 2.7
1924–1925	3.5	2.1	1963–1964	3.5	− 0.4
1925–1926	7.0	4.2	1964–1965	4.0	0.3
1926–1927	− 5.8	− 6.4	1965–1966	4.7	2.8
1927–1928	1.2	− 1.3	1966–1967	− 1.8	− 1.0
1928–1929	7.4	7.9	1967–1968	2.1	0.9
1929–1930	− 5.8	− 8.7	1968–1969	1.8	1.6
1930–1931	− 5.8	− 1.1	1969–1970	1.5	1.1
1931–1932	−18.1	−16.0	1970–1971	1.7	− 3.2
1932–1933	− 0.8	5.9	1971–1972	2.7	− 2.2
1933–1934	0.0	2.9	1972–1973	4.3	1.8
1934–1935	− 5.0	− 3.6	1973–1974	2.9	1.9
1935–1936	− 0.6	2.6	1974–1975	4.0	− 0.5
1936–1937	15.0	12.0	1975–1976	5.6	− 1.3
1937–1938	−12.9	− 9.6	1976–1977	3.7	− 0.9
1938–1939	− 5.9	− 5.0	1977–1978	4.7	4.4
1939–1940	− 6.1	− 1.4	1978–1979	3.4	2.7
1940–1941	8.9	12.5	1979–1980	2.5	0.7
1941–1942	16.5	3.0	1980–1981	4.2	2.3
1942–1943	−11.0	− 3.5	1981–1982	− 2.5	− 5.0
1943–1944	− 9.2	− 5.5	1982–1983	− 2.7	− 3.9
1944–1945	− 6.9	−12.5	1983–1984	3.6	2.5
1945–1946	− 11.5	− 6.7	1984–1985	− 1.9	− 1.9
1946–1947	8.2	6.3	1985–1986	− 7.0	− 2.3
1947–1948	11.4	12.0	1986–1987	− 4.7	− 0.3
1948–1949	0.6	− 0.3	1987–1988	3.5	2.6
1949–1950	7.6	6.8	1988–1989	6.1	3.2
1950–1951	9.6	9.8	1989–1990	1.9	0.4
1951–1952	1.5	9.8	1990–1991	0.4	3.1
1952–1953	4.6	2.9	1991–1992	− 8.9	0.4
1953–1954	− 2.5	− 3.6	1992–1993	− 5.4	4.7

Source: Economic Report of the President; Banking and Monetary Statistics; Citibase databank. Velocities before 1959 are calculated using nominal GNP; for 1959 and after, using nominal GDP.

constant was demonstrably false. The decline in velocity during the Great Depression years was so great, however, that even the crude data available to economists at that time suggested that velocity was not constant. This explains why, after the Great Depression, John Maynard Keynes and other economists began to search for other factors influencing the demand for money that might help explain the large fluctuations in velocity.

Let's now examine the theories of money demand that arose from this search for a better explanation of the behavior of velocity.

KEYNES'S LIQUIDITY PREFERENCE THEORY

In his famous 1936 book *The General Theory of Employment, Interest and Money,* John Maynard Keynes abandoned the classical view that velocity was a constant and developed a theory of money demand that emphasized the importance of interest rates. Keynes, at Cambridge at the time, naturally enough followed the approach developed by his Cambridge predecessors. His theory of the demand for money, which he called **liquidity preference theory,** also asked the question, Why do individuals hold money? But Keynes was far more precise than his predecessors regarding what influences the individuals' decisions. He postulated that there are three motives behind the demand for money: (1) the transactions motive, (2) the precautionary motive, and (3) the speculative motive.

Transactions Motive

In both the Fisher and Cambridge classical approaches, individuals are assumed to hold money because it is a medium of exchange that can be used to carry out everyday transactions. Following the classical tradition, Keynes emphasized that this component of the demand for money is determined primarily by the level of people's transactions. Because he believed that these transactions were proportional to income, like the classical economists, he took the transactions component of the demand for money to be proportional to income.

Precautionary Motive

Keynes went beyond the classical analysis by recognizing that in addition to holding money to carry out current transactions, people hold money as a cushion against an unexpected need. Suppose that you've been thinking about buying a fancy stereo; you walk by a store that is having a 50%-off sale on the one you want. If you are holding money as a precaution for just such an occurrence, you can purchase the stereo right away; if you are not holding precautionary money balances, you cannot take advantage of the sale. Precautionary money balances also come in handy if you are hit with an unexpected bill, say, for a major car repair or hospitalization.

Keynes believed that the amount of precautionary money balances people want to hold is determined primarily by the level of transactions that they expect to make in the future and that these transactions are proportional to income. Therefore, he postulated, the demand for precautionary money balances is proportional to income.

Speculative Motive

If Keynes had ended his theory with the transactions and precautionary motives, income would be the only important determinant of the demand for money, and he would not have added much to the Cambridge approach. However, Keynes agreed with the classical Cambridge economists that money is a store of wealth and called this motive for holding money the speculative motive. Since he also agreed with the classical Cambridge economists that wealth is tied closely to income, the speculative component of money demand would be related to income. However, Keynes looked more carefully at the factors that influence the decisions regarding how much money to hold as a store of wealth. Unlike the classical Cambridge economists, who were willing to treat the wealth component of money demand as proportional to income, Keynes believed that interest rates, too, have an important role to play.

Keynes divided the assets that can be used to store wealth into two categories: money and bonds. He then asked the following question: Why would individuals decide to hold their wealth in the form of money rather than bonds?

Thinking back to the discussion of the theory of asset demand (Chapter 5), you would want to hold money if its expected return was greater than the expected return from holding bonds. Keynes assumed that the expected return on money was zero because in his time, unlike today, most checkable deposits did not earn interest. For bonds, there are two components of the *expected* return: the interest payment and the *expected* rate of capital gains.

You learned in Chapter 4 that when interest rates rise, the price of a bond falls. If you expect interest rates to rise, you expect the price of the bond to fall and therefore suffer a negative capital gain—that is, a capital loss. If you expect the rise in interest rates to be substantial enough, the capital loss might outweigh the interest payment, and your *expected* return on the bond would be negative. In this case, you would want to store your wealth as money because its expected return is higher; its zero return exceeds the negative return on the bond.

Keynes assumed that individuals believe that interest rates gravitate to some normal value (an assumption less plausible in today's world). If interest rates are below this normal value, individuals expect the interest rate on bonds to rise in the future and so expect to suffer capital losses on them. As a result, individuals will be more likely to hold their wealth as money rather than bonds, and the demand for money will be high.

What would you expect to happen to the demand for money when interest rates are above the normal value? In general, people will expect interest rates to fall, bond prices to rise, and capital gains to be realized. At higher interest rates, they are more likely to expect the return from holding a bond to be positive, thus exceeding the expected return from holding money. They will be more likely to hold bonds than money, and the demand for money will be quite low. From Keynes's reasoning we can conclude that as interest rates rise, the demand for money falls, and therefore ***money demand is negatively related to the level of interest rates.***

Putting the Three Motives Together

In putting the three motives for holding money balances together into a demand-for-money equation, Keynes was careful to distinguish between *nominal* quantities and *real* quantities. Money is valued in terms of what it can buy. If, for example, all prices in the economy double (the price level doubles), the same nominal quantity of money will be able to buy only half as many goods. Keynes thus reasoned that people want to hold a certain amount of **real money balances** (the quantity of money in real terms)—an amount that his three motives indicated would be related to *real* income Y and to interest rates i.[5] Keynes wrote down the following demand-for-money equation, known as the *liquidity preference function,* which says that the demand for real money balances M^d/P is a function of (related to) i and Y:

$$\frac{M^d}{P} = f(\underset{-}{i}, \underset{+}{Y}) \tag{4}$$

The minus sign below i in the liquidity preference function means that the demand for real money balances is negatively related to the interest rate i, and the plus sign below Y means that the demand for real money balances and real income Y are positively related: This money demand function has the same implications for money demand as we discussed in Chapter 6.

Keynes's conclusion that the demand for money is related not only to income but also to interest rates is a major departure from Fisher's view of money demand in which interest rates can have no effect on the demand for money, but it is less of a departure from the Cambridge approach, which did not rule out possible effects of interest rates. However, the classical Cambridge economists did not explore the explicit effects of interest rates on the demand for money.

---

[5]The classical economists' money demand equation can also be written in terms of real money balances by dividing both sides of Equation 3 by the price level P to obtain

$$\frac{M}{d} = k \times Y$$

By deriving the liquidity preference function for velocity *PY/M,* we can see that Keynes's theory of the demand for money implies that velocity is not constant but instead fluctuates with movements in interest rates. The liquidity preference equation can be rewritten as

$$\frac{P}{M^d} = \frac{1}{f(i, Y)}$$

Multiplying both sides of this equation by Y and recognizing that M^d can be replaced by M because they must be equal in money market equilibrium, we solve for velocity:

$$V = \frac{PY}{M} = \frac{Y}{f(i, Y)} \tag{5}$$

We know that the demand for money is negatively related to interest rates; when i goes up, $f(i, Y)$ declines, and therefore velocity rises. In other words, a rise in interest rates encourages people to hold fewer real money balances for a given level of income; therefore, the rate of turnover of money (velocity) must be higher. This reasoning implies that because interest rates have substantial fluctuations, the liquidity preference theory of the demand for money indicates that velocity has substantial fluctuations as well.

An interesting feature of Equation 5 is that it explains some of the velocity movements in Figure 1, in which we noted that when recessions occur, velocity falls or its rate of growth declines. What fact regarding the cyclical behavior of interest rates that we discussed in Chapter 6 might help us explain this phenomenon? You might recall that interest rates are procyclical—rising in expansions and falling in recessions. The liquidity preference theory indicates that a rise in interest rates will cause velocity to rise also. The procyclical movements of interest rates should induce procyclical movements in velocity, and that is exactly what we see in Figure 1 and Table 1.

Keynes's model of the speculative demand for money provides another reason why velocity might show substantial fluctuations. What would happen to the demand for money if the view of the normal level of interest rates changes? For example, what if people expect the future normal interest rate to be higher than the current normal interest rate? Because interest rates are then expected to be higher in the future, more people will expect the prices of bonds to fall and will expect capital losses. The expected returns from holding bonds will decline, and money will become more attractive relative to bonds. As a result, the demand for money will increase. This means that $f(i, Y)$ will increase and so velocity will fall. Velocity will change as expectations about future normal levels of interest rates change, and unstable expectations about future movements in normal interest rates can lead to instability of velocity. This is one more reason why Keynes rejected the view that velocity could be treated as a constant.

STUDY GUIDE

Keynes's explanation of how interest rates affect the demand for money will be easier to understand if you think of yourself as an investor who is trying to decide whether to invest in bonds or to hold money. Ask yourself what you would do if you expected the normal interest rate to be lower in the future than it is currently. Would you rather be holding bonds or money?

To sum up, Keynes's liquidity preference theory is an extension of the classical Cambridge approach but is far more precise about the reasons why people hold money. Specifically, Keynes postulated three motives for holding money: (1) the transactions motive, (2) the precautionary motive, and (3) the speculative motive. Although Keynes took the transactions and precautionary components of the demand for money to be proportional to income, he reasoned that the speculative motive would be negatively related to the level of interest rates.

Keynes's model of the demand for money has the important implication that velocity is not constant but instead is positively related to interest rates, which fluctuate substantially. His theory also rejected the constancy of velocity because changes in people's expectations about the normal level of interest rates would cause shifts in the demand for money that would cause velocity to shift as well. Thus Keynes's liquidity preference theory casts doubt on the classical quantity theory that nominal income is determined primarily by movements in the quantity of money.

FURTHER DEVELOPMENTS IN THE KEYNESIAN APPROACH

After World War II, economists began to take the Keynesian approach to the demand for money even further by developing more precise theories to explain the three Keynesian motives for holding money. Because interest rates were viewed as a crucial element in monetary theory, a key focus of this research was to understand better the role of interest rates in the demand for money.

Transactions Demand

William Baumol and James Tobin independently developed similar demand-for-money models, which demonstrated that even money balances held for transactions purposes are sensitive to the level of interest rates.[6] In developing their models, they considered a hypothetical individual who receives a payment once a period and spends it over the course of this period. In their model, money, which earns zero interest, is held only because it can be used to carry out transactions.

To refine this analysis, let's say that Grant Smith receives $1000 at the beginning of the month and spends it on transactions that occur at a constant rate dur-

---

[6]William J. Baumol, "The Transactions Demand for Cash: An Inventory Theoretic Approach," *Quarterly Journal of Economics* 66 (1952): 545–556; James Tobin, "The Interest Elasticity of the Transactions Demand for Cash," *Review of Economics and Statistics* 38 (1956): 241–247.

ing the course of the month. If Grant keeps the $1000 in cash in order to carry out his transactions, his money balances follow the saw-toothed pattern displayed in Figure 2. At the beginning of the month he has $1000, and by the end of the month he has no cash left because he has spent it all. Over the course of the month, his holdings of money will on average be $500 (his holdings at the beginning of the month, $1000, plus his holdings at the end of the month, $0, divided by 2).

At the beginning of the next month, Grant receives another $1000 payment, which he holds as cash, and the same decline in money balances begins again. This process repeats monthly, and his average money balance during the course of the year is $500. Since his yearly nominal income is $12,000 and his holdings of money average $500, the velocity of money ($V = PY/M$) is $12,000/$500 = 24.

Suppose that as a result of taking a money and banking course, Grant realizes that he can improve his situation by not always holding cash. In January, then, he decides to hold part of his $1000 in cash and puts part of it into an income-earning security such as bonds. At the beginning of each month, Grant keeps $500 in cash and uses the other $500 to buy a Treasury bond. As you can see in Figure 3, he starts out each month with $500 of cash and $500 of bonds, and by the middle of the month, his cash balance has run down to zero. Because bonds cannot be used directly to carry out transactions, Grant must sell them and turn them into cash so that he can carry out the rest of the month's transactions. At the middle of the month, then, Grant's bond holdings drop to zero and his cash balance rises back up to $500. By the end of the month, the cash is gone. When he again receives his next $1000 monthly payment, he again divides

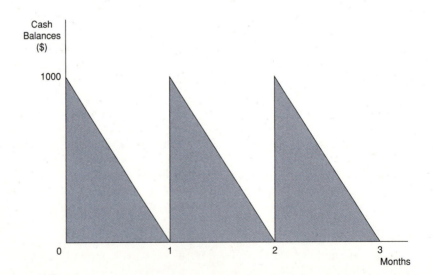

FIGURE 2 Cash Balances for an Individual Who Keeps the Entire Monthly Payment in Cash
The $1000 payment at the beginning of each month is held entirely as cash and is spent at a constant rate until it is exhausted by the end of the month. At this point, a new $1000 payment is received and the whole process begins again.

it into $500 of cash and $500 of bonds, and the process continues. The net result of this process is that the average cash balance held during the month is $500/2 = $250—just half of what it was before. Velocity has doubled to $12,000/$250 = 48.

What has Grant Smith gained from his new strategy? He has earned interest on $500 of bonds that he held for half the month. If the interest rate is 1% per month, he has earned an additional $2.50 (= ½ × $500 × 1%) per month.

Sounds like a pretty good deal, doesn't it? In fact, if he had kept $333.33 in cash at the beginning of the month, he would have been able to hold $666.67 in bonds for the first third of the month. Then he could have sold $333.33 of bonds and held on to $333.34 of bonds for the next third of the month. Finally, two-thirds of the way through the month, he would have had to sell the remaining bonds to raise cash. The net result of this is that Grant would have earned $3.33 per month [= (⅓ × $666.67 × 1%) + (⅓ × $333.34 × 1%)]. This is an even better deal. His average cash holdings in this case would be $333.33/2 = $166.67. Clearly, the lower his average cash balance, the more interest he will earn.

As you might expect, there is a catch to all this. In buying bonds, Grant incurs transactions costs of two types. First, he must pay a straight brokerage fee for the buying and selling of the bonds. These fees increase when average cash balances are lower because Grant will be buying and selling bonds more often. Second, by holding less cash, he will have to make more trips to the bank to get the cash, once he has sold some of his bonds. Because time is money, this must also be counted as part of the transactions costs.

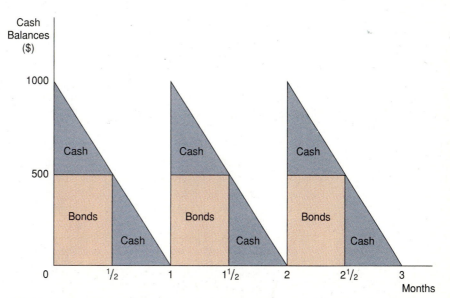

FIGURE 3 Cash and Bond Balances for an Individual Who Keeps Only Half the Monthly Payment in Cash

Half of a monthly $1000 payment is put into bonds and half into cash. At the middle of the month, cash balances are zero and bonds must be sold to bring balances up to $500. By the end of the month, cash balances dwindle to zero.

Grant faces a trade-off. If he holds very little cash, he can earn a lot of interest on bonds, but he will incur greater transactions costs. If the interest rate is high, the benefits of holding bonds will be high relative to the transactions costs, and he will hold more bonds and less cash. Conversely, if interest rates are low, the transactions costs involved in holding a lot of bonds may outweigh the interest payments, and Grant would then be better off holding more cash and fewer bonds.

The conclusion of the Baumol-Tobin analysis may be stated as follows: As interest rates increase, the amount of cash held for transactions purposes will decline, which in turn means that velocity will increase as interest rates increase.[7] Put another way, ***the transactions component of the demand for money is negatively related to the level of interest rates.***

The basic idea in the Baumol-Tobin analysis is that there is an opportunity cost of holding money—the interest that can be earned on other assets. There is also a benefit to holding money—the avoidance of transactions costs. When interest rates increase, people will try to economize on their holdings of money for transactions purposes because the opportunity cost of holding money has increased. By using simple models, Baumol and Tobin revealed something that we might not otherwise have seen: that the transactions demand for money, and not just the speculative demand, will be sensitive to interest rates. The Baumol-Tobin analysis presents a nice demonstration of the value of economic modeling.

STUDY GUIDE

The idea that as interest rates increase, the opportunity cost of holding money increases so that the demand for money falls can be stated equivalently with the terminology of expected returns used earlier. As interest rates increase, the expected return on the other asset, bonds, increases, causing the relative expected return on money to fall, thereby lowering the demand for money. These two explanations are in fact identical because as we saw in Chapter 6, changes in the opportunity cost of an asset are just a description of what is happening to the relative expected return. The opportunity cost terminology was used by Baumol and Tobin in their work on the transactions demand for money, and that is why we used this terminology in the text. To make sure you understand the equivalence of the two terminologies, try to translate the reasoning in the precautionary demand discussion from opportunity cost terminology to expected returns terminology.

---

[7]Similar reasoning leads to the conclusion that as brokerage fees increase, the demand for transactions money balances increases as well. When these fees rise, the benefits from holding transactions money balances increase because by holding these balances, an individual will not have to sell bonds as often, thereby avoiding these higher brokerage costs. The greater benefits to holding money balances relative to the opportunity cost of interest forgone, then, lead to a higher demand for transactions balances.

Precautionary Demand

Models that explore the precautionary motive of the demand for money have been developed along lines similar to the Baumol-Tobin framework, so we will not go into great detail about them here. We have already discussed the benefits of holding precautionary money balances, but weighed against these benefits must be the opportunity cost of the interest forgone by holding money. We therefore have a trade-off similar to the one for transactions balances. As interest rates rise, the opportunity cost of holding precautionary balances rises, and so the holdings of these money balances fall. We then have a result similar to the one found for the Baumol-Tobin analysis.[8] ***The precautionary demand for money is negatively related to interest rates.***

Speculative Demand

Keynes's analysis of the speculative demand for money was open to several serious criticisms. It indicated that an individual holds only money as a store of wealth when the expected return on bonds is less than the expected return on money and holds only bonds when the expected return on bonds is greater than the expected return on money. Solely in the rare instance when people have expected returns on bonds and money that are exactly equal would they hold both. Keynes's analysis therefore implies that practically no one holds a diversified portfolio of bonds and money simultaneously as a store of wealth. Since diversification is apparently a sensible strategy for choosing which assets to hold (recall Chapter 5), the fact that it rarely occurs in Keynes's analysis is a serious shortcoming of his theory of the speculative demand for money.

Tobin developed a model of the speculative demand for money that attempted to avoid this criticism of Keynes's analysis.[9] His basic idea was that not only do people care about the expected return on one asset versus another when they decide what to hold in their portfolio, but they also care about the riskiness of the returns from each asset. Specifically, Tobin assumed that most people are risk-averse—that they would be willing to hold an asset with a lower expected return if it is less risky. An important characteristic of money is that its return is certain; Tobin assumed it to be zero. Bonds, by contrast, can have substantial fluctuations in price, and their returns can be quite risky and even negative. So even if the expected returns on bonds exceed the expected return on

---

[8]These models of the precautionary demand for money also reveal that as uncertainty about the level of future transactions grows, the precautionary demand for money increases. This is so because greater uncertainty means that individuals are more likely to incur transactions costs if they are not holding precautionary balances. The benefit of holding such balances then increases relative to the opportunity cost of forgone interest, and so the demand for them rises.

[9]James Tobin, "Liquidity Preference as Behavior Towards Risk," *Review of Economic Studies* 25 (1958): 65–86.

money, people might still want to hold money as a store of wealth because it has less risk associated with its return than bonds do.

The Tobin analysis also shows that people can reduce the total amount of risk in a portfolio by diversifying, that is, by holding both bonds and money. The model suggests that individuals will hold bonds and money simultaneously as stores of wealth. Since this is probably a more realistic description of people's behavior than Keynes's, Tobin's rationale for the speculative demand for money seems to rest on more solid ground.

Tobin's attempt to improve on Keynes's rationale for the speculative demand for money was only partly successful, however. It is still not clear that the speculative demand even exists. What if there are assets that have no risk—like money—but earn a higher return? Will there be any speculative demand for money? No, because an individual will always be better off holding such an asset rather than money. The resulting portfolio will enjoy a higher expected return yet has no higher risk. Do such assets exist in the American economy? The answer is yes. U.S. Treasury bills, money market mutual fund shares, and other assets that have no default risk provide certain returns that are greater than those available on money. Therefore, why would anyone want to hold money balances as a store of wealth (ignoring for the moment transactions and precautionary reasons)?

Although Tobin's analysis did not explain why money is held as a store of wealth, it was an important development in our understanding of how people should choose among assets. Indeed, his analysis was an important step in the development of the academic field of finance, which examines asset pricing and portfolio choice (the decision to buy one asset over another).

To sum up, further developments of the Keynesian approach have attempted to give a more precise explanation for the transactions, precautionary, and speculative demand for money. The attempt to improve Keynes's rationale for the speculative demand for money has been only partly successful; it is still not clear that this demand even exists. However, the models of the transactions and precautionary demand for money indicate that these components of money demand are negatively related to interest rates. Hence Keynes's proposition that the demand for money is sensitive to interest rates—suggesting that velocity is not constant and that nominal income might be affected by other factors than the quantity of money—is still supported.

FRIEDMAN'S MODERN QUANTITY THEORY OF MONEY

In 1956, Milton Friedman developed a theory of the demand for money in a famous article, "The Quantity Theory of Money: A Restatement."[10] Although Friedman frequently refers to Irving Fisher and the quantity theory, his analysis of the

---

[10]Milton Friedman, "The Quantity Theory of Money: A Restatement," in *Studies in the Quantity Theory of Money,* ed. Milton Friedman (Chicago: University of Chicago Press, 1956), pp. 3–21.

demand for money is actually closer to that of Keynes and the Cambridge economists than it is to Fisher's.

Like his predecessors, Friedman pursued the question of why people choose to hold money. Instead of analyzing the specific motives for holding money, as Keynes did, Friedman simply stated that the demand for money must be influenced by the same factors that influence the demand for any asset. Friedman then applied the theory of asset demand to money.

The theory of asset demand (Chapter 5) indicates that the demand for money should be a function of the resources available to individuals (their wealth) and the expected returns on other assets relative to the expected return on money. Like Keynes, Friedman recognized that people want to hold a certain amount of real money balances (the quantity of money in real terms). From this reasoning, Friedman expressed his formulation of the demand for money as follows:

$$\frac{M^d}{P} = f(\underset{+}{Y_p},\ \underset{-}{r_b - r_m},\ \underset{-}{r_e - r_m},\ \underset{-}{\pi_e - r_m}) \qquad (6)$$

where

M^d/P = demand for real money balances

Y_p = Friedman's measure of wealth, known as *permanent income* (technically, the present discounted value of all expected future income, but more easily described as expected average long-run income)

r_m = expected return on money

r_b = expected return on bonds

r_e = expected return on equity (common stocks)

π^e = expected inflation rate

and the signs underneath the equation indicate whether the demand for money is positively (+) related or negatively (−) related to the terms that are immediately above them.[11]

Let us look in more detail at the variables in Friedman's money demand function and what they imply for the demand for money.

Because the demand for an asset is positively related to wealth, money demand is positively related to Friedman's wealth concept, permanent income (indicated by the plus sign beneath it). Unlike our usual concept of income, permanent income (which can be thought of as expected average long-run income) has much smaller short-run fluctuations because many movements of income are transitory (short-lived). For example, in a business cycle expansion, income in-

---

[11]Friedman also added to his formulation a term *h* that represented the ratio of human to nonhuman wealth. He reasoned that if people had more permanent income coming from labor income and thus from their human capital, they would be less liquid than if they were receiving income from financial assets. In this case, they might want to hold more money because it is a more liquid asset than the alternatives. The term *h* plays no essential role in Friedman's theory and has no important implications for monetary theory. That is why we ignore it in the money demand function.

creases rapidly, but because some of this increase is temporary, average long-run income does not change very much. Hence in a boom, permanent income rises much less than income. During a recession much of the income decline is transitory, and average long-run income (hence permanent income) falls less than income. One implication of Friedman's use of the concept of permanent income as a determinant of the demand for money is that the demand for money will not fluctuate much with business cycle movements.

An individual can hold wealth in several forms besides money; Friedman categorized them into three types of assets: bonds, equity (common stocks), and goods. The incentives for holding these assets rather than money are represented by the expected return on each of these assets relative to the expected return on money, the last three terms in the money demand function. The minus sign beneath each indicates that as each term rises, the demand for money will fall.

The expected return on money r_m, which appears in all three terms, is influenced by two factors:

1. The services provided by banks on deposits included in the money supply, such as provision of receipts in the form of canceled checks or the automatic paying of bills. When these services are increased, the expected return from holding money rises.

2. The interest payments on money balances. NOW accounts and other deposits that are included in the money supply currently pay interest. As these interest payments rise, the expected return on money rises.

The terms $r_b - r_m$ and $r_e - r_m$ represent the expected return on bonds and equity relative to money; as they rise, the relative expected return on money falls, and the demand for money falls. The final term, $\pi^e - r_m$, represents the expected return on goods relative to money. The expected return from holding goods is the expected rate of capital gains that occurs when their prices rise and hence is equal to the expected inflation rate π^e. If the expected inflation rate is 10%, for example, then goods prices are expected to rise at a 10% rate, and their expected return is 10%. When $\pi^e - r_m$ rises, the expected return on goods relative to money rises, and the demand for money falls.

DISTINGUISHING BETWEEN THE FRIEDMAN AND KEYNESIAN THEORIES

There are several differences between Friedman's theory of the demand for money and the Keynesian theories. One is that by including many assets as alternatives to money, Friedman recognized that more than one interest rate is important to the operation of the aggregate economy. Keynes, for his part, lumped financial assets other than money into one big category—bonds—because he felt that their returns generally move together. If this is so, the expected return on bonds will be a good indicator of the expected return on other financial assets, and there will be no need to include them separately in the money demand function.

Also in contrast to Keynes, Friedman viewed money and goods as substitutes; that is, people choose between them when deciding how much money to hold. That is why Friedman included the expected return on goods relative to money as a term in his money demand function. The assumption that money and goods are substitutes indicates that changes in the quantity of money may have a direct effect on aggregate spending.

In addition, Friedman stressed two issues in discussing his demand-for-money function that distinguish it from Keynes's liquidity preference theory. First, Friedman did not take the expected return on money to be a constant, as did Keynes. When interest rates rise in the economy, banks make more profits on their loans, and they want to attract more deposits to increase the volume of their now more profitable loans. If there are no restrictions on interest payments on deposits, banks attract deposits by paying higher interest rates on them. Because the industry is competitive, the expected return on money held as bank deposits then rises with the higher interest rates on bonds and loans. The banks compete to get deposits until there are no excess profits, and in doing so they close the gap between interest earned on loans and interest paid on deposits. The net result of this competition in the banking industry is that $r_b - r_m$ stays relatively constant when the interest rate i rises.[12]

What if there are restrictions on the amount of interest that banks can pay on their deposits? Will the expected return on money be a constant? As interest rates rise, will $r_b - r_m$ rise as well? Friedman thought not. He argued that although banks might be restricted from making pecuniary payments on their deposits, they can still compete on the quality dimension. For example, they can provide more services to depositors by providing more tellers, paying bills automatically, or providing more cash machines at more accessible locations. The result of these improvements in money services is that the expected return from holding deposits will rise. So despite the restrictions on pecuniary interest payments, we might still find that a rise in market interest rates will raise the expected return on money sufficiently so that $r_b - r_m$ will remain relatively constant.[13] ***Unlike Keynes's theory, which indicates that interest rates are an important determinant of the demand for money, Friedman's theory suggests that changes in interest rates should have little effect on the demand for money.***

---

[12]Friedman does suggest that there is some increase in $r_b - r_m$ when i rises because part of the money supply (especially currency) is held in forms that cannot pay interest in a pecuniary or nonpecuniary form. See, for example, Milton Friedman, "Why a Surge of Inflation Is Likely Next Year," *Wall Street Journal,* September 1, 1983, p. 24.

[13]Competing on the quality of services is characteristic of many industries that are restricted from competing on price. For example, in the 1960s and early 1970s, when airfares were set at too high a level by the Civil Aeronautics Board, airlines were not allowed to lower their fares to attract customers. Instead, they improved the quality of their service by providing free wine, fancier food, piano bars, movies, and wider seats.

Therefore, Friedman's money demand function is essentially one in which permanent income is the primary determinant of money demand, and his money demand equation can be approximated by

$$M_d = f(Y_p) \tag{7}$$

In Friedman's view, the demand for money is insensitive to interest rates—not because he viewed the demand for money as insensitive to changes in the incentives for holding other assets relative to money but rather because changes in interest rates should have little effect on these incentive terms in the money demand function. The incentive terms remain relatively constant because any rise in the expected returns on other assets as a result of the rise in interest rates would be matched by a rise in the expected return on money.

The second issue Friedman stressed is the stability of the demand-for-money function. In contrast to Keynes, Friedman suggested that random fluctuations in the demand for money are small and that the demand for money can be predicted accurately by the money demand function. When combined with his view that the demand for money is insensitive to changes in interest rates, this means that velocity is highly predictable. We can see this by writing down the velocity that is implied by the money demand equation (7):

$$V = \frac{Y}{f(Y_p)} \tag{8}$$

Because the relationship between Y and Y_p is usually quite predictable, a stable money demand function (one that does not undergo pronounced shifts so that it predicts the demand for money accurately) implies that velocity is predictable as well. If we can predict what velocity will be in the next period, a change in the quantity of money will produce a predictable change in aggregate spending. Even though velocity is no longer assumed to be constant, the money supply continues to be the primary determinant of nominal income as in the quantity theory of money. Therefore, Friedman's theory of money demand is indeed a restatement of the quantity theory because it leads to the same conclusion about the importance of money to aggregate spending.

You might recall that we said that the Keynesian liquidity preference function (in which interest rates *are* an important determinant of the demand for money) is able to explain the procyclical movements of velocity that we find in the data. Can Friedman's money demand formulation explain this procyclical velocity phenomenon as well?

The key clue to answering this question is the presence of permanent income rather than measured income in the money demand function. What happens to permanent income in a business cycle expansion? Because much of the increase in income will be transitory, permanent income rises much less than income. Friedman's money demand function then indicates that the demand for money rises only a small amount relative to the rise in measured income and, as Equation 8 indicates, velocity rises. Similarly, in a recession, the demand for money falls less than income because the decline in permanent income is small relative to income, and velocity falls. In this way we have the procyclical movement in velocity.

To summarize, Friedman's theory of the demand for money used a similar approach to that of Keynes and the earlier Cambridge economists but did not go into detail about the motives for holding money. Instead, Friedman made use of the theory of asset demand to indicate that the demand for money will be a function of permanent income and the expected returns on alternative assets relative to the expected return on money. There are two major differences between Friedman's theory and Keynes's. Friedman believed that changes in interest rates have little effect on the expected returns on other assets relative to money. Thus, in contrast to Keynes, he viewed the demand for money as insensitive to interest rates. In addition, he differed from Keynes in stressing that the money demand function does not undergo substantial shifts and so is stable. These two differences also indicate that velocity is predictable, yielding a quantity theory conclusion that money is the primary determinant of aggregate spending.

SUMMARY

1. Irving Fisher developed a transactions-based theory of the demand for money in which the demand for real balances is proportional to real income and is insensitive to interest-rate movements. An implication of his theory is that velocity, the rate of turnover of money, is constant. This generates the quantity theory of money, which implies that aggregate spending is determined solely by movements in the quantity of money.

2. The classical Cambridge approach tried to answer the question of how much money individuals want to hold. This approach also viewed the demand for real balances as proportional to real income, but it differs from Fisher's analysis in that it does not rule out interest-rate effects on the demand for money.

3. The classical view that velocity can be effectively treated as a constant is not supported by the data. The nonconstancy of velocity became especially clear to the economics profession after the sharp drop in velocity during the years of the Great Depression.

4. Keynes extended the Cambridge approach by suggesting three motives for holding money: the transactions motive, the precautionary motive, and the speculative motive. His resulting liquidity preference theory views the transactions and pre-

cautionary components of money demand as proportional to income. However, the speculative component of money demand is viewed as sensitive to interest rates as well as to expectations about the future movements of interest rates. This theory, then, implies that velocity is unstable and cannot be treated as a constant.

5. Further developments in the Keynesian approach provided a better rationale for the three Keynesian motives for holding money. Interest rates were found to be important to the transactions and precautionary components of money demand as well as to the speculative component.

6. Milton Friedman's theory of money demand used a similar approach to that of Keynes and the classical Cambridge economists. Treating money like any other asset, Friedman used the theory of asset demand to derive a demand for money that is a function of the expected returns on other assets relative to the expected return on money and permanent income. In contrast to Keynes, Friedman believed that the demand for money is stable and insensitive to interest-rate movements. His belief that velocity is predictable (though not constant) in turn leads to the quantity theory conclusion that money is the primary determinant of aggregate spending.

KEY TERMS

monetary theory

velocity of money

equation of exchange

quantity theory of money

liquidity preference theory

real money balances

QUESTIONS AND PROBLEMS

*1. The money supply M has been growing at 10% per year, and nominal GDP PY has been growing at 20% per year. The data are as follows (in billions of dollars):

	1995	1996	1997
M	100	110	121
PY	1000	1200	1440

Calculate the velocity in each year. At what rate is velocity growing?

2. Calculate what happens to nominal GDP if velocity remains constant at 5 and the money supply increases from $200 billion to $300 billion.

*3. What happens to nominal GDP if the money supply grows by 20% but velocity declines by 30%?

4. If credit cards were made illegal by congressional legislation, what would happen to velocity? Explain your answer.

*5. If velocity and aggregate output are reasonably constant (as the classical economists believed), what happens to the price level when the money supply increases from $1 trillion to $4 trillion?

6. If velocity and aggregate output remain constant at 5 and 1000, respectively, what happens to the price level if the money supply declines from $400 billion to $300 billion?

*7. "Considering that both Fisher and the classical Cambridge economists ended with the same equation for the demand for money, $M^d = kPY$, their theories are equivalent." In this statement true, false, or uncertain? Explain.

8. Using data from the *Economic Report of the President*, calculate velocity for the $M2$ definition of the money supply in the past five years. Does velocity appear to be constant?

*9. In Keynes's analysis of the speculative demand for money, what will happen to money demand if people suddenly decide that the normal level of the interest rate has declined? Why?

10. Why is Keynes's analysis of the speculative demand for money important to his view that velocity will undergo substantial fluctuations and thus cannot be treated as constant?

*11. If interest rates on bonds go to zero, what does the Baumol-Tobin analysis suggest Grant Smith's average holdings of money balances should be?

12. If brokerage fees go to zero, what does the Baumol-Tobin analysis suggest Grant Smith's average holdings of money should be?

*13. "In Tobin's analysis of the speculative demand for money, people will hold both money and bonds, even if bonds are expected to earn a positive return." In this statement true, false, or uncertain? Explain.

14. Both Keynes's and Friedman's theories of the demand for money suggest that as the relative expected return on money falls, demand for it will fall. Why does Friedman think that money demand is unaffected by changes in interest rates, but Keynes thought that it is affected?

*15. Why does Friedman's view of the demand for money suggest that velocity is predictable, whereas Keynes's view suggests the opposite?

Appendix to Chapter 23

EMPIRICAL EVIDENCE ON THE DEMAND FOR MONEY

As we have seen, the alternative theories of the demand for money can have very different implications for our view of the role of money in the economy. Which of these theories is an accurate description of the real world is an important question, and it is the reason why evidence on the demand for money has been at the center of many debates on the effects of monetary policy on aggregate economic activity. Here we examine the empirical evidence on the two primary issues that distinguish the different theories of money demand and that affect their conclusions about whether the quantity of money is the primary determinant of aggregate spending: Is the demand for money sensitive to changes in interest rates, and is the demand-for-money function stable over time?

INTEREST RATES AND MONEY DEMAND

In Chapter 23 we saw that if interest rates do not affect the demand for money, velocity is more likely to be a constant—or at least predictable—so that the quantity theory view that aggregate spending is determined by the quantity of money is more likely to be true. But the more sensitive the demand for money is to interest rates, the more unpredictable velocity will be, and the link between the money supply and aggregate spending will be less clear. Indeed, there is an extreme case of ultrasensitivity of the demand for money to interest rates, called the *liquidity trap,* in which monetary policy has no effect on aggregate spending.

James Tobin conducted one of the earliest studies on the link between interest rates and money demand using U.S. data.[1] Tobin separated out transactions balances from other money balances, which he called *idle balances,* by assuming that transactions balances were proportional to income only and that idle balances were related to interest rates only. He then looked at whether his measure of idle balances was inversely related to interest rates in the period

---

[1]James Tobin, "Liquidity Preference and Monetary Policy," *Review of Economics and Statistics* 29 (1947): 124–131.

1922–1941 by plotting the average level of idle balances in each year against the average interest rate on commercial paper in that year. When he found a clear-cut inverse relationship between interest rates and idle balances, Tobin concluded that the demand for money is sensitive to interest rates.[2]

Additional empirical evidence on the demand for money strongly confirms Tobin's finding.[3] Does this sensitivity ever become so high that we approach the case of the liquidity trap in which monetary policy is ineffective? The answer is almost certainly no. Keynes suggested in his *General Theory* that a liquidity trap might occur when interest rates are extremely low. (However, he did state that he had never seen the occurrence of a liquidity trap.)

Typical of the evidence demonstrating that the liquidity trap has never occurred is that of David Laidler, Karl Brunner, and Allan Meltzer, who looked at whether the interest sensitivity of money demand increased in periods when interest rates were very low.[4] Laidler and Meltzer looked at this question by seeing if the interest sensitivity of money demand differed across periods, especially in periods such as the 1930s when interest rates were particularly low.[5] They found that there was no tendency for interest sensitivity to increase as interest rates fell—in fact, interest sensitivity did not change from period to period. Brunner and Meltzer explored this question by recognizing that a higher interest sensitivity in the 1930s as a result of a liquidity trap implies that a money demand function estimated for this period should not predict well in more normal periods. What Brunner and Meltzer found was that a money demand function, estimated mostly with data from the 1930s, accurately predicted the demand for money in the 1950s. This result provided little evidence in favor of the existence of a liquidity trap during the Great Depression period.

The evidence on the interest sensitivity of the demand for money found by different researchers is remarkably consistent. Neither extreme case is supported

---

[2] A problem with Tobin's procedure is that idle balances are not really distinguishable from transactions balances. As the Baumol-Tobin model of transactions demand for money makes clear, transactions balances will be related to both income and interest rates, just like idle balances.

[3] See David E. W. Laidler, *The Demand for Money: Theories and Evidence,* 3rd ed. (New York: HarperCollins, 1985). Only one major study finds that the demand for money is insensitive to interest rates: Milton Friedman, "The Demand for Money: Some Theoretical and Empirical Results," *Journal of Political Economy* 67 (1959): 327–351. Friedman concluded that the demand for money is not sensitive to interest-rate movements, but as later work by Laidler (using the same data as Friedman) demonstrated, Friedman used a faulty statistical procedure that biased his results: David E. W. Laidler, "The Rate of Interest and the Demand for Money: Some Empirical Evidence," *Journal of Political Economy* 74 (1966): 545–555. When a correct statistical procedure was employed, Laidler found the usual result that the demand for money is sensitive to interest rates. In later work, Friedman has also concluded that the demand for money is sensitive to interest rates.

[4] David E. W. Laidler, "Some Evidence on the Demand for Money," *Journal of Political Economy* 74 (1966): 55–68; Allan H. Meltzer, "The Demand for Money: The Evidence from the Time Series," *Journal of Political Economy* 71 (1963): 219–246; Karl Brunner and Allan H. Meltzer, "Predicting Velocity: Implications for Theory and Policy," *Journal of Finance* 18 (1963): 319–354.

[5] Interest sensitivity is measured by the interest elasticity of money demand, which is defined as the percentage change in the demand for money divided by the percentage change in the interest rate.

by the data: The demand for money is sensitive to interest rates, but there is little evidence that a liquidity trap has ever existed.

STABILITY OF MONEY DEMAND

If the money demand function is unstable and undergoes substantial unpredictable shifts, as Keynes thought, then velocity is unpredictable, and the quantity of money may not be tightly linked to aggregate spending, as in the modern quantity theory. The stability of the money demand function is also crucial to whether the Federal Reserve should target on interest rates or the money supply (see Chapter 25). Thus the question of whether the money demand function is stable or not has important implications for the conduct of monetary policy.

As our discussion of the Brunner and Meltzer article indicates, evidence on the stability of the demand-for-money function is related to the evidence on the existence of a liquidity trap. Brunner and Meltzer's finding that a money demand function estimated using data mostly from the 1930s predicted the demand for money in the postwar period not only suggests that a liquidity trap did not exist in the 1930s but also indicates that the money demand function has been stable over long periods of time. The evidence that the interest sensitivity of the demand for money did not change from period to period also suggests that the money demand function is stable, for a changing interest sensitivity would mean that the demand-for-money function estimated in one period would not be able to predict well in another period.

By the early 1970s, the evidence using quarterly data from the postwar period strongly supported the stability of the money demand function when $M1$ was used as the definition of the money supply. For example, a well-known study by Stephen Goldfeld published in 1973 found not only that the interest sensitivity of $M1$ money demand did not undergo changes in the postwar period but also that the $M1$ money demand function predicted extremely well throughout the postwar period.[6] As a result of this evidence, the $M1$ money demand function became the conventional money demand function used by economists.

The Case of the Missing Money

The stability of the demand for money, then, was a well-established fact when, starting in 1974, the conventional $M1$ money demand function began severely overpredicting the demand for money. Goldfeld labeled this phenomenon of instability in the demand-for-money function the case of the missing money.[7] It

---

[6]Stephen M. Goldfeld, "The Demand for Money Revisited," *Brookings Papers on Economic Activity* (1973): 577–638.

[7]Stephen M. Goldfeld, "The Case of the Missing Money," *Brookings Papers on Economic Activity* (1976): 683–730.

has presented a serious challenge to the usefulness of the money demand function as a tool for understanding how monetary policy affects aggregate economic activity. In addition, it has important implications for the conduct of monetary policy. As a result, the instability of the $M1$ money demand function stimulated an intense search for a solution to the mystery of the missing money so that a stable money demand function could be resurrected.

The search for a stable money demand function has taken two directions. The first focused on whether an incorrect definition of money could be the reason why the demand-for-money function had become so unstable. Because of inflation, high nominal interest rates, and advances in computer technology, the payments mechanism and cash management techniques have undergone rapid changes since 1974. In addition, many new financial instruments have emerged and gained in importance. This led some researchers to suspect that the rapid pace of financial innovation since 1974 means that the conventional definitions of the money supply no longer apply. They searched for a stable money demand function by actually searching directly for the missing money; that is, they looked for financial instruments that have been incorrectly left out of the definition of money.

Overnight repurchase agreements (repos) are one example. These are one-day loans with little default risk because they are structured to provide Treasury bills as collateral. (Chapter 2 gives a more detailed discussion of the structure of this type of loan.) Corporations with demand deposit accounts at commercial banks frequently loan out substantial amounts of their account balances overnight with these repos, lowering the measures of the money supply. However, the amounts loaned out are very close substitutes for money in that the corporation can quickly make a decision to decrease these loans if it needs more money in its demand deposit account to pay its bills. Gillian Garcia and Simon Pak, for example, found that including overnight repos in measures of the money supply substantially reduced the degree to which money demand functions overpredicted the money supply.[8] More recent evidence using later data casts some doubt on whether including overnight repos and other highly liquid assets in measures of the money supply produces money demand functions that are stable.[9]

The second direction of search for a stable money demand function was to look for new variables to include in the money demand function that would make it stable. Michael Hamburger found that including the average dividend-price ratio on common stocks (average dividends divided by the average price) as a measure of their interest rate resulted in a money demand function that is

---

[8]Gillian Garcia and Simon Pak, "Some Clues in the Case of the Missing Money," *American Economic Review* 69 (1979): 330–334.

[9]See the survey in John P. Judd and John L. Scadding, "The Search for a Stable Money Demand Function," *Journal of Economic Literature* 20 (1982): 993–1023.

stable.[10] Other researchers, such as H. Heller and Moshin Khan, added the entire term structure of interest rates to their money demand function and found that this produces a stable money demand function.[11]

These attempts to produce a stable money demand function have been criticized on the grounds that these additional variables do not accurately measure the opportunity cost of holding money, and so the theoretical justification for including them in the money demand function is weak.[12] Also, later research calls into question whether these alterations to the money demand function really do lead to continuing stability in the future.[13]

Velocity Slowdown in the 1980s

The woes of conventional money demand functions increased in the 1980s. We have seen that they overpredicted money demand in the mid- and late 1970s; that is, they underpredicted velocity PY/M, which rose faster than expected. The tables turned beginning in 1982; as is clear from Figure 1 in Chapter 23, economists were now faced with a surprising slowdown in $M1$ velocity, which conventional money demand functions also could not predict. Although researchers have tried to explain this velocity slowdown, they have not been entirely successful.[14]

---

[10]Michael Hamburger, "Behavior of the Money Stock: Is There a Puzzle?" *Journal of Monetary Economics* 3 (1977): 265–288. The stability of his money demand function also depends on his assumption that the income elasticity of the demand for money is unity. This assumption has been strongly criticized by many analysts, including R. W. Hafer and Scott E. Hein, "Evidence on the Temporal Stability of the Demand for Money Relationship in the United States," *Federal Reserve Bank of St. Louis Review*, December 1979, pp. 3–14, who find that this assumption is strongly rejected by the data.

[11]H. Heller and Moshin S. Khan, "The Demand for Money and the Term Structure of Interest Rates," *Journal of Political Economy* 87 (1979): 109–129.

[12]Frederic S. Mishkin, "Discussion of Asset Substitutability and the Impact of Federal Deficits," in *The Economic Consequences of Government Deficits,* ed. Laurence H. Meyer (Boston: Kluwer-Nijhoff, 1983), pp. 117–120; Frederic S. Mishkin, "Discussion of Recent Velocity Behavior, the Demand for Money and Monetary Policy," in *Monetary Targeting and Velocity* (Federal Reserve Bank of San Francisco, 1983), pp. 129–132.

[13]This research is discussed in Judd and Scadding, "Search for a Stable Money Demand Function."

[14]See, for example, Robert H. Rasche, "M1 Velocity and Money-Demand Functions: Do Stable Relationships Exist?" in *Empirical Studies of Velocity, Real Exchange Rates, Unemployment and Productivity,* ed. Karl Brunner and Allan H. Meltzer (Carnegie-Rochester Conference Series on Public Policy, (1987), pp. 9–88.

M2 to the Rescue?

As we saw in Figure 1 in Chapter 23, $M2$ velocity remained far more stable than $M1$ velocity in the 1980s. The relative stability of $M2$ velocity suggests that money demand functions in which the money supply is defined as $M2$ might perform substantially better than those in which the money supply is defined as $M1$. Researchers at the Federal Reserve found that $M2$ money demand functions performed well in the 1980s, with $M2$ velocity moving quite closely with the opportunity cost of holding $M2$ (market interest rates minus an average of the interest paid on deposits and financial instruments that make up $M2$).[15] However, in the early 1990s, $M2$ growth has experienced a dramatic slowdown, which some researchers believe cannot be explained by traditional money demand functions.[16] Doubts persist about the stability of money demand.

Conclusion

The main conclusion from the research on the money demand function seems to be that the most likely cause of its instability is the rapid pace of financial innovation occurring after 1973. The evidence is still somewhat tentative, however; a truly stable and satisfactory money demand function has not yet been found, and so the search for one continues.

The recent instability of the money demand function calls into question whether our theories and empirical analyses are adequate.[17] It also has important implications for the way monetary policy should be conducted because it casts doubt on the usefulness of the money demand function as a tool to provide guidance to policymakers. In particular, because the money demand function has become unstable, velocity is now harder to predict, and setting rigid money supply targets in order to control aggregate spending in the economy may not be an effective way to conduct monetary policy.

---

[15] See David H. Small and Richard D. Porter, "Understanding the Behavior of M2 and V2," *Federal Reserve Bulletin* 75 (1989): 244–254.

[16] See, for example, Bryon Higgins, "Policy Implications of Recent M2 Behavior," in *Federal Reserve Bank of Kansas City Economic Review,* Third Quarter, 1992, pp. 21–36. For a contrary view, see Robert L. Hetzel, "How Useful Is M2 Today?" in *Federal Reserve Bank of Richmond Economic Review,* September-October 1992, pp. 12–26.

[17] Thomas F. Cooley and Stephen F. Le Roy, "Identification and Estimation of Money Demand," *American Economic Review* 71 (1981): 825–844, is especially critical of the empirical research on the demand for money.

Chapter 24

THE KEYNESIAN FRAMEWORK AND THE *ISLM* MODEL

PREVIEW   In the media you often see forecasts of GDP and interest rates by economists and government agencies. At times these forecasts seem to come from a crystal ball, but economists actually make their predictions using a variety of economic models. One model widely used by economic forecasters is the *ISLM* model, which was developed by Sir John Hicks in 1937 and is based on the analysis in John Maynard Keynes's influential book *The General Theory of Employment, Interest and Money,* published in 1936.[1] The *ISLM* model explains how interest rates and total output produced in the economy (aggregate output or, equivalently, aggregate income) are determined, given a fixed price level.

The *ISLM* model is valuable not only because it can be used in economic forecasting but also because it provides a deeper understanding of how government policy can affect aggregate economic activity. In Chapter 25 we use it to evaluate the effects of monetary and fiscal policy on the economy and to learn some lessons about how monetary policy might best be conducted.

In this chapter we begin by developing the simplest framework for determining aggregate output, in which all economic actors (consumers, firms, and others) except the government play a role. Government fiscal policy (spending and taxes) is then added to the framework to see how it can affect the determination of aggregate output. Finally, we achieve a complete picture of the *ISLM* model by adding monetary policy variables: the money supply and the interest rate.

---

[1]John Hicks, "Mr. Keynes and the Classics: A Suggested Interpretation," *Econometrica* (1937):147–159.

DETERMINATION OF AGGREGATE OUTPUT

Keynes was especially interested in understanding movements of aggregate output because he wanted to explain why the Great Depression had occurred and how government policy could be used to increase employment in a similar economic situation. Keynes's analysis started with the recognition that the total quantity demanded of an economy's output was the sum of four types of spending: (1) **consumer expenditure** (C), the total demand for consumer goods and services (hamburgers, stereos, rock concerts, etc.); (2) **planned investment spending** (I), the total planned spending by businesses on new physical capital (machines, computers, factories, raw materials, etc.) plus planned spending on new homes; (3) **government spending** (G), the spending by all levels of government on goods and services (typewriters, aircraft carriers, government workers, red tape, etc.); (4) **net exports** (NX), the net foreign spending on domestic goods and services, equal to exports minus imports.[2] The total quantity demanded of an economy's output, called **aggregate demand** (Y^{ad}), can be written as

$$Y^{ad} = C + I + G + NX \tag{1}$$

Using the commonsense concept from supply and demand analysis, Keynes recognized that equilibrium would occur in the economy when total quantity of output supplied (aggregate output produced, Y) equals quantity of output demanded Y^{ad}, that is, when

$$Y = Y^{ad} \tag{2}$$

When this equilibrium condition is satisfied, producers are able to sell all of their output and have no reason to change their production. Keynes's analysis involves explaining why aggregate output is at a certain level by understanding what factors affect each component of aggregate demand and how the sum of these components could add up to an output smaller than the economy is capable of producing, resulting in less than full employment.

Keynes was especially concerned with explaining the low level of output and employment during the Great Depression. Because inflation was not a serious problem during this period, he assumed that output could change without causing a change in prices. ***Keynes's analysis assumes that the price level is fixed;*** that is, dollar amounts for such variables as consumer expenditure, investment, and aggregate output do not have to be adjusted for changes in the price level to tell us how much the real quantities of these variables change. Because the price level is assumed to be fixed, when we talk in this chapter about changes in nominal quantities, we are talking about changes in real quantities as well.

---

[2]Imports are subtracted from exports in arriving at the net exports component of the total quantity demanded of an economy's output because imports are already counted in *C, I,* and *G* but do not add to the demand for the economy's output.

Our discussion of Keynes's analysis begins with a simple framework of aggregate output determination in which the role of government, net exports, and the possible effects of money and interest rates are ignored. Because we are assuming that government spending and net exports are zero ($G = 0$ and $NX = 0$), we need only examine consumer expenditure and investment spending to explain how aggregate output is determined. This simple framework is unrealistic because both government and monetary policy are left out of the picture, and it makes other simplifying assumptions, such as a fixed price level. Still, the model is worth studying because it provides a simplified view that helps us understand the key factors that explain how the economy works. It also clearly illustrates the Keynesian idea that the economy can come to rest at a level of aggregate output below the full employment level. Once you understand this simple framework, we can proceed to more complex and more realistic models.

Consumer Expenditure and the Consumption Function

Ask yourself what determines how much you spend on consumer goods and services. Your likely response is that your income is the most important factor because if your income rises, you will be willing to spend more. Keynes reasoned similarly that consumer expenditure is related to **disposable income,** the total income available for spending, equal to aggregate income (which is equivalent to aggregate output) minus taxes ($Y - T$). He called this relationship between disposable income Y_D and consumer expenditure C the **consumption function** and expressed it as

$$C = a + (mpc \times Y_D) \tag{3}$$

The term *mpc,* called the **marginal propensity to consume,** is the slope of the consumption function line ($\Delta C / \Delta Y_D$) and reflects the change in consumer expenditure that results from an additional dollar of disposable income. Keynes assumed that *mpc* was a constant between the values of 0 and 1. If, for example, a \$1.00 increase of disposable income leads to an increase in consumer expenditure of \$0.50, then *mpc* = 0.5.

The term *a* stands for **autonomous consumer expenditure,** the amount of consumer expenditure that is independent of disposable income. It tells us how much consumers will spend when disposable income is 0 (they still must have food, clothing, and shelter). If *a* is \$200 billion when disposable income is 0, consumer expenditure will equal \$200 billion.[3]

A numerical example of a consumption function using the values of *mpc* = 0.5 and *a* = 200 will clarify the preceding concept. The \$200 billion of

---

[3]Consumer expenditure can exceed income if people have accumulated savings to tide them over bad times. An alternative is to have parents who will give you money for food (or to pay for school) when you have no income. The situation in which consumer expenditure is greater than disposable income is called *dissaving.*

consumer expenditure at a disposable income of 0 is listed in the first row of Table 1 and is plotted as point E in Figure 1. (Remember that throughout this chapter, dollar amounts for all variables in the figures correspond to real quantities because Keynes assumed that the price level is fixed.) Because $mpc = 0.5$, when disposable income increases by $400 billion, the change in consumer expenditure—ΔC in column 3 of Table 1—is $200 billion ($0.5 \times \$400$ billion). Thus when disposable income is $400 billion, consumer expenditure is $400 billion (initial value of $200 billion when income is 0 plus the $200 billion change in consumer expenditure). This combination of consumer expenditure and disposable income is listed in the second row of Table 1 and is plotted as point F in Figure 1. Similarly, at point G, where disposable income has increased by another $400 billion to $800 billion, consumer expenditure will rise by another $200 billion to $600 billion. By the same reasoning, at point H, at which disposable income is $1200 billion, consumer expenditure will be $800 billion. The line connecting these points in Figure 1 graphs the consumption function.

STUDY GUIDE

The consumption function is an intuitive concept that you can readily understand if you think about how your own spending behavior changes as you receive more disposable income. One way to make yourself more comfortable with this concept is to estimate your marginal propensity to consume (for example, it might be 0.8) and your level of consumer expenditure when your disposable income is 0 (it might be $2000) and then construct a consumption function similar to that in Table 1.

TABLE 1   A Consumption Function: The Schedule of Consumer Expenditure C When $mpc = 0.5$ and $a = 200$ ($ billions)

Point in Figure 1	Disposable income Y_D (1)	Change in Disposable Income ΔY_D (2)	Change in Consumer Expenditure ΔC ($0.5 \times \Delta Y_D$) (3)	Consumer Expenditure C (4)
E	0	—	—	200 (= a)
F	400	400	200	400
G	800	400	200	600
H	1200	400	200	800

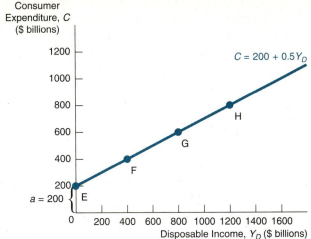

FIGURE 1
A Consumption Function
The consumption function plotted here is from Table 1; *mpc* = 0.5 and *a* = 200.

Investment Spending

It is important to understand that there are two types of investment. The first type, **fixed investment**, is the spending by firms on equipment (machines, computers, airplanes) and structures (factories, office buildings, shopping centers) and planned spending on residential housing. The second type, **inventory investment**, is spending by firms on additional holdings of raw materials, parts, and finished goods, calculated as the change in holdings of these items in a given time period, say, a year. (Box 1 explains how economists' use of the word *investment* differs from everyday use of the term.)

Suppose that Compaq, a company that produces personal computers, has 100,000 computers sitting in its warehouses on December 31, 1994, ready to be shipped to dealers. If each computer has a wholesale price of $1000, Compaq has an inventory worth $100 million. If by December 31, 1995, its inventory of

Box 1

MEANING OF THE WORD *INVESTMENT*

Economists use the word *investment* somewhat differently from other people. When people say that they are making an investment, they are normally referring to the purchase of common stocks or bonds, purchases that do not necessarily involve newly produced goods and services. But when economists speak of *investment spending,* they are referring to the purchase of *new* physical assets such as *new* machines or *new* houses—purchases that add to aggregate demand.

personal computers has risen to $150 million, its inventory investment in 1995 is $50 million, the *change* in the level of its inventory over the course of the year ($150 million minus $100 million). Now suppose that there is a drop in the level of inventories; inventory investment will then be negative.

Compaq may also have additional inventory investment if the level of raw materials and parts that it is holding to produce these computers increases over the course of the year. If on December 31, 1994, it holds $20 million of computer chips used to produce its computers and on December 31, 1995, it holds $30 million, it has an additional $10 million of inventory investment in 1995.

An important feature of inventory investment is that—in contrast to fixed investment, which is always planned—some inventory investment can be unplanned. Suppose that the reason that Compaq finds itself with an additional $50 million of computers on December 31, 1995, is that $50 million less of its computers were sold in 1995 than expected. This $50 million of inventory investment in 1995 was unplanned. In this situation, Compaq is producing more computers than it can sell and will cut production.

Planned investment spending, a component of aggregate demand Y^{ad}, is equal to planned fixed investment plus the amount of inventory investment *planned* by firms. Keynes mentioned two factors that influence planned investment spending: interest rates and businesses' expectations about the future. How these factors affect investment spending is discussed later in this chapter. For now, planned investment spending will be treated as a known value. At this stage we want to see how aggregate output is determined for a given level of planned investment spending; once we understand this, we can examine how interest rates and business expectations influence aggregate output by affecting planned investment spending.

Equilibrium and the Keynesian Cross Diagram

We have now assembled the building blocks (consumer expenditure and planned investment spending) that will enable us to see how aggregate output is determined when we ignore the government. Although unrealistic, this stripped-down analysis clarifies the basic principles of output determination. In the next section, government enters the picture and makes our model more realistic.

The diagram in Figure 2, known as the *Keynesian cross diagram,* shows how aggregate output is determined. The vertical axis measures aggregate demand, and the horizontal axis measures the level of aggregate output. The 45° line shows all the points at which aggregate output Y equals aggregate demand Y^{ad}; that is, it shows all the points at which the equilibrium condition $Y = Y^{ad}$ is satisfied. Since government spending is zero ($G = 0$), aggregate demand is

$$Y^{ad} = C + I$$

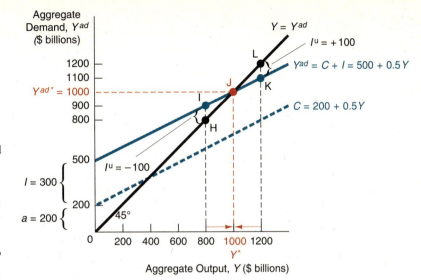

FIGURE 2

Keynesian Cross Diagram

When $I = 300$ and $C = 200 + 0.5Y$, equilibrium output occurs at $Y^* = 1000$, where the aggregate demand function $Y^{ad} = C + I$ intersects with the 45° line $Y = Y^{ad}$.

Because there is no government sector to collect taxes, there are none in our simplified economy; disposable income Y_D then equals aggregate output Y (remember that aggregate income and aggregate output are equivalent; see the appendix to Chapter 1). Thus the consumption function with $a = 200$ and $mpc = 0.5$ plotted in Figure 1 can be written as $C = 200 + 0.5Y$ and is plotted in Figure 2. Given that planned investment spending is $300 billion, aggregate demand can then be expressed as

$$Y^{ad} = C + I = 200 + 0.5Y + 300 = 500 + 0.5Y$$

This equation, plotted in Figure 2, represents the quantity of aggregate demand at any given level of aggregate output and is called the **aggregate demand function.**

The aggregate demand function $Y^{ad} = C + I$ is the vertical sum of the consumption function line ($C = 200 + 0.5Y$) and planned investment spending ($I = 300$). The point at which the aggregate demand function crosses the 45° line $Y = Y^{ad}$ indicates the equilibrium level of aggregate demand and aggregate output. In Figure 2, equilibrium occurs at point J, with both aggregate output Y^* and aggregate demand Y^{ad*} at $1000 billion.

As you learned in Chapter 6, the concept of equilibrium is useful only if there is a tendency for the economy to settle there. To see whether the economy heads toward the equilibrium output level of $1000 billion, let's first look at what happens if the amount of output produced in the economy is $1200 billion and is therefore above the equilibrium level. At this level of output, aggregate demand is $1100 billion (point K), $100 billion less than the $1200 billion of output

can be derived algebraically by solving for the unknown value of Y in terms of a, mpc, and I, resulting in the following equation:[4]

$$Y = (a + I) \times \frac{1}{1 - mpc} \qquad (4)$$

Because I is multiplied by the term $1/(1 - mpc)$, this equation tells us that a $1 change in I leads to a $1/(1 - mpc) change in aggregate output; thus $1/(1 - mpc)$ is the expenditure multiplier. When $mpc = 0.5$, the change in output for a $1 change in I is $2 $[= 1/(1 - 0.5)]$; if $mpc = 0.8$, the change in output for a $1 change in I is $5. The larger the marginal propensity to consume, the higher the expenditure multiplier.

Response to Changes in Autonomous Spending Because a is also multiplied by the term $1/(1 - mpc)$ in Equation 4, a $1 change in autonomous consumer expenditure a also changes aggregate output by $1/(1 - mpc)$, the amount of the expenditure multiplier. Therefore, we see that the expenditure multiplier applies equally well to changes in autonomous consumer expenditure. In fact, Equation 4 can be rewritten as

$$Y = A \times \frac{1}{1 - mpc} \qquad (5)$$

in which A = autonomous spending = $a + I$.

This rewritten equation tells us that any change in autonomous spending, whether from a change in a, in I, or in both, will lead to a multiplied change in Y. If both a and I decrease by $100 billion each and $mpc = 0.5$, the expenditure multiplier is 2 $[= 1/(1 - 0.5)]$, and aggregate output Y will fall by $2 \times $200 billion = $400 billion. Conversely, a rise in I by $100 billion that is offset by a $100 billion decline in a will leave autonomous spending A, and hence Y, unchanged. The expenditure multiplier $1/(1 - mpc)$ can therefore be defined more

---

[4]Substituting the consumption function $C = a + (mpc \times Y)$ into the aggregate demand function $Y^{ad} = C + I$ yields

$$Y^{ad} = a + (mpc \times Y) + I$$

In equilibrium, where aggregate output equals aggregate demand,

$$Y = Y^{ad} = a + (mpc \times Y) + I$$

Subtracting the term $mpc \times Y$ from both sides of this equation in order to collect the terms involving Y on the left side, we have

$$Y - (mpc \times Y) = Y(1 - mpc) = a + I$$

Dividing both sides by $1 - mpc$ to solve for Y leads to Equation 4 in the text.

generally as the ratio of change in aggregate output to a change in autonomous spending ($\Delta Y/\Delta A$).

Another way to reach this conclusion—that any change in autonomous spending will lead to a multiplied change in aggregate output—is to recognize that the shift in the aggregate demand function in Figure 3 did not have to come from an increase in I; it could also have come from an increase in a, which directly raises consumer expenditure and therefore aggregate demand. Alternatively, it could have come from an increase in both a and I. Changes in the attitudes of consumers and firms about the future, which cause changes in their spending, will result in multiple changes in aggregate output.

Keynes believed that changes in autonomous spending are dominated by unstable fluctuations in planned investment spending, which is influenced by emotional waves of optimism and pessimism—factors he referred to as **"animal spirits."** His view was colored by the collapse in investment spending during the Great Depression, which he saw as the primary reason for the economic contraction. We will examine the consequences of this fall in investment spending in the following application.

APPLICATION

THE COLLAPSE OF INVESTMENT SPENDING AND THE GREAT DEPRESSION

From 1929 to 1933, the U.S. economy experienced the largest percentage decline in investment spending ever recorded. One explanation for the investment collapse was the ongoing set of financial crises during this period described in Chapter 9. In 1987 dollars, investment spending fell from $166 billion to $27 billion—a decline of over 80%. What does the Keynesian analysis developed so far suggest should have happened to aggregate output in this period?

Figure 4 demonstrates how the $139 billion drop in planned investment spending would shift the aggregate demand function downward from Y_1^{ad} to Y_2^{ad}, moving the economy from point 1 to point 2. Aggregate output would then fall sharply; real GDP actually fell by $252 billion (a multiple of the $139 billion drop in investment spending), from $847 billion to $595 billion (in 1987 dollars). Because the economy was at full employment in 1929, the fall in output resulted in massive unemployment, with over 25% of the labor force unemployed in 1933.

After witnessing the events in the Great Depression, Keynes took the view that an economy would continually suffer major output fluctuations because of the volatility of autonomous spending, particularly planned investment spending. He was especially worried about sharp declines in autonomous spending, which would inevitably lead to large declines in output and an equilibrium with high unemployment. If autonomous spending fell sharply, as it did during the Great Depression, how could an economy be restored to higher levels of output

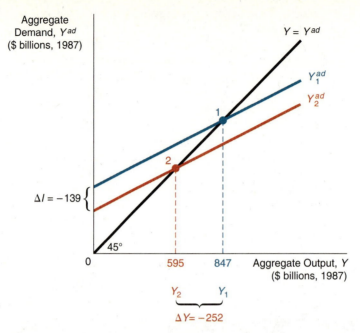

FIGURE 4 Response of Aggregate Output to the Collapse of Investment Spending, 1929–1933
The decline of $139 billion (in 1987 dollars) in planned investment spending from 1929 to 1933 shifted the aggregate demand function down from Y_1^{ad} to Y_2^{ad} and caused the economy to move from point 1 to point 2, where output fell by $252 billion. *Source:* Data from *Economic Report of the President.*

and more reasonable levels of unemployment? Not by an increase in autonomous spending, since the business outlook was so grim. Keynes's answer to this question involved looking at the role of government in determining aggregate output.

Government's Role

Keynes realized that government spending and taxation could also affect the position of the aggregate demand function and hence be manipulated to restore the economy to full employment. As shown in the aggregate demand equation $Y^{ad} = C + I + G + NX$, government spending G adds directly to aggregate demand. Taxes, however, do not affect aggregate demand directly, as government spending does. Instead, taxes lower the amount of income that consumers have available for spending and affect aggregate demand by influencing consumer expenditure; that is, when there are taxes, disposable income Y_D does not equal aggregate output; it equals aggregate output Y minus taxes T: $Y_D = Y - T$. The consumption function $C = a + mpc \times Y_D)$ can be rewritten as follows:

$$C = a + [mpc \times (Y - T)] = a + (mpc \times Y) - (mpc \times T) \qquad (6)$$

This consumption function looks similar to the one used in the absence of taxes, but it has the additional term $- mpc \times T$ on the right side. This term indicates that if taxes increase by \$100, consumer expenditure declines by mpc times this amount; if $mpc = 0.5$, consumer expenditure declines by \$50. This occurs because consumers view \$100 of taxes as equivalent to a \$100 reduction in income and reduce their expenditure by the marginal propensity to consume times this amount.

To see how the inclusion of government spending and taxes modifies our analysis, first we will observe the effect of a positive level of government spending on aggregate output in the Keynesian cross diagram of Figure 5. Let's say that in the absence of government spending or taxes, the economy is at point 1, where the aggregate demand function $Y_1^{ad} = C + I = 500 + 0.5Y$ crosses the 45° line $Y = Y_1^{ad}$. Here equilibrium output is at \$1000 billion. Suppose, however, that the economy reaches full employment at an aggregate output level of \$1800 billion. How can government spending be used to restore the economy to full employment at \$1800 billion of aggregate output?

If government spending is set at \$400 billion, the aggregate demand function shifts upward to $Y_2^{ad} = C + I + G = 900 + 0.5Y$. The economy moves to point 2, and aggregate output rises by \$800 billion to \$1800 billion. Figure 5 indicates that aggregate output is positively related to government spending and that a change in government spending leads to a multiplied change in aggregate output, equal to the expenditure multiplier, $1/(1 - mpc) = 1/(1 - 0.5) = 2$. Therefore, declines in planned investment spending that produce high unemployment (as occurred during the Great Depression) can be offset by raising government spending.

What happens if the government decides that it must collect taxes of \$400 billion to balance the budget? Before taxes are raised, the economy is in equilibrium at the same point 2 found in Figure 5. Our discussion of the consumption function (which allows for taxes) indicates that taxes T reduce consumer expenditure by $mpc \times T$ because there is \$$T$ less income now available for spending. In our example, $mpc = 0.5$, so consumer expenditure and the aggregate demand function shift downward by \$200 billion ($= 0.5 \times 400$); at the new equilibrium, point 3, the level of output has declined by twice this amount (the expenditure multiplier) to \$1400 billion.

Although you can see that aggregate output is negatively related to the level of taxes, it is important to recognize that the change in aggregate output from the \$400 billion increase in taxes ($\Delta Y = - $ \$400 billion) is smaller than the change in aggregate output from the \$400 billion increase in government spending ($\Delta Y = $ \$800 billion). If both taxes and government spending are raised equally by \$400 billion, as occurs in going from point 1 to point 3 in Figure 5, aggregate output will rise.

The Keynesian framework indicates that the government can play an important role in determining aggregate output by changing the level of government spending or taxes. If the economy enters a deep recession, in which output

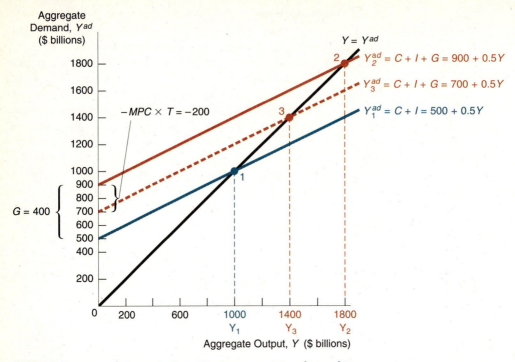

FIGURE 5 Response of Aggregate Output to Government Spending and Taxes
With no government spending or taxes, the aggregate demand function is Y_1^{ad}, and equilibrium output is $Y_1 = 1000$. With government spending of \$400 billion, the aggregate demand function shifts upward to Y_2^{ad}, and aggregate output rises by \$800 billion to $Y_2 = \$1800$ billion. Taxes of \$400 billion lower consumer expenditure and the aggregate demand function by \$200 billion from Y_2^{ad} to Y_3^{ad}, and aggregate output falls by \$400 billion to $Y_3 = \$1400$ billion.

drops severely and unemployment climbs, the analysis we have just developed provides a prescription for restoring the economy to health. The government might raise aggregate output by increasing government spending, or it could lower taxes and reverse the process described in Figure 5 (that is, a tax cut makes more income available for spending at any level of output, shifting the aggregate demand function upward and causing the equilibrium level of output to rise).

Role of International Trade

International trade also plays a role in determining aggregate output because net exports (exports minus imports) are a component of aggregate demand. To analyze the effect of net exports in the Keynesian cross diagram of Figure 6, suppose that initially net exports are equal to zero ($NX_1 = 0$) so that the economy is at point 1, where the aggregate demand function

$Y_1^{ad} = C + I + G + NX_1 = 500 + 0.5Y$ crosses the 45° line $Y = Y_1^{ad}$. Equilibrium output is again at \$1000 billion. Now foreigners suddenly get an urge to buy more American products so that net exports rise to \$100 billion ($NX_2 = 100$). The \$100 billion increase in net exports adds directly to aggregate demand and shifts the aggregate demand function upward to $Y_2^{ad} = C + I + G + NX_2 = 600 + 0.5Y$. The economy moves to point 2, and aggregate output rises by \$200 billion to \$1200 billion (Y_2). Figure 6 indicates that just as we found for planned investment spending and government spending, a rise in net exports leads to a multiplied rise in aggregate output, equal to the expenditure multiplier, $1/(1 - mpc) = 1/(1 - 0.5) = 2$. Therefore, changes in net exports can be another important factor affecting fluctuations in aggregate output.

Summary of the Determinants of Aggregate Output

Our analysis of the Keynesian framework so far has identified five autonomous factors (factors independent of income) that shift the aggregate demand function and hence the level of aggregate output:

1. Changes in autonomous consumer expenditure (a)
2. Changes in planned investment spending (I)
3. Changes in government spending (G)
4. Changes in taxes (T)

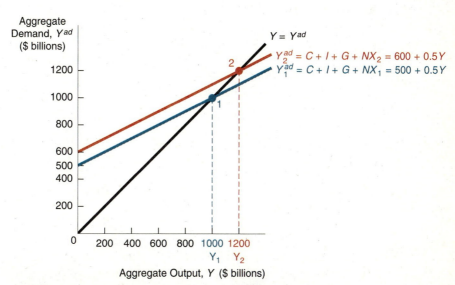

FIGURE 6 Response of Aggregate Output to a Change in Net Exports
A \$100 billion increase in net exports from $NX_1 = 0$ to $NX_2 = 100$ shifts the aggregate demand function upward from Y_1^{ad} to Y_2^{ad}. The equilibrium moves from point 1 to point 2, and equilibrium output rises from $Y_1 = \$1000$ billion to $Y_2 = \$1200$ billion.

5. Changes in net exports (*NX*)

The effects of changes in each of these variables on aggregate output are summarized in Table 2 and discussed next in the text.

Changes in Autonomous Consumer Spending (*a*) A rise in autonomous consumer expenditure *a* (say, because consumers become more optimistic about the economy when the stock market booms) directly raises consumer expenditure and shifts the aggregate demand function upward, resulting in an increase in aggregate output. A decrease in *a* causes consumer expenditure to fall, leading ultimately to a decline in aggregate output. Therefore, ***aggregate output is positively related to autonomous consumer expenditure a.***

Changes in Planned Investment Spending (*I*) A rise in planned investment spending adds directly to aggregate demand, thus raising the aggregate demand function and aggregate output. A fall in planned investment spending lowers aggregate demand and causes aggregate output to fall. Therefore, ***aggregate output is positively related to planned investment spending I.***

Changes in Government Spending (*G*) A rise in government spending also adds directly to aggregate demand and raises the aggregate demand function, raising aggregate output. A fall directly reduces aggregate demand, lowers the aggregate demand function, and causes aggregate output to fall. Therefore, ***aggregate output is positively related to government spending G.***

Changes in Taxes (*T*) A rise in taxes does not affect aggregate demand directly but does lower the amount of income available for spending, reducing consumer expenditure. The decline in consumer expenditure then leads to a fall in the aggregate demand function, resulting in a decline in aggregate output. A lowering of taxes makes more income available for spending, raises consumer expenditure, and leads to higher aggregate output. Therefore, ***aggregate output is negatively related to the level of taxes T.***

Changes in Net Exports (*NX*) A rise in net exports adds directly to aggregate demand and raises the aggregate demand function, increasing aggregate output. A fall directly reduces aggregate demand, lowers the aggregate demand function, and causes aggregate output to fall. Therefore, ***aggregate output is positively related to net exports NX.***

Size of the Effects from the Five Factors The aggregate demand function in the Keynesian cross diagrams shifts vertically by the full amount of the change in *a, I, G,* or *NX,* resulting in a multiple effect on aggregate output through the effects of the expenditure multiplier, $1/(1 - mpc)$. A change in taxes has a smaller effect on aggregate output because consumer expenditure changes only by *mpc* times the

SUMMARY

TABLE 2 Response of Aggregate Output Y to Autonomous Changes in a, I, G, T, and NX

Variable	Change in Variable	Response of Aggregate Output, Y	
a	↑	↑	
I	↑	↑	
G	↑	↑	
T	↑	↓	
NX	↑	↑	

Note: Only increases (↑) in the variables are shown; the effects of decreases in the variables on aggregate output would be the opposite of those indicated in the "Response" column.

change in taxes ($- mpc \times \Delta T$), which in the case of $mpc = 0.5$ means that aggregate demand shifts vertically by only half of the change in taxes.

If there is a change in one of these autonomous factors that is offset by a change in another (say, I rises by $100 billion, but a, G, or NX falls by $100 billion or *T* rises by $200 billion when *mpc* = 0.5), the aggregate demand function will remain in the same position, and aggregate output will remain unchanged.[5]

STUDY GUIDE

To test your understanding of the Keynesian analysis of how aggregate output changes in response to changes in the factors described, see if you can use Keynesian cross diagrams to illustrate what happens to aggregate output when each variable decreases rather than increases. Also, be sure to do the problems at the end of the chapter that ask you to predict what will happen to aggregate output when certain economic variables change.

THE *ISLM* MODEL

So far our analysis has excluded monetary policy. We now include money and interest rates in the Keynesian framework in order to develop the more intricate *ISLM* model of how aggregate output is determined, in which monetary policy plays an important role. Why another complex model? The *ISLM* model is more versatile and allows us to understand economic phenomena that cannot be ana-

---

[5]These results can be derived algebraically as follows. Substituting the consumption function allowing for taxes (Equation 6) into the aggregate demand function (Equation 1), we have

$$Y^{ad} = a - (mpc \times T) + (mpc \times Y) + I + G + NX$$

If we assume that taxes *T* are unrelated to income, we can define autonomous spending in the aggregate demand function to be

$$A = a - (mpc \times T) + I + G + NX$$

and the expenditure equation can be rewritten as

$$Y^{ad} = A + (mpc \times Y)$$

In equilibrium, aggregate demand equals aggregate output,

$$Y = A + (mpc \times Y)$$

which can be solved for *Y*. The resulting equation,

$$Y = A \times \frac{1}{1 - mpc}$$

is the same equation that links autonomous spending and aggregate output in the text (Equation 5), but it now allows for additional components of autonomous spending in *A*. We see that any increase in autonomous expenditure leads to a multiple increase in output. Thus any component of autonomous spending that enters *A* with a positive sign (*a, I, G,* and *NX*) will have a positive relationship with output, and any component with a negative sign (− *mpc* × *T*) will have a negative relationship with output. This algebraic analysis also show us that any rise in a component of *A* that is offset by a movement in another component of *A*, leaving *A* unchanged, will also leave output unchanged.

lyzed with the simpler Keynesian cross framework used earlier. The *ISLM* model will help you understand how monetary policy affects economic activity and interacts with fiscal policy (changes in government spending and taxes) to produce a certain level of aggregate output; how the level of interest rates is affected by changes in investment spending as well as by changes in monetary and fiscal policy; how best to conduct monetary policy; and how it generates the aggregate demand curve, an essential building block for the aggregate supply and demand analysis used in Chapter 26 and later chapters.

Like our simplified Keynesian model, the full Keynesian *ISLM* model examines an equilibrium in which aggregate output produced equals aggregate demand, and since it assumes a fixed price level, real and nominal quantities are the same. The first step in constructing the *ISLM* model is to examine the effect of interest rates on planned investment spending and hence on aggregate demand. Next we use a Keynesian cross diagram to see how the interest rate affects the equilibrium level of aggregate output. The resulting relationship between equilibrium aggregate output and the interest rate is known as the **IS curve.**

Just as a demand curve alone cannot tell us the quantity of goods sold in a market, the *IS* curve by itself cannot tell us what the level of aggregate output will be because the interest rate is still unknown. We need another relationship, called the **LM curve,** which describes the combinations of interest rates and aggregate output for which the quantity of money demanded equals the quantity of money supplied. When the *IS* and *LM* curves are combined in the same diagram, the intersection of the two determines the equilibrium level of aggregate output as well as the interest rate. Finally, we will have obtained a more complete analysis of the determination of aggregate output in which monetary policy plays an important role.

Equilibrium in the Goods Market: The *IS* Curve

In Keynesian analysis, the primary way that interest rates affect the level of aggregate output is through their effects on planned investment spending and net exports. After explaining why interest rates affect planned investment spending and net exports, we will use Keynesian cross diagrams to learn how interest rates affect equilibrium aggregate output.[6]

Interest Rates and Planned Investment Spending Businesses make investments in physical capital (machines, factories, and raw materials) as long as they expect to earn more from the physical capital than the interest cost of a loan to finance the investment. When the interest rate is high, few investments in physical capital will earn more than the cost of borrowed funds, so planned investment spending is

---

[6]More modern Keynesian approaches suggest that consumer expenditure, particularly for consumer durables (cars, furniture, appliances), is influenced by the interest rate. This interest sensitivity of consumer expenditure can be allowed for in the model here by defining planned investment spending more generally to include the interest-sensitive component of consumer expenditure.

low. When the interest rate is low, many investments in physical capital will earn more than the interest cost of borrowed funds. Therefore, when interest rates are lower, business firms are more likely to undertake an investment in physical capital, and planned investment spending will be higher.

Even if a company has surplus funds and does not need to borrow to undertake an investment in physical capital, its planned investment spending will still be affected by the interest rate. Instead of investing in physical capital, it could purchase a security, such as a bond. If the interest rate on this security is high, the opportunity cost (forgone interest earnings) of an investment is high, and planned investment spending will be low because the firm would probably prefer to purchase the security than to invest in physical capital. As the interest rate and the opportunity cost of investing fall, planned investment spending will increase, because investments in physical capital are more likely to earn greater income for the firm than the security.

The relationship between the amount of planned investment spending and any given level of the interest rate is illustrated by the investment schedule in panel (a) of Figure 7. The downward slope of the schedule reflects the negative relationship between planned investment spending and the interest rate. At a low interest rate i_1, the level of planned investment spending I_1 is high; for a high interest rate i_3, planned investment spending I_3 is low.

Interest Rates and Net Exports   As discussed in more detail in Chapter 8, when interest rates rise in the United States (with the price level fixed), U.S. dollar bank deposits become more attractive relative to deposits denominated in foreign currencies, thereby causing a rise in the value of dollar deposits relative to other currency deposits, that is, a rise in the exchange rate. The higher value of the dollar resulting from the rise in interest rates makes domestic goods more expensive than foreign goods, thereby causing a fall in net exports. Therefore, as the interest rate rises, the value of the dollar rises, domestic goods become more expensive, and net exports fall. The resulting negative relationship between interest rates and net exports is shown in panel (b) of Figure 7. At a low interest rate i_1, the exchange rate is low and net exports NX_1 are high; at a high interest rate i_3, the exchange rate is high and net exports NX_3 are low.

Deriving the *IS* Curve   We can now use what we have learned about the relationship of interest rates to planned investment spending and net exports in panels (a) and (b) to examine the relationship between interest rates and the equilibrium level of aggregate output (holding government spending and autonomous consumer expenditure constant). The three levels of planned investment spending and net exports in panels (a) and (b) are represented in the three aggregate demand functions in the Keynesian cross diagram of panel (c). The lowest interest rate i_1 has the highest level of both planned investment spending I_1 and net exports NX_1 and hence the highest aggregate demand function Y_1^{ad}. Point 1 in panel (d) shows the resulting equilibrium level of output Y_1, which corresponds to interest rate i_1. As the interest rate rises to i_2, both planned investment spending and net exports fall to I_2 and NX_2, so equilibrium output falls to Y_2. Point 2 in

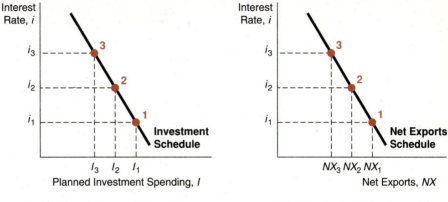

(a) Interest rates and planned investment spending

(b) Interest rates and net exports

FIGURE 7
Deriving the *IS* Curve

The investment schedule in panel (a) shows that as the interest rate rises from i_1 to i_2 to i_3, planned investment spending falls from I_1 to I_2 to I_3, and panel (b) shows that net exports also fall from NX_1 to NX_2 to NX_3 as the interest rate rises. Panel (c) then indicates the levels of equilibrium output Y_1, Y_2, and Y_3 that correspond to those three levels of planned investment and net exports. Finally, panel (d) plots the level of equilibrium output corresponding to each of the three interest rates; the line that connects these points is the *IS* curve.

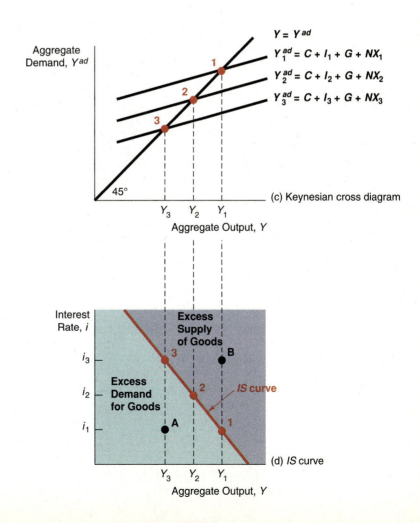

(c) Keynesian cross diagram

(d) *IS* curve

panel (d) shows the lower level of output Y_2, which corresponds to interest rate i_2. Finally, the highest interest rate i_3 leads to the lowest level of planned investment spending and net exports and hence the lowest level of equilibrium output, which is plotted as point 3.

The line connecting the three points in panel (d), the *IS* curve, shows the combinations of interest rates and equilibrium aggregate output for which aggregate output produced equals aggregate demand.[7] The negative slope indicates that higher interest rates result in lower planned investment spending and net exports and hence lower equilibrium output.

What the *IS* Curve Tells Us   The *IS* curve traces out the points at which the total quantity of goods produced equals the total quantity of goods demanded. It describes points at which the goods market is in equilibrium. For each given level of the interest rate, the *IS* curve tells us what aggregate output must equal in order for there to be equilibrium in the goods market. As the interest rate rises, planned investment spending and net exports fall, which in turn lowers aggregate demand; aggregate output must be lower in order for it to equal aggregate demand and satisfy goods market equilibrium.

The *IS* curve is a useful concept because output tends to move toward points on the curve that satisfy goods market equilibrium. If the economy is located in the area to the right of the *IS* curve, it has an excess supply of goods. At point B, for example, aggregate output Y_1 is greater than the equilibrium level of output Y_3 on the *IS* curve. This excess supply of goods results in unplanned inventory accumulation, which causes output to fall toward the *IS* curve. The decline stops only when output is again at its equilibrium level on the *IS* curve.

If the economy is located in the area to the left of the *IS* curve, it has an excess demand for goods. At point A, aggregate output Y_3 is below the equilibrium level of output Y_1 on the *IS* curve. The excess demand for goods results in an unplanned decrease in inventory, which causes output to rise toward the *IS* curve, stopping only when aggregate output is again at its equilibrium level on the *IS* curve.

Significantly, equilibrium in the goods market does not produce a unique equilibrium level of aggregate output. Although we now know where aggregate output will head for a given level of the interest rate, we cannot determine aggregate output because we do not know what the interest rate is. To complete our analysis of aggregate output determination, we need to introduce another market that produces an additional relationship that links aggregate output and interest rates. The market for money fulfills this function with the *LM* curve. When the *LM* curve is combined with the *IS* curve, a unique equilibrium that determines both aggregate output and the interest rate is obtained.

---

[7]The *IS* was so named by Sir John Hicks because in the simplest Keynesian framework with no government sector, equilibrium in the Keynesian cross diagram occurs when investment spending *I* equals saving *S*.

Equilibrium in the Market for Money: The *LM* Curve

Just as the *IS* curve is derived from the equilibrium condition in the goods market (aggregate output equals aggregate demand), the *LM* curve is derived from the equilibrium condition in the market for money, which requires that the quantity of money demanded equal the quantity of money supplied. The main building block in Keynes's analysis of the market for money is the demand for money he called *liquidity preference.* Let us briefly review his theory of the demand for money (discussed at length in Chapters 6 and 23).

Keynes's liquidity preference theory states that the demand for money in real terms M^d/P depends on income Y (aggregate output) and interest rates i. The demand for money is positively related to income for two reasons. First, a rise in income raises the level of transactions in the economy, which in turn raises the demand for money because it is used to carry out these transactions. Second, a rise in income increases the demand for money because it increases the wealth of individuals who want to hold more assets, one of which is money. The opportunity cost of holding money is the interest sacrificed by not holding other assets (such as bonds) instead. As interest rates rise, the opportunity cost of holding money rises, and the demand for money falls. According to the liquidity preference theory, the demand for money is positively related to aggregate output and negatively related to interest rates.

Deriving the *LM* Curve In Keynes's analysis, the level of interest rates is determined by equilibrium in the market for money, at which point the quantity of money demanded equals the quantity of money supplied. Figure 8 depicts what happens to equilibrium in the market for money as the level of output changes. Since the *LM* curve is derived holding the money supply at a fixed level, it is fixed at the level of $\overline{M}$ in panel (a).[8] Each level of aggregate output has its own money demand curve because as aggregate output changes, the level of transactions in the economy changes, which in turn changes the demand for money.

When aggregate output is Y_1, the money demand curve is $M^d(Y_1)$: It slopes downward because a lower interest rate means that the opportunity cost of holding money is lower, so the quantity of money demanded is higher. Equilibrium in the market for money occurs at point 1, at which the interest rate is i_1. When aggregate output is at the higher level Y_2, the money demand curve shifts rightward to $M^d(Y_2)$ because the higher level of output means that at any given interest rate, the quantity of money demanded is higher. Equilibrium in the market for money now occurs at point 2, at which the interest rate is at the higher level of i_2. Similarly, a still higher level of aggregate output Y_3, results in an even higher level of the equilibrium interest rate i_3.

---

[8]As pointed out in earlier chapters on the money supply process, the money supply is positively related to interest rates, and so the M^s curve in panel (a) should actually have a positive slope. The M^s curve is assumed to be vertical in panel (a) in order to simplify the graph, but allowing for a positive slope leads to identical results.

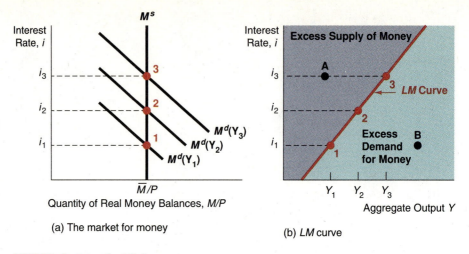

FIGURE 8 Deriving the LM Curve
Panel (a) shows the equilibrium levels of the interest rate in the market for money that arise when aggregate output is at Y_1, Y_2, and Y_3. Panel (b) plots the three levels of the equilibrium interest rate i_1, i_2, and i_3 corresponding to these three levels of output; the line that connects these points is the LM curve.

Panel (b) plots the equilibrium interest rates that correspond to the different output levels, with points 1, 2, and 3 corresponding to the equilibrium points 1, 2, and 3 in panel (a). The line connecting these points is the *LM* curve, which shows the combinations of interest rates and output for which the market for money is in equilibrium.[9] The positive slope arises because higher output raises the demand for money and thus raises the equilibrium interest rate.

What the LM Curve Tells Us   The *LM* curve traces out the points that satisfy the equilibrium condition that the quantity of money demanded equals the quantity of money supplied. For each given level of aggregate output, the *LM* curve tells us what the interest rate must be for there to be equilibrium in the market for money. As aggregate output rises, the demand for money increases and the interest rate rises, so that money demanded equals money supplied and the market for money is in equilibrium.

Just as the economy tends to move toward the equilibrium points represented by the *IS* curve, it also moves toward the equilibrium points on the *LM* curve. If the economy is located in the area to the left of the *LM* curve, there is an excess supply of money. At point A, for example, the interest rate is i_3 and aggregate output is Y_1. The interest rate is above the equilibrium level, and people are holding more money than they want to. To eliminate their excess money balances, they will purchase bonds, which causes the price of the bonds to rise

---

[9]Hicks named this the *LM* curve to indicate that it represents the combinations of interest rates and output for which money demand, which Keynes denoted as *L* to represent liquidity preference, equals money supply *M*.

and their interest rate to fall. (The inverse relationship between the price of a bond and its interest rate is discussed in Chapter 4.) As long as an excess supply of money exists, the interest rate will fall until it comes to rest on the *LM* curve.

If the economy is located in the area to the right of the *LM* curve, there is an excess demand for money. At point B, for example, the interest rate i_1 is below the equilibrium level, and people want to hold more money than they currently do. To acquire this money, they will sell bonds and drive down bond prices, and the interest rate will rise. This process will stop only when the interest rate rises to an equilibrium point on the *LM* curve.

THE *ISLM* APPROACH TO AGGREGATE OUTPUT AND INTEREST RATES

Now that we have derived the *IS* and *LM* curves, we can put them into the same diagram (Figure 9) to produce a model that enables us to determine both aggregate output and the interest rate. The only point at which the goods market and the market for money are in simultaneous equilibrium is at the intersection of the *IS* and *LM* curves, point E. At this point, aggregate output equals aggregate demand (*IS*) and the quantity of money demanded equals the quantity of money supplied (*LM*). At any other point in the diagram, at least one of these equilibrium conditions is not satisfied, and market forces move the economy toward the general equilibrium, point E.

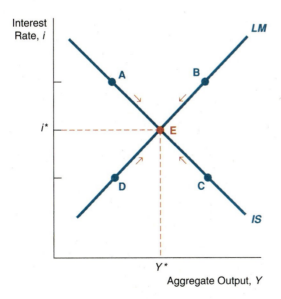

FIGURE 9 *ISLM* Diagram: Simultaneous Determination of Output and the Interest Rate
Only at point E, when the interest rate is i^* and output is Y^*, is there equilibrium simultaneously in both the goods market (as measured by the *IS* curve) and the market for money (as measured by the *LM* curve). At other points, such as A, B, C, or D, one of the two markets is not in equilibrium, and there will be a tendency to head toward the equilibrium, point E.

To learn how this works, let's consider what happens if the economy is at point A, which is on the *IS* curve but not the *LM* curve. Even though at point A the goods market is in equilibrium, so that aggregate output equals aggregate demand, the interest rate is above its equilibrium level, so the demand for money is less than the supply. Because people have more money than they want to hold, they will try to get rid of it by buying bonds. The resulting rise in bond prices causes a fall in interest rates, which in turn causes both planned investment spending and net exports to rise, and thus aggregate output rises. The economy then moves down along the *IS* curve, and the process continues until the interest rate falls to i^* and aggregate output rises to Y^*, that is, until the economy is at equilibrium point E.

If the economy is on the *LM* curve but off the *IS* curve at point B, it will also head toward the equilibrium at point E. At point B, even though money demand equals money supply, output is higher than the equilibrium level and exceeds aggregate demand. Firms are unable to sell all their output, and unplanned inventory accumulates, prompting them to cut production and lower output. The decline in output means that the demand for money will fall, lowering interest rates. The economy then moves down along the *LM* curve until it reaches equilibrium point E.

STUDY GUIDE

To test your understanding of why the economy heads toward equilibrium point E at the intersection of the *IS* and *LM* curves, see if you can provide the reasoning behind the movement to point E from points such as C and D in the figure.

We have finally developed a model, the *ISLM* model, that tells us how both interest rates and aggregate output are determined when the price level is fixed. Although we have demonstrated that the economy will head toward an aggregate output level of Y^*, there is no reason to assume that at this level of aggregate output the economy is at full employment. If the unemployment rate is too high, government policymakers might want to increase aggregate output to reduce it. The *ISLM* apparatus indicates that they can do this by manipulating monetary and fiscal policy. *ISLM* analysis of how monetary and fiscal policy can affect economic activity will be discussed in the next chapter.

SUMMARY

1. In the simple Keynesian framework in which the price level is fixed, output is determined by the equilibrium condition in the goods market that aggregate output equals aggregate demand. Aggregate demand equals the sum of consumer expenditure, planned investment spending, government spending, and net exports. Consumer expenditure is described by the consumption function, which indicates that consumer expenditure will rise as disposable income increases. Keynes's

analysis shows that aggregate output is positively related to autonomous consumer expenditure, planned investment spending, government spending, and net exports and negatively related to the level of taxes. A change in any of these factors leads, through the expenditure multiplier, to a multiple change in aggregate output.

2. The *ISLM* model determines aggregate output and the interest rate for a fixed price level using the *IS* and *LM* curves. The *IS* curve traces out the combinations of the interest rate and aggregate output for which the goods market is in equilibrium, and the *LM* curve traces out the combinations for which the market for money is in equilibrium. The *IS* curve slopes downward because

higher interest rates lower planned investment spending and so lower equilibrium output. The *LM* curve slopes upward because higher aggregate output raises the demand for money and so raises the equilibrium interest rate.

3. The simultaneous determination of output and interest rates occurs at the intersection of the *IS* and *LM* curves, where both the goods market and the market for money are in equilibrium. At any other level of interest rates and output, at least one of the markets will be out of equilibrium, and forces will move the economy toward the general equilibrium point at the intersection of the *IS* and *LM* curves.

KEY TERMS

consumer expenditure

planned investment spending

government spending

net exports

aggregate demand

disposable income

consumption function

marginal propensity to consume

autonomous consumer expenditure

fixed investment

inventory investment

aggregate demand function

expenditure multiplier

"animal spirits"

IS curve

LM curve

QUESTIONS AND PROBLEMS

1. Calculate the value of the consumption function at each level of disposable income in Table 1 if $a = 100$ and $mpc = 0.9$.

*2. Why do companies cut production when they find that their unplanned inventory investment is greater than zero? If they didn't cut production, what effect would this have on their profits? Why?

3. Plot the consumption function $C = 100 + 0.75Y$ on graph paper.
   (a) Assuming no government sector, if planned investment spending is 200, what is the equilibrium level of aggregate output? Show this equilibrium level on the graph you have drawn.
   (b) If businesses become more pessimistic about the profitability of investment and planned investment spending falls by 100, what happens to the equilibrium level of output?

*4. If the consumption function is $C = 100 + 0.8Y$ and planned investment spending is 200, what is the equilibrium level of output? If planned investment falls by 100, how much does the equilibrium level of output fall?

5. Why are the multipliers in problems 3 and 4 different? Explain intuitively why one is higher than the other.

*6. If firms suddenly become more optimistic about the profitability of investment and planned investment spending rises by $100 billion, while consumers become more pessimistic and autonomous consumer spending falls by $100 billion, what happens to aggregate output?

7. "A rise in planned investment spending by $100 billion at the same time that autonomous consumer expenditure falls by $50 billion has the same effect on aggregate output as a rise in autonomous consumer expenditure alone by $50

billion." Is this statement true, false, or uncertain? Explain.

*8. If the consumption function is $C = 100 + 0.75Y$, $I = 200$, and government spending is 200, what will be the equilibrium level of output? Demonstrate your answer with a Keynesian cross diagram. What happens to aggregate output if government spending rises by 100?

9. If the marginal propensity to consume is 0.5, how much would government spending have to rise in order to raise output by $1000 billion?

*10. Suppose that government policymakers decide that they will change taxes to raise aggregate output by $400 billion, and $mpc = 0.5$. By how much will taxes have to be changed?

11. What happens to aggregate output if both taxes and government spending are lowered by $300 billion and $mpc = 0.5$? Explain.

*12. Will aggregate output rise or fall if an increase in autonomous consumer expenditure is matched by an equal increase in taxes?

13. If a change in the interest rate has no effect on planned investment spending, trace out what happens to the equilibrium level of aggregate output as interest rates fall. What does this imply about the slope of the *IS* curve?

*14. Using a supply and demand diagram for the market for money, show what happens to the equilibrium level of the interest rate as aggregate output falls. What does this imply about the slope of the *LM* curve?

15. "If the point describing the combination of the interest rate and aggregate output is not on either the *IS* or *LM* curve, the economy will have no tendency to head toward the intersection of the two curves." Is this statement true, false, or uncertain? Explain.

Chapter 25

MONETARY AND FISCAL POLICY IN THE *ISLM* MODEL

PREVIEW   Since World War II, government policymakers have tried to promote high employment without creating inflation. If the economy experiences a recession such as the one that occurred at the time of Iraq's invasion of Kuwait in 1990, policymakers have two principal sets of tools by which to affect aggregate economic activity: *monetary policy,* the control of interest rates or the money supply, and *fiscal policy,* the control of government spending and taxes.

The *ISLM* model can help policymakers predict what will happen to aggregate output and interest rates if they decide to increase the money supply or increase government spending. In this way, *ISLM* analysis enables us to answer some important questions about the usefulness and effectiveness of monetary and fiscal policy on economic activity.

But which is better? When is monetary policy more effective than fiscal policy at controlling the level of aggregate output, and when is it less effective? Will fiscal policy be more effective if it is conducted by changing government spending rather than changing taxes? Should the monetary authorities conduct monetary policy by manipulating the money supply or interest rates?

In this chapter we use the *ISLM* model to help answer these questions and to learn how the model generates the aggregate demand curve featured prominently in the aggregate demand and supply framework (examined in Chapter 26). Our analysis will show why economists focus so much attention on topics such as the stability of the demand-for-money function and whether the demand for money is strongly influenced by interest rates.

First, however, let's examine the *ISLM* model in more detail to see how the *IS* and *LM* curves developed in Chapter 24 shift and the implications of these shifts. (We continue to assume that the price level is fixed so that real and nominal quantities are the same.)

FACTORS THAT CAUSE THE *IS* CURVE TO SHIFT

You have already learned that the *IS* curve describes equilibrium points in the goods market—the combinations of aggregate output and interest rate for which aggregate output produced equals aggregate demand. The *IS* curve shifts whenever a change in autonomous factors (independent of aggregate output) occurs that is unrelated to the interest rate. (A change in the interest rate that affects equilibrium aggregate output only causes a movement along the *IS* curve.) We have already identified five candidates as autonomous factors that can shift aggregate demand and hence affect the level of equilibrium output. We can now ask how changes in each of these factors affect the *IS* curve.

1. *Changes in Autonomous Consumer Expenditure.* A rise in autonomous consumer expenditure shifts aggregate demand upward and shifts the *IS* curve to the right (see Figure 1). To see how this shift occurs, suppose that the *IS* curve is initially at IS_1 in panel (a) and a huge oil field is discovered in Wyoming, perhaps containing more oil than in Saudi Arabia. Consumers now become more optimistic about the future health of the economy, and autonomous consumer expenditure rises. What happens to the equilibrium level of aggregate output as a result of this rise in autonomous consumer expenditure when the interest rate is held constant at i_A?

The IS_1 curve tells us that equilibrium aggregate output is at Y_A when the interest rate is at i_A (point A). Panel (b) shows that this point is an equilibrium in the goods market because the aggregate demand function Y_1^{ad} at an interest rate i_A crosses the 45° line $Y = Y^{ad}$ at an aggregate output level of Y_A. When autonomous consumer expenditure rises because of the oil discovery, the aggregate demand function shifts upward to Y_2^{ad} and equilibrium output rises to $Y_{A'}$. This rise in equilibrium output from Y_A to $Y_{A'}$ when the interest rate is i_A is plotted in panel (a) as a movement from point A to point A'. The same analysis can be applied to every point on the initial IS_1 curve; therefore, the rise in autonomous consumer expenditure shifts the *IS* curve to the right from IS_1 to IS_2 in panel (a).

A decline in autonomous consumer expenditure reverses the direction of the analysis. For any given interest rate, the aggregate demand function shifts downward, the equilibrium level of aggregate output falls, and the *IS* curve shifts to the left.

2. *Changes in Investment Spending Unrelated to the Interest Rate.* In Chapter 24 we learned that changes in the interest rate affect planned investment spending and hence the equilibrium level of output, but *this* change in investment spending merely causes a movement along the *IS* curve and not a shift. A rise in planned investment spending unrelated to the interest rate shifts the aggregate demand function upward, as in panel (b) of Figure 1 (as when companies become more confident about investment profitability after the Wyoming oil discovery). For any given interest rate, the equilibrium level of aggregate output rises, and the *IS* curve will shift to the right, as in panel (a).

A decrease in investment spending because companies become more pessimistic about investment profitability shifts the aggregate demand function

**FIGURE 1
Shift in the *IS*
Curve**

The *IS* curve will
shift from IS_1 to
IS_2 as a result of
(1) an increase in
autonomous con-
sumer spending,
(2) an increase in
planned invest-
ment spending
due to business
optimism, (3) an
increase in gov-
ernment spending,
(4) a decrease in
taxes, or (5) an in-
crease in net ex-
ports that is unre-
lated to interest
rates. Panel (b)
shows how
changes in these
factors lead to the
rightward shift in
the *IS* curve using
a Keynesian cross
diagram. For any
given interest rate
(here i_A), these
changes shift up
the aggregate de-
mand function up-
ward and raise
equilibrium output
from Y_A to $Y_{A'}$.

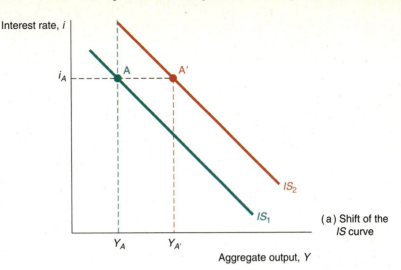

(a) Shift of the
IS curve

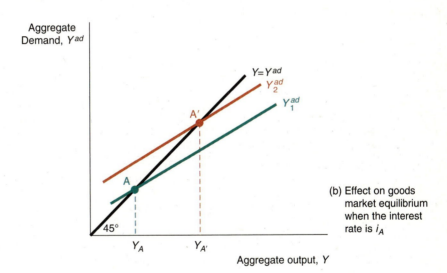

(b) Effect on goods
market equilibrium
when the interest
rate is i_A

downward for any given interest rate; the equilibrium level of aggregate output
falls, shifting the *IS* curve to the left.

    3. Changes in Government Spending. An increase in government spending
will also cause the aggregate demand function at any given interest rate to shift
upward, as in panel (b). The equilibrium level of aggregate output rises at any
given interest rate, and the *IS* curve shifts to the right. Conversely, a decline in
government spending shifts the aggregate demand function downward and the
equilibrium level of output falls, shifting the *IS* curve to the left.

    4. Changes in Taxes. Unlike changes in other factors that directly affect the
aggregate demand function, a decline in taxes shifts the aggregate demand func-

tion by raising consumer expenditure and shifting the aggregate demand function upward at any given interest rate. A decline in taxes raises the equilibrium level of aggregate output at any given interest rate and shifts the *IS* curve to the right (as in Figure 1). Recall, however, that a change in taxes has a smaller effect on aggregate demand than an equivalent change in government spending. So for a given change in taxes, the *IS* curve will shift less than for an equal change in government spending.

A rise in taxes lowers the aggregate demand function and reduces the equilibrium level of aggregate output at each interest rate. Therefore, a rise in taxes shifts the *IS* curve to the left.

5. *Changes in Net Exports Unrelated to the Interest Rate.* As with planned investment spending, changes in net exports arising from a change in interest rates merely causes a movement along the *IS* curve and not a shift. An autonomous rise in net exports unrelated to the interest rate—say, because American-made jeans become more chic than French-made jeans—shifts the aggregate demand function upward and causes the *IS* curve to shift to the right, as in Figure 1. Conversely, an autonomous fall in net exports shifts the aggregate demand function downward and the equilibrium level of output falls, shifting the *IS* curve to the left.

FACTORS THAT CAUSE THE *LM* CURVE TO SHIFT

The *LM* curve describes the equilibrium points in the market for money—the combinations of aggregate output and interest rate for which the quantity of money demanded equals the quantity of money supplied. Whereas five factors can cause the *IS* curve to shift (changes in autonomous consumer expenditure, planned investment spending unrelated to the interest rate, government spending, taxes, and net exports unrelated to the interest rate), only two factors can cause the *LM* curve to shift: autonomous changes in money demand and changes in money supply. How do changes in these two factors affect the *LM* curve?

1. *Changes in the Money Supply.* A rise in the money supply shifts the *LM* curve to the right, as shown in Figure 2. To see how this shift occurs, suppose that the *LM* curve is initially at LM_1 in panel (a) and the Federal Reserve conducts open market purchases that increase the money supply. If we consider point A, which is on the initial LM_1 curve, we can examine what happens to the equilibrium level of the interest rate, holding output constant at Y_A.

Panel (b), which contains a supply and demand diagram for the market for money, depicts the equilibrium interest rate initially as i_A at the intersection of the supply curve for money M_1^s and the demand curve for money M^d. The rise in the quantity of money supplied shifts the supply curve to M_2^s, and, holding output constant at Y_A, the equilibrium interest rate falls to $i_{A'}$. In panel (a), this decline in the equilibrium interest rate from i_A to $i_{A'}$ is shown as a movement from point A to point A'. The same analysis can be applied to every point on the initial LM_1 curve, leading to the conclusion that at any given level of aggregate

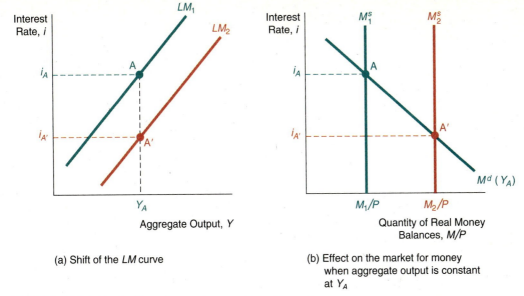

(a) Shift of the *LM* curve

(b) Effect on the market for money
when aggregate output is constant
at Y_A

FIGURE 2 Shift in the *LM* Curve from an Increase in the Money Supply
The *LM* curve shifts to the right from LM_1 to LM_2 when the money supply increases because, as indicated in
panel (b), at any given level of aggregate output (say, Y_A), the equilibrium interest rate falls (point A to A').

output, the equilibrium interest rate falls when the money supply increases. Thus
LM_2 is below and to the right of LM_1.

Reversing this reasoning, a decline in the money supply shifts the *LM* curve
to the left. A decline in the money supply results in a shortage of money at
points on the initial *LM* curve. This condition of excess demand for money can
be eliminated by a rise in the interest rate, which reduces the quantity of money
demanded until it again equals the quantity of money supplied.

2. Autonomous Changes in Money Demand. The theory of asset demand
outlined in Chapter 5 indicates that there can be an autonomous rise in money
demand (not caused by a change in the price level, aggregate output, or the interest rate). For example, an increase in the volatility of bond returns would
make bonds riskier relative to money and would increase the quantity of money
demanded at any given interest rate, price level, or amount of aggregate output.
The resulting autonomous increase in the demand for money shifts the *LM* curve
to the left, as shown in Figure 3. Consider point A on the initial LM_1 curve. Suppose that a massive financial panic occurs, sending many companies into bankruptcy. Because bonds have become a riskier asset, people want to shift from
holding bonds to holding money; they will hold more money at all interest rates
and output levels. The resulting increase in money demand at an output level of
Y_A is shown by the shift of the money demand curve from M_1^d to M_2^d in panel
(b). The new equilibrium in the market for money now indicates that if aggre-

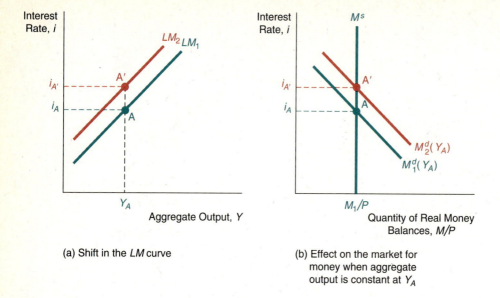

(a) Shift in the *LM* curve

(b) Effect on the market for money when aggregate output is constant at Y_A

FIGURE 3 Shift in the *LM* Curve When Money Demand Increases

The *LM* curve shifts to the left from LM_1 to LM_2 when money demand increases because, as indicated in panel (b), at any given level of aggregate output (say, Y_A), the equilibrium interest rate rises (point A to A').

gate output is constant at Y_A, the equilibrium interest rate will rise to $i_{A'}$, and the point of equilibrium moves from A to A'.

Conversely, an autonomous decline in money demand would lead to a right-ward shift in the *LM* curve. The fall in money demand would create an excess supply of money, which is eliminated by a rise in the quantity of money demanded from a decline in the interest rate.

CHANGES IN EQUILIBRIUM LEVEL OF THE INTEREST RATE AND AGGREGATE OUTPUT

You can now use your knowledge of factors that cause the *IS* and *LM* curves to shift for the purpose of analyzing how the equilibrium levels of the interest rate and aggregate output change in response to changes in monetary and fiscal policies.

Response to a Change in Monetary Policy

Figure 4 illustrates the response of output and interest rate to an increase in the money supply. Initially, the economy is in equilibrium for both the goods market and the market for money at point 1, the intersection of IS_1 and LM_1. Suppose that at the resulting level of aggregate output Y_1, the economy is suffering from an unemployment rate of 20%, and the Federal Reserve decides that it should try to raise output and reduce unemployment by raising the money supply. Will the Fed's change in monetary policy have the intended effect?

The rise in the money supply causes the *LM* curve to shift rightward to LM_2, and the equilibrium point for both the goods market and the market for money moves to point 2 (intersection of IS_1 and LM_2). As a result of an increase in money supply, the interest rate declines to i_2, as we found in Chapter 6, and aggregate output rises to Y_2; the Fed's policy has been successful in improving the health of the economy.

For a clear understanding of why aggregate output rises and the interest rate declines, think about exactly what has happened in moving from point 1 to point 2. When the economy is at point 1, the increase in the money supply (rightward shift of the *LM* curve) creates an excess supply of money, resulting in a decline in the interest rate. The decline causes investment spending and net exports to rise, which in turn raises aggregate demand and causes aggregate output to rise. The excess supply of money is eliminated when the economy reaches point 2 because both the rise in output and the fall in the interest rate have raised the quantity of money demanded until it equals the new higher level of the money supply.

A decline in the money supply reverses the process; it shifts the *LM* curve to the left, causing the interest rate to rise and output to fall. Accordingly, ***aggregate output is positively related to the money supply;*** aggregate output expands when the money supply increases and falls when it decreases.

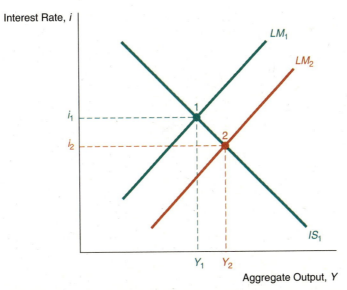

FIGURE 4 Response of Aggregate Output and the Interest Rate to an Increase in the Money Supply
The increase in the money supply shifts the *LM* curve to the right from LM_1 to LM_2; the economy moves to point 2, where output has increased to Y_2 and the interest rate has declined to i_2.

Response to a Change in Fiscal Policy

Suppose that the Federal Reserve is not willing to increase the money supply when the economy is suffering from a 20% unemployment rate at point 1. Can the federal government come to the rescue and manipulate government spending and taxes to raise aggregate output and reduce the massive unemployment?

The *ISLM* model demonstrates that it can. Figure 5 depicts the response of output and the interest rate to an expansionary fiscal policy (increase in government spending or decrease in taxes). An increase in government spending or a decrease in taxes causes the *IS* curve to shift to IS_2, and the equilibrium point for both the goods market and the market for money moves to point 2 (intersection of IS_2 with LM_1). The result of the change in fiscal policy is a rise in aggregate output to Y_2 and a rise in the interest rate to i_2. Note the difference in the effect on the interest rate of an expansionary fiscal policy from an expansionary monetary policy. In the case of an expansionary fiscal policy, the interest rate rises, whereas in the case of an expansionary monetary policy, the interest rate falls.

Why does an increase in government spending or a decrease in taxes move the economy from point 1 to point 2, causing a rise in both aggregate output and the interest rate? An increase in government spending raises aggregate demand directly; a decrease in taxes makes more income available for spending and raises aggregate demand by raising consumer expenditure. The resulting in-

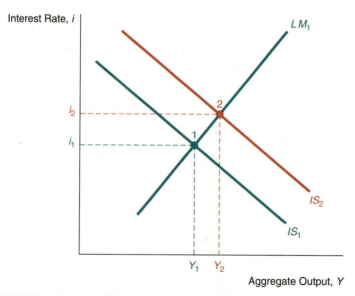

FIGURE 5 Response of Aggregate Output and the Interest Rate to an Expansionary Fiscal Policy

Expansionary fiscal policy (a rise in government spending or a decrease in taxes) shifts the *IS* curve to the right from IS_1 to IS_2; the economy moves to point 2, aggregate output increases to Y_2, and the interest rate rises to i_2.

crease in aggregate demand causes aggregate output to rise. The aggregate output raises the quantity of money demanded, creatin mand for money, which in turn causes the interest rate to rise. At cess demand for money created by a rise in aggregate output nated by a rise in the interest rate, which lowers the quantity ot money demanded.

A contractionary fiscal policy (decrease in government spending or increase in taxes) reverses the process described in Figure 5; it causes aggregate demand to fall, which shifts the *IS* curve to the left and causes both aggregate output and the interest rate to fall. ***Aggregate output and the interest rate are positively related to government spending and negatively related to taxes.***

STUDY GUIDE

As a study aid, Table 1 indicates the effect on aggregate output and interest rates of a change in the seven factors that shift the *IS* and *LM* curves. In addition, the table provides schematics describing the reason for the output and interest-rate response. *ISLM* analysis is best learned by practicing applications. To get this practice, you might try to develop the reasoning for your own Table 1 in which all the factors decrease rather than increase or answer Problems 5–7 and 13–15 at the end of this chapter.

APPLICATION

THE VIETNAM WAR BUILDUP AND THE RISE IN INTEREST RATES, 1965–1966

From early 1965 to the end of 1966, America dramatically increased its involvement in the Vietnam War by increasing the number of troops in Vietnam from under 25,000 to over 350,000. The troop buildup resulted in a substantial rise in military spending, which led to a $55 billion (in 1987 dollars) increase in government spending from 1965 to 1966 (from $567 billion to $622 billion). What does our *ISLM* model predict should have happened to aggregate output and interest rates as a result?

Figure 6 shows that the increase in government spending would have shifted the *IS* curve to the right from IS_1 to IS_2, while the *LM* curve remained unchanged because the money supply (*M*1) remained almost constant in real terms: $591 billion in 1965 and $585 billion (in 1987 dollars) in 1966. The *ISLM* model then predicts that the economy moves from point 1 to point 2 in which both GDP and interest rates rise, and this is exactly what happened from 1965 to 1966: GDP rose by $145 billion (a multiple of the $55 billion increase in government spending), from $2471 billion to $2616 billion, while the interest rate

SUMMARY

TABLE 1 Effects from Factors That Shift the *IS* and *LM* Curves

Factor	Change in Factor	Response	Reason	
C	↑	$Y\uparrow, i\uparrow$	$C\uparrow \to Y^{ad}\uparrow \to$ *IS* shifts right	
I	↑	$Y\uparrow, i\uparrow$	$I\uparrow \to Y^{ad}\uparrow \to$ *IS* shifts right	
G	↑	$Y\uparrow, i\uparrow$	$G\uparrow \to Y^{ad}\uparrow \to$ *IS* shifts right	
T	↑	$Y\downarrow, i\downarrow$	$T\uparrow \to C\downarrow \to Y^{ad}\downarrow \to$ *IS* shifts left	
NX	↑	$Y\uparrow, i\uparrow$	$NX\uparrow \to Y^{ad}\uparrow \to$ *IS* shifts right	
M^s	↑	$Y\uparrow, i\downarrow$	$M^s\uparrow \to i\downarrow \to$ *LM* shifts right	
M^d	↑	$Y\downarrow, i\uparrow$	$M^d\uparrow \to i\uparrow \to$ *LM* shifts left	

Note: Only increases (↑) in the factors are shown. The effect of decreases in the factors would be the opposite of those indicated in the "Response" column.

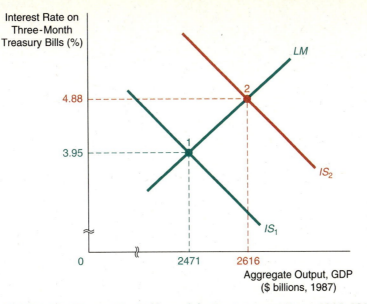

FIGURE 6   The Vietnam War Buildup and the Rise in Interest Rates, 1965–1966
The rise in military spending from 1965 to 1966 led to a rightward shift of the *IS* curve
from IS_1 to IS_2, which moved the economy from point 1 to point 2, thereby raising both
aggregate output and the interest rate.

on three-month Treasury bills rose from 3.95% to 4.88%.[1]

Economists at the time agreed that taxes needed to be increased to keep
the economy from overheating and to reduce interest rates by shifting the *IS*
curve back to the left. Unfortunately, President Lyndon Johnson thought it politically infeasible to raise taxes to pay for what was rapidly becoming America's
most unpopular war. Taxes were not increased until 1968, and by then the
overheated economy had burst into inflation and record-high interest rates.

EFFECTIVENESS OF MONETARY VERSUS FISCAL POLICY

Our discussion of the effects of fiscal and monetary policy suggests that a government can easily lift an economy out of a recession by implementing any of a
number of policies (changing the money supply, government spending, or
taxes). But how can policymakers decide which of these policies to use if faced

---

[1]An alternative explanation of why interest rates rose from 1965 to 1966 is that expected inflation increased over this period, causing nominal interest rates to rise. (See Chapter 6 for an explanation of
why a rise in expected inflation can raise nominal interest rates.) Note that this explanation and the
ISLM explanation are not inconsistent; both the rise in expected inflation and the rightward shift of
the *IS* curve may have contributed to the rise in interest rates in this period.

with too much unemployment? Should they decrease taxes, increase government spending, raise the money supply, or do all three? And if they decide to increase the money supply, by how much? Economists do not pretend to have all the answers, and although the *ISLM* model will not clear the path to aggregate economic bliss, it can help policymakers decide which policies might be most effective under certain circumstances.

Monetary Policy Versus Fiscal Policy: The Case of Complete Crowding Out

The *ISLM* model developed so far in this chapter shows that both monetary and fiscal policy affect the level of aggregate output. To understand when monetary policy is more effective than fiscal policy, we will examine a special case of the *ISLM* model in which money demand is unaffected by the interest rate (money demand is said to be *interest-inelastic*) so that monetary policy affects output but fiscal policy does not.

Consider the slope of the *LM* curve if the demand for money is unaffected by changes in the interest rate. If point 1 in panel (a) of Figure 7 is such that the quantity of money demanded equals the quantity of money supplied, then it is on the *LM* curve. If the interest rate rises to, say, i_2, the quantity of money demanded is unaffected, and it will continue to equal the *unchanged* quantity of money supplied only if aggregate output remains *unchanged* at Y_1 (point 2). Equilibrium in the market for money will occur at the same level of aggregate output regardless of the interest rate, and the *LM* curve will be vertical, as shown in both panels of Figure 7.

Suppose that the economy is suffering from a high rate of unemployment, which policymakers try to eliminate with either expansionary fiscal or monetary policy. Panel (a) depicts what happens when an expansionary fiscal policy (increase in government spending or cut in taxes) is implemented, shifting the *IS* curve to the right from IS_1 to IS_2. As you can see in panel (a), the fiscal expansion has no effect on output; aggregate output remains at Y_1 when the economy moves from point 1 to point 2.

In our earlier analysis, expansionary fiscal policy always increased aggregate demand and raised the level of output. Why doesn't that happen in panel (a)? The answer is that because the *LM* curve is vertical, the rightward shift of the *IS* curve raises the interest rate to i_2, which causes investment spending and net exports to fall sufficiently so as completely to offset increased spending resulting from expansionary fiscal policy. Put another way, increased spending that results from expansionary fiscal policy has *crowded out* investment spending and net exports, which decrease because of the rise in the interest rate. This situation in

FIGURE 7
Effectiveness of Monetary and Fiscal Policy When Money Demand Is Unaffected by the Interest Rate

When the demand for money is unaffected by the interest rate, the *LM* curve is vertical. In panel (a), an expansionary fiscal policy (increase in government spending or cut in taxes) shifts the *IS* curve from IS_1 to IS_2 and leaves aggregate output unchanged at Y_1. In panel (b), an increase in the money supply shifts the *LM* curve from LM_1 to LM_2 and raises aggregate output from Y_1 to Y_2. Therefore, monetary policy is effective but fiscal policy is not.

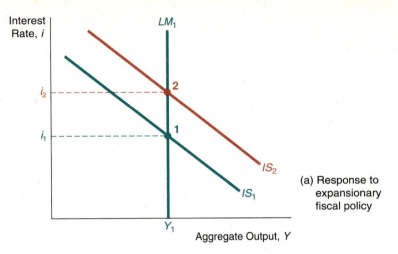

(a) Response to expansionary fiscal policy

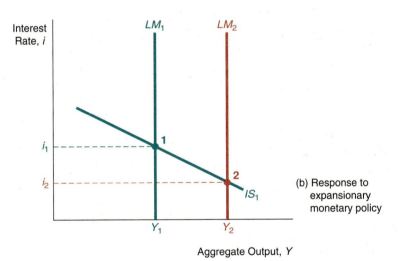

(b) Response to expansionary monetary policy

which expansionary fiscal policy does not lead to a rise in output is frequently referred to as a case of **complete crowding out.**[2]

Panel (b) shows what happens when the Federal Reserve tries to eliminate high unemployment through an expansionary monetary policy (increase in the

---

[2]When the demand for money is affected by the interest rate, the usual case in which the *LM* curve slopes upward but is not vertical, some crowding out occurs. The rightward shift of the *IS* curve also raises the interest rate, which causes investment spending and net exports to fall somewhat. However, as Figure 5 indicates, the rise in the interest rate is not sufficient to reduce investment spending and net exports to the point where aggregate output does not increase. Thus expansionary fiscal policy increases aggregate output, and only partial crowding out occurs.

money supply). Here the *LM* curve shifts to the right from LM_1 to LM_2 because at each interest rate, output must rise so that the quantity of money demanded rises to match the increase in the money supply. Aggregate output rises from Y_1 to Y_2 (the economy moves from point 1 to point 2), and expansionary monetary policy does affect aggregate output in this case.

We conclude from the analysis in Figure 7 that if the demand for money is unaffected by changes in the interest rate (money demand is interest-inelastic), monetary policy is effective but fiscal policy is not. An even more general conclusion can be reached: ***The less interest-sensitive money demand is, the more effective monetary policy is relative to fiscal policy.***

Because the interest sensitivity of money demand is important to policymakers' decisions regarding the use of monetary or fiscal policy to influence economic activity, the subject has been studied extensively by economists and has been the focus of many debates. Findings on the interest sensitivity of money demand are discussed in Chapter 23.

APPLICATION

TARGETING ON MONEY SUPPLY VERSUS INTEREST RATES

The *ISLM* model has important implications for an issue discussed in Chapter 21: Should the Federal Reserve conduct monetary policy by using its policy tools to hit a money supply target (try to make the money supply equal to a target value), or should it try to hit an interest-rate target instead? Our *ISLM* model will answer this question.[3]

As we saw in Chapter 21, when the Federal Reserve attempts to hit a money supply target, it cannot at the same time pursue an interest-rate target; it can hit one target or the other but not both. Consequently, it needs to know which of these two targets will produce more accurate control of aggregate output.

In contrast to the textbook world you have been inhabiting, in which the *IS* and *LM* curves are assumed to be fixed, the real world is one of great uncertainty in which *IS* and *LM* curves shift unexpectedly because of unanticipated changes in autonomous spending and money demand. To understand whether the Fed should use a money supply target or an interest-rate target, we need to look at two cases: first, one in which uncertainty about the *IS* curve is far greater than uncertainty about the *LM* curve and another in which uncertainty about the *LM* curve is far greater than uncertainty about the *IS* curve.

---

[3]The classic paper on this topic is William Poole, "The Optimal Choice of Monetary Policy Instruments in a Simple Macro Model," *Quarterly Journal of Economics* 84 (1970): 192–216. A less mathematical version of his analysis, far more accessible to students, is contained in William Poole, "Rules of Thumb for Guiding Monetary Policy," in *Open Market Policies and Operating Procedures: Staff Studies* (Washington, D.C.: Board of Governors of the Federal Reserve System, 1971).

The *ISLM* diagram in Figure 8 illustrates the outcome of the two targeting strategies for the case in which the *IS* curve is unstable and uncertain while the *LM* curve is stable and certain. If the Fed expects that the *IS* curve will be at *IS** and desires aggregate output of *Y**, it will set its interest-rate target at *i** so that the expected level of output is *Y**. This policy of targeting the interest rate at *i** is labeled "Interest-rate target." (Recall from Chapter 21 that the Fed can hit its interest-rate target by buying and selling bonds when the interest rate differs from *i**. When it is above *i**, the Fed buys bonds to raise the price and lower the interest rate back down to *i**. When the interest rate is below *i**, the Fed sells bonds to lower the price and raise the interest rate back up to *i**.)

If, instead, the Fed pursues a money supply target, it will set the money supply so that the resulting *LM* curve *LM** intersects the *IS** curve at the desired output level of *Y**. This policy of targeting the money supply is labeled "Money Supply Target."

Because the *IS* curve is unstable, it fluctuates between *IS'* and *IS"*, causing aggregate output to fluctuate between Y_I' and Y_I'' for the interest-rate target policy or between Y_M' and Y_M'' for the money supply target policy. As you can see in the figure, the money supply target leads to smaller output fluctuations around the desired level than the interest-rate target. A rightward shift of the *IS* curve to *IS"*, for example, causes the interest rate to rise given a money supply target, and this rise in the interest rate leads to a lower level of investment

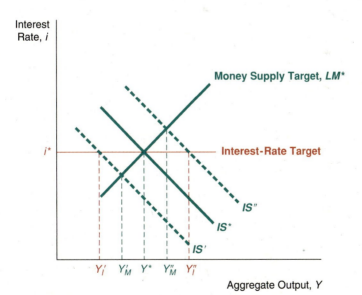

FIGURE 8 Money Supply and Interest-Rate Targets When the *IS* Curve Is Unstable and the *LM* Curve Is Stable

The unstable *IS* curve fluctuates between *IS'* and *IS"*. The money supply target produces smaller fluctuations in output (Y_M' to Y_M'') than the interest rate targets (Y_I' to Y_I''). Therefore, the money supply target is preferred.

spending and net exports and hence to a smaller increase in aggregate output than occurs under an interest-rate target. Because smaller output fluctuations are desirable, the conclusion is that ***if the IS curve is more unstable than the LM curve, a money supply target is preferred.***

The outcome of the two targeting strategies for the case of a stable *IS* curve and an unstable *LM* curve is illustrated in Figure 9. Again, the interest-rate and money supply targets are set so that the expected level of aggregate output equals the desired level Y^*. Because the *LM* curve is now unstable, it fluctuates between *LM'* and *LM"* even when the money supply is fixed, causing aggregate output to fluctuate between Y'_M and Y''_M. The interest-rate target, by contrast, is not affected by uncertainty about the *LM* curve because it is set by the Fed's adjusting the money supply whenever the interest rate tries to depart from i^*. The only effect of the fluctuating *LM* curve, then, is that the money supply fluctuates more as a result of the interest rate target policy. The outcome of the interest-rate target is that output will be exactly at the desired level with no fluctuations. Since smaller output fluctuations are desirable, the conclusion from Figure 9 is that ***if the LM curve is more unstable than the IS curve, an interest-rate target is preferred.***

Milton Friedman and his followers tend to believe that the money demand function, and hence the *LM* curve, is stable, and they conclude that a money supply target is always better than an interest-rate target. Keynesians are much less confident in the stability of the money demand function and are more

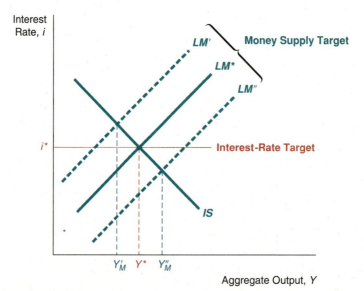

FIGURE 9 Money Supply and Interest-Rate Targets When the *LM* Curve Is Unstable and the *IS* Curve Is Stable

The unstable *LM* curve fluctuates between *LM'* and *LM"*. The money supply target then produces bigger fluctuations in output (Y'_M to Y''_M) than the interest-rate target (which leaves output fixed at Y^*). Therefore, the interest-rate target is preferred.

likely to support an interest-rate target. This was especially true in the 1980s, when the money demand function proved to be highly unstable—a result of the rapid proliferation of new financial instruments whose presence can affect the demand for money (see Chapter 23). It is important to recognize, however, that the crucial factor in deciding which target is preferred is the *relative* instability of the *IS* and *LM* curves. Although the *LM* curve has been unstable recently, the evidence supporting a stable *IS* curve is also weak. The recent instability in the money demand function does not automatically mean that money supply targets should be abandoned for an interest-rate target.[4]

THE *ISLM* MODEL IN THE LONG RUN

So far in our *ISLM* analysis, we have been assuming that the price level is fixed so that nominal values and real values are the same. This is a reasonable assumption for the short run, but in the long run the price level does change. To see what happens in the *ISLM* model in the long run, we make use of the concept of the **natural rate level of output,** which is the rate of output at which the price level has no tendency to rise or fall. When output is above the natural rate level, the booming economy will cause prices to rise; when output is below the natural rate level, the slack in the economy will cause prices to fall.

Because we now want to examine what happens when the price level changes, we can no longer assume that real and nominal values are the same. The spending variables that affect the *IS* curve (consumer expenditure, investment spending, government spending, and net exports) describe the demand for goods and services and are *in real terms;* that is, they describe the physical quantities of goods that people want to buy. Since these quantities do not change when the price level changes, a change in the price level has no effect on the *IS* curve, which describes the combinations of the interest rate and aggregate output *in real terms* that satisfy goods market equilibrium.

Figure 10 shows what happens in the *ISLM* model when output rises above the natural rate level, which is marked by a vertical line at the natural rate level of output Y_n. Suppose that initially the *IS* and *LM* curves intersect at point 1, where output $Y = Y_n$. Panel (a) examines what happens to output and interest rates when there is a rise in the money supply. As we saw earlier in Figure 2, the

---

[4]The analysis so far has been conducted assuming that the price level is fixed. More realistically, when the price level can change so that there is uncertainty about expected inflation, the case for an interest-rate target is even weaker. As we learned in Chapters 4 and 6, the interest rate that is more relevant to investment decisions is the *real* interest rate (the nominal interest rate minus expected inflation) and not the nominal interest rate. Hence, when expected inflation rises, at each given nominal interest rate, the real interest rate falls and investment and net exports rise, shifting the *IS* curve to the right. Similarly, a fall in expected inflation raises the real interest rate at each given nominal interest rate, lowers investment and net exports, and shifts the *IS* curve to the left. Since in the real world, expected inflation undergoes large fluctuations, the *IS* curve in Figure 9 will also have substantial fluctuations, making it less likely that the interest-rate target is better than the money supply target.

rise in the money supply causes the *LM* curve to shift to LM_2, and the equilibrium moves to point 2 (the intersection of IS_1 and LM_2), where the interest rate falls to i_2 and output rises to Y_2. However, as we can see in panel (a), the level of output at Y_2 is greater than the natural rate level Y_n, and so the price level begins to rise.

In contrast to the *IS* curve, which is unaffected by a rise in the price level, the *LM* curve is affected by the price level rise because liquidity preference theory states that the demand for money *in real terms* depends on real income and interest rates. This makes sense because money is valued in terms of what it can buy. However, the money supply that you read about in newspapers is not the money supply in real terms; it is a nominal quantity. As the price level rises, the quantity of money *in real terms* falls, and the effect on the *LM* curve is identical to a fall in the nominal money supply with the price level fixed. The lower value of the real money supply creates an excess demand for money, causing the interest rate to rise at any given level of aggregate output, and the *LM* curve shifts back to the left. As long as the level of output exceeds the natural rate level, the price level will continue to rise, shifting the *LM* curve to the left, until finally output is back at the natural rate level Y_n. This occurs when the *LM* curve has re-

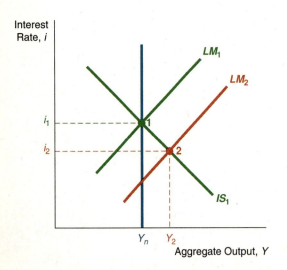

(a) Response to a rise in the money supply (*M*)

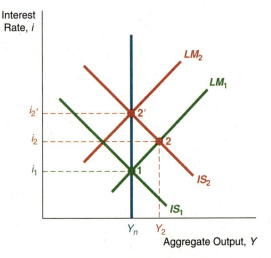

(b) Response to a rise in government spending (*G*)

FIGURE 10 The *ISLM* Model in the Long Run

In panel (a), a rise in the money supply causes the *LM* curve to shift rightward to LM_2, and the equilibrium moves to point 2, where the interest rate falls to i_2 and output rises to Y_2. Because output at Y_2 is above the natural rate level Y_n, the price level rises, the real money supply falls, and the *LM* curve shifts back to LM_1; the economy has returned to the original equilibrium at point 1. In panel (b), an increase in government spending shifts the *IS* curve to the right to IS_2, and the economy moves to point 2, at which the interest rate has risen to i_2 and output has risen to Y_2. Because output at Y_2 is above the natural rate level Y_n, the price level begins to rise, real money balances M/P begin to fall, and the *LM* curve shifts to the left to LM_2. The long-run equilibrium at point 2' has an even higher interest rate at $i_{2'}$, and output has returned to Y_n.

turned to LM_1, where real money balances M/P have returned to the original level and the economy has returned to the original equilibrium at point 1. The result of the expansion in the money supply in the long run is that the economy has the same level of output and interest rates.

The fact that the increase in the money supply has left output and interest rates unchanged in the long run is referred to as **long run monetary neutrality.** The only result of the increase in the money supply is a higher price level, which has increased proportionally to the increase in the money supply so that real money balances M/P are unchanged.

Panel (b) looks at what happens to output and interest rates when there is expansionary fiscal policy such as an increase in government spending. As we saw earlier, the increase in government spending shifts the *IS* curve to the right to IS_2, and in the short run the economy moves to point 2 (the intersection of IS_2 and LM_1), where the interest rate has risen to i_2 and output has risen to Y_2. Because output at Y_2 is above the natural rate level Y_n, the price level begins to rise, real money balances M/P begin to fall, and the *LM* curve shifts to the left. Only when the *LM* curve has shifted to LM_2 and the equilibrium is at point 2', where output is again at the natural rate level Y_n, does the price level stop rising and the *LM* curve comes to rest. The resulting long-run equilibrium at point 2' has an even higher interest rate at $i_{2'}$, and output has not risen from Y_n. Indeed, what has occurred in the long run is complete crowding out: The rise in the price level, which has shifted the *LM* curve to LM_2, has caused the interest rate to rise sufficiently to $i_{2'}$ so that investment and net exports fall sufficiently to offset completely the increased government spending. What we have discovered is that even though complete crowding out does not occur in the short run in the *ISLM* model (when the *LM* curve is not vertical), it does occur in the long run.

Our conclusion from examining what happens in the *ISLM* model from an expansionary monetary or fiscal policy is that ***although monetary and fiscal policy can affect output in the short run, neither affects output in the long run.*** Clearly, an important issue in deciding on the effectiveness of monetary and fiscal policy to raise output is how soon the long run occurs. This is a topic that we explore in the next chapter.

THE *ISLM* MODEL AND THE AGGREGATE DEMAND CURVE

We now examine further what happens in the *ISLM* model when the price level changes. When we conduct the *ISLM* analysis with a changing price level, we find that as the price level falls, the level of aggregate output rises. Thus we obtain a relationship between the price level and quantity of aggregate output for which the goods market and the market for money are in equilibrium, called the **aggregate demand curve.** This aggregate demand curve is a central element in the aggregate supply and demand analysis of Chapter 26, which allows us to explain changes not only in aggregate output but also in the price level.

Deriving the Aggregate Demand Curve

Now that you understand how a change in the price level affects the *IS* and *LM* curves, we can analyze what happens in the *ISLM* diagram when the price level changes. This exercise is carried out in Figure 11. Panel (a) contains an *ISLM* diagram for a given value of the nominal money supply. Let us first consider a price level of P_1. The *LM* curve at this price level is $LM(P_1)$, and its intersection with the *IS* curve is at point 1, where output is Y_1. The equilibrium output level Y_1 that occurs when the price level is P_1 is also plotted in panel (b) as point 1. If the price level rises to P_2, then *in real terms* the money supply has fallen. The effect on the *LM* curve is identical to a decline in the nominal money supply when the price level is fixed: The *LM* curve will shift leftward to $LM(P_2)$. The new equilibrium level of output has fallen to Y_2 because planned investment and net exports fall when the interest rate rises. Point 2 in panel (b) plots this level of output for price level P_2. A further increase in the price level to P_3 causes a further decline in the real money supply, leading to a further decline in planned investment and net exports, and output declines to Y_3. Point 3 in panel (b) plots this level of output for price level P_3.

The line that connects the three points in panel (b) is the aggregate demand curve *AD*, and it indicates the level of aggregate output consistent with equilibrium in the goods market and the market for money at any given price level. This aggregate demand curve has the usual downward slope because a higher

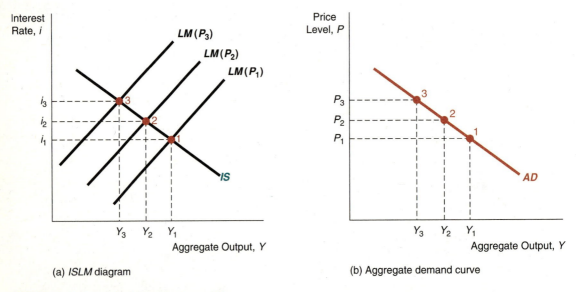

(a) *ISLM* diagram

(b) Aggregate demand curve

FIGURE 11 Deriving the Aggregate Demand Curve

The *ISLM* diagram in panel (a) shows that as the price level rises from P_1 to P_2 to P_3, the *LM* curve shifts to the left, and equilibrium output falls. The combinations of the price level and equilibrium output from panel (a) are then plotted in panel (b), and the line connecting them is the aggregate demand curve *AD*.

price level reduces the money supply in real terms, raises interest rates, and lowers the equilibrium level of aggregate output.

Factors That Cause the Aggregate Demand Curve to Shift

The *ISLM* analysis demonstrates how the equilibrium level of aggregate output changes for a given price level. A change in any factor that causes the *IS* or *LM* curve to shift (except a change in the price level) causes the aggregate demand curve to shift. To see how this works, let's first look at what happens to the aggregate demand curve when the *IS* curve shifts.

Shifts in the Curve Five factors cause the *IS* curve to shift: changes in autonomous consumer spending, changes in investment spending related to business confidence, changes in government spending, changes in taxes, and autonomous changes in net exports. How these factors lead to a shift in the aggregate demand curve is examined in Figure 12.

Suppose that initially the aggregate demand curve is at AD_1 and there is a rise, for example, in government spending. The *ISLM* diagram in panel (b) shows what then happens to equilibrium output, holding the price level constant at P_A. Initially, equilibrium output is at Y_A at the intersection of IS_1 and LM_1. The rise

SUM

1. Th
   to
   in
   de
   ta
   mc
   fac
2. Th
   the
   mc
   the
   mc
3. A
   out
   Exp
   spe
   out
   pol
4. The
   mo
   poli
5. The
   sior
   Whe
   curv

KEY T

comple

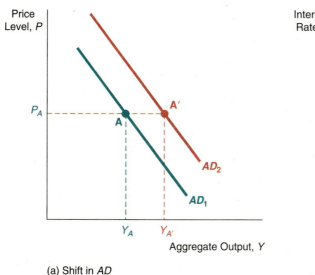

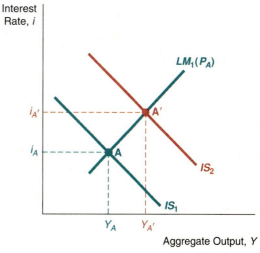

(a) Shift in *AD*   (b) Shift in *IS*

FIGURE 12 Shift in the Aggregate Demand Curve from a Shift in the *IS* Curve
Expansionary fiscal policy, a rise in net exports, or more optimistic consumers and firms shift the *IS* curve to the right in panel (b), and at a price level of P_A, equilibrium output rises from Y_A to $Y_{A'}$. This change in equilibrium output is shown as a movement from point A to point A' in panel (a); hence the aggregate demand curve shifts to the right from AD_1 to AD_2.

QUESTIONS AND PROBLEMS

1. If taxes and government spending rise by equal amounts, what will happen to the position of the *IS* curve? Explain this with a Keynesian cross diagram.

*2. What happened to the *IS* curve during the Great Depression when investment spending collapsed? Why?

3. What happens to the position of the *LM* curve if the Fed decides that it will decrease the money supply to fight inflation and if, at the same time, the demand for money falls?

*4. "An excess demand for money resulting from a rise in the demand for money can be eliminated only by a rise in the interest rate." Is this statement true, false, or uncertain? Explain.

In the remaining problems, demonstrate your answers with an ISLM diagram.

5. In late 1969, the Federal Reserve reduced the money supply while the government raised taxes. What do you think should have happened to interest rates and aggregate output?

*6. "The high level of interest rates and the rapidly growing economy during the second two years of Ronald Reagan's first term as president can be explained by a tight monetary policy that was combined with an expansionary fiscal policy." Do you agree? Why or why not?

7. Suppose that the Federal Reserve wants to keep interest rates from rising when the government sharply increases military spending. How can the Fed do this?

*8. Evidence indicates that lately the demand for money has become quite unstable. Why is this finding important to Federal Reserve policymakers?

9. "As the price level rises, the equilibrium level of output determined in the *ISLM* model also rises." Is this statement true, false, or uncertain? Explain.

*10. What will happen to the position of the aggregate demand curve if the money supply is reduced when government spending increases?

11. An equal rise in government spending and taxes will have what effect on the position of the aggregate demand curve?

*12. If money demand is unaffected by changes in the interest rate, what effect will a rise in government spending have on the position of the aggregate demand curve?

Using Economic Analysis to Predict the Future

13. Predict what will happen to interest rates and output if a stock market crash causes autonomous consumer expenditure to fall.

*14. Predict what will happen to interest rates and aggregate output when there is an autonomous export boom.

15. If a series of defaults in the bond market make bonds riskier and as a result the demand for money rises, predict what will happen to interest rates and aggregate output.

Chapter 26

AGGREGATE DEMAND AND SUPPLY ANALYSIS

PREVIEW   In earlier chapters we focused considerable attention on the money supply and monetary policy because they touch our everyday lives by affecting the prices of the goods we buy and the quantity of available jobs. In this chapter we develop a basic tool, aggregate demand and supply analysis, that will enable us to study the effects of money on output and prices. **Aggregate demand** is the total quantity of an economy's final goods and services demanded at different price levels. **Aggregate supply** is the total quantity of final goods and services that firms in the economy want to sell at different price levels. As with other supply and demand analyses, the actual quantity of output and the price level are determined by equating aggregate demand and aggregate supply.

Aggregate demand and supply analysis will enable us to explore how aggregate output and the price level are determined. Not only will it help us interpret recent episodes in the business cycle, but it will also enable us to understand the debates on how economic policy should be conducted.

AGGREGATE DEMAND

The first building block of aggregate supply and demand analysis is the **aggregate demand curve,** which describes the relationship between the quantity of aggregate output demanded and the price level when all other variables are held constant. **Monetarists** (led by Milton Friedman) view the aggregate demand curve as downward-sloping with one primary factor that causes it to shift—changes in the quantity of money. **Keynesians** (the followers of Keynes) also view the aggregate demand curve as downward-sloping, but they believe that changes in government spending and taxes or in consumer and business willingness to spend can also cause it to shift.

Aggregate Output, Unemployment, and the Price Level

Newspapers periodically report data that provide information on the level of aggregate output, unemployment, and the price level. Here is a list of the relevant data series, their frequency, and when they are published.

Aggregate Output and Unemployment

Real GDP: Quarterly (January–March, April–June, July–September, October–December); published about three weeks after the end of a quarter. A "flash" estimate is reported about a month earlier, just before the end of the quarter, but this estimate is much less accurate.

Industrial production: Monthly. Industrial production is not as comprehensive a measure of aggregate output as real GDP because it measures only manufacturing output; the estimate for the previous month is reported in the middle of the following month.

Unemployment rate: Monthly; previous month's figure is usually published on Friday of the first week of the following month.

Price Level

GDP deflator: Quarterly. This comprehensive measure of the price level (described in the appendix to Chapter 1) is published at the same time as the real GDP data.

Consumer price index (CPI): Monthly. The CPI is a measure of the price level for consumers (also described in the appendix to Chapter 1); the value for the previous month is published in the fourth week of the following month.

Producer price index (PPI): Monthly. The PPI is a measure of the average level of wholesale prices charged by producers and is published at the same time as industrial production data.

Monetarist View of Aggregate Demand

The monetarist view of aggregate demand links the quantity of money M with total nominal spending on goods and services $P \times Y$ (P = price level and Y = aggregate real output or, equivalently, aggregate real income). To do this it uses the concept of **velocity:** the average number of times per year that a dollar is spent on final goods and services. More formally, velocity V is calculated by dividing nominal spending $P \times Y$ by the money supply M:

$$V = \frac{P \times Y}{M}$$

Suppose that the total nominal spending in a year was $2 trillion and the money supply was $1 trillion; velocity would then be $2 trillion/$1 trillion = 2. On average, the money supply supports a level of transactions associated with 2 times its value in final goods and services in the course of a year. By multiplying both sides by *M,* we obtain the **equation of exchange,** which relates the money supply to aggregate spending:

$$M \times V = P \times Y \qquad (1)$$

At this point, the equation of exchange is nothing more than an identity; that is, it is true by definition. It does not tell us that when *M* rises, aggregate spending will rise as well. For example, the rise in *M* could be offset by a fall in *V,* with the result that $M \times V$ does not rise. However, Milton Friedman's analysis of the demand for money (discussed in detail in Chapter 23) suggests that velocity varies over time in a predictable manner unrelated to changes in the money supply. With this analysis, the equation of exchange is transformed into a theory of how aggregate spending is determined and is called the **modern quantity theory of money.**

To see how the theory works, let's look at an example. If velocity is predicted to be 2 and the money supply is $1 trillion, the equation of exchange tells us that aggregate spending will be $2 trillion ($2 \times \$1$ trillion). If the money supply doubles to $2 trillion, Friedman's analysis suggests that velocity will continue to be 2 and aggregate spending will double to $4 trillion ($2 \times \$2$ trillion). Thus Friedman's modern quantity theory of money concludes that *changes in aggregate spending are determined primarily by changes in the money supply.*

Deriving the Aggregate Demand Curve To learn how the modern quantity theory of money generates the aggregate demand curve, let's look at an example in which we measure aggregate output in trillions of 1987 dollars, with the price level in 1987 having a value of 1.0. As shown, with a predicted velocity of 2 and a money supply of $1 trillion, aggregate spending will be $2 trillion. If the price level is given at 2.0, the quantity of aggregate output demanded is $1 trillion because aggregate spending $P \times Y$ then continues to equal $2.0 \times \$1$ trillion = $2 trillion, the value of $M \times V$. This combination of a price level of 2.0 and aggregate output of 1 is marked as point A in Figure 1. If the price level is given as 1.0 instead, aggregate output demanded is $2 trillion (1987 $) (point B), so aggregate spending continues to equal $2 trillion (= 1.0×2 trillion). Similarly, at an even lower price level of 0.5, the quantity of output demanded rises to $4 trillion (1987 $), shown by point C. The curve connecting these points is the aggregate demand curve, given a money supply of $1 trillion, marked AD_1, and as you can see, it has the usual downward slope of a demand curve, indicating that as the price level falls (everything else held constant), the quantity of output demanded rises.

Shifts in the Aggregate Demand Curve In Friedman's modern quantity theory, changes in the money supply are the primary source of the changes in aggregate spending and shifts in the aggregate demand curve. To see how a change in the money supply shifts the aggregate demand curve, let's look at what happens when the money supply increases to $2 trillion. Now aggregate spending rises to $2 \times \$2$ trillion = $4 trillion, and at a price level of 2.0, the quantity of aggregate output demanded will rise to $2 trillion (1987 $) so that 2.0×2 trillion = $4 trillion. Therefore, at a price level of 2.0, the aggregate demand curve moves from

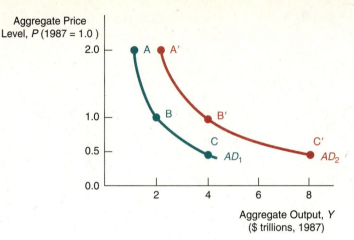

FIGURE 1

Aggregate Demand Curve

The rise in the money supply from $1 trillion to $2 trillion leads to a shift in the aggregate demand curve from AD_1 to AD_2.

point A to A'. At a price level of 1.0, the quantity of output demanded rises from $2 to $4 trillion (from point B to B'), and at a price level of 0.5, output demanded rises from $4 to $8 trillion (from point C to C'). The result is that the rise in the money supply to $2 trillion shifts the aggregate demand curve out to AD_2 in Figure 1.

Similar reasoning indicates that a decline in the money supply lowers aggregate spending proportionally and reduces the quantity of aggregate output demanded at each price level. Thus a decline in the money supply shifts the aggregate demand curve to the left.

Keynesian View of Aggregate Demand

Rather than determining aggregate demand from the equation of exchange, the Keynesian analysis analyzes aggregate demand in terms of its four component parts: **consumer expenditure,** the total demand for consumer goods and services; **planned investment spending,**[1] the total planned spending by business firms on new machines, factories, and other inputs to production, plus planned spending on new homes; **government spending,** spending by all levels of government (federal, state, and local) on goods and services (paper clips, computers, computer programming, missiles, government workers, etc.); and **net exports,** the net foreign spending on domestic goods and services, equal to exports minus imports. Using the symbols C for consumer expenditure, I for planned investment spending, G for government spending, and NX for net exports, we can write the following expression for aggregate demand Y^{ad}:

$$Y^{ad} = C + I + G + NX \qquad (2)$$

---

[1]Recall that economists restrict use of the word *investment* to a purchase of *new* physical capital, such as a new machine or a new house, that adds to expenditure.

Aggregate Demand Curve Keynesian analysis, like monetarist analysis, suggests that the aggregate demand curve is downward sloping because a lower price level ($P\downarrow$), holding the nominal quantity of money constant, leads to a larger quantity of money *in real terms* (in terms of the goods and services that it can buy). The larger quantity of money in real terms ($M/P\uparrow$) that results from the lower price level causes interest rates to fall ($i\downarrow$), as suggested in Chapter 6. The resulting lower cost of financing purchases of new physical capital makes investment more profitable and stimulates planned investment spending ($I\uparrow$). Because, as shown in Equation 2, the increase in planned investment spending adds directly to aggregate demand ($Y^{ad}\uparrow$), the lower price level leads to a higher level of aggregate demand ($P\downarrow \rightarrow Y^{ad}\uparrow$). Schematically, we can write the mechanism just described as follows:

$$P\downarrow \rightarrow \quad \uparrow \rightarrow i\downarrow \rightarrow I\uparrow \ Y^{ad}\uparrow$$

Another mechanism that generates a downward-sloping aggregate demand curve operates through international trade. Because a lower price level ($P\downarrow$) leads to a larger quantity of money in real terms ($M/P\uparrow$) and lower interest rates ($i\downarrow$), U.S. dollar bank deposits become less attractive relative to deposits denominated in foreign currencies, thereby causing a fall in the value of dollar deposits relative to other currency deposits (a decline in the exchange rate, denoted by $E\downarrow$). The lower value of the dollar, which makes domestic goods cheaper relative to foreign goods, then causes net exports to rise, which in turn increases aggregate demand:

$$P\downarrow \rightarrow \quad \uparrow \rightarrow i\downarrow \rightarrow E\downarrow \rightarrow NX\uparrow \rightarrow Y^{ad}\uparrow$$

The mechanisms described also indicate why Keynesian analysis suggests that changes in the money supply shift the aggregate demand curve. For a given price level, a rise in the money supply causes the real money supply to increase ($M/P\uparrow$), which leads to an increase in aggregate demand, as shown. Thus an increase in the money supply shifts the aggregate demand curve to the right (as in Figure 1) because it lowers interest rates and stimulates planned investment spending and net exports. Similarly, a decline in the money supply shifts the aggregate demand curve to the left.[2]

In contrast to monetarists, Keynesians believe that other factors (manipulation of government spending and taxes, changes in net exports, and shifts in consumer and business spending) are also important causes of shifts in the aggregate demand curve. For instance, if the government spends more ($G\uparrow$) or net exports increase ($NX\uparrow$), aggregate demand rises, and the aggregate demand curve shifts to the right. A decrease in government taxes ($T\downarrow$) leaves consumers with more income to spend, so consumer expenditure rises ($C\uparrow$). Aggregate demand also rises, and the aggregate demand curve shifts to the right. Finally, if

---

[2]A complete demonstration of the Keynesian analysis of the aggregate demand curve is given in Chapters 24 and 25.

consumer and business optimism increases, consumer expenditure and planned investment spending rise ($C\uparrow$, $I\uparrow$), again shifting the aggregate demand curve to the right. Keynes described these waves of optimism and pessimism as **"animal spirits"** and considered them a major factor affecting the aggregate demand curve and an important source of business cycle fluctuations.

The Crowding-Out Debate

You have seen that both monetarists and Keynesians agree that the aggregate demand curve is downward-sloping and shifts in response to changes in the money supply. However, monetarists see only one important source of movements in the aggregate demand curve—changes in the money supply—while Keynesians suggest that other factors—fiscal policy, net exports, and "animal spirits"—are equally important sources of shifts in the aggregate demand curve.

Because aggregate demand can be written as the sum of $C + I + G + NX$, it might appear as though any factor that affects one of its components must cause aggregate demand to change. Then it would seem as though a fiscal policy change such as a rise in government spending (holding the money supply constant) would necessarily shift the aggregate demand curve. Because the monetarist framework views changes in the money supply as the only important source of shifts in the aggregate demand curve, they must have an explanation as to why the foregoing reasoning is invalid.

Monetarists agree that an increase in government spending will raise aggregate demand if the other components of aggregate demand, C, I, and NX, remained unchanged after the government spending rise. They contend, however, that the increase in government spending will crowd out private spending (C, I, and NX), which will fall by exactly the amount of the government spending increase. This phenomenon of an exactly offsetting movement of private spending to an expansionary fiscal policy, such as a rise in government spending, is called **complete crowding out.**

How might complete crowding out occur? When government spending increases ($G\uparrow$), the government has to finance this spending by competing with private borrowers for funds in the credit market. Interest rates will rise ($i\uparrow$), increasing the cost of financing purchases of both physical capital and consumer goods and lowering net exports. The result is that private spending will fall ($C\downarrow$, $I\downarrow$, $NX\downarrow$), and so aggregate demand may remain unchanged. This chain of reasoning can be summarized as follows:

$$G\uparrow \rightarrow i\uparrow \rightarrow C\downarrow, I\downarrow, NX\downarrow$$

therefore, $C + I + G + NX = Y^{ad}$ is unchanged.

Keynesians do not deny the validity of the first set of steps. They agree that an increase in government spending raises interest rates, which in turn lowers private spending; indeed, this is a feature of the Keynesian analysis of aggregate demand (Chapters 24 and 25). However, they contend that in the short run only **partial crowding out** occurs, in which there is some decline in private spending that does not completely offset the rise in government spending.

The Keynesian crowding-out picture suggests that when government spending rises, aggregate demand does increase, and the aggregate demand curve shifts to the right. The *extent* to which crowding out occurs is the issue that separates monetarist and Keynesian views of the aggregate demand curve. We will discuss the evidence on this issue in Chapter 27.

The Money View Versus the Credit View

A more recent debate on how monetary policy affects aggregate demand focuses on whether it occurs through a "money channel" or a "credit channel." The money channel is the traditional Keynesian analysis described here in which monetary policy, such as open market operations, works by affecting bank deposits and the money supply, which affects interest rates, which in turn affect spending and hence aggregate demand. In contrast to the money view, which focuses on the liabilities side of banks' balance sheets (deposits) in describing the monetary transmission mechanism, the credit view focuses on the assets side (loans).

The basic story for the credit view of the effect of monetary policy on the economy is as follows. Suppose that the Fed conducts open market purchases to stimulate the economy. As we saw in our discussion of the money supply process, an open market purchase leads to an expansion of loans. If bank loans play a special role in the economy because certain borrowers do not have access to the credit markets unless they borrow from banks (a view that we have taken in Chapters 9 and 11), this increase in loans will enable these firms and consumers to increase spending more than they would without these loans, thereby increasing aggregate demand.[3]

The money and credit views of how monetary policy affects the economy are by no means mutually exclusive. Expansionary open market purchases increase both the money supply and the amount of loans, and so both the money and credit channels are operative. The credit channel is important because it provides an *additional* reason why monetary policy may have potent effects on the economy. Furthermore, the credit channel suggests that interest rates and the money supply may not be the only indicators of the tightness of monetary policy; the amount of bank loans might be too.

---

[3]To be more precise, the credit view requires two assumptions. The first is that when the Fed adds reserves to the banking system, banks increase their lending and do not just increase their holdings of securities. (This will occur as long as loans and securities are not perfect substitutes for banks.) The second assumption is that bank loans are special and are not perfect substitutes for other types of credit for borrowers. If this were not the case, an increase in bank loans would not imply increased spending because borrowers would just reduce their borrowings elsewhere when bank loans increased.

Currently, there is an active debate on the relative importance of the money and credit channels, and much new research is being conducted on this topic.[4] Although the importance of the credit channel has not yet been fully established, research on how money affects the economy, described in Chapter 27, is giving us a much richer view on the channels through which monetary policy affects aggregate demand.

AGGREGATE SUPPLY

The key feature of aggregate supply is that, as the price level increases, the quantity of output supplied increases *in the short run*. Figure 2 illustrates the positive relationship between quantity of output supplied and price level. Suppose that initially the quantity of output supplied at a price level of 1.0 is $4 trillion, represented by point A. A rise in the price level to 2.0 leads, in the short run, to an increase in the quantity of output supplied to $6 trillion (point B). The line AS_1 connecting points A and B describes the relationship between the quantity of output supplied in the short run and the price level and is called the **aggregate supply curve;** as you can see, it is upward-sloping.

To understand why the aggregate supply curve slopes upward, we have to look at the factors that cause the quantity of output supplied to change. Because the goal of business is to maximize profits, the quantity of output supplied is determined by the profit made on each unit of output. If profit rises, more output will be produced, and the quantity of output supplied will increase; if it falls, less output will be produced, and the quantity of output supplied will fall.

Profit on a unit of output equals the price for the unit minus the costs of producing it. In the short run, costs of many factors that go into producing goods

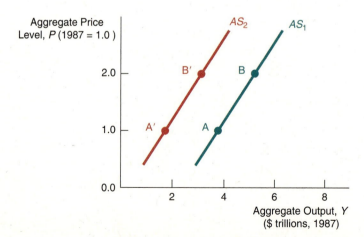

FIGURE 2
Aggregate Supply Curve in the Short Run
A rise in the costs of production shifts the supply curve leftward from AS_1 to AS_2.

---

[4]For an excellent and readable survey of the evidence on the credit view, see Ben Bernanke, "Credit in the Macroeconomy," *Federal Reserve Bank of New York Quarterly Review,* Spring 1993, pp. 50–70.

and services are fixed; wages, for example, are often fixed for periods of time by labor contracts (sometimes as long as three years), and raw materials are often bought by firms under long-term contracts that fix the price. Because these costs of production are fixed in the short run, when the overall price level rises, the price for a unit of output will be rising relative to the costs of producing it, and the profit per unit will rise. Because the higher price level results in higher profits in the short run, firms increase production, and the quantity of aggregate output supplied rises, resulting in an upward-sloping aggregate supply curve.

Frequent mention of the *short run* in the preceding paragraph hints that the aggregate supply curve (AS_1 in Figure 2) may not remain fixed as time passes. To see what happens over time, we need to understand what makes the aggregate supply curve shift.[5]

Shifts in the Aggregate Supply Curve

We have seen that the profit on a unit of output determines the quantity of output supplied. If the cost of producing a unit of output rises, profit on a unit of output falls, and the quantity of output supplied falls. To learn what this implies for the position of the aggregate supply curve, let's consider what happens at a price level of 1.0 when the costs of production increase. Now that firms are earning a lower profit per unit of output, they reduce production, and the quantity of aggregate output supplied falls from $4 (point A) to $2 trillion (point A'). Applying the same reasoning at point B indicates that aggregate output supplied falls to point B'. What we see is that ***the aggregate supply curve shifts to the left when costs of production increase and to the right when costs decrease.***

EQUILIBRIUM IN AGGREGATE SUPPLY AND DEMAND ANALYSIS

The equilibrium level of aggregate output and the price level will occur at the point where the quantity of aggregate output demanded equals the quantity of aggregate output supplied. However, in the context of aggregate supply and demand analysis, there are two types of equilibrium: short-run and long-run.

Equilibrium in the Short Run

Figure 3 illustrates an equilibrium in the short run in which the quantity of aggregate output demanded equals the quantity of output supplied, that is, where the aggregate demand curve *AD* and the aggregate supply curve *AS* intersect at

---

[5]The aggregate supply curve is closely linked to the *Phillips curve* discussed in macroeconomics. The relationship between those two concepts is described in the appendix to this chapter.

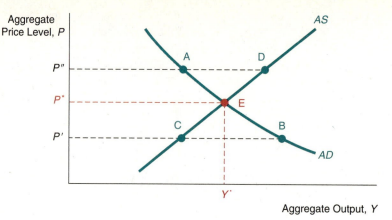

FIGURE 3
Equilibrium in the Short Run
Equilibrium occurs at point E at the intersection of the aggregate demand curve *AD* and the aggregate supply curve *AS*.

point E. The equilibrium level of aggregate output equals Y^*, and the equilibrium price level equals P^*.

As in our earlier supply and demand analyses, equilibrium is a useful concept only if there is a tendency for the economy to head toward it. We can see that the economy heads toward the equilibrium at point E by first looking at what happens when we are at a price level above the equilibrium price level P^*. If the price level is at P', the quantity of aggregate output supplied at point D is greater than the quantity of aggregate output demanded at point A. Because people want to sell more goods and services than others want to buy (a condition of *excess supply*), the prices of goods and services will fall, and the aggregate price level will drop. This decline in the price level will continue until it has reached its equilibrium level of P^* at point E.

When the price level is below the equilibrium price level, say, at P', the quantity of output demanded is greater than the quantity of output supplied. Now the price level will rise because people want to buy more goods than others want to sell (a condition of *excess demand*). This rise in the price level will continue until it has again reached its equilibrium level of P^* at point E.

Equilibrium in the Long Run

Usually in supply and demand analysis, once we find the equilibrium at which the quantity demanded equals the quantity supplied, no need for additional discussion exists. In *aggregate* supply and demand analysis, however, that is not the case. Even when the quantity of aggregate output demanded equals the quantity supplied, forces operate that can cause the equilibrium to move over time. To understand why, we must remember that if costs of production change, the aggregate supply curve will shift.

The most important component of production costs is wage cost (approximately 70% of production costs), which is determined in the labor market. If the economy is booming, employers will find that they have difficulty hiring qualified workers and may even have a hard time keeping their present employees. In this case, the labor market is tight because the demand for labor exceeds the supply; employers will raise wages to attract needed workers, and this raises the costs of production. The higher costs of production lower the profits per unit of output at each price level, and the aggregate supply curve shifts to the left (see Figure 2).

By contrast, if the economy enters a recession and the labor market is slack because demand for labor is less than supply, workers who cannot find jobs will be willing to work for lower wages. In addition, employed workers may be willing to make wage concessions to keep from losing their jobs (as airline and steel workers did in the 1980s).[6] Therefore, in a slack labor market in which the demand for labor is less than the supply, wages and hence costs of production will fall, profits per unit of output will rise, and the aggregate supply curve will shift to the right.

Our analysis suggests that the aggregate supply curve will shift depending on whether the labor market is tight or slack. How do we decide which it is? One helpful concept is the **natural rate of unemployment,** the rate of unemployment when demand for labor equals supply. Many economists believe that the rate is currently around 6%. When unemployment is at, say, 4%, below the natural rate of unemployment of 6%, the labor market is tight; wages will rise, and the aggregate supply curve will shift leftward. When unemployment is at, say, 8%, above the natural rate of unemployment, the labor market is slack; wages will fall, and the aggregate supply curve will shift rightward. Only when unemployment is at the natural rate will no pressure exist from the labor market for wages to rise or fall, so the aggregate supply need not shift.

The level of aggregate output produced at the natural rate of unemployment is called the **natural rate level of output.** Because, as we have seen, the aggregate supply curve will not remain stationary when unemployment and aggregate output differ from their natural rate levels, we need to look at how the short-run equilibrium changes over time in response to two situations: when equilibrium is initially below the natural rate level and when it is initially above the natural rate level.

In panel (a) of Figure 4, the initial equilibrium occurs at point 1, the intersection of the aggregate demand curve (*AD*) and the initial aggregate supply curve AS_1. Because the level of equilibrium output Y_1 is greater than the natural rate level Y_n, unemployment is less than the natural rate, and excessive tightness

---

[6]Airline and steel workers may have lost jobs because of other market forces besides overall high unemployment in the economy, specifically, airline deregulation and a change in the competitiveness of the American auto industry compared to the rest of the world.

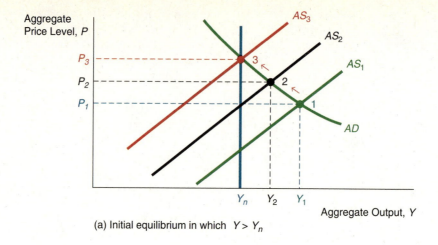

(a) Initial equilibrium in which $Y > Y_n$

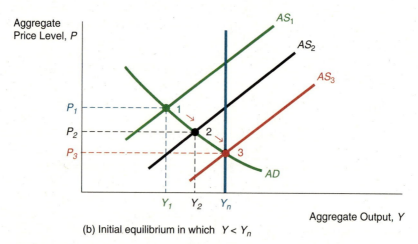

(b) Initial equilibrium in which $Y < Y_n$

FIGURE 4 Adjustment to Long-Run Equilibrium in Aggregate Supply and Demand Analysis
In both panels, the initial equilibrium is at point 1 at the intersection of AD and AS_1. In panel (a), $Y_1 > Y_n$, so the aggregate supply curve keeps shifting to the left until it reaches AS_3, where output has returned to Y_n. In panel (b), $Y_1 < Y_n$, so the aggregate supply curve keeps shifting to the right until output is again returned to Y_n. Hence in both cases the economy displays a self-correcting mechanism that returns it to the natural rate level of output.

exists in the labor market. This tightness drives wages up, raises production costs, and shifts the aggregate supply curve to AS_2. The equilibrium is now at point 2, and output falls to Y_2. Because aggregate output Y_2 is still above the natural rate level, Y_n, wages continue to be driven up, eventually shifting the aggregate supply curve to AS_3. The equilibrium reached at point 3 is on the vertical line at Y_n and is a long-run equilibrium. Because output is at the natural rate level, there is no further pressure on wages to rise and thus no further tendency for the aggregate supply curve to shift.

The movements in panel (a) indicate that the economy will not remain at a level of output higher than the natural rate level because the aggregate supply curve will shift to the left, raise the price level, and cause the economy to slide up along the aggregate demand curve until it comes to rest at a point on the vertical line through the natural rate level of output Y_n. Because the vertical line through Y_n is the only place at which the aggregate supply curve comes to rest, this vertical line indicates the quantity of output supplied in the long run for any given price level. We can characterize this as the **long-run aggregate supply curve.**

In panel (b), the initial equilibrium at point 1 is one at which output Y_1 is below the natural rate level. Because unemployment is higher than the natural rate, wages begin to fall, shifting the aggregate supply curve rightward until it comes to rest at AS_3. The economy slides down along the aggregate demand curve until it reaches the long-run equilibrium point 3, the intersection of the aggregate demand curve AD and the long-run aggregate supply curve at Y_n. Here, as in panel (a), the economy comes to rest when output has again returned to the natural rate level.

A striking feature of both panels of Figure 4 is that regardless of where output is initially, it returns eventually to the natural rate level. This feature is described by saying that the economy has a **self-correcting mechanism.**

An important issue for policymakers is how rapidly this self-correcting mechanism works. Many economists, particularly Keynesians, believe that the self-correcting mechanism takes a long time, so the approach to long-run equilibrium is slow. This view is reflected in John Maynard Keynes's often quoted remark, "In the long run, we are all dead." These economists view the self-correcting mechanism as slow because wages are inflexible, particularly in the downward direction when unemployment is high. The resulting slow wage and price adjustment means that the aggregate supply curve does not move quickly to restore the economy to the natural rate of unemployment. Hence when unemployment is high, these economists (called **activists**) are more likely to see the need for active government policy to restore the economy to full employment.

Other economists, particularly monetarists, believe that wages are sufficiently flexible that the wage and price adjustment process is reasonably rapid. As a result of this flexibility, adjustment of the aggregate supply curve to its long-run position and the economy's return to the natural rate levels of output and unemployment will occur quickly. Thus these economists (called **nonactivists**) see much less need for active government policy to restore the economy to the natural rate levels of output and unemployment when unemployment is high. Indeed, monetarists advocate the use of a rule whereby the money supply or the monetary base grows at a constant rate so as to minimize fluctuations in aggregate demand that might lead to output fluctuations. We will return to the debate about whether active government policy to keep the economy near full employment is beneficial in Chapter 28.

Shifts in Aggregate Demand

You are now ready to analyze what happens when the aggregate demand curve shifts. Our discussion of the Keynesian and monetarist views of aggregate demand indicates that six factors can affect the aggregate demand curve: the money supply, government spending, net exports, taxes, consumer optimism, and business optimism–the last two ("animal spirits") affecting the willingness to spend. The possible effect on the aggregate demand curve of these six factors is summarized in Table 1.

Figure 5 depicts the effect of an outward shift in the aggregate demand curve caused by an increase in the money supply ($M\uparrow$), an increase in government spending ($G\uparrow$), an increase in net exports ($NX\uparrow$), a decrease in taxes ($T\downarrow$), or an increase in the willingness of consumers and businesses to spend because they become more optimistic ($C\uparrow$, $I\uparrow$). The figure has been drawn so that initially the economy is in long-run equilibrium at point 1, where the initial aggregate demand curve AD_1 intersects the aggregate supply AS_1 curve at Y_n. When the aggregate demand curve shifts rightward to AD_2, the economy moves to point 1', and both output and the price level rise. However, the economy will not remain at point 1' because output at Y_1' is above the natural rate level. Wages will rise, eventually shifting the aggregate supply curve leftward to AS_2, where it finally comes to rest. The economy thus slides up the aggregate demand curve from point 1' to point 2, which is the point of long-run equilibrium at the intersection of AD_2 and Y_n. ***Although the initial effect of the rightward shift in the aggregate demand curve is a rise in both the price level and output, the ultimate effect is only a rise in the price level.***

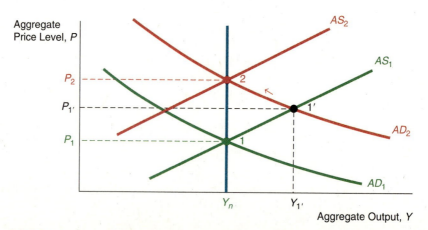

FIGURE 5 Response of Output and the Price Level to a Shift in the Aggregate Demand Curve
A shift in the aggregate demand curve from AD_1 to AD_2 moves the economy from point 1 to point 1'. Because $Y_1' < Y_n$, the aggregate supply curve begins to shift leftward eventually reaching AS_2, where output returns to Y_n and the price level has risen to P_2.

SUMMARY

TABLE 1   Factors That Shift the Aggregate Demand Curve

Factor	Change	Shift in the Aggregate Demand Curve
Money supply	↑	
Government spending	↑	
Taxes	↑	
Net exports	↑	
Consumer optimism	↑	
Business optimism	↑	

Note: Only increases (↑) in the factors are shown. The effect of decreases in the factors would be the opposite of those indicated in the "shift" column. Note that monetarists view only the money supply as an important cause of shifts in the aggregate demand curve.

Shifts in Aggregate Supply

Not only can shifts in aggregate demand be a source of fluctuations in aggregate output (the business cycle), but so can shifts in aggregate supply. Factors that cause the aggregate supply curve to shift are the ones that affect costs of production: (1) tightness of the labor market, (2) expectations of inflation, (3) workers' attempts to push up their real wages, and (4) changes in the production costs that are unrelated to wages (such as energy costs). The first three factors shift the aggregate supply curve by affecting wage costs (approximately 70% of production costs); the fourth affects other costs of production.

Tightness of the Labor Market Our analysis of the approach to long-run equilibrium has shown us that when the labor market is tight ($Y > Y_n$), wages and hence production costs rise, and when the labor market is slack ($Y < Y_n$), wages and production costs fall. The effects on the aggregate supply curve are as follows: *When aggregate output is above the natural rate level, the aggregate supply curve shifts to the left; when aggregate output is below the natural rate level, the aggregate supply curve shifts to the right.*

Expected Price Level Workers and firms care about wages in real terms, that is, in terms of the goods and services that wages can buy. When the price level increases, a worker earning the same nominal wage will be able to buy fewer goods and services. A worker who expects the price level to rise will thus demand a higher nominal wage in order to keep the real wage from falling. For example, if Chuck the Construction Worker expects prices to increase by 5%, he will want a wage increase of at least 5% (possibly more if he thinks he deserves an increase in real wages). Similarly, if Chuck's employer knows that the houses he is building will rise in value at the same rate as inflation (5%), his employer will be willing to pay Chuck 5% more. An increase in the expected price level leads to higher wages, which in turn raise the costs of production, lower the profits per unit of output at each price level, and shift the aggregate supply curve to the left (see Figure 2). Therefore, *a rise in the expected price level causes the aggregate supply curve to shift to the left; the greater the expected increase in price level (that is, the higher the expected inflation), the larger the shift.*

Wage Push Suppose that Chuck and his fellow construction workers decide to strike and succeed in obtaining higher real wages. This *wage push* will then raise the costs of production, and the aggregate supply curve will shift leftward. *A successful wage push by workers will cause the aggregate supply curve to shift to the left.*

Changes in Production Costs Unrelated to Wages Changes in technology and in the supply of raw materials (called **supply shocks**) also can shift the aggregate supply curve. A negative supply shock, such as a reduction in the availability of raw materials (like oil), which raises their price, raises production costs and shifts the aggregate supply curve leftward. A positive supply shock such as unusually good weather that leads to a bountiful harvest and lowers the cost of food, will reduce production costs and shift the aggregate supply curve rightward. Similarly, the development of a new technology that lowers production costs, perhaps by raising worker productivity, can also be considered a positive supply shock that shifts the aggregate supply curve to the right.[7]

The effect on the aggregate supply curve of changes in production costs unrelated to wages can be summarized as follows: ***A negative supply shock that raises production costs shifts the aggregate supply curve to the left; a positive supply shock that lowers production costs shifts the aggregate supply curve to the right.***[7]

As a study aid, factors that shift the aggregate supply curve are listed in Table 2.

Now that we know what factors can affect the aggregate supply curve, we can examine what occurs when they cause the aggregate supply curve to shift leftward, as in Figure 6. Suppose that the economy is initially at the natural rate level of output at point 1 when the aggregate supply curve shifts from AS_1 to AS_2 because of a negative supply shock (a sharp rise in energy prices). The economy will move from point 1 to point 2, where the price level rises but aggregate output *falls*. A situation of a rising price level but a falling level of aggregate output, as pictured in Figure 6, has been labeled *stagflation* (a combination of words *stagnation* and *inflation*). At point 2, output is below the natural rate level, so wages fall and shift the aggregate supply curve back to where it was initially at AS_1. The result is that the economy slides down the aggregate demand curve AD_1 (assuming that the aggregate demand curve remains in the same position), and the economy returns to the long-run equilibrium at point 1. ***Although a leftward shift in the aggregate supply curve initially raises the price level and lowers output, the ultimate effect is that output and price level are unchanged (holding the aggregate demand curve constant).***

Shifts in the Long-Run Aggregate Supply Curve: Real Business Cycle Theory and Hysteresis

To this point we have assumed that the natural rate level of output Y_n and hence the long-run aggregate supply curve (the vertical line through Y_n) are given. However, over time the natural rate level of output clearly increases as a result of economic growth. If the productive capacity of the economy is growing at a steady rate of 3% per year, for example, this means that every year Y_n will grow by 3% and the long-run aggregate supply curve at Y_n will shift to the right by

---

[7]Developments in the foreign exchange market can also shift the aggregate supply curve by changing domestic production costs. As discussed in more detail in Chapter 8, when the dollar increases in value, it makes foreign goods cheaper in the United States. The decline in prices of foreign goods and hence foreign factors of production lowers U.S. production costs and thus raises the profit per unit of output at each price level in the United States. An increase in the value of the dollar therefore shifts the aggregate supply curve to the right. Conversely, a decline in the value of the dollar, which makes foreign factors of production more expensive, shifts the aggregate supply curve to the left.

SUMMARY

TABLE 2 Factors That Shift the Aggregate Supply Curve

Factor	Shift in the Aggregate Supply Curve
Y > Yn	
$Y << Y_n$	
Rise in expected price level	
Wage push	
Positive supply shock	
Negative supply shock	

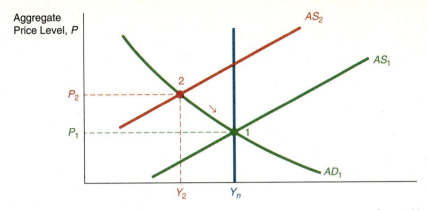

FIGURE 6 Response of Output and the Price Level to a Shift in Aggregate Supply
A shift in the aggregate supply curve from AS_1 to AS_2 moves the economy from point 1 to point 2. Because $Y_2 < Y_n$, the aggregate supply curve begins to shift back to the right, eventually returning to AS_1, where the economy is again at point 1.

3%. To simplify the analysis when Y_n grows at a steady rate, Y_n and the long-run aggregate supply curve are drawn as fixed in the aggregate demand and supply diagrams. Keep in mind, however, that the level of aggregate output pictured in these diagrams is actually best thought of as the level of aggregate output relative to its normal rate of growth (trend).

The usual assumption when conducting aggregate demand and supply analysis is that shifts in either the aggregate demand or aggregate supply curve have no effect on the natural rate level of output (which grows at a steady rate). Movements of aggregate output around the Y_n level in the diagram then describe short-run (business cycle) fluctuations in aggregate output. However, some economists take issue with the assumption that Y_n is unaffected by aggregate demand and supply shocks.

One group, led by Edward Prescott of the University of Minnesota, has developed a theory of aggregate economic fluctuations called **real business cycle theory** in which aggregate supply (real) shocks do affect the natural rate level of output Y_n. This theory views shocks to tastes (workers' willingness to work, for example) and technology (productivity) as the major driving forces behind short-run fluctuations in the business cycle because these shocks lead to substantial short-run fluctuations in Y_n. Shifts in the aggregate demand curve, say, as a result of changes in monetary policy, by contrast, are not viewed as being particularly important to aggregate output fluctuations. Because real business cycle theory views most business cycle fluctuations as resulting from fluctuations in the natural rate level of output, it does not see much need for activist policy to eliminate high unemployment. Real business cycle theory is highly controversial and is currently the subject of intensive research.[8]

---

[8]See Charles Plosser, "Understanding Real Business Cycles," *Journal of Economic Perspectives,* Summer 1989, pp. 51–77, for a detailed review of the literature on real business cycle theory.

Another group of economists disagrees with the assumption that the natural rate level of output Y_n is unaffected by aggregate demand shocks. These economists contend that the natural rate level of unemployment and output are subject to **hysteresis,** a departure from full employment levels as a result of past high unemployment.[9] When unemployment rises because of a reduction of aggregate demand that shifts the *AD* curve inward, the natural rate of unemployment is viewed as rising above the full employment level. This could occur because the unemployed become discouraged and fail to look hard for work or because employers may be reluctant to hire workers who have been unemployed for a long time, thinking that it is a signal that the worker is undesirable. The outcome is that the natural rate of unemployment shifts upward after unemployment has become high, and Y_n falls below the full employment level. In this situation, the self-correcting mechanism will be able to return the economy only to the natural rate levels of output and unemployment, not to the full employment level. Only with expansionary policy to shift the aggregate demand curve to the right and raise aggregate output can the natural rate of unemployment be lowered (Y_n raised) to the full employment level. Proponents of hysteresis are thus more likely to promote activist, expansionary policies to restore the economy to full employment.

STUDY GUIDE

Aggregate supply and demand analysis is best learned by practicing applications. In this section we have traced out what happens to aggregate output when there is an increase in the money supply or a negative supply shock. Make sure that you can also draw the appropriate shifts in the aggregate demand and supply curves and analyze what happens when other variables such as taxes or the expected price level change.

Conclusions

Aggregate demand and supply analysis yields the following conclusions (under the usual assumption that the natural rate level of output is unaffected by aggregate demand and supply shocks):

1. A shift in the aggregate demand curve—which can be caused by changes in monetary policy (the money supply), fiscal policy (government spending or taxes), international trade (net exports), or "animal spirits" (business and consumer optimism)—affects output only in the short run and has no effect in the long run. Furthermore, the initial change in the price level is less than is achieved in the long run, when the aggregate supply curve has fully adjusted.

2. A shift in the aggregate supply curve—which can be caused by changes in expected inflation, workers' attempts to push up real wages, or a supply

---

[9]For a further discussion of hysteresis, see Olivier Blanchard and Lawrence Summers, "Hysteresis in the European Unemployment Problem," *NBER Macroeconomics Annual, 1986,* pp. 15–78.

shock—affects output and prices only in the short run and
long run (holding the aggregate demand curve constant).

   3. The economy has a self-correcting mechanism, which
natural rate levels of unemployment and aggregate output ove.

APPLICATION

EXPLAINING PAST BUSINESS CYCLE EPISODES

Aggregate supply and demand analysis is an extremely useful tool for analyzing
aggregate economic activity; we will apply it to several business cycle episodes.
In addition, since a good economic model must be able to predict the future as
well as explain the past, we will look at how aggregate supply and demand
analysis can be used to predict the response of aggregate output and price level
to events that might happen in the future. To simplify our analysis, we always
assume that aggregate output is initially at the natural rate level.

Vietnam War Buildup, 1964–1970

America's involvement in Vietnam began to escalate in the early 1960s, and
after 1964, the United States was fighting a full-scale war. Beginning in 1965, the
resulting increases in military expenditure raised government spending, while at
the same time the Federal Reserve increased the rate of money growth in an attempt to keep interest rates from rising. What does aggregate supply and demand analysis suggest should have happened to aggregate output and the price
level as a result of the Vietnam War buildup?

   The rise in government spending and the higher rate of money growth
would shift the aggregate demand curve to the right (shown in Figure 5). As a
result, aggregate output would rise, unemployment would fall, and the price
level would rise. Table 3 demonstrates that this is exactly what happened: The
unemployment rate fell steadily from 1964 to 1969, remaining well below what
economists now think was the natural rate of unemployment during that period
(around 5%), and inflation began to rise. As Figure 5 predicts, unemployment
would eventually begin to return to the natural rate level because of the economy's self-correcting mechanism. This is exactly what we saw occurring in
1970, when the inflation rate rose even higher and unemployment increased.

Negative Supply Shocks, 1973–1975 and 1978–1980

In 1973, the U.S. economy was hit by a series of negative supply shocks. As a
result of the oil embargo stemming from the Arab-Israeli war of 1973, the Organization of Petroleum Exporting Countries (OPEC) was able to engineer a qua-
drupling of oil prices by restricting oil production. In addition, a series of crop
failures throughout the world led to a sharp increase in food prices. Another
factor was the termination of wage and price controls in 1973 and 1974, which

TABLE 3 Unemployment and Inflation During the Vietnam War Buildup, 1964–1970		
Year	**Unemployment Rate (%)**	**Inflation (Year to Year) (%)**
1964	5.0	1.3
1965	4.4	1.6
1966	3.7	2.9
1967	3.7	3.1
1968	3.5	4.2
1969	3.4	5.5
1970	4.8	5.7

Source: Economic Report of the President.

led to a push by workers to obtain wage increases that had been prevented by the controls. The triple thrust of these events caused the aggregate supply curve to shift sharply leftward, and as the aggregate demand and supply diagram in Figure 6 predicts, both the price level and unemployment began to rise dramatically (see Table 4).

The 1978–1980 period was almost an exact replay of the 1973–1975 period. By 1978, the economy had just about fully recovered from the 1973–1974 supply shocks when poor harvests and a doubling of oil prices (as a result of the overthrow of the shah of Iran) again led to another sharp leftward shift of the aggregate supply curve. The pattern predicted by Figure 6 played itself out again—inflation and unemployment both shot upward (see Table 4).

Credit Crunch and Slow Recovery from the 1990–1991 Recession

The Iraqi invasion of Kuwait in the summer of 1990 caused a collapse in consumer confidence and threatened to drive oil prices permanently higher. The resulting decline in consumer expenditure caused the aggregate demand curve to shift to the left, and consistent with our aggregate demand and supply analysis, unemployment rose and inflation fell (see Table 5). What is surprising about the resulting recession in 1990–1991 is not that it occurred but that the recovery from it was so sluggish.

After a typical recession, aggregate output grows quite rapidly, with growth rates ordinarily exceeding 4%. A rapid recovery might have been expected to be even more likely after the Western victory in the 1991 Gulf War, which quickly returned oil prices to their previous level. However, recovery from the 1990–1991 recession did not follow the typical pattern. From the middle of 1990, when the recession was officially declared over, until the end of 1992,

TABLE 4 Unemployment and Inflation During the Supply Shock Periods, 1973–1975 and 1978–1980					
Year	Unemployment Rate (%)	Inflation (Year to Year) (%)	Year	Unemployment Rate (%)	Inflation (Year to Year) (%)
1973	4.8	6.2	1978	6.0	7.6
1974	5.5	11.0	1979	5.8	11.3
1975	8.3	9.1	1980	7.0	13.5

Source: Economic Report of the President.

real gross domestic product grew at an anemic rate, less than 2%. This caused the unemployment rate to keep on rising in 1992 as Table 5 indicates. Only in 1993 did the economy begin to pick up steam. Why was the recovery from the recession so sluggish?

The explanation seems to be related to the credit view discussed earlier in the chapter. We saw that a reduction in bank lending could cause a decline in business and consumer spending that would reduce aggregate demand. The period from 1990 to 1992 saw an unprecedented slowdown in the growth of bank lending. In our discussion of the credit view, the reduction might have come about because of tight monetary policy, but in this episode the credit slowdown stemmed from other sources. As we discussed in Chapter 11, banks found themselves with capital shortfalls for two reasons: Huge losses on their loans, particularly in real estate, eroded their capital, and increases in capital requirements in the aftermath of the banking crisis described in Chapter 13 required them to obtain more capital. The resulting capital shortfalls restrained asset growth for banks and hence restricted bank lending. In addition, the deterioration in companies' balance sheets as a result of the huge run-up of debt in the 1980s exacerbated adverse selection and moral hazard problems for lenders such as banks, which made them less likely to make loans. The resulting credit crunch is viewed by most analysts as an important factor in causing the 1990–1991 recession and accounts for the anemic recovery.

TABLE 5 Unemployment and Inflation During the 1990–1992 Credit Crunch		
Year	Unemployment Rate (%)	Inflation (Year to Year) (%)
1990	5.4	5.4
1991	6.6	4.2
1992	7.3	3.0

Source: Economic Report of the President.

APPLICATION

PREDICTING FUTURE ECONOMIC ACTIVITY

Now let's see what will happen to aggregate output and the price level if certain events happen that have a reasonable probability of occurring in the near future.

Elimination of Japanese Trade Barriers

The U.S. and Japanese governments have been engaged in talks about eliminating barriers to exports of U.S. goods to Japan. If the talks are successful in tearing down these barriers, what might we predict would happen to output and the price level in the United States?

Our aggregate supply and demand analysis of the elimination of Japanese trade barriers would be that pictured in Figure 5. The elimination of Japanese trade barriers would cause U.S. net exports to rise, leading to a rightward shift of the aggregate demand curve, which would initially raise aggregate output and the price level (increasing inflation) in the United States. In the long run, however, aggregate output would return to its natural rate level, and the price level would stop rising, so the increase in inflation would be only temporary.

Reduction in the Size of the U.S. Military

The Clinton administration has been talking about significantly downsizing the U.S. military, a move that includes the closing of many military bases. What effect will cuts in military spending have on the economy?

The reduction in military spending would probably lead to less government spending and a leftward shift of the aggregate demand curve. The outcome would be opposite that pictured in Figure 5: The price level would fall, lowering the inflation rate, and aggregate output would also fall at first; in the long run, however, aggregate output would return to the natural rate level.

STUDY GUIDE

Many examples of future events with implications for shifts in the aggregate demand and supply curves come to mind. Try to think of some yourself, and then use aggregate supply and demand analysis to predict what will happen to the economy. Such exercises will help you master aggregate supply and demand analysis (and may even be fun).

SUMMARY

1. The aggregate demand curve indicates the quantity of aggregate output demanded at each price level, and it is downward-sloping. Monetarists view changes in the money supply as the primary source of shifts in the aggregate demand curve. Keynesians believe that not only are changes in the money supply important to shifts in the aggregate demand curve, but so are changes in fiscal policy (government spending and taxes), net exports, and the willingness of consumers and businesses to spend ("animal spirits").

2. In the short run, the aggregate supply curve slopes upward because a rise in the price level raises the profit earned on each unit of production, and the quantity of output supplied rises. Four factors can cause the aggregate supply curve to shift: tightness of the labor market as represented by unemployment relative to the nat-

ural rate, expectations of inflation, workers' attempts to push up their real wages, and supply shocks unrelated to wages that affect production costs.

3. Equilibrium in the short run occurs at the point where the aggregate demand curve intersects the aggregate supply curve. Although this is where the economy heads temporarily, it has a self-correcting mechanism, which leads it to settle permanently at the long-run equilibrium where aggregate output is at its natural rate level. Shifts in either the aggregate demand or the aggregate supply curve can produce changes in aggregate output and the price level.

4. Aggregate supply and demand analysis can be used either to explain past business cycle episodes or to predict the response of aggregate output and the price level to future events.

KEY TERMS

aggregate demand

aggregate supply

aggregate demand curve

monetarists

Keynesians

velocity

equation of exchange

modern quantity theory of money

consumer expenditure

planned investment spending

government spending

net exports

"animal spirits"

complete crowding out

partial crowding out

aggregate supply curve

natural rate of unemployment

natural rate level of output

long-run aggregate supply curve

self-correcting mechanism

activists

nonactivists

supply shock

real business cycle theory

hysteresis

QUESTIONS AND PROBLEMS

1. Given that a monetarist predicts velocity to be 5, graph the aggregate demand curve that results if the money supply is $400 billion. If the money supply falls to $50 billion, what happens to the position of the aggregate demand curve?

*2. Milton Friedman states, "Money is all that matters to nominal income." How is this statement built

into the aggregate demand curve in the monetarist framework?

3. Suppose that government spending is raised at the same time that the money supply is lowered. What will happen to the position of the Keynesian aggregate demand curve? The monetarist aggregate demand curve?

*4. Why does the Keynesian aggregate demand curve shift when "animal spirits" change, but the monetarist aggregate demand curve does not?

5. If the dollar increases in value relative to foreign currencies so that foreign goods become cheaper in the United States, what will happen to the position of the aggregate supply curve? The aggregate demand curve?

*6. "Profit-maximizing behavior on the part of firms explains why the aggregate supply curve is upward-sloping." Is this statement true, false, or uncertain? Explain.

7. If huge budget deficits cause the public to think that there will be higher inflation in the future, what is likely to happen to the aggregate supply curve when budget deficits rise?

*8. If a pill were invented that made workers twice as productive but their wages did not change, what would happen to the position of the aggregate supply curve?

9. When aggregate output is below the natural rate level, what will happen to the price level over time if the aggregate demand curve remains unchanged? Why?

*10. Show how aggregate supply and demand analysis can explain why both aggregate output and the price level fell sharply when investment spending collapsed during the Great Depression.

11. "An important difference between monetarists and Keynesians rests on how long they think the long run actually is." Is this statement true, false, or uncertain? Explain.

Using Economic Analysis to Predict the Future

*12. Predict what will happen to aggregate output and the price level if the Federal Reserve increases the money supply at the same time that Congress implements an income tax cut.

13. Suppose that the public believes that a newly announced anti-inflation program will work and so lowers its expectations of future inflation. What will happen to aggregate output and the price level in the short run?

*14. Proposals have come before Congress that advocate the implementation of a national sales tax. Predict the effect of such a tax on both the aggregate supply and demand curves and on aggregate output and the price level.

15. With the decline in the value of the dollar since 1985, some experts predict a dramatic improvement in the ability of American firms to compete abroad. Predict what would happen to output and the price level in the United States as a result?

Appendix to Chapter 26

AGGREGATE SUPPLY AND THE PHILLIPS CURVE: A HISTORICAL PERSPECTIVE

In this appendix we examine how economists' view of aggregate supply has evolved over the time and how the concept called the **Phillips curve**, which describes the relationship between unemployment and inflation, fits into the analysis of aggregate supply.

The classical economists, who predated Keynes, believed that wages and prices were extremely flexible, so the economy would always adjust quickly to the natural rate level of output Y_n. This view is equivalent to assuming that the aggregate supply curve is vertical at an output level of Y_n even in the short run.

With the advent of the Great Depression in 1929 and the subsequent long period of high unemployment, the classical view of an economy that adjusts quickly to the natural rate level of output became less tenable. The teachings of John Maynard Keynes emerged as the dominant way of thinking about the determination of aggregate output, and the view that aggregate supply is vertical was abandoned. Instead, Keynesians in the 1930s, 1940s, and 1950s assumed that for all practical purposes, the price level could be treated as fixed. They viewed aggregate supply as a horizontal curve along which aggregate output could increase without an increase in the price level.

In 1958, A. W. Phillips published a famous paper that outlined a relationship between unemployment and inflation.[1] This relationship was popularized by Paul Samuelson and Robert Solow of the Massachusetts Institute of Technology in the early 1960s, and naturally enough, it became known as the *Phillips curve*, after its discoverer. The Phillips curve indicates that the rate of change of wages $\Delta w/w$, called *wage inflation*, is negatively related to the difference between the actual unemployment rate U and the natural rate of unemployment U_n:

$$\frac{\Delta w}{w} = -h(U - U_n)$$

---

[1]A. W. Phillips, "The Relationship Between Unemployment and the Rate of Change of Money Wages in the United Kingdom, 1861–1957," *Economica* 25 (1958): 283–299.

where h is a constant that indicates how much wage inflation changes for a given change in $U - U_n$. If h were 2, for example, a 1% increase in the unemployment rate relative to the natural rate would result in a 2% decline in wage inflation.

The Phillips curve provides a view of aggregate supply because it indicates that a rise in aggregate output that lowers the unemployment rate will raise wage inflation and thus lead to a higher level of wages and the price level. In other words, the Phillips curve implies that the aggregate supply curve will be upward-sloping. In addition, it indicates that when $U > U_n$ (the labor market is slack), $\Delta w/w$ is negative and wages decline over time. Hence the Phillips curve supports the view of aggregate supply in Chapter 26 that when the labor market is slack, production costs will fall and the aggregate supply curve will shift to the right.[2]

Figure A1 shows what the Phillips curve relationship looks like for the United States. As we can see from panel (a), the relationship works well until 1969 and seems to indicate an apparent trade-off between unemployment and wage inflation: If the public wants to have a lower unemployment rate, it can "buy" this by accepting a higher rate of wage inflation.

In 1967, however, Milton Friedman pointed out a severe flaw in the Phillips curve analysis: It left out an important factor that affects wage changes, workers' expectations of inflation.[3] Friedman noted that firms and workers are concerned with real wages, not nominal wages; they are concerned with the wage adjusted for any expected increase in the price level—that is, they look at the rate of change of wages minus expected inflation. When unemployment is high relative to the natural rate, real (not nominal) wages should fall ($\Delta w/w - \pi^e < 0$); when unemployment is low relative to the natural rate, real wages should rise ($\Delta w/w - \pi^e > 0$). The Phillips curve relationship thus needs to be modified by replacing $\Delta w/w$ by $\Delta w/w - \pi^e$. This results in an *expectations-augmented Phillips curve*, expressed as

$$\frac{\Delta w}{w} - \pi^e = -h\,(U - U_n) \qquad \text{or} \qquad \frac{\Delta w}{w} = -h\,(U - U_n) + \pi^e$$

The expectations-augmented Phillips curve implies that as expected inflation rises, nominal wages will be increased to prevent real wages from falling, and the Phillips curve will shift upward. The resulting rise in production costs will then shift the aggregate supply curve leftward. The conclusion from Friedman's modification of the Phillips curve is therefore that the higher inflation is ex-

---

[2]Because workers normally become more productive over time as a result of new technology and increases in physical capital, their real wages grow over time, even when the economy is at the natural rate of unepmployment. To reflect this, the Phillips curve should include a term that reflects the growth in real wages due to higher worker productivity. We have left this term out of the equation in the text because higher productivity that results in higher real wages will not cause the aggregate supply curve to shift. If, for example, workers become 3% more productive every year and their real wages grow at 3% per year, the effective cost of workers to the firm (called *unit labor costs*) remains unchanged, and the aggregate supply curve does not shift. Thus the $\Delta w/w$ term in the Phillips curve is more accurately thought of as the change in the unit labor costs.

[3]This criticism of the Phillips curve was outlined in Milton Friedman's famous presidential address to the American Economic Association: Milton Friedman, "The Role of Monetary Policy," *American Economic Review* 58 (1968): 1–17.

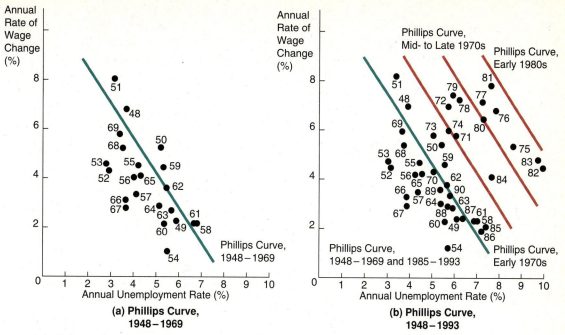

Figure A1   Phillips Curve in the United States

Although the Phillips curve relationship worked fairly well from 1948 to 1969, after this period it appeared to shift upward, as is clear from panel (b). Looking at the whole period after World War II, there is no apparent trade-off between unemployment and inflation. *Source: Economic Report of the President.*

pected to be, the larger the leftward shift in the aggregate supply curve; this conclusion is built into the analysis of the aggregate supply curve in the chapter.

Friedman's modification of the Phillips curve analysis was remarkably clairvoyant: As inflation increased in the late 1960s, the Phillips curve did indeed begin to shift upward, as we can see from panel (b). An important feature of panel (b) is that a trade-off between unemployment and wage inflation is no longer apparent; there is no clear-cut relationship between unemployment and wage inflation—a high rate of wage inflation does not mean that unemployment is low, nor does a low rate of wage inflation mean that unemployment is high. This is exactly what the expectations augmented Phillips curve predicts: A rate of unemployment permanently below the natural rate of unemployment cannot be "bought" by accepting a higher rate of inflation because no long-run trade-off between unemployment and wage inflation exists.[4]

---

[4]This prediction can be derived from the expectations-augmented Phillips curve as follows. When wage inflaction is held at a constant level, inflation and expected inflation will eventually equal wage inflation. Thus in the long run, $\pi^e = \Delta w/w$. Substituting the long-run value of π^e into the expectations-augmented Phillips curve gives

$$\frac{\Delta w}{w} = -b(U - U_n) + \frac{\Delta w}{w}$$

Subtracting $\Delta w/w$ from both sides of the equation gives $0 = -b(U - U_n)$, which implies that $U = U_n$. This tells us that in the long run, for any level of wage inflation, unemployment will settle to its natural rate level; hence the long-run Phillips curve is vertical, and there is no long-run trade-off between unemployment and wage inflation.

A further refinement of the concept of aggregate supply came from research by Milton Friedman, Edmund Phelps, and Robert Lucus, who explored the implications of the expectations augmented Phillips curve for the behavior of unemployment. Solving the expectations-augmented Phillips curve for U leads to the following expression:

$$U = U_n - \frac{\Delta w/w - \pi^e}{b}$$

Because wage inflation and price inflation are closely tied to each other, π can be substituted for $\Delta w/w$ in this expression to obtain

$$U = U_n - \frac{\pi - \pi^e}{b}$$

This expression, often referred to as the *Lucas supply function*, indicates that deviations of unemployment and aggregate output from the natural rate levels respond to unanticipated inflation (actual inflation minus expected inflation, $\pi - \pi^e$). When inflation is greater than anticipated, unemployment will be below the natural rate (and aggregate output above the natural rate). When inflation is below its anticipated value, unemployment will rise above the natural rate level. The conclusion from this view of aggregate supply is that only unanticipated policy can cause deviations from the natural rate of unemployment and output. The implications of this view are explored in detail in Chapter 30.

Chapter 27

MONEY AND ECONOMIC ACTIVITY: THE EMPIRICAL EVIDENCE

PREVIEW Since 1980, the U.S. economy has been on a roller coaster, with output and unemployment undergoing drastic fluctuations. The recession of 1980 was followed by one of the shortest economic expansions on record. After a year, the economy plunged into the 1981–1982 recession, the most severe economic contraction in the postwar era—the unemployment rate climbed to over 10%. The 1981–1982 recession was then followed by a long economic expansion that led to a decline of the unemployment rate below 6% in the 1987–1990 period. With Iraq's invasion of Kuwait and a rise in oil prices in the second half of 1990, the economy again plunged into recession. Subsequent growth in the economy was sluggish, with unemployment rates remaining above 6% in 1993. In light of large fluctuations in aggregate output and the economic instability that accompanies them, policymakers face the following dilemma: What policy or policies should be implemented to reduce output fluctuations in the future?

As you learned in Chapter 26, monetarists believe that there is only one major source of output fluctuations: changes in the money supply. Their solution to reducing output fluctuations is a rule providing a constant rate of money growth. Keynesians, by contrast, believe that there are other sources of output fluctuations (fiscal policy, net exports, "animal spirits," supply shocks), and they doubt that controlling the money supply alone will eliminate them. As you can see, it is extremely important for policymakers to know how important money is as a factor in determining aggregate economic activity.

In this chapter we examine empirical evidence on the effect of money on aggregate output (real GDP) and aggregate spending (nominal GDP) and discuss the disagreement between monetarists and Keynesians on the importance of money to these variables. Amazingly, although there has been some convergence of views, after more than three decades, differences still exist. Debates in the physical sciences are usually resolved more quickly. Why is this not the case in economics?

This chapter provides an answer to this question by focusing on why empirical evidence in economics is much harder to interpret than evidence in the physical sciences. Debates in economics often remain unresolved because there are two different kinds of evidence, which sometimes lead to conflicting conclusions. The analysis in this chapter will not only help you understand the debate on the importance of money to economic activity but, more important, will also provide you with a perspective on how to evaluate other controversies in economics (as well as other scientific disciplines) that are hard to resolve.

TWO TYPES OF EMPIRICAL EVIDENCE

We encounter two types of empirical evidence in economics and other scientific disciplines: **Structural model evidence** examines whether one variable affects another by using data to build a model that explains the channels through which this variable affects the other; **reduced-form evidence** examines whether one variable has an effect on another simply by looking directly at the relationship between the two variables.

Suppose that you were interested in whether drinking coffee leads to heart disease. Structural model evidence would involve developing an empirical model that analyzed data on how coffee is metabolized by the human body, how it affects the operation of the heart, and how its effects on the heart lead to heart attacks. Reduced-form evidence would involve looking directly at whether coffee drinkers tend to experience heart attacks more frequently than non–coffee drinkers.

How you look at the evidence—whether you focus on structural model evidence or reduced-form evidence—can lead to different conclusions. This is particularly true for the debate between monetarists and Keynesians: Monetarists tend to focus on reduced-form evidence and find that changes in the money supply are more important to economic activity than do Keynesians, who focus on structural model evidence. To understand the differences in their views about the importance of monetary policy, we need to look at the nature of the two types of evidence and the advantages and disadvantages of each.

Structural Model Evidence

The Keynesian analysis discussed in Chapter 26 is specific about the channels through which the money supply affects economic activity (called the **transmission mechanisms of monetary policy**). Keynesians typically examine the effect of money on economic activity by building a **structural model,** a description of how the economy operates using a collection of equations that describe the behavior of firms and consumers in many sectors of the economy. These equations then show the channels through which monetary and fiscal policy affect aggregate output and spending. A Keynesian structural model might have behavioral equations that describe the workings of monetary policy with the following schematic diagram:

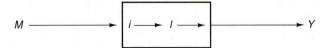

The model describes the transmission mechanism of monetary policy as follows: The money supply M affects interest rates i, which in turn affect investment spending I, which in turn affects aggregate output or aggregate spending Y. The Keynesians examine the relationship between M and Y by looking at empirical evidence (structural model evidence) on the specific channels of monetary influence, such as the link between interest rates and investment spending.

Reduced-Form Evidence

Monetarists do not describe specific ways in which the money supply affects aggregate spending. Instead, they examine the effect of money on economic activity by looking at whether movements in Y are tightly linked to (have a high correlation with) movements in M. Using reduced-form evidence, monetarists analyze the effect of M on Y as if the economy were a black box whose workings cannot be seen. The monetarist way of looking at the evidence can be represented by the following schematic diagram, in which the economy is drawn as a black box with a question mark:

Now that we have seen how monetarists and Keynesians look at the empirical evidence on the link between money and economic activity, we can consider the advantages and disadvantages of a reduced-form versus a structural model approach.

Advantages and Disadvantages of Structural Model Evidence

The structural model approach, used primarily by Keynesians, has the advantage of giving us an understanding of how the economy works. If the structure is correct, that is, if it contains all the transmission mechanisms and channels through which monetary and fiscal policy can affect economic activity, the structural model approach has three major advantages over the reduced-form approach.

1. Because we can evaluate each transmission mechanism separately to see whether it is plausible, we will obtain more pieces of evidence on whether money has an important effect on economic activity. If we find important effects of money on economic activity, for example, we will have more confidence that changes in money actually cause the changes in economic activity; that is, we will have more confidence on the direction of causation between M and Y.

2. Knowing how changes in money affect economic activity may help us predict the effect of M on Y more accurately. Expansions in the money supply might be found to be less effective when interest rates are low. Then, when interest rates are higher, we would be able to predict that an expansion in the money supply would have a larger impact on Y than would otherwise be the case.

3. By knowing how the economy operates, we may be able to predict how institutional changes in the economy might affect the link between M and Y. For instance, before 1980 when Regulation Q was still in effect, restrictions on interest payments on savings deposits meant that the average consumer would not earn more on savings when interest rates rose. With the termination of Regulation Q, the average consumer now earns more on savings when interest rates rise. If we understand how earnings on savings affect consumer spending, we might be able to say that a change in the money supply, which affects interest rates, will have a different effect today than it would have had before 1980. Because of the rapid pace of financial innovation, the advantage of being able to predict how institutional changes affect the link between M and Y may be even more important now than in the past.

These three advantages of the structural model approach suggest that this approach is better than the reduced-form approach *if we know the correct structure of the model.* Put another way, structural model evidence is only as good as the structural model it is based on; it is best only if all the transmission mechanisms are fully understood. This is a big *if,* as failing to include one or two relevant transmission mechanisms for monetary policy in the structural model might result in a serious underestimate of the impact of M on Y.

Monetarists worry that many Keynesian structural models may ignore the transmission mechanisms for monetary policy that are most important. For example, if the most important monetary transmission mechanisms involve consumer spending rather than investment spending, the Keynesian structural model (such as the $M \rightarrow i \rightarrow I \rightarrow Y$ one we used earlier), which focuses on investment spending for its monetary transmission mechanism, may underestimate the importance of money to economic activity. In other words, monetarists reject the interpretation of evidence from many Keynesian structural models because they believe that the channels of monetary influence are too narrowly defined. In a sense, they accuse Keynesians of wearing blinders that prevent them from recognizing the full importance of monetary policy.

Advantages and Disadvantages of Reduced-Form Evidence

The main advantage of reduced-form evidence over structural model evidence is that no restrictions are imposed on the way monetary policy affects the economy. If we are not sure that we know what all the monetary transmission mechanisms are, we may be more likely to spot the full effect of *M* on *Y* by looking at whether movements in *Y* correlate highly with movements in *M*. Monetarists favor reduced-form evidence because they believe that the particular channels through which changes in the money supply affect *Y* are diverse and continually changing. They contend that it may be too difficult to identify all the transmission mechanisms of monetary policy.

The most notable objection to reduced-form evidence is that it may misleadingly suggest that changes in *M* cause changes in *Y* when that is not the case. A basic principle applicable to all scientific disciplines, including economics, states that ***correlation does not necessarily imply causation.*** The fact that the movement of one variable is linked to another doesn't necessarily mean that one variable *causes* the other.

Suppose that you notice that wherever criminal activity abounds, more police patrol the street. Should you conclude that police patrols cause criminal activity and recommend that pulling police off the street would lower the crime rate? The answer is clearly no, because police patrols do not cause criminal activity; criminal activity causes police patrols. This situation is called **reverse causation** and can lead to misleading conclusions when interpreting correlations (see Box 1).

The reverse causation problem may be present when examining the link between money and aggregate output or spending. Our discussion of the conduct of monetary policy in Chapter 21 suggested that when the Federal Reserve has an interest rate or a free reserves target, higher output may lead to a higher money supply. If most of the correlation between *M* and *Y* occurs because of the Fed's interest-rate target, then controlling the money supply will not help control

Box 1

THE PERILS OF REVERSE CAUSATION: SHOULD YOU BECOME A MODERATE DRINKER?

An often cited medical statistic is that moderate drinkers of alcohol have substantially less heart disease and live longer than teetotalers. If you don't currently drink, does this mean that you should start having a glass of whiskey with dinner every night?

The answer is not as clear-cut as the correlation between moderate drinking and a lower risk of heart disease might suggest. Recent research has found that men who were told by their doctors that they had heart disease were more likely to quit drinking than men who were free of heart disease. Thus it might be that heart disease causes less drinking rather than that drinking causes less heart disease.* The possibility of reverse causation indicates that claims that moderate drinking is beneficial to your health might be overstated.

*A. G. Shaper, "Editorial: Alcohol, the Heart, and Health," *American Journal of Public Health* 83 (1993): 799–800.

Box 2

THE PERILS OF IGNORING AN OUTSIDE DRIVING FACTOR: HOW TO LOSE A PRESIDENTIAL ELECTION

The political adviser to a presidential candidate discovers a little town in New Hampshire whose vote for president always exactly matches the national vote; that is, in every election, there has been a perfect correlation between the town's vote and the national vote. The political adviser thus tells the candidate that election will be assured if all the candidate's campaign funds are spent on this one town.

Should the presidential candidate promote or fire this adviser? Why?

aggregate output because it is actually *Y* that is causing *M* rather than the other way around.

Another facet of the correlation-causation question is that an outside factor, yet unknown, could be the driving force behind two variables that move together. Coffee drinking might be associated with heart disease not because coffee drinking causes heart attacks but because coffee drinkers tend to be people who are under a lot of stress and the stress causes heart attacks. Getting people to stop drinking coffee, then, would not lower the incidence of heart disease. Similarly, if there is an unknown outside factor that causes *M* and *Y* to move together, controlling *M* will not improve control of *Y*. (The perils of ignoring an outside driving factor are illustrated in Box 2.)

Conclusions

No clear-cut case can be made that reduced-form evidence is preferable to structural model evidence or vice versa. The structural model approach, used primarily by Keynesians, provides an understanding of how the economy works. If the structure is correct, it predicts the effect of monetary policy more accurately, allows predictions of the effect of monetary policy when institutions change, and provides more confidence in the direction of causation between *M* and *Y*. If the structure of the model is not correctly specified because it leaves out important transmission mechanisms of monetary policy, it could be very misleading.

The reduced-form approach, used primarily by monetarists, does not restrict the way monetary policy affects the economy and may be more likely to spot the full effect of *M* on *Y*. However, reduced-form evidence cannot rule out the possibility of reverse causation, whereby changes in output cause changes in money, or that an outside factor drives changes in both output and money. A high correlation of money and output might then be misleading because controlling the money supply would not help control the level of output.

EARLY KEYNESIAN EVIDENCE ON THE IMPORTANCE OF MONEY

Although Keynes proposed his framework for analyzing aggregate economic activity in 1936, his views reached their peak of popularity among economists in the 1950s and early 1960s, when the majority of economists had accepted his framework. Although Keynesians currently believe that money has important effects on economic activity, the early Keynesians of the 1950s and early 1960s characteristically held the view that *monetary policy does not matter at all* to movements in aggregate output and hence to the business cycle.

Their belief in the ineffectiveness of monetary policy stemmed from three pieces of structural model evidence:

1. During the Great Depression, interest rates on U.S. Treasury securities fell to extremely low levels; the three-month Treasury bill rate, for example, declined to below 1%. Early Keynesians viewed monetary policy as affecting aggregate demand solely through its effect on nominal interest rates, which in turn affect investment spending; they believed that low interest rates during the depression indicated that monetary policy was easy because it encouraged investment spending and so could not have played a contractionary role during this period. Since monetary policy was not capable of explaining why the worst economic contraction in U.S. history had taken place, they concluded that changes in the money supply have no effect on aggregate output—in other words, money doesn't matter.

2. Early empirical studies found no linkage between movements in nominal interest rates and investment spending. Because early Keynesians saw this link as the channel through which changes in the money supply affect aggregate demand, finding that the link was weak also led them to the conclusion that changes in the money supply have no effect on aggregate output.

3. Surveys of businesspeople revealed that their decisions on how much to invest in new physical capital were not influenced by market interest rates. This evidence further confirmed that the link between interest rates and investment spending was weak, strengthening the conclusion that money doesn't matter.

The result of this interpretation of the evidence was that most economists paid only scant attention to monetary policy until the mid-1960s.

STUDY GUIDE

Before reading about the objections that were raised against early Keynesian interpretations of the evidence, use the ideas on the disadvantages of structural model evidence to see if you can come up with some objections yourself. This will help you learn to apply the principles of evaluating evidence discussed earlier.

OBJECTIONS TO EARLY KEYNESIAN EVIDENCE

While Keynesian economics was reaching its ascendancy in the 1950s and 1960s, a small group of economists at the University of Chicago, led by Milton Friedman, adopted what was then an unfashionable view—that money *does* matter to aggregate demand. Friedman and his disciples, who later became known as *monetarists,* objected to the early Keynesian interpretation of the evidence on the grounds that the structural model used by the early Keynesians was severely flawed. Because structural model evidence is only as good as the structural model it is based on, the monetarist critique of this evidence needs to be taken seriously.

In 1963, Friedman and Anna Schwartz published their classic monetary history of the United States,[1] which showed that contrary to the early Keynesian beliefs, monetary policy during the Great Depression was not easy; indeed, it had never been more contractionary. Friedman and Schwartz documented the massive bank failures of this period and the resulting decline in the money supply—the largest ever experienced in the United States (see Chapter 17). Hence monetary policy could explain the worst economic contraction in U.S. history, and the Great Depression could not be singled out as a period that demonstrates the ineffectiveness of monetary policy.

A Keynesian could still counter Friedman and Schwartz's argument that money was contractionary during the Great Depression by citing the low level of interest rates. But were these interest rates really so low? Referring to Figure 1 in Chapter 7, you will note that while interest rates on U.S. Treasury securities and high-grade corporate bonds were low during the Great Depression, interest rates on lower-grade bonds, such as Baa corporate bonds, rose to unprecedented high levels during the sharpest part of the contraction phase (1930–1933). By the standard of these lower-grade bonds, then, interest rates were high and monetary policy was tight.

There is a moral to this story. Although much aggregate economic analysis proceeds as though there is only *one* interest rate, we must always be aware that there are *many* interest rates, some of which may tell different stories. During normal times, most interest rates move in tandem, so lumping them all together and looking at one representative interest rate may not be too misleading. But that is not always so. Unusual periods (like the Great Depression) do occur, when interest rates on different securities begin to diverge. This is exactly the kind of situation in which a structural model (like the early Keynesians') that

---

[1]Milton Friedman and Anna Jacobson Schwartz, *A Momentary History of the United States, 1867–1960* (Princeton, N.J.: Princeton University Press, 1963).

looks at only the interest rates on a low-risk security such as a U.S. Treasury bill or bond can be very misleading.

There is a second, potentially more important reason why the early Keynesian structural model's focus on nominal interest rates provides a misleading picture of the tightness of monetary policy during the Great Depression. In a period of deflation, when there is a declining price level, low *nominal* interest rates do not necessarily indicate that the cost of borrowing is low and that monetary policy is easy—in fact, the cost of borrowing could be quite high. If, for example, the public expects the price level to decline at a 10% rate, then even though nominal interest rates are at zero, the real cost of borrowing would be as high as 10%. [Recall from Chapter 4 that the real rate equals the nominal rate, 0, minus the expected rate of inflation, −10%, so the real rate equals $0 - (-10\%) = 10\%$.]

In Figure 1 you can see that this is exactly what happened during the Great Depression: Real interest rates on U.S. Treasury bills were far higher during the 1931–1933 contraction phase of the depression than was the case throughout the next 40 years.[2] As a result, movements of *real* interest rates indicate that contrary to the early Keynesians' beliefs, monetary policy was extremely tight during the Great Depression. Because an important role for monetary policy during this depressed period could no longer be ruled out, most economists were forced to rethink their position regarding whether money matters.

Monetarists also objected to the early Keynesian structural model's view that a weak link between nominal interest rates and investment spending indicates that investment spending is unaffected by monetary policy. A weak link between *nominal* interest rates and investment spending does not rule out a strong link between *real* interest rates and investment spending. As depicted in Figure 1, nominal interest rates are often a very misleading indicator of real interest rates—not only during the Great Depression but in later periods as well. Because real interest rates more accurately reflect the true cost of borrowing, they should be more relevant to investment decisions than nominal interest rates. Accordingly, the two pieces of early Keynesian evidence indicating that nominal interest rates have little effect on investment spending do not rule out a strong effect of changes in the money supply on investment spending and hence on aggregate demand.

Monetarists also assert that interest-rate effects on investment spending might be only one of many channels through which monetary policy affects aggregate demand. Monetary policy could then have a major impact on aggregate demand even if interest rate effects on investment spending are small, as was suggested by the early Keynesians.

---

[2] In the 1980s, real interest rates rose to exceedingly high levels, approaching those of the Great Depression period. Much current research is trying to explain this phenomenon, some of which points to monetary policy as the source of high real rates in the 1980s. For example, see Oliver J. Blanchard and Lawrence H. Summers, "Perspectives on High World Interest Rates," *Brookings Papers on Economic Activity* 2 (1984): 273–324; and John Huizinga and Frederic S. Mishkin, "Monetary Policy Regime Shifts and the Unusual Behavior of Real Interest Rates," *Carnegie-Rochester Conference Series on Public Policy* 24 (1986): 231–274.

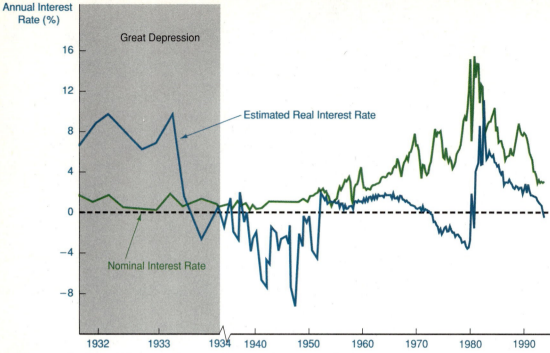

FIGURE 1   Real and Nominal Interest Rates on Three-Month Treasury Bills, 1931–1993
Source: Citibase databank.

STUDY GUIDE

As you read the monetarist evidence presented in the next section, again try to think of objections to the evidence. This time use the ideas on the disadvantages of reduced-form evidence.

EARLY MONETARIST EVIDENCE ON THE IMPORTANCE OF MONEY

In the early 1960s, Milton Friedman and his followers published a series of studies based on reduced-form evidence that promoted the case for a strong effect of money on economic activity. In general, reduced-form evidence can be broken down into three categories: *timing evidence,* which looks at whether the movements in one variable typically occur before another; *statistical evidence,* which performs formal statistical tests on the correlation of the movements of one variable with another; and *historical evidence,* which examines specific historical episodes to see whether movements in one variable appear to cause another.

Now let's look at the monetarist evidence on the importance of money that falls into each of these three categories.

Timing Evidence

Monetarist timing evidence looks at how the rate of money supply growth moves relative to the business cycle. The evidence on this relationship was first presented by Friedman and Schwartz in their famous paper "Money and Business Cycles," published in 1963.[3] nearly a century, the rate at which the money supply is growing always decreases before output does. On average, the peak in the rate of money growth occurs 16 months before the peak in the level of output. However, this lead time is variable, ranging from a few months to more than two years. The conclusion that these authors reached on the basis of this evidence is that money growth causes business cycle fluctuations, but its effect on the business cycle operates with "long and variable lags."

Timing evidence is based on the philosophical principle first stated in Latin as *post hoc, ergo propter hoc,* which means that if one event occurs after another, the second event must have been caused by the first. This principle is valid only if we know that the first event is an *exogenous* event, an event occurring as a result of an independent action that could not possibly be caused by the event following it or by some outside factor that might affect both events. If the first event is exogenous, when the second event follows the first, we can be more confident that the first event is causing the second.

An example of an exogenous event is a controlled experiment. A chemist mixes two chemicals; suddenly his lab blows up and he with it. We can be absolutely sure that the cause of his demise was the act of mixing the two chemicals together. The principle of *post hoc, ergo propter hoc* is extremely useful in scientific experimentation.

Unfortunately, economics does not enjoy the precision of the hard sciences like physics or chemistry. Often we cannot be sure that an economic event, such as a decline in the rate of money growth, is an exogenous event—it could have been caused, itself, by an outside factor, or by the event it is supposedly causing. When another event (such as a decline in output) typically follows the first event (a decline in money growth), we cannot be sure that one caused the other. Timing evidence is clearly of a reduced-form nature because it looks directly at the relationship of the movements of two variables. Money growth could lead output, or both could be driven by an outside factor.

Because timing evidence is of a reduced-form nature, there is also the possibility of reverse causation, in which output growth causes money growth. How can this reverse causation occur while money growth still leads output? There

---

[3]Milton Friedman and Anna Jacobson Schwartz, "Money and Business Cycles," *Review of Economics and Statistics* 45, Suppl. (1963): 32–64.

are several ways in which this can happen, but we will deal with just one example.[4]

Suppose that you are in a hypothetical economy with a very regular business cycle movement, plotted in panel (a) of Figure 2, that is four years long (four years from peak to peak). Let's assume that in our hypothetical economy, there is reverse causation from output to the money supply, so movements in the money supply and output are perfectly correlated; that is, the money supply M and output Y move upward and downward at the same time. The result is that the peaks and troughs of the M and Y series in panels (a) and (b) occur at exactly the same time; therefore, no lead or lag relationship exists between them.

Now let's construct the rate of money supply growth from the money supply series in panel (b). This is done in panel (c). What is the rate of growth of the money supply at its peaks in years 1 and 5? At these points, it is not growing at all; the rate of growth is zero. Similarly, at the trough in year 3, the growth rate is zero. When the money supply is declining from its peak in year 1 to its trough in year 3, it has a negative growth rate, and its decline is fastest sometime between years 1 and 3 (year 2). Translating to panel (c), the rate of money growth is below zero from years 1 to 3, with its most negative value reached at year 2. By similar reasoning, you can see that the growth rate of money is positive in years 0 to 1 and 3 to 5, with the highest values reached in years 0 and 4. When we connect all these points together, we get the money growth series in panel (c), in which the peaks are at years 0 and 4, with a trough in year 2.

Now let's look at the relationship of the money growth series of panel (c) with the level of output in panel (a). As you can see, the money growth series consistently has its peaks and troughs exactly one year before the peaks and troughs of the output series. We conclude that in our hypothetical economy, the rate of money growth always decreases one year before output does. This evidence does not, however, imply that money growth *drives* output. In fact, by assumption, we know that this economy is one in which causation actually runs from output to the level of money supply, and there is no lead or lag relationship between the two. Only by our judicious choice of using the *growth rate* of the money supply rather than its *level* have we found a leading relationship.

This example shows how easy it is to misinterpret timing relationships. Furthermore, by searching for what we hope to find, we might focus on a variable, such as a growth rate, rather than a level, which suggests a misleading relationship. Timing evidence can be a dangerous tool for deciding on causation.

Stated even more forcefully, "one person's lead is another person's lag." For example, you could just as easily interpret the relationship of money growth and output in Figure 2 to say that the money growth rate lags output by three years—after all, the peaks in the money growth series occur three years after the

---

[4]A famous article by James Tobin, "Money and Income: Post Hoc, Ergo Propter Hoc," *Quarterly Journal of Economics* 84 (1970): 301–317, describes an economic system in which changes in aggregate output cause changes in the growth rate of money but changes in the growth rate of money have no effect on output. Tobin shows that such a system with reverse causation could yield timing evidence similar to that found by Friedman and Schwartz.

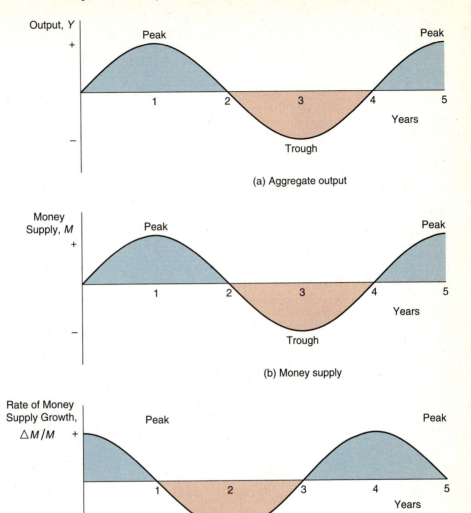

**FIGURE 2
Hypothetical
Example in Which
Money Growth
Leads Output**
Although neither
M nor *Y* leads
each other (that
is, their peaks and
troughs coincide),
$\Delta M/M$ has its
peaks and troughs
one year ahead of
M and *Y*, thus
leading both se-
ries. (Note that *M*
and *Y* in the pan-
els are drawn as
movements
around a positive
average value; a
plus sign indicates
a value above the
average, and a
minus sign indi-
cates a value
below the aver-
age, not a nega-
tive value.)

peaks in the output series. In short, you could say that output leads money growth.

We have seen that timing evidence is extremely hard to interpret. Unless we can be sure that changes in the leading variable are exogenous events, we cannot be sure that the leading variable is actually causing the following variable. And it is all too easy to find what we seek when looking for timing evidence. Perhaps the best way of describing this danger is to say that "timing evidence may be in the eyes of the beholder."

Statistical Evidence

Monetarist statistical evidence examines the correlations between money and aggregate output or aggregate spending by performing formal statistical tests. Again in 1963 (obviously a vintage year for the monetarists), Milton Friedman and David Meiselman published a paper that proposed the following test of a monetarist model against a Keynesian model.[5] In the Keynesian framework, investment and government spending are the sources of fluctuations in aggregate demand, so Friedman and Meiselman constructed a "Keynesian" autonomous expenditure variable A equal to investment spending plus government spending. They characterized the Keynesian model as saying that A should be highly correlated with aggregate spending Y, while the money supply M should not. In the monetarist model, the money supply is the source of fluctuations in aggregate spending, and M should be highly correlated with Y, while A should not.

A logical way to find out which model is better would be to see which is more highly correlated with Y: M or A. When Friedman and Meiselman conducted this test for many different periods of U.S. data, they discovered that *the monetarist model wins!*[6] They concluded that monetarist analysis gives a better description than Keynesian analysis of how aggregate spending is determined.

Several objections were raised against the Friedman-Meiselman evidence.

1. The standard criticisms of this reduced-form evidence are the ones we have already discussed: Reverse causation could occur, or an outside factor might drive both series.

2. The test may not be fair because the Keynesian model is characterized too simplistically. Keynesian structural models commonly include hundreds of equations. The one-equation Keynesian model that Friedman-Meiselman tested may not adequately capture the effects of autonomous expenditure. Furthermore, Keynesian models usually include the effects of other variables. By ignoring them, the effect of monetary policy might be overestimated and the effect of autonomous expenditure underestimated.

3. The Friedman-Meiselman measure of autonomous expenditure A might be constructed poorly, preventing the Keynesian model from performing well. For example, orders for military hardware affect aggregate demand before they appear as spending in the autonomous expenditure variable that Friedman and Meiselman used. A more careful construction of the autonomous expenditure variable should take account of the placing of orders for military hardware. When the autonomous expenditure variable was constructed more carefully by

---

[5]Milton Friedman and David Meiselman, "The Relative Stability of Monetary Velocity and the Investment Multiplier," in *Stabilization Policies*, ed. Commission on Money and Credit (Englewood Cliffs, N.J.: Prentice Hall, 1963), pp. 165–268.

[6]Friedman and Meiselman did not actually run their tests using the Y variable because they felt that this gave an unfair advantage to the Keynesian model in that A is included in Y. Instead, they subtracted A from Y and tested for the correlation of $Y - A$ with M or A.

critics of the Friedman-Meiselman study, they found that the results were reversed: The Keynesian model won.[7] A more recent postmortem on the appropriateness of various ways of determining autonomous expenditure does not give a clear-cut victory to either the Keynesian or the monetarist model.[8]

Historical Evidence

The monetarist historical evidence, found in Friedman and Schwartz's *Monetary History,* has been very influential in gaining support for the monetarist position. We have already seen that the book was extremely important as a criticism of early Keynesian thinking, showing as it did that the Great Depression was not a period of easy monetary policy and that the depression could be attributed to the sharp decline in the money supply from 1930 to 1933 resulting from bank panics. In addition, the book documents in great detail that the growth rate of money leads business cycles because it declines before every recession. This timing evidence is, of course, subject to all the criticisms raised earlier.

The historical evidence, however, contains one feature that makes it different from other monetarist evidence we have discussed so far. Several episodes occur in which changes in the money supply appear to be exogenous events. These episodes are almost like controlled experiments, so the *post hoc, ergo propter hoc* principle is far more likely to be valid: If the decline in the growth rate of the money supply is soon followed by a decline in output in these episodes, much stronger evidence is presented that money growth is the driving force behind the business cycle.

One of the best examples of such an episode is the increase in reserve requirements in 1936–1937 (discussed in Chapter 21) that led to a sharp decline in the money supply and in its rate of growth. The increase in reserve requirements was implemented because the Federal Reserve wanted to improve its control of monetary policy; it was not implemented in response to economic conditions. We can thus rule out reverse causation from output to the money supply. Also, it is hard to think of an outside factor that could have driven the Fed to increase reserve requirements and that could also have directly affected output. Therefore, the decline in the money supply in this episode can probably be classified as an exogenous event with the characteristics of a controlled experiment. Soon after this experiment, the very severe recession of 1937–1938 occurred. We can conclude with confidence that in this episode, the change in the money supply due to the Fed's increase in reserve requirements was indeed the source of the business cycle contraction that followed.

---

[7]See, for example, Albert Ando and Franco Modigliani, "The Relative Stability of Monetary Velocity and the Investment Multiplier," *American Economic Review* 55 (1965): 693–728.

[8]See William Poole and Edith Kornblith, "The Friedman-Meiselman CMC Paper: New Evidence on an Old Controversy," *American Economic Review* 63 (1973): 908–917.

A Monetary History also documents other historical episodes, such as the bank panic of 1907 and other years in which the decline in money growth again appears to have been an exogenous event. The fact that recessions have frequently followed apparently exogenous declines in money growth is very strong evidence that changes in the growth rate of the money supply do have an impact on aggregate output.[9]

OVERVIEW OF THE MONETARIST EVIDENCE

Where does this discussion of the monetarist evidence leave us? We have seen that because of reverse causation and outside-factor possibilities, there are some serious doubts about the conclusions that can be drawn from timing and statistical evidence alone. However, some of the historical evidence in which exogenous declines in money growth are followed by business cycle contractions does provide stronger support for the monetarist position. When historical evidence is combined with timing and statistical evidence, the conclusion that money does matter seems warranted.

As you can imagine, the economics profession was quite shaken by the appearance of the monetarist evidence, as up to that time the majority of the profession believed that money does not matter at all. Monetarists had demonstrated that this early Keynesian position was probably wrong, and it won them a lot of converts. Recognizing the fallacy of the position that money does not matter does not necessarily mean that we must accept the position that money is *all* that matters. Many Keynesian economists shifted their views toward the monetarist position, but not all the way. Instead, they adopted an intermediate position compatible with the Keynesian aggregate supply and demand analysis described in Chapter 26: They believed that money was extremely important but that fiscal policy, net exports, and "animal spirits" also contributed to fluctuations in aggregate demand.

Economic research went in two directions after the successful monetarist attack against the early Keynesian position. One direction was to use more sophisticated monetarist reduced-form models to test for the importance of money to economic activity.[10] The second direction was to pursue a structural model approach and search for other channels of monetary influence on aggregate demand than merely interest-rate effects on investment.

---

[9] For a more recent use of the historical approach to examine the importance of money to the economy, see Christina Romer and David Romer, "Does Monetary Policy Matter? A New Test in the Spirit of Friedman and Schwartz," *NBER Macroeconomics Annual, 1989,* pp. 121–170.

[10] The most prominent example of more sophisticated reduced-form research is the so-called St. Louis model, which was developed at the Federal Reserve Bank of St. Louis in the late 1960s and early 1970s. It provided support for the monetarist position but is subject to the same criticisms of reduced-form evidence outlined in the text. The St. Louis model was first outlined in Leonall Andersen and Jerry Jordan, "Monetary and Fiscal Actions: A Test of Their Relative Importance in Economic Stabilization," *Federal Reserve Bank of St. Louis Review,* November 1968, pp. 11–23.

THE SEARCH FOR NEW MONETARY TRANSMISSION MECHANISMS

The traditional Keynesian view of the monetary transmission mechanism can be characterized as follows:

$$M\uparrow \to i\downarrow \to I\uparrow \to Y\uparrow$$

However, as we have seen, the effect of the interest rate i on investment spending I is usually fairly small. We have mentioned that in response to monetarist evidence that money matters, many economists began to search for new channels of monetary influence on economic activity. These transmission mechanisms fall into three categories, determined by whether they operate through investment spending, consumer expenditure, or international trade. (All these mechanisms are summarized in the schematic diagram in Figure 3.)

Investment Spending

Because Keynes emphasized the role of investment in business cycle fluctuations, the earliest work on new monetary transmission mechanisms first focused on investment spending.

Tobin's *q* Theory Economists have suggested that monetary policy can affect investment spending through its effect on the prices of common stock. James Tobin developed a theory of the link between stock prices and investment spending, referred to as *Tobin's q theory*. Tobin defines q as the market value of firms divided by the replacement cost of capital. If q is high, the market price of firms is high relative to the replacement cost of capital, and new plant and equipment capital is cheap relative to the market value of firms. Companies can then issue stock and get a high price for it relative to the cost of the facilities and equipment they are buying. Investment spending will rise because firms can buy a lot of new investment goods with only a small issue of stock.

Conversely, when q is low, firms will not purchase new investment goods because the market value of firms is low relative to the cost of capital. If companies want to acquire capital when q is low, they can buy another firm cheaply and acquire old capital instead. Investment spending, the purchase of new investment goods, will then be very low. Tobin's q theory gives a good explanation for the extremely low rate of investment spending during the Great Depression. In that period, stock prices collapsed and by 1933 were worth only one-tenth of their value in late 1929; q fell to unprecedented low levels.

The crux of this discussion is that a link exists between Tobin's q and investment spending. But how might monetary policy affect stock prices? Quite simply, when money supply increases, the public finds that it has more money than it wants and so gets rid of it through spending. One place the public spends is in the stock market, increasing the demand for stocks and consequently raising

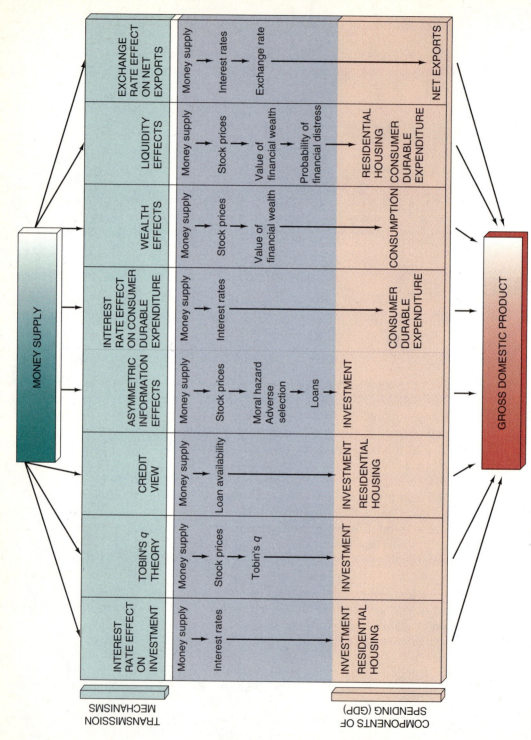

FIGURE 3 The Link Between Money and GDP: Monetary Transmission Mechanisms

their prices.[11] Combining this with the fact that higher stock prices (P_s) will lead to a higher q and thus higher investment spending I leads to the following transmission mechanism of monetary policy:[12]

$$M\uparrow \rightarrow P_s\uparrow \rightarrow q\uparrow \rightarrow I\uparrow \rightarrow Y\uparrow$$

The Credit View The credit view of the monetary transmission mechanism was described in Chapter 26. An open market purchase (which incidentally also raises the monetary base and the money supply) increases the quantity of bank loans available. If bank loans have a special role in the economy because certain borrowers cannot borrow unless they do so from banks, then this increase in loans will cause investment (and possibly consumer) spending to rise. Schematically, the monetary policy effect is

$$\text{Open market purchase} \rightarrow M\uparrow \rightarrow \text{loans}\uparrow \rightarrow I\uparrow \rightarrow Y\uparrow$$

An important implication of the credit view is that monetary policy will have a greater effect on smaller firms that are more dependent on bank loans than it will on large firms that can access the credit markets directly through stock and bond markets without going through banks. This result is exactly what researchers have found in the data.[13]

Asymmetric Information Effects A monetary transmission mechanism that is closely related to the credit view stems from asymmetric information effects. (The credit view requires that bank loans are special, and this will be the case if banks have special expertise in solving asymmetric information problems, as was indicated in Chapter 11.) In our discussion of the impact of asymmetric information on financial markets in Chapter 9, we saw that the higher the net worth of firms, the less severe the adverse selection and moral hazard problems. Higher net worth

---

[11]A somewhat more Keynesian story with the same outcome is that the increase in the money supply lowers interest rates on bonds so that the yields on alternatives to stocks fall. This makes stocks more attractive relative to bonds, so demand for them increases, raises their price, and thereby lowers their yield.

[12]An alternative way of looking at the link between stock prices and investment spending is that higher stock prices lower the yield on stocks and reduce the cost of financing investment spending through issuing equity. This way of looking at the link between stock prices and investment spending is formally equivalent to Tobin's q approach; see Barry Bosworth, "The Stock Market and the Economy," *Brookings Papers on Economic Activity* 2 (1975): 257–290.

[13]For example, see Mark Gertler and Simon Gilchrist, "Monetary Policy, Business Cycles, and the Behavior of Small Manufacturing Firms," *Quarterly Journal of Economics*, May 1994, pp. 309–340, and references in Ben Bernanke, "Credit in the Macroeconomy," *Federal Reserve Bank of New York Quarterly Review*, Spring 1993, pp. 50–70.

means that lenders in effect have more collateral for their loans, and so losses from adverse selection are reduced. A rise in net worth, which reduces the adverse selection problem, thus encourages increased lending to finance investment spending. Higher net worth of firms also reduces the moral hazard problem because it means that owners have a higher equity stake in their firms. With more of an equity stake, owners have less incentive to engage in risky investment projects or to spend company funds on items that benefit them personally but do not add to profits. Because borrowers' taking on less risky investment projects and spending less for personal benefits make it more likely that lenders will be paid back, an increase in firms' net worth leads to an increase in lending and hence in investment spending.

A rise in stock prices raises the net worth of firms and so leads to higher investment spending because of the reduction in adverse selection and moral hazard problems. Because, as we have noted, monetary policy affects stock prices, our asymmetric information analysis provides the following additional monetary transmission mechanism:

$$M\uparrow \to P_s\uparrow \to \text{net worth } \uparrow \to, \text{adverse selection } \downarrow, \text{moral hazard } \downarrow \to \text{loans } \uparrow$$
$$\to I\uparrow \to Y\uparrow$$

Consumer Expenditure

Monetarist reduced-form evidence also suggests that there might be a more direct link between monetary policy and consumer expenditure. The earliest work along these lines focused on possible interest-rate effects on one component of consumer spending, **consumer durable expenditure,** the spending by consumers on durable items such as automobiles and refrigerators.

Interest-Rate Effects on Consumer Durable Expenditure   Because consumer spending on durable items such as automobiles is often financed by borrowing, early Keynesian structural model builders looked for some effect of interest rates on consumer durable expenditure. They reasoned that lower interest rates, which lowered the cost of financing these purchases, would encourage consumers to increase their consumer durable expenditure. The resulting channel of monetary influence on aggregate demand is as follows:

$$M\uparrow \to i\downarrow \to \text{consumer durable expenditure } \uparrow \to Y\uparrow$$

However, the size of this effect was found to be small. Some other channel of monetary influence on consumer spending was needed to explain why monetary policy might affect consumer expenditure.

Wealth Effects   In their search for new monetary transmission mechanisms, researchers looked at how the balance sheet of consumers might affect their spending decisions. Franco Modigliani was the first to take this tack, using his famous life cycle hypothesis of consumption. **Consumption** is spending by consumers on nondurable goods and services.[14] It differs from consumer expenditure in that it does not include spending on consumer durables. The basic premise of Modigliani's theory is that consumers smooth out their consumption over time. Therefore, what determines consumption spending is the lifetime resources of consumers, not just today's income. An important component of consumers' lifetime resources is financial wealth, a major component of which is common stocks. When stock prices rise, the value of financial wealth increases, thereby increasing the lifetime resources of consumers, and consumption should rise. Considering that, as we have seen, expansionary monetary policy can lead to a rise in stock prices, we now have another monetary transmission mechanism:

$$M\uparrow \rightarrow P_s\uparrow \rightarrow \text{wealth} \uparrow \rightarrow \text{lifetime resources} \uparrow \rightarrow \text{consumption} \uparrow \rightarrow Y\uparrow$$

Modigliani's research found this to be an extremely powerful mechanism that adds substantially to the potency of monetary policy.[15]

Liquidity Effects The stock market also affects consumer durable expenditure. The argument for this effect concentrates on the illiquid nature of consumer durables such as automobiles and household appliances. If all of a sudden you needed cash and tried to sell your consumer durables to raise it, you would expect to take a big loss because you could not get their full value in a distress sale. In contrast, if you held financial assets (such as money in the bank, stocks, or bonds), you could easily sell them quickly for their full market value and raise the cash. Now ask yourself this question: If you expected to find yourself in financial distress, would you rather be holding illiquid consumer durables or more liquid financial assets? Naturally, you would rather hold the financial assets. Therefore, if the possibility of financial distress increases, consumers will spend less on consumer durables; if the possibility of financial distress becomes less likely, consumers will spend more on consumer durables.

A consumer's balance sheet should be an important influence on his or her estimate of the likelihood of suffering financial distress. Specifically, when consumers have a lot of financial assets relative to their debts, their estimate of the probability of financial distress is low, and they will be more willing to purchase consumer durables. When stock prices rise, the value of financial assets rises as well; consumer durable expenditure will also increase because consumers have a more secure financial position and a lower estimate of the likelihood of suffering financial distress. We now have another powerful transmission mechanism for monetary policy because of the link between money and stock prices:[16]

---

[14]Consumption also includes another small component, the services that a consumer receives from the ownership of housing and consumer durables.

[15]See Franco Modigliani, "Monetary Policy and Consumption," in *Consumer Spending and Money Policy: The Linkages* (Federal Reserve Bank of Boston, 1971), pp. 9–84.

[16]See Frederic S. Mishkin, "What Depressed the Consumer? The Household Balance Sheet and the 1973–1975 Recession," *Brookings Papers on Economic Activity* 1 (1977): 123–164.

Box 3

CONSUMERS' BALANCE SHEETS AND THE GREAT DEPRESSION

The years between 1929 and 1933 witnessed the worst deterioration in consumers' balance sheets ever seen in the United States. The stock market crash in 1929, which caused a slump that lasted until 1933, reduced the value of consumers' wealth by $371 billion (in 1987 dollars), and as expected, consumption dropped sharply (by over $80 billion). Because of the decline in the price level in that period, the level of real debt consumers owed also increased sharply (by over 20%). Consequently, the value of financial assets relative to the amount of debt declined sharply, increasing the likelihood of financial distress. Not surprisingly, spending on consumer durables and housing fell precipitously: From 1929 to 1933, consumer durable expenditure declined by over 50%, while expenditure on housing declined by 80%.*

*For further discussion of the effect of consumers' balance sheets on spending during the Great Depression, see Frederic S. Mishkin, "The Household Balance Sheet and the Great Depression," *Journal of Economic History* 38 (1978): 918–937.

$$M\uparrow \rightarrow P_s\uparrow \rightarrow \text{financial assets} \uparrow \rightarrow \text{likelihood of financial distress} \downarrow$$
$$\rightarrow \text{consumer durable expenditure} \uparrow \rightarrow Y\uparrow$$

The liquidity argument can also be applied to the demand for housing because, like consumer durables, homes are very illiquid. A rise in stock prices, which improves the health of consumers' balance sheets, will lower the likelihood of financial distress and increase the willingness of consumers to buy new houses. So another channel of monetary influence is

$$M\uparrow \rightarrow P_s\uparrow \rightarrow \text{financial assets} \uparrow \rightarrow \text{likelihood of financial distress} \downarrow$$
$$\rightarrow \text{spending on new housing} \uparrow \rightarrow Y\uparrow$$

The last three monetary transmission mechanisms suggest that monetary policy effects on consumers' balance sheets can have large effects on aggregate demand. One period where these effects might have been extremely important was during the Great Depression (see Box 3).

International Trade

With the growing internationalization of the economy and the advent of flexible exchange rates, an exchange rate effect on net exports has become an important monetary transmission mechanism.

As was discussed in more detail in Chapter 8, when domestic interest rates fall (with inflation unchanged), domestic deposits become less attractive relative to deposits denominated in foreign currencies. The result is a fall in the value of dollar deposits relative to other currency deposits, that is, a fall in the exchange rate (denoted by $E\downarrow$). The lower value of the domestic currency makes domestic goods cheaper than foreign goods, thereby causing a rise in net exports and hence in aggregate output. The monetary transmission mechanism operating through international trade is thus

$$M\uparrow \rightarrow i\downarrow \rightarrow E\downarrow \rightarrow NX\uparrow \rightarrow Y\uparrow$$

OVERVIEW OF THE MONETARIST/KEYNESIAN DEBATE ON MONEY AND ECONOMIC ACTIVITY

The monetarist reduced-form evidence presented a major challenge to the Keynesian view that money does not matter. This led to a more open-minded search for new monetary transmission mechanisms. Once these transmission mechanisms were incorporated into Keynesian structural models such as the one currently in use at the Federal Reserve Board, these models revealed a strong effect of money on economic activity. The result has been a convergence of the Keynesian and monetarist views on the importance of money to economic activity. Keynesians now generally agree that monetary policy is an extremely important source of business cycle fluctuations. However, proponents of a new theory of aggregate fluctuations called the *real business cycle theory* do not accept the monetarist reduced-form evidence that money is important to business cycle fluctuations because they believe there is reverse causation from the business cycle to money (see Box 4).

Although Keynesians now agree that money matters, they do not agree with the monetarist statement that money is *all* that matters. Their structural models still provide strong evidence that fiscal policy has powerful effects. Reduced-form evidence and structural model evidence, then, do not yield similar conclusions on the effectiveness of fiscal policy, and so the monetarist/Keynesian debate on the determinants of aggregate demand is not yet fully resolved.

SUMMARY

1. Monetarists tend to focus on reduced-form evidence and hold that changes in the money supply are important to economic activity. Keynesians, who focus on structural model evidence, tend to discount the role of money. No clear-cut case can be made that one type of evidence is better than the other: Both have advantages and disadvantages. The main advantage of structural model evidence is that it provides us with an understanding of how the economy works and gives us more confidence in the direction of causation between money and output. However, if the structure is not correctly specified because it ignores important monetary transmission mecha-

Box 4

REAL BUSINESS CYCLE THEORY AND THE DEBATE ON MONEY AND ECONOMIC ACTIVITY

New entrants to the debate on money and economic activity are advocates of the *real business cycle theory,* which states that real shocks to tastes and technology (rather than monetary shocks) are the driving forces behind business cycles. Proponents of this theory do not accept the monetarist view that money matters to business cycles because they believe that the correlation of output with money reflects reverse causation; that is, the business cycle drives money, rather than the other way around. An important piece of evidence they offer to support the reverse causation argument is that almost none of the correlation between money and output comes from the monetary base, which is controlled by the monetary authorities.* Instead, the money-output correlation stems from other sources of money supply movements that, as we saw in Chapters 16 and 17, are affected by the actions of banks, depositors, and borrowers from banks and are more likely to be influenced by the business cycle.

Although the real business cycle theory reserves no role for money in the business cycle, it does view money as an important determinant of inflation. So monetary policy still plays a crucial role in the economy.

*Robert King and Charles Plosser, "Money, Credit and Prices in a Real Business Cycle," *American Economic Review* 74 (1984): 363–380; Charles Plosser, "Understanding Real Business Cycles," *Journal of Economic Perspectives* 3, Summer (1989): pp. 51–78.

nisms, it could seriously underestimate the effectiveness of monetary policy. Reduced-form evidence has the advantage of not restricting the way monetary policy affects economic activity and so may be more likely to capture the full effects of monetary policy. However, reduced-form evidence cannot rule out the possibility of reverse causation or an outside driving factor, which could lead to misleading conclusions about the importance of money.

2. The early Keynesians believed that money does not matter because they found weak links between interest rates and investment and because low interest rates on Treasury securities convinced them that monetary policy was easy during the worst economic contraction in U.S. history, the Great Depression. Monetarists objected to this interpretation of the evidence on the grounds that the focus on nominal rather than real interest rates may have obscured any link be-

tween interest rates and investment, interest-rate effects on investment might be only one of many channels through which monetary policy affects aggregate demand, and by the standards of real interest rates and interest rates on lower-grade bonds, monetary policy was extremely contractionary during the Great Depression.

3. Early monetarist evidence falls into three categories: timing, statistical, and historical. Because of reverse causation and outside-factor possibilities, some serious doubts exist regarding conclusions that can be drawn from timing and statistical evidence alone. However, some of the historical evidence in which exogenous declines in money growth are followed by recessions provides stronger support for the monetarist position that money matters.

4. The monetarist evidence stimulated a search for new monetary transmission mechanisms, which include Tobin's *q* theory, the credit view, asym-

metric information effects, interest-rate effects on consumer durable expenditure, wealth effects, liquidity effects, and exchange rate effects on net exports.

5. As a result of empirical research, Keynesian and monetarist opinion has converged to the view that money does matter. However, Keynesians do not agree with the monetarist position that money is *all* that matters.

KEY TERMS

structural model evidence

reduced-form evidence

transmission mechanisms of monetary policy

structural model

reverse causation

consumer durable expenditure

consumption

QUESTIONS AND PROBLEMS

1. Suppose that a researcher is trying to determine whether jogging is good for a person's health. She examines this question in two ways. In method A, she looks to see whether joggers live longer than nonjoggers. In method B, she looks to see whether jogging reduces cholesterol in the bloodstream and lowers blood pressure; then she asks whether lower cholesterol and blood pressure prolong life. Which of these two methods will produce reduced-form evidence and which will produce structural model evidence?

2. If research indicates that joggers do not have lower cholesterol and blood pressure than nonjoggers, is it still possible that jogging is good for your health? Give a concrete example.

3. If research indicates that joggers live longer than nonjoggers, is it possible that jogging is not good for your health? Give a concrete example.

*4. Suppose that you plan to buy a car and want to know whether a General Motors car is more reliable than a Ford. One way to find out is to ask owners of both cars how often their cars go into the shop for repairs. Another way is to visit the factory producing the cars and see which one is built better. Which procedure will provide reduced-form evidence and which structural model evidence?

*5. If the GM car you plan to buy has a better repair record than a Ford, does this mean that the GM

car is necessarily more reliable? (GM car owners might, for example, change their oil more frequently than Ford owners.)

*6. Suppose that when you visit the Ford and GM car factories to examine how the cars are built, you only have time to see how well the engine is put together. If Ford engines are better built than GM engines, does that mean that the Ford will be more reliable than the GM car?

7. How might bank behavior (described in Chapter 17) lead to causation running from output to the money supply? What does this say about evidence that finds a strong correlation between money and output?

*8. What operating procedures of the Fed (described in Chapter 21) might explain how movements in output might cause movements in the money supply?

9. "In every business cycle in the past hundred years, the rate at which the money supply is growing always decreases before output does. Therefore, the money supply causes business cycle movements." Do you agree? What objections can you raise against this argument?

*10. How did the research strategies of Keynesian and monetarist economists differ after they were exposed to the earliest monetarist evidence?

11. In the 1973–1975 recession, the value of common stocks in real terms fell by nearly 50%. How might this decline in the stock market have

affected aggregate demand and thus contributed to the severity of this recession? Be specific about the mechanisms through which the stock market decline affected the economy.

*12. "The cost of financing investment is related only to interest rates; therefore, the only way that monetary policy can affect investment spending is through its effects on interest rates." Is this statement true, false, or uncertain? Explain.

13. Predict what will happen to stock prices if the money supply rises. Explain why you are making this prediction.

*14. Franco Modigliani found that the most important transmission mechanisms of monetary policy involve consumer expenditure. Describe how at least two of these mechanisms work.

15. "The monetarists have demonstrated that the early Keynesians were wrong in saying that money doesn't matter at all to economic activity. Therefore, we should accept the monetarist position that money is all that matters." Do you agree? Why or why not?

Chapter 28

MONEY AND INFLATION

PREVIEW   Since the early 1960s, when the inflation rate hovered between 1% and 2%, the economy has suffered from higher and more variable rates of inflation. By the late 1960s, the inflation rate climbed beyond 5%, and by 1974, it reached the double-digit level. After moderating somewhat during the 1975–1978 period, it skyrocketed above 10% in 1979 and 1980, only to slow to around 5% from 1982 to 1990 and to decline further to near 3% by 1993. Inflation, the condition of a continually rising price level, has become a major concern of politicians and the public, and how to control it frequently dominates the discussion of economic policy.

How do we prevent the inflationary fire from igniting and stop the roller coaster ride in the inflation rate of the past 30 years? Milton Friedman provides an answer in his famous proposition, "Inflation is always and everywhere a monetary phenomenon." He postulates that the source of all inflations is a high growth rate of the money supply: Simply by reducing the growth rate of the money supply to low levels, inflation can be prevented.

In this chapter we use aggregate demand and supply analysis (Chapter 26) to understand the role of monetary policy in creating inflation. You will find that as long as inflation is defined as the condition of a continually and rapidly rising price level, monetarists and Keynesians both agree with Friedman's proposition that inflation is a monetary phenomenon.

But what *causes* inflation? How does inflationary monetary policy come about? You will see that inflationary monetary policy is an offshoot of other government policies: the attempt to hit high employment targets or the running of large budget deficits. Understanding how these policies lead to inflation will provide us with some idea of how to prevent it at minimum cost in terms of unemployment and output loss.

MONEY AND INFLATION: THE EVIDENCE

The evidence for Friedman's statement is straightforward. ***Whenever a country's inflation rate is extremely high for a sustained period of time, its rate of money supply growth is extremely high.***

Consider the inflation experienced in Latin America from 1983 to 1993. A popular belief is that something structural in the Latin American economies (e. g., militant labor unions or unstable political systems) causes high inflation. In reality, the experience of inflation in Latin America is varied; some Latin American countries, such as Honduras, had average annual inflation rates below 10% during this period, while others, such as Argentina, Brazil, and Nicaragua, suffered from inflation rates exceeding 200%.

Box 1, which plots the inflation rates for Latin American countries against the growth rates of their money supply, reveals that the countries with very high inflation also have the highest rates of money growth. Evidence for the Latin American countries as well as countries elsewhere in the world (see Figure 3 in Chapter 1) seems to support the proposition that extremely high inflation is the result of a high rate of money growth. Keep in mind, however, that you are looking at reduced-form evidence, which focuses solely on the correlation of two variables: money growth and the inflation rate. As with all reduced-form evidence, reverse causation (inflation causing money supply growth) or an outside factor that drives both money growth and inflation could be involved.

How might you rule out these possibilities? First, you might look for historical episodes in which an increase in money growth appears to be an exogenous event; a high inflation rate for a sustained period following the increase in money growth would provide strong evidence that high money growth is the driving force behind the inflation. Luckily, such clear-cut historical episodes—hyperinflations (extremely rapid inflations with inflation rates exceeding 50% per month)—do exist. The most notorious example is the German hyperinflation of 1921–1923.

German Hyperinflation, 1921–1923

The German hyperinflation started in 1921 when the need to make reparations and reconstruct the economy after World War I caused government expenditures greatly to exceed revenues. The German government could have raised revenues to pay for this increased expenditure by raising taxes, but that solution was, as always, politically unpopular and would have taken much time to implement. The government could also have financed the expenditure by borrowing from the public, but the amount needed was far in excess of its capacity to borrow. There was only one route left: the printing press. The government could pay for its expenditures simply by printing more currency (increasing the money

A Global Perspective

Box 1

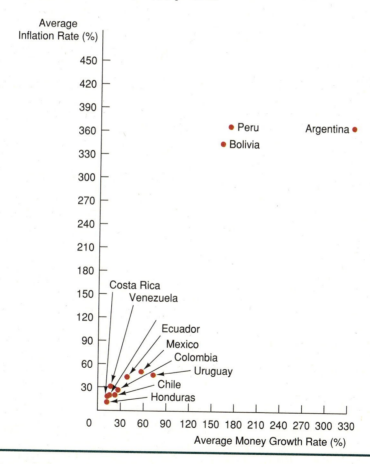

INFLATION AND MONEY GROWTH RATES IN LATIN AMERICA, 1983–1993

This graph plots for a group of Latin American countries the average inflation rate over the ten-year period 1983–1993 against the average money growth rate over the same period. It demonstrates that high inflation in these countries is generally associated with a high rate of money growth. (Countries such as Brazil and Nicaragua do not appear in the graph because their data were unavailable for the 1983–1993 period.)

supply) and using it to make payments to the individuals and companies that were providing it with goods and services. As shown in Figure 1, this is exactly what the German government did; in late 1921, the money supply began to increase rapidly, and so did the price level.

In 1923, the budgetary situation of the German government deteriorated even further. Early that year, the French invaded the Ruhr because Germany had failed to make its scheduled reparations payments. A general strike in the region then ensued to protest the French action, and the German government actively supported this "passive resistance" by making payments to striking workers. As a result, government expenditures climbed dramatically, and the government printed currency at an even faster rate to finance this spending. As displayed in Figure 1, the result of the explosion in the money supply was that the price level blasted off, leading to an inflation rate for 1923 that exceeded 1,000,000%.

The invasion of the Ruhr and the printing of currency to pay striking workers fit the characteristics of an exogenous event. Reverse causation (that the rise in the price level caused the French to invade the Ruhr) is highly implausible, and it is hard to imagine a third factor that could have been a driving force behind both inflation and the explosion in the money supply. Therefore, the Ger-

FIGURE 1

Money Supply and the Price Level in the German Hyperinflation

Source: Frank D. Graham, *Exchange, Prices and Production in Hyperinflation: Germany, 1920–25* (Princeton, N.J.: Princeton University Press, 1930), pp. 105–106.

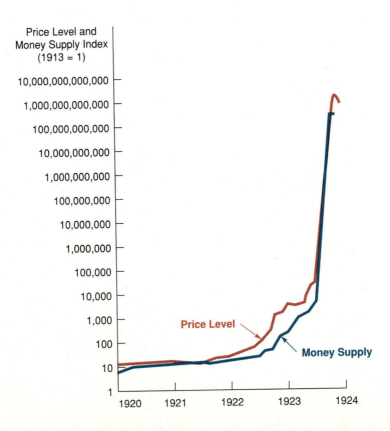

man hyperinflation qualifies as a "controlled experiment" that supports Friedman's proposition that inflation is a monetary phenomenon.

Recent Examples of Rapid Inflation

Although recent rapid inflations have not been as dramatic as the German hyperinflation, many countries in the 1980s and 1990s experienced rapid inflations in which the high rates of money growth can also be classified as exogenous events. For example, of all Latin American countries in the decade from 1983 to 1993, Argentina, Brazil, and Nicaragua had both the highest rates of money growth and the highest average inflation rates. The inflation problem in Brazil and Nicaragua still continues, but a monetary reform plan brought Argentina's inflation rate down to near the 10% level by 1993.

The explanation for the high rates of money growth in these countries is similar to the explanation for Germany during its hyperinflation: The unwillingness of Argentina, Brazil and Nicaragua to finance government expenditures by raising taxes led to large budget deficits (sometimes over 15% of GDP), which were financed by money creation.

That the inflation rate is high in all cases in which the high rate of money growth can be classified as an exogenous event (including episodes in Argentina, Brazil, Nicaragua, and Germany) is strong evidence that high money growth causes high inflation.

THE MEANING OF *INFLATION*

You may have noticed that all the empirical evidence on the relationship of money growth and inflation discussed so far looks only at cases in which the price level is continually rising at a rapid rate. It is this definition of *inflation* that Friedman and other economists use when they make statements such as "Inflation is always and everywhere a monetary phenomenon." This is not what your friendly newscaster means when reporting the monthly inflation rate on the nightly news. The newscaster is only telling you how much, in percentage terms, the price level has changed from the previous month. For example, when you hear that the monthly inflation rate is 1% (12% annual rate), this merely indicates that the price level has risen by 1% in that month. This could be a one-shot change, in which the high inflation rate is merely temporary, not sustained. Only if the inflation rate remains high for a substantial period of time (greater than 1% per month for several years) will economists say that inflation has been high.

Accordingly, Milton Friedman's proposition actually says that upward movements in the price level are a monetary phenomenon *only* if this is a sustained process. When *inflation* is defined as a continuing and rapidly rise in the price level, most economists, be they monetarist or Keynesian, will agree with Friedman's proposition that money alone is to blame.

05

INFLATION

Now that we understand what Friedman's proposition means, we can use the aggregate supply and demand analysis learned in Chapter 26 to show that large and persistent upward movements in the price level (high inflation) can occur only if there is a continually increasing money supply.

Monetarist View

First, let's look at the outcome of a continually increasing money supply using monetarist analysis (see Figure 2). Initially, the economy is at point 1, with output at the natural rate level and the price level at P_1 (the intersection of the aggregate demand curve AD_1 and the aggregate supply curve AS_1). If the money supply increases steadily over the course of the year, the aggregate demand curve shifts rightward to AD_2. At first, for a very brief time, the economy may move to point 1' and output may increase above the natural rate level to Y', but the resulting decline in unemployment below the natural rate level will cause wages to rise and the aggregate supply curve will quickly begin to shift leftward. It will stop shifting only when it reaches AS_2, at which time the economy has returned to the natural rate level of output on the long-run aggregate supply curve.[1] At the new equilibrium, point 2, the price level has increased from P_1 to P_2.

If the money supply increases the next year, the aggregate demand curve will shift to the right again to AD_3, and the aggregate supply curve will shift from AS_2 to AS_3; the economy will then move to point 2' and then 3, where the price level has risen to P_3. If the money supply continues to grow in subsequent years, the economy will continue to move to higher and higher price levels. As long as the money supply grows, this process will continue, and inflation will occur.

Do monetarists believe that a continually rising price level can be due to any source other than money supply growth? The answer is no. In monetarist analysis, the money supply is viewed as the sole source of shifts in the aggregate demand curve, so there is nothing else that can move the economy from point 1 to 2 to 3 and beyond. ***Monetarist analysis indicates that rapid inflation must be driven by high money supply growth.***

---

[1] In monetarist analysis, the aggregate supply curve may immediately shift in toward AS_2 because workers and firms may expect the increase in the money supply, so expected inflation will be higher. In this case, the movement to point 2 will be very rapid, and output need not rise above the natural rate level. (Further support for this scenario, from the theory of rational expectations, is discussed in Chapter 30.)

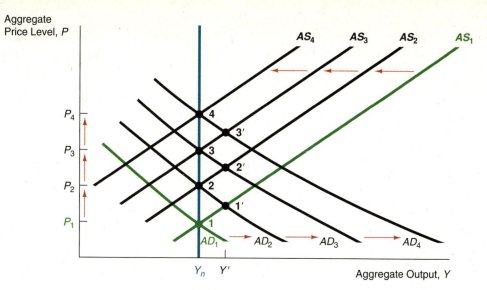

FIGURE 2 Response to a Continually Rising Money Supply
A continually rising money supply shifts the aggregate demand curve to the right from AD_1 to AD_2 to AD_3 to AD_4, while the supply curve shifts to the left from AS_1 to AS_2 to AS_3 to AS_4. The result is that the price level rises continually from P_1 to P_2 to P_3 to P_4.

Keynesian View

Keynesian analysis indicates that the continually increasing money supply will have the same effect on the aggregate demand and supply curves that we see in Figure 2: The aggregate demand curve will keep on shifting to the right and the aggregate supply curve will keep shifting to the left.[2] The conclusion is the same one that the monetarists reach: A rapidly growing money supply will cause the price level to rise continually at a high rate, thus generating inflation.

Could a factor other than money generate high inflation in the Keynesian analysis? The answer is no. This result probably surprises you, for in Chapter 26 you learned that Keynesian analysis allows other factors besides changes in the money supply (such as fiscal policy and supply shocks) to affect the aggregate demand and supply curves. To see why Keynesians also view high inflation as a monetary phenomenon, let's examine whether their analysis allows other factors to generate high inflation in the absence of a high rate of money growth.

---

[2]The only difference in the two analyses is that Keynesians believe that the aggregate supply curve would shift leftward more slowly than monetarists do. Thus Keynesian analysis suggests that output might tend to stay above the natural rate longer than monetarist analysis does.

Can Fiscal Policy by Itself Produce Inflation? To examine this question, let's look at Figure 3, which demonstrates the effect of a one-shot permanent increase in government expenditure (say, from $500 billion to $600 billion) on aggregate output and the price level. Initially we are at point 1, where output is at the natural rate level and the price level is P_1. The increase in government expenditure shifts the aggregate demand curve to AD_2, and we move to point 1', where output is above the natural rate level at $Y_{1'}$. The aggregate supply curve will begin to shift leftward, eventually reaching AS_2, where it intersects the aggregate demand curve AD_2 at point 2, at which output is again at the natural rate level and the price level has risen to P_2.

The net result of a one-shot permanent increase in government expenditure is a one-shot permanent increase in the price level. What happens to the inflation rate? When we move from point 1 to 1' to 2, the price level rises, and we have a positive inflation rate. But when we finally get to point 2, the inflation rate returns to zero. We see that the one-shot increase in government expenditure leads to only a *temporary* increase in the inflation rate, not to an inflation in which the price level is continually rising.

If, however, government spending increased continually, we *could* get a continuing rise in the price level. It appears, then, that Keynesian analysis could

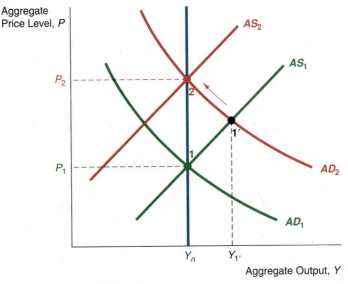

FIGURE 3 Response to a One-Shot Permanent Increase in Government Expenditure
A one-shot permanent increase in government expenditure shifts the aggregate demand curve rightward from AD_1 to AD_2, moving the economy from point 1 to point 1'. Because output now exceeds the natural rate level Y^n, the aggregate supply curve eventually shifts leftward to AS_2, and the price level rises from P_1 to P_2, a one-shot permanent increase but not a continuing increase.

reject Friedman's proposition that inflation is always the result of money growth. The problem with this argument is that a continually increasing level of government expenditure is not a feasible policy. There is a limit on the total amount of possible government expenditure; the government cannot spend more than 100% of GDP. In fact, well before this limit is reached, the political process would stop the increases in government spending. As revealed in the continual debates in Congress over balanced budgets and government spending, both the public and politicians have a particular target level of government spending they deem appropriate; although small deviations from this level might be tolerated, large deviations would not. Indeed, public and political perceptions impose tight limits on the degree to which government expenditures can increase.

What about the other side of fiscal policy, taxes? Could continual tax cuts generate an inflation? Again the answer is no. The analysis in Figure 3 also describes the price and output response to a one-shot decrease in taxes. There will be a one-shot increase in the price level, but the increase in the inflation rate will be only temporary. We can increase the price level by cutting taxes even more, but this process would have to stop—when taxes are at zero, they can't be reduced further. We must conclude, then, that *Keynesian analysis indicates that high inflation cannot be driven by fiscal policy alone.*[3]

Can Supply-Side Phenomena by Themselves Produce Inflation? Because supply shocks and workers' attempts to increase their wages can shift the aggregate supply curve leftward, you might suspect that these supply-side phenomena by themselves could stimulate inflation. Again, we can show that this suspicion is incorrect.

Suppose that there is a negative supply shock—for example, an oil embargo—that raises oil prices (or workers could have successfully pushed up their wages). As displayed in Figure 4, the negative supply shock shifts the aggregate supply curve from AS_1 to AS_2. If the money supply remains unchanged, leaving the aggregate demand curve at AD_1, we move to point 1', where output $Y_{1'}$ is below the natural rate level and the price level $P_{1'}$ is higher. The aggregate supply curve will now shift back to AS_1 because unemployment is above the natural rate, and the economy slides down AD_1 from point 1' to point 1. The net result of the supply shock is that we return to full employment at the initial price level, and inflation does not result. Additional negative supply shocks that again shift the aggregate supply curve leftward will lead to the same outcome: The price level will temporarily rise, but inflation will not result. The conclusion that we

---

[3]The argument here demonstrates that "animal spirits" also cannot be the source of inflation. Although consumer and business optimism, which stimulates their spending, can produce a one-shot shift in the aggregate demand curve and a *temporary* inflation, it cannot produce continuing shifts in the aggregate demand curve and inflation in which the price level rises continually. The reasoning is the same as before: Consumers and businesses cannot continue to raise their spending without limit because their spending cannot exceed 100% of GDP.

and the price level will not continue to rise. Hence the one-shot increase in the money supply from the temporary deficit generates only a one-shot increase in the price level, and no inflation develops.

To summarize, *a deficit can be the source of a sustained inflation only if it is persistent and not temporary and if the government finances it by creating money rather than by issuing bonds to the public.*

If inflation is the result, why do governments frequently finance persistent deficits by creating money? The answer is the key to understanding how budget deficits may lead to inflation.

Budget Deficits and Money Creation in Other Countries Although the United States has well-developed money and capital markets in which huge quantities of its government bonds, both short- and long-term, can be sold, this is not the situation in many developing countries. If developing countries run budget deficits, they cannot finance them by issuing bonds and must resort to their only other alternative, printing money. As a result, when they run large deficits relative to GDP, the money supply grows at substantial rates, and inflation results.

Earlier we cited Latin American countries with high inflation rates and high money growth as evidence that inflation is a monetary phenomenon. The Latin American countries with high money growth are precisely the ones that have persistent and extremely large budget deficits relative to GDP. The only way to finance the deficits is to print more money, so the ultimate source of their high inflation rates is their large budget deficits. Other countries experiencing high budget deficits and high inflation recently are Russia and other former members of the Soviet Union (see Box 2).

In all episodes of hyperinflation, huge government budget deficits are also the ultimate source of inflationary monetary policies. The budget deficits during hyperinflations are so large that even if a capital market exists to issue government bonds, it does not have sufficient capacity to handle the quantity of bonds that the government wishes to sell. In this situation, the government must also resort to the printing press to finance the deficits.

Budget Deficits and Money Creation in the United States So far we have seen why budget deficits in some countries must lead to money creation and inflation. Either the deficit is huge, or the country does not have sufficient access to capital markets in which it can sell government bonds. But neither of these scenarios seems to describe the situation in the United States. True, the United States' deficits have increased in the recent past, but even so, the magnitude of these deficits relative to GDP is small compared to the deficits of countries that have experienced hyperinflations: The U.S. deficit as a percent of GDP reached a peak of 6% in 1983, whereas Argentina's budget deficit has often exceeded 15% of GDP. Furthermore, since the United States has the best-developed government bond market of any country in the world, it can issue large quantities of bonds to finance its deficit.

Although it appears that moderate deficits in the United States need not lead to inflation, do not assume that deficits in the United States present *no* inflation-

A Global Perspective

Box 2

THE BUDGET DEFICIT AND HIGH INFLATION IN RUSSIA AND OTHER FORMER MEMBERS OF THE SOVIET UNION

The high inflation experienced in Russia in the aftermath of the breakup of the Soviet Union is the result of severe fiscal problems for the Russian government. As a result of subsidies to state enterprises and to other republics that used to be a part of the Soviet Union, the Russian government found itself facing a huge budget deficit, estimated at 20% of GDP in 1991. Unable to finance this deficit by any other means, the Russian government had to resort to its only option, printing money. Contributing further to the rapid rate of money growth was the fact that the Russian central bank readily granted credits to state enterprises. Not surprisingly given the rapid money growth, inflation took off, averaging close to 1000% in 1992 and 1993.

Russia is not the only former member of the Soviet Union that has suffered high budget deficits and hyperinflation in recent years. In 1992 and 1993, Ukraine had inflation rates averaging nearly 2000%, and Kazakhstan, Turkmenistan, Armenia, and Kyrgyzstan also experienced inflation rates greater than in Russia. However, some former members of the Soviet Union, including Estonia and Latvia, have been more successful in keeping their budget deficits under control, holding inflation to less than 100%.

ary danger. To understand why moderate budget deficits might be inflationary, recall that the Fed might have a goal of preventing high interest rates (Chapter 18). When the government issues bonds to finance a deficit, this might put upward pressure on interest rates, and the Fed may buy bonds to prop their price up and prevent interest rates from rising. Because the Fed's open market purchases lead to an increase in high-powered money, the net effect of government financing of the deficit by issuing bonds is an increase in the money supply. If the budget deficit persists so that the quantity of bonds supplied keeps on growing, the upward pressure on interest rates will continue, the Fed will purchase bonds again and again, and the money supply will continually rise, resulting in inflation.

Not all economists agree that deficits in and of themselves lead to continuing upward pressure on interest rates. Much research is now being done to assess the importance of budget deficits to the inflation process. Many economists, however, do worry that large deficits in the United States may lead to higher inflation.

To sum up, although high inflation is "always and everywhere a monetary phenomenon" in the sense that it cannot occur without a high rate of money growth, there are reasons why this inflationary monetary policy comes about. The two underlying reasons are the adherence of policymakers to a high employment target and the presence of persistent government budget deficits.

APPLICATION

EXPLAINING THE RISE IN U.S. INFLATION, 1960–1980

Now that we have examined the underlying sources of inflation, let's apply this knowledge to understanding the underlying causes of the rise in U.S. inflation from 1960 to 1980.

Figure 7 documents the rise in inflation in those years. At the beginning of the period, the inflation rate is close to 1% at an annual rate; by the late 1970s, it is averaging around 8%. How does the analysis of this chapter explain this rise in inflation?

The conclusion that inflation is a monetary phenomenon is given a fair amount of support by the period from 1960 through 1980. As Figure 7 shows, in this period there is a close correspondence between movements in the inflation rate and the monetary growth rate from two years earlier. (The money growth rates are from two years earlier because research indicates that a change in money growth takes that long to affect the inflation rate.) The rise in inflation from 1960 to 1980 can be attributed to the rise in the money growth rate over this period. But you have probably noticed that in 1974–1975 and 1979–1980, the inflation rate is well above the money growth rate from two years earlier. You may recall from Chapter 26 that temporary upward bursts of the inflation rate in those years can be attributed to supply shocks from oil and food price increases that occurred in 1973–1975 and 1978–1980.

However, the linkage between money growth and inflation after 1980 is not at all evident in Figure 7. This is the result of substantial gyrations in velocity in

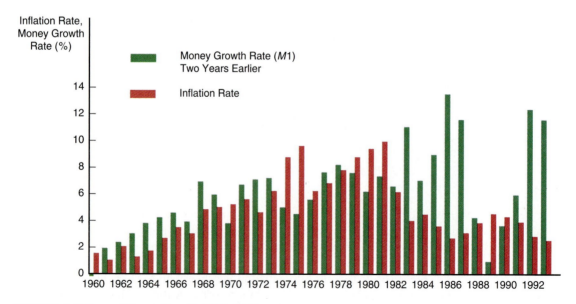

FIGURE 7 Inflation and Money Growth, 1960–1993
Source: Economic Report of the President.

the 1980s (documented in Chapter 23). Indeed, the early 1980s was a period of rapid disinflation (a substantial fall in the inflation rate), yet the money growth rates in Figure 7 do not display a visible downward trend until after the disinflation was over. (The disinflationary process in the 1980s will be discussed in another application later in this chapter.) Although some economists see the 1980s as evidence against the money-inflation link, others view the 1980s as an unusual period with large fluctuations in interest rates and rapid financial innovation that made the correct measurement of money far more difficult (see Chapter 3). In their view, the 1980s was an aberration, and the close correspondence of money and inflation is sure to reassert itself.

What is the underlying cause of the increased rate of money growth that we see occurring from 1960 to 1980? We have identified two possible sources of inflationary monetary policy: government adherence to a high employment target and budget deficits. Let's see if budget deficits can explain the move to an inflationary monetary policy by plotting the ratio of government debt to GDP in Figure 8. This ratio provides a reasonable measure of whether government budget deficits put upward pressure on interest rates. Only if this ratio is rising might there be tendency for budget deficits to raise interest rates, because the public is then being asked to hold more government bonds relative to their capacity to buy them. Surprisingly, over the course of the 20-year period from 1960 to 1980, this ratio was falling, not rising. Thus U.S. budget deficits in this period did not raise interest rates and so could not have encouraged the Fed to expand the money supply by buying bonds. Therefore, Figure 8 tells us that we can rule out budget deficits as a source of the rise in inflation in this period.

Because politicians were frequently bemoaning the budget deficits in this period, why did deficits not lead to an increase in the debt-GDP ratio? The reason is that in this period, U.S. budget deficits were sufficiently small that the increase in the stock of government debt was still slower than the growth in nom-

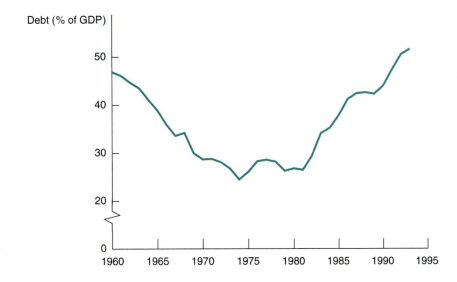

FIGURE 8
Government Debt-to-GDP Ratio, 1960–1993
Source: Economic Report of the President.

inal GDP, and the ratio of debt to GDP declined. You can see that interpreting budget deficit numbers is a tricky business.[6]

We have ruled out budget deficits as the instigator; what else could be the underlying cause of the higher rate of money growth and more rapid inflation in the 1960s and 1970s? Figure 9, which compares the unemployment rate to the natural rate of unemployment, shows that the economy was experiencing unemployment below the natural rate in all but one year between the 1965 and 1973. This suggests that in 1965–1973, the American economy was experiencing the demand-pull inflation described in Figure 6.

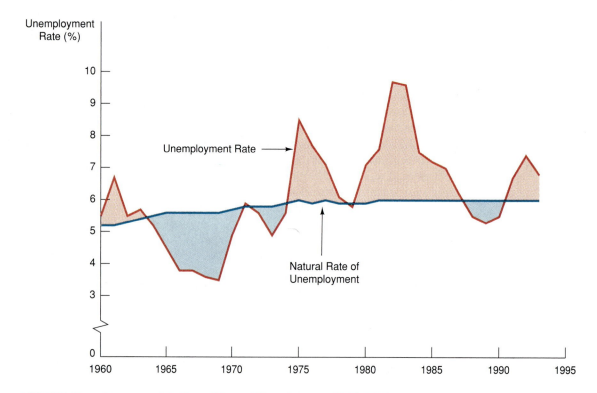

FIGURE 9 Unemployment and the Natural Rate of Unemployment, 1960–1993
Sources: Economic Report of the President; Robert Gordon, *Macroeconomics,* 6th ed. (New York: Harper-Collins, 1993).

_____

[6]Another way of understanding the decline in the debt-GDP ratio is to recognize that a rise in the price level reduces the value of the outstanding government debt *in real terms,* that is, in terms of the goods and services it can buy. So even though budget deficits did lead to a somewhat higher *nominal* amount of debt in this period, the continually rising price level (inflation) produced a lower *real* value of the government debt. The decline in the real amount of debt at the same time that real GDP was rising in this period then resulted in the decline in the debt-GDP ratio. For a fascinating discussion of how tricky it is to interpret deficit numbers, see Robert Eisner and Paul J. Pieper, "A New View of the Federal Debt and Budget Deficits," *American Economic Review* 74 (1984), 11–29.

Apparently policymakers pursued policies that continually shifted the aggregate demand curve to the right in trying to achieve an output target that was too high, thus causing the continual rise in the price level outlined in Figure 6. This occurred because policymakers, economists, and politicians had become committed in the mid-1960s to a target unemployment rate of 4%, the level of unemployment they thought was consistent with price stability. In hindsight, most economists today agree that the natural rate of unemployment was substantially higher in this period, on the order of 5% to 6% (see Figure 9). The result of the inappropriate 4% unemployment target was the beginning of the most sustained inflationary episode in American history.

After 1975, the unemployment rate was regularly above the natural rate of unemployment, yet inflation continued. It appears that we have the phenomenon of a cost-push inflation described in Figure 5 (the impetus for which was the earlier demand-pull inflation). The persistence of inflation can be explained by the public's knowledge that government policy continued to be concerned with achieving high employment. With a higher rate of expected inflation arising initially from the demand-pull inflation, the aggregate supply curve in Figure 5 continued to shift leftward, causing a rise in unemployment that policymakers would try to eliminate by shifting the aggregate demand curve to the right. The result was a continuation of the inflation that had started in the 1960s.

THE ACTIVIST/NONACTIVIST POLICY DEBATE

All economists have similar policy goals—they want to promote high employment and price stability—and yet they often have very different views on how policy should be conducted. Activists regard the self-correcting mechanism through wage and price adjustment (see Chapter 26) as very slow and hence see the need for the government to pursue active, accommodating, discretionary policy to eliminate high unemployment whenever it develops. Nonactivists, by contrast, believe that the performance of the economy would be improved if the government avoided active policy to eliminate unemployment. We will explore the activist/nonactivist policy debate by first looking at what the policy responses might be when the economy experiences high unemployment.

Responses to High Unemployment

Suppose that policymakers confront an economy that has moved to point 1' in Figure 10. At this point, aggregate output $Y_{1'}$ is lower than the natural rate level, and the economy is suffering from high unemployment. Policymakers have two viable choices: If they are nonactivists and do nothing, the aggregate supply curve will eventually shift rightward over time, driving the economy from point

1' to point 1, where full employment is restored. The accommodating, activist alternative is to try to eliminate the high unemployment by attempting to shift the aggregate demand curve rightward to AD_2 by pursuing expansionary policy (an increase in the money supply, increase in government spending, or lowering of taxes). If policymakers could shift the aggregate demand curve to AD_2 instantaneously, the economy would immediately move to point 2, where there is full employment. However, several types of lags exist that prevent this immediate movement from occurring.

1. The *data lag* is the time it takes for policymakers to obtain the data that tell them what is happening in the economy. Accurate data on GDP, for example, are not available until several months after a given quarter is over.

2. The *recognition lag* is the time it takes for policymakers to be sure of what the data are signaling about the future course of the economy. For example, to minimize errors, the National Bureau of Economic Research (the organization that officially dates business cycles) will not declare the economy to be in recession until at least six months after it has determined that one has begun.

3. The *legislative lag* represents the time it takes to pass legislation to implement a particular policy. The legislative lag does not exist for most monetary policy actions such as open market operations. It can, however, be quite important for the implementation of fiscal policy, when it can sometimes take six months to a year to get legislation passed to change taxes or government spending.

4. The *implementation lag* is the time it takes for policymakers to change policy instruments once they have decided on the new policy. Again, this lag is unimportant for the conduct of open market operations because the Fed's trading desk can purchase or sell bonds almost immediately upon being told to do

FIGURE 10
The Choice Between Activist and Nonactivist Policy
When the economy has moved to point 1', the policymaker has two choices of policy: the nonactivist policy of doing nothing and letting the economy return to point 1 or the activist policy of shifting the aggregate demand curve to AD_2 to move the economy to point 2.

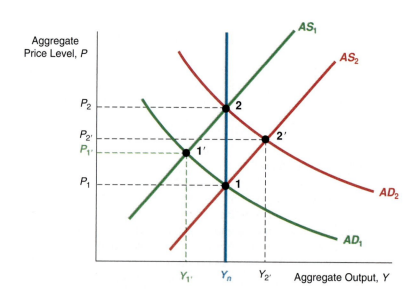

so by the Federal Open Market Committee. Actually implementing fiscal policy may take time, however; for example, getting government agencies to change their spending habits takes time, as does changing tax tables.

5. The *effectiveness lag* is the time it takes for the policy actually to have an impact on the economy. An important element of the monetarist viewpoint is that the effectiveness lag for changes in the money supply is long and variable (from several months to several years). Keynesians usually view fiscal policy as having a shorter effectiveness lag than monetary policy (fiscal policy takes approximately a year until its full effect is felt), but there is substantial uncertainty about how long this lag is.

Activist and Nonactivist Positions

Now that we understand the considerations that affect decisions by policymakers on whether to pursue an activist or nonactivist policy, we can examine when each of these policies would be preferable.

The Case for an Activist Policy Activists, such as the Keynesians, view the wage and price adjustment process as extremely slow. They consider a nonactivist policy costly because the slow movement of the economy back to full employment results in a large loss of output. However, even though the five lags described result in delay of a a year or two before the aggregate demand curve shift to AD_2, the aggregate supply curve moves very little during this time. The appropriate path for policymakers to pursue is thus an activist policy of moving the economy to point 2 in Figure 10.

The Case for a Nonactivist Policy Nonactivists, such as the monetarists, view the wage and price adjustment process as more rapid than activists and consider nonactivist policy less costly because output is soon back at the natural rate level. They suggest that an activist, accommodating policy of shifting the aggregate demand curve to AD_2 is costly because it produces more volatility in both the price level and output. The reason for this volatility is that the time it takes to shift the aggregate demand curve to AD_2 is substantial, while the wage and price adjustment process is more rapid. Hence before the aggregate demand curve shifts to the right, the aggregate supply curve will have shifted rightward to AS_2, and the economy will have moved from point 1' to point 1, where it has returned to the natural rate level of output Y_n. After adjustment to the AS_2 curve is complete, the shift of the aggregate demand curve to AD_2 finally takes effect, leading the economy to point 2' at the intersection of AD_2 and AS_2. Aggregate output at $Y_{2'}$ is now greater than the natural rate level ($Y_{2'} > Y_n$), so the aggregate supply curve will now shift leftward back to AS_1, moving the economy to point 2, where output is again at the natural rate level.

Although the activist policy eventually moves the economy to point 2 as policymakers intended, it leads to a sequence of equilibrium points—1', 1, 2', and 2—at which both output and the price level have been highly variable: Output overshoots its target level of Y_n, and the price level falls from $P_{1'}$ to P_1 and then rises to $P_{2'}$ and eventually to P_2. Because this variability is undesirable, policymakers would be better off pursuing the nonactivist policy, which moved the economy to point 1 and left it there.

Expectations and the Activist/Nonactivist Debate

Our analysis of inflation in the 1970s demonstrated that expectations about policy can be an important element in the inflation process. Allowing for expectations about policy to affect how wages are set (the wage-setting process) provides an additional reason for pursuing a nonactivist policy.

Do Expectations Favor a Nonactivist Approach?   Does the possibility that expectations about policy matter to the wage-setting process strengthen the case for a nonactivist policy? The case for an activist policy states that with slow wage and price adjustment, the activist policy returns the economy to full employment at point 2 far more quickly than it takes to get to full employment at point 1 under nonactivist policy. However, the activist argument does not allow for the possibility (1) that expectations about policy matter to the wage-setting process and (2) that the economy might initially have moved from point 1 to point 1' because an attempt by workers to raise their wages or a negative supply shock shifted the aggregate supply curve from AS_2 to AS_1. We must therefore ask the following question about activist policy: Will the aggregate supply curve continue to shift to the left after the economy has reached point 2, leading to cost-push inflation?

The answer to this question is yes *if* expectations of policy matter. Our discussion of cost-push inflation in Figure 5 suggested that if workers know that policy will be accommodating in the future, they will continue to push their wages up, and the aggregate supply curve will keep on shifting leftward. As a result, policymakers are forced to accommodate the cost push by continuing to shift the aggregate demand curve to the right to eliminate the unemployment that develops. The accommodating, activist policy with its high employment target has the hidden cost or disadvantage that it may well lead to inflation.[7]

The main advantage of a nonaccommodating, nonactivist policy, in which policymakers do not try to shift the aggregate demand curve in response to the cost push, is that it will prevent inflation. As depicted in Figure 4, the result of an

---

[7]The issue that is being described here is the *dynamic inconsistency of policy* described by Finn Kydland and Edward Prescott, "Rules Rather than Discretion: The Inconsistency of Optimal Plans," *Journal of Political Economy* 85 (1977): 473–491. A much less technical discussion of this subject can be found in Edward Prescott, "Should Control Theory Be Used for Economic Stabilization?" in *Optimal Policies, Control Theory and Technology Exports,* ed. Karl Brunner and Allan H. Meltzer, *Carnegie-Rochester Conference Series on Public Policy* 7 (1977): 13–38.

upward push on wages in the face of a nonaccommodating, nonactivist policy will be a period of unemployment above the natural rate level, which will eventually shift the aggregate supply curve and the price level back to their initial positions. The main criticism of this nonactivist policy is that the economy will suffer protracted periods of unemployment when the aggregate supply curve shifts leftward. Workers, however, would probably not push for higher wages to begin with if they knew that policy would be nonaccommodating, because their wage gains will lead to a protracted period of unemployment. A nonaccommodating, nonactivist policy may have not only the advantage of preventing inflation but also the hidden benefit of discouraging inward shifts in the aggregate supply curve that lead to excessive unemployment.

In conclusion, ***if workers' opinions about whether policy is accommodating or nonaccommodating matter to the wage-setting process, the case for a nonactivist policy is much stronger and the case for an activist policy is much weaker.***

Do Expectations About Policy Matter to the Wage-setting Process? The answer to this question is crucial to deciding whether activist or nonactivist policy is preferred and so has become a major topic of current research for economists, but the evidence is not yet conclusive. We can ask, however, whether expectations about policy do affect people's behavior in other contexts. This information will help us know if expectations regarding whether or not policy is accommodating are important to the wage-setting process.

As any good negotiator knows, convincing your opponent that you will be nonaccommodating is crucial to getting a good deal. If you are bargaining with a car dealer over price, for example, you must convince him that you can just as easily walk away from the deal and buy a car from a dealer on the other side of town. This principle also applies to conducting foreign policy—it is to your advantage to convince your opponent that you will go to war (be nonaccommodating) if your demands are not met. Similarly, if your opponent thinks that you will be accommodating, he will almost certainly take advantage of you. (For an example, see Box 3.) Finally, anyone who has dealt with a 2-year-old child knows that the more you give in (pursue an accommodating policy), the more demanding the child becomes. In conclusion, people's expectations about policy *do* affect their behavior. Consequently, it is quite plausible that expectations about policy also affect the wage-setting process.[8]

_____

[8]A recent development in monetary theory, new classical macroeconomics, strongly suggests that expectations about policy are crucial to the wage-setting process and the movements of the aggregate supply curve. We will explore why new classical macroeconomics comes to this conclusion when we discuss the implications of the rational expectations hypothesis (Chapters 29 and 30), which states that expectations are formed using all available information, including expectations about policy.

Box 3

THE PERILS OF ACCOMMODATING POLICY: THE TERRORISM DILEMMA

A major dilemma confronting our foreign policy in recent years is whether to cave in to the demands of terrorists when they are holding American hostages. Because our hearts go out to the hostages and their families, we might be tempted to pursue an accommodating policy of giving in to the terrorists to bring the hostages safely back home. However, pursuing this accommodating policy is likely to encourage terrorists to take additional hostages in the future.

The terrorism dilemma illustrates the principle that opponents are more likely to take advantage of you in the future if you accommodate them now. Recognition of this principle, which demonstrates the perils of accommodating policy, explains why governments in countries such as the United States and Israel have been reluctant to give in to terrorist demands even though it has sometimes resulted in the death of hostages.

Rules Versus Discretion: Conclusions

The following conclusions can be generated from our analysis: Activists believe in the use of discretionary policy to eliminate excessive unemployment whenever it develops because they view the wage and price adjustment process as sluggish and unresponsive to expectations about policy. Nonactivists, by contrast, believe that a discretionary policy that reacts to excessive unemployment is counterproductive because wage and price adjustment is rapid and because expectations about policy can matter to the wage-setting process. Nonactivists thus advocate the use of a policy rule to keep the aggregate demand curve from fluctuating away from the trend rate of growth of the natural rate level of output. Monetarists, who adhere to the nonactivist position and who also see money as the sole source of fluctuations in the aggregate demand curve, therefore advocate a policy rule whereby the Federal Reserve keeps the money supply growing at a constant rate. This monetarist rule is referred to as a **constant-money-growth-rate rule.**

As our analysis indicates, an important element for the success of a nonaccommodating policy rule is that it be *credible:* The public must believe that policymakers will be tough and not accede to a cost push by shifting the aggregate demand curve to the right to eliminate unemployment. In other words, government policymakers need credibility as inflation fighters in the eyes of the public. Otherwise, workers will be more likely to push for higher wages, which will shift the aggregate supply curve leftward after the economy reaches full employment at a point such as point 2 in Figure 10 and lead to unemployment or inflation (or both). Alternatively, a credible, nonaccommodating policy rule has the benefit that it makes a cost push less likely and thus helps prevent inflation and potential increases in unemployment. The following application suggests that recent historical experience is consistent with the importance of credibility to successful policymaking.

APPLICATION

THE IMPORTANCE OF CREDIBILITY TO VOLCKER'S VICTORY OVER INFLATION

In the period from 1965 through the 1970s, policymakers had little credibility as inflation fighters—a well-deserved reputation, as they pursued an accommodating policy to achieve high employment. As we have seen, the outcome was not a happy one. Inflation soared to double-digit levels, while the unemployment rate remained high. To wring inflation out of the system, the Federal Reserve under Chairman Paul Volcker put the economy through two back-to-back recessions in 1980 and 1981–1982 (see Chapter 21). (The data on inflation, money growth, and unemployment in this period are shown in Figures 7 and 9.) Only after the 1981–1982 recession—the most severe in the postwar period, with unemployment above the 10% level—did Volcker establish credibility for the Fed's anti-inflation policy. By the end of 1982, inflation was running at a rate of less than 5%.

One indication of Volcker's credibility came in 1983 when the money growth rate accelerated dramatically and yet inflation did not rise. Workers and firms were convinced that if inflation reared its head, Volcker would pursue a nonaccommodating policy of quashing it. They did not raise wages and prices, which would have shifted the aggregate supply curve leftward and would have led to both inflation and unemployment. The success of Volcker's anti-inflation policy continued throughout the rest of his term as chairman, which ended in 1987; unemployment fell steadily, while the inflation rate remained below 5%. Volcker's triumph over inflation was achieved because he obtained credibility the hard way; he earned it.

SUMMARY

1. Milton Friedman's famous proposition that "inflation is always and everywhere a monetary phenomenon" is supported by the following evidence: Every country that has experienced a sustained, high inflation has also experienced a high rate of money growth.

2. Aggregate demand and supply analysis shows that Keynesian and monetarist views of the inflation process are not very different. Both believe that high inflation can occur only if there

is a high rate of money growth. As long as we recognize that by inflation we mean a rapid and continuing increase in the price level, almost all economists agree with Friedman's proposition.

3. Although high inflation is "always and everywhere a monetary phenomenon" in the sense that it cannot occur without a high rate of money growth, there are reasons why inflationary monetary policy comes about. The two underlying rea-

sons are the adherence of policymakers to a high employment target and the presence of persistent government budget deficits.

4. Activists believe in the use of discretionary policy to eliminate excessive unemployment whenever it occurs because they view wage and price ad-justment as sluggish and unresponsive to expectations about policy. Nonactivists take the opposite view and believe that discretionary policy is counterproductive. In addition, they regard the credibility of a nonaccommodating (nonactivist) anti-inflation policy as crucial to its success.

KEY TERMS

cost-push inflation

demand-pull inflation

accommodating policy

constant-money-growth-rate rule

QUESTIONS AND PROBLEMS

1. "There are frequently years when the inflation rate is high and yet money growth is quite low. Therefore, the statement that inflation is a monetary phenomenon cannot be correct." Comment.

*2. Why do economists focus on historical episodes of hyperinflation to decide whether inflation is a monetary phenomenon?

3. "Since increases in government spending raise the aggregate demand curve in Keynesian analysis, fiscal policy by itself can be the source of inflation." Is this statement true, false, or uncertain? Explain.

*4. "A cost-push inflation occurs as a result of workers' attempts to push up their wages. Therefore, inflation does not have to be a monetary phenomenon." Is this statement true, false, or uncertain? Explain.

5. "Because government policymakers do not consider inflation desirable, their policies cannot be the source of inflation." Is this statement true, false, or uncertain? Explain

*6. "A budget deficit that is only temporary cannot be the source of inflation." Is this statement true, false, or uncertain? Explain.

7. How can the Fed's desire to prevent high interest rates lead to inflation?

*8. "If the data and recognition lags could be reduced, activist policy would more likely be beneficial to the economy." Is this statement true, false, or uncertain? Explain.

9. "The more sluggish wage and price adjustment is, the more variable output and the price level are when an activist policy is pursued." Is this statement true, false, or uncertain? Explain.

*10. "If the public believes that the monetary authorities will pursue an accommodating policy, a cost-push inflation is more likely to develop." Is this statement true, false, or uncertain? Explain.

11. Why are activist policies to eliminate unemployment more likely to lead to inflation than nonactivist policies?

*12. "The less important expectations about policy are to movements of the aggregate supply curve, the stronger the case is for activist policy to eliminate unemployment." Is this statement true, false, or uncertain? Explain.

13. If the economy's self-correcting mechanism works slowly, should the government necessarily pursue an activist policy to eliminate unemployment?

*14. "To prevent inflation, the Fed should follow Teddy Roosevelt's advice: 'Speak softly and carry a big stick.'" What would the Fed's "big stick" be? What is the statement trying to say?

15. In a speech early in the Iraq-Kuwait crisis, President George Bush stated that although his heart went out to the hostages held by Saddam Hussein, he would not let this hostage taking deter the United States from insisting on the withdrawal of Iraq from Kuwait. Do you think that Bush's position made sense? Explain why or why not.

Chapter 29

THE THEORY OF RATIONAL EXPECTATIONS AND EFFICIENT CAPITAL MARKETS

PREVIEW   Throughout our discussion of the many facets of money, banking, and financial markets, you may have noticed that the subject of expectations keeps cropping up again and again. If consumers expect that they will be richer in the future, for example, they spend more today, and aggregate output will increase; if banks expect deposit outflows to occur, they increase their holdings of excess reserves, which causes the money supply to fall; and if participants in the capital markets expect interest rates to rise and anticipate capital losses on long-term bonds, they will decrease their demand for long-term bonds, and the bond prices will fall. Expectations influence the behavior of all participants in the economy and have a major impact on economic activity.

The *theory of rational expectations* attempts to explain how economic agents form their expectations. It is at the center of many recent debates about how monetary policy and fiscal policy should be conducted (discussed in Chapter 30). In addition, when this theory is applied to financial markets, where it is called the *theory of efficient capital markets* (or, more simply, *efficient markets theory*), it has important implications about what factors determine securities prices and how these prices move over time.

In this present chapter we examine the basic reasoning behind the theory of rational expectations and apply it to financial markets. In addition to helping us understand the factors that influence the formation of business and consumer expectations, rational expectations theory explains some puzzling features of the operation and behavior of financial markets. You will see, for example, that it explains why changes in stock prices are unpredictable and why listening to a stock broker's hot tips may not be a good idea.

Theoretically, rational expectations theory should be a powerful tool for analyzing behavior. But to establish that it is *in reality* a useful tool, we must compare the theory with the data. Does the empirical evidence support it? Although the verdict is not yet in, the available evidence indicates that for many purposes, this theory is a good starting point for analyzing expectations.

THE ROLE OF EXPECTATIONS IN ECONOMIC ACTIVITY

It is difficult to think of any sector of the economy in which expectations exert no influence on the effects of policy and the way markets behave. To point up the critical role of expectations in influencing economic activity, it might be useful to list the various avenues in which they have come into play in our study of money, banking, and financial markets.

STUDY GUIDE

Before you read on, try to list examples from this book in which expectations influence economic behavior and then compare your list to the examples that follow. This is an excellent way for you to review how the material we have studied so far fits together.

---

1. *Asset Demand and the Determination of Interest Rates.* Because expectations of returns are an important factor in determining the quantity of an asset people demand, expectations are central to the behavior of asset prices in a financial market (Chapters 5 and 6). For example, we have seen that expectations of inflation have a major impact on bond prices and interest rates through the Fisher effect. The speed with which expectations of inflation respond to a higher rate of money growth is an important factor determining whether interest rates rise or fall when money growth increases.

2. *Risk and Term Structure of Interest Rates.* Expectations are also central in the determination of the risk and term structure of interest rates (Chapter 7). Expectations about the likelihood of bankruptcy are probably the most important factors in determining the risk structure of interest rates. Expectations of future short-term interest rates play a central role in determining long-term interest rates.

3. *Foreign Exchange Rates.* Recall that the exchange rate is the price of one asset (deposits denominated in the domestic currency) in terms of another (deposits denominated in the foreign currency). Thus the expected returns on foreign deposits relative to domestic deposits are a central element in the determination of foreign exchange rates (Chapter 8). Because expected appreciation or depreciation of the domestic currency affects the expected return on foreign deposits relative to domestic deposits, expectations about the price level, inflation, tariffs and quotas, import and export demand, and the money supply play an important role in determining the exchange rate. In addition, expectations that a central bank is about to devalue or revalue its domestic currency are a key feature of a speculative attack on a currency (Chapter 22).

4. *Asymmetric Information and Financial Structure.* Expectations are what make the asymmetric information problems of adverse selection and moral hazard we encountered in Part III important in determining financial structure. Financial intermediaries engage in the important task of information collection because they have expectations that adverse selection will occur; that is, the least desirable credit risks will be the most likely to seek loans. Similarly, expectations that borrowers will increase moral hazard by taking on too much risk are what drives financial institutions to take steps to limit moral hazard through monitoring and enforcement of restrictive covenants. The greater the expectations of the effects of adverse selection and moral hazard, the greater the efforts of financial institutions to engage in activities to reduce these asymmetric information problems and hence the greater the impact of asymmetric information on our financial structure.

5. *Financial Innovation.* Because financial institutions are concerned with the future profitability of the new financial instruments they issue, expectations about interest-rate movements and the nature of the regulatory environment in the future affect financial innovation (Chapter 10). Furthermore, in deciding on which regulations to impose on financial markets, regulators must guess how financial institutions will behave in response to new regulation. The result can be a complicated game between regulators and regulated in which each tries to outguess the other.

6. *Bank Asset and Liability Management.* Banks' decisions about which assets to hold are influenced by their expectations about the returns, risk, and liquidity of various assets (Chapter 11). Their decisions about which liabilities to assume are influenced by their expectations about the future cost of taking on various liabilities. In addition, because banks must manage liquidity to remain solvent, expectations about deposit outflows will affect their decisions about whether to hold more or fewer liquid assets.

7. *The Money Supply Process.* As you should recall from Chapters 15 to 17, depositor behavior and bank behavior are important in the money supply process. Depositors' decisions to hold currency versus demand or time deposits are affected primarily by expectations of the relative returns on these assets. Banks' decisions about excess reserves and borrowing from the Fed are influenced by their expectations of the returns they can earn on loans. In addition, the amount of excess reserves is affected by bankers' expectations concerning depositor outflows.

The role of expectations in bank panics and the resulting declines in the money supply are especially important (Chapter 17). Depositors' expectations that a bank or banks are in trouble cause them to withdraw deposits, which in turn causes banks to fail, which causes more banks to fail. Bankers' expectations of deposit outflows make the situation even worse because their scramble for liquidity and the resulting increase in excess reserves can lead to more bank failures. The net result of this process is that the currency–checkable deposits ratio and excess reserves rise, causing a sharp drop in the money supply.

8. *The Federal Reserve.* The Fed's expectations of inflation and the state of the economy affect the targets it sets for monetary policy. Its expectations of short-term interest rates can be a factor in the procedures it uses to control the money supply (Chapter 21).

9. *Demand for Money.* Because money is just another asset, its expected return relative to other assets is an important factor in determining its demand

(Chapter 23). Expectations about the level of lifetime resources (usually represented by permanent income) are frequently thought to be another major determinant of the demand for money.

10. Aggregate Demand. Expectations play a prominent role in determining aggregate demand. Our discussion of the *ISLM* model (Chapters 24 and 25) and the transmission mechanisms of monetary policy (Chapter 27) reveals that consumer expenditure is related to consumers' expectations of the future resources available to them and of the likelihood of financial distress. Investment spending depends on firms' expectations of future profits from investment projects as well as expectations about the cost of financing the project. It is no wonder that Keynes emphasized "animal spirits" (expectations) as a major factor driving aggregate demand and the business cycle.

11. Aggregate Supply and Inflation. Analysis of the aggregate supply curve (Chapter 26) indicated that workers' expectations about inflation and the likely response of government policy to unemployment affect the position of the aggregate supply curve. Expectations about inflation and government policy influence workers' willingness to push wages higher, and so these expectations play a central role in cost-push inflation, whereby the aggregate supply curve shifted farther and farther to the left (Chapter 28). The public's expectations of government policy, which are affected by the credibility of government policymakers, have implications for the desirability of pursuing activist or nonactivist policies.

In conclusion, expectations are important in every sector of the economy through their effects on policy and market behavior. Next we outline the theory of rational expectations, currently the most widely used theory to describe the formation of business and consumer expectations.

THEORY OF RATIONAL EXPECTATIONS

In the 1950s and 1960s, economists regularly viewed expectations as formed from past experience only. Expectations of inflation, for example, were typically viewed as being an average of past inflation rates. This view of expectation formation, called **adaptive expectations,** suggests that changes in expectations will occur slowly over time as past data change.[1] So if inflation had formerly been steady at a 5% rate, expectations of future inflation would be 5% too. If inflation rose to a steady rate of 10%, expectations of future inflation would rise to-

---

[1]More specifically, adaptive expectations, say, of inflation, are written as a weighted average of past inflation rates:

$$\pi_t^e = (1 - \lambda) \sum_{j=0}^{\infty} \lambda^j \pi_{t-j}$$

where
$\quad \pi_t^e \quad$ = adaptive expectation of inflation at time t
$\quad \pi_{t-j} \quad$ = inflation at time $t - j$
$\quad \lambda \quad$ = a constant between the values of 0 and 1

ward 10%, but slowly: In the first year, expected inflation might rise only to 6%; in the second year, to 7%; and so on.

Adaptive expectations have been faulted on the grounds that people use more information than just past data on a single variable to form their expectations of that variable. Their expectations of inflation will almost surely be affected by their predictions of future monetary policy as well as by current and past monetary policy. In addition, people often change their expectations quickly in the light of new information. To meet these objections to adaptive expectations, John Muth developed an alternative theory of expectations, called **rational expectations,** which can be stated as follows: ***Expectations will not differ from optimal forecasts (the best guess of the future) using all available information.***[2]

What exactly does this mean? To explain it more clearly, let's use the theory of rational expectations to examine how expectations are formed in a situation that most of us encounter at some point in our lifetime: our drive to work. Suppose that when Joe Commuter does not travel during rush hour, it takes an average of 30 minutes for his trip. Sometimes it takes him 35 minutes, other times 25 minutes, but the average non-rush-hour driving time is 30 minutes. If, however, Joe leaves for work during the rush hour, it takes him, on average, an additional 10 minutes to get to work. Given that he leaves for work during the rush hour, the best guess of the driving time—the **optimal forecast**—is 40 minutes.

If the only information available to Joe before he leaves for work that would have a potential effect on his driving time is that he is leaving during the rush hour, what does rational expectations theory allow you to predict about Joe's expectations of his driving time? Since the best guess of his driving time using all available information is 40 minutes, Joe's expectation should also be the same. Clearly, an expectation of 35 minutes would not be rational because it is not equal to the optimal forecast, the best guess of the driving time.

Suppose that the next day, given the same conditions and the same expectations, it takes Joe 45 minutes to drive, and the day after that, it takes Joe only 35 minutes. Do these variations mean that Joe's 40-minute expectation is irrational? No, an expectation of 40 minutes' driving time is still a rational expectation. In both cases, the forecast is off by 5 minutes, so the expectation has not been perfectly accurate. However, the forecast does not have to be perfectly accurate to be rational—it need only be the *best possible* given the available information; that is, it has to be correct *on average,* and the 40-minute expectation meets this requirement. Since there is bound to be some randomness in Joe's driving time regardless of driving conditions, an optimal forecast will never be completely accurate.

The example makes the following important point about rational expectations: ***Even though a rational expectation equals the optimal forecast using all available information, a prediction based on it may not always be perfectly accurate.***

---

[2]John Muth, "Rational Expectations and the Theory of Price Movements," *Econometrica* 29 (1961): 315–335.

What if an item of information relevant to predicting driving time is unavailable or ignored? Suppose that on Joe's usual route to work there is an accident that causes a two-hour traffic jam. If Joe has no way of ascertaining this information, his rush-hour expectation of 40 minutes' driving time is still rational because the accident information is not available to him for incorporation into his optimal forecast. However, if there was a radio or TV traffic report about the accident that Joe did not hear or heard but ignored, his 40-minute expectation is no longer rational. In light of the availability of this information, Joe's optimal forecast should have been two hours and 40 minutes.

Accordingly, there are two reasons why an expectation may fail to be rational:

1. People might be aware of all available information but too lazy to make their expectation the best guess possible.

2. People might be unaware of some available relevant information, so their best guess of the future will not be accurate.

Nonetheless, it is important to recognize that if an additional factor is important but information about it is not available, an expectation that does not take account of it can still be rational.

Formal Statement of the Theory

We can state the theory of rational expectations somewhat more formally. If X stands for the variable that is being forecast (in our example, it is Joe Commuter's driving time), X^e for the expectation of this variable (Joe's expectation of his driving time), and X^{of} for the optimal forecast of X using all available information (the best guess possible of his driving time), the theory of rational expectations then simply says

$$X^e = X^{of} \tag{1}$$

That is, the expectation of X equals the optimal forecast using all available information.

Rationale Behind the Theory

Why do people try to make their expectations match their best possible guess of the future using all available information? The simplest explanation is that it is costly for people not to do so. Joe Commuter has a strong incentive to make his expectations of the time it takes him to drive to work as accurate as possible. If he underpredicts his driving time, he will often be late to work and risk being fired. If he overpredicts, he will, on average, get to work too early and will have given up sleep or leisure time unnecessarily. Accurate expectations are desirable, and there are strong incentives for people to try to make them equal to optimal forecasts by using all available information.

The same principle applies to businesses. Suppose that an appliance manufacturer, say, General Electric, knows that interest-rate movements are important to the sales of appliances. If GE makes poor forecasts of interest rates, it will earn less profit because it might either produce too many appliances or too few. There are strong incentives for GE to acquire all available information to help it forecast interest rates and use the information to make the best possible guess of future interest-rate movements.

The incentives for equating expectations with optimal forecasts are especially strong in financial markets. In these markets, people with better forecasts of the future get rich. The application of the theory of rational expectations to financial markets (where it is called *efficient markets theory*) is thus particularly useful.

Implications of the Theory

Rational expectations theory leads to two commonsense implications for the forming of expectations that are important in the analysis of the aggregate economy.

  1. If there is a change in the way a variable moves, the way in which expectations of this variable are formed will change as well. This tenet of rational expectations theory can be most easily understood through a concrete example. Suppose that, as Keynes thought (Chapter 23), interest rates move in such a way that they tend to return to a "normal" level in the future. If today's interest rate is high relative to the normal level, an optimal forecast of the interest rate in the future is that it will decline to the normal level. Rational expectations theory would imply that when today's interest rate is high, the expectation is that it will fall in the future.

Suppose now that the way in which the interest rate moves changes so that when the interest rate is high, it stays high. In this case, when today's interest rate is high, the optimal forecast of the future interest rate, and hence the rational expectation, is that it will stay high. Expectations of the future interest rate will no longer indicate that the interest rate will fall. The change in the way the interest-rate variable moves has therefore led to a change in the way that expectations of future interest rates are formed. The rational expectations analysis here is generalizable to expectations of any variable. Hence when there is a change in the way any variable moves, the way in which expectations of this variable are formed will change too.

  2. The forecast errors of expectations will on average be zero and cannot be predicted ahead of time. The forecast error of an expectation is $X - X^e$, the difference between the realization of a variable X and the expectation of the variable; that is, if Joe Commuter's driving time on a particular day is 45 minutes and his expectation of the driving time is 40 minutes, the forecast error is 5 minutes.

Suppose that in violation of the rational expectations tenet, Joe's forecast error is not, on average, equal to zero; instead, it equals 5 minutes. The forecast error is now predictable ahead of time because Joe will soon notice that he is, on average, 5 minutes late for work and can improve his forecast by increasing it by 5 minutes. Rational expectations theory implies that this is exactly what Joe will do because he will want his forecast to be the best guess possible. When Joe has revised his forecast upward by 5 minutes, on average, the forecast error will equal zero so that it cannot be predicted ahead of time. Rational expectations theory implies that forecast errors of expectations cannot be predicted.

EFFICIENT MARKETS THEORY: RATIONAL EXPECTATIONS IN FINANCIAL MARKETS

While the theory of rational expectations was being developed by monetary economists, financial economists were developing a parallel theory of expectation formation in financial markets. It led them to the same conclusion as the rational expectations theorists: Expectations in financial markets are equal to optimal forecasts using all available information.[3] Although financial economists gave their theory another name, calling it the *theory of efficient capital markets* or *efficient markets theory,* in fact their theory is just an application of rational expectations to the pricing of securities.

Efficient markets theory is based on the assumption that prices of securities in financial markets fully reflect all available information. You may recall from Chapter 4 that the rate of return from holding a security equals the sum of the capital gain on the security (the change in the price) plus any cash payments, divided by the initial purchase price of the security:

$$RET = \frac{P_{t+1} - P_t + C}{P_t} \tag{2}$$

where *RET* = rate of return on the security held from time t to $t + 1$
(say, the end of 1994 to the end of 1995)

P_{t+1} = price of the security at time $t + 1$, the end of the holding period

P_t = price of the security at time t, the beginning of the holding period

C = cash payment (coupon or dividend payments) made in the period t to $t + 1$

---

[3]The development of efficient markets theory was not wholly independent of the development of rational expectations theory in that financial economists were aware of Muth's work.

Let's look at the expectation of this return at time t, the beginning of the holding period. Because the current price P_t and the cash payment C are known at the beginning, the only variable in the definition of the return that is uncertain is the price next period P_{t+1}.[4] Denoting the expectation of the security's price at the end of the holding period as P^e_{t+1}, the expected return RET^e is

$$RET^e = \frac{P^e_{t+1} - P_t + C}{P_t}$$

Efficient markets theory also views expectations of future prices as equal to optimal forecasts using all currently available information. In other words, the market's expectations of future securities prices are rational, so that

$$P^e_{t+1} = P^{of}_{t+1}$$

which in turn implies that the expected return on the security will equal the optimal forecast of the return:

$$RET^e = RE^{of} \tag{3}$$

Unfortunately, we cannot observe either RET^e or P^e_{t+1}, so the rational expectations equations by themselves do not tell us much about how the financial market behaves. However, if we can devise some way to measure the value of RET^e, these equations will have important implications for how prices of securities change in financial markets.

The supply and demand analysis of the bond market developed in Chapter 6 shows us that the expected return on a security (the interest rate in the case of the bond examined) will have a tendency to head toward the equilibrium return that equates the quantity demanded to the quantity supplied. Supply and demand analysis enables us to determine the expected return on a security with the following equilibrium condition: The expected return on a security RET^e equals the equilibrium return RET^*, which equates the quantity of the security demanded to the quantity supplied; that is,

$$RET^e = RET^* \tag{4}$$

The academic field of finance explores the factors (risk and liquidity, for example) that influence the equilibrium returns on securities. For our purposes, it is sufficient to know that we can determine the equilibrium return and thus determine the expected return with the equilibrium condition.

---

[4]There are cases where C might not be known at the beginning of the period, but that does not make a substantial difference to the analysis. We would in that case assume that not only price expectations but also the expectations of C are optimal forecasts using all available information.

We can derive an equation to describe pricing behavior in an efficient market by using the equilibrium condition to replace RET^e with RET^* in the rational expectations equation (Equation 3). In this way we obtain

$$RET^{of} = RET^* \tag{5}$$

This equation tells us that **current prices in a financial market will be set so that the optimal forecast of a security's return using all available information equals the security's equilibrium return.** Financial economists state it more simply: A security's price fully reflects all available information in an efficient market.

Rationale Behind the Theory

Let's see what the efficient markets condition means in practice and why it is a sensible characterization of pricing behavior. Suppose that the equilibrium return on a security, say, Exxon common stock, is 10% at an annual rate, and its current price P_t is lower than the optimal forecast of tomorrow's price P^{of}_{t+1} so that the optimal forecast of the return at an annual rate is 50%, which is greater than the equilibrium return of 10%. We are now able to predict that, on average, Exxon's return would be abnormally high. This situation is called an **unexploited profit opportunity** because, on average, people would be earning more than they should, given the characteristics of that security. Knowing that, on average, you can earn such an abnormally high rate of return on Exxon because $RET^{of} > RET^*$, you would buy more, which would in turn drive up its current price (P_t relative to the expected future price P^{of}_{t+1}, thereby lowering RET^{of}. When the current price had risen sufficiently so that RET^{of} equals RET^* and the efficient markets condition (Equation 5) is satisfied, the buying of Exxon will stop, and the unexploited profit opportunity will have disappeared.

Similarly, a security for which the optimal forecast of the return is −5% while the equilibrium return is 10% ($RET^{of} < RET^*$) would be a poor investment because, on average, it earns less than the equilibrium return. In such a case, you would sell the security and drive down its current price relative to the expected future price until RET^{of} rose to the level of RET^* and the efficient markets condition is again satisfied. What we have shown can be summarized as follows:

$$RET^{of} > RET^* \rightarrow P_t\uparrow \rightarrow RET^{of}\downarrow$$
$$RET^{of} < RET^* \rightarrow P_t\downarrow \rightarrow RET^{of}\uparrow$$
$$\text{until}$$
$$RET^{of} = RET^*$$

Another way to state the efficient markets condition is this: **In an efficient market, all unexploited profit opportunities will be eliminated.**

An extremely important factor in this reasoning is that **not everyone in a financial market must be well informed about a security or have rational expectations for its price to be driven to the point at which the efficient**

markets condition holds. Financial markets are structured so that many participants can play. As long as a few keep their eyes open for unexploited profit opportunities, they will eliminate the profit opportunities that appear because in so doing, they make a profit. The theory of efficient markets makes sense because it does not require everyone in a market to be cognizant of what is happening to every security.

A PRACTICAL GUIDE TO INVESTING IN THE STOCK MARKET

Efficient markets theory is not esoteric, without applications to the real world. It is extremely valuable because it can be applied directly to an issue that concerns many of us: how to get rich (or at least not get poor) in the stock market. (The "Following the Financial News" box shows how stock prices are reported daily.) A practical guide to investing in the stock market, which we develop here, provides a better understanding of the use and implications of efficient markets theory. In addition, we examine evidence concerning these implications.

How Valuable Are Published Reports of Investment Advisers?

Suppose that you have just read in the "Heard on the Street" column of the *Wall Street Journal* that investment advisers are predicting a boom in oil stocks because an oil shortage is developing. Should you proceed to withdraw all your hard-earned savings from the bank and invest it in oil stocks?

Efficient markets theory tells us that when purchasing a security, we cannot expect to earn an abnormally high return, a return greater than the equilibrium return. Information in newspapers and in the published reports of investment advisers is readily available to many market participants and is already reflected in market prices. So acting on this information will not yield abnormally high returns, on average. How valuable, then, are published reports of investment advisers? The answer is "not very."

THE EVIDENCE: DO INVESTMENT ADVISERS BEAT THE MARKET? The implication of efficient markets theory that published reports of investment advisers are not valuable indicates that their published recommendations cannot help us outperform the general market. Many studies shed light on whether investment advisers and mutual funds (some of which charge steep sales commissions to people who purchase them) beat the market. One common test that has been performed is to take buy and sell recommendations from a group of advisers or mutual funds and compare the performance of the resulting selection of stocks with the market as a whole. Sometimes the advisers' choices have even been compared to a group of stocks chosen by putting a copy of the financial page of the newspaper on a dartboard and throwing darts. The *Wall Street Journal,* for example, has a regular feature called "Investment Dartboard," which compares how well

FOLLOWING THE FINANCIAL NEWS

Stock Prices

Stock prices are published daily, and in the *Wall Street Journal* they are reported in the sections "NYSE—Composite Transactions," "Amex—Composite Transactions," and "Over-the-Counter Markets." The New York Stock Exchange (NYSE) and American Stock Exchange (Amex) stocks' prices are quoted in the following format:

52 Weeks Hi	Lo	Stock	Sym	Div	Yld %	PE	Vol 100s	Hi	Lo	Close	Net Chg
28	21⅜	IntAlum	IAL	1.00	3.7	27	49	27⅜	26⅞	26⅞	− ½
60	40⅝	IBM	IBM	1.00	1.9	dd	41325	55	52½	53½	+ ⅞
26⅜	24¼	IBM dep pf		1.88	7.8	...	968	24⅜	23⅞	24⅛	− ¼
21⅜	10⅜	IntColnEngy	KCN	p	...	...	234	13⅜	12¾	12¾	− ⅝
25⅛	13⅞	IntFamEntn B	FAM		...	34	372	17½	16⅝	17½	+ ⅝

Source: *Wall Street Journal,* March 31, 1994, p. C4.

The following information is included in each column. International Business Machines (IBM) common stock is used as an example.

52 Weeks Hi: Highest price of a share in the past 52 weeks: 60 for IBM stock

52 Weeks Lo: Lowest price of a share in the past 52 weeks: 40⅝ for IBM stock

Stock: Company name; IBM for International Business Machines

Sym: Symbol that identifies company

Div: Annual dividends: $1.00 for IBM

Yld %: Yield for stock expressed as annual dividends divided by today's closing price: 1.9% (= 1.00 ÷ 53½) for IBM stock

PE: Price-earnings ratio; the stock price divided by the annual earnings per share: "dd" entry indicates negative earnings, so the PE ratio is not calculated for IBM stock

Vol 100s: Number of shares (in hundreds) traded that day: 4,132,500 shares for IBM

Hi: Highest price of a share that day: 55

Lo: Lowest price of a share that day: 52½

Close: Closing price (last price) that day: 53½

Net Chg: Change in the closing price from the previous day: +⅞

Prices quoted for shares traded over-the-counter (through dealers rather than on an organized exchange) are sometimes quoted with the same information, but in many cases only the bid price (the price the dealer is willing to pay for the stock) and the asked price (the price the dealer is willing to sell the stock for) are quoted.

stocks picked by investment advisers do relative to stocks picked by throwing darts. (An interesting variant on the dartboard is described in Box 1.) Do the advisers win? To their embarrassment, on average they do not. The dartboard or the overall market does just as well even when the comparison includes only advisers who have been successful in the past in predicting the stock market.[5]

In studies of mutual fund performance, mutual funds are separated into groups according to whether they had the highest or lowest profits in a chosen period. When their performance is compared to a subsequent period, the mu-

[5]There is one important exception to the usual finding that investment advisers do not beat the market: the Value Line Survey. See Fischer Black, "Yes, Virginia, There Is Hope: Tests of the Value Line Ranking System," *Financial Analysts Journal* 29 (September-October 1973): 10–14, and Gur Huberman and Shmuel Kandel, "Market Efficiency and Value Line's Record," *Journal of Business* 63 (1990): 187–216.

| Box 1 | |

SHOULD YOU HIRE AN APE AS YOUR INVESTMENT ADVISER?

The *San Francisco Chronicle* has come up with an amusing way of evaluating how successful investment adivsers are at picking stocks. They ask eight analysts to pick five stocks at the beginning of the year and then compare the performance of their stock picks to those chosen by Jolyn, an orangutan living at Marine World/Africa USA in Vallejo, California. Consistent with the results found in the "Investment Dartboard" feature of the *Wall Street Journal,* Jolyn beats the investment advisers as often as they beat her. Given this result, you might be just as well off hiring an orangutan as your investment adviser as you would hiring a human being!

tual funds that did well in the first period do not beat the market in the second.[6]

The conclusion from the study of investment advisers and mutual fund performance is this: ***Having performed well in the past does not indicate that an investment adviser or a mutual fund will perform well in the future.*** This is not pleasing news to investment advisers, but it is exactly what the theory of efficient markets predicts. It says that some advisers will be lucky and some will be unlucky. Being lucky does not mean that a forecaster actually has the ability to beat the market. (An exception that proves the rule is discussed in Box 2.)

Probably no other conclusion is met with more skepticism by students than this when they first hear it. We all know or have heard of somebody who has been successful in the stock market for a period of many years. We wonder, how could someone be so consistently successful if he or she did not really know how to predict when returns would be abnormally high? The following story, reported in the press, illustrates why such anecdotal evidence is not reliable.

A get-rich-quick artist invented a clever scam. Every week he wrote two letters. In letter A he would pick team A to win a particular football game, and in letter B he would pick the opponent, team B. A mailing list would then be separated into two groups, and he would send letter A to the people in one group and letter B to the people in the other. The following week he would do the same thing but would send these letters only to the group who had received the first letter with the correct prediction. After doing this for ten games, he had

---

[6]An early study that found that mutual funds do not outperform the market is Michael C. Jensen, "The Performance of Mutual Funds in the Period 1945–64," *Journal of Finance* 23 (1968): 389–416. More recent studies on mutual fund performance are Mark Grimblatt and Sheridan Titman, "Mutual Fund Performance: An Analysis of Quarterly Portfolio Holdings," *Journal of Business* 62 (1989): 393–416, and R. A. Ippolito, "Efficiency with Costly Information: A Study of Mutual Fund Performance, 1965–84," *Quarterly Journal of Economics* 104 (1989): 1–23.

Box 2

AN EXCEPTION THAT PROVES THE RULE: IVAN BOESKY

Efficient markets theory indicates that investment advisers should not have the ability to beat the market. Yet that is exactly what Ivan Boesky was able to do until 1986, when he was charged by the Securities and Exchange Commission with making unfair profits (rumored to be in the hundreds of millions of dollars) by trading on inside information. In an out-of-court settlement, Boesky was banned from the securities business, fined $100 million, and sentenced to three years in jail. (After serving his sentence, Boesky was released from jail in 1990.) If the stock market is efficient, can the SEC legitimately claim that Boesky was able to beat the market? The answer is yes.

Ivan Boesky was the most successful of the so-called *arbs* (short for *arbitrageurs*) who made hundreds of millions in profits for himself and his clients by investing in the stocks of firms that were about to be taken over by other firms at an above-market price. Boesky's continuing success was assured by an arrangement in which he paid cash (sometimes in a suitcase) to Dennis Levine, an investment banker who had inside information about when a takeover was to take place because his firm was arranging the financing of the deal. When Levine found out that a firm was planning a takeover, he would inform Boesky, who would then buy the stock of the company being taken over and sell it after the stock had risen.

Boesky's ability to make millions year after year in the 1980s is an exception that proves the rule that financial analysts cannot continually outperform the market; yet it supports the efficient markets claim that only information *unavailable* to the market enables an investor to do so. Boesky profited from knowing about takeovers before the rest of the market; this information was known to him but unavailable to the market.

a small cluster of people who had received letters predicting the correct winning team for every game. He then mailed a final letter to them, declaring that since he was obviously an expert predictor of the outcome of football games (he had picked winners ten weeks in a row) and since his predictions were profitable for the recipients who bet on the games, he would continue to send his predictions only if he were paid a substantial amount of money. When one of his clients figured out what he was up to, the con man was prosecuted and thrown in jail!

What is the lesson of the story? Even if no forecaster is an accurate predictor of the market, there will always be a group of consistent winners. A person who has done well regularly in the past cannot guarantee that he or she will do well in the future. Note that there will also be a group of persistent losers, but you rarely hear about them because no one brags about a poor forecasting record.

Should You Be Skeptical of Hot Tips?

Suppose that your broker phones you with a hot tip to buy stock in the Happy Feet Corporation (HFC) because it has just developed a product that is completely effective in curing athlete's foot. The stock price is sure to go up. Should you follow this advice and buy HFC stock?

Efficient markets theory indicates that you should be skeptical of such news. If the stock market is efficient, it has already priced HFC stock so that its expected return will equal the equilibrium return. The hot tip is not particularly valuable and will not enable you to earn an abnormally high return.

You might wonder, though, if the hot tip is based on new information and would give you an edge on the rest of the market. If other market participants have gotten this information before you, the answer is no. As soon as the information hits the street, the unexploited profit opportunity it creates will be quickly eliminated. The stock's price will already reflect the information, and you should expect to realize only the equilibrium return. But if you are one of the first to know the new information (as Ivan Boesky was—see Box 2), it can do you some good. Only then can you be one of the lucky ones who, on average, will earn an abnormally high return by helping eliminate the profit opportunity by buying HFC stock.

EVIDENCE Because most hot tips are whispered from ear to ear, it is not possible to collect data on the frequency with which they allow people to earn abnormally high returns. Because it is unlikely that investment advisers' hot tips are any better than their published recommendations, the evidence we have presented indicates that investment advisers do not beat the market and that hot tips are unlikely to be very valuable.

Do Stock Prices Follow a Random Walk?

The term **random walk** describes the movements of a variable whose future changes cannot be predicted (are random) because, given today's value, the variable is just as likely to fall as to rise. An important implication of efficient markets theory is that stock prices should approximately follow a random walk; that is, ***future changes in stock prices should, for all practical purposes, be unpredictable.*** The random-walk implication of efficient markets theory is the one most commonly mentioned in the press because it is the most readily comprehensible to the public. In fact, when people mention the "random-walk theory of stock prices," they are in reality referring to efficient markets theory.

The case for random-walk stock prices can be demonstrated. Suppose that people could predict that the price of HFC stock would rise 1% in the coming week. The predicted rate of capital gains and rate of return on HFC stock would then be over 50% at an annual rate. Since this is very likely to be far higher than the equilibrium rate of return on HFC stock ($RET^{of} > RET^*$), the theory of efficient markets indicates that people would immediately buy this stock and bid up its current price. The action would stop only when the predictable change in the price dropped to near zero so that $RET^{of} = RET^*$.

Similarly, if people could predict that the price of HFC stock would fall by 1%, the predicted rate of return would be negative ($RET^{of} < RET^*$), and people would immediately sell. The current price would fall until the predictable change in the price rose back to near zero, where the efficient markets condition again holds. Efficient markets theory suggests that the predictable change in stock prices will be near zero, leading to the conclusion that stock prices will generally follow a random walk.[7] (Similar reasoning indicates that foreign exchange rates will also follow a random walk; see Box 3.)

THE EVIDENCE Economists have used two types of tests to explore the hypothesis that stock prices follow a random walk. In the first, economists examine stock market records to see if changes in stock prices are systematically related to

A Global Perspective

Box 3

WHY FOREIGN EXCHANGE RATES SHOULD FOLLOW A RANDOM WALK

Efficient markets theory implies that foreign exchange rates, like stock prices, should generally follow a random walk. To see why this is the case, consider what would happen if people could predict that a currency would appreciate by 1% in the coming week. By buying this currency, they could earn a greater than 50% return at an annual rate, which is likely to be far above the equilibrium return for holding a currency. As a result, people would immediately buy the currency and bid up its current price, thereby reducing the expected return. The process would stop only when the predictable change in the exchange rate dropped to near zero so that the optimal forecast of the return no longer differed from the equilibrium return. Likewise, if people could predict that the currency would depreciate by 1% in the coming week, they would sell it until the predictable change in the exchange rate was again near zero. Efficient markets theory therefore implies that future changes in exchange rates should, for all practical purposes, be unpredictable; in other words, exchange rates should approximately follow random walks. This is exactly what empirical evidence finds.*

*See Richard A. Meese and Kenneth Rogoff, "Empirical Exchange Rate Models of the Seventies: Do They Fit out of Sample?" *Journal of International Economics* 14 (1983): pp. 3–24.

[7]Note that the random-walk behavior of stock prices is only an *approximation* derived from efficient markets theory. It would hold exactly only for a stock for which an unchanged price leads to its having the equilibrium return. Then, when the predictable change in the stock price is exactly zero, $RET^{of} = RET^*$.

past changes and hence could have been predicted on that basis. The second type of test examines the data to see if publicly available information other than past stock prices could have been used to predict changes. These tests are somewhat more stringent because additional information (money supply growth, government spending, interest rates, corporate profits) might be used to help forecast stock returns.

Initial results from both types of tests generally confirmed the efficient markets view that stock prices are not predictable and follow a random walk.[8] However, more recent research does find some departures from random-walk stock market behavior. Stock prices tend to experience an abnormal price rise from December to January that is predictable and hence inconsistent with random-walk behavior. This so-called **January effect** seems to have diminished in recent years for shares of large companies but still occurs for shares of small companies.[9] Some researchers have also found that stock returns display **mean reversion:** Stocks with low returns today tend to have high returns in the future, and vice versa. Hence stocks that have done poorly in the past are more likely to do well in the future because mean reversion indicates that there will be a predictable positive change in the future price, suggesting that stock prices are not a random walk. Other researchers have found that mean reversion is not nearly as strong in data after World War II and so have raised doubts about whether it is currently an important phenomenon. Even though the evidence on whether stock prices follow a random walk is somewhat mixed and is currently quite controversial, deviations from random-walk behavior appear to be small.[10] So for most investors, the random-walk assumption is a reasonable one.

---

[8]The first type of test, using only stock market data, is referred to as a test of *weak-form efficiency* because the information that can be used to predict stock prices is restricted solely to past price data. The second type of test is referred to as a test of *semistrong-form efficiency* because the information set is expanded to include all publicly available information, not just past stock prices. A third type of test is called a test of *strong-form efficiency* because the information set includes insider information, known only to the owners of the corporation, as when they plan to declare a high dividend. Strong-form tests do sometimes indicate that insider information can be used to predict changes in stock prices. This finding does not contradict efficient markets theory because the information is not available to the market and hence cannot be reflected in market prices. In fact, there are strict laws against using insider information to trade in financial markets. For an early survey on the three forms of tests, see Eugene F. Fama, "Efficient Capital Markets: A Review of Theory and Empirical Work," *Journal of Finance* 25 (1970): 383–416.

[9]For example, see D. B. Keim, "The CAPM and Equity Return Regularities," *Financial Analysts Journal* 42 (May-June 1986): 19–34.

[10]Evidence for mean reversion has been reported by James M. Poterba and Lawrence H. Summers, "Mean Reversion in Stock Prices: Evidence and Implications," *Journal of Financial Economics* 22 (1988): 27–59; Eugene F. Fama and Kenneth R. French, "Permanent and Temporary Components of Stock Prices," *Journal of Political Economy* 96 (1988): 246–273; and Andrew W. Lo and A. Craig MacKinlay, "Stock Market Prices Do Not Follow Random Walks: Evidence from a Simple Specification Test," *Review of Financial Studies* 1 (1988): 41–66. However, Myung Jig Kim, Charles R. Nelson, and Richard Startz, "Mean Reversion in Stock Prices? A Reappraisal of the Evidence," *Review of Economic Studies* 58 (1991): 515–528, question whether some of these findings are valid. For an excellent summary of this evidence, see Charles Engel and Charles S. Morris, "Challenges to Stock Market Efficiency: Evidence from Mean Reversion Studies," *Federal Reserve Bank of Kansas City Economic Review,* September-October 1991, pp. 21–35.

Do Stock Prices Always Rise When There Is Good News?

If you follow the stock market, you might have noticed a puzzling phenomenon: When good news about a stock such as a particularly favorable earnings report, is announced, the price of the stock frequently does not rise. Efficient markets theory and the random-walk behavior of stock prices explain this phenomenon.

Because changes in stock prices are unpredictable, when information is announced that has already been expected by the market, the stock price will remain unchanged. The announcement does not contain any new information that should lead to a change in stock prices. If this were not the case and the announcement led to a change in stock prices, it would mean that the change was predictable. Because this is ruled out in an efficient market, **stock prices will respond to announcements only when the information being announced is new and unexpected.** If the news is expected, there will be no stock price response.

Sometimes a stock price declines when good news is announced. Although this seems somewhat peculiar, it is completely consistent with the workings of an efficient market. Suppose that although the announced news is good, it is not as good as expected. HFC's earnings may have risen 15%, but if the market expected earnings to rise by 20%, the new information is actually unfavorable, and the stock price declines.

THE EVIDENCE   The evidence cited that stock prices follow a random walk suggests that stock prices will frequently not rise when good news is announced. The evidence that this occurs is even more straightforward. We often see headlines like the following one in the *New York Times* on October 15, 1987 (shortly before the Black Monday crash):

Trade Gap Shrinks Less than
Hoped: Markets Plunge,
Dow Falls Record 95.46

In this case, the good news that the trade deficit shrank led to a decline in stock prices because the shrinkage was less than expected.

Is Technical Analysis Worthwhile?

A popular technique used to predict stock prices is to study past stock price data and search for patterns such as trends and regular cycles. Rules for when to buy and sell stocks are then established on the basis of the patterns that emerge. This forecasting procedure is called *technical analysis,* and 20 or 25 years ago it had a very large following in the financial community. Its following is smaller now because the increasingly popular theory of efficient markets suggests that technical analysis is a waste of time. The simplest way to understand why is to use the random-walk result derived from efficient markets theory that holds that past stock price data cannot help predict changes. Therefore, technical analysis, which relies on such data to produce its forecasts, cannot successfully predict changes in stock prices.

THE EVIDENCE Two types of tests bear directly on the value of technical analysis. The first performs the empirical analysis described earlier to evaluate the performance of any financial analyst, technical or otherwise. The results are exactly what efficient markets theory predicts: Technical analysts fare no better than other financial analysts; on average, they do not outperform the market, and successful past forecasting does not imply that their forecasts will outperform the market in the future. The second type of test (first performed by Sidney Alexander) takes the rules developed in technical analysis for when to buy and sell stocks and applies them to new data.[11] The performance of these rules is then evaluated by the profits that would have been made using them. These tests also discredit technical analysis: It does not outperform the overall market.

Efficient Markets Prescription for the Investor

What does the theory of efficient markets recommend for investing in the stock market? It tells us that hot tips, investment advisers' published recommendations, and technical analysis—all of which make use of publicly available information—cannot help an investor outperform the market. Indeed, it indicates that anyone without better information than other market participants cannot expect to beat the market. So what is an investor to do?

Efficient markets theory leads to the conclusion that such an investor (and almost all of us fit into this category) should not try to outguess the market by constantly buying and selling securities. This process does nothing but boost the income of brokers, who earn commissions on each trade.[12] Instead, the investor should pursue a "buy and hold" strategy—purchase stocks and hold them for long periods of time. This will lead to the same returns, on average,

---

[11]Sidney Alexander, "Price Movements in Speculative Markets: Trends or Random Walks?" *Industrial Management Review,* May 1961, pp. 7–26; Sidney Alexander, "Price Movements in Speculative Markets: Trends or Random Walks? No. 2," in *The Random Character of Stock Prices,* ed. Paul Cootner (Cambridge, Mass.: MIT Press, 1964), pp. 338–372.

[12]The investor may also have to pay Uncle Sam capital gains taxes on any profits that are realized when a security is sold—an additional reason why continual buying and selling does not make sense.

but the investor's net profits will be higher because fewer brokerage commissions will have to be paid.[13]

It is frequently a sensible strategy for a small investor, whose costs of managing a portfolio may be high relative to its size, to buy into a mutual fund rather than individual stocks. Because efficient markets theory indicates that no mutual fund can consistently outperform the market, an investor should not buy into one that has high management fees or that pays sales commissions to brokers but rather should purchase a no-load (commission-free) mutual fund that has low management fees.

As we have seen, the evidence provides a great deal of scientific support for efficient markets theory in the stock market and for the basic prescription for the investor outlined here. However, efficient markets theory remains controversial (as Box 4 indicates) and continues to be the subject of substantial research.

EVIDENCE ON RATIONAL EXPECTATIONS IN OTHER MARKETS

Evidence in other financial markets also supports efficient markets theory and hence the rationality of expectations. For example, there is little evidence that financial analysts are able to outperform the bond market.[14] The returns on bonds appear to conform to the efficient markets condition of Equation 5.

Rationality of expectations is, however, much harder to test in markets other than financial markets because price data that reflect expectations are not as readily available. The most common tests of rational expectations in these markets make use of survey data on the forecasts of market participants. For example, one well-known study by James Pesando used a survey of inflation expectations collected from prominent economists and inflation forecasters.[15] In that survey, these people were asked what they predicted the inflation rate would be over the next six months and over the next year. Because rational expectations theory implies that forecast errors should on average be zero and cannot be predicted, tests of the theory involve asking whether the forecast errors in a survey could be predicted ahead of time using publicly available information. The evidence from Pesando's and other subsequent studies is mixed. Sometimes the forecast errors cannot be predicted, and at other times they can. The evidence is

---

[13]As we saw in Chapter 5, the investor can also minimize risk by holding a diversified portfolio. The investor will be better off by pursuing a buy-and-hold strategy with a diversified portfolio or with a mutual fund that has a diversified portfolio.

[14]See the discussion in Frederic S. Mishkin, "Efficient Markets Theory: Implications for Monetary Policy," *Brookings Papers on Economic Activity* 3 (1978): 707–768, of the results in Michael J. Prell, "How Well Do the Experts Forecast Interest Rates?" *Federal Reserve Bank of Kansas City Monthly Review*, September-October 1973, pp. 3–15.

[15]James Pesando, "A Note on the Rationality of the Livingston Price Expectations," *Journal of Political Economy* 83 (1975): 845–858.

Box 4

WHAT DOES THE STOCK MARKET CRASH OF 1987 TELL US ABOUT RATIONAL EXPECTATIONS AND EFFICIENT MARKETS?

Some economists have suggested that the October 19, 1987, stock market crash should make us question the validity of efficient markets and rational expectations. They do not believe that a rational marketplace could have produced such a massive swing in share prices. To what degree should the stock market crash make us doubt the validity of rational expectations and efficient markets theory?

Nothing in rational expectations and efficient markets theory rules out large one-day changes in stock prices. A large change in stock prices can result from a dramatic change in optimal forecasts of the future valuation of firms. There are many possible explanations for why rational expectations of the future value of firms dropped dramatically on October 19, 1987: moves in Congress to restrict corporate takeovers, the disappointing performance of the trade deficit, congressional failure to reduce the budget deficit substantially, increased fears of inflation, the decline of the dollar, and increased fears of financial distress in the banking industry. There is, however, a lingering suspicion that factors other than market fundamentals (items that have a direct impact on future earnings prospects for the firms) may have had an effect on stock prices. Analysts often attribute a large role to market psychology, for example.

One lesson from the crash might be that the stock market is not entirely driven by market fundamentals and that market psychology or the institutional structure of the marketplace can influence stock prices. However, nothing in this view obviates the basic reasoning behind rational expectations or efficient markets theory—that market participants eliminate unexploited profit opportunities. Even though stock market prices may not always solely reflect market fundamentals, the basic implications of rational expectations and efficient markets theory are still likely to hold.

not as supportive of rational expectations theory as the evidence from financial markets.

Does the fact that forecast errors from surveys are often predictable suggest that we should reject rational expectations theory in these other markets? The answer is not necessarily. One problem with this evidence is that the expectations data are obtained from surveys rather than from actual economic decisions of market participants. That is a serious criticism of this evidence. Survey responses are not always reliable because there is little incentive for participants to tell the truth. For example, when people are asked in surveys how much television they watch, it is well known that responses greatly underestimate the actual time spent. Neither are people very truthful about the shows they watch. Often they say they watch ballet on public television. We actually know they are watching Vanna White turn letters on *Wheel of Fortune* instead, because it, not ballet, gets high Nielsen ratings. Truly, how many people will admit to being regular watchers of *Wheel of Fortune?*

A second problem with survey evidence is that a market's behavior may not be equally influenced by the expectations of all the survey participants, making survey evidence a poor guide to market behavior. For example, we have already seen that prices in financial markets *behave* as if expectations are rational even though many of the market participants do not have rational expectations.[16]

Proof is not yet conclusive on the validity of rational expectations theory in markets other than financial markets. One important conclusion, however, that is supported by the survey evidence is that ***if there is a change in the way a variable moves, there will be a change in the way expectations of this variable are formed as well.***

---

[16] There is some fairly strong evidence for this proposition. For example, Frederic S. Mishkin, "Are Market Forecasts Rational?" *American Economic Review* 71 (1981): 295–306, finds that although survey forecasts of short-term interest rates are not rational, the bond market *behaves* as if the expectations of these interest rates are rational.

SUMMARY

1. A review of the topics covered in the study of money, banking, and financial markets shows that expectations are important to almost all economic behavior.

2. The theory of rational expectations states that expectations will not differ from optimal forecasts (the best guesses of the future) using all available information. Rational expectations theory makes sense because it is costly for people not to have the best forecast of the future. The theory has two important implications: (a) If there is a change in the way a variable moves, there will be a change in the way expectations of this variable are formed, too, and (b) the forecast errors of expectations are unpredictable.

3. Efficient markets theory is the application of rational expectations to the pricing of securities in financial markets. Current securities prices will fully reflect all available information because in an efficient market, all unexploited profit opportunities are eliminated. The elimination of unex-

ploited profit opportunities necessary for a financial market to be efficient does not require that all market participants be well informed and have rational expectations.

4. Efficient markets theory indicates that hot tips, investment advisers' published recommendations, and technical analysis cannot help an investor outperform the market. The prescription for investors is to pursue a buy-and-hold strategy—purchase stocks and hold them for long periods of time. Empirical evidence generally supports efficient markets theory in the stock market.

5. Although the evidence supporting rational expectations in financial markets is strong, the evidence in other markets is more mixed. However, even for these other markets, there is support for the rational expectations conclusion that a change in the way a variable moves will change the way that expectations of the variable are formed.

KEY TERMS

adaptive expectations

rational expectations

optimal forecast

unexploited profit opportunity

random walk

January effect

mean reversion

QUESTIONS AND PROBLEMS

*1. "Forecasters' predictions of inflation are notoriously inaccurate, so their expectations of inflation cannot be rational." Is this statement true, false, or uncertain? Explain.

2. "Whenever it is snowing when Joe Commuter gets up in the morning, he misjudges how long it will take him to drive to work. Otherwise, his expectations of the driving time are perfectly accurate. Considering that it snows only once every ten years where Joe lives, Joe's expectations are almost always perfectly accurate." Are Joe's expectations rational? Why or why not?

*3. If a forecaster spends hours every day studying data to forecast interest rates but his expectations are not as accurate as predicting that tomorrow's interest rates will be identical to today's interest rate, are his expectations rational?

4. "If stock prices did not follow a random walk, there would be unexploited profit opportunities in the market." Is this statement true, false, or uncertain? Explain.

*5. In Chapter 27 you studied why stock prices might rise when the money supply rises. Does this mean that when you see that the money supply has risen sharply in the past week, you should go out and buy stocks? Why or why not?

6. If the public expects a corporation to lose $5 a share this quarter and it actually loses $4, which is still the largest loss in the history of the company, what does efficient markets theory say will happen to the price of the stock when its $4 loss is announced?

*7. If I read in the *Wall Street Journal* that the "smart money" on Wall Street expects stock prices to fall, should I take their advice and sell all my stocks?

8. If my broker has been right in her five previous buy and sell recommendations, should I start listening to her advice?

*9. Can a person expect the price of IBM to rise by 10% in the next month if his or her expectations are rational?

10. "If most participants in the stock market do not follow what is happening to the monetary aggregates, prices of common stocks will not fully reflect information about them." Is this statement true, false, or uncertain? Explain.

*11. "An efficient market is one in which no one ever profits from having better information than the rest." Is this statement true, false, or uncertain? Explain.

12. If higher money growth is associated with higher future inflation and if announced money growth turns out to be extremely high but is still less than the market expected, what do you think would happen to long-term bond prices?

*13. "Foreign exchange rates, like stock prices, should follow a random walk." Is this statement true, false, or uncertain? Explain.

14. Can we expect the value of the dollar to rise by 2% next week if our expectations are rational?

*15. "Human fear is the source of stock market crashes, so these crashes indicate that expectations in the stock market cannot be rational." In this statement true, false, or uncertain? Explain.

Chapter 30

RATIONAL EXPECTATIONS: IMPLICATIONS FOR POLICY

PREVIEW   After World War II, economists, armed with Keynesian models (the *ISLM* model, for example) that described how government policies could be used to manipulate employment and output, felt that activist policies could reduce the severity of business cycle fluctuations without creating inflation. In the 1960s and 1970s, these economists got their chance to put their policies into practice (see Chapter 28), but the results were not what they had anticipated. The economic record from that period was not a happy one: Inflation accelerated, the rate often climbing above 10%, while unemployment figures deteriorated from those of the 1950s.[1]

In the 1970s and 1980s, economists such as Robert Lucas of the University of Chicago and Thomas Sargent of Stanford University and the University of Chicago used the rational expectations theory to examine why activist policies appear to have performed so poorly. Their analysis casts doubt on whether macroeconomic models can be used to evaluate the potential effects of policy or whether policy can be effective if the public *expects* that it will be implemented. Because the analysis of Lucas and Sargent has such strong implications for the way policy should be conducted, it has been labeled the *rational expectations revolution*.[2]

This chapter examines the analysis behind the rational expectations revolution. We start first with the Lucas critique, which indicates that because expectations are important in economic behavior, it may be quite difficult to predict what the outcome of an activist policy will be. We then discuss the effect of rational expectations on the aggregate demand and supply analysis developed in

---

[1]Some of the deterioration can be attributed to supply shocks in 1973–1975 and 1978–1980.

[2]Other economists who have been active in promoting the rational expectations revolution are Robert Barro of Harvard University, Bennett McCallum of Carnegie-Mellon University, and Edward Prescott and Neil Wallace of the University of Minnesota.

Chapter 26 by exploring three models that incorporate expectations in different ways.

A comparison of all three models indicates that the existence of rational expectations makes activist policies less likely to be successful and raises the issue of credibility as an important element affecting policy outcomes. With rational expectations, an essential ingredient to a successful anti-inflation policy is the credibility of the policy in the eyes of the public. The rational expectations revolution is now at the center of many of the current debates in monetary theory that have major implications for how monetary and fiscal policy should be conducted.

THE LUCAS CRITIQUE OF POLICY EVALUATION

In his famous paper "Econometric Policy Evaluation: A Critique," Robert Lucas presented an argument that had devastating implications for the usefulness of conventional **econometric models** (models whose equations are estimated with statistical procedures) for evaluating policy.[3] Economists developed these models for two purposes: to forecast economic activity and to evaluate the effects of different policies. Although Lucas's critique had nothing to say about the usefulness of these models as forecasting tools, he argued that they could not be relied on to evaluate the potential impact of particular policies on the economy.

Econometric Policy Evaluation

To understand Lucas's argument, we must first understand econometric policy evaluation: how econometric models are used to evaluate policy. For example, we can examine how the Federal Reserve uses its econometric model in making decisions about the future course of monetary policy. The model contains equations that describe the relationships among hundreds of variables. These relationships are assumed to remain constant and are estimated using past data. Let's say that the Fed wants to know the effect on unemployment and inflation of an increase in the rate of money growth from 5% to 10%. It feeds the new higher rate of money growth into a computer that contains the model, and the model then provides an answer about how much unemployment will fall as a result of the higher money growth and how much the inflation rate will rise. Other possible policies, such as a decline in money growth to 1%, might also be fed into the model. After a series of these policies have been tried out, the policymakers at the Fed can see which policies produce the most desirable outcome for unemployment and inflation.

---

[3]Robert Lucas, Jr., "Econometric Policy Evaluation: A Critique," in *The Phillips Curve and Labor Markets,* ed. Karl Brunner and Allan H. Meltzer, *Carnegie-Rochester Conference Series on Public Policy* 1 (1976): 19–46.

Lucas's challenge to this procedure for evaluating policies is based on a simple principle of rational expectations theory: *The way in which expectations are formed (the relationship of expectations to past information) changes when the behavior of forecasted variables changes.* So when policy changes, the relationship between expectations and past information will change, and because expectations affect economic behavior, the relationships in the econometric model will change. The econometric model, which has been estimated with past data, is then no longer the correct model for evaluating the response to this policy change and may consequently prove highly misleading.

An Example: The Term Structure of Interest Rates

The best way to understand Lucas's argument is to look at a concrete example involving only one equation typically found in econometric models: the term structure equation. The equation relates the long-term interest rate to current and past values of the short-term interest rate. It is one of the most important equations in Keynesian econometric models because the long-term interest rate, not the short-term rate, is the one believed to have an impact on aggregate demand.

In Chapter 7 we learned that the long-term interest rate is related to an average of expected future short-term interest rates. Suppose that in the past, when the short-term rate rose, it quickly fell back down again; that is, any increase was temporary. Because the rational expectations theory suggests that any rise in the short-term interest rate is expected to be only temporary, a rise should have only a minimal effect on the average of expected future short-term rates. It will cause the long-term interest rate to rise by a negligible amount. The term structure relationship estimated using past data will then show only a weak effect on the long-term interest rate of changes in the short-term rate.

Suppose that the Fed wants to evaluate what will happen to the economy if it pursues a policy that is likely to raise the short-term interest rate from a current value of 5% to a permanently higher level of 8%. The term structure equation that has been estimated using past data will indicate that there will be just a small change in the long-term interest rate. However, if the public recognizes that the short-term rate is rising to a permanently higher level, the rational expectations theory indicates that people will no longer expect a rise in the short-term rate to be temporary. Instead, when they see the interest rate rise to 8%, they will expect the average of future short-term interest rates to rise substantially, and so the long-term interest rate will rise greatly, not minimally as the estimated term structure equation suggests. You can see that evaluating the likely outcome of the change in Fed policy with an econometric model can be highly misleading.

The term structure example also demonstrates another aspect of the Lucas critique. The effects of a particular policy depend critically on the public's expectations about the policy. If the public expects the rise in the short-term interest rate to be merely temporary, the response of long-term interest rates, as we have seen, will be negligible. If, however, the public expects the rise to be more permanent, the response of long-term rates will be far greater. ***The Lucas critique points out not only that conventional econometric models cannot be used for policy evaluation but also that the public's expectations about a policy will influence the response to that policy.***

The term structure equation discussed here is only one of many equations in econometric models to which the Lucas critique applies. In fact, Lucas uses the examples of consumption and investment equations in his paper. One attractive feature of the term structure example is that it deals with expectations in a financial market, a sector of the economy for which the theory and empirical evidence supporting rational expectations are very strong. The Lucas critique should also apply, however, to sectors of the economy for which the rational expectations theory is more controversial because the basic principle of the Lucas critique is not that expectations are always rational but rather that the formation of expectations changes when the behavior of a forecasted variable changes. This less stringent principle is supported by the evidence in other sectors of the economy besides financial markets.

THE NEW CLASSICAL MACROECONOMIC MODEL

We now turn to the implications of rational expectations for the aggregate demand and supply analysis we studied in Chapter 26. The first model we examine that views expectations as rational is the *new classical macroeconomic model* developed by Lucas and Sargent, among others. In the new classical model, all wages and prices are completely flexible with respect to expected changes in the price level; that is, a rise in the expected price level results in an immediate and equal rise in wages and prices because workers try to keep their *real* wages from falling when they expect the price level to rise.

This view of how wages and prices are set indicates that a rise in the expected price level causes an immediate leftward shift in the aggregate supply curve, which leaves real wages unchanged and aggregate output at the natural rate (full-employment) level if expectations are realized. This model then suggests that anticipated policy has no effect on aggregate output and unemployment; only unanticipated policy has an effect.

Effect of Unanticipated and Anticipated Policy

First, let us look at the short-run response to an unanticipated (unexpected) policy such as an unexpected increase in the money supply.

In Figure 1 the aggregate supply curve AS_1 is drawn for an expected price level P_1. The initial aggregate demand curve AD_1 intersects AS_1 at point 1, where the realized price level is at the expected price level P_1 and aggregate output is at the natural rate level Y_n. Because point 1 is also on the long-run aggregate supply curve at Y_n, there is no tendency for the aggregate supply to shift. The economy remains in long-run equilibrium.

Suppose that Fed suddenly decides that the unemployment rate is too high and so makes a large bond purchase that is unexpected by the public. The money supply increases, and the aggregate demand curve shifts rightward to AD_2. Because this shift is unexpected, the expected price level remains at P_1 and the aggregate supply curve remains at AS_1. Equilibrium is now at point 2', the intersection of AD_2 and AS_1. Aggregate output increases above the natural rate level to Y_2, and the realized price level increases to $P_{2'}$.

If, by contrast, the public expects that the Fed will make these open market purchases in order to lower unemployment because they have seen it done in the past, the expansionary policy will be anticipated. The outcome of such anticipated expansionary policy is illustrated in Figure 2. Because expectations are rational, workers and firms recognize that an expansionary policy will shift the aggregate demand curve to the right and will expect the aggregate price level to rise to P_2. Workers will demand higher wages so that their real earnings will remain the same when the price level rises. The aggregate supply curve then shifts

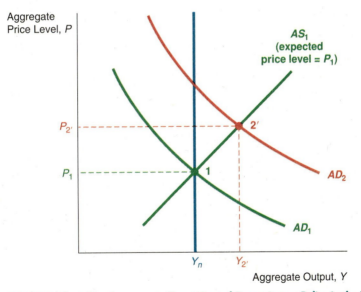

FIGURE 1 Short-Run Response to Unanticipated Expansionary Policy in the New Classical Model

Initially the economy is at point 1 at the intersection of AD_1 and AS_1 (expected price level = P_1). An expansionary policy shifts the aggregate demand curve to AD_2, but because this is unexpected, the aggregate supply curve remains fixed at AS_1. Equilibrium now occurs at point 2'—aggregate output has increased above the natural rate level to $Y_{2'}$, and the price level has increased to $P_{2'}$.

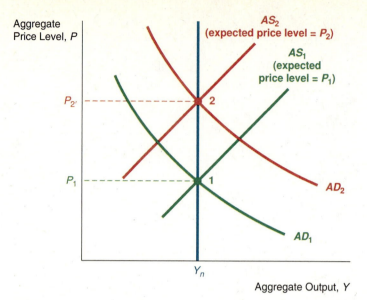

FIGURE 2 Short-Run Response to Anticipated Expansionary Policy in the New Classical Model
The expansionary policy shifts the aggregate demand curve rightward to AD_2, but because this policy is expected, the aggregate supply curve shifts leftward to AS_2. The economy moves to point 2, where aggregate output is still at the natural rate level but the price level has increased to P_2.

leftward to AS_2 and intersects AD_2 at point 2, an equilibrium point where aggregate output is at the natural rate level Y_n and the price level has risen to P_2.

The new classical macroeconomic model demonstrates that aggregate output does not increase as a result of anticipated expansionary policy and that the economy immediately moves to a point of long-run equilibrium (point 2) where aggregate output is at the natural rate level. Although Figure 2 suggests why this occurs, we have not yet proved why an anticipated expansionary policy shifts the aggregate supply curve to exactly AS_2 (corresponding to an expected price level of P_2) and hence why aggregate output *necessarily* remains at the natural rate level. The proof is somewhat difficult and is dealt with in Box 1.

The new classical model has the word *classical* associated with it because when policy is anticipated, the new classical model has a property that is associated with the classical economists of the nineteenth and early twentieth centuries: Aggregate output remains at the natural rate level. Yet the new classical model allows aggregate output to fluctuate away from the natural rate level as a result of *unanticipated* movements in the aggregate demand curve. The conclusion from the new classical model is a striking one: ***Anticipated policy has no effect on the business cycle; only unanticipated policy matters.***[4]

_____

[4]Note that the new classical view in which anticipated policy has no effect on the business cycle does not imply that anticipated policy has no effect on the overall health of the economy. For example, the new classical analysis does not rule out possible effects of anticipated policy on the natural rate of output Y_n, which can benefit the public.

Box 1

A PROOF OF THE POLICY INEFFECTIVENESS PROPOSITION

The proof that in the new classical macroeconomic model aggregate output *necessarily* remains at the natural rate level when there is anticipated expansionary policy is as follows. In the new classical model, the expected price level for the aggregate supply curve occurs at its intersection with the long-run aggregate supply curve (see Figure 2). The optimal forecast of the price level is given by the intersection of the aggregate supply curve with the anticipated aggregate demand curve AD_2. If the aggregate supply curve is to the right of AS_2 in Figure 2, it will intersect AD_2 at a price level lower than the expected level (at the intersection of this aggregate supply curve and the Y_n line). The optimal forecast of the price level will then not equal the expected price level, thereby violating the rationality of expectations. A similar argument can be made to show that when the aggregate supply curve is to the left of AS_2, the assumption of rational expectations is violated. Only when the aggregate supply curve is at AS_2 (corresponding to an expected price level of P_2) are expectations rational because the optimal forecast equals the expected price level. As we see in Figure 2, the AS_2 curve implies that aggregate output remains at the natural rate level as a result of the anticipated expansionary policy.

This conclusion has been called the **policy ineffectiveness proposition** because it implies that one anticipated policy is just like any other; it has no effect on output fluctuations. You should recognize that this proposition does not rule out output effects from policy changes. If the policy is a surprise (unanticipated), it will have an effect on output.[5]

Can an Expansionary Policy Lead to a Decline in Aggregate Output?

Another important feature of the new classical model is that an expansionary policy, such as an increase in the rate of money growth, can lead to a *decline* in aggregate output if the public expects an even more expansionary policy than the one actually implemented. There will be a surprise in the policy, but it will be negative and drive output down. Policymakers cannot be sure if their policies will work in the intended direction.

To see how an expansionary policy can lead to a decline in aggregate output, let us turn to the aggregate supply and demand diagram in Figure 3. Initially

---

[5]Thomas Sargent and Neil Wallace, "'Rational' Expectations, the Optimal Monetary Instrument, and the Optimal Money Supply Rule," *Journal of Political Economy* 83 (1975): 241–254, first demonstrated the full implications of the policy ineffectiveness proposition.

we are at point 1, the intersection of AD_1 and AS_1; output is Y_n, and the price level is P_1. Now suppose that the public expects the Fed to increase the money supply in order to shift the aggregate demand curve to AD_2. As we saw in Figure 2, the aggregate supply curve shifts leftward to AS_2 because the price level is expected to rise to P_2. Suppose that the expansionary policy engineered by the Fed actually falls short of what was expected so that the aggregate demand curve shifts only to $AD_{2'}$. The economy will move to point 2', the intersection of the aggregate supply curve AS_2 and the aggregate demand curve $AD_{2'}$. The result of the mistaken expectation is that output falls to $Y_{2'}$, while the price level rises to $P_{2'}$ rather than P_2. An expansionary policy that is less expansionary than anticipated leads to an output movement directly opposite to that intended.

STUDY GUIDE

Mastering the new classical macroeconomic model, as well as the new Keynesian model in the next section, requires practice. Make sure that you can draw the aggregate demand and supply curves that explain what happens in each model when there is a contractionary policy that is (1) unanticipated, (2) anticipated, and (3) less contractionary than anticipated.

Implications for Policymakers

The new classical model, with its policy ineffectiveness proposition, has two important lessons for policymakers: (1) It illuminates the distinction between the effects of anticipated versus unanticipated policy actions, and (2) it demonstrates that policymakers cannot know the outcome of their decisions without knowing the public's expectations regarding them.

At first you might think that policymakers can still use policy to stabilize the economy. Once they figure out the public's expectations, they can know what effect their policies will have. There are two catches to such a conclusion. First, it may be nearly impossible to find out what the public's expectations are, given that the public consists of more than 250 million U.S. citizens. Second, even if it were possible, policymakers would run into further difficulties in that because the public has rational expectations, it will try to guess what policymakers plan to do. Public expectations do not remain fixed while policymakers are plotting a surprise—the public will revise its expectations, and policies will have no predictable effect on output.[6]

---

[6]This result follows from one of the implications of rational expectations: The forecast error of expectations about policy (the deviation of actual policy from expectations of policy) must be unpredictable. Because output is affected only by unpredictable (unanticipated) policy changes in the new classical model, policy effects on output must be unpredictable as well.

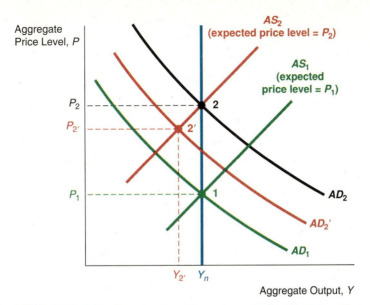

FIGURE 3   Short-Run Response to an Expansionary Policy That Is Less Expansionary than Expected in the New Classical Model
Because the public expects the aggregate demand curve to shift to AD_2, the aggregate supply curve shifts to AS_2 (expected price level = P_2). When the actual expansionary policy falls short of the public's expectation (the aggregate demand curve merely shifts to $AD_{2'}$), the economy ends up at point 2', at the intersection of $AD_{2'}$ and AS_2. Despite the expansionary policy, aggregate output falls to $Y_{2'}$.

Where does this lead us? Should the Fed and other policymaking agencies pack up, lock the doors, and go home? In a sense, the answer is yes. The new classical model implies that discretionary stabilization policy cannot be effective and might have undesirable effects on the economy. Policymakers' attempts to use discretionary policy may create a fluctuating policy stance that leads to unpredictable policy surprises, which in turn cause undesirable fluctuations around the natural rate level of aggregate output. To eliminate these undesirable fluctuations, the Fed and other policymaking agencies should abandon discretionary policy and generate as few policy surprises as possible.

As we have seen in Figure 2, even though anticipated policy has no effect on aggregate output in the new classical model, it *does* have an effect on the price level. The new classical macroeconomists care about anticipated policy and suggest that policy rules be designed so that the price level will remain stable. One natural suggestion for achieving this goal, as well as for reducing uncertainty about policy, is for the monetary authorities to follow a constant money growth rule in which the rate of money growth is consistent with price stability. Many adherents of the new classical macroeconomics in the end support this monetarist policy prescription (see Chapter 28).

THE NEW KEYNESIAN MODEL

In the new classical model, all wages and prices are completely flexible with respect to expected changes in the price level; that is, a rise in the expected price level results in an immediate and equal rise in wages and prices. Many economists who accept rational expectations as a working hypothesis do not accept the characterization of wage and price flexibility in the new classical model. These critics of the new classical model, the so-called *new Keynesians,* object to complete wage and price flexibility and identify factors in the economy that prevent some wages and prices from rising fully with a rise in the expected price level.

Long-term labor contracts are one source of rigidity that prevent wages and prices from fully responding to changes in the expected price level (called *wage-price stickiness*). For example, workers might find themselves at the end of the first year of a three-year wage contract that specifies the wage rate for the coming two years. Even if new information appeared that would make them raise their expectations of the inflation rate and the future price level, they could not do anything about it because they are locked into a wage agreement. Even with a high expectation about the price level, the wage rate will not adjust. In two years, when the contract is renegotiated, both workers and firms may build the expected inflation rate into their agreement, but they cannot do so immediately.

Another source of rigidity is that firms may be reluctant to change wages frequently even when there are no explicit wage contracts because it may affect the work effort of the labor force. For example, a firm may not want to lower workers' wages when unemployment is high because this might result in poorer worker performance. Price stickiness may also occur because firms engage in fixed-price contracts with their suppliers or because it is costly for firms to change prices frequently. All of these rigidities (which diminish wage and price flexibility), even if they are not present in all wage and price arrangements, suggest that an increase in the expected price level might not translate into an immediate and complete adjustment of wages and prices.

Although the new Keynesians do not agree with the complete wage and price flexibility of the new classical macroeconomics, they nevertheless recognize the importance of expectations to the determination of aggregate supply and are willing to accept rational expectations theory as a reasonable characterization of how expectations are formed. The model they have developed, the *new Keynesian model,* assumes that expectations are rational but does not assume complete wage and price flexibility; instead, it assumes that wages and prices are sticky. Its basic conclusion is that unanticipated policy has a larger effect on aggregate output than anticipated policy (as in the new classical model). However, in contrast to the new classical model, the policy ineffectiveness proposition does not hold: Anticipated policy *does* affect aggregate output and the business cycle.

Effects of Unanticipated and Anticipated Policy

In panel (a) of Figure 4, we look at the short-run response to an unanticipated expansionary policy for the new Keynesian model. The analysis is identical to that of the new classical model. We again start at point 1, where the aggregate demand curve AD_1 intersects the aggregate supply curve AS_1 at the natural rate level of output and price level P_1. When the Fed pursues its expansionary policy of purchasing bonds and raising the money supply, the aggregate demand curve shifts rightward to AD_2. Because the expansionary policy is unanticipated, the expected price level remains unchanged, leaving the aggregate supply curve unchanged. Thus the economy moves to point U, where aggregate output has increased to Y_U and the price level has risen to P_U.

In panel (b), we see what happens when the Fed's expansionary policy that shifts the aggregate demand curve from AD_1 to AD_2 is anticipated. Because the expansionary policy is anticipated and expectations are rational, the expected price level increases, causing wages to increase and the aggregate supply curve to shift to the left. Because of rigidities that do not allow *complete* wage and price adjustment, the aggregate supply curve does not shift all the way to AS_2 as it does in the new classical model. Instead, it moves to AS_A, and the economy settles at point A, the intersection of AD_2 and AS_A. Aggregate output has risen above the natural rate level to Y_A, while the price level has increased to P_A. ***Unlike in the new classical model, anticipated policy does have an effect on aggregate output in the new Keynesian model.***

We can see in Figure 4 that Y_U is greater than Y_A, meaning that the output response to unanticipated policy is larger than it is to anticipated policy. It is larger because the aggregate supply curve does not shift when policy is unanticipated, causing a lower price level and hence a higher level of output. We see that ***like the new classical model, the new Keynesian model distinguishes between the effects of anticipated versus unanticipated policy, with unanticipated policy having a greater effect.***

Implications for Policymakers

Because the new Keynesian model indicates that anticipated policy has an effect on aggregate output, it does not rule out beneficial effects from activist stabilization policy, in contrast to the new classical model. It does warn the policymaker that designing such a policy will not be an easy task because the effects of anticipated and unanticipated policy can be quite different. As in the new classical model, to predict the outcome of their actions, policymakers must be aware of the public's expectations about those actions. Policymakers face similar difficulties in devising successful policies in both the new classical and new Keynesian models.

FIGURE 4
Short-Run Response to Expansionary Policy in a New Keynesian Model

The expansionary policy that shifts aggregate demand to AD_2 has a bigger effect on output when it is unanticipated than when it is anticipated. When the expansionary policy is unanticipated in panel (a), the short-run aggregate supply curve does not shift, and the economy moves to point U so that aggregate output increases to Y_U and the price level rises to P_U. When the policy is anticipated in panel (b), the short-run aggregate supply curve shifts to AS_A (but not all the way to AS_2 because rigidities prevent complete wage and price adjustment), and the economy moves to point A so that aggregate output rises to Y_A (which is less than Y_U and the price level rises to P_A (which is higher than P_U).

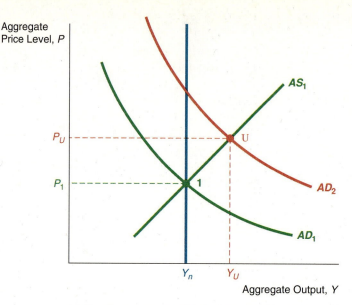

(a) Response to an unanticipated expansionary policy

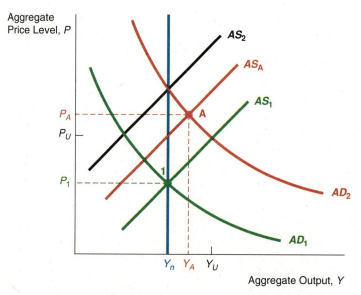

(b) Response to an anticipated expansionary policy

COMPARISON OF THE TWO NEW MODELS WITH THE TRADITIONAL MODEL

To obtain a clearer picture of the impact of the rational expectations revolution on our analysis of the aggregate economy, we can compare the two rational expectations models (the new classical macroeconomic model and the new Keynesian model) to a model we call, for lack of a better name, the *traditional model*. In it expectations are *not* rational. The traditional model uses adaptive expectations (mentioned in Chapter 29), expectations based solely on past experience. The traditional model views expected inflation as an average of past inflation rates. This average is not affected by the public's predictions of future policy; hence predictions of future policy do not affect the aggregate supply curve.

First we will examine the short-run output and price responses in the three models. Then we will examine the implications of these models for both stabilization and anti-inflation policies.

STUDY GUIDE

As a study aid, the comparison of the three models is summarized in Table 1. You may want to refer to the table as we proceed with the comparison.

Short-Run Output and Price Responses

Figure 5 compares the response of aggregate output and the price level to an expansionary policy in the three models. Initially the economy is at point 1, the intersection of the aggregate demand curve AD_1 with the aggregate supply curve AS_1. When the expansionary policy occurs, the aggregate demand curve shifts to AD_2. If the expansionary policy is *unanticipated,* all three models show the same short-run output response. The traditional model views the aggregate supply curve as given in the short run, while the other two view it as remaining at AS_1 because there is no change in the expected price level when the policy is a surprise. Hence when policy is *unanticipated,* all three models indicate a movement to point 1', where the AD_2 and AS_1 curves intersect and where aggregate output and the price level have risen to $Y_{1'}$ and $P_{1'}$, respectively.

The response to the *anticipated* expansionary policy is, however, quite different in the three models. In the traditional model in panel (a), the aggregate supply curve remains at AS_1 even when the expansionary policy is anticipated because adaptive expectations imply that anticipated policy has no effect on expectations and hence on aggregate supply. It indicates that the economy moves to point 1', which is where it moved when the policy was unanticipated. The traditional model does not distinguish between the effects of anticipated and unanticipated policy: Both have the same effect on output and prices.

SUMMARY

TABLE 1 The Three Models

Model	Response to Unanticipated Expansionary Policy	Response to Anticipated Expansionary Policy	Can Activist Policy Be Beneficial?	Response to Unanticipated Anti-inflation Policy	Response to Anticipated Anti-inflation Policy	Is Credibility Important to Successful Anti-inflation Policy?
Traditional model	$Y\uparrow$, $P\uparrow$	$Y\uparrow$, $P\uparrow$ by same amount as when policy is unanticipated	Yes	$Y\downarrow$, $\pi\downarrow$	$Y\downarrow$, $\pi\downarrow$ by same amount as when policy is unanticipated	No
New classical macroeconomic model	$Y\uparrow$, $P\uparrow$	Y unchanged, $P\uparrow$ by more than when policy is unanticipated	No	$Y\downarrow$, $\pi\downarrow$	Y unchanged, $\pi\downarrow$ by more than when policy is unanticipated	Yes
New Keynesian model	$Y\uparrow$, $P\uparrow$	$Y\uparrow$ by less than when policy is unanticipated, $P\uparrow$ by more than when policy is unanticipated	Yes, but designing a beneficial policy is difficult	$Y\downarrow$, $\pi\downarrow$	$Y\downarrow$ by less than when policy is unanticipated, $\pi\downarrow$ by more than when policy is unanticipated	Yes

Note: π represents the inflation rate.

In the new classical model in panel (b), the aggregate supply curve shifts leftward to AS_2 when policy is anticipated because when expectations of the higher price level are realized, aggregate output will be at the natural rate level. Thus it indicates that the economy moves to point 2; aggregate output does not rise, but prices do, to P_2. This outcome is quite different from the move to point 1' when policy is unanticipated. The new classical model distinguishes between the short-run effects of anticipated and unanticipated policies: Anticipated policy has no effect on output, but unanticipated policy does. However, anticipated policy has a bigger impact than unanticipated policy on price level movements.

The new Keynesian model in panel (c) is an intermediate position between the traditional and new classical models. It recognizes that anticipated policy af-

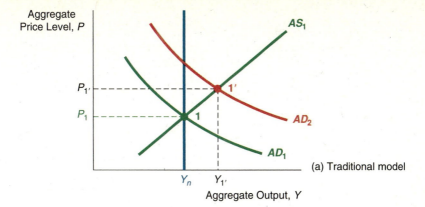

(a) Traditional model

FIGURE 5
Comparison of the Short-Run Response to Expansionary Policy in the Three Models

Initially the economy is at point 1. The expansionary policy shifts the aggregate demand curve from AD_1 to AD_2. In the traditional model, the expansionary policy moves the economy to point 1' whether the policy is anticipated or not. In the new classical model, the expansionary policy moves the economy to point 1' if it is unanticipated and to point 2 if it is anticipated. In the new Keynesian model, the expansionary policy moves the economy to point 1' if it is unanticipated and to point 2' if it is anticipated.

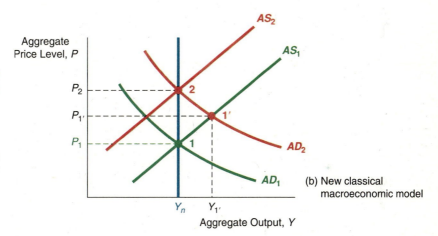

(b) New classical macroeconomic model

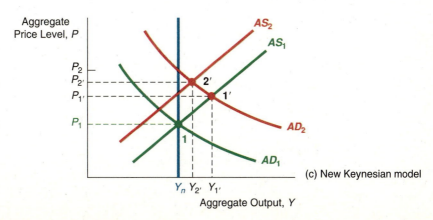

(c) New Keynesian model

fects the aggregate supply curve, but due to rigidities such as long-term contracts, wage and price adjustment is not as complete as in the new classical model. Hence the aggregate supply curve shifts only to AS_2 in response to anticipated policy, and the economy moves to point 2', where output at $Y_{2'}$ is lower than the $Y_{1'}$ level reached when the expansionary policy is unanticipated. But the price level at $P_{2'}$ is higher than the level $P_{1'}$ that resulted from the unanticipated policy. Like the new classical model, the new Keynesian model distinguishes between the effects of anticipated and unanticipated policies: Anticipated policy has a smaller effect on output than unanticipated policy but a larger effect on the price level. However, in contrast to the new classical model, anticipated policy does affect output fluctuations.

Stabilization Policy

The three models have different views of the effectiveness of *stabilization policy,* policy intended to reduce output fluctuations. Because the effects of anticipated and unanticipated policy are identical in the traditional model, policymakers do not have to concern themselves with the public's expectations. This makes it easier for them to predict the outcome of their policy, an essential matter if their policies are to have the intended effect. In the traditional model, it is possible for an activist policy to stabilize output fluctuations.

The new classical model takes the extreme position that activist stabilization policy serves to aggravate output fluctuations. In this model, only unanticipated policy affects output; anticipated policy does not matter. Policymakers can affect output only by surprising the public. Because the public is assumed to have rational expectations, it will always try to guess what policymakers plan to do.

In the new classical model, the conduct of policy can be viewed as a game in which the public and the policymakers are always trying to outfox each other by guessing the other's intentions and expectations. The sole possible outcome of this process is that an activist stabilization policy will have no predictable effect on output and cannot be relied on to stabilize economic activity. Instead it may create a lot of uncertainty about policy that will increase random output fluctuations around the natural rate level of output. Such an undesirable effect is exactly the opposite of what the activist stabilization policy is trying to achieve. The outcome in the new classical view is that policy should follow a nonactivist rule in order to promote as much certainty about policy actions as possible.

The new Keynesian model again takes an intermediate position between the traditional and the new classical models. Contrary to the new classical model, it indicates that anticipated policy *does* matter to output fluctuations. Policymakers can count on some output response from their anticipated policies and can use them to stabilize the economy.

In contrast to the traditional model, however, the new Keynesian model recognizes that the effects of anticipated and unanticipated policy will not be the same. Policymakers will encounter more uncertainty about the outcome of their actions because they cannot be sure to what extent the policy is anticipated or not. Hence an activist policy is less likely to operate always in the intended direction and is less likely to achieve its goals. The new Keynesian model raises the possibility that an activist policy could be beneficial, but uncertainty about the outcome of policies in this model may make the design of such a beneficial policy extremely difficult.

Anti-inflation Policies

So far we have focused on the implications of these three models for policies whose intent is to eliminate fluctuations in output. By the end of the 1970s, the high inflation rate (which exceeded 10%) helped shift the primary concern of policymakers to the reduction of inflation. What do these models have to say about anti-inflation policies designed to eliminate upward movements in the price level? The aggregate demand and supply diagrams in Figure 6 will help us answer the question.

Suppose that the economy has settled into a sustained 10% inflation rate caused by a high rate of money growth that shifts the aggregate demand curve so that it moves up by 10% every year. If this inflation rate has been built into wage and price contracts, the aggregate supply curve shifts so as to rise at the same rate. We see this in Figure 6 as a shift in the aggregate demand curve from AD_1 in year 1 to AD_2 in year 2, while the aggregate supply curve moves from AS_1 to AS_2. (Note that the figure is not drawn to scale.) In year 1, the economy is at point 1 (intersection of AD_1 and AS_1); in the second year the economy moves to point 2 (intersection of AD_2 and AS_2), and the price level has risen 10% from P_1 to P_2.

Now suppose that a new Federal Reserve chairman is appointed who decides that inflation must be stopped. He convinces the Board of Governors to stop the high rate of money growth so that the aggregate demand curve will not rise from AD_1. The policy of halting money growth immediately could be costly if it led to a fall in output. Let's use our three models to explore the degree to which aggregate output will fall as a result of an anti-inflation policy.

First, look at the outcome of this policy in the traditional model's view of the world in panel (a). The movement of the aggregate supply curve to AS_2 is already set in place and is unaffected by the new policy of keeping the aggregate demand curve at AD_1 (whether the effort is anticipated or not). The economy moves to point 2' (the intersection of the AD_1 and AS_2 curves), and the inflation rate slows down because the price level increases only to $P_{2'}$ rather than P_2. The reduction in inflation has not been without cost: Output has declined to $Y_{2'}$, which is well below the natural rate level.

The late Arthur Okun of the Brookings Institution estimated that in the traditional model, the cost in terms of lost output for each 1% reduction in the inflation rate is 9% of a year's real GDP. The high cost of reducing inflation in the traditional model is one reason why some economists are reluctant to advocate an anti-inflation policy of the sort tried here. They question whether the cost of high unemployment is worth the benefits of a reduced inflation rate.

If you adhere to the new classical philosophy, you would not be as pessimistic about the high cost of reducing the inflation rate. If the public *expects*

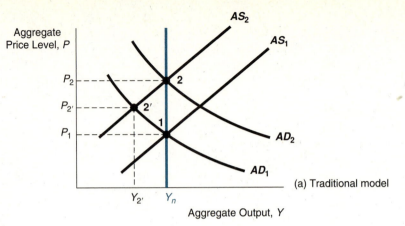

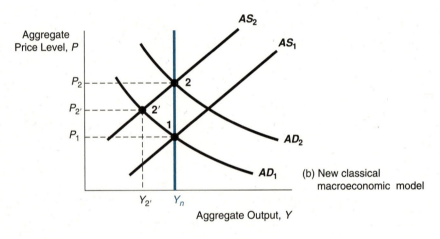

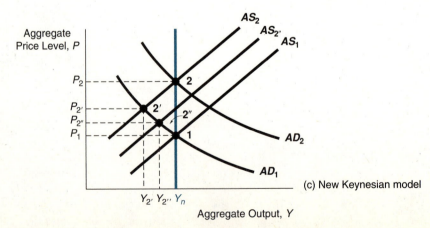

FIGURE 6
Anti-inflation Policy in the Three Models

With an ongoing inflation in which the economy is moving from point 1 to point 2, the aggregate demand curve is shifting from AD_1 to AD_2 and the short-run aggregate supply curve from AS_1 to AS_2. The anti-inflation policy, when implemented, prevents the aggregate demand curve from rising, holding it at AD_1. In the traditional model, the economy moves to point 2' whether the anti-inflation policy is anticipated or not. In the new classical model, the economy moves to point 2' if the policy is unanticipated and point 1 if it is anticipated. In the new Keynesian model, the economy moves to point 2' if the policy is unanticipated and point 2" if it is anticipated.

the monetary authorities to stop the inflationary process by ending the high rate of money growth, it will occur without any output loss. In panel (b), the aggregate demand curve will remain at AD_1, but because this is expected, wages and prices can be adjusted so that they will not rise, and the aggregate supply curve will remain at AS_1 instead of moving to AS_2. The economy will stay put at point 1 (the intersection of AD_1 and AS_1), and aggregate output will remain at the natural rate level while inflation is stopped because the price level is unchanged.

An important element in the story is that the anti-inflation policy be anticipated by the public. If the policy is *not* expected, the aggregate demand curve remains at AD_1, but the aggregate supply curve continues its shift to AS_2. The outcome of the unanticipated anti-inflation policy is a movement of the economy to point 2'. Although the inflation rate slows in this case, it is not entirely eliminated as it was when the anti-inflation policy was anticipated. Even worse, aggregate output falls below the natural rate level to $Y_{2'}$. An anti-inflation policy that is unanticipated, then, is far less desirable than one that is.

The new Keynesian model in panel (c) also leads to the conclusion that an unanticipated anti-inflation policy is less desirable than an anticipated one. If the policy of keeping the aggregate demand curve at AD_1 is *not* expected, the aggregate supply curve will continue its shift to AS_2, and the economy moves to point 2', at the intersection of AD_1 and AS_2. The inflation rate slows, but output declines to $Y_{2'}$, well below the natural rate level.

If, by contrast, the anti-inflation policy is *expected,* the aggregate supply curve will not move all the way to AS_2. Instead it will shift only to $AS_{2''}$ because some wages and prices (but not all) can be adjusted, so wages and the price level will not rise at their previous rates. Instead of moving to point 2' (as occurred when the anti-inflation policy was not expected), the economy moves to point 2", the intersection of the AD_1 and $AS_{2''}$ curves. The outcome is more desirable than when the policy is unanticipated—the inflation rate is lower (the price level rises only to $P_{2''}$ and not $P_{2'}$), and the output loss is smaller as well ($Y_{2''}$ is higher than $Y_{2'}$).

The Role of Credibility in Fighting Inflation

Both the new classical and new Keynesian models indicate that for an anti-inflation policy to be successful in reducing inflation at the lowest output cost, the public must believe (expect) that it will be implemented. In the new classical view of the world, the best anti-inflation policy (when it is credible) is to go "cold turkey." The rise in the aggregate demand curve from AD_1 should be stopped immediately. Inflation would be eliminated at once with no loss of output *if the policy were credible.* In a new Keynesian world, the "cold turkey" policy, *even if credible,* is not as desirable because it will produce some output loss.

John Taylor, a proponent of the new Keynesian model, has demonstrated that a more gradual approach to reducing inflation may be able to eliminate inflation without producing a substantial output loss.[7] An important catch here is that this gradual policy must somehow be made credible, which may be harder to achieve than a "cold turkey" anti-inflation policy, which demonstrates immediately that the policymakers are serious about fighting inflation. Taylor's contention that inflation can be reduced with little output loss may be overoptimistic.

Incorporating rational expectations into aggregate supply and demand analysis indicates that a successful anti-inflation policy must be credible. Evidence that credibility plays an important role in successful anti-inflation policies is provided by the dramatic end of the Bolivian hyperinflation in 1985 (see Box 2). Establishing credibility is easier said than done. You might think that an announcement by policymakers at the Federal Reserve that they plan to pursue an anti-inflation policy might do the trick. The public would expect this policy and would act accordingly. However, it implies that the public will believe the policymakers' announcement.

Unfortunately, that is not how the real world works.

Our historical review of Federal Reserve policymaking in Chapter 21 suggests that the Fed has never exercised tight control over the money supply. In fact, during the 1970s, the chairman of the Federal Reserve Board, Arthur Burns, repeatedly announced that the Fed would pursue a vigorous anti-inflation policy. The actual policy pursued, however, had quite a different outcome as the rate of growth of the money supply increased rapidly during the period. Such episodes have reduced the credibility of the Federal Reserve in the eyes of the public and, as predicted by the new classical and new Keynesian models, have had serious consequences. The reduction of inflation that occurred from 1981 to 1984 was bought at a very high cost; the 1981–1982 recession that helped bring the inflation rate down was the most severe recession in the post–World War II period. Unless some method of restoring credibility to anti-inflation policy is achieved, eliminating inflation will be a costly affair because such policy will be unanticipated.

The U.S. government can play an important role in establishing the credibility of anti-inflation policy. We have seen that large budget deficits may help stimulate inflationary monetary policy, and when the government and the Fed announce that they will pursue a restrictive anti-inflation policy, it is less likely that they will be believed *unless* the federal government demonstrates fiscal responsibility. Another way to say this is to use the old cliché "actions speak louder than words." When the government takes actions that will help the Fed adhere to anti-inflation policy, the policy will be more credible. Unfortunately, this lesson has sometimes been ignored by politicians in the United States and in other countries.

---

[7]John Taylor, "The Role of Expectations in the Choice of Monetary Policy," in *Monetary Policy Issues in the 1980s* (Federal Reserve Bank of Kansas City, 1982), pp. 47–76.

A Global Perspective

Box 2

ENDING THE BOLIVIAN HYPERINFLATION: CASE STUDY OF A SUCCESSFUL ANTI-INFLATION PROGRAM

The most remarkable anti-inflation program in recent years was that of Bolivia. In the first half of 1985, Bolivia's inflation rate was running at 20,000% and rising. Indeed, the inflation rate was so high that the price of a movie ticket often rose while people waited in line to buy it. In August 1985, Bolivia's new president announced his anti-inflation program, the New Economic Policy. To rein in money growth and establish credibility, the new government took drastic actions to slash the budget deficit by shutting down many state-owned enterprises, eliminating subsidies, freezing public sector salaries, and collecting a new wealth tax. The finance ministry was put on a new footing; the budget was balanced on a day-by-day basis. Without exceptions, the finance minister would not authorize spending in excess of the amount of tax revenue that had been collected the day before.

Arthur Okun's rule of thumb that a reduction of 1% in the inflation rate requires a 9% loss of a year's aggregate output indicates that ending the Bolivian hyperinflation would have required halving Bolivian aggregate output for 400 years! Instead, the Bolivian inflation was stopped in its tracks within one month, and the output loss was minor (less than 5% of GDP).

Certain hyperinflations before World War II were also ended with small losses of output using policies similar to Bolivia's,* and a more recent anti-inflation program in Israel that also involved substantial reductions in budget deficits sharply reduced inflation without any clear loss of output. There is no doubt that credible anti-inflation policies can be highly successful in eliminating inflation.

*For an excellent discussion of the end of four hyperinflations in the 1920s, see Thomas Sargent, "The Ends of Four Big Inflations," in *Inflation: Causes and Consequences,* ed. Robert E. Hall (Chicago: University of Chicago Press, 1982), pp. 41–98.

APPLICATION

CREDIBILITY AND THE REAGAN BUDGET DEFICITS

The Reagan administration was strongly criticized for creating huge budget deficits by cutting taxes in the early 1980s. In the Keynesian framework, we usually think of tax cuts as stimulating aggregate demand and increasing aggregate output. Could the expectation of large budget deficits have helped create a more severe recession in 1981–1982 after the Federal Reserve implemented an anti-inflation monetary policy?

Some economists answer yes, using diagrams like panels (b) and (c) of Figure 6. They claim that the prospect of large budget deficits made it harder for the public to believe that an anti-inflationary policy would actually be pursued when the Fed announced its intention to do so. Consequently the aggregate supply curve would continue to rise from AS_1 to AS_2 as in panels (b) and (c). When the Fed actually kept the aggregate demand curve from rising to AD_2 by slowing the rate of money growth in 1980–1981 and allowing interest rates to rise, the economy moved to a point like 2' in panels (b) and (c), and much unemployment resulted. As our analysis in panels (b) and (c) of Figure 6 predicts, the inflation rate did slow substantially, falling below 5% by the end of 1982, but this was very costly: Unemployment reached a peak of 10.7%.

If the Reagan administration had actively tried to reduce deficits instead of raising them by cutting taxes, what might have been the outcome of the anti-inflation policy? Instead of moving to point 2', the economy might have moved to point 2" in panel (c)—or even to point 1 in panel (b) if the new classical macroeconomists are right. We would have had an even more rapid reduction in inflation and a smaller loss of output. No wonder some economists were so hostile to Reagan's budget policies!

Reagan is not the only head of state who ran large budget deficits while espousing an anti-inflation policy. Britain's Margaret Thatcher preceded Reagan in this activity, and economists such as Thomas Sargent assert that the reward for her policy was a climb of unemployment in Britain to unprecedented levels.[8]

Although many economists agree that the Fed's anti-inflation program lacked credibility, especially in its initial phases, not all of them agree that the Reagan budget deficits were the cause of that lack of credibility. The conclusion that the Reagan budget deficits helped create a more severe recession in 1981–1982 is controversial.

IMPACT OF THE RATIONAL EXPECTATIONS REVOLUTION

The theory of rational expectations has caused a revolution in the way most economists now think about the conduct of monetary and fiscal policies and their effects on economic activity. One result of this revolution is that economists are now far more aware of the importance of expectations to economic decision making and to the outcome of particular policy actions. Although the rationality of expectations in all markets is still controversial, most economists now accept the following principle suggested by rational expectations: Expectation formation will change when the behavior of forecasted variables changes. As a result,

---

[8]Thomas Sargent, "Stopping Moderate Inflations: The Methods of Poincaré and Thatcher," in *Inflation, Debt and Indexation,* ed. Rudiger Dornbusch and M. H. Simonsen (Cambridge, Mass.: MIT Press, 1983), pp. 54–96, discusses the problems that Thatcher's policies caused and contrasts them with more successful anti-inflation policies pursued by the Poincaré government in France during the 1920s.

the Lucas critique of policy evaluation using conventional econometric models is now taken seriously by most economists. The Lucas critique also demonstrates that the effect of a particular policy depends critically on the public's expectations about that policy. This observation has made economists much less certain that policies will have their intended effect. An important result of the rational expectations revolution is that economists are no longer as confident in the success of activist stabilization policies as they once were.

Has the rational expectations revolution convinced economists that there is no role for activist stabilization policy? Those who adhere to the new classical macroeconomics think so. Because anticipated policy does not affect aggregate output, activist policy can lead only to unpredictable output fluctuations. Pursuing a nonactivist policy in which there is no uncertainty about policy actions is then the best that we can do. Such a position is not accepted by many economists because the empirical evidence on the policy ineffectiveness proposition is mixed. Some studies find that only unanticipated policy matters to output fluctuations, while other studies find a significant impact of anticipated policy on output movements.[9] In addition, some economists question whether the degree of wage and price flexibility required in the new classical model actually exists.

The result is that many economists take an intermediate position that recognizes the distinction between the effects of anticipated versus unanticipated policy but believe that anticipated policy can affect output. They are still open to the possibility that activist stabilization policy can be beneficial, but they recognize the difficulties of designing it.

The rational expectations revolution has also highlighted the importance of credibility to the success of anti-inflation policies. Economists now recognize that if an anti-inflation policy is not believed by the public, it may be less effective in reducing the inflation rate when it is actually implemented and may lead to a larger loss of output than is necessary. Achieving credibility (not an easy task in that policymakers often say one thing then do another) should then be an important goal for policymakers. To achieve credibility, policymakers must be consistent in their course of action.

The rational expectations revolution has caused major rethinking about the way economic policy should be conducted and has forced economists to recognize that we may have to accept a more limited role for what policy can do for us. Rather than attempting to fine-tune the economy so that all output fluctua-

---

[9]Studies with findings that only unanticipated policy matters include Thomas Sargent, "A Classical Macroeconometric Model for the United States," *Journal of Political Economy* 84 (1976): 207–237; Robert J. Barro, "Unanticipated Money Growth and Unemployment in the United States," *American Economic Review* 67 (1977): 101–115; and Robert J. Barro and Mark Rush, "Unanticipated Money and Economic Activity," in *Rational Expectations and Economic Policy*, ed. Stanley Fischer (Chicago: University of Chicago Press, 1980), pp. 23–48. Studies that find a significant impact of anticipated policy are Frederic S. Mishkin, "Does Anticipated Monetary Policy Matter? An Econometric Investigation," *Journal of Political Economy* 90 (1982): 22–51; and Robert J. Gordon, "Price Inertia and Policy Effectiveness in the United States, 1890–1980," *Journal of Political Economy* 90 (1982): 1087–1117.

tions are eliminated, we may have to settle for policies that create less uncertainty and thereby promote a more stable economic environment.

SUMMARY

1 The simple principle (derived from rational expectations theory) that expectation formation changes when the behavior of forecasted variables changes leads to the famous Lucas critique of econometric policy evaluation. Lucas argued that when policy changes, expectation formation changes; hence the relationships in an econometric model will change. An econometric model that has been estimated on the basis of past data will no longer be the correct model for evaluating the effects of this policy change and may prove to be highly misleading. The Lucas critique also points out that the effects of a particular policy depend critically on the public's expectations about the policy.

2. The new classical macroeconomic model assumes that expectations are rational and that wages and prices are completely flexible with respect to the expected price level. It leads to the policy ineffectiveness proposition that anticipated policy has no effect on output; only unanticipated policy matters.

3. The new Keynesian model also assumes that expectations are rational but views wages and prices as sticky. Like the new classical model, the new Keynesian model distinguishes between the effects from anticipated versus unanticipated policy: Anticipated policy has a smaller effect on ag-

gregate output than unanticipated policy. However, anticipated policy does matter to output fluctuations.

4. The new classical model indicates that activist policy can only be counterproductive, while the new Keynesian model suggests that activist policy might be beneficial. However, since both indicate that there is uncertainty about the outcome of a particular policy, the design of a beneficial activist policy may be very difficult. A traditional model in which expectations about policy have no effect on the aggregate supply curve does not distinguish between the effects of anticipated versus unanticipated policy. This model favors activist policy because the outcome of a particular policy is less uncertain.

5. If expectations about policy affect the aggregate supply curve, as they do in the new classical and new Keynesian models, then an anti-inflation policy will be more successful (will produce a faster reduction in inflation with smaller output loss) if it is credible.

6. The rational expectations revolution has forced economists to be less optimistic about the effective use of activist stabilization policy and has made them more aware of the importance of credibility to successful policymaking.

KEY TERMS

econometric models

policy ineffectiveness proposition

QUESTIONS AND PROBLEMS

1. If the public expects the Fed to pursue a policy that is likely to raise short-term interest rates permanently to 12% but the Fed does not go

through with this policy change, what will happen to long-term interest rates? Explain your answer.

*2. If consumer expenditure is related to consumers' expectations of their average income in the future, will an income tax cut have a larger effect on consumer expenditure if the public expects the tax cut to last for one year or for ten years?

Use an aggregate supply and demand diagram to illustrate your answer in all the following questions.

3. Having studied the new classical model, the new chairman of the Federal Reserve Board has thought up a surefire plan for reducing inflation and lowering unemployment. He announces that the Fed will lower the rate of money growth from 10% to 5% and then persuades the FOMC to keep the rate of money growth at 10%. If the new classical view of the world is correct, can his plan achieve the goals of lowering inflation and unemployment? How? Do you think his plan will work? If the traditional model's view of the world is correct, will the Fed chairman's surefire plan work?

*4. "The costs of fighting inflation in the new classical and new Keynesian models are lower than in the traditional model." Is this statement true, false, or uncertain? Explain.

5. The new classical model is sometimes characterized as an offshoot of the monetarist model because the two models have similar views of aggregate supply. What are the differences and similarities between the monetarist and new classical views of aggregate supply?

*6. "The new classical model does not eliminate policymakers' ability to reduce unemployment because they can always pursue policies that are more expansionary than the public expects." Is this statement true, false, or uncertain? Explain.

7. What principle of rational expectations theory is used to prove the proposition that stabilization policy can have no predictable effect on aggregate output in the new classical model?

*8. "The Lucas critique by itself casts doubt on the ability of activist stabilization policy to be beneficial." Is this statement true, false, or uncertain? Explain.

9. "The more credible the policymakers who pursue an anti-inflation policy, the more successful that policy will be." Is this statement true, false, or uncertain? Explain.

*10. Many economists are worried that a high level of budget deficits may lead to inflationary monetary policies in the future. Could these budget deficits have an effect on the current rate of inflation?

Using Economic Analysis to Predict the Future

11. Suppose that a treaty is signed limiting armies throughout the world. The result of the treaty is that the public expects military and hence government spending to be reduced. If the new classical view of the economy is correct and government spending does affect the aggregate demand curve, predict what will happen to aggregate output and the price level when government spending is reduced in line with the public's expectations.

12. How would your prediction differ in Problem 11 if the new Keynesian model provides a more realistic description of the economy? What if the traditional model provides the most realistic description of the economy?

*13. The chairman of the Federal Reserve Board announces that over the next year, the rate of money growth will be reduced from its current rate of 10% to a rate of 2%. If the chairman is believed by the public but the Fed actually reduces the rate of money growth to 5%, predict what will happen to the inflation rate and aggregate output if the new classical view of the economy is correct.

*14. How would your prediction differ in Problem 13 if the new Keynesian model provides a more accurate description of the economy? What if the traditional model provides the most realistic description of the economy?

15. If, in a surprise victory, a new administration is elected to office that the public believes will pursue inflationary policy, predict what might happen to the level of output and inflation even before the new administration comes into power. Would your prediction differ depending on which of the traditional, new classical, and new Keynesian models you believed in?

A MATHEMATICAL TREATMENT OF THE BAUMOL-TOBIN AND TOBIN MEAN-VARIANCE MODELS

BAUMOL-TOBIN MODEL OF TRANSACTIONS DEMAND FOR MONEY

The basic idea behind the Baumol-Tobin model was laid out in the chapter. Here we explore the mathematics that underlie their model. The assumptions of the model are as follows:

1. An individual receives income of T_0 at the beginning of every period.

2. An individual spends this income at a constant rate, so at the end of the period, all income T_0 has been spent.

3. There are only two assets—cash and bonds. Cash earns a nominal return of zero, and bonds earn an interest rate i.

4. Every time an individual buys or sells bonds to raise cash, a fixed brokerage fee of b is incurred.

Let us denote the amount of cash that the individual raises for each purchase or sale of bonds as C, and n = the number of times the individual conducts a transaction in bonds. As we saw in Figure 3 in the chapter, where $T_0 = 1000$, $C = 500$, and $n = 2$,

$$n = \frac{T_0}{C}$$

Because the brokerage cost of each bond transaction is b, the total brokerage costs for a period are

$$nb = \frac{bT_0}{C}$$

Not only are there brokerage costs, but there is also an opportunity cost to holding cash rather than bonds. This opportunity cost is the bond interest rate i times average cash balances held during the period, which, from the discussion in the chapter, we know is equal to $C/2$. The opportunity cost is then

$$\frac{iC}{2}$$

Combining these two costs, we have the total costs for an individual equal to

$$COSTS = \frac{bT_0}{C} + \frac{iC}{2}$$

The individual wants to minimize costs by choosing the appropriate level of C. This is accomplished by taking the derivative of costs with respect to C and setting it to zero.[1] That is,

$$\frac{d\ COSTS}{dC} = \frac{-bT_0}{C^2} + \frac{i}{2} = 0$$

Solving for C yields the optimal level of C:

$$C = \sqrt{\frac{2bT_0}{i}}$$

Because money demand M^d is the average desired holding of cash balances $C/2$,

$$M^d = \frac{1}{2}\sqrt{\frac{2bT_0}{i}} = \sqrt{\frac{bT_0}{2i}} \tag{1}$$

This is the famous *square root rule*.[2] It has these implications for the demand for money:

----

[1] To minimize costs, the second derivative must be greater than zero. We find that it is, because

$$\frac{d^2 COSTS}{dC^2} = \frac{-2}{C^3}(-bT_0) = \frac{2bT_0}{C^3} > 0$$

[2] An alternative way to get Equation 1 is to have the individual maximize profits, which equal the interest on bonds minus the brokerage costs. The average holding of bonds over a period is just

$$\frac{T_0}{2} - \frac{C}{2}$$

Thus profits are

$$PROFITS = -\frac{i}{2}(T_0 - C) - \frac{bT_0}{C}$$

Then

$$\frac{d\ PROFITS}{dC} = \frac{-i}{2} + \frac{bT_0}{C^2} = 0$$

This equation yields the same square root rule as Equation 1.

1. The transactions demand for money is negatively related to the interest rate i.

2. The transactions demand for money is positively related to income, but there are economies of scale in money holdings—that is, the demand for money rises less than proportionally with income. For example, if T_0 quadruples in Equation (1), the demand for money only doubles.

3. A lowering of the brokerage costs due to technological improvements would decrease the demand for money.

4. There is no money illusion in the demand for money. If the price level doubles, both T_0 and b will double. Equation (1) then indicates that M will double as well. Thus the demand for real money balances remains unchanged, which makes sense because neither the interest rate nor real income has changed.

TOBIN MEAN-VARIANCE MODEL

Tobin's mean-variance analysis of money demand is just an application of the basic ideas in the theory of asset demand outlined in Chapter 5. Tobin assumes that the utility people derive from their assets is positively related to the expected return on their portfolio of assets and is negatively related to the riskiness of this portfolio as represented by the variance (or standard deviation) of its returns. This framework implies that an individual has indifference curves that can be drawn as in Figure 1. Notice that these indifference curves are upward-sloping because an individual is willing to accept more risk if offered a higher expected return. In addition, as we go to higher indifference curves, utility is higher because for the same level of risk, the expected return is higher.

FIGURE 1
Indifference Curves in a Mean-Variance Model
The indifference curves are up-ward-sloping, and higher indifference curves indicate that utility is higher. In other words, $U_3 > U_2 > U_1$.

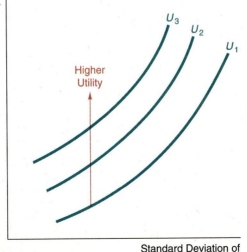

Tobin looks at the choice of holding money, which earns a certain zero return, or bonds, whose return

$$R_B = i + g$$

where i = interest rate on the bond

$\quad\ g$ = capital gain

Tobin also assumes that the expected capital gain is zero[3] and its variance is σ_g^2. That is,

$$E(g) = 0 \quad \text{and so} \quad E(R_B) = i + 0 = i$$

$$Var(g) = E[g - E(g)]^2 = E(g^2) = \sigma_g^2$$

where E = expectation of the variable inside the parentheses

$\qquad Var$ = variance of the variable inside the parentheses

If A is the fraction of the portfolio put into bonds ($0 \leq A \leq 1$) and $1 - A$ is the fraction of the portfolio held as money, the return R on the portfolio can be written as

$$R = AR_B + (1 - A)(0) = AR_B = A(i + g)$$

Then the mean and variance of the return on the portfolio, denoted respectively as μ and σ^2, can be calculated as follows:

$$\mu = E(R) = E(AR_B) = AE(R_B) = Ai$$

$$\sigma^2 = E(R - \mu)^2 = E[A(i + g) - Ai]^2 = E(Ag)^2 = A^2 E(g^2) = A^2 \sigma_g^2$$

Taking the square root of both sides of the equation directly above and solving for A yields

$$A = \frac{1}{\sigma_g} \sigma \tag{2}$$

Substituting for A in the equation $\mu = Ai$ using the preceding equation gives us

$$\mu = \frac{i}{\sigma_g} \sigma \tag{3}$$

---

[3] This assumption is not critical to the results. If $E(g) \neq 0$, then it can be added to the interest term i, and the analysis proceeds as indicated.

FIGURE 2
Optimal Choice of the Fraction of the Portfolio in Bonds
The highest indifference curve is reached at a point B, the tangency of the indifference curve with the opportunity locus. This point determines the optimal risk σ*, and using Equation 2 in the bottom half of the figure, we solve for the optimal fraction of the portfolio in bonds A*.

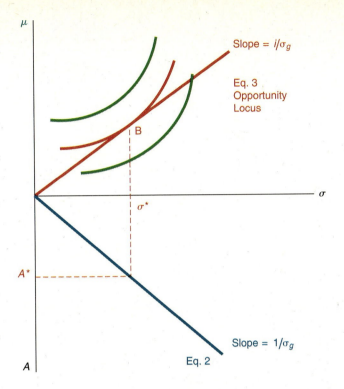

Equation 3 is known as the *opportunity locus* because it tells us the combinations of μ and σ that are feasible for the individual. This equation is written in a form in which the μ variable corresponds to the Y axis and the σ variable to the X axis. The opportunity locus is a straight line going through the origin with a slope of i/σ_g. It is drawn in the top half of Figure 2 along with the indifference curves from Figure 1.

The highest indifference curve is reached at point B, the tangency of the indifference curve and the opportunity locus. This point determines the optimal level of risk σ^* in the figure. As Equation 2 indicates, the optimal level of A, A*, is

$$A^* = \frac{\sigma^*}{\sigma_g}$$

This equation is solved in the bottom half of Figure 2. Equation 2 for A is a straight line through the origin with a slope of $1/\sigma_g$. Given σ^*, the value of A read off this line is the optimal value A^*. Notice that the bottom part of the figure is drawn so that as we move down, A is increasing.

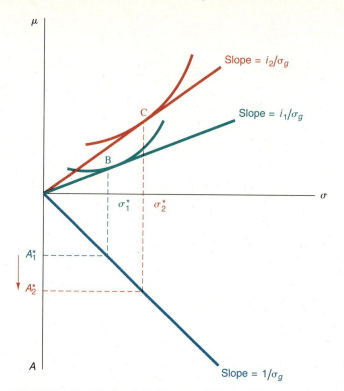

FIGURE 3 Optimal Choice of the Fraction of the Portfolio in Bonds as the Interest Rate Rises

The interest rate on bonds rises from i_1 to i_2, rotating the opportunity locus upward. The highest indifference curve is now at point C, where it is tangent to the new opportunity locus. The optimal level of risk rises from σ_1^* to σ_2^*, and then Equation 2, in the bottom half of the figure, shows that the optimal fraction of the portfolio in bonds rises from A_1^* to A_2^*.

Now let's ask ourselves what happens when the interest rate increases from i_1 to i_2. This situation is shown in Figure 3. Because σ_g is unchanged, the Equation 2 line in the bottom half of the figure does not change. However, the slope of the opportunity locus does increase as i increases. Thus the opportunity locus rotates up and we move to point C at the tangency of the new opportunity locus and the indifference curve. As you can see, the optimal level of risk increases from σ_1^* to σ_2^*, and the optimal fraction of the portfolio in bonds rises from A_1^* to A_2^*. The result is that as the interest rate on bonds rises, the demand for money falls; that is, $1 - A$, the fraction of the portfolio held as money, declines.[4]

---

[4] The indifference curves have been drawn so that the usual result is obtained that as i goes up, A^* goes up as well. However, there is a subtle issue of income versus substitution effects. If, as people get wealthier, they are willing to bear less risk, and if this income effect is larger than the substitution effect, then it is possible to get the opposite result that as i increases, A^* declines. This set of conditions is unlikely, which is why the figure is drawn so that the usual result is obtained. For a discussion of income versus substitution effects, see David Laidler, *The Demand for Money: Theories and Evidence*, 3rd ed. (New York: HarperCollins, 1985).

Tobin's model then yields the same result as Keynes's analysis of the speculative demand for money: It is negatively related to the level of interest rates. This model, however, makes two important points that Keynes's model does not:

1. Individuals diversify their portfolios and hold money *and* bonds at the same time.
2. Even if the expected return on bonds is greater than the expected return on money, individuals will still hold money as a store of wealth because its return is more certain.

Mathematical Appendix to Chapter 25

ALGEBRA OF THE *ISLM* MODEL

The use of algebra to analyze the *ISLM* model allows us to extend the multiplier analysis in Chapter 24 and to obtain many of the results of Chapters 24 and 25 very quickly.

BASIC CLOSED-ECONOMY *ISLM* MODEL

The goods market can be described by the following equations:

Consumption function:	$C = \overline{C} + mpc\,(Y - T)$	(1)
Investment function:	$I = \overline{I} - di$	(2)
Taxes:	$T = \overline{T}$	(3)
Government spending:	$G = \overline{G}$	(4)
Goods market equilibrium condition:	$Y = Y^{ad} = C + I + G$	(5)

The money market is described by these equations:

Money demand function:	$M^d = \overline{M}^d + eY - fi$	(6)
Money supply:	$M^s = \overline{M}$	(7)
Money market equilibrium condition	$M^d = M^s$	(8)

The uppercase terms are the variables of the model; $\overline{G}$, $\overline{T}$, and $\overline{M}$ are the values of the policy variables that are set exogenously (outside the model); and $\overline{C}$, $\overline{I}$, and $\overline{M}^d$ are autonomous components of consumer expenditure, investment spending, and money demand that are also determined exogenously (outside the model). Except for the interest rate i, the lowercase terms are the parameters, the givens of the model, and all are assumed to be positive. The definitions of these variables and parameters are as follows:

C = consumer spending
I = investment spending
$G = \overline{G}$ = government spending
Y = output
$T = \overline{T}$ = taxes

$$M^d = \text{money demand}$$
$$M^s = \overline{M} = \text{money supply}$$
$$i = \text{interest rate}$$
$$\overline{C} = \text{autonomous consumer spending}$$
$$d = \text{interest sensitivity of investment spending}$$
$$\overline{I} = \text{autonomous investment spending related to business confidence}$$
$$\overline{M}^d = \text{autonomous money demand}$$
$$e = \text{income sensitivity of money demand}$$
$$f = \text{interest sensitivity of money demand}$$
$$mpc = \text{marginal propensity to consume}$$

IS and LM Curves

Substituting for C, I, and G in the goods market equilibrium condition and then solving for Y, we obtain the *IS* curve:

$$Y = \frac{1}{1 - mpc} (\overline{C} + \overline{I} - mpc\,\overline{T} + \overline{G} - di) \tag{9}$$

Solving for i from Equations 6, 7, and 8, we obtain the *LM* curve:

$$i = \frac{\overline{M}^d - \overline{M} + eY}{f} \tag{10}$$

Solution of the Model

The solution to the model occurs at the intersection of the *IS* and *LM* curves, which involves solving for Y and i simultaneously, using Equations 9 and 10, as follows:

$$Y = \frac{1}{1 - mpc + de/f} \left(\overline{C} + \overline{I} - mpc\,\overline{T} + \overline{G} - \frac{d\overline{M}^d}{f} + \frac{d\overline{M}}{f} \right) \tag{11}$$

$$i = \frac{1}{f(1 - mpc) + d} \left[e(\overline{C} + \overline{I} - mpc\,\overline{T} + \overline{G}) + \overline{M}^d(1 - mpc) - \overline{M}(1 - mpc) \right]$$

(12)

Implications

The conclusions reached with these algebraic solutions are the same as those reached in Chapters 24 and 25; for example:

1. Because all the coefficients are positive, Equation 11 indicates that a rise in $\bar{C}$, $\bar{I}$, $\bar{G}$, and $\bar{M}$ leads to a rise in Y and that a rise in $\bar{T}$ or $\bar{M}^d$ leads to a fall in Y.

2. Equation 12 indicates that a rise in $\bar{C}$, $\bar{I}$, $\bar{G}$, and $\bar{M}^d$ leads to a rise in i and that a rise in $\bar{M}$ or $\bar{T}$ leads to a fall in i.

3. As f, the interest sensitivity of money demand, increases, the multiplier term

$$\frac{1}{1 - mpc + de/f}$$

increases, and so fiscal policy ($\bar{G}$, $\bar{T}$) has more effect on output; conversely, the term multiplying $\bar{M}$,

$$\frac{d}{f}\left(\frac{1}{1 - mpc + de/f}\right) = \frac{d}{f(1 - mpc) + de}$$

declines, so monetary policy has less effect on output.

4. By similar reasoning, as d, the interest sensitivity of investment spending, increases, monetary policy has more effect on output and fiscal policy has less effect on output.

OPEN-ECONOMY *ISLM* MODEL

To make the basic *ISLM* model into an open-economy model, we need to include net exports in the goods market equilibrium condition so that Equation 5 becomes Equation 5':

$$Y = Y^{ad} = C + I + G + NX \tag{5'}$$

As the discussion in Chapter 25 suggests, the net exports and exchange rate relations can be written

$$NX = \overline{NX} - hE \tag{13}$$
$$E = \bar{E} + ji \tag{14}$$

where NX = net exports
  $\overline{NX}$ = autonomous net exports
  h = exchange rate sensitivity of net exports
  E = exchange rate (value of domestic currency)

$\overline{E}$ = autonomous exchange rate

j = interest sensitivity of exchange rate

Substituting for net exports in the goods market equilibrium condition (Equation 5') using the net exports and exchange rate relations and then solving for Y as in the basic model, we obtain the open-economy *IS* curve:

$$Y = \frac{1}{1 - mpc} [\overline{C} + \overline{I} - mpc\,\overline{T} + \overline{G} + \overline{NX} - b\overline{E} - (d + bj)i] \qquad (15)$$

The *LM* curve is the same as in the basic model, and so the solutions for Y and i are as follows:

$$Y = \frac{1}{1 - mpc + (d + bj)e/f}$$

$$\times (\overline{C} + \overline{I} - mpc\,\overline{T} + \overline{G} - \frac{d + bj}{f}\overline{M}^d + \frac{d + bj}{f}\overline{M} + \overline{NX} - b\overline{E}) \qquad (16)$$

$$i = \frac{1}{f(1 - mpc) + (d + bj)e}$$

$$\times [e(\overline{C} + \overline{I} - mpc\,\overline{T} + \overline{G} + \overline{NX} - b\overline{E}) + \overline{M}^d(1 - mpc) - \overline{M}(1 - mpc)] \qquad (17)$$

Implications

1. As the *IS* curve in Equation 15 indicates, including net exports in aggregate demand provides an additional reason for the negative relationship between Y and i (the downward slope of the *IS* curve). This additional reason for the negative relationship of Y and i is represented by bj in the term $-(d + bj)i$.

2. Equations 16 and 17 indicate that all the results we found for the basic model still hold.

3. Equation 16 indicates that a rise in $\overline{NX}$ leads to a rise in Y, and an autonomous rise in the value of the domestic currency $\overline{E}$ leads to a decline in Y.

4. Equation 17 indicates that a rise in $\overline{NX}$ leads to a rise in i, and a rise in $\overline{E}$ leads to a decline in i.

GLOSSARY

accommodating policy   An activist policy in pursuit of a high employment target. **692**

activist   An economist who views the self-correcting mechanism through wage and price adjustment to be very slow and hence sees the need for the government to pursue active, discretionary policy to eliminate high unemployment whenever it develops. **537**

adaptive expectations   Expectations of a variable based on an average of past values of the variable. **712**

adverse selection   The problem created by asymmetric information *before* a transaction occurs: The people who are the most undesirable from the other party's point of view are the ones who are most likely to want to engage in the financial transaction. **35**

aggregate demand   The total quantity of output demanded in the economy at different price levels. **574, 625**

aggregate demand curve   A relationship between the price level and the quantity of aggregate output demanded when the goods and money markets are in equilibrium. **619, 625**

aggregate demand function   The relationship between aggregate output and aggregate demand that shows the quantity of aggregate output demanded for each level of aggregate output. **579**

aggregate income   The total income of factors of production (land, labor, capital) in the economy. **17**

aggregate output   The total production of final goods and services in the economy. **4**

aggregate price level   The average price of goods and services in an economy. **5**

aggregate supply   The quantity of aggregate output supplied by the economy at different price levels. **625**

aggregate supply curve   The relationship between the quantity of output supplied in the short run and the price level. **632**

"animal spirits"   Waves of optimism and pessimism that affect consumers' and businesses' willingness to spend. **583, 630**

appreciation   Increase in a currency's value. **175**

asset   A financial claim or piece of property that is a store of value. **11, 95**

asset management   The acquisition of assets that have a low rate of default and diversification of asset holdings to increase profits. **260**

asset market approach   Determin asset prices using stocks of assets rather than flows. **113**

asymmetric information   The inequality of knowledge that each party to a transaction has about the other party. **35**

autonomous consumer expenditure   The amount of consumer expenditure that is independent of disposable income. **575**

balance of payments   A bookkeeping system for recording all payments that have a direct bearing on the movement of funds between a country and foreign countries. **524**

balance sheet   A list of the assets and liabilities of a bank (or firm) that balances—total assets equal total liabilities plus capital. **251**

bank failure   A situation in which a bank cannot satisfy its obligations to pay its depositors and other creditors and thus goes out of business. **265**

bank holding companies Companies that own one or more banks. **286**

bank panic The simultaneous failure of many banks, as during a financial crisis. **225**

banks Financial institutions that accept money deposits and make loans (such as commercial banks, savings and loan associations, and credit unions). **9**

basis point One one-hundredth of a percentage point. **85**

beta A measure of the sensitivity of an asset's return to changes in the value of the market portfolio, which is also a measure of the asset's marginal contribution to the risk of the market portfolio. **103**

Board of Governors of the Federal Reserve System A board with seven governors (including the chairman) that plays an essential role in decision making within the Federal Reserve System. **438**

bond A debt security that promises to make payments periodically for a specified period of time. **11**

branches Additional offices of banks that conduct banking operations. **287**

Bretton Woods system The international monetary system in use from 1945 to 1971 in which exchange rates were fixed and the U.S. dollar was freely convertible into gold (by foreign governments and central banks only). **530**

brokerage firms Firms that participate in all three securities markets as brokers, dealers, and investment bankers. **361**

brokered deposits Deposits that enable depositors to circumvent the $100,000 limit on federal deposit insurance by breaking up a large deposit into smaller packages of less than $100,000 at each bank so the total amount deposited is fully insured. **322**

brokers Agents for investors who match buyers with sellers. **25**

budget deficit The excess of government expenditure over tax revenues. **8**

business cycles The upward and downward movement of aggregate output produced in the economy. **4**

call option An option contract that provides the right to buy a security at a specified price. **236**

capital account An account that describes the flow of capital between the United States and other countries. **527**

capital market A financial market in which longer-term debt (maturity of greater than one year) and equity instruments are traded. **26**

capital mobility A situation in which foreigners can easily purchase a country's assets and the country's residents can easily purchase foreign assets. **185**

central bank The government agency that oversees the banking system and is responsible for the amount of money and credit supplied in the economy; in the United States, the Federal Reserve System. **284, 367**

closed-end fund A mutual fund in which a fixed number of nonredeemable shares are sold at an initial offering, then traded in the over-the-counter market like common stock. **356**

coinsurance A situation in which only a portion of losses are covered by insurance, so that the insured suffers a percentage of the losses along with the insurance agency. **334**

collateral Property that is pledged to the lender to guarantee payment in the event that the borrower should be unable to make debt payments. **208**

commodity money Money made up of precious metals or another valuable commodity. **56**

compensating balance A required minimum amount of funds that a firm receiving a loan must keep in a checking account at the lending bank. **274**

complete crowding out The situation in which expansionary fiscal policy, such as an increase in government spending, does not lead to a rise in output because there is an exactly offsetting movement of private spending. **613, 630**

consol A perpetual bond with no maturity date and no repayment of principal that periodically makes fixed coupon payments. **78**

constant-money-growth-rate rule A policy rule advocated by monetarists whereby the Federal Reserve keeps the money supply growing at a constant rate. **706**

consumer durable expenditure Spending by consumers on durable items such as automobiles and household appliances. **674**

consumer expenditure The total demand for (spending on) consumer goods and services. **574, 628**

consumption Spending by consumers on non-durable goods and services (including services related to the ownership of homes and consumer durables). **675**

consumption function The relationship between disposable income and consumer expenditure. **575**

costly state verification Monitoring a firm's activities, an expensive process in both time and money. **219**

cost-push inflation Inflation that occurs because of the push by workers to obtain higher wages. **691**

coupon bond A credit market instrument that pays the owner a fixed interest payment every year until the maturity date, when a specified final amount is repaid. **70**

coupon rate The dollar amount of the yearly coupon payment expressed as a percentage of the face value of a coupon bond. **70**

credit rationing A lender's refusing to make loans even though borrowers are willing to pay the stated interest rate or even a higher rate or restricting the size of loans made to less than the full amount sought. **274**

credit risk The risk arising from the possibility that the borrower will default. **260**

currency Paper money (such as dollar bills) and coins. **27**

current account An account that shows international transactions involving currently produced goods and services. **524**

current yield An approximation of the yield to maturity that equals the yearly coupon payment divided by the price of a coupon bond. **80**

dealers People who link buyers with sellers by buying and selling securities at stated prices. **25**

debt deflation A situation in which a substantial decline in the price level sets in, leading to a further deterioration in firms' net worth because of the increased burden of indebtedness. **226**

deductible The fixed amount by which the insured's loss is reduced when a claim is paid off. **346**

default A situation in which the party issuing a debt instrument is unable to make interest payments or pay off the amount owed when the instrument matures. **27**

default-free bonds Bonds with no default risk, such as U.S. government bonds. **150**

default risk The chance that the issuer of a debt instrument will be unable to make interest payments or pay off the face value when the instrument matures. **150**

defensive open market operations Open market operations intended to offset movements in other factors that affect the monetary base (such as changes in Treasury deposits with the Fed or changes in float). **477**

demand curve A curve depicting the relationship between quantity demanded and price when all other economic variables are held constant. **107**

demand-pull inflation Inflation that results when policymakers pursue policies that shift the aggregate demand curve. **691**

deposit outflows Losses of deposits when depositors make withdrawals or demand payment. **260**

deposit rate ceilings Restrictions on the maximum interest rates payable on deposits. **245**

depreciation Decrease in a currency's value. **175**

devaluation Resetting of the par value of a currency at a lower level. **532**

dirty float See *managed float regime*. **519**

discount bond A credit market instrument that is bought at a price below its face value and whose face value is repaid at the maturity date; it does not make any interest payments. Also called a *zero-coupon bond*. **70**

discount loans A bank's borrowing from the Federal Reserve System; also known as *advances*. **254**

discount rate The interest rate that the Federal Reserve charges banks on discount loans. **262, 370**

discount window The Federal Reserve facility at which discount loans are made to banks. **480**

discount yield See *yield on a discount basis*. **81**

disintermediation A reduction in the flow of funds into the banking system that causes the amount of financial intermediation to decline. **245**

disposable income Total income available for spending, equal to aggregate income minus taxes. **575**

diversification The holding of many risky assets. **100**

dividends Periodic payments made by equities to shareholders. **24**

dual banking system The system in the United States in which banks supervised by the federal government and banks supervised by the states operate side by side. **285**

duration analysis A measurement of the sensitivity of the market value of a bank's assets and liabilities to changes in interest rates. **276**

dynamic open market operations Open market operations that are intended to change the level of reserves and the monetary base. **477**

econometric model A model whose equations are estimated using statistical procedures. **734**

economies of scale The reduction in transactions costs per dollar of transaction as the size (scale) of transactions increases. **34**

Edge Act corporation A special subsidiary of a U.S. bank that is engaged primarily in international banking. **295**

effective exchange rate index An index reflecting the value of a basket of representative foreign currencies. **197**

equation of exchange The equation $MV = PY$, which relates nominal income to the quantity of money. **544, 627**

equities Claims to share in the net income and assets of a corporation (such as common stock). **24**

equity capital See *net worth*. **215**

equity multiplier The amount of assets per dollar of equity capital. **257**

Eurobonds Bonds denominated in a currency other than that of the country in which they are sold. **47**

Eurodollars U.S. dollars that are deposited in foreign banks outside of the United States or in foreign branches of U.S. banks. **30**

excess demand A situation in which quantity demanded is greater than quantity supplied. **111**

excess reserves Reserves in excess of required reserves. **254, 370**

excess supply A situation in which quantity supplied is greater than quantity demanded. **110**

exchange rate The price of one currency in terms of another. **173**

exchange rate overshooting A phenomenon whereby the exchange rate changes by more in the short run than it does in the long run when the money supply changes. **195**

exchanges Secondary markets in which buyers and sellers of securities (or their agents or brokers) meet in one central location to conduct trades. **25**

expectations hypothesis The proposition that the interest rate on a long-term bond will equal the average of the short-term interest rates that people expect to occur over the life of the long-term bond. **159**

expected return The return on an asset expected over the next period. **96**

expenditure multiplier The ratio of the change in aggregate output to a change in investment spending (or autonomous spending). **581**

face value A specified final amount paid to the owner of a coupon bond at the maturity date. Also called *par value*. **70**

federal funds rate The interest rate on overnight loans of deposits at the Federal Reserve. **30**

Federal Open Market Committee (FOMC) The committee that makes decisions regarding the conduct of open market operations; composed of the seven members of the Board of Governors of the Federal Reserve System, the president of the Federal Reserve Bank of New York, and the presidents of four other Federal Reserve banks on a rotating basis. **438**

Federal Reserve banks The 12 district banks in the Federal Reserve System. **438**

Federal Reserve System (the Fed) The central banking authority responsible for monetary policy in the United States. **7, 368**

fiat money Paper currency decreed by a government as legal tender but not convertible into coins or precious metal. **56**

financial crisis A major disruption in financial markets that is characterized by sharp declines in asset prices and the failures of many financial and nonfinancial firms. **223**

financial engineering The process of researching and developing new financial products and services that would meet customer needs and prove profitable. **232**

financial futures contract A futures contract in which the standardized commodity is a particular type of financial instrument. **234**

financial intermediaries Institutions (such as banks, insurance companies, mutual funds, pension funds, and finance companies) that borrow funds from people who have saved and then make loans to others. **9**

financial intermediation The process of indirect finance whereby financial intermediaries link lender-savers and borrower-spenders. **34**

financial markets Markets in which funds are transferred from people who have a surplus of available funds to people who have a shortage of available funds. **11**

financial panic The widespread collapse of financial markets and intermediaries in an economy. **43**

Fisher effect The outcome that when expected inflation occurs, interest rates will rise; named after economist Irving Fisher. **121**

fixed exchange rate regime A regime in which central banks buy and sell their own currencies to keep their exchange rates fixed at a certain level. **529**

fixed investment Spending by firms on equipment (computers, airplanes) and structures (factories, office buildings) and planned spending on residential housing. **577**

fixed-payment loan A credit market instrument that provides a borrower with an amount of money that is repaid by making a fixed payment periodically (usually monthly) for a set number of years. **70**

float Cash items in process of collection at the Fed minus deferred-availability cash items. **460**

foreign bonds Bonds sold in a foreign country and denominated in that country's currency. **46**

foreign exchange intervention An international financial transaction in which a central bank buys or sells currency to influence foreign exchange rates. **175**

foreign exchange market The market in which exchange rates are determined. **173**

foreign exchange rate See *exchange rate*. **13**

forward exchange rate The exchange rate for a forward transaction. **175**

forward transaction An exchange rate transaction that involves the exchange of bank deposits denominated in different currencies at some specified future date. **175**

free reserves Excess reserves in the banking system minus the volume of discount loans. **506**

free-rider problem The problem that occurs when people who do not pay for information take advantage of the information that other people have paid for. **214**

fully funded Describing a pension plan in which the contributions to the plan and their earnings over the years are sufficient to pay out the defined benefits when they come due. **351**

futures contract A contract in which the seller agrees to provide a certain standardized commodity to the buyer on a specified future date at an agreed-on price. **234**

gap analysis A measurement of the sensitivity of bank profits to changes in interest rates, calculated by subtracting the amount of rate-sensitive liabilities from the amount of rate-sensitive assets. **276**

gold standard A regime under which a currency is directly convertible into gold. **528**

government budget constraint The requirement that the government budget deficit equal the sum of the change in the monetary base and the change in government bonds held by the public. **467**

government spending Spending by all levels of government on goods and services. **574, 628**

gross domestic product (GDP) The value of all final goods and services produced in the economy during the course of a year. **17**

hedge To protect oneself against risk. **234**

high-powered money The monetary base. **384**

hyperinflation An extreme inflation in which the inflation rate exceeds 50% per month. **55**

hysteresis A departure from full employment levels as a result of past high unemployment. **644**

incentive-compatible Aligning the incentives of both parties to a contract. **221**

income The flow of earnings. **52**

inflation The condition of a continually rising price level. **5**

inflation rate The rate of change of the price level, usually measured as a percentage change per year. **6**

insolvent A situation in which the value of a firm's or bank's assets have fallen below its liabilities; bankrupt. **266**

interest parity condition The observation that the domestic interest rate equals the foreign interest rate plus the expected appreciation in the foreign currency. **185**

interest rate   The cost of borrowing or the price paid for the rental of funds (usually expressed as a percentage per year). **6**

interest-rate risk   The possible reduction in returns that is associated with changes in interest rates. **88**

intermediate target   Any of a number of variables, such as monetary aggregates or interest rates, that have a direct effect on employment and the price level and that the Fed seeks to influence. **497**

intermediate-term   With Reference to a debt instrument, having a maturity of between one and ten years. **24**

international banking facilities (IBFs)   Banking establishments in the United States that can accept time deposits from foreigners but are not subject to either reserve requirements or restrictions on interest payments. **295**

International Monetary Fund (IMF)   The international organization created by the Bretton Woods agreement whose objective is to promote the growth of world trade by making loans to countries experiencing balance-of-payments difficulties. **530**

international policy coordination   Agreements among countries to enact policies cooperatively. **513**

international reserves   Central bank holdings of assets denominated in foreign currencies. **519**

inventory investment   Spending by firms on additional holdings of raw materials, parts, and finished goods. **577**

investment banks   Firms that assist in the initial sale of securities in the primary market. **25**

IS **curve**   The relationship that describes the combinations of aggregate output and interest rates for which the total quantity of goods produced equals the total quantity demanded (goods market equilibrium). **591**

January effect   An abnormal rise in stock prices from December to January. **725**

junk bonds   Bonds with ratings below Baa (or BBB) that have a high default risk. **152**

Keynesian   A follower of John Maynard Keynes who believes that movements in the price level

and aggregate output are driven by changes not only in the money supply but also in government spending and fiscal policy and who does not regard the economy as inherently stable. **625**

L   A measure of highly liquid assets that adds to *M3* short-term Treasury securities, commercial paper, long-term Eurodollars, savings bonds, and banker's acceptances. **60**

law of one price   The principle that if two countries produce an identical good, the price of this good should be the same throughout the world no matter which country produces it. **178**

lender of last resort   Provider of reserves to financial institutions when no one else would provide them in order to prevent a financial crisis. **427**

leverage ratio   A bank's capital divided by its assets. **311**

liabilities   IOUs or debts. **22**

liability management   The acquisition of funds at low cost to increase profits. **260**

liquid   Easily converted into cash. **25**

liquidity   The relative ease and speed with which an asset can be converted into cash. **55, 96**

liquidity management   The decisions made by a bank to maintain sufficient liquid assets to meet the bank's obligations to depositors. **260**

liquidity preference framework   A model developed by John Maynard Keynes that predicts the equilibrium interest rate on the basis of the supply of and demand for money. **125**

liquidity preference theory   John Maynard Keynes's theory of the demand for money. **551**

liquidity premium theory   The theory that the interest rate on a long-term bond will equal an average of short-term interest rates expected to occur over the life of the long-term bond plus a positive term (liquidity) premium. **164**

LM **curve**   The relationship that describes the combinations of interest rates and aggregate output for which the quantity of money demanded equals the quantity of money supplied (money market equilibrium). **591**

load funds   Open-end mutual funds sold by salespeople who receive a commission that is paid at the time of purchase and is immediately subtracted from the redemption value of the shares. **356**

loanable funds The quantity of loans. **112**

loanable funds framework Determining the equilibrium interest rate by analyzing the supply of and demand for bonds (loanable funds). **112**

loan commitment A bank's commitment (for a specified future period of time) to provide a firm with loans up to a given amount at an interest rate that is tied to some market interest rate. **272**

loan sale The sale under a contract (also called a *secondary loan participation*) of all or part of the cash stream from a specific loan, thereby removing the loan from the bank's balance sheet. **279**

long-run aggregate supply curve The quantity of output supplied in the long run at any given price level. **637**

long-run monetary neutrality See *monetary neutrality*. **619**

long-term With reference to a debt instrument, having a maturity of ten years or more. **24**

luxury An asset for which the wealth elasticity of demand is greater than 1. **97**

M1 A measure of money that includes currency, traveler's checks, and checkable deposits. **60**

M2 A measure of money that adds to M1 money market deposit accounts, money market mutual fund shares, small-denomination time deposits, savings deposits, overnight repurchase agreements, and overnight Eurodollars. **60**

M3 A measure of money that adds to M2 large-denomination time deposits, long-term repurchase agreements, and institutional money market fund shares. **60**

managed float regime The current international financial environment in which exchange rates fluctuate from day to day, but central banks attempt to influence their countries' exchange rates by buying and selling currencies. Also known as a *dirty float*. **00**

managing capital adequacy The maintainence and acquisition of needed capital. **260**

marginal propensity to consume The slope of the consumption function line that measures the change in consumer expenditure resulting from an additional dollar of disposable income. **575**

market equilibrium A situation occurring when the quantity that people are willing to buy (demand) equals the quantity that people are willing to sell (supply). **110**

matched sale-purchase transaction An arrangement whereby the Fed sells securities and the buyer agrees to sell them back to the Fed in the near future; sometimes called a *reverse repo*. **479**

maturity Time to the expiration date (maturity date) of a debt instrument. **24**

mean reversion The phenomenon that stocks with low returns today tend to have high returns in the future, and vice versa. **725**

medium of exchange Anything that is used to pay for goods and services. **52**

modern quantity theory of money The theory that changes in aggregate spending are determined primarily by changes in the money supply. **627**

monetarist A follower of Milton Friedman who sees changes in the money supply as the primary source of movements in the price level and aggregate output and who views the economy as inherently stable. **625**

monetary aggregates The various measures of the money supply used by the Federal Reserve System (M1, M2, M3, and L). **60**

monetary base The sum of the Fed's monetary liabilities (currency in circulation and reserves) and the U.S. Treasury's monetary liabilities (Treasury currency in circulation, primarily coins). **369**

monetary neutrality A proposition that in the long run, a percentage rise in the money supply is matched by the same percentage rise in the price level, leaving unchanged the real money supply and all other economic variables such as interest rates. **194**

monetary policy The management of the money supply and interest rates. **7**

monetary theory The theory that relates changes in the quantity of money to changes in economic activity. **5, 543**

monetizing the debt A method of financing government spending whereby the government debt issued to finance government spending is removed from the hands of the public and is replaced by high-powered money instead. Also called *printing money*. **471**

money Anything that is generally accepted in payment for goods or services or in the repayment of debts. **3**

money center banks   Large banks in key financial centers. **265**

money market   A financial market in which only short-term debt instruments (maturity of less than one year) are traded. **26**

money multiplier   A ratio that relates the change in the money supply to a given change in the monetary base. **383**

money supply   See *money*. **3**

moral hazard   The risk that one party to a transaction will engage in behavior that is undesirable from the other party's point of view. **36**

multiple deposit creation   The process whereby, when the Fed supplies the banking system with $1 of additional reserves, deposits increase by a multiple of this amount. **370**

national banks   Federally chartered banks. **285**

natural rate level of output   The level of aggregate output produced at the natural rate of unemployment at which there is no tendency for wages or prices to change. **617, 649**

natural rate of unemployment   The rate of unemployment consistent with full employment at which the demand for labor equals the supply of labor. **494, 635**

necessity   An asset for which as wealth grows, the percentage increase in demand is less than the percentage increase in wealth—in other words, an asset with wealth elasticity less than one. **96**

net exports   The net foreign spending on domestic goods and services, equal to exports minus imports. **574**

net worth   The difference between a firm's assets (what it owns or is owed) and its liabilities (what it owes). Also called *equity capital*. **216**

no-load funds   Mutual funds sold directly to the public on which no sales commissions are charged. **356**

nominal interest rate   An interest rate that does not take inflation into account. **91**

nonactivist   An economist who believes that the performance of the economy would be improved if the government avoided active policy to eliminate unemployment. **637**

nonbank banks   Limited-service banks that either do not make commercial loans or do not take in deposits. **290**

nonborrowed monetary base   The monetary base minus discount loans. **390**

nonsystematic risk   The component of an asset's risk that is unique to the asset and so can be eliminated by diversification. **101**

off-balance-sheet activities   Bank activities that involve trading financial instruments and the generation of income from fees and loan sales, all of which affect bank profits but are not visible on bank balance sheets. **279**

official reserve transactions balance   The current account balance plus items in the capital account. **527**

open-end fund   A mutual fund in which shares can be redeemed at any time at a price that is tied to the asset value of the fund. **356**

open market operation   The Fed's buying or selling of bonds in the open market. **371**

open market purchase   A purchase of bonds by the Fed. **384**

open market sale   A sale of bonds by the Fed. **384**

operating target   Any of a set of variables, such as reserve aggregates or interest rates, that the Fed seeks to influence and that are responsive to its policy tools. **497**

opportunity cost   The amount of interest (expected return) sacrificed by not holding an alternative asset. **126**

optimal forecast   The best guess of the future using all available information. **713**

over-the-counter (OTC) market   A secondary market in which dealers at different locations who have an inventory of securities stand ready to buy and sell securities "over the counter" to anyone who comes to them and is willing to accept their prices. **25**

partial crowding out   The situation in which an increase in government spending leads to a decline in private spending that does not completely offset the rise in government spending. **631**

par value   See *face value*. **70**

payments system   The method of conducting transactions in the economy. **55**

Phillips curve   A relationship between unemployment and inflation discovered by A. W. Phillips. **651**

planned investment spending   Total planned spending by businesses on new physical capital (machines, computers, apartment buildings) plus planned spending on new homes. **574, 628**

policy ineffectiveness proposition The conclusion from the new classical model that anticipated policy has no effect on output fluctuations. **756**

political business cycle A business cycle caused by expansionary policies before an election. **451**

preferred habitat theory The theory that the interest rate on a long-term bond will equal the average of the short-term interest rates expected to occur over the life of the long-term bond plus a term premium that responds to supply and demand conditions for that bond. **164**

present discounted value See *present value.* **72**

present value Today's value of a payment to be received in the future when the interest rate is *i.* Also called *present discounted value.* **71**

primary market A financial market in which new issues of a security are sold to initial buyers. **24**

principal-agent problem A moral hazard problem that occurs when the managers in control (the agents) act in their own interest rather than in the interest of the owners (the principals) due to different sets of incentives. **217**

printing money See *monetizing the debt.* **471**

put option An option contract that provides the right to sell a security at a specified price. **236**

quantity theory of money The theory that nominal income is determined solely by movements in the quantity of money. **545**

quotas Restrictions on the quantity of foreign goods that can be imported. **180**

random walk The movements of a variable whose future changes cannot be predicted (are random) because, given today's value, the variable is just as likely to fall as to rise. **723**

rate of capital gain The change in a security's price relative to the initial purchase price. **87**

rate of return See *return.* **86**

rational expectations Expectations that reflect optimal forecasts (the best guess of the future) using all available information. **713**

real bills doctrine A guiding principle (now discredited) for the conduct of monetary policy that states that as long as loans are made to support the production of goods and services, providing reserves to the banking system to make these loans will not be inflationary. **503**

real business cycle theory A theory that views real shocks to tastes and technology as the major driving force behind short-run business cycle fluctuations. **643**

real interest rate The interest rate adjusted for expected changes in the price level (inflation) so that it more accurately reflects the true cost of borrowing. **91**

real money balances The quantity of money in real terms. **553**

real terms Terms reflecting actual goods and services one can buy. **91**

recession A period when aggregate output is declining. **4**

reduced-form evidence Evidence that examines whether one variable has an effect on another by simply looking directly at the relationship between the two variables. **656**

Regulation Q The regulation under which the Federal Reserve System has the power to set maximum interest rates that banks can pay on savings and time deposits. **46**

regulatory forbearance Regulators' refraining from exercising their right to put an insolvent bank out of business. **323**

repurchase agreement (repo) An arrangement whereby the Fed purchases securities with the understanding that the seller will repurchase them in a short period of time, usually less than a week. **479**

required reserve ratio The fraction of deposits that the Fed requires be kept as reserves. **254, 370**

required reserves Reserves that are held to meet the Feds requirement that for every dollar of deposits at a bank, a certain fraction must be kept as reserves. **254, 370**

reserve currency A currency, such as the U.S. dollar, that is used by other countries to denominate the assets they hold as international reserves. **530**

reserve requirements Regulation making it obligatory for depository institutions to keep a certain fraction of their deposits in accounts with the Fed. **46**

reserves Banks' holding of deposits in accounts with the Fed, plus currency that is physically held by banks (vault cash). **254, 369**

restrictive covenants Provisions that restrict and specify certain activities that a borrower can engage in. **209**

return The payments to the owner of a security plus the change in the security's value, expressed as a fraction of its purchase price. More precisely called the *rate of return*. **86**

return on assets (ROA) Net profit after taxes per dollar of assets. **266,**

return on equity (ROE) Net profit after taxes per dollar of equity capital. **267**

revaluation Resetting of the par value of a currency at a higher level. **532**

reverse causation A situation in which one variable is said to cause another variable when in reality the reverse is true. **659**

reverse repo See *matched sale-purchase transaction*. **479**

risk The degree of uncertainty associated with the return on an asset. **96**

risk premium The spread between the interest rate on bonds with default risk and the interest rate on default-free bonds. **150**

risk structure of interest rates The relationship among the various interest rates on bonds with the same term to maturity. **149**

secondary market A financial market in which securities that have previously been issued (and are thus secondhand) can be resold. **24**

secondary reserves Short-term U.S. government and agency securities held by banks. **256**

secured debt Debt guaranteed by collateral. **208**

securitization The process of transforming illiquid financial assets into marketable capital market instruments. **240**

security A claim on the borrower's future income that is sold by the borrower to the lender. Also called a *financial instrument*. **11**

segmented markets theory A theory of term structure that sees markets for different-maturity bonds as completely separated and segmented such that the interest rate for bonds of a given maturity is determined solely by supply of and demand for bonds of that maturity. **162**

self-correcting mechanism A characteristic of the economy that causes output to return eventually to the natural rate level regardless of where it is initially. **637**

share draft accounts Accounts at credit unions that are similar to NOW accounts. **246**

short-term With reference to a debt instrument, having a maturity of one year or less. **24**

simple deposit multiplier The multiple increase in deposits generated from an increase in the banking system's reserves in a simple model in which the behavior of depositor and bank plays no role. **376**

simple loan A credit market instrument providing the borrower with an amount of funds that must be repaid to the lender at the maturity date along with an additional payment (interest). **70**

sources of the base The factors that determine the monetary base. **459**

special drawing rights (SDRs) An IMF-issued paper substitute for gold that functions as international reserves. **534**

specialist A dealer-broker operating in an exchange who maintains orderly trading of the securities for which he or she is responsible. **361**

spot exchange rate The exchange rate for a spot transaction. **175**

spot transaction The predominant type of exchange rate transaction involving the immediate exchange of bank deposits denominated in different currencies. **175**

state banks State-chartered banks. **285**

sterilized foreign exchange intervention A foreign exchange intervention with an offsetting open market operation that leaves the monetary base unchanged. **521**

store of value A repository of purchasing power over time. **54**

structural model A description of how the economy operates using a collection of equations that describe the behavior of firms and consumers in many sectors of the economy. **656**

structural model evidence Evidence that examines whether one variable affects another by using data to build a model illustrating the channels through which this variable affects the other. **656**

supply curve A curve depicting the relationship between quantity supplied and price when all other economic variables are held constant. **109**

supply shock Any change in technology or the supply of raw materials that can shift the aggregate supply curve. **640**

systematic risk The component of an asset's risk that cannot be eliminated by diversification. **101**

T-account   A simplified balance sheet with lines in the form of a T that lists only the changes that occur in balance sheet items starting from some initial balance sheet position. **257**

tariffs   Taxes on imported goods. **180**

term structure of interest rates   The relationship among interest rates on bonds with different terms to maturity. **149**

theory of asset demand   The theory that the quantity demanded of an asset is (1) usually positively related to wealth, (2) positively related to its expected return relative to alternative assets, (3) negatively related to the risk of its return relative to alternative assets, and (4) positively related to its liquidity relative to alternative assets. **99**

theory of purchasing power parity (PPP)   The theory that exchange rates between any two currencies will adjust to reflect changes in the price levels of the two countries. **178**

thrift institutions (thrifts)   Savings and loan associations, mutual savings banks, and credit unions. **39**

trade balance   The difference between merchandise exports and imports. **524**

transactions costs   The time and money spent trying to exchange financial assets, goods, or services. **34**

transmission mechanisms of monetary policy   The channels through which the money supply affects economic activity. **656**

underfunded   Describing a pension plan in which the contributions and their earnings are not sufficient to pay out the defined benefits when they come due. **351**

underground economy   Unreported economic activity. **412**

underwriters   Investment banks that guarantee prices on securities to corporations and then sell the securities to the public. **359**

underwriting   Guaranteeing prices on securities to corporations and then selling the securities to the public. **25**

unemployment rate   The percentage of the labor force not working. **4**

unexploited profit opportunity   A situation in which an investor can earn a higher than normal return. **718**

unit of account   Anything used to measure value in an economy. **53**

unsecured debt   Debt not guaranteed by collateral. **208**

unsterilized foreign exchange intervention   A foreign exchange intervention in which a central bank allows the purchase or sale of domestic currency to affect the monetary base. **521**

uses of the base   The items accounting for use of the monetary base (Federal Reserve notes, reserves, and Treasury currency outstanding not held by the Fed). **459**

vault cash   Currency that is physically held by banks and stored in vaults overnight. **254**

velocity of money   The rate of turnover of money; the average number of times per year that a dollar is spent in buying the total amount of final goods and services produced in the economy. **544, 626**

venture capital firm   A financial intermediary that pools the resources of its partners and uses the funds to help entrepreneurs start up new businesses. **219**

wealth   All resources owned by an individual, including all assets. **52, 96**

wealth elasticity of demand   The measure of how much, with everything else unchanged, demand for an asset changes in percentage terms in response to a percentage change in wealth. **96**

World Bank   The International Bank for Reconstruction and Redevelopment, an international organization that provides long-term loans to assist developing countries in building dams, roads, and other physical capital that would contribute to their economic development. **530**

yield curve   A plot of the interest rates for particular types of bonds with different terms to maturity. **157**

yield on a discount basis   The measure of interest rates by which dealers in bill markets quote the interest rate on U.S. Treasury bills; formally defined in Equation 8 of Chapter 4. Also known as the *discount yield*. **81**

yield to maturity   The interest rate that equates the present value of payments received from a credit market instrument with its value today. **73**

zero-coupon bond   See *discount bond*. **70**

ANSWERS TO SELECTED QUESTIONS AND PROBLEMS

Chapter 1

2. The data in Figures 1, 2, 3, and 4 suggest that real output, the inflation rate, and interest rates would all fall.

4. You might be more likely to buy a house or a car because the cost of financing them would fall, or you might be less likely to save because you earn less on your savings.

6. No. It is true that people who borrow to purchase a house or a car are worse off because it costs them more to finance their purchase; however, savers benefit because they can earn higher interest rates on their savings.

8. They channel funds from people who do not have a productive use for them to people who do, thereby resulting in higher economic efficiency.

10. The lower price for a firm's shares means that it can raise a smaller amount of funds, and so investment in facilities and equipment will fall.

12. It makes foreign goods more expensive, so British consumers will buy fewer foreign goods and more domestic goods.

14. In the mid- to late 1970s and in the late 1980s and early 1990s, the value of the dollar was low, making travel abroad relatively more expensive; thus it was a good time to vacation in the United States and see the Grand Canyon. With the rise of the dollar's value in the early 1980s, travel abroad became relatively cheaper, making it a good time to visit the Tower of London.

Chapter 2

1. The share of IBM stock is an asset for its owner because it entitles the owner to a share of the earnings and assets of IBM. The share is a liability for IBM because it is a claim on its earnings and assets by the owner of the share.

3. Yes, because the absence of financial markets means that funds cannot be channeled to people who have the most productive use for them. Entrepreneurs then cannot acquire funds to set up businesses that would help the economy grow rapidly.

5. This statement is false. Prices in secondary markets determine the prices that firms issuing securities receive in primary markets. In addition, secondary markets make securities more liquid and thus easier to sell in the primary markets. Therefore, secondary markets are, if anything, more important than primary markets.

7. Because you know your family member better than a stranger, you know more about the borrower's honesty, propensity for risk taking, and other traits. There is less asymmetric information than with a stranger and less likelihood of an adverse selection problem, with the result that you are more likely to lend to the family member.

9. Loan sharks can threaten their borrowers with bodily harm if borrowers take actions that might jeopardize their paying off the loan. Hence borrowers from a loan shark are less likely to increase moral hazard.

11. Yes because even if you know that a borrower is taking actions that might jeopardize paying off the loan, you must still stop the borrower from doing so. Because that may be costly, you may not spend the time and effort to reduce moral hazard, and so the problem of moral hazard still exists.

13. Because the costs of making the loan to your neighbor are high (legal fees, fees for a credit check, and so on), you will probably not be able to earn 5% on the loan after your expenses even though it has a 10% interest rate. You are better off depositing your savings with a financial intermediary and earning 5% interest. In addition, you are likely to bear less risk by depositing your savings at the bank rather than lending them to your neighbor.

15. Increased discussion of foreign financial markets in the U.S. press and the growth in markets for international financial instruments such as Eurodollars and Eurobonds.

Chapter 3

2. Since the orchard owner likes only bananas but the banana grower doesn't like apples, the banana grower will not want apples in exchange for his bananas, and they will not trade. Similarly, the chocolatier will not be willing to trade with the banana grower because she does not like bananas. The orchard owner will not trade with the chocolatier because he doesn't like chocolate. Hence in a barter economy, trade among these three people may well not take place because in no case is there a double coincidence of wants. However, if money is introduced into the economy, the orchard owner can sell his apples to the chocolatier and then use the money to buy bananas from the banana grower. Similarly, the banana grower can use the money she receives from the orchard owner to buy chocolate from the chocolatier, and the chocolatier can use the money to buy apples from the orchard owner. The result is that the necessity of a double coincidence of wants is eliminated, and everyone is better off because all three producers are now able to eat what they like best.

4. Because money was losing value at a slower rate (the inflation rate was lower) in the 1950s than in the 1970s, it was then a better store of value, and you would have been willing to hold more of it.

6. Money loses its value at an extremely rapid rate in hyperinflation, so you want to hold it for as short a time as possible. Thus money is like a hot potato that is quickly passed from one person to another.

8. Not necessarily. Although the total amount of debt has predicted inflation and the business cycle better than $M1$, $M2$, or $M3$, it may not be a better predictor in the future. Without some theoretical reason for believing that the total amount of debt will continue to predict well in the future, we may not want to define money as the total amount of debt.

10. $M1$ contains the most liquid assets. $M3$ is the largest measure.

12. Revisions are not a serious problem for long-run movements of the money supply because revisions for short-run (one-month) movements tend to cancel out. Revisions for long-run movements, such as one-year growth rates, are thus typically quite small.

14. Because a check was so much easier to transport than gold, people would frequently rather be paid by check even if there were a possibility that the check might bounce. In other words, the lower transactions costs involved in handling checks made people more willing to accept them.

Chapter 4

1. Less. It would be worth $1/(1 + 0.20) = \$0.83$ when the interest rate is 20%, rather than $1/(1 + 0.10) = \$0.91$ when the interest rate is 10%.

3. $\$1100/(1 + 0.10) + \$1210/(1 + 0.10)^2 + \$1331/(1 + 0.10)^3 = \$3000$.

5. $\$2000 = \$100/(1 + i) + \$100/(1 + i)^2 + \ldots + \$100/(1 + i)^{20} + \$1000/(1 + i)^{20}$

7. 14.9%, derived as follows: The present value of the $2 million payment five years from now is $\$2/(1 + i)^5$ million which equals the $1 million loan. Thus $1 = 2/(1 + i)^5$. Solving for i, $(1 + i)^5 = 2$, so that $i = \sqrt[5]{2} - 1 = 0.149 = 14.9\%$.

9. If the one-year bond did not have a coupon payment, its yield to maturity would be ($1000 − $800)/$800 = $200/$800 = 0.25 = 25%. Since it does have a coupon payment, its yield to maturity must be greater than 25%. On the other hand, because the current yield is a good approximation of the yield to maturity for a twenty-year bond, we know that the yield to maturity on this bond is approximately 15%. Therefore, the one-year bond has a higher yield to maturity.

11. You would rather own the Treasury bill because it has a higher yield to maturity. As the example in the text indicates, the discount yield's understatement of the yield to maturity for a one-year bond is substantial, exceeding one percentage point. Thus the yield to maturity on the one-year bill would be greater than 9%, the yield to maturity on the one-year Treasury bond.

13. No. If interest rates rise sharply in the future, long-term bonds may suffer such a sharp fall in price that their return might be quite low, possibly even negative.

15. The economists are right. They reason that nominal interest rates were below expected rates of inflation in the late 1970s, making real interest rates negative. The expected inflation rate, however, fell much faster than nominal interest rates in the mid-1980s, so nominal interest rates were above the expected inflation rate and real rates became positive.

Chapter 5

2. (a) More, because your wealth has increased; (b) more, because it has become more liquid; (c) less, because its expected return has fallen relative to Polaroid stock; (d) more, because it has become less risky relative to stocks; (e) less, because its expected return has fallen.

4. (a) More, because they have become more liquid; (b) more, because their expected return has risen relative to stocks; (c) less, because they have become less liquid relative to stocks; (d) less, because their expected return has fallen; (e) more, because they have become more liquid.

6. Yes. The higher expected return on stocks, holding everything else constant, would mean a lower relative expected return on bonds. Thus the demand for bonds would decrease.

8. Purchasing shares in the pharmaceutical company is more likely to reduce my overall risk because the correlation of returns on my investment in a football team with the returns on the pharmaceutical company should be low. By contrast, the correlation of returns on an investment in a football team and an investment in a basketball team are probably pretty high, so in this case there would be little risk reduction if I invested in both.

10. True. When an asset's beta is higher, its systematic risk is higher. Since this systematic risk cannot be diversified away, the asset is less desirable, everything else being equal, and the demand for the asset will be lower. (Note that we assume that investors are risk-averse and hence do not like risk.)

12. It wouldn't matter from a risk point of view because both stocks have a beta of 0.5 and have the same amount of systematic risk.

14. Risk premium = $R^e - R_f = \beta(R^e_m - R_f) = 3(8\% - 5\%) = 9\%$.

Chapter 6

1. When the Fed sells bonds to the public, it increases the supply of bonds, thus shifting the supply curve B^s to the right. The result is that the intersection of the supply and demand curves B^s and B^d occurs at a higher equilibrium interest rate, and the interest rate rises. With the liquidity preference framework, the decrease in the money supply shifts the money supply curve M^s to the left, and the equilibrium interest rate rises. The answer from the loanable funds framework is consistent with the answer from the liquidity preference framework.

3. When the price level rises, the quantity of money in real terms falls (holding the nominal supply of money constant); to restore their holdings of money in real terms to their former level, people will want to hold a greater nominal quantity of money. Thus the money demand curve M^d shifts to the right, and the interest rate rises.

6. Interest rates would rise. A sudden increase in people's expectations of future real estate prices raises the expected return on real estate relative to bonds, so the demand for bonds falls. The demand curve B^d shifts to the left, and the equilibrium interest rate rises.

8. In the loanable funds framework, the increased riskiness of bonds lowers the demand for bonds. The demand curve B^d shifts to the left, and the equilibrium interest rate rises. The same answer is found in the liquidity preference framework. The increased riskiness of bonds relative to money increases the demand for money. The money demand curve M^d shifts to the right, and the equilibrium interest rate rises.

10. Yes, interest rates will rise. The lower commission on stocks makes them more liquid relative to bonds, and the demand for bonds will fall. The demand curve B^d will therefore shift to the left, and the equilibrium interest rate will rise.

12. The interest rate on the AT&T bonds will rise. Because people now expect interest rates to rise, the expected return on long-term bonds such as AT&T's will fall, and the demand for these bonds will decline. The demand curve B^d will therefore shift to the left, and the equilibrium interest rate will rise.

14. Interest rates will rise. When bond prices become volatile and bonds become riskier, the demand for bonds will fall. The demand curve B^d will shift to the left, and the equilibrium interest rate will rise.

Chapter 7

2. U.S. Treasury bills have lower default risk and more liquidity than negotiable CDs. Consequently, the demand for Treasury bills is higher, and they have a lower interest rate.

4. True. When bonds of different maturities are close substitutes, a rise in interest rates for one bond causes the interest rates for others to rise because the expected returns on bonds of different maturities cannot get too far out of line.

6. (a) The yield to maturity would be 5% for a one-year bond, 6% for a two-year bond, 6.33% for a three-year bond, 6.5% for a four-year bond, and 6.6% for a five-year bond. (b) The yield to maturity would be 5% for a one-year bond, 4.5% for a two-year bond, 4.33% for a three-year bond, 4.25% for a four-year bond, and 4.2% for a five-year bond. The upward-sloping yield curve in (a) would be even steeper if people preferred short-term bonds over long-term bonds because long-term bonds would then have a positive risk premium. The downward-sloping yield curve in (b) would be less steep and might even have a slight positive upward slope if the long-term bonds have a positive risk premium.

8. The flat yield curve at shorter maturities suggests that short-term interest rates are expected to fall moderately in the near future, while the steep upward slope of the yield curve at longer maturities indicates that interest rates further into the future are expected to rise. Because interest rates and expected inflation move together, the yield curve suggests that the market expects inflation to fall moderately in the near future but to rise later on.

10. The reduction in income tax rates would make the tax-exempt privilege for municipal bonds less valuable, and they would be less desirable than taxable Treasury bonds. The resulting decline in the demand for municipal bonds and increase in demand for Treasury bonds would raise interest rates on municipal bonds while causing interest rates on Treasury bonds to fall.

12. Lower brokerage commissions for corporate bonds would make them more liquid and thus increase their demand, which would lower their risk premium.

14. You would raise your predictions of future interest rate because the higher long-term rates imply that the average of the expected future short-term rate is higher.

Chapter 8

2. False. Although a weak currency has the negative effect of making it more expensive to buy foreign goods or to travel abroad, it may help domestic industry. Domestic goods become cheaper relative to foreign goods, and the demand for domestically produced goods increases. The resulting higher sales of domestic products may lead to higher employment, a beneficial effect on the economy.

4. It predicts that the value of the French franc will fall 5% in terms of dollars.

6. Even though the Japanese price level rose relative to the American, the yen appreciated because the increase in Japanese productivity relative to American productivity made it possible for the Japanese to continue to sell their goods at a profit at a high value of the yen.

8. The pound depreciates but overshoots, declining by more in the short run than in the long run. Consider Britain the domestic country. The rise in the money supply leads to a higher domestic price level in the long run, which leads to a higher expected future exchange rate. The resulting expected depreciation of the pound raises the expected return on foreign deposits, shifting RET^F to the right. The rise in the money supply lowers the interest rate on pound deposits in the short run, which shifts $RET^{\pounds}$ to the left. The short-run outcome is a lower equilibrium exchange rate. However, in the long run, the domestic interest rate returns to its previous value, and $RET^{\pounds}$ shifts back to its original position. The exchange rate rises to some extent, although it still remains below its initial position.

10. The dollar will depreciate. A rise in nominal interest rates but a decline in real interest rates implies a rise in expected inflation that produces an expected depreciation of the dollar that is larger than the increase in the domestic interest rate. As a result, the expected return on foreign deposits rises by more than the expected return on domestic deposits. RET^F shifts rightward more than $RET^{\$}$, so the equilibrium exchange rate falls.

12. The dollar will depreciate. An increased demand for imports would lower the expected future exchange rate and result in an expected appreciation of the foreign currency. The higher resulting expected return on foreign deposits shifts the RET^F schedule to the right, and the equilibrium exchange rate falls.

14. The contraction of the German money supply will increase German interest rates and raise the future value of the mark, both of which will shift RET^F (with Germany as the foreign country) to the right. The result is a decline in the value of the dollar.

Chapter 9

2. Financial intermediaries develop expertise in such areas as computer technology so that they can inexpensively provide liquidity services such as checking accounts that lower transactions costs for depositors. Financial intermediaries can also take advantage of economies of scale and engage in large transactions that have a lower cost per dollar per transaction.

4. Standard accounting principles make profit verification easier, thereby reducing adverse selection and moral hazard problems in financial markets and hence making them operate better. Standard accounting principles make it easier for investors to screen out good firms from bad firms, thereby reducing the adverse selection problem in financial markets. In addition, they make it harder for managers to understate prof-

its, thereby reducing the principal-agent (moral hazard) problem.

6. Smaller firms that are not well known are the most likely to use bank financing. Since it is harder for investors to acquire information about these firms, it will be hard for the firms to sell securities in the financial markets. Banks that specialize in collecting information about smaller firms will then be the only outlet these firms have for financing their activities.

8. Yes. The person who is putting her life savings into her business has more to lose if she takes on too much risk or engages in personally beneficial activities that don't lead to higher profits. So she will act more in the interest of the lender, making it more likely that the loan will be paid off.

10. True. If the borrower turns out to be a bad credit risk and goes broke, the lender loses less because the collateral can be sold to make up any losses on the loan. Thus adverse selection is not as severe a problem.

12. The separation of ownership and control creates a principal-agent problem. The managers (the agents) do not have as strong an incentive to maximize profits as the owners (the principals). Thus the managers might not work hard, might engage in wasteful spending on personal perks, or might pursue business strategies that enhance their personal power but do not increase profits.

14. A stock market crash reduces the net worth of firms and so increases the moral hazard problem. With less of an equity stake, owners have a greater incentive to take on risky projects and spend corporate funds on items that benefit them personally. A stock market crash, which increases the moral hazard problem, thus makes it less likely that lenders will be paid back. So lending and investment will decline, creating a financial crisis in which financial markets do not work well and the economy suffers.

Chapter 10

1. Financial innovation is driven by the search for profits—in other words, by greed. Since financial innovation is usually beneficial, greed can be viewed as a positive force in our society.

3. You can sell a contract that delivers three-month CDs or T-bills in nine months' time. If the interest rate rises, the price of the contract will fall, and the profits you make will offset the higher interest payments on your loan.

5. Probably not, because the costs of servicing these credit cards would not have been as high, making it easier for the banks to earn a profit on them.

7. True. Banks have increased their borrowing in the Eurodollar market, causing it to grow faster, because it allowed them to avoid the restrictions on raising funds arising from Regulation Q and because the funds acquired in the Eurodollar market were not initially subject to reserve requirements.

9. Advances in telecommunications and computers have made it easier for investors to screen out good from bad credit risks in securities markets, thereby making it easier for corporations to issue securities. Thus less well known corporations with lower credit ratings were now able to sell their junk bonds, making it possible for this market to develop.

11. If the Fed pays an interest rate of i_{Fed} on reserves, the tax on deposits imposed by reserve requirements will fall to $(i - i_{Fed}) \times r_D$. The result of the lower tax on deposits would be that banks could now pay a higher interest rate on deposits and so make them more competitive with money market funds. Depositors would now find deposits more attractive relative to money market funds, deposits would rise, and money market funds would decline.

13. If inflation became more variable, interest rates would also probably become more variable, and interest-rate risk would increase. Trading in financial futures and options markets would then increase because it enables people to avoid some of the increased interest-rate risk.

15. If Regulation Q ceilings were reimposed, banks would not be able to compete as effectively for funds, causing funds to flow from banks into money market mutual funds. In addition, it would stimulate the commercial paper market because banks would then try to obtain funds by having their holding companies issue commercial paper on which there are no interest-rate ceilings.

Chapter 11

2. The rank from most to least liquid is (c), (b), (a), (d).

4. Reserves drop by $500. The T-account for the First National Bank is as follows:

First National Bank	
Assets	Liabilities
Reserves	Checkable deposits
−$500	−$500

6. The bank would rather have the balance sheet shown in this problem because after it loses $50 million due to deposit outflow, the bank would still have excess reserves of $5 million: $50 million in reserves minus required reserves of $45 million (10% of the $450 million of deposits). Thus the bank would not have to alter its balance sheet further and would not incur any costs as a result of the deposit outflow. By contrast, with the balance sheet in Problem 5, the bank would have a shortfall of reserves of $20 million ($25 million in reserves minus the required reserves of $45 million). In this case the bank will incur costs when it raises the necessary reserves through the methods described in the text.

8. No. When you turn a customer down, you may lose that customer's business forever, which is extremely costly. Instead, you might go out and borrow from other banks, corporations, or the Fed to obtain funds so that you can make the customer's loans. Alternatively, you might sell negotiable CDs or some of your securities to acquire the necessary funds.

10. It can raise $1 million of capital by issuing new stock. It can cut its dividend payments by $1 million, thereby increasing its retained earnings by $1 million. It can decrease the amount of its assets so that the amount of its capital relative to its assets increases, thereby meeting the capital requirements.

12. Compensating balances can act as collateral. They also help establish long-term customer relationships, which make it easier for the bank to collect information about prospective borrowers, thus reducing the adverse selection problem. Compensating balances help the bank monitor the activities of a borrowing firm so that it can

prevent the firm from taking on too much risk, thereby not acting in the interest of the bank.

14. The assets fall in value by 8% (= − 2% × 4 years), while the liabilities fall in value by 12% (= − 2% × 6 years). Since the liabilities fall in value by 4% more than the assets do, the net worth of the bank rises by 4%, that is, by $3 million (= 4% × $75 million). The interest-rate risk can be reduced by shortening the maturity of the liabilities to a duration of four years or lengthening the maturity of the assets to a duration of six years. Alternatively, you could engage in an interest-rate swap, in which you swap the interest earned on your assets with the interest on another bank's assets that have a duration of six years.

Chapter 12

2. (a) Office of the Controller of the Currency; (b) the Federal Reserve; (c) state banking authorities and the FDIC; (d) the Federal Reserve.

4. New technologies such as electronic banking facilities are frequently shared by several banks, so these facilities are not classified as branches. Thus they can be used by banks to escape limitations to offering services in other states and, in effect, to escape limitations from restrictions on branching.

6. Because restrictions on branching are stricter for commercial banks than for savings and loans. Thus small commercial banks have greater protection from competition and are more likely to survive than small savings and loans.

8. International banking has been encouraged by giving special tax treatment and relaxed branching regulations to Edge Act corporations and to international banking facilities (IBFs); this was done to make American banks more competitive with foreign banks. The hope is that it will create more banking jobs in the United States.

10. No, because the Saudi-owned bank is subject to the same regulations as the American-owned bank.

12. The rise of inflation and the resulting higher interest rates on alternatives to checkable deposits meant that banks had a big shrinkage in this low-cost way of raising funds. The innovation of money market mutual funds also meant that the

banks lost checking account business. The abolishment of Regulation Q and the appearance of NOW accounts did help decrease disintermediation but raised the cost of funds for American banks, which now had to pay higher interest rates on checkable and other deposits. Foreign banks were also able to tap a large pool of domestic savings, thereby lowering their cost of funds relative to American banks.

14. The growth of the commercial paper market and the development of the junk bond market meant that corporations were now able to issue securities rather than borrow from banks, thus eroding the competitive advantage of banks on the lending side. Securitization has enabled other financial institutions to originate loans, again taking away some of the banks' loan business.

Chapter 13

2. There would be adverse selection because people who might want to burn their property for some personal gain would actively try to obtain substantial fire insurance policies. Moral hazard could also be a problem because a person with a fire insurance policy has less incentive to take measures to prevent a fire.

4. Regulations that restrict banks from holding risky assets directly decrease the moral hazard of risk taking by the bank. Requirements that force banks to have a large amount of capital also decrease the banks' incentives for risk taking because banks now have more to lose if they fail. Such regulations will not completely eliminate the moral hazard problem because bankers have incentives to hide their holdings of risky assets from the regulators and to overstate the amount of their capital.

6. The S&L crisis did not occur until the 1980s because interest rates stayed low before then, so S&Ls were not subjected to losses from high interest rates. Also, the opportunities for risk taking were not available until the 1980s, when legislation and financial innovation made it easier for S&Ls to take on more risk, thereby greatly increasing the adverse selection and moral hazard problems.

8. FIRREA provided funds for the S&L bailout, created the Resolution Trust Corporation to manage

the resolution of insolvent thrifts, eliminated the Federal Home Loan Bank Board and gave its regulatory role to the Office of Thrift Supervision, eliminated the FSLIC and turned its insurance role and regulatory responsibilities over to the FDIC, imposed restrictions on thrift activities similar to those in effect before 1982, increased the capital requirements to those adhered to by commercial banks, and increased the enforcement powers of thrift regulators.

10. If political candidates receive campaign funds from the government and are restricted in the amount they spend, they will have less need to satisfy lobbyists to win elections. As a result, they may have greater incentives to act in the interest of taxpayers (the principals), and so the political process might improve.

12. Eliminating or limiting the amount of deposit insurance would help reduce the moral hazard of excessive risk taking on the part of banks. It would, however, make bank failures and panics more likely, so it might not be a very good idea.

14. The economy would benefit from reduced moral hazard; that is, banks would not want to take on too much risk because doing so would increase their deposit insurance premiums. The problem is, however, that it is difficult to monitor the degree of risk in bank assets because often only the bank making the loans knows how risky they are.

Chapter 14

1. Because there would be more uncertainty about how much they would have to pay out in any given year, life insurance companies would tend to hold shorter-term assets that are more liquid.

3. Because benefits paid out are set to equal contributions to the plan and their earnings.

5. False. Government pension plans are often underfunded. Many pension plans for both federal and state employees are not fully funded.

7. Because the bigger the policy, the greater the moral hazard—the incentive for the policyholder to engage in activities that make the insurance payoff more likely. Because payoffs are costly, the insurance company will want to reduce moral hazard by limiting the amount of insurance.

9. Because interest rates on loans are typically lower at banks than at finance companies.

11. Because you do not have to pay a commission on a no-load fund, it is cheaper than a load fund, which does require a commission.

13. Government loan guarantees may be very costly because like any insurance, they increase moral hazard. Because the banks and other institutions making the guaranteed loans do not suffer any losses if the loans default, these institutions have little incentive not to make bad loans. The resulting losses to the government can be substantial, as has been the case in recent years.

15. No. Investment banking is a risky business because if the investment bank cannot sell a security it is underwriting for the price it promised to pay the issuing firm, the investment bank can suffer substantial losses.

Chapter 15

1. False. A bank's cash holdings are already counted as reserves, so depositing them with the Fed leaves the bank's reserves unchanged.

3. Reserves at the First National Bank remain unchanged as the following T-accounts indicate:

First National Bank			
Assets		**Liabilities**	
Reserves	0	Discount	
Securities	+$1 million	loans	+$1 million

Federal Reserve System			
Assets		**Liabilities**	
Securities	−$1 million		
Discount loans	+$1 million		

5. The T-accounts are identical to those in the sections "Deposit Creation: The Single Bank" and "Deposit Creation: The Banking System" except that all the entries are multiplied by 10,000 (that is, $100 becomes $1 million). The net result is that checkable deposits rise by $10 million.

7. The $1 million Fed purchase of bonds increases reserves in the banking system by $1 million, and the total increase in checkable deposits is $10 million. The fact that banks buy securities rather than make loans with their excess re-

serves makes no difference in the multiple deposit creation process.

9. Reserves in the banking system fall by $1000 and a multiple contraction occurs, reducing checkable deposits by $10,000.

11. The level of checkable deposits falls by $50 million. The T-account of the banking system in equilibrium is as follows:

Banking System

Assets		Liabilities	
Reserves	−$5 million	Checkable	
Securities	+$5 million	deposits	−$50 million
Loans	−$50 million		

13. The $1 million holdings of excess reserves means that the bank has to reduce its holdings of loans or securities, thus starting the multiple contraction process. Because the required reserve ratio is 10%, checkable deposits must decline by $10 million.

15. The deposit of $100 in the bank increases its reserves by $100. This starts the process of multiple deposit expansion, leading to an increase in checkable deposits of $1000.

Chapter 16

2. Reserves are unchanged, but the monetary base falls by $2 million as indicated by the following T-accounts:

Irving the Investor

Assets		Liabilities
Currency	−$2 million	
Securities	+$2 Million	

Federal Reserve System

Assets		Liabilities	
Securities	−$2 million	Currency	−$2 million

4. Uncertain. As the formula in Equation 4 indicates, if $r_D + \{ER/D\}$ is greater than 1, the money multiplier can be less than 1. In practice, however, $\{ER/D\}$ is so small that $r_D + \{ER/D\}$ is less than 1 and the money multiplier is greater than 1.

6. The money supply fell sharply because when $\{C/D\}$ rose, there was a shift from one component of the money supply (checkable deposits) with more multiple expansion to another (currency) with less. Overall multiple deposit expansion fell, leading to a decline in the money supply.

8. There is a shift from one component of the money supply (checkable deposits) with less multiple expansion to another (traveler's checks) with more. Multiple expansion therefore increases, and the money supply increases.

10. Yes, because with no reserve requirements on time deposits, a shift from checkable deposits (with less multiple expansion) to time deposits (with more multiple expansion) increases the total amount of deposits and raises $M2$. However, if reserve requirements were equal for both types of deposits, they would both undergo the same amount of multiple expansion, and a shift from one to the other would have no effect on $M2$. Thus control of $M2$ would be better because random shifts from time deposits to checkable deposits or vice versa would not affect $M2$.

12. Both the Fed's purchase of $100 million of bonds (which raises the monetary base) and the lowering of r_D (which increases the amount of multiple expansion and raises the money multiplier) lead to a rise in the money supply.

14. The Fed's sale of $1 million of bonds shrinks the monetary base by $1 million, and the reduction of discount loans also lowers the monetary base by another $1 million. The resulting $2 million decline in the monetary base leads to a decline in the money supply.

Chapter 17

2. The rise in interest rates in a boom increases the cost of holding excess reserves and the incentives to borrow from the Fed. Therefore, $\{ER/D\}$ falls, which increases the amount of reserves available to support checkable deposits, and the volume of discount loans increases, which raises the monetary base. The result is a higher money supply during a boom. Similarly, when interest rates fall during a recession, the money supply also has a tendency to fall because $\{ER/D\}$ rises and the volume of discount loans falls.

4. Using deposits for illegal transactions would no longer increase the probability of being caught by the government. The expected return on checkable deposits relative to currency would therefore rise, and the current ratio would fall.

6. Because the wealth elasticity of currency is lower than that of checkable deposits, the demand for currency will rise less than the demand for checkable deposits, and the currency ratio will fall.

8. The level of {ER/D} would rise because excess reserves would be more attractive to hold because of the interest they would earn.

10. A rise in expected inflation would increase interest rates (through the Fisher effect), which would in turn cause {ER/D} to fall and the volume of discount loans to rise. As the answer to Problem 2 suggests, the result would be an increase in the money supply.

12. The money supply would fall because if the discount window were eliminated, banks would need to hold more excess reserves, making fewer reserves available to support deposits. Moreover, abolishing discounting would reduce the volume of discount loans, which would also cause the monetary base and the money supply to fall.

14. The congressional action would probably lead to more check forgery, which leads to losses for depositors with checking accounts. The expected return on checkable deposits relative to currency would fall, and the currency ratio would rise. Because there had been a movement toward currency, which does not undergo multiple deposit expansion, overall multiple deposit expansion would decrease, and the money supply would fall.

Chapter 18

1. Because of traditional American hostility to a central bank and centralized authority, the system of 12 regional banks was set up to diffuse power along regional lines.

3. Like the U.S. Constitution, the Federal Reserve System, originally established by the Federal Reserve Act, has many checks and balances and is a peculiarly American institution. The ability of the 12 regional banks to affect discount policy was viewed as a check on the centralized power of the Board of Governors, just as states' rights are a check on the centralized power of the federal government. The provision that there be three types of directors (A, B, and C) representing different groups (professional bankers, businesspeople, and the public) was again intended to prevent any group from dominating the Fed. The Fed's independence of the federal government and the setting up of the Federal Reserve banks as incorporated institutions were further intended to restrict government power over the banking industry.

5. The Board of Governors sets reserve requirements and the discount rate; the FOMC directs open market operations. In practice, however, the FOMC helps make decisions about reserve requirements and the discount rate.

7. The Board of Governors has clearly gained power at the expense of the regional Federal Reserve banks. This trend toward ever more centralized power is a general one in American government, but in the case of the Fed it was a natural outgrowth of the Fed's having been given the responsibility for promoting a stable economy. This responsibility has required greater central direction of monetary policy, the role taken over the years by the Board of Governors and by the FOMC, which the board controls.

9. The threat that Congress will acquire greater control over the Fed's finances and budget.

11. False. Maximizing one's welfare does not rule out altruism. Operating in the public interest is clearly one objective of the Fed. The theory of bureaucratic behavior only points out that other objectives, such as maximizing power, also influence Fed decision making.

13. False. The Fed is still subject to political pressure because Congress can pass legislation limiting the Fed's power. If the Fed is performing badly, Congress can therefore make the Fed accountable by passing legislation that the Fed does not like.

15. The argument for not releasing the FOMC directives immediately is that it keeps Congress off the Fed's back, thus enabling the Fed to pursue an independent monetary policy that is less subject to inflation and political business cycles. The argument for releasing the directive immediately is that it would make the Fed more accountable.

Chapter 19

2. In both cases, the monetary base declines by $200 billion. The T-accounts when the bonds are sold to banks are as follows:

Federal Reserve	
Assets	Liabilities
Securities −$200 million	Reserves −$200 million

Banks	
Assets	Liabilities
Securities +$200 million	
Reserves −$200 Million	

The T-accounts when the bonds are sold to private investors are as follows:

Federal Reserve	
Assets	Liabilities
Securities −$200 million	Currency −$200 million

Irving the Investor	
Assets	Liabilities
Securities +$200 million	
Currency −$200 Million	

5. The Fed would not be able to present checks for payment to California banks as quickly as it normally would, so float would go up. As the T-accounts in the text indicate, this would lead to a rise in the monetary base.

7. When contractors receive $100 million from the Fed for the new building, they will deposit their checks in local banks. The resulting T-accounts for the Fed and the local banks are as follows:

Federal Reserve	
Assets	Liabilities
New building +$100 million	Reserves +$100 million

Local Bank	
Assets	Liabilities
Reserves +$100 million	Deposits +$100 million

The result is that reserves and hence the monetary base will rise by $100 million.

9. Because the Treasury is better able to predict when it needs to make payments, it can keep fewer deposits with the Fed. The result of a decline in Treasury deposits with the Fed would be a rise in reserves and hence in the monetary base (see in the text the fourth T-account in the section "Treasury Deposits with the Fed").

11. When the $200 billion deficit is financed by selling bonds to the public or to banks, the monetary base will remain unchanged. However, when the bonds are sold to the Fed, the monetary base rises by $200 billion. The T-accounts are the same as those in the text in the sections "Debt Financing (ΔB)" and "Financing with Money Creation (ΔMB)," with the entries multiplied by 2000 (that is, $100 million becomes $200 billion).

13. The monetary base need not be affected because the Fed is not required to help the Treasury finance deficits by buying Treasury bonds. However, if deficits cause interest rates to rise and the Fed tries to prevent higher interest rates by buying bonds, a higher deficit might lead to a higher monetary base. The fall in the deficit from $200 billion to $100 billion might then cause a smaller increase in the monetary base than would otherwise occur.

15. Because it indicates that changes in the deficit should have no effect on the level of interest rates. Thus there will be no need for the Fed to conduct open market operations and affect the monetary base to keep interest rates from changing when the deficit changes.

Chapter 20

1. The snowstorm would cause float to increase, which would increase the monetary base. To counteract this effect, the manager will undertake a defensive open market sale.

3. As we saw in Chapter 19, when the Treasury's deposits at the Fed fall, the monetary base increases. To counteract this increase, the manager would undertake an open market sale.

5. It suggests that defensive open market operations are far more common than dynamic operations because repurchase agreements are used primarily to conduct defensive operations to counteract temporary changes in the monetary base.

7. The monetary base and the money supply would increase indefinitely. Banks could borrow at the lower discount rate and then lend the proceeds at a higher interest rate. Hence banks would make a profit on every dollar borrowed from the Fed, so they would continue to borrow indefinitely—which would in turn increase the monetary base indefinitely.

9. This statement is incorrect. The FDIC would not be effective in eliminating bank panics without Fed discounting to troubled banks in order to keep bank failures from spreading.

11. Usually not, since most declines in the Fed discount rate occur because market interest rates have fallen and the Fed does not want to let the discount rate get too far out of line with market rates. Hence a reduction in the discount rate frequently says nothing about the future direction of Fed policy.

13. Abolishing discounting would provide tighter control over the money supply because no fluctuation in the volume of discount loans would be possible. By contrast, the proposal to tie the discount rate to market interest rates may be more desirable because it has the advantage that the Fed could still perform its role as lender of last resort.

15. Open market operations are more flexible, reversible, and faster to implement than the other two tools. Discount policy is more flexible, reversible, and faster to implement than changing reserve requirements, but it is less effective than either of the other two tools.

Chapter 21

1. Disagree. Some unemployment is beneficial to the economy because the availability of vacant jobs makes it more likely that a worker will find the right job and that the employer will find the right worker for the job.

3. True. In such a world, hitting a monetary target would mean that the Fed would also hit its interest target, or vice versa. Thus the Fed could pursue both a monetary target and an interest-rate target at the same time.

5. The Fed can control the interest rate on three-month Treasury bills by buying and selling them in the open market. When the bill rate rises above the target level, the Fed would buy bills, which would bid up their price and lower the interest rate to its target level. Similarly, when the bill rate falls below the target level, the Fed would sell bills to raise the interest rate to the target level. The resulting open market operations would of course affect the money supply and cause it to change. The Fed would be giving up control of the money supply to pursue its interest-rate target.

7. Disagree. Although *nominal* interest rates are measured more accurately and more quickly than the money supply, the interest-rate variable that is of more concern to policymakers is the *real* interest rate. Because the measurement of real interest rates requires estimates of inflation, it is not true that real interest rates are necessarily measured more accurately and more quickly than the money supply. Interest-rate targets are therefore not necessarily better than money supply targets.

9. Because the Fed did not lend to troubled banks during this period, massive bank failures occurred, leading to a decline in the money supply when depositors increased their holdings of currency relative to deposits and banks increased their excess reserves to protect themselves against runs. As the money supply model presented in Chapters 15–17 indicates, these decisions by banks and depositors led to a sharp contraction of the money supply.

11. When the economy enters a recession, interest rates usually fall. If the Fed is targeting interest rates, it tries to prevent a decline in interest rates by selling bonds, thereby lowering their prices and raising interest rates to the target level. The open market sale would then lead to a decline in the monetary base and in the money supply. The decline in interest rates would also cause excess reserves to rise and the volume of discount loans to fall, thereby raising free reserves. With a free reserve target, the Fed would find monetary policy easy and would pursue contractionary policy. Therefore, neither interest-rate nor free reserve targets are very satisfactory because both can lead to a slower rate of money supply growth during a recession, just when the Fed would not want to slow money supply growth.

13. A borrowed reserves target will produce smaller fluctuations in the federal funds rate. In contrast to when there is a nonborrowed reserves target, when the federal funds rate rises with a borrowed reserves target, the Fed prevents the tendency of discount borrowings to rise by buying bonds to lower interest rates. The result is smaller fluctuations in the federal funds rate with a borrowed reserves target.

15. The Fed may prefer to control interest rates rather than the money supply because it wishes to avoid the conflict with Congress that occurs when interest rates rise. The Fed might also believe that interest rates are actually a better guide to future economic activity.

Chapter 22

2. The purchase of dollars involves a sale of foreign assets, which means that international reserves fall and the monetary base falls. The resulting fall in the money supply causes interest rates to rise and $RET^\$$ to shift to the right while it lowers the future price level, thereby raising the future expected exchange rate, causing RET^F to shift to the left. The result is a rise in the exchange rate. However, in the long run, the $RET^\$$ curve returns to its original position, and so there is overshooting.

4. Because other countries often intervene in the foreign exchange market when the United States has a deficit so that U.S. holdings of international reserves do not change. By contrast, when the Netherlands has a deficit, it must intervene in the foreign exchange market and buy guilders, which results in a reduction of international reserves for the Netherlands.

6. Two francs per dollar.

8. A large balance-of-payments surplus may require a country to finance the surplus by selling its currency in the foreign exchange market, thereby gaining international reserves. The result is that the central bank will have supplied more of its currency to the public, and the monetary base will rise. The resulting rise in the money supply can cause the price level to rise, leading to a higher inflation rate.

10. Countries may implement a contractionary monetary policy when they decide to intervene in the foreign exchange market and buy domestic currency to finance the deficit. The result is that

they sell off international reserves and their monetary base falls, leading to a decline in the money supply.

12. When other countries buy U.S. dollars to keep their exchange rates from changing vis-à-vis the dollar because of the U.S. deficits, they gain international reserves and their monetary base increases. The outcome is that the money supply in these countries grows faster and leads to higher inflation throughout the world.

14. There are no direct effects on the money supply because there is no central bank intervention in a pure flexible exchange rate regime; therefore, changes in international reserves that affect the monetary base do not occur. However, monetary policy can be affected by the foreign exchange market because monetary authorities may want to manipulate exchange rates by changing the money supply and interest rates.

Chapter 23

1. Velocity is approximately 10 in 1995, 11 in 1996, and 12 in 1997. The rate of velocity growth is approximately 10% per year.

3. Nominal GDP declines by approximately 10%.

5. The price level quadruples.

7. False. The two approaches differ in that Fisher's rules out any possible effect of interest rates on the demand for money, whereas the Cambridge approach does not.

9. The demand for money will decrease. People would be more likely to expect interest rates to fall and therefore more likely to expect bond prices to rise. The increase in the expected return on bonds relative to money will then mean that people would demand less money.

11. Money balances should average one-half of Grant's monthly income because he would hold no bonds, since holding them would entail additional brokerage costs but would not provide him with any interest income.

13. True. Because bonds are riskier than money, risk-averse people would be likely to want to hold both.

15. In Keynes's view, velocity is unpredictable because interest rates, which have large fluctuations, affect the demand for money and hence velocity. In addition, Keynes's analysis suggests that if people's expectations of the normal level

of interest rates change, the demand for money changes. Keynes thought that these expectations moved unpredictably, meaning that money demand and velocity are also unpredictable. Friedman sees the demand for money as stable, and because he also believes that changes in interest rates have only small effects on the demand for money, his position is that the demand for money, and hence velocity, is predictable.

Chapter 24

2. Companies cut production when their unplanned inventory investment is greater than zero because they are then producing more than they can sell. If they continue at current production, profits will suffer because they are building up unwanted inventory, which is costly to store and finance.

4. The equilibrium level of output is 1500. When planned investment spending falls by 100, the equilibrium level of output falls by 500 to 1000.

6. Nothing. The $100 billion increase in planned investment spending is exactly offset by the $100 billion decline in autonomous consumer expenditure, and autonomous spending and aggregate output remain unchanged.

8. Equilibrium output of 2000 occurs at the intersection of the 45° line $Y = Y^{ad}$ and the aggregate demand function $Y^{ad} = C + I + G = 500 + 0.75Y$. If government spending rises by 100, equilibrium output will rise by 400 to 2400.

10. Taxes should be reduced by $400 billion because the increase in output for a $T decrease in taxes is $T; that is, it equals the change in autonomous spending $mpc \times T$ times the multiplier $1/(1 - mpc) = (mpc \times T)[1/(1 - mpc)] = 0.5T[1/(1 - 0.5)] = 0.5T/0.5 = T$.

12. Rise. The fall in autonomous spending from an increase in taxes is always less than the change in taxes because the marginal propensity to consume is less than 1. By contrast, autonomous spending rises one-for-one with a change in autonomous consumer expenditure. So if taxes and autonomous consumer expenditure rise by the same amount, autonomous spending must rise, and aggregate output also rises.

14. When aggregate output falls, the demand for money falls, shifting the money demand curve to the left, which causes the equilibrium interest rate to fall. Because the equilibrium interest rate falls when aggregate output falls, there is a positive association between aggregate output and the equilibrium interest rate, and the *LM* curve slopes up.

Chapter 25

2. When investment spending collapsed, the aggregate demand function in the Keynesian cross diagram fell, leading to a lower level of equilibrium output for any given interest rate. The fall in equilibrium output for any given interest rate implies that the *IS* curve shifted to the left.

4. False. It can also be eliminated by a fall in aggregate output, which lowers the demand for money and brings it back into equality with the supply of money.

6. The *ISLM* model gives exactly this result. The tax cuts shifted the *IS* curve to the right, while tight money shifted the *LM* curve to the left. The interest rate at the intersection of the new *IS* and *LM* curves is necessarily higher than at the initial equilibrium, and aggregate output can be higher.

8. Because it suggests that an interest-rate target is better than a money supply target. The reason is that unstable money demand increases the volatility of the *LM* curve relative to the *IS* curve, and as demonstrated in the text, this makes it more likely that an interest-rate target is preferred to a money supply target.

10. The effect on the aggregate demand curve is uncertain. A rise in government spending would shift the *IS* curve to the right, raising equilibrium output for a given price level. But the reduction in the money supply would shift the *LM* curve to the left, lowering equilibrium output for a given price level. Depending on which of these two effects on equilibrium output is stronger, the aggregate demand curve could shift either to the right or to the left.

12. No effect. The *LM* curve would be vertical in this case, meaning that a rise in government spending and a rightward shift in the *IS* curve would not lead to higher aggregate output but rather only to a rise in the interest rate. For any given price level, therefore, equilibrium output would remain the same, and the aggregate demand curve would not shift.

14. The increase in net exports shifts the *IS* curve to the right, and the equilibrium level of interest rates and aggregate output will rise.

Chapter 26

2. Because the position of the aggregate demand curve is fixed if nominal income ($P \times Y$) is fixed, Friedman's statement implies that the position of the aggregate demand curve is completely determined by the quantity of money. This is built into the monetarist aggregate demand curve because it shifts only when the money supply changes.

4. The Keynesian aggregate demand curve shifts because a change in "animal spirits" causes consumer expenditure or planned investment spending to change, which then causes the quantity of aggregate output demanded to change at any given price level. In the monetarist view, by contrast, a change in "animal spirits" has little effect on velocity, and aggregate spending ($P \times Y$) remains unchanged; hence the aggregate demand curve does not shift.

6. True. Given fixed production costs, firms can earn higher profits by producing more when prices are higher. Profit-maximizing behavior on the part of firms thus leads them to increase production when prices are higher.

8. The aggregate supply curve would shift to the right because production costs would fall.

10. The collapse in investment spending during the Great Depression reduced the quantity of output demanded at any given price level and shifted the aggregate demand curve to the left. In an aggregate demand and supply diagram, the equilibrium price level and aggregate output would then fall, which explains the decline in aggregate output and the price level that occurred during the Great Depression.

12. Both the increase in the money supply and the income tax cut will increase the quantity of output demanded at any given price level and so will shift the aggregate demand curve to the right. The intersection of the aggregate demand and aggregate supply curve will be at a higher level of both output and price level in the short run. However, in the long run, the aggregate supply curve will shift leftward, leaving output

at the natural rate level, but the price level will be even higher.

14. Because goods would cost more, the national sales tax would raise production costs, and the aggregate supply curve would shift to the left. The intersection of the aggregate supply curve with the aggregate demand curve would then be at a higher level of prices and a lower level of aggregate output; aggregate output would fall, and the price level would rise.

Chapter 27

4. Seeing which car is built better produces structural model evidence because it explains why one car is better than the other (that is, how the car is built). Asking owners how often their cars undergo repairs produces reduced-form evidence because it looks only at the correlation of reliability with the manufacturer of the car.

5. Not necessarily. If GM car owners change their oil more frequently than Ford owners, GM cars would have better repair records even though they are not more reliable cars. In this case, it is a third factor, the frequency of oil changes, that leads to the better repair record for GM cars.

6. Not necessarily. Although the Ford engine might be built better than the GM engine, the rest of the GM car might be better made than the Ford. The result could be that the GM car is more reliable than the Ford.

8. If the Fed has interest-rate targets, a rise in output that raises interest rates might cause the Fed to buy bonds and bid up their price in order to drive interest rates back down to their target level (see Chapter 6). The result of these open market purchases would be that the increase in output would cause an increase in the monetary base and hence an increase in the money supply. In addition, a rise in output and interest rates would cause free reserves to fall (because excess reserves would fall and the volume of discount loans would rise). If the Fed has a free reserves target, the increase in aggregate output will then cause the Fed to increase the money supply because it believes that money is tight.

10. Monetarists went on to refine their reduced-form models with more sophisticated statistical procedures, one outcome of which was the St. Louis model. Keynesians began to look for transmission mechanisms of monetary policy that they may have ignored.

12. False. Monetary policy can affect stock prices, which affect Tobin's q, thereby affecting investment spending. In addition, monetary policy can affect loan availability, which may also influence investment spending.

14. There are three mechanisms involving consumer expenditure. First, a rise in the money supply lowers interest rates and reduces the cost of financing purchases of consumer durables, and consumer durable expenditure rises. Second, a rise in the money supply causes stock prices and wealth to rise, leading to greater lifetime resources for consumers and causing them to increase their consumption. Third, a rise in the money supply that causes stock prices and the value of financial assets to rise also lowers people's probability of financial distress, and so they spend more on consumer durables.

Chapter 28

2. Because hyperinflations appear to be examples in which the increase in money supply growth is an exogenous event, the fact that hyperinflation occurs when money growth is high is powerful evidence that a high rate of money growth causes inflation.

4. False. Although workers' attempts to push up their wages can lead to inflation if the government has a high employment target, inflation is still a monetary phenomenon because it cannot occur without accommodating monetary policy.

6. True. If financed with money creation, a temporary budget deficit can lead to a one-time rightward shift in the aggregate demand curve and hence to a one-time increase in the price level. However, once the budget deficit disappears, there is no longer any reason for the aggregate demand curve to shift. Thus a temporary deficit cannot lead to a continuing rightward shift of the aggregate demand curve and therefore cannot produce inflation, a continuing increase in the price level.

8. True. The monetarist objection to activist policy would no longer be as serious. The aggregate demand curve could be quickly moved to AD_2 in Figure 10, and the economy would move quickly to point 2 because the aggregate supply

curve would not have as much time to shift. The scenario of a highly variable price level and output would not occur, making an activist policy more desirable.

10. True, if expectations about policy affect the wage-setting process. In this case, workers and firms are more likely to push up wages and prices because they know that if they do so and unemployment develops as a result, the government will pursue expansionary policies to eliminate the unemployment. Therefore, the cost of pushing up wages and prices is lower, and workers and firms will be more likely to do it.

12. True. If expectations about policy have no effect on the aggregate supply curve, a cost-push inflation is less likely to develop when policymakers pursue an activist accommodating policy. Furthermore, if expectations about policy do not matter, pursuing a nonaccommodating, nonactivist policy does not have the hidden benefit of making it less likely that workers will push up their wages and create unemployment. The case for an activist policy is therefore stronger.

14. The Fed's big stick is the ability to let unemployment develop as a result of a wage push by not trying to eliminate unemployment with expansionary monetary policy. The statement proposes that the Fed should pursue a nonaccommodating policy because this will prevent cost-push inflation and make it less likely that unemployment develops because of workers' attempts to push up their wages.

Chapter 29

1. False. Expectations can be highly inaccurate and still be rational because optimal forecasts are not necessarily accurate: A forecast is optimal if it is the best possible even if the forecast errors are large.

3. No, because he could improve the accuracy of his forecasts by predicting that tomorrow's interest rates will be identical to today's. His forecasts are therefore not optimal, and he does not have rational expectations.

5. No, you shouldn't buy stocks because the rise in the money supply is publicly available information that will be already incorporated into stock prices. So you cannot expect to earn more than

the equilibrium return on stocks by acting on the money supply information.

7. No, because this is publicly available information and is already reflected in stock prices. The optimal forecast of stock returns will equal the equilibrium return, so there is no benefit from selling your stocks.

9. No, if the person has no better information than the rest of the market. An expected price rise of 10% over the next month implies over a 100% annual return on IBM stock, which certainly exceeds its equilibrium return. This would mean that there is an unexploited profit opportunity in the market, which would have been eliminated in an efficient market. The only time that the person's expectations could be rational is if the person had information unavailable to the market that allowed him or her to beat the market.

11. False. The people with better information are exactly those who make the market more efficient by eliminating unexploited profit opportunities. These people can profit from their better information.

13. True in principle. Foreign exchange rates are a random walk over a short interval such as a week because changes in the exchange rate are unpredictable. If a change were predictable, large unexploited profit opportunities would exist in the foreign exchange market. If the foreign exchange market is efficient, these unexploited profit opportunities cannot exist, and so the foreign exchange rate will approximately follow a random walk.

15. False. Although human fear may be the source of stock market crashes, that does not imply that there are unexploited profit opportunities in the market. Nothing in rational expectations theory rules out large changes in stock prices as a result of fears on the part of the investing public.

Chapter 30

2. A tax cut that is expected to last for ten years will have a larger effect on consumer expenditure than the one that is expected to last only one year. The reason is that the longer the tax cut is expected to last, the greater its effect on expected average income and consumer expenditure.

4. True, if the anti-inflation policy is credible. As shown in Figure 6, if anti-inflation policy is believed (and hence expected), there is no output loss in the new classical model [the economy stays at point 1 in panel (b)], and there is a smaller output loss than would otherwise be the case in the new Keynesian model [the economy goes to point 2" rather than point 2' in panel (c)].

6. Uncertain. It is true that policymakers can reduce unemployment by pursuing a more expansionary policy than the public expects. However, the rational expectations assumption indicates that the public will attempt to anticipate policymakers' actions. Policymakers cannot be sure whether expansionary policy will be more or less expansionary than the public expects and hence cannot use policy to make a predictable impact on unemployment.

8. True, because the Lucas critique indicates that the effect of policy on the aggregate demand curve depends on the public's expectations about that policy. The outcome of a particular policy is therefore less certain in Lucas's view than if expectations about it do not matter, and it is harder to design a beneficial activist stabilization policy.

10. Yes, if budget deficits are expected to lead to an inflationary monetary policy and expectations about monetary policy affect the aggregate supply curve. In this case, a large budget deficit would cause the aggregate supply curve to shift more to the left because expected inflation would be higher. The result is that the increase in the price level (the inflation rate) would be higher.

13. The aggregate supply curve would shift to the left less than the aggregate demand curve shifts to the right; hence at their intersection, aggregate output would rise and the price level would be higher than it would have been if money growth had been reduced to a rate of 2%.

14. Using the traditional model, the aggregate supply curve would continue to shift leftward at the same rate, and the smaller rightward shift of the aggregate demand curve because money supply growth has been reduced would mean a smaller increase in the price level and a reduction of aggregate output. In the new Keynesian model, the effect of this anti-inflation policy on aggregate output is uncertain. The aggregate supply

curve would not shift leftward by as much as in the traditional model because the anti-inflation policy is expected, but it would shift to the left by more than in the new classical model. Hence inflation falls, but aggregate output may rise or fall, depending on whether the aggregate supply curve shifts to the left more or less than the aggregate demand curve shifts to the right.

CREDITS

Page 28: **Following the Financial News: Money Market Rates.** "Money Rates" from *The Wall Street Journal,* March 2, 1994. Reprinted by permission of The Wall Street Journal. Copyright © 1994 Dow Jones & Company, Inc. All Rights Reserved Worldwide.

Page 47: **Following the Financial News: Foreign Stock Market Indexes.** "Stock Market Indexes" from *The Wall Street Journal,* March 2, 1994. Reprinted by permission of The Wall Street Journal. Copyright © 1994 Dow Jones & Company, Inc. All Rights Reserved Worldwide.

Page 62: **Following the Financial News: The Monetary Aggregates.** "Federal Reserve Data" from *The Wall Street Journal,* March 18, 1994. Reprinted by permission of The Wall Street Journal. Copyright © 1994 Dow Jones & Company, Inc. All Rights Reserved Worldwide.

Page 84: **Following the Financial News: Bond Prices and Interest Rates.** "Government Bonds, Treasury Bills, Corporation Bonds" from *The Wall Street Journal,* March 2, 1994. Reprinted by permission of The Wall Street Journal. Copyright © 1994 Dow Jones & Company, Inc. All Rights Reserved Worldwide.

Page 124: **Following the Financial News: Money Market Rates.** "Sharp Increase in National Purchasing Index Fuels Inflation Fears, Pushing Down Bond Prices" by Thomas D. Lauricella from *The Wall Street Journal,* March 2, 1994. Reprinted by permission of The Wall Street Journal. Copyright © 1994 Dow Jones & Company, Inc. All Rights Reserved Worldwide.

Pages 134-135: **Following the Financial News: Forecasting Interest Rates.** "A Sampling of Interest-Rate, Economic and Currency Forecasts"

from *The Wall Street Journal,* January 3, 1994. Reprinted by permission of The Wall Street Journal. Copyright © 1994 Dow Jones & Company, Inc. All Rights Reserved Worldwide.

Page 146: **Following the Financial News: The Commodities Column.** "Prices of Precious Metals Rise Amid Concerns Over U.S.-Serbia Clash, Prospect for Inflation" by Jeffrey Taylor from *The Wall Street Journal,* March 1, 1994. Reprinted by permission of The Wall Street Journal. Copyright © 1994 Dow Jones & Company, Inc. All Rights Reserved Worldwide.

Page 158: **Following the Financial News: Yield Curve.** "Treasury Yield Curve" from *The Wall Street Journal,* March 3, 1994. Reprinted by permission of The Wall Street Journal. Copyright © 1994 Dow Jones & Company, Inc. All Rights Reserved Worldwide.

Page 176: **Following the Financial News: Current Exchange Rates.** "Currency Trading" from *The Wall Street Journal,* March 3, 1994. Reprinted by permission of The Wall Street Journal. Copyright © 1994 Dow Jones & Company, Inc. All Rights Reserved Worldwide.

Page 200: **Following the Financial News: The Foreign Exchange Column.** "Dollar Falls Against Major Currencies on Concern Over U.S. Rates and Trade" by Gary Rosenberger from *The Wall Street Journal,* February 2, 1994. Reprinted by permission of The Wall Street Journal. Copyright © 1994 Dow Jones & Company, Inc. All Rights Reserved Worldwide.

Page 235: **Following the Financial News: Financial Features.** "Interest Rate" from *The Wall Street Journal,* March 3, 1994. Reprinted by permission of The Wall Street Journal. Copyright ©

Page 360: **Following the Financial News: New Securities Issues.** "New Securities Issues" from *The Wall Street Journal,* March 14, 1994, p. C19.

Page 468: **Following the Financial News: Reserves and Sources of Change in the Monetary Base.** "Federal Reserve Data" from *The Wall Street Journal,* March 4, 1994. Reprinted by permission of The Wall Street Journal. Copyright © 1994 Dow Jones & Company, Inc. All Rights Reserved Worldwide.

Page 720: **Following the Financial News: Stock Prices.** "Stock Prices" from *The Wall Street Journal,* March 31, 1994. Reprinted by permission of The Wall Street Journal. Copyright © 1994 Dow Jones & Company, Inc. All Rights Reserved Worldwide.

INDEX

Abedi, Agha Hasan, 317
Acceptances, bankers', 28
Accommodating policy, 692
Accord between Federal
    Reserve and Treasury, 506
Accounts
    automatic transfer from sav-
        ings, 60, 246–247,
        318–319, 488
    capital, 459, 466, 527
    cash management, 361
    current, 524–526
    money market deposit,
        252–253
    negotiable order of with-
        drawal, 10, 60 231, 246,
        252, 318–319, 488, 509
    savings, 253–254
    share draft, 246
    sweep, 246–247
    T-, 257–259
    tax and loan, 465, 469
    unit of, 53–54
Accrual ("Z") bonds, 241
Activist policy, 637, 701–707
Adaptive expectations, 712
Adjustable-rate mortgages, 233
Adjustment credit, 481
Advances, 254
Adverse selection, 34–37,
    212–217
    and banking regulations,
        305–314, 333, 337–338
    defined, 35, 211

and financial crises, 223–228
and financial intermediation,
    710–712
influence on financial struc-
    ture, 212–217
and insurance companies,
    344–347
lemons in stock/bond mar-
    kets, 212–213
in loan market, 269–275
solutions to problems,
    213–217
After-tax real interest rate, 92
Agents, 217–220
Aggregate demand, 625
    crowding out effect, 630–631
    defined, 574, 625
    Keynesian view of, 625,
        628–630
    monetarist view of, 625–628
    money versus credit,
        631–632
    role of expectations, 712
    shifts in, 638
Aggregate demand and supply
    analysis
    of anti-inflation policy,
        749–751
    equilibrium in, 633–645
    of inflation, 686–690
    of inflationary policy,
        691–695
    monetarist versus Keynesian,
        625–630

with new classical macro-
    economic model, 736–741
with new Keynesian model,
    742–744
in predicting future eco-
    nomic activity, 647–648
with traditional model,
    745–752
Aggregate demand curve
    defined, 619, 625
    derivation of, 620–621, 627
    and *ISLM* model, 619–623
    in Keynesian analysis,
        629–630
    in monetarist analysis,
        627–628
    shifts in, 579–580
Aggregate demand function,
    579–580
Aggregate income, 17
Aggregate output, 17, 543
    and autonomous spending,
        580–583, 587–588
    and business cycles, 4,
        645–647
    defined, 4
    in demand and supply
        analysis, 625–633
    determination of, 574–590
    equilibrium level of,
        578–580; changes in,
        606–609; demand and
        supply analysis of,
        633–645

Aggregate output (*Continued*)
  and expansionary policy,
    736–740, 743
  and expenditure multiplier,
    580–583
  and fiscal policy, 608–609
  and government spending,
    574, 584–588
  and interest rate, 606–609
  and international trade, 574,
    586–588
  and investment spending,
    577–578, 580–583,
    587–588
  ISLM approach to, 590–598
  Keynesian cross diagram,
    578–580
  and monetary policy,
    606–608
  natural rate level of, 617, 635
  and net exports, 574,
    587–588
  newspaper data on, 626
  short-run, and price
    responses, 745–748
  and taxes, 584–588, 608–609
Aggregate price level, 4, 6,
  17–19
Aggregate supply, 632–633
  defined, 625
  and Phillips curve, 651–654
  role of expectations, 712
  shifts in, 638, 640–641
Aggregate supply and demand
  analysis. *See* Aggregate
  demand and supply
  analysis
Aggregate supply curve,
  632–633
  defined, 632
  long-run, 634–637
  shifts in, 633, 638, 640–641,
    643–644
  short-run, 633–634
Agricultural Adjustment Act
  (1933), 504

Akerlof, George 212
Alesina, Alberto, 452n
Alexander, Sidney, 727
Allstate Insurance Co., 349
American Express, 238
American Stock Exchange
  (AMEX), 25, 85, 360
Amortization schedule, for
  mortgage loans, 75
Andersen, Leonall, 670n
Ando, Albert, 669n
Angell, Wayne, 199
"Animal spirits"
  aggregate demand curve,
    622, 630
  autonomous spending,
    582–583
  defined, 583
  inflation, 689n
Announcement effect,
  485–486
Anti-inflationary policy 510-
  511, 707, 749–754
Anticipated policy, 736–739,
  743
Appreciation, of currency, 175,
  177, 533
Arbitrage, 244, 722
Arbitrage pricing theory, 104
Argentina
  inflation in, 682–683, 685
  loans made to, 296
Armenia, inflation in, 697
Asset demand
  and demand for money,
    560–562
  determinants of, 95–99
  and diversification benefits,
    99–101
  for domestic assets, 183–185
  and interest rates, 710
  and risk premiums, 103–104
  shifts in demand curves for
    bonds, 113–117
  and systematic risk, 101–103
  theory of, 99

Asset management, 260–264,
  711
Asset market approach, 113
Asset transformation, 257
Assets
  of bank, 251–252, 254–257,
    301–302
  beta of, 103
  defined, 11, 95
  diversification of, 99–101,
    103–104, 264
  of Fed, 370, 457–458
  inferior, 96
  liquidity of, 24.
  as luxury, 97
  as necessity, 96–97
  real, 116
  restrictions on, 309–311
Asymmetric information,
  34–37, 211–212. *See also*
  Adverse selection; Moral
  hazard
  and banking regulation,
    305–314
  defined, 34–35
  and financial structure,
    710–711
  and investment spending,
    673–674
  in loan markets, 273
Australia
  banking system in, 303, 315,
    452
  reserve requirements in, 490
Automated teller machines
  (ATMs), 291
Automatic transfer from savings (ATS) accounts, 60,
  246–247, 318–319, 488
Automobile insurance, 349–350
Automobile loans, 209, 241
Autonomous spending,
  575–577
  and aggregate output,
    582–583, 587–588, 590n
  defined, 575

Friedman-Meiselman measure of, 668–669
and *ISLM* model, 601

Bacon, Kenneth H., 310*n*
Bahamas, banking in, 295
Balance
  compensating, 274
  official reserve transactions, 527
Balance of payments, 524–528
  defined, 524
  methods of financing, 527–528
  monetary policy for, 537–538
Balance of payments deficit, 527
  in Bretton Woods system, 529–533
  in managed float system, 533–534
  monetary policy for, 537–538
Balance of payments surplus, 528–533
Balance sheets
  of bank, 251–257
  defined, 251
  of Fed, 368–370, 457–461
Banc One Corp., 289
Bankamerica Corp., 289, 291, 296, 301
Bankamericard, 238
Bank capital, 254
  management of, 268
  managing capital adequacy, 260, 265–268
  physical, 257
  and prevention of bank failure, 266
  required, 268, 309–311
  and returns to equity holders, 266–268
  risk-based, 311–312
Bank credit cards, 238
Bankers' acceptances, 28
Bankers Trust Corp., 289, 296

Bank examiners, 313
Bank failures, 265–266, 284–285, 306–309
Bank holding companies, 286, 289–291, 295
Bank Holding Company Act (1956), 321
Banking
  and money supply, 10
  universal, 315
  why study, 9–11
Banking Act (1933), 285, 293, 314–315, 321, 337–339, 444
Banking Act (1935), 504–505
Banking regulation. *See also* Financial regulation
  of commercial banks, 287–291
  of credit unions, 292–293
  international, 314–317
  of mutual savings banks, 292
  recent, 320, 322–339
  reforms in, 291, 316–321
  of savings and loan associations, 291–292
Banking system, 283–303
  bank panics in, 426–427
  crisis in, 223–228
  in deposit creation, 373–376
  dual, 284–285
  how Fed provides reserves to, 371–372
  international, 293–297
  nationwide, 335
  separated from securities industry, 314–315, 337–339
Bank Insurance Fund (BIF), 327–329
Bank Merger Acts (1960, 1966), 321
Banknotes, 284–285
Bank of Canada, 515
Bank of Credit and Commerce International (BCCI), 315, 317, 330

Bank of England, 317, 514, 536
Bank of Japan, 516–517
Bank of New England, 309–310, 424
Bank of North America, 284
Bank of the United States, 226, 284
Bank panics, 43, 45, 438, 669
  anatomy of, 423–429
  and currency-checkable deposits ratio, 410, 413
  defined, 225, 410
  expectations in, 711
  and Federal Reserve System, 421, 496
  and financial crises, 225
  and money supply, 421, 427
Bankruptcy, 226, 266
Banks
  assets of, 251–252, 254–257, 264, 301–302
  balance sheet of, 251–257
  basic operations, 257–260
  behavior of, 415–418
  branching restrictions, 287–288
  cash items in process of collection, 255–256
  central. *See* Central banks
  charters of, 311, 313
  commercial, 38–39, 256, 284–291, 441
  decline of industry, 298–303
  defined, 9, 38
  deposits of: in Federal Reserve banks. *See* Reserves; offshore, 294–295; in other banks, 256
  electronic facilities, 291
  examination of, 311, 313
  excess reserves, 254–255, 261–264, 370, 416–417
  failure of. *See* Bank failures
  Federal Reserve, 438–443
  as financial intermediaries, 9–10

Banks (*Continued*)
    foreign, 293–297
    importance in business
        financing, 208
    investment, 25, 359–360
    liabilities of, 251–254,
        264–265, 299–301
    liquidity management by,
        260–264
    loan management by,
        255–257, 269–275
    loans from Fed. *See* Dis-
        count loans
    members of Federal Reserve,
        441–442
    in money supply model,
        368, 370–379
    money center, 265
    narrow/wide, 334–335
    national, 284–286, 441
    nationwide, 335
    nonbank, 290
    off-balance-sheet activities
        of, 279–280
    open market purchase from,
        384–386
    problems, 290–303
    runs on, 425–426
    savings. *See* Mutual savings
        banks; Savings and loan
        associations
    securities held by, 256
    state, 285–286
    vault cash of, 254, 369–370,
        458
    wire transfers by, 57–58
Banks for Cooperatives, 357
Barnett, William, 63n
Barro, Robert J., 473, 733n,
    755n
Barter economy, 53–55
Base drift, 449
Basel Agreement (1988), 297,
    311–312, 315–317, 332
Basis points, 85

Baumol, William, 555–559
Baumol-Tobin model of trans-
    actions demand, 555–558,
    568n, 759–760
Bent, Bruce, 247
Bernanke, Ben S., 228n, 673n
Beta, of asset, 103
BfG Bank, 303
Black, Fischer, 720n
"Black Monday." *See* Stock
    market crash of 1987
Blanchard, Oliver J., 644n,
    663n
Bliss, Robert, 167n
Board of Governors. *See* Fed-
    eral Reserve System,
    Board of Governors
Boesky, Ivan, 722–723
Bolivia, inflation in, 752–753
Bond contracts, 209
Bond market, 11
    demand and supply in,
        107–125
    international, 47
    investing in, 728–730
    "lemon problems" in,
        212–213
    rational expectations in,
        728–730
    volatility of, 88–90
Bond prices, 82–86
    discount yield negatively
        related to, 82
    and interest rates, 79, 89, 710
    published in newspapers,
        82–86
Bonds
    accrual ("Z"), 241
    consols, 78–79
    convertible, 31–32
    corporate, 11. 31–32
    and corporate financing,
        207–208
    coupon, 70, 75–79
    default-free, 150–152

    default risk on, 150–153
    defined, 11, 22
    discount, 70, 79
    Eurobonds, 47
    foreign, 47
    "gilt-edged," 89
    interest rates on, 11–12, 89
    junk, 152–154, 238–239
    liquidity of, 153–155
    long-term, 89
    municipal, 32, 155–156, 256,
        264
    tax-exempt, 155–156, 256
    U.S. government. *See* Secu-
        rities, U.S. government
    zero-coupon, 70
Borrowers, in money supply
    process, 368
Borrowing by banks. *See* Dis-
    count loans
Bosworth, Barry, 673n
Boyd, J., 308n
Bracket creep, 411, 414
Brady Commission, 244
Branches, 287
Branching regulations
    commercial banks, 287–288
    credit unions, 293
    mutual savings banks, 292
    savings and loan associa-
        tions, 292
Branson, William H., 523n
Brazil
    inflation in, 5, 682–683, 685
    loans made to, 296
Bretton Woods Agreement
    (1945), 529–530
Bretton Woods system,
    529–534, 537–538
Bridge banks, 309–310
Britain
    banking system in, 303,
        314–315
    budget deficits in, 754
    business financing in, 207

inflation in, 754
monetary policy in, 513–514
pound and exchange rates, 13, 535–536, 538
securities industry in, 33, 47
Brokerage fees, 242, 558*n*
Brokerage firms, 242–243, 361
Brokered deposits, 322
Brokers, 25, 242–243, 359–361
Brown, Henry, 247
Brunner, Karl, 507, 568–569, 571*n*, 704*n*, 734*n*
Bubble economy, 516–517
Budget constraints, government, 457–458
Budget deficits
  and bond supply, 118
  credibility about, 753–754
  defined, 8–9
  and inflation, 695–697
  and interest rates, 156–157, 472–474
  and monetary base, 467–474
  and money creation, 696–697
Bundesbank, 515, 535–536
Bureaucratic behavior, theory of, 447–450, 513*n*
"Bureaucratic gambling," 325
Bureau of Engraving and Printing, 369*n*
Burns, Arthur, 445, 507, 752
Bush, George, 286, 326, 335
Business cycle expansion
  and demand for money, 131
  effect on interest rates, 121–123
Business cycles
  aggregate demand and supply analysis, 645–647
  defined, 4
  and money, 4, 629–630
  real, 641, 643–644, 677–678

Business finance companies, 355
Business optimism, 638–639

Call option, 236–237
Cambridge model, 547–548, 551–553, 555, 561, 565
CAMEL rating, 311
Campbell, John Y., 167*n*
Canada
  banking system in, 315, 448
  business financing in, 207
  monetary policy in, 513–515
  reserve requirements in, 490
  securities industry in, 33
Cancellation, of insurance policy, 346
Capital
  bank. *See* Bank capital
  equity, 216–217
  venture, 219–220
Capital accounts, 459, 466, 527
Capital asset pricing model (CAPM), 103–104
Capital controls, 294
Capital gains
  and long-term bonds, 89
  rate of, 87
  taxes on, 727*n*
Capital loss
  and long-term bonds, 89
  as "paper loss," 88
Capital markets
  defined, 26
  instruments of, 30–32
  theory of efficient. *See* Efficient markets theory
Capital mobility, 185
Carte Blanche, 238
Carter, Jimmy, 447
Cash
  items in process of collection, 255–256, 458–460, 463–464
  vault, 254, 369–370, 458

Cash management accounts (CMAs), 361
Casualty insurance, 40–41, 349–350
Causation-correlation question, 659–660
Cayman Islands, banking in, 295
Central banks, 284, 367–368, 427, 438, 441, 448, 452, 495, 529–530
Certificates for amortizing revolving debts (CARDs), 241
Certificates of accrual on Treasury securities (CATS), 241
Certificates of automobile receivables (CARs), 241
Certificates of deposit (CDs), 27–28, 322
  negotiable, 265
  as nontransaction deposits, 253–254
Ceteris paribus, 107
Charles Schwab and Co., 242
Charters, 311, 313
  commercial banks, 288, 313
  credit unions, 292–293
  mutual savings banks, 292
  savings and loan associations, 291
Chase Manhattan Corp., 289, 291, 296
Checkable deposits
  current level of, 488
  defined, 252–253
  interest rates on, 409–410, 415, 421
  and multiple deposit creation, 370–379
  ratio of currency to. *See* Currency-checkable deposits ratio
  ratio of excess reserves to, 394–395, 404–405

Checkable deposits (*Continued*)
 ratio of money market funds
  to, 404–405
 ratio of time deposits to,
  404–405, 421
 required reserve ratio,
  420–421
 shifts into currency, 387–388
Checks
 clearing of, 459, 462–464
 and float, 462–464
 payments system based on,
  56–58
Chemical Bank Corp., 289, 296
Chicago Board Options
  Exchange (CBOE), 237
Chicago Board of Trade (CBT),
  25, 235, 242
Chicago Mercantile Exchange
  (CME), 236, 242
Christiano, Lawrence, 138n
Chrysler Corp., 150
Chrystal, K. Alec, 63n
Cirrus, 291
Citibank, 28, 536
Citicorp, 270, 289, 291, 293,
  296, 301, 355, 361
Civil Aeronautics Board, 563n
Clearing House Inter-bank Pay-
  ment Systems (CHIPS), 58
Clift, Eleanor, 327n
Clinton, Bill, 8, 156–157, 199,
  286, 291, 335–336, 353,
  648
Closed-economy *ISLM* model,
  767–769
Closed-end funds, 356
Coins, 458–459, 465n, 471n
Coinsurance
 for federal deposit insur-
  ance, 334
 in insurance policies, 346
Collateral, 208–209, 222
 defined, 208
 and loan management, 274
 and net worth, 216–217

Collateralized debt, 208–209
Collateralized mortgage obligations (CMOs), 241–242
Commerce Department, U.S.,
  125
Commercial banks, 256,
  284–291
 branching restrictions on,
  287–288
 charters, 288, 313
 as financial intermediaries,
  38–39
 largest in the United States,
  289
 number in the United States,
  287
 regulation of, 286
 size distribution, 288
 structure of industry,
  286–291
Commercial loans, 256
 as capital market instruments, 32
 as simple loans, 70
Commercial mortgages, 209
Commercial paper, 28, 239,
  245, 249
"Commodities" column in
  newspapers, 145–147
Commodities Futures Trading
  Commission (CFTC), 44
Commodity exchanges, 25
Commodity money, 56
Compensating balances, 274
Competitive Equality Banking
  Act (CEBA, 1987), 321,
  324–325
Complete crowding out,
  612–614, 630
Comptroller of the Currency.
  See Office of the Comp-
  troller of the Currency
Congress, U.S., and Federal
  Reserve, 445–447,
  449–451, 453
Consols, 78–79

Constant-money-growth-rate
  rule, 706
Constitution, U.S., 437
Consumer debt, collateralized,
  208–209
Consumer durable expendi-
  ture, 674–676
Consumer expenditure, 574
 autonomous, 575–576; and
  aggregate output,
  582–583, 587–588, 590n;
  defined, 575; Friedman-
  Meiselman measure,
  668–669; and *IS* curve, 601
 changes in, 602
 and consumption function,
  575–577
 defined, 574, 628
 as monetary transmission
  mechanism, 674–676
Consumer finance companies,
  355
Consumer loans, 32, 256
Consumer optimism, 638–639
Consumer price index (CPI),
  19, 626
Consumer Reports, 215
Consumption, 674–675
Consumption function,
  575–577
Contagion effect, 306
Continental Illinois National
  Bank, 311, 424, 481, 483,
  485–486
Contracts
 debt, 220–223
 equity, 217–220
Contractual savings institutions,
  40–41
Convertible bonds, 31–32
Cooke, Jay, & Co., 226
Cooley, Thomas F., 572n
Cootner, Paul, 727n
Corporate bonds
 as capital market instru-
  ments, 31–32

default risk on, 150–153
liquidity of, 153–154
yield on, 149–150
Corporate financing
   access to securities markets, 208
   through collateralized debt, 208–209
   external sources of, 205–209
   and stock issuance, 206
Correlation-causation question, 659–660
Correspondent banking, 256
Corrigan, E. Gerald, 484
Cost-push inflation, 691–693, 712
Costly state verification, 219
Costs
   opportunity, 126–127
   transaction, 34, 209–211
Coupon bonds, 70, 75–79, 161, 163
Coupon rate, 70
Covenants. *See* Restrictive covenants
CPI *See* Consumer price index
Cranston, Alan, 327
Credibility, and inflation, 706–707, 751–754
Credit, 481
   and investment spending, 673
   letters of, 280
Credit agencies, federal, 357–358
Credit cards, bank, 238
Credit Control Act (1969), 443
Credit crunch, 268–269
Crédit Lyonnais, 303
"Credit markets" column in newspapers, 123–125
Credit rationing, 274–275
Credit risk, 255–257, 260, 269–275
   collateral, 274
   and credit rationing, 274–275

loan commitments, 272–273
long-term customer relationships, 271–272
screening/monitoring, 270–271
Credit unions
   branching restrictions on, 293
   charters, 292–293
   consumer loans by, 257
   as financial intermediaries, 40
   regulation of, 291–292
Crises. *See* Financial crises
Crow, John, 515
Crowding out, 630–631
   complete, 612–614, 631
   partial, 631
Currency
   appreciation/depreciation, 175, 177, 522–523
   banknotes, 284–285
   in circulation, 369, 384
   commodity/fiat money, 56
   and crime, 410–411, 421
   defined, 51
   federal government issuance of, 27
   foreign exchange rates for. *See* Exchange rates
   paper, 55–56
   reserve, 530, 537
   shift from deposits, 387–388
   single European, 57, 536
   Treasury, 369n, 384n, 459n, 465n
Currency-checkable deposits ratio
   and bank panics, 410, 413
   behavior of, 407–415
   future of, 414–415
   historical record, 407–408, 412–414
   and interest rates, 409–412
   and money multiplier, 395–396, 404–405

and money supply, 428–429
and risk, 409–412
and taxes, 411–412, 415
underground economy, 412, 414
and wealth, 409
Current account, 524–526
Current yield, 80–81

Dai-Ichi Kangyo, 297
Data lag, 702
Dealers, 25, 359–361
Dean Witter Reynolds, 361
Debt
   collateralized, 208–209
   monetizing, 471
   Third World, 296
Debt contracts, 209, 220–223
Debt deflation, 226, 228
Debt financing, of government spending, 470–471
Debt instruments, 24, 255–257
Debt market, 24, 220
DeConcini, Dennis, 327
Deductible, in insurance, 346
Default, 27
Default-free bonds, 150–155
Default risk, 150–153, 570
Defensive open market operations, 477
Deferred availability cash items, 459–460, 463–464
Deficits, budget. *See* Budget deficits
Defined benefit plans, 351
Defined contribution plans, 351
Demand
   aggregate. *See* Aggregate demand
   analysis of, 111–113
   asset. *See* Asset demand
   in bond market, 107, 111–114, 116–117
   excess, 111, 634
   in gold market, 141–142

Demand (*Continued*)
 for innovative financial products, 232–237
 money. *See* Money demand
 in money market, 128–129
 wealth elasticity of, 96
Demand curve
 aggregate. *See* Aggregate demand curve
 for bonds, 108–109
 defined, 107
 for gold, 141–144
 for money, 128–129
 movements along, 113
 shifts in, 113–117, 128–129, 143–144
Demand-pull inflation, 691, 693–694
Deposit insurance
 federal. *See* Federal deposit insurance
 privately provided, 335
 state funds for, 292–293
Deposit multiplier, simple, 377–378
Depositors, in money supply process, 368
Depository Institutions Act (1982), 319–321
Depository Institutions Deregulation and Monetary Control Act (DIDMCA, 1980), 318–319, 321, 442, 488
Deposit outflows, 260–264
 defined, 260
 expected, and excess reserve ratio, 416–417
 and money supply, 421
Deposit rate ceilings, 245, 316–320
Deposits
 brokered, 322
 certificates of. *See* Certificates of deposit
 checkable. *See* Checkable deposits

domestic, 183–185, 190–191
 at Federal Reserve. *See* Reserves
 foreign, 183–185, 188–190, 459, 466
 multiple, creation of, 370–379
 nontransaction, 253–254
 offshore, 253–254
 returns on domestic and foreign compared, 183–185
 shifts to currency from. *See* Currency-checkable deposits ratio
 time, 253–254
Depreciation, of currency, 175, 177, 522
Devaluation, 532
Diners Club, 238
Direct finance, 208
Dirty float, 519
Discount bonds, 70, 79, 161, 163
Discount brokers, 25, 242–243
Discounting the future, 72
Discount loans, 262–263
 in control of monetary base, 370–371, 388–389, 440, 444, 457, 461–462, 480–481
 defined, 254
 interest rate. *See* Discount rate
 and market interst rate, 417–418
 money supply related to, 396–397
 types, 481
Discount policy
 advantages/disadvantages, 486
 and announcement effect, 485–486
 historical perspective, 503–504
 in monetary policy, 480–488

 proposed reforms, 487–488
Discount rate
 defined, 254, 370, 457, 503
 and discount loans, 262–263, 417–418, 440, 444
 and market interest rates, 481–482, 487–488
 and money supply, 420
 penalty, 487
Discounts, 503
Discount window, 480–482
Discount yield, 81–82
Discover card, 238
Discretionary policy, 706–707, 740–741
Discretion versus rules, 706–707
Disequilibrium, fundamental, 532
Disintermediation, 245
Disposable income, 575
Diversification
 by banks to reduce risk, 264
 benefits, 99–101
 defined, 100
 in market portfolio, 103–104
Dividends, 24
Dollar
 Canadian, 174
 fluctuations in, 13–14
 and interest rates, 196–198
 as reserve currency, 530, 537
 role in exchange market, 173–201
Domestic deposits, expected returns in, 183–185, 190–191
Domestic goods, preferences for, 180–181
Dornbusch, Rudiger, 193n, 754n
Dow Jones Industrial Average (DJIA), 12–13, 47, 243–244
Drexel Burnham, 239, 241
Drug Enforcement Agency, 411n

Dual banking system, 284–285
Duration analysis, 276–277
Dynamic open market operations, 477

Earthquake insurance, 349–350
Eccles, Marriner S., 445
Econometric models, 734–736
Economic activity
    expectations, 710–712
    and financial crises, 223–228
    and money: early Keynesian evidence on, 661–664; early monetarist evidence on, 664–670; overview of Keynesian-monetarist debate, 677–678; search for new transmission mechanisms, 671–677; types of empirical evidence, 656–661
Economically relevant money supply, 491
Economic growth, as monetary policy goal, 494–495
Economies of scale, 34, 210
Economy
    barter, 53–55
    underground, 412, 414
Edge Act (1919), 295
Edge Act corporations, 295, 297
Education Department, U.S., 358
Effective exchange rate index, 197
Effectiveness lag, 703
Efficient markets theory, 716–719
    in bond market, 728–730
    in stock market, 719–729
Eichenbaum, Martin, 138n
Eisenhower, Dwight, 447n, 506
Electronic banking facilities, 291

Electronic funds transfer system (EFTS), 57–58
Eligible paper, 503
Empirical evidence, reduced form/structural model, 656–661
Employee Retirement Income Security Act (ERISA, 1974), 352
Employment Act (1946), 493, 691
Employment targets, high
    and inflation, 691–695
    as monetary policy goal, 493–494
Engel, Charles, 725n
Equation of exchange, 544–545, 627
Equilibrium
    in aggregate output, 578–580, 633–645
    in bond market, 109–111
    in foreign exchange market, 186–188
    in gold market, 143
    in goods market, 591–594
    long-run, 634–637
    in money market, 127–128, 595–597
    short-run, 633–634
Equilibrium exchange rate, 191, 193–194
Equilibrium interest rate
    and aggregate output, 606–609
    changes in, 113, 119–123, 129–131
    in money market, 125–129
    and supply and demand for bonds, 110–111, 113–123
Equilibrium price, 110–111, 144
Equities, 24
Equity capital, 216–217
Equity contracts, 217–220
Equity holders, and bank capital, 266–268

Equity market, 24
Equity multiplier, 267
Estonia, inflation in, 697
EU. *See* European Union
Eurobonds, 47
Eurodollars
    defined, 29
    futures market in, 236
    market for, 245, 249, 254, 293–294
    as "offshore" deposits, 295
Eurofranc, 294n
Euromark, 294n
Euromoney, exchange rate forecasts in, 197
Euronotes, 280
European-American Bank, 483
European currency unit (ECU), 57, 534
European Monetary System (EMS), 534–536
European System of Central Banks, 495
European Union (EU)
    banking in, 287, 448, 495
    financial regulation by, 43
    monetary union, 57
European Union Treaty (1991), 495, 536
Euroyen, 236
Ex ante real interest rate, 90
Excess demand, 111, 634
Excess reserves, 254–255, 261–264, 370, 416–417
Excess reserves ratio
    to checkable deposits, 396, 404–405
    determinants of, 416–417
    and money supply, 428–429
Excess supply, 110, 634
Exchange rate index, 197
Exchange rates
    changes in, 188–196
    defined, 13, 173, 175

Exchange rates (*Continued*)
   determinants of: long-run,
      178–182; short-run,
      182–188
   effect on net exports,
      676–677
   equilibrium, 191, 193–194
   expectations, 189–190, 523n,
      710
   fixed, 529–533
   flexible, 533
   forecasting, 197
   importance of, 175, 177
   and interest rates, 193–194
   interventions in foreign
      exchange market, 462,
      519–524, 530–533, 538
   and monetary policy,
      537–538
   and money supply, 194–195,
      537
   overshooting, 194–196
   and random walks, 724
   shifts in expected-return
      schedules, 188–191
   and trading, 177
   volatility of, 173, 196
Exercise price, 236
Exogenous event, 665
Expansionary policy, 739–740
Expectations
   adaptive, 712
   and forecast errors, 715–716,
      729
   in foreign exchange market,
      189–190
   on monetary policy,
      704–705
   rational, 713
   role in economic activity,
      710–712
Expectations-augmented
      Phillips curve, 652
Expectations hypothesis,
      159–162

Expected inflation, 117,
      120–121, 133, 136–137
Expected profits, 117
Expected returns, 96–98, 114,
      116, 183–191
Expenditure multiplier,
      580–583
Expertise, 211, 215–216,
      219–220
Exports. *See* Net exports
Ex post real interest rate, 90
Extended credit, 481

Face value, 70
Factoring, 355
"Fallen angels," 239
Fama, Eugene F., 167n, 725n
Farm Credit System, 357–358
Farmers' Home Administration,
      358
Farm mortgages, 209
FDIC. *See* Federal Deposit In-
      surance Corporation
Fed. *See* Federal Reserve Sys-
      tem
Federal Advisory Council, 438,
      441, 445
Federal Banking Commission,
      286, 335–336
Federal credit agencies,
      357–358
Federal deposit insurance,
      44–45, 483, 485, 487
   and adverse selection,
      306–309, 333
   creation of, 285, 410, 413,
      427
   for credit unions, 293
   and moral hazard, 306–309,
      333
   for mutual savings banks,
      292
   proposed changes, 333–335
   recent developments,
      329–339

   for savings and loan associa-
      tions, 291–292, 327–329
Federal Deposit Insurance Cor-
      poration (FDIC)
   and bank panics, 410, 413,
      427, 487
   deposits with Fed, 459
   establishment of, 285, 410,
      413, 427
   regulation by, 44–46,
      306–308, 313, 319,
      327–331, 338–339, 483,
      485, 487
   supervision of banks by, 286
   "too big to fail" policy,
      308–310, 334
Federal Deposit Insurance Cor-
      poration Improvement Act
      (FDICIA, 1991), 321,
      329–336
Federal funds, as money mar-
      ket instruments, 29, 31
Federal funds rate, 29, 416–417
Federal Home Loan Bank
      Board (FHLBB), 323–324,
      326–327
Federal Home Loan Bank Sys-
      tem (FHLBS), 291–292,
      424, 459
Federal Home Loan Mortgage
      Corp. (FHLMC), 31, 357
Federal Housing Administra-
      tion (FHA), 358
Federal Insurance Contribution
      Act (FICA), 352–354
Federal National Mortgage
      Association (FNMA), 30,
      357
Federal Open Market Commit-
      tee (FOMC), 441–444, 449,
      478–479, 508, 703
Federal Reserve Act (1931),
      321, 438, 444, 451n, 503
Federal Reserve Banks, 438,
      443

Federal Reserve Board. *See* Federal Reserve System, Board of Governors
Federal Reserve System (Fed), 311–312, 335–336, 711
  ability to monitor foreign banks, 332
  accountability, 446–447, 513*n*
  balance sheet of, 368–370; assets, 370, 457–458; liabilities, 369–370, 458–459; monetary base, 369, 459–461
  bank examination by, 313
  and bank panics, 424–429, 482–483, 485, 496
  behavior of, 447–449
  Board of Governors, 199, 329, 368, 439–445, 447, 449, 504, 507, 512
  capital account, 459, 466
  as central bank, 367–368, 444
  check-clearing process, 459, 461–465
  congressional control over, 445–447, 449–451, 453
  creation of, 285, 437–438
  defined, 7, 60, 368
  deposits with, 254, 465–466
  discount loans by. *See* Discount loans
  discount policy, 480–488, 503–504
  discount rate. *See* Discount rate
  discount window, 480–482
  emergency powers, 330
  in foreign exchange market, 519–524
  functions, 368
  games played by, 449
  independence of, 445–447, 450–453

international banking facilities, 295–297
as lender of last resort, 427, 453, 482–483, 485
member banks, 285, 441–442
monetary policy, 447–480; anti-inflationary, 510–511, 707, 751–754; basis of, 407; and complete crowding out, 613–615; constant-money-growth-rate rule, 706; Federal Reserve Banks in, 441–442; goals, 493–497; international considerations, 512; open market operations, 477–480; procedures, 502–512; use of money targets, 449, 497–502, 614–617
in money supply process, 130–131, 368–370, 543, 614–617; control of monetary base, 369, 384–390, 396–397, 512–514; and money multiplier, 390–396; multiple deposit creation, 370–379; shift from deposits to currency, 387–388
open market operations, 371–372, 384–387, 443–445, 449, 477–480
overview, 368–370
power, 444–445, 447–450
presidential control over, 445–447, 449–451, 453, 504–505
regulation by, 44, 46, 285–286, 484, 495–496; Regulation K, 295; Regulation Q, 46, 245–247, 299–300, 316, 318–319, 443; Regulation Y, 289

reserve requirements. *See* Reserve requirements
stock in, 459
structure, 368, 438–445
telecommunications system, 57–58
Federal Savings and Loan Insurance Corp. (FSLIC), 319, 323–324, 327
Fedwire, 57–58
Fiat money, 56
Finance companies, 41, 354–355
Financial crises
  anatomy of, 225–228
  case study, 228
  defined, 223
  factors causing, 224–225
Financial engineering, 232
Financial futures contracts, 234–235, 248
Financial futures market, 234–236
Financial innovation, 10–11, 231
  to avoid existing regulations, 243–247
  due to changing demand conditions, 232–23
  due to changing supply conditions, 237–243
  economic analysis of, 231–232
  expectations, 711
  future directions, 247–249
Financial Institutions Reform, Recovery, and Enforcement Act (FIRREA, 1989), 321, 326–329
Financial instruments, 11, 22
Financial intermediaries
  asymmetric information problems, 34–37, 211, 710–711
  contractual savings institutions, 40–41

Financial intermediaries
    (*Continued*)
    defined, 9–10
    depository institutions, 38–40
    economies of scale by, 210
    expertise, 41–42, 211,
        215–216, 219–220
    functions, 32–37
    importance of, 33–34,
        210–211
    as investment intermediaries,
        41–42
    and restrictive covenants,
        222–223
    soundness of, regulation to
        ensure, 43–46, 208
    types, 37–42
Financial intermediation, 9–10,
    33, 357–359
Financial markets
    debt/equity, 24
    defined, 11
    economies of scale in, 34,
        210
    exchanges/over-the-counter,
        25–26
    functions, 21–23
    instruments traded in, 26–32
    intermediaries in. *See* Finan-
        cial intermediaries
    money/capital, 26
    primary/secondary, 24–25
    rational expectations theory
        in, 716–719
    regulation of. *See* Financial
        regulation
    stability, as monetary policy
        goal, 496
    structure, 23–26
    and technology, 239–240
    uncertainty during financial
        crises, 225
    why study, 11–14
Financial options market,
    236–237

Financial panics. *See* Bank
    panics
Financial regulation
    agencies responsible for, 44
    to ensure soundness of fi-
        nancial intermediaries,
        43–46, 208
    financial innovation to
        avoid, 243–247
    in foreign countries, 43, 208
    to improve monetary policy,
        46
    to provide information,
        42–43, 208, 214–215, 219
Financial system
    flow of funds through, 22
    future of, 247–249
    innovation in. *See* Financial
        innovation
    regulation of. *See* Financial
        regulation
    structure: and asymmetric in-
        formation, 211–223; basic
        puzzles about, 205–209;
        and transaction costs,
        209–211
Financial Times-Stock
    Exchange 100-Share
    Index, 47
Fire insurance, 40–41, 349–350
First automotive short-term
    bonds and certificates
    (FASTBAGs), 241
First Bank of the United States,
    437
First Boston Corp., 285, 359
First Chicago, 296
First National Bank of Boston,
    285
First Republic Bank of Texas,
    424
Fiscal policy
    and aggregate output,
        608–609
    defined, 601

effectiveness versus mone-
    tary policy, 611–614
    and inflation, 687–690
    and interest rates, 608–609
    in *ISLM* model, 601–624
    lags in, 701–703
Fischer, Stanley, 755*n*
Fisher, Irving, 91, 543–548,
    551, 553, 560–561, 565
Fisher effect, 120–121, 245,
    248, 710
Fisher equation, 91, 193
Fixed exchange rate, 529–533
Fixed investment, 577–578
Fixed payment loans, 70,
    74–75
Flexible exchange rate, 533
Float, 460–464, 519, 533–534
Forecasts
    errors, 715–716, 729
    exchange rates, 197
    interest rates, 134–135
    ISLM model in, 573
    optimal, 713
Foreign Bank Supervision
    Enhancement Act
    (FBSEA), 330
Foreign banking. *See* Interna-
    tional banking
Foreign bonds, 47
Foreign deposits, 183–185,
    188–190, 459, 466
"Foreign exchange" column in
    newspapers, 199–201
Foreign exchange market,
    13–14, 173–177
    and aggregate supply, 641*n*
    defined, 173
    equilibrium in, 186–188
    exchange rates. *See*
        Exchange rates
    intervention in, 462,
        519–524; under fixed
        exchange rate, 529–533;
        under flexible exchange

rate, 533; and money supply, 519–521; sterilized, 523–524; unsterilized, 521–523
and monetary policy, 537–538
and money supply, 537
stability, as pricing goal, 496
trading on, 177
Foreign exchange rates. *See* Exchange rates
Foreign goods, preferences for, 180–181
Forward exchange rates, 175
Forward transactions, 175
France
banking system in, 448
business financing in, 207
franc and exchange rates, 538
monetary policy in, 513
securities industry in, 33
Franklin National Bank, 279, 483, 486
Fraud, insurance, 345–346
Freedom National Bank, 309–310
Free reserves, 506–507
Free-rider problem, 214–216, 223
French, Kenneth R., 725*n*
Frenkel, Jacob A., 523*n*
Frictional unemployment, 494
Friedman, Benjamin M., 498*n*
Friedman, Milton, 5, 131–132, 428, 453*n*, 487, 490–491, 505*n*, 543, 560–565, 568*n*, 597, 625, 627, 652–653, 662, 664–665, 668–669, 670*n*, 681, 685–686, 689–690
Full Employment and Balanced Growth Act (1978), 447, 493, 691

Fully funded plans, 351–352
Fundamental disequilibrium, 532
Futures contracts, 234
Futures market, 234–236
bank use to reduce interest rate risk, 277–278
in stock price indexes, 242

Gap analysis, 276–277
Garcia, Gillian, 570
Garn-St. Germain Act (1982), 319–321
GDP. *See* Gross domestic product
General Accounting Office (GAO), 328, 332, 358, 445
General Agreement on Tariffs and Trade (GATT), 530*n*
General Motors Acceptance Corp., 355
Germany
banking system in, 273, 303, 315, 448, 452
business financing in, 207
inflation in , 55, 495, 682, 684–685
mark and exchange rates, 173–174, 535–536, 538
monetary policy in, 513, 515
securities industry in, 33
Gertler, Mark, 211*n*, 308*n*, 673*n*
Gilchrist, Simon, 673
Glass-Steagall Act (1933), 285, 293, 314–315, 321, 337–339, 444
Glenn, John, 327
Globex, 236
Gold, 285
Gold certificate accounts, 458, 462
Goldfeld, Stephen, 569–570
Goldman Sachs, 359

Gold market
and changes in equilibrium price of gold, 143–144
supply and demand in, 141–143
Gold standard, 503*n*, 528–529
Goldstein, Morris, 523*n*
Gonzalez, Henry B., 447
Goodfriend, Marvin, 487*n*
Goods market, equilibrium in, 591–594
Goodwill, 323
Gordon, David B., 138*n*
Gordon, Robert J., 755*n*
Government activities, and bond supply, 118–119
Government agency securities, 32, 85
Government budget constraints, 467–468
Government deficits. *See* Budget deficits
Government loan guarantees, 358–359
Government National Mortgage Association (GNMA), 30–31, 85, 235, 240–241, 357
Government regulation of financial system. *See* Banking regulation; Financial regulation
Government securities. *See* Securities, U.S. government
Government spending
and aggregate demand, 638–639
and aggregate output, 584–588, 608–609
changes in, 603
defined, 574, 628
financing of, 469–472
and inflation, 687–689
and *IS* curve, 603
Grant & Ward, 226

Gray, Edwin, 326–327
Great Depressions (1930s),
    228, 676
  bank panics, 410, 413, 424,
    427–429, 482–483
  bank failures, 285, 444, 483
  bond market, 150, 152, 155
  currency-checkable deposits
    ratio during, 410, 413, 424,
    427–429
  excess reserves ratio during,
    427–429
  and Fed policy, 504–505
  investment spending,
    314–315, 583–590,
    661–663
  liquidity trap during, 569
  unemployment, 494
  velocity of money during,
    548–551
Greece, banking system in, 448
Greenspan, Alan, 339, 445,
    484, 512
Greenwald, Bruce, 212n
Grimblatt, Mark, 721n
Gross domestic product (GDP)
  defined, 17
  deflator, 18–19, 626
  and employment, 494
  and inflation, 698–701
  nominal, 18, 655
  real, 18, 626
Gross national product, 17n
Guaranteed Student Loan Pro-
    gram, 357
Gulf War, recession from,
    646–647

Hafer, R. W., 571n
Hall, Robert E., 753n
Hamburger, Michael, 570–571
Hamilton, Alexander, 284
Hedging, 234
Hein, Scott E., 571n
Heller, H., 571

Hetzel, Robert L., 572n
Hicks, John, 573, 594n, 596n
Higgins, Bryon, 572n
High employment, as monetary
    policy goal, 493–494
Highly leveraged transaction
    loans, 320
High-powered money, 384,
    457
Home mortgages, 209
Home State Savings Bank of
    Cincinnati, 424
Hong Kong, banking in, 295
House Current Resolution 133
    (1975), 446–447, 449
Household Finance Corp., 355
Housing and Urban Develop-
    ment Department, U.S.,
    358–359
Hubbard, R. Glenn, 33n,
    206–207
Huberman, Gur, 720n
Huizinga, John, 663n
Humphrey-Hawkins Act
    (1978), 447, 493, 691
Hyperinflation, 55, 495,
    682–685, 752–753
Hysteresis, 641, 643–645

Implementation lag, 702–703
Imports, 180–181, 183
Incentive compatibility, 221
Income
  aggregate, 17
  changes in, and money mar-
    ket, 129
  defined, 52
  disposable, 575
  and money demand, 551,
    563–564
Income effect, 128, 132,
    136–137
Income taxes. *See* Taxes
Indifference curves, 761–765
Indirect finance, 208

Industrial production, 626
Inferior assets, 96
Inflation
  activist-nonactivist debate,
    701–707
  and bond supply and
    demand, 116–121
  and budget deficits,
    695–697
  cost-push, 691–693
  credibility concerning,
    706–707, 751–754
  defined, 4, 685
  demand-pull, 691, 693–694
  expectations, 712
  expected, 117, 120–121, 133,
    136–137
  and fiscal policy, 687–690
  in future, 248–249
  and government spending,
    687–688
  hyperinflation, 55, 495,
    682–685, 752–753
  and interest rates, 120–121,
    710
  Keynesian view of, 687–690
  monetarist view of, 686–687
  and monetary policy,
    510–511, 749–751
  money creation in, 696–697
  and money supply, 4–6,
    681–707
  Phillips curve for, 651–654
  and supply shocks, 645–647,
    689–690
  and taxes, 688–689, 753–754
  and unemployment,
    651–654, 701–703
  wage, 651
Inflationary policy, 691–697
Inflation rate, 5
Information
  asymmetric, 34–37, 211–212,
    305–314, 673–674,
    710–711

and free-rider problem, 214–216, 223

insider, 361

monitoring firm production of, 219

sale of private, 213–214

Innovation. *See* Financial innovatio*n*

Insider information, 361

Insiders, 43

Insolvent banks, 266, 323

Installment loans, 70

Institut Monétaire Luxembourgeois, 317

Insurance

adverse selection problem, 344–347

automobile, 349–350

casualty, 40–41, 349–350

deposit. *See* Federal deposit insurance

fire, 40–41

life, 40, 347–349

malpractice, 349–350

management principles concerning, 344–347

moral hazard problem, 344–347

portfolio, 244

property, 349–350

Insurance companies, 343–350

Interbank Card Association, 238

Interest parity condition, 185–186

Interest rate risk, 88–90

defined, 88, 233

in future, 248

increases, and financial innovation, 233–237

in loan management, 260

management of, 275–279

Interest rates

and aggregate output, 606–609

and bond prices, 12, 79, 82–86, 107–113

and budget deficit, 472–473

during business cycle expansion, 121–123

ceiling on. *See* Regulation Q

changes in, 602–603

on checkable deposits, 245, 409–410, 415, 421

and consumer expenditure, 674

and currency-checkable deposits ratio, 409–412

current yield as, 80–81

defined, 6

and discount loans, 417–418

and discount rate, 481–482, 487–488

domestic, 190–191

equilibrium. *See* Equilibrium interest rate

and excess reserve ratio, 416–417

and exchange rates, 193–194, 196–198

and fiscal policy, 608–609

forecasting, 134–135

foreign, 189

for government securities, 8, 11, 29

increases, and financial crises, 224

and inflation, 120–121, 136–138

and investment spending, 590–594, 602–603

ISLM approach, 597–598

in liquidity preference framework, 125–128

in loanable funds framework, 107–113

market, 416–418, 421–422, 481–482, 487–488

measurement of, 70–82

and monetary policy, 606–608

and money, 6–7, 131–133, 136–138

and money demand: asset demand in, 562–563, 710; and crowding out effect, 612–614; empirical evidence on, 567–569; *ISLM* model, 597–598; Keynesian approach, 555–560, 562–565; in liquidity preference theory, 551–555; monetarist approach, 560–565

in money market, 125–138

and money supply, 131–138, 421–422

and net exports, 592

nominal, 91–93, 107, 198

pegging of, 505–506

and present value, 71–72

prime, 29

rate of return distinguished from, 86–90

real, 91–93, 198, 662–664

risk structure, 149–157, 710

for savings deposits, 46

simple, 71

stability of, 496

targeting, 498–500, 569, 614–617

and taxes, 92, 155–156

term structure, 149, 157–167, 710, 735–736

yield on discount basis as, 81–82

yield to maturity, 72–80

Interest rate swap, 233*n*, 278–279

Intermediaries. *See* Financial intermediaries

Intermediate targets, 497

Intermediate-term debt instruments, 24

Internal rate of return, 76
Internal Revenue Service (IRS),
     92, 242, 413, 453
International Bank for Recon-
     struction and Develop-
     ment. See World Bank
International banking, 293–297,
     314–317, 330
International Banking Act
     (1978), 297
International banking facilities
     (IBFs), 295–297
International Development
     Association (IDA), 530n
International financial system,
     528–538
   balance of payments,
     524–528
   bond market, 47
   Bretton Woods system,
     529–533
   crises in, 535–536
   and European Monetary Sys-
     tem, 534–535
   exchange rates. See
     Exchange rates
   futures market, 236
   gold standard, 503n,
     528–529
   intervention in, 519–524
   managed float, 533–534
   monetary policy, 512–513,
     537–537
   stock market, 47–48
   and technology, 239–240
International Monetary Fund
     (IMF), 296, 458, 530,
     532–534
International Monetary Market
     (IMM), 236
International policy coordina-
     tion, 512–513
International reserves, 519–521,
     530, 532, 537
Inventory investment, 577–578

Investment
   in bond market, 728–730
   defined, 577, 628n
   fixed, 577–578
   government regulation. See
     Financial regulation
   inventory, 577–578
   planned, 578
   in stock market, 719–729
Investment advisers, reports of,
     719–722
Investment banks, 25, 359–360
Investment Company Act
     (1940), 356
Investment intermediaries,
     41–42
Investment opportunities, and
     bond supply, 117
Investment spending, 577–578
   changes in, 602–603
   as monetary transmission
     mechanism, 671, 673–674
   planned: and aggregate out-
     put, 580–583; defined,
     574, 628; and interest
     rates, 591–594, 602–603,
     662–664; IS curve for,
     602–603
   and stock prices, 675
   Tobin's q theory for, 671,
     673
Investors, 42–43, 98, 727–728
Ippolito, R. A., 721n
IRS. See Internal Revenue Ser-
     vice
IS curve, 591–594
   defined, 591
   derivation of, 592, 594
   shifts in, 602–604, 621–623
ISLM model, 573, 590–598, 733
   and aggregate demand
     curve, 619–620
   algebra of, 767–770
   closed-economy, 767–769
   in long run, 617–619

open-economy, 769–770
Italy
   banking system in, 452
   lira and exchange rates, 174
   securities industry in, 33

Jackson, Andrew, 284, 438
January effect, 725
Japan
   banking system in, 273, 287,
     297, 300–301, 303,
     314–315, 448
   business financing in, 207
   monetary policy in, 513,
     516–517
   securities industry in, 33,
     46–48
   trade barriers, 648
   yen and exchange rates,
     173–174, 538
Jensen, Michael, 721n
Johannes, James, 514n
Johnson, Lyndon, 611
Joint Chiefs of Staff, 453
Jordan, Jerry, 670n
Judd, John P., 570n, 571
Junk bonds, 152–154, 238–239
Justice Department, U.S., 328

Kandel, Shmuel, 720n
Kane, Edward J., 243, 323, 325
Kansas City Board of Trade
     (KCBT), 242
Kazakhstan, inflation in, 697
Keating, Charles H., Jr., 311,
     326–327
Keim, D. B., 725n
Keiretsu, 273
Kennedy, John, 447n
Keynes, John Maynard,
     125–126, 128, 543, 548,
     551–555, 559–565, 568–569,
     573–576, 578, 581,
     583–587, 590–592, 595,
     616, 625, 637, 651, 715

Keynesian cross diagram, 578
Keynesians, 376*n*, 733
  on aggregate output,
    573–590
  on aggregate supply and
    demand, 625, 628–630,
    651
  on importance of money:
    early evidence, 661–664;
    versus monetarists,
    677–678; structural model
    evidence, 656–661
  on inflation, 687–690
  on money demand, 555–560,
    616–617
  new Keynesian model,
    742–744
Khan, Moshin S., 571
Kim, Myung Jig, 725*n*
Kimball, Ralph C., 411*n*
King, Robert, 487*n*, 678*n*
Knickerbocker Trust Co., 226
Korean War, 505
Kornblith, Edith, 669*n*
Krugman, Paul, 182*n*, 524*n*
Kydland, Finn, 704*n*
Kyrgyzstan, inflation in, 697

L, 60–61
Labor costs, unit, 652*n*
Labor Department, U.S., 352
Labor market, tightness of, 638
Laidler, David, 568, 764*n*
Latvia, inflation in, 697
Leeper, Eric M., 138*n*
Legislative lag, 702
"Lemons problem," 212-217
Lender of last resort, 427, 453,
    482–483, 485
LeRoy, Stephen F., 572*n*
Letters of credit, 280
Leveraged transaction loans,
    320
Leverage ratio, 311
Levine, Dennis, 722

Liabilities
  of bank, 251–254, 299–301
  defined, 22
  of Fed, 369–370, 458–459
Liability management, 260,
    264–265, 711
Life insurance, 40, 347–349
Limits, on insurance amounts,
    346
Lincoln Savings & Loan Associ-
    ation, 326–327
Lindsey, David, 509*n*
Line of credit, 271–272,
    279–280
Liquidity
  and asset demand, 96,
    98–99, 117
  of bonds, 153–155
  defined, 25, 55
  and interest rates, 153–155
  management by banks,
    261–264
  provided by financial inter-
    mediaries, 211
Liquidity effect, 132, 136–137,
    675–676
Liquidity preference theory,
    551–555, 595
  additional developments,
    555–560
  Friedman's theory distin-
    guished from, 560–562
Liquidity premium, 155
Liquidity premium theory,
    164–167
Liquidity services, 211
Liquidity trap, 569
Liquid-yield option notes
    (LYONs), 241
Litner, John, 103
Lloyd, Edward, 350
Lloyd's of London, 350
LM curve, 595–597
  defined, 591
  derivation of, 596–597

  shifts in, 604–606, 622–623
Lo, Andrew W., 725*n*
Load funds, 356
Loan commitments, 272–273
Loanable funds, 112
Loanable funds framework,
    107–113
Loans
  automobile, 209, 241
  by banks, 209, 256–257
  commercial, 32, 70, 256
  consumer, 32, 256
  contracts for, 209
  discount. *See* Discount loans
  fixed-payment, 70, 74–75
  by government, 357–358
  installment, 70
  management of, 269–275
  mortgages. *See* Mortgages
  selling of, 279
  simple, 70–73
  to Third World countries,
    530*n*
Loan sales, 279
Local bonds, 32
London International Financial
    Futures Exchange, 236
Long-term customer relation-
    ships, 271–272
Long-term debt instruments,
    24, 89–90
"Loophole mining," 243
Loss, capital, 88
Louvre Accord (1987), 512–513
LTV Steel Co., 353
Lucas, Robert, 653, 733–736
Lucas critique, 734–736, 755
Lucas supply function, 654
Luxembourg, banking system
    in, 317
Luxury, 97

*M*1
  defined, 60–61, 253, 449
  growth rate, 61–63, 508–511

M1 (*Continued*)
  money multiplier, 383–384
  stability of, 569–572
  velocity, 548–550, 572
M2
  defined, 60–61, 449, 512
  growth rate, 61–65
  money multiplier, 384,
    403–405
  velocity, 549–550, 572
M3
  defined, 60–61, 449
  growth rate, 61–63
Maastricht Treaty (1991), 495,
    536
Macaulay's concept of dura-
    tion, 276
McCain, John, 327
McCallum, Bennett, 733n
McFadden Act (1927), 287–288,
    290–291
MacKinlay, A. Craig, 725n
Macroeconomic model, new
    classical, 705n, 736–741
Majluf, N. S., 212n
Malpractice insurance, 349–350
Managed float system, 519,
    533–534
Mankiw, N. Gregory, 167n
Manufacturers Hanover, 296
Marché à Terme des Instru-
    ments Financiers, 236
Marginal propensity to con-
    sume, 575
Market-clearing interest rate.
    See Equilibrium interest
    rate
Market-clearing price, 110–111
Market equilibrium, 110–111
Market portfolio, 95–105
Market-value accounting for
    bank capital, 336–337
Marshall, Alfred, 543, 547
Martin, William McChesney, Jr.,
    442n, 445, 447n, 506

Maryland Savings-Share Insur-
    ance Corp., 424–425
MasterCard, 238
Matched sale-purchase transac-
    tion, 479
Maturity
  of debt instrument, 24, 70,
    88–90
  yield to. See Yield to maturity
Maturity buckets, 276
Mayer, Colin, 33n, 206–207
Mean reversion, 725
Mean-variance model of trans-
    action demand, 761–765
Medicare, 353–354
Medium of exchange, money
    as, 52–53, 547
Meehan, John, 309n
Meese, Richard A., 724n
Meiselman, David, 668–669
Meltzer, Allan H., 507,
    568–569, 571n, 704n, 734n
Merrill Lynch, 241, 359, 361
Metropolitan Life Insurance
    Co., 347
Mexico, loans made to, 296
Meyer, Laurence H., 509n,
    571n
Military, reduction of size of,
    648
Milken, Michael, 239
Miller, Merton, 244
Mishkin, Frederic S., 92n,
    121n, 193n, 571n, 663n,
    675n, 676n, 728n, 730n,
    755n
Modern quantity theory of
    money, 560–565, 627
Modigliani, Franco, 669n,
    674–675
Monetarists
  on aggregate supply and
    demand, 625, 627–630
  on importance of money:
    early evidence, 664–670;

reduced form evidence,
    656–661
  on inflation, 686–687
  versus Keynesians,
    677–678
Monetary aggregates, 60–63
  defined, 60
  measures of, 61
  targeting, 449
Monetary base
  and budget deficit, 467–474
  control over, 384–390,
    396–397
  defined, 369
  factors affecting, 461–467
  and Fed's balance sheet,
    459–461
  foreign exchange rate inter-
    vention, 462
  and international reserves,
    519–521
  nonborrowed portion of,
    390, 396–397
  and open market purchases,
    384–386
  sources, 459
  uses, 459
Monetary neutrality, 194–195,
    619
Monetary policy
  and aggregate output,
    606–608
  basis of, 407
  and budget deficits, 8
  conduct of, 7–8
  and consumer expenditure,
    674–676
  defined, 7, 601
  discount policy in, 480–488
  discretionary, 706–707,
    740–741
  early Keynesians on,
    661–664
  early monetarists on,
    664–670

expectations, 704–705, 710–712, 740–741
versus fiscal policy, 611–614
goals, 493–497
historical perspective, 502–512
improved control of, 46
and independence of Fed, 445–447, 450–453
inflationary, 691–697
and interest rates, 606–609
international considerations, 537–538
in *ISLM* model, 601–624
lags in, 701–703
monetary targets, 497–502
neutral, 194–195
open market operations, 477–480
procedures, 502–512
reserve requirements, 488–491
transmission mechanisms, 656–661, 671–677
Monetary targets
choosing, 498–502
intermediate, 500–502
operating, 502
use of, 449, 497–498
Monetary theory, 4, 543
Monetary union, European, 57
Monetizing the debt, 471
Money
and business cycles, 4
case of missing, 569–571
commodity, 56
defined, 3, 51–52, 59–60
demand. *See* Money demand
and economic activity, 655–678
evolution of payments system, 55–58
fiat, 56
functions, 52–55

high-powered, 384, 457
versus income, 52
and inflation, 4–6, 681–707
and interest rates, 6–7, 131–133, 136–138
measurement of, 58–63
as medium of exchange, 52–53, 547
opportunity costs, 126–127
printing, 471, 473, 696–697
quantity theory, 544–547, 560–562
reliability of data, 63–65
as store of value, 54–55, 547
supply and demand, 125–131
as unit of account, 53–54
velocity. *See* Velocity of money
versus wealth, 52
as weighted aggregate, 62–63
why study, 3–9
Money aggregates
targeting, 507–509, 511–512
weighted, 62–63
Money center banks, 265
Money creation, 471–472, 696–697
Money demand, 543
Cambridge approach, 547–548
changes in, 605–606
expectations, 711–712
Friedman's theory, 560–565
and interest rates, 567–569; crowding out effect, 612–614; in liquidity preference framework, 125–131
Keynesian theories, 551–560, 562–565
liquidity preference theory, 551–555, 595
and *LM* curve, 604–606

quantity theory, 544–547
stability of, 569–572
velocity as constant, 548–551
Money market certificates (MMCs), 318
Money market conditions, targeting, 506–507
Money market deposit accounts (MMDAs), 252–253, 319
Money market fund-checkable accounts ratio, 404–405
Money market mutual funds, 10, 41–42, 247, 356–357
Money markets
defined, 26
equilibrium in, 127–128, 595–597
instruments, 26–29
supply and demand, 125–138
Money multiplier, 383–396, 403–405
Money supply
and aggregate demand, 638–639
and aggregate output, 606–608
and banking, 10
during bank panics, 427
changes in, 130–131, 604–605
complete model for, 407, 418–423
control by Fed, 46
currency-checkable deposits ratio, 428–429
defined, 3, 51
determinants, 383–405, 420–422
economically relevant, 491
excess reserves ratio, 428–429
expectations, 711

Money supply (*Continued*)
  explaining movements in,
    398–401
  and foreign exchange rate,
    194–195, 519–524
  growth in, 136–138
  and inflation, 686–690,
    695–697
  and interest rates, 131–138
  and *LM* curve, 604–606
  model for, 390–398, 418–423
  official, 491
  targeting, 498–500
Money supply process
  agents, 367–368
  bank behavior, 415–418
  Federal Reserve System in,
    368–370, 512–514, 543
  monetary base, 384–390,
    396–397
  money multiplier, 390–396
  multiple deposit creation,
    370–379
  overview, 397–398
  reserve requirements,
    488–491, 504–505
Monitoring
  of production of informa-
    tion, 219
  of restrictive covenants,
    221–222, 271
Moody's, 153, 213
Moral hazard, 34–37, 217–223
  and banking regulation,
    305–314, 333, 337–338
  in debt contracts, 221–223
  defined, 35–36, 211–212
  in equity contracts, 217–220
  and financial crises, 223–228
  and financial intermediation,
    710–712
  and insurance, 344–347
  in loan market, 269–275
  solutions to problems,
    219–220
Moral suasion, 481

Morgan, J. P., & Co., 285, 289,
    296, 339
Morgan Stanley & Co., 285, 359
Morganthau, Tom, 327*n*
Morris, Charles S., 725*n*
Mortgages
  adjustable-rate, 233
  amortization schedule, 75
  as capital market instru-
    ments, 31–32
  commercial, 209
  farm, 209
  government-guaranteed,
    240–242
  home, 209
  market for, 30–31
  as percentage of business
    borrowing, 209
  as simple loans, 70
  yield to maturity on, 74–75
Mullins, David, 199
Multiple deposit contraction,
    377–378
Multiple deposit creation,
    370–380
Municipal bonds, 32, 155–156,
    256, 264
Muth, John, 713, 716*n*
Mutual funds, 355–357
  as investment intermediaries,
    41
  lower transaction costs, 210
  money market, 10, 41–42,
    247, 356–357
Mutual savings banks
  branching restrictions, 292
  charters, 292
  as financial intermediaries, 40
  mortgage loans by, 257
  regulation of, 292
Myers, Stewart, 212*n*

Narrow banks, 334
National Association of Pur-
    chasing Management
    (NAPM), 124–125

National Association of Securi-
    ties Dealers' Automated
    Quotation System (NAS-
    DAQ), 362
National Banking Act (1863),
    285
National banks, 284–286, 441
National Bureau of Economic
    Research, 702
National Cordage Co., 226
National Credit Union Adminis-
    tration (NCUA), 44,
    292–293
National Credit Union Share
    Insurance Fund (NCUSIF),
    45, 293
National Urban League, 310
Nations Bank, 289
Natural rate level of output,
    617, 635
Natural rate of unemployment,
    494, 635
Navy Federal Credit Union, 293
NCNB Corp., 291
Necessity, 96–97
Negligence insurance,
    349–350
Negotiable certificates of
    deposit, 265
Negotiable order of withdrawal
    (NOW) accounts, 10, 60,
    231, 246, 252, 318–319,
    488, 509
Nelson, Charles R., 725*n*
Net exports, 587–588
  and aggregate demand,
    638–639
  changes in, 604
  defined, 574, 628
  exchange rate effect on,
    676–677
  and interest rates, 592
  and *IS* curve, 604
Netherlands, banking system
    in, 315, 448
Net worth, 216–217, 221

New York Futures Exchange (NYFE), 242

New York Stock Exchange (NYSE), 25–26, 85, 177, 242, 244, 360

New Zealand
banking system in, 452
reserve requirements in, 490

Nicaragua, inflation in, 682–683, 685

Nikkei Average, 47, 236

Nixon, Richard, 447n

No-load funds, 356

Nominal GDP, 18, 655

Nominal interest rates, 91–93, 107, 198

Nominal money balances, 553

Nonaccommodating policy, 704–705

Nonactivist policy, 637, 701–707

Nonbank banks, 290

Nonborrowed monetary base, 390, 396–397, 420

Nonsystematic risk, 101–102

Nontransaction deposits, 253–254

Northern Pacific Railroad, 226

Note-issuance facilities (NIFs), 280

NYCE, 291

NYSE. *See* New York Stock Exchange

Obstfeld, Maurice, 182n, 523n, 524n

Off-balance-sheet activities, 279–280

Offenbacher, Edward, 63n

Office of the Comptroller of the Currency, 44–45, 285–286, 308, 3311, 313, 327, 335, 441

Office of Thrift Supervision (OTS), 44, 292, 327, 332, 335

Official money supply, 491

Official reserve transaction balance, 527

Offshore deposits, 294–295

Ohio Deposit Guarantee Fund, 424

Ohio Life Insurance & Trust Co., 226

Okun, Arthur, 749, 753

Old Age and Survivors Insurance Fund, 352

Open-economy *ISLM* model, 769–770

Open-end funds, 356

Open market operations, 371–372, 384–387, 443–445. 449, 477–480

Open market purchases, 384–386

Operating targets, 497

Opportunity costs, 126–127

Opportunity locus, 763–765

Optimal forecast, 713

Option contracts, 236–237

Options market
bank trading in, 278–279
for debt instruments, 236–237

Organization of Petroleum Exporting Countries (OPEC), 296, 645

Osaka Securities Exchange, 236

Outflows, deposit, 260–264

Output
aggregate. *See* Aggregate output
natural rate level of, 617, 635

Overnight repurchase agreements, 246–247

Overshooting, exchange rate, 194–196

Over-the-counter (OTC) markets, 25–26

Overvaluation, 531–533

Paine Webber, 361

Pak, Simon, 570

Panics. *See* Bank panics

Paper currency, 55–56, 284–285

Partial crowding out, 631

Par value, 70

Payments, balance of. *See* Balance of payments

Payments system, 55–58

Payoff method, 307

Pegging
of currency, in international financial system, 533–534
of interest rates, 505–506

Penalty discount rate, concept of, 487

Pension Benefit Guaranty Corp. (PBGC), 352–353

Pension funds, 41, 350–354

Perfect substitutes, 159

Permanent life insurance, 347–348

Person-to-Person Finance Co., 355

Pesando, James, 728

Phelps, Edmund, 653

Phillips, A. W., 651

Phillips curve, 651–654

Pigou, A. C., 543, 547

Planned investment spending. *See* Investment spending, planned

Plaza Agreement (1985), 512–513, 538

Plosser, Charles, 643n, 678n

PNC Financial Corp., 289

Point-of-sale (POS) systems, 57

Policy. *See also* Fiscal policy; Monetary policy
accommodating versus nonaccommodating, 704–705
activist versus nonactivist, 637, 701–707
anticipated versus unanticipated, 736–739, 743

Policy (*Continued*)
  anti-inflationary, 707,
    749–752
  discretionary, 706–707,
    740–741
  expansionary, 739–740
  inflationary, 691–697
  lags in, 701–703
  stabilization, 748–749
Policy evaluation, 733–734,
    754–756
  Lucas critique, 734–736, 755
  new classical macroeco-
    nomic model, 736–741
  new Keynesian model,
    742–744
  traditional model, 745–752
Policy ineffectiveness proposi-
    tion, 739
Political business cycles, 451
Poole, William, 614n, 669n
Porter, Richard D., 572n
Portfolio
  insurance for, 244
  market, 95–105
Portugal, banking system in,
    448
Poterba, James M., 725n
PPI. *See* Producer price index
Precautionary demand for
    money, 551–552, 559
Preferred habitat theory,
    164–167
Prell, Michael J., 728n
Premiums, 237
  life insurance, 345, 347–349
  liquidity, 155
  risk, 103–104, 150–152,
    154–155
Presbyterian Ministers' Fund,
    347
Prescott, Edward, 643, 704n,
    733n
Present value (PV), 71–72
Present discounted value, 72

President, and Federal Reserve,
    445–447, 449–451, 453,
    504–505
Price
  in barter economy, 53–55
  of bonds. *See* Bond prices
  equilibrium, 110–111, 144
  law of one price, 178
  market-clearing, 110–111
  of stocks. *See* Stock prices
Price level
  aggregate, 4, 17–19
  in aggregate demand and
    supply analysis, 640
  changes in, and money mar-
    ket, 129–130
  data in newspapers, 626
  and exchange rates, 180
  during financial crises, 225
  in rational expectations
    theory, 745–748
  and value of money, 55
Price level effect, 128–129, 132,
    136–137
Price stability, 495
Primary markets, 24–25
Prime rate, 29
Principal, 217–220
Principal-agent problem,
    217–220, 324–326
Printing of money, 471, 473,
    696–697
Private deposit insurance, 335
Private pension plans, 352
Private production, and sale of
    information, 213–214
Producer price index (PPI),
    626
Production costs, 640–641
Productivity, 181
Profit opportunity, unex-
    ploited, 718–719
Profits, expected, 117
Program trading, 244
Property insurance, 349–350

Prudential Insurance Co., 347
Public interest view, 447
Public pension plans, 352–354
Purchase and assumption
    method, 307
Purchasing power parity (PPP),
    theory of, 178–180
Put option, 236–237

q theory, 671, 673
Quantity theory of money,
    544–547, 560–562, 627
Quantity theory of money
    demand, 546–547
Quotas, 180

Radford, R. A., 53n
Random walks, 723–725
Rasche, Robert H., 514n, 571n
Rate of capital gain, 87
Rate of return
  defined, 86
  distinguished from interest
    rate, 86–90
  expected: and asset demand,
    96–98, 107, 113–117; and
    currency-checkable de-
    posits, 409–412; domestic
    versus foreign deposits,
    183–191; and money de-
    mand, 553–555, 559–560
  internal, 76
  standard deviation, 101
  and taxes, 92, 155–156
Rational expectations, 713
Rational expectations theory,
    709, 712–716, 733–734
  as basis for Lucas critique,
    734–736
  in bond market, 728–730
  in financial markets, 716–719
  new classical macroeco-
    nomic model, 736–741
  new Keynesian model,
    742–744

in stock market, 719–729
in traditional model, 745–752
Reagan, Ronald, 322, 324, 447,
    753–754
Real assets, 116
Real bills doctrine, 503
Real business cycle theory,
    641, 643–644, 677–678
Real estate mortgage invest-
    ment conduits (REMICs),
    242
Real GDP, 18, 626, 655
Real interest rate, 91–93, 198,
    662–664
Real money balances, 553
Real terms, 91, 617–618, 620,
    629
Recessions, 4, 646–647
Recognition lag, 702
Rediscounting, 503
Reduced form evidence,
    656–661
Regulation. *See* Banking regu-
    lation; Financial regulation
Regulation K, 295
Regulation Q, 46, 245–247,
    299–300, 316, 318–319,
    322, 443
Regulation Y, 289
Regulatory forbearance,
    323–324
Reinsurance, 350
Reinvestment risk, 90
Repurchase agreements (RPs),
    28, 246–247, 479, 570
Required reserve ratio
    on checkable deposits, 420
    defined, 254, 370
    and money multiplier,
        394–395, 404–405
Reserve currency, 530, 537
Reserve requirements, 46
    accounts not subject to,
        252–253
    and bank liquidity, 489

defined, 254–255, 370
and financial innovation,
    243–244
as policy tool, 488–491,
    504–505
revision of, 441–442,
    490–491
Reserves, 255, 369–370
    accounting for, 257–260,
        457–458, 465–466
    defined, 254–255, 369
    excess, 254–255, 261–264,
        370, 416–417
    free, 506–507
    how Fed provides to bank-
        ing system, 371–372
    international, 519–521, 530,
        532, 537
    liquidity management,
        260–264
    and open market purchases,
        384–386
    required. *See* Reserve
        requirements
    secondary, 256
Residual claimants, 24
Resolution Funding Corp., 328
Resolution Trust Corp.,
    327–328
Restrictive covenants
    defined, 209
    in insurance policies, 345
    monitoring/enforcing,
        221–223, 271
Retirement funds, 41, 350–354
Return on assets (ROA),
    266–267
Return on equity (ROE), 267
Returns. *See* Rate of return
Revaluation, 532
Reverse causation, 659
Reverse repurchase agree-
    ments, 479
Revolving underwriting facili-
    ties (RUFs), 280

Rhode Island Share & Deposit
    Indemnity Corp., 424–425
Ricardian equivalence, 472–473
Ricardo, David, 473
Risk
    and asset demand, 96, 98,
        116–117
    aversion to, 98
    credit, 260, 269–275
    default, 150–153, 569–571
    interest-rate, 88–90, 233–237,
        248, 260, 275–279
    nonsystematic, 101–102
    preference for, 98
    reinvestment, 90
    and speculative demand for
        money, 559–560
    systematic, 101–103
Risk-based capital require-
    ments, 311–312, 332
Risk-based premiums, 345
Risk premiums, 103–104,
    150–152, 154–155
Risk structure of interest rates,
    149–157, 710
Robinson, Jackie, 310
Rogoff, Kenneth, 724n
Rohaytn, Felix, 484
Roosevelt, Franklin, 426
Ross, Stephen, 104
Rules versus discretion,
    706–707
Runs on banks, 425–426
Rush, Mark, 755n
Russia
    forms of money in, 53
    inflation in, 697

Sales finance companies, 355
Salomon Brothers, 241, 359
Samuelson, Paul, 651
San Francisco Chronicle, in-
    vestment advising in, 721
Sargent, Thomas, 733, 736,
    739n, 753n, 754, 755n

Savings accounts, 253–254

Savings Association Insurance Fund (SAIF), 45, 292, 327–328

Savings institutions, contractual, 40–41

Savings and loan associations (S&Ls)
  bailouts, 73
  branching restrictions, 292
  charters, 291
  crises concerning, 322–329
  as financial intermediaries, 39–40
  loans to, 292
  mortgage loans by, 257
  regulation of, 291–292
  zombie, 323–324

Scadding, John L., 570*n*, 571*n*

Schoenholtz, Kermit L., 167*n*

Schwartz, Anna J., 328, 505*n*, 662, 665, 669, 670*n*

Screening
  by banks, for credit risk, 270–271
  by insurance companies, 344–345

Sears Roebuck, 339

Sears Roebuck Acceptance Corp., 355

Seasonal credit, 481

Secondary markets, 24–25
  exchanges, 25
  over-the-counter, 25–26

Secondary reserves, 256

Second Bank of the United States, 284, 438

Secured debt, 208

Securities. *See also* Bonds; Stocks
  bank holding of, 256
  defined, 11, 22
  "gilt-edged," 89
  international, 46–47
  municipal, 155–156, 256, 264

primary/secondary markets for, 24–25
  underwriting, 25
  U.S. government, 26, 32, 471–474, 505; default-free, 150–155; futures market in, 235; held by banks, 256; held by Fed, 370–372, 457, 461, 477–480; Treasury bills, 11, 27–28, 70, 84, 98–99, 121, 123, 158–159, 169, 232–234, 236–237, 246–247, 254, 316, 478, 487; Treasury bonds, 78, 83–85, 89, 118, 149–159, 168, 235–237, 451
  U.S. government agency, 32, 85

Securities Act (1933), 42, 360

Securities Amendment Act (1975), 362

Securities brokers/dealers, 25, 359–361

Securities Exchange Act (1934), 360

Securities and Exchange Commission (SEC), 42–44, 214, 326, 338, 356, 360–362, 722

Securities industry
  institutions in, 359–362
  separated from banking industry, 314–315, 337–339

Securities market
  access to, 208
  foreign, 33
  free-rider problem in, 214–216, 223
  importance of, 33

Securitization, 240–242

Segmented markets theory, 162–164

Seidman, William, 309–310

Self-correcting mechanism, 637

Semistrong-form efficiency, 725*n*

Shaper, A. G., 659*n*

Share draft accounts, 246

Sharpe, William, 103

Shiller, Robert J., 167*n*

Short-term debt instruments, 24

Simons, Henry, 491*n*

Simonsen, M. H., 754*n*

Simple deposit multiplier, 376

Simple interest rate, 71

Simple loans, 70, 72–74

Singapore, banking in, 295

Small, David H., 572*n*

Smith Barney Shearson, 361

Smithsonian Agreement (1971), 533

Social Security, 353–354

Solow, Robert, 651

Soros, George, 536

Sources of funds, 251–252, 299–301. *See also* Liabilities

Sources of monetary base, 459

Soviet Union, 37, 294, 697. *See also* Russia

Spain, banking system in, 448, 452

Special drawing rights (SDRs), 458, 462, 534

Specialists, 271, 360

Speculative demand, 552–553, 559–560

Spindt, Paul, 63*n*

Spot exchange rates, 175

Spot transactions, 175

Spread, 83

Stabilization policy, 748–749

Stagflation, 641

Standard and Poor, 153, 213

Standard deviation of returns, 101

Standby letters of credit, 280

Startz, Richard, 725*n*

State banking and insurance commissions, 45–46

State banks, 285–286
State bonds, 32
State Farm Insurance Co., 349
Statistical evidence, monetarist, 664, 668–669
Sterilized foreign exchange intervention, 521, 523–524
Stiglitz, Joseph F., 212n
Stock exchanges, 25–26, 47–48, 85, 242, 361–362
Stock index futures, 242–243
Stock market, 11–13, 25, 206
    effect on consumer expenditure, 675
    foreign, 47–48
    investing in, 719–729
    "lemons problem" in, 212–213
    and rational expectations theory, 719–729
    sharp declines during financial crises, 224–225
Stock market crash of 1929, 224, 228, 676
Stock market crash of 1987, 12, 153–154, 224n, 240, 243–244, 484–486, 729
Stock price indexes, 47–48, 242
Stock prices
    and good news, 726
    investment advisers' reports on, 719–722
    and investment spending, 547
    published in newspapers, 720
    random walks, 723–725
    technical analysis of, 726–727
    volatility of, 12
Stocks
    as capital market instruments, 30
    and corporate financing, 206–207
"Stop-go" policy, 538

Store of value, money as, 54–55
Store of wealth, 547
Strike price, 236
Strong-form efficiency, 725n
Strongin, Steven, 138n
Structural model, 656
Structural model evidence, 656–661
Student Loan Marketing Association, 357–358
Sumitomo Trust & Banking Co., 303
Summers, Lawrence H., 167n, 193n, 452n, 644n, 663n, 725n
Supply
    analysis of, 111–113
    in bond market, 107, 111–113, 117–119
    excess, 110, 634
    in gold market, 142–143
    of innovative financial products, 237–243
    in money market, 129
Supply curve
    for bonds, 109–110
    defined, 109
    for gold, 142–144
    for money, 129
    movements along, 113
    shifts in, 117–119, 129, 144
Supply shocks, 733n
    aggregate supply and demand analysis of, 638, 640–641, 645–647
    and inflation, 689–690
    and unemployment, 645–647
Sweep accounts, 246–247
Swiss National Bank, 515–516
Switzerland
    banking system in, 303, 315, 448, 452
    franc and exchange rates, 173–174

    inflation in, 5
    monetary policy in, 515–516
    reserve requirements in, 490
Systematic risk, 101–103

T-accounts, 257–259
Targets. *See* Monetary targets
Tariffs, 180
Tax and loan accounts, 465, 469
Tax code, 220n
Taxes
    and aggregate demand, 638–639
    and aggregate output, 584–588, 603–604
Taxes (*Continued*)
    bracket creep, 411, 414
    capital gains, 727n
    changes in, 603–604
    and currency-checkable deposits ratio, 411–414
    evasion of, and money supply, 421
    to finance government spending, 469–471
    and inflation, 688–689, 753–754
    and interest rates, 92, 155–156
    and *IS* curve, 603–604
    and mutual funds, 356
    underground economy, 412, 414
Taylor, John, 751–752
Technical analysis, 726–727
Technological advances, and financial innovation, 239–240
Temporary life insurance, 347–348
Term insurance, 347–348
Term structure of interest rates, 149, 157–167, 710, 735–736

Thatcher, Margaret, 514, 754

Theft insurance, 349–350

Third World, debt crisis of, 296, 530*n*

Thomas, Rich, 327*n*

Thrift industry, 38, 291–293

Time deposits, 253–254

Time deposits-checkable deposits ratio, 404–405

Timing evidence, monetarist, 664–667

Tips, investment, 723

Titman, Sheridan, 721*n*

Tobin, James, 193*n*, 555, 558–560, 567–568, 666*n*, 671

Tobin's mean-variance model, 761–765

Tobin's q theory, 671, 673

Tokyo Stock Exchange, 236

Trade balance, 524–525

Trade barriers, 648

Trading
    foreign exchange, 177
    program, 244

Trading desks, 478–479

Traditional model, 745–752

Tranches, 241

Transactions, spot/forward, 175

Transactions balances, 527

Transactions costs, 34, 209–211

Transactions demand, 551, 555–558, 759–761

Transmission mechanisms of monetary policy
    early Keynesian evidence, 661–664
    early monetarist evidence, 664–670
    monetarist-Keynesian debate, 677–678
    reduced form evidence, 656–661
    structural model evidence, 656–661

Treasury Department, U.S.
    currency of, 369*n*, 384*n*, 459*n*, 465*n*
    regulation by, 285, 316, 327–329, 352, 451
    securities. *See* Securities, U.S. government

Treasury investment growth receipts (TIGRs), 241

Treynor, Jack, 103

Truman, Harry, 447*n*

Trump, Donald, 102

Turkmenistan, inflation in, 697

Ukraine, inflation in, 697

Unanticipated policy, 736–739, 743

Uncertainty, and financial crises, 225

Underfunded plans, 351–352

Underground economy, 412, 414

Undervaluation, 531–533

Underwriters, 25, 359–360

Unemployment, frictional, 494

Unemployment rate
    activist-nonactivist debate, 637, 701–707
    data in newspapers, 626
    defined, 4
    high, responses to, 701–703
    and inflation, 651–654, 701–703
    natural, 494, 635
    and supply shocks, 645–647

Unexploited profit opportunity, 718–719

United Nations, 459

United Negro College Fund, 310

Unit labor costs, 652*n*

Unit of account, money as, 53–54

Universal banking, 315

Universal life insurance, 347–348

Unsecured debt, 208

Unsterilized foreign exchange intervention, 521–523

Uses of funds, 251–252, 301–302. *See also* Assets

Uses of monetary base, 459

Value
    face (par), 70
    present, 71–72
    store of, money as, 54–55

Value Line, 213

Variable life insurance, 347–348

Vault cash, 254, 369–370, 458

Velocity of money, 548–551
    defined, 544–545
    fluctuations in, 548–549, 551, 554–555
    and interest rates, 554–555
    in monetarist view of aggregate demand, 626–628
    predictability of, 565
    slowdowns, 571–572

Venture capital, 219–220

Venture capital firms, 219–220

Vesting, of pension plans, 351

Veterans Administration, 358

Vietnam War, 609, 611, 645

VISA card, 238

Volatility, 88–90, 173, 196

Volcker, Paul A., 445, 447, 509–510, 512, 707

Wage inflation, 651

Wage-price stickiness, 742

Wage push, 640

Wage-setting process, 705

Wall, M. Danny, 327

Wall Street Journal
    banking industry, 301
    bond listings, 82–86
    commodities, 145–147
    credit markets, 123–125
    exchange rates, 176, 197, 199–201

Federal Reserve data, 468
financial futures contracts, 235
foreign stock market indexes, 47
insurance, 350
interest rates, 29, 134–135
investments, 719–721
monetary aggregates, 62
new security issues, 360
stock market crash of 1987, 484
stock prices, 720
yield curves, 157–158
Wallace, Neil, 733n, 739n
War finance, 505–506, 609, 611
Washington State Public Power Supply System bonds, 155
Weak-form efficiency, 725n
Wealth
  and asset demand, 96–97, 114, 561–562
  changes in, and currency-checkable deposits ratio, 409
  and consumer expenditures, 674–675
  money as store of, 547
  and money supply, 409, 420–421
Wealth elasticity of demand, 96
Weighted money aggregates, 62–63
Weintraub, Robert E., 453n
Weiss, Andrew, 212n
Wells Fargo & Co., 289, 291
Whole life insurance, 347–348
Wide banks, 335
Williamson, John, 530n
Wire transfers, 57–58
World Bank (International Bank for Reconstruction and Development), 85, 459, 530
World War I, 503, 529
World War II, 505–506, 529–530
Wriston, Walter, 270, 361

Yield
  current, 80–81
  discount, 81–82
Yield curve, 157–158
  defined, 157
  in expectations theory, 161–162
  and expected interest rates, 168–169
  in liquidity premium theory, 165–167
  in preferred habitat theory, 165–167
  in segmented markets theory, 163
Yield to maturity, 72–80
  for consols, 78–79
  for coupon bonds, 75–79
  defined, 72
  for discount bonds, 79
  as measure of interest rates, 108
  for fixed-payment loans, 74–75
  negatively related to bond prices, 82
  and rate of return, 86–90
  for simple loans, 72–73

"Z" (accrual) bonds, 241
Zero-coupon bonds, 70
Zombie S&Ls, 323–324

Guide to Commonly Used Symbols

Symbol	Page Where Introduced	Term
β	103	beta
Δ	376	change in a variable
π^e	91	expected inflation
a	575	autonomous consumer expenditure
AD	620	aggregate demand curve
AS	632	aggregate supply curve
B^d	109	demand for bonds
B^s	110	supply of bonds
C	76	yearly coupon payment
C	384	currency
C	574	consumer expenditure
$\{C/D\}$	391	currency ratio
D	151	demand curve
D	376	checkable deposits
DL	390	discount loans
E	181	exchange (spot) rate
$(E^e_{t+1} - E_t) E_t$	183	expected appreciation of domestic currency
EM	267	equity multiplier
ER	391	excess reserves
$\{ER/D\}$	391	excess reserves ratio
G	574	government spending
i	71	interest rate (yield to maturity)
i_d	418	discount rate
$i^\$$	183	interest rate on dollar assets
i^F	183	interest rate on foreign assets
i_r	91	real interest rate
I	574	investment spending
IS	591	IS curve
LM	591	LM curve
m	390	money multiplier